# Great Britain
# Northern Ireland
# AZ Road Atlas

## Journey Route Planning maps

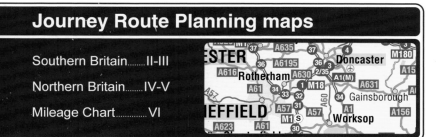

Southern Britain ........ II-III

Northern Britain ........ IV-V

Mileage Chart ........ VI


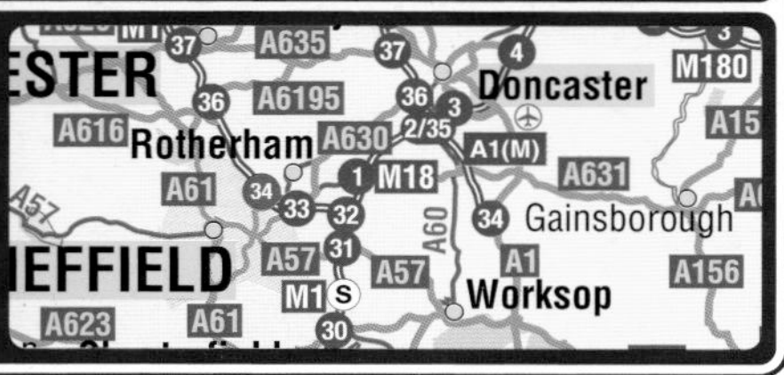

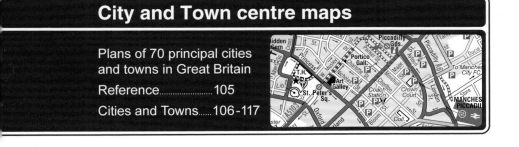

## Sea Port & Channel Tunnel plans

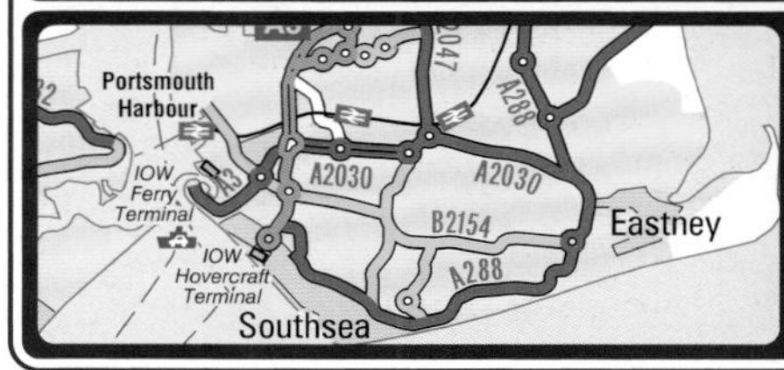

Access maps to principal sea ports in Britain ........ 118

Folkestone and Calais Terminals ........ 13


## Motorway Junctions


Details of motorway junctions with limited interchange ........ VII

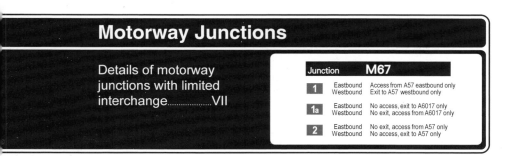

| Junction | M67 | |
|---|---|---|
| 1 | Eastbound<br>Westbound | Access from A57 eastbound only<br>Exit to A57 westbound only |
| 1a | Eastbound<br>Westbound | No access, exit to A6017 only<br>No exit, access from A6017 only |
| 2 | Eastbound<br>Westbound | No exit, access from A57 only<br>No access, exit to A57 only |

## Airport plans

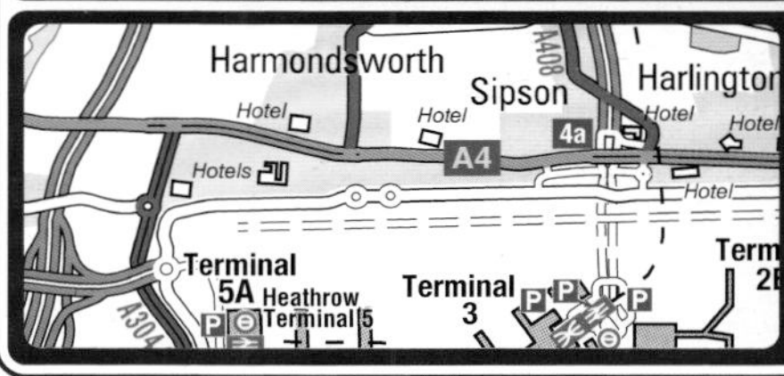

Access maps to principal Airports in Great Britain ........ 119


## Road map section


Key to map pages inside front cover

Reference ........ 2

Britain ........ 3-91

Northern Ireland ........ 92-93


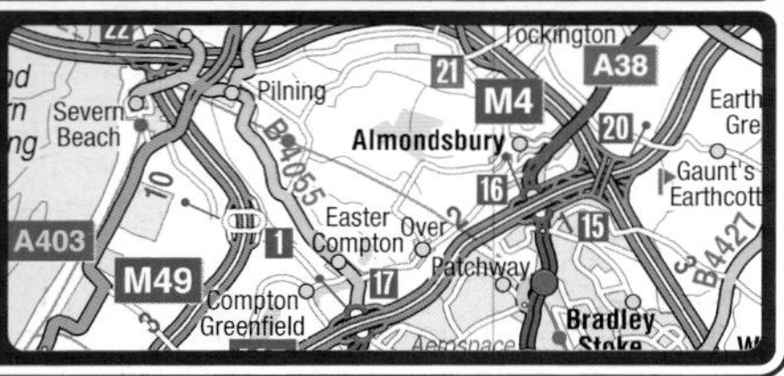


## Over 32,000 Index References

| A | |
|---|---|
| Abbas Combe. *Som* .........3F 8 | Abingdon-on-Thames. *Oxon* ............ |
| Abberley. *Worc* ............5F 26 | Abinger Common. *Surr* ... |
| Abberley Common. *Worc* ................5F 26 | Abinger Hammer. *Surr* ... |
| Abberton. *Essx* ............2G 23 | Abington. *S Lan* ........ |
| Abberton. *Worc* ............6H 27 | Abington Pigotts. *Cambs* . |
| Abberwick. *Nmbd* ..........8J 61 | Ab Kettleby. *Leics* ...... |
| Abbess Roding. *Essx* .......2B 22 | Ab Lench. *Worc* ........ |
| | Ablington. *Glos* ........ |
| | Ablington. *Wilts* ........ |
| | Abney. *Derbs* ........ |

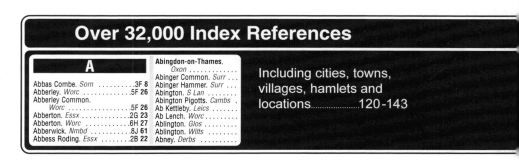

Including cities, towns, villages, hamlets and locations ........ 120-143

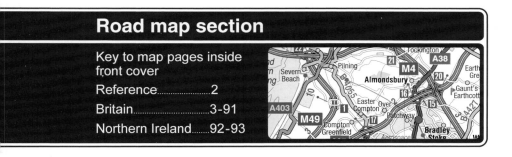

## Detailed Main Route maps


London ........ 94-101

Birmingham ........ 102-103

Manchester ........ 104

## Index to Places of Interest

**L**

Lacock Abbey (SN15 2LG) ................. 7H **19**
Lady Lever Art Gallery (CH62 5EQ) ........... 1B **34**
Lady of the North (NE23 8AU) ............... 4F **54**
Laing Art Gallery
(NE1 8AG) ........... **Newcastle upon Tyne 111**
Lake District Nat. Pk. (LA9 7RL) ............ 4B **46**
Lakeside & Haverthwaite Railway


Full postcodes to easily locate popular places of interest on your SatNav ........ 144-146

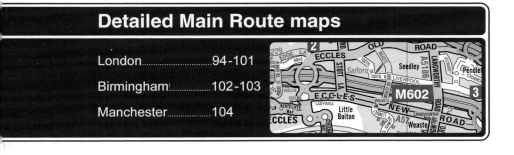

## City and Town centre maps


Plans of 70 principal cities and towns in Great Britain

Reference ........ 105

Cities and Towns ........ 106-117


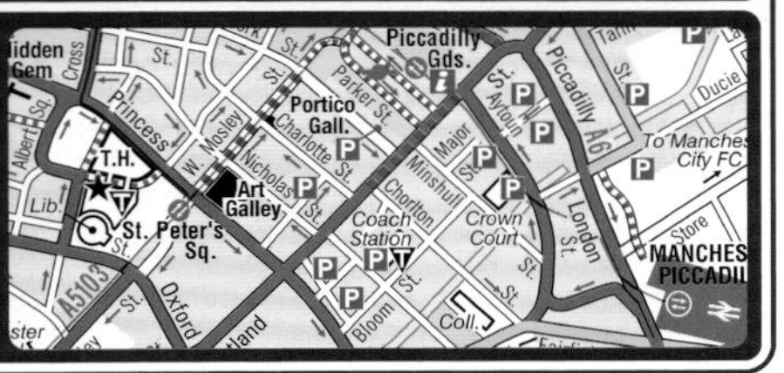





EDITION 37 2023

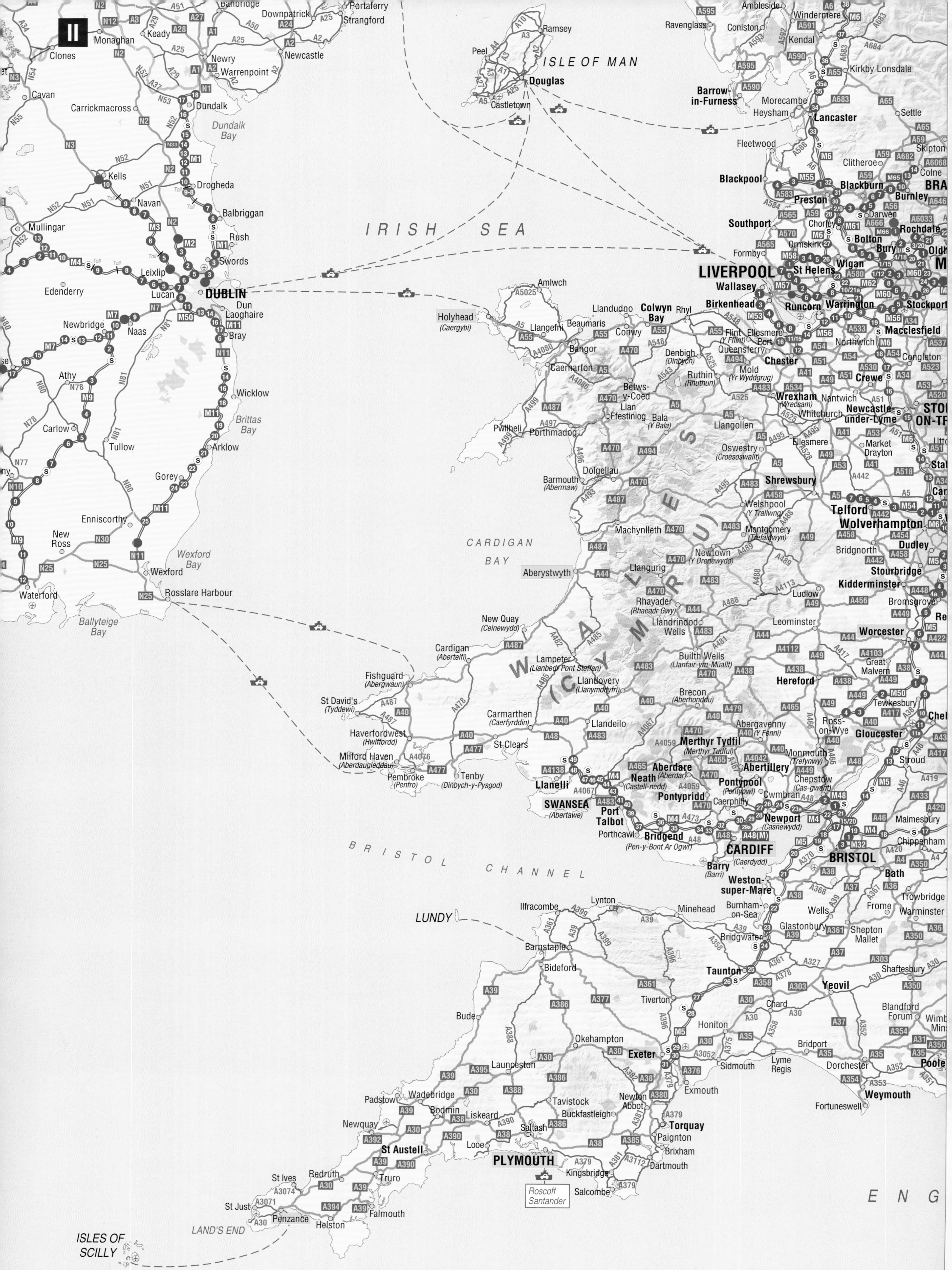
IRISH SEA
ISLE OF MAN
Ramsey
Peel
Douglas
Castletown
Dundalk Bay
Wexford Bay
Brittas Bay
Ballyteige Bay
Banbridge
Downpatrick
Portaferry
Strangford
Monaghan
Keady
Clones
Newry
Warrenpoint
Newcastle
Cavan
Carrickmacross
Dundalk
Kells
Drogheda
Navan
Balbriggan
Mullingar
Rush
Swords
Leixlip
DUBLIN
Lucan
Edenderry
Dun Laoghaire
Newbridge
Naas
Bray
Athy
Wicklow
Carlow
Tullow
Arklow
Gorey
Enniscorthy
New Ross
Wexford
Rosslare Harbour
Waterford
Ravenglass
Coniston
Ambleside
Windermere
Kendal
Kirkby Lonsdale
Barrow-in-Furness
Morecambe
Heysham
Lancaster
Settle
Fleetwood
Skipton
Clitheroe
Colne
Blackpool
Blackburn
Burnley
Preston
Southport
Chorley
Darwen
Bolton
Rochdale
Ormskirk
Bury
Formby
St Helens
Wigan
LIVERPOOL
Wallasey
Birkenhead
Runcorn
Warrington
Stockport
Amlwch
Holyhead (Caergybi)
Llangefni
Beaumaris
Llandudno
Colwyn Bay
Rhyl
Conwy
Bangor
Flint (Y Fflint)
Ellesmere Port
Macclesfield
Denbigh (Dinbych)
Queensferry
Northwich
Congleton
Caernarfon
Ruthin (Rhuthun)
Mold (Yr Wyddgrug)
Chester
Crewe
Betws-y-Coed
Wrexham (Wrecsam)
Nantwich
Llan Ffestiniog
Bala (Y Bala)
Whitchurch
Newcastle-under-Lyme
Pwllheli
Porthmadog
Llangollen
Oswestry (Croesoswallt)
Ellesmere
Market Drayton
Dolgellau
Barmouth (Abermaw)
Shrewsbury
Welshpool (Y Trallwng)
Telford
Wolverhampton
Machynlleth
Montgomery (Trefaldwyn)
Dudley
CARDIGAN BAY
Newtown (Y Drenewydd)
Bridgnorth
Stourbridge
Aberystwyth
Llangurig
Kidderminster
Ludlow
Rhayader (Rhaeadr Gwy)
Bromsgrove
New Quay (Ceinewydd)
Llandrindod Wells
Leominster
Worcester
Cardigan (Aberteifi)
Lampeter (Llanbedr Pont Steffan)
Builth Wells (Llanfair-ym-Muallt)
Great Malvern
WALES (CYMRU)
Fishguard (Abergwaun)
Llandovery (Llanymddyfri)
Hereford
St David's (Tyddewi)
Brecon (Aberhonddu)
Tewkesbury
Carmarthen (Caerfyrddin)
Llandeilo
Abergavenny (Y Fenni)
Ross-on-Wye
Gloucester
Haverfordwest (Hwlffordd)
St Clears
Merthyr Tydfil (Merthyr Tudful)
Milford Haven (Aberdaugleddau)
Monmouth (Trefynwy)
Stroud
Pembroke (Penfro)
Tenby (Dinbych-y-Pysgod)
Aberdare (Aberdar)
Abertillery
Chepstow (Cas-gwent)
Llanelli
Neath (Castell-nedd)
Pontypool (Pontypwl)
SWANSEA (Abertawe)
Pontypridd
Cwmbran
Caerphilly
Port Talbot
Newport (Casnewydd)
Malmesbury
Porthcawl
Bridgend (Pen-y-Bont Ar Ogwr)
Chippenham
CARDIFF (Caerdydd)
BRISTOL
BRISTOL CHANNEL
Barry (Barri)
Bath
Weston-super-Mare
Trowbridge
Frome
Warminster
LUNDY
Ilfracombe
Lynton
Minehead
Burnham-on-Sea
Wells
Glastonbury
Shepton Mallet
Barnstaple
Bridgwater
Bideford
Taunton
Shaftesbury
Yeovil
Tiverton
Chard
Bude
Blandford Forum
Honiton
Okehampton
Exeter
Bridport
Launceston
Sidmouth
Lyme Regis
Dorchester
Poole
Exmouth
Weymouth
Padstow
Wadebridge
Tavistock
Newton Abbot
Fortuneswell
Bodmin
Liskeard
Buckfastleigh
Newquay
Saltash
Torquay
Paignton
St Austell
Looe
PLYMOUTH
Brixham
Kingsbridge
Dartmouth
Roscoff Santander
Salcombe
St Ives
Redruth
Truro
St Just
Penzance
Falmouth
Helston
LAND'S END
ISLES OF SCILLY
ENG

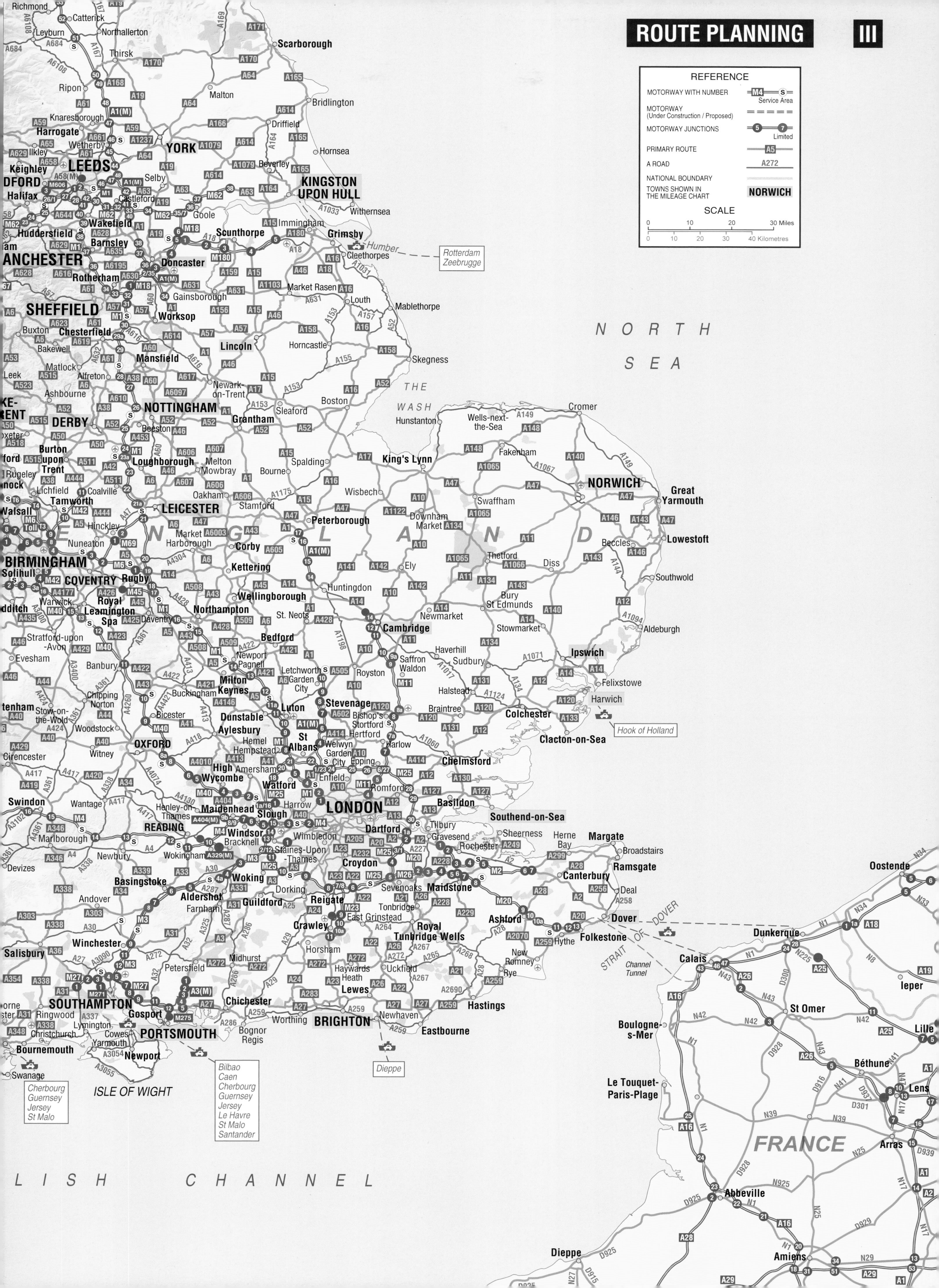
REFERENCE
MOTORWAY WITH NUMBER
Service Area
MOTORWAY (Under Construction / Proposed)
MOTORWAY JUNCTIONS
Limited
PRIMARY ROUTE
A ROAD
NATIONAL BOUNDARY
TOWNS SHOWN IN THE MILEAGE CHART
NORWICH
SCALE
0 10 20 30 Miles
0 10 20 30 40 Kilometres
NORTH SEA
THE WASH
ENGLISH CHANNEL
STRAIT OF DOVER
FRANCE
ISLE OF WIGHT
LEEDS
YORK
KINGSTON UPON HULL
SHEFFIELD
NOTTINGHAM
DERBY
LEICESTER
BIRMINGHAM
COVENTRY
OXFORD
READING
LONDON
SOUTHAMPTON
PORTSMOUTH
BRIGHTON
NORWICH
Scarborough
Bridlington
Grimsby
Scunthorpe
Doncaster
Lincoln
Boston
Skegness
King's Lynn
Peterborough
Cambridge
Ipswich
Colchester
Chelmsford
Southend-on-Sea
Great Yarmouth
Lowestoft
Cromer
Canterbury
Dover
Folkestone
Ashford
Maidstone
Hastings
Eastbourne
Bournemouth
Salisbury
Winchester
Swindon
Northampton
Bedford
Luton
Milton Keynes
Calais
Dunkerque
Boulogne-s-Mer
Le Touquet-Paris-Plage
Abbeville
Amiens
Arras
Lille
Lens
Béthune
St Omer
Ieper
Oostende
Dieppe
Rotterdam
Zeebrugge
Hook of Holland
Bilbao
Caen
Cherbourg
Guernsey
Jersey
Le Havre
Santander
St Malo
Channel Tunnel

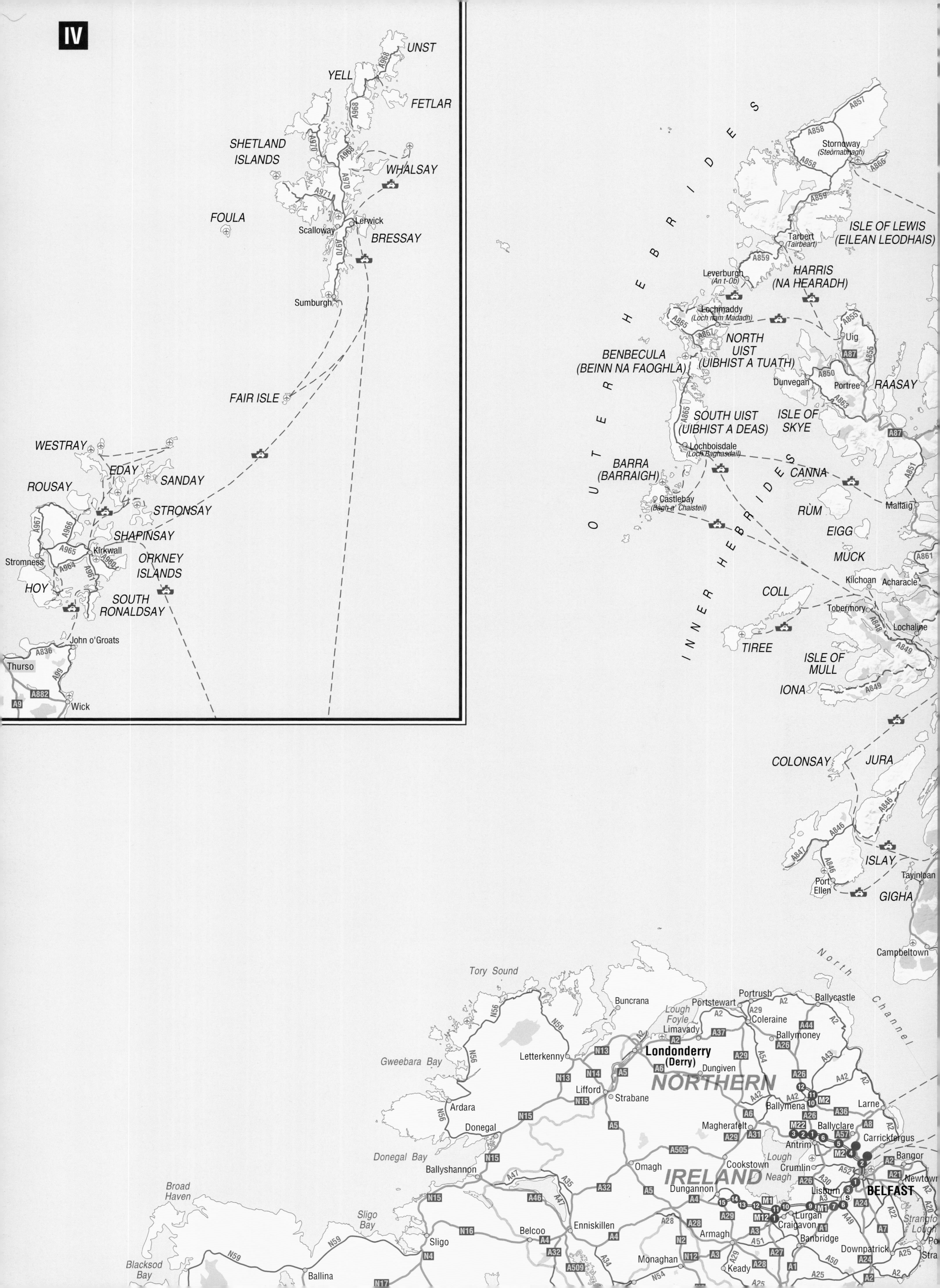

IV
UNST
YELL
FETLAR
SHETLAND ISLANDS
WHALSAY
FOULA
Lerwick
Scalloway
BRESSAY
Sumburgh
FAIR ISLE
WESTRAY
EDAY
SANDAY
ROUSAY
STRONSAY
SHAPINSAY
Kirkwall
Stromness
ORKNEY ISLANDS
HOY
SOUTH RONALDSAY
John o'Groats
Thurso
Wick
A968
A970
A971
A967
A966
A965
A964
A961
A960
A836
A99
A882
A9
OUTER HEBRIDES
Stornoway
(Steòrnabhagh)
A857
A858
A866
A859
ISLE OF LEWIS
(EILEAN LEODHAIS)
Tarbert
(Tairbeart)
Leverburgh
(An t-Ob)
HARRIS
(NA HEARADH)
Lochmaddy
(Loch nam Madadh)
A865
A867
NORTH UIST
(UIBHIST A TUATH)
BENBECULA
(BEINN NA FAOGHLA)
A855
Uig
A87
A850
Dunvegan
Portree
A863
RAASAY
SOUTH UIST
(UIBHIST A DEAS)
ISLE OF SKYE
Lochboisdale
(Loch Baghasdail)
BARRA
(BARRAIGH)
CANNA
A851
Mallaig
Castlebay
(Bàgh a' Chaisteil)
RÙM
EIGG
MUCK
A861
INNER HEBRIDES
Kilchoan
Acharacle
COLL
Tobermory
A848
Lochaline
A849
TIREE
ISLE OF MULL
IONA
COLONSAY
JURA
A846
A847
ISLAY
Port Ellen
Tayinloan
GIGHA
Campbeltown
North Channel
Tory Sound
Buncrana
Lough Foyle
Portstewart
Portrush
Coleraine
Ballycastle
Limavady
Ballymoney
Letterkenny
Londonderry
(Derry)
Dungiven
Gweebara Bay
NORTHERN
IRELAND
Lifford
Strabane
Ardara
Ballymena
Larne
Donegal
Magherafelt
Ballyclare
Carrickfergus
Antrim
Bangor
Donegal Bay
Lough Neagh
Ballyshannon
Omagh
Cookstown
Crumlin
Newtown
Broad Haven
Dungannon
Lisburn
BELFAST
Sligo Bay
Lurgan
Craigavon
Strangford Lough
Enniskillen
Armagh
Banbridge
Belcoo
Sligo
Downpatrick
Blacksod Bay
Monaghan
Ballina
Keady
N56
N13
N14
N15
N16
N59
N4
N17
N54
N12
N2
A2
A29
A37
A44
A26
A54
A6
A5
A42
A43
M2
A36
M22
A57
A8
A31
A505
A52
A21
A30
A32
A3
A1
A24
A20
A22
A7
A50
A25
A27
A28
A4
A46
A47
A35
A509
A34
A51
M1
M12

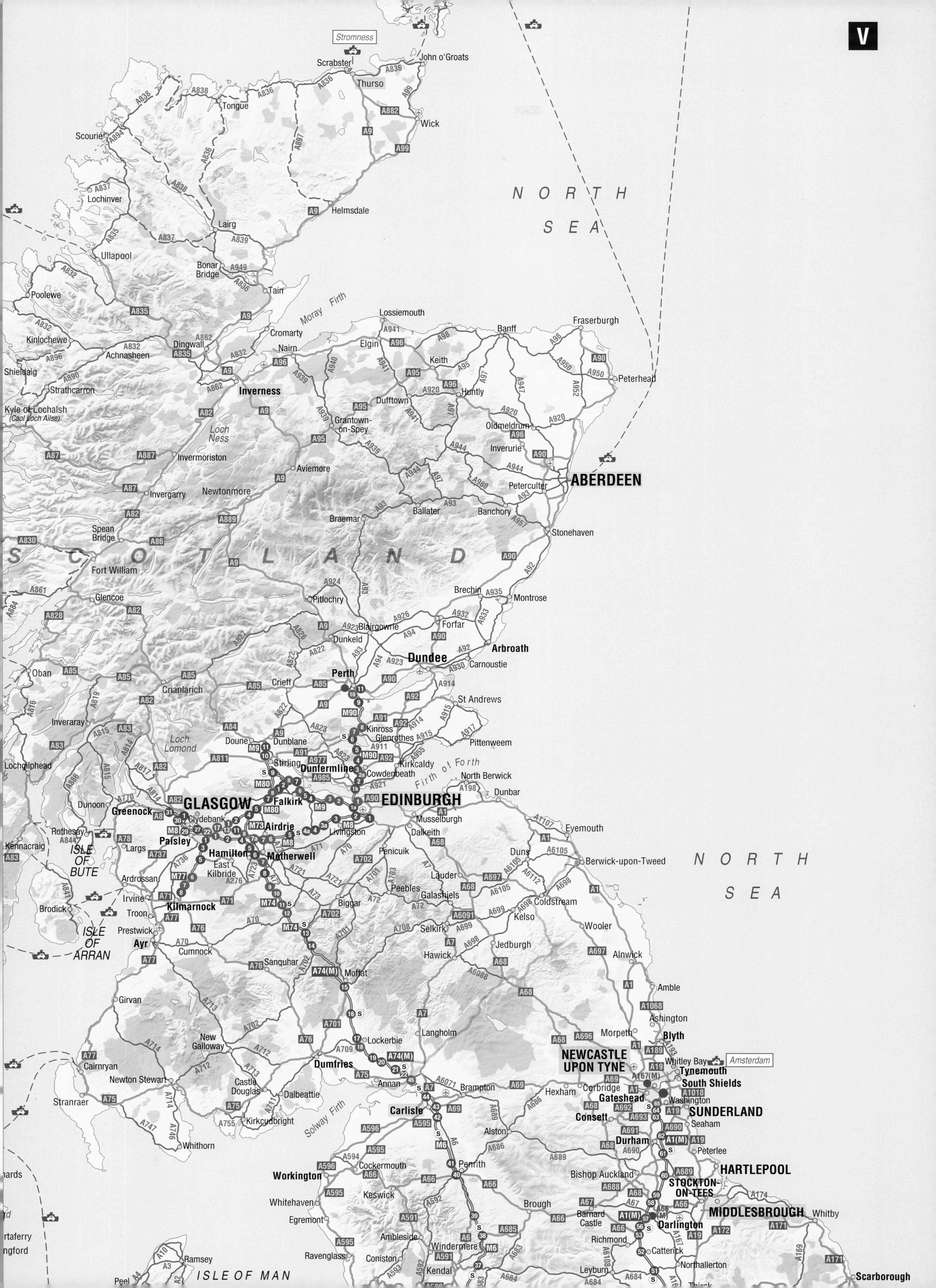
Stromness
Scrabster
John o'Groats
Thurso
Tongue
Wick
Scourie
Lochinver
Helmsdale
NORTH SEA
Lairg
Ullapool
Bonar Bridge
Tain
Poolewe
Moray Firth
Lossiemouth
Cromarty
Kinlochewe
Dingwall
Achnasheen
Nairn
Elgin
Banff
Fraserburgh
Keith
Shieldaig
Strathcarron
Inverness
Huntly
Peterhead
Dufftown
Kyle of Lochalsh
(Caol Loch Ailse)
Loch Ness
Grantown-on-Spey
Oldmeldrum
Inverurie
Invermoriston
Aviemore
ABERDEEN
Invergarry
Newtonmore
Peterculter
Ballater
Banchory
Braemar
Spean Bridge
Stonehaven
SCOTLAND
Fort William
Glencoe
Pitlochry
Brechin
Montrose
Blairgowrie
Forfar
Dunkeld
Arbroath
Dundee
Carnoustie
Oban
Perth
Crieff
Crianlarich
St Andrews
Inveraray
Kinross
Glenrothes
Pittenweem
Loch Lomond
Doune
Dunblane
Lochgilphead
Stirling
Kirkcaldy
Dunfermline
Cowdenbeath
Firth of Forth
North Berwick
Dunbar
Dunoon
Greenock
GLASGOW
Falkirk
EDINBURGH
Clydebank
Musselburgh
Airdrie
Rothesay
Paisley
Livingston
Dalkeith
Eyemouth
Kennacraig
ISLE OF BUTE
Largs
Hamilton
Motherwell
Penicuik
Duns
Berwick-upon-Tweed
East Kilbride
Lauder
Ardrossan
Peebles
Galashiels
Coldstream
Brodick
Irvine
Kilmarnock
Biggar
Kelso
Troon
Prestwick
Selkirk
Wooler
ISLE OF ARRAN
Ayr
Cumnock
Hawick
Jedburgh
Alnwick
Sanquhar
Moffat
Amble
Girvan
Ashington
Lockerbie
Langholm
Morpeth
Blyth
New Galloway
NEWCASTLE UPON TYNE
Whitley Bay
Amsterdam
Tynemouth
Cairnryan
Dumfries
South Shields
Newton Stewart
Castle Douglas
Annan
Brampton
Hexham
Corbridge
Gateshead
Dalbeattie
Stranraer
Carlisle
Washington
SUNDERLAND
Consett
Seaham
Kirkcudbright
Solway Firth
Alston
Durham
Peterlee
Whithorn
Cockermouth
Penrith
Workington
Bishop Auckland
HARTLEPOOL
STOCKTON-ON-TEES
Keswick
Whitehaven
Brough
MIDDLESBROUGH
Egremont
Barnard Castle
Darlington
Whitby
Ambleside
Richmond
Ravenglass
Windermere
Catterick
Ramsey
Coniston
Northallerton
Kendal
Leyburn
Scarborough
ISLE OF MAN
Peel
Thirsk
Portaferry
Longford

# Mileage Chart and Journey Times

This chart shows the distance in miles and journey time between two cities or towns in Great Britain. Each route has been calculated using a combination of motorways, primary routes and other major roads. This is normally the quickest, though not always the shortest route.

Average journey times are calculated whilst driving at the maximum speed limit. These times are approximate and do not include traffic congestion or convenience breaks.

To find the distance and journey time between two cities or towns, follow a horizontal line and vertical column until they meet each other.

For example, the 285 mile journey from London to Penzance is approximately 4 hours and 59 minutes.

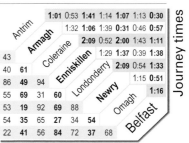

## Northern Ireland

Journey times

| | Armagh | Coleraine | Enniskillen | Londonderry | Newry | Omagh | Belfast |
|---|---|---|---|---|---|---|---|
| Antrim | 1:01 | 0:53 | 1:41 | 1:14 | 1:07 | 1:13 | 0:30 |
| Armagh | | 1:32 | 1:06 | 1:39 | 0:31 | 0:46 | 0:57 |
| Coleraine | | | 2:09 | 0:52 | 2:00 | 1:43 | 1:11 |
| Enniskillen | | | | 1:29 | 1:37 | 0:39 | 1:38 |
| Londonderry | | | | | 2:09 | 0:54 | 1:33 |
| Newry | | | | | | 1:15 | 0:51 |
| Omagh | | | | | | | 1:16 |

Distance in miles

| | Antrim | Armagh | Coleraine | Enniskillen | Londonderry | Newry | Omagh |
|---|---|---|---|---|---|---|---|
| Armagh | 43 | | | | | | |
| Coleraine | 40 | 61 | | | | | |
| Enniskillen | 86 | 49 | 94 | | | | |
| Londonderry | 55 | 69 | 31 | 60 | | | |
| Newry | 53 | 19 | 92 | 69 | 88 | | |
| Omagh | 54 | 35 | 65 | 27 | 34 | 54 | |
| Belfast | 22 | 41 | 56 | 84 | 72 | 37 | 68 |

Belfast to London = 440m / 9:46h (excluding ferry)
Belfast to Glasgow = 104m / 4:46h (excluding ferry)

## Great Britain

Journey times

| | Aberystwyth | Ayr | Birmingham | Bradford | Brighton | Bristol | Cambridge | Cardiff | Carlisle | Coventry | Derby | Doncaster | Dover | Edinburgh | Exeter | Fort William | Glasgow | Gloucester | Harwich | Holyhead | Inverness | Ipswich | Kendal | Kingston upon Hull | Leeds | Leicester | Lincoln | Liverpool | Manchester | Middlesbrough | Newcastle upon Tyne | Norwich | Nottingham | Oxford | Penzance | Perth | Plymouth | Portsmouth | Reading | Salisbury | Sheffield | Shrewsbury | Southampton | Southend-on-Sea | Stoke-on-Trent | Swansea | Thurso | Worcester | York | London |
|---|---|---|---|---|---|---|---|---|---|---|---|---|---|---|---|---|---|---|---|---|---|---|---|---|---|---|---|---|---|---|---|---|---|---|---|---|---|---|---|---|---|---|---|---|---|---|---|---|---|---|
| Aberdeen | 8:21 | 3:31 | 7:13 | 6:28 | 9:56 | 8:26 | 8:15 | 8:55 | 4:08 | 7:27 | 7:09 | 6:25 | 10:16 | 2:39 | 9:38 | 3:38 | 2:50 | 7:55 | 9:32 | 7:41 | 2:30 | 9:08 | 4:55 | 6:51 | 6:16 | 7:40 | 7:07 | 6:13 | 6:01 | 5:16 | 4:39 | 9:18 | 7:14 | 8:18 | 11:22 | 1:48 | 10:16 | 9:33 | 8:57 | 9:21 | 6:42 | 7:07 | 9:25 | 9:22 | 6:28 | 9:31 | 4:52 | 7:35 | 6:07 | 9:03 |
| Aberystwyth | | 6:34 | 2:34 | 3:27 | 5:21 | 2:44 | 4:00 | 2:29 | 4:24 | 2:52 | 2:56 | 3:45 | 5:41 | 6:20 | 3:51 | 8:13 | 5:53 | 2:34 | 5:17 | 2:29 | 8:39 | 4:53 | 3:40 | 4:20 | 3:29 | 3:18 | 4:11 | 2:39 | 2:54 | 4:34 | 5:07 | 5:03 | 3:17 | 3:43 | 5:35 | 6:41 | 4:29 | 4:27 | 3:50 | 4:01 | 3:41 | 1:47 | 4:18 | 4:56 | 2:48 | 1:48 | 11:00 | 2:19 | 4:00 | 4:28 |
| Ayr | | | 5:28 | 4:28 | 8:11 | 6:42 | 6:31 | 7:10 | 2:24 | 5:43 | 5:25 | 4:41 | 8:32 | 1:48 | 7:54 | 3:03 | 0:48 | 6:11 | 7:48 | 5:56 | 3:51 | 7:24 | 3:10 | 5:06 | 4:32 | 5:55 | 5:22 | 4:29 | 4:16 | 3:56 | 3:28 | 7:34 | 5:29 | 6:34 | 9:37 | 1:53 | 8:31 | 7:49 | 7:13 | 7:37 | 4:57 | 5:23 | 7:40 | 7:37 | 4:43 | 7:46 | 6:12 | 5:50 | 4:22 | 7:16 |
| Birmingham | | | | 2:15 | 3:04 | 1:41 | 1:43 | 2:09 | 3:16 | 0:36 | 1:01 | 1:40 | 3:25 | 5:12 | 2:53 | 7:05 | 4:45 | 1:10 | 3:01 | 2:59 | 7:31 | 2:37 | 2:32 | 2:21 | 2:05 | 1:01 | 1:55 | 1:49 | 1:46 | 2:55 | 3:28 | 2:46 | 1:08 | 1:27 | 4:36 | 5:33 | 3:30 | 2:42 | 2:06 | 2:39 | 1:36 | 0:59 | 2:33 | 2:39 | 1:02 | 2:44 | 9:52 | 0:49 | 2:21 | 2:11 |
| Bradford | | | | | 4:30 | 3:34 | 2:43 | 4:03 | 2:17 | 2:19 | 1:34 | 0:53 | 4:37 | 4:17 | 4:46 | 6:06 | 3:46 | 3:03 | 4:01 | 2:49 | 6:31 | 3:37 | 1:32 | 1:18 | 0:28 | 2:02 | 1:35 | 1:22 | 0:57 | 1:32 | 2:06 | 3:46 | 1:37 | 3:05 | 6:29 | 4:33 | 5:24 | 4:20 | 3:44 | 4:18 | 1:00 | 2:15 | 4:12 | 3:50 | 1:36 | 4:38 | 8:52 | 2:42 | 0:59 | 3:32 |
| Brighton | | | | | | 2:49 | 2:09 | 3:26 | 6:00 | 2:42 | 3:15 | 3:53 | 1:53 | 7:53 | 3:41 | 9:49 | 7:29 | 2:47 | 2:19 | 5:39 | 10:14 | 2:20 | 5:15 | 4:35 | 4:19 | 2:57 | 3:43 | 4:32 | 4:29 | 5:08 | 5:42 | 3:05 | 3:21 | 1:58 | 5:24 | 8:16 | 4:18 | 1:14 | 1:39 | 1:54 | 3:49 | 3:45 | 1:35 | 1:41 | 3:45 | 4:01 | 12:35 | 3:07 | 4:35 | 1:27 |
| Bristol | | | | | | | 3:02 | 0:56 | 4:31 | 1:44 | 2:21 | 2:59 | 3:18 | 6:27 | 1:37 | 8:20 | 6:00 | 0:47 | 3:27 | 4:13 | 8:45 | 3:28 | 3:46 | 3:41 | 3:25 | 2:17 | 3:11 | 3:03 | 3:01 | 4:15 | 4:48 | 3:58 | 2:28 | 1:30 | 3:20 | 6:48 | 2:14 | 2:03 | 1:26 | 1:37 | 2:56 | 2:14 | 1:54 | 2:58 | 2:17 | 1:30 | 11:07 | 1:07 | 3:41 | 2:07 |
| Cambridge | | | | | | | | 3:28 | 4:20 | 1:30 | 1:52 | 2:03 | 2:06 | 6:04 | 4:11 | 8:09 | 5:49 | 2:29 | 1:28 | 4:20 | 8:35 | 1:04 | 3:56 | 2:37 | 2:34 | 1:25 | 1:47 | 3:12 | 3:10 | 3:19 | 3:52 | 1:13 | 1:41 | 1:55 | 5:54 | 6:37 | 4:49 | 2:34 | 1:51 | 2:47 | 2:15 | 2:26 | 2:35 | 1:19 | 2:26 | 4:03 | 10:56 | 2:08 | 2:45 | 1:17 |
| Cardiff | | | | | | | | | 4:58 | 2:15 | 2:48 | 3:27 | 3:54 | 6:54 | 2:02 | 8:47 | 6:27 | 1:16 | 4:03 | 4:23 | 9:13 | 4:03 | 4:14 | 4:09 | 3:53 | 2:46 | 3:39 | 3:31 | 3:28 | 4:42 | 5:16 | 4:31 | 2:55 | 2:05 | 3:46 | 7:15 | 2:40 | 2:38 | 2:01 | 2:12 | 3:23 | 2:24 | 2:29 | 3:33 | 2:44 | 0:53 | 11:34 | 1:35 | 4:09 | 2:43 |
| Carlisle | | | | | | | | | | 3:30 | 3:12 | 2:28 | 6:19 | 2:08 | 5:41 | 4:01 | 1:41 | 3:58 | 5:35 | 3:44 | 4:27 | 5:11 | 0:58 | 2:54 | 2:19 | 3:43 | 3:10 | 2:16 | 2:04 | 1:44 | 1:15 | 5:21 | 3:17 | 4:21 | 7:25 | 2:29 | 6:19 | 5:36 | 5:00 | 5:24 | 2:45 | 3:10 | 5:28 | 5:25 | 2:31 | 5:34 | 6:48 | 3:38 | 2:10 | 5:07 |
| Coventry | | | | | | | | | | | 1:03 | 1:41 | 3:05 | 5:29 | 2:55 | 7:22 | 5:02 | 1:12 | 2:49 | 3:13 | 7:48 | 2:21 | 2:49 | 2:23 | 2:06 | 0:45 | 1:39 | 2:06 | 2:03 | 2:56 | 3:30 | 2:31 | 1:09 | 1:04 | 4:38 | 5:50 | 3:32 | 2:19 | 1:43 | 2:17 | 1:37 | 1:18 | 2:11 | 2:20 | 1:19 | 2:49 | 10:09 | 0:56 | 2:22 | 1:53 |
| Derby | | | | | | | | | | | | 0:57 | 3:33 | 4:58 | 3:31 | 7:02 | 4:42 | 1:48 | 3:09 | 2:52 | 7:27 | 2:45 | 2:28 | 1:39 | 1:23 | 0:49 | 1:24 | 1:45 | 1:42 | 2:13 | 2:46 | 2:55 | 0:33 | 1:51 | 5:14 | 5:29 | 4:08 | 3:06 | 2:30 | 3:04 | 0:54 | 1:21 | 2:58 | 2:48 | 0:53 | 3:22 | 9:49 | 1:27 | 1:39 | 2:19 |
| Doncaster | | | | | | | | | | | | | 3:58 | 4:13 | 4:12 | 6:19 | 3:59 | 2:30 | 3:21 | 3:17 | 6:44 | 2:57 | 2:16 | 0:56 | 0:43 | 1:27 | 0:55 | 1:48 | 1:25 | 1:28 | 2:02 | 3:07 | 1:02 | 2:30 | 5:56 | 4:46 | 4:50 | 3:45 | 3:09 | 3:43 | 0:30 | 2:13 | 3:36 | 3:11 | 1:44 | 4:04 | 9:05 | 2:09 | 0:54 | 2:57 |
| Dover | | | | | | | | | | | | | | 7:56 | 4:14 | 10:08 | 7:48 | 3:16 | 2:16 | 5:59 | 10:34 | 2:17 | 5:35 | 4:29 | 4:26 | 3:14 | 3:40 | 4:52 | 4:49 | 5:11 | 5:45 | 3:02 | 3:34 | 2:27 | 5:57 | 8:36 | 4:51 | 2:23 | 2:08 | 2:50 | 4:06 | 4:05 | 2:38 | 1:37 | 4:05 | 4:29 | 12:55 | 3:36 | 4:38 | 1:34 |
| Edinburgh | | | | | | | | | | | | | | | 7:38 | 3:01 | 1:05 | 5:55 | 7:20 | 5:41 | 3:02 | 6:56 | 2:55 | 4:38 | 4:04 | 5:26 | 4:54 | 4:13 | 4:00 | 3:00 | 2:23 | 7:06 | 5:01 | 6:18 | 9:21 | 1:02 | 8:16 | 7:33 | 6:57 | 7:21 | 4:29 | 5:07 | 7:25 | 7:09 | 4:28 | 7:30 | 5:24 | 5:34 | 3:54 | 6:57 |
| Exeter | | | | | | | | | | | | | | | | 9:31 | 7:11 | 1:58 | 4:36 | 5:24 | 9:56 | 4:37 | 4:57 | 4:52 | 4:36 | 3:28 | 4:22 | 4:14 | 4:12 | 5:26 | 5:59 | 5:07 | 3:39 | 2:46 | 1:54 | 7:59 | 0:53 | 2:38 | 2:43 | 1:55 | 4:07 | 3:25 | 2:27 | 4:02 | 3:28 | 2:37 | 12:18 | 2:18 | 4:52 | 3:16 |
| Fort William | | | | | | | | | | | | | | | | | 2:26 | 7:49 | 9:26 | 7:35 | 1:32 | 9:02 | 4:49 | 6:44 | 6:10 | 7:34 | 7:00 | 6:07 | 5:54 | 5:34 | 5:06 | 9:12 | 7:07 | 8:12 | 11:15 | 2:09 | 10:10 | 9:27 | 8:51 | 9:15 | 6:35 | 7:01 | 9:19 | 9:16 | 6:22 | 9:24 | 4:04 | 7:28 | 6:01 | 8:56 |
| Glasgow | | | | | | | | | | | | | | | | | | 5:28 | 7:05 | 5:13 | 3:08 | 6:41 | 2:28 | 4:23 | 3:49 | 5:12 | 4:39 | 3:46 | 3:33 | 3:13 | 2:45 | 6:51 | 4:46 | 5:51 | 8:54 | 1:10 | 7:48 | 7:06 | 6:30 | 6:54 | 4:14 | 4:40 | 6:57 | 6:55 | 4:01 | 7:03 | 5:29 | 5:07 | 3:40 | 6:36 |
| Gloucester | | | | | | | | | | | | | | | | | | | 3:25 | 3:42 | 8:14 | 3:22 | 3:15 | 3:10 | 2:54 | 1:46 | 2:39 | 2:32 | 2:29 | 3:43 | 4:17 | 3:31 | 1:56 | 1:11 | 3:39 | 6:16 | 2:33 | 2:00 | 1:24 | 1:42 | 2:24 | 1:42 | 1:52 | 2:56 | 1:45 | 1:49 | 10:35 | 0:36 | 3:10 | 2:05 |
| Harwich | | | | | | | | | | | | | | | | | | | | 5:38 | 9:53 | 0:42 | 5:13 | 3:55 | 3:52 | 2:43 | 3:05 | 4:30 | 4:28 | 4:37 | 5:10 | 1:32 | 2:59 | 2:26 | 6:20 | 7:55 | 5:14 | 2:49 | 2:17 | 3:12 | 3:33 | 3:44 | 3:01 | 1:09 | 3:44 | 4:38 | 12:14 | 3:26 | 4:03 | 1:42 |
| Holyhead | | | | | | | | | | | | | | | | | | | | | 7:58 | 5:16 | 2:59 | 3:39 | 2:49 | 3:23 | 3:52 | 1:53 | 2:13 | 3:53 | 4:26 | 5:25 | 3:15 | 4:06 | 7:06 | 6:00 | 6:00 | 5:21 | 4:45 | 5:05 | 3:06 | 2:10 | 5:12 | 5:18 | 2:11 | 4:33 | 10:19 | 3:19 | 3:19 | 4:47 |
| Inverness | | | | | | | | | | | | | | | | | | | | | | 9:27 | 5:14 | 7:10 | 6:35 | 7:59 | 7:26 | 6:32 | 6:20 | 5:41 | 5:04 | 9:37 | 7:33 | 8:37 | 11:41 | 2:10 | 10:35 | 9:52 | 9:16 | 9:40 | 7:01 | 7:26 | 9:44 | 9:41 | 6:47 | 9:50 | 2:31 | 7:54 | 6:26 | 9:21 |
| Ipswich | | | | | | | | | | | | | | | | | | | | | | | 4:50 | 3:31 | 3:28 | 2:20 | 2:41 | 4:06 | 4:04 | 4:13 | 4:46 | 1:08 | 2:35 | 2:27 | 6:21 | 7:31 | 5:15 | 2:50 | 2:18 | 3:13 | 3:09 | 3:20 | 3:02 | 1:10 | 3:20 | 4:39 | 11:50 | 3:02 | 3:39 | 1:43 |
| Kendal | | | | | | | | | | | | | | | | | | | | | | | | 2:44 | 1:53 | 3:02 | 3:00 | 1:36 | 1:23 | 1:38 | 1:59 | 5:00 | 2:54 | 3:41 | 6:44 | 3:13 | 5:38 | 4:56 | 4:20 | 4:44 | 2:22 | 2:30 | 4:47 | 4:53 | 1:50 | 4:53 | 7:32 | 2:57 | 2:04 | 4:22 |
| Kingston upon Hull | | | | | | | | | | | | | | | | | | | | | | | | | 1:08 | 2:08 | 0:58 | 2:13 | 1:49 | 1:54 | 2:27 | 3:18 | 1:43 | 3:10 | 6:36 | 5:12 | 5:30 | 4:25 | 3:49 | 4:23 | 1:11 | 2:53 | 4:17 | 3:43 | 2:25 | 4:44 | 9:31 | 2:49 | 1:02 | 3:39 |
| Leeds | | | | | | | | | | | | | | | | | | | | | | | | | | 1:53 | 1:25 | 1:23 | 0:58 | 1:20 | 1:53 | 3:37 | 1:27 | 2:55 | 6:21 | 4:38 | 5:15 | 4:10 | 3:34 | 4:08 | 0:50 | 2:16 | 4:02 | 3:40 | 1:37 | 4:29 | 8:57 | 2:34 | 0:46 | 3:23 |
| Leicester | | | | | | | | | | | | | | | | | | | | | | | | | | | 1:16 | 2:17 | 2:14 | 2:42 | 3:15 | 2:27 | 0:46 | 1:32 | 5:11 | 6:01 | 4:05 | 2:47 | 2:11 | 2:45 | 1:23 | 1:43 | 2:39 | 2:29 | 1:24 | 3:20 | 10:20 | 1:25 | 2:08 | 2:01 |
| Lincoln | | | | | | | | | | | | | | | | | | | | | | | | | | | | 2:31 | 2:02 | 2:11 | 2:44 | 2:20 | 0:59 | 2:28 | 6:07 | 5:29 | 5:01 | 3:43 | 3:07 | 3:41 | 1:07 | 2:33 | 3:34 | 2:54 | 2:10 | 4:16 | 9:48 | 2:21 | 1:35 | 2:51 |
| Liverpool | | | | | | | | | | | | | | | | | | | | | | | | | | | | | 0:48 | 2:28 | 3:01 | 4:16 | 2:10 | 2:56 | 6:00 | 4:33 | 4:54 | 4:11 | 3:35 | 3:59 | 1:52 | 1:25 | 4:03 | 4:09 | 1:06 | 3:48 | 8:53 | 2:13 | 1:54 | 3:39 |
| Manchester | | | | | | | | | | | | | | | | | | | | | | | | | | | | | | 2:03 | 2:36 | 4:12 | 1:51 | 2:52 | 5:55 | 4:22 | 4:49 | 4:07 | 3:30 | 3:55 | 1:14 | 1:41 | 3:58 | 4:04 | 1:01 | 4:04 | 8:41 | 2:08 | 1:29 | 3:37 |
| Middlesbrough | | | | | | | | | | | | | | | | | | | | | | | | | | | | | | | 0:55 | 4:20 | 2:15 | 3:43 | 7:09 | 3:40 | 6:03 | 4:58 | 4:22 | 4:56 | 1:43 | 3:20 | 4:50 | 4:24 | 2:40 | 5:17 | 8:02 | 3:22 | 1:05 | 4:12 |
| Newcastle upon Tyne | | | | | | | | | | | | | | | | | | | | | | | | | | | | | | | | 4:54 | 2:49 | 4:17 | 7:43 | 3:03 | 6:37 | 5:32 | 4:56 | 5:30 | 2:17 | 3:54 | 5:24 | 4:58 | 3:14 | 5:51 | 7:25 | 3:56 | 1:43 | 4:46 |
| Norwich | | | | | | | | | | | | | | | | | | | | | | | | | | | | | | | | | 2:44 | 2:58 | 6:51 | 7:40 | 5:45 | 3:31 | 2:48 | 3:43 | 3:18 | 3:29 | 3:32 | 2:00 | 3:28 | 5:06 | 11:59 | 3:10 | 3:48 | 2:13 |
| Nottingham | | | | | | | | | | | | | | | | | | | | | | | | | | | | | | | | | | 1:57 | 5:23 | 5:34 | 4:17 | 3:12 | 2:36 | 3:10 | 0:57 | 1:44 | 3:04 | 2:49 | 1:18 | 3:31 | 9:53 | 1:36 | 1:42 | 2:25 |
| Oxford | | | | | | | | | | | | | | | | | | | | | | | | | | | | | | | | | | | 4:30 | 6:40 | 3:24 | 1:28 | 0:45 | 1:25 | 2:25 | 2:08 | 1:19 | 1:56 | 2:09 | 2:40 | 10:59 | 1:31 | 3:10 | 1:15 |
| Penzance | | | | | | | | | | | | | | | | | | | | | | | | | | | | | | | | | | | | 9:43 | 1:41 | 4:22 | 4:27 | 3:39 | 5:51 | 5:09 | 4:11 | 5:46 | 5:12 | 4:20 | 14:02 | 4:02 | 6:36 | 4:59 |
| Perth | | | | | | | | | | | | | | | | | | | | | | | | | | | | | | | | | | | | | 8:37 | 7:54 | 7:18 | 7:42 | 5:03 | 5:28 | 7:46 | 7:43 | 4:49 | 7:52 | 4:30 | 5:55 | 4:28 | 7:24 |
| Plymouth | | | | | | | | | | | | | | | | | | | | | | | | | | | | | | | | | | | | | | 3:16 | 3:20 | 2:32 | 4:44 | 4:02 | 3:04 | 4:39 | 4:05 | 3:14 | 12:55 | 2:55 | 5:29 | 3:54 |
| Portsmouth | | | | | | | | | | | | | | | | | | | | | | | | | | | | | | | | | | | | | | | 1:18 | 0:52 | 3:39 | 3:23 | 0:32 | 2:11 | 3:23 | 3:13 | 12:13 | 2:20 | 4:25 | 1:39 |
| Reading | | | | | | | | | | | | | | | | | | | | | | | | | | | | | | | | | | | | | | | | 1:22 | 3:01 | 2:45 | 1:09 | 1:46 | 2:45 | 2:37 | 11:35 | 1:44 | 3:47 | 0:56 |
| Salisbury | | | | | | | | | | | | | | | | | | | | | | | | | | | | | | | | | | | | | | | | | 3:37 | 3:09 | 0:40 | 2:37 | 3:12 | 2:47 | 12:02 | 2:02 | 4:22 | 1:52 |
| Sheffield | | | | | | | | | | | | | | | | | | | | | | | | | | | | | | | | | | | | | | | | | | 2:08 | 3:32 | 3:22 | 1:40 | 3:59 | 9:22 | 2:04 | 1:11 | 2:53 |
| Shrewsbury | | | | | | | | | | | | | | | | | | | | | | | | | | | | | | | | | | | | | | | | | | | 3:16 | 3:22 | 1:04 | 2:45 | 9:46 | 1:23 | 2:46 | 2:53 |
| Southampton | | | | | | | | | | | | | | | | | | | | | | | | | | | | | | | | | | | | | | | | | | | | 2:26 | 3:15 | 3:05 | 12:05 | 2:12 | 4:16 | 1:40 |
| Southend-on-Sea | | | | | | | | | | | | | | | | | | | | | | | | | | | | | | | | | | | | | | | | | | | | | 3:21 | 4:09 | 12:02 | 3:03 | 3:51 | 1:07 |
| Stoke-on-Trent | | | | | | | | | | | | | | | | | | | | | | | | | | | | | | | | | | | | | | | | | | | | | | 3:18 | 9:08 | 1:23 | 2:09 | 2:53 |
| Swansea | | | | | | | | | | | | | | | | | | | | | | | | | | | | | | | | | | | | | | | | | | | | | | | 12:11 | 2:10 | 4:44 | 3:18 |
| Thurso | | | | | | | | | | | | | | | | | | | | | | | | | | | | | | | | | | | | | | | | | | | | | | | | 10:15 | 8:47 | 11:43 |
| Worcester | | | | | | | | | | | | | | | | | | | | | | | | | | | | | | | | | | | | | | | | | | | | | | | | | 2:49 | 2:24 |
| York | | | | | | | | | | | | | | | | | | | | | | | | | | | | | | | | | | | | | | | | | | | | | | | | | | 3:39 |

Distance in miles

| | Aberdeen | Aberystwyth | Ayr | Birmingham | Bradford | Brighton | Bristol | Cambridge | Cardiff | Carlisle | Coventry | Derby | Doncaster | Dover | Edinburgh | Exeter | Fort William | Glasgow | Gloucester | Harwich | Holyhead | Inverness | Ipswich | Kendal | Kingston upon Hull | Leeds | Leicester | Lincoln | Liverpool | Manchester | Middlesbrough | Newcastle upon Tyne | Norwich | Nottingham | Oxford | Penzance | Perth | Plymouth | Portsmouth | Reading | Salisbury | Sheffield | Shrewsbury | Southampton | Southend-on-Sea | Stoke-on-Trent | Swansea | Thurso | Worcester | York |
|---|---|---|---|---|---|---|---|---|---|---|---|---|---|---|---|---|---|---|---|---|---|---|---|---|---|---|---|---|---|---|---|---|---|---|---|---|---|---|---|---|---|---|---|---|---|---|---|---|---|---|
| Aberystwyth | 471 |
| Ayr | 181 | 324 |
| Birmingham | 423 | 114 | 272 |
| Bradford | 377 | 159 | 196 | 124 |
| Brighton | 596 | 258 | 441 | 169 | 263 |
| Bristol | 505 | 122 | 375 | 88 | 215 | 129 |
| Cambridge | 487 | 198 | 366 | 102 | 156 | 117 | 167 |
| Cardiff | 525 | 106 | 377 | 106 | 233 | 168 | 42 | 201 |
| Carlisle | 229 | 232 | 89 | 183 | 107 | 345 | 286 | 256 | 288 |
| Coventry | 442 | 134 | 297 | 18 | 124 | 157 | 102 | 84 | 129 | 200 |
| Derby | 418 | 137 | 269 | 41 | 88 | 188 | 134 | 99 | 159 | 180 | 43 |
| Doncaster | 371 | 192 | 239 | 95 | 40 | 232 | 184 | 117 | 210 | 150 | 94 | 57 |
| Dover | 620 | 315 | 477 | 195 | 284 | 81 | 194 | 118 | 233 | 393 | 180 | 208 | 244 |
| Edinburgh | 126 | 340 | 75 | 284 | 198 | 466 | 377 | 326 | 379 | 91 | 303 | 266 | 212 | 444 |
| Exeter | 581 | 199 | 425 | 161 | 282 | 170 | 75 | 323 | 107 | 336 | 166 | 213 | 257 | 244 | 439 |
| Fort William | 159 | 430 | 136 | 391 | 305 | 568 | 478 | 456 | 486 | 198 | 415 | 387 | 345 | 591 | 131 | 549 |
| Glasgow | 146 | 322 | 36 | 291 | 203 | 468 | 378 | 355 | 384 | 96 | 313 | 282 | 245 | 491 | 46 | 449 | 100 |
| Gloucester | 473 | 109 | 317 | 53 | 171 | 152 | 35 | 132 | 53 | 228 | 59 | 93 | 149 | 189 | 331 | 107 | 435 | 324 |
| Harwich | 568 | 258 | 411 | 170 | 224 | 130 | 203 | 64 | 234 | 323 | 152 | 167 | 185 | 129 | 397 | 262 | 524 | 419 | 171 |
| Holyhead | 452 | 96 | 315 | 151 | 158 | 330 | 204 | 252 | 209 | 226 | 167 | 156 | 169 | 358 | 316 | 279 | 423 | 323 | 189 | 331 |
| Inverness | 105 | 492 | 198 | 449 | 353 | 620 | 536 | 490 | 558 | 260 | 458 | 421 | 369 | 601 | 157 | 607 | 63 | 162 | 496 | 554 | 481 |
| Ipswich | 538 | 268 | 420 | 156 | 210 | 125 | 206 | 54 | 240 | 311 | 138 | 155 | 171 | 127 | 381 | 264 | 510 | 409 | 177 | 21 | 307 | 538 |
| Kendal | 280 | 182 | 139 | 151 | 62 | 324 | 235 | 215 | 232 | 50 | 170 | 136 | 99 | 344 | 141 | 307 | 248 | 146 | 200 | 279 | 180 | 310 | 268 |
| Kingston upon Hull | 398 | 235 | 255 | 139 | 68 | 243 | 228 | 134 | 239 | 165 | 123 | 94 | 37 | 254 | 230 | 290 | 367 | 255 | 195 | 204 | 218 | 387 | 189 | 127 |
| Leeds | 359 | 171 | 198 | 119 | 9 | 256 | 209 | 144 | 226 | 111 | 117 | 74 | 32 | 275 | 190 | 279 | 309 | 208 | 167 | 217 | 162 | 345 | 197 | 72 | 60 |
| Leicester | 445 | 155 | 294 | 43 | 99 | 163 | 118 | 70 | 140 | 214 | 24 | 30 | 73 | 183 | 282 | 189 | 412 | 312 | 83 | 146 | 182 | 431 | 125 | 166 | 98 | 97 |
| Lincoln | 411 | 208 | 249 | 87 | 80 | 207 | 170 | 88 | 192 | 178 | 76 | 53 | 41 | 206 | 247 | 241 | 376 | 274 | 135 | 152 | 204 | 402 | 124 | 140 | 46 | 72 | 52 |
| Liverpool | 354 | 120 | 199 | 99 | 67 | 267 | 180 | 179 | 169 | 110 | 113 | 90 | 89 | 294 | 201 | 240 | 308 | 213 | 142 | 265 | 95 | 370 | 236 | 75 | 126 | 73 | 110 | 118 |
| Manchester | 349 | 128 | 204 | 87 | 37 | 252 | 167 | 159 | 188 | 117 | 99 | 58 | 51 | 273 | 208 | 239 | 315 | 215 | 132 | 230 | 120 | 363 | 211 | 72 | 96 | 42 | 95 | 87 | 34 |
| Middlesbrough | 289 | 233 | 181 | 174 | 69 | 316 | 265 | 196 | 287 | 92 | 175 | 130 | 84 | 316 | 147 | 337 | 279 | 192 | 230 | 266 | 226 | 306 | 253 | 77 | 88 | 64 | 154 | 127 | 134 | 106 |
| Newcastle upon Tyne | 252 | 266 | 146 | 209 | 98 | 345 | 300 | 232 | 312 | 58 | 209 | 165 | 115 | 350 | 104 | 369 | 237 | 153 | 263 | 297 | 257 | 263 | 287 | 88 | 130 | 96 | 188 | 153 | 167 | 136 | 40 |
| Norwich | 536 | 270 | 348 | 163 | 185 | 174 | 234 | 62 | 256 | 280 | 142 | 146 | 142 | 169 | 351 | 284 | 478 | 378 | 193 | 72 | 289 | 505 | 44 | 249 | 145 | 178 | 112 | 103 | 222 | 177 | 221 | 252 |
| Nottingham | 416 | 155 | 267 | 54 | 78 | 191 | 140 | 84 | 165 | 188 | 52 | 15 | 48 | 210 | 256 | 218 | 386 | 286 | 108 | 165 | 177 | 410 | 140 | 141 | 92 | 72 | 27 | 37 | 107 | 68 | 128 | 159 | 118 |
| Oxford | 497 | 151 | 335 | 68 | 167 | 106 | 73 | 92 | 106 | 267 | 57 | 101 | 138 | 142 | 358 | 151 | 465 | 365 | 47 | 134 | 208 | 515 | 128 | 223 | 175 | 162 | 76 | 123 | 168 | 157 | 218 | 253 | 159 | 104 |
| Penzance | 688 | 301 | 552 | 269 | 394 | 279 | 184 | 343 | 218 | 463 | 278 | 316 | 369 | 355 | 551 | 109 | 663 | 561 | 217 | 374 | 388 | 715 | 375 | 419 | 412 | 391 | 310 | 359 | 353 | 344 | 449 | 481 | 393 | 323 | 261 |
| Perth | 86 | 366 | 85 | 336 | 245 | 509 | 412 | 370 | 422 | 134 | 346 | 309 | 254 | 485 | 43 | 487 | 103 | 59 | 362 | 439 | 360 | 113 | 424 | 184 | 273 | 233 | 326 | 290 | 244 | 254 | 191 | 148 | 394 | 299 | 404 | 598 |
| Plymouth | 619 | 232 | 461 | 203 | 325 | 206 | 111 | 274 | 159 | 372 | 209 | 254 | 300 | 286 | 485 | 43 | 592 | 490 | 150 | 305 | 322 | 648 | 305 | 348 | 326 | 323 | 231 | 284 | 299 | 281 | 379 | 412 | 327 | 255 | 193 | 75 | 529 |
| Portsmouth | 579 | 231 | 440 | 147 | 274 | 50 | 95 | 132 | 138 | 357 | 132 | 184 | 231 | 137 | 448 | 127 | 555 | 455 | 114 | 161 | 303 | 603 | 158 | 308 | 268 | 245 | 166 | 209 | 254 | 237 | 315 | 360 | 200 | 191 | 83 | 235 | 486 | 170 |
| Reading | 538 | 180 | 399 | 103 | 213 | 79 | 77 | 90 | 112 | 309 | 90 | 138 | 184 | 115 | 402 | 141 | 506 | 406 | 75 | 129 | 264 | 554 | 126 | 263 | 209 | 207 | 113 | 168 | 193 | 197 | 264 | 295 | 152 | 129 | 25 | 251 | 445 | 184 | 60 |
| Salisbury | 538 | 178 | 383 | 121 | 245 | 82 | 53 | 140 | 101 | 312 | 113 | 159 | 207 | 158 | 400 | 91 | 510 | 408 | 73 | 177 | 262 | 569 | 177 | 265 | 251 | 230 | 132 | 187 | 213 | 208 | 287 | 318 | 200 | 162 | 65 | 201 | 443 | 132 | 43 | 57 |
| Sheffield | 390 | 173 | 235 | 79 | 40 | 225 | 163 | 121 | 193 | 154 | 75 | 35 | 21 | 268 | 230 | 245 | 352 | 250 | 139 | 185 | 164 | 387 | 176 | 102 | 66 | 33 | 68 | 46 | 74 | 40 | 102 | 133 | 144 | 37 | 137 | 361 | 273 | 293 | 228 | 160 | 203 |
| Shrewsbury | 419 | 73 | 260 | 47 | 100 | 216 | 116 | 140 | 107 | 171 | 64 | 67 | 114 | 249 | 262 | 175 | 369 | 267 | 77 | 215 | 104 | 424 | 195 | 125 | 163 | 102 | 79 | 123 | 59 | 67 | 166 | 203 | 196 | 86 | 105 | 286 | 309 | 218 | 195 | 147 | 150 | 85 |
| Southampton | 564 | 213 | 401 | 128 | 235 | 64 | 75 | 129 | 122 | 330 | 114 | 167 | 201 | 150 | 433 | 106 | 528 | 426 | 98 | 157 | 287 | 590 | 162 | 276 | 249 | 230 | 136 | 189 | 235 | 215 | 288 | 320 | 190 | 162 | 66 | 217 | 476 | 149 | 20 | 47 | 23 | 206 | 175 |
| Southend-on-Sea | 549 | 258 | 431 | 152 | 220 | 85 | 177 | 64 | 211 | 342 | 129 | 168 | 185 | 89 | 395 | 226 | 548 | 438 | 152 | 57 | 303 | 549 | 57 | 283 | 200 | 213 | 139 | 156 | 255 | 225 | 262 | 299 | 99 | 160 | 105 | 337 | 439 | 269 | 117 | 98 | 132 | 197 | 173 | 126 |
| Stoke-on-Trent | 381 | 108 | 243 | 47 | 75 | 217 | 127 | 137 | 140 | 150 | 64 | 36 | 74 | 236 | 241 | 202 | 348 | 248 | 95 | 201 | 122 | 410 | 179 | 121 | 117 | 78 | 55 | 87 | 56 | 36 | 142 | 173 | 171 | 55 | 118 | 311 | 287 | 241 | 201 | 147 | 168 | 50 | 35 | 183 | 199 |
| Swansea | 529 | 76 | 368 | 124 | 220 | 209 | 80 | 236 | 41 | 279 | 150 | 184 | 244 | 264 | 370 | 154 | 477 | 375 | 91 | 279 | 172 | 578 | 279 | 249 | 262 | 229 | 174 | 226 | 168 | 187 | 293 | 323 | 286 | 178 | 144 | 266 | 446 | 196 | 175 | 147 | 136 | 202 | 124 | 159 | 245 | 159 |
| Thurso | 212 | 584 | 304 | 557 | 461 | 728 | 644 | 589 | 640 | 352 | 552 | 529 | 475 | 706 | 262 | 715 | 169 | 268 | 604 | 657 | 589 | 108 | 654 | 402 | 492 | 453 | 544 | 510 | 463 | 471 | 410 | 367 | 613 | 519 | 621 | 823 | 220 | 758 | 709 | 662 | 664 | 506 | 523 | 682 | 659 | 502 | 631 |
| Worcester | 448 | 96 | 309 | 29 | 135 | 162 | 62 | 119 | 73 | 220 | 46 | 68 | 124 | 197 | 306 | 136 | 418 | 311 | 28 | 168 | 151 | 480 | 174 | 169 | 166 | 146 | 72 | 118 | 108 | 101 | 203 | 229 | 180 | 85 | 57 | 244 | 350 | 177 | 146 | 95 | 101 | 103 | 49 | 124 | 150 | 65 | 97 | 572 |
| York | 345 | 193 | 201 | 129 | 34 | 269 | 227 | 151 | 237 | 116 | 129 | 84 | 33 | 269 | 187 | 289 | 314 | 214 | 181 | 232 | 185 | 344 | 200 | 81 | 38 | 24 | 108 | 76 | 96 | 65 | 48 | 83 | 176 | 84 | 174 | 400 | 230 | 331 | 257 | 217 | 244 | 54 | 132 | 244 | 214 | 114 | 268 | 450 | 164 |
| London | 537 | 228 | 440 | 118 | 203 | 53 | 118 | 61 | 151 | 309 | 97 | 129 | 171 | 76 | 403 | 179 | 511 | 404 | 116 | 86 | 277 | 562 | 82 | 263 | 214 | 195 | 103 | 155 | 211 | 209 | 251 | 283 | 117 | 128 | 59 | 285 | 451 | 216 | 84 | 41 | 92 | 166 | 161 | 82 | 43 | 161 | 187 | 669 | 136 | 211 |

## Scales to Map Pages

BRITAIN
1:221,760 = 3.5 miles to 1 inch (2.54 cm)
2.2 km to 1 cm

0 1 2 3 4 5 10 15 20 25 Miles
0 1 2 3 4 5 10 15 20 25 30 35 40 Kilometres

NORTHERN IRELAND
1:380,160 = 6 miles to 1 inch (2.54 cm)
3.8 km to 1 cm

0 1 2 3 4 5 10 15 20 25 Miles
0 1 2 3 4 5 10 15 20 25 30 35 40 Kilometres

# Limited Interchange Motorway Junctions



Limited Interchange Motorway Junctions are shown on the mapping pages by red junction indicators 2

## M1

| Junction | Direction | Restriction |
|---|---|---|
| 2 | Northbound | No exit, access from A1 only |
| | Southbound | No access, exit to A1 only |
| 4 | Northbound | No exit, access from A41 only |
| | Southbound | No access, exit to A41 only |
| 6a | Northbound | No exit, access from M25 only |
| | Southbound | No access, exit to M25 only |
| 17 | Northbound | No access, exit to M45 only |
| | Southbound | No exit, access from M45 only |
| 19 | Northbound | Exit to M6 only, access from A14 only |
| | Southbound | Access from M6 only, exit to A14 only |
| 21a | Northbound | No access, exit to A46 only |
| | Southbound | No exit, access from A46 only |
| 24a | Northbound | No exit |
| | Southbound | Access from A50 only |
| 35a | Northbound | No access, exit to A616 only |
| | Southbound | No exit, access from A616 only |
| 43 | Northbound | Exit to M621 only |
| | Southbound | Access from M621 only |
| 48 | Eastbound | Exit to A1(M) northbound only |
| | Westbound | Access from A1(M) southbound only |

## M2

| Junction | Direction | Restriction |
|---|---|---|
| 1 | Eastbound | Access from A2 eastbound only |
| | Westbound | Exit to A2 westbound only |

## M3

| Junction | Direction | Restriction |
|---|---|---|
| 8 | Eastbound | No exit, access from A303 only |
| | Westbound | No access, exit to A303 only |
| 10 | Northbound | No access from A31 |
| | Southbound | No exit to A31 |
| 13 | Southbound | No access from A335 to M3 leading to M27 Eastbound |

## M4

| Junction | Direction | Restriction |
|---|---|---|
| 1 | Eastbound | Exit to A4 eastbound only |
| | Westbound | Access from A4 westbound only |
| 21 | Eastbound | No exit to M48 |
| | Westbound | No access from M48 |
| 23 | Eastbound | No access from M48 |
| | Westbound | No exit to M48 |
| 25 | Eastbound | No exit |
| | Westbound | No access |
| 25a | Eastbound | No exit |
| | Westbound | No access |
| 29 | Eastbound | No exit, access from A48(M) only |
| | Westbound | No access, exit to A48(M) only |
| 38 | Westbound | No access, exit to A48 only |
| 39 | Eastbound | No access or exit |
| | Westbound | No exit, access from A48 only |
| 42 | Eastbound | No access from A48 |
| | Westbound | No exit to A48 |

## M5

| Junction | Direction | Restriction |
|---|---|---|
| 10 | Northbound | No exit, access from A4019 only |
| | Southbound | No access, exit to A4019 only |
| 11a | Southbound | No exit to A417 westbound |
| 18a | Northbound | No access from M49 |
| | Southbound | No exit to M49 |

## M6

| Junction | Direction | Restriction |
|---|---|---|
| 3a | Eastbound | No exit to M6 Toll |
| | Westbound | No access from M6 Toll |
| 4 | Northbound | No exit to M42 northbound<br>No access from M42 southbound |
| | Southbound | No exit to M42<br>No access from M42 southbound |
| 4a | Northbound | No exit, access from M42 S'bound only |
| | Southbound | No access, exit to M42 only |
| 5 | Northbound | No access, exit to A452 only |
| | Southbound | No exit, access from A452 only |
| 10a | Northbound | No access, exit to M54 only |
| | Southbound | No exit, access from M54 only |
| 11a | Northbound | No exit to M6 Toll |
| | Southbound | No access from M6 Toll |
| 20 | Northbound | No exit to M56 eastbound |
| | Southbound | No access from M56 westbound |
| 24 | Northbound | No exit, access from A58 only |
| | Southbound | No access, exit to A58 only |
| 25 | Northbound | No access, exit to A49 only |
| | Southbound | No exit, access from A49 only |
| 30 | Northbound | No exit, access from M61 N'bound only |
| | Southbound | No access, exit to M61 S'bound only |
| 31a | Northbound | No access, exit to B6242 only |
| | Southbound | No exit, access from B6242 only |
| 45 | Northbound | No access onto A74(M) |
| | Southbound | No exit from A74(M) |

## M6 Toll

| Junction | Direction | Restriction |
|---|---|---|
| T1 | Northbound | No exit |
| | Southbound | No access |
| T2 | Northbound | No access or exit |
| | Southbound | No access |
| T5 | Northbound | No exit |
| | Southbound | No access |
| T7 | Northbound | No access from A5 |
| | Southbound | No exit |
| T8 | Northbound | No exit to A460 northbound |
| | Southbound | No exit |

## M8

| Junction | Direction | Restriction |
|---|---|---|
| 6 | Eastbound | No exit, access only |
| | Westbound | No access, exit only |
| 6a | Eastbound | No access, exit only |
| | Westbound | No exit, access only |
| 7 | Eastbound | No access, exit only |
| | Westbound | No exit, access only |
| 7a | Eastbound | No exit, access from A725 Northbound only |
| | Westbound | No access, exit to A725 Southbound only |
| 8 | Eastbound | No exit to M73 northbound |
| | Westbound | No access from M73 southbound |
| 9 | Eastbound | No access, exit only |
| | Westbound | No exit, access only |
| 13 | Eastbound | No access from M80 southbound |
| | Westbound | No exit to M80 northbound |
| 14 | Eastbound | No access, exit only |
| | Westbound | No exit, access only |
| 16 | Eastbound | No exit, access only |
| | Westbound | No access, exit only |
| 17 | Eastbound | No exit, access from A82 only |
| | Westbound | No access, exit to A82 only |
| 18 | Westbound | No exit, access only |
| 19 | Eastbound | No exit to A814 eastbound |
| | Westbound | No access from A814 westbound |
| 20 | Eastbound | No exit, access only |
| | Westbound | No access, exit only |
| 21 | Eastbound | No access, exit only |
| | Westbound | No exit, access only |
| 22 | Eastbound | No exit, access from M77 only |
| | Westbound | No access, exit to M77 only |
| 23 | Eastbound | No exit, access from B768 only |
| | Westbound | No access, exit to B768 only |
| 25 | Eastbound & Westbound | Access from A739 southbound only<br>Exit to A739 northbound only |
| 25a | Eastbound | Access only |
| | Westbound | Exit only |
| 28 | Eastbound | No exit, access from airport only |
| | Westbound | No access, exit to airport only |
| 29a | Eastbound | No exit, access only |
| | Westbound | No access, exit only |

## M9

| Junction | Direction | Restriction |
|---|---|---|
| 2 | Northbound | No exit, access from B8046 only |
| | Southbound | No access, exit to B8046 only |
| 3 | Northbound | No access, exit to A803 only |
| | Southbound | No exit, access from A803 only |
| 6 | Northbound | No exit, access only |
| | Southbound | No access, exit to A905 only |
| 8 | Northbound | No access, exit to M876 only |
| | Southbound | No exit, access from M876 only |

## M11

| Junction | Direction | Restriction |
|---|---|---|
| 4 | Northbound | No exit, access from A406 E'bound only |
| | Southbound | No access, exit to A406 W'bound only |
| 5 | Northbound | No access, exit to A1168 only |
| | Southbound | No exit, access from A1168 only |
| 8a | Northbound | No access, exit only |
| | Southbound | No exit, access only |
| 9 | Northbound | No access, exit only |
| | Southbound | No exit, access only |
| 13 | Northbound | No access, exit only |
| | Southbound | No exit, access only |
| 14 | Northbound | No access from A428 eastbound<br>No exit to A428 westbound |
| | Southbound | No exit, access from A428 E'bound only |

## M20

| Junction | Direction | Restriction |
|---|---|---|
| 2 | Eastbound | No access, exit to A20 only (access via M26 Junction 2a) |
| | Westbound | No exit, access only (exit via M26 J2a) |
| 3 | Eastbound | No exit, access from M26 E'bound only |
| | Westbound | No access, exit to M26 W'bound only |
| 10 | Eastbound | No access, exit only |
| | Westbound | No exit, access only |
| 11a | Eastbound | No access from Channel Tunnel |
| | Westbound | No exit to Channel Tunnel |

## M23

| Junction | Direction | Restriction |
|---|---|---|
| 7 | Northbound | No exit to A23 southbound |
| | Southbound | No access from A23 northbound |

## M25

| Junction | Direction | Restriction |
|---|---|---|
| 5 | Clockwise | No exit to M26 eastbound |
| | Anti-clockwise | No access from M26 westbound |
| Spur to A21 | Northbound | No exit to M26 eastbound |
| | Southbound | No access from M26 westbound |
| 19 | Clockwise | No access, exit only |
| | Anti-clockwise | No exit, access only |
| 21 | Clockwise & Anti-clockwise | No exit to M1 southbound<br>No access from M1 northbound |
| 31 | Northbound | No access, exit only (access via J.30) |
| | Southbound | No exit, access only (exit via J.30) |

## M26

**Junction with M25** (M25 Jun.5)

| Direction | Restriction |
|---|---|
| Eastbound | No access from M25 clockwise or spur from A21 northbound |
| Westbound | No exit to M25 anti-clockwise or spur to A21 southbound |

**Junction with M20** (M20 Jun.3)

| Direction | Restriction |
|---|---|
| Eastbound | No exit to M20 westbound |
| Westbound | No access from M20 eastbound |

## M27

| Junction | Direction | Restriction |
|---|---|---|
| 4 | Eastbound & Westbound | No exit to A33 S'bound (Southampton)<br>No access from A33 northbound |
| 10 | Eastbound | No exit, access from A32 only |
| | Westbound | No access, exit to A32 only |

## M40

| Junction | Direction | Restriction |
|---|---|---|
| 3 | North-Westbound | No access, exit to A40 only |
| | South-Eastbound | No exit, access from A40 only |
| 7 | N.W bound | No access, exit only |
| | S.E bound | No exit, access only |
| 13 | N.W bound | No access, exit only |
| | S.E bound | No exit, access only |
| 14 | N.W bound | No exit, access only |
| | S.E bound | No access, exit only |
| 16 | N.W bound | No exit, access only |
| | S.E bound | No access, exit only |

## M42

| Junction | Direction | Restriction |
|---|---|---|
| 1 | Eastbound | No exit |
| | Westbound | No access |
| 7 | Northbound | No access, exit to M6 only |
| | Southbound | No exit, access from M6 N'bound only |
| 8 | Northbound | No exit, access from M6 S'bound only |
| | Southbound | Exit to M6 nothbound only<br>Access from M6 southbound only |

## M45

**Junction with M1** (M1 Jun.17)

| Direction | Restriction |
|---|---|
| Eastbound | No exit to M1 northbound |
| Westbound | No access from M1 southbound |

**Junction with A45 east of Dunchurch**

| Direction | Restriction |
|---|---|
| Eastbound | No access, exit to A45 only |
| Westbound | No exit, access from A45 N'bound only |

## M48

**Junction with M4** (M4 Jun.21)

| Direction | Restriction |
|---|---|
| Eastbound | No exit to M4 westbound |
| Westbound | No access from M4 eastbound |

**Junction with M4** (M4 Jun.23)

| Direction | Restriction |
|---|---|
| Eastbound | No access from M4 westbound |
| Westbound | No exit to M4 eastbound |

## M53

| Junction | Direction | Restriction |
|---|---|---|
| 11 | Northbound & Southbound | No access from M56 eastbound, no exit to M56 westbound |

## M56

| Junction | Direction | Restriction |
|---|---|---|
| 1 | Eastbound | No exit to M60 N.W bound<br>No exit to A34 southbound |
| | S.E bound | No access from A34 northbound |
| | Westbound | No access from M60 |
| 2 | Eastbound | No exit, access from A560 only |
| | Westbound | No access, exit to A560 only |
| 3 | Eastbound | No access, exit only |
| | Westbound | No exit, access only |
| 4 | Eastbound | No exit, access only |
| | Westbound | No access, exit only |
| 7 | Westbound | No access, exit only |
| 8 | Eastbound | No access or exit |
| | Westbound | No exit, access from A556 only |
| 9 | Eastbound | No access from M6 northbound |
| | Westbound | No exit to M60 southbound |
| 10a | Northbound | No exit, access only |
| | Southbound | No access, exit only |
| 15 | Eastbound | No exit to M53 |
| | Westbound | No access from M53 |

## M57

| Junction | Direction | Restriction |
|---|---|---|
| 3 | Northbound | No exit, access only |
| | Southbound | No access, exit only |
| 5 | Northbound | No exit, access from A580 W'bound only |
| | Southbound | No access, exit to A580 E'bound only |

## M60

| Junction | Direction | Restriction |
|---|---|---|
| 2 | N.E bound | No access, exit to A560 only |
| | S.W bound | No exit, access from A560 only |
| 3 | Eastbound | No access from A34 southbound |
| | Westbound | No exit to A34 northbound |
| 4 | Eastbound | No exit to M56 S.W bound<br>No exit to A34 northbound |
| | Westbound | No access from A34 southbound<br>No access from M56 eastbound |
| 5 | N.W bound | No access from or exit to A5103 S'bound |
| | S.E bound | No access from or exit to A5103 N'bound |
| 14 | Eastbound | No exit to A580<br>No access from A580 westbound |
| | Westbound | No exit to A580 eastbound<br>No access from A580 |
| 16 | Eastbound | No exit, access from A666 only |
| | Westbound | No access, exit to A666 only |
| 20 | Eastbound | No access from A664 |
| | Westbound | No exit to A664 |
| 22 | Westbound | No access from A62 |
| 25 | S.W bound | No access from A560 / A6017 |
| 26 | N.E bound | No access or exit |
| 27 | N.E bound | No access, exit only |
| | S.W bound | No exit, access only |

## M61

| Junction | Direction | Restriction |
|---|---|---|
| 2&3 | N.W bound | No access from A580 eastbound |
| | S.E bound | No exit to A580 westbound |

**Junction with M6** (M6 Jun.30)

| Direction | Restriction |
|---|---|
| N.W bound | No exit to M6 southbound |
| S.E bound | No access from M6 northbound |

## M62

| Junction | Direction | Restriction |
|---|---|---|
| 23 | Eastbound | No access, exit to A640 only |
| | Westbound | No exit, access from A640 only |

## M65

| Junction | Direction | Restriction |
|---|---|---|
| 9 | N.E bound | No access, exit to A679 only |
| | S.W bound | No exit, access from A679 only |
| 11 | N.E bound | No exit, access only |
| | S.W bound | No access, exit only |

## M66

| Junction | Direction | Restriction |
|---|---|---|
| 1 | Northbound | No access, exit to A56 only |
| | Southbound | No exit, access from A56 only |

## M67

| Junction | Direction | Restriction |
|---|---|---|
| 1 | Eastbound | Access from A57 eastbound only |
| | Westbound | Exit to A57 westbound only |
| 1a | Eastbound | No access, exit to A6017 only |
| | Westbound | No exit, access from A6017 only |
| 2 | Eastbound | No exit, access from A57 only |
| | Westbound | No access, exit to A57 only |

## M69

| Junction | Direction | Restriction |
|---|---|---|
| 2 | N.E bound | No exit, access from B4669 only |
| | S.W bound | No access, exit to B4669 only |

## M73

| Junction | Direction | Restriction |
|---|---|---|
| 1 | Southbound | No exit to A721 eastbound |
| 2 | Northbound | No access from M8 eastbound<br>No exit to A89 eastbound |
| | Southbound | No exit to M8 westbound<br>No access from A89 westbound |
| 3 | Northbound | No exit to A80 S.W bound |
| | Southbound | No access from A80 N.E bound |

## M74

| Junction | Direction | Restriction |
|---|---|---|
| 1 | Eastbound | No access from M8 Westbound |
| | Westbound | No exit to M8 Westbound |
| 3 | Eastbound | No exit |
| | Westbound | No access |
| 7 | Northbound | No exit, access from A72 only |
| | Southbound | No access, exit to A72 only |
| 9 | Northbound | No access or exit |
| | Southbound | No access, exit to B7078 only |
| 10 | Southbound | No exit, access from B7078 only |
| 11 | Northbound | No exit, access from B7078 only |
| | Southbound | No access, exit to B7078 only |
| 12 | Northbound | No access, exit to A70 only |
| | Southbound | No exit, access from A70 only |

## M77

**Junction with M8** (M8 Jun.22)

| Direction | Restriction |
|---|---|
| Northbound | No exit to M8 westbound |
| Southbound | No access from M8 eastbound |

| Junction | Direction | Restriction |
|---|---|---|
| 4 | Northbound | No exit |
| | Southbound | No access |
| 6 | Northbound | No exit to A77 |
| | Southbound | No access from A77 |
| 7 | Northbound | No access from A77<br>No exit to A77 |

## M80

| Junction | Direction | Restriction |
|---|---|---|
| 1 | Northbound | No access from M8 westbound |
| | Southbound | No exit to M8 eastbound |
| 4a | Northbound | No access |
| | Southbound | No exit |
| 6a | Northbound | No exit |
| | Southbound | No access |
| 8 | Northbound | No access from M876 |
| | Southbound | No exit to M876 |

## M90

| Junction | Direction | Restriction |
|---|---|---|
| 1 | Northbound | No exit |
| | Southbound | No Access from A90 |
| 2a | Northbound | No access, exit to A92 only |
| | Southbound | No exit, access from A92 only |
| 7 | Northbound | No exit, access from A91 only |
| | Southbound | No access, exit to A91 only |
| 8 | Northbound | No access, exit to A91 only |
| | Southbound | No exit, access from A91 only |
| 10 | Northbound | No access from A912<br>Exit to A912 northbound only |
| | Southbound | No exit to A912<br>Access from A912 southbound only |

## M180

| Junction | Direction | Restriction |
|---|---|---|
| 1 | Eastbound | No access, exit only |
| | Westbound | No exit, access from A18 only |

## M606

| Junction | Direction | Restriction |
|---|---|---|
| 2 | Northbound | No access, exit only |

## M621

| Junction | Direction | Restriction |
|---|---|---|
| 2a | Eastbound | No exit, access only |
| | Westbound | No access, exit only |
| 4 | Southbound | No exit |
| 5 | Northbound | No access, exit to A61 only |
| | Southbound | No exit, access from A61 only |
| 6 | Northbound | No exit, access only |
| | Southbound | No access, exit only |
| 7 | Eastbound | No access, exit only |
| | Westbound | No exit, access only |
| 8 | Northbound | No access, exit only |
| | Southbound | No exit, access only |

## M876

**Junction with M80** (M80 Jun.5)

| Direction | Restriction |
|---|---|
| N.E bound | No access from M80 southbound |
| S.W bound | No exit to M80 northbound |

**Junction with M9** (M9 Jun.8)

| Direction | Restriction |
|---|---|
| N.E bound | No exit to M9 northbound |
| S.W bound | No access from M9 southbound |

## A1(M)

**Hertfordshire Section**

| Junction | Direction | Restriction |
|---|---|---|
| 2 | Northbound | No access, exit only |
| | Southbound | No exit, access from A1001 only |
| 3 | Southbound | No access, exit only |
| 5 | Northbound | No exit, access only |
| | Southbound | No access or exit |

**Cambridgeshire Section**

| Junction | Direction | Restriction |
|---|---|---|
| 14 | Northbound | No exit, access only |
| | Southbound | No access, exit only |

**Leeds Section**

| Junction | Direction | Restriction |
|---|---|---|
| 40 | Southbound | Exit to A1 southbound only |
| 43 | Northbound | Access from M1 eastbound only |
| | Southbound | Exit to M1 westbound only |

**Durham Section**

| Junction | Direction | Restriction |
|---|---|---|
| 57 | Northbound | No access, exit to A66(M) only |
| | Southbound | No exit, access from A66(M) |
| 65 | Northbound | Exit to A1 N.W bound and to A194(M) only |
| | Southbound | Access from A1 S.E bound and from A194(M) only |

## A3(M)

| Junction | Direction | Restriction |
|---|---|---|
| 4 | Northbound | No access, exit only |
| | Southbound | No exit, access only |

## Aston Expressway A38(M)

**Junction with Victoria Road, Aston**

| Direction | Restriction |
|---|---|
| Northbound | No exit, access only |
| Southbound | No access, exit only |

## A48(M)

**Junction with M4** (M4 Jun.29)

| Direction | Restriction |
|---|---|
| N.E bound | Exit to M4 eastbound only |
| S.W bound | Access from M4 westbound only |

| Junction | Direction | Restriction |
|---|---|---|
| 29a | N.E bound | Access from A48 eastbound only |
| | S.W bound | Exit to A48 westbound only |

## Mancunian Way A57(M)

**Junction with A34 Brook Street, Manchester**

| Direction | Restriction |
|---|---|
| Eastbound | No access, exit to A34 Brook Street, southbound only |
| Westbound | No exit, access only |

## Leeds Inner Ring Road A58(M)

**Junction with Park Lane / Westgate**

| Direction | Restriction |
|---|---|
| Southbound | No access, exit only |

## Leeds Inner Ring Road A64(M) (continuation of A58(M))

**Junction with A58 Clay Pit Lane**

| Direction | Restriction |
|---|---|
| Eastbound | No access |
| Westbound | No exit |

## A66(M)

**Junction with A1(M)** (A1(M) Jun.57)

| Direction | Restriction |
|---|---|
| N.E bound | Access from A1(M) N'bound only |
| S.W bound | Exit to A1(M) southbound only |

## A74(M)

| Junction | Direction | Restriction |
|---|---|---|
| 18 | Northbound | No access |
| | Southbound | No exit |

## Newcastle Central Motorway A167(M)

**Junction with Camden Street**

| Direction | Restriction |
|---|---|
| Northbound | No exit, access only |
| Southbound | No access or exit |

## A194(M)

**Junction with A1(M)** (A1(M) Jun.65) **and A1 Gateshead Western By-Pass**

| Direction | Restriction |
|---|---|
| Northbound | Access from A1(M) only |
| Southbound | Exit to A1(M) only |

# Northern Ireland

## M1

| Junction | Direction | Restriction |
|---|---|---|
| 3 | Northbound | No exit, access only |
| | Southbound | No access, exit only |
| 7 | Westbound | No access, exit only |

## M2

| Junction | Direction | Restriction |
|---|---|---|
| 2 | Eastbound | No access to M5 northbound |
| | Westbound | No exit to M5 southbound |

## M5

| Junction | Direction | Restriction |
|---|---|---|
| 2 | Northbound | No access from M2 eastbound |
| | Southbound | No exit to M2 westbound |

# Reference

Légende
Zeichenerklärung

**Motorway** M1
Autoroute
Autobahn

**Motorway Under Construction**
Autoroute en construction
Autobahn im Bau

**Motorway Proposed**
Autoroute prévue
Geplante Autobahn

**Motorway Junctions with Numbers**
Unlimited Interchange 4
Limited Interchange 5
Autoroute échangeur numéroté
Echangeur complet
Echangeur partiel
Autobahnanschlußstelle mit Nummer
Unbeschränkter Fahrtrichtungswechsel
Beschränkter Fahrtrichtungswechsel

**Motorway Service Area** (with fuel station)
with access from one carriageway only
Aire de services d'autoroute (avec station service)
accessible d'un seul côté
Rastplatz oder Raststätte (mit tankstelle)
Einbahn

**Major Road Service Area** (with fuel station) with 24 hour facilities
Primary Route — Class A Road
Aire de services sur route prioriataire (avec station service) Ouverte 24h sur 24
Route à grande circulation — Route de type A
Raststätte (mit tankstelle) Durchgehend geöffnet
Hauptverkehrsstraße — A- Straße

**Major Road Junctions** — Detailed / Détaillé / Ausführlich
Jonctions grands routiers
Hauptverkehrsstraße Kreuzungen
Other Autre Andere

**Truckstop** (selection of)
Sélection d'aire pour poids lourds
Auswahl von Fernfahrerrastplatz

**Primary Route** A41
Route à grande circulation
Hauptverkehrsstraße

**Primary Route Junction with Number** 5
Echangeur numéroté
Hauptverkehrsstraßenkreuzung mit Nummer

**Primary Route Destination** DOVER
Route prioritaire, direction
Hauptverkehrsstraße Richtung

**Dual Carriageways** (A & B roads)
Route à double chaussées séparées (route A & B)
Zweispurige Schnellstraße (A- und B- Straßen)

**Class A Road** A129
Route de type A
A-Straße

**Class B Road** B177
Route de type B
B-Straße

**Narrow Major Road** (passing places)
Route prioritaire étroite (possibilité de dépassement)
Schmale Hauptverkehrsstaße (mit Überholmöglichkeit)

**Major Roads Under Construction**
Route prioritaire en construction
Hauptverkehrsstaße im Bau

**Major Roads Proposed**
Route prioritaire prévue
Geplante Hauptverkehrsstaße

**Gradient 1:7** (14%) **& steeper**
(descent in direction of arrow)
Pente égale ou supérieure à 14% (dans le sens de la descente)
14% Steigung und steiler (in Pfeilrichtung)

**Toll** Toll
Barrière de péage
Gebührenpflichtig

**Dart Charge**
www.gov.uk/pay-dartford-crossing-charge

**Park & Ride** P+R
Parking avec Service Navette
Parken und Reisen

**Mileage between markers** 8
Distence en miles entre les flèches
Strecke zwischen Markierungen in Meilen

**Airport**
Aéroport
Flughafen

**Airfield**
Terrain d'aviation
Flugplatz

**Heliport**
Héliport
Hubschrauberlandeplatz

**Ferry** — Bac — Fähre
(vehicular, sea) — (véhicules, mer) — (auto, meer)
(vehicular, river) — (véhicules, rivière) — (auto, fluß)
(foot only) — (piétons) — (nur für Personen)

**Railway and Station**
Voie ferrée et gare
Eisenbahnlinie und Bahnhof

**Level Crossing and Tunnel**
Passage à niveau et tunnel
Bahnübergang und Tunnel

**River or Canal**
Rivière ou canal
Fluß oder Kanal

**County or Unitary Authority Boundary**
Limite de comté ou de division administrative
Grafschafts- oder Verwaltungsbezirksgrenze

**National Boundary**
Frontière nationale
Landesgrenze

**Built-up Area**
Agglomération
Geschloßene Ortschaft

**Town, Village or Hamlet**
Ville, Village ou hameau
Stadt, Dorf oder Weiler

**Wooded Area**
Zone boisée
Waldgebiet

**Spot Height in Feet** • 813
Altitude (en pieds)
Höhe in Fuß

**Relief above 400'** (122m)
Relief par estompage au-dessus de 400' (122m)
Reliefschattierung über 400' (122m)

**National Grid Reference** (kilometres) [1]00
Coordonnées géographiques nationales (Kilomètres)
Nationale geographische Koordinaten (Kilometer)

**Page Continuation** 48
Suite à la page indiquée
Seitenfortsetzung

**Area covered by Main Route map** MAIN ROUTE 94
Repartition des cartes des principaux axes routiers
Von Karten mit Hauptverkehrsstrecken

**Area covered by Town Plan** PAGE 109
Ville ayant un plan à la page indiquée
Von Karten mit Stadtplänen erfaßter Bereich

# Tourist Information

Information
Touristeninformationen

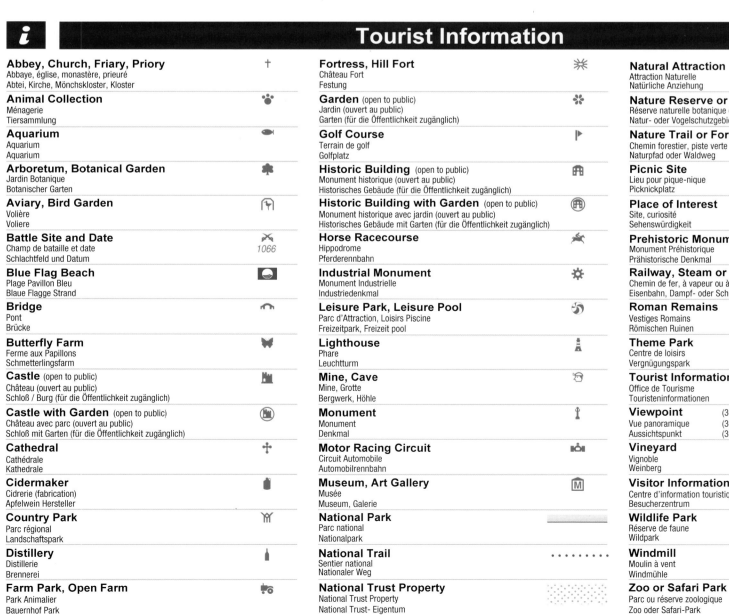

**Abbey, Church, Friary, Priory**
Abbaye, église, monastère, prieuré
Abtei, Kirche, Mönchskloster, Kloster

**Animal Collection**
Ménagerie
Tiersammlung

**Aquarium**
Aquarium
Aquarium

**Arboretum, Botanical Garden**
Jardin Botanique
Botanischer Garten

**Aviary, Bird Garden**
Volière
Voliere

**Battle Site and Date** 1066
Champ de bataille et date
Schlachtfeld und Datum

**Blue Flag Beach**
Plage Pavillon Bleu
Blaue Flagge Strand

**Bridge**
Pont
Brücke

**Butterfly Farm**
Ferme aux Papillons
Schmetterlingsfarm

**Castle** (open to public)
Château (ouvert au public)
Schloß / Burg (für die Öffentlichkeit zugänglich)

**Castle with Garden** (open to public)
Château avec parc (ouvert au public)
Schloß mit Garten (für die Öffentlichkeit zugänglich)

**Cathedral**
Cathédrale
Kathedrale

**Cidermaker**
Cidrerie (fabrication)
Apfelwein Hersteller

**Country Park**
Parc régional
Landschaftspark

**Distillery**
Distillerie
Brennerei

**Farm Park, Open Farm**
Park Animalier
Bauernhof Park

**Fortress, Hill Fort**
Château Fort
Festung

**Garden** (open to public)
Jardin (ouvert au public)
Garten (für die Öffentlichkeit zugänglich)

**Golf Course**
Terrain de golf
Golfplatz

**Historic Building** (open to public)
Monument historique (ouvert au public)
Historisches Gebäude (für die Öffentlichkeit zugänglich)

**Historic Building with Garden** (open to public)
Monument historique avec jardin (ouvert au public)
Historisches Gebäude mit Garten (für die Öffentlichkeit zugänglich)

**Horse Racecourse**
Hippodrome
Pferderennbahn

**Industrial Monument**
Monument Industrielle
Industriedenkmal

**Leisure Park, Leisure Pool**
Parc d'Attraction, Loisirs Piscine
Freizeitpark, Freizeit pool

**Lighthouse**
Phare
Leuchtturm

**Mine, Cave**
Mine, Grotte
Bergwerk, Höhle

**Monument**
Monument
Denkmal

**Motor Racing Circuit**
Circuit Automobile
Automobilrennbahn

**Museum, Art Gallery**
Musée
Museum, Galerie

**National Park**
Parc national
Nationalpark

**National Trail**
Sentier national
Nationaler Weg

**National Trust Property**
National Trust Property
National Trust- Eigentum

**Natural Attraction**
Attraction Naturelle
Natürliche Anziehung

**Nature Reserve or Bird Sanctuary**
Réserve naturelle botanique ou ornithologique
Natur- oder Vogelschutzgebiet

**Nature Trail or Forest Walk**
Chemin forestier, piste verte
Naturpfad oder Waldweg

**Picnic Site**
Lieu pour pique-nique
Picknickplatz

**Place of Interest** Craft Centre •
Site, curiosité
Sehenswürdigkeit

**Prehistoric Monument**
Monument Préhistorique
Prähistorische Denkmal

**Railway, Steam or Narrow Gauge**
Chemin de fer, à vapeur ou à voie étroite
Eisenbahn, Dampf- oder Schmalspurbahn

**Roman Remains**
Vestiges Romains
Römischen Ruinen

**Theme Park**
Centre de loisirs
Vergnügungspark

**Tourist Information Centre**
Office de Tourisme
Touristeninformationen

**Viewpoint** — (360 degrees) (360 degrés) (360 Grade) — (180 degrees) (180 degrés) (180 Grade)
Vue panoramique
Aussichtspunkt

**Vineyard**
Vignoble
Weinberg

**Visitor Information Centre**
Centre d'information touristique
Besucherzentrum

**Wildlife Park**
Réserve de faune
Wildpark

**Windmill**
Moulin à vent
Windmühle

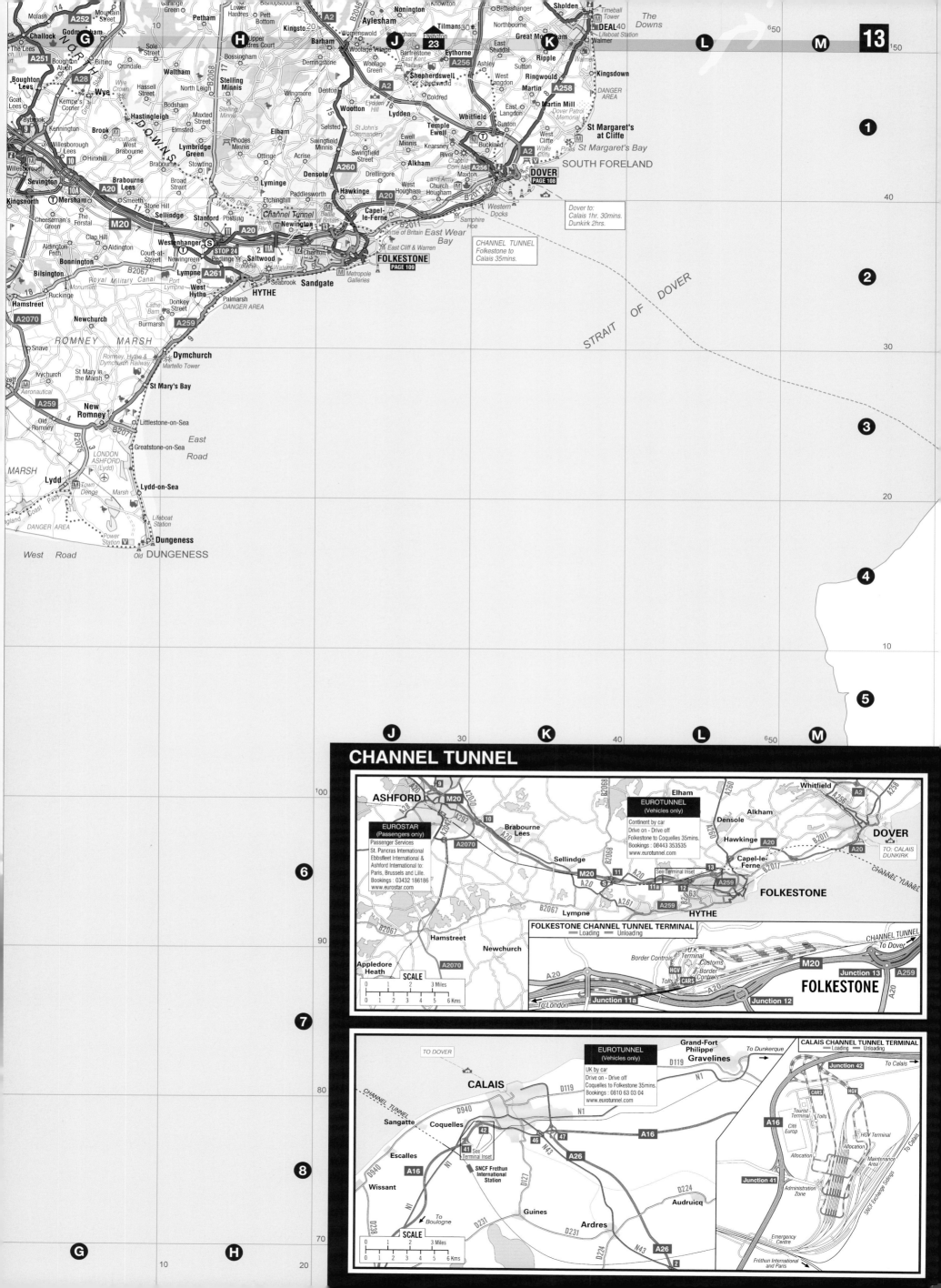

**Zoo or Safari Park**
Parc ou réserve zoologique
Zoo oder Safari-Park

G
H
J
K
L
M
ISLES OF SCILLY
Round Island
St Helen's
White Island
BRYHER
Tean
Lower Town
Middle Town
Day Mark
Old Grimsby
Higher Town
ST MARTIN'S
Gweal
New Grimsby
TRESCO
Maiden Bower
Valhalla Ships' Figurehead Collection
EASTERN ISLES
Mincarlo
Samson
Maypole
ISLES OF SCILLY
Hugh Town
ST MARY'S
North West Passage
Crim Rocks
Broad Sound
Annet
Old Town
Gugh
Western Rocks
ST AGNES
Bishop Rock
Hugh Town to Penzance 2hrs. 40mins. (Seasonal)
The Isles of Scilly lie 28 miles WSW of Land's End
ATLANTIC OCEAN
TREVOSE HEAD
Gulland Rock
Quies
Constantine Bay
Treyarnon
Porthcothan
Park Head
Bedruthan Steps
Berryl's Point
Trenance
Mawgan Porth
St Mawgan
Watergate Bay
Towan Head
NEWQUAY
Newquay Bay
Fistral Bay
Kelsey Head
Pentire
Crantock
Holywell Bay
Penhale Point
Cubert
Ligger or Perran Bay
St Newlyn East
Perranporth
Goonhavern
Mitchell
Bawden Rocks
St Agnes Head
St Agnes
Mithian
Porthtowan
Portreath
Crane Islands
Navax Point
Godrevy Island
Chacewater
Redruth
St Day
TRURO
Carharrack
The Carracks
St Ives Bay
St Ives
Gurnard's Head
Zennor
Hayle
Lelant
Copperhouse
CAMBORNE
Pendeen Watch
Pendeen
CORNWALL
Stithians
Penryn
FALMOUTH
St Mawes
Cape Cornwall
St Just
The Brisons
Madron
Newbridge
Sancreed
PENZANCE
Newlyn
Marazion
Perranuthnoe
Praa Sands
Germoe
Breage
Helston
Porthleven
Constantine
Mawnan
Pendennis Point
Falmouth Bay
Rosemullion Head
Nare Point
Manaccan
St Keverne
Manacle Point
The Manacles
Coverack
Whitesand Bay
Sennen
Longships
LAND'S END
St Buryan
St Clement's Isle
Cudden Point
Trewavas Head
Loe Bar
MOUNT'S BAY
Porthcurno
Treen
Cribba Head
Gwennap Head
Runnel Stone
Penzance to Hugh Town 2hrs. 40mins. (Seasonal)
Poldhu Point
Mullion
Mullion Cove
Mullion Island
Cury
Ruan Major
Ruan Minor
Cadgwith
Black Head
Vellan Head
Kynance Cove
Lizard
Hot Point
LIZARD POINT
A30
A39
A390
A393
A394
A3083
A3071
A3074
A3075
A3076
A3058
A3059
A3078
A392
1
2
3
4
5
6
7
8

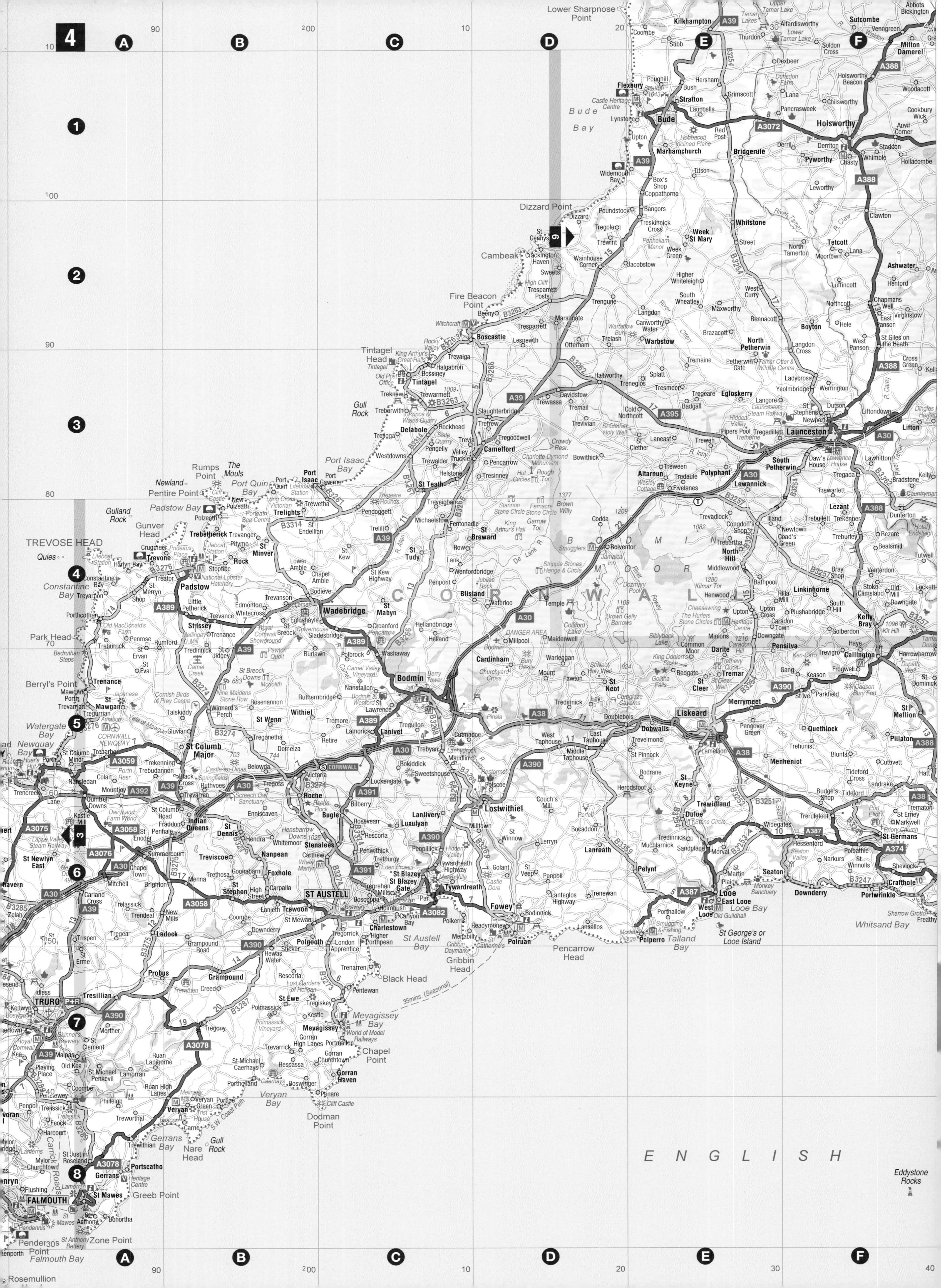

Lower Sharpnose Point
Kilkhampton
Sutcombe
Milton Damerel
Flexbury
Stratton
Bude
Bude Bay
Holsworthy
Marhamchurch
Bridgerule
Pyworthy
Widemouth Bay
Dizzard Point
Whitstone
Week St Mary
Cambeak
Crackington Haven
Tetcott
Ashwater
Fire Beacon Point
Boscastle
Warbstow
North Petherwin
Boyton
Tintagel Head
Tintagel
Gull Rock
Delabole
Camelford
Egloskerry
Launceston
Lifton
Port Isaac Bay
Port Isaac
Rumps Point
The Mouls
Pentire Point
Padstow Bay
Polzeath
Trebetherick
St Teath
Altarnun
South Petherwin
Polyphant
Lewannick
Gulland Rock
TREVOSE HEAD
Trevone
Padstow
Rock
St Minver
St Breward
BODMIN MOOR
CORNWALL
Constantine Bay
Wadebridge
St Mabyn
Blisland
Bolventor
North Hill
Linkinhorne
Park Head
St Issey
Bodmin
Cardinham
St Neot
Darite
Pensilva
Callington
Berryl's Point
Mawgan Porth
St Mawgan
Watergate Bay
Newquay Bay
St Columb Major
Lanivet
Liskeard
Dobwalls
Menheniot
St Mellion
Pillaton
Indian Queens
Roche
Bugle
Lostwithiel
St Keyne
Duloe
St Germans
St Newlyn East
Mitchell
Summercourt
St Dennis
Nanpean
Stenalees
St Blazey
Tywardreath
Fowey
Polruan
Lanreath
Pelynt
Looe
East Looe
West Looe
Seaton
Downderry
Crafthole
Portwrinkle
Whitsand Bay
ST AUSTELL
St Austell Bay
Charlestown
Par
Polperro
Talland Bay
Looe Bay
St George's or Looe Island
Pencarrow Head
Gribbin Head
Black Head
Mevagissey
Mevagissey Bay
Gorran Haven
Chapel Point
Dodman Point
Veryan Bay
Veryan
Probus
Grampound
Tregony
Ladock
TRURO
Tresillian
Portscatho
Gerrans
Gerrans Bay
Nare Head
Gull Rock
St Mawes
St Just in Roseland
FALMOUTH
Greeb Point
Zone Point
Pendennis Point
Falmouth Bay
Rosemullion
ENGLISH
Eddystone Rocks
A39
A30
A38
A388
A3072
A395
A389
A390
A391
A387
A374
A3058
A3059
A3075
A3076
A3078
A3082
A392
B3254
B3263
B3266
B3314
B3274
B3276
B3268
B3269
B3359
B3252
B3253
B3247
B3287
B3273
B3275
B3257
B3251
A
B
C
D
E
F
1
2
3
4
5
6
7
8
10
90
200
20
30
40
100
80
70
35mins. (Seasonal)

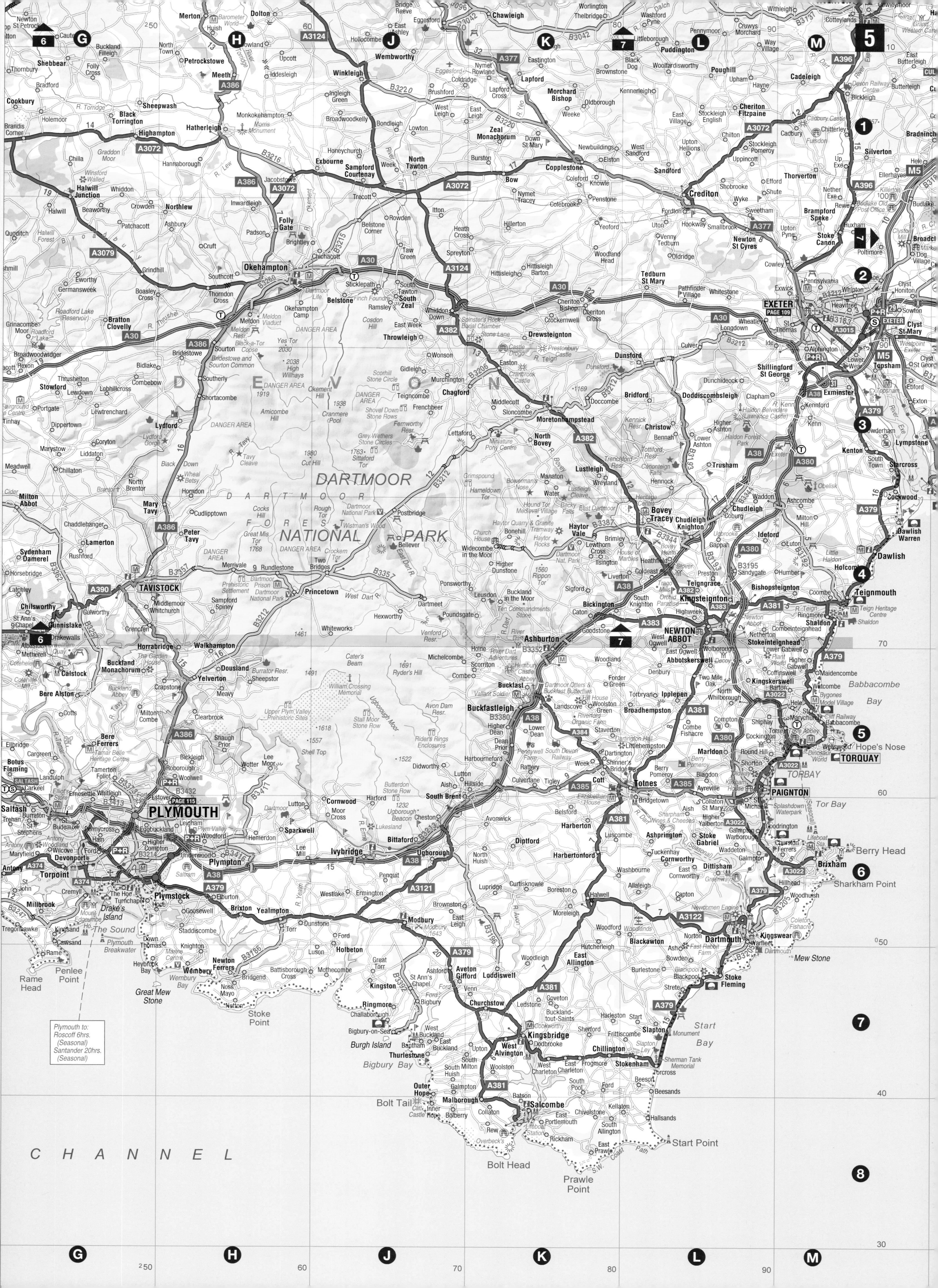
5
DEVON
DARTMOOR
DARTMOOR FOREST
NATIONAL PARK
DANGER AREA
CHANNEL
TORBAY
Tor Bay
Babbacombe Bay
Start Bay
Bigbury Bay
Plymouth Sound
The Sound
EXETER
PAGE 109
PLYMOUTH
PAGE 115
TORQUAY
PAIGNTON
NEWTON ABBOT
TAVISTOCK
Okehampton
Crediton
Teignmouth
Dawlish
Exmouth
Totnes
Dartmouth
Kingsbridge
Salcombe
Brixham
Ivybridge
Ashburton
Buckfastleigh
Moretonhampstead
Chagford
Bovey Tracey
Princetown
Yelverton
Plympton
Plymstock
Saltash
Torpoint
Hatherleigh
Tiverton
Silverton
Bow
Copplestone
Sandford
Kenton
Starcross
Chudleigh
Kingsteignton
Kingskerswell
Modbury
Yealmpton
Stoke Fleming
Slapton
Thurlestone
Bolt Tail
Bolt Head
Prawle Point
Start Point
Berry Head
Sharkham Point
Hope's Nose
Mew Stone
Rame Head
Penlee Point
Great Mew Stone
Stoke Point
Burgh Island
Plymouth to:
Roscoff 6hrs.
(Seasonal)
Santander 20hrs.
(Seasonal)
A30
A38
A379
A380
A381
A382
A383
A384
A385
A386
A390
A3072
A3079
A3121
A3122
A3124
A377
A396
A374
A3022
M5
G
H
J
K
L
M
1
2
3
4
5
6
7
8
250
60
70
80
90
30
40
50

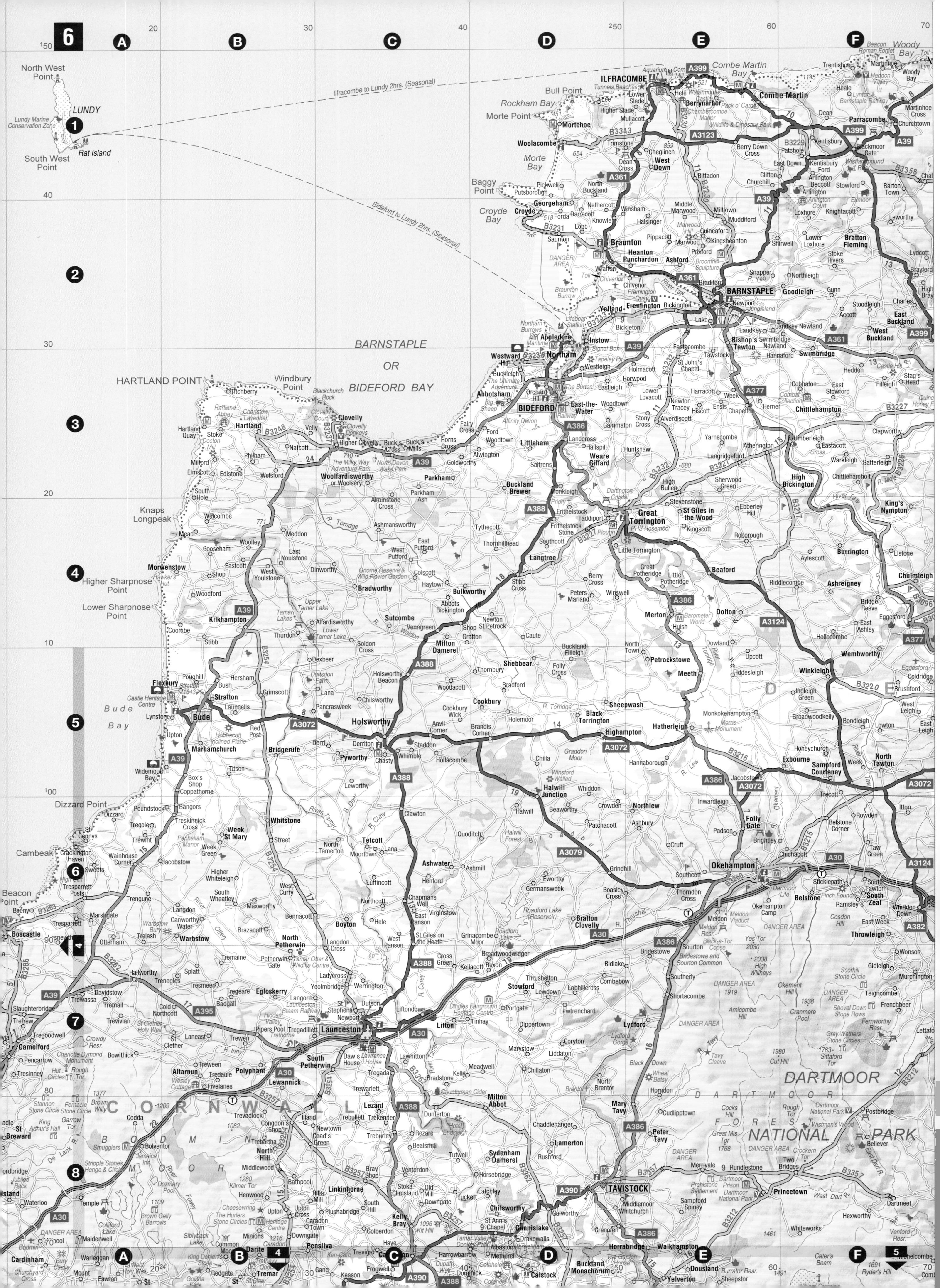

LUNDY
North West Point
South West Point
Rat Island
Lundy Marine Conservation Zone
Ilfracombe to Lundy 2hrs. (Seasonal)
Bideford to Lundy 2hrs. (Seasonal)
ILFRACOMBE
Combe Martin Bay
Combe Martin
Woody Bay
Bull Point
Rockham Bay
Morte Point
Mortehoe
Woolacombe
Morte Bay
Baggy Point
Croyde Bay
Croyde
Georgeham
Braunton
Heanton Punchardon
Ashford
BARNSTAPLE
Fremington
Bickington
Instow
Appledore
Westward Ho!
Northam
BIDEFORD
East-the-Water
BARNSTAPLE OR BIDEFORD BAY
HARTLAND POINT
Windbury Point
Clovelly
Hartland
Hartland Quay
Woolfardisworthy or Woolsery
Parkham
Littleham
Buckland Brewer
Great Torrington
St Giles in the Wood
Knaps Longpeak
Morwenstow
Higher Sharpnose Point
Lower Sharpnose Point
Kilkhampton
Bradworthy
Sutcombe
Milton Damerel
Shebbear
Merton
Dolton
Beaford
Winkleigh
Flexbury
Stratton
Bude
Bude Bay
Widemouth Bay
Marhamchurch
Bridgerule
Holsworthy
Pyworthy
Black Torrington
Sheepwash
Highampton
Hatherleigh
Exbourne
Sampford Courtenay
North Tawton
Dizzard Point
Week St Mary
Whitstone
Tetcott
Ashwater
Halwill Junction
Northlew
Folly Gate
Okehampton
Belstone
South Zeal
Cambeak
Crackington Haven
Beacon Point
Boscastle
Warbstow
North Petherwin
Bratton Clovelly
Bridestowe
Lydford
Launceston
Lifton
Camelford
Altarnun
Polyphant
Lewannick
South Petherwin
Milton Abbot
Mary Tavy
Peter Tavy
Lamerton
Sydenham Damerel
TAVISTOCK
Princetown
Two Bridges
Postbridge
Chilsworthy
Gunnislake
Calstock
Callington
Kelly Bray
Linkinhorne
North Hill
Bolventor
St Breward
Cardinham
Buckland Monachorum
Yelverton
Horrabridge
Walkhampton
Dousland
CORNWALL
BODMIN MOOR
DARTMOOR
DARTMOOR FOREST
NATIONAL PARK
DANGER AREA
A39
A361
A399
A3123
A386
A388
A377
A3072
A3124
A3079
A30
A395
A390
A382
B3233
B3231
B3343
B3230
B3227
B3232
B3217
B3216
B3248
B3237
B3254
B3263
B3262
B3257
B3362
B3357
B3212

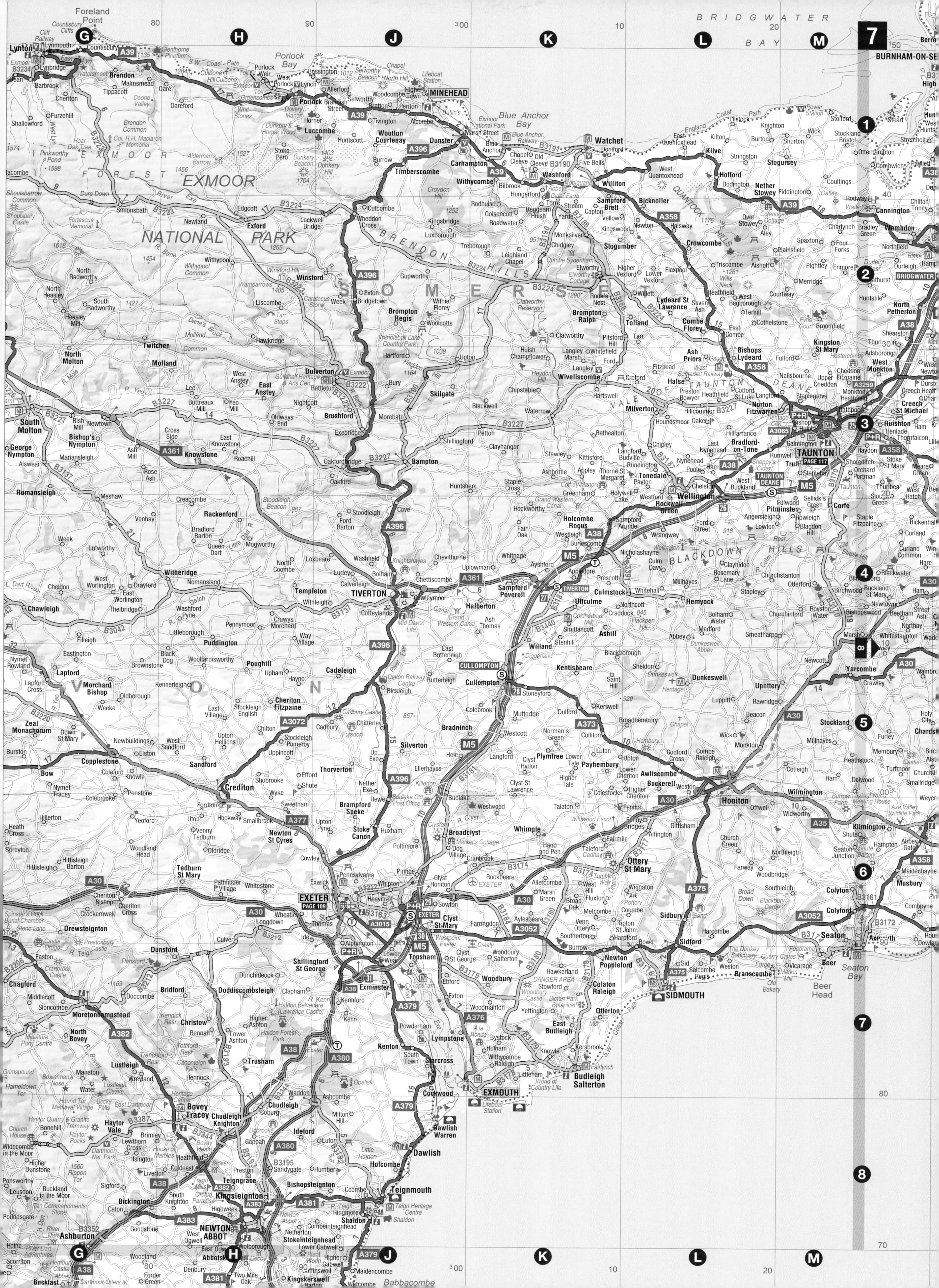
BRIDGWATER BAY
BURNHAM-ON-SEA
Foreland Point
Lynton
Lynmouth
Countisbury
Porlock Bay
Porlock
MINEHEAD
Blue Anchor Bay
Watchet
Dunster
Carhampton
Washford
Williton
EXMOOR
NATIONAL PARK
EXMOOR FOREST
BRENDON HILLS
QUANTOCK HILLS
S O M E R S E T
Exford
Simonsbath
Winsford
Dulverton
Bampton
Wiveliscombe
Milverton
Nether Stowey
Stogursey
Cannington
BRIDGWATER
North Petherton
TAUNTON
PAGE 117
TAUNTON DEANE
Wellington
Bishops Lydeard
BLACKDOWN HILLS
South Molton
TIVERTON
Witheridge
Uffculme
Culmstock
Hemyock
CULLOMPTON
Cullompton
Dunkeswell
Yarcombe
Upottery
Stockland
Honiton
Crediton
Copplestone
Morchard Bishop
Cheriton Fitzpaine
Silverton
Bradninch
Feniton
Ottery St Mary
Whimple
EXETER
PAGE 109
Topsham
Exmouth
Budleigh Salterton
Otterton
SIDMOUTH
Sidford
Colyton
Seaton
Seaton Bay
Beer
Beer Head
Axminster
Musbury
Kilmington
Chard
Moretonhampstead
Chagford
Lustleigh
Bovey Tracey
Chudleigh
Chudleigh Knighton
Haytor Vale
Kingsteignton
Teignmouth
Dawlish
Dawlish Warren
Starcross
Kenton
Lympstone
Shaldon
NEWTON ABBOT
Ashburton
Buckfast
Kingskerswell
Babbacombe
Maidencombe
Bishopsteignton
M5
A30
A38
A39
A358
A361
A373
A375
A376
A377
A379
A380
A381
A382
A383
A396
A3052
A3072
G H J K L M
80 90 300 10 20
1 2 3 4 5 6 7 8
150 100 90 80 70

BURNHAM-ON-SEA
BRIDGWATER
TAUNTON
PAGE 117
Glastonbury
Street
Wells
Shepton Mallet
FROME
Bruton
Wincanton
Castle Cary
Somerton
Langport
Ilchester
YEOVIL
Sherborne
Crewkerne
Chard
Ilminster
Axminster
Lyme Regis
Charmouth
Bridport
Beaminster
DORCHESTER
WEYMOUTH
Fortuneswell
ISLE OF PORTLAND
BILL OF PORTLAND
LYME BAY
Weymouth Bay
Portland Harbour
Chesil Beach
Seaton
Seaton Bay
Beer Head
POLDEN HILLS
SOMERSET
DEVON
DORSET
BLACKMOOR VALE
M5
A39
A303
A30
A35
A37
A358
A361
A371
A372
A352
A354
A3066
A3088
A359
A357
A362
A367
A3052
A378
A356
A353
A3030
A3259
A3065
18
7
A
B
C
D
E
F
1
2
3
4
5
6
7
8

9
G
H
J
K
L
M
SALISBURY PLAIN
WILTSHIRE
HAMPSHIRE
NEW FOREST NATIONAL PARK
DORSET
ENGLISH CHANNEL
POOLE BAY
WARMINSTER
ANDOVER
SALISBURY
PAGE 115
Amesbury
Wilton
Shaftesbury
Blandford Forum
Wimborne Minster
POOLE
BOURNEMOUTH
PAGE 106
CHRISTCHURCH
Ringwood
Fordingbridge
Romsey
TOTTON
LYMINGTON
Lyndhurst
Wareham
Swanage
Highcliffe
New Milton
Ferndown
Tidworth
Ludgershall
Stockbridge
Westbury
Gillingham
Yarmouth
Freshwater
Brownsea Island
Sandbanks
Studland Bay
ISLE OF PURBECK
Durlston Head
St Aldhelm's or St Alban's Head
Hengistbury Head
Christchurch Bay
The Needles
Totland Bay
Alum Bay
Colwell Bay
Kimmeridge Bay
Worbarrow Bay
Lulworth Cove
The Foreland or Handfast Point
Poole Harbour
Poole to:
Cherbourg 4hrs. 30mins.
Guernsey 3hrs.
(Fast Ferry, Seasonal)
Jersey 4hrs. 30mins.
(Fast Ferry, Seasonal)
St Malo 6hrs.
(Fast Ferry, Seasonal)
DANGER AREA
Black Heath
19
10
A36
A303
A30
A338
A350
A354
A31
A35
A337
A27
M27
A3057
A345
A360
A343
A3090
A326
A348
A341
A349
A347
A351
A352
A357
A3054
A3055
80
70
90
400
10
20
30

A
B
C
D
E
F
1
2
3
4
5
6
7
8
BASINGSTOKE
20
ALDERSHOT
FARNHAM
NORTH
ANDOVER
Tangley
Tarrant
Lower Chute
Enham Alamein
Penton Mewsey
Weyhill
Abbotts Ann
Monxton
Upper Clatford
Goodworth Clatford
Middleton
Longparish
Hurstbourne Priors
Whitchurch
Overton
Oakley
Laverstoke
Freefolk Priors
Cole Henley
St Mary Bourne
Swampton
Stoke
Egbury
Quidhampton
Ashe
Steventon
North Waltham
Dummer
Cliddesden
Farleigh Wallop
Ellisfield
Herriard
Winslade
Tunworth
Upton Grey
South Warnborough
Long Sutton
North Warnborough
Greywell
Mapledurwell
Crookham Village
Crondall
Lower Froyle
Upper Froyle
Bentley
Weston Patrick
Lower Common
Southrope
Lasham
Shalden
Golden Pot
Holybourne
Alton
Chawton
Beech
Medstead
Bentworth
Bradley
Preston Candover
Axford
Chilton Candover
Brown Candover
Woodmancott
Popham
Micheldever
Micheldever Station
East Stratton
West Stratton
Hunton
Upper Bullington
Lower Bullington
Egypt
Barton Stacey
Newton Stacey
Bransbury
Wherwell
Chilbolton
Fullerton
Longstock
Leckford
Stockbridge
Nether Wallop
Middle Wallop
Danebury Hill Fort
Houghton
Broughton
King's Somborne
Little Somborne
Up Somborne
Ashley
Sparsholt
Crawley
Littleton
South Wonston
Sutton Scotney
Wonston
Stoke Charity
Kings Worthy
Headbourne Worthy
Abbots Worthy
Martyr Worthy
Itchen Abbas
Itchen Stoke
Avington
Easton
Chilland
Ovington
New Alresford
Old Alresford
Bighton
Swarraton
Northington
WINCHESTER
PAGE 117
Weeke
Fulflood
Stanmore
Pitt
Farley Mount
Standon
Hursley
Oliver's Battery
Compton
Twyford
Morestead
Owslebury
Baybridge
Upham
Colden Common
Otterbourne
Brambridge
Shawford
Hiltingbury
Chandler's Ford
Ampfield
Knapp
Braishfield
Michelmersh
Timsbury
Mottisfont
Kent's Oak
Awbridge
Cupernham
Romsey
Whitenap
North Baddesley
Chilworth
EASTLEIGH
Bishopstoke
Fair Oak
Crowdhill
Lower Upham
Durley
Horton Heath
Bishop's Waltham
Droxford
Dundridge
Swanmore
Shirrell Heath
Soberton
Soberton Heath
Meonstoke
Exton
Corhampton
Warnford
West Meon
East Meon
Clanfield
Hambledon
HORNDEAN
Cowplain
WATERLOOVILLE
Denmead
Purbrook
HAVANT
Emsworth
Westbourne
Chichester
CHICHESTER
SOUTH DOWNS
NATIONAL PARK
HAMPSHIRE
PETERSFIELD
Steep
Sheet
Liss
Liphook
Greatham
Selborne
East Tisted
Ropley
Four Marks
Bishop's Sutton
Tichborne
Cheriton
New Cheriton
Hinton Ampner
Bramdean
West Tisted
Kilmeston
Beauworth
Lane End
Privett
Froxfield Green
Stroud
Langrish
Buriton
South Harting
West Harting
East Harting
Rogate
Trotton
Midhurst
Cocking
Singleton
West Dean
Mid Lavant
East Lavant
Funtington
Bosham
Fishbourne
Chidham
Nutbourne
Southbourne
Hermitage
Hayling Island
SOUTH HAYLING
HAYLING ISLAND
Hayling Bay
Thorney Island
West Thorney
Itchenor
Birdham
Shipton Green
West Wittering
East Wittering
Bracklesham
Bracklesham Bay
Selsey
SELSEY BILL
Sidlesham
Hunston
North Mundham
Merston
Runcton
Donnington
Apuldram
Norton
Earnley
Almodington
Somerley
Church Norton
Highleigh
SOUTHAMPTON
PAGE 116
HYTHE
Totton
TOTTON
Marchwood
Netley
Netley Abbey
Hamble-le-Rice
Bursledon
Swanwick
Sarisbury Green
Park Gate
Locks Heath
Warsash
Titchfield
Fareham
FAREHAM
Portchester
GOSPORT
PORTSMOUTH
PAGE 115
PORTSEA ISLAND
Cosham
Wymering
Hilsea
Southsea
Eastney
Stubbington
Lee-on-the-Solent
Hill Head
Bridgemary
Rowner
West End
Hedge End
Botley
Curdridge
Wickham
Shedfield
Waltham Chase
Fawley
Calshot
Holbury
Hardley
Blackfield
Langley
Beaulieu
Dibden Purlieu
Dibden
Applemore
Lyndhurst
Ashurst
Woodlands
Netley Marsh
Cadnam
Bartley
Lymington
LYMINGTON
Boldre
Pilley
East Boldre
South Baddesley
Walhampton
Keyhaven
Milford on Sea
Needs Ore Point
THE SOLENT
COWES
East Cowes
Gurnard
Northwood
Osborne Bay
Ryde Roads
RYDE
Wootton
Wootton Bridge
Fishbourne
Whippingham
Binstead
Havenstreet
Seaview
Nettlestone
St Helens
Bembridge
Bembridge Point
FORELAND
Whitecliff Bay
Culver Cliff
Brading
Sandown
SANDOWN
Lake
SHANKLIN
Luccombe Village
DUNNOSE
Bonchurch
VENTNOR
St Lawrence
Niton
Whitwell
Wroxall
Godshill
Rookley
Chillerton
Gatcombe
NEWPORT
Carisbrooke
Shide
Arreton
Newchurch
Shalfleet
Yarmouth
Freshwater
Totland
Colwell Bay
Compton Bay
Brook
Brighstone
Brighstone Bay
Shorwell
Calbourne
Chale
Chale Bay
Atherfield Point
ST CATHERINE'S POINT
Thorness Bay
Newtown Bay
SPITHEAD
Stokes Bay
Gilkicker Point
Portsmouth to:
Bilbao 24hrs.
Caen 6hrs.
(Seasonal)
Cherbourg 3hrs.
(Fast Ferry, Seasonal)
Guernsey 7hrs.
Jersey 8hrs.
Le Havre 5hrs. 30mins.
St Malo 9hrs.
Santander 24hrs.
Nab Tower
M3
M27
M271
M275
A3(M)
A30
A303
A34
A31
A32
A33
A35
A36
A27
A3
A272
A286
A259
A3054
A3055
A3020
A3021
A3056
40
50
60
70
80
90

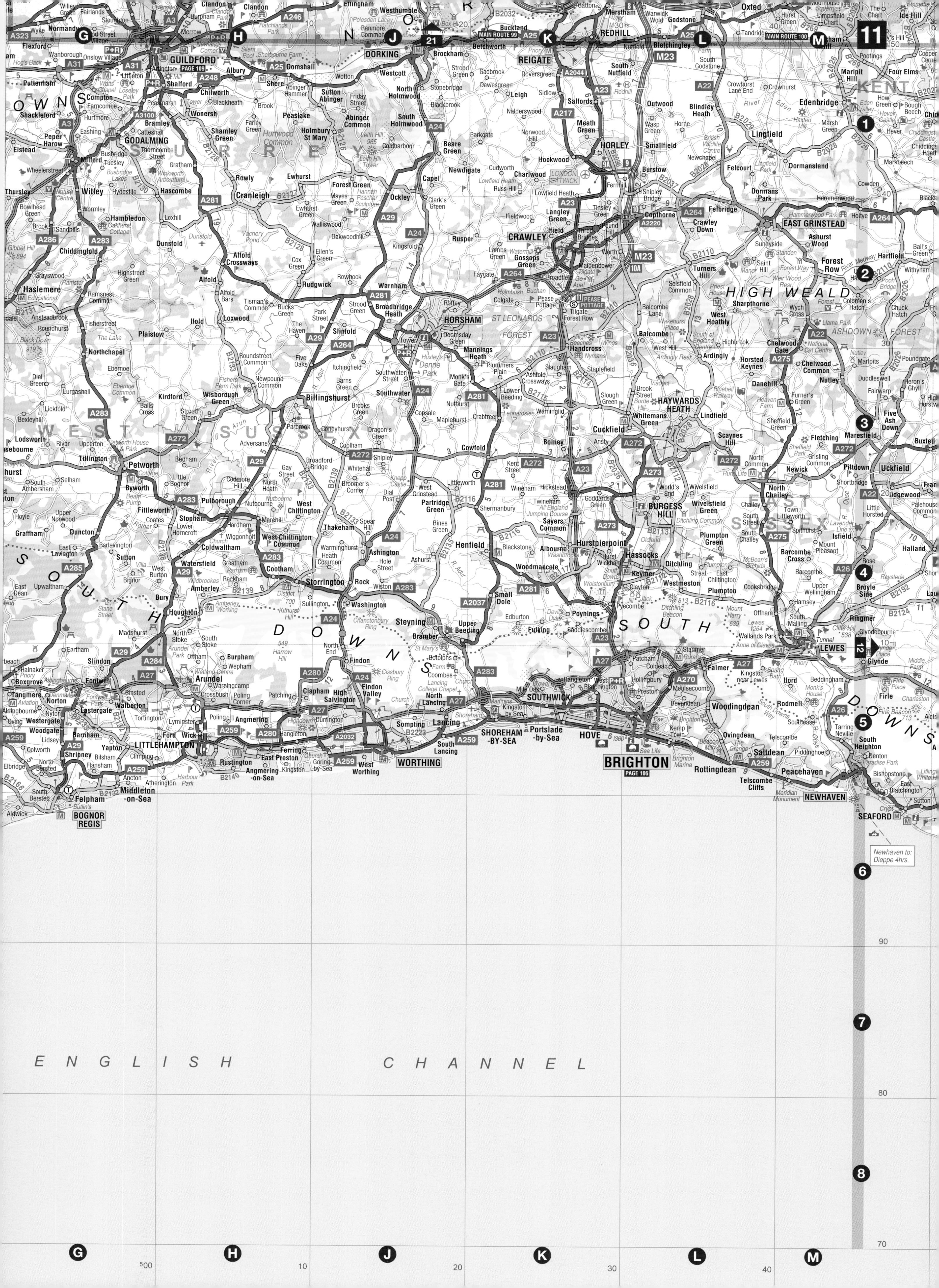
11
MAIN ROUTE 99
MAIN ROUTE 100
GUILDFORD
PAGE 109
DORKING
REIGATE
REDHILL
GODALMING
HORLEY
CRAWLEY
EAST GRINSTEAD
HORSHAM
HAYWARDS HEATH
BURGESS HILL
SURREY
WEST SUSSEX
EAST SUSSEX
KENT
HIGH WEALD
ASHDOWN FOREST
ST LEONARDS FOREST
SOUTH DOWNS
LONDON GATWICK
ARUNDEL
STORRINGTON
STEYNING
LEWES
WORTHING
LITTLEHAMPTON
BOGNOR REGIS
SHOREHAM -BY-SEA
SOUTHWICK
Portslade -by-Sea
HOVE
BRIGHTON
PAGE 106
Peacehaven
NEWHAVEN
SEAFORD
Newhaven to: Dieppe 4hrs.
ENGLISH CHANNEL
G
H
J
K
L
M
500
10
20
30
40
90
80
70
1
2
3
4
5
6
7
8

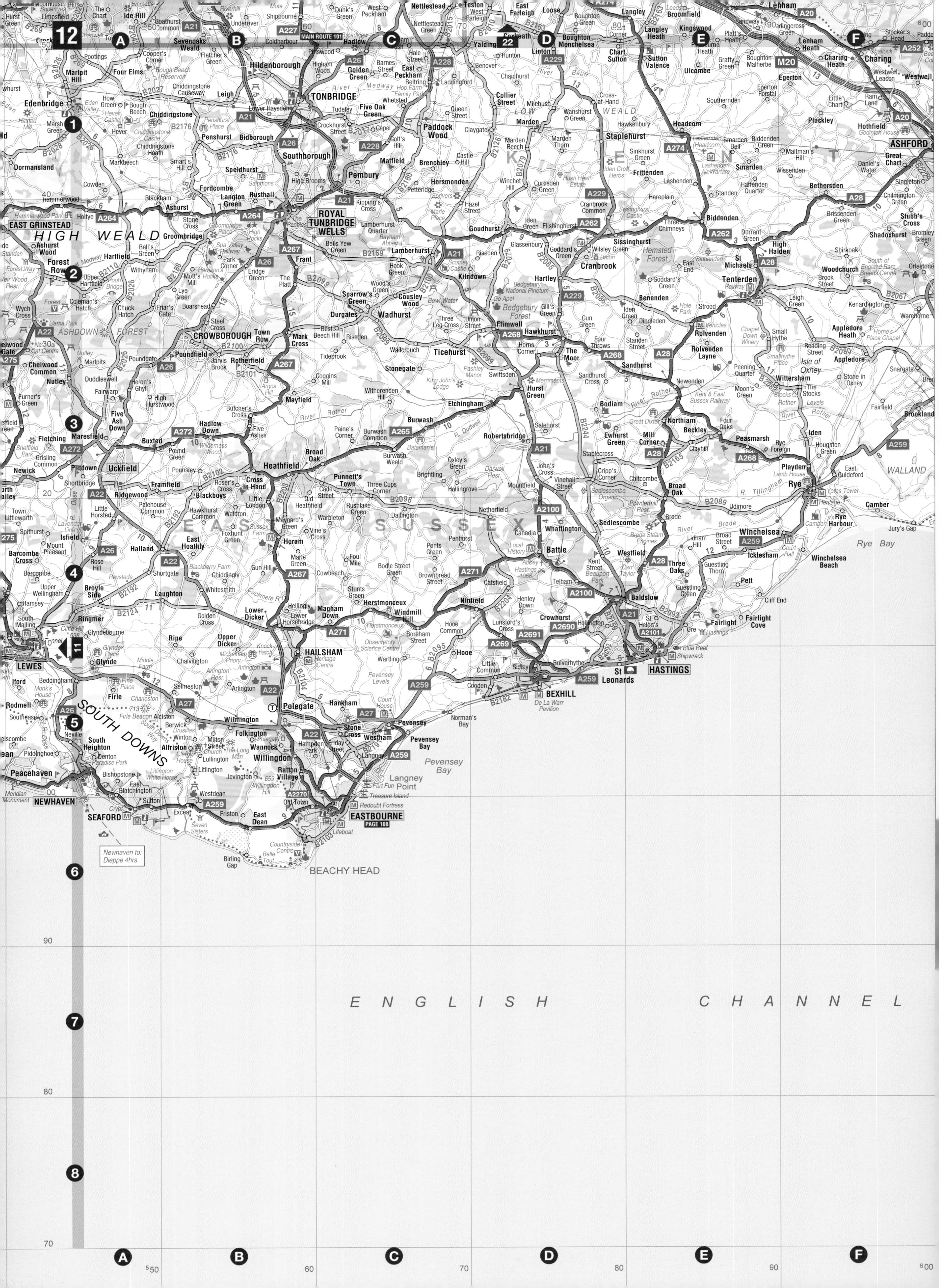
12
MAIN ROUTE 101
22
11
PAGE 108
HIGH WEALD
ASHDOWN FOREST
SOUTH DOWNS
LOW WEALD
KENT
EAST SUSSEX
ENGLISH CHANNEL
Rye Bay
Pevensey Bay
WALLAND
BEACHY HEAD
Newhaven to: Dieppe 4hrs.
TONBRIDGE
ROYAL TUNBRIDGE WELLS
Southborough
Hildenborough
Edenbridge
EAST GRINSTEAD
CROWBOROUGH
Uckfield
LEWES
NEWHAVEN
SEAFORD
EASTBOURNE
HAILSHAM
Polegate
BEXHILL
HASTINGS
St Leonards
Battle
Rye
Tenterden
Cranbrook
ASHFORD
Heathfield
Wadhurst
Mayfield
Hawkhurst
Lamberhurst
Paddock Wood
Pembury
Staplehurst
Headcorn
Biddenden
Charing
Lenham
Sevenoaks Weald
Hadlow
Yalding
Linton
Boughton Monchelsea
Sutton Valence
Marden
Goudhurst
Ticehurst
Flimwell
Northiam
Robertsbridge
Burwash
Etchingham
Winchelsea
Winchelsea Beach
Camber
Fairlight
Herstmonceux
Pevensey
Westham
Willingdon
Peacehaven
Alfriston
Ringmer
Maresfield
Forest Row
Hartfield
Groombridge
Frant
Rotherfield
Crowhurst
Ninfield
Sedlescombe
Westfield
Icklesham
Appledore
Wittersham
Woodchurch
Bethersden
Smarden
Pluckley
Egerton
A21
A26
A22
A264
A267
A268
A272
A265
A271
A27
A259
A28
A262
A229
A228
A274
A2100
A2690
A2691
A269
A2270
A20
A252
M20
A227
A2101
Langney Point
Treasure Island
Redoubt Fortress
Fort Fun
Bodiam
Bateman's
Bedgebury Forest
Bedgebury National Pinetum
Scotney Castle
Sissinghurst
Penshurst
Hever

# CHANNEL TUNNEL

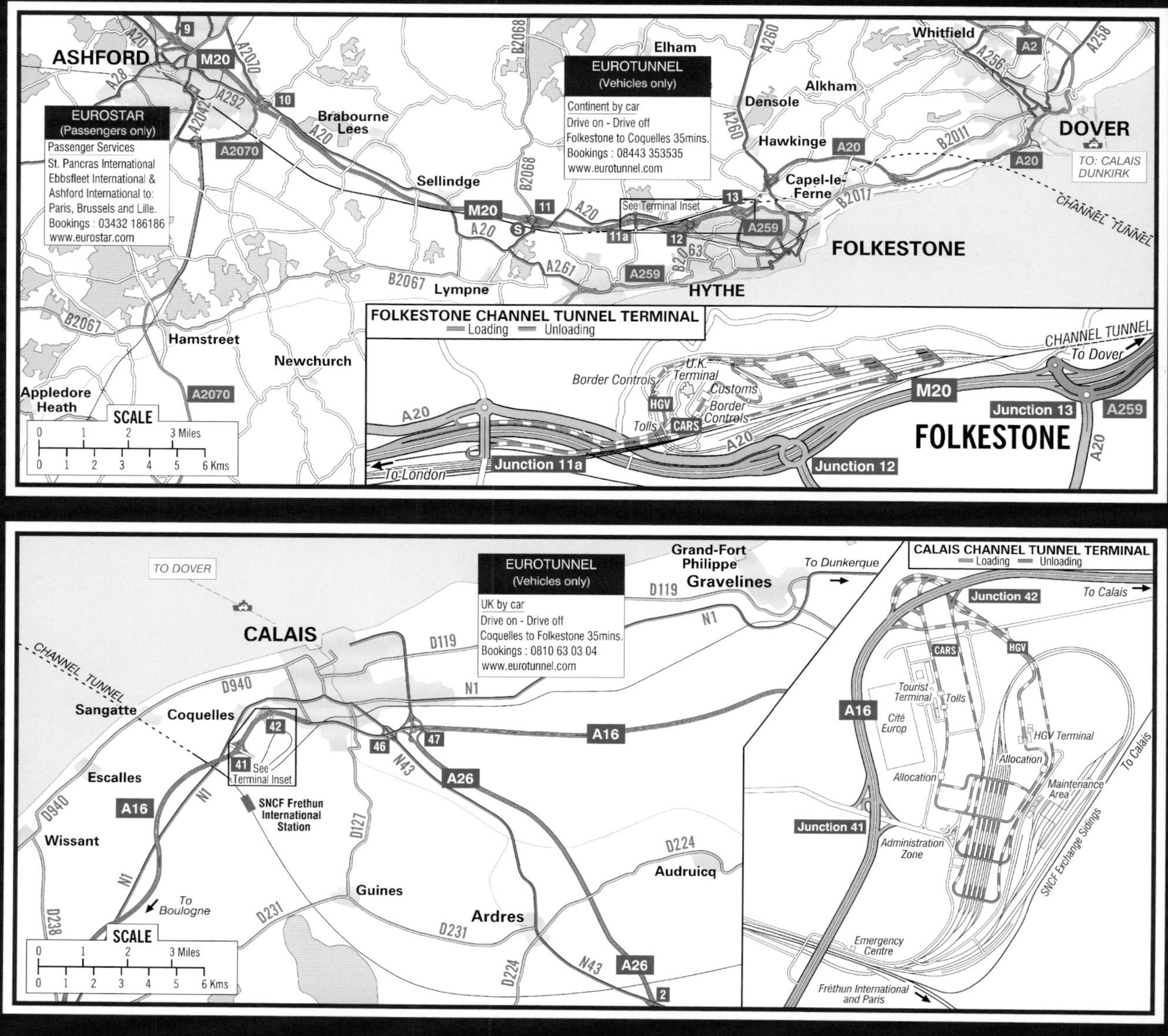

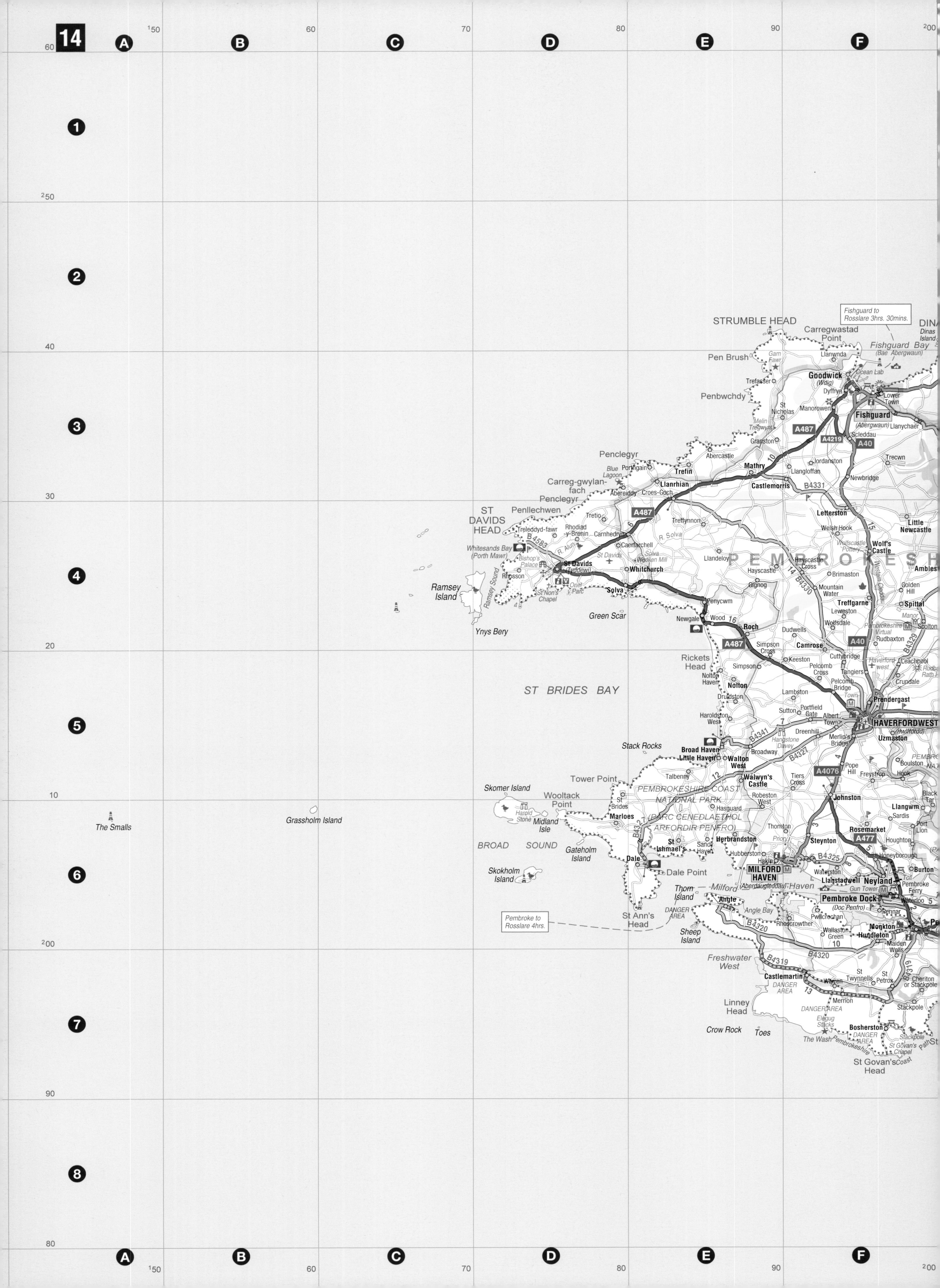

A
B
C
D
E
F
1
2
3
4
5
6
7
8
STRUMBLE HEAD
Fishguard to Rosslare 3hrs. 30mins.
Carregwastad Point
Fishguard Bay
(Bae Abergwaun)
Dinas Island
Pen Brush
Llanwnda
Goodwick
(Wdig)
Dyffryn
Ocean Lab
Lower Town
Trefasser
Penbwchdy
St Nicholas
Manorowen
Fishguard
(Abergwaun)
Llanychaer
Scleddau
A487
A4219
A40
Granston
Abercastle
Jordanston
Trecwn
Penclegyr
Porthgain
Blue Lagoon
Trefin
Mathry
Llangloffan
Newbridge
Carreg-gwylan-fach
Abereiddy
Croes-Goch
Llanrhian
Castlemorris
B4331
Penclegyr
ST DAVIDS HEAD
Penllechwen
Tretio
Treffynnon
Letterston
Little Newcastle
Treleddyd-fawr
Rhodiad y-Brenin
Carnhedryn
R. Solva
Welsh Hook
Whitesands Bay
(Porth Mawr)
B4583
R. Alun
Caerfarchell
St Davids
Solva Woollen Mill
Llandeloy
Wolf's Castle
PEMBROKESH
Bishop's Palace
St Davids
(Tyddewi)
Whitchurch
Hayscastle
Hayscastle Cross
Brimaston
Ambleston
Ramsey Island
Ramsey Sound
Ramsey Island
Porthsgain
Caerbwdy
Rhosson
St Non's Chapel
Solva
Eglwys
Mountain Water
Golden Hill
Treffgarne
Spittal
Penycwm
Leweston
Newgale
Wood
Green Scar
Ynys Bery
Roch
Dudwells
Wolfsdale
Pembrokeshire Virtual
Scolton
Rudbaxton
A487
Simpson Cross
Camrose
A40
B4329
Rickets Head
Keeston
Cuttybridge
Haverfordwest
Leachpool
Simpson
Pelcomb Cross
Tangiers
Crundale
Nolton Haven
Nolton
Pelcomb Bridge
ST BRIDES BAY
Druidston
Lambston
Prendergast
Haroldston West
Sutton
Portfield Gate
Albert Town
HAVERFORDWEST
(Hwlffordd)
Dreenhill
Merlin's Bridge
Uzmaston
Stack Rocks
Broad Haven
Little Haven
Walton West
B4341
Broadway
Hangstone Davey
B4327
Boulston
Talbenny
A4076
Pope Hill
Freystrop
Hook
Tower Point
Walwyn's Castle
Tiers Cross
Skomer Island
Wooltack Point
PEMBROKESHIRE COAST
St Brides
Robeston West
Johnston
NATIONAL PARK
Hasguard
Llangwm
Harold Stone
Midland Isle
Marloes
(PARC CENEDLAETHOL ARFORDIR PENFRO)
Sardis
B4327
Thornton
Rosemarket
BROAD SOUND
Gateholm Island
St Ishmael's
Sandy Haven
Herbrandston
Steynton
A477
Houghton
Hubberston
Hakin
B4325
Honeyborough
Dale
Dale Point
MILFORD HAVEN
Waterston
Burton
Skokholm Island
Thorn Island
Milford
(Aberdaugleddau)
Haven
Llanstadwell
Neyland
Gun Tower
Pembroke Ferry
Angle
DANGER AREA
Pembroke Dock
(Doc Penfro)
Waterloo
Angle Bay
Pwllcrochan
Pennar
Pembroke to Rosslare 4hrs.
St Ann's Head
B4320
Rhoscrowther
Wallaston Green
Monkton
Hundleton
Sheep Island
Maiden Wells
B4320
Freshwater West
B4319
St Twynnells
St Petrox
Cheriton or Stackpole
Castlemartin
DANGER AREA
Warren
Merrion
Linney Head
DANGER AREA
Stackpole
Elegug Stacks
Crow Rock
Toes
Bosherston
DANGER AREA
Stackpole
The Wash
Pembrokeshire Coast
St Govan's Chapel
Path
St Govan's Head
Grassholm Island
The Smalls
150
60
70
80
90
200
260
250
40
30
20
10
200
90
80

CEREDIGION
CARMARTHENSHIRE
PEMBROKESHIRE COAST NATIONAL PARK
(PARC CENEDLAETHOL ARFORDIR PENFRO)
MYNYDD PRESELI
FOREST OF BRECHFA
CARMARTHEN BAY
(BAE CAERFYRDDIN)
GOWER
SWANSEA
Aberaeron
New Quay (Ceinewydd)
Cwmtudu
Ynys-Lochtyn
Llangranog
Penbryn
Aberporth
Cardigan Island
Cemaes Head
Cardigan (Aberteifi)
St Dogmaels (Llandudoch)
Moylgrove (Trewyddel)
Trwyn-y-bwa
Nevern (Nanhyfer)
Newport (Trefdraeth)
Dinas Cross
Newcastle Emlyn (Castell Newydd Emlyn)
Llandysul
Lampeter
Llanybydder
Crymych
Maenclochog
Puncheston (Cas-Mael)
Henry's Moat (Castell Hendre)
Whitland
St Clears
Narberth (Arberth)
Templeton
Kilgetty (Cilgeti)
Saundersfoot
Tenby (Dinbych-y-Pysgod)
Penally (Penalum)
Manorbier
Lamphey
Carew
Caldey Island
Caldey Sound
Giltar Point
St Margaret's Island
Old Castle Head
Trewent Point
Monkstone Point
Amroth
Pendine (Pentywyn)
Laugharne
Llansteffan
Ferryside
Ginst Point
CARMARTHEN (Caerfyrddin)
Kidwelly (Cydweli)
Pembrey
Burry Port (Porth Tywyn)
LLANELLI
GORSEINON
Whiteford Point
Burry Holms
WORMS HEAD (Penrhyn-gwyr)
Rhossili
Port-Eynon
Port-Eynon Point
Oxwich Point
Pwlldu Head
Brechfa
Nantgaredig
Cross Hands
Tumble (Y Tymbl)
Llandybie
Synod Inn (Post-Mawr)
Talgarreg
Rhydowen
Capel Dewi
Cynwyl Elfed
Bronwydd Arms
Meidrim
Llanboidy
Efailwen
Llangolman
Clynderwen
Robeston Wathen
Martletwy
Cresselly
Milton
DANGER AREA
24
16
G
H
J
K
L
M
10
20
30
40
50
60
80

16
PEMBROKESHIRE
PEMBROKESHIRE COAST NATIONAL PARK (PARC CENEDLAETHOL ARFORDIR PENFRO)
CARMARTHENSHIRE
FOREST OF BRECHFA
SWANSEA
GOWER
CARMARTHEN BAY (BAE CAERFYRDDIN)
Swansea Bay (Bae Abertawe)
BRISTOL
Newcastle Emlyn (Castell Newydd Emlyn)
Cenarth
Llandyfriog
Penrhiw-llan
Llandysul
Llanfihangel-ar-Arth
Eglwyswrw
Crymych
Boncath
Whitland
St Clears
Laugharne
Llansteffan
Pendine (Pentywyn)
Llanmiloe
CARMARTHEN (Caerfyrddin)
Pen-sarn
Llangunnor
Cwmffrwd
Nantgaredig
Llandeilo
Ffairfach
Ammanford (Rhydaman)
Llandybie
Cross Hands
Gorslas
Tumble (Y Tymbl)
Pontyberem
Kidwelly (Cydweli)
Ferryside
Burry Port (Porth Tywyn)
Pembrey
LLANELLI
GORSEINON
Pontarddulais
Loughor
Gowerton
Penllergaer
Morriston
Clydach
SWANSEA (Abertawe)
Mumbles (Mwmbwls)
Port-Eynon
Reynoldston
Rhossili
WORMS HEAD (Penrhyn-gwyr)
Burry Holms
Whiteford Point
Tenby (Dinbych-y-Pysgod)
Saundersfoot
Kilgetty (Cilgeti)
Caldey Island
St Margaret's Island
Giltar Point
Monkstone Point
Narberth
Talley
Brechfa
Llansawel
Pencader
Abernant
Meidrim
Llangynog
A40
A48
A478
A484
A485
A476
A483
A4138
M4

G
H
J
K
L
M
25
Hay-on-Wye
(Y Gelli Gandryll)
Llandovery
(Llanymddyfri)
Brecon
(Aberhonddu)
P O W Y S
BRECON BEACONS
NATIONAL PARK
(PARC CENEDLAETHOL
BANNAU BRYCHEINIOG)
PEN Y FAN
2906
BRECON BEACONS
BLACK
MOUNTAINS
Crickhowell
(Crughywel)
Abergavenny
Llangadog
Llanwrda
Trecastle
Sennybridge
Talgarth
Bronllys
Glasbury
Llyswen
Llangorse
Ystradgynlais
Ystalyfera
Pontardawe
Glyn-neath
Hirwaun
ABERDARE
(Aberdâr)
MERTHYR
TYDFIL
(Merthyr Tudful)
RHYMNEY
(Rhymni)
TREDEGAR
EBBW
VALE
(Glyn Ebwy)
Brynmawr
Nantyglo
Blaenavon
Blaina
ABERTILLERY
(Abertyleri)
Abersychan
NEATH
(Castell-Nedd)
NEATH
PORT TALBOT
Skewen
Briton Ferry
Baglan
Aberavon
PORT TALBOT
Cymmer
(Cymer)
Treherbert
Treorchy
(Treorci)
Ferndale
Tonypandy
Porth
PONTYPRIDD
MOUNTAIN ASH
(Aberpennar)
Abercynon
MAESTEG
BRIDGEND
(Pen-y-Bont Ar Ogwr)
Pencoed
Pyle
PORTHCAWL
Porthcawl
Point
Sker Point
Ogmore-by-Sea
Tusker
Rock
Cowbridge
(Y Bont-Faen)
Llantwit
Major
(Llanilltud Fawr)
Nash Point
St Athan
(Sain Tathan)
Rhoose
(Y Rhws)
BARRY
(Y Barri)
Barry Island
(Ynys y Barri)
Sully
Sully
Island
Penarth
Dinas
Powys
CARDIFF
(Caerdydd)
PAGE 107
Llantrisant
Talbot Green
Pontyclun
Caerphilly
(Caerffili)
CAERPHILLY
Bargoed
Blackwood
Newbridge
(Trecelyn)
Crumlin
Oakdale
Risca
Rogerstone
CWMBRAN
Pontypool
Ystrad Mynach
Hengoed
GELLIGAER
Nelson
Treharris
Bedlinog
New
Tredegar
Radyr
Tongwynlais
Rumney
Marshfield
Castleton
St Mellons
Lavernock
Point
Flat Holm
Steep Holm
C H A N N E L
Breaksea
Point
THE VALE OF
GLAMORGAN
RHONDDA
CYNON
TAF
BRIDGEND
WESTON-SUPER-M
A40
A470
A465
A4059
A4061
A4107
A48
M4
A4232
A4050
A4055
A4226
A4119
A4054
A469
A467
A4043
A472
A4046
A4048
A4063
A4064
A4093
A4222
A4229
A4106
A473
A4109
A4067
A4069
A4068
A474
A483
A4221
A4215
A4058
A4233
A4241
A438
A479
A4078
A4077
A4042
A468
A4160
1
2
3
4
5
6
7
8
18
26
80
90
300
10
20
70
60

A
B
C
D
E
F
26
1
2
3
4
5
6
7
8
17
BLACK MOUNTAINS
HEREFORDSHIRE
MONMOUTHSHIRE
TORFAEN
NEWPORT
CARDIFF
PAGE 107
PAGE 114
ENGLAND
WALES
FOREST OF DEAN
SOUTH GLOUCESTERSHIRE
NORTH SOMERSET
BATH & N.E. SOMERSET
SOMERSET
MENDIP
THE SEVERN
MOUTH OF THE SEVERN
RIVER SEVERN
BRIDGWATER BAY
Portland Grounds
Flat Holm
Steep Holm
Sand Point
Sand Bay
Weston Bay
Portishead Point
Abbey Dore
Ewyas Harold
Pontrilas
Kentchurch
Grosmont
Skenfrith
Much Dewchurch
Hoarwithy
King's Caple
Ross-on-Wye
Newent
Dymock
Kempley
Gorsley
Pandy
Llanvihangel Crucorney
Crickhowell (Crughywel)
Gilwern
ABERGAVENNY (Y Fenni)
Govilon
Blaenavon
Nantyglo
Blaina
Abersychan
ABERTILLERY (Abertyleri)
PONTYPOOL (Pontypwl)
Griffithstown
CWMBRAN
Newbridge (Trecelyn)
Crosskeys
Risca
Rogerstone
Caerleon (Caerllion)
NEWPORT (Casnewydd)
St Mellons
Rumney
CARDIFF (Caerdydd)
Raglan
Usk
Llantrisant
Shirenewton
Caerwent
Caldicot
Magor (Magwyr)
Undy
Rogiet
Portskewett
CHEPSTOW (Cas-gwent)
Tutshill
Sedbury
St Arvans
Tintern
Llandogo
Whitebrook
MONMOUTH (Trefynwy)
Wyesham
Staunton
Coleford
Cinderford
Mitcheldean
Drybrook
Lydney
Aylburton
Blakeney
Newnham
Berkeley
Sharpness
Dursley
Cam
Wotton-under-Edge
Thornbury
Oldbury-on-Severn
Alveston
Almondsbury
Winterbourne
Yate
Chipping Sodbury
Filton
MANGOTSFIELD
Kingswood
BRISTOL
Avonmouth
Portishead
Portbury
Easton-in-Gordano
Clevedon
Nailsea
Backwell
Long Ashton
Keynsham
Saltford
BATH
PAGE 106
Whitchurch
Chew Magna
Pensford
Congresbury
Yatton
WESTON-SUPER-MARE
Banwell
Winscombe
Sandford
Blagdon
Cheddar
Axbridge
Wedmore
Burnham-on-Sea
Highbridge
Midsomer Norton
Radstock
Paulton
Chilcompton
Farmborough
Timsbury
FROME
Mells
Wookey Hole
Severn Bridge
Second Severn Crossing
Severn Tunnel
M4
M5
M32
M48
M49
M50
A40
A48
A38
A4
A465
A466
A449
A4042
A369
A370
A371
A368
A37
A39
A36
A46
A420
A431
A432
A4174
A4175
A367
A362
A366
A4136
A4151
A417
A419
A4135
A403
A4018
A4810
A468
A467
A472
A4043
A4051
A4077
A4137
A449
SEVERN VIEW
MAGOR
MICHAELWOOD
GORDANO
SEDGEMOOR
CARDIFF GATE
ROSS SPUR
8

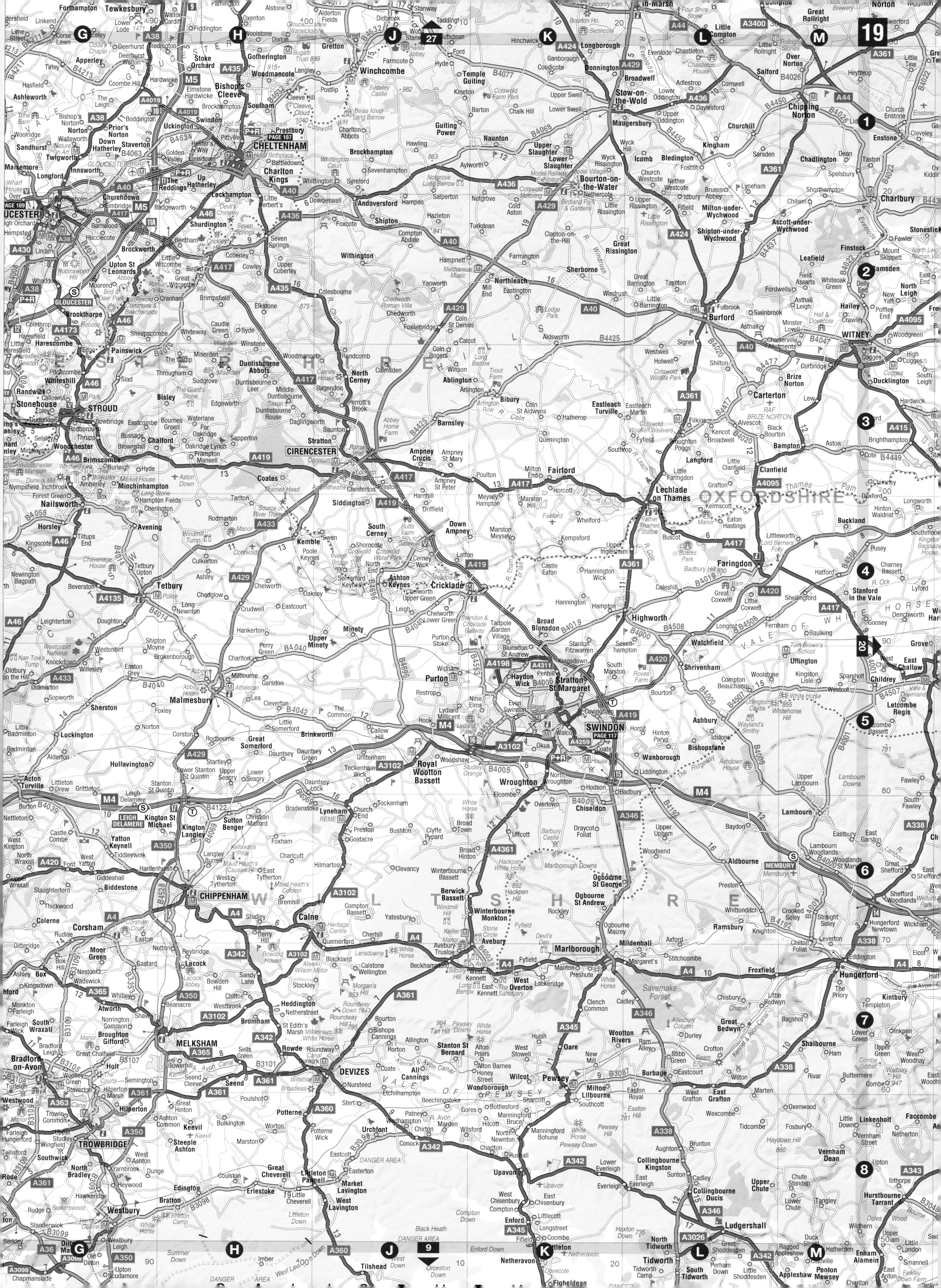
CHELTENHAM
PAGE 107
GLOUCESTER
PAGE 109
STROUD
CIRENCESTER
Tetbury
Malmesbury
CHIPPENHAM
Calne
Corsham
MELKSHAM
TROWBRIDGE
Westbury
DEVIZES
Marlborough
Hungerford
SWINDON
PAGE 117
Royal Wootton Bassett
Cricklade
Highworth
Faringdon
Lechlade on Thames
Fairford
Burford
WITNEY
Carterton
Charlbury
Chipping Norton
Stow-on-the-Wold
Bourton-on-the-Water
Winchcombe
Tewkesbury
Northleach
Wroughton
Pewsey
Ludgershall
Tidworth
Nailsworth
Bishop's Cleeve
OXFORDSHIRE
W I L T S H I R E
G
H
J
K
L
M
1
2
3
4
5
6
7
8
9
10
20
27

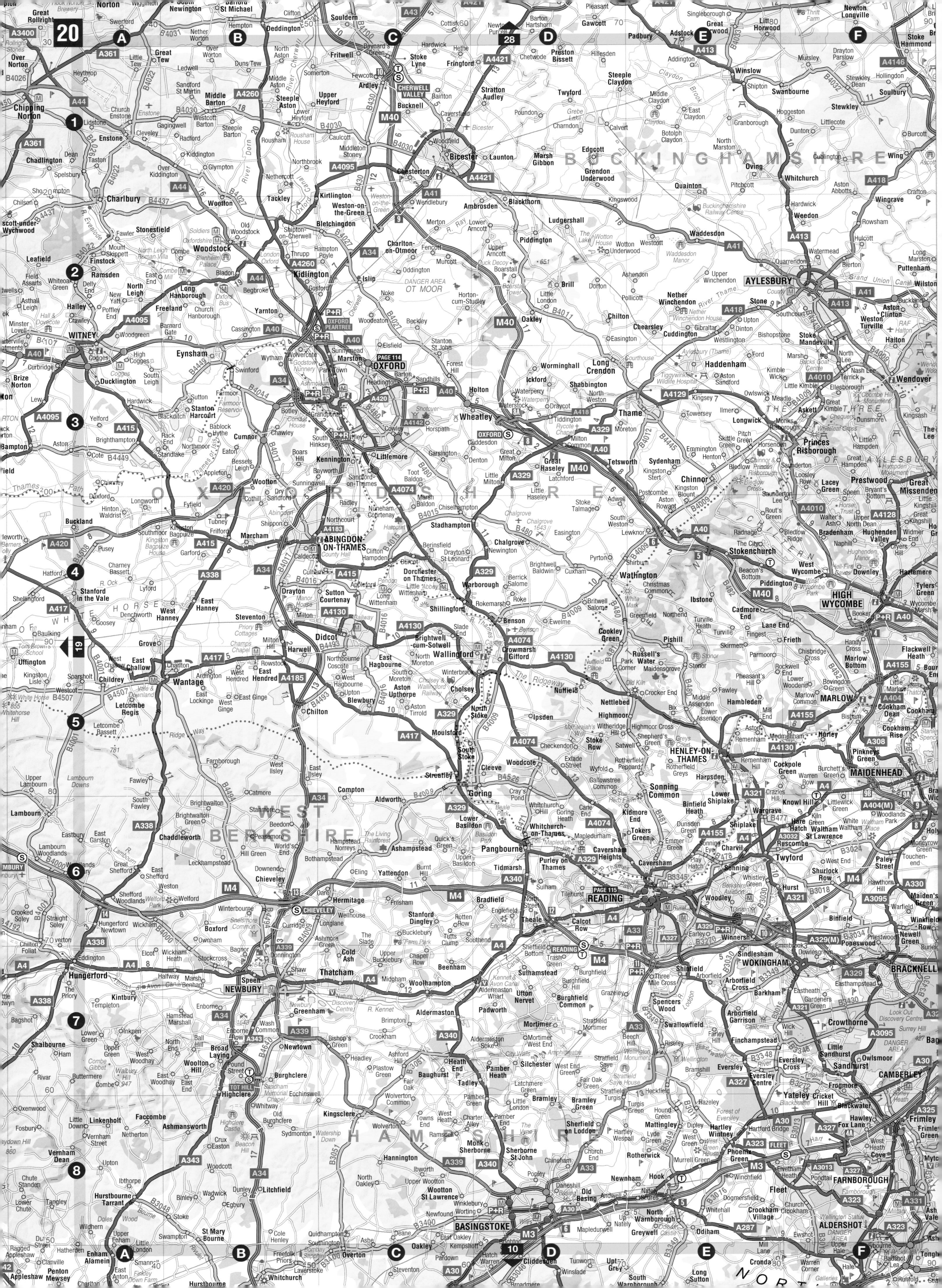

20
A
B
C
D
E
F
1
2
3
4
5
6
7
8
28
19
10
BUCKINGHAMSHIRE
OXFORDSHIRE
WEST BERKSHIRE
HAMPSHIRE
Chipping Norton
Charlbury
Woodstock
Kidlington
Bicester
Witney
OXFORD
PAGE 114
Abingdon-on-Thames
Didcot
Wallingford
Wantage
Thame
Aylesbury
Princes Risborough
High Wycombe
Marlow
Henley-on-Thames
Maidenhead
Reading
PAGE 115
Wokingham
Bracknell
Newbury
Hungerford
Thatcham
Basingstoke
Camberley
Farnborough
Fleet
Aldershot
Goring
Pangbourne
Wendover
Chinnor
Watlington
Hook
Odiham
Kingsclere
Whitchurch
Overton
Tadley
M40
M4
M3
A34
A40
A44
A41
A4
A329
A338
A413
A418
A4074
A4130
Cherwell Valley
Oxford
Chieveley
Reading
Fleet
Tot Hill

HERTFORDSHIRE
LONDON
PAGE 112-113
MAIN ROUTE 94
MAIN ROUTE 95
MAIN ROUTE 96
MAIN ROUTE 98
MAIN ROUTE 99
MAIN ROUTE 100
PAGE 117
PAGE 109
29
11
22
NORTH DOWNS
LUTON
DUNSTABLE
TODDINGTON
HITCHIN
STEVENAGE
BISHOP'S STORTFORD
HARPENDEN
WELWYN GARDEN CITY
HERTFORD
WARE
HARLOW
ST ALBANS
HATFIELD
HEMEL HEMPSTEAD
BERKHAMSTED
HODDESDON
CHESHAM
AMERSHAM
WATFORD
BOREHAMWOOD
POTTERS BAR
CHESHUNT
WALTHAM ABBEY
EPPING
LOUGHTON
ENFIELD
BARNET
CHORLEYWOOD
RICKMANSWORTH
BEACONSFIELD
NORTHWOOD
STANMORE
EDGWARE
HARROW
PINNER
CHINGFORD
CHIGWELL
WOODFORD
WALTHAMSTOW
UXBRIDGE
RUISLIP
WEMBLEY
SLOUGH
HAYES
SOUTHALL
EALING
ACTON
ILFORD
STRATFORD
DAGENHAM
WINDSOR
HOUNSLOW
RICHMOND
WOOLWICH
ELTHAM
STAINES UPON THAMES
EGHAM
TWICKENHAM
KINGSTON UPON THAMES
CROYDON
BROMLEY
SIDCUP
ORPINGTON
WEYBRIDGE
ESHER
EPSOM
SUTTON
PURLEY
WOKING
LEATHERHEAD
CATERHAM
GUILDFORD
DORKING
REIGATE
REDHILL
OXTED
SEVENOAKS

A
B
C
D
E
F
30
1
2
3
4
5
6
7
8
21
12
BISHOP'S STORTFORD
Stansted Mountfitchet
Sawbridgeworth
HARLOW
EPPING
Theydon Bois
LOUGHTON
Chigwell
ILFORD
BARKING
DAGENHAM
ROMFORD
HORNCHURCH
UPMINSTER
BRENTWOOD
BILLERICAY
CHELMSFORD
BRAINTREE
Great Dunmow
Halstead
Coggeshall
WITHAM
MALDON
Kelvedon
Tiptree
Danbury
Great Baddow
Chipping Ongar
Ingatestone
BASILDON
Wickford
Rayleigh
Hockley
Rochford
Hadleigh
SOUTHEND-ON-SEA
Shoeburyness
SHOEBURY NESS
CANVEY ISLAND
Burnham-on-Crouch
Tolleshunt Knights
Tollesbury
Osea Island
Northey Island
Mersea
WOOLWICH
ERITH
Purfleet-on-Thames
GRAYS
TILBURY
Stanford-le-Hope
Corringham
DARTFORD
GRAVESEND
Northfleet
Swanscombe
Bexleyheath
Bexley
SIDCUP
CHISLEHURST
BROMLEY
ORPINGTON
Swanley
Farningham
West Kingsdown
STROOD
ROCHESTER
CHATHAM
GILLINGHAM
Rainham
Walderslade
SHEERNESS
Minster
Queenborough
ISLE OF
Isle of Grain
SITTINGBOURNE
Teynham
MAIDSTONE
Bearsted
Harrietsham
Lenham
Charing
Snodland
Aylesford
West Malling
SEVENOAKS
Otford
Kemsing
Westerham
Biggin Hill
Hildenborough
Wrotham
Borough Green
Ightham
Mereworth
Yalding
River Thames
Thamesport
MEDWAY
N O R T H D O W N S
ESSEX
Rayne
Felsted
Great Leighs
Writtle
Epping Forest
M11
M25
M20
M26
M2
A12
A13
A120
A127
A130
A2
A20
A21

Harwich to:
Hook of Holland 7hrs. 15mins.
NORTH SEA
Dedham
Mistley
Manningtree
Lawford
Langham
Harwich
Harwich Harbour
Parkeston
Dovercourt
Ramsey
Wrabness
Bradfield
Little Oakley
Great Oakley
Hamford Water
Horsey Island
The Naze
Walton-on-the-Naze
Kirby-le-Soken
Kirby Cross
Frinton-on-Sea
Great Holland
Holland-on-Sea
Holland Haven
COLCHESTER
Elmstead Market
Wivenhoe
Alresford
Rowhedge
Fingringhoe
Abberton
Langenhoe
Great Bentley
Weeley
Thorpe-le-Soken
Weeley Heath
Little Clacton
Great Clacton
Brightlingsea
St Osyth
Point Clear
CLACTON-ON-SEA
Jaywick
Seawick
Colne Point
MERSEA ISLAND
West Mersea
East Mersea
Virley Channel
Sales Point
Bradwell-on-Sea
Holliwell Point
Foulness Sands
Foulness Point
Courtsend
Churchend
Maplin Sands
Warden Point
Leysdown-on-Sea
SHEPPEY
Isle of Harty
Shell Ness
Whitstable Bay
WHITSTABLE
Herne Bay
HERNE BAY
Reculver
Birchington
South Channel
MARGATE
Westgate on Sea
Foreness Point
NORTH FORELAND
BROADSTAIRS
ISLE OF THANET
RAMSGATE
Pegwell Bay
Minster
Monkton
Manston
Cliffsend
Richborough Port
Sandwich Bay
Sandwich
The Small Downs
Sholden
DEAL
The Downs
Walmer
Kingsdown
FAVERSHAM
CANTERBURY
PAGE 107
Harbledown
Sturry
Fordwich
Bridge
Bekesbourne
Littlebourne
Wingham
Ash
Eastry
Aylesham
Nonington
Chartham
Chilham
Challock
Godmersham
Boughton under Blean
Selling
Sheldwich
Stelling Minnis
Shepherdswell or Sibertswold
Ringwould
Ripple
Great Mongeham
Eythorne

Bardsey Island (Ynys Enlli)
Abbey
Trwyn Cilan
32
15
16
CARDIGAN BAY
(BAE CEREDIGION)
GWYNE
CADAIR
Llanddwywe
Dyffryn Ardudwy Burial Chamber
Irddyn
Mynach
Llawlech
y-bont
A496
Bontddu
Llanaber
Caerdeon
Cutiau
Penmaenpool
Afon Mawddach
A493
Barmouth (Abermaw)
Barmouth Bay (Bae Bermo)
Lifeboat
FB (Toll)
The Bar
Fairbourne Steam Railway
Fairbourne
Nature Centre
Arthog
Waterfalls
Friog
2040
Mynydd Pennant
Mary Jones Monument (Tyn-y-ddol)
Llanfihangel-y-pennant
Castell y Bere
Abergynolwyn
Esgair Berfa
Dysynni
Llwyngwril
Llangelynin
Rhoslefain
Peniarth
Llanegryn
B4405
Dolgoch
Talyllyn Railway
Dolgoch Falls
2076
Torrenhendre
Llanfendigaid
Tonfanau
Bryncrug
Pandy
Aber Dysynni
Broad Water
Rhyd-yr-onen
Trum Gelli
Tywyn
Narrow Gauge Railway
Corlan-fraith
Cwrt
Penhelig
Aberdovey (Aberdyfi)
Snowdonia National Park
Glandyfi
Eglwys Fach
Dyfi Furnace
Furnace
A487
Dyfi
Ynyslas
B4353
Llancynfelyn
Tre'r-ddol
Tre Taliesin
Borth
Station
Animal Kingdom
Upper Borth
Tal-y-bont
Afon Leri
Dol-y-Bont
Rhyd-meirionydd
Llandre
Bontgoch
B4572
Bow Street
Pen-y-garn
Garth
Salem
Cwmsymlog
Llangorwen
Penrhyn-coch
Camera Obscura
Cliff Railway
National Library
A4159
Cefn Llwyd
Pen-bont Rhydybeddau
ABERYSTWYTH
Waun Fawr
Comins Coch
Capel Dewi
Llanbadarn Fawr
Blaen-geuffordd
Dollwen
The Bar
Penparcau
Southgate
Afon Rheidol
Capel Bangor
A44
Aberffrwd
Vale of Rheidol
Rhydyfelin
Moriah
Capel Seion
Llanfarian
Gors
A4120
Chancery
New Cross
Llanfihangel-y-Creuddyn
Blaenplwyf
Llanilar
B4340
Cnwch Coch
B4576
B4575
Rhos-y-garth
Crosswood (Trawsgoed)
Llanafan
Wenallt
Llanddeiniol
Carreg Ti-pw
Llangwyryfon
Lledrod
Llanrhystud
A485
Tynygraig
Trefenter
1183
Rhyd-Rosser
Rhydfudr
Bronnant
Llansantffraed
Llan-non
Swyddffynnon
B4337
MYNYDD BACH
Bontnewydd
Rhos Haminiog
Nebo
Aberarth
B4577
Cross Inn
Bethania
Blaenpennal
Aberaeron
Pennant
Monachty
Penuwch
B4577
Ty'n-yr-eithin
Cors Caron
A482
Ffos-y-ffin
Llanerchaeron
Llanaeron
Cilcennin
Llangeitho
Tregaron
Newbridge
B4342
Llwyncelyn
Ciliau Aeron
Bwlch-Llan
Capel Betws Lleucu
New Quay (Ceinewydd)
Marine Wildlife Centre
Gilfachreda
Maen-y-groes
Llanarth
Oakford (Derwen Gam)
Trefilan
Cwmtudu
Cross Inn
Geneva
Ystrad Aeron
Abermeurig
Gartheli
Nanternis
Caerwedros
New Quay Honey Farm
Pen-cae
Talsarn
Llundain-fach
Llwyn-y-groes
A486
Dihewyd
Felinfach
Olmarch
Ynys-Lochtyn
Blaen Celyn
Llwyndafydd
Synod Inn (Post-Mawr)
Mydroilyn
Llanddewi Brefi
Llangranog
Pontgarreg
Ffynnon-oer
Morfa
Penbryn
Bettws Bledrws
Cardigan Island
Llangybi
Brynhoffnant
Pentregat
Plwmp
Rainforest Centre
Tresaith
Aberporth
Parcllyn
Cardigan Island Coastal Farm Park
Felinwynt
Talgarreg
Gorsgoch
Cribyn
Silian
Llanfair Clydogau
Cemaes Head
West Wales (Aberporth)
Sarnau
Gwbert
Internal Fire
Allt-y-goed
Y Ferwig
Blaenannerch
Capel Cynon
Bwlch-y-fadfa
B4338
Maestir
Cellan
Tan-y-groes
Llygranant
Cippyn
Tremain
Blaenporth
Glynarthen
Lampeter (Llanbedr Pont Steffan)
Pentrefelin
Craig Twrch
Cardigan (Aberteifi)
Penparc
Felin Wnda
Brithdir
Aber
Cwrtnewydd
A475
St Dogmaels (Llandudoch)
Noyadd Trefawr
Bettws Ifan
Curlew Weavers Woollen Mill
Rhydlewis
Ffostrasol
Pont-Sian
Cwmsychpant
Llanwnnen
Pentre-bach
Cwmann
Moylgrove (Trewyddel)
Abbey
Pantgwyn
B4570
Beulah
Hawen
Drefach
Alltyblacca
Watermill
Castle
Llangoedmor
Troedyraur
Penrhiw-pal
Llanwenog
Pencarreg
Ffaldybrenin
Farmers
Monington
A487
Ponthirwaun
Brongest
Maes Llyn
Rhydowen
Glan Duar
Cwrt-y-Cadno
A484
Llechryd
Llandygwydd
Brongwyn
Coed-y-bryn
Croes-lan
Tre-groes
Llanybydder
Mynydd Pencarreg
1360
Welsh Wildlife Centre
National Coracle Centre
Pren-gwyn
Capel Dewi
Glanrhyd
Pen-y-bryn
Cilgerran
Cwm Plysgog
Cenarth
Aber-banc
Horeb
Rhuddlan
Bridell
Cenarth Falls
Cwm-cou
Penrhiw-llan
Afon Ceri
Llandyfriog
Rock Mill Woollen Mill
Maesycrugiau
A485
Five Saints Stone
Llantood
A478
Teifi Valley
Pumsaint
Rhos-hill
Abercych
Newchapel (Capel Newydd)
Penrhiw
Adpar
Aberarad
Pentrecagal
Henllan
Llandysul
Pontwelly
Llanfihangel-ar-Arth
Notwood
Aber-Giâr
Dolaucothi Gold Mines
Caio
Felindre Farchog
Castell Henllys Iron Age Fort
Pengelli Forest
Newcastle Emlyn (Castell Newydd Emlyn)
Waungilwen
Llangeler
Drefach
Llanllwni
1339
Eglwyswrw
Llanfair-Nant-Gwyn
Cilwendeg Shell House
Penrherber
National Wool Museum
Felindre
Pentre-cwrt
Mynydd Llanllwni
Rhydcymerau
Crugybar
Boncath
Cwmhiraeth
Bancyffordd
Llidiad-Nenog
A B C D E F
1 2 3 4 5 6 7 8

G
H
J
K
L
M
33
34
26
17
Dolgellau
Llanelltyd
Llanfachreth
Brithdir
Cross Foxes
Dinas Mawddwy
Mallwyd
Cwm-Cewydd
Aber-Cywarch
Cywarch
Llanymawddwy
Pennant
Lake Vyrnwy
Llanwddyn
Abertridwr
Dolanog
Pont Llogel
Llanfyllin
Tycrwyn
Llanfihangel-yng-Ngwynfa
Nant-y-meichiaid
Bwlch-y-cibau
Meifod
Llanfechain
Llansantffraid-ym-Mechain
Llanyblodwel
Llanymynech
Llandysilio
Four Crosses
Llandrinio
Ardleen
Guilsfield (Cegidfa)
Pool Quay
Welshpool (Y Trallwng)
Buttington
Castle Caereinion
Llanfair Caereinion
Heniarth
Neuadd
Melin-y-ddol
Llangadfan
Llanerfyl
Foel
Nant-y-dugoed
Wern
Four Crosses
Sychtyn
Pen Coed
Cemmaes
Cemmaes Road
Aberangell
Clipiau
Cwm-Llinau
Corris
Corris Uchaf
Aberllefenni
Esgairgeiliog
Centre for Alternative Technology
Tal-y-llyn
Pantperthog
DYFI FOREST
CADAIR IDRIS
Machynlleth
Penegoes
Abercegir
Commins Coch
Darowen
Tal-y-Wern
Llanwrin
Forge
Derwenlas
Pennal
Glaspwll
Llanbrynmair
Tafolwern
Llan
Bont Dolgadfan
Dol-fâch
Talerddig
Pandy
Carno
Trannon
Pennant
Aberhosan
Dylife
Staylittle (Penffordd-Lâs)
Llwynygog
Pencarreggopa
Llyn Clywedog (Reservoir)
Llanidloes
Glan-y-nant
Glynbrochan
Cwmbelan
Van
Bryn y Fan
Trefeglwys
Cerist
Oakley Park
Llandinam
Clatter
Pontdolgoch
Caersws
Llanwnog
Bwlch y Garreg
Llanllugan
Manafon
New Mills (Felin Newydd)
Berriew (Aberriw)
Garthmyl
Forden (Ffodun)
Kingswood
Fron
Leighton (Tre'r llai)
Trelystan
Montgomery (Trefaldwyn)
Chirbury
Hendomen
Abermule (Aber-miwl)
Bettws Cedewain
Tregynon
Newtown (Y Drenewydd)
Aberhafesp
Llanllwchaiarn
Milford
Kerry (Ceri)
Glanmule
Sarn
Church Stoke
Llandyssil
Llanmerwig
Hodley
Mochdre
Little London
Dolfor
Kerry Hill
Anchor
Newcastle
Felindre
Beguildy
Llanbadarn Fynydd
Llananno
Llanbister
Knucklas
Llangunllo
Llanfair Waterdine
Lloyney
Knighton (Tref-y-clawdd)
WALES
ENGLAND
Clun Forest
Bleddfa
Heartsease
Llanddewi Ystradenni
Dolau
Llanfihangel Rhydithon
Penybont
Crossgates
Llandegley
RADNOR FOREST
Kinnerton
Presteigne (Llanandras)
New Radnor
Old Radnor
Walton
Llanfihangel-Nant-Melan
Gladestry
Kington
Huntington
Llandrindod Wells (Llandrindod)
Howey
Crossway
Disserth
Newbridge on Wye
Llanyre
Rhayader (Rhaeadr Gwy)
Llansantffraed Cwmdeuddwr
Elan Village
Nantmel
St Harmon
Pant-y-dwr
Bwlch-y-sarnau
Abbey-cwm-hir
Tylwch
Llangurig
Devil's Bridge (Pontarfynach)
Ponterwyd
Pont-rhyd-y-groes
Pontrhydfendigaid
Strata Florida
Cwmystwyth
Elan Valley
PLYNLIMON (PUMLUMON FAWR)
CAMBRIAN MOUNTAINS
POWYS
Builth Wells (Llanfair-ym-Muallt)
Builth Road
Llanelwedd
Cilmery
Garth
Beulah
Llanwrtyd Wells (Llanwrtud)
Abergwesyn
Rhandirmwyn
Cilycwm
Cynghordy
Llanafan-fawr
Llangammarch Wells
Aberedw
Llandeilo Graban
Erwood
Gwenddwr
Crickadarn
Llansantffraed-in-Elwel
Frank's Bridge
Glascwm
Newchurch
Painscastle
Clyro
Hay-on-Wye (Y Gelli Gandryll)
Glasbury
Llowes
Whitney-on-Wye
Clifford
Rhydspence
MYNYDD EPPYNT
Upper Chapel
Merthyr Cynog
A470
A458
A487
A489
A44
A483
A488
A490
A495
A481
A438
A4081

A
B
C
D
E
F
1
2
3
4
5
6
7
8
PAGE 116
34
25
17
18
SHREWSBURY
TELFORD
Wellington
Hadley
Oakengates
Shifnal
Welshpool
Montgomery
Church Stoke
Chirbury
Minsterley
Pontesbury
Condover
Dawley
Madeley
Ironbridge
Much Wenlock
Bridgnorth
Church Stretton
Bishop's Castle
Clun
Craven Arms
Knighton
Presteigne
Kington
Ludlow
Cleobury Mortimer
Bewdley
Tenbury Wells
Leominster
Bromyard
Hereford
Ledbury
Hay-on-Wye
Clifford
Longtown
S H R O P S H I R E
H E R E F O R D S H I R E
WALES
ENGLAND
M54
M50
A5
A49
A458
A488
A489
A4113
A4117
A456
A44
A438
A465
A4103
A480
A4110

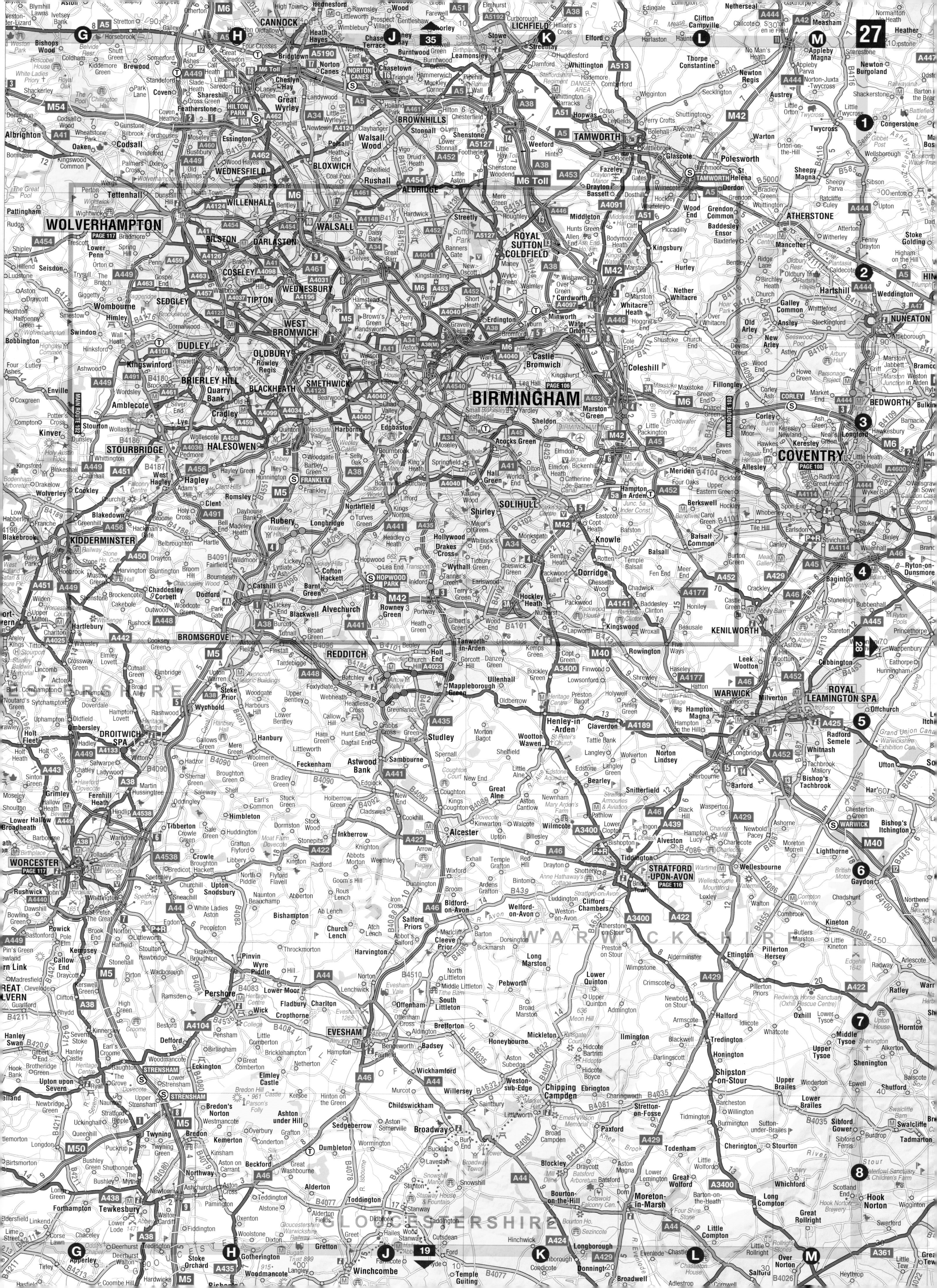
35
28
19
G
H
J
K
L
M
1
2
3
4
5
6
7
8
WOLVERHAMPTON
PAGE 117
BIRMINGHAM
PAGE 106
COVENTRY
PAGE 108
WORCESTER
PAGE 117
STRATFORD -UPON-AVON
PAGE 116
MAIN ROUTE 102
MAIN ROUTE 103
CANNOCK
LICHFIELD
TAMWORTH
WALSALL
ROYAL SUTTON COLDFIELD
DUDLEY
WEST BROMWICH
NUNEATON
ATHERSTONE
BEDWORTH
KIDDERMINSTER
STOURBRIDGE
HALESOWEN
BROMSGROVE
REDDITCH
SOLIHULL
KENILWORTH
WARWICK
ROYAL LEAMINGTON SPA
DROITWICH SPA
EVESHAM
ALCESTER
STUDLEY
SHIPSTON -ON-STOUR
CHIPPING CAMPDEN
MORETON -IN-MARSH
TEWKESBURY
PERSHORE
BROADWAY
WINCHCOMBE
WARWICKSHIRE
GLOUCESTERSHIRE
WORCESTERSHIRE
M5
M6
M6 Toll
M40
M42
M50
M54

A
B
C
D
E
F
36
1
2
3
4
5
6
7
8
27
20
LEICESTER
PAGE 110
COVENTRY
PAGE 108
NORTHAMPTON
PAGE 114
MILTON KEYNES
PAGE 114
LEICESTERSHIRE
WARWICKSHIRE
WEST NORTHAMPTONSHIRE
OXFORDSHIRE
BUCKINGHAMSHIRE
RUTLAND
ATHERSTONE
NUNEATON
HINCKLEY
BEDWORTH
RUGBY
ROYAL LEAMINGTON SPA
DAVENTRY
BANBURY
Brackley
Buckingham
Towcester
Stony Stratford
Wolverton
NEWPORT PAGNELL
BLETCHLEY
WELLINGBOROUGH
KETTERING
CORBY
MARKET HARBOROUGH
Desborough
Rothwell
Uppingham
Oakham
WIGSTON
Oadby
Lutterworth
Ibstock
Earl Shilton
Market Bosworth
WARWICK
WATFORD GAP
LEICESTER FOREST EAST
CORLEY
M1
M6
M40
M45
M69
A5
A6
A14
A43
A45
A47
A361
A422
A423
A426
A428
A508
A5199

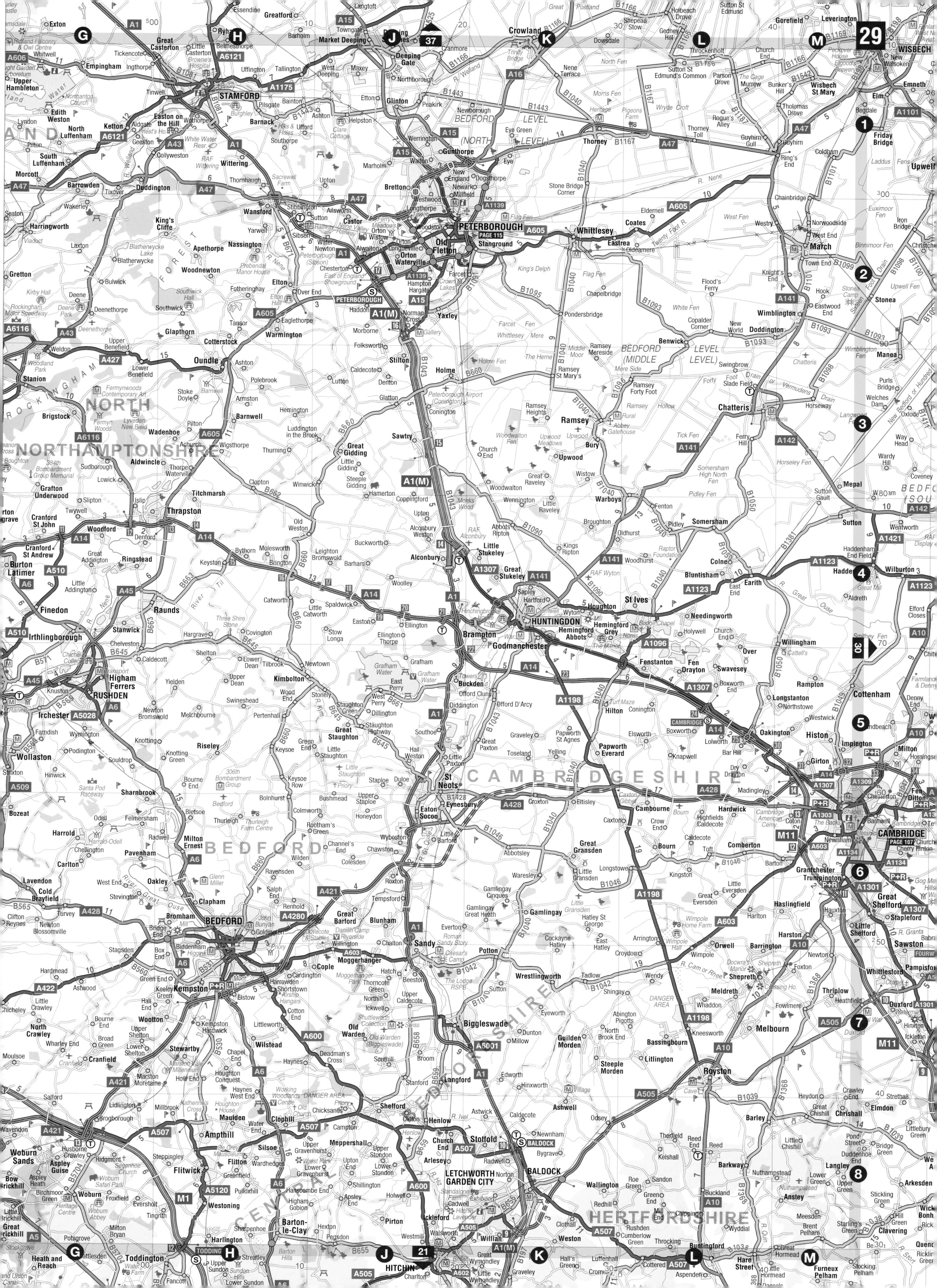

29
37
30
21
G
H
J
K
L
M
1
2
3
4
5
6
7
8
WISBECH
Wisbech St Mary
March
Chatteris
Ramsey
Warboys
Somersham
St Ives
HUNTINGDON
Godmanchester
Brampton
St Neots
Eaton Socon
Eynesbury
CAMBRIDGESHIRE
CAMBRIDGE
Cottenham
Histon
Girton
Sawston
Great Shelford
Royston
Melbourn
Sandy
Biggleswade
Potton
Gamlingay
BEDFORD
Kempston
Ampthill
Flitwick
Shefford
Stotfold
BALDOCK
LETCHWORTH GARDEN CITY
HITCHIN
Arlesey
Henlow
Toddington
Woburn
Woburn Sands
HERTFORDSHIRE
Buntingford
PETERBOROUGH
Old Fletton
Orton Waterville
Yaxley
Whittlesey
Thorney
Crowland
Market Deeping
Deeping St James
STAMFORD
Great Casterton
Wansford
Oundle
Thrapston
Raunds
Rushden
Higham Ferrers
Irthlingborough
Finedon
Burton Latimer
Wollaston
Irchester
NORTH NORTHAMPTONSHIRE
Sawtry
Alconbury
Kimbolton
Somersham
Fenstanton
Swavesey
Papworth Everard
Cambourne
Wilburton
Haddenham
Sutton
Mepal
Manea
Stonea
Doddington
Wimblington
PAGE 115
PAGE 107
A1
A1(M)
A14
A15
A16
A47
A141
A142
A428
A421
A505
A507
A603
A600
A6
A10
A1198
M1
M11

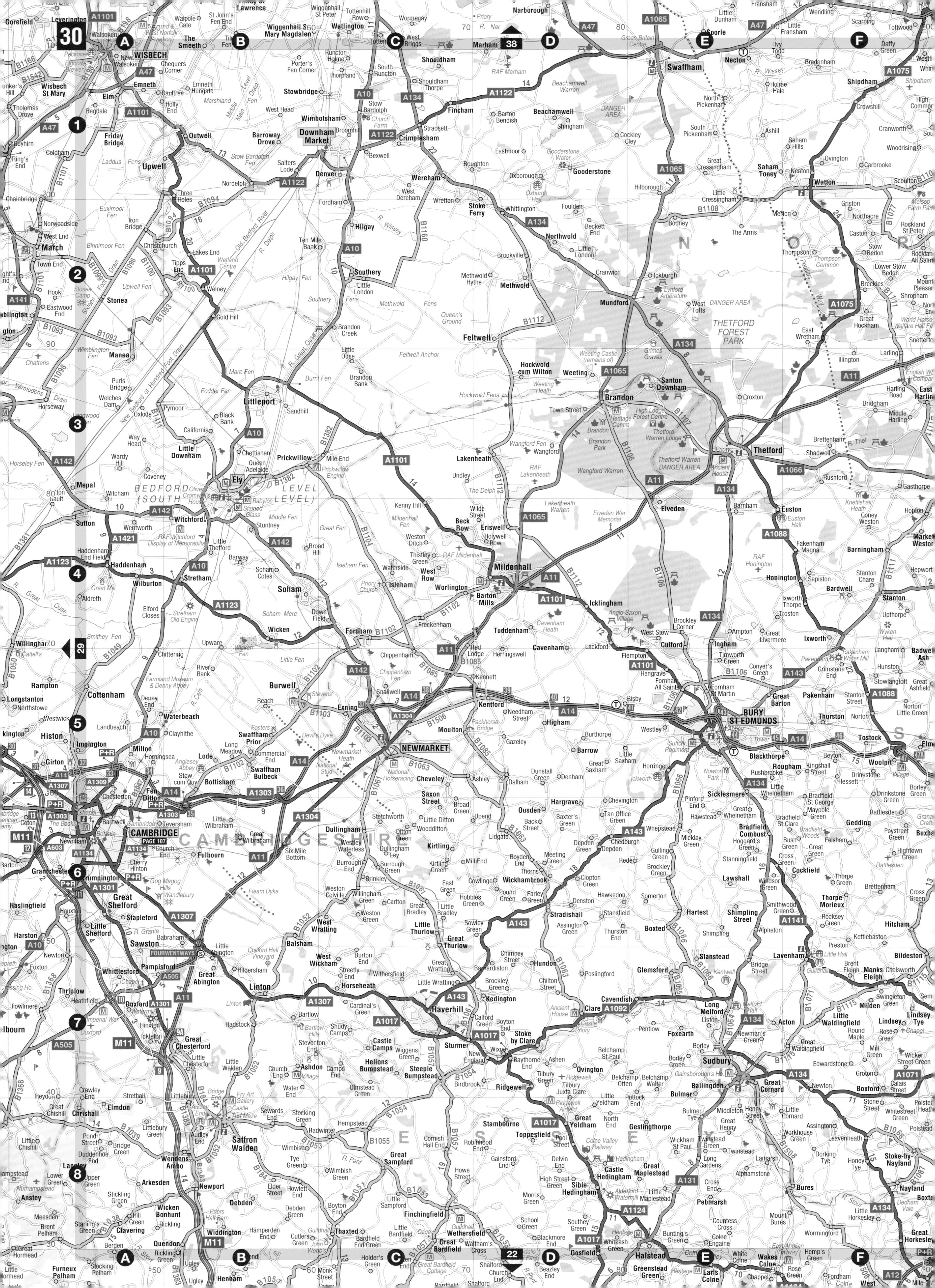

30
A
B
C
D
E
F
38
29
22
1
2
3
4
5
6
7
8
WISBECH
Downham Market
Swaffham
Upwell
March
Littleport
Ely
Mildenhall
Brandon
Thetford
Mundford
Feltwell
Methwold
Watton
NEWMARKET
CAMBRIDGE
PAGE 107
BURY ST EDMUNDS
Haverhill
Sudbury
Saffron Walden
Halstead
Linton
Soham
Chatteris
Lavenham
Clare
THETFORD FOREST PARK
BEDFORD (SOUTH LEVEL)
CAMBRIDGESHIRE
ESSEX
FOURWENTWAYS
M11
A10
A11
A14
A47
A134
A142
A143
A1065
A1101
A1122
A1307
A1017
A1092
A131
A1124

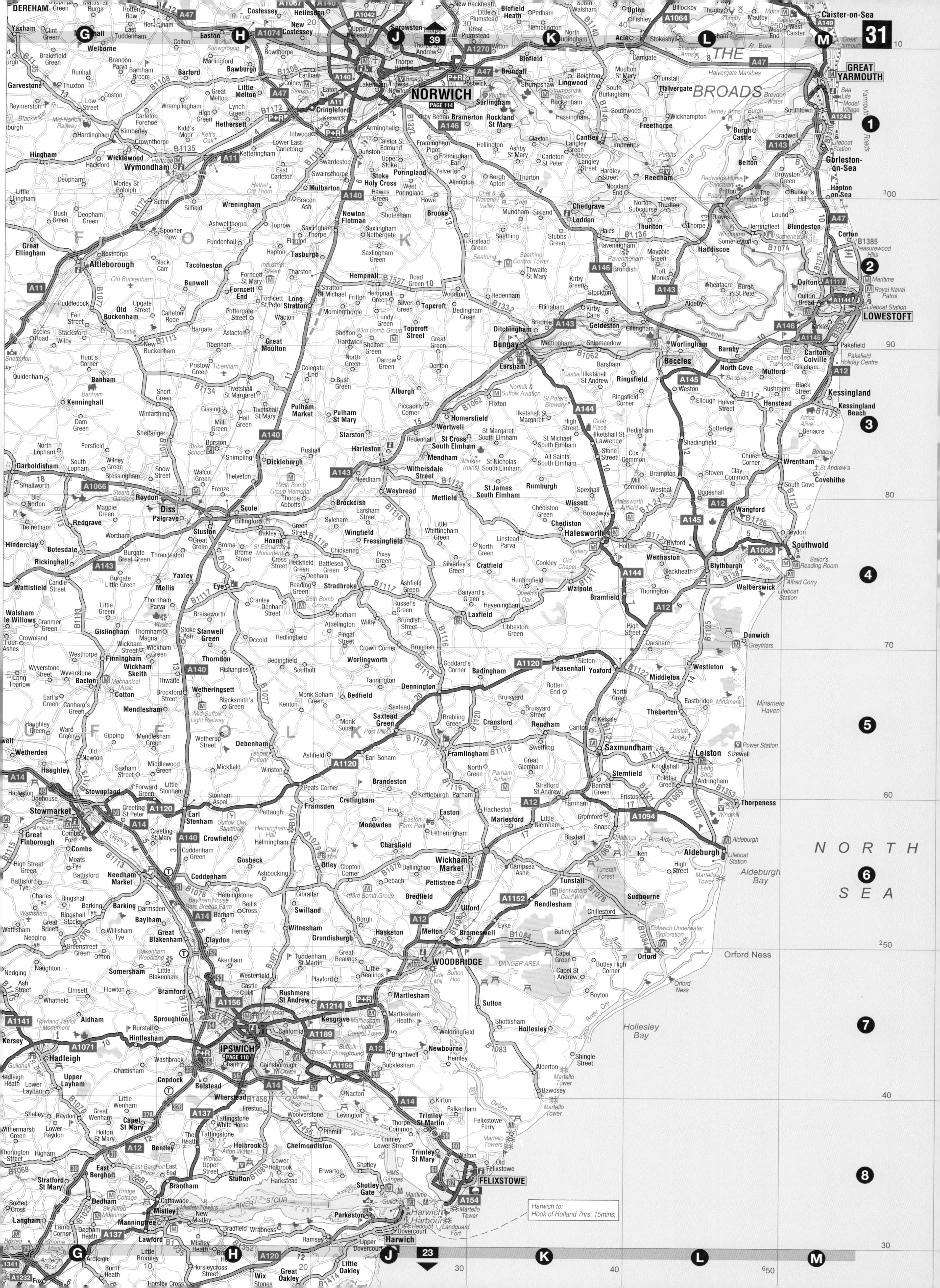
NORWICH
PAGE 114
GREAT YARMOUTH
LOWESTOFT
IPSWICH
PAGE 110
FELIXSTOWE
WOODBRIDGE
THE BROADS
NORTH SEA
Caister-on-Sea
Gorleston-on-Sea
Hopton on Sea
Corton
Carlton Colville
Kessingland
Southwold
Walberswick
Dunwich
Aldeburgh
Thorpeness
Leiston
Saxmundham
Halesworth
Beccles
Bungay
Harleston
Diss
Eye
Attleborough
Wymondham
Hethersett
Hingham
Stowmarket
Needham Market
Hadleigh
Manningtree
Mistley
Harwich
Dovercourt
Wickham Market
Framlingham
Orford
Orford Ness
Hollesley Bay
Aldeburgh Bay
Minsmere Haven
Harwich to: Hook of Holland 7hrs. 15mins.
A47
A140
A146
A143
A144
A145
A12
A14
A1120
A1094
A1152
A1156
A1214
A1189
A137
A120
A1066
A11
A154
DEREHAM
Garboldisham
Botesdale
Rickinghall
Haughley
Coddenham
Claydon
Capel St Mary
East Bergholt
Dedham
Lawford
Brantham
Stutton
Holbrook
Shotley Gate
Trimley St Martin
Trimley St Mary
Kesgrave
Martlesham
Melton
Ufford
Tunstall
Rendlesham
Sudbourne
Butley
Hollesley
Alderton
Bawdsey
Shottisham
Sutton
Reedham
Acle
Loddon
Brundall
Blofield
Poringland
Long Stratton
Dickleburgh
Scole
Hoxne
Stradbroke
Laxfield
Fressingfield
Wrentham
Blythburgh
Wenhaston
Yoxford
Peasenhall
Middleton
Westleton
Theberton
Wangford
Reydon
Covehithe
Benacre
Henstead
Pakefield
Oulton Broad
Oulton
Haddiscoe
Belton
Fritton
Bradwell
Burgh Castle
Halvergate
Freethorpe
Cantley
Lingwood
Cringleford
Costessey
New Costessey
Hellesdon
Sprowston
Thorpe St Andrew
Easton
Barford
Mulbarton
Newton Flotman
Tasburgh
Hempnall
Pulham Market
Pulham St Mary
Alburgh
Earsham
Ditchingham
Geldeston
Gillingham
Barnby
Mutford
Worlingham
Wortwell
Homersfield
Mendham
Weybread
Brockdish
Wingfield
Mellis
Gislingham
Finningham
Bacton
Cotton
Mendlesham
Debenham
Otley
Grundisburgh
Witnesham
Westerfield
Rushmere St Andrew
Bramford
Sproughton
Belstead
Wherstead
Freston
Woolverstone
Chelmondiston
Pin Mill
Nacton
Levington
Bucklesham
Brightwell
Newbourne
Waldringfield
Copdock
Chattisham
Washbrook
Hintlesham
Aldham
Kersey
Layham
Raydon
Holton St Mary
Bentley
Tattingstone
Ardleigh
Great Oakley
Little Oakley
Wix
Ramsey
Wrabness
Bradfield
Mistley Heath

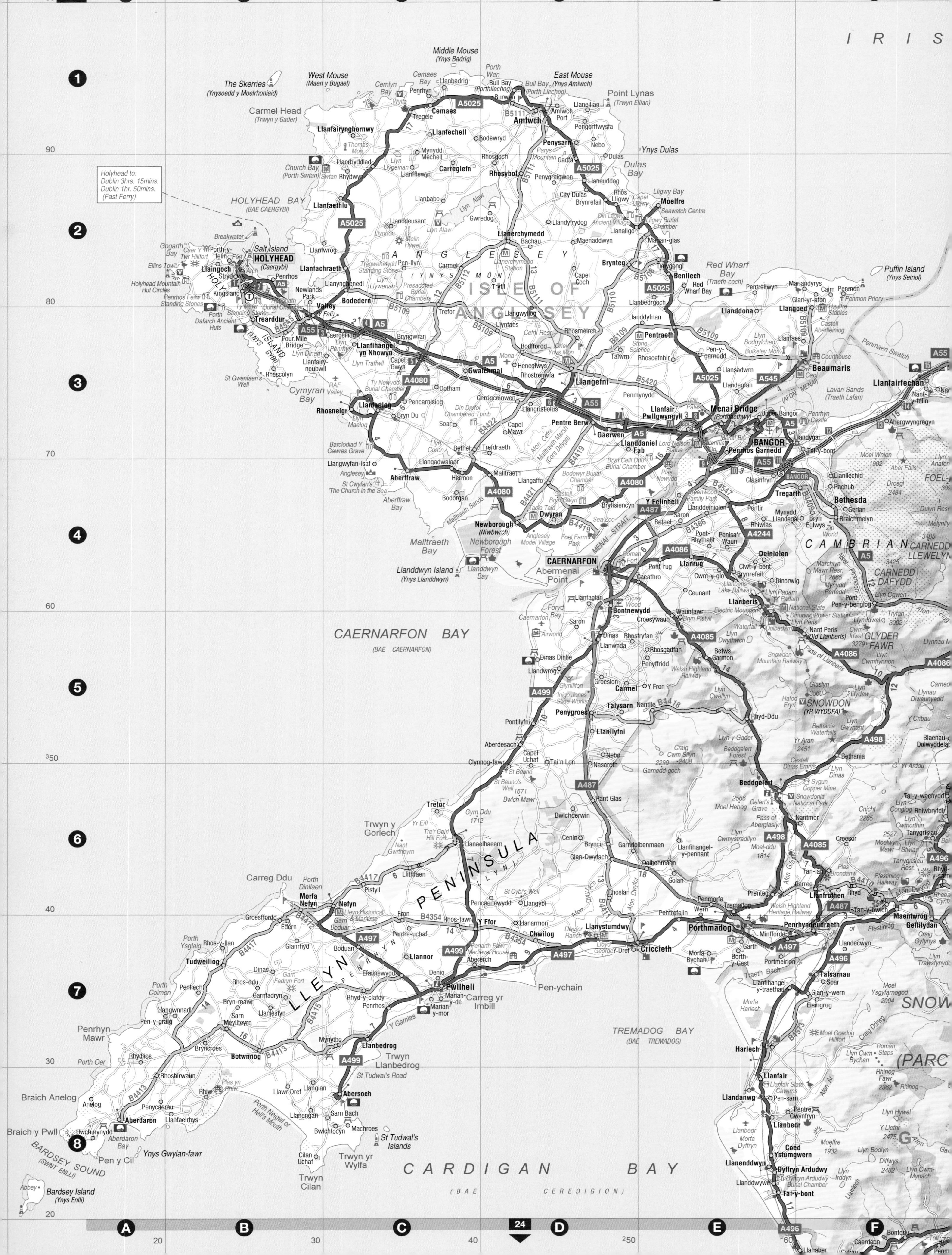
A B C D E F
1 2 3 4 5 6 7 8
IRISH SEA
Middle Mouse (Ynys Badrig)
West Mouse (Maen y Bugael)
East Mouse (Ynys Amlwch)
The Skerries (Ynysoedd y Moelrhoniaid)
Carmel Head (Trwyn y Gader)
Point Lynas (Trwyn Eilian)
Ynys Dulas
Dulas Bay
Holyhead to:
Dublin 3hrs. 15mins.
Dublin 1hr. 50mins.
(Fast Ferry)
HOLYHEAD BAY (BAE CAERGYBI)
HOLYHEAD (Caergybi)
Salt Island
HOLY ISLAND (YNYS GYBI)
Cemaes
Amlwch
Llanfairynghornwy
Llanfechell
Penysarn
Moelfre
Rhosybol
Carreglefn
Llanfaethlu
Llanerchymedd
Benllech
Red Wharf Bay (Traeth-coch)
Puffin Island (Ynys Seiriol)
ANGLESEY (YNYS MÔN)
ISLE OF ANGLESEY
Valley
Trearddur
Bodedern
Llangefni
Gwalchmai
Pentraeth
Beaumaris
Menai Bridge (Porthaethwy)
BANGOR
Llanfair Pwllgwyngyll
Pentre Berw
Gaerwen
Rhosneigr
Llanfaelog
Aberffraw
Cymyran Bay
Malltraeth Bay
Newborough (Niwbwrch)
Newborough Forest
Llanddwyn Island (Ynys Llanddwyn)
Abermenai Point
CAERNARFON
Y Felinheli
Bethesda
Llanberis
Llanfairfechan
CAMBRIAN
CARNEDD LLEWELYN
CARNEDD DAFYDD
GLYDER FAWR
SNOWDON (YR WYDDFA)
CAERNARFON BAY (BAE CAERNARFON)
Penygroes
Beddgelert
Nefyn
Morfa Nefyn
LLEYN PENINSULA (PENRHYN LLYN)
Pwllheli
Criccieth
Porthmadog
Penrhyndeudraeth
Tremadog
Harlech
Llanbedr
Dyffryn Ardudwy
Tudweiliog
Aberdaron
Abersoch
Llanbedrog
Botwnnog
Braich Anelog
Braich y Pwll
Bardsey Island (Ynys Enlli)
BARDSEY SOUND (SWNT ENLLI)
Ynys Gwylan-fawr
St Tudwal's Islands
Porth Neigwl or Hell's Mouth
Carreg Ddu
Trwyn y Gorlech
Pen-ychain
TREMADOG BAY (BAE TREMADOG)
CARDIGAN BAY (BAE CEREDIGION)
A5 A55 A5025 A4080 A487 A499 A497 A498 A4085 A4086 A496 A4244 A545
24

SEA
LIVERPOOL BAY
Liverpool to Dublin 8hrs.
Liverpool to Douglas 2hrs. 30mins. (Fast Ferry, Seasonal)
Birkenhead to: Belfast 8hrs. Douglas 4hrs. 15mins. (Seasonal)
40
34
25
Great Ormes Head (Pen-y-Gogarth)
Little Ormes Head
CONWY BAY
Colwyn Bay
Abergele Roads
Point of Ayr
LLANDUDNO
COLWYN BAY (Bae Colwyn)
Rhôs-on-Sea (Llandrillo-yn-Rhos)
Penrhyn Bay (Bae Penrhyn)
Deganwy
Conwy
Llandudno Junction
Mochdre
Old Colwyn
Llanddulas
Abergele
Kinmel Bay (Bae Cinmel)
Towyn
RHYL
Prestatyn
Meliden (Gallt Melyd)
Gronant
Gwespyr
Talacre
Rhuddlan
Dyserth
Trelawnyd
Mostyn
Greenfield (Maes-glas)
Holywell (Treffynnon)
Bagillt
Flint (Y Fflint)
CONNAH'S QUAY
Northop
BUCKLEY (Bwcle)
Mold (Yr Wyddgrug)
HOYLAKE
West Kirby
Hilbre Islands
HESWALL
NESTON
WALLASEY
Parkgate
Penmaenmawr
Dwygyfylchi
Llanfairfechan
Bodelwyddan
St Asaph (Llan-Elwy)
Trefnant
Denbigh (Dinbych)
Henllan
Llansannan
Llanfair Talhaiarn
Llangernyw
Betws-yn-Rhos
Llansanffraid Glan Conwy
Eglwysbach
Dolgarrog
Trefriw
Llanrwst
Betws-y-Coed
Capel Curig
Pentrefoelas
Cerrigydrudion
Bylchau
Nantglyn
Ruthin (Rhuthun)
Llanrhaeadr
Llandegla
Cyffylliog
Clocaenog
Derwen
Llanelidan
Bettws Gwerfil Goch
Gwyddelwern
Corwen
Cynwyd
Llangollen
Glyn Ceiriog
Chirk
Bala (Y Bala)
Llanuwchllyn
Llandderfel
Llandrillo
Llanarmon Dyffryn Ceiriog
Llanrhaeadr-ym-Mochnant
Llangynog
Llansilin
Llangedwyn
Llanfyllin
Llanymynech
Blaenau Ffestiniog
Llan Ffestiniog
Trawsfynydd
Dolgellau
Llanelltyd
Llanymawddwy
Dolwyddelan
Penmachno
CONWY
FLINTSHIRE
DENBIGHSHIRE
GWYNEDD
POWYS
ENGLAND
WALES
SNOWDONIA NATIONAL PARK
PARC CENEDLAETHOL ERYRI
CAMBRIAN MOUNTAINS
BERWYN
CLOCAENOG FOREST
GWYDYR FOREST PARK
COED Y BRENIN FOREST PARK
Llyn Celyn
Llyn Brenig
Alwen Resr.
Bala Lake
Lake Vyrnwy
A55
A470
A5
A548
A547
A525
A543
A541
A494
A5104
A539
A483
A495
A490
A4212
A544
A5151
A5026
A5119
A540
A551
A553
G
H
J
K
L
M
1
2
3
4
5
6
7
8
80
90
300
10
20
400

LIVERPOOL
PAGE 111
BIRKENHEAD
WARRINGTON
WIDNES
RUNCORN
HUYTON
ELLESMERE PORT
FRODSHAM
CHESTER
PAGE 108
NORTHWICH
WINSFORD
KNUTSFORD
MIDDLEWICH
SANDBACH
CREWE
NANTWICH
WREXHAM
Whitchurch
OSWESTRY
MARKET DRAYTON
SHREWSBURY
PAGE 116
TELFORD
ALTRINCHAM
HOYLAKE
West Kirby
BEBINGTON
HESWALL
NESTON
Flint
CONNAH'S QUAY
BUCKLEY
Mold
Helsby
Kelsall
Tarporley
Malpas
Ellesmere
Wem
Chirk
Ruabon
Llangollen
Hawarden
Saltney
Audlem
Holt
Gresford
Overton
Hodnet
Newport
Wellington
Oakengates
Donnington
Shifnal
Shawbury
Baschurch
Welshampton
Rossett
Llay
Caergwrle
Coedpoeth
Brymbo
Rhosllanerchrugog
Lymm
Audley
Madeley
Woore
Holmes Chapel
Goostrey
Runcorn
Speke
Garston
Hale
Weaverham
Sandiway
Cuddington
Delamere
Tarvin
Christleton
Waverton
Farndon
Hanmer
Prees
Loppington
Cockshutt
Myddle
Hadnall
Upton Magna
Atcham
Bayston Hill
Ford
Alberbury
Llanymynech
Four Crosses
Welshpool
ENGLAND
WALES
WREXHAM
CHESHIRE WEST & CHESTER
CHESHIRE
SHROPSHIRE
RIVER MERSEY
RIVER DEE
Manchester Ship Canal
Shropshire Union Canal
M6
M53
M56
M54
M62
A49
A41
A5
A483
A51
A54
A556
A534
A525
A528
A495
A442
A53
A529
A530
A500
33
40
26
25
A
B
C
D
E
F
1
2
3
4
5
6
7
8

41
35
36
27
PEAK DISTRICT NATIONAL PARK
HIGH PEAK
Kinder Scout 2088
DERBYSHIRE
STAFFORDSHIRE
CANNOCK CHASE
NEEDWOOD FOREST
THE NATIONAL FOREST
SHEFFIELD
PAGE 116
STOCKPORT
CHEADLE
Cheadle Hulme
Gatley
Hazel Grove
Marple
New Mills
Hayfield
Whaley Bridge
Chapel-en-le-Frith
Castleton
Hope
Bamford
Hathersage
Bradwell
Tideswell
Eyam
Stoney Middleton
Baslow
Bakewell
Ashford in the Water
Buxton
Macclesfield
Bollington
Wilmslow
Alderley Edge
Congleton
Biddulph
Kidsgrove
Leek
Cheadle
Ashbourne
Matlock
Darley Dale
Wirksworth
Cromford
Belper
Duffield
Derby
PAGE 108
Dronfield
Chesterfield
Clay Cross
Stoke-on-Trent
Newcastle-under-Lyme
Hanley
Burslem
Tunstall
Longton
Stone
Stafford
Uttoxeter
Rugeley
Cannock
Lichfield
Burton upon Trent
Swadlincote
Ashby-de-la-Zouch
Penkridge
Eccleshall
Tutbury
Mickleover
Hednesford
Barton-under-Needwood
Alrewas
Melbourne
Appleby Magna
Measham
MAIN ROUTE 104
M6
M6 Toll
M1
M42
M60
A6
A50
A38
A52
A53
A515
A523
A54
A34
A57
A61
A619
A623
A625
A5
G
H
J
K
L
M

36
42
35
28
A
B
C
D
E
F
1
2
3
4
5
6
7
8
NOTTINGHAMSHIRE
LEICESTERSHIRE
SHEFFIELD
ROTHERHAM
MALTBY
GAINSBOROUGH
WORKSOP
RETFORD
DRONFIELD
CHESTERFIELD
MATLOCK
MANSFIELD
MANSFIELD WOODHOUSE
SUTTON IN ASHFIELD
KIRKBY-IN-ASHFIELD
ALFRETON
NEWARK-ON-TRENT
BELPER
HEANOR
EASTWOOD
HUCKNALL
ARNOLD
ILKESTON
NOTTINGHAM
CARLTON
DERBY
STAPLEFORD
BEESTON
WEST BRIDGFORD
LONG EATON
LOUGHBOROUGH
MELTON MOWBRAY
COALVILLE
Ashby-de-la-Zouch
Oakham

LINCOLNSHIRE
THE WASH
LINCOLN
PAGE 111
GRANTHAM
BOSTON
SPALDING
LOUTH
WISBECH
Sleaford
Horncastle
Market Rasen
Woodhall Spa
Spilsby
Alford
Bourne
Holbeach
Long Sutton
Market Deeping
Crowland
Coningsby
Tattershall
Wragby
Donington
Sutton Bridge
Skegness
Kirton
Swineshead
Billinghay
Ruskington
Navenby
Waddington
Colsterworth
Corby Glen
Dunsby
Deeping St James
Deeping St Nicholas
Moulton
Whaplode
Pinchbeck
Surfleet
Gosberton
Quadring
Fosdyke
Sutterton
Wigtoft
Bicker
Heckington
Helpringham
Digby
Metheringham
Nocton
Branston
Washingborough
Nettleham
Welton
Dunholme
Saxilby
Ingham
Spridlington
Hemswell
Bishop Norton
Middle Rasen
Tealby
Ludford
Kelstern
Legbourne
Saltfleetby St Peter
Grimoldby
Manby
Withern
Maltby le Marsh
Bilsby
Partney
Candlesby
Hundleby
Halton Holegate
Toynton All Saints
Great Steeping
Firsby
Friskney
Wrangle
Old Leake
Sibsey
Frithville
Stickney
Leverton
Benington
Butterwick
Freiston
Wyberton
Fleet Hargate
Gedney
Lutton
Tydd Gote
Newton
Leverington
Crowland
Thurlby
Baston
Greatford
Ryhall
Great Casterton
Empingham
Clipsham
Castle Bytham
Little Bytham
Witham on the Hill
Edenham
Swinstead
Swayfield
North Witham
South Witham
Burton Coggles
Ropsley
Old Somerby
Folkingham
Billingborough
Horbling
Osbournby
Welby
Barkston
Honington
Wilsford
Ancaster
Leasingham
North Rauceby
South Rauceby
Caythorpe
Fulbeck
Leadenham
Welbourn
Wellingore
Coleby
Harmston
Bassingham
North Hykeham
Skellingthorpe
A15
A46
A17
A16
A52
A153
A158
A157
A631
A1
A607
A151
A1175
A1104
A1028
A155
A1121
A1101
A6121
A152
A1500
A57
A1192
A1434
A1103
A47
B1398
B1202
B1225
B1200
B1191
B1188
B1183
B1192
B1184
B1397
B1357
B1165
B1166
B1168
B1176
B1177
B1394
43
29
38
G
H
J
K
L
M
1
2
3
4
5
6
7
8

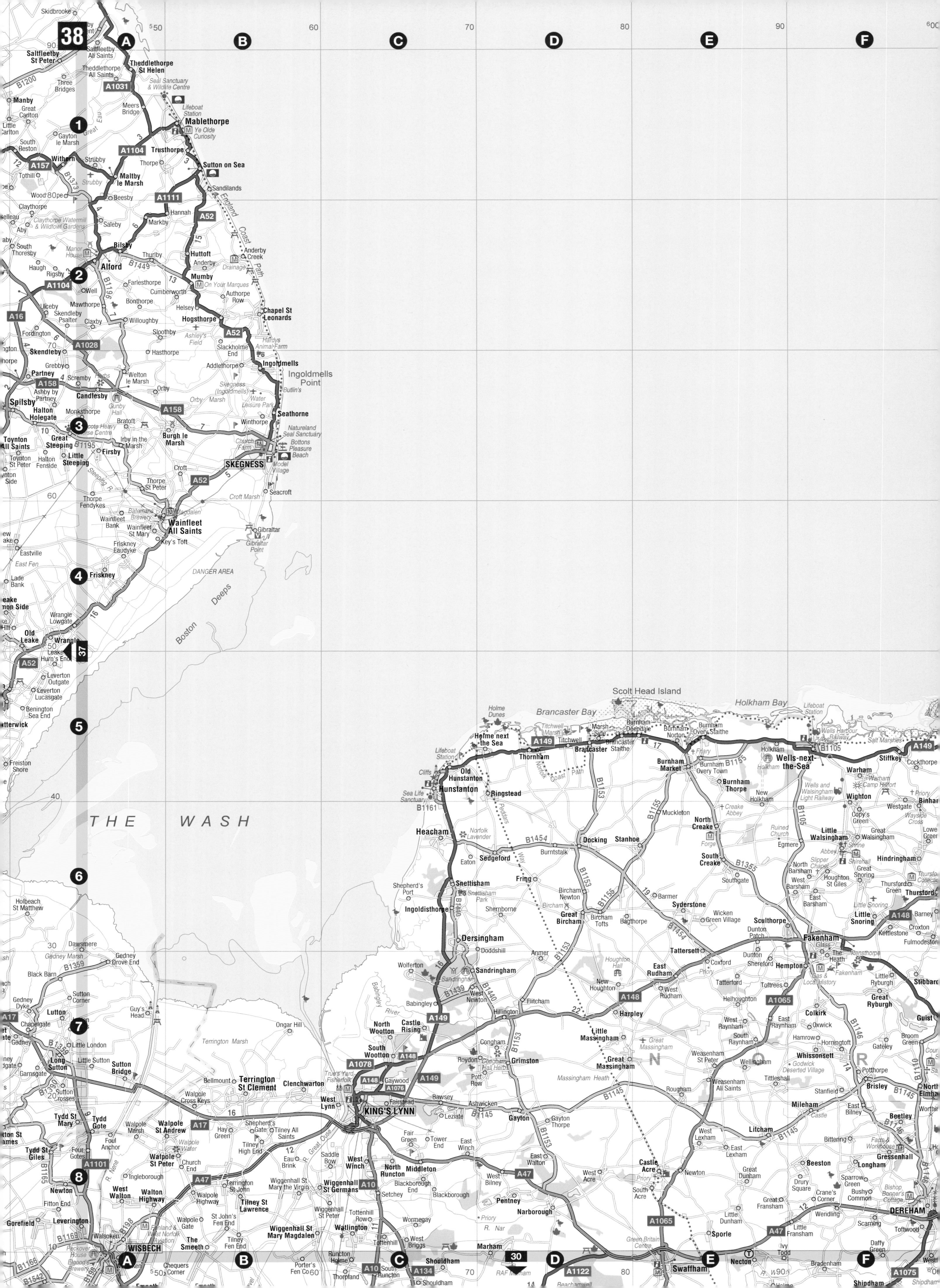
A
B
C
D
E
F
1
2
3
4
5
6
7
8
50
60
70
80
90
Skidbrooke
Saltfleetby St Peter
Saltfleetby All Saints
Theddlethorpe St Helen
Theddlethorpe All Saints
Three Bridges
A1031
Seal Sanctuary & Wildlife Centre
Lifeboat Station
Manby
Great Carlton
Little Carlton
Meers Bridge
Mablethorpe
Ye Olde Curiosity
South Reston
Gayton le Marsh
Great Eau
A1104
Trusthorpe
Withern
A157
Strubby
Thorpe
Sutton on Sea
Tothill
Maltby le Marsh
Sandilands
Wood Thorpe
Beesby
A1111
England Coast Path
Claythorpe
Claythorpe Watermill & Wildfowl Gardens
Hannah
A52
Aby
Saleby
Markby
South Thoresby
Manor House
Bilsby
Thurlby
Huttoft
Anderby Creek
Haugh
Alford
B1449
Anderby
Drainage
Rigsby
Mumby
On Your Marques
A1104
Farlesthorpe
Well
B1196
Cumberworth
Authorpe Row
Mawthorpe
Bonthorpe
Helsey
A16
Ulceby
Skendleby Psalter
Claxby
Willoughby
Hogsthorpe
Chapel St Leonards
Fordington
Sloothby
Ashley's Field
A52
A1028
Hardys Animal Farm
Skendleby
Slackholme End
Grebby
Hasthorpe
Ingoldmells
Addlethorpe
Ingoldmells Point
Partney
Scremby
Welton le Marsh
Butlin's
A158
Skegness (Ingoldmells)
Ashby by Partney
Candlesby
Orby
Orby Marsh
Water Leisure Park
Spilsby
Gunby Hall
A158
Seathorne
Halton Holegate
Monksthorpe
Bratoft
Winthorpe
Natureland Seal Sanctuary
Great Steeping
Irby in the Marsh
Burgh le Marsh
Church Farm
Bottons Pleasure Beach
Toynton All Saints
B1195
Little Steeping
Firsby
SKEGNESS
Model Village
Toynton St Peter
Halton Fenside
Croft
A52
Steeping R.
Thorpe St Peter
Seacroft
Thorpe Fendykes
Croft Marsh
Batemans Brewery
Magdalen
Wainfleet Bank
Wainfleet All Saints
Wainfleet St Mary
Gibraltar
Key's Toft
Gibraltar Point
Friskney Eaudyke
Eastville
East Fen
DANGER AREA
Friskney
Lade Bank
Boston Deeps
Wrangle Lowgate
Old Leake
Wrangle
Leake Hurn's End
37
A52
Leverton Outgate
Leverton Lucasgate
Benington Sea End
Freiston Shore
THE WASH
Holbeach St Matthew
Dawsmere
Gedney Marsh
Gedney Drove End
B1359
Black Barn
Sutton Corner
Gedney Dyke
Lutton
Guy's Head
Chapelgate
Gedney
Little London
Ongar Hill
Terrington Marsh
Long Sutton
Little Sutton
Sutton Bridge
Garnsgate
Sutton Crosses
Bellmount
Terrington St Clement
Clenchwarton
True's Yard Fisherfolk
Walpole Cross Keys
West Lynn
KING'S LYNN
Tydd St Mary
Tydd Gote
Walpole Marsh
Walpole St Andrew
A17
Hay Green
Shepherd's Gate
Tilney All Saints
Tilney High End
Tydd St Giles
Four Gotes
Foul Anchor
Walpole Water
A1101
Walpole St Peter
Church End
R. Great Ouse
Eau Brink
Saddle Bow
West Winch
Ingleborough
A47
Terrington St John
Wiggenhall St Mary the Virgin
Wiggenhall St Germans
A10
Newton
West Walton
Walton Highway
Walpole Highway
Tilney St Lawrence
Wiggenhall St Peter
Fitton End
Gorefield
Leverington
Walpole Gate
St John's Fen End
Wiggenhall St Mary Magdalen
Walsoken
WISBECH
Fenland & West Norfolk Aviation
The Smeeth
Tilney Fen End
Peckover House
Elgood's Brewery
Chequers Corner
Porter's Fen Co
Scolt Head Island
Brancaster Bay
Holkham Bay
Holme Dunes
Lifeboat Station
Titchwell Marsh
Marsh Side
Burnham Deepdale
Burnham Norton
Burnham Overy Staithe
Wells Harbour Railway
Holme next the Sea
A149
Titchwell
Brancaster
Brancaster Staithe
Thornham
Norfolk Coast Path
B1105
Holkham
Wells-next-the-Sea
Salt Marshes
Stiffkey
Cockthorpe
Cliffs
Old Hunstanton
Burnham Market
Burnham Overy Town
B1155
Friary
Hunstanton
Ringstead
B1153
Burnham Thorpe
Warham
Warham Camp Hillfort
Sea Life Sanctuary
B1161
Peddars Way
Muckleton
New Holkham
Wells and Walsingham Light Railway
Wighton
Westgate
Binham
Priory
Creake Abbey
North Creake
Ruined Church
Copy's Green
Wayside Cross
Heacham
Norfolk Lavender
B1454
Docking
Stanhoe
Little Walsingham
Great Walsingham
Burntstalk
Forge
Egmere
Abbey
Shrine
Sedgeford
Eaton
South Creake
B1355
Slipper Chapel
Shirehall
Hindringham
Fring
North Barsham
Great Snoring
Snettisham
Snettisham Park
Southgate
West Barsham
Houghton St Giles
Thursford Collection
Shepherd's Port
Bircham Newton
Barmer
East Barsham
Thursford Green
Thursford
Bircham
Syderstone
Little Snoring
Ingoldisthorpe
Shernborne
Great Bircham
Bircham Tofts
Bagthorpe
Wicken Green Village
Sculthorpe
A148
Barney
Little Snoring
Dunton Patch
Kettlestone
Croxton
Dersingham
Doddshill
Anmer
Tattersett
Fakenham
Fulmodeston
Dunton
Coxford
Pensthorpe
Wolferton
Sandringham
Houghton Hall
East Rudham
Shereford
Hempton
The Heath
Little Ryburgh
Stibbard
Priory
Tatterford
Gas & Local History
Fakenham
New Houghton
West Rudham
Toftrees
Babingley
West Newton
Flitcham
A148
Helhoughton
A1065
Great Ryburgh
Babingley River
Hillington
Harpley
East Raynham
Colkirk
Guist
North Wootton
Castle Rising
West Raynham
Oxwick
Little Massingham
South Raynham
Hamrow
Horningtoft
Broom Green
South Wootton
Congham
Great Massingham
Gateley
A1078
Roydon
Congham Hall Herbs
Grimston
Great Massingham
Weasenham St Peter
Wellingham
Whissonsett
Godwick Deserted Village
Potthorpe
Pott Row
Massingham Heath
Tittleshall
Brisley
Gaywood
Weasenham All Saints
Stanfield
A1076
Bawsey
Rougham
B1145
North Elmham
Fairstead
Ashwicken
Mileham
Leziate
Gayton
Gayton Thorpe
East Bilney
Beetley
Fair Green
Tower End
East Winch
West Lexham
Litcham
Worthing
Bittering
Farm & Workhouse
East Lexham
Gressenhall
North Runcton
Middleton
East Walton
Castle Acre
Beeston
Longham
Setchey
Blackborough End
West Bilney
West Acre
Newton
Great Dunham
Drury Square
Sparrow Green
Blackborough
Pentney
South Acre
Crane's Corner
Bushy Common
Bishop Bonner's Cottage
Tottenhill Row
Wormegay
Narborough
Great Fransham
Wendling
DEREHAM
Tottenhill
Wallington
Priory
Little Dunham
Scarning
R. Nar
A1065
Little Fransham
Tottwood
West Briggs
Sporle
A47
Runcton Holme
Marham
Green Britain Centre
Ivy Todd
Daffy Green
Shouldham
30
RAF Marham
A1122
Swaffham
Necton
Bradenham
A10
South Runcton
A134
Thorpland
Shipdham
A1075
Holme
Beachamwell
NORFOLK

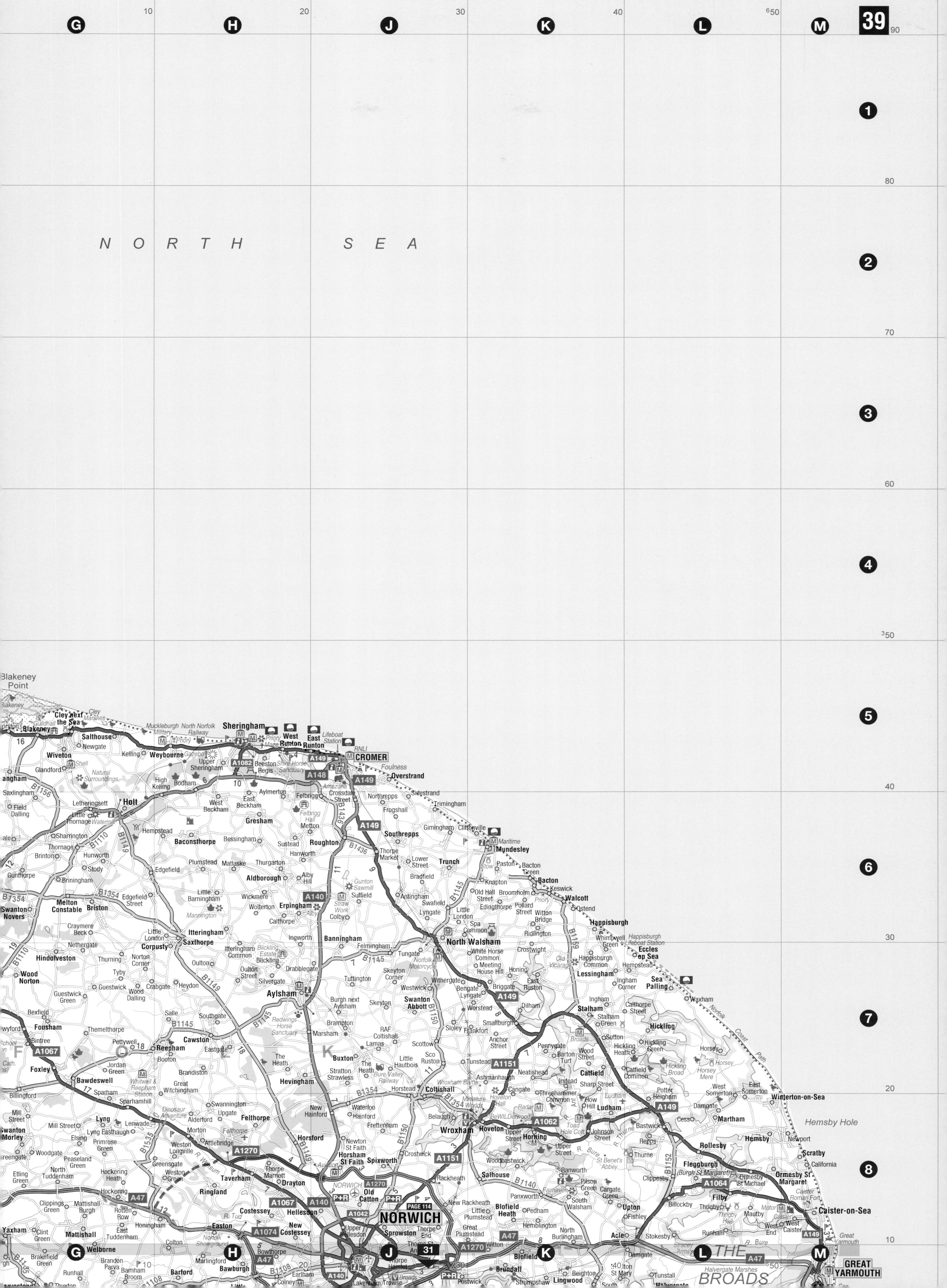
G
H
J
K
L
M
1
2
3
4
5
6
7
8
NORTH SEA
Blakeney Point
Cley next the Sea
Blakeney
Salthouse
Sheringham
West Runton
East Runton
CROMER
Overstrand
Weybourne
Wiveton
Holt
Sidestrand
Trimingham
Mundesley
Bacton
Walcott
Happisburgh
Eccles on Sea
Sea Palling
Waxham
North Walsham
Aylsham
Reepham
Cawston
Foulsham
Melton Constable
Briston
Corpusty
Saxthorpe
Itteringham
Erpingham
Roughton
Gresham
Baconsthorpe
Stalham
Hickling
Ludham
Horning
Hoveton
Wroxham
Coltishall
Horstead
Buxton
Hevingham
Horsford
Drayton
Taverham
Costessey
Hellesdon
NORWICH
Sprowston
Rackheath
Salhouse
Blofield
Acle
Upton
Filby
Ormesby St Margaret
Caister-on-Sea
Martham
Hemsby
Scratby
Winterton-on-Sea
Rollesby
Fleggburgh
GREAT YARMOUTH
THE BROADS
Mattishall
Welborne
Easton
Barford
Bawburgh
Lyng
Swanton Morley
Hempstead
Edgefield
Hindolveston
Wood Norton
Bawdeswell
Foxley
Felthorpe
Attlebridge
Ringland
A149
A148
A140
A1067
A1151
A1062
A1064
A47
A1270
A1074
A1042
A1082
B1145
B1354
B1149
PAGE 114
Hemsby Hole
Lingwood
Brundall

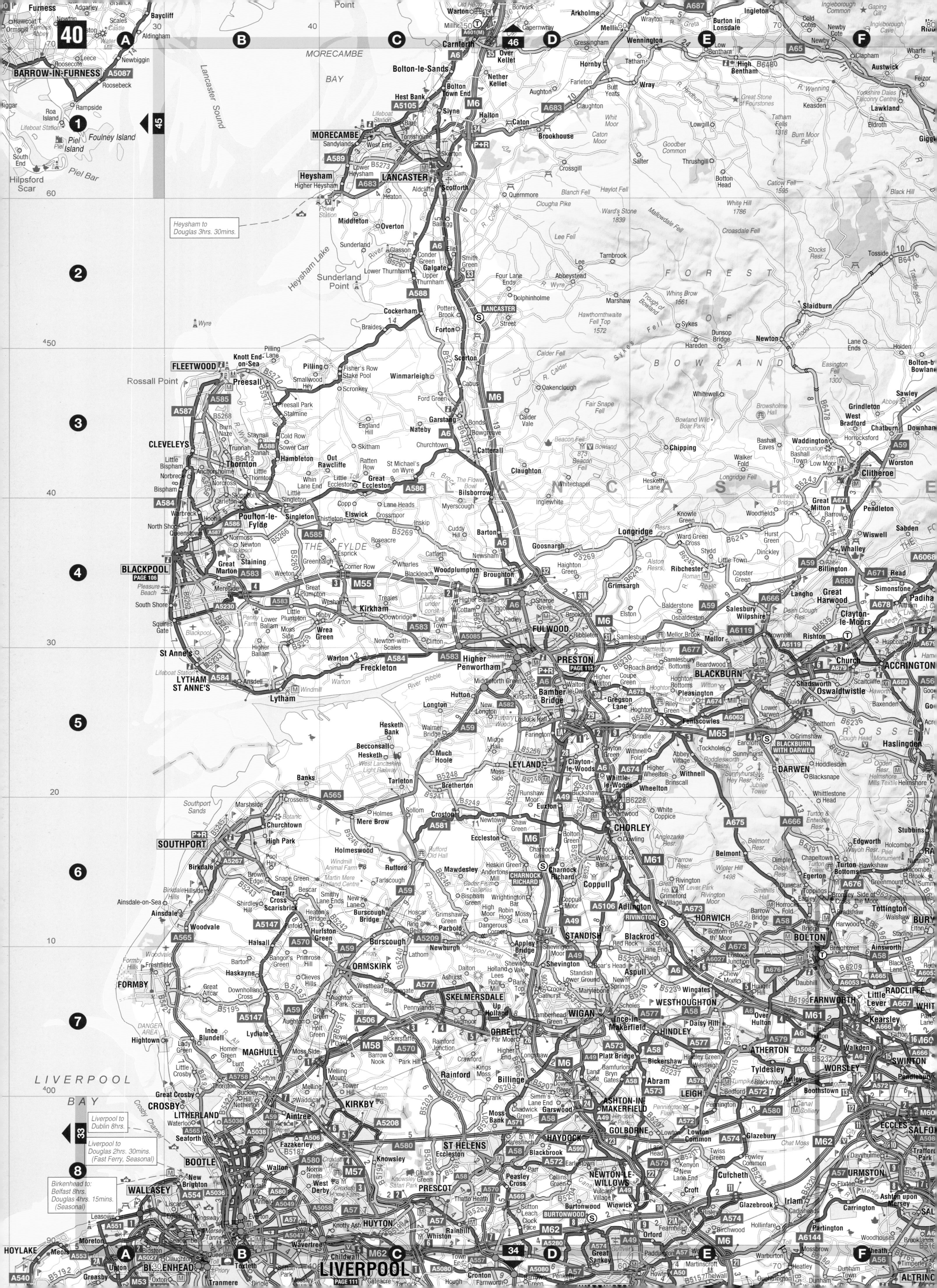

40
BARROW-IN-FURNESS
Foulney Island
Piel Island
MORECAMBE BAY
Lancaster Sound
MORECAMBE
Heysham
LANCASTER
Carnforth
Bolton-le-Sands
Heysham to Douglas 3hrs. 30mins.
Heysham Lake
Sunderland Point
Galgate
Cockerham
Garstang
FLEETWOOD
Knott End-on-Sea
Rossall Point
Preesall
Pilling
CLEVELEYS
Thornton
Poulton-le-Fylde
Singleton
BLACKPOOL
PAGE 106
St Anne's
LYTHAM ST ANNE'S
Lytham
Kirkham
Freckleton
THE FYLDE
FOREST OF BOWLAND
LANCASHIRE
Longridge
Clitheroe
Ribchester
PRESTON
PAGE 115
FULWOOD
BLACKBURN
ACCRINGTON
Oswaldtwistle
DARWEN
Haslingden
LEYLAND
CHORLEY
Tarleton
Banks
SOUTHPORT
Southport Sands
Ormskirk
Burscough
Formby
SKELMERSDALE
WIGAN
STANDISH
HORWICH
BOLTON
FARNWORTH
WESTHOUGHTON
HINDLEY
LEIGH
ATHERTON
Tyldesley
WORSLEY
SWINTON
ECCLES
MAGHULL
KIRKBY
ST HELENS
CROSBY
LITHERLAND
BOOTLE
WALLASEY
BIRKENHEAD
HOYLAKE
LIVERPOOL
PAGE 111
LIVERPOOL BAY
Liverpool to Dublin 8hrs.
Liverpool to Douglas 2hrs. 30mins. (Fast Ferry, Seasonal)
Birkenhead to: Belfast 8hrs. Douglas 4hrs. 15mins. (Seasonal)
HUYTON
PRESCOT
NEWTON-LE-WILLOWS
HAYDOCK
ASHTON-IN-MAKERFIELD
GOLBORNE
URMSTON
Irlam
M6
M55
M61
M65
M58
M57
M62
A6
A59
A565
A583
A584
A585
A586
A587
A588
A589
A683
A675
A666
A677
A580
45
46
33
34

47
NORTH
YORKSHIRE
LEEDS
PAGE 110
BRADFORD
PAGE 106
HARROGATE
PAGE 110
MANCHESTER
PAGE 111
MAIN ROUTE 104
HUDDERSFIELD
HALIFAX
KEIGHLEY
SKIPTON
ILKLEY
OTLEY
WAKEFIELD
BARNSLEY
DEWSBURY
BATLEY
MORLEY
ROCHDALE
OLDHAM
BURNLEY
NELSON
STOCKPORT
STALYBRIDGE
GLOSSOP
DERBYSHIRE
PEAK DISTRICT
PEAK DISTRICT NATIONAL PARK
HIGH PEAK
KNARESBOROUGH
RIPON
WETHERBY
PUDSEY
SHIPLEY
BINGLEY
BRIGHOUSE
CLECKHEATON
MIRFIELD
PENISTONE
STOCKSBRIDGE
THE PENNINES
RUMBALDS MOOR
KEIGHLEY MOOR
THE FOREST OF TRAWDEN
FOREST OF ROSSENDALE
SADDLEWORTH
42
35

A
B
C
D
E
F
1
2
3
4
5
6
7
8
48
36
NORTH YORKSHIRE
EAST YORKSHIRE
NOTTINGHAMSHIRE
HOWARDIAN HILLS
ISLE OF AXHOLME
RIPON
HARROGATE
PAGE 110
KNARESBOROUGH
Wetherby
WETHERBY
LEEDS
PAGE 110
YORK
PAGE 117
SELBY
Tadcaster
CASTLEFORD
PONTEFRACT
KNOTTINGLEY
FERRYBRIDGE
WAKEFIELD
NORMANTON
FEATHERSTONE
GOOLE
Howden
Malton
Norton-on-Derwent
Easingwold
Pocklington
Market Weighton
BARNSLEY
WOMBWELL
HOYLAND
MEXBOROUGH
CONISBROUGH
DONCASTER
ROTHERHAM
MALTBY
Thorne
Crowle
Bawtry
GAINSBOROUGH
ADWICK LE STREET
BENTLEY
WATH UPON DEARNE
SWINTON
RAWMARSH
Tickhill
A1(M)
A64
A19
A59
A61
M62
M1
M18
M180
A614
A63
A162
A1079
A166
A163
A631
A638
A18
A161

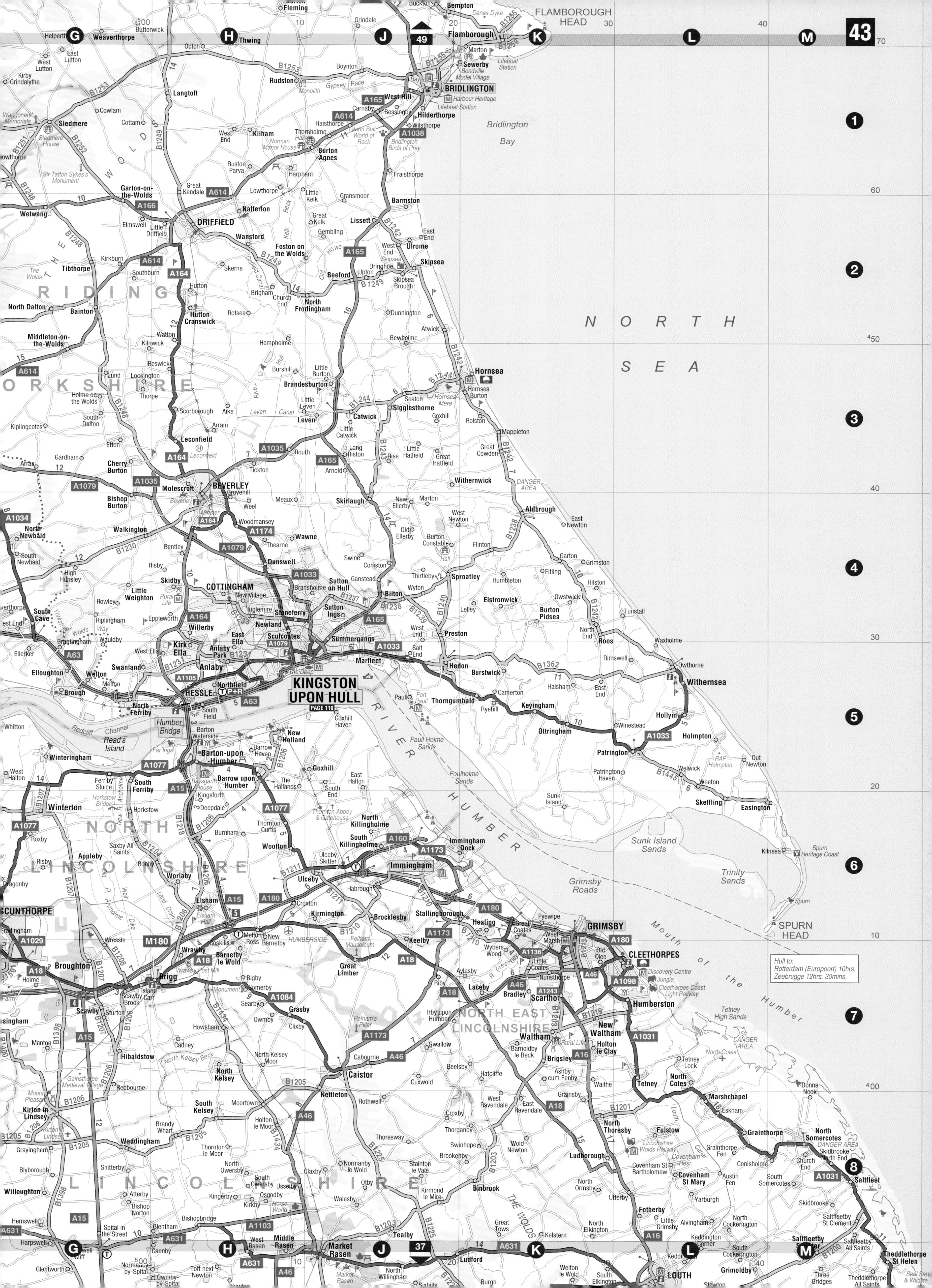
FLAMBOROUGH HEAD
Flamborough
Bempton
Sewerby
BRIDLINGTON
Bridlington Bay
Hilderthorpe
Wilsthorpe
Fraisthorpe
Barmston
Lissett
Ulrome
Skipsea
Atwick
Hornsea
Mappleton
Aldbrough
Withernsea
Holmpton
Patrington
Easington
Kilnsea
SPURN HEAD
NORTH SEA
Humber Bridge
KINGSTON UPON HULL
PAGE 110
Hessle
Cottingham
Beverley
Driffield
Nafferton
Wansford
Kilham
Rudston
Langtoft
Sledmere
Thwing
Weaverthorpe
Helperthorpe
Garton-on-the-Wolds
Hutton Cranswick
Leconfield
Molescroft
Walkington
Skidby
Willerby
Anlaby
Kirk Ella
Swanland
Welton
Elloughton
Brough
North Ferriby
Hedon
Burstwick
Keyingham
Ottringham
Paull
Preston
Sproatley
Bilton
Skirlaugh
Leven
Brandesburton
Sigglesthorne
Catwick
Barton-upon-Humber
Barrow upon Humber
New Holland
Goxhill
Winteringham
Winterton
South Ferriby
Immingham
Immingham Dock
Killingholme
Ulceby
Habrough
Stallingborough
Healing
GRIMSBY
CLEETHORPES
Humberston
New Waltham
Waltham
Scartho
Laceby
Keelby
Brocklesby
Kirmington
Great Limber
Caistor
Nettleton
Brigg
Broughton
Scawby
SCUNTHORPE
Barnetby le Wold
Grasby
Binbrook
Ludborough
North Thoresby
Fulstow
Tetney
North Cotes
Marshchapel
Grainthorpe
North Somercotes
Saltfleet
Saltfleetby St Peter
Theddlethorpe St Helen
LOUTH
Market Rasen
Middle Rasen
Tealby
Ludford
NORTH EAST LINCOLNSHIRE
NORTH LINCOLNSHIRE
LINCOLNSHIRE
EAST RIDING OF YORKSHIRE
RIVER HUMBER
Mouth of the Humber
Sunk Island Sands
Trinity Sands
Grimsby Roads
Hull to: Rotterdam (Europoort) 10hrs. Zeebrugge 12hrs. 30mins.
A165
A614
A1038
A166
A164
A1035
A1079
A1174
A1033
A1105
A63
A15
A1077
A160
A1173
A180
A18
M180
A1084
A46
A1136
A1098
A1243
A16
A1031
A1103
A631
A1029
A1034
B1249
B1242
B1238
B1362
B1445
B1206
B1205
B1225
B1203
B1200
49
37

Port Logan
Kilstay Bay
Kirkmaiden
Drummore
Cailiness Point
Maryport Bay
Port Kemin
MULL OF GALLOWAY
Scares
Barsalloch Point
Monreith
Point of Cairndoon
Craiglemine
Glasserton
Fell of Carleton
St Ninian's Cave
Port Castle Bay
Bishopton
Whithorn
Portyerrock Bay
Cairn Head
Isle of Whithorn
BURROW HEAD
Little Ross
I R I S H
S E A
POINT OF AYRE
Rue Point
The Ayres
Cranstal
The Lhen
Bride
Andreas
Shellag Point
Jurby Head
Jurby West
Jurby East
Ballasalla
Sandygate
Regaby
The Cronk
St Judes
Dhoor
Ramsey Bay
Ramsey
Sulby
Churchtown
Glen Auldyn
Port e Vullen
Maughold Head
Ballajora
Port Mooar
Orrisdale
Orrisdale Head
Ballaugh
Ravensdale
Kirk Michael
Glen Wyllin
Glen Mooar
Ballaleigh
Ballacarnane Beg
Barregarrow
SNAEFELL
North Barrule
Corrany
Glen Mona
Port Cornaa
Dhoon
Bulgham Bay
Gob y Deigan
Knocksharry
Cronk-y-Voddy
St Patrick's Isle
Ballagyr
Lambfell Moar
ISLE OF MAN
Peel
Contrary Head
Patrick
Ballig
St John's
Greeba Castle
Baldwin
Laxey
Old Laxey Head
Ballacannell
Laxey Bay
Baldrine
Clay Head
Glen Maye
Dalby Point
Dalby
Niarbyl Bay
Lower Foxdale
Foxdale
Crosby
Glen Vine
Union Mills
Strang
Willaston
Onchan
Port Groudle
Onchan Head
DOUGLAS
Douglas Bay
Douglas Head
Spring Valley
Braaid
Close Clark
Kewaigue
Stroin Vuigh
Fleshwick Bay
Ballamodha
St Mark's
Newtown
Quine's Hill
Keristal
Little Ness
Lingague
Ronague
Grenaby
Port Soderick
Surby
Ballabeg
Santon Head
Bradda Head
Bradda
Colby
Ballasalla
Port Erin
Four Roads
Port St Mary
Castletown
Derbyhaven
St Michael's Island
Cregneash
Kitterland
SPANISH HEAD
Calf of Man
Dreswick Point
Douglas to:
Belfast 2hrs.45mins. (Fast Ferry, Seasonal)
Birkenhead 4hrs. 15mins. (Seasonal)
Heysham 3hrs. 30mins.
Dublin 2hrs. 45mins. (Fast Ferry, Seasonal)
Liverpool 2hrs. 30mins. (Fast Ferry, Seasonal)

SOLWAY FIRTH
IRISH SEA
CUMBRIA
CUMBRIAN
SKIDDAW FOREST
SKIDDAW 3054
WHINLATTER FOREST PARK
COPELAND FOREST
SCAFELL PIKE 3209
SCAFELL 3162
FURNESS
THE OLD MAN OF CONISTON 2635
Allonby Bay
Aspatria
Hayton
Mealsgate
Blennerhasset
Prospect
Oughterside
Harriston
Kirkland Guards
Westmoor End
Allerby
Crosscanonby
Crosby
Threapland
Plumbland
Parsonby
Torpenhow
Whitrigg
Ireby
Bothel
Gilcrux
Bullgill
Greengill
Maryport
Dearham
Tallentire
Moota Hill
Sunderland
Blindcrake
Bewaldeth
Orthwaite
Longlands
Ellenborough
Fothergill
Flimby
Broughton Moor
Dovenby
Bridekirk
Redmain
Isel Hall
Bassenthwaite
North Row
Kilnhill
Chapel
Seaton
Camerton
Great Broughton
Papcastle
Belle Vue
Cockermouth
Embleton
Wythop Mill
Siddick
North Side
Great Clifton
Brigham
Stainburn
WORKINGTON
Moss Bay
Harrington
Greysouthen
Bridgefoot
Little Clifton
Eaglesfield
Deanscales
Winscales
High Harrington
Branthwaite
Dean
Ullock
Pardshaw
Low Lorton
High Lorton
Thornthwaite
Keswick
Braithwaite
Portinscale
Millbeck
Applethwaite
Ormathwaite
Distington
Gilgarran
Common End
Lowca
Pica
Kidburngill
Mockerkin
Loweswater
Lamplugh
Asby
Parton
Moresby Parks
Arlecdon
Rowrah
Kirkland
WHITEHAVEN
Frizington
Cleator Moor
Hensingham
Keekle
Ennerdale Bridge
Buttermere
Gatesgarth
Seatoller
Rosthwaite
Stonethwaite
Grange
Saltom Bay
Mirehouse
Sandwith
St Bees Head
Moor Row
Wath Brow
Bigrigg
Cleator
Egremont
Rottington
St Bees
Wilton
Carleton
Thornhill
Haile
Coulderton
Middletown
Nethertown
Beckermet
Braystones
Calder Bridge
Wasdale Head
Nether Wasdale
Wellington
Gosforth
Seascale
Santon
Santon Bridge
Boot
Eskdale Green
Beckfoot
Cockley Beck
Holmrook
Drigg
Saltcoats
Ravenglass
Hall Waberthwaite
Broad Oak
Newbiggin
Waberthwaite
Woodend
Hall Dunnerdale
Seathwaite
Torver
Ulpha
Corney
Hycemoor
Bootle
Hyton
Annaside
Selker Bay
Broughton Mills
Beckfoot
Duddon Bridge
Broughton in Furness
Broadgate
Lady Hall
Foxfield
Hallthwaites
Grizebeck
Whitbeck
Dunningwell
The Green
The Hill
Chapels
Gawthwaite
Kirkby-in-Furness
Whicham
Silecroft
Millom
Kirksanton
Haverigg
Soutergate
ULVERSTON
Pennington
Askam in Furness
Ireleth
Marton
Lindal in Furness
Swarthmoor
Urswick
Bardsea
Dalton-in-Furness
Stainton with Adgarley
Little Urswick
Hawcoat
Ormsgill
Newton
Gleaston
Scales
Dendron
Aldingham
North Walney
North Scale
Vickerstown
BARROW-IN-FURNESS
Leece
Newbiggin
Roosecote
Roosebeck
Rampside
Biggar
Roa Island
Walney Island
South End
Piel Island
Foulney Island
Piel Bar
Hilpsford Scar
A596
A594
A595
A66
A597
A5086
A591
A593
A5092
A5093
A590
A5087
52
53
46
40
G
H
J
K
L
M
80
90
300
10
20
60

46
A
B
C
D
E
F
1
2
3
4
5
6
7
8
53
45
40
NOR
CUMBRIA
CUMBRIAN MOUNTAINS
LAKE DISTRICT NATIONAL PARK
SKIDDAW FOREST
SKIDDAW 3054
HELVELLYN 3117
SCAFELL PIKE 3209
THE OLD MAN OF CONISTON 2635
FURNESS FELLS
GRIZEDALE FOREST
HOWGILL FELLS
INGLEWOOD FOREST
GILDERDALE FOREST
MILBURN FOREST
WHERNSIDE 2414
Cross Fell 2930
MORECAMBE BAY
Humphrey Head Point
Chapel Island
Leven Viaduct
Kent Viaduct
Holme Island
Wigton
Thursby
Dalston
Cotehill
Caldbeck
Ireby
Mealsgate
Bassenthwaite
Keswick
Braithwaite
Threlkeld
Mungrisdale
Greystoke
Penruddock
Penrith
Newbiggin
Stainton
Dacre
Eamont Bridge
Clifton
Askham
Alston
Nenthead
Kirkoswald
Lazonby
Glassonby
Gamblesby
Melmerby
Great Salkeld
Langwathby
Culgaith
Temple Sowerby
Kirkby Thore
Appleby-in-Westmorland
Long Marton
Dufton
Bolton
Morland
Great Strickland
Shap
Bampton
Glenridding
Patterdale
Grasmere
Ambleside
Windermere
Bowness-on-Windermere
Hawkshead
Coniston
Troutbeck
Staveley
Kendal
Burneside
Crook
Grayrigg
Tebay
Orton
Kirkby Stephen
Ravenstonedale
Sedbergh
Dent
Kirkby Lonsdale
Casterton
Barbon
Milnthorpe
Heversham
Levens
Beetham
Arnside
Silverdale
Carnforth
Burton-in-Kendal
Grange-over-Sands
Cartmel
Flookburgh
Lindale
Newby Bridge
Haverthwaite
Ulverston
Dalton-in-Furness
Broughton in Furness
Kirkby-in-Furness
Askam in Furness
Great Urswick
Bardsea
Baycliff
Ingleton
Burton in Lonsdale
Bentham
Austwick
Bolton-le-Sands
Over Kellet
Hornby
Warcop
Brough
Soulby
Winton
Hartle
M6
A6
A66
A591
A592
A593
A595
A590
A65
A683
A684
A685
A686
A687
A689
A596
A5074
A5084
A5091
A5092
A6070
A601(M)
A5087
SOUTHWAITE
TEBAY (EAST)
TEBAY (WEST)
KILLINGTON LAKE
BURTON-IN-KENDAL
RROW-IN-FURNESS

47
54
55
48
41
G
H
J
K
L
M
1
2
3
4
5
6
7
8
THUMBERLAND
DURHAM
THE PENNINES
NORTH YORKSHIRE
YORKSHIRE DALES NATIONAL PARK
Consett
Stanley
Annfield Plain
Chester-le-Street
Lanchester
Durham
PAGE 108
Stanhope
Wolsingham
Tow Law
Crook
Willington
Spennymoor
Ferryhill
Bishop Auckland
Sedgefield
Shildon
Newton Aycliffe
Middleton-in-Teesdale
Eggleston
Staindrop
Barnard Castle
Bowes
Darlington
Scotch Corner
Richmond
Catterick Garrison
Catterick
Leyburn
Hawes
Askrigg
Aysgarth
Middleham
Bedale
Masham
Northallerton
Ripon
Kettlewell
Horton in Ribblesdale
Allenheads
Cowshill
Hamsterley Forest
Stainmore Forest
Lune Forest
Great Whernside
A1(M)
A66
A67
A68
A689
A690
A167
A684
A6108
A6055
A61
A688
A177
A691
A692
A693
A6072
A6136
A1150
A168

48
55
47
42
A
B
C
D
E
F
1
2
3
4
5
6
7
8
DURHAM
REDCAR & CLEVELAND
NORTH YORK MOORS NATIONAL PARK
NORTH YORKSHIRE
CLEVELAND HILLS
HAMBLETON HILLS
HOWARDIAN HILLS
SEAHAM
PETERLEE
HARTLEPOOL
Hartlepool Bay
Tees Bay
TEESSIDE
REDCAR
STOCKTON-ON-TEES
MIDDLESBROUGH
BILLINGHAM
DARLINGTON
GUISBOROUGH
NORTHALLERTON
Thirsk
RIPON
Helmsley
Pickering
Malton
Norton-on-Derwent
Kirkbymoorside
Saltburn-by-the-Sea
Marske-by-the-Sea
Loftus
Staithes
Runswick Bay
Sandsend
Whitby
Stokesley
Great Ayton
Yarm
Sedgefield
Osmotherley
Beacon Point
Horden Point
Dene Mouth
A19
A1(M)
A66
A67
A167
A168
A169
A170
A171
A172
A173
A174
A178
A179
A684

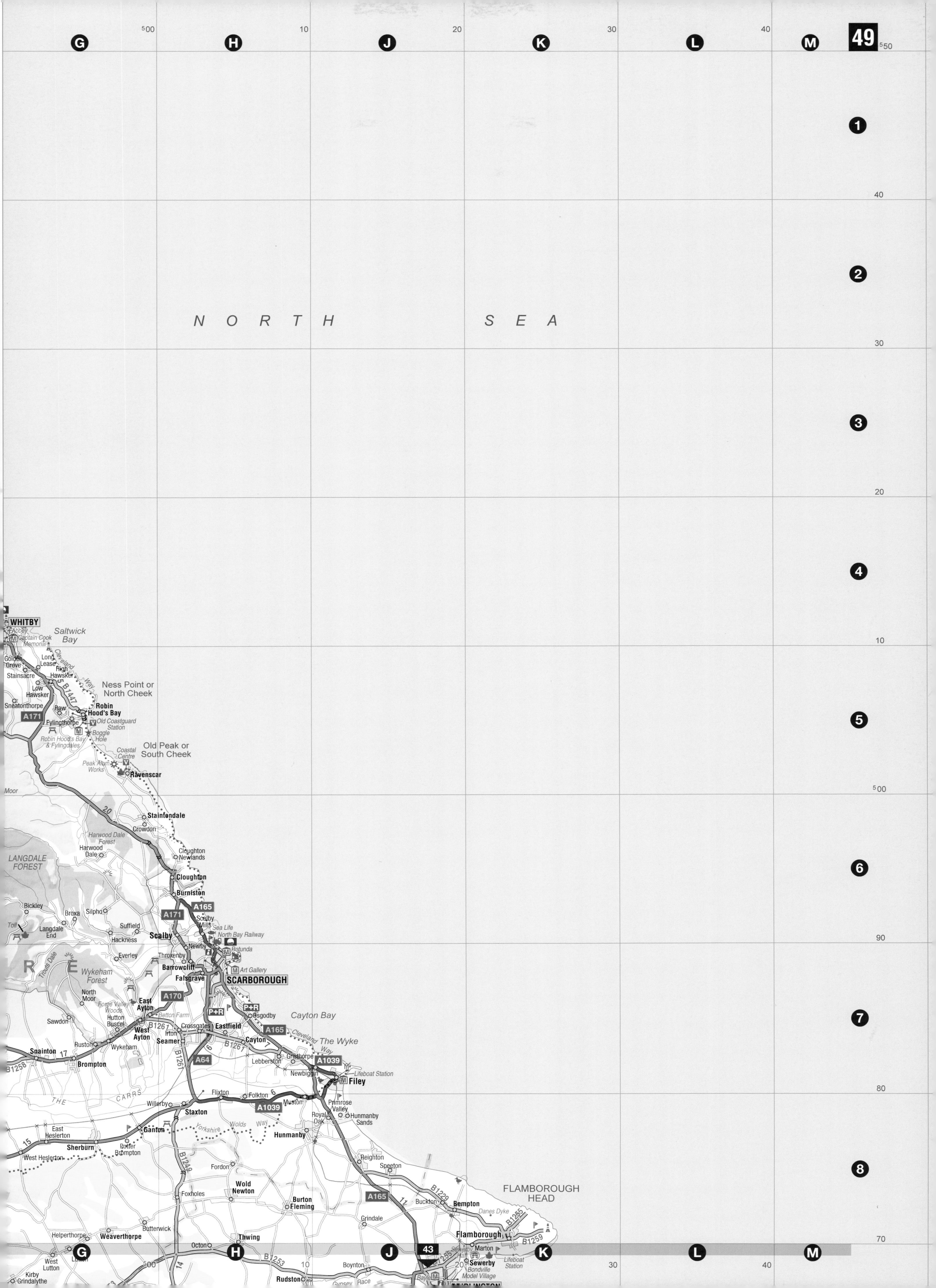
G
H
J
K
L
M
1
2
3
4
5
6
7
8
NORTH SEA
WHITBY
Saltwick Bay
Ness Point or North Cheek
Robin Hood's Bay
Old Peak or South Cheek
Ravenscar
Stainsacre
Sneatonthorpe
Fylingthorpe
Old Coastguard Station
Boggle Hole
Coastal Centre
Peak Alum Works
Staintondale
Harwood Dale
LANGDALE FOREST
Cloughton
Burniston
Scalby
SCARBOROUGH
Falsgrave
Barrowcliff
Sea Life
North Bay Railway
Rotunda
Art Gallery
Cayton Bay
Osgodby
Eastfield
Cayton
The Wyke
Cleveland Way
East Ayton
West Ayton
Seamer
Wykeham Forest
Snainton
Brompton
Filey
Lifeboat Station
Hunmanby
Hunmanby Sands
Primrose Valley
Staxton
Ganton
Sherburn
Reighton
Speeton
FLAMBOROUGH HEAD
Bempton
Buckton
Danes Dyke
Flamborough
Sewerby
Marton
Bondville Model Village
Lifeboat Station
Wold Newton
Burton Fleming
Thwing
Weaverthorpe
Rudston
Kirby Grindalythe
West Lutton
A171
A165
A170
A64
A1039
B1261
B1249
B1253
B1229
B1255
B1259
B1258
B1447
43

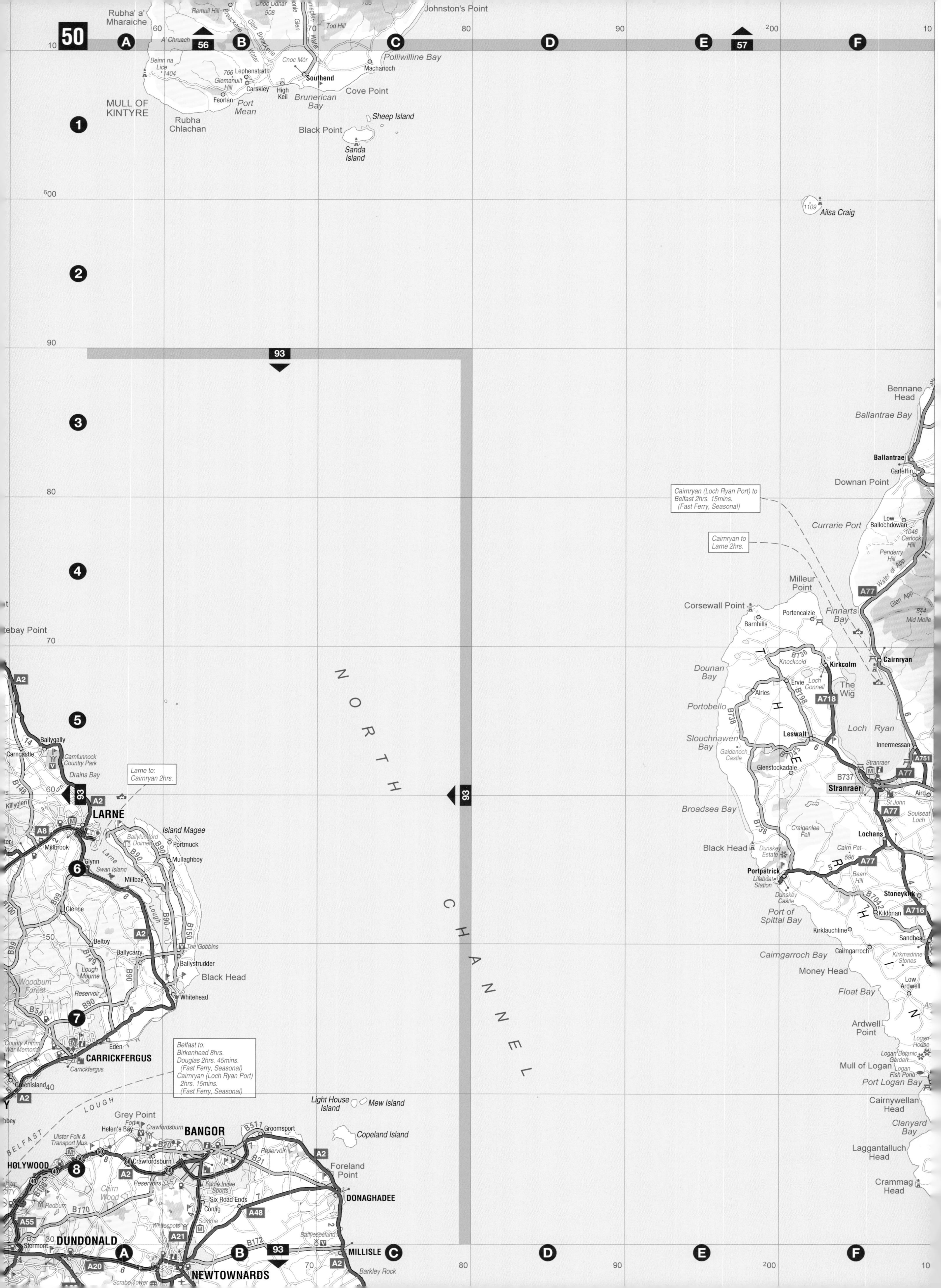
Rubha' a' Mharaiche
A' Chruach
56
Johnston's Point
57
Beinn na Lice
1404
Lephenstrath
Glemanuilt Hill
Carskiey
High Keil
Southend
Polliwilline Bay
Macharioch
Cove Point
Feorlan
Port Mean
Brunerican Bay
MULL OF KINTYRE
Rubha Chlachan
Sheep Island
Black Point
Sanda Island
Ailsa Craig
93
Bennane Head
Ballantrae Bay
Ballantrae
Downan Point
Cairnryan (Loch Ryan Port) to Belfast 2hrs. 15mins. (Fast Ferry, Seasonal)
Cairnryan to Larne 2hrs.
Currarie Port
Milleur Point
Corsewall Point
Portencalzie
Barnhills
Finnarts Bay
Cairnryan
Dounan Bay
Kirkcolm
The Wig
Portobello
Loch Ryan
Leswalt
Slouchnawen Bay
Innermessan
Stranraer
Broadsea Bay
Lochans
Black Head
Portpatrick
Port of Spittal Bay
Stoneykirk
Kirklauchline
Sandhead
Cairngarroch Bay
Money Head
Float Bay
Ardwell Point
Mull of Logan
Port Logan Bay
Cairnywellan Head
Clanyard Bay
Laggantalluch Head
Crammag Head
NORTH CHANNEL
Ballygally
Carncastle
Drains Bay
Larne to: Cairnryan 2hrs.
LARNE
Island Magee
Portmuck
Mullaghboy
Millbrook
Glynn
Millbay
Glenoe
Beltoy
Ballycarry
Ballystrudder
Black Head
Whitehead
Woodburn Forest
Eden
CARRICKFERGUS
Greenisland
Belfast to: Birkenhead 8hrs. Douglas 2hrs. 45mins. (Fast Ferry, Seasonal) Cairnryan (Loch Ryan Port) 2hrs. 15mins. (Fast Ferry, Seasonal)
BELFAST LOUGH
Grey Point
Helen's Bay
Crawfordsburn
BANGOR
Groomsport
Light House Island
Mew Island
Copeland Island
HOLYWOOD
Foreland Point
DONAGHADEE
Six Road Ends
Conlig
DUNDONALD
MILLISLE
NEWTOWNARDS
Barkley Rock
Stormont
A B C D E F
1 2 3 4 5 6 7 8

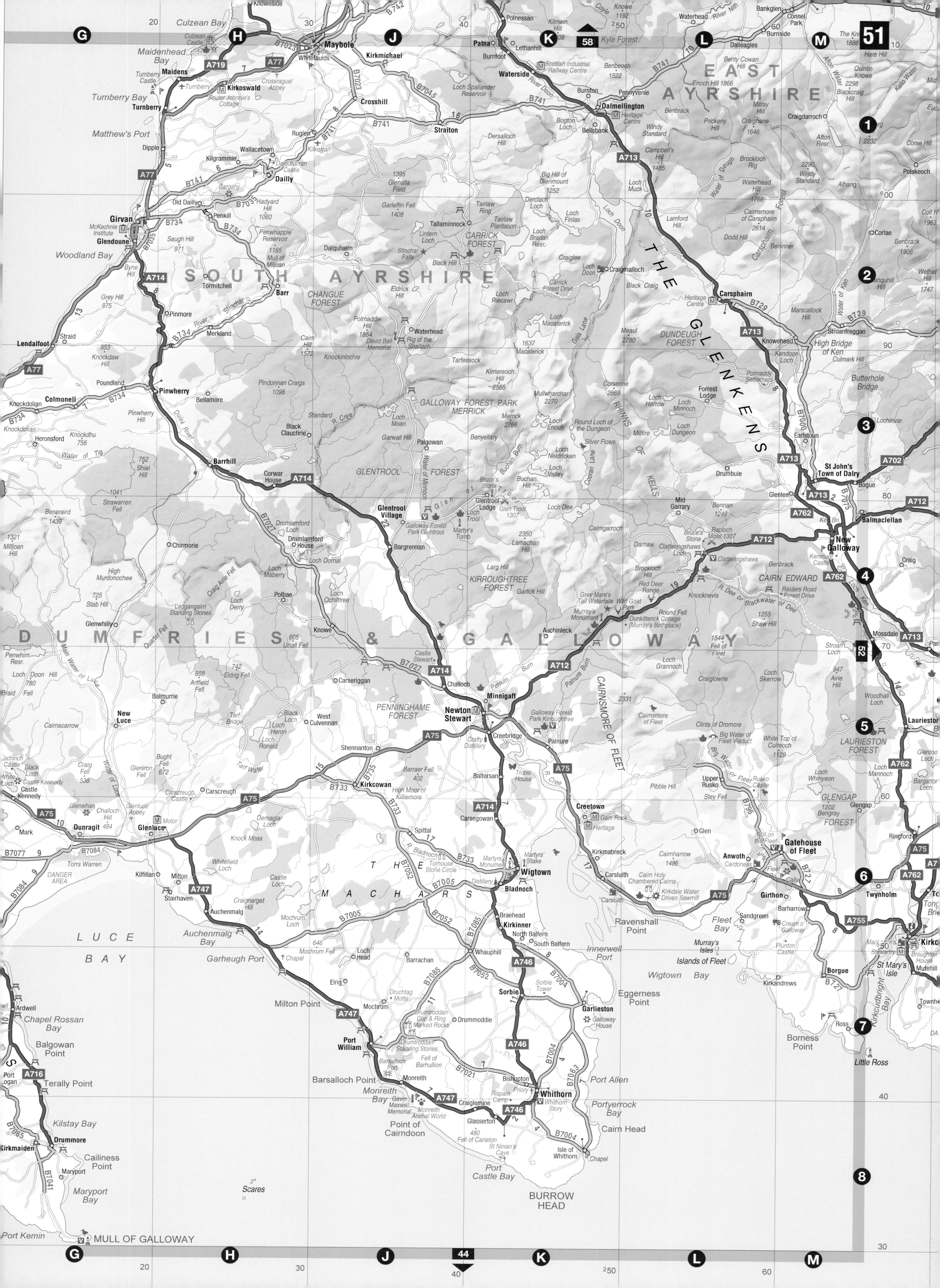
EAST AYRSHIRE
SOUTH AYRSHIRE
DUMFRIES & GALLOWAY
THE GLENKENS
THE MACHARS
GALLOWAY FOREST PARK
MERRICK
CARRICK FOREST
CHANGUE FOREST
DUNDEUGH FOREST
GLENTROOL FOREST
KIRROUGHTREE FOREST
PENNINGHAME FOREST
LAURIESTON FOREST
GLENGAP FOREST
CAIRN EDWARD
CAIRNSMORE OF FLEET
RHINNS OF KELLS
Culzean Bay
Maidenhead Bay
Turnberry Bay
Matthew's Port
Woodland Bay
LUCE BAY
Maybole
Kirkmichael
Crosshill
Straiton
Maidens
Turnberry
Kirkoswald
Dailly
Girvan
Glendoune
Barr
Pinmore
Pinwherry
Colmonell
Lendalfoot
Barrhill
Patna
Waterside
Dalmellington
Bellsbank
Carsphairn
St John's Town of Dalry
New Galloway
Balmaclellan
Mossdale
Laurieston
Ringford
Gatehouse of Fleet
Twynholm
Borgue
Glentrool Village
Bargrennan
Newton Stewart
Minnigaff
Creebridge
Palnure
Kirkcowan
Wigtown
Bladnoch
Kirkinner
Sorbie
Garlieston
Whithorn
Isle of Whithorn
Port William
Monreith
Glenluce
Dunragit
New Luce
Drummore
Port Logan
MULL OF GALLOWAY
BURROW HEAD
Port Castle Bay
Wigtown Bay
Fleet Bay
Islands of Fleet
Little Ross
Kirkcudbright Bay
A77
A719
A713
A714
A712
A702
A762
A75
A747
A746
A716
A755
B741
B734
B7027
B7052
B7004
B7005
B733
B7084
58
52
44
G
H
J
K
L
M
1
2
3
4
5
6
7
8
20
30
40
50
60
70
80
90

A
B
C
D
E
F
58
59
51
44
45
PAGE 108
WORKINGTON
NITHSDALE
LOWTHER HILLS
ANNANDALE
DUMFRIES & GAL
SOLWAY FIRTH
FOREST OF AE
LAURIESTON FOREST
GLENGAP FOREST
DALBEATTIE FOREST
Garcrogo Forest
Mabie Forest
Kirkconnel
Crawick
Sanquhar
Wanlockhead
Nunnerie
Moffat
Beattock
Mennock
Enterkinfoot
Durisdeer
Enoch
Carronbridge
Thornhill
Penpont
Tynron
Closeburn
Moniaive
Kirkland
Auldgirth
Dunscore
St John's Town of Dalry
Balmaclellan
New Galloway
Corsock
Crocketford or Ninemile Bar
Springholm
Kirkpatrick Durham
Dumfries
Lochmaben
Lockerbie
Torthorwald
Tinwald
Locharbriggs
Kirkton
Holywood
Templand
Ecclefechan
Brydekirk
Annandale Water
New Abbey
Kirkbean
Dalbeattie
Castle Douglas
Crossmichael
Laurieston
Mossdale
Parton
Gatehouse of Fleet
Twynholm
Tongland
Kirkcudbright
Borgue
Dundrennan
Auchencairn
Kippford or Scaur
Rockcliffe
Palnackie
Southerness
Southerness Point
Abbey Head
Little Ross
Borness Point
Silloth
Abbeytown
Allonby
Maryport
Aspatria
Cockermouth
Dearham
Flimby
Seaton
Great Clifton
Crosby
Gilcrux
Plumbland
Blennerhasset
Westnewton
A76
A702
A701
A708
A74(M)
A75
A709
A710
A711
A712
A713
A745
A755
A762
A780
A596
A594
A595
A66
A5086
B729
B7076
B7020

SCOTTISH BORDERS
NORTHUMBERLAND
CUMBRIA
TEVIOTDALE
ESKDALE
LIDDESDALE
CRAIK FOREST
ESKDALEMUIR FOREST
CASTLE O'ER FOREST
WAUCHOPE FOREST
KIELDER FOREST
REDESDALE FOREST
KIELDER WATER & FOREST PARK
KERSHOPE FOREST
WARK FOREST
INGLEWOOD FOREST
GILDERDALE FOREST
MILBURN FOREST
SKIDDAW FOREST
CUMBRIAN MOUNTAINS
SCOTLAND
ENGLAND
Langholm
Canonbie
Longtown
Gretna
Gretna Green
Eastriggs
ANNAN
CARLISLE
PAGE 107
Brampton
Haltwhistle
Alston
Penrith
Wigton
Dalston
Caldbeck
Kielder
Bonchester Bridge
Southdean
Newcastleton or Copshaw Holm
Bewcastle
Gilsland
Greenhead
Kirkoswald
Lazonby
Langwathby
Greystoke
Hesket Newmarket
Bassenthwaite
Mungrisdale
Skiddaw 3054
Cross Fell 2930
Carter Bar
Byrness
Catcleugh
Kielder Castle
Butteryhaugh
Falstone
Stannersburn
Deadwater
Saughtree
Hermitage
Teviothead
Mosspaul
Eskdalemuir
Bentpath
Kirtleton
Waterbeck
Eaglesfield
Kirtlebridge
Springfield
Burgh by Sands
Port Carlisle
Bowness-on-Solway
Kirkbride
Thursby
Sebergham
Hutton Roof
Newbiggin
Culgaith
Milburn
Nenthead
Garrigill
Lambley
Slaggyford
Knarsdale
Halton Lea Gate
Hallbankgate
Castle Carrock
Wetheral
Warwick Bridge
Hayton
Scotby
Houghton
Stanwix
Cummersdale
Plumpton
Calthwaite
Armathwaite
Ainstable
Croglin
Renwick
Gamblesby
Melmerby
Hunsonby
Glassonby
Skirwith
Ousby
Great Salkeld
Catterlen
Skelton
Hadrian's Wall
Solway Moss 1542
Torduff Point
Redkirk Point
A7
A74(M)
A75
A6071
A689
A69
A595
A596
A591
A686
A6
A66
A6088
A68
M6
B6357
B6318
B709
B7068
B6399

A
B
C
D
E
F
60
61
53
46
47
1
2
3
4
5
6
7
8
SCOTLAND
ENGLAND
NORTHUMBERLAND NATIONAL PARK
REDESDALE FOREST
KIELDER FOREST
WARK FOREST
HARWOOD FOREST
NORTHUMBERLAND
DURHAM
MILBURN FOREST
HAMSTERLEY FOREST
Slaley Forest
Alnmouth Bay
Carter Bar
Catcleugh
Byrness
Rochester
Otterburn
Elsdon
Alwinton
Rothbury
Whittingham
Alnmouth
Warkworth
Amble
Felton
Longhorsley
Morpeth
Ashington
Bedlington
Cramlington
Ponteland
Bellingham
Wark
Kirkwhelpington
Cambo
Hexham
Corbridge
Haltwhistle
Haydon Bridge
Prudhoe
Ryton
NEWCASTLE UPON TYNE
GATESHEAD
GOSFORTH
FELLING
WHICKHAM
BLAYDON
NEWBURN
CONSETT
STANLEY
CHESTER-LE-STREET
DURHAM
PAGE 108
Lanchester
Allendale Town
Allenheads
Alston
Nenthead
Stanhope
Wolsingham
Tow Law
Crook
Willington
Spennymoor
BISHOP AUCKLAND
Blanchland
A68
A69
A1
A696
A697
A6079
A686
A689
A692
A691
A690
A167

G
H
J
K
L
M
40
450
60
70
80
10
1
600
2
90
3
80
4
70
5
60
6
550
7
40
48
8
30
Beacon Point
Heritage
Newbiggin-by-the-Sea
Seaton
Cambois
North Blyth
BLYTH
B1329
South Newsham
Seaton Sluice
Hartley
St Mary's Lighthouse
St Mary's or Bait Island
Seaton Delaval Hall
B1325
Holywell
A190
A192
A193
A1148
Earsdon
WHITLEY BAY
Lifeboat Station
Monkseaton
Shiremoor
New York
Cullercoats
Blue Reef Aquarium
A186
A19
A191
TYNEMOUTH
Newcastle to: Amsterdam (IJmuiden) 15hrs.
North Shields
Willington
A193
Arbeia Roman Fort
SOUTH SHIELDS
Tyne Tunnel
A187
A183
A185
Marsden Bay
Westoe
Marsden
JARROW
West Harton
Harton
A1300
Souter
Lizard Point
Whitburn Colliery
Whitburn
A1018
Boldon Colliery
Boldon
Cleadon
B1299
A194
A184
A183
South Bents
Seaburn
A195
Southwick
A1290
Fulwell
Roker
Castletown
WASHINGTON
A1231
National Glass Centre
Monkwearmouth
South Hylton
Pennywell
SUNDERLAND
PAGE 116
Hendon
Offerton
A183
A690
High Newport
Ryhope Colliery
Penshaw
New Herrington
Herrington
Tunstall
A1018
Philadelphia
Silksworth
Ryhope
Ryhope Engines
A19
Newbottle
HOUGHTON-LE-SPRING
Fence Houses
Seaton
Deneside
SEAHAM
A1052
Colliery Row
A182
Great Eppleton
Dawdon
Hetton-le-Hole
Murton
Dalton-le-Dale
Cold Hesledon
West Rainton
East Rainton
Middle Rainton
A182
EASINGTON
Beacon Point
A690
Moorsley
Easington Lane
South Hetton
Hawthorn
Easington Colliery
Pittington
High Haswell
Carrville
Hallgarth
Littletown
Haswell
Easington
Horden Point
Sherburn
Sherburn Hill
Haswell Plough
Horden
Shotton Colliery
PETERLEE
A1086
Dene Mouth
A181
Shadforth
Ludworth
Castle Eden Dene
Blackhall Colliery
A688
Thornley
Wheatley Hill
Shotton
Old Cassop
Castle Eden
Blackhall Rocks
Quarrington
Wingate
High Hesleden
Hesleden
Crimdon Park
Quarrington Hill
Cassop
Deaf Hill
Eden Vale
Town Kelloe
Station Town
Monk Hesleden
Hart Station
A19
Kelloe
Coxhoe
Trimdon Grange
Trimdon Colliery
Hutton Henry
A1086
Hart
A1049
Garmondsway
Sheraton
West View
Trimdon
A179
High Throston
Middleton
Maritime Experience
A1(M)
A177
Fishburn
Elwick
Dalton Piercy
West Park
Rift House
HARTLEPOOL
Hartlepool Bay
Bishop Middleham
Summerhill
A178
Butterwick
Embleton
Brierton
Owton Manor
Sedgefield
Seaton Carew
A689
A689
Bradbury
Newton Bewley
Greatham
Graythorp
North Gate
Tees Bay
N O R T H
S E A

63
93
Rathlin Island
Bull Point
Doonmore
Bruce's
ORONSAY
Eilean Leathann
Dubh Eilean
Eilean Ghaoideamal
Eilean nan Ron
Ceann Riobha
Garvard
Rubha Dubh
Colonsay to Port Askaig 1hr. 10mins. (Seasonal)
Corpach Bay
Shian Bay
Rubh'an t-Sailein
Rubh' a' chrois-aoinidh
Post Rocks
RUBHA A'MHAIL
Rubha Bholsa
Nave Island
Eilean Beag
Ardnave Point
Tòn Mhór
Sanaigmore
Braigo
Rubha Lamanais
Saligo Bay
Saligo
Grulinbeg
Gruinart
Kilnave
Leckgruinart
Gortantaoid
Coul Point
Machir Bay
Kilchoman
Kilchiaran Bay
Kilchiaran
Conisby
Bruichladdich
Carraigo Dhubh
Blackrock
Carnain
Bridgend (Beul an Atha)
Bowmore
Octomore
Port Charlotte
Natural History Centre
Lossit
Lossit Bay
Neribus
Octofad
Portnahaven
Port Wemyss
Orsay
RHINNS POINT
Port Gleann na Gaoidh
RHINNS OF ISLAY
Loch Indaal
Laggan
Laggan Point
Laggan Bay
Laggan Bri.
Glenegedale
Glenegedale Lots
Torra
Mulindry
Port Alsaig
Kintra
Slugaide Glas
Cragabus
Dùn Mór Ghil
THE OA
Risabus
Lower Killeyan
American Monument
MULL OF OA
Rubha nan Leacan
Rubha na Meise Bàine
Port Ellen
Laphroaig
Lagavulin
Ardbeg
Dunyvaig Castle
Texa
Eilean Imersay
Rubha na Gainmhich
Eilean Bhride
Eilean a' Chuirn
Eilean Craobhach
Kildalton Cross
Ardmore Point
Kintour
Aros Bay
Claggain Bay
Ardtalla
Carraig Mhór
McArthur's Head
Port Ellen to Ballycastle 1hr. (Seasonal)
Kennacraig to Port Ellen 2hrs. 20mins.
Kennacraig to Port Askaig 2hrs.
Ballygrant
Keills
Port Askaig (Port Asgaig)
Feolin Ferry
Caol Ila
Bunnahabhain
Finlaggan
Esknish
Kilmeny
Redhouses
Eallabus
Sound of Islay
ARGYLL
ISLAY
JURA
JURA FOREST
PAPS OF JURA
Glas Eilean
Ardfin
Am Fraoch Eilean
Brosdale Island
Rubha na Tràille
Cabrach
Craighouse
Small Isles
Port na Birlinne
Na Cùiltean
Keils
Knockrome
Ardfernal
Leargybreck
Skervuile
An Dùnan
Port Doir' a' Chrorain
Lagg
Tarbert
Loch Tarbert
Lussagiven
Inverlussa
Ardlussa
Ardlussa Bay
Lussa Point
Gob Dubh
Lealt
Eilean Mor
Bàgh na Dojde
Island of Dann
Keillmore
Point of Knap
Kilberry Head
Craighouse to Tayvallich 1hr. (Seasonal)
SOUND OF JURA
An Dubh-sgeir
Gamhna Gigha
Eilean Garbh
West Tarbert Bay
East Tarbert Bay
ISLE OF GIGHA
Druimyeon Bay
Ardminish
Ardminish Bay
Craro Island
Gigalum Island
Cara Island
Mull of Cara
Tayinloan
Killean
A' Chleit
Muasdale
Glenacardoch Point
Glenbarr
Port a' Bhorrain
Glenbarr Abbey
Bellochantuy Bay
Bellochantuy
Port Corbert
Kilchenzie
Machrihanish Bay
Machrihanish
CAMPBELTOWN
Drumlemble
Stewarton
Earadale Point
Rubha Dùin Bhàin
Rubha' a' Mharaiche
Killellan
Dalsmirren
A' Chruach
Lephenstrath
Southend
A846
A847
B8016
B8017
B8018
A83
B843
B842

KNAPDALE
FOREST
Lochgilphead
Ardrishaig
Tayvallich
Eilean Dubh
Carsaig Bay
Eilean Loain
Kilmichael of Inverlussa
Daltot
Taynish
Dunrostan
Loch Caolisport
Ellary
Kilmory
Achahoish
Clachbreck
Erines
Bàgh an Tailleir
Inverneil House
Eilean Mór
Liath Eilean
Castleton
Port Ann
LOCH FYNE
Largiemore
Otter Ferry
Kilfinan
Kilfinan Bay
Port Leathan
Auchalick Bay
Ardmarnock Bay
Barmore Island
Tarbert
East Loch Tarbert
West Tarbert
Portavadie
Eilean Aoidhe
Asgog Bay
Kilbride Bay
Fionn Phort
Ardlamont Bay
Ardlamont Point
Camas na Ceardaich
Rubha Leathan
Tighnabruaich
Kames
Millhouse
Auchenlochan
Kyles of Bute
Colintraive
Rhubodach
Glendaruel Forest
Clachan of Glendaruel
Craig Lodge
Glenmassan
Benmore Forest
Ardentinny
Glenlean
Clachaig
Invereck
Rashfield
Ardbeg
Kilmun
Sandbank
Strone
Blairmore
Strone Point
Hunter's Quay
DUNOON
Kilcreggan
Gourock
Cove
Rosneath
HELENSBURGH
Rhu
Clynder
Shandon
Gare Loch
Loch Long
Cloch Point
Bullwood
Corlarach Forest
Innellan
Toward
Toward Point
Wemyss Bay
Inverkip
Skelmorlie
Largs
GREAT CUMBRAE ISLAND
Millport
Little Cumbrae Island
Fairlie
Port Bannatyne
ISLE OF BUTE
ROTHESAY
Bogany Point
Kames Bay
Ettrick Bay
St Colmac
Strone Point
Port Lamont
Inchmarnock
Ardscalpsie Point
Scoulag Point
Kilchattan Bay
Kingarth
Stravanan Bay
Dunagoil Bay
Garroch Head
SOUND OF BUTE
Kennacraig
Whitehouse
Dunmore
Ardpatrick
Ardpatrick Point
Clachan
Ronachan Point
Skipness
Skipness Point
Claonaig
Claonaig Bay
Eascairt Point
Rubha Creagan Dubha
Cock of Arran
Lochranza
Catacol
Millstone Point
Rubha Airigh Bheirg
North Sannox
Sannox
Sannox Bay
Corrie
NORTH AYRSHIRE
ISLE OF ARRAN
Goatfell 2866
Merkland Point
Brodick
Brodick Bay
Whitefarland Point
Dougarie Point
Machrie Bay
Lamlash
Lamlash Bay
Holy Island
Clauchlands Point
Kingscross Point
Whiting Bay
Largybeg Point
Dippin Head
Sound of Pladda
Pladda
Bennan Head
Kildonan
Blackwaterfoot
Drumadoon Point
Drumadoon Bay
Brown Head
Lagg
Kilmory
KILBRANNAN SOUND
Carradale
Port Righ
Carradale Point
Rubha nan Sgarbh
Saddell
Saddell Bay
Ugadale Point
Black Bay
Ardnacross Bay
Campbeltown
Island Davaar
Achinhoan Head
Johnston's Point
Polliwilline Bay
Cove Point
Machrioch
FIRTH OF CLYDE
Ardrossan
Saltcoats
Stevenston
Horse Isle
West Kilbride
Portencross
Farland Head
Ardneil Bay
Lady Isle
Heads of Ayr
Dunure
Culzean Bay
Maidenhead Bay
Maidens
Ardrossan to Brodick 55mins.
Campbeltown to Brodick 2hrs. 20mins. (Seasonal)
Ardrossan to Campbeltown 2hrs. 40mins. (Seasonal)
Tarbert to Lochranza 1hr. 25mins. (Seasonal)
Campbeltown to Ballycastle 1hr. 30 mins. (Seasonal)
G
H
J
K
L
M
1
2
3
4
5
6
7
8

64
65
58
50
51

65
51
57
PAGE 109
PAGE 110
ARGYLL & BUTE
STIRLING
WEST DUNBARTONSHIRE
EAST DUNBARTONSHIRE
INVERCLYDE
RENFREWSHIRE
EAST RENFREWSHIRE
NORTH AYRSHIRE
SOUTH AYRSHIRE
EAST AYRSHIRE
NORTH LANARK
SOUTH
DUMFRIES & GALLOWAY
GLASGOW
HELENSBURGH
GREENOCK
PORT GLASGOW
DUMBARTON
CLYDEBANK
RENFREW
PAISLEY
JOHNSTONE
RUTHERGLEN
BEARSDEN
MILNGAVIE
KIRKINTILLOCH
CUMBERNAULD
COATBRIDGE
AIRDRIE
MOTHERWELL
HAMILTON
EAST KILBRIDE
BARRHEAD
BOTHWELL
IRVINE
KILMARNOCK
AYR
Alexandria
Balloch
Gourock
Largs
Kilbirnie
Beith
Dalry
Kilwinning
Stevenston
Saltcoats
Ardrossan
Troon
Prestwick
Stewarton
Galston
Newmilns
Darvel
Strathaven
Mauchline
Catrine
Auchinleck
Cumnock
New Cumnock
Maybole
Dalrymple
Muirkirk
Kilsyth
Lennoxtown
Balfron
Drymen
Killearn
Strathblane
Bishopbriggs
Stepps
Uddingston
Bellshill
Wishaw
Larkhall
Stonehouse
Neilston
Newton Mearns
Eaglesham
Fenwick
Kilmaurs
Dundonald
Symington
Tarbolton
Ochiltree
Drongan
Coylton
Sanquhar
Kirkconnel
Lochwinnoch
Bridge of Weir
Kilmacolm
Erskine
Inchmurrin
Inchcailloch
Whitelee Forest
Kyle Forest
Carron Valley Forest
Irvine Bay
Culzean Bay
Heads of Ayr
Lady Isle
Horse Isle
CLYDE MUIRSHIEL REGIONAL PARK
M8
M73
M74
M77
M80
M898
A70
A71
A76
A77
A78
A82
A737
A736
A760

EDINBURGH
PAGE 109
FIRTH OF FORTH
KIRKCALDY
DUNFERMLINE
ALLOA
GRANGEMOUTH
FALKIRK
BO'NESS
Linlithgow
LIVINGSTON
BATHGATE
WEST LOTHIAN
FALKIRK
MIDLOTHIAN
Dalkeith
Musselburgh
Prestonpans
Penicuik
PENTLAND HILLS
MOORFOOT HILLS
SCOTTISH BORDERS
Peebles
Innerleithen
LANARKSHIRE
Lanark
Carluke
Biggar
Abington
DUMFRIES & GALLOWAY
ETTRICK FOREST
SOUTHERN UPLANDS
CRAIK FOREST
Queensferry Crossing
Forth Road Bridge
Kincardine Bridge
Clackmannanshire Bridge
HEART OF SCOTLAND
CAIRN LODGE SERVICES
ABINGTON
66
67
60
52
53

FIRTH OF FORTH
Bass Rock
Fidra
Lamb
Craigleith
Eyebroughy
North Berwick
Scottish Seabird Centre
Tantallon
Dirleton
North Berwick Law
Gullane Bay
Gullane
Fenton Barns
Kingston
Whitekirk
Aberlady Bay
Aberlady
Craigielaw
Myreton Motor
Drem
East Fortune
Tyninghame
Gosford Bay
Ballencrieff
Preston
Knowes
Dunbar
Town House
John Muir
West Barns
Belhaven
Barns Ness
Spittal
Camptoun
Athelstaneford
Cockenzie and Port Seton
Longniddry
East Linton
Broxburn
East Barns
Pinkerton
Skateraw
Power Station
Thorntonloch
EDINBURGH
PAGE 109
Prestonpans
Prestongrange
Portobello
Joppa
MUSSELBURGH
Fisherrow
Inveresk
Newcraighall
Wallyford
Levenhall
Cuthill
Meadowmill
Tranent
Elvingston
Huntington
Haddington
Hailes
Spott
Doonhill Homestead
Pitcox
Luggate Burn
Stenton
Innerwick
Macmerry
Bladsmuir
Penston
Whitecraig
Elphinstone
New Winton
New Town
Samuelston
Bolton
Colstoun House
Morham
Whitelaw Hill
Papple
Garvald
EAST LOTHIAN
Reed Point
Cove
Siccar Point
Fast Castle Head
Cocklaw Hill
Cockburnspath
Oldhamstocks
Crossgatehall
Ormiston
Pencaitland
Cousland
DALKEITH
Eskbank
Easthouses
Newbattle
Bonnyrigg
Mayfield
Newtongrange
Gilford
Yester Castle
Longyester
Gilchriston
East Saltoun
West Saltoun
Peastonbank
Pathhead
Peaston
Nunraw Abbey
White Castle Hillfort
Clints Dod
Dunbar Common
Lumsdaine
Coldingham Moor
Grantshouse
Blackburn Rig
Houndwood
Reston
Auchencrow
Abbey St Bathans
Cranshaws
Whiteadder Resr.
Ellemford
Edin's Hall Broch
Hunterfield
Arniston
Gorebridge
Crichton
Humbie
Fala Dam
Fala
Lammer Law
Hopes Resr.
Meikle Says Law
Stobshiel Resr.
MIDLOTHIAN
Carrington
Borthwick
North Middleton
Tynehead
Middleton
Temple
Fala Moor
Soutra Aisle
Crib Law
LAMMERMUIR
Hunt Law
Blythe Edge
Mutiny Stones
Whitchester
Longformacus
Millburn Bridge
Preston
Cumledge Mill
Chirnside
Chirnsidebridge
Edrom
Manderston
Allanton
Rosebery Reservoir
Gilston
Carfrae
Hogs Law
Watch Water Resr.
Dirrington Great Law
Jim Clark Room
Duns
Torfichen Hill
Heriot
MOORFOOT HILLS
Oxton
Addinston
Cleekhimin Bridge
Edgarhope Wood
Dirrington Little Law
Gavinton
Nisbet Hill
Whitsome
Gladhouse Resr.
Collie Law
Scoured Rig
Westruther
Polwarth
Fogo
Fogorig
Hornden
Blackhope Scar
Dun Law
Fountainhall
Thirlestane
Lauder
Houndslow
Halliburton
Swinton
Ladykirk
Ladyside Height
SOUTHERN UPLANDS
LAUDERDALE
Bassendean
Greenlaw
Simprim
Upsettlington
Killochyett
Stow
SCOTTISH BORDERS
Whitehope Law
Windlestraw Law
Legerwood
Huntlywood
Greenknowe Tower
Gordon
Leitholm
Nether Blainslie
MERSE
Black Law
Great Law
Hume
Lambden
Eccles
Lennel
Coldstream
Hirsel
Cornhill-on-Tweed
Melkington
Priesthorpe Hill
Fans
Hume Castle
Sweethope Hill
Birgham
Wark Castle
Wark
Carham
Barelees
Branxton
Horsbrugh Ford
Lee Pen
St Ronan's Wells
Pirn Hill Fort
Knowes Hill
William Law
Langshaw
Buckholm
Earlston
Mellerstain House
Nenthorn
Stichill
Ednam
West Learmouth
East Learmouth
Flodden Field Monument
Innerleithen
Walkerburn
Robert Smail's Printing Works
Traquair House
Traquair
Elibank and Traquair Forest
Ashiestiel Hill
Clovenfords
Peel
Caddonfoot
Meigle Hill
Old Gala House
GALASHIELS
Tweedbank
Lowood
Gattonside
Newstead
Darnick
Melrose
Leaderfoot
Redpath
Smailholm
Smailholm Tower
James Thomson Obelisk
Kelso
Floors
Roxburgh Castle
Maxwellheugh
Hadden
Sprouston
Pressen
Kirkhouse
Minch Moor
Yair Hill Forest
Boleside
Abbotsford
Dingleton
Eildon
Newtown St Boswells
Bemersyde
Clintmains
Dryburgh Abbey
Mertoun Bridge
Makerstoun
Downham
Thornington
Lempitlaw
Mindrum
Pawston
Kilham
Broomy Law
Lindean
Cauldshiels Hill
Eildon Hills
Bowden
St Boswells
Maxton
Roxburgh
Heiton
Hoselaw Loch
Shotton
Yarrow Ford
Newark Castle
Linglie Hill
Lochcarron Mill
Sir Walter Scott's Courtroom
Longnewton Forest
Bowmount Forest
Linton Hill
Town Yetholm
Kirk Yetholm
Hethpool
Yarrow
Bowhill House & Country Estate
Bowhill
Fastheugh Hill
Philiphaugh
Selkirk
Halliwell's House
Longnewton
Ancrum Moor
Peniel Heugh
Waterloo Monument
Sandystones
Midlem
Nisbet
Eckford
Linton
Primsidemill
White Law
Yarrow Feus
Lilliesleaf
Bloomfield
Ancrum
Monteviot House
Harestanes Countryside
Crailing
Morebattle
Steer Rig
Brockhill
Ettrickbridge
ETTRICK FOREST
Cessford
Castle
Bowmont Water
The Schil
The Curr
ENGLAND
SCOTLAND
Black Knowe Head
Ashkirk
Bonjedward
Crailinghall
Whitton
Hownam Law
Caver's Hill
Minto Hills
Fatlips
Mary, Queen of Scots' House
Lanton
Jedburgh
Castle Jail
Abbey
Sourhope
Gilmanscleuch
Essenside Loch
Akermoor Loch
Shaws Under Loch
Hassendean
Minto
Spittal-on-Rule
Newton
Whitton Loch
Mowhaugh
Drinkstone Hill
Horsleyhill
Clarilaw
Leyden Monument
Denholm
Bedrule
Dunion Hill
Hownam
Craik Moor
Tushielaw
Dun Knowe
Appletreehall
Fernihirst
Oxnam
Swinside Hall
Cock Law
Hellmoor Loch
Smasha Hill
Scottish Borders Art Glass
Burnfoot
Cauldmill
Rubers Law
Mossburnford
Mozie Law
Windy Gyle
Redfordgreen
Alemoor Loch
TEVIOTDALE
Wilton
HAWICK
Borders Textile Towerhouse
Kirkton
Leyden Obelisk
Camptown
Whitestone Hill
Beefstand Hill
Buccleuch
Roberton
Burnfoot
Jedforest Deer & Farm Park
Woden Law
Loft Hill
Deanburnhaugh
Branxholme
White Hill
Bonchester Bridge
Hobkirk
Blindburn
Barrowburn
Saughie Law
Redcleuch Edge
Newmill
Hott Hill
Chesters
Jed Water
CRAIK FOREST
Southdean
Deerlee Knowe
Leithope Forest
Upper Hindhope
Redeswire Fray
Grindstone Law
DANGER AREA
Bell Hill
Shillmoor
Craik
Dryden Fell
Stobs Castle
Hungry
CHEVIOT HILLS
LAMMERMUIR HILLS
A1
A198
A199
A6137
A1087
A6093
A6124
A6106
A720
A68
A7
A697
A6105
A6112
A1107
A6089
A72
A707
A6091
A699
A708
A698
A6088
B6355
B6368
B6456
B6460
B6461
B6470
B6437
B6438
B6362
B6397
B6364
B6350
B6396
B6352
B6401
B6400
B6359
B6358
B6357
B6453
B6404
B709
B710
B7009
B711
B7007
B6367
B6458
B6372
B6414
B6363
B6371
B6471
B1347
B1345
B1343
B1377
B1348
B6370
B6369
B6365
B6355
B6361
B6360
B6374
B7060
B6398
B6436
B6405
B6399
53
59
67
A
B
C
D
E
F
1
2
3
4
5
6
7
8
40
50
60
70
80
90
30
20
10

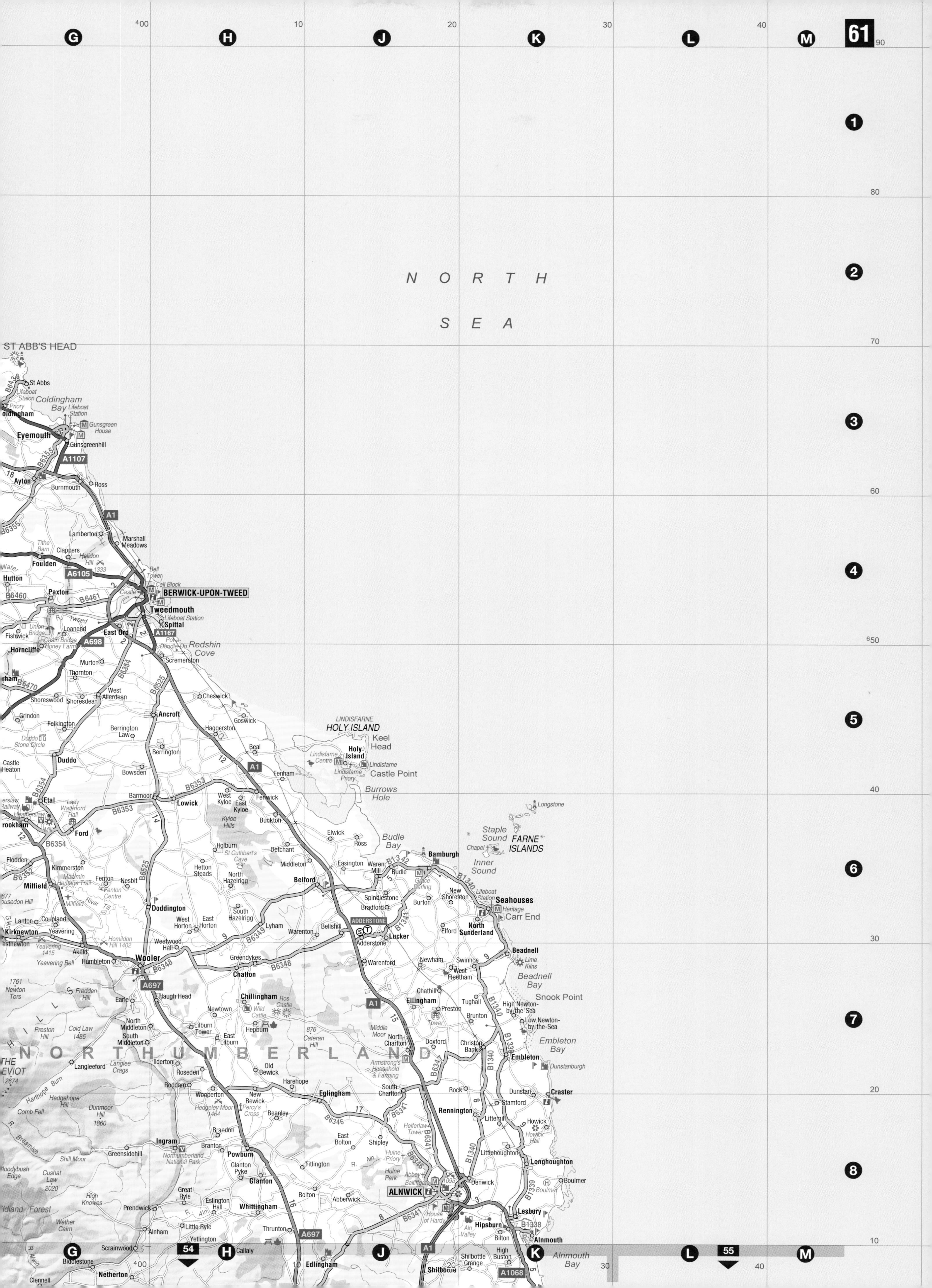
NORTH SEA
ST ABB'S HEAD
St Abbs
Coldingham Bay
Eyemouth
Gunsgreen House
Gunsgreenhill
A1107
Ayton
Burnmouth
Ross
A1
Lamberton
Marshall Meadows
Foulden
Hutton
Paxton
A6105
B6461
BERWICK-UPON-TWEED
Tweedmouth
Spittal
A1167
Lifeboat Station
East Ord
Loanend
Fishwick
Horncliffe
A698
Redshin Cove
Scremerston
Murton
Thornton
West Allerdean
Shoreswood
Shoresdean
Grindon
Felkington
Cheswick
Goswick
Haggerston
Ancroft
Berrington Law
Berrington
Duddo
Duddo Stone Circle
Castle Heaton
Bowsden
Beal
Fenham
LINDISFARNE
HOLY ISLAND
Keel Head
Holy Island
Lindisfarne Centre
Lindisfarne Priory
Lindisfarne Castle
Castle Point
Burrows Hole
Barmoor
Lowick
West Kyloe
East Kyloe
Fenwick
Kyloe Hills
Buckton
Etal
Ford
Lady Waterford Hall
Heatherslaw
B6353
B6354
B6525
Holburn
St Cuthbert's Cave
Detchant
Elwick
Ross
Budle Bay
Bamburgh
Longstone
Staple Sound
FARNE ISLANDS
Inner Sound
Flodden
Kimmerston
Milfield
Maelmin Heritage Trail
Fenton
Nesbit
Fenton Centre
Hetton Steads
North Hazelrigg
Middleton
Belford
Easington
Waren Mill
Budle
Grace Darling
Spindlestone
Bradford
New Shoreston
Burton
Seahouses
Heritage Carr End
Lifeboat Station
Doddington
South Hazelrigg
Lyham
West Horton
East Horton
Warenton
Bellshill
ADDERSTONE
Adderstone
Lucker
Elford
North Sunderland
Beadnell
Lime Kilns
Beadnell Bay
Lanton
Coupland
Kirknewton
Yeavering
Yeavering Bell
Akeld
Humbleton
Homildon Hill 1402
Wooler
A697
B6348
B6349
Weetwood Hall
Greendykes
Chatton
Warenford
Newham
Swinhoe
West Fleetham
Chathill
Ellingham
Preston
Preston Tower
Tughall
Brunton
High Newton-by-the-Sea
Low Newton-by-the-Sea
Snook Point
Embleton Bay
Fredden Hill
Newton Tors
Earle
Haugh Head
Chillingham
Wild Cattle
Ros Castle
Newtown
Lilburn Tower
East Lilburn
Hepburn
Cateran Hill
Middle Moor
North Charlton
Doxford
Christon Bank
Embleton
Dunstanburgh
Preston Hill
Cold Law 1485
North Middleton
South Middleton
NORTHUMBERLAND
Ilderton
Langleeford
Langlee Crags
Roseden
Old Bewick
Armstrong's Household & Farming
THE CHEVIOT 2674
Hedgehope Hill
Comb Fell
Dunmoor Hill 1860
Roddam
Wooperton
Hedgeley Moor 1464
New Bewick
Percy's Cross
Harehope
Eglingham
Beanley
South Charlton
Rock
Dunstan
Craster
Rennington
Stamford
Littlemill
Howick
Howick Hall
B6346
B6341
B6347
Heiferlaw Tower
Brandon
Branton
Ingram
Powburn
Greensidehill
Northumberland National Park
Shill Moor
Cushat Law 2020
Bloodybush Edge
Glanton Pyke
Glanton
East Bolton
Shipley
Titlington
Hulne Priory
Hulne Park
Abbey
Bailiffgate
Littlehoughton
Longhoughton
Boulmer
Denwick
ALNWICK
Great Ryle
High Knowes
Eslington Hall
Whittingham
Bolton
Abberwick
Prendwick
Kidland Forest
Wether Cairn
Little Ryle
Alnham
Yetlington
Thrunton
House of Hardy
Aln Valley
Hipsburn
Lesbury
Bilton
Alnmouth
Alnmouth Bay
B1338
B1339
B1340
B1341
B1342
Scrainwood
Callaly
Biddlestone
Netherton
Clennell
Edlingham
Shilbottle
Shilbottle Grange
High Buston
A1068
54
55

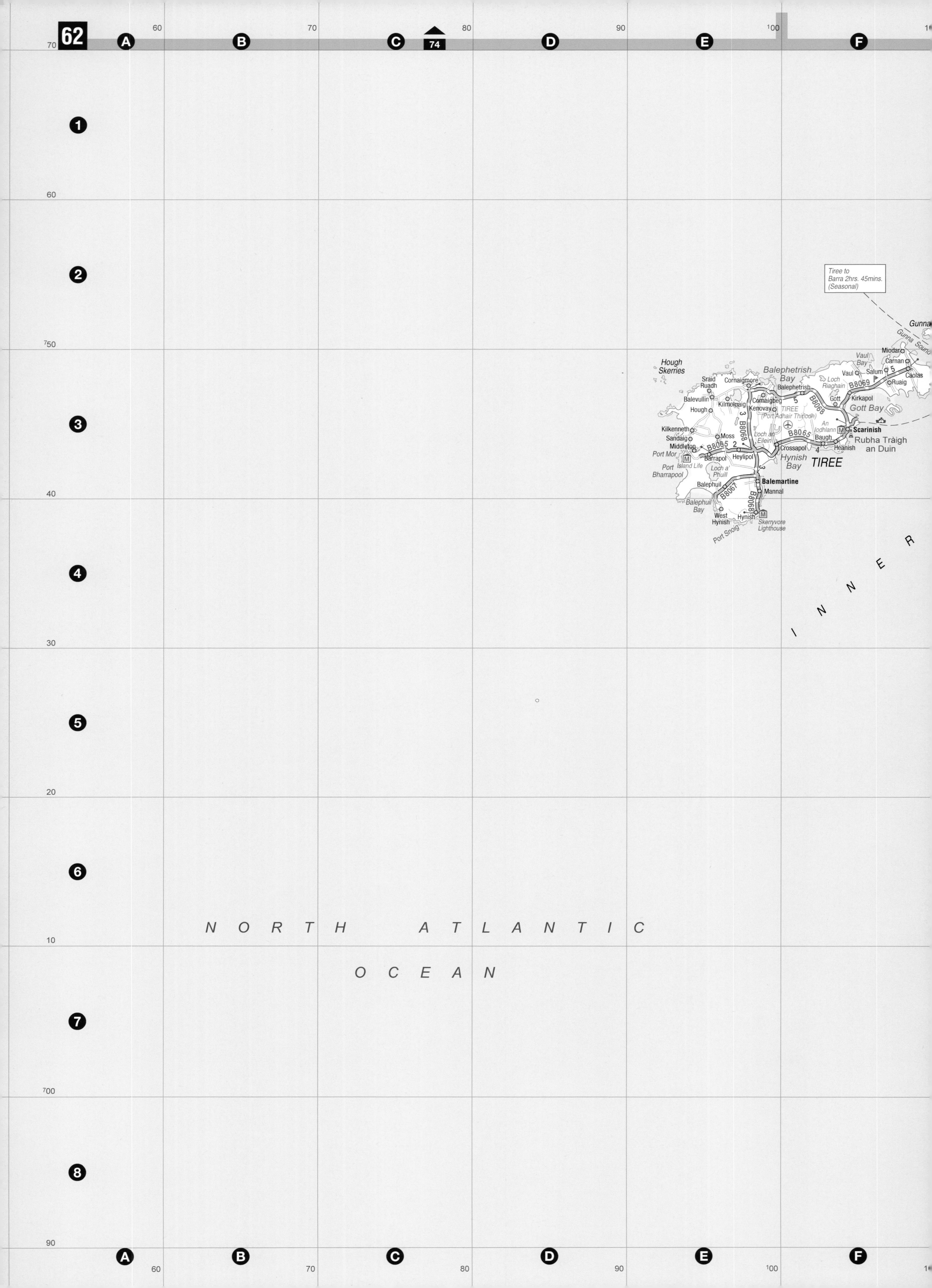
74
Tiree to
Barra 2hrs. 45mins.
(Seasonal)
Gunna
Gunna Sound
Hough Skerries
Sraid Ruadh
Cornaigmore
Balephetrish Bay
Balephetrish
Loch Riaghain
Vaul Bay
Vaul
Salum
Miodar
Carnan
Caolas
Ruaig
B8069
Balevullin
Kilmoluaig
Cornaigbeg
Kenovay
TIREE
(Port Adhair Thiriodh)
B8068
Gott
Kirkapol
Gott Bay
Hough
Kilkenneth
Sandaig
Middleton
Moss
Loch an Eilein
An Iodhlann
Scarinish
Rubha Tràigh an Duin
B8065
Baugh
Heanish
Crossapol
Heylipol
Barrapol
Port Mor
Island Life
Port Bharrapool
Loch a' Phuill
Hynish Bay
TIREE
Balemartine
Mannal
Balephuil
B8067
Balephuil Bay
West Hynish
Hynish
Skerryvore Lighthouse
Port Snoig
INNER
NORTH ATLANTIC
OCEAN

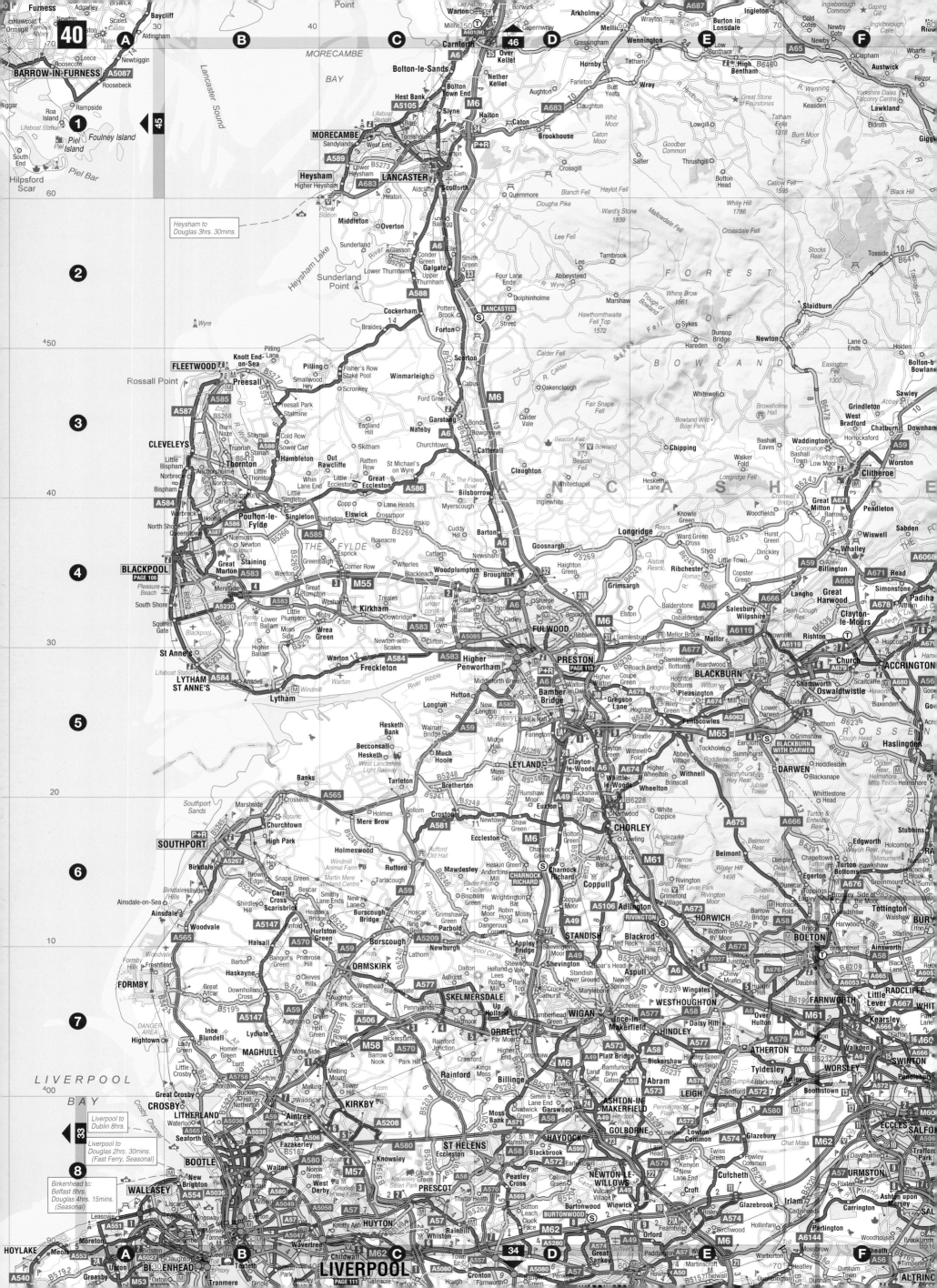

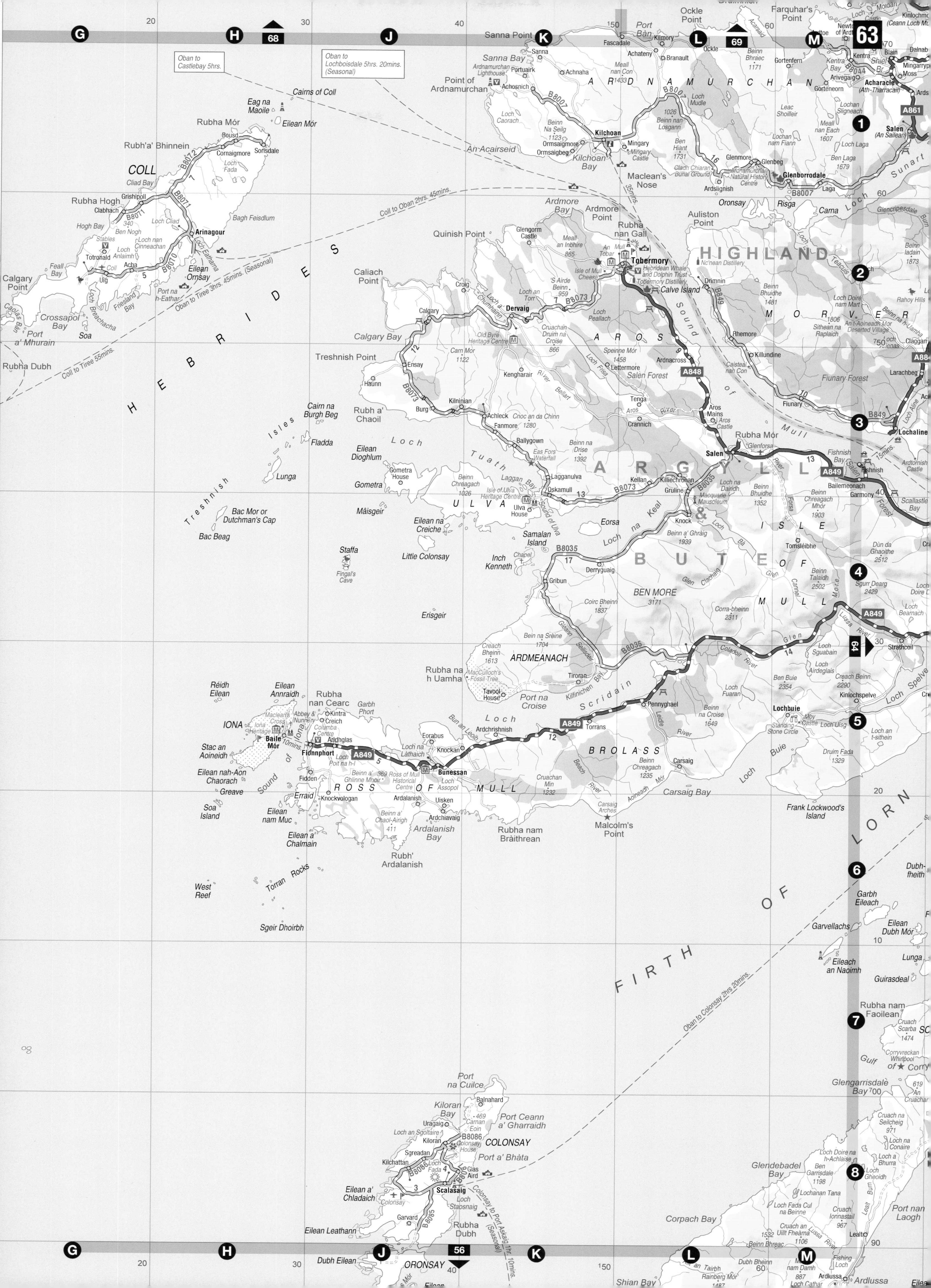

Oban to Castlebay 5hrs.
Oban to Lochboisdale 5hrs. 20mins. (Seasonal)
Sanna Point
Ockle Point
Farquhar's Point
Cairns of Coll
Eag na Maoile
Eilean Mór
Rubha Mór
Rubh'a' Bhinnein
COLL
Cliad Bay
Rubha Hogh
Hogh Bay
Arinagour
Bagh Feisdlum
Eilean Ornsay
Calgary Point
Crossapol Bay
Port a' Mhurain
Soa
Rubha Dubh
Coll to Tiree 55mins.
Oban to Tiree 3hrs. 45mins. (Seasonal)
Coll to Oban 2hrs. 45mins.
HEBRIDES
Sanna Bay
Point of Ardnamurchan
ARDNAMURCHAN
Kilchoan
Kilchoan Bay
An Acairseid
Maclean's Nose
Glenborrodale
Oronsay
Risga
Carna
Loch Sunart
Acharacle
Salen
Ardmore Bay
Ardmore Point
Rubha nan Gall
Quinish Point
Auliston Point
HIGHLAND
MORVERN
Tobermory
Calve Island
Caliach Point
Dervaig
Calgary
Calgary Bay
Treshnish Point
Sound of Mull
AROS
Salen Forest
Fiunary Forest
Lochaline
Cairn na Burgh Beg
Rubh a' Chaoil
Fladda
Lunga
Treshnish Isles
Eilean Dioghlum
Gometra
Loch Tuath
ULVA
ARGYLL
Salen
Bac Mor or Dutchman's Cap
Bac Beag
Màisgeir
Eilean na Creiche
Staffa
Fingal's Cave
Little Colonsay
Inch Kenneth
Samalan Island
Eorsa
Loch na Keal
& BUTE
ISLE OF MULL
BEN MORE 3171
Erisgeir
Rubha na h Uamha
ARDMEANACH
Loch Scridain
Réidh Eilean
Eilean Annraidh
IONA
Baile Mòr
Fionnphort
Bunessan
ROSS OF MULL
BROLASS
Carsaig Bay
Lochbuie
Loch Spelve
Stac an Aoineidh
Eilean nah-Aon Chaorach
Soa Island
Eilean nam Muc
Eilean a' Chalmain
Ardalanish Bay
Rubh' Ardalanish
Rubha nam Bràithrean
Malcolm's Point
Frank Lockwood's Island
West Reef
Torran Rocks
Sgeir Dhoirbh
FIRTH OF LORN
Garvellachs
Eileach an Naoimh
Lunga
Guirasdeal
Rubha nam Faoilean
Gulf of Corry
Corryvreckan Whirlpool
Oban to Colonsay 2hrs 20mins.
Port na Cuilce
Kiloran Bay
Port Ceann a' Gharraidh
COLONSAY
Port a' Bhàta
Scalasaig
Eilean a' Chladaich
Rubha Dubh
Eilean Leathann
Colonsay to Port Askaig 1hr. 10mins. (Seasonal)
Glengarrisdale Bay
Glendebadel Bay
Corpach Bay
Port nan Laogh
Dubh Eilean
ORONSAY
Shian Bay

69

A
B
C
D
E
F
1
2
3
4
5
6
7
8
Farquhar's Point
Kinlochmoidart
Ardmolich
Brunery
Shielfoot
Kentra
Kentra Bay
Blain
Dalnabreck
Langal
Dalelia
Mingarrypark
Moss
Arivegaig
Gorteneorn
Gortenfern
Acharacle
(Ath-Tharracail)
Ardshealach
A861
Salen
(An Sailean)
Resipole
Ardery
Glenborrodale
Laga
Risga
Carna
Loch Sunart
SUNART
HIGHLAND
ARDGOUR
Polloch
Loch Doilet
Glenhurich
Scotstown
Ariundle
Anaheilt
Strontian
(Sron an t-Sithein)
Ardnastang
Glen Tarbert
River Tarbert
Inversanda
Inversanda Bay
Sallachan
Clovullin
Ardgour
Corran
Corran Narrows
Sallachan Point
Onich
Inchree
Inchree Falls
Bunree
Glenrigh Forest
Conaglen
Inverscaddle Bay
Blarmachfoldach
Achriabhach
Glen Nevis
BEN NEVIS
4411
Nevis Forest
North Ballachulish
Bridge of Coe
Glencoe
Kinlochleven
South Ballachulish
Ballachulish
Clachaig
The Three Sisters
Kentallen
Duror
Achindarroch
Glenduror Forest
A828
A82
B863
Laudale House
A884
Lochuisge
Kinloch
MORVERN
Kingairloch
Camasnacroise
Loch a' Choire
Kilmalieu
Loch Linnhe
Bun Allt na Criche
Rubha Mor
Camas Chil-Mhalieu
Eilean Bainagowan
Cuil Bay
Dalnatrat
Creran Forest
Dalness
Claggan
Larachbeg
Ardtornish
Achranich
Loch Aline
Fiunary Forest
Fiunary
Lochaline
B849
Sound of Mull
Fishnish Bay
Fishnish
A849
Bailemeonach
Garmony
Scallastle Bay
Craignure Bay
Craignure
ISLE OF MULL
Duart Point
Duart Bay
Lochdon
Oakbank
Strathcoil
Glensanda
Port a' Chaisteil
Eignaig
Shuna Island
Castle Shuna
Sound of Shuna
Portnacroish
Appin
Eilean nan Caorach
Eilean Loch Oscair
Port Ramsay
Port Appin
Clachan
LISMORE
Balliveolan
Achnacroish
Kilcheran
Bernera Island
Eilean Dubh
Creag Island
Pladda Island
Eriska
North Shian
Creagan
South Creagan
Loch Creran
Barcaldine
Benderloch
Ledaig
South Ledaig
Rubha Garbh-àird
Eilean Musdile
Oban to Craignure 45mins.
Oban to Lismore 50mins.
Dunstaffnage
Connel
Achaleven
Stonefield
A85
Ganavan
Dunbeg
Dunollie
PAGE 115
OBAN
KERRERA
Eilean nan Gramhna
Grass Point
Balliemore
Bach Island
Pulpit Hill
Dalintart
Taynuilt
Airdeny
Bonawe
Inveresragan
Glen Etive
Loch Etive
BEN CRUACHAN
Bridge of Awe
Pass of Brander
Lochawe
Kilchurn
Dalmally
Stronmilchan
Edendonich
Loch Awe
Kilchrenan
Annat
North Port
Portsonachan
South Port
Cladich
A819
Loch Spelve
Croggan
Lochbuie
Loch Uisg
Firth of Lorn
Dubh Sgeir
Rubha Seanach
Minard Point
Kilbride
Cleigh
Kilmore
Loch Feochan
A816
Kilninver
Eilean Dùin
Insh Island
SEIL
Clachan-Seil
Easdale
Ellenabeich
Balvicar
Frank Lockwood's Island
Oban to Colonsay 2hrs. 20 mins.
SLATE ISLANDS
Cuan
Cullipool
Dubh-fheith
Belnahua
Fladda
LUING
Torsa
Garbh Eileach
Garvellachs
Eilean Dubh Mór
Lunga
Eileach an Naoimh
Guirasdeal
Shuna
Toberonochy
Melfort
Kilmelford
Loch Melfort
Arduaine
Rubh' a' Chnaip
Craobh Haven
Barravullin
Kintraw
Ardfern
Rubha nam Faoilean
SCARBA
Gulf of Corryvreckan
Eilean Ona
Rèisa Mhic Phaidean
Eilean Mhic Chrion
Eilean Righ
Carnasserie
Kilmartin
Glengarrisdale Bay
Island Mcaskin
Garbh Rèisa
Rèisa an t-Sruith
Rubh' a' Bhacain
Rubha Garbh-ard
Crinan
Loch Crinan
Ardnoe Point
Ruadh Sgeir
Rubha nam Bàrr
Port nan Laogh
Kilmahumaig
Bellanoch
Cairnbaan
Lochgilphead
KNAPDALE FOREST
Tayvallich
Ardlussa
Eilean Dubh
Kilmichael Glassary
Bridgend
KILMICHAEL FOREST
Ford
Fincharn
Inverliever Lodge
Dalavich
Lochavich
Inverinan
Ardchonnell
Portinnisherrich
Eredine
Durran
Braevallich
Eredine Forest
Achnagoul
Inveraray
Auchindrain
Furnace
Minard Forest
Minard
Crarae
Tullochgorm
Castle Lachlan
Lachan Bay
Loch Fyne
Lephinmore
Lephinchapel
Strachur
Clachan Strachur
Creggans
St Catherines
Glenbranter
Tombuidhe
ARGYLL FOREST PARK
Lochgoilhead
Cairndow
A815
A83
A886
B840
B8000
ARGYLL & BUTE
Garvie
Conchra
Ardentinny
Craigbrack
Carrick Castle

63

56

57

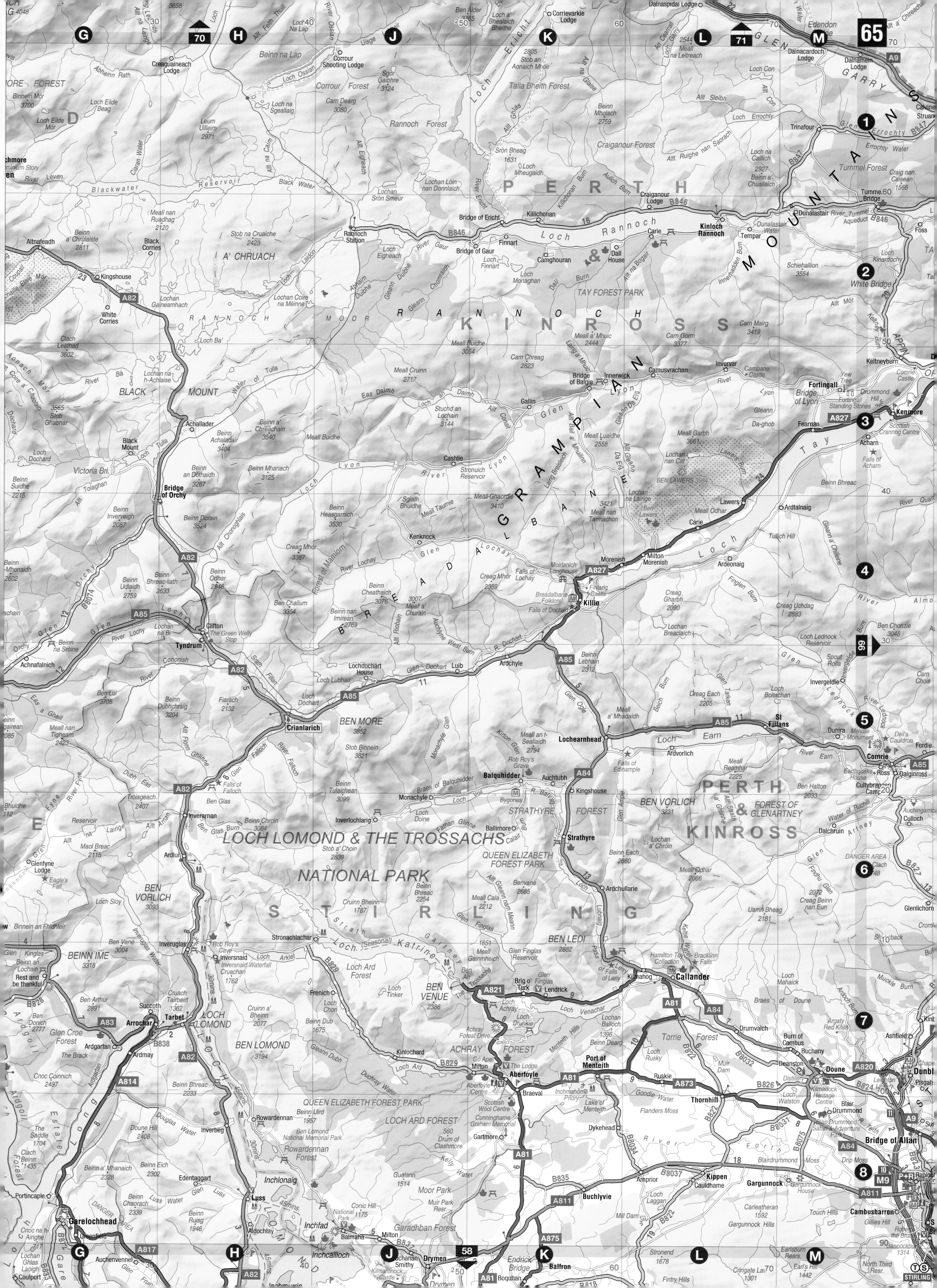
PERTH
KINROSS
RANNOCH MOOR
GRAMPIAN MOUNTAINS
BREADALBANE
LOCH LOMOND & THE TROSSACHS
NATIONAL PARK
STIRLING
PERTH & KINROSS
BLACK MOUNT
A' CHRUACH
TAY FOREST PARK
QUEEN ELIZABETH FOREST PARK
LOCH ARD FOREST
BEN LOMOND
BEN VORLICH
BEN LEDI
BEN MORE
BEN VENUE
BEINN IME
Loch Rannoch
Loch Tay
Loch Earn
Loch Katrine
Loch Ossian
Loch Laidon
Loch Tulla
Loch Venachar
Loch Lubnaig
Loch Voil
Loch Ard
Loch Long
Corrour Forest
Rannoch Forest
Talla Bheith Forest
Craiganour Forest
Tummel Forest
Achray Forest
Glen Lyon
Glen Lochay
Glen Dochart
Glen Ogle
Glen Errochty
Glen Garry
Rannoch Station
Kinloch Rannoch
Bridge of Gaur
Bridge of Ericht
Kingshouse
Altnafeadh
Achallader
Bridge of Orchy
Tyndrum
Clifton
Crianlarich
Killin
Kenmore
Fortingall
Fearnan
Lawers
Lochearnhead
St Fillans
Comrie
Balquhidder
Strathyre
Callander
Kilmahog
Aberfoyle
Port of Menteith
Thornhill
Doune
Deanston
Bridge of Allan
Kippen
Gargunnock
Buchlyvie
Drymen
Balfron
Luss
Tarbet
Arrochar
Ardlui
Inverarnan
Inversnaid
Stronachlachar
Garelochhead
Trinafour
Tummel Bridge
Keltneyburn
A82
A85
A827
A84
A81
A821
A873
A811
A875
A9
A820
A83
A814
A817
B846
B847
B829
B8074
M9
70
71
58
66

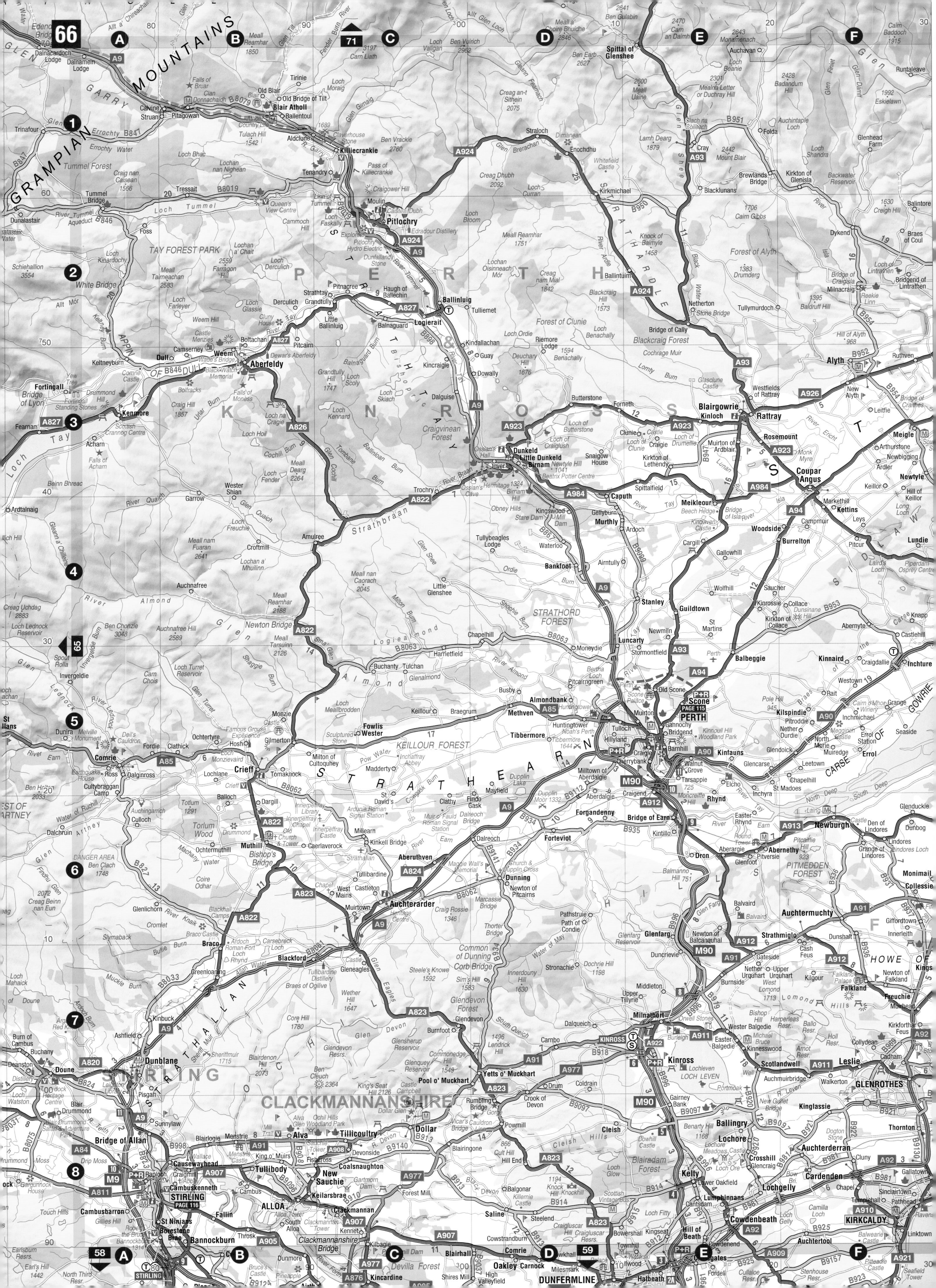
GRAMPIAN MOUNTAINS
71
58
59
65
PERTH & KINROSS
STRATHEARN
STIRLING
CLACKMANNANSHIRE
Blair Atholl
Killiecrankie
Pitlochry
Ballinluig
Logierait
Aberfeldy
Kenmore
Fortingall
Tummel Bridge
Spittal of Glenshee
Kirkmichael
Bridge of Cally
Alyth
Blairgowrie
Rattray
Coupar Angus
Meigle
Dunkeld
Birnam
Caputh
Murthly
Bankfoot
Stanley
Luncarty
Scone
PERTH
PAGE 115
Methven
Almondbank
Crieff
Comrie
Muthill
Auchterarder
Dunning
Bridge of Earn
Abernethy
Newburgh
Auchtermuchty
Falkland
Glenfarg
Milnathort
Kinross
Leslie
GLENROTHES
Kinglassie
Lochgelly
Cowdenbeath
Kelty
Ballingry
Lochore
Cardenden
Auchterderran
KIRKCALDY
DUNFERMLINE
Oakley
Saline
Dollar
Tillicoultry
Alva
Menstrie
Tullibody
ALLOA
Clackmannan
Kincardine
Bridge of Allan
STIRLING
PAGE 116
Bannockburn
Dunblane
Doune
Braco
Blackford
Gleneagles
Amulree
Trochry
Tay Forest Park
Loch Tay
Loch Tummel
Loch Leven
A9
A93
A94
A85
A90
A91
A92
A822
A823
A824
A827
A923
A924
A926
A977
A984
M9
M90

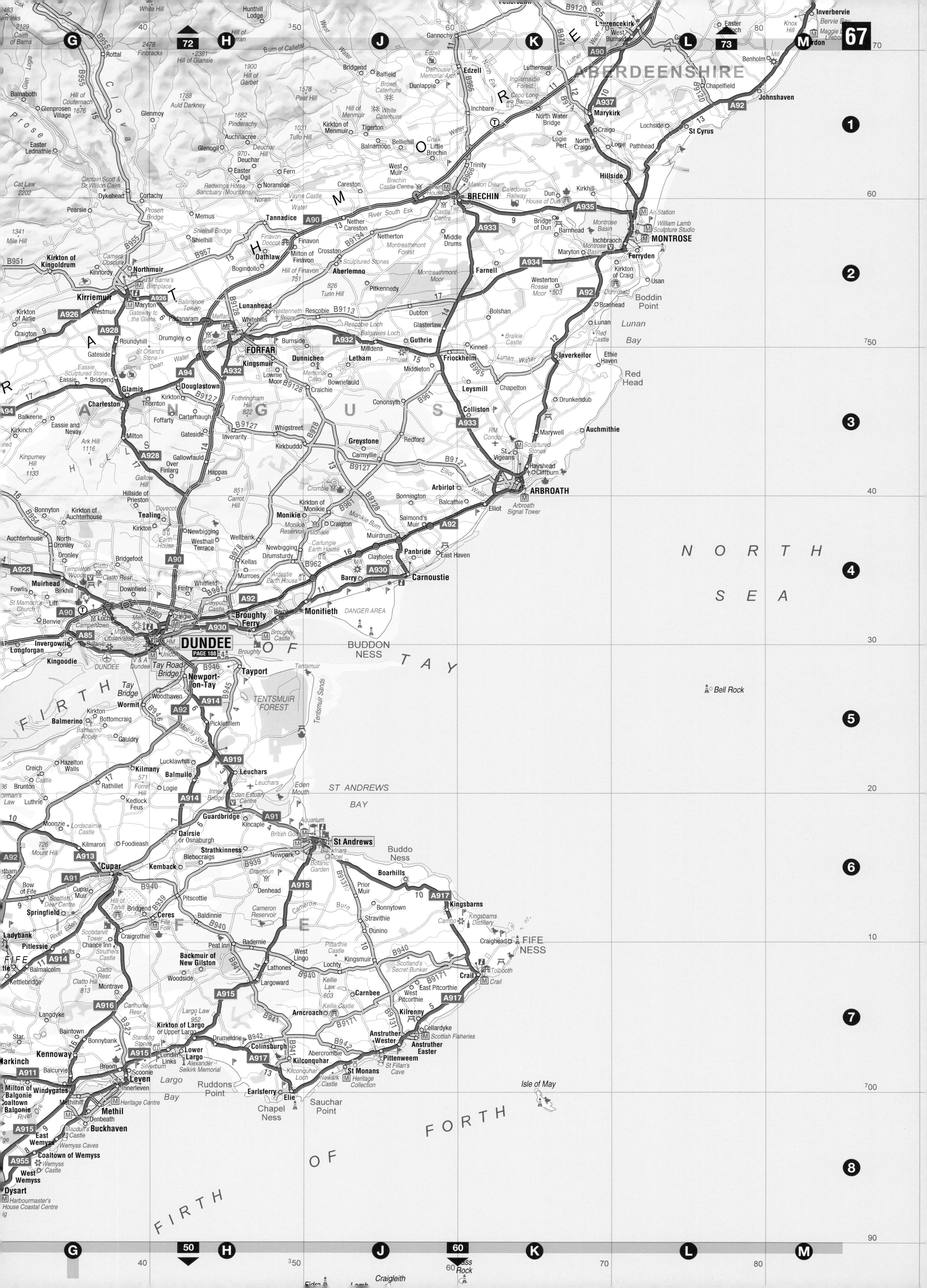
G
72
H
J
K
73
L
M
ABERDEENSHIRE
Inverbervie
Laurencekirk
Johnshaven
St Cyrus
Marykirk
Edzell
Brechin Castle Centre
BRECHIN
MONTROSE
Ferryden
Hillside
Boddin Point
Lunan Bay
Inverkeilor
Red Head
Auchmithie
Friockheim
Letham
Guthrie
FORFAR
Kirriemuir
Glamis
Tannadice
Aberlemno
Carmyllie
Arbirlot
ARBROATH
Arbroath Signal Tower
Carnoustie
Monifieth
Broughty Ferry
DUNDEE
PAGE 108
Tay Road Bridge
Newport-on-Tay
Tayport
Tentsmuir Forest
Tay Bridge
Wormit
Balmerino
Leuchars
Guardbridge
St Andrews
St Andrews Bay
Cupar
Ceres
Kingsbarns
Fife Ness
Crail
Anstruther Easter
Anstruther Wester
Pittenweem
St Monans
Colinsburgh
Kilconquhar
Earlsferry
Elie
Lower Largo
Leven
Methil
Buckhaven
Kennoway
Dysart
Isle of May
Bell Rock
Buddon Ness
Firth of Tay
Firth of Forth
North Sea
Largo Bay
Chapel Ness
Saucher Point
Ruddons Point
1
2
3
4
5
6
7
8
50
60
Craigleith

A
B
C
D
E
F
1
2
3
4
5
6
7
8
76
74
62
63
An Ceannaich
Loch Pooltiel
Lower Milovaig
Upper Milovaig
Oisgill Bay
Waterstein
Borrodale
Feriniquarrie
Glendale
Lephin
Holmisdale
Colbost
Totaig
Uig
Ben Ettow
Skinidin
Dunvegan
Kilmuir
Lonmore
Giant Angus Macaskill
Dun Fiadhairt
Souterrain
Suardal Hut Circle
Fairy Bridge
Annait
Flashader
Edinbane
Blackhill
Bernisdale
Glen Bernisdale
A850
A863
A87
A855
B884
B885
B8009
Kensaleyre
Rhenetra
Haultin
Borve
Borve Standing Stones
Carbost
Crepkill
Tote
Skeabost
St Columba's Isle
Uigshader
Drumuie
Achachork
Portree
Torvaig
Glengrasco
Shulishadermor
Heatherfield
Penifiler
Loch Portree
Moonen Bay
Ramasaig
Hoe Rape
The Hoe 759
HEALABHAL MHOR 1538
HEALABHAL BHEAG 1600
Loch Glen Ionadal
Ben Conan 799
Hoe Point
Orbost
Roskhill
Roag
Ardroag
Vatten
Harlosh
Balmore
Ose
Loch Caroy
Harlosh Point
Colbost Point
Harlosh Island
Tarner Island
Wiay
Oronsay
Loch Bracadale
Bracadale
Ullinish
Struan
Struanmore
Coillore
Totardor
Am Bi-bogha Mór
An Dubh-sgeir
Macleod's Maidens
IDRIGILL POINT
Ben Idrigill
Beinn na Boineid 1207
Portnalong
Fiskavaig
Fernilea
Rubha nan Clach
Carbost
Drynoch
Talisker Distillery
Merkadale
Talisker
Talisker Bay
Sligachan
Loch Harport
Roineval 1442
Meall an Fhuarain
Beinn nan Cuithean
Loch Sleadale
Eynort River
Beinn Bhreac 1468
Eynort
Glen Brittle Forest
ISLE OF
M I N G I N I S H
Loch Eynort
An Dubh-sgeir
Stac an Tuill
Bualintur
Glenbrittle
Loch Brittle
Sgurr nan Gillean 3167
Sgurr a' Ghreadaidh 3197
CUILLIN HILLS
Sgurr Alasdair 3257
Loch Coruisk
Ceann na Beinne 736
Rubh' an Dùnain Chambered Cairn
Soay Sound
Beinn Bhreac 464
Mol-chlach
SOAY
Loch Scavaig
S E A  O F  T H E  H E B R I D E S
I N N E R  H E B R I D E S
CANNA
Carn a' Ghaill 693
Castle
Ceann Creag-airighe 426
Garrisdale Point
A' Chill
An Coroghon
Canna Harbour
Sanday
Rùm to Canna 55mins.
Rubha Shamhnan Insir
Mallaig to Canna 2hrs. (Seasonal)
Kilmory
Camas Pliasgaig
Guirdil Bay
Sound of Canna
Sgorr Mhòr 1273
Mullach Mòr 997
Kinloch Castle
Kinloch
Loch Scresort
Mallaig to Rùm 1hr. 20mins.
Muck to Canna 1hr. 35mins. (Seasonal)
Orval 1874
Long Loch
Loch Gainmhich
Schooner Point
Oigh-sgeir
Glen Harris
Hallival
Askival 2663
Loch Fiachanis
RÙM
NATIONAL NATURE RESERVE
Ainshval 2552
Ruinsival
Sgurr nan Gillean
Loch Papadil
Rubha nam Meirleach
SOUND OF RÙM
Rùm to Muck 1hr. 10mins. (Seasonal)
Bay of Laig
Cleadale
Loch Beinn Tighe
Rubha an Fhasaidh
EIGG
An Sgurr 1292
Sandavore
Kildonan
Galmisdale
Sgeir Eskernish
Sound of Eigg
Eilean nan Each
Gòdag
Eigg to Muck 35mins.
Mallaig to Muck
Port Mor
MUCK
Dubh Sgeir
Sanna Point
Fascadale
Sanna Bay
Ardnamurchan Lighthouse
Portuairk
Achnaha
Achosnich
Point of Ardnamurchan
100
10
20
30
40
850
40
30
20
10
800
90
80
70

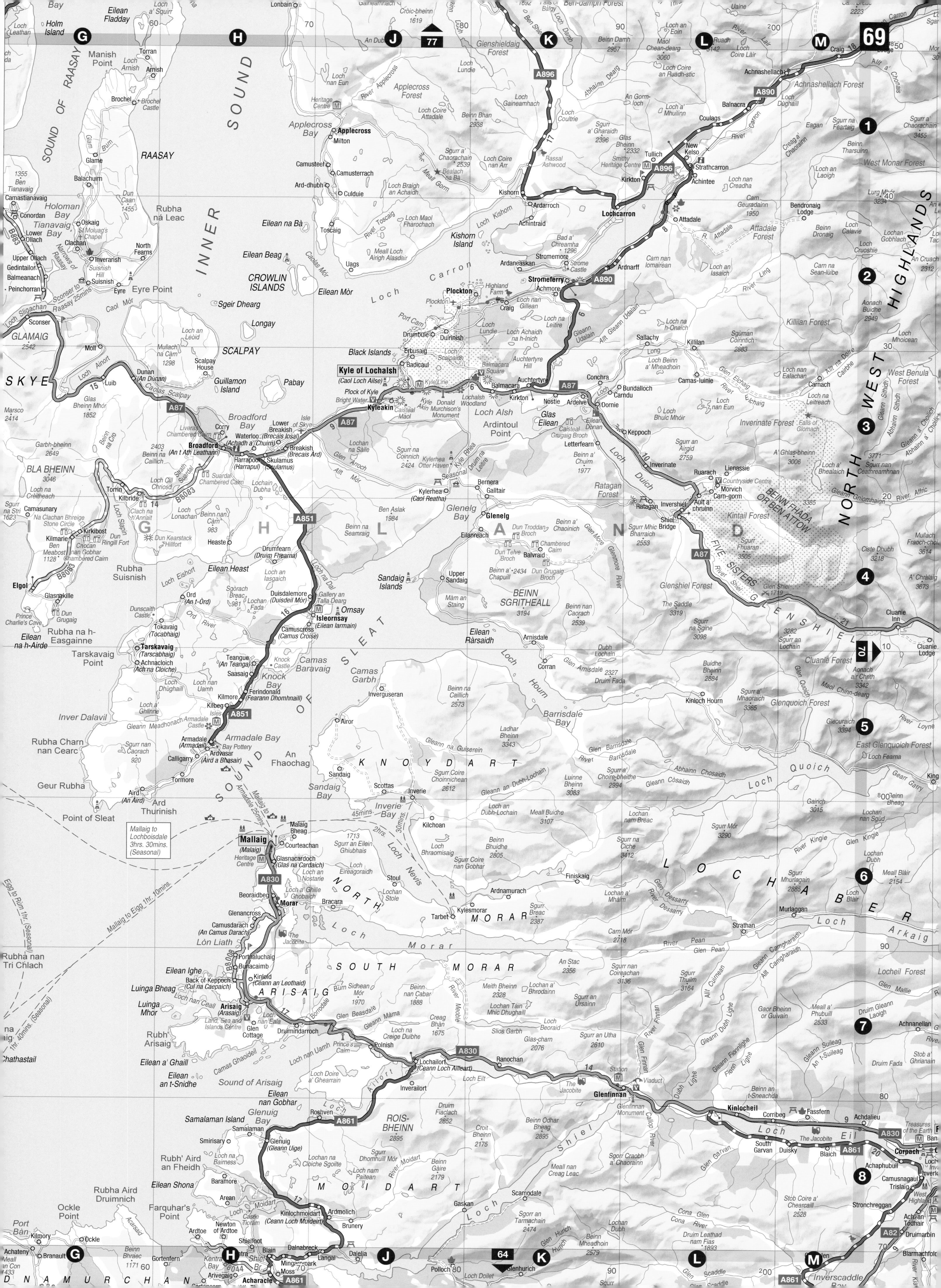
77
70
64
G
H
J
K
L
M
1
2
3
4
5
6
7
8
SOUND OF RAASAY
INNER SOUND
RAASAY
SKYE
SCALPAY
CROWLIN ISLANDS
H I G H L A N D
NORTH WEST HIGHLANDS
K N O Y D A R T
L O C H A B E R
SOUTH MORAR
NORTH MORAR
ARISAIG
M O I D A R T
ROIS-BHEINN
SOUND OF SLEAT
A R D N A M U R C H A N
GLENSHIEL
FIVE SISTERS
BEINN FHADA OR BEN ATTOW
BEINN SGRITHEALL
BLA BHEINN
Holm Island
Eilean Fladday
Manish Point
Torran
Arnish
Brochel
Brochel Castle
Glame
Balachuirn
Holoman Bay
Tianavaig Bay
Camastianavaig
Conordan
Lower Ollach
Upper Ollach
Gedintailor
Balmeanach
Peinchorran
Clachan
Raasay
Inverarish
Suisnish
Suisnish Hill
North Fearns
Rubha na Leac
Dun Caan 1455
Eyre
Eyre Point
Sconser
Sconser to Raasay 25mins.
Loch Sligachan
GLAMAIG 2542
Moll
Loch Ainort
Luib
Dunan (An Dùnan)
Caolas Scalpay
Scalpay House
Guillamon Island
Pabay
Mullach na Càrn 1298
Longay
Sgeir Dhearg
Caol Mòr
Eilean Beag
Eilean na Bà
Eilean Mòr
Applecross
Applecross Bay
Applecross Forest
Milton
Camusteel
Camusterrach
Ard-dhubh
Culduie
Toscaig
Uags
Kishorn Island
Kishorn
Ardarroch
Achintraid
Lochcarron
Strathcarron
Achintee
Attadale
Attadale Forest
Stromeferry
Stromemore
Ardaneaskan
Achmore
Craig
Plockton
Duirinish
Drumbuie
Erbusaig
Badicaul
Black Islands
Kyle of Lochalsh (Caol Loch Ailse)
Plock of Kyle
Kyleakin
Balmacara
Balmacara Square
Auchtertyre
Kirkton
Nostie
Ardelve
Dornie
Eilean Donan
Conchra
Bundalloch
Carndu
Camas-luinie
Killilan
Sallachy
Keppoch
Letterfearn
Inverinate
Ruarach
Lienassie
Morvich
Carn-gorm
Ault a' chruinn
Shiel Bridge
Invershiel
Ratagan
Ratagan Forest
Kintail Forest
Glenshiel Forest
Inverinate Forest
Falls of Glomach
Loch Duich
Loch Alsh
Glas Eilean
Ardintoul Point
Broadford
Broadford Bay
Corry
Waterloo
Lower Breakish
Breakish
Harrapool
Skulamus
Isle of Skye
Kylerhea
Bernera
Galltair
Glenelg
Glenelg Bay
Eilanreach
Balvraid
Beinn a' Chapuill
Upper Sandaig
Sandaig Islands
Arnisdale
Corran
Loch Hourn
Kinloch Hourn
Barrisdale Bay
Torrin
Kilbride
Camasunary
Kilmarie
Kirkibost
Elgol
Glasnakille
Rubha Suisnish
Eilean Heast
Heaste
Drumfearn
Duisdalemore
Isleornsay
Ornsay
Camuscross
Teangue
Saasaig
Knock Bay
Ferindonald
Kilmore
Kilbeg
Armadale
Armadale Bay
Ardvasar
Calligarry
Tormore
Aird
Ard Thurinish
Point of Sleat
Tarskavaig
Tarskavaig Point
Tokavaig
Achnacloich
Ord
Inver Dalavil
Rubha Charn nan Cearc
Geur Rubha
Rubha na h-Easgainne
Eilean na h-Airde
Prince Charlie's Cave
Camas Baravaig
Camas Garbh
Inverguseran
Airor
Sandaig
Sandaig Bay
Scottas
Inverie
Inverie Bay
Kilchoan
Loch Nevis
Tarbet
Kylesmorar
Ardnamurach
Finiskaig
Stoul
Mallaig
Mallaig Bheag
Courteachan
Glasnacardoch
Mallaig to Lochboisdale 3hrs. 30mins. (Seasonal)
Mallaig to Eigg 1hr. 10mins.
Beoraidbeg
Morar
Bracara
Glenancross
Camusdarach
Lòn Liath
Portnaluchaig
Bunacaimb
Back of Keppoch
Kinloid
Arisaig
Eilean Ighe
Luinga Bheag
Luinga Mhor
Rubh' Arisaig
Eilean a' Ghaill
Eilean an t-Snidhe
Sound of Arisaig
Camas Ghaoideil
Druimindarroch
Polnish
Lochailort
Inveraillort
Ranochan
Glenfinnan
Glenfinnan Monument
Kinlocheil
Corribeg
Fassfern
Achdalieu
Loch Eil
South Garvan
Duisky
Blaich
Corpach
Achaphubuil
Camusnagaul
Trislaig
Stronchreggan
Druimarbin
Blarmachfoldach
Inverscaddle Bay
Achnanellan
Roshven
Samalaman Island
Samalaman
Glenuig
Glenuig Bay
Smirisary
Rubh' Aird an Fheidh
Eilean Shona
Rubha Aird Druimnich
Baramore
Arean
Farquhar's Point
Ockle Point
Ockle
Port Bàn
Kilmory
Achateny
Branault
Ardtoe
Newton of Ardtoe
Shielfoot
Kinlochmoidart
Ardmolich
Brunery
Dalnabreck
Langal
Dalelia
Blain
Mingarrypark
Moss
Acharacle
Arivegaig
Kentra Bay
Gortenfern
Scamodale
Gaskan
Polloch
Glenhurich
Loch Shiel
Glen Finnan
Strathan
Murlaggan
Loch Arkaig
Loch Quoich
Loch Morar
Loch Carron
Loch Kishorn
Cluanie Inn
Cluanie Lodge
Cluanie Forest
Glenquoich Forest
East Glenquoich Forest
Locheil Forest
West Monar Forest
Killilan Forest
Achnashellach
Achnashellach Forest
Balnacra
Coulags
New Kelso
Tullich
Glenshieldaig Forest
Lonbain
Craig
Bendronaig Lodge
A87
A851
A890
A896
A830
A861
A82
B8083
B8008
B883
B8044
Isle of Skye
Skulamus

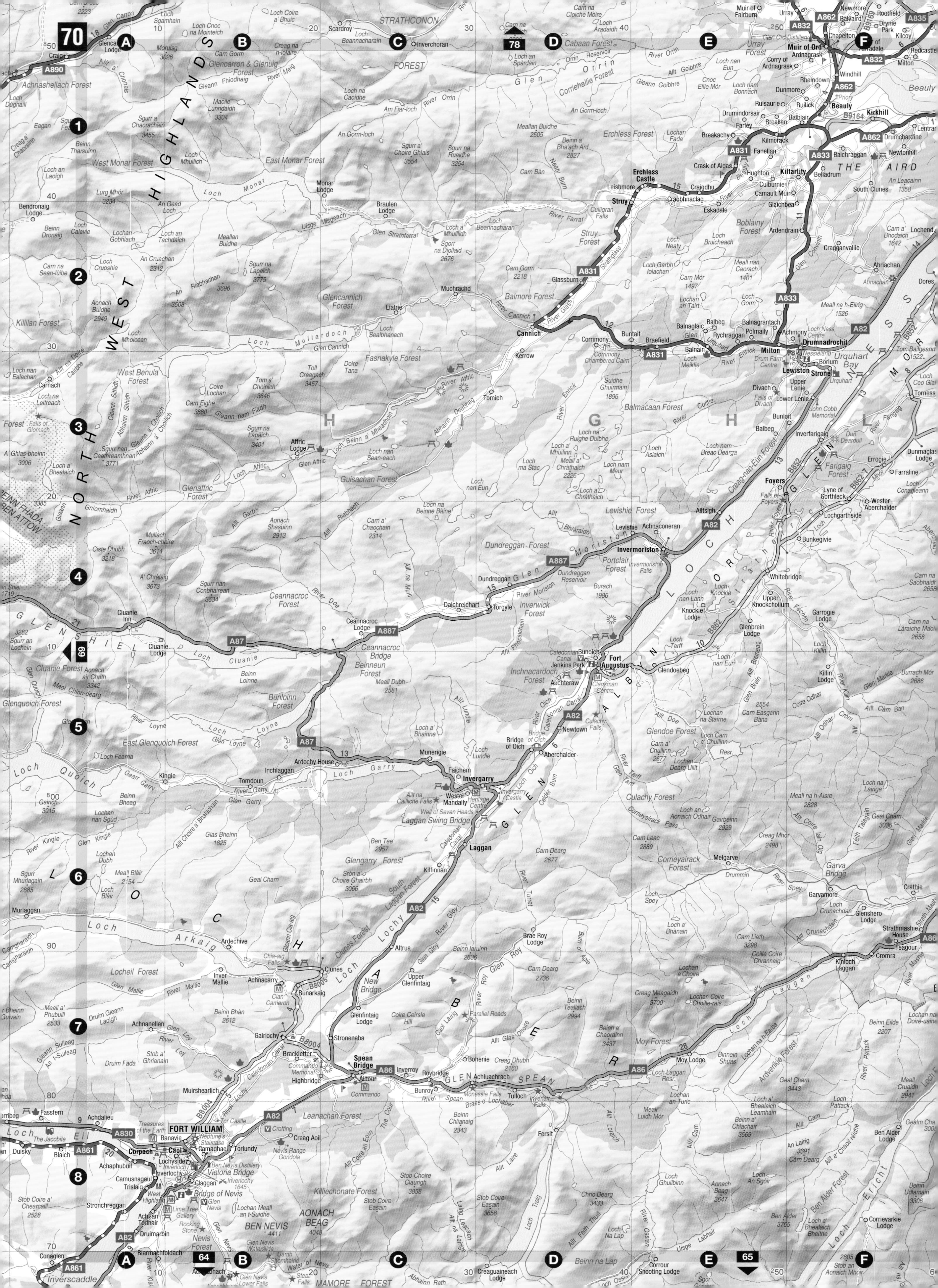
STRATHCONON
NORTH WEST HIGHLANDS
Glencarron & Glenuig Forest
Achnashellach Forest
West Monar Forest
East Monar Forest
Loch Monar
Monar Lodge
Braulen Lodge
Glen Strathfarrar
Struy
Erchless Castle
Muir of Ord
Beauly
Kirkhill
Kiltarlity
THE AIRD
Drumnadrochit
Milton
Lewiston
Strone
Urquhart Bay
Cannich
Glencannich Forest
Loch Mullardoch
Fasnakyle Forest
Tomich
Glen Affric
Affric Lodge
Guisachan Forest
Glenaffric Forest
Balmacaan Forest
Foyers
Invermoriston
Glen Moriston
Dundreggan Forest
Levishie Forest
Torgyle
Ceannacroc Forest
Cluanie Inn
Loch Cluanie
GLEN SHIEL
Fort Augustus
LOCH NESS
Inchnacardoch Forest
Glendoe Forest
Bridge of Oich
Invergarry
Loch Garry
Glen Garry
Tomdoun
Loch Quoich
Laggan
Laggan Swing Bridge
Glengarry Forest
Corrieyairack Forest
Garva Bridge
Loch Arkaig
Loch Lochy
Clunes Forest
Gairlochy
Spean Bridge
GLEN SPEAN
Roybridge
Tulloch
Loch Laggan
Moy Lodge
Kinloch Laggan
Ardverikie Forest
Ben Alder Forest
Loch Ericht
Moy Forest
FORT WILLIAM
Corpach
Caol
Banavie
Loch Eil
Inverlochy
Bridge of Nevis
BEN NEVIS 4411
AONACH BEAG 4048
Killiechonate Forest
Leanachan Forest
Nevis Forest
MAMORE FOREST
Fersit
Loch Treig
Corrour Shooting Lodge
Inverscaddle
A82
A86
A87
A887
A831
A862
A833
A830
A861
B852
B8004
B8005
A B C D E F
1 2 3 4 5 6 7 8

78
69
64
65

MORAY FIRTH
INVERNESS
PAGE 110
Cawdor
79
Nairn
Dallas
Darnaway Forest
Logie Steading
Newtyle Forest
Drumine Forest
North Kessock
Charlestown
Culloden
Smithton
Balloch
Westhill
Croy
Clephanton
Littlemill
Ferness
Relugas
Dunphail
Glenernie
M O R A Y
Upper Knockando
Knockando
Dava
Carn Kitty 1712
Lochindorb
Lochindorb Lodge
Daviot
Craggiemore
Moy
Inverarnie
Farr
Strathnairn Forest
Dunlichity Lodge
Ruthven
Balvraid Lodge
Tomatin
Findhorn Bridge
Corrybrough
Raigbeg
Clune
Corrievorrie
Slochd
Carrbridge
Ellan
Sluggan
Duthil
Dulnain Bridge
Grantown-on-Spey
Cromdale
Speybridge
Advie
Cragganmore
Bridge of Avon
Dalvey
Glaschoil
Cottartown
Upper Derraid
Auchnagallin
Dellefure
Achnahannet
Craggan
Skye of Curr
Broomhill
Boat of Garten
Nethy Bridge
Abernethy Forest
Loch Garten
Tulloch
Chapelton
Kinveachy
Avielochan
Granish
Aviemore
West Croftmore
Coylumbridge
GLENMORE FOREST PARK
Glenmore
Lynwilg
Inverdruie
Doune
Alvie
Delfour
Polchar
Loch Morlich
Kincraig
Speybank
Feshiebridge
Lagganlia
Insh
Inshriach Forest
Kingussie
Lynchat
Strone
Newtonmore
Ralia
Ruthven
Drumguish
Glentromie Lodge
Glentruim House
Etteridge
Crubenmore Lodge
Catlodge
Drumgask
Laggan
Balgowan
Cuaich
Dalwhinnie
Gaick Lodge
Gaick Forest
MONADHLIATH MOUNTAINS
Coignafearn Forest
Coignafearn Lodge
Dalmigavie
Glenmazeran Lodge
CAIRNGORMS NATIONAL PARK
CAIRN GORM 4085
CAIRNGORM MOUNTAINS
BRAERIACH 4248
BEN MACDUI 4296
CAIRN TOUL
BEINN A' BHUIRD
BEN AVON 3843
HILLS OF CROMDALE
Tomintoul
Tomnavoulin
Bridge of Brown
Tomachlaggan
Dorback Lodge
Braes of Abernethy
Glenfeshie Lodge
GLENFESHIE FOREST
FOREST OF MAR
ABERDEENSHIRE
BRAEMAR
Braemar
Castleton
Mar Lodge
Inverey
Keiloch
Invercauld Bridge
Morrone or Morven
Baddoch
AN SOCACH 3073
GLAS MAOL 3504
Devil's Elbow
Spittal of Glenshee
GRAMPIAN
PERTH & KINROSS
BEINN DEARG 3307
Bruar Lodge
Forest Lodge
Glenlochsie Lodge
Sronphadruig Lodge
Dalnamein Forest
FOREST OF ATHOLL
Dalnacardoch Forest
Dalnaspidal Lodge
Edendon Bridge
Dalnacardoch Lodge
Dalnacardoch
GLEN GARRY
A9
A96
A82
A862
A8082
A939
A940
A938
A95
A86
A889
A93
B9006
B9154
B9153
B9152
B970
B9007
B9102
B9136
B851
B862
66
72

Dallas
Rothes
Keith
Aberchirder
Milltown of Rothiemay
Archiestown
Craigellachie
Charlestown of Aberlour
Dufftown
Ruthven
Cairnie
Huntly
STRATHBOGIE
Marypark
Advie
Bridge of Avon
BEN RINNES
M O R A Y
Glenlivet
Tomnavoulin
Cabrach
Rhynie
Insch
Old Rayne
Leslie
Auchleven
CORREEN HILLS
Lumsden
Tomintoul
LADDER HILLS
Kildrummy
Alford
HOWE OF ALFORD
PITFICHIE FOREST
Monymusk
Tillyfourie
Strathdon
A B E R D E E N S H I R E
Cock Bridge
Corgarff
Leochel Cushnie
CAIRNGORMS NATIONAL PARK
MOUNTAINS
GRAMPIAN
Logie Coldstone
Tarland
Lumphanan
Torphins
Kincardine O'Neil
Aboyne
Dinnet
Ballater
Crathie
Balmoral Castle
Braemar
Bridge of Canny
Banchory
Strachan
B R A E M A R
LOCHNAGAR
Spittal of Glenmuick
Mount Keen
Mount Battock
Tarfside
GLAS MAOL
A N G U S
Clova
Fettercairn
Edzell
HOWE OF THE
A93
A97
A939
A944
A941
A920
A96
A95
A980

BUCHAN
FORMARTINE
Turriff
Cuminestown
New Deer
Maud
Mintlaw
Old Deer
Longside
Peterhead
Buchanhaven
Keith Inch
Burnhaven
Boddam
St Fergus
Rora
Stuartfield
Fyvie
Methlick
Auchnagatt
Rothienorman
Tarves
Ellon
Hatton
Cruden Bay
Port Erroll
Bay of Cruden
Collieston
Hackley Head or Forvie Ness
Newburgh
Newburgh Bar
Oldmeldrum
Pitmedden
Inverurie
Port Elphinstone
Newmachar
Balmedie
Kintore
Kemnay
Blackburn
Dyce
Bridge of Don
Bankhead
Bucksburn
Westhill
Kirkton of Skene
Dunecht
Echt
ABERDEEN
PAGE 106
Aberdeen to:
Kirkwall (Hatston) 6hrs.
Lerwick (Holmsgarth) 12hrs. 30mins.
Nigg Bay
Cults
Souter Head
Cove Bay
Peterculter
Portlethen
Cammachmore Bay
Muchalls
Doonie Point
Garron Point
Stonehaven
Castle Haven
Drumlithie
Todhead Point
Inverbervie
Bervie Bay
Gourdon
Laurencekirk
NORTH SEA
A90
A92
A93
A947
A948
A950
A952
A975
A981
A982
A920
A944
A956
A957
A96
A9119
A937
P+R
81

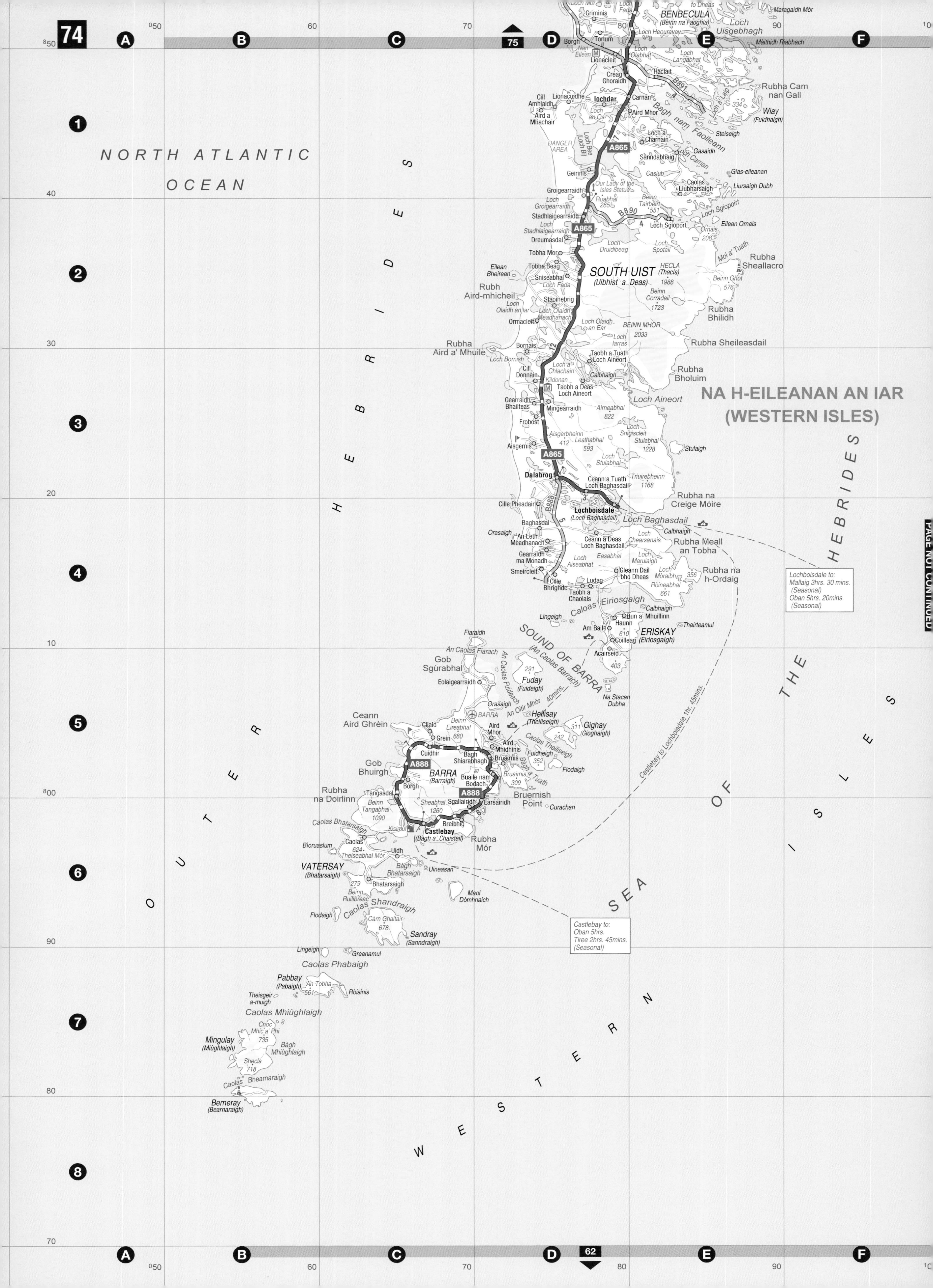
NORTH ATLANTIC OCEAN
OUTER HEBRIDES
SEA OF THE HEBRIDES
SEA OF THE WESTERN ISLES
NA H-EILEANAN AN IAR (WESTERN ISLES)
BENBECULA (Beinn na Faoghla)
SOUTH UIST (Uibhist a Deas)
BARRA (Barraigh)
ERISKAY (Eiriosgaigh)
VATERSAY (Bhatarsaigh)
SOUND OF BARRA (An Caolas Barrach)
Loch Uisgebhagh
Rubha Cam nan Gall
Wiay (Fuidhaigh)
Bagh nam Faoileann
Iochdar
Lionacleit
Creag Ghoraidh
Carnan
Haclait
Borgh
Torlum
Griminis
Cill Amhlaidh
Lionacuidhe
Aird a Mhachair
Aird Mhor
Loch a Charnain
Sanndabhaig
Gasaidh
Steiseigh
Geirinis
Glas-eileanan
Caolas Liubharsaigh
Liursaigh Dubh
Our Lady of the Isles Statue
Groigearraidh
Stadhlaigearraidh
Loch Sgioport
Eilean Ornais
Dreumasdal
Tobha Mor
Tobha Beag
Sniseabhal
Eilean Bheirean
Rubh Aird-mhicheil
HECLA (Thacla) 1988
Beinn Corradail 1723
Rubha Shealacro
Rubha Bhilidh
Staoinebrig
Ormacleit
BEINN MHOR 2033
Rubha Sheileasdail
Rubha Aird a' Mhuile
Bornais
Taobh a Tuath Loch Aineort
Cill Donnain
Taobh a Deas Loch Aineort
Rubha Bholuim
Loch Aineort
Gearraidh Bhailteas
Mingearraidh
Frobost
Aisgernis
Stulaigh
Dalabrog
Ceann a Tuath Loch Baghasdail
Triuirebheinn 1168
Cille Pheadair
Lochboisdale (Loch Baghasdail)
Loch Baghasdail
Rubha na Creige Móire
Baghasdal
Orasaigh
An Leth Meadhanach
Ceann a Deas Loch Baghasdail
Calbhaigh
Rubha Meall an Tobha
Gearraidh ma Monadh
Smeircleit
Gleann Dail bho Dheas
Rubha na h-Ordaig
Cille Bhrighde
Ludag
Taobh a Chaolais
Caolas Eiriosgaigh
Lochboisdale to: Mallaig 3hrs. 30 mins. (Seasonal) Oban 5hrs. 20mins. (Seasonal)
Lingeigh
Bun a' Mhuillinn
Haunn
Am Baile
Thairteamul
Coilleag
Acairseid
Fiaraidh
Gob Sgùrabhal
Eolaigearraidh
Fuday (Fuideigh)
Na Stacan Dubha
Orasaigh
Hellisay (Theiliseigh)
Gighay (Gioghaigh)
Ceann Aird Ghrèin
Cliaid
Grein
Aird Mhor
Aird Mhidhinis
Bruairnis
Cuidhir
Bagh Shiarabhagh
Flodaigh
Gob Bhuirgh
Buaile nam Bodach
Bruernish Point
Curachan
Rubha na Doirlinn
Tangasdal
Borgh
Sgallairidh
Earsairidh
Castlebay (Bàgh a' Chaisteil)
Breibhig
Rubha Mór
Castlebay to Lochboisdale 1hr. 45mins.
Caolas Bhatarsaigh
Bioruaslum
Caolas
Uidh
Uineasan
Bhatarsaigh
Maol Dòmhnaich
Caolas Shandraigh
Flodaigh
Sandray (Sanndraigh)
Castlebay to: Oban 5hrs. Tiree 2hrs. 45mins. (Seasonal)
Lingeigh
Greanamul
Caolas Phabaigh
Pabbay (Pabaigh)
Ròisinis
Theisgeir a-muigh
Caolas Mhiùghlaigh
Mingulay (Miùghlaigh)
Bàgh Mhiùghlaigh
Caolas Bhearnaraigh
Berneray (Bearnaraigh)
A865
A888
B890
B891
B888
75
62
PAGE NOT CONTINUED

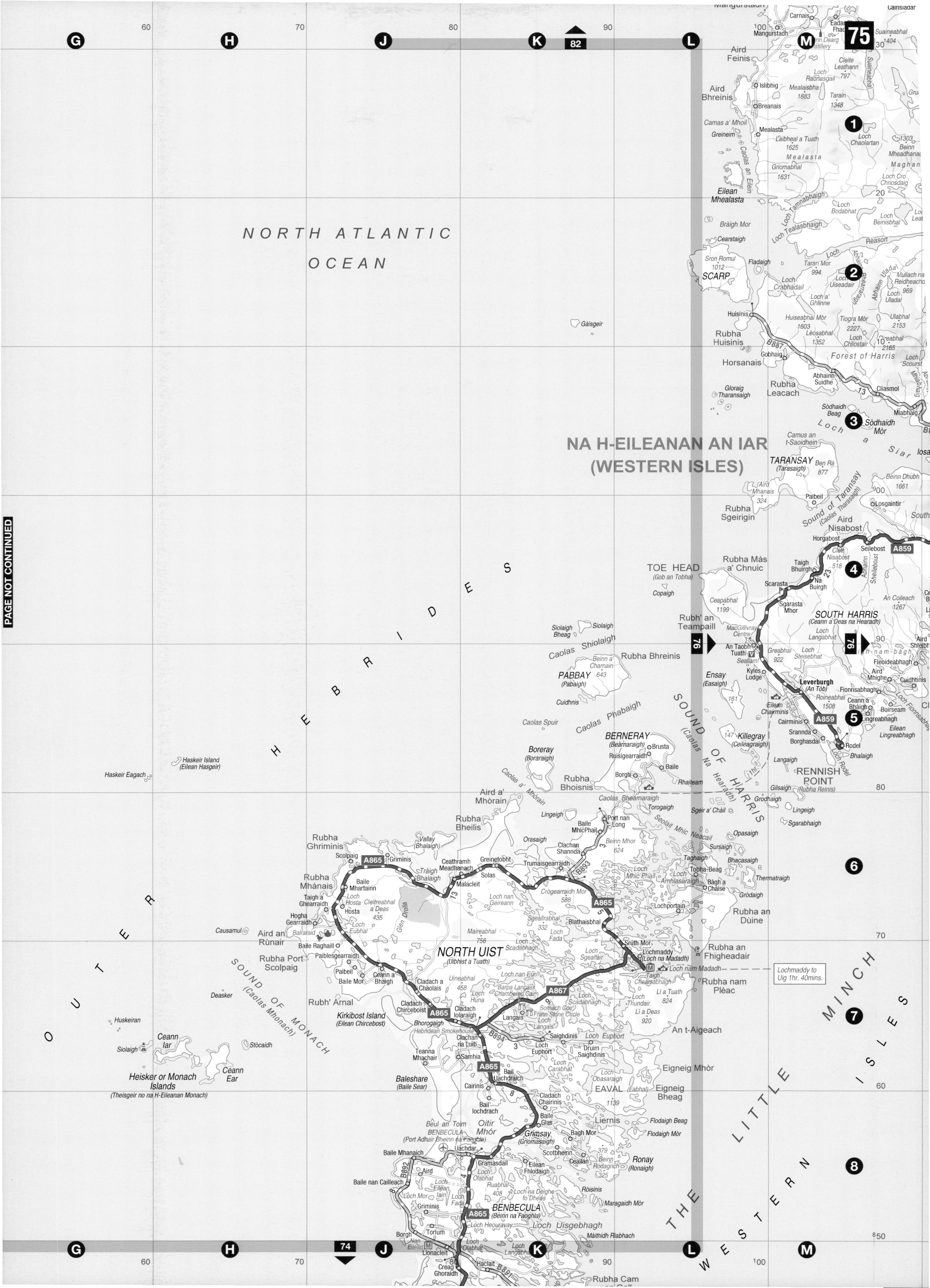
PAGE NOT CONTINUED
G
H
J
K
L
M
82
74
76
60
70
80
90
100
NORTH ATLANTIC
OCEAN
NA H-EILEANAN AN IAR
(WESTERN ISLES)
OUTER HEBRIDES
THE LITTLE MINCH
WESTERN ISLES
SOUND OF HARRIS
(Caolas na Hearadh)
SOUND OF MONACH
(Caolas Mhonach)
Mangurstadh
Carnais
Aird Feinis
Aird Bhreinis
Islibhig
Breanais
Camas a' Mhoil
Greineim
Mealasta
Caolas an Eilein
Eilean Mhealasta
Làibheal a Tuath 1625
Mealasta
Griomabhal 1631
Suaineabhal 1404
Loch Raonasgail
Mealaisbha 1883
Tarain 1348
Cleite Leathann 797
Loch Chaolartan
Beinn Mheadhanach
Loch Tamnabhaigh
Loch Teàlasbhaigh
Loch Bodabhat
Loch Beinisbhal
Bràigh Mor
Cearstaigh
Sron Romul 1012
SCARP
Fladaigh
Taran Mor 994
Loch Crabhadail
Loch Uiseadair
Loch a' Ghlinne
Mullach na Reidheachd 969
Loch Uladal
Huisinis
Rubha Huisinis
Huiseabhal Mòr 1603
Tiorga Mòr 2227
Ulabhal 2153
Leòsabhal 1352
Loch Chliostair
B887
Gobhaig
Horsanais
Forest of Harris
Abhainn Suidhe
Rubha Leacach
Gloraig Tharansaigh
Cliasmol
Miabhaig
Sòdhaidh Beag
Sòdhaidh Mòr
Loch a Siar
Gàisgeir
Camus an t-Saoidhein
TARANSAY (Tarasaigh)
Ben Rà 877
Aird Mhanais 324
Paibeil
Sound of Taransay (Caolas Tharasaigh)
Beinn Dhubh 1661
Losgaintir
Rubha Sgeirigin
Aird Nisabost
Horgabost
Seilebost
A859
Rubha Màs a' Chnuic
TOE HEAD (Gob an Tobha)
Copaigh
Taigh Bhuirgh
Scarasta
Na Buirgh
Sgarasta Mhor
Ceapabhal 1199
An Coileach 1267
SOUTH HARRIS (Ceann a Deas na Hearadh)
Rubh' an Teampaill
MacGillivray Centre
An Taobh Tuath
Seallam!
Greabhal 922
Loch Langabhat
Loch Steisebhat
Fleoideabhagh
Aird Mhighe
Kyles Lodge
Leverburgh (An Tòb)
Roineabhal 1508
Fionnsabhagh
Ceann a Bhàigh
Borseam
Lingreabhagh
Eilean Lingreabhagh
Eilean Chàirminis
Cairminis
Srannda
Borghasdal
Rodel
Bhalaigh
Langaigh
RENNISH POINT (Rubha Reinis)
Gilsaigh
Grodhaigh
Lingeigh
Sgarabhaigh
Siolaigh Bheag
Siolaigh
Caolas Shiolaigh
Rubha Bhreinis
Beinn a' Charnain 643
PABBAY (Pabaigh)
Ensay (Easaigh)
Cuidhnis
Caolas Phabaigh
Caolas Spuir
Killegray (Ceileagraigh)
BERNERAY (Beàrnaraigh)
Brusta
Ruisigearraidh
Baile
Borgh
Rhaiteam
Boreray (Boraraigh)
Rubha Bhoisnis
Caolas a' Mhòrain
Caolas Bheàrnaraigh
Torogaigh
Sgeir a' Chàil
Aird a' Mhòrain
Lingeigh
Port nan Long
Baile MhicPhail
Orasaigh
Beinn Mhor 624
Clachan Shannda
Rubha Bheilis
Vallay (Bhalaigh)
Rubha Ghriminis
Scolpaig
Griminis
A865
Ceathramh Meadhanach
Greinetobht
Trumaisgearraidh
B893
Tràigh Bhalaigh
Malacleit
Solas
Loch Mhic Phàil
Loch Amhlasaraigh
Bàgh a Chàise
Opasaigh
Sursaigh
Taghaigh
Bhacasaigh
Tobha-Beag
Thernatraigh
Gròdaigh
Rubha Mhànais
Baile Mhartainn
Loch Hosta
Cleitreabhal a Deas 435
Hosta
Taigh a Ghearraidh
Hogha Gearraidh
Loch Eubhal
Glen Drolla
Loch nan Geireann
Crogearraidh Mor 588
Sgealrabhal 332
Blathaisbhal
Lochportain
Rubha an Dùine
Causamul
Aird an Rùnair
Balaraid
Baile Raghaill
Paiblesgearraidh
Maireabhal 756
Loch Fada
Loch Scadabhagh
Sruth Mor
Lochmaddy (Loch na Madadh)
Rubha an Fhigheadair
NORTH UIST (Uibhist a Tuath)
Loch Sgealtair
Taigh Chearsabhagh
Loch nam Madadh
Lochmaddy to Uig 1hr. 40mins.
Rubha nam Plèac
Rubha Port Scolpaig
Paibeil
Baile Mor
Ceann a Bhàigh
Cladach a Chaolais
Uineabhal 458
Loch Hunna
Loch nan Eun
Barpa Langass Chambered Cairn
A867
Loch Scadabhagh
Loch Thundair
Lì a Tuath 824
Lì a Deas 920
Deasker
Rubh' Arnal
Kirkibost Island (Eilean Chirceboist)
Cladach Chirceboist
Cladach Iolaraigh
Langais
Sornach Coir Fhinn Stone Circle
Loch Langais
An t-Aigeach
Huskeiran
Ceann Iar
Siolaigh
Stòcaidh
Ceann Ear
Heisker or Monach Islands (Theisgeir no na H-Eileanan Monach)
Bhorogaigh
Hebridean Smokehouse
Clachan na Luib
B894
Saighdinis
Loch Euphort
Druim Saighdinis
Teanna Mhachair
Samhla
Loch Carabhat
Loch Obasaraigh
Eigneig Mhòr
Baleshare (Baile Sear)
Bail Uachdraich
Cairinis
EAVAL (Eabhal) 1139
Eigneig Bheag
Cladach Chairinis
Bail' Iochdrach
Baile Glas
Liernis
Flodaigh Beag
Flodaigh Mòr
Beul an Toim
BENBECULA (Port Adhair Bheinn na Faoghla)
Oitir Mhór
Grimsay (Griomasaigh)
Bagh Mor
Scotbheinn
Ceallan
Beinn Rodagrich 379
Ronay (Ronaigh)
Baile Mhanaich
Uachdar
Gramasdail
Eilean Fhlodaigh
Aird
Loch Olabhat
Rueabhal 408
Loch na Deighe fo Dheas
Baile nan Cailleach
Loch Eilean Iain
Loch Mor
Loch Fada
Ròisinis
Maragaidh Mòr
Griminis
A865
BENBECULA (Beinn na Faoghla)
Loch Heouravay
Loch Uisgebhagh
Màithidh Rìabhach
Borgh
Torlum
Nan Eilean
Lionacleit
Loch Olabhat
Loch Langabhat
Creag Ghoraidh
Haclait
B891
B892
Rubha Cam
1
2
3
4
5
6
7
8

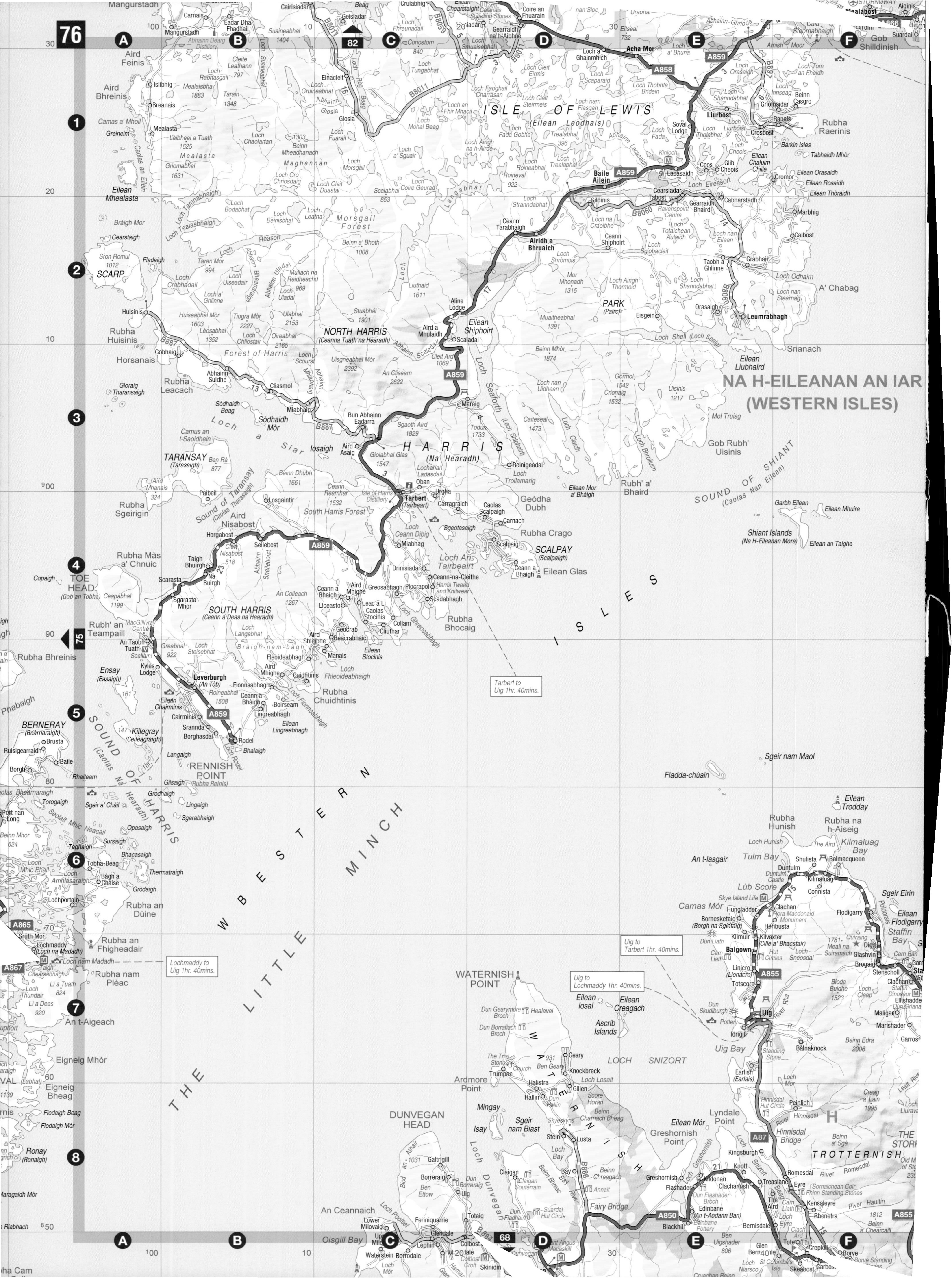
ISLE OF LEWIS
(Eilean Leodhais)
NORTH HARRIS
(Ceanna Tuath na Hearadh)
HARRIS
(Na Hearadh)
SOUTH HARRIS
(Ceann a Deas na Hearadh)
NA H-EILEANAN AN IAR
(WESTERN ISLES)
PARK
(Pairc)
SCARP
TARANSAY
(Tarasaigh)
SCALPAY
(Scalpaigh)
BERNERAY
(Bearnaraigh)
Shiant Islands
(Na h-Eileanan Mora)
SOUND OF SHIANT
(Caolas Nan Eilean)
SOUND OF HARRIS
(Caolas na Hearadh)
Sound of Taransay
(Caolas Tharasaigh)
Loch a Siar
Loch Seaforth
(Loch Shiphoirt)
Loch Shell (Loch Sealg)
Loch Roag
Loch Erisort
Forest of Harris
South Harris Forest
Morsgail Forest
WESTERN ISLES
THE LITTLE MINCH
TOE HEAD
(Gob an Tobha)
RENNISH POINT
(Rubha Reinis)
Rubha Huisinis
Huisinis
Horsanais
Rubha Leacach
Rubha Sgeirigin
Rubha Màs a' Chnuic
Rubh' an Teampaill
Rubha Bhreinis
Rubha Chuidhtinis
Rubha Bhocaig
Rubha Crago
Eilean Glas
Gob Rubh' Uisinis
Rubh' a' Bhaird
Eilean Mhealasta
Aird Feinis
Aird Bhreinis
Mangurstadh
Mealasta
Breanais
Islibhig
Tarbert
(Tairbeart)
Leverburgh
(An t-Ob)
Rodel
Scalpaigh
Ceann a Bhaigh
Scarasta
Seilebost
Horgabost
Losgaintir
Aird Asaig
Bun Abhainn Eadarra
Miabhaig
Cliasmol
Abhainn Suidhe
Gobhaig
Maraig
Reinigeadal
Urgha
Caolas Scalpaigh
Drinisiadar
Ceann-na-Cleithe
Plocrapol
Scadabhagh
Greosabhagh
Manais
Fionnsabhagh
Lingreabhagh
Srannda
Sgarasta Mhor
An Taobh Tuath
Kyles Lodge
Killegray
(Ceilegraigh)
Ensay
(Easaigh)
Aline Lodge
Airidh a Bhruaich
Ceann Tarabhaigh
Baile Ailein
Lacasaidh
Liurbost
Soval Lodge
Acha Mor
Leumrabhagh
Orasaigh
Eisgein
Ranais
Crosbost
Grimsiadar
Cromor
Marbhig
Calbost
Rubha Raerinis
A' Chabag
Srianach
Eilean Liubhaird
Eilean Shiphoirt
Clisham / An Cliseam 2622
Uisgneabhal Mòr 2392
Tarbert to Uig 1hr. 40mins.
Uig to Tarbert 1hr. 40mins.
Uig to Lochmaddy 1hr. 40mins.
Lochmaddy to Uig 1hr. 40mins.
Lochmaddy
(Loch na Madadh)
Rubha nam Plèac
Rubha an Fhigheadair
Rubha an Dùine
Eigneig Mhòr
Eigneig Bheag
An t-Aigeach
Ronay
(Ronaigh)
Fladda-chùain
Sgeir nam Maol
Eilean Trodday
Rubha Hunish
Rubha na h-Aiseig
Kilmaluag Bay
Tulm Bay
Duntulm
Kilmaluag
Lùb Score
Camas Mòr
Skye Island Life
Flodigarry
Eilean Flodigarry
Staffin Bay
Balgown
Uig
Uig Bay
LOCH SNIZORT
WATERNISH POINT
WATERNISH
Eilean Iosal
Eilean Creagach
Ascrib Islands
Ardmore Point
Mingay
Isay
Sgeir nam Biast
DUNVEGAN HEAD
Loch Dunvegan
Lyndale Point
Greshornish Point
Eilean Mòr
TROTTERNISH
Fairy Bridge
An Ceannaich
Oisgill Bay
A859
A858
A865
A867
A855
A850
A87
B887
B8011
B8060
B897
82
75
68
A B C D E F
1 2 3 4 5 6 7 8

Pabail Uarach
Pabail Iarach
Bagh Phabail Iarach
Stornoway to Ullapool 2hrs. 40mins.
Ullapool to Stornoway 2hrs. 40mins.
G
H
J
K
L
M
83
84
69
60
70
80
90
200
Rhubha Stoer
Achnacarnin
Clashnessie Bay
Balchladich
Stoer
Bay of Stoer
Clachtoll
Achmelvich Bay
Achmelvich
Rhicarn
Rubha Rodha
Baddidarach
Lochinver
Soyea Island
Loch Inver
Kirkaig Point
A' Chleit
Badnaban
Strathan
Inverkirkaig
Loch Kirkaig
Rubha Coigeach
Loch na Totaig
Camas Coille
Eilean Mór
Enard Bay
Camas Eilean Ghlais
Rubha Mór
Brae of Achnahaird
Reiff
Inverpolly Lodge
Eilean Mullagrach
Altandhu
Isle Ristol
Polbain
Badentarbat
Badentarbat Bay
Glas-leac Mór
Achiltibuie
Polglass
Badenscallie
Tanera Beg
Tanera Mór
Summer Isles
Horse Sound
Horse Island
COIGACH
Glas-leac Beag
Eilean Dubh
Culnacraig
Achduart
Ben More Coigach
Priest Island
Bottle Island
Carn nan Sgeir
Cailleach Head
Leac Dhonn
Isle Martin
Greenstone Point
Rubha Beag
Opinan
Mellon Udrigle
Scoraig
Achmore
Annat Bay
Gruinard Island
Stattic Point
Little Loch Broom
Badluarach
Rireavach
Eilean Furadh Mór
Slaggan Bay
Beinn Dearg Mhór
Achgarve
Gruinard Bay
Laide
Gruinard House
Mungasdale
Durnamuck
Badcaul
Badrallach
Rubha Reidh
Camas Mór
Rubha nan Sasan
Mellon Charles
Sand
Second Coast
First Coast
Ardessie
Camusnagaul
A832
Cove
Ormiscaig
Loch an Draing
An Cuaidh 972
Mellangaun
Aultbea
Isle of Ewe
Drumchork
Sàil Mhòr 2508
Ardessie Falls
Dundonnell
B8057
Melvaig
Aultgrishan
B8021
Loch Sguod
Midtown
Brae
Loch Ewe
AN TEALLACH
Seana Chamas
Cnoc Breac 962
Naast
Inverewe
Peterburn
Londubh
Port Erradale
North Erradale
Big Sand
Poolewe
Fisherfield Forest
Caolas Beag
Longa Island
Lonemore
Mial
Strath
Tollie Farm
Smithstown
Gairloch
Loch Gairloch
Eilean Horrisdale
Charlestown
Port Henderson
Aird
Badachro
Opinan
South Erradale
Shieldaig
Eilean Subhainn
Letterewe
Letterewe Forest
Loch Maree
Redpoint
Victoria Falls
Talladale
SLIOCH 3215
W E S T E R   R O S S
Sgeir Ghlas
Flowerdale Forest
Bridge of Grudie
Sgeir na Trian
Shieldaig Forest
Baosbheinn 2869
Beinn Bhreac 2031
Kinlochewe Forest
Heights of Kinlochewe
Craig
Kinlochewe
Incheril
Rubha na Fearn
Fearnmore
Fearnbeg
Lower Diabaig
Upper Diabaig
Beinn Alligin 3232
BEINN EIGHE
Rubha Chuaig
Arinacrinachd
Kenmore
Alligin Shuas
Rechullin
Torridon Forest
LIATHACH
Cuaig
Inveralligin
Fasag
Torridon
Glen Torridon
A896
Ardheslaig
Upper Loch Torridon
Shieldaig Island
Coulin Lodge
Balgy
Annat
Callakille
Shieldaig
Ben-damph Forest
Coulin Forest
Lonbain
Croic-bheinn 1619
Beinn Damh 2957
Maol Chean-dearg 3060
Sgorr Ruadh 3142
A890
Glencarron Lodge
Glenshieldaig Forest
An Dubh-loch
Craig
Achnashellach
Achnashellach Forest
Applecross
Kilt Rock
Mealt Falls
Valtos
Rubha nam Brathairean
A855
Culnacnoc
Lealt Falls
Leac Tressirnish
Port an Fhearainn
RONA
SOUND OF RAASAY
Eilean Garbh
Eilean Tigh
Garbh Eilean
INNER SOUND
Bearreraig Bay
Eilean Fladday
Holm Island
Manish Point
Torran
Loch Arnish
Arnish

A B C D E F
1 2 3 4 5 6 7 8

84
77
70

BEN KLIBRECK 3152
85
86
G
H
J
K
L
M
70
80
90
00
10
Kinbrace
B871
River Helmsdale
Loch Achnamoine
Loch an Altan Fhearna
Loch na Gaineimh
Cnoc an Liath-bhaid Mhóir 1423
Creag na h-Iolaire 2278
Loch Choire Forest
Meall a' Bhata 1907
Ben Armine 2311
Gorm-Loch Beag
Borrobol Forest
Cnoc na Breun-choille 1194
Altanduin
Borrobol Lodge
Loch Ascaig
Creag nam Fiadh 1271
A897
Kildonan
Creag Mhór 2338
Gorm-Loch Mór
Garvary Burn
Creag Riabhach na Greighe 1506
Ben Armine Forest
Ben Armine Lodge
Glas-Loch Mór
1407 Meallan Liath Mór
Strath na Seilge
Tuarie Burn
Craggie
Craggie Water
Cnoc Meadhonach 1134
Strath of Kildonan or Strath Ullie
Torrish
Beinn Dubhain 1365
Cnoc Coire na Feàrna 1434
Gobernuisgeach
Cnoc an Eireannaich 1699
Morven 2313
1587 Maiden Pap
Berriedale Water
Braemore
Scaraben 2055
Meall na Caorach 1301
Wag
Creag Scalabsdale 1819
Langwell Forest
Langwell Water
Alltibea
Ramscraigs
Borgue
Newport
Berriedale
Berriedale Castle
Balnabruich
Knockally
Portormin
Laidhay Croft
Heritage Centre
Latheronwheel
Knockinnon
Smerral
Badnabay
A9
Cnoc na Maoile 1315
Ousdale
Ousdale Broch
Badbea Clearance Village
Boch-ailean
Ord Point
Eldrable Hill 1338
Marrel
Navidale
East Helmsdale
West Helmsdale
Gartymore
Helmsdale
Timespan
Portgower
Beinn Dhorain 2060
Meallan Liath Beag 1512
Glen Sletdale
Glen Loth
Lothmore
Kilmote
Lothbeg
Crackaig
Lothbeg Point
Dalnessie
Loch Bad an t-Sean-tighe
Coirefrois Burn
1230 Meall a' Phiobaire
Sidhean Achadh nan Eun 1040
Loch Beannach
A N D
River Brora
Loch na Gaineimh
Cnoc Leamhnachd 961
Loch Beannach
Balnacoil
Black Water
Col-bheinn 1765
Gordonbush
Loch Tigh na Creige
Loch Preas nan Sgiathanach
978 Grumby Rock
West Langwell
Strath Brora
Dalreavoch
Rhilochan
Knockarthur
Kilbraur Hill 1063
Loch Brora
Loch an Tubairnaich
Achrimsdale
East Clyne
West Clyne
Clynelish
Distillery
Dalchalm
Badnellan
Brora
Heritage Centre
Loch Craggie
East Langwell
Torbreck Burn
Achvoan
Loch Horn
Ben Horn 1706
A839
Tomich
Rhian Breck
Strath Fleet
River Fleet
Muie
Tressady
Little Rogart
Rogart
Cagar Feosaig 1239
Uppat
Doll
Ardachu
Dalmore
Pittentrail
An Stoc-bheinn 1104
Loch Cracail Mór
Creagan Glas 1028
Beinn Lunndaidh 1463
Beinn a' Bhragaidh 1293
Backies
Golspie Burn
Orcadian Stone Company
Carn Liath
Dunrobin
Duke of Sutherland Monument
Morvich
Mound Rock
Golspie
Loch Laro
Lochan na Gaoithe
Loch Buidhe
Abhainn an t-Stratha Charnaig
Little Torboll
Kirkton
928 Sròn Ach a' Bhacaidh
Beinn Domhnaill 1144
Loch an Lagain
Loch Laoigh
Loch Fleet
Skelbo
Littleferry
Meall Moraig 1090
Creag Liath 930
Achvaich
Badninish
Skelbo Street
Embo
Airdens
Tulloch
Loch a' Ghobhair
River Evelix
Lednabirichen
Birichen
Poles
Migdale
Loch Migdale
Rearquhar
Astle
Fleuchary
Embo Street
Bonar Bridge
A949
Evelix
B9168
Pitgrudy
Bardnabeinne
Clashmore Wood
Ardgay
Kincardine
Little Creich
Spinningdale
Ospisdale
Clashmore
Camore
Dornoch
Littletown
Historylinks
Carnegie Courthouse
Archronie
Dun Creich
Whiteface
Loch Evelix
Lonemore
A836
Easter Fearn
Wester Fearn
Fearn Burn
Ardmore
Doune
Edderton
Clach Biorach
Cambuscurrie Bay
DORNOCH FIRTH
Struie 1218
TARBAT NESS
Wilkhaven
Bindal
Portmahomack
Tarbat Discovery Centre
Seafield
Rockfield
Glenmorangie Distillery
Morangie
Tarlogie
B9174
Tain
Tain Through Time
DANGER AREA
Inver
Lower Arboll
Toulvaddie
Tarrel
B9165
Loch Muigh-bhlàraidh
1792 Cnoc Muigh-bhlàraidh
Aultnamain Inn
Easter Fearn Burn
B9176
O S S
Morangie Forest
Hilton
Lochslin
Lower Pitkerrie
Geanies
Beinn Tharsuinn 2270
Loch Sheilah
Cnoc an t-Sabhail 1243
Glen Aldie
Hartmount Holdings
Loch Eye
Hill of Fearn
Fearn
B9166
Hilton of Cadboll Chapel
Hilton of Cadboll
Balintore
Shandwick
Strath Rory
Lamington
Brenachie
Scotsburn
Marybank
Pitmaduthy
Arabella
Strathy
Cnoc Corr Guinie 1301
Kinrive Hill 1056
Kinrhive
Kildary
Loanreoch
Ardross Forest
Ardross
Easter Ardross
Stittenham
Dalnavie
Tullich Muir
Milton
Ankerville
Wester Rarichie
Clach a' Charridh
Port an Righ
Badachonacher
River Averon
Delny
Kilmuir
B9175
Bayfield Loch
Achandunie
Newmore
Coillemore
Nigg Bay
Nonikiln
Rhicullen
Polio
Barbaraville
Pitcalnie
Hill of Nigg 665
Nigg
Contullich
Fyrish Monument
Crosshills
Obsdale
Achnagarron
Tomich
Broomhill
Balintraid
B817
Balnabruaich
Balnapaling
Castlecraig
Rosskeen
Saltburn
Nigg Ferry
Alness
Distillery
Dalmore
Invergordon
FIRTH
Cromarty
High Miller
Blue Head
Sutors of Cromarty
Courthouse
(Seasonal)
Alness Bay
Ferryton
Balblair
Udale Bay
Cromarty Bay
Newton
A832
Evanton
Drummond
CROMARTY
Alnessferry
Resolis
Newmills
Jemimaville
B9163
Davidston
Cromarty Brewing
Muirton
McFarquhar's Cave
Cullicudden
Springfield
Mount High
Findon Mains
Kinbeachie
Easter Brae
Wester Brae
Millbuie
Forest
B9160
B9169
Culbo
Braefindon
Culbokie
Whitebog
Mount Eagle
BLACK ISLE
FIRTH
Whiteness Head
Findon Forest
Killen
Rosemarkie
Rosemarkie Bay
Fortrose
Groam House
Knockbain
Easter Suddie
Avoch
A832
Chanonry Point
Fort George
DANGER AREA
Belmaduthy
Avoch Bay
Ardersier
Connage Highland Dairy
B9006
B9092
Munlochy
Munlochy Bay
MORAY
Milton of Gollanfield
Gollanfield
Highland Aviation
Fisherton
B9039
Inverness
Lochside
Loch Flemington
Black Isle
Tore
Arpafeelie
Bogallan
Artafallie
A9
B9161
Alturlie Point
Kilmuir
Craigton
Lifeboat Station
Charlestown
North Kessock
Craigrory
Firth
A96
Newton
Ballo...
Tornagrain
Croy
Dalcross
Cantraywood
Easter Galcantray
Cawdor
Clephanton
B9090
Brackla
River Nairn
B9091
Piperhill
Culcharry
Regoul
Geddes
Foynesfield
Laiken Forest
A939
Littlemill
Kingsteps
Drum
Moss-side
Househill
B9101
Boath Doocot
Auldearn
1645
Blackhills
NAIRN
Tradespark
Loch Loy
Culbin Forest
Cran Loch
Cloddymoss
Kintessack
Dyke
Rodney Stone
Brodie
Broom of Moy
Benromach Distillery
Sueno's Stone
FORRES
Nelson Tower
Lochaber
Balnageith
Whiterow
Falconer
Dallas Dhu Historic Distillery
Loch of Blairs
Rafford
Califer
Moor of Granary
Muckle Burn
River Findhorn
Whitemire
Conicaval
A940
MORAY
Altyre Woods
Romach Loch
Darnaway Forest
Logie Steading
Logie
Drumine Forest
Newtyle Forest
Branchill
Dallas
Mill Buie 1218
Hill of Tomechole 1129
Randolph's Leap
Relugas
Dunphail
Carnach
Findhorn
Heritage Centre
Findhorn Foundation
Findhorn Bay
Kinloss
Kinloss Abbey
Morayvia
B9011
B9089
A96
Burghead
Burghead Bay
Roseisle Forest
College of Roseisle
Roseisle
Cummingstown
Hopeman
B9040
Covesea
Caves
Duffus
St Peter's Kirk
Duffus
B9012
B9013
Quarrywood
Elgin
Newton
Coltfield
Alves
Quarrel Wood Woodland Park
Glen Moray Distillery
Miltonduff
Muir of Miltonduff
Monaughty Forest
Foresterseat
Heldon Hill
Pluscarden Abbey
Barnhill
Black Burn
Pluscarden
Hill of the Wangie 1046
Dallas Forest
Kellas
Meikle Hill 932
Carn Uish 1197
Lochindorb...
NORTH SEA
80
90
20
10
900
80
70
60
50
1 2 3 4 5 6 7 8
71

Smerral
Latheronwheel
Clan Gunn Heritage Centre
Knockinnon
Dunbeath
Balnabruich
Laidhay Croft
Portormin
Knockally
Heritage Centre
Ramscraigs
A9
Borgue
Newport
Berriedale
Berriedale Castle
Boch-ailean
A
B
C
D
E
F
1
2
3
4
5
6
7
8
86
79
72
20
30
40
350
60
70
10
900
90
80
N O R T H
Covesea
Caves
Fisheries & Community
Branderburgh
Stotfield
Seatown
Hopeman
Lossiemouth
Burghead
B9040
Cummingstown
Duffus
St Peter's Kirk
Roseisle
Roseisle Forest
Loch Spynie
Lossie Forest
Spynie Palace
College of Roseisle
Quarrywood
Elgin
Bishopmill
Moray Motor Museum
Newton
Quarrel Wood Woodland Park
Coltfield
Alves
A96
Glen Moray Distillery
Ashgrove
New Elgin
Linkwood
Glassgreen
Moss of Barmuckity
Miltonduff
Muir of Miltonduff
Monaughty Forest
Heldon Hill
Pluscarden Abbey
Foresterseat
Barnhill
Thornhill
Upper Bogside
Longmorn
Whitewreath
Coleburn
Kellas
Dallas Forest
Hill of Wangie 1046
Dallas
Meikle Hill 932
Cairn Uish 1197
Glenlatterach Reservoir
Pikey Hill 1164
Glen of Rothes
Rothes
Glen Grant Distillery
Ben Aigan 1546
A941
Lhanbryde
Sheriffston
Urquhart
Urquhart Stone Circle
Lochhill
Scotsburn
Cranloch
Clackmarras
Teindland
Teindland Forest
M O R A Y
Spey Bay
Tugnet Ice House
Scottish Dolphin Centre
DANGER AREA
Kingston
Garmouth
Spey Viaduct
Bogmoor
Cowfords
Mosstodloch
Baxters
Crofts of Dipple
Fochabers
Folk Museum
Inchberry
Ordiquish
Wood of Ordiequish
Speymouth Forest
Whiteash Hill Wood
River Spey
Auchroisk Distillery
Orton
Malcolmburn
Mulben
A95
Hill of Mulderie 1019
Mount Pleasant
Nether Dallachy
Upper Dallachy
Lower Auchenreath
Auchenhalrig
Newlands of Tynet
A98
Porttannachy
Portgordon
Buckpool
A990
Buckie
A942
Portessie
Ianstown
Rathven
Findochty
Findochty Castle
B9020
B9021
Portknockie
Bauds of Cullen
Bin of Cullen 1051
Slackhead
Drybridge
Broadley
Clochan
Shiel Muir
Aultmore
Millstone Hill 987
Forgie
A96
Broadrashes
Aultmore
Newmill
Keith
Strathisla Distillery
ISLA
Mains of Auchindachy
Deerhill
Grange Crossroads
Crannoch
Bracobrae
Cullen Bay
Logie Head
Seatown
Cullen
Marcat Cross
Lintmill
Findlater Castle
Sandend Bay
Sandend
Milton
Kirktown of Deskford
Deskford Church
Berryhillock
Joiner's Workshop
Durn Hill 653
Fordyce
1028 Lurg Hill
Mains of Edingight
1412 Knock Hill
Sillyearn
Knock
Drumnagorrach
Farmtown
Nethermills
Upper Cuttlehill
The Bin Forest
Redhythe Point
Portsoy
Salmon Bothy
Boyne Bay
Boyne Castle
Brodiesord
Drums of Park
Gordonstown
Cornhill
Ramsburn
Milltown of Rothiemay
Marnoch
Dubiton
Turtory
Hillbrae
Knock Head
Whitehills
Boyndie Bay
Inverboyndie
Boyndie
Banff
Wester Culbeuchly
Kirktown of Alvah
Itlaw
Finnygaud
Knowes of Elrick
Aberchirder
Newton of Mountblairy
Bogton
A97
Deveron
Eden Castle
B9139
B9023
B9025
B9022
B9018
B9017
B9016
B9015
B9013
B9012
B9010
B9089
B9135
B9117
B9121
B9038
A B E

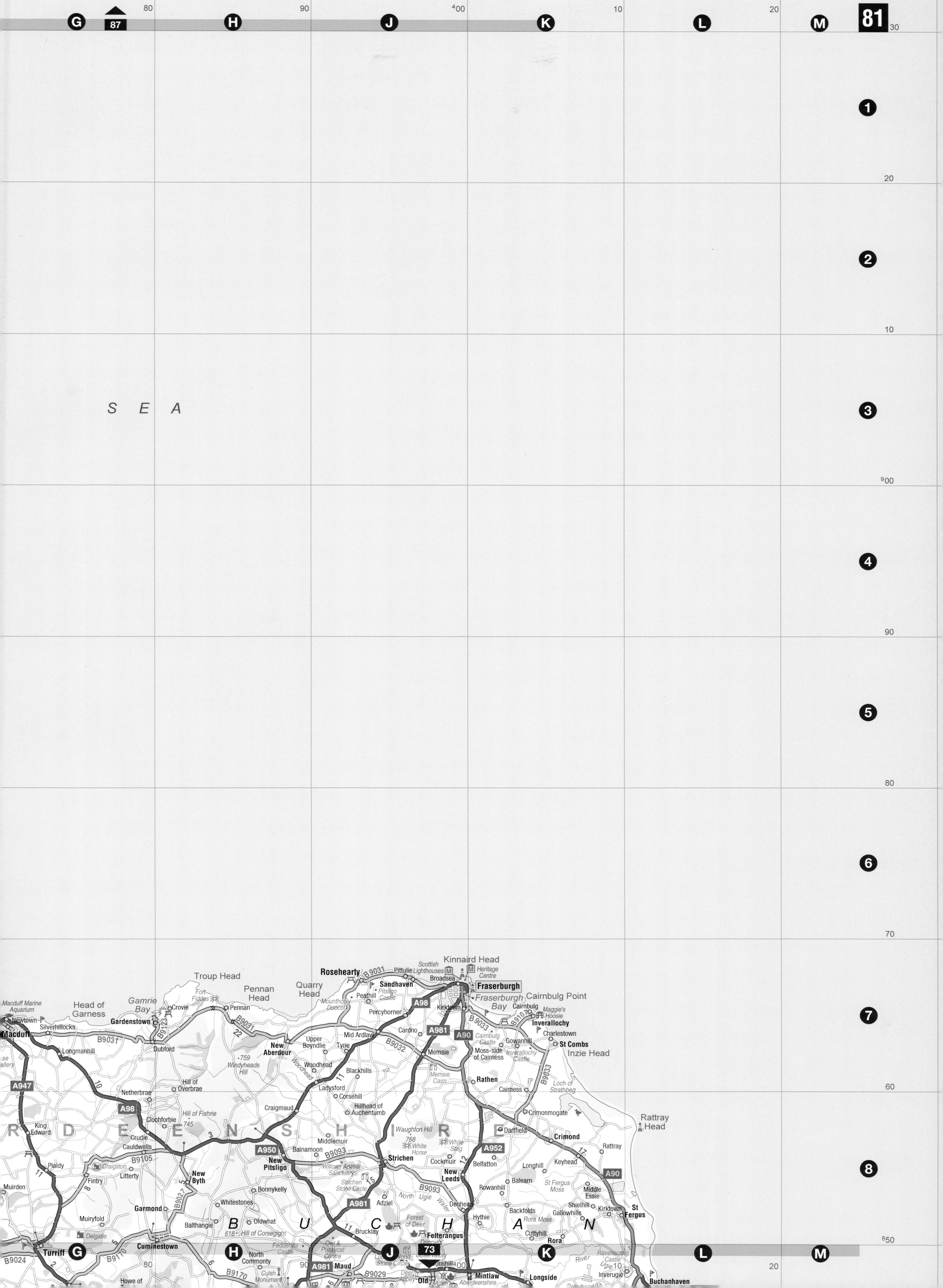

SEA
Troup Head
Pennan Head
Quarry Head
Rosehearty
Pittulie
Sandhaven
Broadsea
Kinnaird Head
Scottish Lighthouses
Heritage Centre
Fraserburgh
Fraserburgh Bay
Cairnbulg Point
Cairnbulg
Inverallochy
Charlestown
St Combs
Inzie Head
Macduff Marine Aquarium
Head of Garness
Gamrie Bay
Gardenstown
Crovie
Fort Fiddes
Pennan
Newtown
Silverhillocks
Macduff
Longmanhill
Dubford
New Aberdour
Upper Boyndlie
Tyrie
Mid Ardlaw
Peathill
Pitsligo Castle
Percyhorner
Cardno
Kirkton
Memsie
Memsie Cairn
Rathen
Cairness
Loch of Strathbeg
Crimonmogate
Dartfield
Crimond
Rattray Head
Rattray
Windyheads Hill
Woodhead
Blackhills
Ladysford
Corsehill
Hillhead of Auchentumb
Netherbrae
Hill of Overbrae
Craigmaud
Hill of Fishrie
Clochforbie
King Edward
Crudie
Cauldwells
Plaidy
Craigston
Fintry
Litterty
New Byth
Middlemuir
Balnamoon
New Pitsligo
Waughton Hill
White Horse
White Stag
Strichen
Cockmuir
New Leeds
Belfatton
Longhill
Keyhead
Balearn
St Fergus Moss
Middle Essie
Rowanhill
Backfolds
Rora Moss
Gallowhills
Shielhill
Kirktown
St Fergus
Hythie
Denhead
Adziel
Strichen Stone Circle
Willows Animal Sanctuary
Bonnykelly
Whitestones
Muiryfold
Delgatie
Garmond
Oldwhat
Balthangie
Hill of Corsegight
Brucklay
Forest of Deer
Fetterangus
Cuttyhill
Rora
Muirden
Turriff
Cuminestown
North Commonty
Maud
Howe of
Mintlaw
Longside
Inverugie
Buchanhaven
Ravenscraig Castle
Aberdeenshire
ABERDEENSHIRE
BUCHAN
A98
A947
A950
A981
A90
A952
B9031
B9032
B9033
B9093
B9105
B9123
B9170
B9024
B9029
B9107
87
73
G
H
J
K
L
M
1
2
3
4
5
6
7
8

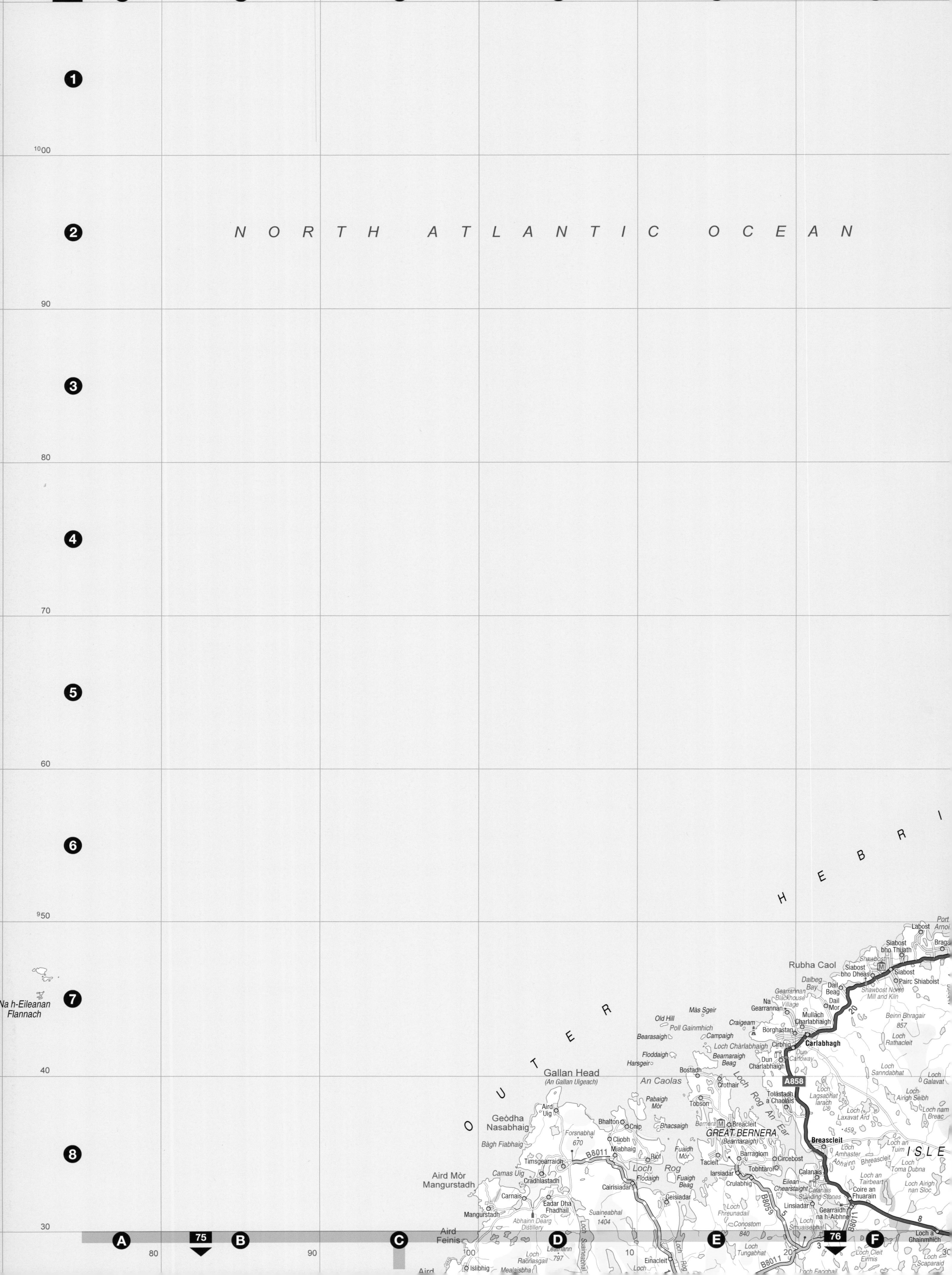
NORTH ATLANTIC OCEAN
OUTER HEBRI
ISLE
Na h-Eileanan Flannach
Gallan Head
(An Gallan Uigeach)
Geòdha Nasabhaig
Bàgh Fiabhaig
Aird Uig
Aird Mòr Mangurstadh
Camas Uig
Mangurstadh
Carnais
Cradhlastadh
Timsgearraidh
Forsnabhal 670
Eadar Dha Fhadhail
Abhainn Dearg Distillery
Suaineabhal 1404
Loch Suaineabhal
Aird Feinis
Aird
Islibhig
Loch Raonasgail
Mealaisbha
Leathann 797
Bhaltos
Cnip
Cliobh
Miabhaig
Riof
Loch Rog
Flodaigh
Cairisiadar
Geisiadar
Fuaigh Mòr
Fuaigh Beag
Bhacsaigh
Pabaigh Mòr
An Caolas
Harsgeir
Floddaigh
Bearasaigh
Old Hill
Poll Gainmhich
Màs Sgeir
Craigeam
Campaigh
Loch Chàrlabhaigh
Bearnaraigh Beag
Bostadh
Tobson
Crothair
Loch Rog An Ear
GREAT BERNERA
(Bearnaraigh)
Breacleit
Barraglom
Tacleit
Iarsiadar
Crulabhig
Tobhtarol
Circebost
B8059
B8011
Loch Fhreunadail
Conostom 840
Einacleit
Loch Tungabhat
Loch Smuaisabhal
Rubha Caol
Dalbeg Bay
Gearrannan Blackhouse Village
Na Gearrannan
Mullach Charlabhaigh
Borghastan
Cirbhig
Carlabhagh
Dun Charlabhaigh
Dun Carloway
A858
Tolàstadh a Chaolais
Loch Lagsabhat Iarach
Loch Laxavat Ard
Breascleit
Loch Amhaster
Abhainn Bhreascleit
Calanais
Eilean Chearstaigh
Calanais Standing Stones
Linsiadar
Gearraidh na h-Aibhne
Coire an Fhuarain
Loch an Tairbeart
Loch a Ghainmhich
Loch Cleit Eirmis
Loch Scaparaid
Loch Faoghail
Labost
Port Arnol
Braga
Siabost bho Thuath
Shawbost
Siabost bho Dheas
Siabost
Pairc Shiaboist
Shawbost Norse Mill and Kiln
Dail Beag
Dail Mòr
Beinn Bhragair 857
Loch Rathacleit
Loch Sanndabhat
Loch Galavat
Loch Airigh Seibh
Loch nam Breac
Loch an Tuim
Loch Toma Dubna
Loch Airigh nan Sloc
459
75
76
A B C D E F
1 2 3 4 5 6 7 8

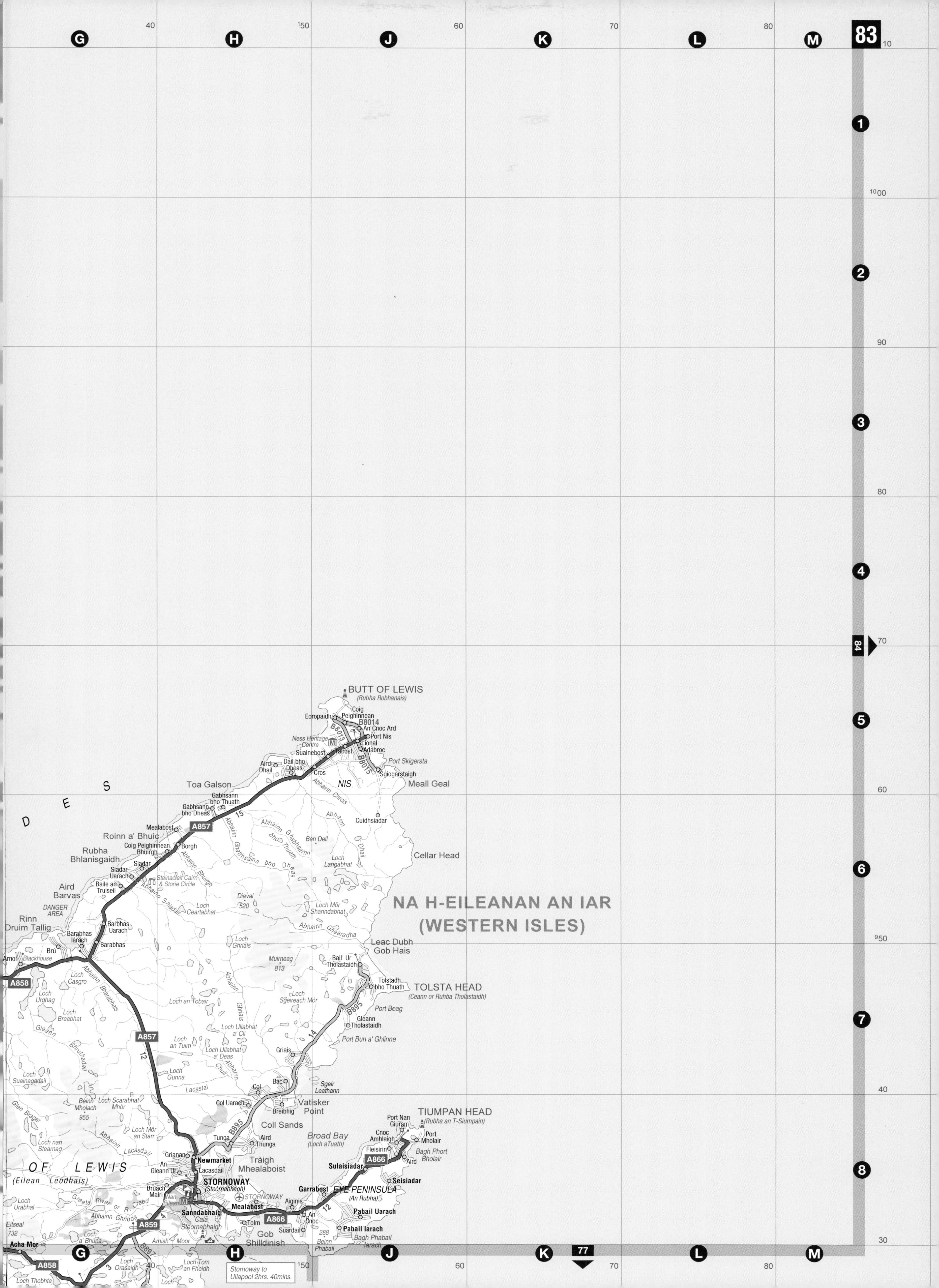
BUTT OF LEWIS
(Rubha Robhanais)
Coig Peighinnean
Eoropaidh
B8014
An Cnoc Ard
Port Nis
Ness Heritage Centre
Lional
Adabroc
Suainebost
Tabost
B8013
B8015
Port Skigersta
Sgiogarstaigh
Aird Dhail
Dail bho Dheas
Cros
NIS
Meall Geal
Toa Galson
Gabhsann bho Thuath
Gabhsann bho Dheas
Cuidhsiadar
Mealabost
A857
Roinn a' Bhuic
Coig Peighinnean Bhuirgh
Borgh
Rubha Bhlanisgaidh
Siadar
Siadar Uarach
Baile an Truiseil
Steinacleit Cairn & Stone Circle
Ben Dell
Loch Langabhat
Cellar Head
Aird Barvas
DANGER AREA
Loch Ceartabhat
Diaval 520
Loch Mòr Shanndabhat
NA H-EILEANAN AN IAR
(WESTERN ISLES)
Rinn Druim Tallig
Barbhas Uarach
Barabhas Iarach
Barabhas
Brù
Arnol
Blackhouse
Loch Ghriais
Muirneag 813
Leac Dubh
Gob Hais
Bail' Ur Tholastaidh
Tolstadh bho Thuath
TOLSTA HEAD
(Ceann or Rubha Tholastaidh)
A858
Loch Casgro
Loch Urghag
Loch an Tobair
Loch Sgeireach Mòr
Port Beag
B895
Loch Breabhat
Gleann Tholastaidh
Port Bun a' Ghlinne
Loch Ullabhat a' Cli
Loch an Tuim
Loch Ullabhat a' Deas
Griais
Loch Suainagadail
Loch Gunna
Lacastal
Bac
Col
Sgeir Leathann
Vatisker Point
Beinn Mholach 955
Loch Scarabhat Mhòr
Col Uarach
Breibhig
Coll Sands
Port Nan Giuran
TIUMPAN HEAD
(Rubha an T-Siumpain)
Glen Bragar
Loch Mòr an Starr
Tunga
Aird Thunga
Broad Bay
(Loch aTuath)
Cnoc Amhlaigh
Port Mholair
Loch nan Stearnag
Griانan
Newmarket
Tràigh Mhealaboist
Fleisirin
A866
Bagh Phort Bholair
Aird
OF LEWIS
(Eilean Leodhais)
An Gleann Ur
Lacasdail
Sulaisiadar
Seisiadar
STORNOWAY
(Steòrnabhagh)
Bruach Mairi
Garrabost
EYE PENINSULA
(An Rubha)
Loch Urabhal
Greeta River
Nan Eilean
STORNOWAY
Mealabost
Aiginis
Sanndabhaig
Pabail Uarach
Eitseal 732
A859
Cala Steòrnabhaigh
Tolm
An Cnoc
Suardail
288 Beinn Phabail
Pabail Iarach
Bagh Phabail Iarach
Acha Mor
Amish
Moor
Gob Shilldinish
77
Loch Tom an Fheidh
Stornoway to Ullapool 2hrs. 40mins.
A858
Loch Thobhta
Loch Orasaigh
B897
84
G
H
J
K
L
M
1
2
3
4
5
6
7
8
40
150
60
70
80
1000
90
80
70
60
950
40
30

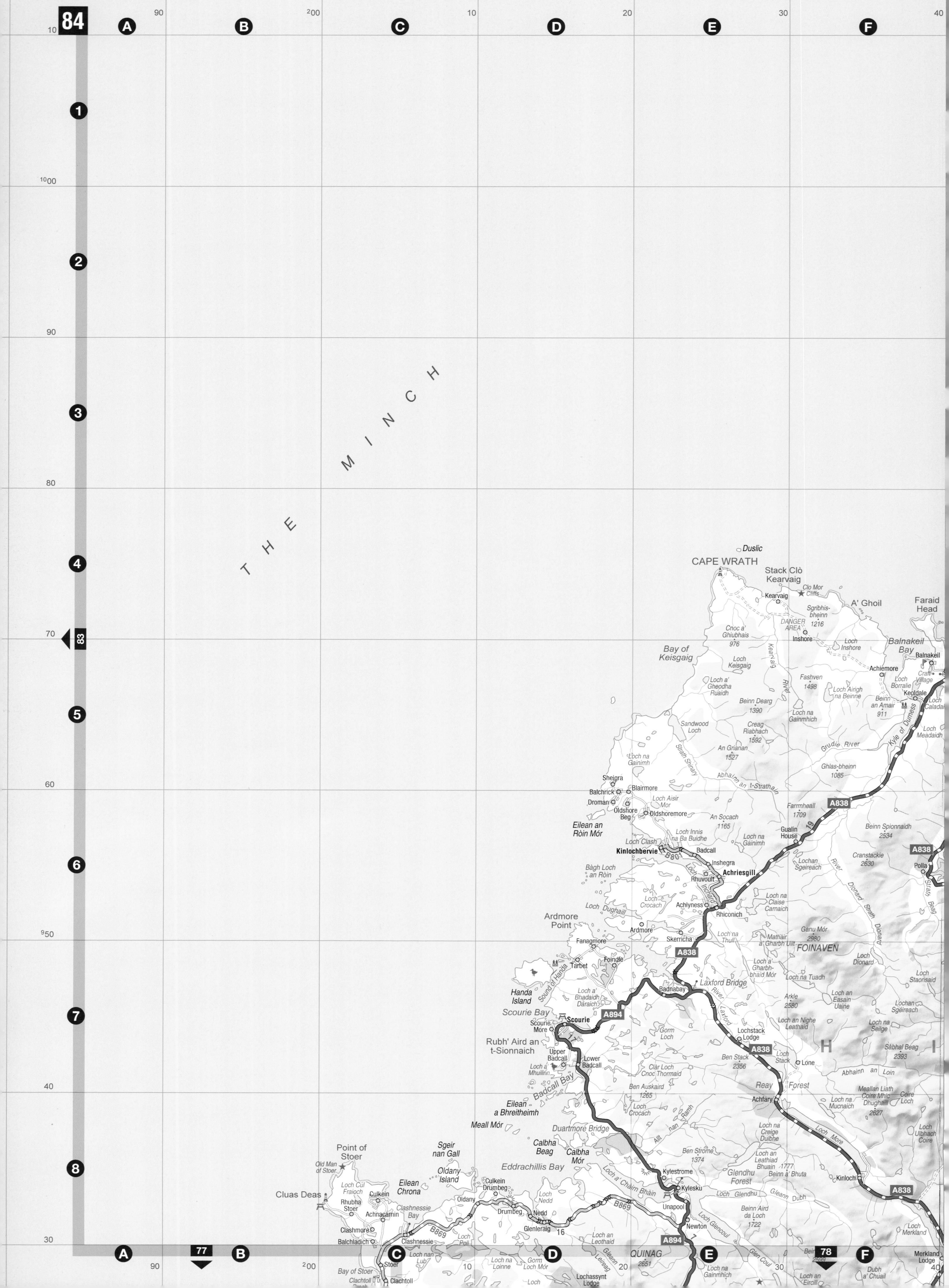
A
B
C
D
E
F
1
2
3
4
5
6
7
8
90
200
10
20
30
40
1000
80
70
60
950
30
83
77
78
THE MINCH
Duslic
CAPE WRATH
Stack Clò Kearvaig
Kearvaig
Clo Mor Cliffs
A' Ghoil
Faraid Head
Sgribhis-bheinn 1216
DANGER AREA
Inshore
Cnoc a' Ghiubhais 976
Loch Inshore
Balnakeil Bay
Balnakeil
Bay of Keisgaig
Loch Keisgaig
Kearvaig River
Achiemore
Craft Village
Fashven 1498
Loch Airigh na Beinne
Loch Borralie
Keoldale
Loch a' Gheodha Ruaidh
Beinn an Amair 911
Beinn Dearg 1390
Loch na Gainmhich
Kyle of Durness
Sandwood Loch
Creag Riabhach 1592
Loch Meadaidh
Strath Shinary
An Grianan 1527
Grudie River
Loch na Gainimh
Ghlas-bheinn 1085
Sheigra
Abhainn an t-Strathain
Balchrick
Blairmore
Droman
Loch Aisir Mor
Oldshore Beg
Oldshoremore
A838
Farrmheall 1709
An Socach 1165
Eilean an Ròin Mór
Loch Innis na Ba Buidhe
Gualin House
Beinn Spionnaidh 2534
Loch Clash
Loch na Gainimh
Kinlochbervie
Badcall
B801
Cranstackie 2630
Inshegra
Lochan Sgeireach
Polla
Bàgh Loch an Ròin
Achriesgill
Rhuvoult
Loch Inchard
Strath Beag
Loch Crocach
Achlyness
Loch na Claise Carnaich
Loch Dughaill
Rhiconich
Dionard River
Strath Dionard
Ardmore Point
Ardmore
Skerricha
Loch na Thull
Mathair a' Gharbh Uilt
Ganu Mór 2980
Fanagmore
FOINAVEN
Tarbet
Foindle
Loch Dionard
Loch a' Gharbh-bhaid Mór
Loch Staonsaid
Sound of Handa
Badnabay
Laxford Bridge
Loch na Tuadh
Handa Island
Loch a' Bhadaidh Daraich
Arkle 2580
Loch an Easain Uaine
Lochan Sgeireach
Scourie Bay
A894
River Laxford
Scourie More
Scourie
Gorm Loch
Loch an Nighe Leathaid
Loch na Seilge
Lochstack Lodge
Rubh' Aird an t-Sionnaich
A838
H
I
Sàbhal Beag 2393
Upper Badcall
Lower Badcall
Ben Stack 2356
Loch Stack
Lone
Loch a' Mhuilinn
Clàr Loch
Cnoc Thormaid
Abhainn an Loin
Badcall Bay
Reay Forest
Ben Auskaird 1265
Achfary
Meallan Liath Coire Mhic Dhughaill 2627
Coire Loch
Eilean a Bhreitheimh
Loch Crocach
Loch na Mucnaich
Meall Mór
Loch More
Duartmore Bridge
Loch na Creige Duibhe
Loch Ulbhach Coire
Calbha Beag
Calbha Mór
Allt nan Ramh
Point of Stoer
Sgeir nan Gall
Ben Strome 1374
Loch an Leathiad Bhuain
Old Man of Stoer
Eddrachillis Bay
Oldany Island
QUINAG
Kylestrome
Glendhu Forest
Beinn a' Bhuta
Loch Cùl Fraioch
Eilean Chrona
Culkein Drumbeg
Kylesku
Kinloch
Cluas Deas
Culkein
Loch a' Chàirn Bhàin
A838
Rhubha Stoer
Clashnessie Bay
Oldany
Loch Nedd
Unapool
Loch Glendhu
Gleann Dubh
Achnacarnin
Drumbeg
Nedd
B869
Newton
Loch Glencoul
Beinn Aird da Loch 1722
Clashmore
Glenleraig
Loch an Leothaid
Loch Merkland
Balchladich
Clashnessie
Loch Poll
Loch nan Lub
Loch na Loinne
Gorm Loch Mór
Gleann Leireag
A894
Glen Coul
Merkland Lodge
Bay of Stoer
Stoer
Clachtoll
Loch
Lochassynt Lodge
2651
Loch na Gainmhich
Loch an Eircill
Dubh a' Chuail

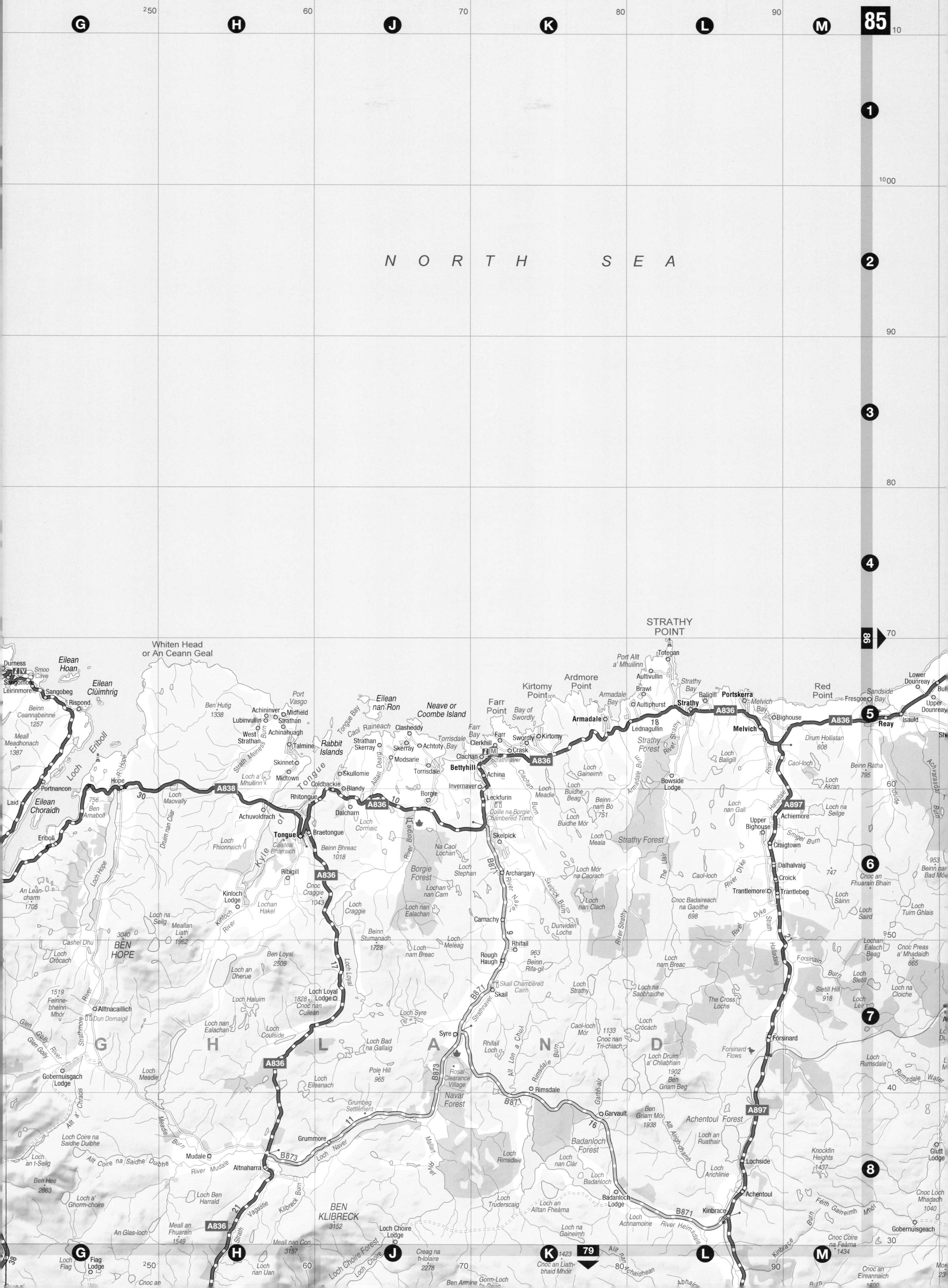
NORTH SEA
STRATHY POINT
Whiten Head or An Ceann Geal
Durness
Smoo Cave
Sangomore
Leirinmore
Sangobeg
Eilean Hoan
Eilean Cluimhrig
Rispond
Loch Eriboll
Portnancon
Laid
Eilean Choraidh
Eriboll
Hope
Ben Hutig
Port Vasgo
Achininver
Lubinvullin
Midfield
Strathan
Achinahuagh
West Strathan
Talmine
Skinnet
Midtown
Rabbit Islands
Eilean nan Ron
Neave or Coombe Island
Tongue Bay
Kyle of Tongue
Tongue
Rhitongue
Coldbackie
Blandy
Skullomie
Strathan Skerray
Clasheddy
Skerray
Achtoty
Modsarie
Torrisdale
Torrisdale Bay
Borgie
Dalcharn
Braetongue
Farr Point
Farr Bay
Farr
Clerkhill
Clachan
Bettyhill
Achina
Invernaver
Leckfurin
Swordly
Kirtomy
Kirtomy Point
Crask
Ardmore Point
Armadale
Armadale Bay
Port Allt a' Mhuilinn
Totegan
Aultivullin
Brawl
Aultiphurst
Strathy
Strathy Bay
Baligill
Portskerra
Melvich Bay
Melvich
Bighouse
Red Point
Fresgoe
Sandside Bay
Lower Dounreay
Upper Dounreay
Reay
Isauld
A836
A838
A897
B871
B873
Ben Hope
Ben Loyal
Ben Klibreck
Borgie Forest
Strathy Forest
Naver Forest
Badanloch Forest
Achentoul Forest
Forsinard Flows
Forsinard
Forsinain
Achiemore
Upper Bighouse
Craigtown
Dalhalvaig
Croick
Trantlemore
Trantlebeg
Skelpick
Archargary
Carnachy
Rhifail
Rough Haugh
Skail
Syre
Rosal Clearance Village
Grummore
Mudale
Altnaharra
Rimsdale
Garvault
Badanloch Lodge
Kinbrace
Achentoul
Lochside
Kinloch Lodge
Ribigill
Alltnacaillich
Gobernuisgach Lodge
Loch Choire Lodge
Flag Lodge
Loch Naver
Loch Loyal
Loch Hope
Strathnaver
River Naver
Halladale
Gobernuisgeach
Glutt Lodge
HIGHLAND

86
79

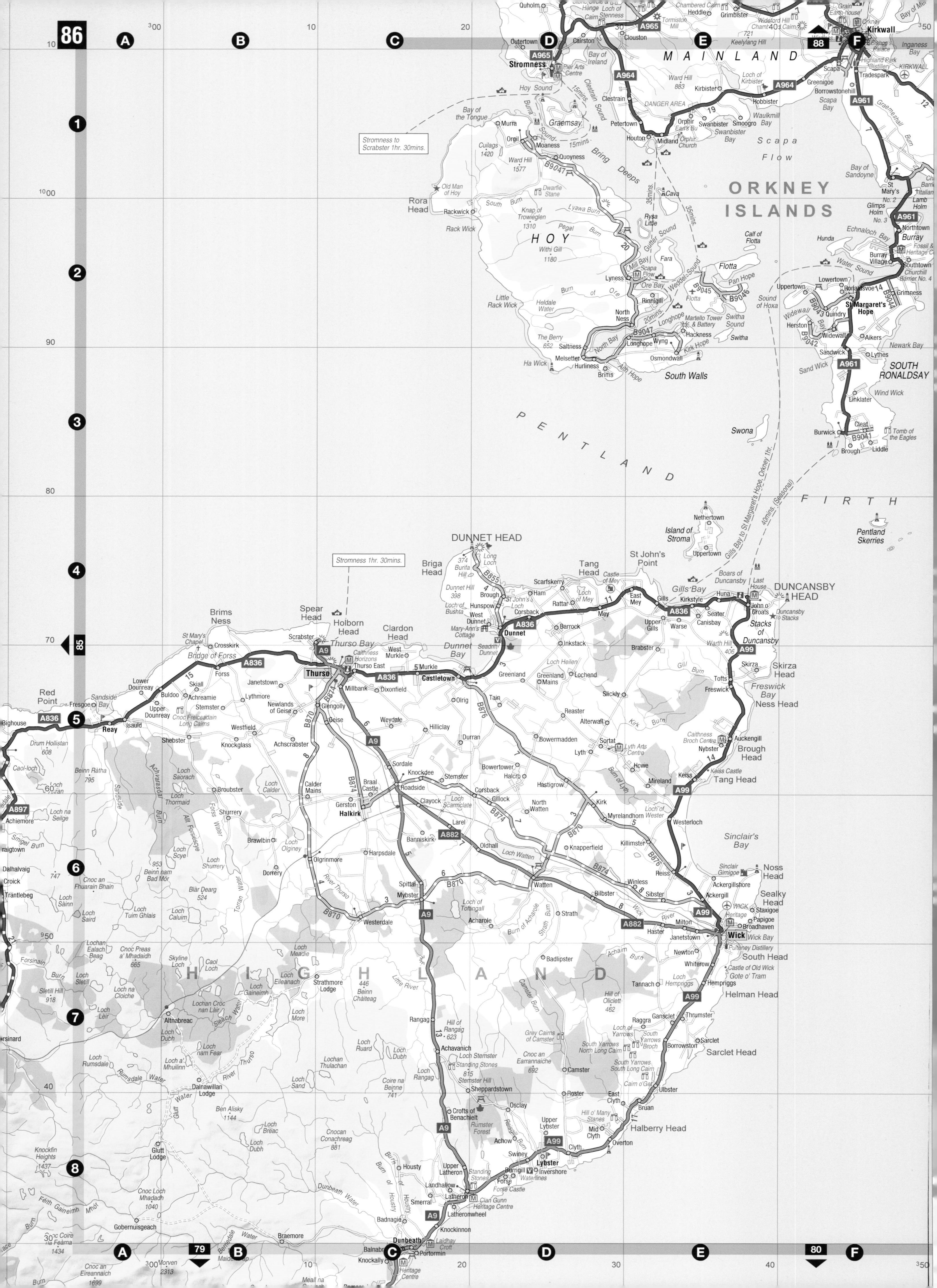
A
B
C
D
E
F
1
2
3
4
5
6
7
8
85
79
80
88
MAINLAND
ORKNEY ISLANDS
HOY
Kirkwall
Stromness
Stromness to Scrabster 1hr. 30mins.
Stromness 1hr. 30mins.
Scapa Flow
Bring Deeps
Flotta
South Walls
SOUTH RONALDSAY
Burray
St Margaret's Hope
Swona
Island of Stroma
Pentland Skerries
Gills Bay to St Margaret's Hope, Orkney 1hr.
40mins. (Seasonal)
PENTLAND FIRTH
DUNNET HEAD
DUNCANSBY HEAD
John o' Groats
Dunnet
Castletown
Thurso
Scrabster
Thurso Bay
Holborn Head
Dunnet Bay
Tang Head
St John's Point
Brims Ness
Red Point
Reay
Halkirk
Watten
Wick
Sinclair's Bay
Noss Head
South Head
Helman Head
Sarclet Head
Halberry Head
Lybster
Dunbeath
Latheron
Altnabreac
HIGHLAND
Freswick Bay
Ness Head
Brough Head
Keiss
A9
A99
A836
A882
B870
B874
B876
B855
A961
A964
A965
A897

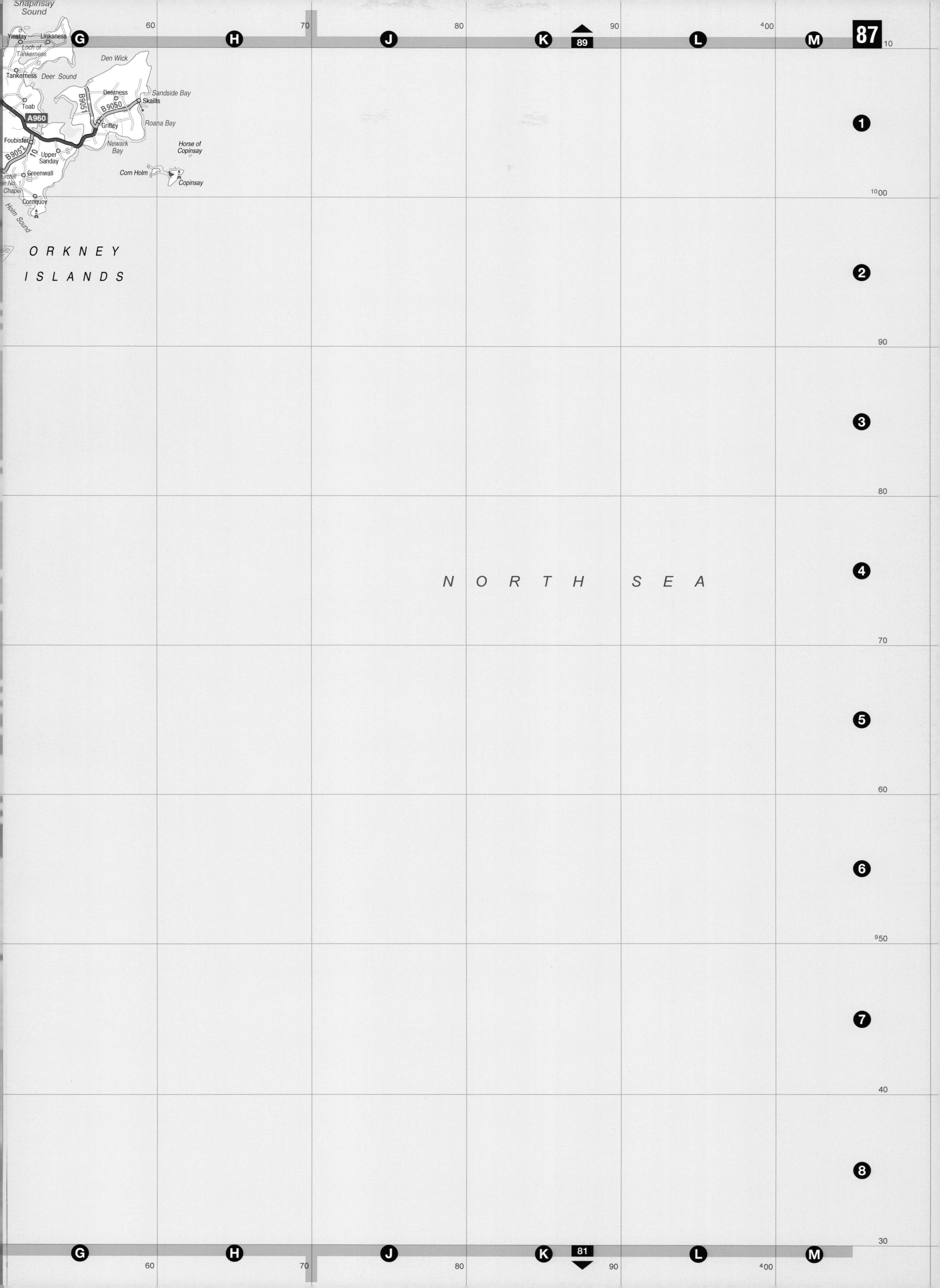

Shapinsay Sound
Yinstay
Linksness
Loch of Tankerness
Tankerness
Deer Sound
Den Wick
Deerness
Sandside Bay
Skaills
Toab
A960
B9051
B9050
Gritley
Roana Bay
Foubister
B9052
Upper Sanday
Newark Bay
Horse of Copinsay
Greenwall
Corn Holm
Copinsay
Corriquoy
Holm Sound
ORKNEY ISLANDS
NORTH SEA
G
H
J
K
L
M
89
81
60
70
80
90
400
10
1000
90
80
70
60
950
40
30
1
2
3
4
5
6
7
8

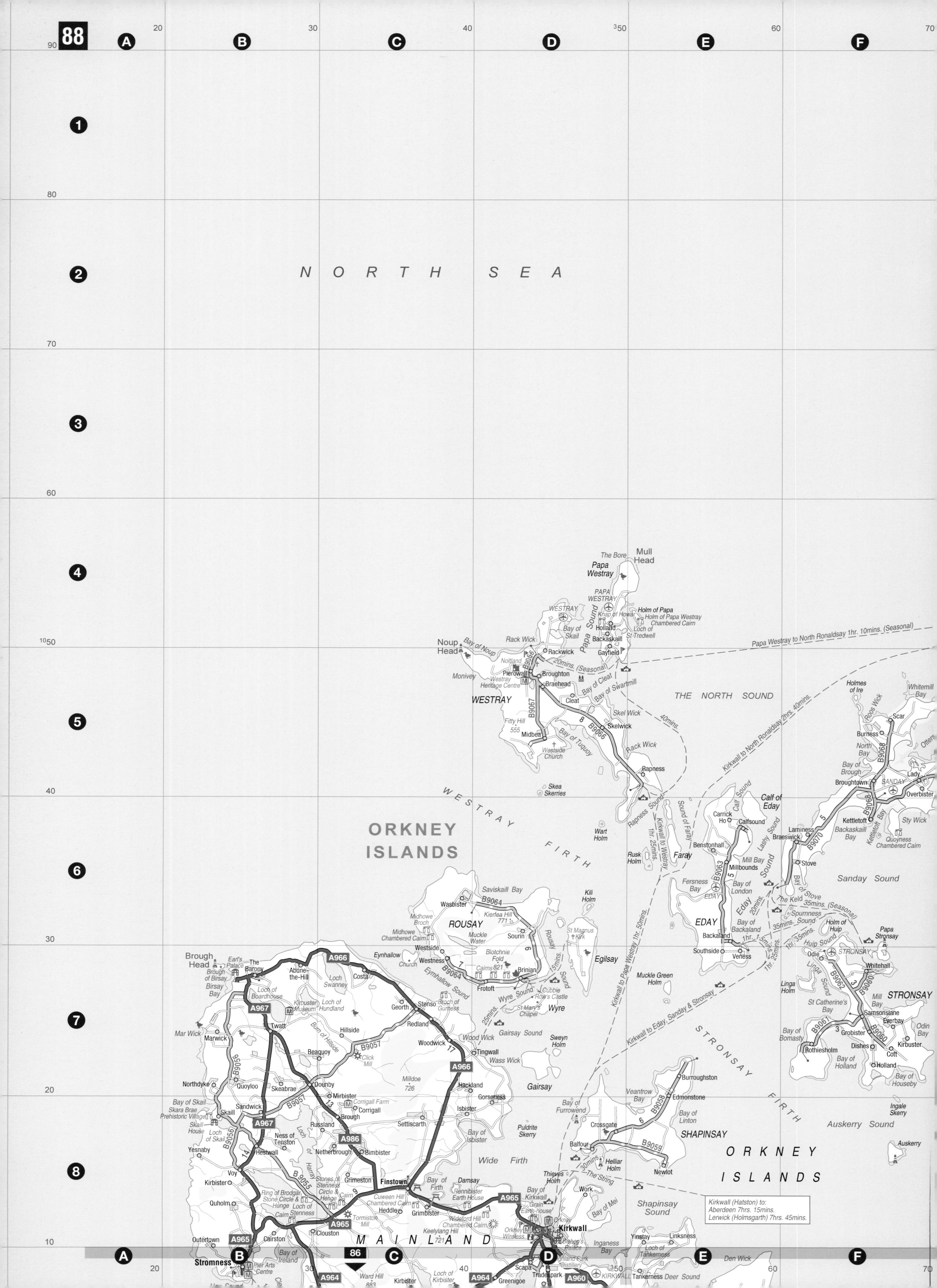

NORTH SEA
ORKNEY ISLANDS
WESTRAY FIRTH
THE NORTH SOUND
STRONSAY FIRTH
Sanday Sound
Auskerry Sound
Wide Firth
Shapinsay Sound
Gairsay Sound
Papa Sound
Papa Westray to North Ronaldsay 1hr. 10mins. (Seasonal)
Kirkwall to North Ronaldsay 2hrs. 40mins.
Kirkwall to Westray 1hr. 25mins.
Kirkwall to Papa Westray 1hr. 50mins.
Kirkwall to Eday, Sanday & Stronsay
Kirkwall (Hatston) to:
Aberdeen 7hrs. 15mins.
Lerwick (Holmsgarth) 7hrs. 45mins.
Papa Westray
Mull Head
The Bore
Holm of Papa
Holm of Papa Westray Chambered Cairn
Knap of Howar
Holland
Backaskaill
Gayfield
Loch of St Tredwell
Noup Head
Bay of Noup
Rack Wick
Rackwick
Noltland
Pierowall
Westray Heritage Centre
Broughton
Braehead
Bay of Cleat
Bay of Swartmill
Cleat
Monivey
WESTRAY
Fitty Hill 555
Midbea
Skelwick
Skel Wick
Bay of Tuquoy
Westside Church
Rack Wick
Rapness
Skea Skerries
Wart Holm
Rusk Holm
Faray
Sound of Faray
Rapness Sound
Calf of Eday
Carrick Ho
Calfsound
Calf Sound
Lashy Sound
Benstonhall
Millbounds
Mill Bay
Bay of London
Fersness Bay
EDAY
Eday Sound
Bay of Backaland
Backaland
Southside
Veness
Holmes of Ire
Whitemill Bay
Roos Wick
Scar
Burness
North Bay
Bay of Brough
Broughtown
SANDAY
Lady
Overbister
Otters
Lamimess
Braeswick
Kettletoft
Kettletoft Bay
Backaskaill Bay
Sty Wick
Quoyness Chambered Cairn
Stove
Bay of Stove
The Keld 35mins. (Seasonal)
Spurness Sound
Holm of Huip
Huip Sound
Papa Stronsay
Odie
Whitehall
Linga Sound
Linga Holm
STRONSAY
Mill Bay
St Catherine's Bay
Samsonslane
Everbay
Bay of Bomasty
Grobister
Dishes
Kirbuster
Odin Bay
Rothiesholm
Bay of Holland
Cott
Holland
Bay of Houseby
Ingale Skerry
Auskerry
Saviskaill Bay
Wasbister
ROUSAY
Kierfea Hill 771
Muckle Water
Midhowe Broch
Midhowe Chambered Cairn
Sourin
Westside
Westness
Blotchnie Fold 821
Brinian
Frotoft
Eynhallow Sound
Eynhallow Church
Rousay Sound
Kili Holm
St Magnus Kirk
Egilsay
Muckle Green Holm
Wyre Sound
Cubbie Row's Castle
St Mary's Chapel
Wyre
Sweyn Holm
Gairsay
Puldrite Skerry
Burroughston
Veantrow Bay
Edmonstone
Bay of Linton
Bay of Furrowend
Crossgate
SHAPINSAY
Balfour
Helliar Holm
Newlot
The String
Thieves Holm
Brough Head
Earl's Palace
The Barony
Brough of Birsay
Birsay Bay
Loch of Boardhouse
Abune-the-Hill
Loch Swannay
Costa
Kirbuster Museum
Loch of Hundland
Mar Wick
Marwick
Twatt
Burn of Hillside
Hillside
Georth
Stenso
Broch of Gurness
Redland
Woodwick
Beaquoy
Click Mill
Wood Wick
Tingwall
Wass Wick
Northdyke
Quoyloo
Skeabrae
Dounby
Milldoe 726
Hackland
Gorseness
Bay of Skaill
Skara Brae Prehistoric Village
Skaill House
Skaill
Sandwick
Loch of Skaill
Mirbister
Corrigall Farm
Corrigall
Brough
Isbister
Bay of Isbister
Settiscarth
Russland
Ness of Tenston
Netherbrough
Bimbister
Yesnaby
Hestwall
Voy
Loch of Harray
Stones of Stenness Circle & Henge
Grimeston
Finstown
Bay of Firth
Damsay
Rennibister Earth House
Kirbister
Ring of Brodgar Stone Circle & Henge
Loch of Stenness
Cairn
Cuween Hill Chambered Cairn
Heddle
Grimbister
Bay of Kirkwall
Grain Earth-house
Work
Bay of Meil
Quholm
Tormiston Mill
Wideford Hill Chambered Cairn
Orkney Wireless
Kirkwall
Outertown
Cairston
Clouston
MAINLAND
Keelylang Hill 721
Inganess Bay
Yinstay
Linksness
Loch of Tankerness
Stromness
Pier Arts Centre
Bay of Ireland
Ward Hill 883
Kirbister
Loch of Kirbister
Scapa
Tradespark
Greenigoe
Highland Park Distillery
Bishop's Palace
KIRKWALL
Tankerness
Deer Sound
Den Wick
A966
A967
A965
A986
A964
A960
B9057
B9055
B9056
B9064
B9066
B9067
B9063
B9068
B9069
B9070
B9062
B9060
B9061
B9058
B9059
86

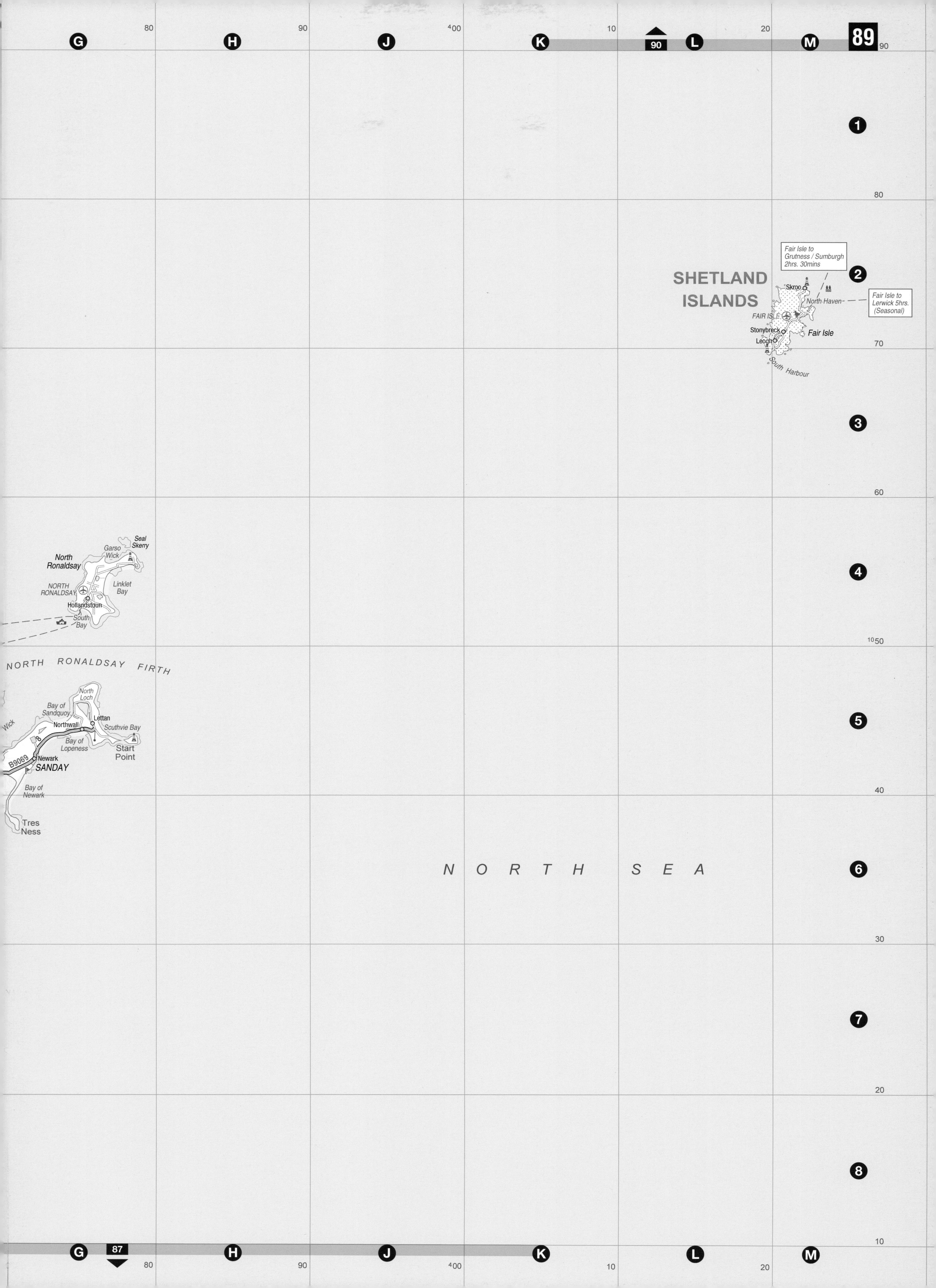

SHETLAND ISLANDS
Fair Isle to Grutness / Sumburgh 2hrs. 30mins
Fair Isle to Lerwick 5hrs. (Seasonal)
Skroo
North Haven
FAIR ISLE
Stonybreck
Fair Isle
Leogh
South Harbour
Seal Skerry
Garso Wick
North Ronaldsay
NORTH RONALDSAY
Linklet Bay
Hollandstoun
South Bay
NORTH RONALDSAY FIRTH
North Loch
Bay of Sandquoy
Lettan
Wick
Northwall
Scuthvie Bay
Bay of Lopeness
Start Point
B9069
Newark
SANDAY
Bay of Newark
Tres Ness
N O R T H S E A
90
87

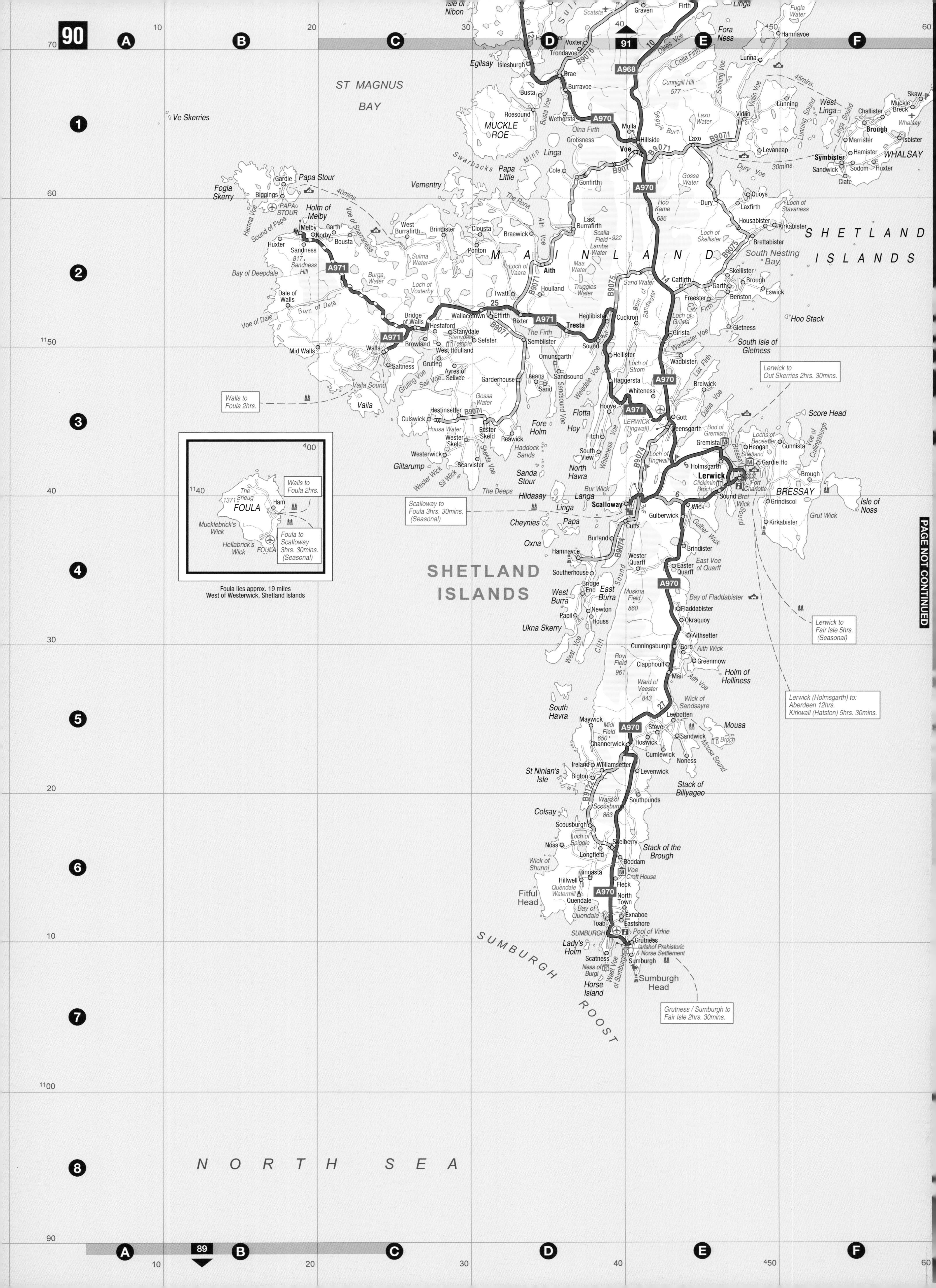
ST MAGNUS BAY
Ve Skerries
Papa Stour
Fogla Skerry
PAPA STOUR
Holm of Melby
Melby
Norby
Garth
Bousta
Huxter
Sandness
Sandness Hill
Bay of Deepdale
Dale of Walls
Voe of Dale
Burn of Dale
Mid Walls
Walls
Bridge of Walls
Hestaford
Browland
Stanydale
Sefster
West Houlland
Saltness
Gruting
Ayres of Selivoe
Vaila Sound
Vaila
Walls to Foula 2hrs.
West Burrafirth
Brindister
Clousta
Ponton
Braewick
Vementry
Papa Little
Swarbacks Minn
Linga
MUCKLE ROE
Egilsay
Islesburgh
Brae
Busta
Roesound
Burravoe
Wetherstal
Olna Firth
Grobsness
Voe
Mulla
Hillside
Cole
Gonfirth
East Burrafirth
Aith
Houlland
Twatt
Wallacetown
Effirth
Bixter
Tresta
Heglibister
Cuckron
Semblister
The Firth
Sound
Omunsgarth
Sandsound
Leeans
Sand
Garderhouse
Hestinsetter
Culswick
Easter Skeld
Wester Skeld
Reawick
Westerwick
Giltarump
Scarvister
Fore Holm
Hoy
Flotta
Sanda Stour
The Deeps
Hildasay
Linga
Langa
Scalloway
Scalloway to Foula 3hrs. 30mins. (Seasonal)
Cheynies
Papa
Oxna
Burland
Hamnavoe
Southerhouse
West Burra
East Burra
Bridge End
Papil
Newton
Houss
Ukna Skerry
Trondavoe
Voxter
Graven
Firth
Fora Ness
Hamnavoe
Lunna
Dales Voe
Colla Firth
Cunnigill Hill 577
Laxo
Vidlin
Lunning
West Linga
Levaneap
Symbister
Sandwick
Marrister
Hamister
Sodom
Hulter
Clate
Isbister
Brough
Challister
Muckle Breck
Skaw
WHALSAY
Gossa Water
Dury
Quoys
Laxfirth
Housabister
Kirkabister
Brettabister
SHETLAND ISLANDS
South Nesting Bay
Catfirth
Skellister
Eswick
Benston
Freester
Garth
Girlsta
Gletness
South Isle of Gletness
Hoo Stack
Wadbister
Lerwick to Out Skerries 2hrs. 30mins.
Breiwick
Whiteness
Haggersta
Hellister
Gott
Veensgarth
Score Head
Gremista
Heogan
Gunnista
Gardie Ho
Brough
Lerwick
Holmsgarth
Fort Charlotte
Sound
BRESSAY
Grindiscol
Isle of Noss
Kirkabister
Gulberwick
Wick
Cutts
Brindister
Wester Quarff
Easter Quarff
East Voe of Quarff
Bay of Fladdabister
Fladdabister
Okraquoy
Aithsetter
Cunningsburgh
Gord
Clapphoull
Greenmow
Holm of Helliness
Lerwick to Fair Isle 5hrs. (Seasonal)
Lerwick (Holmsgarth) to: Aberdeen 12hrs. Kirkwall (Hatston) 5hrs. 30mins.
MAINLAND
SHETLAND ISLANDS
South Havra
Maywick
Channerwick
Stove
Hoswick
Sandwick
Mousa
Cumlewick
Noness
Ireland
Williamsetter
Bigton
Levenwick
St Ninian's Isle
Southpunds
Stack of Billyageo
Colsay
Scousburgh
Noss
Longfield
Skelberry
Stack of the Brough
Boddam
Ringasta
Hillwell
Fleck
Quendale
North Town
Fitful Head
Exnaboe
Toab
Eastshore
SUMBURGH
Pool of Virkie
Grutness
Lady's Holm
Scatness
Sumburgh
Sumburgh Head
Horse Island
SUMBURGH ROOST
Grutness / Sumburgh to Fair Isle 2hrs. 30mins.
FOULA
The Sneug
Ham
Mucklebrick's Wick
Hellabrick's Wick
Walls to Foula 2hrs.
Foula to Scalloway 3hrs. 30mins. (Seasonal)
Foula lies approx. 19 miles West of Westerwick, Shetland Islands
NORTH SEA
A971
A970
A968
B9071
B9074
B9075
B9076
B9122
91
89
PAGE NOT CONTINUED

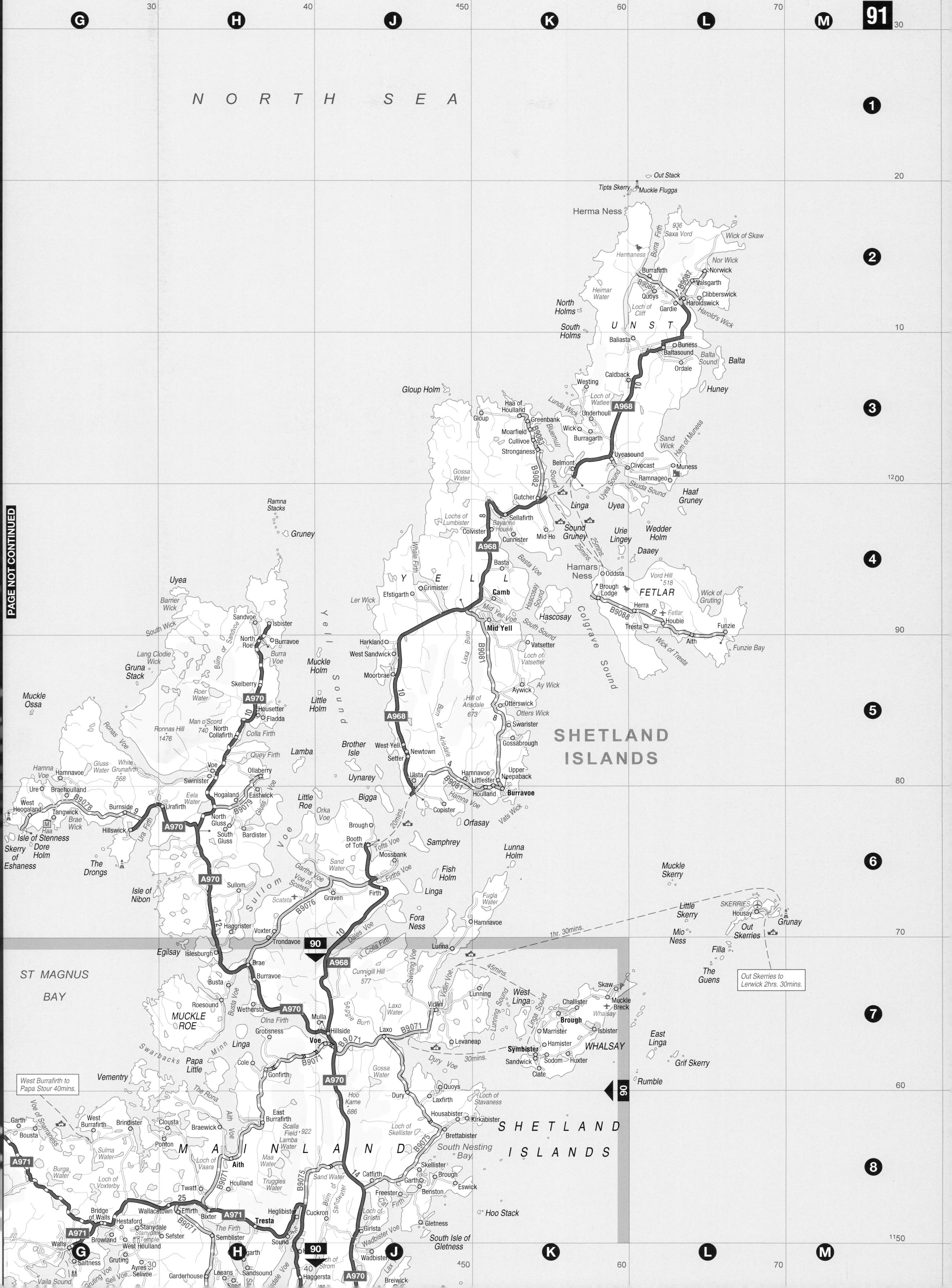
NORTH SEA
PAGE NOT CONTINUED
SHETLAND ISLANDS
UNST
YELL
FETLAR
WHALSAY
MAINLAND
MUCKLE ROE
ST MAGNUS BAY
Out Stack
Tipta Skerry
Muckle Flugga
Herma Ness
Hermaness
Burra Firth
936
Saxa Vord
Wick of Skaw
Nor Wick
Norwick
Burrafirth
Valsgarth
Clibberswick
Haroldswick
Harold's Wick
Heimar Water
Quoys
Loch of Cliff
Gardie
North Holms
South Holms
Baliasta
Buness
Baltasound
Balta Sound
Balta
Ordale
Caldback
Huney
Westing
Loch of Watlee
Gloup Holm
Haa of Houlland
Gloup
Lunda Wick
Underhoull
A968
Greenbank
Moarfield
Cullivoe
Bluemull
Wick
Burragarth
Sand Wick
Ham of Muness
Stronganess
Gossa Water
Belmont
Uyeasound
Clivocast
Muness
Ramnageo
Skuda Sound
Uyea Sound
Haaf Gruney
Gutcher
Linga
Uyea
Lochs of Lumbister
Sellafirth
Bayanne House
Colvister
Cunnister
Mid Ho
Sound Gruney
Urie Lingey
Wedder Holm
Daaey
25mins.
Basta
Basta Voe
Hamars Ness
Oddsta
Vord Hill
518
Brough Lodge
Herra
Fetlar
Houbie
Wick of Gruting
Tresta
Aith
Funzie
Funzie Bay
Wick of Tresta
Colgrave Sound
Efstigarth
Grimister
Camb
Ler Wick
Hascosay Sound
Hascosay
Mid Yell Voe
Mid Yell
South Sound
Harkland
West Sandwick
Vatsetter
Loch of Vatsetter
Whale Firth
Laxa Burn
Moorbrae
Ay Wick
Aywick
Yell Sound
Muckle Holm
Little Holm
Hill of Arisdale
673
Burn of Arisdale
Otterswick
Otters Wick
Swarister
Gossabrough
Brother Isle
West Yell
Newtown
Setter
Lamba
Uynarey
Ulsta
Hamnavoe
Littlester
Upper Neepaback
Houlland
Burravoe
Hamna Voe
Copister
Vats Wick
Orfasay
Bigga
Little Roe
Orka Voe
20mins.
Brough
Booth of Toft
Tofts Voe
Samphrey
Mossbank
Lunna Holm
Sand Water
Firths Voe
Fish Holm
Linga
Firth
Graven
Scatsta
Fugla Water
Fora Ness
Hamnavoe
Ramna Stacks
Gruney
Uyea
Barrier Wick
South Wick
Sandvoe
Isbister
North Roe
Burravoe
Burra Voe
Lang Clodie Wick
Gruna Stack
Skelberry
Muckle Ossa
Roer Water
A970
Housetter
Fladda
Man o' Scord
740
Ronnas Hill
1476
North Collafirth
Colla Firth
Ronas Voe
Quey Firth
Hamna Voe
Hamnavoe
Gluss Water
White Grunafirth
568
Voe
Ollaberry
Swinister
Ure
Braehoulland
B9078
West Heogaland
Tangwick
Haa
Brae Wick
Burnside
Urafirth
Eela Water
Hogaland
Eastwick
Hillswick
Ura Firth
North Gluss
South Gluss
Bardister
Isle of Stenness
Dore Holm
Skerry of Eshaness
The Drongs
Sullom
Sullom Voe
Isle of Nibon
Garths Voe
Voe of Scatsta
B9076
Haggrister
Voxter
Trondavoe
Dales Voe
Egilsay
Islesburgh
Brae
Busta
Busta Voe
Burravoe
Roesound
Wetherstа
Olna Firth
Grobsness
Mulla
Hillside
Voe
Cunnigill Hill
577
Colla Firth
Lunna
Swining Voe
Vidlin Voe
Vidlin
Laxo Water
Laxo
B9071
Lunning
Lunning Sound
West Linga
Linga Sound
Challister
Skaw
Muckle Breck
Whalsay
Brough
Marrister
Isbister
Hamister
Symbister
Sandwick
Sodom
Huxter
Clate
Levaneap
45mins.
30mins.
Dury Voe
East Linga
Grif Skerry
Rumble
Muckle Skerry
Little Skerry
Mio Ness
Filla
The Guens
SKERRIES
Housay
Grunay
Out Skerries
1hr. 30mins.
Out Skerries to Lerwick 2hrs. 30mins.
Minn
Linga
Papa Little
Swarbacks
Vementry
Cole
Gonfirth
Gossa Water
West Burrafirth to Papa Stour 40mins.
The Rona
Hoo Kame
686
Dury
Quoys
Laxfirth
Loch of Stavaness
Housabister
Kirkabister
Brettabister
South Nesting Bay
Garth
West Burrafirth
Brindister
Clousta
Braewick
East Burrafirth
Scalla Field
922
Lamba Water
Loch of Skellister
Voe of Snarraness
Bousta
Sulma Water
Ponton
Aith Voe
Loch of Vaara
Aith
Maa Water
Sand Water
B9075
Skellister
Catfirth
Brough
Eswick
A971
Burga Water
Loch of Voxterby
Houlland
Truggles Water
Twatt
Burn of Sandwater
Freester
Cat Firth
Benston
Bridge of Walls
Wallacetown
Effirth
Bixter
Tresta
Heglibister
Cuckron
Loch of Girlsta
Hoo Stack
Hestaford
Stanydale
B9071
Sefster
The Firth
Semblister
Girlsta
Gletness
Browland
West Houlland
Sound
Wadbister Voe
South Isle of Gletness
Walls
Saltness
Gruting
Ayres
Selivoe
Gruting Voe
Sandsound
Loch of Strom
Wadbister
Vaila Sound
Sell Voe
Garderhouse
Leeans
Haggersta
Breiwick
A970
90
G H J K L M
1 2 3 4 5 6 7 8
30 40 50 60 70
20 10 00 90 80 70 60 50

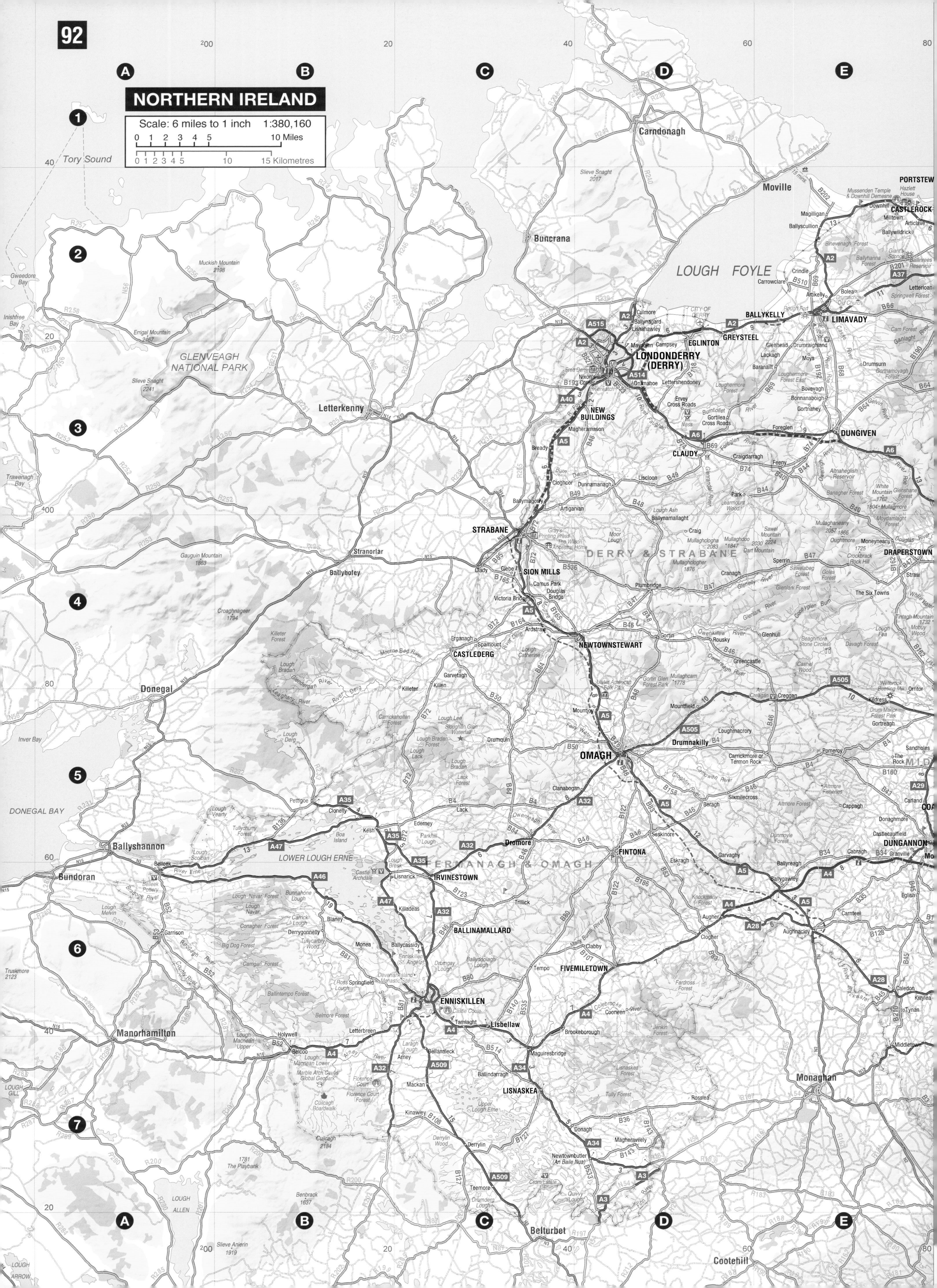
NORTHERN IRELAND
Scale: 6 miles to 1 inch 1:380,160
0 1 2 3 4 5 10 Miles
0 1 2 3 4 5 10 15 Kilometres
Tory Sound
GLENVEAGH NATIONAL PARK
LOUGH FOYLE
Carndonagh
Moville
Buncrana
PORTSTEWART
CASTLEROCK
Letterkenny
LONDONDERRY (DERRY)
BALLYKELLY
LIMAVADY
EGLINTON
GREYSTEEL
NEW BUILDINGS
CLAUDY
DUNGIVEN
STRABANE
SION MILLS
Stranorlar
Ballybofey
DERRY & STRABANE
DRAPERSTOWN
NEWTOWNSTEWART
CASTLEDERG
Donegal
OMAGH
Drumnakilly
DONEGAL BAY
Ballyshannon
Bundoran
LOWER LOUGH ERNE
FERMANAGH & OMAGH
IRVINESTOWN
Dromore
FINTONA
DUNGANNON
BALLINAMALLARD
FIVEMILETOWN
ENNISKILLEN
Lisbellaw
Manorhamilton
LISNASKEA
Monaghan
LOUGH ALLEN
Belturbet
Cootehill
A
B
C
D
E
1
2
3
4
5
6
7

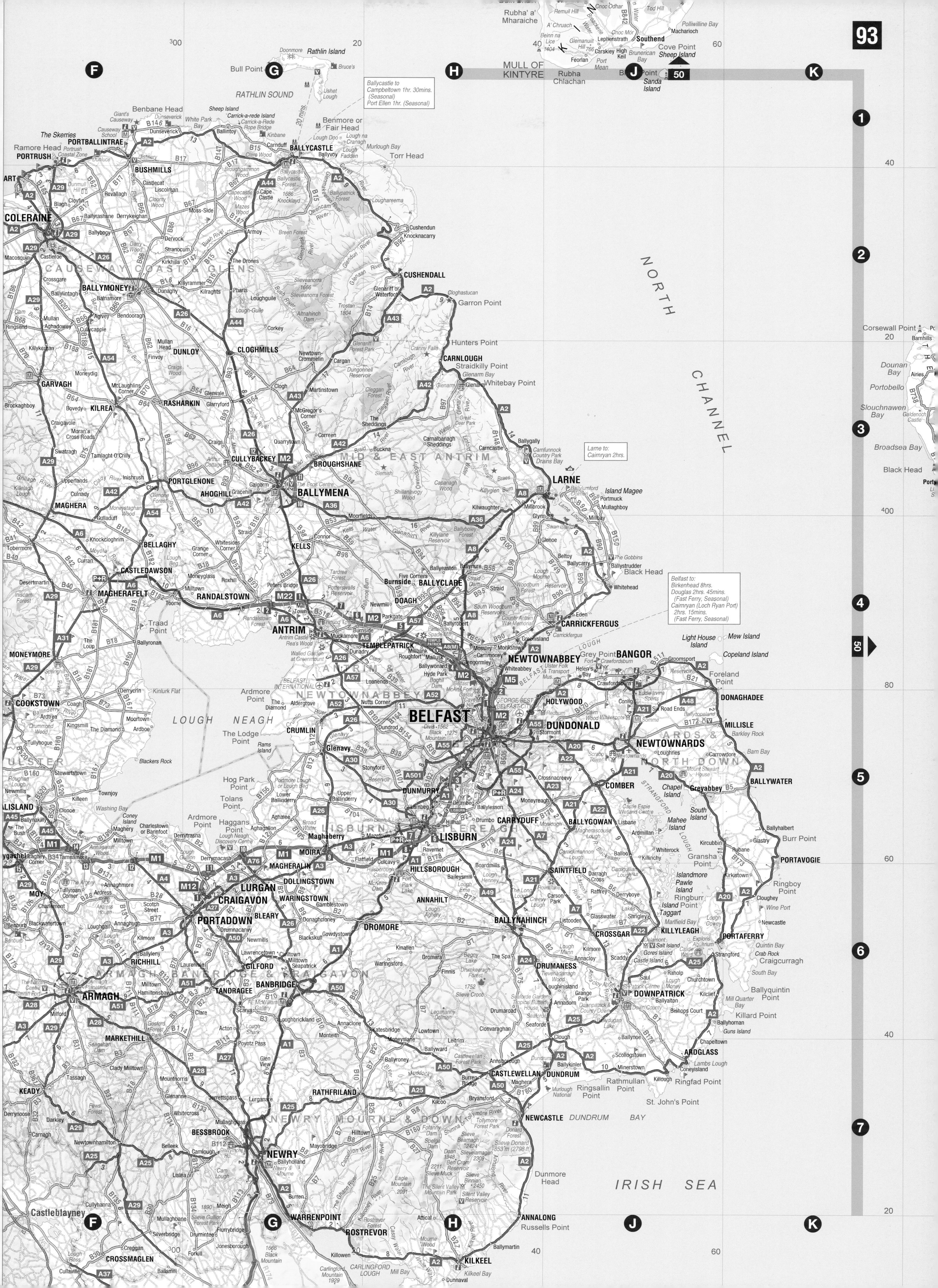
RATHLIN SOUND
Rathlin Island
Bull Point
MULL OF KINTYRE
NORTH CHANNEL
Ballycastle to Campbeltown 1hr. 30mins. (Seasonal) Port Ellen 1hr. (Seasonal)
Larne to: Cairnryan 2hrs.
Belfast to: Birkenhead 8hrs. Douglas 2hrs. 45mins. (Fast Ferry, Seasonal) Cairnryan (Loch Ryan Port) 2hrs. 15mins. (Fast Ferry, Seasonal)
CAUSEWAY COAST & GLENS
MID & EAST ANTRIM
ANTRIM & NEWTOWNABBEY
ARDS & NORTH DOWN
LISBURN & CASTLEREAGH
ARMAGH, BANBRIDGE & CRAIGAVON
NEWRY, MOURNE & DOWN
PORTRUSH
PORTBALLINTRAE
BUSHMILLS
BALLYCASTLE
COLERAINE
BALLYMONEY
CUSHENDALL
CLOGHMILLS
DUNLOY
GARVAGH
KILREA
RASHARKIN
CARNLOUGH
CULLYBACKEY
BROUGHSHANE
BALLYMENA
PORTGLENONE
AHOGHILL
LARNE
MAGHERA
BELLAGHY
CASTLEDAWSON
MAGHERAFELT
RANDALSTOWN
KELLS
BALLYCLARE
DOAGH
ANTRIM
TEMPLEPATRICK
CARRICKFERGUS
NEWTOWNABBEY
BANGOR
MONEYMORE
COOKSTOWN
HOLYWOOD
DONAGHADEE
BELFAST
DUNDONALD
MILLISLE
NEWTOWNARDS
CRUMLIN
LOUGH NEAGH
DUNMURRY
COMBER
BALLYWATER
CARRYDUFF
BALLYGOWAN
LISBURN
PORTAVOGIE
MOIRA
MAGHERALIN
HILLSBOROUGH
SAINTFIELD
LURGAN
DOLLINGSTOWN
CRAIGAVON
WARINGSTOWN
ANNAHILT
PORTADOWN
BLEARY
DROMORE
BALLYNAHINCH
CROSSGAR
KILLYLEAGH
PORTAFERRY
RICHHILL
GILFORD
DRUMANESS
ARMAGH
TANDRAGEE
BANBRIDGE
DOWNPATRICK
MARKETHILL
ARDGLASS
CASTLEWELLAN
DUNDRUM
KEADY
RATHFRILAND
NEWCASTLE
DUNDRUM BAY
BESSBROOK
NEWRY
IRISH SEA
Castleblayney
WARRENPOINT
ROSTREVOR
ANNALONG
CROSSMAGLEN
KILKEEL
CARLINGFORD LOUGH
Strangford Lough
Copeland Island
Mew Island
Black Head
Island Magee
Garron Point
Torr Head
Fair Head
Benbane Head
Ramore Head
Giant's Causeway
Corsewall Point
Black Head
Southend
Sanda Island
St. John's Point
Killard Point
Dunmore Head
Russells Point
Slieve Donard 853m (2798 ft.)
Slieve Croob
Slieve Gullion
Mourne Mountains

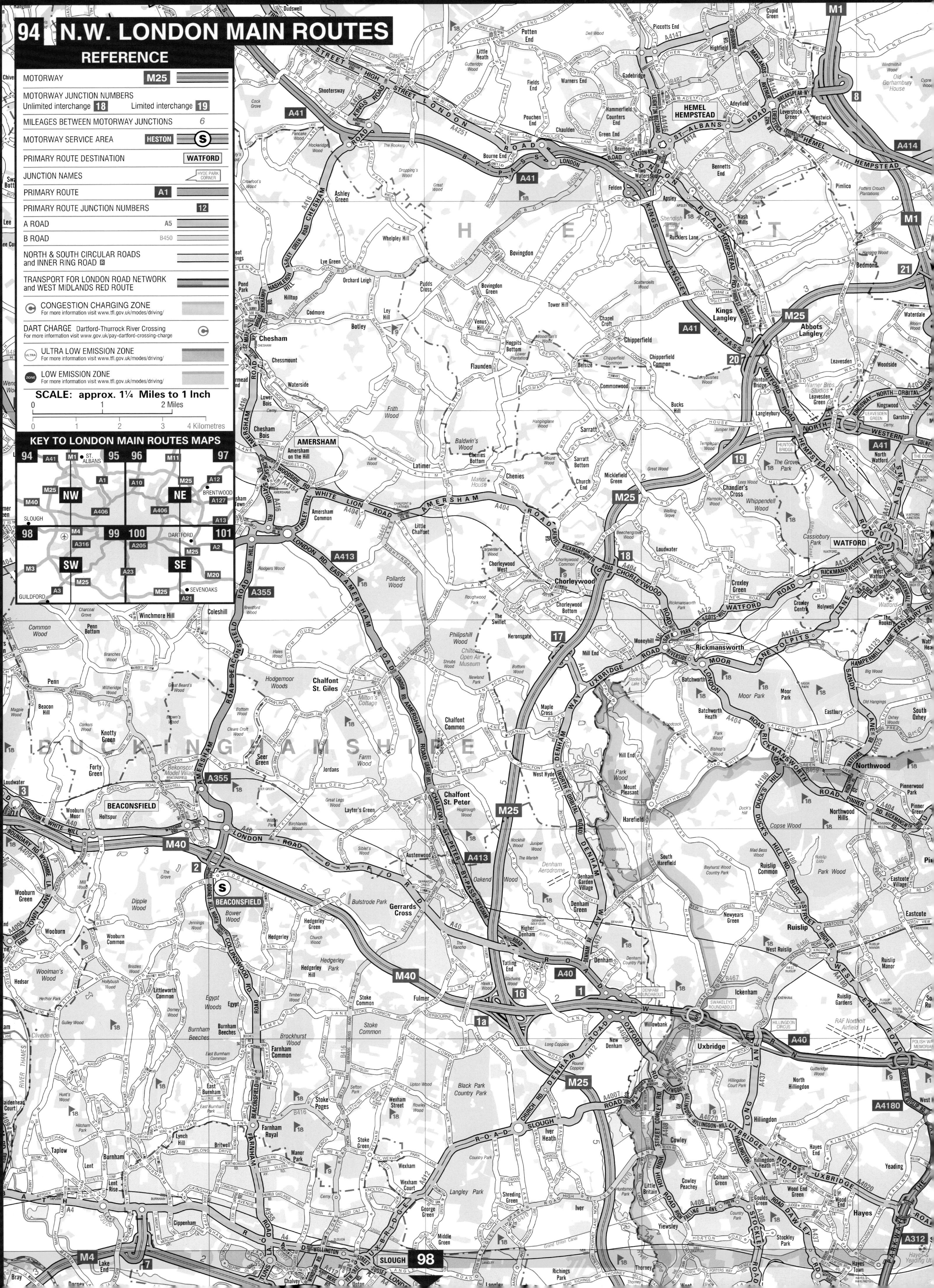
REFERENCE
MOTORWAY M25
MOTORWAY JUNCTION NUMBERS
Unlimited interchange 18 Limited interchange 19
MILEAGES BETWEEN MOTORWAY JUNCTIONS 6
MOTORWAY SERVICE AREA HESTON S
PRIMARY ROUTE DESTINATION WATFORD
JUNCTION NAMES HYDE PARK CORNER
PRIMARY ROUTE A1
PRIMARY ROUTE JUNCTION NUMBERS 12
A ROAD A5
B ROAD B450
NORTH & SOUTH CIRCULAR ROADS and INNER RING ROAD R
TRANSPORT FOR LONDON ROAD NETWORK and WEST MIDLANDS RED ROUTE
CONGESTION CHARGING ZONE For more information visit www.tfl.gov.uk/modes/driving/
DART CHARGE Dartford-Thurrock River Crossing For more information visit www.gov.uk/pay-dartford-crossing-charge
ULTRA LOW EMISSION ZONE For more information visit www.tfl.gov.uk/modes/driving/
LOW EMISSION ZONE For more information visit www.tfl.gov.uk/modes/driving/
SCALE: approx. 1¼ Miles to 1 Inch
0 1 2 Miles
0 1 2 3 4 Kilometres
KEY TO LONDON MAIN ROUTES MAPS
94 95 96 97 98 99 100 101
NW NE SW SE
ST. ALBANS
BRENTWOOD
SLOUGH
DARTFORD
GUILDFORD
SEVENOAKS
HEMEL HEMPSTEAD
WATFORD
AMERSHAM
BEACONSFIELD
Chesham
Chorleywood
Rickmansworth
Northwood
Ruislip
Uxbridge
Gerrards Cross
Chalfont St. Peter
Chalfont St. Giles
Kings Langley
Abbots Langley
Bovingdon
Denham
Iver
Hillingdon
Hayes
Yiewsley
Burnham
Farnham Royal
Stoke Poges
Beaconsfield Services
BUCKINGHAMSHIRE
HERTS
SLOUGH 98

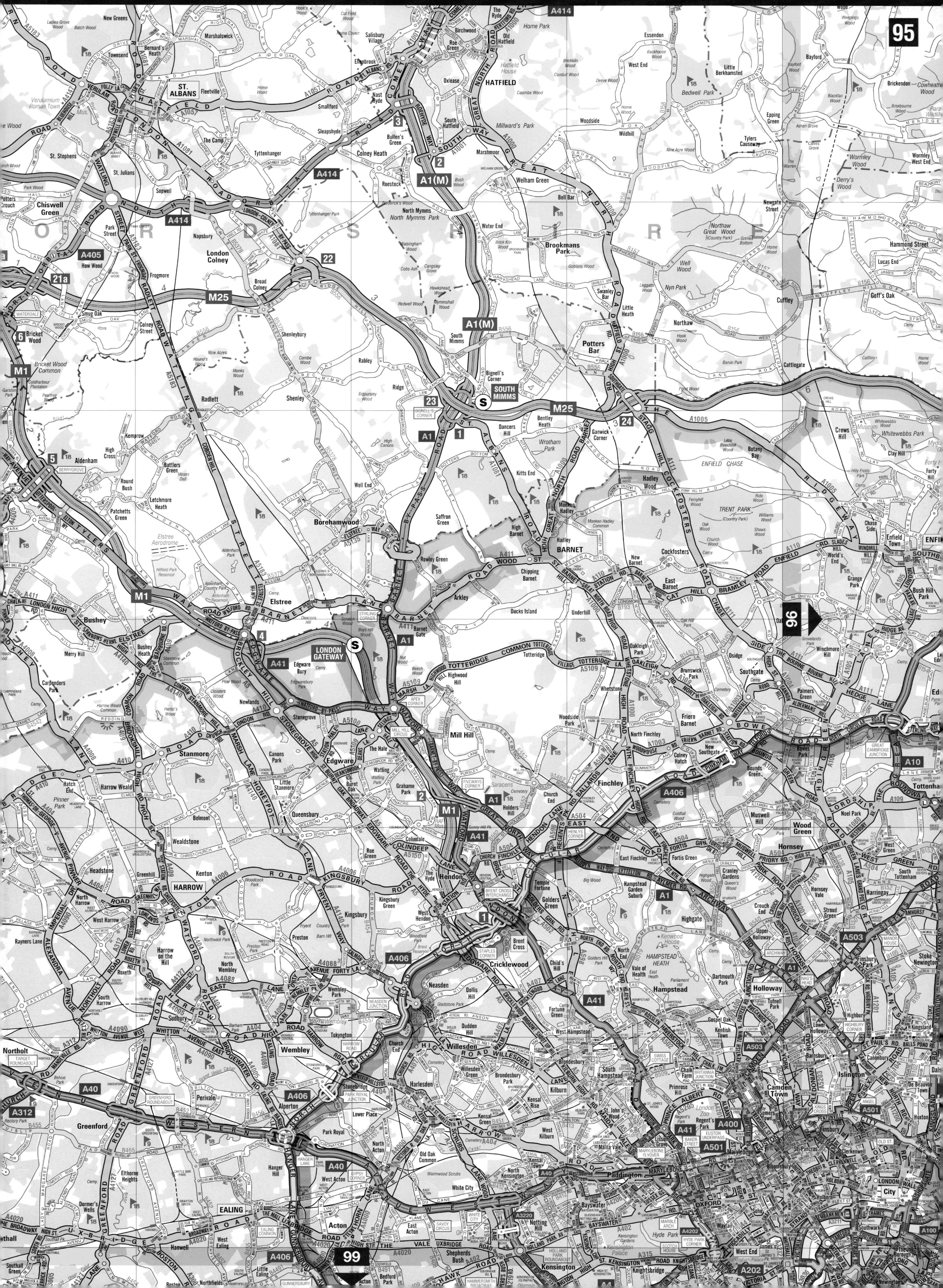
ST. ALBANS
HATFIELD
London Colney
Colney Heath
Welham Green
Brookmans Park
Potters Bar
Cuffley
Northaw
Radlett
Shenley
South Mimms
Borehamwood
Elstree
Bushey
BARNET
Hadley Wood
Cockfosters
East Barnet
New Barnet
Southgate
Mill Hill
Edgware
Stanmore
Harrow Weald
Whetstone
Finchley
Hendon
HARROW
Kenton
Wembley
Kingsbury
Neasden
Willesden
Harlesden
Cricklewood
Hampstead
Highgate
Hornsey
Holloway
Islington
Camden Town
Kilburn
Paddington
Marylebone
Greenford
Perivale
Alperton
Northolt
EALING
Acton
Hanwell
Kensington
Notting Hill
Bayswater
Mayfair
Soho
City
Tottenham
Wood Green
Enfield Town
M25
M1
A1(M)
A406
A41
A40


96

99

HERTFORDSHIRE
HARLOW
Hoddesdon
Broxbourne
Cheshunt
Waltham Cross
Waltham Abbey
Epping
Theydon Bois
Loughton
Chigwell
ENFIELD
Cockfosters
Southgate
Edmonton
Chingford
Tottenham
Walthamstow
Woodford
Wood Green
Hornsey
Highgate
Hampstead
Holloway
Islington
Camden Town
Hackney
Stratford
Leyton
Ilford
BARKING
East Ham
West Ham
Poplar
Bermondsey
Rotherhithe
City
Woolwich
M25
M11
A10
A406
A12
A13
A11
A1
A503
A501
A400
A41
A414
A1020
A117
A200
A202
A101
A102
A100
A1400
Cuffley
Northaw
Crews Hill
Goff's Oak
Nazeing
Upshire
Sewardstone
Hainault
Barkingside
Redbridge
Wanstead
Leytonstone
Clapton
Dalston
Stoke Newington
Finsbury Park
Canning Town
Beckton
Wapping
Shadwell
Stepney
Bow
Marylebone
Oxford
Hyde Park
West End
Knightsbridge
Thamesmead
LONDON CITY AIRPORT

95
100

Threshers Bush
Little Laver
Blackcat
Birds Green
Roxwell
Foster Street
Tilegate Green
High Laver
Magdalen Laver
Norwood End
Moreton Mill
Newhouse
Miller's Green
Shellow Bowells
Skreens Park
Hastingwood
Moreton
Fyfield
Willingale
Clatterford End
Spains Wood
Wall's Green
Newney Green
Great Oxney Green
Writtle
Pedlars End
Cannon's Green
Pigstye Green
Cooksmill Green
Little Oxney Green
Tyler's Green
Bovinger
Bobbingworth
Lower Bobbingworth Green
Shelley
Norton Mandeville
Radley Green
Widford
Edney Common
North Weald Airfield
North Weald Bassett
Norton Heath
Highwood
Loves Green
Hylands Park
High Ongar
Chipping Ongar
Greensted Green
Greensted
King Street
High Woods
Toot Hill
Marden Ash
Nine Ashes
Paslow Wood Common
Blackmore
Elkins Green
Handley Green
Colliers Hatch
Clatterford End
Tawney Common
Littlebury
Beggar Hill
Mill Green
Margaretting
Margaretting Tye
Mount End
Stanford Rivers
Stondon Massey
Clapgate
Little End
Hare Street
Tip's Cross
Hay Green
Green Street
Fryerning
Theydon Mount
Stapleford Tawney
Hook End
Doddinghurst
Wyatt's Green
Ingatestone
Tye Green
Secret Nuclear Bunker
Beacon Hill
Kelvedon Hatch
Kelvedon Common
Swallows Cross
Peartree Green
TRUELOVES INTERCHANGE
Heybridge
Buttsbury
Stock
Fox Hatch
Mountnessing
Passingford Bridge
Navestock
Navestock Side
Bentley
Padhams Green
Stapleford Tawney Airfield
Curtismill Green
Crow Green
MARYLANDS INTERCHANGE
Sabine's Green
Horseman Side
Coxtie Green
Queen's Park
Stapleford Abbotts
Pilgrims Hatch
Gooseberry Green
Hutton
Navestock Common
Watton's Green
Waterhales
Nuper's Hatch
Weald Country Park
Shenfield
Lambourne End
Bournebridge
St. Vincent's Hamlet
South Weald
BRENTWOOD
Hutton Mount
Havering's Grove
BILLERICAY
Sunnymede
Tye Common
Noak Hill
Havering-atte-Bower
Dagnam Park
Thrift Wood
South Green
Ingrave Common
Great Burstead
Brook Street
BROOK STREET INTERCHANGE
Harold Hill
Brentwood Museum
Warley
Little Burstead
Bedfords Park
Chase Cross
Ingrave
Noak Hill
Thorndon Country Park
Collier Row
Harold Park
Herongate
Rise Park
GALLOWS CORNER
Harold Wood
Great Warley
Steeple View
Little Warley
Mawney
Gidea Park
Squirrel's Heath
Southfields
Laindon
ROMFORD
Ardleigh Green
Childerditch
West Horndon
Lee Chapel North
Crowlands
Heath Park
Emerson Park
Great Berry
Langdon Hills
Hornchurch
Cranham
Lee Chapel South
Beacontree Heath
Rush Green
St. Leonards Hamlet
Harrow Lodge Park
Central Park
Upminster
Dry Street
Dagenham & Redbridge
Dagenham
Elm Park
Corbets Tey
Thames Chase Forest Centre
Bulphan
Hacton
North Ockendon
Hornchurch Country Park
PROPOSED
Horndon on the Hill
South Hornchurch
Belhus Woods Country Park
ORSETT FEN
DOVERS CORNER
CHANDLERS CORNER
Rainham
Orsett
Stanford-le-Hope
HORNCHURCH MARSHES
South Ockendon
Belhus Park
Baker Street
Mardyke Country Park
Southfields
Mucking
RAINHAM MARSHES
Wennington
North Stifford
MUCKING MARSHES
Aveley
Brannett's Wood
THURROCK
WENNINGTON MARSHES
Orsett Heath
Linford
Thamesmead East
AVELEY MARSHES
Muckingford
ERITH MARSHES
A414
A12
A127
A13
A128
A129
A1089
M25
101

94
Slough
Iver
Yiewsley
Hayes
Langley
Richings Park
West Drayton
BUCKS.
M4
M25
M3
A30
A4
A312
A308
A316
A322
A3
Eton
Windsor
Datchet
Colnbrook
Harmondsworth
Sipson
Harlington
Cranford
London Heathrow Airport
Stanwell
Wraysbury
Old Windsor
Runnymede
Egham
Staines-upon-Thames
Ashford
Feltham
Laleham
Sunbury
Shepperton
Chertsey
Addlestone
Weybridge
Walton-on-Thames
Ascot
Sunninghill
Sunningdale
Virginia Water
Windsor Great Park
Bagshot
Windlesham
Lightwater
Chobham
Ottershaw
Byfleet
West Byfleet
Woking
Knaphill
Brookwood
Pirbright
Worplesdon
Send
Ripley
Ockham
Wisley
Cobham
East Horsley
West Horsley
West Clandon
East Clandon
Burpham
Guildford

95
99
100
EALING
Acton
Bayswater
OXFORD
Notting Hill
Kensington
Knightsbridge
Hyde Park
West End
Westminster
Lambeth
Chelsea
Hammersmith
Chiswick
Brentford
Hanwell
Southall
Osterley
Heston
HOUNSLOW
Isleworth
RICHMOND
Mortlake
Barnes
Putney
Fulham
Battersea
Clapham
Brixton
Camberwell
Wandsworth
Balham
Tooting
Streatham
Twickenham
Teddington
Ham
Petersham
RICHMOND PARK
Roehampton
WIMBLEDON COMMON
Wimbledon
Merton
Morden
Mitcham
Hampton
BUSHY PARK
Hampton Court
HAMPTON COURT PARK
KINGSTON UPON THAMES
New Malden
Surbiton
Tolworth
Worcester Park
SUTTON
Carshalton
Wallington
Croydon
Purley
Coulsdon
Esher
Claygate
Chessington
Ewell
Cheam
EPSOM
Epsom Common
Oxshott
Ashtead
LEATHERHEAD
Banstead
Tadworth
Kingswood
Burgh Heath
Walton on the Hill
Headley
Mickleham
Great Bookham
Fetcham
Merstham
Redhill
REIGATE
Caterham
Kenley
Old Coulsdon
Chipstead
Hooley
Westhumble
Box Hill
Buckland
Betchworth
Nutfield
M4
M25
M23
A4
A3
A23
A24
A205
A217
A240
A243
A316
A308
A309
A232

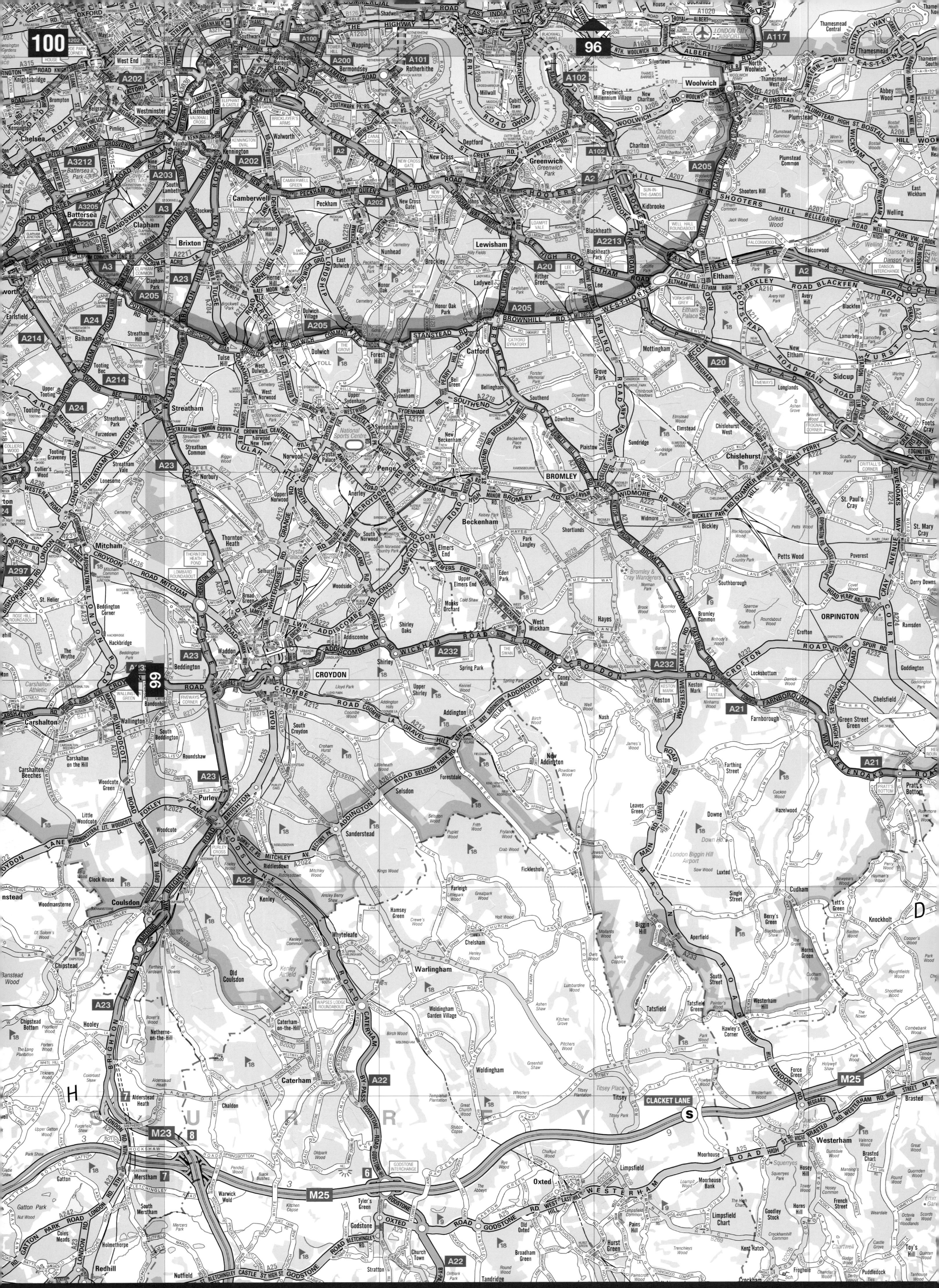

96
99
Oxford
West End
Westminster
Lambeth
Chelsea
Battersea
Clapham
Brixton
Camberwell
Peckham
Walworth
Kennington
Vauxhall
Bermondsey
Rotherhithe
Wapping
Millwall
Deptford
New Cross
Greenwich
Woolwich
North Woolwich
London City Airport
Thamesmead
Plumstead
Charlton
Blackheath
Kidbrooke
Lewisham
Eltham
Welling
Falconwood
Lee
Hither Green
Catford
Brockley
Nunhead
East Dulwich
Dulwich
Forest Hill
Sydenham
Penge
Beckenham
Bromley
Chislehurst
Sidcup
Mottingham
Grove Park
Downham
Plaistow
Sundridge
Shortlands
Bickley
Widmore
Petts Wood
Orpington
St. Paul's Cray
St. Mary Cray
Hayes
Keston
West Wickham
Eden Park
Elmers End
Shirley
Addiscombe
Croydon
Norwood
Crystal Palace
Anerley
Norbury
Streatham
Tooting
Balham
Mitcham
Thornton Heath
Selhurst
Waddon
Beddington
Wallington
Carshalton
Purley
Coulsdon
Kenley
Whyteleafe
Caterham
Warlingham
Sanderstead
Selsdon
Addington
New Addington
Biggin Hill
London Biggin Hill Airport
Downe
Cudham
Knockholt
Westerham
Tatsfield
Titsey
Oxted
Limpsfield
Godstone
Merstham
Redhill
Chipstead
Hooley
Farnborough
Chelsfield
Green Street Green
Pratt's Bottom
Brasted
Clacket Lane
M25
M23
A23
A22
A21
A20
A2
A205
A232
A233
A25
S U R R E Y

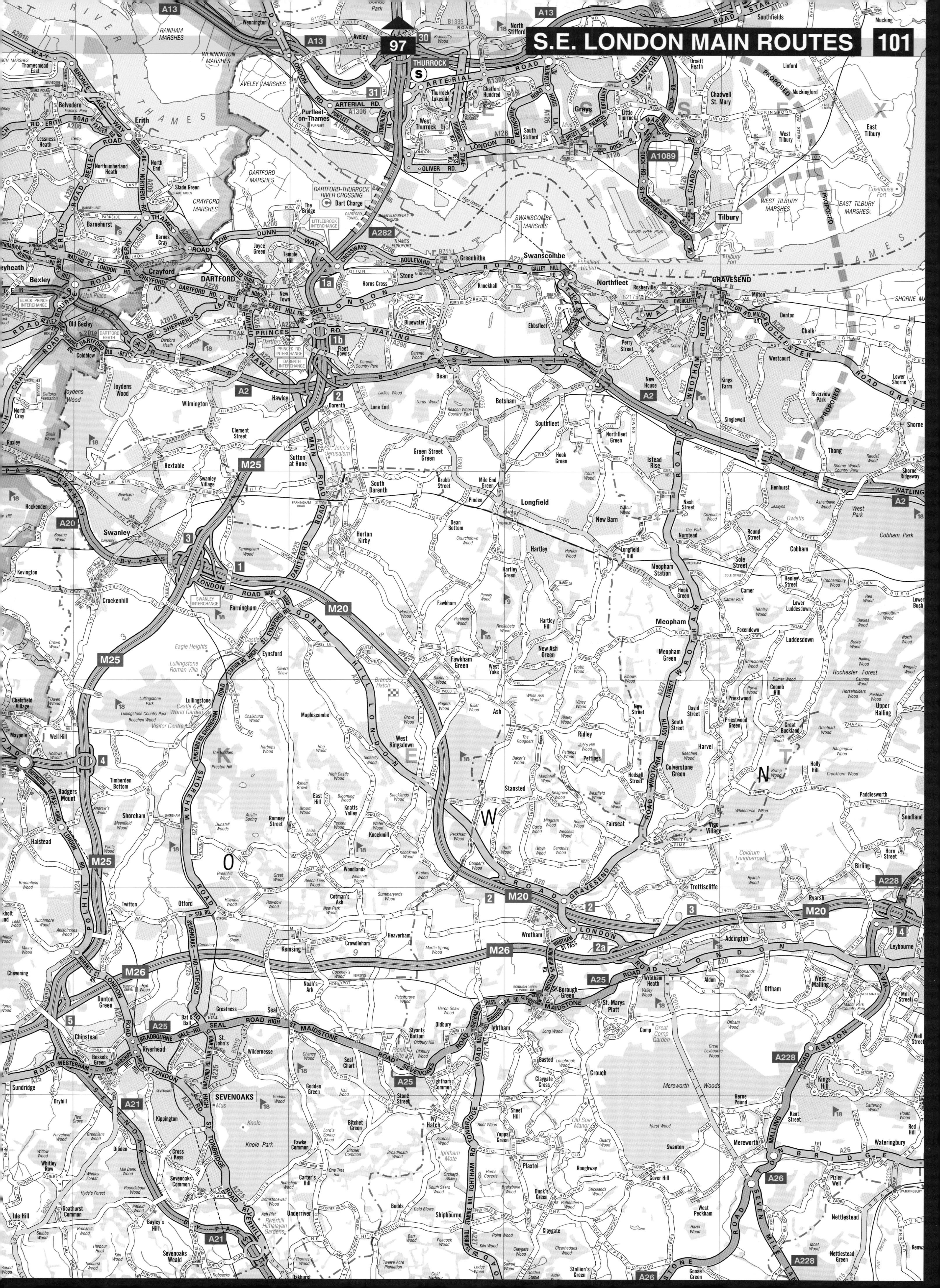
97
30
31
THURROCK
RAINHAM MARSHES
WENNINGTON MARSHES
AVELEY MARSHES
DARTFORD MARSHES
CRAYFORD MARSHES
SWANSCOMBE MARSHES
WEST TILBURY MARSHES
EAST TILBURY MARSHES
DARTFORD-THURROCK RIVER CROSSING
Dart Charge
RIVER THAMES
Wennington
Aveley
North Stifford
Purfleet-on-Thames
West Thurrock
Chafford Hundred
South Stifford
Grays
Little Thurrock
Orsett Heath
Chadwell St. Mary
Linford
Mucking
West Tilbury
East Tilbury
Tilbury
Thamesmead East
Belvedere
Erith
Lessness Heath
Northumberland Heath
North End
Slade Green
Barnehurst
Barnes Cray
Crayford
Bexley
Old Bexley
Dartford
Joyce Green
Temple Hill
Stone
Greenhithe
Swanscombe
Northfleet
Rosherville
GRAVESEND
Milton
Denton
Chalk
Horns Cross
Knockhall
Ebbsfleet
Perry Street
Westcourt
Lower Shorne
Shorne
Riverview Park
Kings Farm
Singlewell
Thong
Shorne Ridgeway
Bluewater
Princes
Fleet Downs
New Town
Joydens Wood
Wilmington
Hawley
Darenth
Lane End
Bean
Betsham
Southfleet
New House
Northfleet Green
Istead Rise
Hextable
Swanley Village
Clement Street
Sutton at Hone
Green Street Green
South Darenth
Brubb Street
Mile End Green
Pinden
Longfield
New Barn
Nash Street
Henhurst
West Park
Cobham Park
Hockenden
Swanley
Kevington
Crockenhill
Horton Kirby
Dean Bottom
Hartley
Hartley Green
Longfield Hill
Nurstead
Round Street
Sole Street
Cobham
Meopham Station
Henley Street
Camer
Farningham
Eynsford
Fawkham
Hartley Hill
Meopham
Hook Green
Foxendown
Lower Luddesdown
Luddesdown
Meopham Green
New Ash Green
Fawkham Green
West Yoke
Ash
Rochester Forest
Chelsfield Village
Lullingstone Park
Lullingstone Roman Villa
Castle & World Garden
Maplescombe
West Kingsdown
New Street
Ridley
David Street
Priestwood
Priestwood Green
South Street
Coomb Hill
Great Buckland
Upper Halling
Holly Hill
Maypole
Well Hill
Timberden Bottom
Badgers Mount
Shoreham
Halstead
Romney Street
East Hill
Knatts Valley
Stansted
Pettings
Hodsoll Street
Culverstone Green
Harvel
Vigo Village
Fairseat
Paddlesworth
Snodland
Knockmill
Woodlands
Cotman's Ash
Trottiscliffe
Birling
Horn Street
Ryarsh
Leybourne
Twitton
Otford
Heaverham
Kemsing
Crowdleham
Wrotham
Addington
Chevening
Dunton Green
Noah's Ark
Seal
Borough Green
Wrotham Heath
St. Marys Platt
Aldon
Offham
West Malling
Mill Street
Chipstead
Bat & Ball
Greatness
Riverhead
St. John's
Wildernesse
Seal Chart
Styants Bottom
Oldbury
Ightham
Ightham Common
Basted
Claygate Cross
Crouch
Mereworth Woods
Comp
Bessels Green
Sundridge
SEVENOAKS
Godden Green
Stone Street
Kings Hill
Kippington
Dryhill
Knole Park
Bitchet Green
Ivy Hatch
Sheet Hill
Yopps Green
Herne Pound
Kent Street
Fawke Common
Carter's Hill
Plaxtol
Roughway
Swanton
Mereworth
Wateringbury
Dibden
Cross Keys
Sevenoaks Common
Whitley Row
Goathurst Common
Ide Hill
Bayley's Hill
Underriver
Budds
Shipbourne
Dunk's Green
Gover Hill
West Peckham
Pizien Well
Nettlestead
Claygate
Sevenoaks Weald
Nettlestead Green
Goose Green
Stallion's Green
A13
A2
A20
A21
A25
A26
A225
A227
A228
A282
A1089
M20
M25
M26
K E N T
E S S E X
PROPOSED

# BIRMINGHAM MAIN ROUTES

## REFERENCE

BIRMINGHAM
Sutton Coldfield
SUTTON PARK
Erdington
Castle Bromwich
Kingsbury
Coleshill
Solihull
Knowle
Dorridge
Hockley Heath
Meriden
Berkswell
Balsall Common
Hampton in Arden
Shirley
Yardley
Saltley
Aston
Acock's Green
Hall Green
Moseley
Kings Heath
Sheldon
Elmdon
Chelmsley Wood
Kingshurst
Marston Green
Water Orton
Minworth
Curdworth
Wishaw
Middleton
Drayton Bassett
Dosthill
Hockley
Wood End
Lapworth
Wroxall
Earlswood
Hollywood
Wythall
Tanworth-in-Arden
Honiley
BIRMINGHAM AIRPORT
NATIONAL EXHIBITION CENTRE
National Motorcycle Museum
Forest of Arden
Packington Park
Maxstoke Castle
Shustoke Reservoir
WARWICKSHIRE
M6
M6 TOLL
M42
M40
A38
A45
A452
A446
A34
A41
A435
A4177
A453
A5

# MANCHESTER MAIN ROUTES

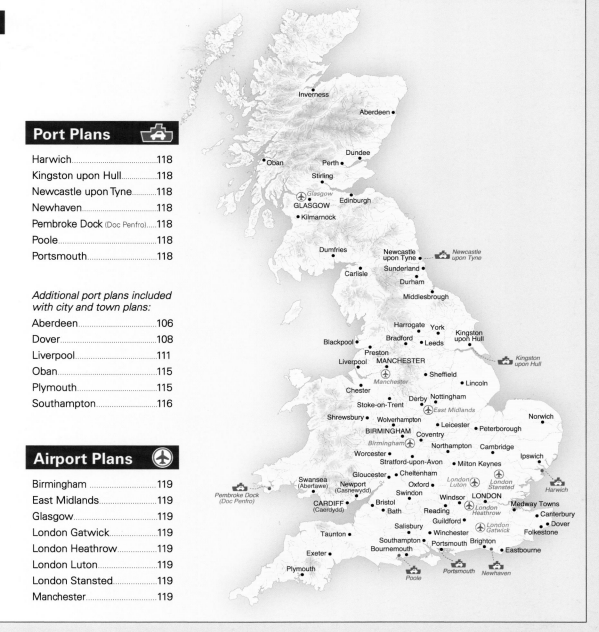

## City & Town Centre Plans


Aberdeen ... 106
Bath ... 106
Birmingham ... 106
Blackpool ... 106
Bournemouth ... 106
Bradford ... 106
Brighton & Hove ... 106
Bristol ... 107
Cambridge ... 107
Canterbury ... 107
Cardiff (Caerdydd) ... 107
Carlisle ... 107
Cheltenham ... 107
Chester ... 108
Coventry ... 108
Derby ... 108
Dover ... 108
Dumfries ... 108
Dundee ... 108
Durham ... 108
Eastbourne ... 108
Edinburgh ... 109
Exeter ... 109
Folkestone ... 109
Glasgow ... 109
Gloucester ... 109
Guildford ... 109
Harrogate ... 110
Inverness ... 110
Ipswich ... 110
Kilmarnock ... 110
Kingston upon Hull ... 110
Leeds ... 110
Leicester ... 110
Lincoln ... 111
Liverpool ... 111
London ... 112-113
Manchester ... 111
Medway Towns ... 111
Middlesbrough ... 111
Milton Keynes ... 114
Newcastle upon Tyne ... 111
Newport (Casnewydd) ... 114
Northampton ... 114
Norwich ... 114
Nottingham ... 114
Oban ... 115
Oxford ... 114
Perth ... 115
Peterborough ... 115
Plymouth ... 115
Portsmouth ... 115
Preston ... 115
Reading ... 115
Salisbury ... 115
Sheffield ... 116
Shrewsbury ... 116
Southampton ... 116
Stirling ... 116
Stoke-on-Trent ... 116
Stratford-upon-Avon ... 116
Sunderland ... 116
Swansea (Abertawe) ... 117
Swindon ... 117
Taunton ... 117
Winchester ... 117
Windsor ... 117
Wolverhampton ... 117
Worcester ... 117
York ... 117


## Port Plans


Harwich ... 118
Kingston upon Hull ... 118
Newcastle upon Tyne ... 118
Newhaven ... 118
Pembroke Dock (Doc Penfro) ... 118
Poole ... 118
Portsmouth ... 118


*Additional port plans included with city and town plans:*


Aberdeen ... 106
Dover ... 108
Liverpool ... 111
Oban ... 115
Plymouth ... 115
Southampton ... 116


## Airport Plans


Birmingham ... 119
East Midlands ... 119
Glasgow ... 119
London Gatwick ... 119
London Heathrow ... 119
London Luton ... 119
London Stansted ... 119
Manchester ... 119

## Reference to City & Town Plans — Légende — Zeichenerklärung

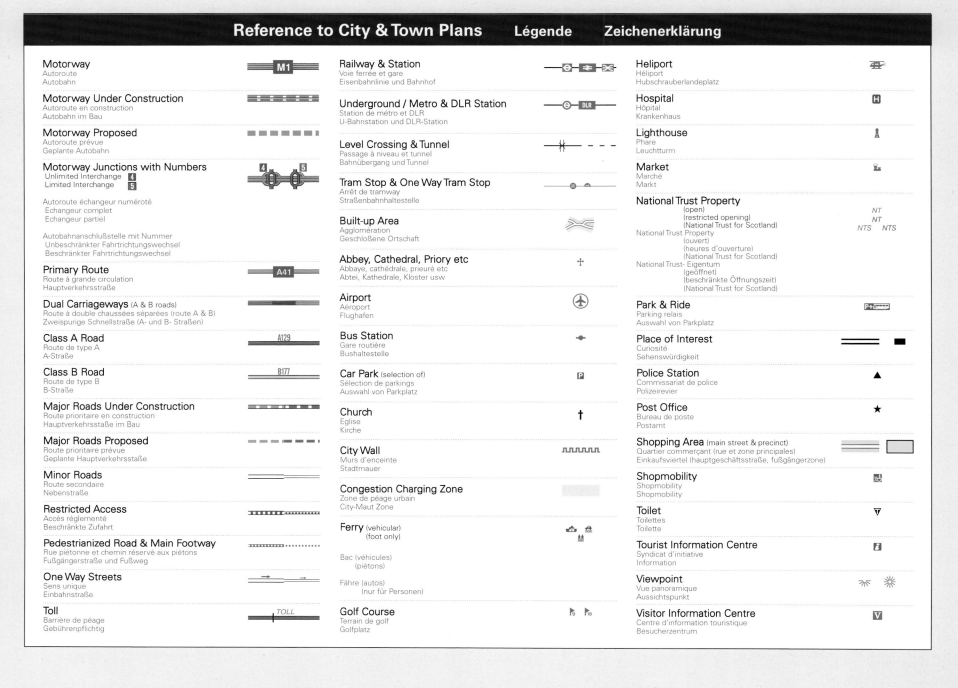

- **Motorway** — Autoroute — Autobahn (M1)
- **Motorway Under Construction** — Autoroute en construction — Autobahn im Bau
- **Motorway Proposed** — Autoroute prévue — Geplante Autobahn
- **Motorway Junctions with Numbers** — Unlimited Interchange 4 — Limited Interchange 5
  - Autoroute échangeur numéroté — Echangeur complet — Echangeur partiel
  - Autobahnanschlußstelle mit Nummer — Unbeschränkter Fahrtrichtungswechsel — Beschränkter Fahrtrichtungswechsel
- **Primary Route** — Route à grande circulation — Hauptverkehrsstraße (A41)
- **Dual Carriageways** (A & B roads) — Route à double chaussées séparées (route A & B) — Zweispurige Schnellstraße (A- und B- Straßen)
- **Class A Road** — Route de type A — A-Straße (A129)
- **Class B Road** — Route de type B — B-Straße (B177)
- **Major Roads Under Construction** — Route prioritaire en construction — Hauptverkehrsstaße im Bau
- **Major Roads Proposed** — Route prioritaire prévue — Geplante Hauptverkehrsstaße
- **Minor Roads** — Route secondaire — Nebenstraße
- **Restricted Access** — Accès réglementé — Beschränkte Zufahrt
- **Pedestrianized Road & Main Footway** — Rue piétonne et chemin réservé aux piétons — Fußgängerstraße und Fußweg
- **One Way Streets** — Sens unique — Einbahnstraße
- **Toll** — Barrière de péage — Gebührenpflichtig (TOLL)
- **Railway & Station** — Voie ferrée et gare — Eisenbahnlinie und Bahnhof
- **Underground / Metro & DLR Station** — Station de métro et DLR — U-Bahnstation und DLR-Station (DLR)
- **Level Crossing & Tunnel** — Passage à niveau et tunnel — Bahnübergang und Tunnel
- **Tram Stop & One Way Tram Stop** — Arrêt de tramway — Straßenbahnhaltestelle
- **Built-up Area** — Agglomération — Geschloßene Ortschaft
- **Abbey, Cathedral, Priory etc** — Abbaye, cathédrale, prieuré etc — Abtei, Kathedrale, Kloster usw
- **Airport** — Aéroport — Flughafen
- **Bus Station** — Gare routière — Bushaltestelle
- **Car Park** (selection of) — Sélection de parkings — Auswahl von Parkplatz
- **Church** — Eglise — Kirche
- **City Wall** — Murs d'enceinte — Stadtmauer
- **Congestion Charging Zone** — Zone de péage urbain — City-Maut Zone
- **Ferry** (vehicular) (foot only) — Bac (véhicules) (piétons) — Fähre (autos) (nur für Personen)
- **Golf Course** — Terrain de golf — Golfplatz
- **Heliport** — Héliport — Hubschrauberlandeplatz
- **Hospital** — Hôpital — Krankenhaus
- **Lighthouse** — Phare — Leuchtturm
- **Market** — Marché — Markt
- **National Trust Property** (open) NT (restricted opening) NT (National Trust for Scotland) NTS NTS
  - National Trust Property (ouvert) (heures d'ouverture) (National Trust for Scotland)
  - National Trust- Eigentum (geöffnet) (beschränkte Öffnungszeit) (National Trust for Scotland)
- **Park & Ride** — Parking relais — Auswahl von Parkplatz (P+R)
- **Place of Interest** — Curiosité — Sehenswürdigkeit
- **Police Station** — Commissariat de police — Polizeirevier
- **Post Office** — Bureau de poste — Postamt
- **Shopping Area** (main street & precinct) — Quartier commerçant (rue et zone principales) — Einkaufsviertel (hauptgeschäftsstraße, fußgängerzone)
- **Shopmobility** — Shopmobility — Shopmobility
- **Toilet** — Toilettes — Toilette
- **Tourist Information Centre** — Syndicat d'initiative — Information
- **Viewpoint** — Vue panoramique — Aussichtspunkt
- **Visitor Information Centre** — Centre d'information touristique — Besucherzentrum

## ABERDEEN

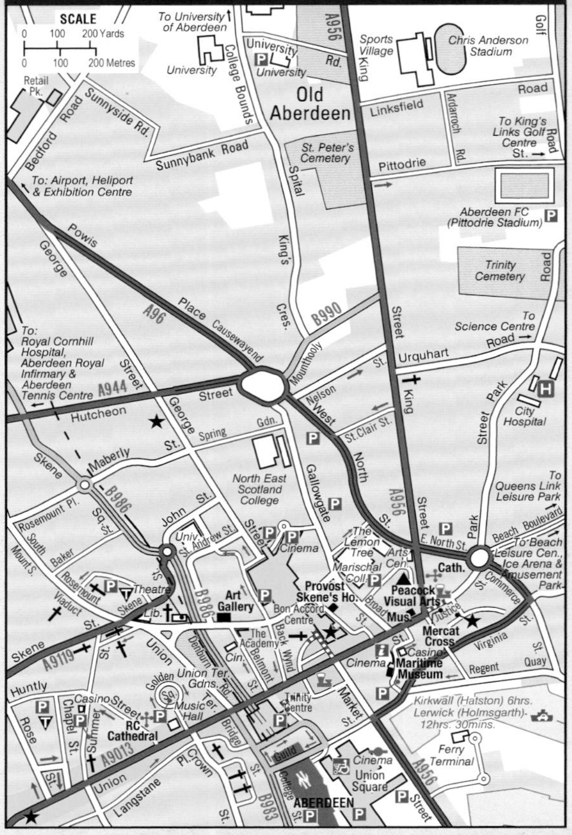


## BATH

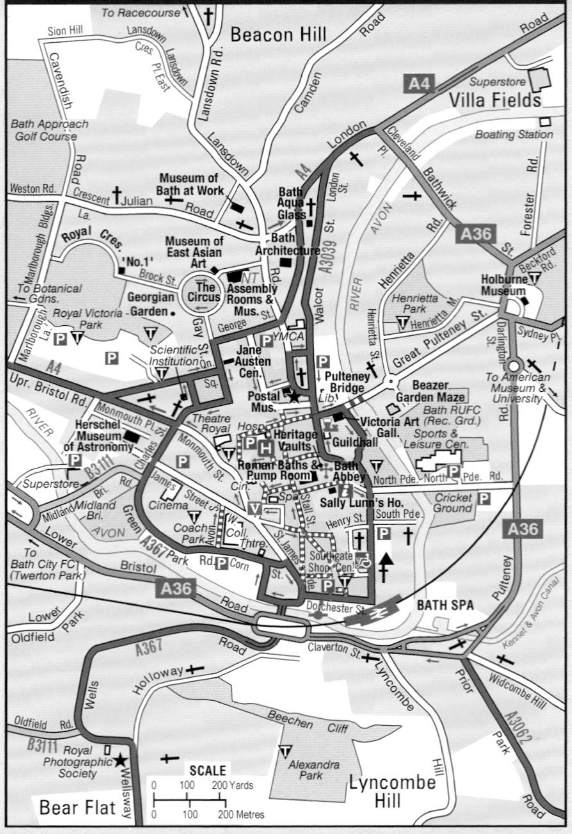


## BLACKPOOL

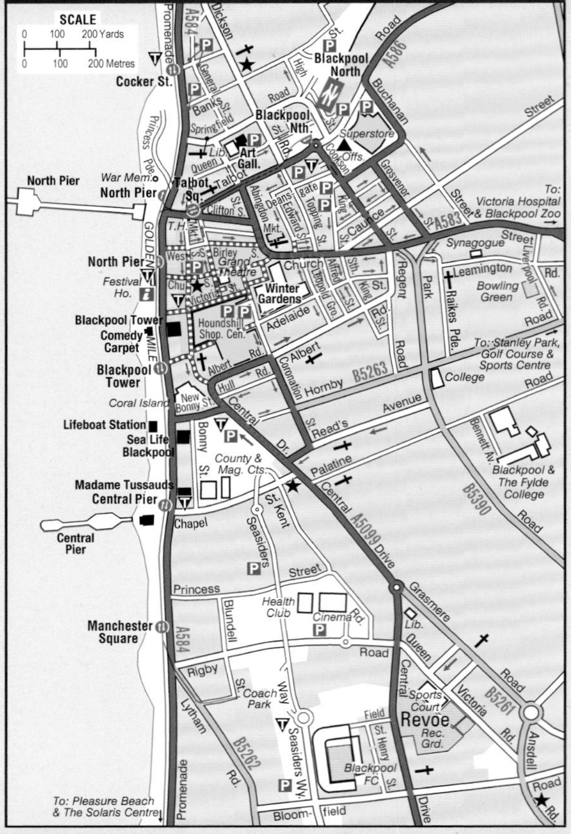


## BIRMINGHAM (CITY CENTRE)

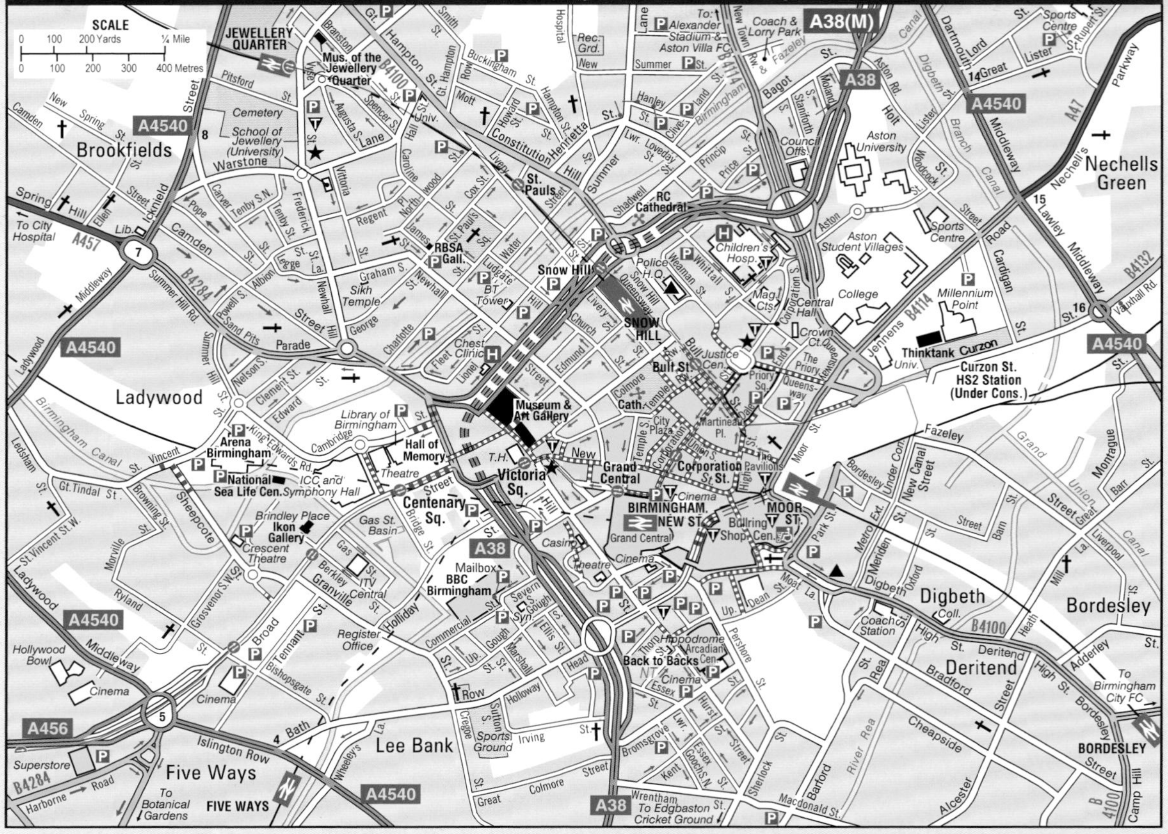


## BOURNEMOUTH

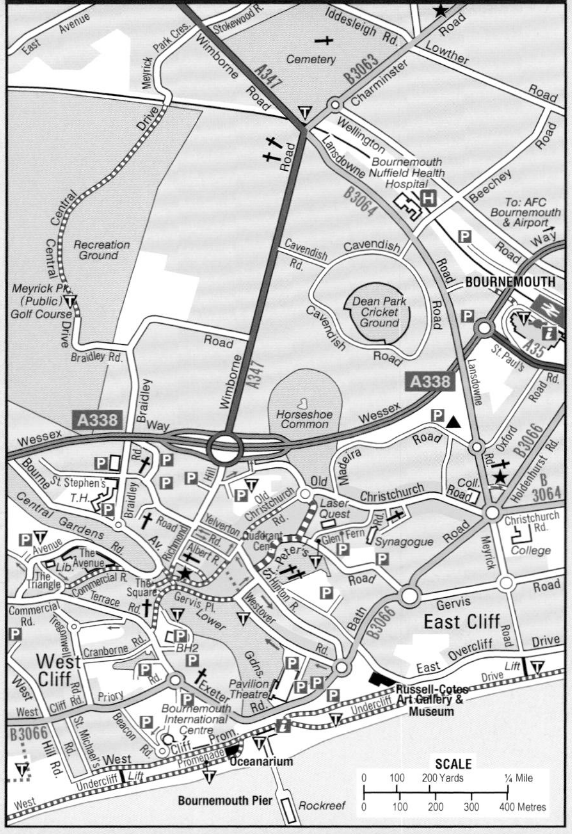


## BRADFORD

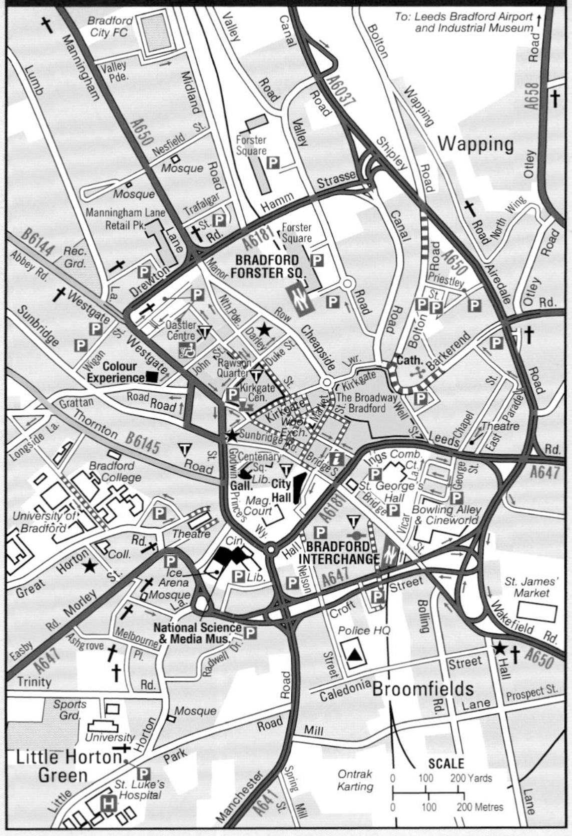


## BRIGHTON and HOVE

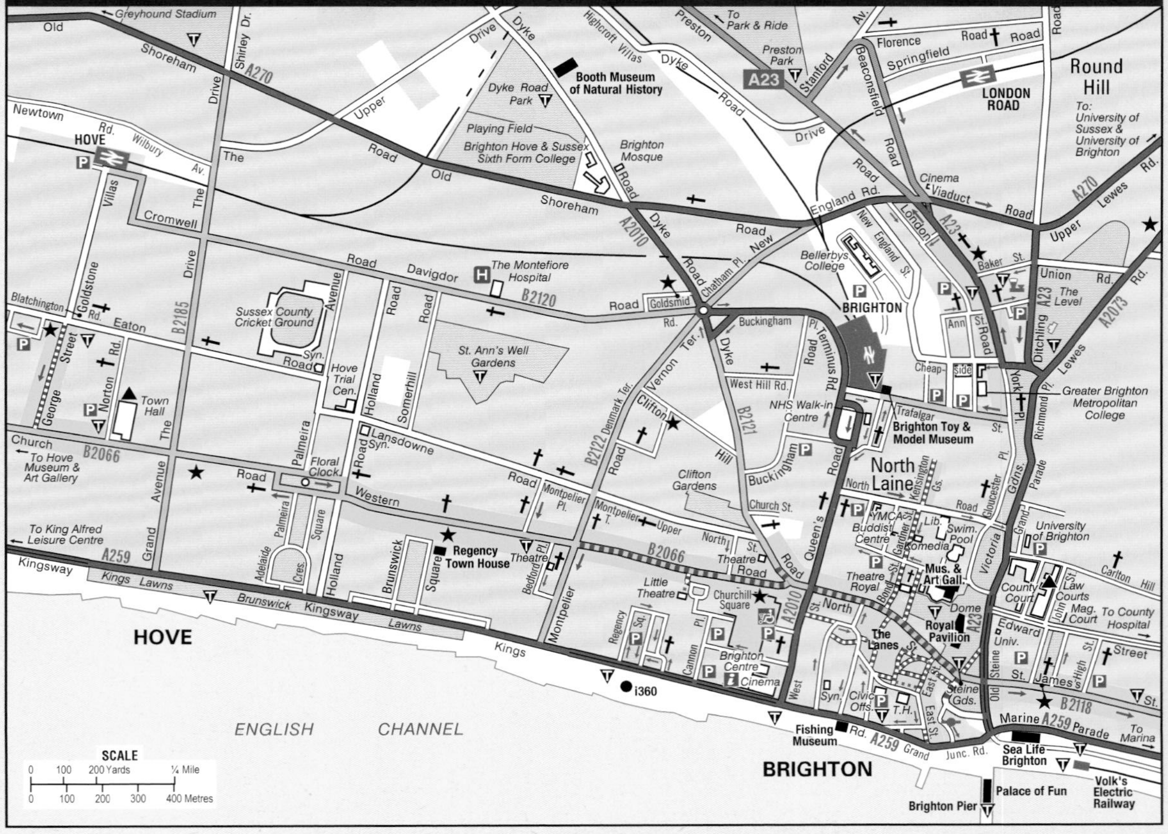

## BRISTOL

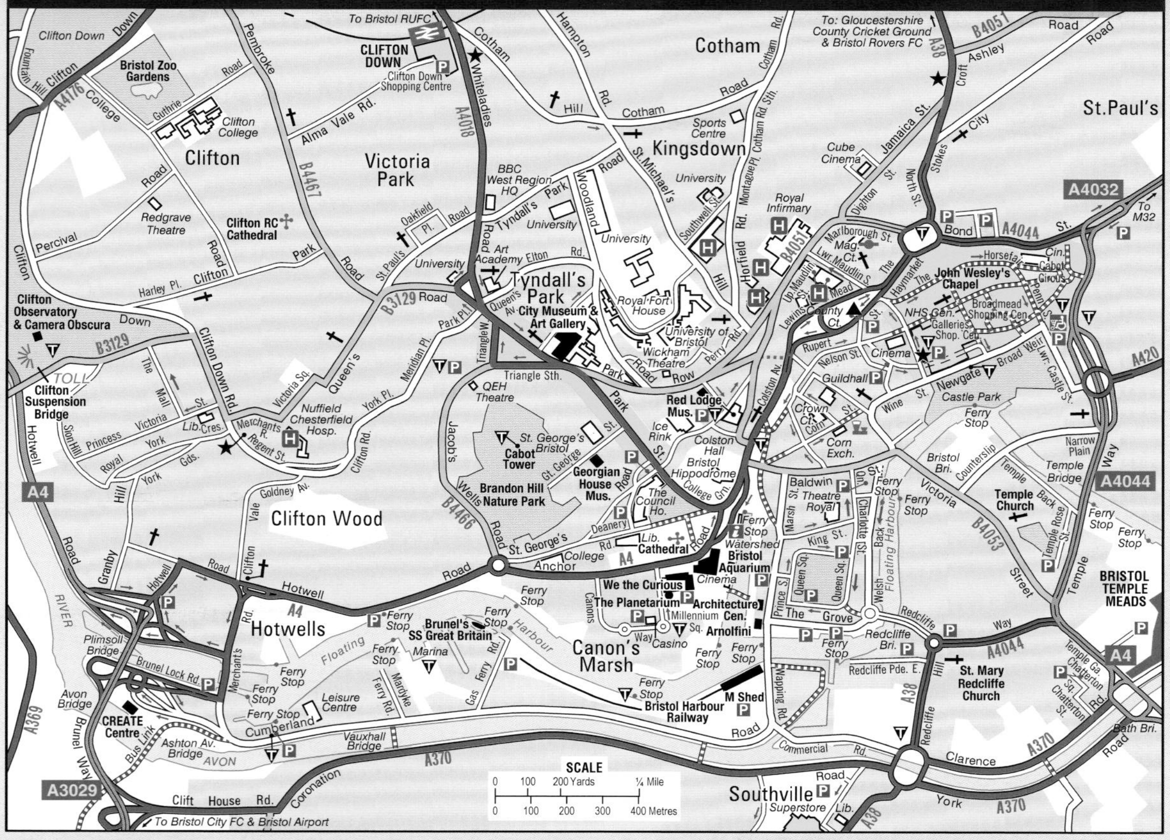


## CANTERBURY

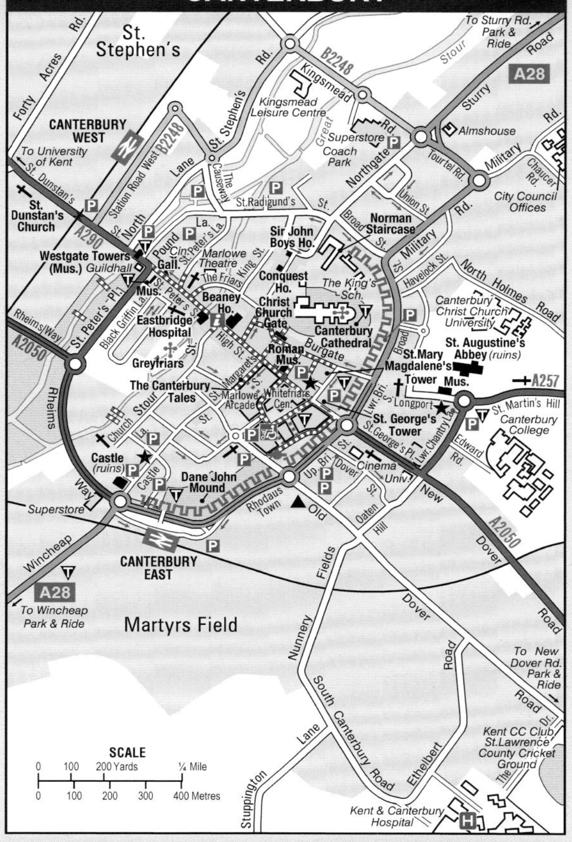


## CAMBRIDGE

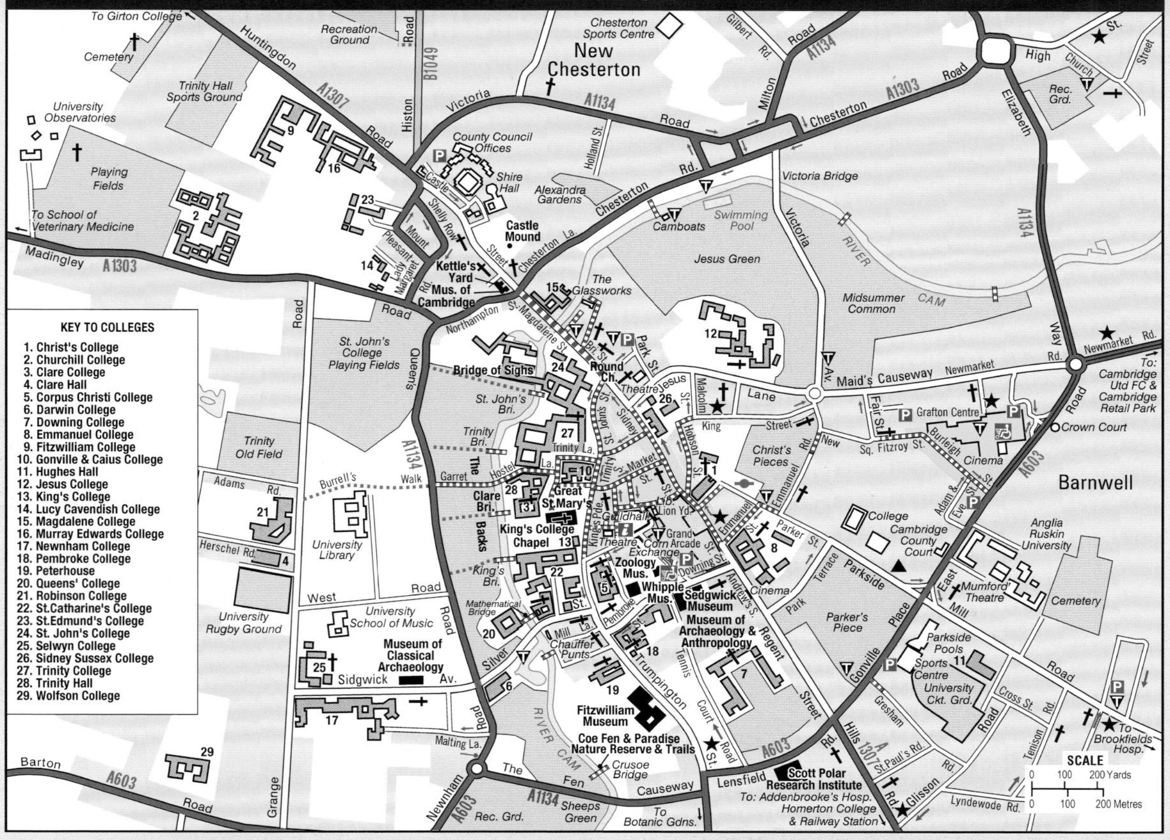


## CARLISLE

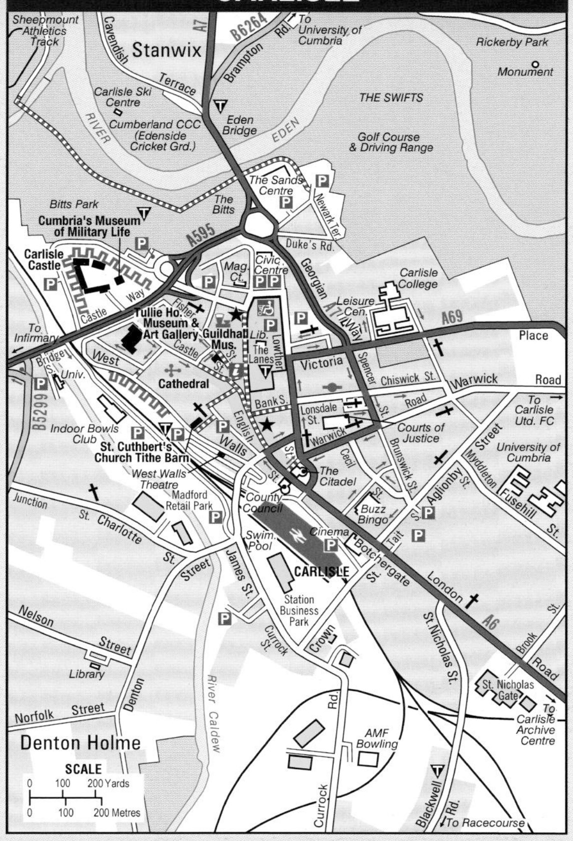


## CARDIFF (CAERDYDD)

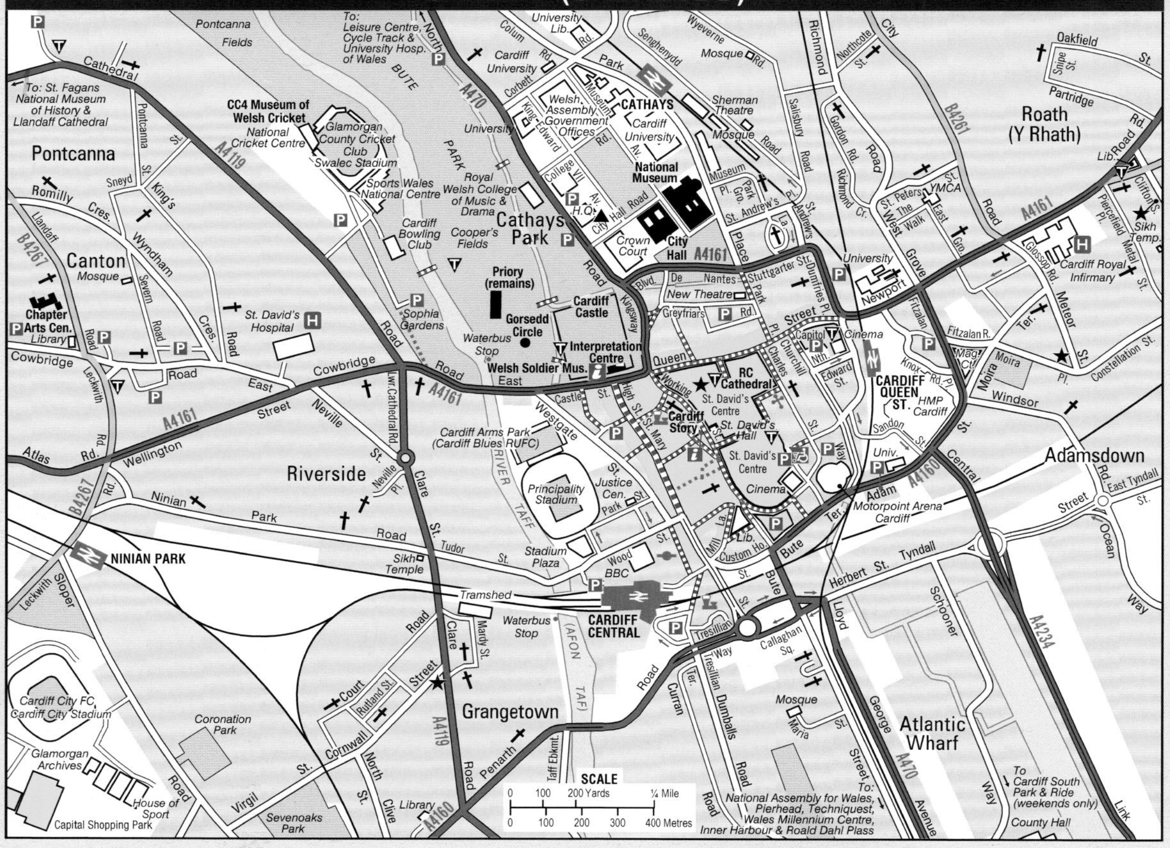


## CHELTENHAM

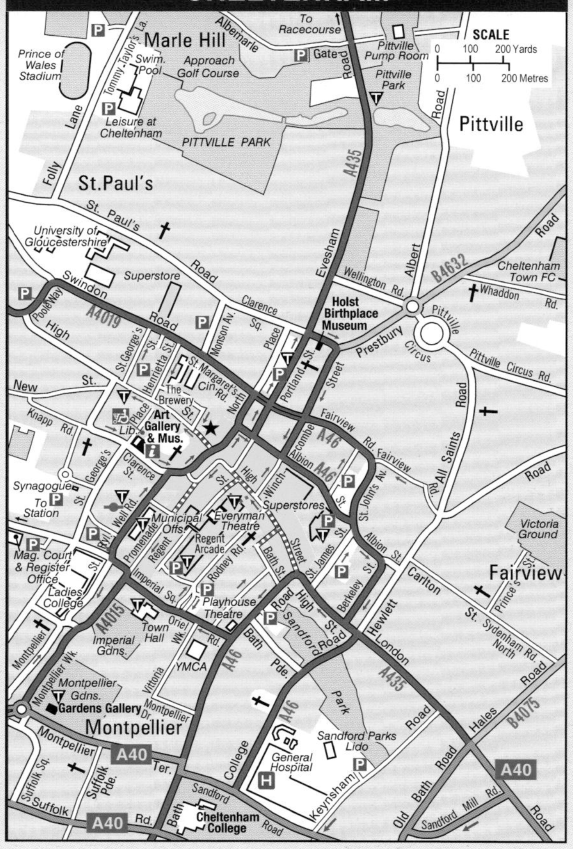

## CHESTER

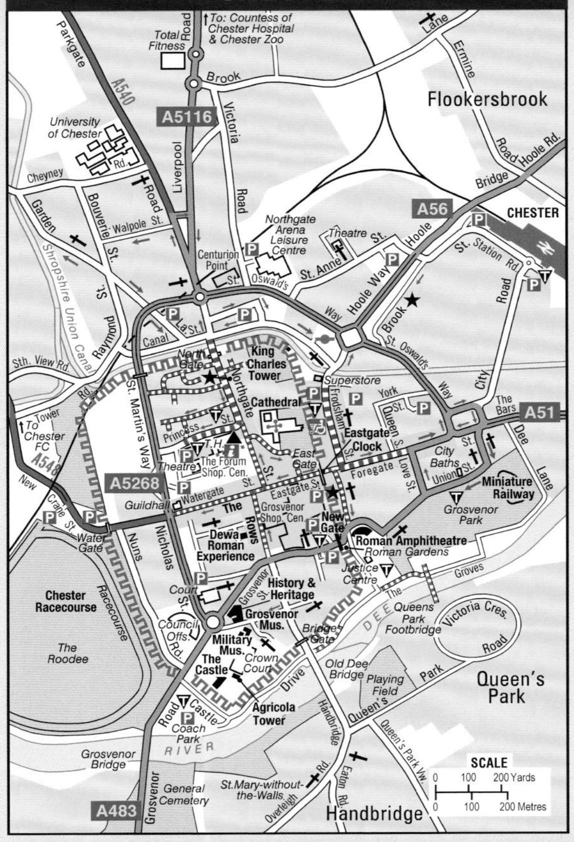


## COVENTRY

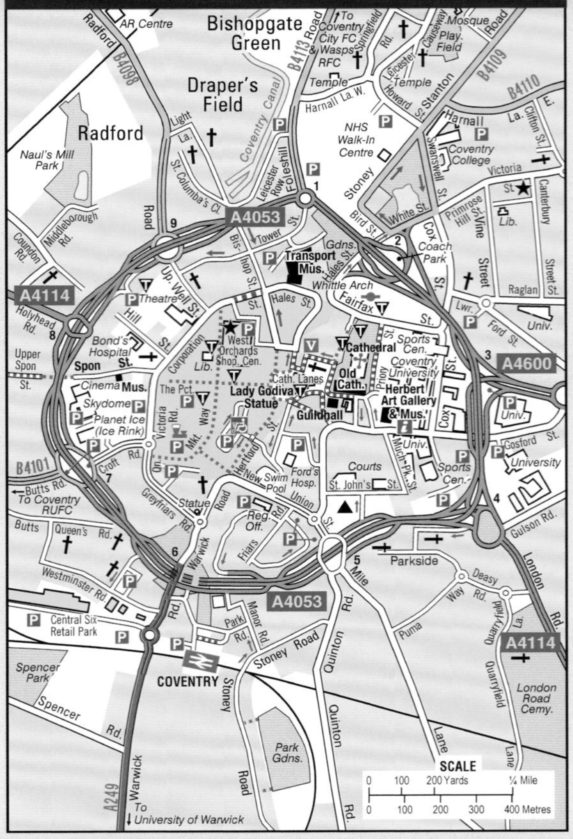


## DERBY

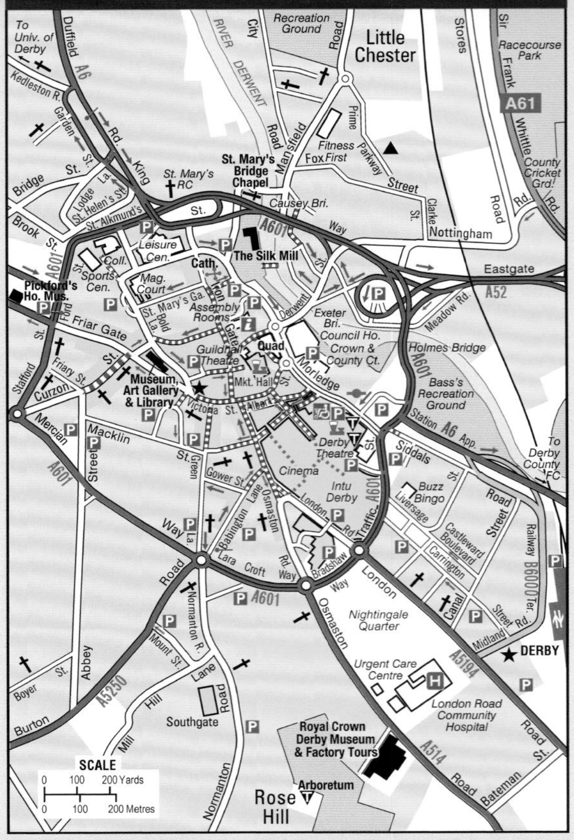


## DOVER

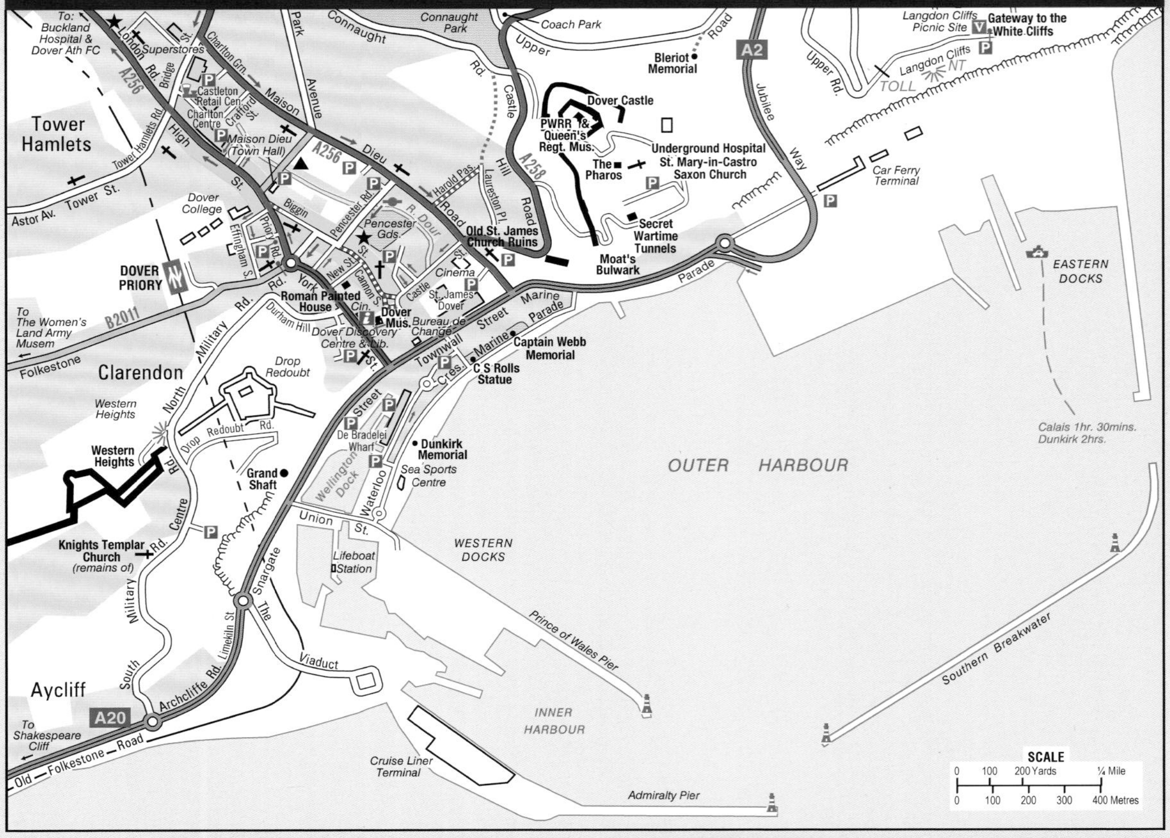


## DUMFRIES

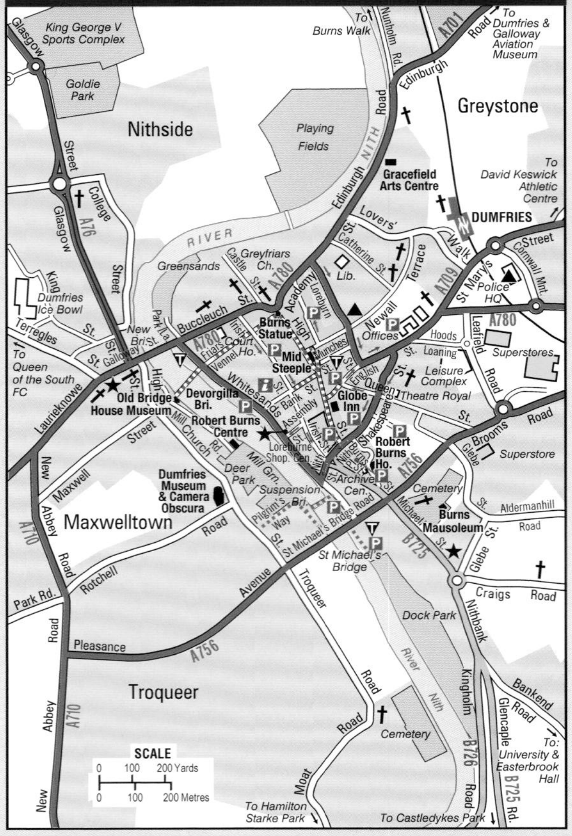


## DUNDEE

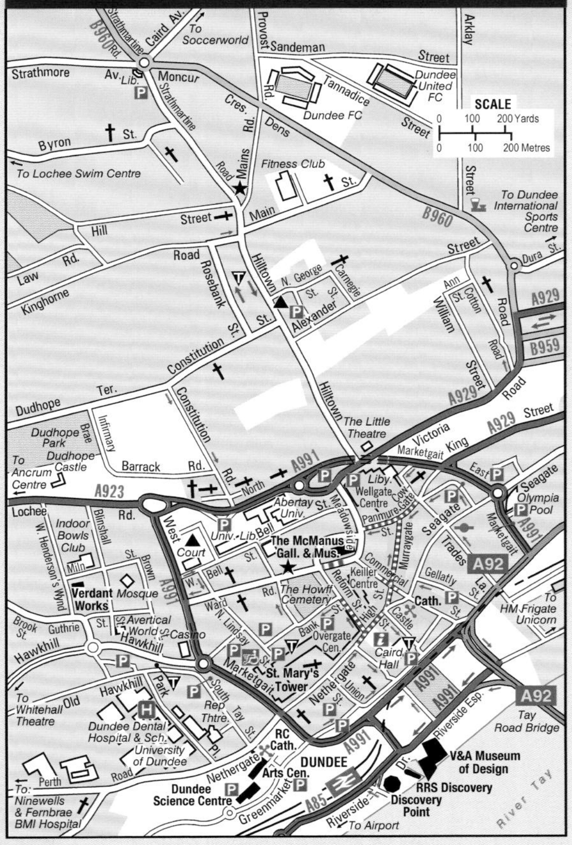


## DURHAM

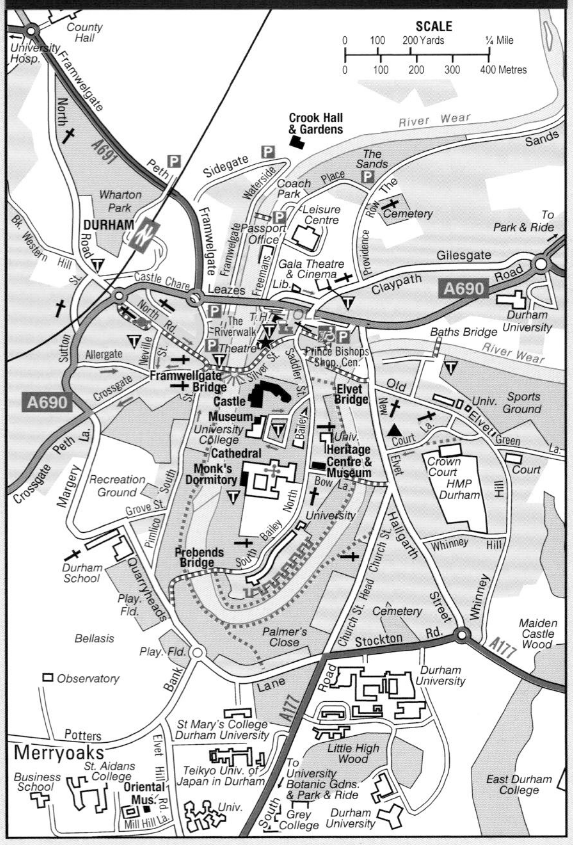


## EASTBOURNE

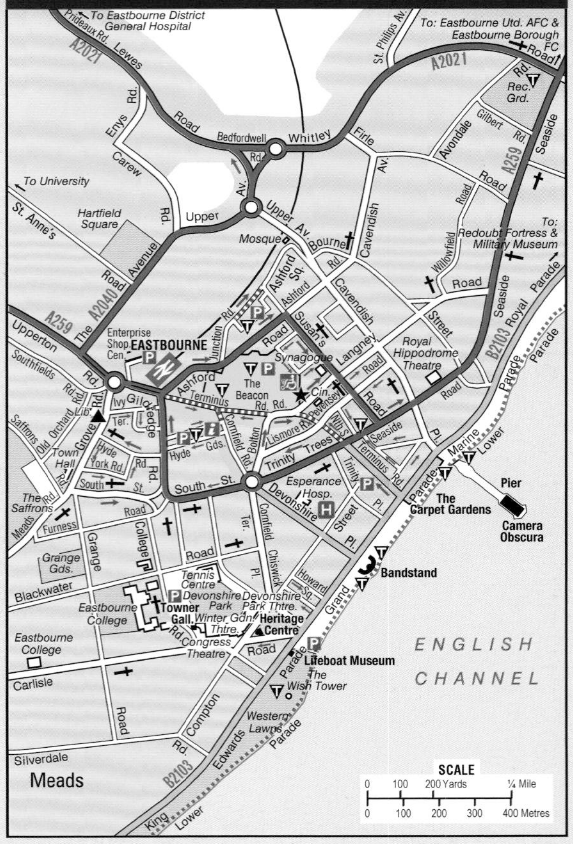

## EDINBURGH

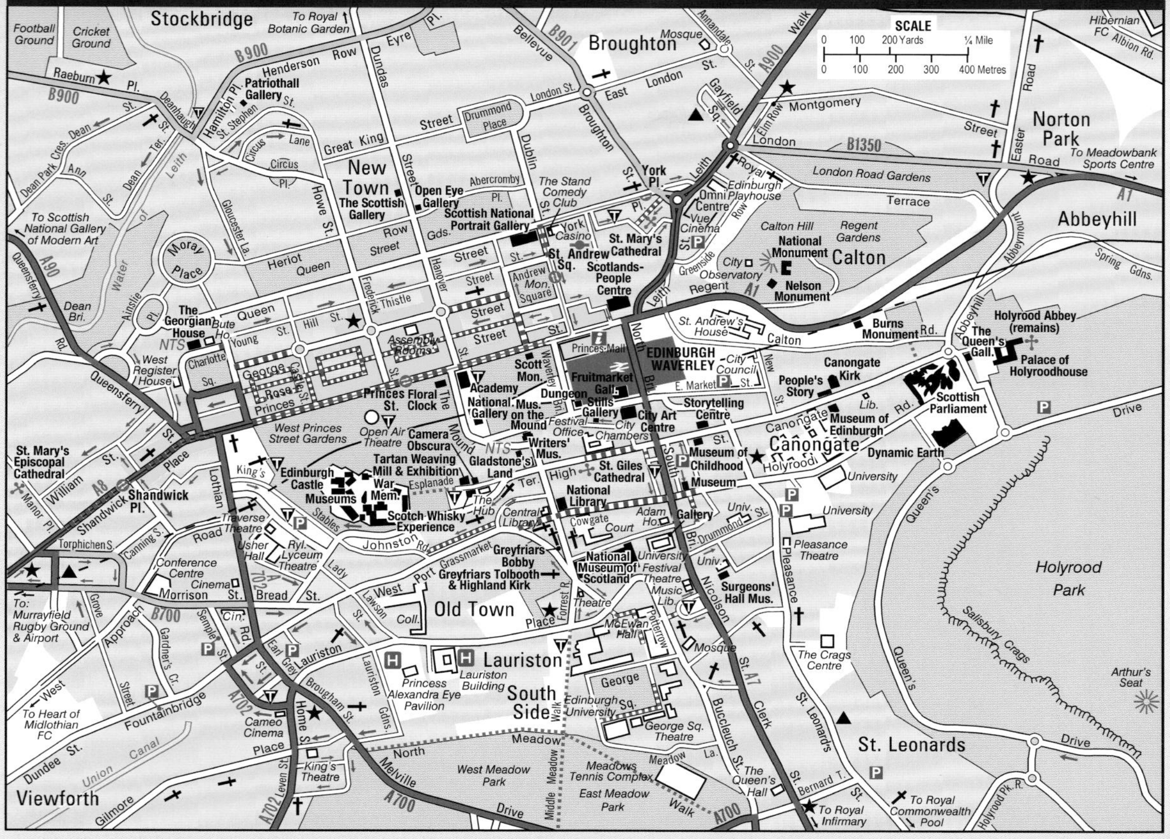


## FOLKESTONE

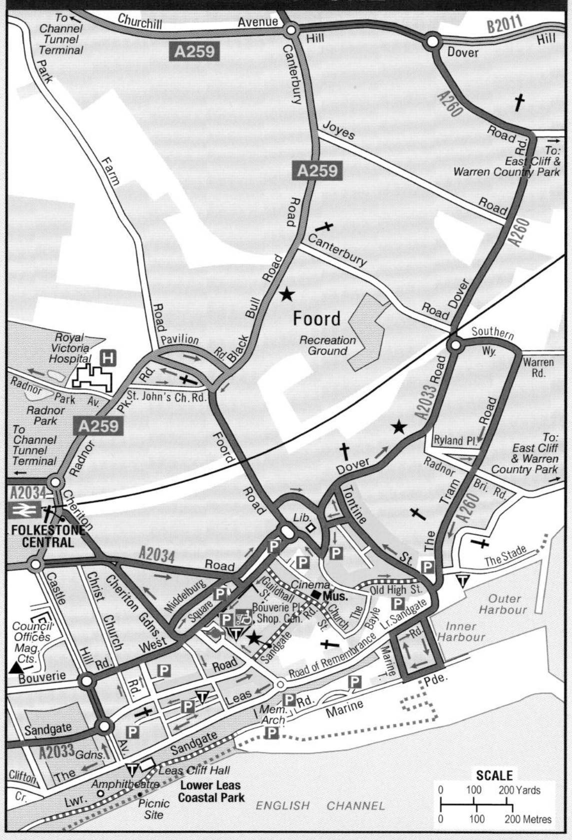


## EXETER

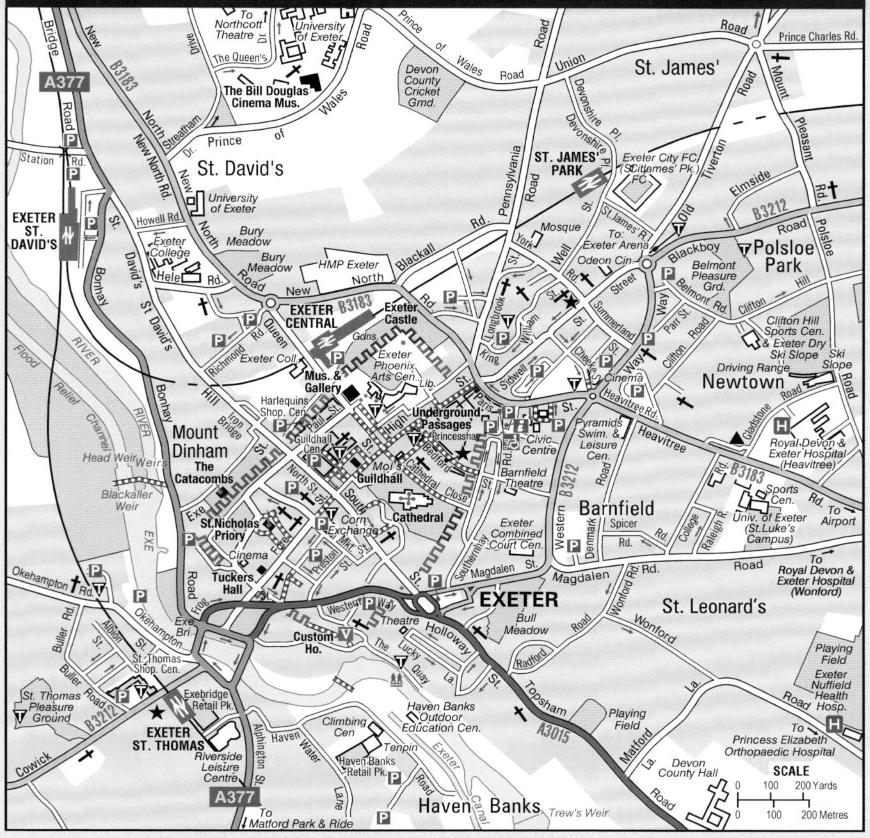


## GUILDFORD

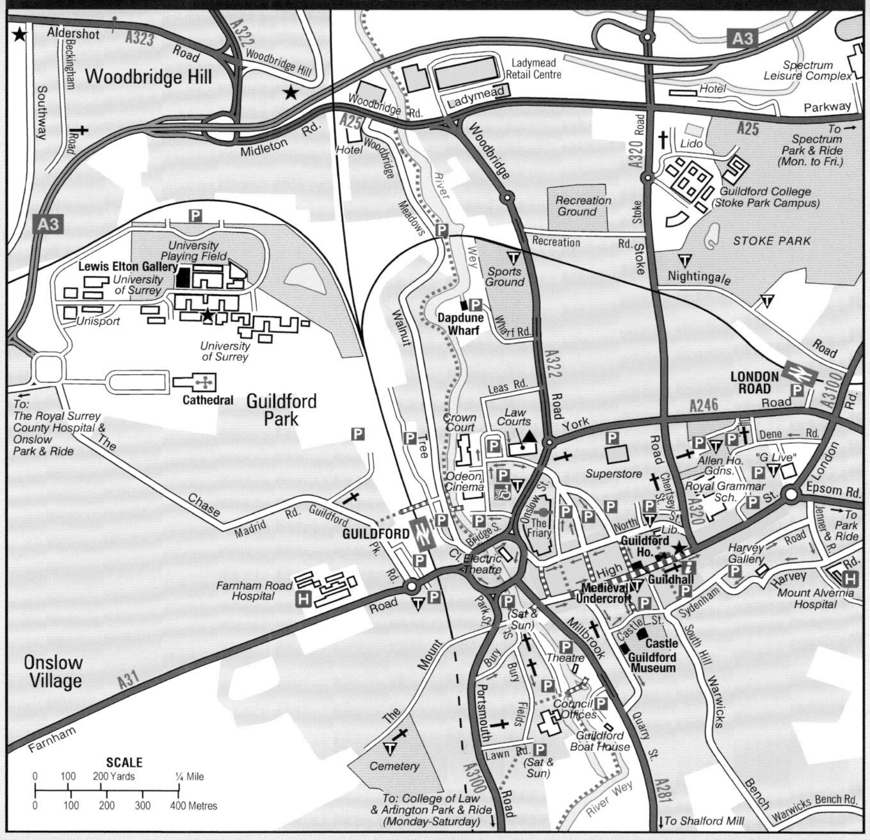


## GLASGOW

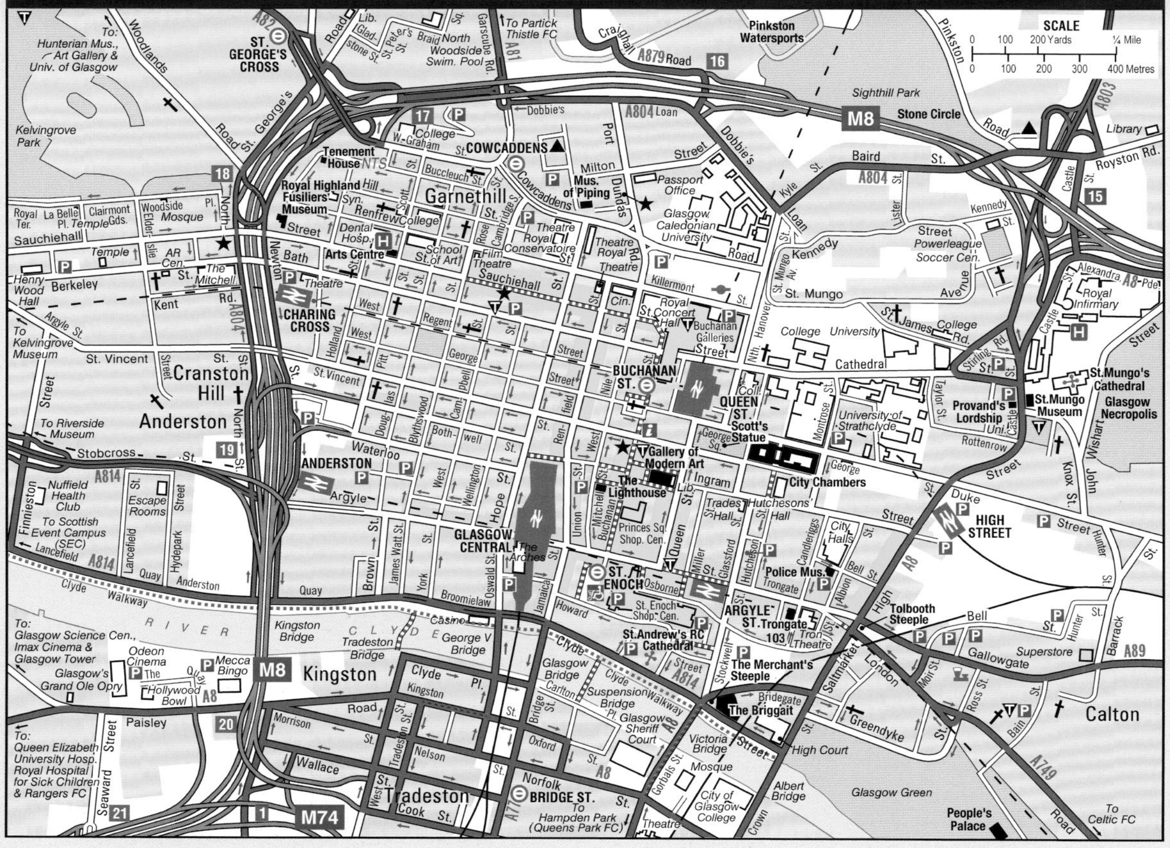


## GLOUCESTER

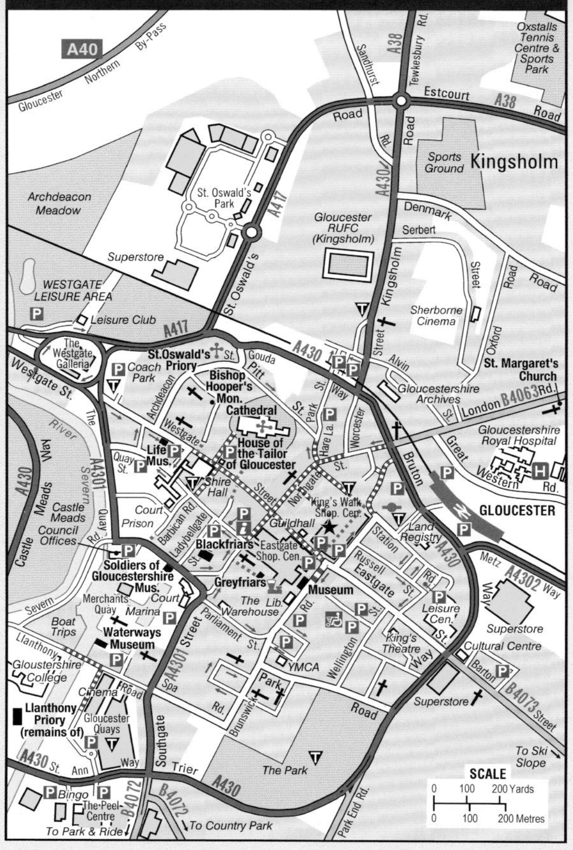

## HARROGATE

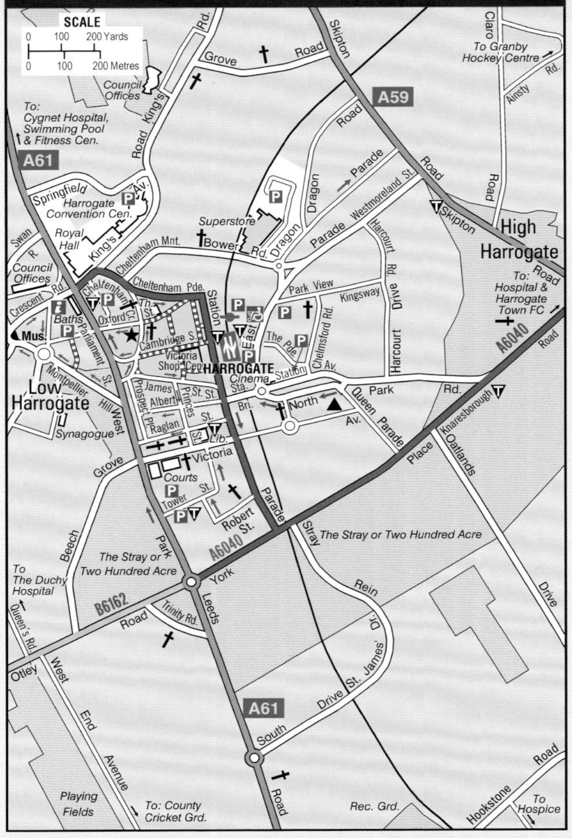


## INVERNESS

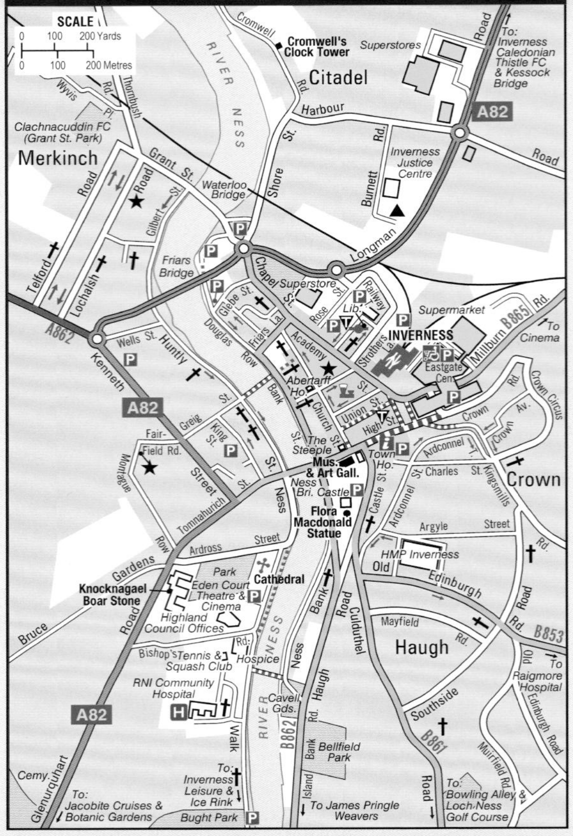


## IPSWICH

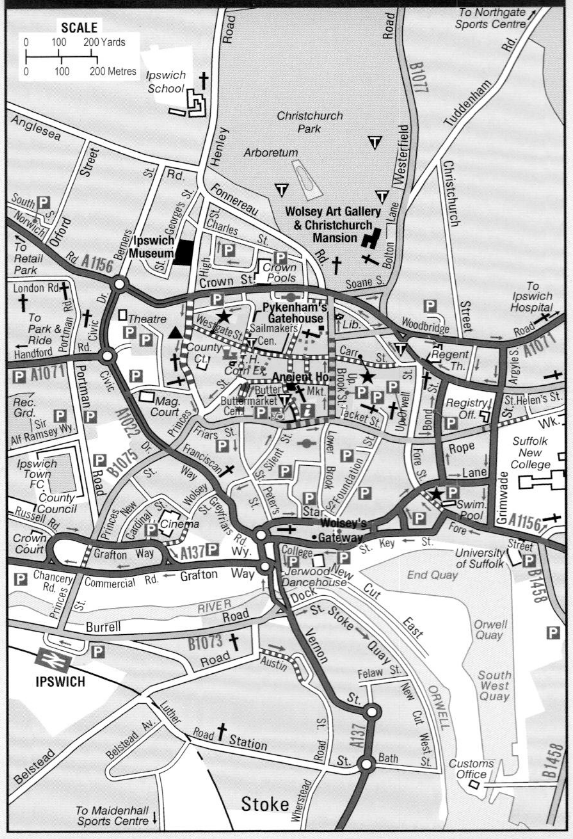


## KILMARNOCK

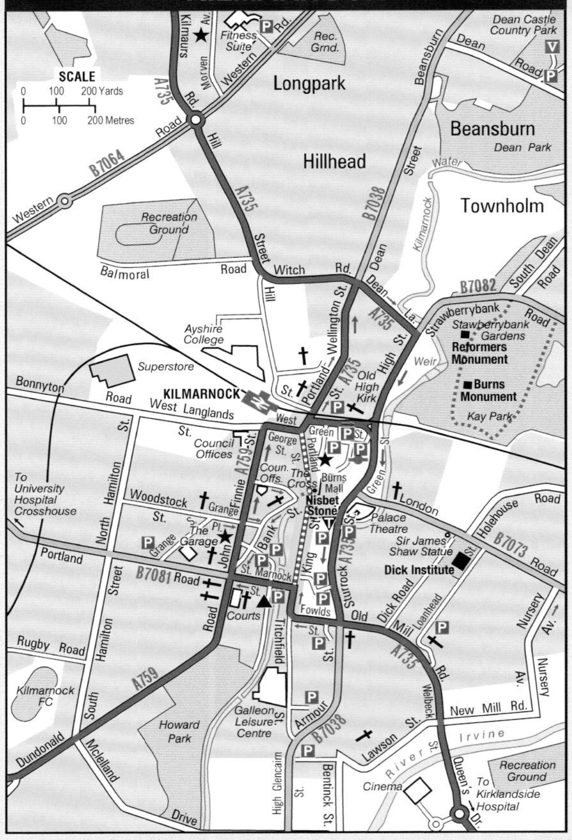


## LEEDS

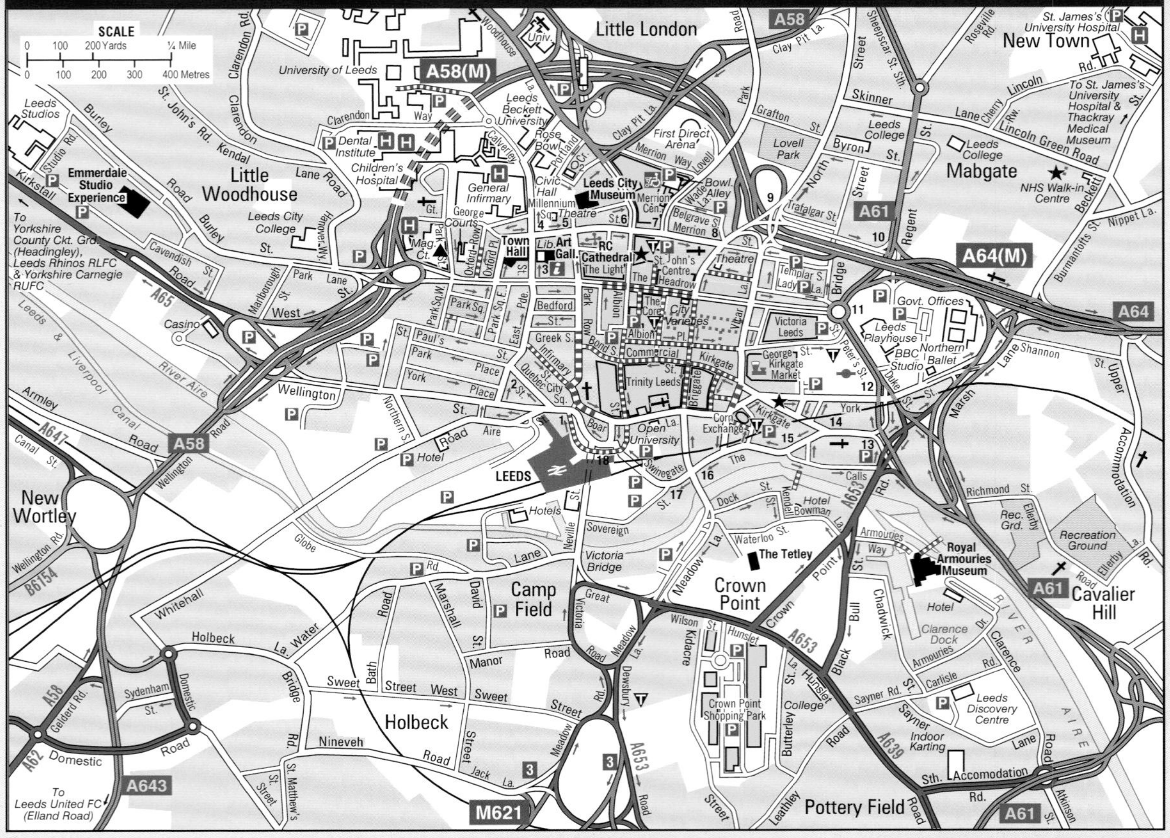


## KINGSTON UPON HULL

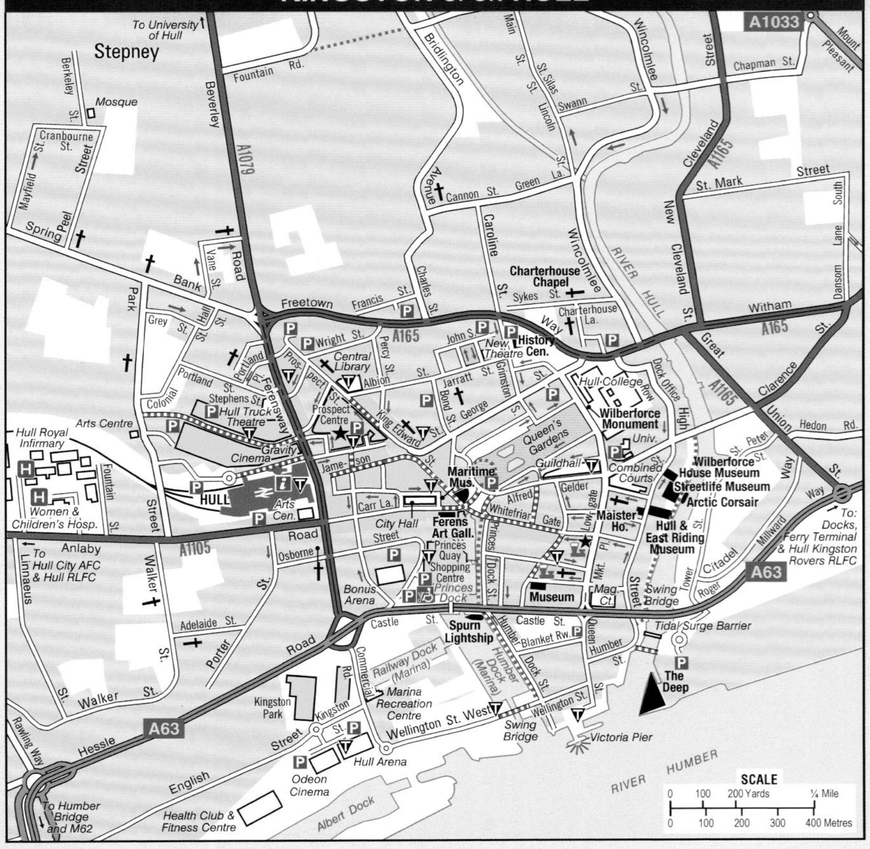


## LEICESTER

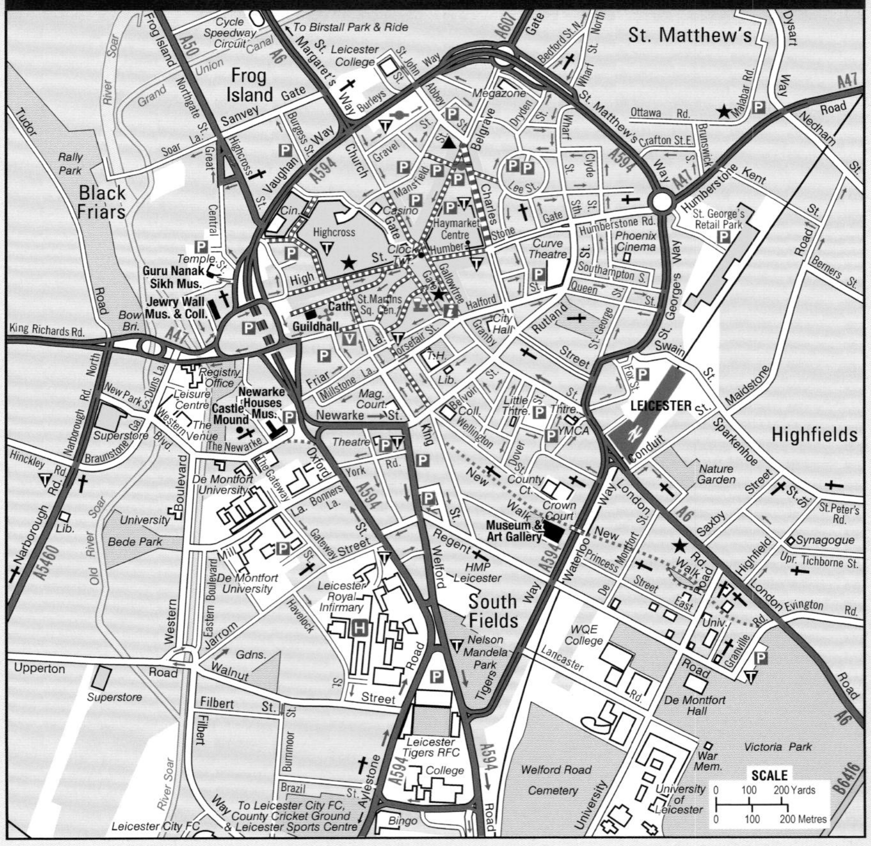

## LINCOLN

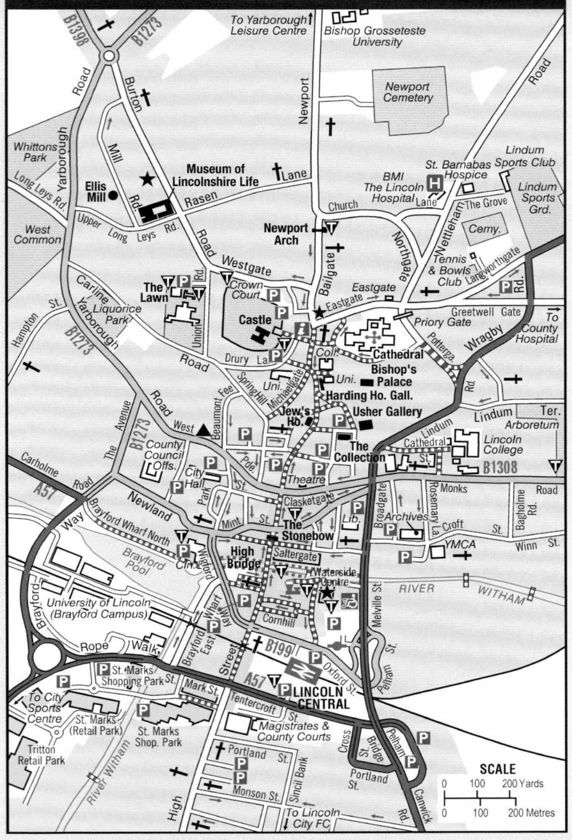


## LIVERPOOL

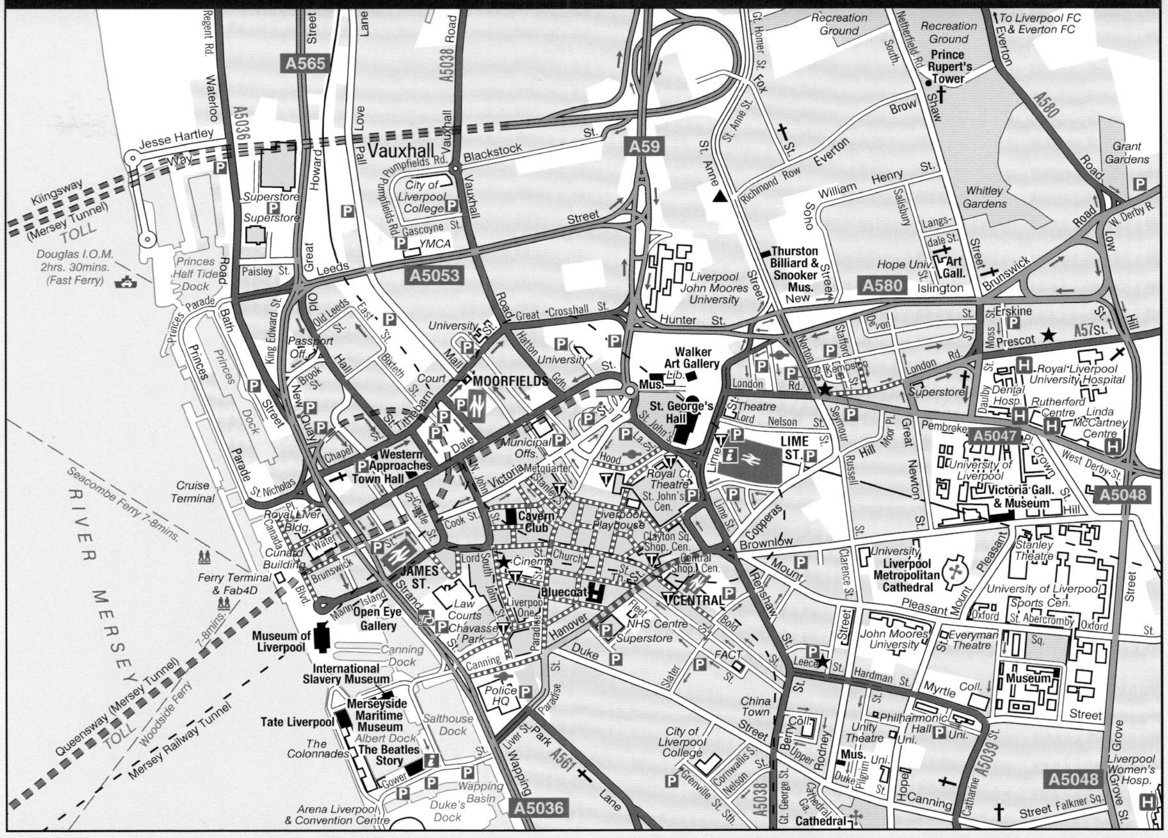


## MANCHESTER (CITY CENTRE)

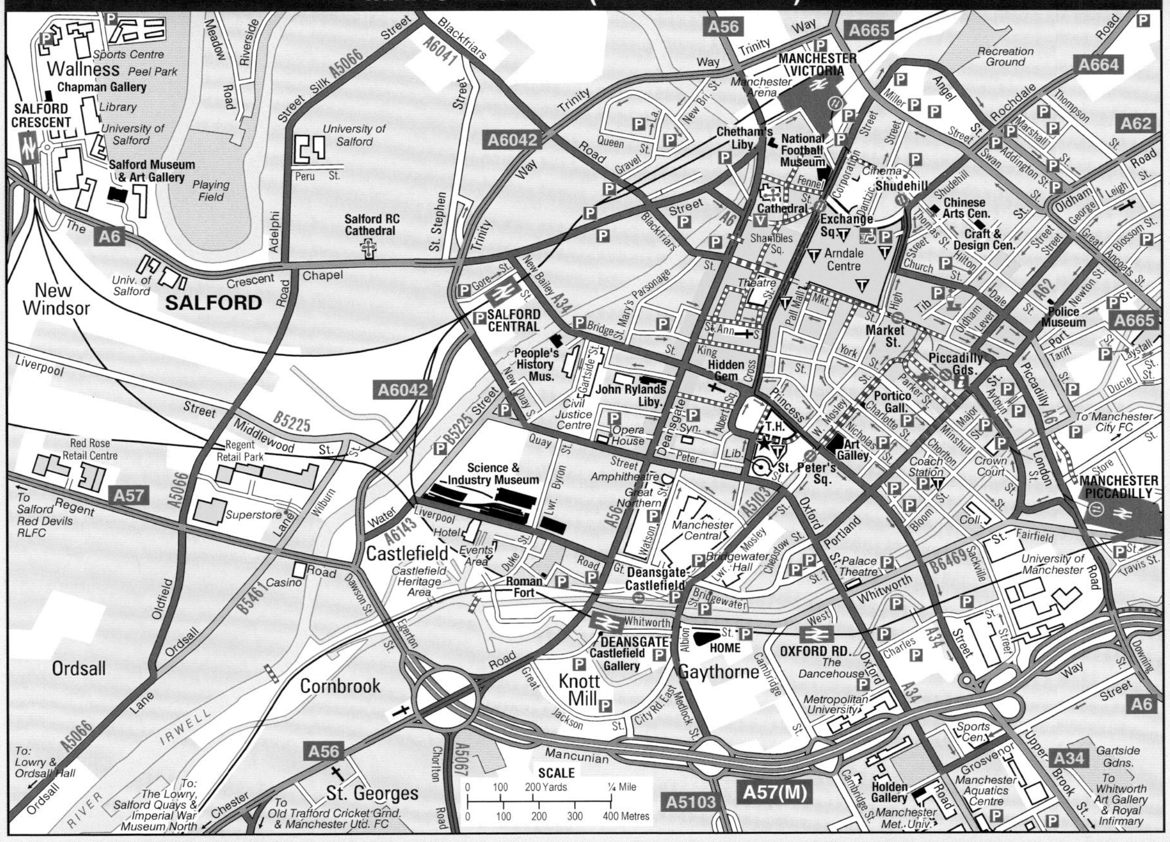


## MIDDLESBROUGH

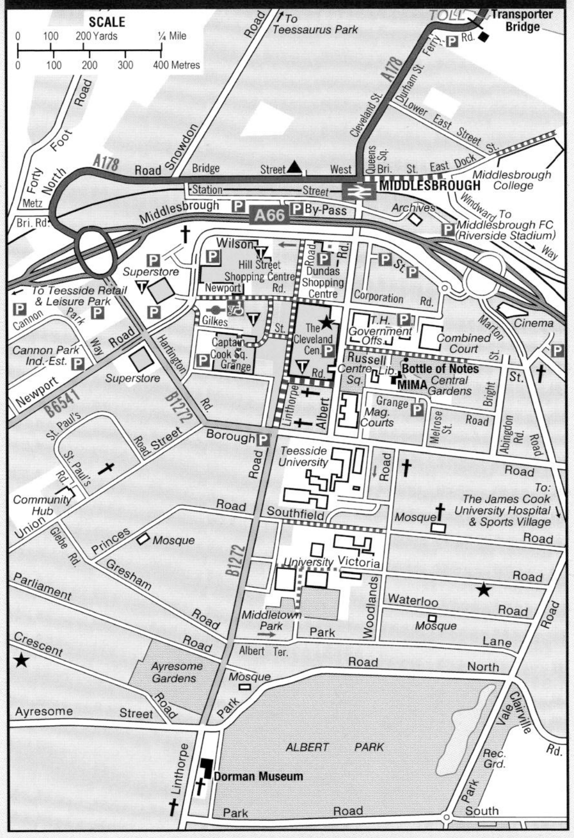


## MEDWAY TOWNS

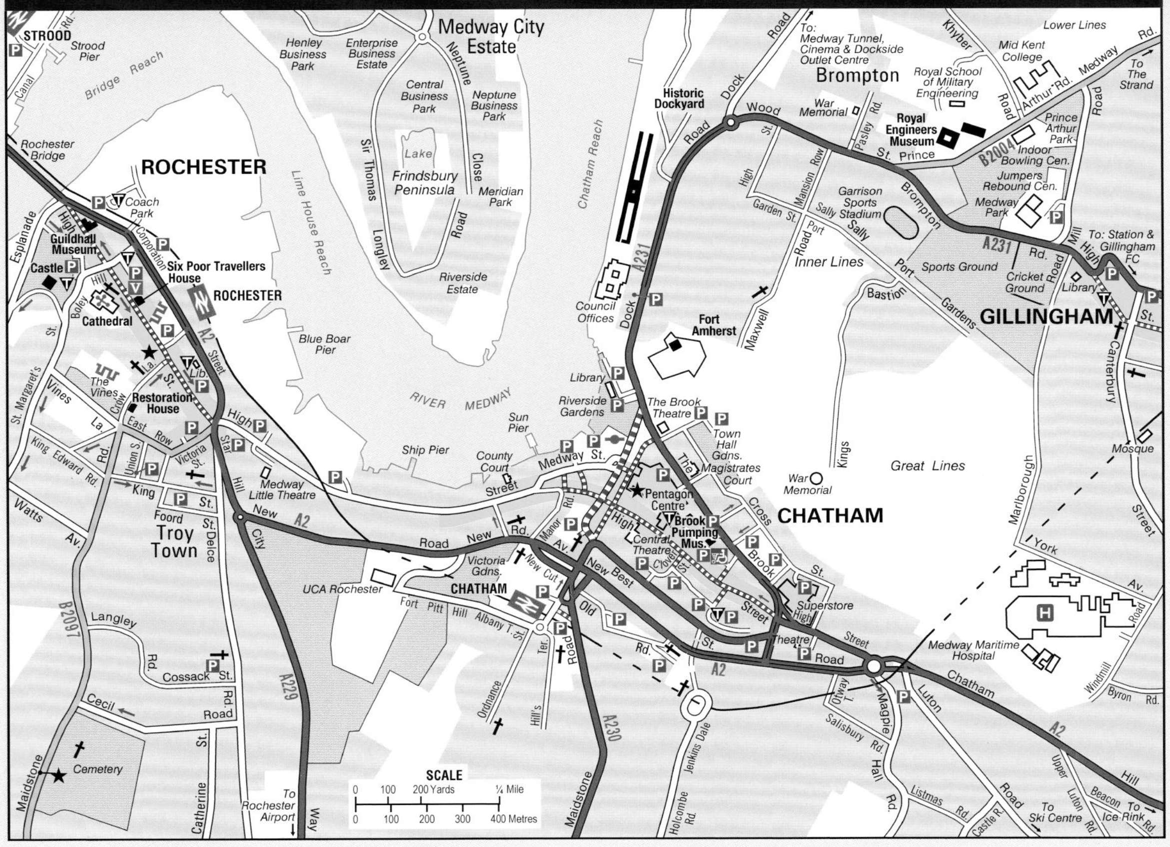


## NEWCASTLE UPON TYNE

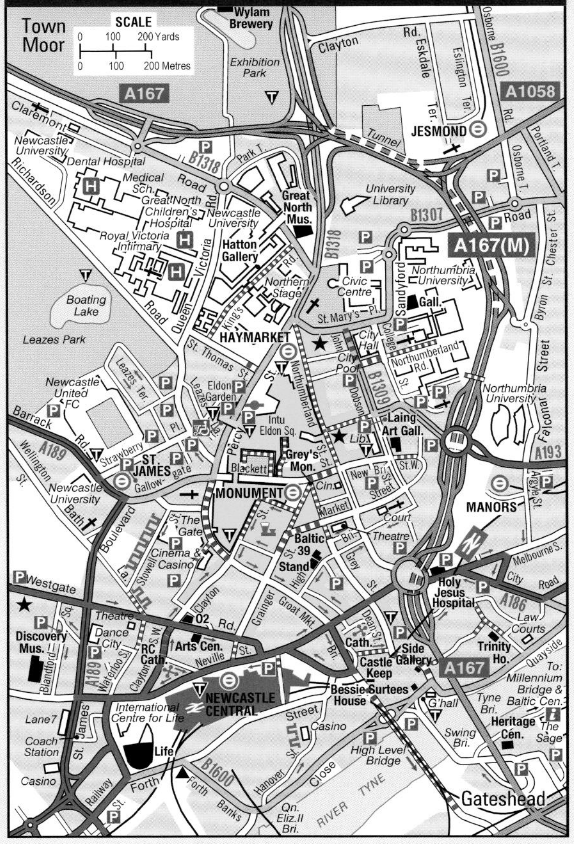

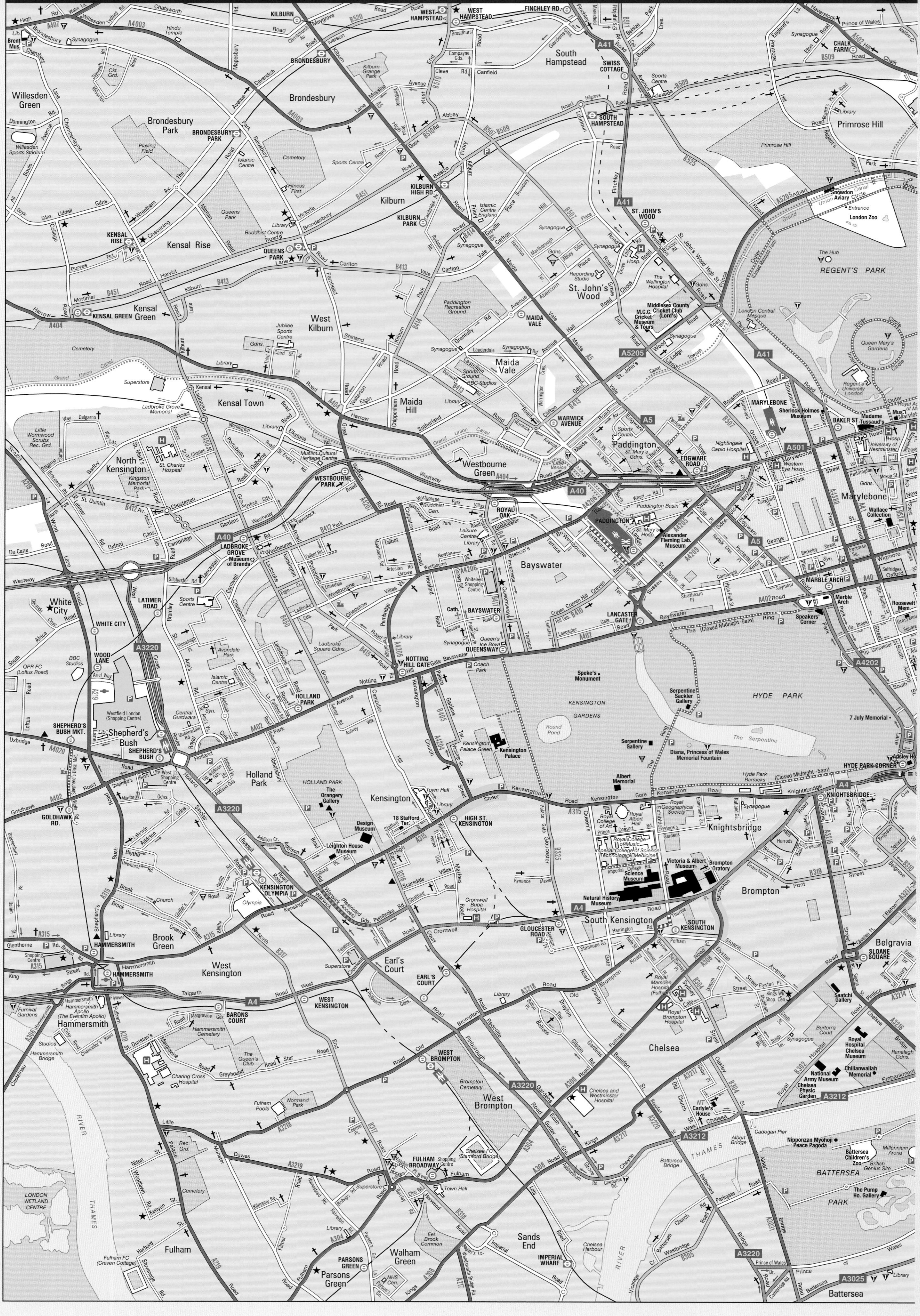
Willesden Green
Brondesbury Park
Brondesbury
Kilburn
Kensal Rise
Kensal Green
Kensal Town
West Kilburn
South Hampstead
St. John's Wood
Primrose Hill
REGENT'S PARK
London Zoo
Maida Vale
Maida Hill
Paddington
Marylebone
North Kensington
Westbourne Green
Bayswater
White City
Shepherd's Bush
Holland Park
Kensington
KENSINGTON GARDENS
HYDE PARK
The Serpentine
Knightsbridge
Brompton
Belgravia
South Kensington
Brook Green
West Kensington
Earl's Court
Hammersmith
West Brompton
Chelsea
Fulham
Walham Green
Parsons Green
Sands End
BATTERSEA PARK
Battersea
RIVER THAMES

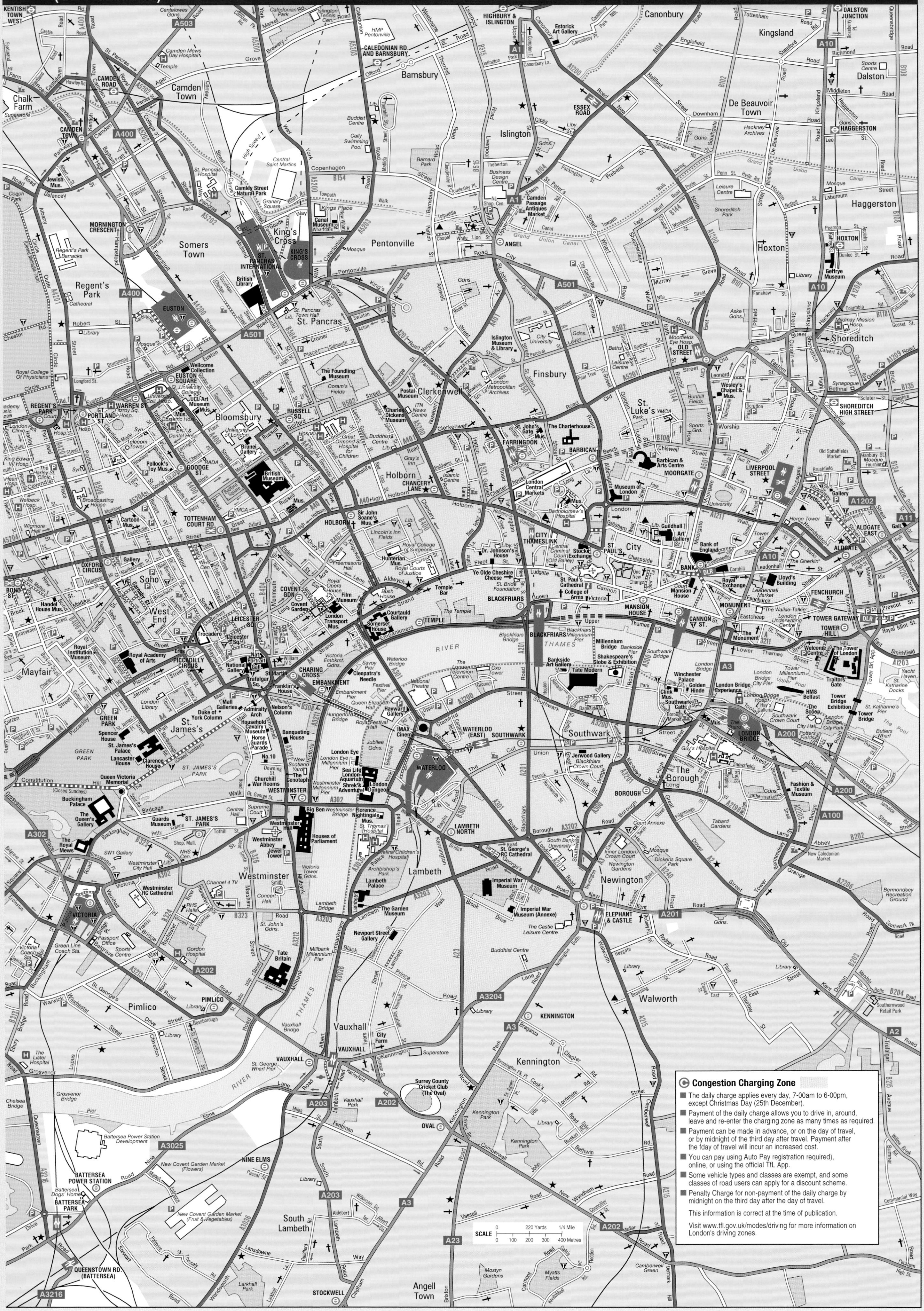
Congestion Charging Zone
The daily charge applies every day, 7-00am to 6-00pm, except Christmas Day (25th December).
Payment of the daily charge allows you to drive in, around, leave and re-enter the charging zone as many times as required.
Payment can be made in advance, or on the day of travel, or by midnight of the third day after travel. Payment after the fday of travel will incur an increased cost.
You can pay using Auto Pay registration required), online, or using the official TfL App.
Some vehicle types and classes are exempt, and some classes of road users can apply for a discount scheme.
Penalty Charge for non-payment of the daily charge by midnight on the third day after the day of travel.
This information is correct at the time of publication.
Visit www.tfl.gov.uk/modes/driving for more information on London's driving zones.
SCALE
0 220 Yards 1/4 Mile
0 100 200 300 400 Metres

## MILTON KEYNES

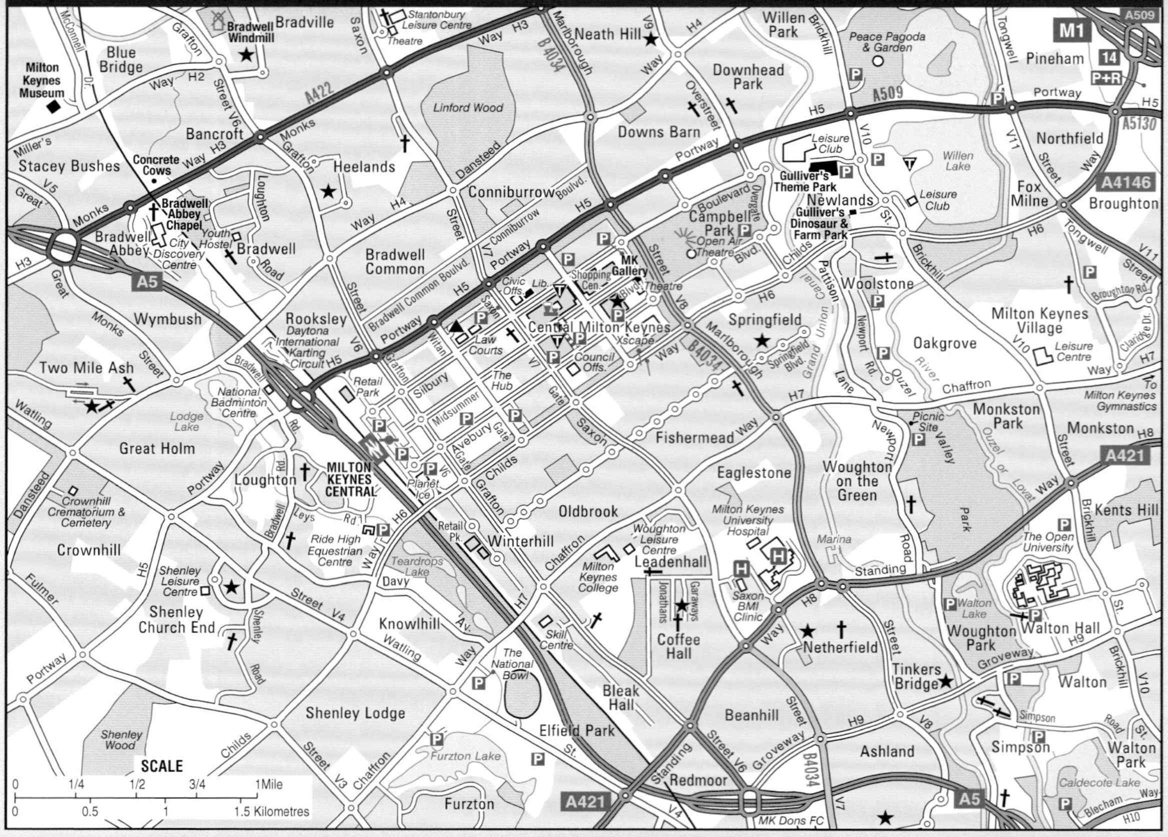


## NEWPORT (CASNEWYDD)

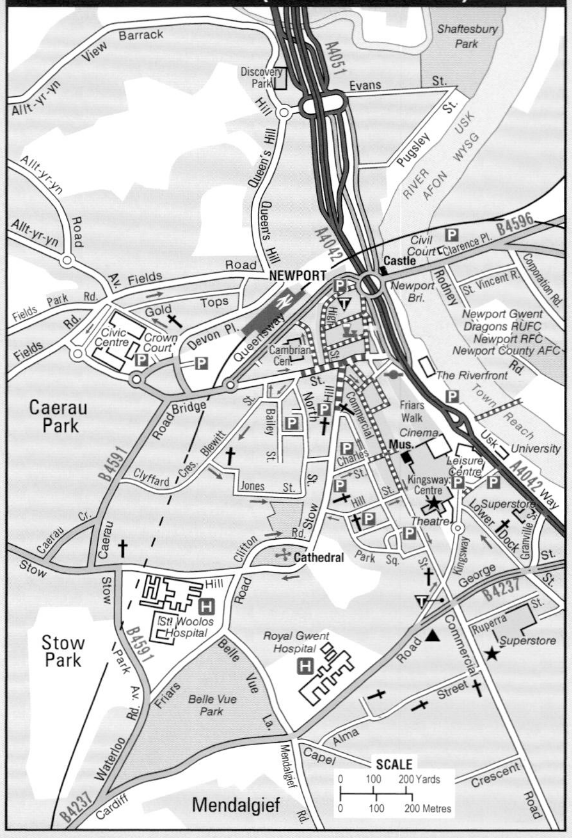


## NORWICH

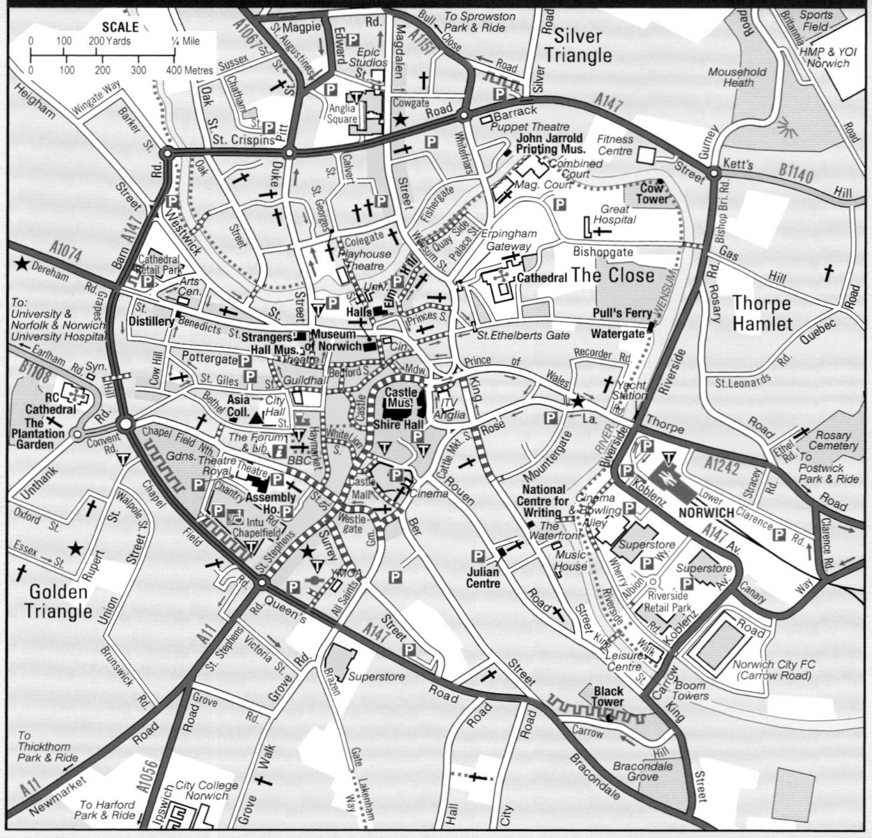


## NOTTINGHAM

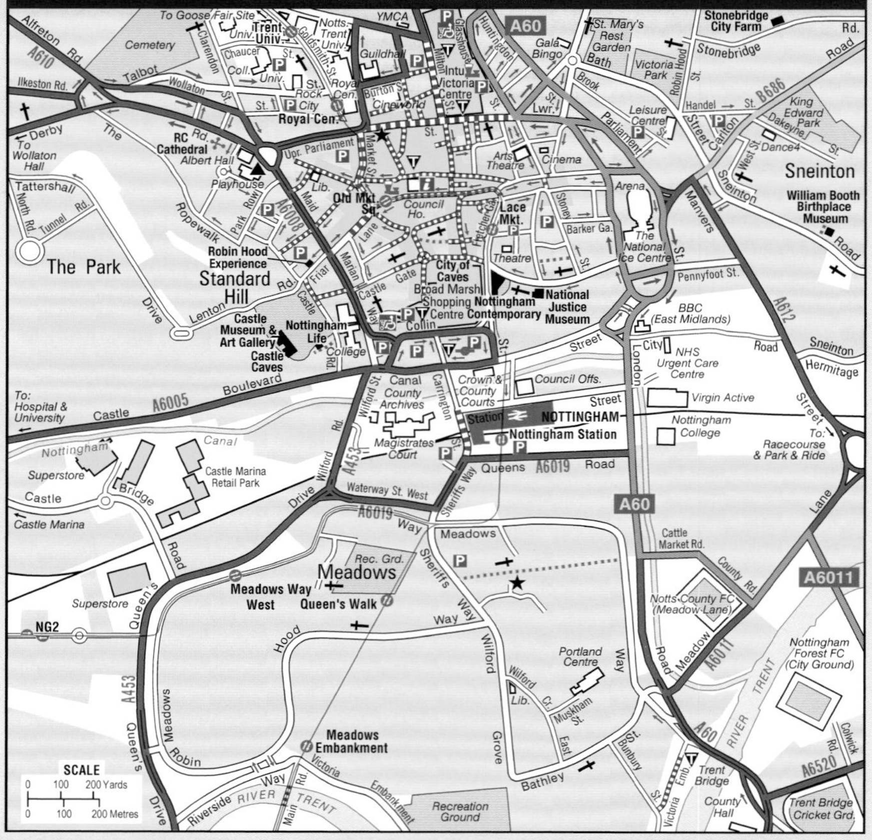


## NORTHAMPTON

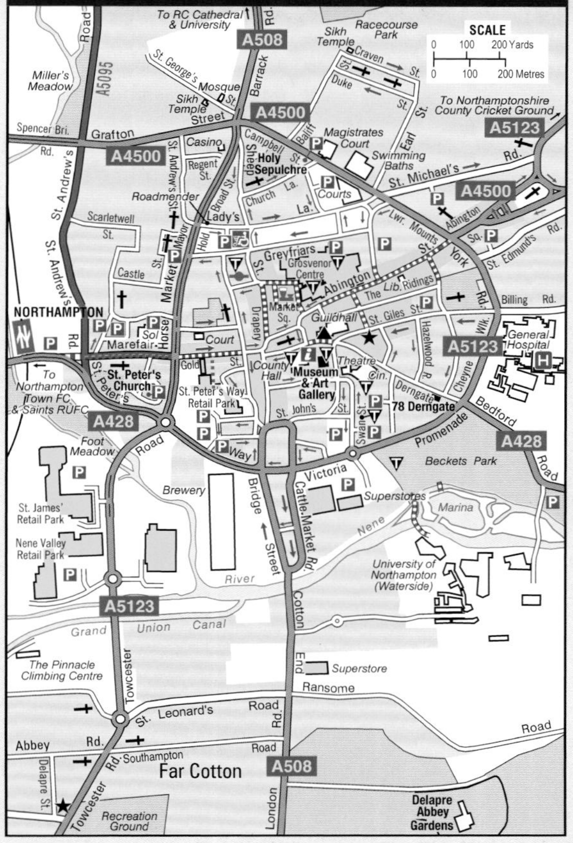


## OXFORD

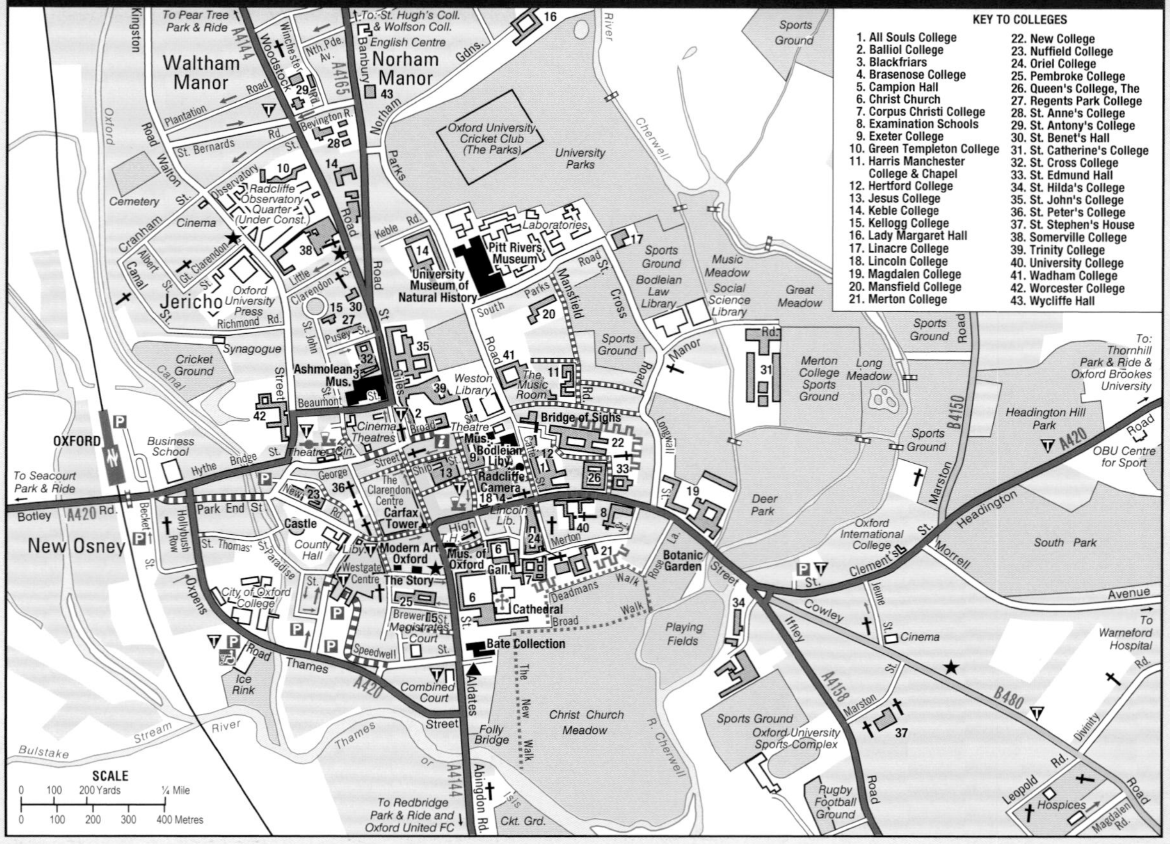

## OBAN

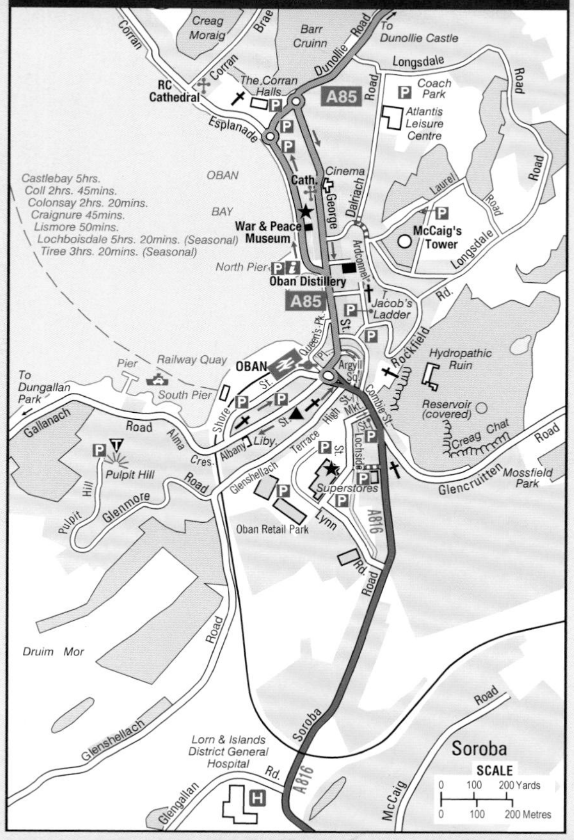


## PERTH

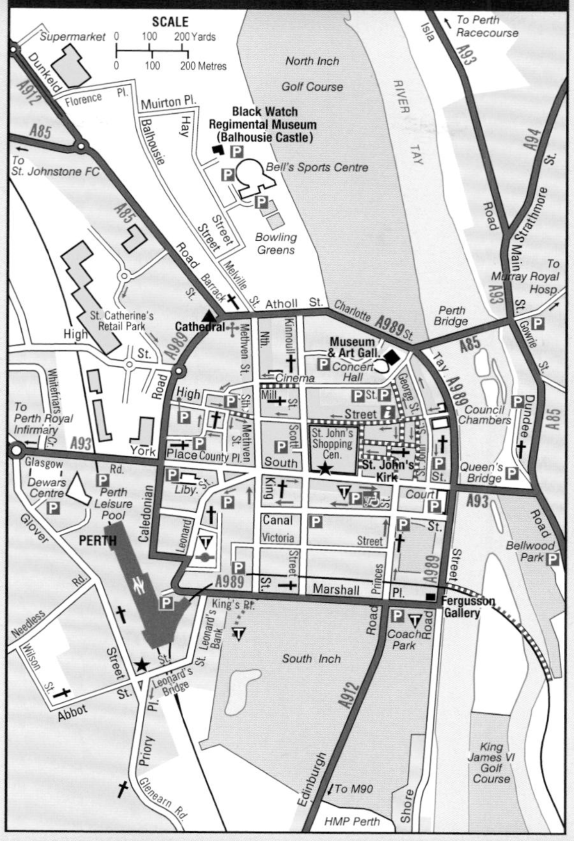


## PETERBOROUGH

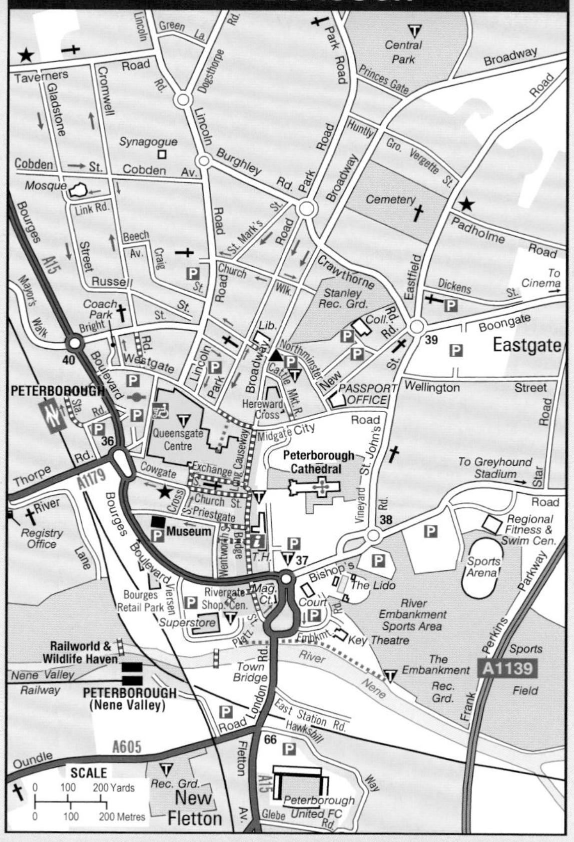


## PLYMOUTH

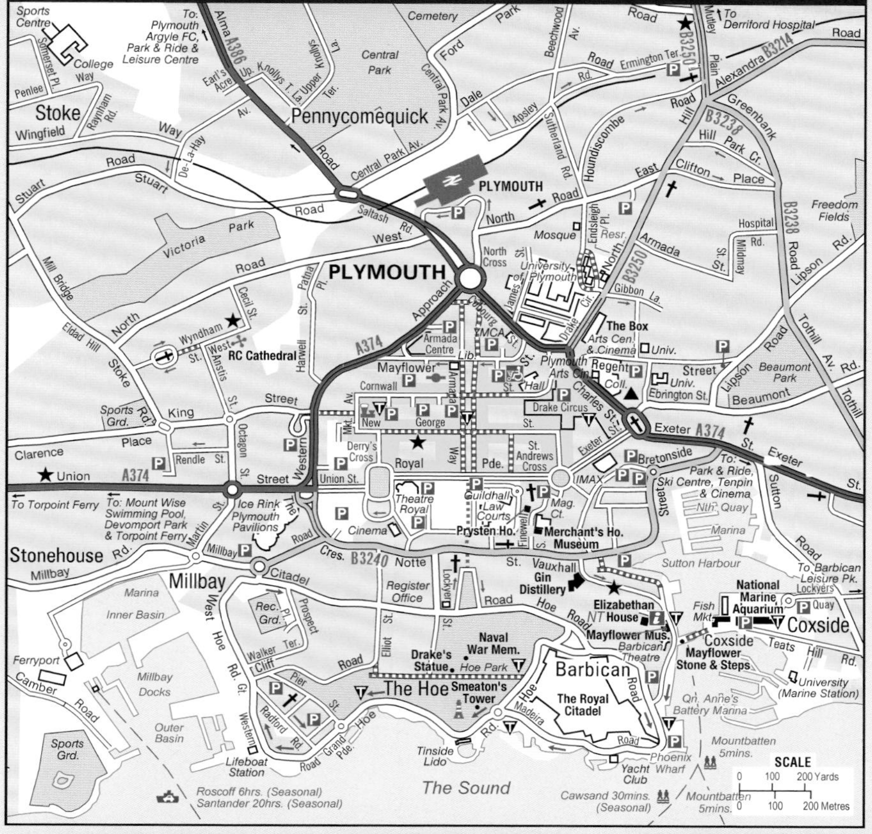


## PORTSMOUTH

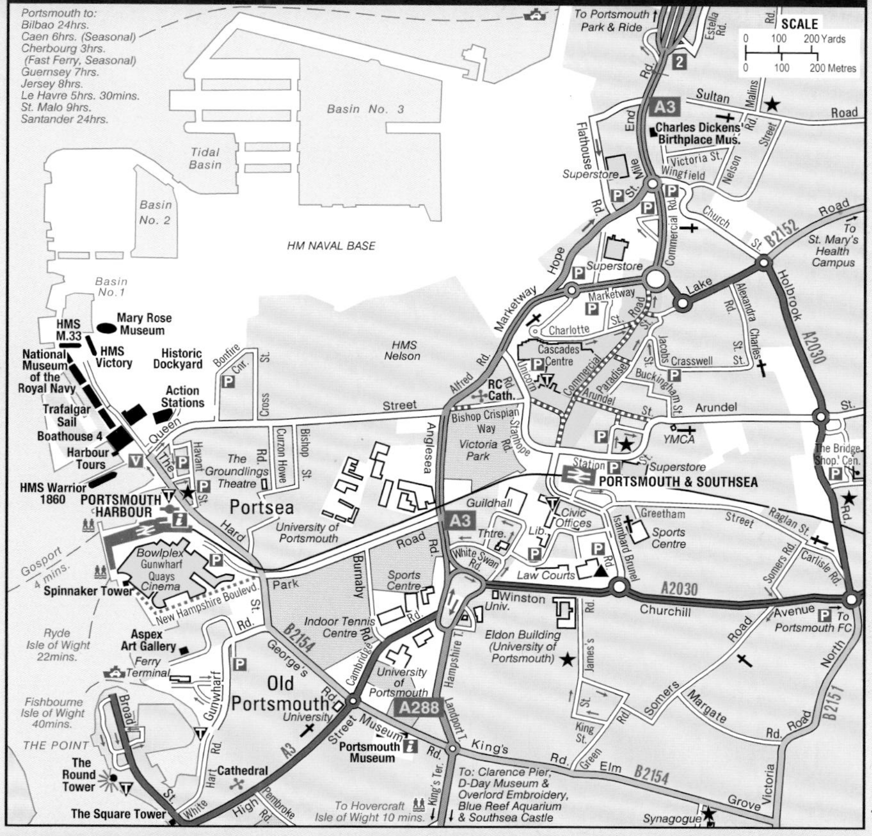


## PRESTON

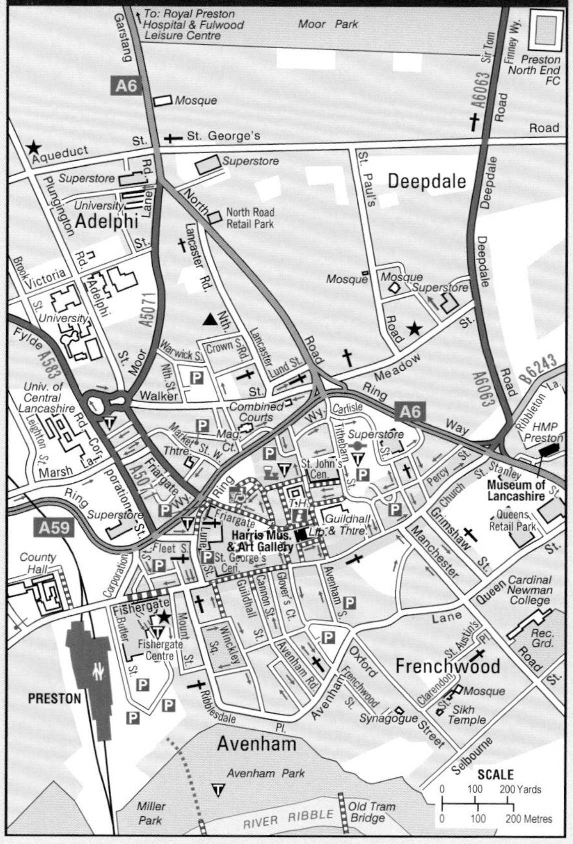


## READING

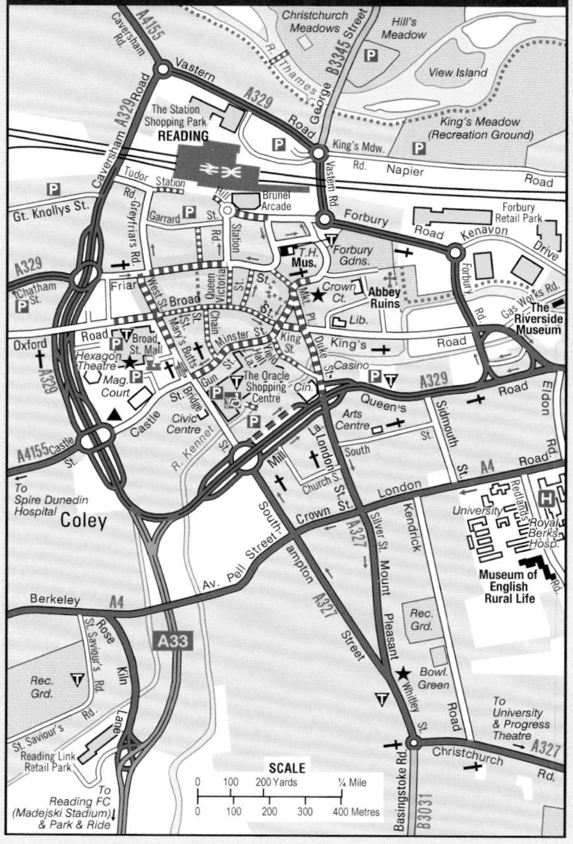


## SALISBURY

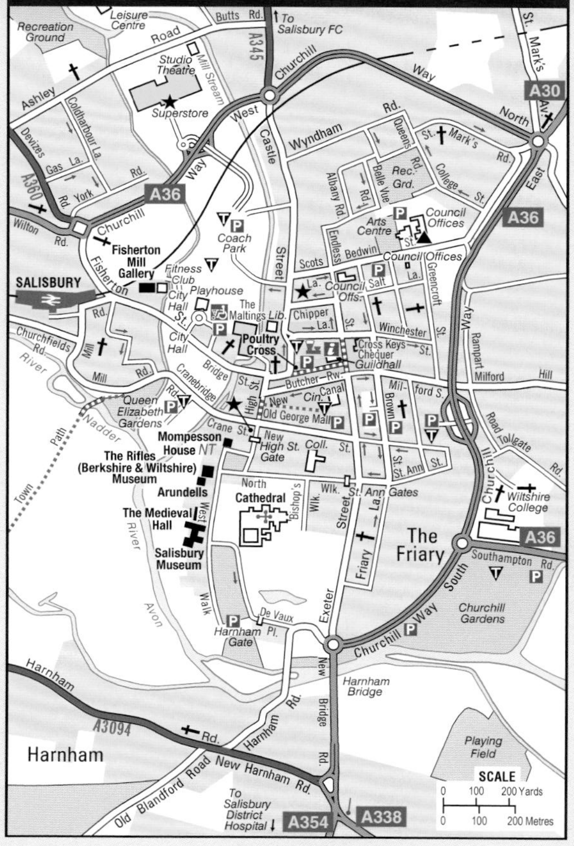

## SHEFFIELD

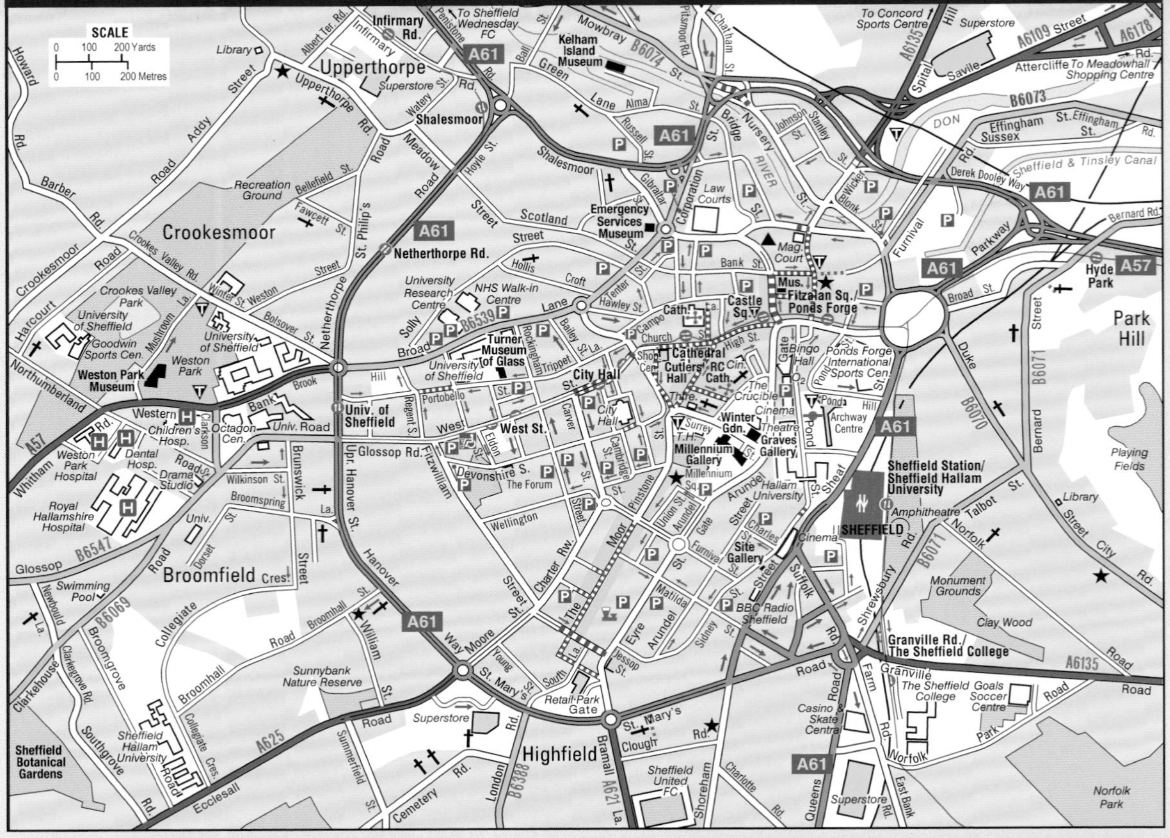


## SHREWSBURY

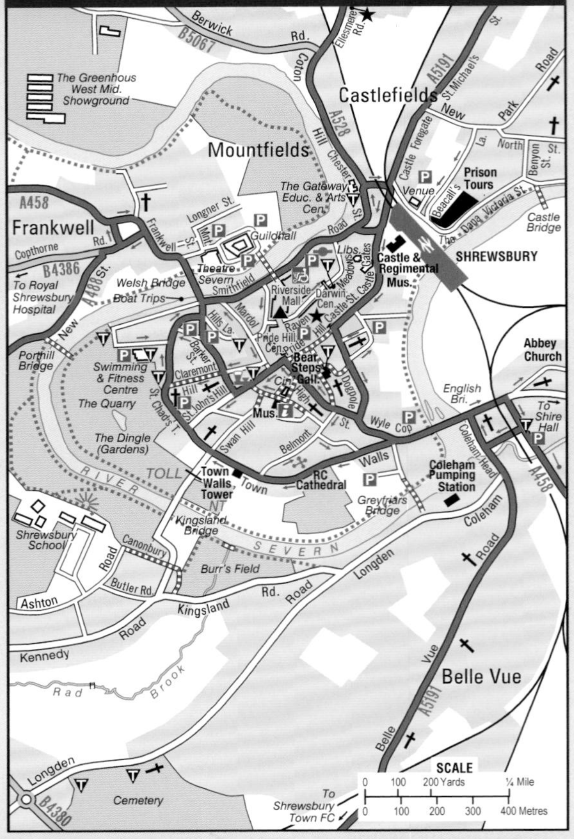


## SOUTHAMPTON

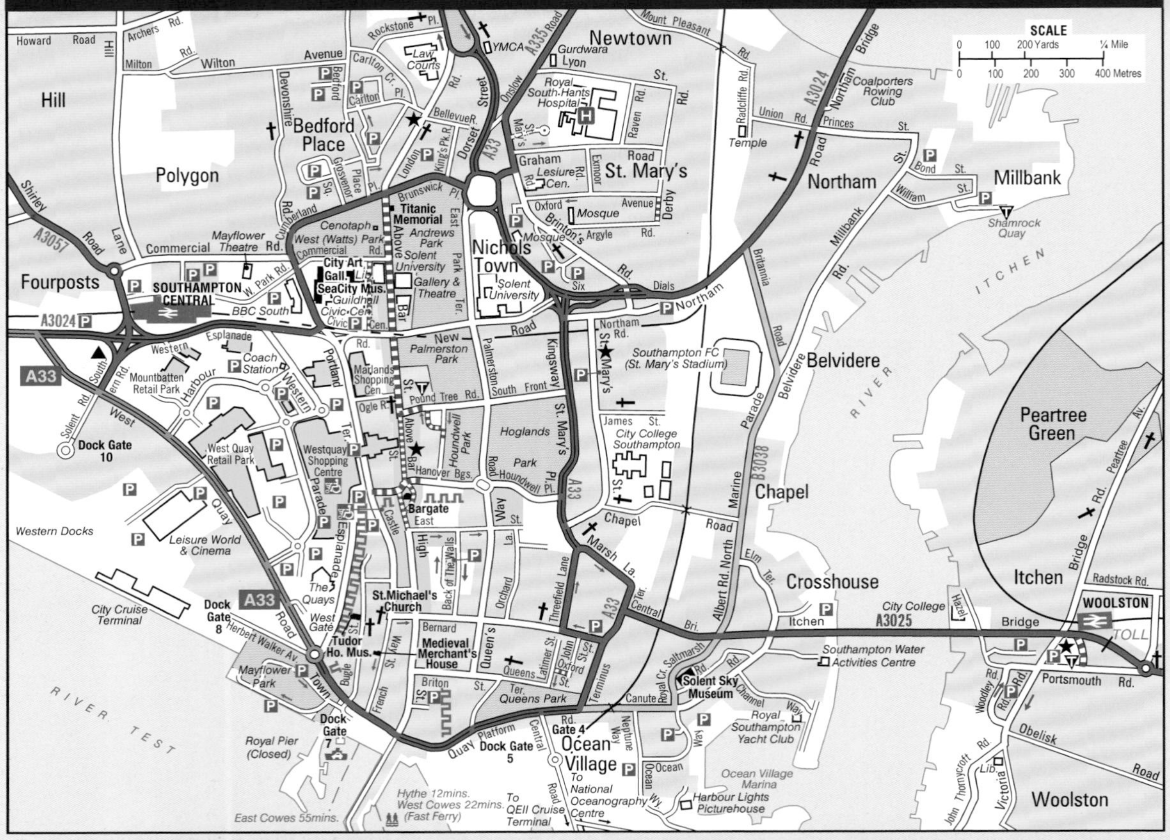


## STIRLING

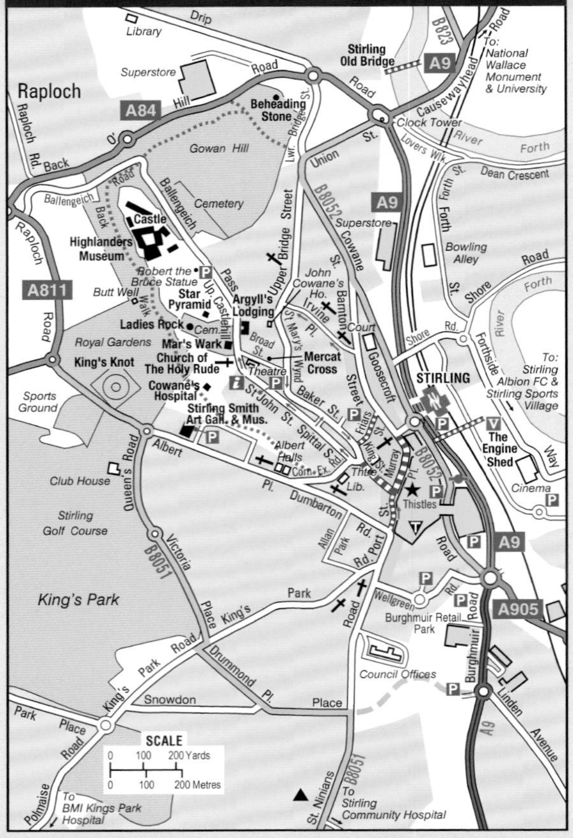


## STOKE-ON-TRENT

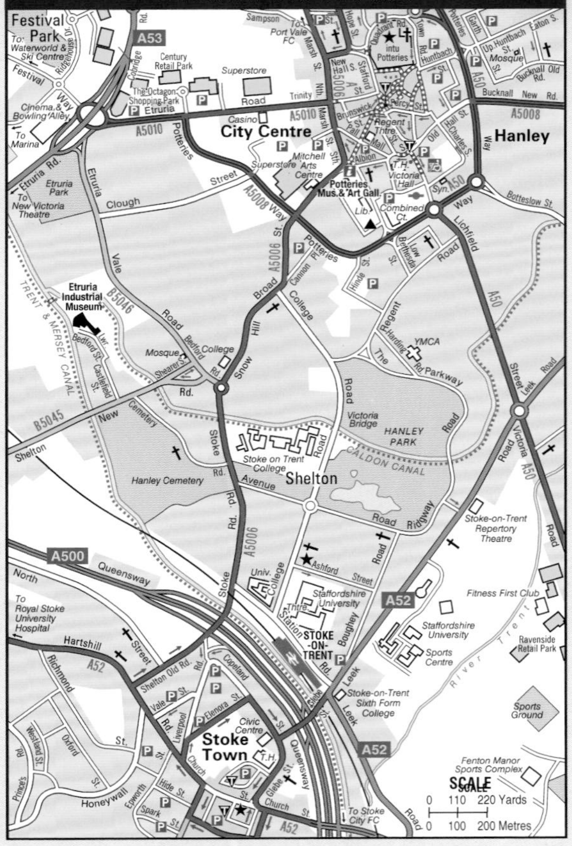


## STRATFORD UPON AVON

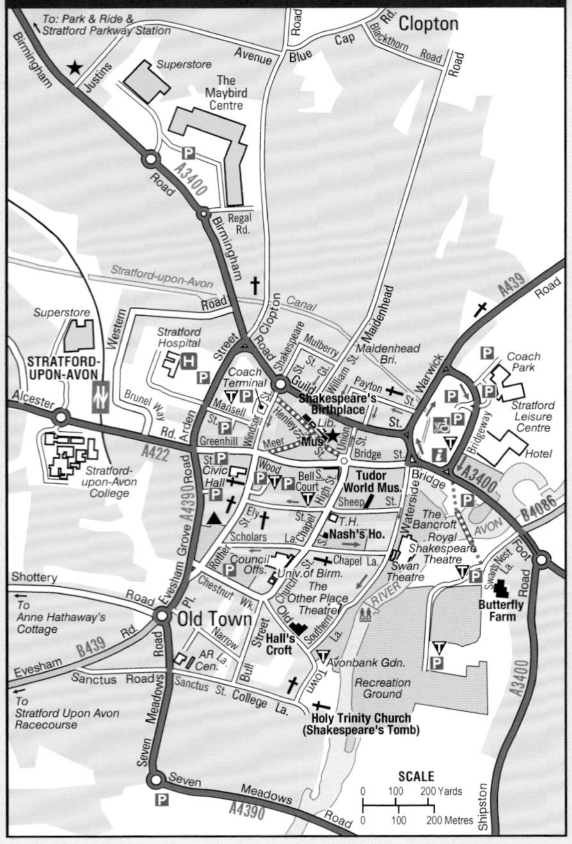


## SUNDERLAND

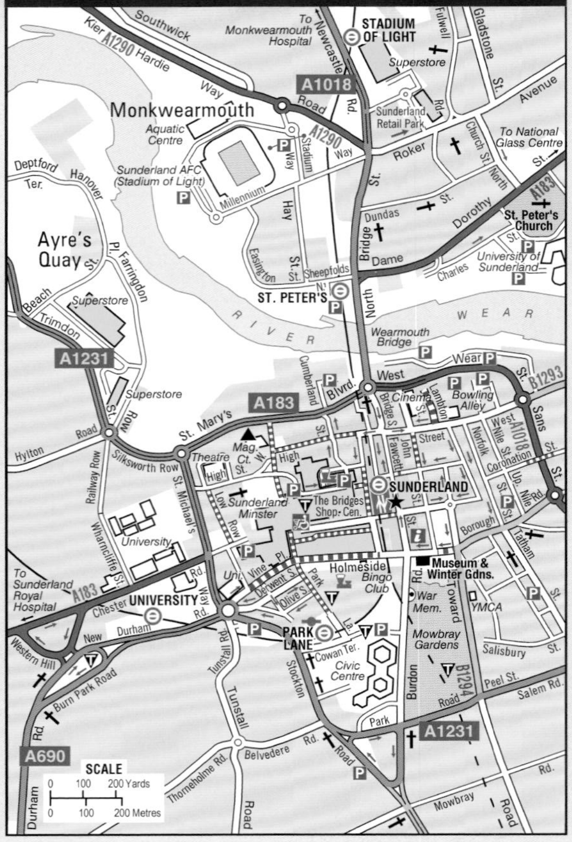

## SWANSEA (ABERTAWE)

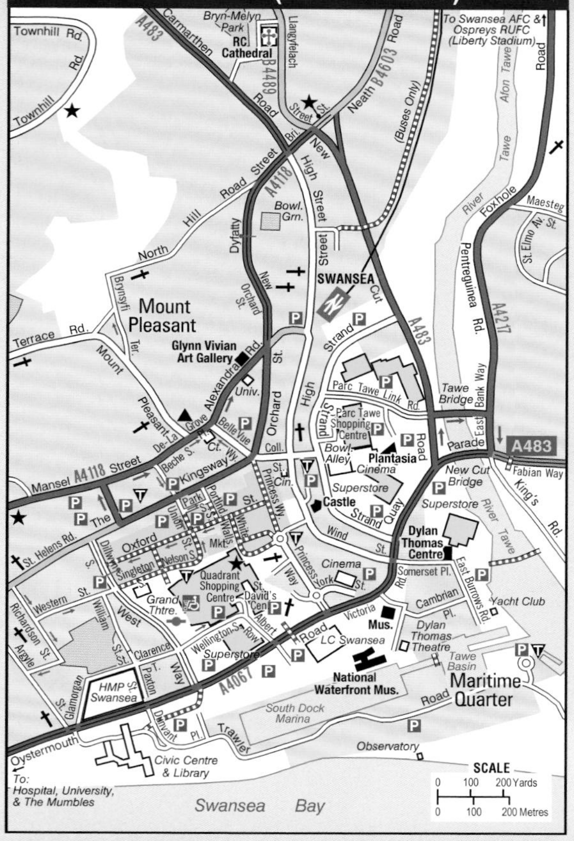


## SWINDON

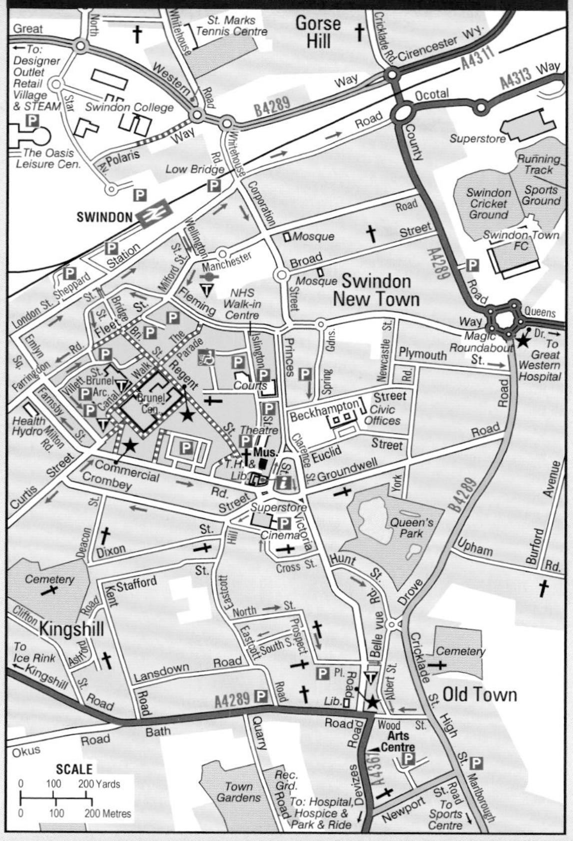


## TAUNTON

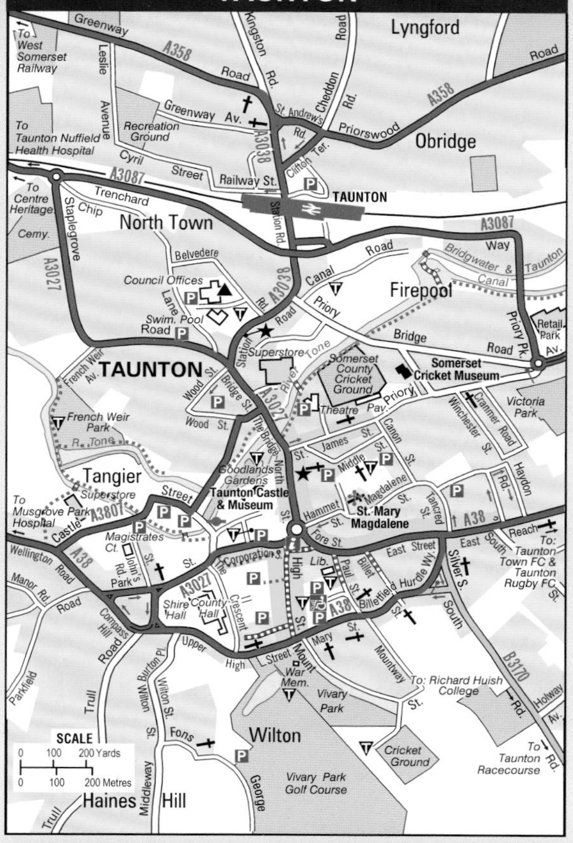


## WINCHESTER

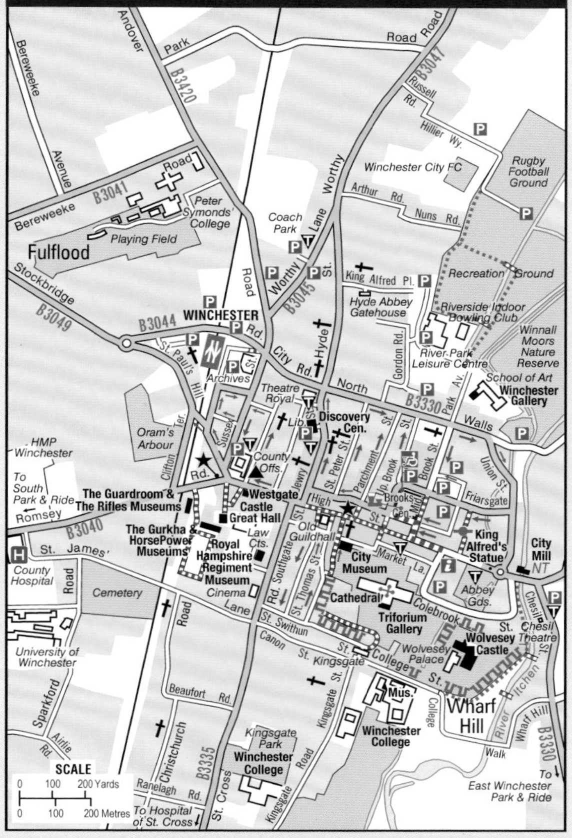


## WINDSOR

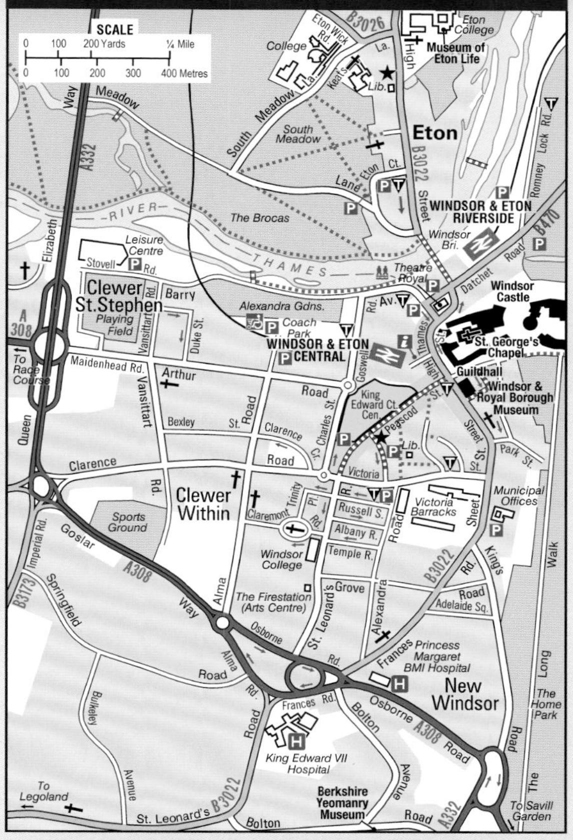


## WOLVERHAMPTON

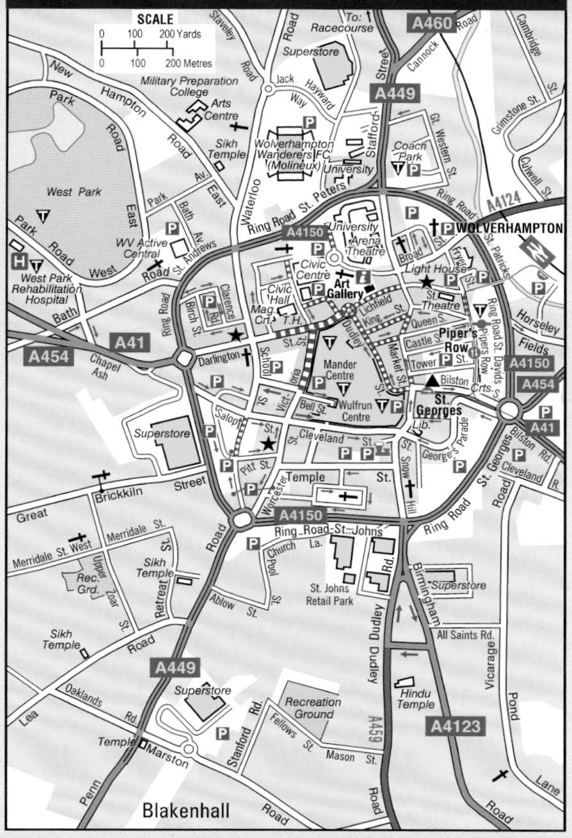


## WORCESTER

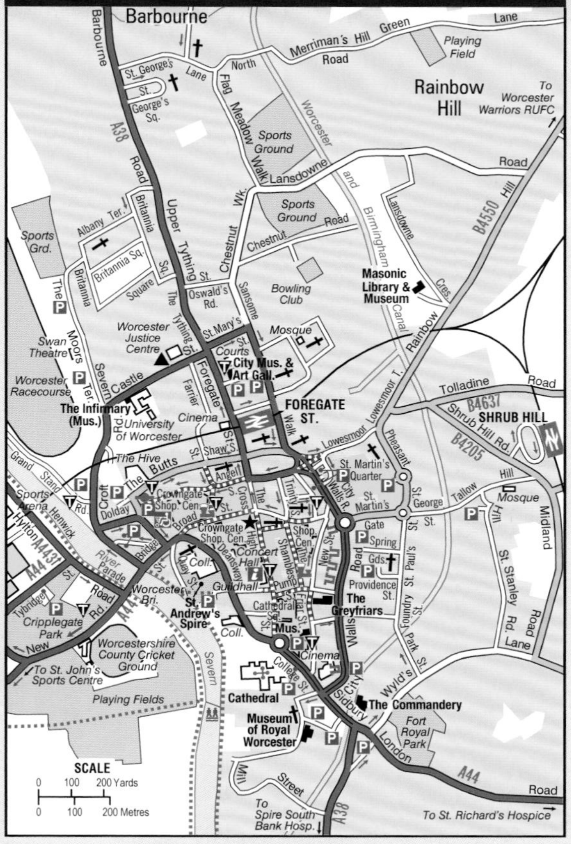


## YORK

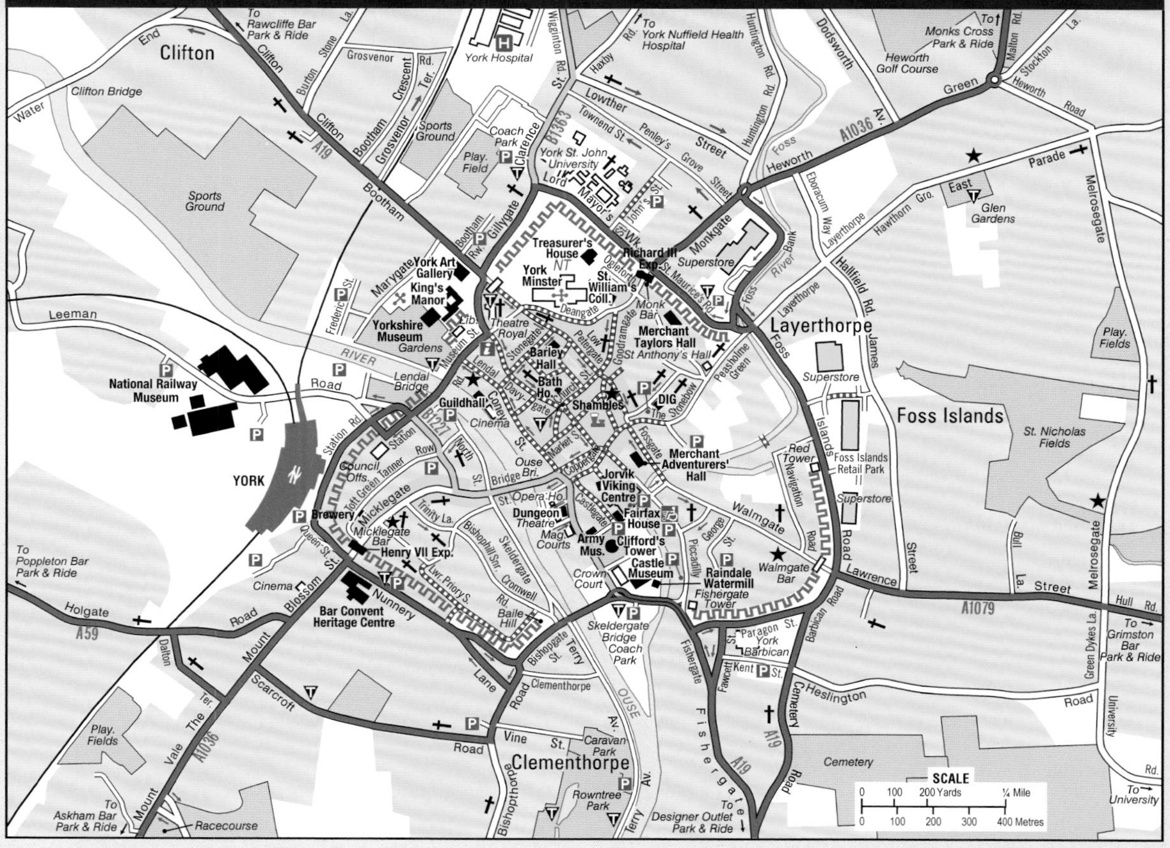

# PORT PLANS

## HARWICH

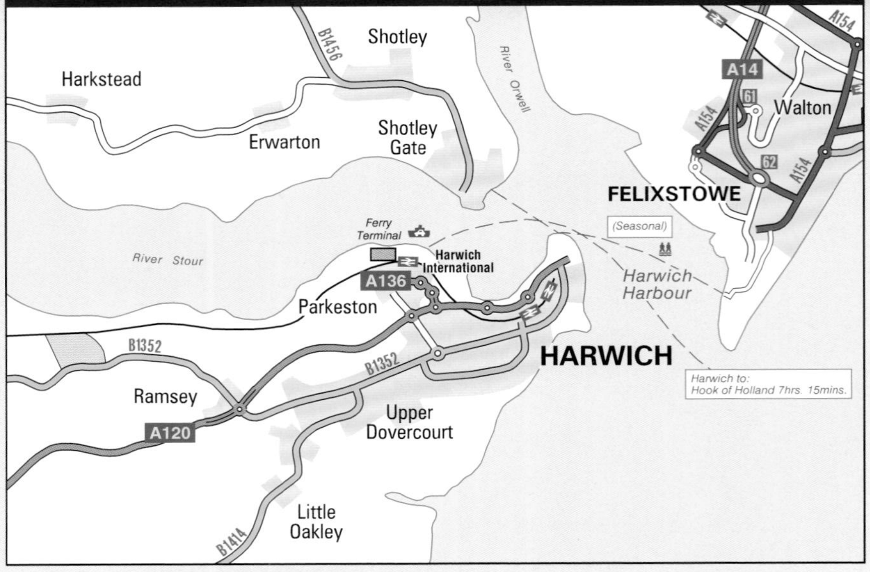


## KINGSTON UPON HULL

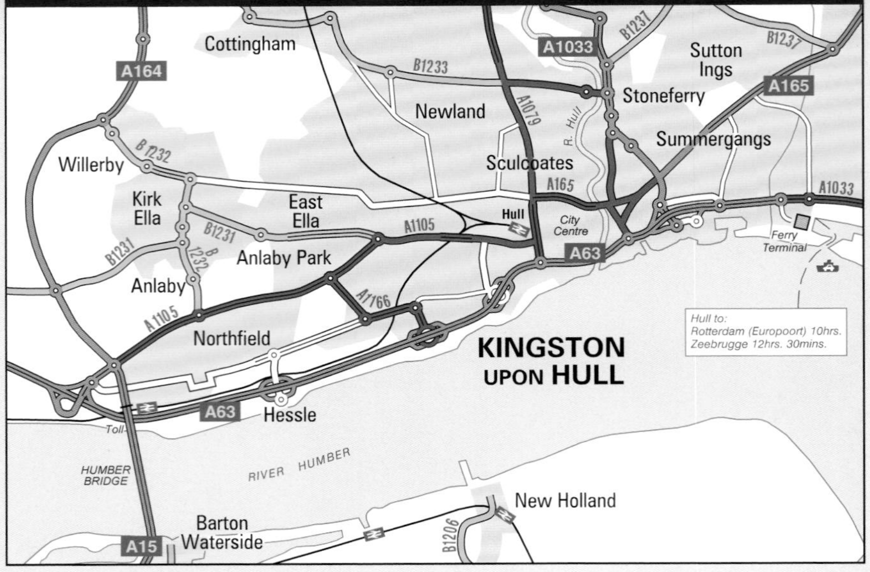


## NEWCASTLE UPON TYNE

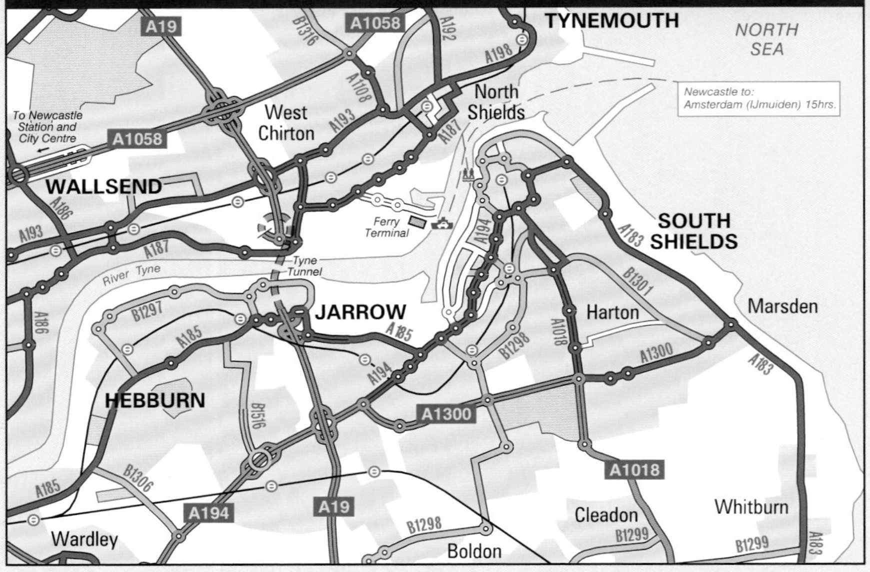


## NEWHAVEN

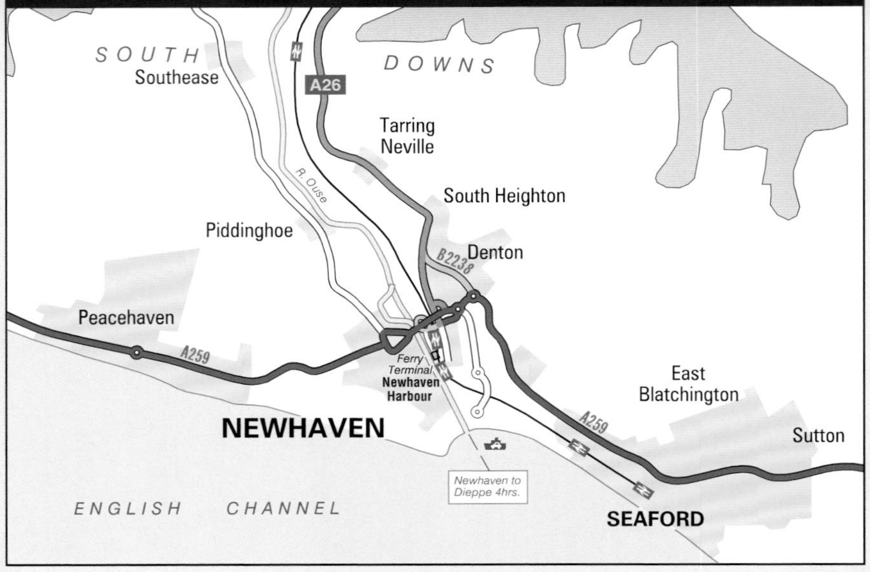


## PEMBROKE DOCK (DOC PENFRO)

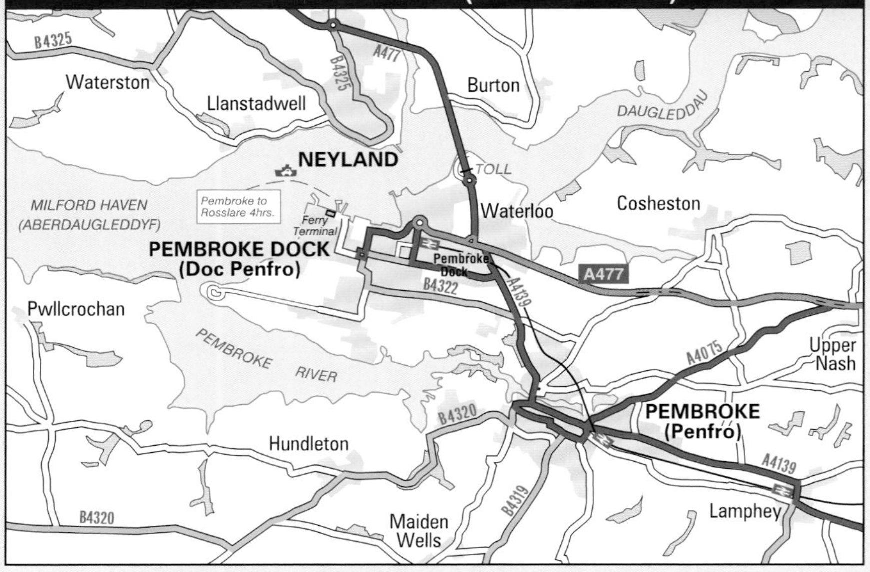


## POOLE

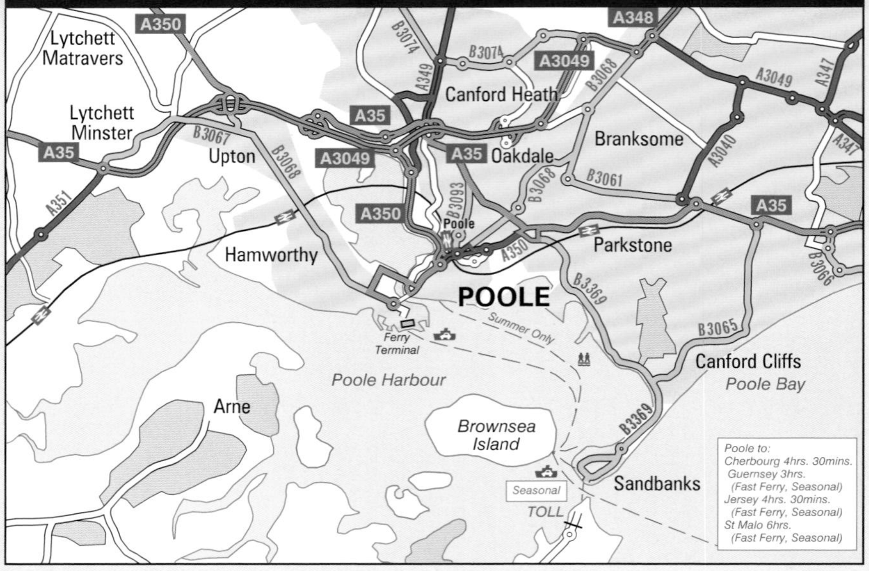


## PORTSMOUTH

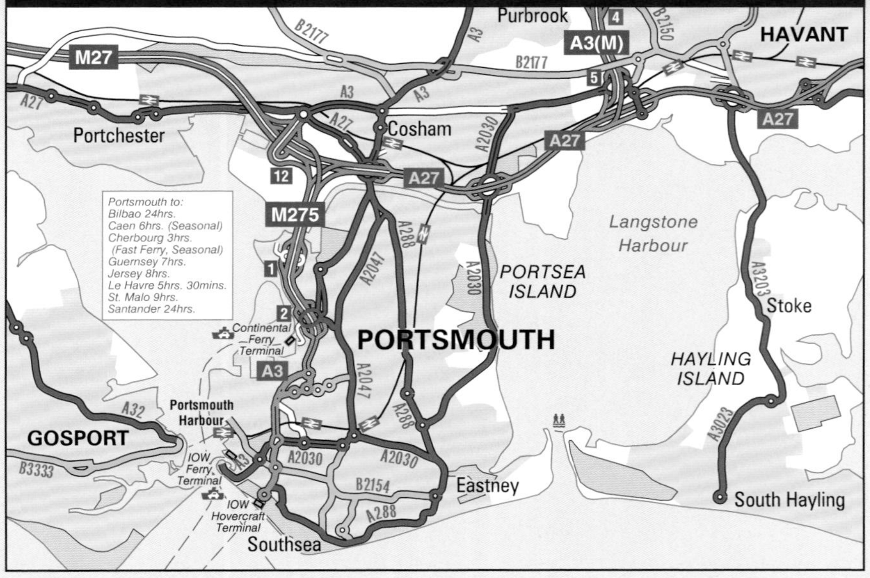


## Other Port Plans

**Please refer to Town Plans for detailed plans of the following Ports:**

**Dover - page 108**

**Plymouth - page 115**

**Southampton - page 116**

# AIRPORT PLANS

## BIRMINGHAM

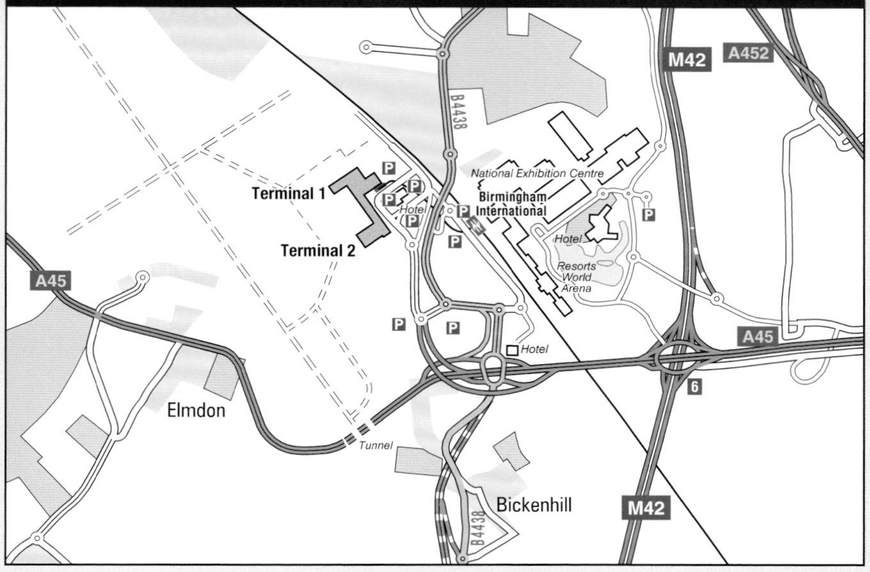


## EAST MIDLANDS

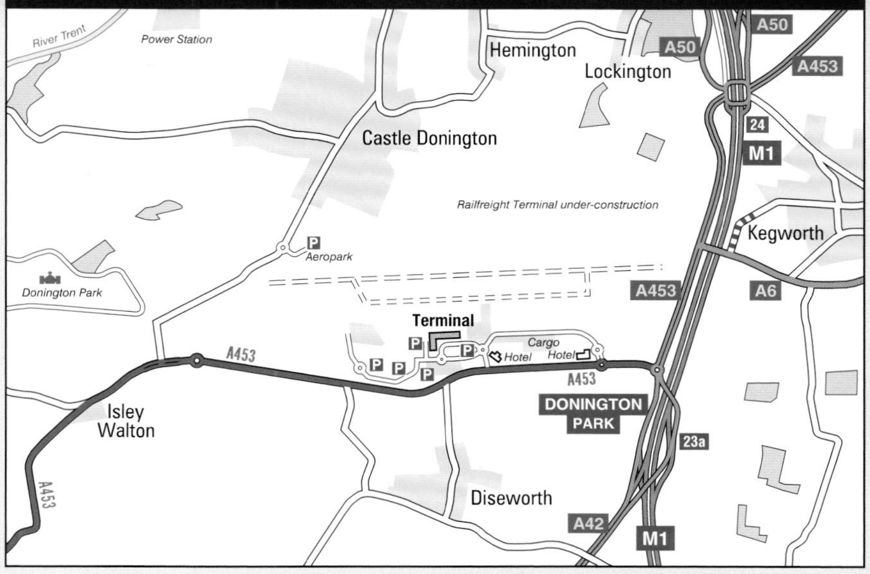


## GLASGOW

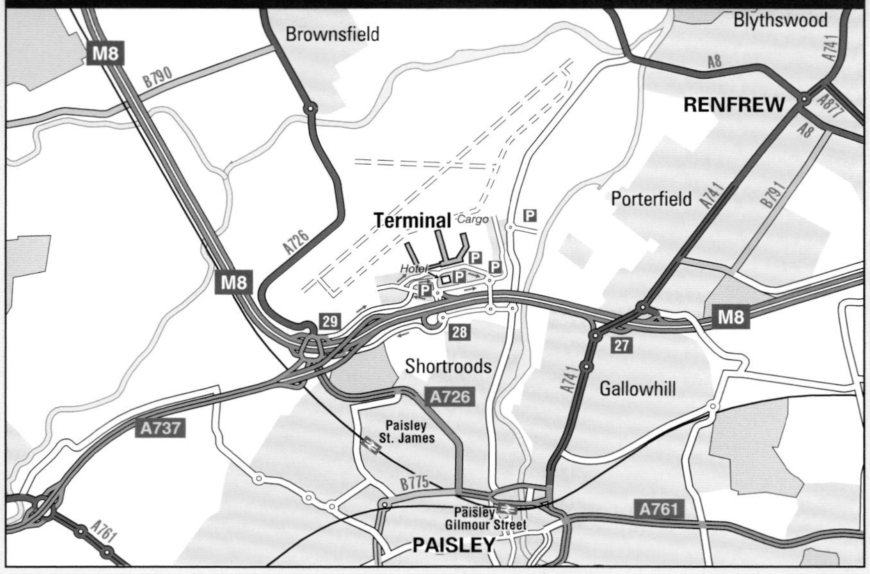


## LONDON GATWICK

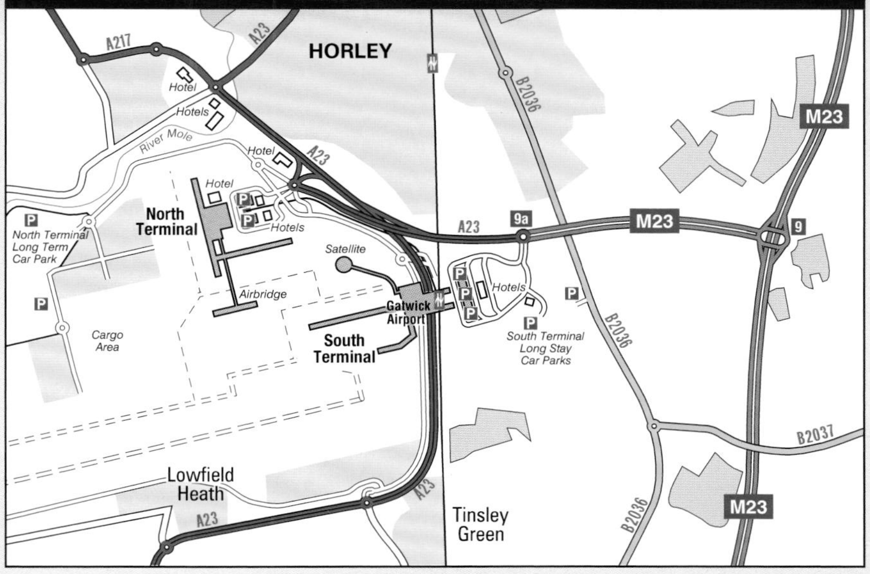


## LONDON HEATHROW

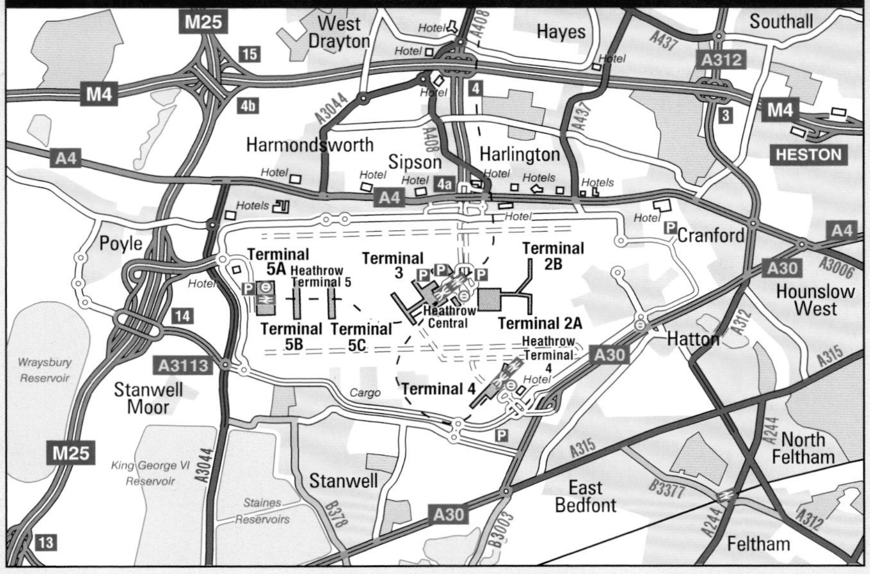


## LONDON LUTON

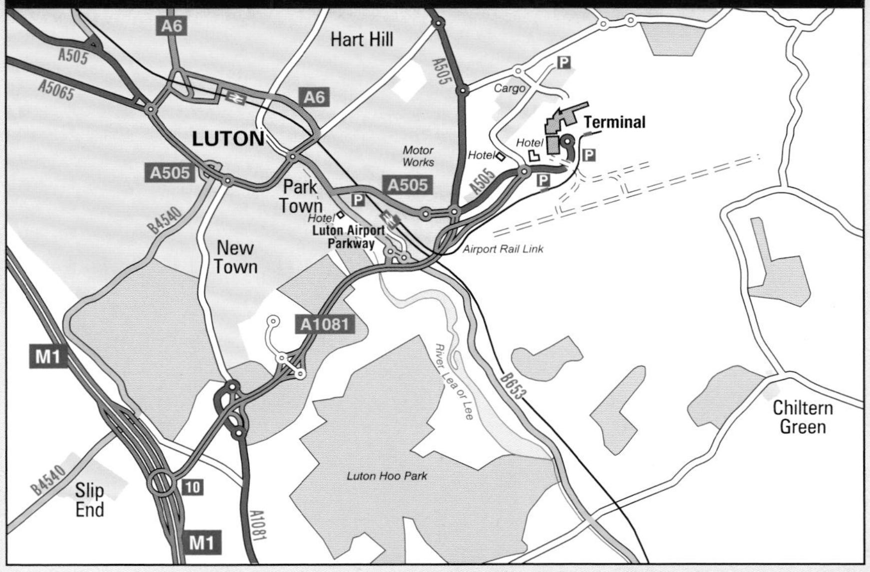


## LONDON STANSTED

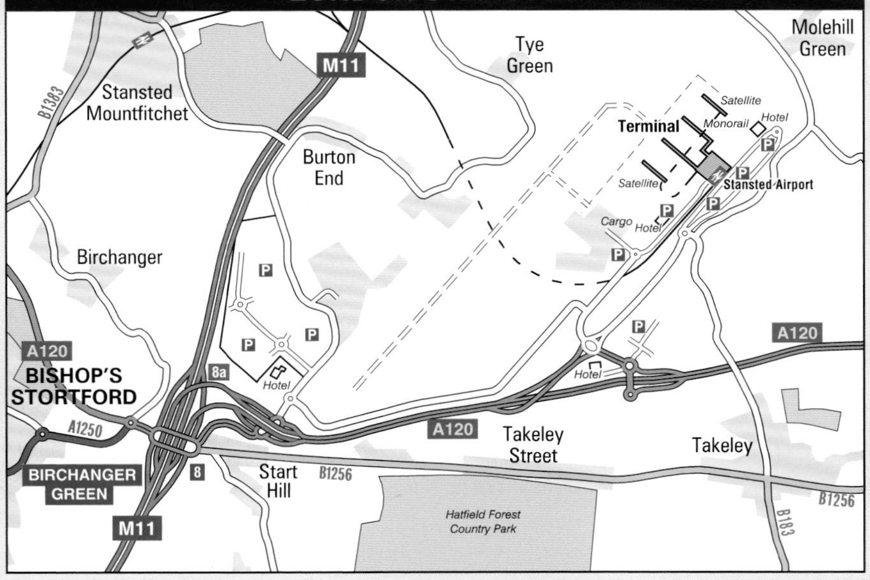


## MANCHESTER

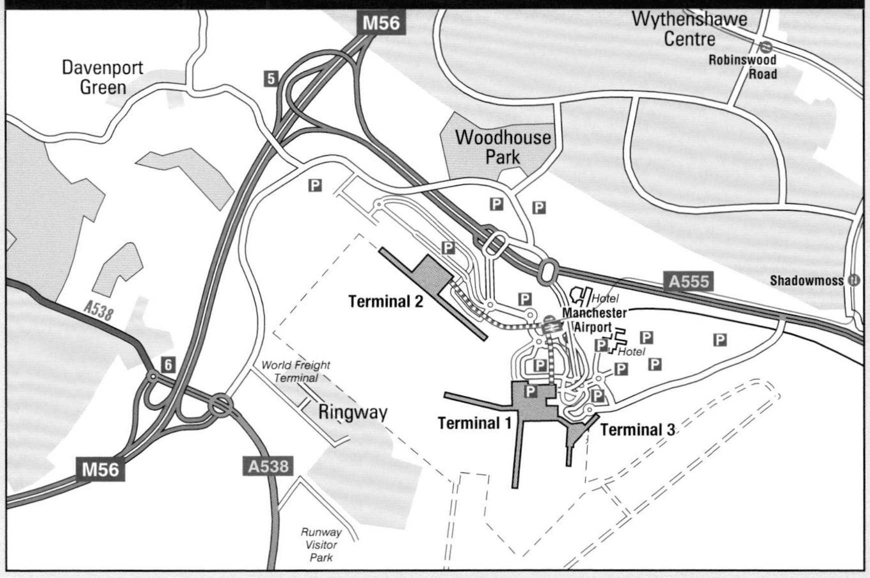

# INDEX TO CITIES, TOWNS, VILLAGES, HAMLETS, LOCATIONS, AIRPORTS & PORTS

(1) A strict alphabetical order is used e.g. An Dùnan follows Andreas but precedes Andwell.

(2) The map reference given refers to the actual map square in which the town spot or built-up area is located and not to the place name.

(3) Major towns and destinations are shown in bold, i.e. **Aberdeen**. *Aber* . . . . **106** (5J **73**)
Page references for Town Plan entries are shown first.

(4) Where two or more places of the same name occur in the same County or Unitary Authority, the nearest large town is also given; e.g. Achiemore. *High* nr. Durness . . . . 5F **84** indicates that Achiemore is located in square 5F on page **84** and is situated near Durness in the Unitary Authority of Highland.

(5) Only one reference is given although due to page overlaps the place may appear on more than one page.

## COUNTIES and UNITARY AUTHORITIES with the abbreviations used in this index

Aberdeen : *Aber*
Aberdeenshire : *Abers*
Angus : *Ang*
Antrim & Newtownabbey : *Ant*
Ards & North Down : *Ards*
Argyll & Bute : *Arg*
Armagh, Banbridge & Craigavon : *Arm*
Bath & N E Somerset : *Bath*
Bedford : *Bed*
Belfast : *Bel*
Blackburn with Darwen : *Bkbn*
Blackpool : *Bkpl*
Blaenau Gwent : *Blae*
Bournemouth : *Bour*
Bracknell Forest : *Brac*
Bridgend : *B'end*
Brighton & Hove : *Brig*
Bristol : *Bris*
Buckinghamshire : *Buck*
Caerphilly : *Cphy*
Cambridgeshire : *Cambs*
Cardiff : *Card*
Carmarthenshire : *Carm*
Causeway Coast & Glens : *Caus*
Central Bedfordshire : *C Beds*
Ceredigion : *Cdgn*
Cheshire East : *Ches E*
Cheshire West & Chester : *Ches W*
Clackmannanshire : *Clac*
Conwy : *Cnwy*
Cornwall : *Corn*
Cumbria : *Cumb*
Darlington : *Darl*
Denbighshire : *Den*
Derby : *Derb*
Derbyshire : *Derbs*
Derry & Strabane : *Derr*
Devon : *Devn*
Dorset : *Dors*
Dumfries & Galloway : *Dum*
Dundee : *D'dee*
Durham : *Dur*
East Ayrshire : *E Ayr*
East Dunbartonshire : *E Dun*
East Lothian : *E Lot*
East Renfrewshire : *E Ren*
East Riding of Yorkshire : *E Yor*
East Sussex : *E Sus*
Edinburgh : *Edin*
Essex : *Essx*
Falkirk : *Falk*
Fermanagh & Omagh : *Ferm*
Fife : *Fife*
Flintshire : *Flin*
Glasgow : *Glas*
Gloucestershire : *Glos*
Greater London : *G Lon*
Greater Manchester : *G Man*
Gwynedd : *Gwyn*
Halton : *Hal*
Hampshire : *Hants*
Hartlepool : *Hart*
Herefordshire : *Here*
Hertfordshire : *Herts*
Highland : *High*
Inverclyde : *Inv*
Isle of Anglesey : *IOA*
Isle of Man : *IOM*
Isle of Wight : *IOW*
Isles of Scilly : *IOS*
Kent : *Kent*
Kingston upon Hull : *Hull*
Lancashire : *Lanc*
Leicester : *Leic*
Leicestershire : *Leics*
Lincolnshire : *Linc*
Lisburn & Castlereagh : *Lis*
Luton : *Lutn*
Medway : *Medw*
Merseyside : *Mers*
Merthyr Tydfil : *Mer T*
Mid & East Antrim : *ME Ant*
Middlesbrough : *Midd*
Midlothian : *Midl*
Mid Ulster : *M Ulst*
Milton Keynes : *Mil*
Monmouthshire : *Mon*
Moray : *Mor*
Neath Port Talbot : *Neat*
Newport : *Newp*
Newry, Mourne & Down : *New M*
Norfolk : *Norf*
Northamptonshire : *Nptn*
North Ayrshire : *N Ayr*
North East Lincolnshire : *NE Lin*
North Lanarkshire : *N Lan*
North Lincolnshire : *N Lin*
North Somerset : *N Som*
Northumberland : *Nmbd*
North Yorkshire : *N Yor*
Nottingham : *Nott*
Nottinghamshire : *Notts*
Orkney : *Orkn*
Oxfordshire : *Oxon*
Pembrokeshire : *Pemb*
Perth & Kinross : *Per*
Peterborough : *Pet*
Plymouth : *Plym*
Poole : *Pool*
Portsmouth : *Port*
Powys : *Powy*
Reading : *Read*
Redcar & Cleveland : *Red C*
Renfrewshire : *Ren*
Rhondda Cynon Taff : *Rhon*
Rutland : *Rut*
Scottish Borders : *Bord*
Shetland : *Shet*
Shropshire : *Shrp*
Slough : *Slo*
Somerset : *Som*
Southampton : *Sotn*
South Ayrshire : *S Ayr*
Southend-on-Sea : *S'end*
South Gloucestershire : *S Glo*
South Lanarkshire : *S Lan*
South Yorkshire : *S Yor*
Staffordshire : *Staf*
Stirling : *Stir*
Stockton-on-Tees : *Stoc T*
Stoke-on-Trent : *Stoke*
Suffolk : *Suff*
Surrey : *Surr*
Swansea : *Swan*
Swindon : *Swin*
Telford & Wrekin : *Telf*
Thurrock : *Thur*
Torbay : *Torb*
Torfaen : *Torf*
Tyne & Wear : *Tyne*
Vale of Glamorgan, The : *V Glam*
Warrington : *Warr*
Warwickshire : *Warw*
West Berkshire : *W Ber*
West Dunbartonshire : *W Dun*
Western Isles : *W Isl*
West Lothian : *W Lot*
West Midlands : *W Mid*
West Sussex : *W Sus*
West Yorkshire : *W Yor*
Wiltshire : *Wilts*
Windsor & Maidenhead : *Wind*
Wokingham : *Wok*
Worcestershire : *Worc*
Wrexham : *Wrex*
York : *York*

## INDEX

### A


Abbas Combe. *Som* 3F **8**
Abberley. *Worc* 5F **26**
Abberley Common. *Worc* 5F **26**
Abberton. *Essx* 2G **23**
Abberton. *Worc* 6H **27**
Abberwick. *Nmbd* 8J **61**
Abbess Roding. *Essx* 2B **22**
Abbey. *Devn* 4L **7**
Abbey-cwm-hir. *Powy* 5K **25**
Abbeydale. *S Yor* 1M **35**
Abbeydale Park. *S Yor* 1M **35**
Abbey Dore. *Here* 8B **26**
Abbey Gate. *Devn* 6A **8**
Abbey Hulton. *Stoke* 5H **35**
Abbey St Bathans. *Bord* 3E **60**
Abbeystead. *Lanc* 2D **40**
Abbeytown. *Cumb* 6F **52**
Abbey Village. *Lanc* 5E **40**
Abbey Wood. *G Lon* 6A **22**
Abbots Bickington. *Devn* 4C **6**
Abbots Bromley. *Staf* 7J **35**
Abbotsbury. *Dors* 7D **8**
Abbotsham. *Devn* 3D **6**
Abbotskerswell. *Devn* 5L **5**
Abbots Langley. *Herts* 3H **21**
Abbots Leigh. *N Som* 6D **18**
Abbotsley. *Cambs* 6K **29**
Abbots Morton. *Worc* 6J **27**
Abbots Ripton. *Cambs* 4K **29**
Abbot's Salford. *Warw* 6J **27**
Abbotstone. *Hants* 2C **10**
Abbots Worthy. *Hants* 2B **10**
Abbotts Ann. *Hants* 1M **9**
Abcott. *Shrp* 4B **26**
Abdon. *Shrp* 3D **26**
Abenhall. *Glos* 2E **18**
Aber. *Cdgn* 2L **15**
Aberaeron. *Cdgn* 6D **24**
Aberafan. *Neat* 5G **17**
Aberaman. *Rhon* 4K **17**
Aberangell. *Gwyn* 1H **25**
Aberarad. *Carm* 3K **15**
Aberarder. *High* 3G **71**
Aberargie. *Per* 6E **66**
Aberarth. *Cdgn* 6D **24**
Aberavon. *Neat* 5G **17**
Aber-banc. *Cdgn* 2K **15**
Aberbargoed. *Cphy* 5L **17**
Aberbechan. *Powy* 4L **25**
Aberbeeg. *Blae* 4M **17**
Aberbowlan. *Carm* 1F **16**
Aberbran. *Powy* 2J **17**
Abercanaid. *Mer T* 4K **17**
Abercarn. *Cphy* 5M **17**
Abercastle. *Pemb* 3E **14**
Abercegir. *Powy* 2H **25**
Aberchalder. *High* 5D **70**
Aberchirder. *Abers* 8F **80**
Aberchwiler. *Den* 4K **33**
Abercorn. *W Lot* 2J **59**
Abercraf. *Powy* 3H **17**
Abercregan. *Neat* 5H **17**
Abercrombie. *Fife* 7J **67**
Abercwmboi. *Rhon* 5K **17**
Abercych. *Pemb* 2J **15**
**Abercynon**. *Rhon* 5K **17**
Aber-Cywarch. *Gwyn* 1H **25**
Aberdalgie. *Per* 5D **66**
**Aberdar**. *Rhon* 4J **17**
**Aberdare**. *Rhon* 4J **17**
Aberdaron. *Gwyn* 8A **32**
**Aberdaugleddau**. *Pemb* 6F **14**
**Aberdeen**. *Aber* **106** (5J **73**)
Aberdeen International Airport. *Aber* 4H **73**
Aberdesach. *Gwyn* 5D **32**
Aberdour. *Fife* 1K **59**
Aberdovey. *Gwyn* 3F **24**
Aberdulais. *Neat* 4G **17**
Aberdyfi. *Gwyn* 3F **24**
Aberedw. *Powy* 8K **25**
Abereiddy. *Pemb* 3D **14**
Abererch. *Gwyn* 7C **32**
Aberfan. *Mer T* 4K **17**
Aberfeldy. *Per* 3B **66**
Aberffraw. *IOA* 4C **32**
Aberffrwd. *Cdgn* 5F **24**
Aberford. *W Yor* 4B **42**
Aberfoyle. *Stir* 7K **65**
Abergarw. *B'end* 6J **17**
Abergarwed. *Neat* 4H **17**
**Abergavenny**. *Mon* 2B **18**
Abergele. *Cnwy* 3J **33**
Aber-Giâr. *Carm* 2M **15**
Abergorlech. *Carm* 1E **16**
Abergwaun. *Pemb* 3F **14**
Abergwesyn. *Powy* 7H **25**
Abergwili. *Carm* 4L **15**
Abergwynfi. *Neat* 5H **17**
Abergwyngregyn. *Gwyn* 3F **32**
Abergynolwyn. *Gwyn* 2F **24**
Aberhafesp. *Powy* 3K **25**
Aberhonddu. *Powy* 2K **17**
Aberhosan. *Powy* 3H **25**
Aberkenfig. *B'end* 6H **17**
Aberlady. *E Lot* 1B **60**
Aberlemno. *Ang* 2J **67**
Aberllefenni. *Gwyn* 2G **25**
Abermaw. *Gwyn* 1F **24**
Abermeurig. *Cdgn* 7E **24**
Aber-miwl. *Powy* 3L **25**
Abermule. *Powy* 3L **25**
Abernant. *Carm* 4K **15**
Abernant. *Rhon* 4K **17**
Abernethy. *Per* 6E **66**
Abernyte. *Per* 4F **66**
Aber-oer. *Wrex* 5A **34**
**Aberpennar**. *Rhon* 5K **17**
Aberporth. *Cdgn* 1J **15**
Aberriw. *Powy* 2L **25**
Abersoch. *Gwyn* 8C **32**
Abersychan. *Torf* 3A **18**
**Abertawe**. *Swan* **117** (5F **16**)
Aberteifi. *Cdgn* 2H **15**
Aberthin. *V Glam* 7K **17**
**Abertillery**. *Blae* 4M **17**
Abertridwr. *Cphy* 6L **17**
**Abertyleri**. *Blae* 4M **17**
Abertysswg. *Cphy* 4L **17**
Aberuthven. *Per* 6C **66**
Aber Village. *Powy* 2L **17**
Aberwheeler. *Den* 4K **33**
Aberyscir. *Powy* 2J **17**
**Aberystwyth**. *Cdgn* 4E **24**
Abhainn Suidhe. *W Isl* 3B **76**
**Abingdon-on-Thames**. *Oxon* 4B **20**
Abinger Common. *Surr* 1J **11**
Abinger Hammer. *Surr* 1H **11**
Abington. *S Lan* 7H **59**
Abington Pigotts. *Cambs* 7L **29**
Ab Kettleby. *Leics* 7E **36**
Ab Lench. *Worc* 6J **27**
Ablington. *Glos* 3K **19**
Ablington. *Wilts* 1K **9**
Abney. *Derbs* 2K **35**
Aboyne. *Abers* 6E **72**
**Abram**. *G Man* 7E **40**
Abriachan. *High* 2F **70**
Abridge. *Essx* 4A **22**
Abronhill. *N Lan* 2F **58**
Abson. *S Glo* 6F **18**
Abthorpe. *Nptn* 7D **28**
Abune-the-Hill. *Orkn* 7B **88**
Aby. *Linc* 2M **37**
Acairseid. *W Isl* 5C **74**
Acaster Malbis. *York* 3C **42**
Acaster Selby. *N Yor* 3C **42**
Accott. *Devn* 2F **6**
**Accrington**. *Lanc* 5F **40**
Acha. *Arg* 2G **63**
Achachork. *High* 1F **68**
Achadh a' Chuirn. *High* 3H **69**
Achahoish. *Arg* 2G **57**
Achaleven. *Arg* 4D **64**
Achallader. *Arg* 3H **65**
Acha Mor. *W Isl* 1E **76**
Achanalt. *High* 7C **78**
Achandunie. *High* 6G **79**
Ach' an Todhair. *High* 8A **70**
Achany. *High* 3F **78**
Achaphubuil. *High* 8A **70**
Acharacle. *High* 1A **64**
Acharn. *Ang* 8B **72**
Acharn. *Per* 3A **66**
Acharole. *High* 6D **86**
Achateny. *High* 1L **63**
Achavanich. *High* 8C **86**
Achdalieu. *High* 8A **70**
Achduart. *High* 3M **77**
Achentoul. *High* 8L **85**
Achfary. *High* 8E **84**
Achfrish. *High* 2F **78**
Achgarve. *High* 4K **77**
Achiemore. *High*
nr. Durness 5F **84**
nr. Thurso 6L **85**
A' Chill. *High* 5D **68**
Achiltibuie. *High* 3M **77**
Achina. *High* 5K **85**
Achinahuagh. *High* 5H **85**
Achindarroch. *High* 2E **64**
Achinduich. *High* 3F **78**
Achinduin. *Arg* 4C **64**
Achininver. *High* 5H **85**
Achintee. *High* 6M **77**
Achintraid. *High* 2K **69**
Achleck. *Arg* 3K **63**
Achlorachan. *High* 8D **78**
Achluachrach. *High* 7C **70**
Achlyness. *High* 6E **84**
Achmelvich. *High* 1A **78**
Achmony. *High* 2F **70**
Achmore. *High*
nr. Stromeferry 2K **69**
nr. Ullapool 4M **77**
Achnacarnin. *High* 8C **84**
Achnacarry. *High* 7B **70**
Achnaclerach. *High* 7E **78**
Achnacloich. *High* 5G **69**
Ach na Cloiche. *High* 5G **69**
Achnaconeran. *High* 4E **70**
Achnacroish. *Arg* 3C **64**
Achnafalnich. *Arg* 5G **65**
Achnagarron. *High* 6G **79**
Achnagoul. *Arg* 7E **64**
Achnaha. *High* 1K **63**
Achnahanat. *High* 4F **78**
Achnahannet. *High* 3K **71**
Achnairn. *High* 2F **78**
Achnamara. *Arg* 1G **57**
Achnanellan. *High* 7A **70**
Achnasheen. *High* 8B **78**
Achnashellach. *High* 1M **69**
Achosnich. *High* 1K **63**
Achow. *High* 8D **86**
Achranich. *High* 3B **64**
Achreamie. *High* 5B **86**
Achriabhach. *High* 1F **64**
Achriesgill. *High* 6E **84**
Achrimsdale. *High* 3K **79**
Achscrabster. *High* 5B **86**
Achtoty. *High* 5J **85**
Achurch. *Nptn* 3H **29**
Achuvoldrach. *High* 6H **85**
Achvaich. *High* 4H **79**
Achvoan. *High* 3H **79**
Ackenthwaite. *Cumb* 7D **46**
Ackergill. *High* 6E **86**
Ackergillshore. *High* 6E **86**
Acklam. *Midd* 4B **48**
Acklam. *N Yor* 1E **42**
Ackleton. *Shrp* 2F **26**
Acklington. *Nmbd* 1F **54**
Ackton. *W Yor* 5B **42**
Ackworth Moor Top. *W Yor* 6B **42**
Acle. *Norf* 8L **39**
Acocks Green. *W Mid* 3K **27**
Acol. *Kent* 7K **23**
Acomb. *Nmbd* 5C **54**
Acomb. *York* 2C **42**
Aconbury. *Here* 8D **26**
Acre. *G Man* 7H **41**
Acre. *Lanc* 5F **40**
Acrefair. *Wrex* 5A **34**
Acrise. *Kent* 1H **13**
Acton. *Arm* 6G **93**
Acton. *Ches E* 4E **34**
Acton. *Dors* 8H **9**
**Acton**. *G Lon* 5J **21**
Acton. *Shrp* 3B **26**
Acton. *Staf* 5G **35**
Acton. *Suff* 7E **30**
Acton. *Worc* 5G **27**
Acton. *Wrex* 4B **34**
Acton Beauchamp. *Here* 6E **26**
Acton Bridge. *Ches W* 2D **34**
Acton Burnell. *Shrp* 1D **26**
Acton Green. *Here* 6E **26**
Acton Pigott. *Shrp* 1D **26**
Acton Round. *Shrp* 2E **26**
Acton Scott. *Shrp* 3C **26**
Acton Trussell. *Staf* 8H **35**
Acton Turville. *S Glo* 5G **19**
Adabroc. *W Isl* 5J **83**
Adam's Hill. *Worc* 4H **27**
Adbaston. *Staf* 7F **34**
Adber. *Dors* 3E **8**
Adderbury. *Oxon* 8B **28**
Adderley. *Shrp* 6E **34**
Adderstone. *Nmbd* 6J **61**
Addiewell. *W Lot* 3H **59**
Addingham. *W Yor* 3J **41**
Addington. *Buck* 1E **20**
Addington. *G Lon* 7L **21**
Addington. *Kent* 8C **22**
Addinston. *Bord* 4C **60**
Addiscombe. *G Lon* 7L **21**
**Addlestone**. *Surr* 7H **21**
Addlethorpe. *Linc* 3B **38**
Adeney. *Telf* 8F **34**
Adfa. *Powy* 2K **25**
Adforton. *Here* 4C **26**
Adgestone. *IOW* 7C **10**
Adisham. *Kent* 8J **23**
Adlestrop. *Glos* 1L **19**
Adlingfleet. *E Yor* 5F **42**
Adlington. *Ches E* 1H **35**
Adlington. *Lanc* 6E **40**
Admaston. *Staf* 7J **35**
Admaston. *Telf* 8E **34**
Admington. *Warw* 7L **27**
Adpar. *Cdgn* 2K **15**
Adsborough. *Som* 3A **8**
Adstock. *Buck* 8E **28**
Adstone. *Nptn* 6C **28**
Adversane. *W Sus* 3H **11**
Advie. *High* 2M **71**
Adwalton. *W Yor* 5L **41**
Adwell. *Oxon* 4D **20**
**Adwick le Street**. *S Yor* 7C **42**
Adwick upon Dearne. *S Yor* 7B **42**
Adziel. *Abers* 8J **81**
Ae. *Dum* 3D **52**
Affleck. *Abers* 3H **73**
Affpuddle. *Dors* 6G **9**
Affric Lodge. *High* 3B **70**
Afon-wen. *Flin* 3L **33**
Agglethorpe. *N Yor* 7J **47**
Aghagallon. *Arm* 5G **93**
Aghalee. *Lis* 5G **93**
Aglionby. *Cumb* 6J **53**
Ahoghill. *ME Ant* 3G **93**
Aigburth. *Mers* 1B **34**
Aiginis. *W Isl* 8H **83**
Aike. *E Yor* 3H **43**
Aikers. *Orkn* 2F **86**
Aiketgate. *Cumb* 7J **53**
Aikhead. *Cumb* 7G **53**
Aikton. *Cumb* 6G **53**
Ailey. *Here* 7B **26**
Ailsworth. *Pet* 2J **29**
Ainderby Quernhow. *N Yor* 7M **47**
Ainderby Steeple. *N Yor* 6M **47**
Aingers Green. *Essx* 1H **23**
Ainsdale. *Mers* 6B **40**
Ainsdale-on-Sea. *Mers* 6B **40**
Ainstable. *Cumb* 7K **53**
Ainsworth. *G Man* 6F **40**
Ainthorpe. *N Yor* 5E **48**
Aintree. *Mers* 8B **40**
Aird. *Arg* 7B **64**
Aird. *Dum* 5F **50**
Aird. *High*
nr. Port Henderson 6J **77**
nr. Tarskavaig 5G **69**
Aird. *W Isl*
on Benbecula 8J **75**
on Isle of Lewis 8J **83**
The Aird. *High* 8F **76**
Àird a Bhasair. *High* 5H **69**
Aird a Mhachair. *W Isl* 1D **74**
Aird a Mhulaidh. *W Isl* 2C **76**
Aird Asaig. *W Isl* 3C **76**
Aird Dhail. *W Isl* 5H **83**
Airdens. *High* 4G **79**
Aird Mhidhinis. *W Isl* 5D **74**
Aird Mhighe. *W Isl*
nr. Ceann a Bhaigh 4C **76**
nr. Fionnsabhagh 5B **76**
Aird Mhor. *W Isl*
on Barra 5D **74**
on South Uist 1E **74**
**Airdrie**. *N Lan* 3F **58**
Aird Shleibhe. *W Isl* 5C **76**
Aird Thunga. *W Isl* 8H **83**
Aird Uig. *W Isl* 8D **82**
Airedale. *W Yor* 5B **42**
Airidh a Bhruaich. *W Isl* 2D **76**
Airies. *Dum* 5E **50**
Airmyn. *E Yor* 5E **42**
Airntully. *Per* 4D **66**
Airor. *High* 5J **69**
Airth. *Falk* 1H **59**
Airton. *N Yor* 2H **41**
Aisby. *Linc*
nr. Gainsborough 8F **42**
nr. Grantham 6H **37**
Aisgernis. *W Isl* 3D **74**
Aish. *Devn*
nr. Buckfastleigh 6L **5**
nr. Totnes 6L **5**
Aisholt. *Som* 2L **7**
Aiskew. *N Yor* 7L **47**
Aislaby. *N Yor*
nr. Pickering 7E **48**
nr. Whitby 5F **48**
Aislaby. *Stoc T* 4B **48**
Aisthorpe. *Linc* 1G **37**
Aith. *Shet*
on Fetlar 5L **91**
on Mainland 2D **90**
Aithsetter. *Shet* 4E **90**
Akeld. *Nmbd* 7H **61**
Akeley. *Buck* 8E **28**
Akenham. *Suff* 7H **31**
Albaston. *Corn* 8D **6**
Alberbury. *Shrp* 8B **34**
Albert Town. *Pemb* 5F **14**
Albert Village. *Leics* 8M **35**
Albourne. *W Sus* 4K **11**
Albrighton. *Shrp*
nr. Shrewsbury 8C **34**
nr. Telford 1G **27**
Alburgh. *Norf* 3J **31**
Albury. *Herts* 1M **21**
Albury. *Surr* 1H **11**
Albyfield. *Cumb* 7K **53**
Alby Hill. *Norf* 6H **39**
Alcaig. *High* 8F **78**
Alcaston. *Shrp* 3C **26**
Alcester. *Warw* 6J **27**
Alciston. *E Sus* 5B **12**
Alcombe. *Som* 1J **7**
Alconbury. *Cambs* 4J **29**
Alconbury Weston. *Cambs* 4J **29**
Aldborough. *Norf* 6H **39**
Aldborough. *N Yor* 1B **42**
Aldbourne. *Wilts* 6L **19**
Aldbrough. *E Yor* 4K **43**
Aldbrough St John. *N Yor* 4L **47**
Aldbury. *Herts* 2G **21**
Aldcliffe. *Lanc* 1C **40**
Aldclune. *Per* 1C **66**
Aldeburgh. *Suff* 6L **31**
Aldeby. *Norf* 2L **31**
Aldenham. *Herts* 4J **21**
Alderbury. *Wilts* 3K **9**
Aldercar. *Derbs* 5B **36**
Alderford. *Norf* 8H **39**
Alderholt. *Dors* 4K **9**
Alderley. *Glos* 4F **18**
Alderley Edge. *Ches E* 2G **35**
Aldermaston. *W Ber* 7C **20**
Aldermaston Soke. *Hants* 7D **20**
Aldermaston Wharf. *W Ber* 7D **20**
Alderminster. *Warw* 7L **27**
Alder Moor. *Staf* 7L **35**
Aldersey Green. *Ches W* 4C **34**
**Aldershot**. *Hants* 8F **20**
Alderton. *Glos* 8J **27**
Alderton. *Nptn* 7E **28**
Alderton. *Shrp* 7C **34**
Alderton. *Suff* 7K **31**
Alderton. *Wilts* 5G **19**
Alderton Fields. *Glos* 8J **27**
Alderwasley. *Derbs* 4M **35**
Aldfield. *N Yor* 1L **41**
Aldford. *Ches W* 4C **34**
Aldgate. *Rut* 1G **29**
Aldham. *Essx* 1F **22**
Aldham. *Suff* 7G **31**
Aldingbourne. *W Sus* 5G **11**
Aldingham. *Cumb* 8A **46**
Aldington. *Kent* 2G **13**
Aldington. *Worc* 7J **27**
Aldington Frith. *Kent* 2G **13**
Aldochlay. *Arg* 8H **65**
Aldon. *Shrp* 4C **26**
Aldoth. *Cumb* 7F **52**
Aldreth. *Cambs* 4M **29**
**Aldridge**. *W Mid* 1J **27**
Aldringham. *Suff* 5L **31**
Aldsworth. *Glos* 2K **19**
Aldsworth. *W Sus* 5E **10**
Aldwark. *Derbs* 4L **35**
Aldwark. *N Yor* 1B **42**
Aldwick. *W Sus* 6G **11**
Aldwincle. *Nptn* 3H **29**
Aldworth. *W Ber* 6C **20**
Alexandria. *W Dun* 1B **58**
Aley. *Som* 2L **7**
Aley Green. *C Beds* 2H **21**
Alfardisworthy. *Devn* 4B **6**
Alfington. *Devn* 6L **7**
Alfold. *Surr* 2H **11**
Alfold Bars. *W Sus* 2H **11**
Alfold Crossways. *Surr* 2H **11**
Alford. *Abers* 4E **72**
Alford. *Linc* 2A **38**
Alford. *Som* 2E **8**
**Alfreton**. *Derbs* 4B **36**
Alfrick. *Worc* 6F **26**
Alfrick Pound. *Worc* 6F **26**
Alfriston. *E Sus* 5B **12**
Algarkirk. *Linc* 6K **37**
Alhampton. *Som* 2E **8**
Aline Lodge. *W Isl* 2C **76**
Alkborough. *N Lin* 5F **42**
Alkerton. *Oxon* 7A **28**
Alkham. *Kent* 1J **13**
Alkington. *Shrp* 6D **34**
Alkmonton. *Derbs* 6L **35**
Alladale Lodge. *High* 5E **78**
Allaleigh. *Devn* 6L **5**
Allanbank. *N Lan* 4G **59**
Allanton. *N Lan* 4G **59**
Allanton. *Bord* 4F **60**
Allaston. *Glos* 3E **18**
Allbrook. *Hants* 3B **10**
All Cannings. *Wilts* 7J **19**
Allendale Town. *Nmbd* 6B **54**
Allen End. *Warw* 2K **27**
Allenheads. *Nmbd* 7B **54**
Allen's Green. *Herts* 2A **22**
Allensmore. *Here* 8C **26**
Allenton. *Derb* 6A **36**
Aller. *Som* 3C **8**
Allerby. *Cumb* 8E **52**
Allercombe. *Devn* 6K **7**
Allerford. *Som* 1J **7**
Allerston. *N Yor* 7F **48**
Allerthorpe. *E Yor* 3E **42**
Allerton. *Mers* 1C **34**
Allerton. *W Yor* 4K **41**
Allerton Bywater. *W Yor* 5B **42**
Allerton Mauleverer. *N Yor* 2B **42**
Allesley. *W Mid* 3L **27**
Allestree. *Derb* 6M **35**
Allet. *Corn* 4L **3**
Allexton. *Leics* 1F **28**
Allgreave. *Ches E* 3H **35**
Allhallows. *Medw* 6E **22**
Allhallows-on-Sea. *Medw* 6E **22**
Alligin Shuas. *High* 8K **77**
Allimore Green. *Staf* 8G **35**
Allington. *Kent* 8D **22**
Allington. *Linc* 5F **36**
Allington. *Wilts*
nr. Amesbury 2L **9**
nr. Devizes 7J **19**
Allithwaite. *Cumb* 8B **46**
**Alloa**. *Clac* 8C **66**
Allonby. *Cumb* 7E **52**
Allostock. *Ches W* 2F **34**
Alloway. *S Ayr* 8B **58**
Allowenshay. *Som* 4B **8**
All Saints South Elmham. *Suff* 3K **31**
Allscott. *Shrp* 2F **26**
Allscott. *Telf* 8E **34**
All Stretton. *Shrp* 2C **26**
Allt. *Carm* 4E **16**
Alltami. *Flin* 3A **34**
Alltgobhlach. *N Ayr* 5H **57**
Alltmawr. *Powy* 8K **25**
Alltnacaillich. *High* 7G **85**
Allt na h' Airbhe. *High* 4B **78**
Alltour. *High* 7C **70**
Alltsigh. *High* 4E **70**
Alltwalis. *Carm* 3L **15**
Alltwen. *Neat* 4G **17**
Alltyblacca. *Cdgn* 2M **15**
Allt-y-goed. *Pemb* 2H **15**
Almeley. *Here* 6B **26**
Almeley Wootton. *Here* 6B **26**
Almer. *Dors* 6H **9**
Almholme. *S Yor* 7C **42**
Almington. *Staf* 6F **34**
Alminstone Cross. *Devn* 3C **6**
Almodington. *W Sus* 6F **10**
Almondbank. *Per* 5D **66**
Almondbury. *W Yor* 6K **41**
Almondsbury. *S Glo* 5E **18**
Alne. *N Yor* 1B **42**
Alness. *High* 7G **79**
Alnessferry. *High* 7G **79**
Alnham. *Nmbd* 8G **61**
Alnmouth. *Nmbd* 8K **61**
Alnwick. *Nmbd* 8J **61**
Alphamstone. *Essx* 8E **30**
Alpheton. *Suff* 6E **30**
Alphington. *Devn* 6J **7**
Alpington. *Norf* 1J **31**
Alport. *Derbs* 3L **35**
Alport. *Powy* 2A **26**
Alpraham. *Ches E* 4D **34**
Alresford. *Essx* 1G **23**
Alrewas. *Staf* 8K **35**
**Alsager**. *Ches E* 4F **34**
Alsagers Bank. *Staf* 5G **35**
Alsop en le Dale. *Derbs* 4K **35**
Alston. *Cumb* 7M **53**
Alston. *Devn* 5B **8**
Alstone. *Glos* 8H **27**
Alstone. *Som* 1B **8**
Alstonefield. *Staf* 4K **35**
Alston Sutton. *Som* 8C **18**
Alswear. *Devn* 3G **7**
Altandhu. *High* 2L **77**
Altanduin. *High* 1J **79**
Altarnun. *Corn* 7B **6**
Altass. *High* 3E **78**
Alterwall. *High* 5D **86**
Altgaltraig. *Arg* 2K **57**
Altham. *Lanc* 4F **40**
Althorne. *Essx* 4F **22**
Althorpe. *N Lin* 7F **42**
Altnabreac. *High* 7B **86**
Altnacealgach. *High* 2C **78**
Altnafeadh. *High* 2G **65**
Altnaharra. *High* 8H **85**
Altofts. *W Yor* 5A **42**
Alton. *Derbs* 3A **36**
**Alton**. *Hants* 2E **10**
Alton. *Staf* 5K **35**
Alton Barnes. *Wilts* 7K **19**
Altonhill. *E Ayr* 6C **58**
Alton Pancras. *Dors* 5F **8**
Alton Priors. *Wilts* 7K **19**
**Altrincham**. *G Man* 1F **34**
Altrua. *High* 6C **70**
Alva. *Clac* 8B **66**
Alvanley. *Ches W* 2C **34**
Alvaston. *Derb* 6A **36**
Alvechurch. *Worc* 4J **27**
Alvecote. *Warw* 1L **27**
Alvediston. *Wilts* 3H **9**
Alveley. *Shrp* 3F **26**
Alverdiscott. *Devn* 3E **6**
Alverstoke. *Hants* 6C **10**
Alverstone. *IOW* 7C **10**
Alverthorpe. *W Yor* 5M **41**
Alverton. *Notts* 5E **36**
Alves. *Mor* 7M **79**
Alvescot. *Oxon* 3L **19**
Alveston. *S Glo* 5E **18**
Alveston. *Warw* 6L **27**
Alvie. *High* 5J **71**
Alvingham. *Linc* 8L **43**
Alvington. *Glos* 3E **18**
Alwalton. *Cambs* 2J **29**
Alweston. *Dors* 4E **8**
Alwington. *Devn* 3D **6**
Alwinton. *Nmbd* 1C **54**
Alwoodley. *W Yor* 3L **41**
Alyth. *Per* 3F **66**
Amatnatua. *High* 4E **78**
Am Baile. *W Isl* 4D **74**
Ambaston. *Derbs* 6B **36**
Ambergate. *Derbs* 4M **35**
Amber Hill. *Linc* 5K **37**
Amberley. *Glos* 3G **19**
Amberley. *W Sus* 4H **11**
Amble. *Nmbd* 1F **54**
Amblecote. *W Mid* 3G **27**
Ambler Thorn. *W Yor* 5J **41**
Ambleside. *Cumb* 5B **46**
Ambleston. *Pemb* 4G **15**
Ambrosden. *Oxon* 2D **20**
Amcotts. *N Lin* 6F **42**
**Amersham**. *Buck* 4G **21**
Amerton. *Staf* 7H **35**
Amesbury. *Wilts* 1K **9**
Amisfield. *Dum* 3D **52**
Amlwch. *IOA* 1D **32**
Amlwch Port. *IOA* 1D **32**
**Ammanford**. *Carm* 3F **16**
Amotherby. *N Yor* 8E **48**
Ampfield. *Hants* 3B **10**
Ampleforth. *N Yor* 8C **48**
Ampleforth College. *N Yor* 8C **48**
Ampney Crucis. *Glos* 3J **19**
Ampney St Mary. *Glos* 3J **19**
Ampney St Peter. *Glos* 3J **19**
Amport. *Hants* 1L **9**
Ampthill. *C Beds* 8H **29**
Ampton. *Suff* 4E **30**
Amroth. *Pemb* 6J **15**
Amulree. *Per* 4C **66**
Amwell. *Herts* 2J **21**
Anaheilt. *High* 1C **64**
An Aird. *High* 5G **69**
An Baile Nua. *Ferm* 7D **92**
An Camus Darach. *High* 6H **69**
Ancaster. *Linc* 5G **37**
Anchor. *Shrp* 4L **25**
Anchorsholme. *Lanc* 3B **40**
Anchor Street. *Norf* 7K **39**
An Cnoc. *W Isl* 8H **83**
An Cnoc Ard. *W Isl* 5J **83**
An Coroghon. *High* 5D **68**
Ancroft. *Nmbd* 5H **61**
Ancrum. *Bord* 7D **60**
Ancton. *W Sus* 5G **11**
Anderby. *Linc* 2B **38**
Anderby Creek. *Linc* 2B **38**
Anderson. *Dors* 6G **9**
Anderton. *Ches W* 2E **34**
Andertons Mill. *Lanc* 6D **40**
**Andover**. *Hants* 1A **10**
Andover Down. *Hants* 1A **10**
Andoversford. *Glos* 2J **19**
Andreas. *IOM* 5D **44**
An Dùnan. *High* 3G **69**
Andwell. *Hants* 8D **20**
Anelog. *Gwyn* 8A **32**
Anfield. *Mers* 8B **40**
Angarrack. *Corn* 5J **3**
Angelbank. *Shrp* 4D **26**
Angersleigh. *Som* 4L **7**
Angerton. *Cumb* 6G **53**
Angle. *Pemb* 6E **14**
An Gleann Ur. *W Isl* 8H **83**
Angmering. *W Sus* 5H **11**
Angmering-on-Sea. *W Sus* 5H **11**
Angram. *N Yor*
nr. Keld 6G **47**
nr. York 3C **42**
Anick. *Nmbd* 5C **54**
Ankerbold. *Derbs* 3A **36**
Ankerville. *High* 6J **79**
Anlaby. *E Yor* 5H **43**
Anlaby Park. *Hull* 5H **43**
An Leth Meadhanach. *W Isl* 4D **74**
Anmer. *Norf* 7D **38**
Anmore. *Hants* 4D **10**
Annahilt. *Lis* 6H **93**
Annalong. *New M* 7H **93**
Annan. *Dum* 5G **53**
Annaside. *Cumb* 6K **45**
Annat. *Arg* 5E **64**
Annat. *High* 8K **77**
Annathill. *N Lan* 2F **58**
Anna Valley. *Hants* 1M **9**
Annbank. *S Ayr* 7C **58**
Annesley. *Notts* 4C **36**
Annesley Woodhouse. *Notts* 4C **36**
**Annfield Plain**. *Dur* 6E **54**
Annsborough. *New M* 7H **93**
Annscroft. *Shrp* 1C **26**
An Sailean. *High* 1A **64**
Ansdell. *Lanc* 5B **40**
Ansford. *Som* 2E **8**
Ansley. *Warw* 2L **27**
Anslow. *Staf* 7L **35**
Anslow Gate. *Staf* 7K **35**
Ansteadbrook. *Surr* 2G **11**
Anstey. *Herts* 8M **29**
Anstey. *Leics* 1C **28**
Anston. *S Lan* 5J **59**
Anstruther Easter. *Fife* 7J **67**
Anstruther Wester. *Fife* 7J **67**
Ansty. *Warw* 3A **28**
Ansty. *W Sus* 3K **11**
Ansty. *Wilts* 3H **9**
An Taobh Tuath. *W Isl* 5A **76**
An t-Aodann Ban. *High* 8E **76**
An t Ath Leathann. *High* 3H **69**
An Teanga. *High* 5H **69**
Anthill Common. *Hants* 4D **10**
Anthorn. *Cumb* 6F **52**
Antingham. *Norf* 6J **39**
An t-Ob. *W Isl* 5B **76**
Anton's Gowt. *Linc* 5K **37**
Antony. *Corn* 6G **5**
An t-Òrd. *High* 5H **69**
**Antrim**. *Ant* 4G **93**
Antrobus. *Ches W* 2E **34**
Anvil Corner. *Devn* 5C **6**
Anwick. *Linc* 4J **37**
Anwoth. *Dum* 6L **51**
Apethorpe. *Nptn* 2H **29**
Apeton. *Staf* 8G **35**
Apley. *Linc* 2J **37**
Apperknowle. *Derbs* 2A **36**
Apperley. *Glos* 1G **19**
Apperley Dene. *Nmbd* 6D **54**
Appersett. *N Yor* 6G **47**
Appin. *Arg* 3D **64**
Appleby. *N Lin* 6G **43**
Appleby-in-Westmorland. *Cumb* 3E **46**
Appleby Magna. *Leics* 1M **27**
Appleby Parva. *Leics* 1M **27**
Applecross. *High* 1J **69**
Appledore. *Devn*
nr. Bideford 2D **6**
nr. Tiverton 4K **7**
Appledore. *Kent* 3F **12**
Appledore Heath. *Kent* 2F **12**
Appleford. *Oxon* 4C **20**
Applegarthtown. *Dum* 4F **52**
Applemore. *Hants* 5A **10**
Appleshaw. *Hants* 1M **9**
Applethwaite. *Cumb* 3A **46**
Appleton. *Hal* 1D **34**
Appleton. *Oxon* 3B **20**
Appleton-le-Moors. *N Yor* 7E **48**
Appleton-le-Street. *N Yor* 8E **48**
Appleton Roebuck. *N Yor* 3C **42**
Appleton Thorn. *Warr* 1E **34**
Appleton Wiske. *N Yor* 5A **48**
Appletree. *Nptn* 7B **28**
Appletreehall. *Bord* 8C **60**
Appletreewick. *N Yor* 1J **41**
Appley. *Som* 3K **7**
Appley Bridge. *Lanc* 6D **40**
Apse Heath. *IOW* 7C **10**
Apsley End. *C Beds* 8J **29**
Apuldram. *W Sus* 5F **10**
Arabella. *High* 6J **79**
Arasaig. *High* 7H **69**
Arbeadie. *Abers* 6F **72**
Arberth. *Pemb* 5H **15**
Arbirlot. *Ang* 3K **67**
Arborfield. *Wok* 7E **20**
Arborfield Cross. *Wok* 7E **20**
Arborfield Garrison. *Wok* 7E **20**
Arbourthorne. *S Yor* 1A **36**
**Arbroath**. *Ang* 3K **67**
Arbuthnott. *Abers* 8H **73**
Arcan. *High* 8F **78**
Archargary. *High* 6K **85**
Archdeacon Newton. *Darl* 4L **47**
Archiestown. *Mor* 1B **72**
Arclid. *Ches E* 3F **34**
Arclid Green. *Ches E* 3F **34**
Ardachu. *High* 3G **79**
Ardalanish. *Arg* 6J **63**
Ardaneaskan. *High* 2K **69**
Ardarroch. *High* 2K **69**
Ardbeg. *Arg*
nr. Dunoon 1L **57**
on Islay 5D **56**
on Isle of Bute 3K **57**
Ardboe. *M Ulst* 5F **93**
Ardcharnich. *High* 5B **78**
Ardchiavaig. *Arg* 6J **63**
Ardchonnell. *Arg* 6D **64**
Ardchrishnish. *Arg* 5K **63**
Ardchronie. *High* 5G **79**
Ardchullarie. *Stir* 6K **65**
Ardchyle. *Stir* 5K **65**
Ard-dhubh. *High* 1J **69**
Arddleen. *Powy* 8A **34**
Arddlîn. *Powy* 8A **34**
Ardechive. *High* 6B **70**
Ardeley. *Herts* 1L **21**
Ardelve. *High* 3K **69**
Arden. *Arg* 1B **58**
Ardendrain. *High* 2F **70**
Arden Hall. *N Yor* 6C **48**
Ardens Grafton. *Warw* 6K **27**
Ardentinny. *Arg* 1L **57**
Ardeonaig. *Stir* 4L **65**
Ardersier. *High* 8H **79**
Ardery. *High* 1B **64**
Ardessie. *High* 5A **78**
Ardfern. *Arg* 7C **64**
Ardfernal. *Arg* 2E **56**
Ardfin. *Arg* 3D **56**
Ardgartan. *Arg* 7G **65**
Ardgay. *High* 4G **79**
Ardglass. *New M* 7J **93**
Ardgour. *High* 1E **64**
Ardheslaig. *High* 8J **77**
Ardindrean. *High* 5B **78**
Ardingly. *W Sus* 3L **11**
Ardington. *Oxon* 5B **20**
Ardlamont House. *Arg* 3J **57**
Ardleigh. *Essx* 1G **23**
Ardler. *Per* 3F **66**
Ardley. *Oxon* 1C **20**
Ardlui. *Arg* 6H **65**
Ardlussa. *Arg* 1F **56**
Ardmair. *High* 4B **78**
Ardmay. *Arg* 7G **65**
Ardmillan. *Ards* 5J **93**
Ardminish. *Arg* 5F **56**
Ardmolich. *High* 8J **69**
Ardmore. *High*
nr. Kinlochbervie 6E **84**
nr. Tain 5H **79**
Ardnacross. *Arg* 3L **63**
Ardnadam. *Arg* 1L **57**
Ardnagrask. *High* 1F **70**
Ardnamurach. *High* 6K **69**
Ardnarff. *High* 2K **69**
Ardnastang. *High* 1C **64**
Ardoch. *Per* 4D **66**
Ardochy House. *High* 5C **70**
Ardpatrick. *Arg* 3G **57**
Ardrishaig. *Arg* 1H **57**
Ardroag. *High* 1D **68**
Ardross. *High* 6G **79**
**Ardrossan**. *N Ayr* 5M **57**
Ardshealach. *High* 1A **64**
Ardsley. *S Yor* 7A **42**
Ardslignish. *High* 1L **63**
Ardstraw. *Derr* 4C **92**
Ardtalla. *Arg* 4D **56**
Ardtalnaig. *Per* 4M **65**
Ardtoe. *High* 8H **69**
Arduaine. *Arg* 6B **64**
Ardullie. *High* 7F **78**
Ardvasar. *High* 5H **69**
Ardvorlich. *Per* 5L **65**
Ardwell. *Dum* 7G **51**
Ardwell. *Mor* 2C **72**
Arean. *High* 8H **69**
Areley Common. *Worc* 4G **27**
Areley Kings. *Worc* 4G **27**
Arford. *Hants* 2F **10**
Argoed. *Cphy* 5L **17**
Argoed Mill. *Powy* 6J **25**
Aridhglas. *Arg* 5J **63**
Arinacrinachd. *High* 8J **77**
Arinagour. *Arg* 2H **63**
Arisaig. *High* 7H **69**
Ariundle. *High* 1C **64**
Arivegaig. *High* 1A **64**
Arkendale. *N Yor* 1A **42**
Arkesden. *Essx* 8A **30**
Arkholme. *Lanc* 8D **46**
Arkle Town. *N Yor* 5J **47**
Arkley. *G Lon* 4K **21**
Arksey. *S Yor* 7C **42**
Arkwright Town. *Derbs* 2B **36**
Arlecdon. *Cumb* 3K **45**
Arlescote. *Warw* 7A **28**
Arlesey. *C Beds* 8J **29**
Arleston. *Telf* 8E **34**
Arley. *Ches E* 1E **34**
Arlingham. *Glos* 2F **18**
Arlington. *Devn* 1F **6**
Arlington. *E Sus* 5B **12**
Arlington. *Glos* 3K **19**
Arlington Beccott. *Devn* 1F **6**
Armadail. *High* 5H **69**
Armadale. *High*
nr. Isleornsay 5H **69**
nr. Strathy 5K **85**
Armadale. *W Lot* 3H **59**
**Armagh**. *Arm* 6F **93**
Armathwaite. *Cumb* 7K **53**
Arminghall. *Norf* 1J **31**
Armitage. *Staf* 8J **35**
Armitage Bridge. *W Yor* 6K **41**
Armley. *W Yor* 4L **41**
Armoy. *Caus* 2G **93**
The Arms. *Norf* 2E **30**
Armscote. *Warw* 7L **27**
Armston. *Nptn* 3H **29**
**Armthorpe**. *S Yor* 7D **42**
Arncliffe. *N Yor* 8H **47**
Arncliffe Cote. *N Yor* 8H **47**
Arncroach. *Fife* 7J **67**
Arne. *Dors* 7H **9**
Arnesby. *Leics* 2D **28**
Arnicle. *Arg* 6G **57**
Arnisdale. *High* 4K **69**
Arnish. *High* 1H **69**
Arniston. *Midl* 3M **59**
Arnol. *W Isl* 7G **83**
Arnold. *E Yor* 3J **43**
**Arnold**. *Notts* 5C **36**
Arnprior. *Stir* 8L **65**
Arnside. *Cumb* 8C **46**
Aros Mains. *Arg* 3L **63**
Arpafeelie. *High* 8G **79**
Arrad Foot. *Cumb* 7B **46**
Arram. *E Yor* 3H **43**
Arras. *E Yor* 3G **43**
Arrathorne. *N Yor* 6K **47**
Arreton. *IOW* 7C **10**
Arrington. *Cambs* 6L **29**
Arrochar. *Arg* 7G **65**
Arrow. *Warw* 6J **27**
Arscaig. *High* 2F **78**
Artafallie. *High* 1G **71**
Arthington. *W Yor* 3L **41**
Arthingworth. *Nptn* 3E **28**
Arthog. *Gwyn* 1F **24**
Arthrath. *Abers* 2J **73**
Arthurstone. *Per* 3F **66**
Articlave. *Caus* 2E **92**
Artigarvan. *Derr* 3C **92**
Artikelly. *Caus* 2E **92**
Artington. *Surr* 1G **11**
Arundel. *W Sus* 5H **11**
Asby. *Cumb* 2K **45**
Ascog. *Arg* 3L **57**
**Ascot**. *Wind* 7G **21**
Ascott-under-Wychwood. *Oxon* 2M **19**
Asenby. *N Yor* 8A **48**
Asfordby. *Leics* 8E **36**
Asfordby Hill. *Leics* 8E **36**
Asgarby. *Linc*
nr. Horncastle 3L **37**
nr. Sleaford 5J **37**
Ash. *Devn* 7L **5**
Ash. *Dors* 4G **9**
Ash. *Kent*
nr. Sandwich 8J **23**
nr. Swanley 7C **22**
Ash. *Som* 3C **8**
Ash. *Surr* 8F **20**
Ashampstead. *W Ber* 6C **20**
Ashbocking. *Suff* 6H **31**
Ashbourne. *Derbs* 5K **35**
Ashbrittle. *Som* 3K **7**
Ashbrook. *Shrp* 2C **26**
Ashburton. *Devn* 5K **5**
Ashbury. *Devn* 6E **6**
Ashbury. *Oxon* 5L **19**
Ashby. *N Lin* 7F **42**
Ashby by Partney. *Linc* 3M **37**
Ashby cum Fenby. *NE Lin* 7K **43**
Ashby de la Launde. *Linc* 4H **37**
**Ashby-de-la-Zouch**. *Leics* 8A **36**
Ashby Folville. *Leics* 8E **36**
Ashby Magna. *Leics* 2C **28**
Ashby Parva. *Leics* 3C **28**
Ashby Puerorum. *Linc* 2L **37**
Ashby St Ledgers. *Nptn* 5C **28**
Ashby St Mary. *Norf* 1K **31**
Ashchurch. *Glos* 8H **27**
Ashcombe. *Devn* 7L **5**
Ashcott. *Som* 2C **8**
Ashdon. *Essx* 7B **30**
Ashe. *Hants* 1C **10**
Asheldham. *Essx* 3F **22**
Ashen. *Essx* 7D **30**
Ashendon. *Buck* 2E **20**
Ashey. *IOW* 7C **10**
Ashfield. *Hants* 4A **10**
Ashfield. *Here* 1D **18**
Ashfield. *Shrp* 3D **26**
Ashfield. *Stir* 7A **66**
Ashfield. *Suff* 5J **31**
Ashfield Green. *Suff* 4J **31**
Ashfold Crossways. *W Sus* 3K **11**
Ashford. *Devn*
nr. Barnstaple 2E **6**
nr. Kingsbridge 7J **5**
Ashford. *Hants* 4K **9**
**Ashford**. *Kent* 1G **13**
Ashford. *Surr* 6H **21**
Ashford Bowdler. *Shrp* 4D **26**
Ashford Carbonel. *Shrp* 4D **26**
Ashford Hill. *Hants* 7C **20**
Ashford in the Water. *Derbs* 3K **35**
Ashgill. *S Lan* 5F **58**
Ash Green. *Warw* 3M **27**
Ashgrove. *Mor* 7B **80**
Ashill. *Devn* 4K **7**
Ashill. *Norf* 1E **30**
Ashill. *Som* 4B **8**
Ashingdon. *Essx* 4E **22**
**Ashington**. *Nmbd* 3F **54**
Ashington. *W Sus* 4J **11**
Ashkirk. *Bord* 7B **60**
Ashleworth. *Glos* 1G **19**
Ashley. *Cambs* 5C **30**
Ashley. *Ches E* 1G **35**
Ashley. *Dors* 5K **9**
Ashley. *Glos* 4H **19**
Ashley. *Hants*
nr. New Milton 6L **9**
nr. Winchester 2A **10**
Ashley. *Kent* 1K **13**
Ashley. *Nptn* 2E **28**
Ashley. *Staf* 6F **34**
Ashley. *Wilts* 7G **19**
Ashley Green. *Buck* 3G **21**
Ashley Heath. *Dors* 5K **9**
Ashley Heath. *Staf* 6F **34**
Ashley Moor. *Here* 5C **26**
Ash Magna. *Shrp* 6D **34**
Ashmanhaugh. *Norf* 7K **39**
Ashmansworth. *Hants* 8B **20**
Ashmansworthy. *Devn* 4C **6**
Ashmead Green. *Glos* 4F **18**
Ash Mill. *Devn* 3H **7**
Ashmill. *Devn* 6C **6**
Ashmore. *Dors* 4H **9**
Ashmore Green. *W Ber* 7C **20**
Ashorne. *Warw* 6M **27**
Ashover. *Derbs* 3M **35**
Ashow. *Warw* 4M **27**
Ash Parva. *Shrp* 6D **34**
Ashperton. *Here* 7E **26**
Ashprington. *Devn* 6L **5**
Ash Priors. *Som* 3L **7**
Ashreigney. *Devn* 4F **6**
Ash Street. *Suff* 7G **31**
Ashtead. *Surr* 8J **21**
Ash Thomas. *Devn* 4K **7**
Ashton. *Corn* 6K **3**
Ashton. *Here* 5D **26**
Ashton. *Inv* 2M **57**
Ashton. *Nptn*
nr. Oundle 3H **29**
nr. Roade 7E **28**
Ashton. *Pet* 1J **29**
Ashton Common. *Wilts* 8G **19**
Ashton Hayes. *Ches W* 3D **34**
**Ashton-in-Makerfield**. *G Man* 8D **40**
Ashton Keynes. *Wilts* 4J **19**
Ashton under Hill. *Worc* 8H **27**
**Ashton-under-Lyne**. *G Man* 8H **41**
Ashton upon Mersey. *G Man* 8F **40**
Ashurst. *Hants* 4M **9**

Ashurst. Kent 2B 12
Ashurst. Lanc 7C 40
Ashurst. W Sus 4J 11
Ashurst Wood. W Sus 2M 11
Ash Vale. Surr 8F 20
Ashwater. Devn 6C 6
Ashwell. Herts 8K 29
Ashwell. Rut 8F 36
Ashwellthorpe. Norf 2H 31
Ashwick. Som 1E 8
Ashwicken. Norf 8D 38
Ashwood. Staf 3G 27
Askam in Furness. Cumb 7M 45
Askern. S Yor 6C 42
Askerswell. Dors 6D 8
Askett. Buck 3F 20
Askham. Cumb 3D 46
Askham. Notts 2E 36
Askham Bryan. York 3C 42
Askham Richard. York 3C 42
Askrigg. N Yor 6H 47
Askwith. N Yor 3K 41
Aslackby. Linc 6H 37
Aslacton. Norf 2H 31
Aslockton. Notts 5E 36
Aspatria. Cumb 7F 52
Aspenden. Herts 1L 21
Asperton. Linc 6K 37
Aspley Guise. C Beds 8G 29
Aspley Heath. C Beds 8G 29
Aspull. G Man 7E 40
Asselby. E Yor 5E 42
Assington. Suff 8F 30
Assington Green. Suff 6D 30
Astbury. Ches E 3G 35
Astcote. Nptn 6D 28
Asterby. Linc 2K 37
Asterley. Shrp 1B 26
Asterton. Shrp 2B 26
Asthall. Oxon 2L 19
Asthall Leigh. Oxon 2M 19
Astle. High 4H 79
Astley. G Man 7F 40
Astley. Shrp 8D 34
Astley. Warw 3M 27
Astley. Worc 5F 26
Astley Abbotts. Shrp 2F 26
Astley Bridge. G Man 6F 40
Astley Cross. Worc 5G 27
Aston. Ches E 5E 34
Aston. Ches W 2D 34
Aston. Derbs
nr. Hope 1K 35
nr. Sudbury 6K 35
Aston. Flin 3B 34
Aston. Here 5C 26
Aston. Herts 1K 21
Aston. Oxon 3M 19
Aston. Shrp
nr. Bridgnorth 2G 27
nr. Wem 7D 34
Aston. S Yor 1B 36
Aston. Staf 5F 34
Aston. Telf 1E 26
Aston. W Mid 2J 27
Aston. Wok 5E 20
Aston Abbotts. Buck 1F 20
Aston Botterell. Shrp 3E 26
Aston-by-Stone. Staf 6H 35
Aston Cantlow. Warw 6K 27
Aston Clinton. Buck 2F 20
Aston Crews. Here 1E 18
Aston Cross. Glos 8H 27
Aston End. Herts 1K 21
Aston Eyre. Shrp 2E 26
Aston Fields. Worc 5H 27
Aston Flamville. Leics 2B 28
Aston Ingham. Here 1E 18
Aston juxta Mondrum.
Ches E 4E 34
Astonlane. Shrp 2E 26
Aston le Walls. Nptn 6B 28
Aston Magna. Glos 8K 27
Aston Munslow. Shrp 3D 26
Aston on Carrant. Glos 8H 27
Aston on Clun. Shrp 3B 26
Aston-on-Trent. Derbs 7B 36
Aston Pigott. Shrp 1B 26
Aston Rogers. Shrp 1B 26
Aston Rowant. Oxon 4E 20
Aston Sandford. Buck 3E 20
Aston Somerville. Worc 8J 27
Aston Subedge. Glos 7K 27
Aston Tirrold. Oxon 5C 20
Aston Upthorpe. Oxon 5C 20
Astrop. Nptn 8C 28
Astwick. C Beds 8K 29
Astwood. Mil 7G 29
Astwood Bank. Worc 5J 27
Aswarby. Linc 6H 37
Aswardby. Linc 2L 37
Atcham. Shrp 1D 26
Atch Lench. Worc 6J 27
Athelhampton. Dors 6F 8
Athelington. Suff 4J 31
Athelney. Som 3B 8
Athelstaneford. E Lot 2C 60
Atherfield Green. IOW 8B 10
Atherington. Devn 3E 6
Atherington. W Sus 5H 11
Athersley. S Yor 7A 42
**Atherstone**. Warw 2M 27
Atherstone on Stour. Warw 6L 27
**Atherton**. G Man 7E 40
Ath-Tharracail. High 1A 64
Atlow. Derbs 5L 35
Attadale. High 2L 69
Attenborough. Notts 6C 36
Atterby. Linc 8G 43
Atterley. Shrp 2E 26
Atterton. Leics 2A 28
Attical. New M 7H 93
Attleborough. Norf 2G 31
Attleborough. Warw 2A 28
Attlebridge. Norf 8H 39
Atwick. E Yor 2J 43
Atworth. Wilts 7G 19
Auberrow. Here 7C 26
Aubourn. Linc 3G 37
Aucharnie. Abers 1F 72
Auchattie. Abers 6F 72
Auchavan. Ang 1E 66
Auchbreck. Mor 3B 72
Auchenback. E Ren 4D 58
Auchenblae. Abers 8G 73
Auchenbrack. Dum 2B 52
Auchenbreck. Arg 1K 57
Auchencairn. Dum
nr. Dalbeattie 6B 52
nr. Dumfries 3D 52
Auchencarroch. W Dun 1C 58
Auchencrow. Bord 3F 60
Auchendennan. Arg 1B 58
Auchendinny. Midl 3L 59
Auchengray. S Lan 4H 59
Auchenhalrig. Mor 7C 80
Auchenheath. S Lan 5G 59
Auchenlochan. Arg 2J 57
Auchenmade. N Ayr 5B 58
Auchenmalg. Dum 6H 51
Auchentiber. N Ayr 5B 58
Auchenvennel. Arg 1A 58
Auchindrain. Arg 7E 64
Auchininna. Abers 1F 72
Auchinleck. Dum 4K 51
Auchinleck. E Ayr 7D 58
Auchinloch. N Lan 2E 58
Auchinstarry. N Lan 2F 58
Auchleven. Abers 3F 72
Auchlochan. S Lan 6G 59
Auchlunachan. High 5B 78
Auchmillan. E Ayr 7D 58
Auchmithie. Ang 3K 67
Auchmuirbridge. Fife 7F 66
Auchmull. Ang 8E 72
Auchnacree. Ang 1H 67
Auchnafree. Per 4B 66
Auchnagallin. High 2L 71
Auchnagatt. Abers 1J 73
Aucholzie. Abers 6C 72
Auchreddie. Abers 1H 73
Auchterarder. Per 6C 66
Auchteraw. High 5D 70
Auchterderran. Fife 8F 66
Auchterhouse. Ang 4G 67
Auchtermuchty. Fife 6F 66
Auchterneed. High 8E 78
Auchtertool. Fife 8F 66
Auchtertyre. High 3K 69
Auchtubh. Stir 5K 65
Auckengill. High 5E 86
Auckley. S Yor 7D 42
**Audenshaw**. G Man 8H 41
Audlem. Ches E 5E 34
Audley. Staf 4F 34
Audley End. Essx 8B 30
Audmore. Staf 7G 35
Auds. Abers 7F 80
Augher. M Ulst 6D 92
Aughertree. Cumb 8G 53
Aughnacloy. M Ulst 6E 92
Aughton. E Yor 4E 42
Aughton. Lanc
nr. Lancaster 1D 40
nr. Ormskirk 7B 40
**Aughton**. S Yor 1B 36
Aughton. Wilts 8L 19
Aughton Park. Lanc 7C 40
Auldearn. High 8K 79
Aulden. Here 6C 26
Auldgirth. Dum 3D 52
Auldhouse. S Lan 4E 58
Ault a' chruinn. High 3L 69
Aultbea. High 5K 77
Aultdearg. High 7C 78
Aultgrishan. High 5J 77
Aultguish Inn. High 6D 78
Ault Hucknall. Derbs 3B 36
Aultibea. High 1L 79
Aultiphurst. High 5L 85
Aultivullin. High 5L 85
Aultmore. Mor 8D 80
Aultnamain Inn. High 5G 79
Aunby. Linc 8H 37
Aunsby. Linc 6H 37
Aust. S Glo 5D 18
Austerfield. S Yor 8D 42
Austin Fen. Linc 8L 43
Austrey. Warw 1L 27
Austwick. N Yor 1F 40
Authorpe. Linc 1M 37
Authorpe Row. Linc 2B 38
Avebury. Wilts 7K 19
Avebury Trusloe. Wilts 7J 19
Aveley. Thur 5B 22
Avening. Glos 4G 19
Averham. Notts 4E 36
Aveton Gifford. Devn 7J 5
Avielochan. High 4K 71
Aviemore. High 4J 71
Avington. Hants 2C 10
Avoch. High 8H 79
Avon. Hants 6K 9
Avonbridge. Falk 2H 59
Avon Dassett. Warw 6B 28
Avonmouth. Bris 6D 18
Avonwick. Devn 6K 5
Awbridge. Hants 3M 9
Awliscombe. Devn 5L 7
Awre. Glos 3F 18
Awsworth. Notts 5B 36
Axbridge. Som 8C 18
Axford. Hants 1D 10
Axford. Wilts 7L 19
Axminster. Devn 6B 8
Axmouth. Devn 6A 8
Aycliffe Village. Dur 3L 47
Aydon. Nmbd 5D 54
Aykley Heads. Dur 7F 54
Aylburton. Glos 3E 18
Aylburton Common. Glos 3E 18
Ayle. Nmbd 7M 53
Aylesbeare. Devn 6K 7
**Aylesbury**. Buck 2F 20
Aylesby. NE Lin 7K 43
Aylescott. Devn 4F 6
**Aylesford**. Kent 8D 22
Aylesham. Kent 8J 23
Aylestone. Leic 1C 28
Aylmerton. Norf 6H 39
Aylsham. Norf 7H 39
Aylton. Here 8E 26
Aylworth. Glos 1K 19
Aymestrey. Here 5C 26
Aynho. Nptn 8C 28
Ayot Green. Herts 2K 21
Ayot St Lawrence. Herts 2J 21
Ayot St Peter. Herts 2K 21
**Ayr**. S Ayr 7B 58
Ayres of Selivoe. Shet 3C 90
Ayreville. Torb 5L 5
Aysgarth. N Yor 7J 47
Ayshford. Devn 4K 7
Ayside. Cumb 7B 46
Ayston. Rut 1F 28
Ayton. Bord 3G 61
Aywick. Shet 5K 91
Azerley. N Yor 8L 47

## B

Babbacombe. Torb 5M 5
Babbinswood. Shrp 6B 34
Babbs Green. Herts 2L 21
Babcary. Som 3D 8
Babel. Carm 1H 17
Babell. Flin 3L 33
Babingley. Norf 7C 38
Bablock Hythe. Oxon 3B 20
Babraham. Cambs 6B 30
Babworth. Notts 1D 36
Bac. W Isl 7H 83
Bachau. IOA 2D 32
Bacheldre. Powy 3M 25
Bachymbyd Fawr. Den 4K 33
Backaland. Orkn 6E 88
Backaskaill. Orkn 4D 88
Backbarrow. Cumb 7B 46
Backe. Carm 5J 15
Backfolds. Abers 8K 81
Backford. Ches W 2C 34
Backhill. Abers 2G 73
Backhill of Clackriach.
Abers 1J 73
Backies. High 3J 79
Backmuir of New Gilston.
Fife 7H 67
Back of Keppoch. High 7H 69
Back Street. Suff 6D 30
Backwell. N Som 7C 18
Backworth. Tyne 4G 55
Bacon End. Essx 2C 22
Baconsthorpe. Norf 6H 39
Bacton. Here 8B 26
Bacton. Norf 6K 39
Bacton. Suff 5G 31
Bacton Green. Norf 6K 39
**Bacup**. Lanc 5G 41
Badachonacher. High 6G 79
Badachro. High 6J 77
Badanloch Lodge. High 8K 85
Badavanich. High 8B 78
Badbury. Swin 5K 19
Badby. Nptn 6C 28
Badcall. High 6E 84
Badcaul. High 4M 77
Baddeley Green. Stoke 4H 35
Baddesley Clinton. W Mid 4L 27
Baddesley Ensor. Warw 2L 27
Baddidarach. High 1A 78
Baddoch. Abers 7M 71
Badenscallie. High 3M 77
Badenscoth. Abers 2G 73
Badentarbat. High 2M 77
Badgall. Corn 7B 6
Badgers Mount. Kent 7A 22
Badgeworth. Glos 2H 19
Badgworth. Som 8B 18
Badicaul. High 3J 69
Badingham. Suff 5K 31
Badlesmere. Kent 8G 23
Badlipster. High 7D 86
Badluarach. High 4L 77
Badminton. S Glo 5G 19
Badnaban. High 1A 78
Badnabay. High 7E 84
Badnagie. High 8C 86
Badnellan. High 3J 79
Badninish. High 4H 79
Badrallach. High 4A 78
Badsey. Worc 7J 27
Badshot Lea. Surr 1F 10
Badsworth. W Yor 6B 42
Badwell Ash. Suff 5F 30
Bae Cinmel. Cnwy 2J 33
**Bae Colwyn**. Cnwy 3H 33
Bae Penrhyn. Cnwy 2H 33
Bagby. N Yor 7B 48
Bag Enderby. Linc 2L 37
Bagendon. Glos 3J 19
Bagginswood. Shrp 3E 26
Bàgh a Chàise. W Isl 6A 76
Bàgh a' Chaisteil. W Isl 6C 74
Bagham. Kent 8G 23
Baghasdal. W Isl 4D 74
Bagh Mor. W Isl 8K 75
Bagh Shiarabhagh. W Isl 5D 74
Bagillt. Flin 3M 33
Baginton. Warw 4M 27
Baglan. Neat 5G 17
Bagley. Shrp 7C 34
Bagley. Som 1C 8
Bagnall. Staf 4H 35
Bagnor. W Ber 7B 20
Bagshot. Surr 7G 21
Bagshot. Wilts 7M 19
Bagstone. S Glo 5E 18
Bagthorpe. Norf 6D 38
Bagthorpe. Notts 4B 36
Bagworth. Leics 1B 28
Bagwy Llydiart. Here 1C 18
**Baildon**. W Yor 4K 41
Baildon Green. W Yor 4K 41
Baile. W Isl 5L 75
Baile Ailein. W Isl 1D 76
Baile an Truiseil. W Isl 6G 83
Baile Boidheach. Arg 2G 57
Baile Glas. W Isl 8K 75
Bailemeonach. Arg 3A 64
Baile Mhanaich. W Isl 8J 75
Baile Mhartainn. W Isl 6J 75
Baile MhicPhail. W Isl 6K 75
Baile Mor. W Isl 7J 75
Baile Mór. Arg 5H 63
Baile nan Cailleach. W Isl 8J 75
Baile Raghaill. W Isl 7J 75
Bailey Green. Hants 3D 10
Baileyhead. Cumb 3K 53
Baileysmill. Lis 6H 93
Bailiesward. Abers 2D 72
Bail' Iochdrach. W Isl 8K 75
Baillieston. Glas 3E 58
Bailrigg. Lanc 2C 40
Bail Uachdraich. W Isl 7K 75
Bail' Ur Tholastaidh. W Isl 7J 83
Bainbridge. N Yor 6H 47
Bainsford. Falk 1G 59
Bainshole. Abers 2F 72
Bainton. E Yor 2G 43
Bainton. Oxon 1C 20
Bainton. Pet 1H 29
Baintown. Fife 7G 67
Baker Street. Thur 5C 22
Bakewell. Derbs 3L 35
Bala. Gwyn 7J 33
Y Bala. Gwyn 7J 33
Balachuirn. High 1G 69
Balbeg. High
nr. Cannich 2E 70
nr. Loch Ness 3E 70
Balbeggie. Per 5E 66
Balblair. High
nr. Bonar Bridge 4F 78
nr. Invergordon 7H 79
nr. Inverness 1F 70
Balby. S Yor 7C 42
Balcathie. Ang 4K 67
Balchladich. High 8C 84
Balchraggan. High 1F 70
Balchrick. High 6D 84
Balcombe. W Sus 2L 11
Balcombe Lane. W Sus 2L 11
Balcurvie. Fife 7G 67
Baldersby. N Yor 8A 48
Baldersby St James. N Yor 8A 48
Balderstone. Lanc 4E 40
Balderton. Ches W 3B 34
Balderton. Notts 4F 36
Baldinnie. Fife 6H 67
Baldock. Herts 8K 29
Baldrine. IOM 6D 44
Baldslow. E Sus 4E 12
Baldwin. IOM 6C 44
Baldwinholme. Cumb 6H 53
Baldwin's Gate. Staf 6F 34
Bale. Norf 6G 39
Balearn. Abers 8K 81
Balemartine. Arg 3E 62
Balephetrish. Arg 3F 62
Balephuil. Arg 3E 62
Balerno. Edin 3K 59
Balevullin. Arg 3E 62
Balfield. Ang 1J 67
Balfour. Orkn 8D 88
Balfron. Stir 1D 58
Balgaveny. Abers 1F 72
Balgonar. Fife 8D 66
Balgowan. High 6G 71
Balgown. High 7E 76
Balgrochan. E Dun 2E 58
Balgy. High 8K 77
Balhalgardy. Abers 3G 73
Baliasta. Shet 3L 91
Baligill. High 5L 85
Balintore. Ang 2F 66
Balintore. High 6J 79
Balintraid. High 6H 79
Balk. N Yor 7B 48
Balkeerie. Ang 3G 67
Balkholme. E Yor 5E 42
Ball. Shrp 7B 34
Ballabeg. IOM 7B 44
Ballacannell. IOM 6D 44
Ballacarnane Beg. IOM 6C 44
Ballachulish. High 2E 64
Ballagyr. IOM 6B 44
Ballajora. IOM 5D 44
Ballaleigh. IOM 6C 44
Ballamodha. IOM 7B 44
Ballantrae. S Ayr 3F 50
Ballards Gore. Essx 4F 22
Ballasalla. IOM
nr. Castletown 7B 44
nr. Kirk Michael 5C 44
Ballater. Abers 6C 72
Ballaugh. IOM 5C 44
Ballencrieff. E Lot 2B 60
Ballencrieff Toll. W Lot 2H 59
Ballentoul. Per 1B 66
Ball Hill. Hants 7B 20
Ballidon. Derbs 4L 35
Balliemore. Arg
nr. Dunoon 1K 57
nr. Oban 5C 64
Ballieward. High 2L 71
Ballig. IOM 6B 44
Ballimore. Stir 6K 65
Ballinamallard. Ferm 6C 92
Ballindarragh. Ferm 7C 92
Ballingdon. Suff 7E 30
Ballinger Common. Buck 3G 21
Ballingham. Here 8D 26
Ballingry. Fife 8E 66
Ballinluig. Per 2C 66
Ballintoy. Caus 1G 93
Ballintuim. Per 2E 66
Balliveolan. Arg 3C 64
Balloan. High 3F 78
Balloch. High 1H 71
Balloch. N Lan 2F 58
Balloch. Per 6B 66
Balloch. W Dun 1B 58
Ballochan. Abers 6E 72
Ballochgoy. Arg 3K 57
Ballochmyle. E Ayr 7D 58
Ballochroy. Arg 4G 57
Balloo. Ards 5J 93
Balls Cross. W Sus 3G 11
Ball's Green. E Sus 2A 12
Ballsmill. New M 7F 93
Ballyalton. New M 6J 93
Ballybogy. Caus 2F 93
Ballycarry. ME Ant 4J 93
Ballycassidy. Ferm 6C 92
Ballycastle. Caus 1G 93
Ballyclare. Ant 4H 93
Ballyeaston. Ant 4H 93
Ballygally. ME Ant 3H 93
Ballygawley. M Ulst 6E 92
Ballygowan. Ards 5J 93
Ballygown. Arg 3K 63
Ballygrant. Arg 3C 56
Ballyhalbert. Ards 5K 93
Ballyholland. New M 7G 93
Ballyhornan. New M 6J 93
Ballykelly. Caus 2E 92
Ballykinler. New M 7J 93
Ballylesson. Lis 5H 93
Ballymagorry. Derr 3C 92
Ballymartin. New M 7H 93
**Ballymena**. ME Ant 3G 93
Ballymichael. N Ayr 6J 57
**Ballymoney**. Caus 2F 93
Ballynagard. Derr 2D 92
Ballynahinch. New M 6H 93
Ballynakilly. M Ulst 5F 93
Ballynoe. New M 6J 93
Ballynure. Ant 4H 93
Ballyrashane. Caus 2F 93
Ballyrobert. Ant 4H 93
Ballyronan. M Ulst 4F 93
Ballyroney. Arm 7H 93
Ballyscullion. Caus 2E 92
Ballystrudder. ME Ant 4J 93
Ballyvoy. Caus 1G 93
Ballyward. New M 7H 93
Ballywater. Ards 5K 93
Ballywonard. Ant 4H 93
Balmacara. High 3K 69
Balmaclellan. Dum 4A 52
Balmacqueen. High 6F 76
Balmaha. Stir 8J 65
Balmalcolm. Fife 7G 67
Balmalloch. N Lan 2F 58
Balmeanach. High 2G 69
Balmedie. Abers 4J 73
Balmerino. Fife 5G 67
Balmerlawn. Hants 5M 9
Balmore. E Dun 2E 58
Balmore. High 1D 68
Balmullo. Fife 5H 67
Balmurrie. Dum 5H 51
Balnaboth. Ang 1G 67
Balnabruaich. High 6H 79
Balnabruich. High 1A 80
Balnacoil. High 2J 79
Balnacra. High 1L 69
Balnacroft. Abers 6B 72
Balnageith. Mor 8L 79
Balnaglaic. High 2E 70
Balnagrantach. High 2E 70
Balnaguard. Per 2C 66
Balnahard. Arg 8K 63
Balnain. High 2E 70
Balnakeil. High 5F 84
Balnaknock. High 7F 76
Balnamoon. Abers 8J 81
Balnamoon. Ang 1J 67
Balnamore. Caus 2F 93
Balnapaling. High 7H 79
Balornock. Glas 3E 58
Balquhidder. Stir 5K 65
Balsall. W Mid 4L 27
Balsall Common. W Mid 4L 27
Balscote. Oxon 7A 28
Balsham. Cambs 6B 30
Balstonia. Thur 5C 22
Baltasound. Shet 3L 91
Balterley. Staf 4F 34
Baltersan. Dum 5K 51
Balthangie. Abers 8H 81
Baltonsborough. Som 2D 8
Balvaird. High 8F 78
Balvaird. Per 6E 66
Balvenie. Mor 1C 72
Balvicar. Arg 6B 64
Balvraid. High 4K 69
Balvraid Lodge. High 2J 71
Bamber Bridge. Lanc 5D 40
Bamber's Green. Essx 1B 22
Bamburgh. Nmbd 6J 61
Bamford. Derbs 1L 35
Bamfurlong. G Man 7D 40
Bampton. Cumb 4D 46
Bampton. Devn 3J 7
Bampton. Oxon 3M 19
Bampton Grange. Cumb 4D 46
Banavie. High 8B 70
**Banbridge**. Arm 6G 93
**Banbury**. Oxon 7B 28
Bancffosfelen. Carm 5L 15
Banchory. Abers 6F 72
Banchory-Devenick. Abers 5J 73
Bancycapel. Carm 5L 15
Bancyfelin. Carm 5K 15
Banc-y-ffordd. Carm 3L 15
Banff. Abers 7F 80
**Bangor**. Ards 4J 93
**Bangor**. Gwyn 3E 32
Bangor-is-y-coed. Wrex 5B 34
Bangors. Corn 6B 6
Bangor's Green. Lanc 7B 40
Banham. Norf 3G 31
Bank. Hants 5L 9
The Bank. Ches E 4G 35
The Bank. Shrp 2E 26
Bankend. Dum 5E 52
Bankfoot. Per 4D 66
Bankglen. E Ayr 8E 58
Bankhead. Aber 4H 73
Bankhead. Abers 5F 72
Bankhead. S Lan 5G 59
Bankland. Som 3B 8
Bank Newton. N Yor 2H 41
Banknock. Falk 2F 58
Banks. Cumb 5K 53
Banks. Lanc 5B 40
Bankshill. Dum 3F 52
Bank Street. Worc 5E 26
Bank Top. Lanc 7D 40
Banners Gate. W Mid 2J 27
Banningham. Norf 7J 39
Banniskirk. High 6C 86
Bannister Green. Essx 1C 22
Bannockburn. Stir 8B 66
**Banstead**. Surr 8K 21
Bantham. Devn 7J 5
Banton. N Lan 2F 58
Banwell. N Som 8B 18
Banyard's Green. Suff 4K 31
Bapchild. Kent 7F 22
Bapton. Wilts 2H 9
Barabhas. W Isl 6G 83
Barabhas Iarach. W Isl 7G 83
Baramore. High 8H 69
Barassie. S Ayr 6B 58
Baravullin. Arg 3D 64
Barbaraville. High 6H 79
Barber Booth. Derbs 1K 35
Barber Green. Cumb 7B 46
Barbhas Uarach. W Isl 6G 83
Barbieston. S Ayr 8C 58
Barbon. Cumb 7E 46
Barbourne. Worc 6G 27
Barbridge. Ches E 4E 34
Barbrook. Devn 1G 7
Barby. Nptn 4C 28
Barby Nortoft. Nptn 4C 28
Barcaldine. Arg 3D 64
Barcheston. Warw 8L 27
Barclose. Cumb 5J 53
Barcombe. E Sus 4M 11
Barcombe Cross. E Sus 4M 11
Barden. N Yor 6K 47
Barden Scale. N Yor 2J 41
Bardfield End Green. Essx 8C 30
Bardfield Saling. Essx 1C 22
Bardister. Shet 6H 91
Bardnabeinne. High 4H 79
Bardney. Linc 3J 37
Bardon. Leics 8B 36
Bardon Mill. Nmbd 5A 54
Bardowie. E Dun 2D 58
Bardrainney. Inv 2B 58
Bardsea. Cumb 8B 46
Bardsey. W Yor 3A 42
Bardsley. G Man 7H 41
Bardwell. Suff 4F 30
Bare. Lanc 1C 40
Barelees. Nmbd 6F 60
Barewood. Here 6B 26
Barford. Hants 2F 10
Barford. Norf 1H 31
Barford. Warw 5L 27
Barford St John. Oxon 8B 28
Barford St Martin. Wilts 2J 9
Barford St Michael. Oxon 8B 28
Barfrestone. Kent 8J 23
Bargeddie. N Lan 3E 58
**Bargod**. Cphy 5L 17
**Bargoed**. Cphy 5L 17
Bargrennan. Dum 4J 51
Barham. Cambs 4J 29
Barham. Kent 8J 23
Barham. Suff 6H 31
Barharrow. Dum 6M 51
Bar Hill. Cambs 5L 29
Barholm. Linc 8H 37
Barkby. Leics 1D 28
Barkestone-le-Vale. Leics 6E 36
Barkham. Wok 7E 20
**Barking**. G Lon 5M 21
Barking. Suff 6G 31
Barkingside. G Lon 5A 22
Barking Tye. Suff 6G 31
Barkisland. W Yor 6J 41
Barkston. Linc 5G 37
Barkston Ash. N Yor 4B 42
Barkway. Herts 8L 29
Barlanark. Glas 3E 58
Barlaston. Staf 6G 35
Barlavington. W Sus 4G 11
Barlborough. Derbs 2B 36
Barlby. N Yor 4D 42
Barlestone. Leics 1B 28
Barley. Herts 8L 29
Barley. Lanc 3G 41
Barley Mow. Tyne 6F 54
Barleythorpe. Rut 1F 28
Barling. Essx 5F 22
Barlings. Linc 2H 37
Barlow. Derbs 2M 35
Barlow. N Yor 5D 42
Barlow. Tyne 5E 54
Barmby Moor. E Yor 3E 42
Barmby on the Marsh.
E Yor 5D 42
Barmer. Norf 6E 38
Barming. Kent 8D 22
Barming Heath. Kent 8D 22
Barmoor. Nmbd 6H 61
Barmouth. Gwyn 1F 24
Barmpton. Darl 4M 47
Barmston. E Yor 2J 43
Barmulloch. Glas 3E 58
Barnack. Pet 1H 29
Barnacle. Warw 3A 28
Barnard Castle. Dur 4J 47
Barnard Gate. Oxon 2B 20
Barnardiston. Suff 7D 30
Barnbarroch. Dum 6C 52
Barnburgh. S Yor 7B 42
Barnby. Suff 3L 31
Barnby Dun. S Yor 7D 42
Barnby in the Willows.
Notts 4F 36
Barnby Moor. Notts 1D 36
**Barnes**. G Lon 6K 21
Barnes Street. Kent 1C 12
**Barnet**. G Lon 4K 21
Barnetby le Wold. N Lin 7H 43
Barney. Norf 6F 38
Barnham. Suff 4E 30
Barnham. W Sus 5G 11
Barnham Broom. Norf 1G 31
Barnhead. Ang 2K 67
Barnhill. D'dee 4H 67
Barnhill. Mor 8M 79
Barnhill. Per 5E 66
Barnhills. Dum 4E 50
Barningham. Dur 4J 47
Barningham. Suff 4F 30
Barnoldby le Beck. NE Lin 7K 43
**Barnoldswick**. Lanc 3G 41
Barns Green. W Sus 3J 11
Barnsley. Glos 3J 19
Barnsley. Shrp 2F 26
**Barnsley**. S Yor 7M 41
**Barnstaple**. Devn 2E 6
Barnston. Essx 2C 22
Barnston. Mers 1A 34
Barnstone. Notts 6E 36
Barnt Green. Worc 4J 27
Barnton. Ches W 2E 34
Barnwell. Cambs 6A 30
Barnwell. Nptn 3H 29
Barnwood. Glos 2G 19
Barons Cross. Here 6C 26
The Barony. Orkn 7B 88
Barr. Dum 1B 52
Barr. S Ayr 2H 51
Barra Airport. W Isl 5C 74
Barrachan. Dum 7J 51
Barraglom. W Isl 8E 82
Barrahormid. Arg 1G 57
Barrapol. Arg 3E 62
Barrasford. Nmbd 4C 54
Barravullin. Arg 7C 64
Barregarrow. IOM 6C 44
**Barrhead**. E Ren 4D 58
Barrhill. S Ayr 3H 51
**Barri**. V Glam 8L 17
Barrington. Cambs 7L 29
Barrington. Som 4B 8
Barripper. Corn 5K 3
Barrmill. N Ayr 4B 58
Barrock. High 4D 86
Barrow. Lanc 4F 40
Barrow. Rut 8F 36
Barrow. Shrp 1E 26
Barrow. Som 2F 8
Barrow. Suff 5D 30
Barroway Drove. Norf 1B 30
Barrow Bridge. G Man 6E 40
Barrowburn. Nmbd 8F 60
Barrowby. Linc 6F 36
Barrowcliff. N Yor 7H 49
Barrow Common. N Som 7D 18
Barrowden. Rut 1G 29
Barrowford. Lanc 4G 41
Barrow Gurney. N Som 7D 18
Barrow Haven. N Lin 5H 43
Barrow Hill. Derbs 2B 36
**Barrow-in-Furness**. Cumb 8M 45
Barrow Nook. Lanc 7C 40
Barrow's Green. Hal 1D 34
Barrows Green. Cumb 7D 46
Barrow Street. Wilts 2G 9
Barrow upon Humber.
N Lin 5H 43
Barrow upon Soar. Leics 8C 36
Barrow upon Trent. Derbs 7A 36
Barry. Ang 4J 67
**Barry**. V Glam 8L 17
Barry Island. V Glam 8L 17
Barsby. Leics 8D 36
Barsham. Suff 3K 31
Barston. W Mid 4L 27
Bartestree. Here 7D 26
Barthol Chapel. Abers 2H 73
Bartholomew Green. Essx 1D 22
Barthomley. Ches E 4F 34
Bartley. Hants 4M 9
Bartley Green. W Mid 3J 27
Bartlow. Cambs 7B 30
Barton. Cambs 6M 29
Barton. Ches W 4C 34
Barton. Cumb 3C 46
Barton. Glos 1K 19
Barton. IOW 7C 10
Barton. Lanc
nr. Ormskirk 7B 40
nr. Preston 4D 40
Barton. N Som 8B 18
Barton. N Yor 5L 47
Barton. Oxon 3C 20
Barton. Torb 5M 5
Barton. Warw 6K 27
Barton Bendish. Norf 1D 30
Barton Gate. Staf 8K 35
Barton Green. Staf 8K 35
Barton Hartsthorn. Buck 8D 28
Barton Hill. N Yor 1E 42
Barton in Fabis. Notts 6C 36
Barton in the Beans. Leics 1A 28
Barton-le-Clay. C Beds 8H 29
Barton-le-Street. N Yor 8E 48
Barton-le-Willows. N Yor 1E 42
Barton Mills. Suff 4D 30
**Barton on Sea**. Hants 6L 9
Barton-on-the-Heath. Warw 8L 27
Barton St David. Som 2D 8
Barton Seagrave. Nptn 4F 28
Barton Stacey. Hants 1B 10
Barton Town. Devn 1F 6
Barton Turf. Norf 7K 39
Barton-Under-Needwood.
Staf 8K 35
Barton-upon-Humber.
N Lin 5H 43
Barton Waterside. N Lin 5H 43
Barugh Green. S Yor 7M 41
Barway. Cambs 4B 30
Barwell. Leics 2B 28
Barwick. Herts 2L 21
Barwick. Som 4D 8
Barwick in Elmet. W Yor 4A 42
Baschurch. Shrp 7C 34
Bascote. Warw 5B 28
Basford Green. Staf 4H 35
Bashall Eaves. Lanc 3E 40
Bashall Town. Lanc 3F 40
Bashley. Hants 6L 9
**Basildon**. Essx 5D 22
**Basingstoke**. Hants 8D 20
Baslow. Derbs 2L 35
Bason Bridge. Som 1B 8
Bassaleg. Newp 5A 18
Bassendean. Bord 5D 60
Bassenthwaite. Cumb 8G 53
Bassett. Sotn 4B 10
Bassingbourn. Cambs 7L 29
Bassingfield. Notts 6D 36
Bassingham. Linc 3G 37
Bassingthorpe. Linc 7G 37
Bassus Green. Herts 1L 21
Basta. Shet 4K 91
Baston. Linc 8J 37
Bastonford. Worc 6G 27
Bastwick. Norf 8L 39
Batchley. Worc 5J 27
Batchworth. Herts 4H 21
Batcombe. Dors 5E 8
Batcombe. Som 2E 8
Bate Heath. Ches E 2E 34
**Bath**. Bath 106 (7F 18)
Bathampton. Bath 7F 18
Bathealton. Som 3K 7
Batheaston. Bath 7F 18
Bathford. Bath 7F 18
**Bathgate**. W Lot 3H 59
Bathley. Notts 4E 36
Bathpool. Corn 8B 6
Bathpool. Som 3A 8
Bathville. W Lot 3H 59
Bathway. Som 8D 18
**Batley**. W Yor 5L 41
Batsford. Glos 8K 27
Batson. Devn 8K 5
Battersby. N Yor 5C 48
**Battersea**. G Lon 6K 21
Battisborough Cross. Devn 7J 5
Battisford. Suff 6G 31
Battisford Tye. Suff 6G 31
Battle. E Sus 4D 12
Battle. Powy 1K 17
Battleborough. Som 8B 18
Battledown. Glos 1H 19
Battlefield. Shrp 8D 34
Battlesbridge. Essx 4D 22
Battlesden. C Beds 1G 21
Battlesea Green. Suff 4J 31
Battleton. Som 3J 7
Battram. Leics 1B 28
Battramsley. Hants 6M 9
Batt's Corner. Surr 1F 10
Bauds of Cullen. Mor 7D 80
Baugh. Arg 3F 62
Baughton. Worc 7G 27
Baughurst. Hants 7C 20
Baulking. Oxon 4M 19
Baumber. Linc 2K 37
Baunton. Glos 3J 19
Baverstock. Wilts 2J 9
Bawburgh. Norf 1H 31
Bawdeswell. Norf 7G 39
Bawdrip. Som 2B 8
Bawdsey. Suff 7K 31
Bawsey. Norf 8C 38
Bawtry. S Yor 8D 42
Baxenden. Lanc 5F 40
Baxterley. Warw 2L 27
Baxter's Green. Suff 6D 30
Bay. High 8D 76
Baybridge. Hants 3C 10
Baybridge. Nmbd 6C 54
Baycliff. Cumb 8A 46
Baydon. Wilts 6L 19
Bayford. Herts 3L 21
Bayford. Som 3F 8
Bayles. Cumb 7M 53
Baylham. Suff 6H 31
Baynard's Green. Oxon 1C 20
Bayston Hill. Shrp 1C 26
Baythorne End. Essx 7D 30
Baythorpe. Linc 5K 37
Bayton. Worc 4E 26
Bayton Common. Worc 4F 26
Bayworth. Oxon 3C 20
Beach. S Glo 6F 18
Beachampton. Buck 8E 28
Beachamwell. Norf 1D 30
Beachley. Glos 4D 18
Beacon. Devn 5L 7
Beacon End. Essx 1F 22
Beacon Hill. Surr 2F 10
Beacon's Bottom. Buck 4E 20
**Beaconsfield**. Buck 4G 21
Beacrabhaic. W Isl 4C 76
Beadlam. N Yor 7D 48
Beadnell. Nmbd 7K 61
Beaford. Devn 4E 6
Beal. Nmbd 5H 61
Beal. N Yor 5C 42
Bealsmill. Corn 8C 6
Beam Hill. Staf 7L 35
Beamhurst. Staf 6J 35
Beaminster. Dors 5C 8
Beamish. Dur 6F 54
Beamond End. Buck 4G 21
Beamsley. N Yor 2J 41
Bean. Kent 6B 22
Beanacre. Wilts 7H 19
Beanley. Nmbd 8H 61
Beaquoy. Orkn 7C 88
Beardwood. Bkbn 5E 40
Beare Green. Surr 1J 11
Bearley. Warw 5K 27
Bearpark. Dur 7F 54
Bearsbridge. Nmbd 6A 54
**Bearsden**. E Dun 2D 58
Bearsted. Kent 8D 22
Bearstone. Shrp 6F 34
Bearwood. Pool 6J 9
Bearwood. W Mid 3J 27
Beattock. Dum 1E 52
Beauchamp Roding. Essx 2B 22
Beauchief. S Yor 1M 35
Beaufort. Blae 3L 17
Beaulieu. Hants 5A 10
Beauly. High 1F 70
Beaumaris. IOA 3F 32
Beaumont. Cumb 6H 53
Beaumont. Essx 1H 23
Beaumont Hill. Darl 4L 47
Beaumont Leys. Leic 1C 28
Beausale. Warw 4L 27
Beauvale. Notts 5B 36
Beauworth. Hants 3C 10
Beaworthy. Devn 6D 6
Beazley End. Essx 1D 22
**Bebington**. Mers 1B 34
Bebside. Nmbd 3F 54
**Beccles**. Suff 3L 31
Becconsall. Lanc 5C 40
Beckbury. Shrp 1F 26
**Beckenham**. G Lon 7L 21
Beckermet. Cumb 4K 45
Beckett End. Norf 2D 30
Beck Foot. Cumb 6E 46
Beckfoot. Cumb
nr. Broughton in Furness 6L 45
nr. Seascale 4L 45
nr. Silloth 7E 52
Beckford. Worc 8H 27
Beckhampton. Wilts 7J 19
Beck Hole. N Yor 5F 48
Beckingham. Linc 4F 36
Beckingham. Notts 8E 42
Beckington. Som 8G 19
Beckley. E Sus 3E 12
Beckley. Hants 6L 9
Beckley. Oxon 2C 20
Beck Row. Suff 4C 30
Beck Side. Cumb
nr. Cartmel 7B 46
nr. Ulverston 6M 45
Beckside. Cumb 7E 46
Beckton. G Lon 5M 21
Beckwithshaw. N Yor 2L 41
Becontree. G Lon 5A 22
Bedale. N Yor 7L 47
Bedburn. Dur 8E 54
Bedchester. Dors 4G 9
Beddau. Rhon 6K 17
Beddgelert. Gwyn 6E 32
Beddingham. E Sus 5M 11
Beddington. G Lon 7L 21
Bedfield. Suff 5J 31
**Bedford**. Bed 7H 29
Bedford. G Man 8E 40
Bedham. W Sus 3H 11
Bedhampton. Hants 5E 10
Bedingfield. Suff 5H 31
Bedingham Green. Norf 2J 31
Bedlam. N Yor 1L 41
Bedlar's Green. Essx 1B 22
**Bedlington**. Nmbd 3F 54
Bedlinog. Mer T 4K 17
Bedminster. Bris 6D 18
Bedmond. Herts 3H 21
Bednall. Staf 8H 35
Bedrule. Bord 8D 60
Bedstone. Shrp 4B 26
Bedwas. Cphy 6L 17
Bedwellty. Cphy 4L 17
**Bedworth**. Warw 3A 28
Beeby. Leics 1D 28
Beech. Hants 2D 10
Beech. Staf 6G 35
Beechcliffe. W Yor 3J 41
Beech Hill. W Ber 7D 20
Beechingstoke. Wilts 8J 19
Beedon. W Ber 6B 20
Beeford. E Yor 2J 43
Beeley. Derbs 3L 35
Beelsby. NE Lin 7K 43
Beenham. W Ber 7C 20
Beeny. Corn 2D 4
Beer. Devn 7M 7
Beer. Som 2C 8
Beercrocombe. Som 3B 8
Beer Hackett. Dors 4E 8
Beesands. Devn 7L 5
Beesby. Linc 1A 38
Beeson. Devn 7L 5
Beeston. C Beds 7J 29
Beeston. Ches W 4D 34
Beeston. Norf 8F 38
**Beeston**. Notts 6C 36
Beeston. W Yor 4L 41
Beeston Regis. Norf 5H 39
Beeswing. Dum 5C 52
Beetham. Cumb 8C 46
Beetham. Som 4A 8
Beetley. Norf 8F 38
Beffcote. Staf 8G 35
Began. Card 6M 17
Begbroke. Oxon 2B 20
Begdale. Cambs 1A 30
Begelly. Pemb 6H 15
Beggar Hill. Essx 3C 22
Beggar's Bush. Powy 5A 26
Beggearn Huish. Som 2K 7
Beguildy. Powy 5L 25
Beighton. Norf 1K 31
**Beighton**. S Yor 1B 36
Beighton Hill. Derbs 4L 35
Beinn Casgro. W Isl 1F 76
Beith. N Ayr 4B 58
Bekesbourne. Kent 8H 23
Belaugh. Norf 8J 39
Belbroughton. Worc 4H 27
Belchalwell. Dors 5F 8
Belchalwell Street. Dors 5F 8
Belchamp Otten. Essx 7E 30
Belchamp St Paul. Essx 7D 30
Belchamp Walter. Essx 7E 30
Belchford. Linc 2K 37
Belcoo. Ferm 7B 92
**Belfast**. Bel 5H 93
Belfast City George Best Airport.
Bel 5H 93
Belfast International Airport.
Ant 4G 93
Belfatton. Abers 8K 81
Belford. Nmbd 6J 61
Belgrano. Cnwy 3J 33
Belhaven. E Lot 2D 60
Belhelvie. Abers 4J 73
Belhinnie. Abers 3D 72
Bellabeg. Abers 4C 72
Belladrum. High 1F 70
Bellaghy. M Ulst 4F 93
Bellamore. S Ayr 3H 51
Bellanaleck. Ferm 7C 92
Bellanoch. Arg 8C 64
Bell Busk. N Yor 2H 41
Belleau. Linc 2M 37
Belleek. Ferm 6A 92
Belleek. New M 7F 93
Belleheiglash. Mor 2A 72
Bell End. Worc 4H 27
Bellerby. N Yor 6K 47
Bellerby Camp. N Yor 6J 47
Bellever. Devn 8F 6
Belle Vue. Cumb 8F 52
Belle Vue. Shrp 8C 34
Bellfield. S Lan 6G 59
Belliehill. Ang 1J 67
Bellingdon. Buck 3G 21
Bellingham. Nmbd 3B 54
Bellmount. Norf 7B 38
Bellochantuy. Arg 6F 56
Bellsbank. E Ayr 1K 51
Bell's Cross. Suff 6H 31
**Bellshill**. N Lan 4F 58
Bellshill. Nmbd 6J 61
Bellside. N Lan 4G 59
Bellspool. Bord 6K 59
Bellsquarry. W Lot 3J 59
Bells Yew Green. E Sus 2C 12
Belmaduthy. High 8G 79
Belmesthorpe. Rut 8H 37
Belmont. Bkbn 6E 40
Belmont. Shet 3K 91
Belmont. S Ayr 7B 58
Belnacraig. Abers 4C 72
Belnie. Linc 6K 37
Belowda. Corn 5B 4
**Belper**. Derbs 5A 36
Belper Lane End. Derbs 5M 35
Belph. Derbs 2C 36
Belsay. Nmbd 4E 54
Belsford. Devn 6K 5
Belsize. Herts 3H 21
Belstead. Suff 7H 31
Belston. S Ayr 7B 58
Belstone. Devn 6F 6
Belstone Corner. Devn 6F 6
Belthorn. Lanc 5F 40
Beltinge. Kent 7H 23
Beltoft. N Lin 7F 42
Belton. Leics 7B 36
Belton. Linc 6G 37
Belton. Norf 1L 31
Belton. N Lin 7E 42
Belton-in-Rutland. Rut 1F 28
Beltring. Kent 1C 12
Belts of Collonach. Abers 6F 72
Belvedere. G Lon 6A 22
Belvoir. Leics 6F 36
Bembridge. IOW 7D 10
Bemersyde. Bord 6C 60
Bemerton. Wilts 2K 9
Bempton. E Yor 8J 49
Benacre. Suff 3M 31
Ben Alder Lodge. High 8F 70
Ben Armine Lodge. High 2H 79
Benbecula Airport. W Isl 8J 75
Benbuie. Dum 2B 52
Benburb. M Ulst 6F 93
Benchill. G Man 1G 35
Benderloch. Arg 4D 64
Bendish. Herts 1J 21
Bendooragh. Caus 2F 93
Bendronaig Lodge. High 2M 69
Benenden. Kent 2E 12
Benfieldside. Dur 6D 54
Bengate. Norf 7K 39
Bengeworth. Worc 7J 27
Benhall Green. Suff 5K 31
Benholm. Abers 1M 67
Beningbrough. N Yor 2C 42
Benington. Herts 1K 21
Benington. Linc 5L 37
Benington Sea End. Linc 5M 37
Benllech. IOA 2E 32
Benmore Lodge. High 2D 78
Bennacott. Corn 6B 6
Bennah. Devn 7H 7
Bennecarrigan. N Ayr 7J 57
Bennethead. Cumb 3C 46
Benniworth. Linc 1K 37
Benover. Kent 1D 12
Benson. Oxon 4D 20
Benston. Shet 2E 90
Benstonhall. Orkn 6E 88
Bent. Abers 8F 72
Benthall. Shrp 1E 26
Bentham. Glos 2H 19
Bentlawnt. Shrp 1B 26
Bentley. E Yor 4H 43
Bentley. Hants 1E 10
**Bentley**. S Yor 7C 42
Bentley. Suff 8H 31
Bentley. Warw 2L 27
Bentley. W Mid 2H 27
Bentley Heath. Herts 4K 21
Bentley Heath. W Mid 4K 27
Bentpath. Dum 2H 53
Bents. W Lot 3H 59
Bentworth. Hants 1D 10
Benvie. D'dee 4G 67
Benville. Dors 5D 8
Benwell. Tyne 5F 54
Benwick. Cambs 2L 29
Beoley. Worc 5J 27
Beoraidbeg. High 6H 69
Bepton. W Sus 4F 10
Beragh. Ferm 5D 92
Berden. Essx 1A 22
Bere Alston. Devn 5G 5
Bere Ferrers. Devn 5G 5
Berepper. Corn 6K 3
Bere Regis. Dors 6G 9
Bergh Apton. Norf 1K 31
Berinsfield. Oxon 4C 20
Berkeley. Glos 4E 18
**Berkhamsted**. Herts 3G 21
Berkley. Som 1G 9
Berkswell. W Mid 4L 27
**Bermondsey**. G Lon 6L 21
Bernera. High 3K 69
Bernice. Arg 8F 64
Bernisdale. High 8F 76
Berrick Salome. Oxon 4D 20
Berriedale. High 1M 79
Berrier. Cumb 3B 46
Berriew. Powy 2L 25
Berrington. Nmbd 5H 61
Berrington. Shrp 1D 26
Berrington. Worc 5D 26
Berrington Green. Worc 5D 26
Berrington Law. Nmbd 5G 61
Berrow. Som 8B 18
Berrow Green. Worc 6F 26
Berry Cross. Devn 4D 6
Berry Down Cross. Devn 1E 6
Berry Hill. Glos 2D 18
Berry Hill. Pemb 2G 15
Berryhillock. Mor 7E 80
Berrynarbor. Devn 1E 6
Berry Pomeroy. Devn 5L 5
Berryscaur. Dum 2F 52
Berry's Green. G Lon 8M 21
Bersham. Wrex 5B 34
Berthengam. Flin 3L 33
Berwick. E Sus 5B 12
Berwick Bassett. Wilts 6K 19
Berwick Hill. Nmbd 4E 54
Berwick St James. Wilts 2J 9
Berwick St John. Wilts 3H 9
Berwick St Leonard. Wilts 2H 9
**Berwick-upon-Tweed**.
Nmbd 4G 61
Berwyn. Den 6L 33
Bescaby. Leics 7F 36
Bescar. Lanc 6B 40
Besford. Worc 7H 27
**Bessacarr**. S Yor 7D 42
Bessbrook. New M 7G 93
Bessels Leigh. Oxon 3B 20
Bessingby. E Yor 1J 43
Bessingham. Norf 6H 39
Best Beech Hill. E Sus 2C 12
Besthorpe. Norf 2G 31
Besthorpe. Notts 3F 36
Bestwood Village. Notts 5C 36
Beswick. E Yor 3H 43
Betchworth. Surr 8K 21
Bethania. Cdgn 6E 24
Bethania. Gwyn
nr. Blaenau Ffestiniog 6G 33
nr. Caernarfon 5F 32
Bethel. Gwyn
nr. Bala 7J 33
nr. Caernarfon 4E 32
Bethel. IOA 3C 32
Bethersden. Kent 1F 12
Bethesda. Gwyn 4F 32
Bethesda. Pemb 5G 15
Bethlehem. Carm 2F 16
**Bethnal Green**. G Lon 5L 21
Betley. Staf 5F 34
Betsham. Kent 6C 22
Betteshanger. Kent 8K 23
Bettiscombe. Dors 6C 8
Bettisfield. Wrex 6C 34
Betton. Shrp 6E 34
Betton Strange. Shrp 1D 26
Bettws. B'end 6J 17
Bettws. Newp 4A 18
Bettws Bledrws. Cdgn 7E 24
Bettws Cedewain. Powy 3L 25
Bettws Gwerfil Goch. Den 6K 33
Bettws Ifan. Cdgn 2K 15
Bettws Newydd. Mon 3B 18
Bettyhill. High 5K 85
Betws. Carm 3F 16
Betws Garmon. Gwyn 5E 32
Betws-y-Coed. Cnwy 5G 33
Betws-yn-Rhos. Cnwy 3J 33
Beulah. Cdgn 2J 15
Beulah. Powy 7J 25
Beul an Atha. Arg 3C 56
Bevendean. Brig 5L 11
Bevercotes. Notts 2E 36
**Beverley**. E Yor 4H 43
Beverston. Glos 4G 19
Bevington. Glos 4E 18
Bewaldeth. Cumb 8G 53

Bewcastle. Cumb. 4K 53
Bewdley. Worc. 4F 26
Bewerley. N Yor 1K 41
Bewholme. E Yor 2J 43
Bexfield. Norf 7G 39
**Bexhill**. E Sus 5D 12
**Bexley**. G Lon 6A 22
**Bexleyheath**. G Lon 6A 22
Bexleyhill. W Sus 3G 11
Bexwell. Norf 1C 30
Beyton. Suff 5F 30
Bhalton. W Isl 8D 82
Bhatarsaigh. W Isl 6C 74
Bibbington. Derbs 2J 35
Bibury. Glos 3K 19
**Bicester**. Oxon 1C 20
Bickenhall. Som 4A 8
Bickenhill. W Mid 3K 27
Bicker. Linc 6K 37
Bicker Bar. Linc 6K 37
Bicker Gauntlet. Linc 6K 37
Bickershaw. G Man 7E 40
Bickerstaffe. Lanc 7C 40
Bickerton. Ches E 4D 34
Bickerton. Nmbd 1C 54
Bickerton. N Yor 2B 42
Bickford. Staf 8G 35
Bickington. Devn
nr. Barnstaple 2E 6
nr. Newton Abbot 8G 7
Bickleigh. Devn
nr. Plymouth 5H 5
nr. Tiverton 5J 7
Bickleton. Devn 2E 6
Bickley. N Yor 6G 49
Bickley Moss. Ches W 5D 34
Bickmarsh. Worc 7K 27
Bicknacre. Essx 3D 22
Bicknoller. Som 2L 7
Bicknor. Kent 8E 22
Bickton. Hants 4K 9
Bicton. Here 5C 26
Bicton. Shrp
nr. Bishop's Castle 3A 26
nr. Shrewsbury 8C 34
Bicton Heath. Shrp 8C 34
Bidborough. Kent 1B 12
Biddenden. Kent 2E 12
Biddenden Green. Kent 1E 12
Biddenham. Bed 6H 29
Biddestone. Wilts 6G 19
Biddisham. Som 8B 18
Biddlesden. Buck 7D 28
Biddlestone. Nmbd 1C 54
**Biddulph**. Staf 4G 35
Biddulph Moor. Staf 4H 35
**Bideford**. Devn 3D 6
Bidford-on-Avon. Warw 6J 27
Bidlake. Devn 7E 6
Bidston. Mers 1A 34
Bielby. E Yor 3E 42
Bieldside. Aber 5H 73
Bierley. IOW 8C 10
Bierley. W Yor 4K 41
Bierton. Buck 2F 20
Bigbury. Devn 7J 5
Bigbury-on-Sea. Devn 7J 5
Bigby. Linc 7H 43
Biggar. Cumb 8L 45
Biggar. S Lan 6J 59
Biggin. Derbs
nr. Hartington 4K 35
nr. Hulland 5L 35
Biggin. N Yor 4C 42
Biggings. Shet 1B 90
**Biggin Hill**. G Lon 8M 21
**Biggleswade**. C Beds 7J 29
Bighouse. High 5L 85
Bighton. Hants 2D 10
Biglands. Cumb 6G 53
Bignall End. Staf 4G 35
Bignor. W Sus 4G 11
Bigrigg. Cumb 3K 45
Big Sand. High 6J 77
Bigton. Shet 5D 90
Bilberry. Corn 6C 4
Bilborough. Nott 5C 36
Bilbrook. Som 1K 7
Bilbrook. Staf 1G 27
Bilbrough. N Yor 3C 42
Bilbster. High 6D 86
Bilby. Notts 1D 36
Bildershaw. Dur 3L 47
Bildeston. Suff 7F 30
**Billericay**. Essx 4C 22
Billesdon. Leics 1E 28
Billesley. Warw 6K 27
Billingborough. Linc 6J 37
Billinge. Mers 7D 40
Billingford. Norf
nr. Dereham 7G 39
nr. Diss 4H 31
**Billingham**. Stoc T 3B 48
Billinghay. Linc 4J 37
Billingley. S Yor 7B 42
Billingshurst. W Sus 3H 11
Billingsley. Shrp 3F 26
Billington. C Beds 1G 21
Billington. Lanc 4F 40
Billington. Staf 7G 35
Billockby. Norf 8L 39
Billy Row. Dur 8E 54
Bilsborrow. Lanc 3D 40
Bilsby. Linc 2A 38
Bilsham. W Sus 5G 11
Bilsington. Kent 2G 13
Bilson Green. Glos 2E 18
Bilsthorpe. Notts 3D 36
Bilston. Midl 3L 59
Bilston. W Mid 2H 27
Bilstone. Leics 1A 28
Bilting. Kent 1G 13
Bilton. E Yor 4J 43
Bilton. Nmbd 8K 61
Bilton. N Yor 2M 41
Bilton. Warw 4B 28
Bilton in Ainsty. N Yor 3B 42
Bimbister. Orkn 8C 88
Binbrook. Linc 8K 43
Binchester. Dur 8F 54
Bincombe. Dors 7E 8
Bindal. High 5K 79
Binegar. Som 1E 8
Bines Green. W Sus 4J 11
Binfield. Brac 6F 20
Binfield Heath. Oxon 6E 20
Bingfield. Nmbd 4C 54
Bingham. Notts 6E 36
Bingham's Melcombe. Dors 5F 8
**Bingley**. W Yor 4K 41
Bings Heath. Shrp 8D 34
Binham. Norf 6F 38
Binley. Hants 8B 20
Binley. W Mid 4A 28
Binnegar. Dors 7G 9
Binniehill. Falk 2G 59
Binsoe. N Yor 8L 47
Binstead. IOW 6C 10
Binsted. Hants 1E 10
Binsted. W Sus 5G 11
Binton. Warw 6K 27
Bintree. Norf 7G 39
Binweston. Shrp 1B 26
Birch. Essx 2F 22
Birch. G Man 7G 41
Birchall. Staf 4H 35
Bircham Newton. Norf 6D 38
Bircham Tofts. Norf 6D 38
Birchanger. Essx 1B 22
Birchburn. N Ayr 7J 57
Birch Cross. Staf 6K 35
Bircher. Here 5C 26
Birch Green. Essx 2F 22
Birchgrove. Card 6L 17
Birchgrove. Swan 5G 17
Birch Heath. Ches W 3D 34
Birch Hill. Ches W 2D 34
Birchill. Devn 5B 8
Birchington. Kent 7J 23
Birchley Heath. Warw 2L 27
Birchmoor. Warw 1L 27
Birchmoor Green. C Beds 8G 29
Birchover. Derbs 3L 35
Birch Vale. Derbs 1J 35
Birchview. Mor 2A 72
**Birchwood**. Linc 3G 37
Birchwood. Som 4M 7
Birchwood. Warr 8E 40
Bircotes. Notts 8D 42
Birdbrook. Essx 7D 30
Birdham. W Sus 5F 10
Birdholme. Derbs 3A 36
Birdingbury. Warw 5B 28
Birdlip. Glos 2H 19
Birdsall. N Yor 1F 42
Birds Edge. W Yor 7L 41
Birds Green. Essx 3B 22
Birdsgreen. Shrp 3F 26
Birdsmoorgate. Dors 5B 8
Birdston. E Dun 2E 58
Birdwell. S Yor 7M 41
Birdwood. Glos 2F 18
Birgham. Bord 6E 60
Birichen. High 4H 79
Birkby. Cumb 8E 52
Birkby. N Yor 5M 47
Birkdale. Mers 6B 40
**Birkenhead**. Mers 1B 34
Birkenhills. Abers 1G 73
Birkenshaw. N Lan 3E 58
Birkenshaw. W Yor 5L 41
Birkhall. Abers 6C 72
Birkhill. Ang 4G 67
Birkholme. Linc 7G 37
Birkin. N Yor 5C 42
Birley. Here 6C 26
Birling. Kent 7C 22
Birling. Nmbd 1F 54
Birling Gap. E Sus 6B 12
Birlingham. Worc 7H 27
**Birmingham**. W Mid 106 (3J 27)
Birmingham Airport.
W Mid 119 (3K 27)
Birnam. Per 3D 66
Birse. Abers 6E 72
Birsemore. Abers 6E 72
**Birstall**. Leics 1C 28
Birstall. W Yor 5L 41
Birstall Smithies. W Yor 5L 41
Birstwith. N Yor 2L 41
Birthorpe. Linc 6J 37
Birtle. G Man 6G 41
Birtley. Here 5B 26
Birtley. Nmbd 4B 54
Birtley. Tyne 6F 54
Birtsmorton. Worc 8G 27
Birts Street. Worc 8F 26
Bisbrooke. Rut 2F 28
Bisham. Wind 5F 20
Bishampton. Worc 6H 27
Bish Mill. Devn 3G 7
Bishop Auckland. Dur 3L 47
Bishopbridge. Linc 8H 43
**Bishopbriggs**. E Dun 2E 58
Bishop Burton. E Yor 4G 43
Bishopdown. Wilts 2K 9
Bishop Middleham. Dur 8G 55
Bishopmill. Mor 7B 80
Bishop Monkton. N Yor 1M 41
Bishop Norton. Linc 8G 43
Bishopsbourne. Kent 8H 23
Bishops Cannings. Wilts 7J 19
Bishop's Castle. Shrp 3B 26
Bishop's Caundle. Dors 4E 8
**Bishop's Cleeve**. Glos 1H 19
Bishops Court. New M 6J 93
Bishop's Down. Dors 4E 8
Bishop's Frome. Here 7E 26
Bishop's Green. Essx 2C 22
Bishop's Green. Hants 7C 20
Bishop's Hull. Som 3M 7
Bishops Itchington. Warw 6A 28
Bishops Lydeard. Som 3L 7
Bishop's Norton. Glos 1G 19
Bishop's Nympton. Devn 3G 7
Bishop's Offley. Staf 7F 34
**Bishop's Stortford**. Herts 1A 22
Bishop's Sutton. Hants 2D 10
Bishop's Tachbrook. Warw 5M 27
Bishop's Tawton. Devn 2E 6
Bishopsteignton. Devn 8J 7
**Bishopstoke**. Hants 4B 10
Bishopston. Swan 6E 16
Bishopstone. Buck 2F 20
Bishopstone. E Sus 5A 12
Bishopstone. Here 7C 26
Bishopstone. Swin 5L 19
Bishopstone. Wilts 3J 9
Bishopstrow. Wilts 1G 9
Bishop Sutton. Bath 8D 18
Bishop's Waltham. Hants 4C 10
Bishops Wood. Staf 1G 27
Bishopswood. Som 4A 8
Bishopsworth. Bris 7D 18
Bishop Thornton. N Yor 1L 41
Bishopthorpe. York 3C 42
Bishopton. Darl 3A 48
Bishopton. Dum 7K 51
Bishopton. N Yor 8L 47
Bishopton. Ren 2C 58
Bishopton. Warw 6K 27
Bishop Wilton. E Yor 2E 42
Bishton. Newp 5B 18
Bishton. Staf 7J 35
Bisley. Glos 3H 19
Bisley. Surr 8G 21
Bispham. Bkpl 3B 40
Bispham Green. Lanc 6C 40
Bissoe. Corn 4L 3
Bisterne. Hants 5K 9
Bisterne Close. Hants 5L 9
Bitchfield. Linc 7G 37
Bittadon. Devn 1E 6
Bittaford. Devn 6J 5
Bittering. Norf 8F 38
Bitterley. Shrp 4D 26
Bitterne. Sotn 4B 10
Bitteswell. Leics 3C 28
Bitton. S Glo 7E 18
Bix. Oxon 5E 20
Bixter. Shet 2D 90
Blaby. Leics 2C 28
Blackawton. Devn 6L 5
Black Bank. Cambs 3B 30
Black Barn. Linc 7M 37
Blackborough. Devn 5K 7
Blackborough. Norf 8C 38
Blackborough End. Norf 8C 38
Black Bourton. Oxon 3L 19
Blackboys. E Sus 3B 12
Blackbrook. Derbs 5M 35
Blackbrook. Mers 8D 40
Blackbrook. Staf 6F 34
Blackbrook. Surr 1J 11
Blackburn. Abers 4H 73
**Blackburn**. Bkbn 5E 40
Blackburn. W Lot 3H 59
Black Callerton. Tyne 5E 54
Black Carr. Norf 2G 31
Black Clauchrie. S Ayr 3H 51
Black Corries. High 2G 65
Black Crofts. Arg 4D 64
Black Cross. Corn 5B 4
Blackden Heath. Ches E 2F 34
Blackditch. Oxon 3B 20
Black Dog. Devn 5H 7
Blackdog. Abers 4J 73
Blackdown. Dors 5B 8
Blackdyke. Cumb 6F 52
Blacker Hill. S Yor 7A 42
Blackfen. G Lon 6A 22
Blackfield. Hants 5B 10
Blackford. Cumb 5H 53
Blackford. Per 7B 66
Blackford. Shrp 3D 26
Blackford. Som
nr. Burnham-on-Sea 1C 8
nr. Wincanton 3E 8
Blackfordby. Leics 8M 35
Blackgang. IOW 8B 10
Blackhall. Edin 2L 59
Blackhall. Ren 3C 58
Blackhall Colliery. Dur 8H 55
Blackhall Mill. Tyne 6E 54
Blackhall Rocks. Dur 8H 55
Blackham. E Sus 2A 12
Blackheath. Essx 1G 23
Blackheath. G Lon 6L 21
Blackheath. Suff 4L 31
Blackheath. Surr 1H 11
Blackheath. W Mid 3H 27
Black Heddon. Nmbd 4D 54
Blackhill. Abers 1K 73
Blackhill. High 8E 76
Blackhills. Abers 7J 81
Blackhills. High 8K 79
Blackjack. Linc 6K 37
Blackland. Wilts 7J 19
Black Lane. G Man 7F 40
Blackleach. Lanc 4C 40
Blackley. G Man 7G 41
Blackley. W Yor 6K 41
Blacklunans. Per 1E 66
Blackmill. B'end 6J 17
Blackmoor. G Man 7E 40
Blackmoor. Hants 2E 10
Blackmoor Gate. Devn 1F 6
Blackmore. Essx 3C 22
Blackmore End. Essx 8D 30
Blackmore End. Herts 2J 21
Black Mount. Arg 3G 65
Blackness. Falk 2J 59
Blacknest. Hants 1E 10
Blackney. Dors 6C 8
Blacknoll. Dors 7G 9
Black Notley. Essx 1D 22
Blacko. Lanc 3G 41
Black Pill. Swan 5F 16
**Blackpool**. Bkpl 106 (4B 40)
Blackpool. Devn 7L 5
Blackpool Corner. Dors 6B 8
Blackpool Gate. Cumb 4K 53
Blackridge. W Lot 3G 59
Blackrock. Arg 3C 56
Blackrock. Mon 3M 17
Blackrod. G Man 6E 40
Blackshaw. Dum 5E 52
Blackshaw Head. W Yor 5H 41
Blackshaw Moor. Staf 4J 35
Blackskull. Arm 6G 93
Blacksmith's Green. Suff 5H 31
Blacksnape. Bkbn 5F 40
Blackstone. W Sus 4K 11
Black Street. Suff 3M 31
Black Tar. Pemb 6F 14
Blackthorn. Oxon 2D 20
Blackthorpe. Suff 5F 30
Blacktoft. E Yor 5F 42
Blacktop. Aber 5H 73
Black Torrington. Devn 5D 6
Blacktown. Newp 5A 18
**Blackwall Tunnel**. G Lon 5L 21
Blackwater. Corn 4L 3
Blackwater. Hants 8F 20
Blackwater. IOW 7C 10
Blackwater. Som 4A 8
Blackwaterfoot. N Ayr 7H 57
Blackwatertown. Arm 6F 93
Blackwell. Darl 4L 47
Blackwell. Derbs
nr. Alfreton 4B 36
nr. Buxton 2K 35
Blackwell. Som 3K 7
Blackwell. Warw 7L 27
Blackwell. Worc 4H 27
**Blackwood**. Cphy 5L 17
Blackwood. Dum 3D 52
Blackwood. S Lan 5F 58
Blackwood Hill. Staf 4H 35
Blacon. Ches W 3B 34
Bladnoch. Dum 6K 51
Bladon. Oxon 2B 20
Blaenannerch. Cdgn 2J 15
Blaenau Dolwyddelan.
Cnwy 5F 32
Blaenau Ffestiniog. Gwyn 6G 33
Blaenavon. Torf 3A 18
Blaenawey. Mon 2A 18
Blaen Celyn. Cdgn 1K 15
Blaen Clydach. Rhon 5J 17
Blaencwm. Rhon 5J 17
Blaendulais. Neat 4H 17
Blaenffos. Pemb 3H 15
Blaengarw. B'end 5J 17
Blaen-geuffordd. Cdgn 4F 24
Blaengwrach. Neat 4H 17
Blaengwynfi. Neat 5H 17
Blaenllechau. Rhon 5K 17
Blaenpennal. Cdgn 6F 24
Blaenplwyf. Cdgn 5E 24
Blaenporth. Cdgn 2J 15
Blaenrhondda. Rhon 4J 17
Blaenwaun. Carm 4J 15
Blaen-y-coed. Carm 4K 15
Blagdon. N Som 8C 18
Blagdon. Torb 5L 5
Blagdon Hill. Som 4M 7
Blagill. Cumb 7M 53
Blaguegate. Lanc 7C 40
Blaich. High 8M 69
Blain. High 1A 64
Blaina. Blae 4M 17
Blair Atholl. Per 1C 66
Blair Drummond. Stir 8M 65
Blairgowrie. Per 3E 66
Blairhall. Fife 1J 59
Blairingone. Per 8C 66
Blairlogie. Stir 8B 66
Blairmore. Abers 2D 72
Blairmore. Arg 1L 57
Blairmore. High 6D 84
Blairquhanan. W Dun 1C 58
Blaisdon. Glos 2F 18
Blakebrook. Worc 4G 27
Blakedown. Worc 4G 27
Blake End. Essx 1D 22
Blakemere. Here 7B 26
Blakeney. Glos 3E 18
Blakeney. Norf 5G 39
Blakenhall. Ches E 5F 34
Blakenhall. W Mid 2H 27
Blakeshall. Worc 3G 27
Blakesley. Nptn 6D 28
Blanchland. Nmbd 6C 54
Blandford Camp. Dors 5H 9
Blandford Forum. Dors 5G 9
Blandford St Mary. Dors 5G 9
Bland Hill. N Yor 2L 41
Blandy. High 5J 85
Blanefield. Stir 2D 58
Blankney. Linc 3H 37
**Blantyre**. S Lan 4E 58
Blarmachfoldach. High 1E 64
Blarnalearoch. High 4B 78
Blashford. Hants 5K 9
Blaston. Leics 2F 28
Blatchbridge. Som 1F 8
Blathaisbhal. W Isl 6K 75
Blatherwycke. Nptn 2G 29
Blawith. Cumb 7A 46
Blaxhall. Suff 6K 31
Blaxton. S Yor 8D 42
**Blaydon**. Tyne 5E 54
Bleadney. Som 1C 8
Bleadon. N Som 8B 18
Blean. Kent 7H 23
Bleary. Arm 6G 93
Bleasby. Linc 1J 37
Bleasby. Notts 5E 36
Bleasby Moor. Linc 1J 37
Blebocraigs. Fife 6H 67
Bleddfa. Powy 6M 25
Bledington. Glos 1L 19
Bledlow. Buck 3E 20
Bledlow Ridge. Buck 4E 20
Blencarn. Cumb 8L 53
Blencogo. Cumb 7F 52
Blendworth. Hants 4E 10
Blennerhasset. Cumb 7F 52
Bletchingdon. Oxon 2C 20
Bletchingley. Surr 8L 21
**Bletchley**. Mil 8F 28
Bletchley. Shrp 6E 34
Bletherston. Pemb 4G 15
Bletsoe. Bed 6H 29
Blewbury. Oxon 5C 20
Blickling. Norf 7H 39
Blidworth. Notts 4C 36
Blindburn. Nmbd 8F 60
Blindcrake. Cumb 8F 52
Blindley Heath. Surr 1L 11
Blindmoor. Som 4A 8
Blisland. Corn 4D 4
Blissford. Hants 4K 9
Bliss Gate. Worc 4F 26
Blists Hill. Telf 1E 26
Blisworth. Nptn 6E 28
Blithbury. Staf 7J 35
Blitterlees. Cumb 6F 52
Blockley. Glos 8K 27
Blofield. Norf 1K 31
Blofield Heath. Norf 8K 39
Blo' Norton. Norf 4G 31
Bloomfield. Bord 7C 60
Blore. Staf 5K 35
Blount's Green. Staf 6J 35
Bloxham. Oxon 8B 28
Bloxholm. Linc 4H 37
Bloxwich. W Mid 1H 27
Bloxworth. Dors 6G 9
Blubberhouses. N Yor 2K 41
Blue Anchor. Som 1K 7
Blue Anchor. Swan 5E 16
Blue Bell Hill. Kent 7D 22
Blue Row. Essx 2G 23
Bluetown. Kent 8F 22
Blundeston. Suff 2M 31
Blunham. C Beds 6J 29
Blunsdon St Andrew. Swin 5K 19
Bluntington. Worc 4G 27
Bluntisham. Cambs 4L 29
Blunts. Corn 5F 4
Blurton. Stoke 5G 35
Blyborough. Linc 8G 43
Blyford. Suff 4L 31
Blymhill. Staf 8G 35
Blymhill Lawns. Staf 8G 35
**Blyth**. Nmbd 3G 55
Blyth. Notts 1D 36
Blyth. Bord 5K 59
Blyth Bank. Bord 5K 59
Blyth Bridge. Bord 5K 59
Blythburgh. Suff 4L 31
The Blythe. Staf 7J 35
Blythe Bridge. Staf 5H 35
Blythe Marsh. Staf 5H 35
Blyton. Linc 8F 42
Boardmills. Lis 6H 93
Boarhills. Fife 6J 67
Boarhunt. Hants 5D 10
Boar's Head. G Man 7D 40
Boarshead. E Sus 2B 12
Boars Hill. Oxon 3B 20
Boarstall. Buck 2D 20
Boasley Cross. Devn 6E 6
Boath. High 6F 78
Boat of Garten. High 4K 71
Bobbing. Kent 7E 22
Bobbington. Staf 2G 27
Bobbingworth. Essx 3B 22
Bocaddon. Corn 6E 4
Bocking. Essx 1D 22
Bocking Churchstreet. Essx 1D 22
Boddam. Abers 1L 73
Boddam. Shet 6D 90
Boddington. Glos 1G 19
Bodedern. IOA 2C 32
Bodelwyddan. Den 3K 33
Bodenham. Here 6D 26
Bodenham. Wilts 3K 9
Bodewryd. IOA 1C 32
Bodfari. Den 3K 33
Bodffordd. IOA 3D 32
Bodham. Norf 5H 39
Bodiam. E Sus 3D 12
Bodicote. Oxon 8B 28
Bodieve. Corn 4B 4
Bodinnick. Corn 6D 4
Bodle Street Green. E Sus 4C 12
**Bodmin**. Corn 5C 4
Bodnant. Cnwy 3H 33
Bodney. Norf 2E 30
Bodorgan. IOA 4C 32
Bodrane. Corn 5E 4
Bodsham. Kent 1H 13
Boduan. Gwyn 7C 32
Bodymoor Heath. Warw 2K 27
The Bog. Shrp 2B 26
Bogallan. High 8G 79
Bogbrae Croft. Abers 2K 73
Bogend. S Ayr 6B 58
Boghall. Midl 3L 59
Boghall. W Lot 3H 59
Boghead. S Lan 5F 58
Bogindollo. Ang 2H 67
Bogmoor. Mor 7D 80
Bogniebrae. Abers 1E 72
**Bognor Regis**. W Sus 6G 11
Bograxie. Abers 4G 73
Bogside. N Lan 4G 59
Bogton. Abers 8F 80
Bogue. Dum 3M 51
Bohenie. High 7C 70
Bohortha. Corn 8A 4
Boirseam. W Isl 5B 76
Bokiddick. Corn 5C 4
Bolam. Dur 3K 47
Bolam. Nmbd 3D 54
Bolberry. Devn 8J 5
Bold Heath. Mers 1D 34
**Boldon**. Tyne 5G 55
Boldon Colliery. Tyne 5G 55
Boldre. Hants 6M 9
Boldron. Dur 4J 47
Bole. Notts 1E 36
Bolehall. Staf 1L 27
Bolehill. Derbs 4L 35
Bolenowe. Corn 5K 3
Boleside. Bord 6B 60
Bolham. Devn 4J 7
Bolham Water. Devn 4L 7
Bolingey. Corn 3L 3
Bollington. Ches E 2H 35
Bolney. W Sus 3K 11
Bolnhurst. Bed 6H 29
Bolshan. Ang 2K 67
**Bolsover**. Derbs 2B 36
Bolsterstone. S Yor 8L 41
Bolstone. Here 8D 26
Boltachan. Per 2B 66
Boltby. N Yor 7B 48
Bolton. Cumb 3F 46
Bolton. E Lot 2C 60
Bolton. E Yor 2E 42
**Bolton**. G Man 7F 40
Bolton. Nmbd 8J 61
Bolton Abbey. N Yor 2J 41
Bolton-by-Bowland. Lanc 3F 40
Boltonfellend. Cumb 5J 53
Boltongate. Cumb 7G 53
Bolton Green. Lanc 6D 40
Bolton-le-Sands. Lanc 1C 40
Bolton Low Houses. Cumb 7G 53
Bolton New Houses. Cumb 7G 53
Bolton-on-Swale. N Yor 6L 47
Bolton Percy. N Yor 3C 42
Bolton Town End. Lanc 1C 40
Bolton upon Dearne. S Yor 7B 42
Bolton Wood Lane. Cumb 7G 53
Bolventor. Corn 8A 6
Bomarsund. Nmbd 3F 54
Bomere Heath. Shrp 8C 34
Bonar Bridge. High 4G 79
Bonawe. Arg 4E 64
Bonby. N Lin 6H 43
Boncath. Pemb 3J 15
Bonchester Bridge. Bord 8C 60
Bonchurch. IOW 8C 10
Bond End. Staf 8K 35
Bondleigh. Devn 5F 6
Bonds. Lanc 3C 40
Bonehill. Devn 8G 7
Bonehill. Staf 1K 27
**Bo'ness**. Falk 1H 59
Boney Hay. Staf 8J 35
Bonham. Wilts 2F 8
**Bonhill**. W Dun 2B 58
Boningale. Shrp 1G 27
Bonjedward. Bord 7D 60
Bonkle. N Lan 4G 59
Bonnanaboigh. Caus 3E 92
Bonnington. Ang 4J 67
Bonnington. Edin 3K 59
Bonnington. Kent 2G 13
Bonnybank. Fife 7G 67
**Bonnybridge**. Falk 1G 59
Bonnykelly. Abers 8H 81
**Bonnyrigg**. Midl 3M 59
Bonnyton. Ang 4G 67
Bonnytown. Fife 6J 67
Bonsall. Derbs 4L 35
Bont. Mon 2B 18
Bontddu. Gwyn 1F 24
Bont Dolgadfan. Powy 2H 25
Y Bont-Faen. V Glam 7J 17
Bontgoch. Cdgn 4F 24
Bonthorpe. Linc 2A 38
Bont Newydd. Gwyn 6G 33
Bont-newydd. Cnwy 3K 33
Bontnewydd. Cdgn 6F 24
Bontnewydd. Gwyn 4D 32
Bontuchel. Den 5K 33
Bonvilston. V Glam 7K 17
Bon-y-maen. Swan 5F 16
Booker. Buck 4F 20
Booley. Shrp 7D 34
Boorley Green. Hants 4C 10
Boosbeck. Red C 4D 48
Boot. Cumb 4L 45
Booth. W Yor 5J 41
Boothby Graffoe. Linc 4G 37
Boothby Pagnell. Linc 6G 37
Booth Green. Ches E 1H 35
Booth of Toft. Shet 6J 91
Boothstown. G Man 7F 40
Boothville. Nptn 5E 28
Bootle. Cumb 6L 45
**Bootle**. Mers 8B 40
Booton. Norf 7H 39
Booze. N Yor 5J 47
Boquhan. Stir 1D 58
Boraston. Shrp 4E 26
Borden. Kent 7E 22
Borden. W Sus 3F 10
Bordlands. Bord 5K 59
Bordley. N Yor 1H 41
**Bordon**. Hants 2E 10
Boreham. Essx 3D 22
Boreham. Wilts 1G 9
Boreham Street. E Sus 4C 12
**Borehamwood**. Herts 4J 21
Boreland. Dum 2F 52
Boreston. Devn 6K 5
Borestone Brae. Stir 8A 66
Boreton. Shrp 1D 26
Borgh. W Isl
on Barra 5C 74
on Benbecula 8J 75
on Berneray 5L 75
on Isle of Lewis 6H 83
Borghasdal. W Isl 5B 76
Borghastan. W Isl 7E 82
Borgh na Sgiotaig. High 6E 76
Borgie. High 6J 85
Borgue. Dum 7M 51
Borgue. High 1M 79
Borley. Essx 7E 30
Borley Green. Essx 7E 30
Borley Green. Suff 5F 30
Borlum. High 3F 70
Bornais. W Isl 3D 74
Bornesketaig. High 6E 76
Boroughbridge. N Yor 1A 42
Borough Green. Kent 8C 22
Borreraig. High 8C 76
Borrobol Lodge. High 1J 79
Borrodale. High 1C 68
Borrowash. Derbs 6B 36
Borrowby. N Yor
nr. Northallerton 7B 48
nr. Whitby 4F 48
Borrowston. High 7E 86
Borrowstonehill. Orkn 1F 86
Borrowstoun. Falk 1H 59
Borstal. Medw 7D 22
Borth. Cdgn 4F 24
Borthwick. Midl 4A 60
Borth-y-Gest. Gwyn 7E 32
Borve. High 1F 68
Borwick. Lanc 8D 46
Bosbury. Here 7E 26
Boscastle. Corn 2D 4
Boscombe. Bour 6K 9
Boscombe. Wilts 2L 9
Boscoppa. Corn 6C 4
Bosham. W Sus 5F 10
Bosherston. Pemb 7F 14
Bosley. Ches E 3H 35
Bossall. N Yor 1E 42
Bossiney. Corn 3C 4
Bossingham. Kent 1H 13
Bossington. Som 1H 7
Bostadh. W Isl 7E 82
Bostock Green. Ches W 3E 34
**Boston**. Linc 5L 37
Boston Spa. W Yor 3B 42
Boswarthen. Corn 5H 3
Boswinger. Corn 7B 4
Botany Bay. G Lon 4K 21
Botcheston. Leics 1B 28
Botesdale. Suff 4G 31
Bothal. Nmbd 3F 54
Bothampstead. W Ber 6C 20
Bothamsall. Notts 2D 36
Bothel. Cumb 8F 52
Bothenhampton. Dors 6C 8
Bothwell. S Lan 4F 58
Botley. Buck 3G 21
Botley. Hants 4C 10
Botley. Oxon 3B 20
Botloe's Green. Glos 1F 18
Botolph Claydon. Buck 1E 20
Botolphs. W Sus 5J 11
Bottacks. High 7E 78
Bottesford. Leics 6F 36
Bottesford. N Lin 7F 42
Bottisham. Cambs 5B 30
Bottlesford. Wilts 8K 19
Bottomcraig. Fife 5G 67
Bottom o' th' Moor. G Man 6E 40
Botton. N Yor 5E 48
Botton Head. Lanc 1E 40
Bottreaux Mill. Devn 3H 7
Botus Fleming. Corn 5G 5
Botwnnog. Gwyn 7B 32
Bough Beech. Kent 1A 12
Boughrood. Powy 1L 17
Boughspring. Glos 4D 18
Boughton. Norf 1C 30
Boughton. Nptn 5E 28
Boughton. Notts 3D 36
Boughton Aluph. Kent 1G 13
Boughton Green. Kent 8D 22
Boughton Lees. Kent 1G 13
Boughton Malherbe. Kent 1E 12
Boughton Monchelsea.
Kent 8D 22
Boughton under Blean.
Kent 8G 23
Boulby. Red C 4E 48
Bouldnor. IOW 7A 10
Bouldon. Shrp 3D 26
Boulmer. Nmbd 8K 61
Boulston. Pemb 5F 14
Boultham. Linc 3G 37
Boulton. Derb 6A 36
Boundary. Staf 5H 35
Bounds. Here 8E 26
Bourn. Cambs 6L 29
Bournbrook. W Mid 3J 27
Bourne. Linc 7H 37
The Bourne. Surr 1F 10
Bourne End. Bed 5H 29
Bourne End. Buck 5F 20
Bourne End. C Beds 7G 29
Bourne End. Herts 3H 21
**Bournemouth**. Bour 106 (6J 9)
Bournemouth Airport. Dors 6K 9
Bournes Green. Glos 3H 19
Bournes Green. S'end 5F 22
Bournheath. Worc 4H 27
Bournmoor. Dur 6G 55
Bournville. W Mid 3J 27
Bourton. Dors 2F 8
Bourton. N Som 7B 18
Bourton. Oxon 5L 19
Bourton. Shrp 2D 26
Bourton. Wilts 7J 19
Bourton on Dunsmore.
Warw 4B 28
Bourton-on-the-Hill. Glos 8K 27
Bourton-on-the-Water. Glos 1K 19
Bousd. Arg 1H 63
Bousta. Shet 2C 90
Boustead Hill. Cumb 6G 53
Bouth. Cumb 7B 46
Bouthwaite. N Yor 8K 47
Boveney. Buck 6G 21
Boveridge. Dors 4J 9
Boverton. V Glam 8J 17
Bovey Tracey. Devn 8H 7
Bovingdon. Herts 3H 21
Bovingdon Green. Buck 5F 20
Bovinger. Essx 3B 22
Bovington Camp. Dors 7G 9
Bow. Devn 5G 7
Bowbank. Dur 3H 47
Bow Brickhill. Mil 8G 29
Bowbridge. Glos 3G 19
Bowburn. Dur 8G 55
Bowcombe. IOW 7B 10
Bowd. Devn 7L 7
Bowden. Devn 7L 5
Bowden. Bord 6C 60
Bowden Hill. Wilts 7H 19
Bowdens. Som 3C 8
Bowderdale. Cumb 5E 46
Bowdon. G Man 1F 34
Bower. Nmbd 3A 54
Bowerchalke. Wilts 3J 9
Bowerhill. Wilts 7H 19
Bower Hinton. Som 4C 8
Bowermadden. High 5D 86
Bowers. Staf 6G 35
Bowers Gifford. Essx 5D 22
Bowershall. Fife 8D 66
Bowertower. High 5D 86
Bowes. Dur 4H 47
Bowgreave. Lanc 3C 40
Bowhousebog. N Lan 4G 59
Bowithick. Corn 7A 6
Bowland Bridge. Cumb 7C 46
Bowlees. Dur 3H 47
Bowley. Here 6D 26
Bowlhead Green. Surr 2G 11
Bowling. W Dun 2C 58
Bowling. W Yor 4K 41
Bowling Bank. Wrex 5B 34
Bowling Green. Worc 6G 27
Bowlish. Som 1E 8
Bowmanstead. Cumb 6B 46
Bowmore. Arg 4C 56
Bowness-on-Solway.
Cumb 5G 53
Bowness-on-Windermere.
Cumb 6C 46
Bow of Fife. Fife 6G 67
Bowriefauld. Ang 3J 67
Bowscale. Cumb 8H 53
Bowsden. Nmbd 5G 61
Bowside Lodge. High 5L 85
Bowston. Cumb 6C 46
Bow Street. Cdgn 4F 24
Bowthorpe. Norf 1H 31
Box. Glos 3G 19
Box. Wilts 7G 19
Boxbush. Glos 1E 18
Box End. Bed 7H 29
Boxford. Suff 7F 30
Boxford. W Ber 6B 20
Boxgrove. W Sus 5G 11
Box Hill. Wilts 7G 19
Boxley. Kent 8D 22
Boxmoor. Herts 3H 21
Box's Shop. Corn 5B 6
Boxted. Essx 8F 30
Boxted. Suff 6E 30
Boxted Cross. Essx 8G 31
Boxworth. Cambs 5L 29
Boxworth End. Cambs 5L 29
Boyden End. Suff 6D 30
Boyden Gate. Kent 7J 23
Boylestone. Derbs 6K 35
Boylestonfield. Derbs 6K 35
Boyndie. Abers 7F 80
Boynton. E Yor 1J 43
Boys Hill. Dors 4E 8
Boythorpe. Derbs 3A 36
Boyton. Corn 6C 6
Boyton. Suff 7K 31
Boyton. Wilts 2H 9
Boyton Cross. Essx 3C 22
Boyton End. Essx 8C 30
Boyton End. Suff 7D 30
Bozeat. Nptn 6G 29
Braaid. IOM 7C 44
Braal Castle. High 5C 86
Brabling Green. Suff 5J 31
Brabourne. Kent 1H 13
Brabourne Lees. Kent 1G 13
Brabster. High 5E 86
Bracadale. High 2E 68
Bracara. High 6J 69
Braceborough. Linc 8H 37
Bracebridge. Linc 3G 37
Bracebridge Heath. Linc 3G 37
Braceby. Linc 6H 37
Bracewell. Lanc 3G 41
Brackenber. Cumb 4F 46
Brackenfield. Derbs 4A 36
Brackenlands. Cumb 7G 53
Brackenthwaite. Cumb 7G 53
Brackenthwaite. N Yor 2L 41
Brackla. B'end 7J 17
Brackla. High 8J 79
Bracklesham. W Sus 6F 10
Brackletter. High 7B 70
Brackley. Nptn 8C 28
Brackley Hatch. Nptn 7D 28
Brackloch. High 1B 78
**Bracknell**. Brac 7F 20
Braco. Per 7B 66
Bracobrae. Mor 8E 80
Bracon. N Lin 7E 42
Bracon Ash. Norf 2H 31
Bradbourne. Derbs 4L 35
Bradbury. Dur 3M 47
Bradda. IOM 7A 44
Bradden. Nptn 7D 28
Bradenham. Buck 4F 20
Bradenham. Norf 1F 30
Bradenstoke. Wilts 6J 19
Bradfield. Essx 8H 31
Bradfield. Norf 6J 39
Bradfield. W Ber 6D 20
Bradfield Combust. Suff 6E 30
Bradfield Green. Ches E 4E 34
Bradfield Heath. Essx 1H 23
Bradfield St Clare. Suff 6F 30
Bradfield St George. Suff 5F 30
Bradford. Derbs 3L 35
Bradford. Devn 5D 6
Bradford. Nmbd 6J 61
**Bradford**. W Yor 106 (4K 41)
Bradford Abbas. Dors 4D 8
Bradford Barton. Devn 4H 7
Bradford Leigh. Wilts 7G 19
Bradford-on-Avon. Wilts 7G 19
Bradford-on-Tone. Som 3L 7
Bradford Peverell. Dors 6E 8
Bradiford. Devn 2E 6
Brading. IOW 7D 10
Bradley. Ches W 2D 34
Bradley. Derbs 5L 35
Bradley. Glos 4F 18
Bradley. Hants 1D 10
Bradley. NE Lin 7K 43
Bradley. N Yor 7J 47
Bradley. Staf 8G 35
Bradley. W Mid 2H 27
Bradley. W Yor 5K 41
Bradley. Wrex 4B 34
Bradley Cross. Som 8C 18
Bradley Green. Ches W 5D 34
Bradley Green. Som 2A 8
Bradley Green. Warw 1L 27
Bradley Green. Worc 5H 27
Bradley in the Moors. Staf 5J 35
Bradley Mount. Ches E 2H 35
Bradley Stoke. S Glo 5E 18
Bradlow. Here 8F 26
Bradmore. Notts 6C 36
Bradmore. W Mid 2G 27
Bradninch. Devn 5K 7
Bradnop. Staf 4J 35
Bradpole. Dors 6C 8
Bradshaw. G Man 6F 40
Bradstone. Devn 7C 6
Bradwall Green. Ches E 3F 34
Bradway. S Yor 1M 35
Bradwell. Derbs 1K 35
Bradwell. Essx 1E 22
Bradwell. Mil 8F 28
Bradwell. Norf 1M 31
Bradwell-on-Sea. Essx 3G 23
Bradwell Waterside. Essx 3F 22
Bradworthy. Devn 4C 6
Brae. High 5K 77
Brae. Shet 1D 90
Braeantra. High 6F 78
Braefield. High 2E 70
Braefindon. High 8G 79
Braegrum. Per 5D 66
**Braehead**. Ang 2K 67
Braehead. Dum 6K 51
Braehead. Mor 1B 72
Braehead. Orkn 5D 88
Braehead. S Lan
nr. Coalburn 6G 59
nr. Forth 4H 59
Braehoulland. Shet 6G 91
Braemar. Abers 6A 72
Braemore. High
nr. Dunbeath 8B 86
nr. Ullapool 6B 78
Brae of Achnahaird. High 2M 77
Brae Roy Lodge. High 6D 70
Braeside. Abers 2J 73
Braeside. Inv 2M 57
Braes of Coul. Ang 2G 67
Braeswick. Orkn 6F 88
Braetongue. High 6H 85
Braeval. Stir 7K 65
Braevallich. Arg 7D 64
Braewick. Shet 2D 90
Brafferton. Darl 3L 47
Brafferton. N Yor 8B 48
Brafield-on-the-Green. Nptn 6F 28
Bragar. W Isl 7F 82
Bragbury End. Herts 1K 21
Bragleenbeg. Arg 5D 64
Braichmelyn. Gwyn 4F 32
Braides. Lanc 2C 40
Braidwood. S Lan 5G 59
Braigo. Arg 3B 56
Brailsford. Derbs 5L 35
**Braintree**. Essx 1D 22
Braiseworth. Suff 4H 31
Braishfield. Hants 3A 10
Braithwaite. Cumb 2M 45
Braithwaite. S Yor 6D 42
Braithwaite. W Yor 3J 41
Braithwell. S Yor 8C 42
Brakefield Green. Norf 1G 31
Bramber. W Sus 4J 11
Brambridge. Hants 3B 10
Bramcote. Notts 6C 36
Bramcote. Warw 3B 28
Bramdean. Hants 3D 10
Bramerton. Norf 1J 31
Bramfield. Herts 2K 21
Bramfield. Suff 4K 31
Bramford. Suff 7H 31
**Bramhall**. G Man 1G 35
Bramham. W Yor 3B 42
Bramhope. W Yor 3L 41
Bramley. Hants 8D 20
Bramley. S Yor 8B 42
Bramley. Surr 1H 11
Bramley. W Yor 4L 41
Bramley Green. Hants 8D 20
Bramley Head. N Yor 2K 41
Bramley Vale. Derbs 3B 36
Bramling. Kent 8J 23
Brampford Speke. Devn 6J 7
Brampton. Cambs 4K 29
Brampton. Cumb
nr. Appleby-in-Westmorland 3E 46
nr. Carlisle 5K 53
Brampton. Linc 2F 36
Brampton. Norf 7J 39
Brampton. S Yor 7B 42
Brampton. Suff 3L 31
Brampton Abbotts. Here 1E 18
Brampton Ash. Nptn 3E 28
Brampton Bryan. Here 4B 26
Brampton en le Morthen.
S Yor 1B 36
Bramshall. Staf 6J 35
Bramshaw. Hants 4L 9
Bramshill. Hants 7E 20
Bramshott. Hants 2F 10
Branault. High 1L 63
Brancaster. Norf 5D 38
Brancaster Staithe. Norf 5D 38
Brancepeth. Dur 8F 54
Branch End. Nmbd 5D 54
Branchill. Mor 8L 79
Brand End. Linc 5L 37
Branderburgh. Mor 6B 80
Brandesburton. E Yor 3J 43
Brandeston. Suff 5J 31
Brand Green. Glos 1F 18
Brandhill. Shrp 4C 26
Brandis Corner. Devn 5D 6
Brandish Street. Som 1J 7
Brandiston. Norf 7H 39
Brandon. Dur 8F 54
Brandon. Linc 5G 37
Brandon. Nmbd 8H 61
Brandon. Suff 3D 30
Brandon. Warw 4B 28
Brandon Bank. Cambs 3C 30
Brandon Creek. Norf 2C 30
Brandon Parva. Norf 1G 31
Brandsby. N Yor 8C 48
Brandy Wharf. Linc 8H 43
Brane. Corn 6H 3
Bran End. Essx 1C 22
Branksome. Pool 6J 9
Bransbury. Hants 1B 10
Bransby. Linc 2F 36
Branscombe. Devn 7L 7
Bransford. Worc 6F 26
Bransgore. Hants 6K 9
Bransholme. Hull 4J 43
Bransley. Shrp 4E 26
Branston. Leics 7F 36
Branston. Linc 3H 37
Branston. Staf 7L 35
Branston Booths. Linc 3H 37
Branstone. IOW 7C 10
Bransty. Cumb 3J 45
Brant Broughton. Linc 4G 37
Brantham. Suff 8H 31
Branthwaite. Cumb
nr. Caldbeck 8G 53
nr. Workington 2K 45
Brantingham. E Yor 5G 43
Branton. Nmbd 8H 61
Branton. S Yor 7D 42
Branton Green. N Yor 1B 42
Branxholme. Bord 8B 60
Branxton. Nmbd 6F 60
Brassington. Derbs 4L 35
Brasted. Kent 8A 22
Brasted Chart. Kent 8A 22
The Bratch. Staf 2G 27
Brathens. Abers 6F 72
Bratoft. Linc 3A 38
Brattleby. Linc 1G 37
Bratton. Som 1J 7
Bratton. Telf 8E 34
Bratton. Wilts 8H 19
Bratton Clovelly. Devn 6D 6
Bratton Fleming. Devn 2F 6
Bratton Seymour. Som 3E 8
Braughing. Herts 1L 21
Braulen Lodge. High 2C 70
Braunston. Nptn 5C 28
Braunstone Town. Leics 1C 28
Braunston-in-Rutland. Rut 1F 28
Braunton. Devn 2D 6
Brawby. N Yor 8E 48
Brawl. High 5L 85
Brawlbin. High 6B 86
Bray. Wind 6G 21
Braybrooke. Nptn 3E 28
Brayford. Devn 2F 6
Bray Shop. Corn 8C 6
Braystones. Cumb 4K 45
Brayton. N Yor 4D 42
Bray Wick. Wind 6F 20
Brazacott. Corn 6B 6
Brea. Corn 4K 3
Breach. W Sus 5E 10
Breachwood Green. Herts 1J 21
Breacleit. W Isl 8E 82
Breaden Heath. Shrp 6C 34
Breadsall. Derbs 5A 36
Breadstone. Glos 3F 18
Breage. Corn 6K 3
Breakachy. High 1E 70
Breakish. High 3H 69
Bream. Glos 3E 18
Breamore. Hants 4K 9
Bream's Meend. Glos 3E 18
Brean. Som 8A 18
Breanais. W Isl 1A 76
Brearton. N Yor 1M 41
Breascleit. W Isl 8F 82
Breaston. Derbs 6B 36
Brecais Ard. High 3H 69
Brecais Iosal. High 3H 69
Brechfa. Carm 3M 15
Brechin. Ang 2K 67
Breckles. Norf 2F 30
Brecon. Powy 2K 17
**Bredbury**. G Man 8H 41
Brede. E Sus 4E 12
Bredenbury. Here 6E 26
Bredfield. Suff 6J 31
Bredgar. Kent 7E 22
Bredhurst. Kent 7D 22
Bredicot. Worc 6H 27
Bredon. Worc 8H 27
Bredon's Norton. Worc 8H 27
Bredwardine. Here 7B 26
Breedon on the Hill. Leics 7B 36
Breibhig. W Isl
on Barra 6C 74
on Isle of Lewis 8H 83
Breich. W Lot 3H 59
Breightmet. G Man 7F 40
Breighton. E Yor 4E 42
Breinton. Here 8C 26
Breinton Common. Here 8C 26
Breiwick. Shet 3E 90
Breston Green. Here 1D 18
Bremhill. Wilts 6H 19
Brenachie. High 6H 79
Brenchley. Kent 1C 12
Brendon. Devn 1G 7
**Brent Cross**. G Lon 5K 21
Brent Eleigh. Suff 7F 30
**Brentford**. G Lon 6J 21
Brentingby. Leics 8E 36
Brent Knoll. Som 8B 18
Brent Pelham. Herts 8M 29
**Brentwood**. Essx 4B 22
Brenzett. Kent 3G 13
Brereton. Staf 8J 35
Brereton Cross. Staf 8J 35
Brereton Green. Ches E 3F 34
Brereton Heath. Ches E 3G 35
Bressingham. Norf 3G 31
Bretby. Derbs 7L 35
Bretford. Warw 4B 28
Bretforton. Worc 7J 27
Bretherdale Head. Cumb 5D 46
Bretherton. Lanc 5C 40
Brettabister. Shet 2E 90
Brettenham. Norf 3F 30
Brettenham. Suff 6F 30
Bretton. Flin 3B 34
Bretton. Pet 1J 29
Brewlands Bridge. Ang 1E 66
Brewood. Staf 1G 27
Briantspuddle. Dors 6G 9
Bricket Wood. Herts 3J 21
Bricklehampton. Worc 7H 27
Bride. IOM 4D 44
Bridekirk. Cumb 8F 52
Bridell. Pemb 2H 15
Bridestowe. Devn 7E 6
Brideswell. Abers 2E 72
Bridford. Devn 7H 7
Bridge. Corn 4K 3
Bridge. Kent 8H 23
Bridge. Som 5B 8
Bridge End. Bed 6H 29
Bridge End. Cumb
nr. Broughton in Furness 5M 45
nr. Dalston 7H 53
Bridge End. Linc 6J 37
Bridge End. Shet 4D 90
Bridgefoot. Ang 4G 67
Bridgefoot. Cumb 2K 45
Bridge Green. Essx 8A 30
Bridgehampton. Som 3D 8
Bridge Hewick. N Yor 8M 47
Bridgehill. Dur 6D 54
Bridgemary. Hants 5C 10
Bridgemere. Ches E 5F 34
Bridgemont. Derbs 1J 35
Bridgend. Abers
nr. Huntly 2E 72
nr. Peterhead 2K 73
Bridgend. Ang
nr. Brechin 1J 67
nr. Kirriemuir 3G 67
Bridgend. Arg
nr. Lochgilphead 8C 64
on Islay 3C 56
**Bridgend**. B'end 6J 17
Bridgend. Cumb 4B 46
Bridgend. Devn 7H 5
Bridgend. Fife 6G 67
Bridgend. High 8D 78
Bridgend. Mor 2D 72
Bridgend. Per 5E 66
Bridgend. W Lot 2J 59
Bridgend of Lintrathen. Ang 2F 66
Bridgeness. Falk 1J 59
Bridge of Alford. Abers 4E 72
Bridge of Allan. Stir 8A 66
Bridge of Avon. Mor 4A 72
Bridge of Awe. Arg 5E 64
Bridge of Balgie. Per 3M 65
Bridge of Brown. High 3M 71
Bridge of Cally. Per 2E 66
Bridge of Canny. Abers 6F 72
Bridge of Dee. Dum 5B 52
Bridge of Don. Aber 4J 73
Bridge of Dun. Ang 2K 67
Bridge of Dye. Abers 7F 72
Bridge of Earn. Per 6E 66
Bridge of Ericht. Per 2K 65
Bridge of Feugh. Abers 6G 73
Bridge of Gairn. Abers 6D 72
Bridge of Gaur. Per 2K 65
Bridge of Muchalls. Abers 6H 73
Bridge of Oich. High 5E 70
Bridge of Orchy. Arg 4H 65
Bridge of Walls. Shet 2C 90
Bridge of Weir. Ren 3B 58
Bridge Reeve. Devn 4F 6
Bridgerule. Devn 5B 6
Bridge Sollers. Here 7C 26
Bridge Street. Suff 7E 30
Bridge Town. Warw 6L 27
Bridgetown. Devn 5L 5
Bridgetown. Som 2J 7
Bridge Trafford. Ches W 2C 34
Bridgeyate. S Glo 6E 18
Bridgham. Norf 3F 30
**Bridgnorth**. Shrp 2F 26
Bridgtown. Staf 1H 27
**Bridgwater**. Som 2B 8
**Bridlington**. E Yor 1J 43

**Bridport**. Dors 6C 8
Bridstow. Here 1D 18
**Brierfield**. Lanc 4G 41
Brierley. Glos 2E 18
Brierley. Here 6C 26
Brierley. S Yor 6B 42
Brierley Hill. W Mid 3H 27
Brierton. Hart 8H 55
Briestfield. W Yor 6L 41
Brigg. N Lin 7H 43
Briggate. Norf 7K 39
Briggswath. N Yor 5F 48
Brigham. Cumb 8E 52
Brigham. E Yor 2H 43
**Brighouse**. W Yor 5K 41
Brighstone. IOW 7B 10
Brightgate. Derbs 4L 35
Brighthampton. Oxon 3A 20
Brightholmlee. S Yor 8L 41
Brightley. Devn 6F 6
Brightling. E Sus 3C 12
Brightlingsea. Essx 2G 23
**Brighton**. Brig 106 (5L 11)
Brighton. Corn 6B 4
Brighton Hill. Hants 1D 10
Brightons. Falk 2H 59
Brightwalton. W Ber 6B 20
Brightwalton Green. W Ber 6B 20
Brightwell. Suff 7J 31
Brightwell Baldwin. Oxon 4D 20
Brightwell-cum-Sotwell. Oxon 4C 20
Brigmerston. Wilts 1K 9
Brignall. Dur 4J 47
Brig o' Turk. Stir 7K 65
Brigsley. NE Lin 7K 43
Brigsteer. Cumb 7C 46
Brigstock. Nptn 3G 29
Brill. Buck 2D 20
Brill. Corn 6L 3
Brilley. Here 7A 26
Brimaston. Pemb 4F 14
Brimfield. Here 5D 26
Brimington. Derbs 2B 36
Brimley. Devn 8H 7
Brimpsfield. Glos 2H 19
Brimpton. W Ber 7C 20
Brims. Orkn 3D 86
Brimscombe. Glos 3G 19
Brimstage. Mers 1B 34
Brincliffe. S Yor 1M 35
Brind. E Yor 4E 42
Brindister. Shet
nr. West Burrafirth 2C 90
nr. West Lerwick 4E 90
Brindle. Lanc 5D 40
Brindley. Ches E 4D 34
Brindley Ford. Stoke 4G 35
Brineton. Staf 8G 35
Bringhurst. Leics 2F 28
Bringsty Common. Here 6E 26
Brington. Cambs 4H 29
Brinian. Orkn 7D 88
Briningham. Norf 6G 39
Brinkhill. Linc 2L 37
Brinkley. Cambs 6C 30
Brinklow. Warw 4B 28
Brinkworth. Wilts 5J 19
Brinscall. Lanc 5E 40
Brinscombe. Som 8C 18
Brinsley. Notts 5B 36
Brinsworth. S Yor 1B 36
Brinton. Norf 6G 39
Brisco. Cumb 6J 53
Brisley. Norf 7F 38
Brislington. Bris 6E 18
Brissenden Green. Kent 2F 12
**Bristol**. Bris 107 (6D 18)
Bristol Airport. N Som 7D 18
Briston. Norf 6G 39
Britannia. Lanc 5G 41
Britford. Wilts 3K 9
Brithdir. Cphy 4L 17
Brithdir. Cdgn 2K 15
Brithdir. Gwyn 1G 25
Briton Ferry. Neat 5G 17
Britwell Salome. Oxon 4D 20
**Brixham**. Torb 6M 5
Brixton. Devn 6H 5
**Brixton**. G Lon 6L 21
Brixton Deverill. Wilts 2G 9
Brixworth. Nptn 4E 28
Brize Norton. Oxon 3M 19
The Broad. Here 5C 26
Broad Alley. Worc 5G 27
Broad Blunsdon. Swin 4K 19
Broadbottom. G Man 8H 41
Broadbridge. W Sus 5F 10
Broadbridge Heath. W Sus 2J 11
Broad Campden. Glos 8K 27
Broad Chalke. Wilts 3J 9
Broadclyst. Devn 6J 7
Broadfield. Inv 2B 58
Broadfield. Pemb 6H 15
Broadfield. W Sus 2K 11
Broadford. High 3H 69
Broadford Bridge. W Sus 3H 11
Broadgate. Cumb 6L 45
Broad Green. Cambs 6C 30
Broad Green. C Beds 7G 29
Broad Green. Worc
nr. Bromsgrove 4H 27
nr. Worcester 6F 26
Broad Haven. Pemb 5E 14
Broadhaven. High 6E 86
Broad Heath. Staf 7G 35
Broadheath. G Man 1F 34
Broadheath. Worc 5E 26
Broadheath Common. Worc 6G 27
Broadhembury. Devn 5L 7
Broadhempston. Devn 5L 5
Broad Hill. Cambs 4B 30
Broad Hinton. Wilts 6K 19
Broadholme. Derbs 5A 36
Broadholme. Linc 2F 36
Broadlay. Carm 6K 15
Broad Laying. Hants 7B 20
Broadley. Lanc 6G 41
Broadley. Mor 7C 80
Broadley Common. Essx 3M 21
Broad Marston. Worc 7K 27
Broadmayne. Dors 7F 8
Broadmere. Hants 1D 10
Broadmoor. Pemb 6G 15
Broad Oak. Carm 2E 16
Broad Oak. Cumb 5L 45
Broad Oak. Devn 6K 7
Broad Oak. Dors 4F 8
Broad Oak. E Sus
nr. Hastings 4E 12
nr. Heathfield 3C 12
Broad Oak. Here 1C 18
Broad Oak. Kent 7H 23
Broadoak. Dors 6C 8
Broadoak. Glos 2E 18
Broadoak. Hants 4C 10
Broadrashes. Mor 8D 80
Broadsea. Abers 7J 81
Broad's Green. Essx 2C 22
Broadshard. Som 4C 8
**Broadstairs**. Kent 7K 23
Broadstone. Pool 6J 9
Broadstone. Shrp 3D 26
Broad Street. E Sus 4E 12
Broad Street. Kent
nr. Ashford 1H 13
nr. Maidstone 8E 22
Broad Street Green. Essx 3E 22
Broad Town. Wilts 6J 19
Broadwas. Worc 6F 26
Broadwath. Cumb 6J 53
Broadway. Carm
nr. Kidwelly 6K 15
nr. Laugharne 6J 15
Broadway. Pemb 5E 14
Broadway. Som 4B 8
Broadway. Suff 4K 31
Broadway. Worc 8J 27
Broadwell. Glos
nr. Cinderford 2D 18
nr. Stow-on-the-Wold 1L 19
Broadwell. Oxon 3L 19
Broadwell. Warw 5B 28
Broadwell House. Nmbd 6C 54
Broadwey. Dors 7E 8
Broadwindsor. Dors 5C 8
Broadwoodkelly. Devn 5F 6
Broadwoodwidger. Devn 7D 6
Broallan. High 1E 70
Brobury. Here 7B 26
Brochel. High 1G 69
Brockaghboy. Caus 3F 93
Brockamin. Worc 6F 26
Brockbridge. Hants 4D 10
Brockdish. Norf 4J 31
Brockencote. Worc 4G 27
Brockenhurst. Hants 5L 9
Brocketsbrae. S Lan 6G 59
Brockford Street. Suff 5H 31
Brockhall. Nptn 5D 28
Brockham. Surr 1J 11
Brockhampton. Glos
nr. Bishop's Cleeve 1H 19
nr. Sevenhampton 1J 19
Brockhampton. Here 8D 26
Brockhill. Bord 7A 60
Brockholes. W Yor 6K 41
Brockhurst. Hants 5C 10
Brocklesby. Linc 6J 43
Brockley. N Som 7C 18
Brockley Corner. Suff 4E 30
Brockley Green. Suff
nr. Bury St Edmunds 7D 30
nr. Haverhill 6E 30
Brockleymoor. Cumb 8J 53
Brockmoor. W Mid 3H 27
Brockton. Shrp
nr. Bishop's Castle 3B 26
nr. Madeley 1F 26
nr. Much Wenlock 2D 26
nr. Pontesbury 1B 26
Brockton. Staf 6G 35
Brockton. Telf 8F 34
Brockweir. Glos 3D 18
Brockworth. Glos 2G 19
Brocton. Staf 8H 35
Brodick. N Ayr 6K 57
Brodie. Mor 8K 79
Brodiesord. Abers 8E 80
Brodsworth. S Yor 7C 42
Brogaig. High 7F 76
Brogborough. C Beds 8G 29
Brokenborough. Wilts 5H 19
Broken Cross. Ches E 2G 35
Bromborough. Mers 1B 34
Bromdon. Shrp 3E 26
Brome. Suff 4H 31
Brome Street. Suff 4H 31
Bromeswell. Suff 6K 31
Bromfield. Cumb 7F 52
Bromfield. Shrp 4C 26
Bromford. W Mid 2K 27
Bromham. Bed 6H 29
Bromham. Wilts 7H 19
**Bromley**. G Lon 7M 21
Bromley. Herts 1M 21
Bromley. Shrp 2F 26
Bromley Cross. G Man 6F 40
Bromley Green. Kent 2F 12
Bromley Wood. Staf 7K 35
Brompton. Medw 7D 22
Brompton. N Yor
nr. Northallerton 6A 48
nr. Scarborough 7G 49
Brompton. Shrp 1D 26
Brompton-on-Swale. N Yor 6L 47
Brompton Ralph. Som 2K 7
Brompton Regis. Som 2J 7
Bromsash. Here 1E 18
Bromsberrow. Glos 8F 26
Bromsberrow Heath. Glos 8F 26
**Bromsgrove**. Worc 4H 27
Bromstead Heath. Staf 8F 34
Bromyard. Here 6E 26
Bromyard Downs. Here 6E 26
Bronaber. Gwyn 7G 33
Broncroft. Shrp 3D 26
Brongest. Cdgn 2K 15
Brongwyn. Cdgn 2J 15
Bronington. Wrex 6C 34
Bronllys. Powy 1L 17
Bronnant. Cdgn 6F 24
Bronwydd Arms. Carm 4L 15
Bronydd. Powy 8M 25
Bronygarth. Shrp 6A 34
Brook. Carm 6J 15
Brook. Hants
nr. Cadnam 4L 9
nr. Romsey 3M 9
Brook. IOW 7A 10
Brook. Kent 1G 13
Brook. Surr
nr. Guildford 1H 11
nr. Haslemere 2G 11
Brooke. Norf 2J 31
Brooke. Rut 1F 28
Brookeborough. Ferm 6C 92
Brookenby. Linc 8K 43
Brook End. Worc 7G 27
Brookend. Glos 3E 18
Brookfield. Lanc 4D 40
Brookfield. Ren 3C 58
Brookhouse. Lanc 1D 40
Brookhouse. S Yor 1C 36
Brookhouse Green. Ches E 3G 35
Brookhouses. Staf 5H 35
Brookhurst. Mers 1B 34
Brookland. Kent 3F 12
Brooklands. G Man 8F 40
Brooklands. Shrp 5D 34
Brookmans Park. Herts 3K 21
Brooks. Powy 3L 25
Brooksby. Leics 8D 36
Brooks Green. W Sus 3J 11
Brook Street. Essx 4B 22
Brook Street. Kent 2F 12
Brook Street. W Sus 3L 11
Brookthorpe. Glos 2G 19
Brookville. Norf 2D 30
Brookwood. Surr 8G 21
Broom. C Beds 7J 29
Broom. Fife 7G 67
Broom. Warw 6J 27
Broome. Norf 2K 31
Broome. Shrp
nr. Cardington 2D 26
nr. Craven Arms 3C 26
Broome. Worc 4H 27
Broomedge. Warr 1F 34
Broomend. Abers 4G 73
Broomer's Corner. W Sus 3J 11
Broomfield. Abers 2J 73
Broomfield. Essx 2D 22
Broomfield. Kent
nr. Herne Bay 7H 23
nr. Maidstone 8E 22
Broomfield. Som 2M 7
Broomfleet. E Yor 5F 42
Broom Green. Norf 7F 38
Broomhall. Ches E 5E 34
Broomhall. Wind 7G 21
Broomhaugh. Nmbd 5D 54
Broom Hill. Dors 5J 9
Broom Hill. Worc 4H 27
Broomhill. High
nr. Grantown-on-Spey 3K 71
nr. Invergordon 6H 79
Broomhill. Norf 1C 30
Broomhill. S Yor 7B 42
Broomhillbank. Dum 2F 52
Broomholm. Norf 6K 39
Broomlands. Dum 1E 52
Broomley. Nmbd 5D 54
Broom of Moy. Mor 8L 79
Broompark. Dur 7F 54
Broom's Green. Glos 8F 26
Brora. High 3K 79
Broseley. Shrp 1E 26
Brotherhouse Bar. Linc 8K 37
Brotheridge Green. Worc 7G 27
Brotherlee. Dur 8C 54
Brothertoft. Linc 5K 37
Brotherton. N Yor 5B 42
Brotton. Red C 4D 48
Broubster. High 5B 86
Brough. Cumb 4F 46
Brough. Derbs 1K 35
Brough. E Yor 5G 43
Brough. High 4D 86
Brough. Notts 4F 36
Brough. Orkn
nr. Finstown 8C 88
nr. St Margaret's Hope 3F 86
Brough. Shet
nr. Benston 2E 90
nr. Booth of Toft 6J 91
on Bressay 3F 90
on Whalsay 1F 90
Broughall. Shrp 5D 34
Brougham. Cumb 3D 46
Brough Lodge. Shet 4K 91
Broughshane. ME Ant 3G 93
Brough Sowerby. Cumb 4F 46
Broughton. Cambs 4K 29
Broughton. Flin 3B 34
Broughton. Hants 2M 9
Broughton. Lanc 4D 40
Broughton. Mil 8F 28
Broughton. Nptn 4F 28
Broughton. N Lin 7G 43
Broughton. N Yor
nr. Malton 8E 48
nr. Skipton 2H 41
Broughton. Orkn 5D 88
Broughton. Oxon 8B 28
Broughton. Bord 6K 59
Broughton. Staf 6F 34
Broughton. V Glam 7J 17
Broughton Astley. Leics 2C 28
Broughton Beck. Cumb 7A 46
Broughton Cross. Cumb 8E 52
Broughton Gifford. Wilts 7G 19
Broughton Green. Worc 5H 27
Broughton Hackett. Worc 6H 27
Broughton in Furness. Cumb 6M 45
Broughton Mills. Cumb 5M 45
Broughton Moor. Cumb 8E 52
Broughton Park. G Man 7G 41
Broughton Poggs. Oxon 3L 19
Broughtown. Orkn 5F 88
Broughty Ferry. D'dee 4H 67
Browland. Shet 2C 90
Brownbread Street. E Sus 4C 12
Brown Candover. Hants 2C 10
Brown Edge. Lanc 6B 40
Brown Edge. Staf 4H 35
Brownhill. Bkbn 4E 40
Brownhill. Shrp 7C 34
Brownhills. Shrp 6E 34
**Brownhills**. W Mid 1J 27
Brown Knowl. Ches W 4C 34
Brownlow. Ches E 3G 35
Brownlow Heath. Ches E 3G 35
Brown's Green. W Mid 2J 27
Brownshill. Glos 3G 19
Brownston. Devn 6J 5
Brownstone. Devn 5G 7
Browston Green. Norf 1L 31
Broxa. N Yor 6G 49
Broxbourne. Herts 3L 21
Broxburn. E Lot 2D 60
**Broxburn**. W Lot 2J 59
Broxholme. Linc 2G 37
Broxted. Essx 1B 22
Broxton. Ches W 4C 34
Broxwood. Here 6B 26
Broyle Side. E Sus 4A 12
Brù. W Isl 7G 83
Bruach Mairi. W Isl 8H 83
Bruairnis. W Isl 5D 74
Bruan. High 8E 86
Bruar Lodge. Per 8J 71
Brucehill. W Dun 2B 58
Brucklay. Abers 8J 81
Bruera. Ches W 3C 34
Bruern Abbey. Oxon 1L 19
Bruichladdich. Arg 3B 56
Bruisyard. Suff 5K 31
Bruisyard Street. Suff 5K 31
Brund. Staf 3K 35
Brundall. Norf 1K 31
Brundish. Norf 2K 31
Brundish. Suff 5J 31
Brundish Street. Suff 4J 31
Brunery. High 8J 69
Brunswick Village. Tyne 4F 54
Brunthwaite. W Yor 3J 41
Bruntingthorpe. Leics 2D 28
Brunton. Fife 5G 67
Brunton. Nmbd 7K 61
Brunton. Wilts 8L 19
Brushford. Devn 5F 6
Brushford. Som 3J 7
Brusta. W Isl 5L 75
Bruton. Som 2E 8
Bryansford. New M 7H 93
Bryanston. Dors 5G 9
Bryant's Bottom. Buck 4F 20
Brydekirk. Dum 4F 52
Brymbo. Cnwy 3H 33
**Brymbo**. Wrex 4A 34
Brympton D'Evercy. Som 4D 8
Bryn. Carm 6M 15
Bryn. G Man 7D 40
Bryn. Neat 5H 17
Bryn. Shrp 3A 26
Brynamman. Carm 3G 17
Brynberian. Pemb 3H 15
Brynbryddan. Neat 5G 17
Bryncae. Rhon 6J 17
Bryncethin. B'end 6J 17
Bryncir. Gwyn 6D 32
Bryncoch. Neat 5G 17
Bryncroes. Gwyn 7B 32
Bryncrug. Gwyn 2F 24
Bryn Du. IOA 3C 32
Bryn Eden. Gwyn 8G 33
Bryn Eglwys. Gwyn 4F 32
Bryneglwys. Den 6L 33
Brynford. Flin 3L 33
Bryn Gates. G Man 7D 40
Bryn Golau. Rhon 6K 17
Bryngwran. IOA 3C 32
Bryngwyn. Mon 3B 18
Bryngwyn. Powy 8L 25
Bryn-henllan. Pemb 3G 15
Brynhoffnant. Cdgn 1K 15
Bryn-llwyn. Den 2K 33
Brynllywarch. Powy 4L 25
Bryn-mawr. Gwyn 7B 32
**Brynmawr**. Blae 3L 17
Brynmenyn. B'end 6J 17
Brynmill. Swan 5F 16
Brynna. Rhon 6J 17
Brynrefail. Gwyn 4E 32
Brynrefail. IOA 2D 32
Brynsadler. Rhon 6K 17
Bryn-Saith Marchog. Den 5K 33
Brynsiencyn. IOA 4D 32
Brynteg. IOA 2D 32
Brynteg. Wrex 4B 34
Brynygwenyn. Mon 2B 18
Bryn-y-maen. Cnwy 3H 33
Buaile nam Bodach. W Isl 5D 74
Bualintur. High 3F 68
Bubbenhall. Warw 4A 28
Bubwith. E Yor 4E 42
Buccleuch. Bord 8M 59
Buchanan Smithy. Stir 1C 58
Buchanhaven. Abers 1L 73
Buchanty. Per 5C 66
Buchany. Stir 7M 65
Buchley. E Dun 2D 58
Buchlyvie. Stir 8K 65
Buckabank. Cumb 7H 53
Buckden. Cambs 5J 29
Buckden. N Yor 8H 47
Buckenham. Norf 1K 31
Buckerell. Devn 5L 7
Buckfast. Devn 5K 5
Buckfastleigh. Devn 5K 5
**Buckhaven**. Fife 8G 67
Buckholm. Bord 6B 60
Buckholt. Here 2D 18
Buckhorn Weston. Dors 3F 8
Buckhurst Hill. Essx 4M 21
Buckie. Mor 7D 80
**Buckingham**. Buck 8D 28
Buckland. Buck 2F 20
Buckland. Glos 8J 27
Buckland. Here 6D 26
Buckland. Herts 8L 29
Buckland. Kent 1K 13
Buckland. Oxon 4M 19
Buckland. Surr 8K 21
Buckland Brewer. Devn 3D 6
Buckland Common. Buck 3G 21
Buckland Dinham. Som 8F 18
Buckland Filleigh. Devn 5D 6
Buckland in the Moor. Devn 8G 7
Buckland Monachorum. Devn 5G 5
Buckland Newton. Dors 5E 8
Buckland Ripers. Dors 7E 8
Buckland St Mary. Som 4A 8
Buckland-tout-Saints. Devn 7K 5
Bucklebury. W Ber 6C 20
Bucklegate. Linc 6L 37
Buckleigh. Devn 3D 6
Buckler's Hard. Hants 6B 10
Bucklesham. Suff 7J 31
**Buckley**. Flin 3A 34
Buckley Green. Warw 5K 27
Buckley Hill. Mers 8B 40
Bucklow Hill. Ches E 1F 34
Buckminster. Leics 7F 36
Bucknall. Linc 3J 37
Bucknall. Stoke 5H 35
Bucknell. Oxon 1C 20
Bucknell. Shrp 4B 26
Buckpool. Mor 7D 80
Bucksburn. Aber 5H 73
Buck's Cross. Devn 3C 6
Bucks Green. W Sus 2H 11
Buckshaw Village. Lanc 5D 40
Bucks Hill. Herts 3H 21
Bucks Horn Oak. Hants 1F 10
Buck's Mills. Devn 3C 6
Buckton. E Yor 8J 49
Buckton. Here 4B 26
Buckton. Nmbd 6H 61
Buckton Vale. G Man 7H 41
Buckworth. Cambs 4J 29
Budby. Notts 3D 36
Bude. Corn 5B 6
Budge's Shop. Corn 6F 4
Budlake. Devn 5J 7
Budle. Nmbd 6J 61
Budleigh Salterton. Devn 7K 7
Budock Water. Corn 5L 3
Buerton. Ches E 5E 34
Buffler's Holt. Buck 8D 28
Bugbrooke. Nptn 6D 28
Buglawton. Ches E 3G 35
Bugle. Corn 6C 4
Bugthorpe. E Yor 2E 42
Buildwas. Shrp 1E 26
Builth Road. Powy 7K 25
Builth Wells. Powy 7K 25
Bulbourne. Herts 2G 21
Bulby. Linc 7H 37
Bulcote. Notts 5D 36
Buldoo. High 5A 86
Bulford. Wilts 1K 9
Bulford Camp. Wilts 1K 9
Bulkeley. Ches E 4D 34
Bulkington. Warw 3A 28
Bulkington. Wilts 8H 19
Bulkworthy. Devn 4C 6
Bullamoor. N Yor 6A 48
Bull Bay. IOA 1D 32
Bullbridge. Derbs 4A 36
Bullgill. Cumb 8E 52
Bull Hill. Hants 6M 9
Bullinghope. Here 8D 26
Bull's Green. Herts 2K 21
Bullwood. Arg 2L 57
Bulmer. Essx 7E 30
Bulmer. N Yor 1D 42
Bulmer Tye. Essx 8E 30
Bulphan. Thur 5C 22
Bulverhythe. E Sus 5D 12
Bulwark. Abers 1J 73
Bulwell. Nott 5C 36
Bulwick. Nptn 2G 29
Bumble's Green. Essx 3M 21
Bun Abhainn Eadarra. W Isl 3C 76
Bunacaimb. High 7H 69
Bun a' Mhuillinn. W Isl 4D 74
Bunarkaig. High 7B 70
Bunbury. Ches E 4D 34
Bunchrew. High 1G 71
Bundalloch. High 3K 69
Buness. Shet 3L 91
Bunessan. Arg 5J 63
Bungay. Suff 3K 31
Bunkegivie. High 4F 70
Bunker's Hill. Cambs 1M 29
Bunker's Hill. Suff 1M 31
Bunkers Hill. Linc 4K 37
Bunloit. High 3F 70
Bunnahabhain. Arg 2D 56
Bunny. Notts 7C 36
Bunoich. High 5D 70
Bunree. High 1E 64
Bunroy. High 7C 70
Buntait. High 2E 70
Buntingford. Herts 1L 21
Bunting's Green. Essx 8E 30
Bunwell. Norf 2H 31
Burbage. Derbs 2J 35
Burbage. Leics 2B 28
Burbage. Wilts 7L 19
Burcher. Here 5B 26
Burchett's Green. Wind 5F 20
Burcombe. Wilts 2J 9
Burcot. Oxon 4C 20
Burcot. Worc 4H 27
Burcote. Shrp 2F 26
Burcott. Buck 1F 20
Burcott. Som 1D 8
Burdale. N Yor 1F 42
Burdrop. Oxon 8A 28
Bures. Suff 8F 30
The Burf. Worc 5G 27
Burford. Oxon 2L 19
Burford. Shrp 5D 26
Burg. Arg 3J 63
Burgate Great Green. Suff 4G 31
Burgate Little Green. Suff 4G 31
**Burgess Hill**. W Sus 4L 11
Burgh. Suff 6J 31
Burgh by Sands. Cumb 6H 53
Burgh Castle. Norf 1L 31
Burghclere. Hants 7B 20
Burghead. Mor 7M 79
Burghfield. W Ber 7D 20
Burghfield Common. W Ber 7D 20
Burghfield Hill. W Ber 7D 20
Burgh Heath. Surr 8K 21
Burghill. Here 7C 26
Burgh le Marsh. Linc 3B 38
Burgh Muir. Abers 4G 73
Burgh next Aylsham. Norf 7J 39
Burgh on Bain. Linc 1K 37
Burgh St Margaret. Norf 8L 39
Burgh St Peter. Norf 2L 31
Burghwallis. S Yor 6C 42
Burham. Kent 7D 22
Buriton. Hants 3E 10
Burland. Ches E 4E 34
Burland. Shet 4D 90
Burlawn. Corn 5B 4
Burleigh. Glos 3G 19
Burleigh. Wind 6F 20
Burlescombe. Devn 4K 7
Burleston. Dors 6F 8
Burlestone. Devn 7L 5
Burley. Hants 5L 9
Burley. Rut 8F 36
Burley. W Yor 4L 41
Burleydam. Ches E 5E 34
Burley Gate. Here 7D 26
Burley in Wharfedale. W Yor 3K 41
Burley Street. Hants 5L 9
Burley Woodhead. W Yor 3K 41
Burlingjobb. Powy 6A 26
Burlington. Shrp 8F 34
Burlton. Shrp 7C 34
Burmantofts. W Yor 4M 41
Burmarsh. Kent 2H 13
Burmington. Warw 8L 27
Burn. N Yor 5C 42
Burnage. G Man 8G 41
Burnaston. Derbs 6L 35
Burnbanks. Cumb 4D 46
Burnby. E Yor 3F 42
Burncross. S Yor 8M 41
Burneside. Cumb 6D 46
Burness. Orkn 5F 88
Burneston. N Yor 7M 47
Burnett. Bath 7E 18
Burnfoot. E Ayr 1K 51
Burnfoot. Per 7C 66
Burnfoot. Bord
nr. Hawick 8C 60
nr. Roberton 8B 60
Burngreave. S Yor 1A 36
Burnham. Buck 5G 21
Burnham. N Lin 6H 43
Burnham Deepdale. Norf 5E 38
Burnham Green. Herts 2K 21
Burnham Market. Norf 5E 38
Burnham Norton. Norf 5E 38
Burnham-on-Crouch. Essx 4F 22
**Burnham-on-Sea**. Som 1B 8
Burnham Overy Staithe. Norf 5E 38
Burnham Overy Town. Norf 5E 38
Burnham Thorpe. Norf 5E 38
Burnhaven. Abers 1L 73
Burnhead. Dum 2C 52
Burnhervie. Abers 4G 73
Burnhill Green. Staf 1F 26
Burnhope. Dur 7E 54
Burnhouse. N Ayr 4B 58
Burniston. N Yor 6H 49
Burnlee. W Yor 7K 41
**Burnley**. Lanc 4G 41
Burnmouth. Bord 3G 61
Burn Naze. Lanc 3B 40
Burn of Cambus. Stir 7M 65
Burnopfield. Dur 6E 54
Burnsall. N Yor 1J 41
Burnside. Ang 2J 67
Burnside. Ant
nr. Antrim 4G 93
nr. Ballyclare 4H 93
Burnside. E Ayr 8D 58
Burnside. Per 7E 66
Burnside. Shet 6G 91
Burnside. S Lan 4E 58
Burnside. W Lot
nr. Broxburn 2J 59
nr. Winchburgh 2J 59
Burntcommon. Surr 8H 21
Burnt Heath. Essx 1G 23
Burntheath. Derbs 6L 35
Burnt Hill. W Ber 6C 20
Burnt Houses. Dur 3K 47
Burntisland. Fife 1L 59
Burnt Oak. G Lon 4K 21
Burnton. E Ayr 1K 51
Burntstalk. Norf 6D 38
**Burntwood**. Staf 1J 27
Burntwood Green. Staf 1J 27
Burnt Yates. N Yor 1L 41
Burnwynd. Edin 3K 59
Burpham. Surr 8H 21
Burpham. W Sus 5H 11
Burradon. Nmbd 1C 54
Burradon. Tyne 4F 54
Burrafirth. Shet 2L 91
Burragarth. Shet 3K 91
Burras. Corn 5K 3
Burraton. Corn 6G 5
Burravoe. Shet
nr. North Roe 5H 91
on Mainland 1D 90
on Yell 6K 91
Burray Village. Orkn 2F 86
Burrells. Cumb 4E 46
Burrelton. Per 4E 66
Burren. New M 7G 93
Burren Bridge. New M 7H 93
Burridge. Hants 4C 10
Burridge. Som 5B 8
Burrigill. High 8D 86
Burrill. N Yor 7L 47
Burringham. N Lin 7F 42
Burrington. Devn 4F 6
Burrington. Here 4C 26
Burrington. N Som 8C 18
Burrough End. Cambs 6C 30
Burrough Green. Cambs 6C 30
Burrough on the Hill. Leics 8E 36
Burroughston. Orkn 7E 88
Burrow. Devn 7K 7
Burrow. Som 1J 7
Burrowbridge. Som 3B 8
Burrowhill. Surr 7G 21
Burry. Swan 7L 15
Burry Green. Swan 7L 15
Burry Port. Carm 6L 15
Burscough. Lanc 6C 40
Burscough Bridge. Lanc 6C 40
Bursea. E Yor 4F 42
Burshill. E Yor 3H 43
Bursledon. Hants 5B 10
Burslem. Stoke 5G 35
Burstall. Suff 7G 31
Burstock. Dors 5C 8
Burston. Devn 5G 7
Burston. Norf 3H 31
Burston. Staf 6H 35
Burstow. Surr 1L 11
Burstwick. E Yor 5K 43
Burtersett. N Yor 7G 47
Burtholme. Cumb 5K 53
Burthorpe. Suff 5D 30
Burthwaite. Cumb 7J 53
Burtle. Som 1C 8
Burtoft. Linc 6K 37
Burton. Ches W
nr. Kelsall 3D 34
nr. Neston 2B 34
Burton. Dors
nr. Christchurch 6K 9
nr. Dorchester 6E 8
Burton. Nmbd 6J 61
Burton. Pemb 6F 14
Burton. Som 1L 7
Burton. Wilts
nr. Chippenham 6G 19
nr. Warminster 2G 9
Burton. Wrex 4B 34
Burton Agnes. E Yor 1J 43
Burton Bradstock. Dors 7C 8
Burton-by-Lincoln. Linc 2G 37
Burton Coggles. Linc 7G 37
Burton Constable. E Yor 4J 43
Burton Corner. Linc 5L 37
Burton End. Cambs 7C 30
Burton End. Essx 1B 22
Burton Fleming. E Yor 8H 49
Burton Green. Warw 4L 27
Burton Green. Wrex 4B 34
Burton Hastings. Warw 3B 28
Burton-in-Kendal. Cumb 8D 46
Burton in Lonsdale. N Yor 8E 46
Burton Joyce. Notts 5D 36
Burton Latimer. Nptn 4G 29
Burton Lazars. Leics 8E 36
Burton Leonard. N Yor 1M 41
Burton on the Wolds. Leics 7C 36
Burton Overy. Leics 2D 28
Burton Pedwardine. Linc 5J 37
Burton Pidsea. E Yor 4K 43
Burton Salmon. N Yor 5B 42
Burton's Green. Essx 1E 22
Burton Stather. N Lin 6F 42
Burton upon Stather. N Lin 6F 42
**Burton upon Trent**. Staf 7L 35
Burton Wolds. Leics 7D 36
Burtonwood. Warr 8D 40
Burwardsley. Ches W 4D 34
Burwarton. Shrp 3E 26
Burwash. E Sus 3C 12
Burwash Common. E Sus 3C 12
Burwash Weald. E Sus 3C 12
Burwell. Cambs 5B 30
Burwell. Linc 2L 37
Burwen. IOA 1D 32
Burwick. Orkn 3F 86
Bury. Cambs 3K 29
**Bury**. G Man 6G 41
Bury. Som 3J 7
Bury. W Sus 4H 11
Burybank. Staf 6G 35
Bury End. Worc 8J 27
Bury Green. Herts 1A 22
**Bury St Edmunds**. Suff 5E 30
Burythorpe. N Yor 1E 42
Busbridge. Surr 1G 11
Busby. E Ren 4D 58
Busby. Per 5D 66
Buscot. Oxon 4L 19
Bush. Corn 5B 6
The Bush. M Ulst 5F 93
Bush Bank. Here 6C 26
Bushbury. W Mid 1H 27
Bushby. Leics 1D 28
Bushey. Dors 7H 9
**Bushey**. Herts 4J 21
Bushey Heath. Herts 4J 21
Bush Green. Norf
nr. Attleborough 2G 31
nr. Harleston 3J 31
Bush Green. Suff 6F 30
Bushley. Worc 8G 27
Bushley Green. Worc 8G 27
Bushmead. Bed 5J 29
Bushmills. Caus 1F 93
Bushmoor. Shrp 3C 26
Bushton. Wilts 6J 19
Bushy Common. Norf 8F 38
Busk. Cumb 7L 53
Buslingthorpe. Linc 1H 37
Bussage. Glos 3G 19
Bussex. Som 2B 8
Busta. Shet 1D 90
Butcher's Cross. E Sus 3B 12
Butcombe. N Som 7D 18
Bute Town. Cphy 4L 17
Butleigh. Som 2D 8
Butleigh Wootton. Som 2D 8
Butlers Marston. Warw 7M 27
Butley. Suff 6K 31
Butley High Corner. Suff 7K 31
Butlocks Heath. Hants 5B 10
Butterburn. Cumb 4L 53
Buttercrambe. N Yor 2E 42
Butterknowle. Dur 3K 47
Butterleigh. Devn 5J 7
Buttermere. Cumb 3L 45
Buttermere. Wilts 7M 19
Buttershaw. W Yor 5K 41
Butterstone. Per 3D 66
Butterton. Staf
nr. Leek 4J 35
nr. Stoke-on-Trent 5G 35
Butterwick. Dur 3A 48
Butterwick. Linc 5L 37
Butterwick. N Yor
nr. Malton 8E 48
nr. Weaverthorpe 8G 49
Butteryhaugh. Nmbd 2L 53
Butt Green. Ches E 4E 34
Buttington. Powy 1A 26
Buttonbridge. Shrp 4F 26
Buttonoak. Shrp 4F 26
Buttsash. Hants 5B 10
Butt's Green. Essx 3D 22
Butt Yeats. Lanc 1D 40
Buxhall. Suff 6G 31
Buxted. E Sus 3A 12
**Buxton**. Derbs 2J 35
Buxton. Norf 7J 39
Buxworth. Derbs 1J 35
**Bwcle**. Flin 3A 34
Bwlch. Powy 2L 17
Bwlchderwin. Gwyn 6D 32
Bwlchgwyn. Wrex 4A 34
Bwlch-Llan. Cdgn 7E 24
Bwlchnewydd. Carm 4K 15
Bwlchtocyn. Gwyn 8C 32
Bwlch-y-cibau. Powy 1L 25
Bwlchyddar. Powy 8L 33
Bwlch-y-fadfa. Cdgn 2L 15
Bwlch-y-ffridd. Powy 3K 25
Bwlch y Garreg. Powy 3K 25
Bwlch-y-groes. Pemb 3J 15
Bwlch-y-sarnau. Powy 5K 25
Bybrook. Kent 1G 13
Byermoor. Tyne 6E 54
Byers Garth. Dur 7G 55
Byers Green. Dur 8F 54
Byfield. Nptn 6C 28
**Byfleet**. Surr 7H 21
Byford. Here 7B 26
Bygrave. Herts 8K 29
Byker. Tyne 5F 54
Byland Abbey. N Yor 8C 48
Bylchau. Cnwy 4J 33
Byley. Ches W 3F 34
Bynea. Carm 7M 15
Byram. N Yor 5B 42
Byrness. Nmbd 1A 54
Bystock. Devn 7K 7
Bythorn. Cambs 4H 29
Byton. Here 5B 26
Bywell. Nmbd 5D 54
Byworth. W Sus 3G 11

## C

Cabharstadh. W Isl 2E 76
Cabourne. Linc 7J 43
Cabrach. Arg 3D 56
Cabrach. Mor 3C 72
Cabragh. M Ulst 5E 92
Cabus. Lanc 3C 40
Cadbury. Devn 5J 7
Cadder. E Dun 2E 58
Caddington. C Beds 2H 21
Caddonfoot. Bord 6B 60
Cadeby. Leics 1B 28
Cadeby. S Yor 7C 42
Cadeleigh. Devn 5J 7
Cade Street. E Sus 3C 12
Cadgwith. Corn 7L 3
Cadham. Fife 7F 66
Cadishead. G Man 8F 40
Cadle. Swan 5F 16
Cadley. Lanc 4D 40
Cadley. Wilts
nr. Ludgershall 8L 19
nr. Marlborough 7L 19
Cadmore End. Buck 4E 20
Cadnam. Hants 4L 9
Cadney. N Lin 7H 43
Cadole. Flin 4M 33
Cadoxton-juxta-Neath. Neat 5G 17
Cadwell. Herts 8J 29
Cadwst. Den 7K 33
Caeathro. Gwyn 4E 32
Caehopkin. Powy 3H 17
Caenby. Linc 1H 37
Caerau. B'end 5H 17
Caerau. Card 7L 17
Cae'r-bont. Powy 3H 17
Cae'r-bryn. Carm 3E 16
Caerdeon. Gwyn 1F 24
**Caerdydd**. Card 107 (7L 17)
Caerfarchell. Pemb 4D 14
**Caerffili**. Cphy 6L 17
**Caerfyrddin**. Carm 5L 15
Caergeiliog. IOA 3C 32
Caergwrle. Flin 4B 34
**Caergybi**. IOA 2B 32
Caerlaverock. Per 6B 66
Caerleon. Newp 4B 18
Caerlleon. Carm 4J 15
Caerllion. Newp 4B 18
**Caernarfon**. Gwyn 4D 32
**Caerphilly**. Cphy 6L 17
Caersws. Powy 3K 25
Caerwedros. Cdgn 1K 15
Caerwent. Mon 4C 18
Caerwys. Flin 3L 33
Caim. IOA 2F 32
Caio. Carm 1F 16
Cairinis. W Isl 7K 75
Cairisiadar. W Isl 8D 82
Cairminis. W Isl 5B 76
Cairnbaan. Arg 8C 64
Cairnbulg. Abers 7K 81
Cairncross. Ang 8D 72
Cairndow. Arg 6F 64
Cairness. Abers 7K 81
Cairneyhill. Fife 1J 59
Cairngarroch. Dum 7F 50
Cairnhill. Abers 2F 72
Cairnie. Abers 1D 72
Cairnorrie. Abers 1H 73
Cairnryan. Dum 5F 50
Cairston. Orkn 8B 88
Caister-on-Sea. Norf 8M 39
Caistor. Linc 7J 43
Caistor St Edmund. Norf 1J 31
Caistron. Nmbd 1C 54
Cakebole. Worc 4G 27
Calais Street. Suff 7F 30
Calanais. W Isl 8F 82
Calbost. W Isl 2F 76
Calbourne. IOW 7B 10
Calceby. Linc 2L 37
Calcot. Glos 2J 19
Calcot Row. W Ber 6D 20
Calcott. Kent 7H 23
Calcott. Shrp 8C 34
Caldback. Shet 3L 91
Caldbeck. Cumb 8H 53
Caldbergh. N Yor 7J 47
Caldecote. Cambs
nr. Cambridge 6L 29
nr. Peterborough 3J 29
Caldecote. Herts 8K 29
Caldecote. Nptn 6D 28
Caldecote. Warw 2A 28
Caldecott. Nptn 5G 29
Caldecott. Oxon 4B 20
Caldecott. Rut 2F 28
Calderbank. N Lan 3F 58
Calder Bridge. Cumb 4K 45
Calderbrook. G Man 6H 41
Caldercruix. N Lan 3G 59
Calder Grove. W Yor 6M 41
Calder Mains. High 6B 86
Caldermill. S Lan 5E 58
Calder Vale. Lanc 3D 40
Calderwood. S Lan 4E 58
**Caldicot**. Mon 5C 18
Caldwell. Derbs 8L 35
Caldwell. N Yor 4K 47
Caldy. Mers 2M 33
Calebrack. Cumb 8H 53
Caledon. M Ulst 6E 92
Calf Heath. Staf 1H 27
Calford Green. Suff 7C 30
Calfsound. Orkn 6E 88
Calgary. Arg 2J 63
Califer. Mor 8L 79
California. Cambs 3B 30
California. Falk 2H 59
California. Norf 8M 39
California. Suff 7H 31
Calke. Derbs 7A 36
Callakille. High 8H 77
Callaly. Nmbd 1D 54
Callander. Stir 7L 65
Callaughton. Shrp 2E 26
Callendoun. Arg 1B 58
Callestick. Corn 3L 3
Calligarry. High 5H 69
Callington. Corn 5F 4
Callingwood. Staf 7K 35
Callow. Here 8C 26
Callowell. Glos 3G 19
Callow End. Worc 7G 27
Callow Hill. Wilts 5J 19
Callow Hill. Worc
nr. Bewdley 4F 26
nr. Redditch 5J 27
Calmore. Hants 4M 9
Calmsden. Glos 3J 19
**Calne**. Wilts 6H 19
Calow. Derbs 2B 36
Calshot. Hants 5B 10
Calstock. Corn 5G 5
Calstone Wellington. Wilts 7J 19
Calthorpe. Norf 6H 39
Calthorpe Street. Norf 7L 39
Calthwaite. Cumb 7J 53
Calton. N Yor 2H 41
Calton. Staf 4K 35
Calveley. Ches E 4D 34
Calver. Derbs 2L 35
Calverhall. Shrp 6E 34
Calverleigh. Devn 4J 7
Calverley. W Yor 4L 41
Calvert. Buck 1D 20
Calverton. Mil 8E 28
Calverton. Notts 5D 36
Calvine. Per 1B 66
Calvo. Cumb 6F 52
Cam. Glos 4F 18
Camaghael. High 8B 70
Camas-luinie. High 3L 69
Camasnacroise. High 2C 64
Camastianavaig. High 2G 69
Camasunary. High 4G 69
Camault Muir. High 1F 70
Camb. Shet 4K 91
Camber. E Sus 4F 12
**Camberley**. Surr 7F 20
**Camberwell**. G Lon 6L 21
Camblesforth. N Yor 5D 42
Cambo. Nmbd 3D 54
Cambois. Nmbd 3G 55
**Camborne**. Corn 5K 3
Cambourne. Cambs 6L 29
**Cambridge**. Cambs 107 (6A 30)
Cambridge. Glos 3F 18
Cambrose. Corn 4K 3
Cambus. Clac 8B 66
Cambusbarron. Stir 8A 66
Cambuskenneth. Stir 8B 66
**Cambuslang**. S Lan 3E 58
Cambusnethan. N Lan 4G 59
Cambus o' May. Abers 6D 72
**Camden Town**. G Lon 5K 21
Cameley. Bath 8E 18
Camelford. Corn 3D 4
Camelon. Falk 1G 59
Camelsdale. W Sus 2F 10
Camer's Green. Worc 8F 26
Camerton. Bath 8E 18
Camerton. Cumb 8E 52
Camerton. E Yor 5K 43
Camghouran. Per 2K 65
Camlough. New M 7G 93
Cammachmore. Abers 6J 73
Cammeringham. Linc 1G 37
Camore. High 4H 79
The Camp. Glos 3H 19
Campbelton. N Ayr 4L 57
Campbeltown. Arg 7G 57
Campbeltown Airport. Arg 7F 56
Cample. Dum 2C 52
Campmuir. Per 4F 66
Campsall. S Yor 6C 42
Campsea Ashe. Suff 6K 31
Camps End. Cambs 7C 30
Campsey. Derr 2D 92
Campton. C Beds 8J 29
Camptoun. E Lot 2C 60
Camptown. Bord 8D 60
Camrose. Pemb 4F 14
Camserney. Per 3B 66
Camster. High 7D 86
Camus Croise. High 4H 69
Camuscross. High 4H 69
Camusdarach. High 6H 69
Camusnagaul. High
nr. Fort William 8A 70
nr. Little Loch Broom 5A 78
Camus Park. Derr 4C 92
Camusteel. High 1J 69
Camusterrach. High 1J 69
Camusvrachan. Per 3L 65
Canada. Hants 4L 9
Canadia. E Sus 4D 12
Canaston Bridge. Pemb 5G 15
Candlesby. Linc 3A 38
Candle Street. Suff 4G 31
Candy Mill. S Lan 5J 59
Cane End. Oxon 6D 20
Canewdon. Essx 4F 22
Canford Cliffs. Pool 7J 9
Canford Heath. Pool 6J 9
Canford Magna. Pool 6J 9
Cangate. Norf 8K 39
Canham's Green. Suff 5G 31
Canholes. Derbs 2J 35
Canisbay. High 4E 86
Canley. W Mid 4M 27
Cann. Dors 3G 9
Cann Common. Dors 3G 9
Cannich. High 2D 70
Cannington. Som 2A 8
**Cannock**. Staf 8H 35
Cannock Wood. Staf 8J 35
Canonbie. Dum 4H 53
Canon Bridge. Here 7C 26
Canon Frome. Here 7E 26
Canon Pyon. Here 7C 26
Canons Ashby. Nptn 6C 28
Canonstown. Corn 5J 3
**Canterbury**. Kent 107 (8H 23)
Cantley. Norf 1K 31
Cantley. S Yor 7D 42
Cantlop. Shrp 1D 26
Canton. Card 7L 17
Cantray. High 1H 71
Cantraybruich. High 1H 71
Cantraywood. High 1H 71
Cantsdam. Fife 8E 66
Cantsfield. Lanc 8E 46
**Canvey Island**. Essx 5D 22
Canwick. Linc 3G 37
Canworthy Water. Corn 6B 6
Caol. High 8B 70
Caolas. Arg 3F 62
Caolas. W Isl 6C 74
Caolas Liubharsaigh. W Isl 1E 74
Caolas Scalpaigh. W Isl 4D 76
Caolas Stocinis. W Isl 4C 76
Caol Ila. Arg 2D 56
Caol Loch Ailse. High 3J 69
Caol Reatha. High 3J 69
Capel. Kent 1C 12
Capel. Surr 1J 11
Capel Bangor. Cdgn 4F 24
Capel Betws Lleucu. Cdgn 7F 24
Capel Coch. IOA 2D 32
Capel Curig. Cnwy 5G 33
Capel Cynon. Cdgn 2K 15
Capel Dewi. Carm 4L 15
Capel Dewi. Cdgn
nr. Aberystwyth 4F 24
nr. Llandysul 2L 15
Capel Garmon. Cnwy 5H 33
Capel Green. Suff 7K 31
Capel Gwyn. IOA 3C 32
Capel Gwynfe. Carm 2G 17
Capel Hendre. Carm 3E 16
Capel Isaac. Carm 2E 16
Capel Iwan. Carm 3J 15
Capel-le-Ferne. Kent 2J 13
Capel Llanilltern. Card 7K 17
Capel Mawr. IOA 3D 32
Capel Newydd. Pemb 3J 15
Capel St Andrew. Suff 7K 31
Capel St Mary. Suff 8G 31
Capel Seion. Carm 5M 15
Capel Seion. Cdgn 5F 24
Capel Uchaf. Gwyn 6D 32
Capel-y-ffin. Powy 8A 26
Capenhurst. Ches W 2B 34
Capernwray. Lanc 8D 46
Capheaton. Nmbd 3D 54
Cappagh. M Ulst 5E 92
Cappercleuch. Bord 7L 59
Capplegill. Dum 1F 52
Capton. Devn 6L 5
Capton. Som 2K 7
Caputh. Per 4D 66
Caradon Town. Corn 8B 6
Carbis Bay. Corn 5J 3
Carbost. High
nr. Loch Harport 2E 68
nr. Portree 1F 68
Carbrook. S Yor 1A 36
Carbrooke. Norf 1F 30
Carburton. Notts 2D 36
Carcluie. S Ayr 8B 58
Car Colston. Notts 5E 36
Carcroft. S Yor 7C 42
Cardenden. Fife 8F 66
Cardeston. Shrp 8B 34
Cardewlees. Cumb 6H 53
**Cardiff**. Card 107 (7L 17)
Cardiff Airport. V Glam 8K 17
Cardigan. Cdgn 2H 15
Cardinal's Green. Cambs 7C 30
Cardington. Bed 7H 29
Cardington. Shrp 2D 26
Cardinham. Corn 5D 4
Cardno. Abers 7J 81
Cardow. Mor 1A 72
Cardross. Arg 2B 58
Cardurnock. Cumb 6F 52
Careby. Linc 8H 37
Careston. Ang 1J 67
Carew. Pemb 6G 15
Carew Cheriton. Pemb 6G 15
Carew Newton. Pemb 6G 15
Carey. Here 8D 26
Carfin. N Lan 4F 58
Carfrae. Bord 4C 60
Cargan. ME Ant 3G 93
Cargate Green. Norf 8K 39
Cargenbridge. Dum 4D 52
Cargill. Per 4E 66
Cargo. Cumb 6H 53
Cargreen. Corn 5G 5
Carham. Nmbd 6F 60
Carhampton. Som 1K 7
Carharrack. Corn 4L 3
Carie. Per
nr. Loch Rannah 2L 65
nr. Loch Tay 4L 65
Carisbrooke. IOW 7B 10
Cark. Cumb 8B 46
Carkeel. Corn 5G 5
Carlabhagh. W Isl 7F 82
Carland Cross. Corn 3M 3
Carlbury. Darl 4L 47
Carlby. Linc 8H 37
Carlecotes. S Yor 7K 41
Carleen. Corn 6K 3
Carlesmoor. N Yor 8K 47
Carleton. Cumb
nr. Carlisle 6J 53
nr. Egremont 4K 45
nr. Penrith 3D 46
Carleton. Lanc 3B 40
Carleton. N Yor 3H 41
Carleton. W Yor 5B 42
Carleton Forehoe. Norf 1G 31
Carleton Rode. Norf 2H 31
Carleton St Peter. Norf 1K 31
Carlidnack. Corn 6L 3
Carlingcott. Bath 8E 18
Carlin How. Red C 4E 48
**Carlisle**. Cumb 107 (6J 53)
Carloonan. Arg 6E 64
Carlops. Bord 4K 59
Carlton. Bed 6G 29
Carlton. Cambs 6C 30
Carlton. Leics 1A 28
Carlton. N Yor
nr. Helmsley 7D 48
nr. Middleham 7J 47
nr. Selby 5D 42
**Carlton**. Notts 5D 36
Carlton. S Yor 6A 42
Carlton. Stoc T 3A 48
Carlton. Suff 5K 31
Carlton. W Yor 5M 41
Carlton Colville. Suff 2M 31
Carlton Curlieu. Leics 2D 28
Carlton Husthwaite. N Yor 8B 48
Carlton in Cleveland. N Yor 5C 48
Carlton in Lindrick. Notts 1C 36
Carlton-le-Moorland. Linc 4G 37
Carlton Miniott. N Yor 7A 48
Carlton-on-Trent. Notts 3F 36

Carlton Scroop. Linc 5G 37
**Carluke**. S Lan 4G 59
Carlyon Bay. Corn 6C 4
**Carmarthen**. Carm 5L 15
Carmel. Carm 3E 16
Carmel. Flin 3L 33
Carmel. Gwyn 5D 32
Carmel. IOA 2C 32
Carmichael. S Lan 6H 59
Carmunnock. Glas 4E 58
Carmyle. Glas 3E 58
Carmyllie. Ang 3J 67
Carnaby. E Yor 1J 43
Carnach. High
nr. Lochcarron 3M 69
nr. Ullapool 4M 77
Carnach. Mor 1L 71
Carnach. W Isl 4D 76
Carnachy. High 6K 85
Carnain. Arg 3C 56
Carnais. W Isl 8D 82
Carnan. Arg 3F 62
Carnan. W Isl 1D 74
Carnbee. Fife 7J 67
Carnbo. Per 7D 66
Carn Brea Village. Corn 4K 3
Carndu. High 3K 69
Carnduff. Caus 1G 93
Carne. Corn 8B 4
Carnell. S Ayr 6C 58
Carnforth. Lanc 8D 46
Carn-gorm. High 3L 69
Carnhedryn. Pemb 4E 14
Carnhell Green. Corn 5K 3
Carnie. Abers 5H 73
Carnkie. Corn
nr. Falmouth 5L 3
nr. Redruth 5K 3
Carnkief. Corn 3L 3
Carnlough. ME Ant 3H 93
Carnmoney. Ant 4H 93
Carno. Powy 3J 25
Carnock. Fife 1J 59
Carnon Downs. Corn 4L 3
**Carnoustie**. Ang 4J 67
Carnteel. M Ulst 6E 92
Carntyne. Glas 3E 58
Carnwath. S Lan 5H 59
Carnyorth. Corn 5G 3
Carol Green. W Mid 4L 27
Carpalla. Corn 6B 4
Carperby. N Yor 7J 47
Carradale. Arg 6H 57
Carragraich. W Isl 4C 76
Carrbridge. High 3K 71
Carr Cross. Lanc 6B 40
Carreglefn. IOA 2C 32
Carrhouse. N Lin 7E 42
Carrick Castle. Arg 8F 64
**Carrickfergus**. ME Ant 4J 93
Carrick Ho. Orkn 6E 88
Carrickmore. Ferm 5E 92
Carriden. Falk 1J 59
Carrington. G Man 8F 40
Carrington. Linc 4L 37
Carrington. Midl 3M 59
Carrog. Cnwy 6G 33
Carrog. Den 6L 33
Carron. Falk 1G 59
Carron. Mor 1B 72
Carronbridge. Dum 2C 52
Carronshore. Falk 1G 59
Carrowclare. Caus 2E 92
Carrowdore. Ards 5J 93
Carrow Hill. Mon 4C 18
Carr Shield. Nmbd 7B 54
Carrutherstown. Dum 4F 52
Carr Vale. Derbs 3B 36
Carrville. Dur 7G 55
Carryduff. Lis 5H 93
Carsaig. Arg 5L 63
Carscreugh. Dum 5H 51
Carsegowan. Dum 6K 51
Carse House. Arg 3G 57
Carseriggan. Dum 5J 51
Carsethorn. Dum 6D 52
**Carshalton**. G Lon 7K 21
Carsington. Derbs 4L 35
Carskiey. Arg 1B 50
Carsluith. Dum 6K 51
Carson Park. New M 6J 93
Carsphairn. Dum 2L 51
Carstairs. S Lan 5H 59
Carstairs Junction. S Lan 5H 59
Cartbridge. Surr 8H 21
Carterhaugh. Ang 3H 67
Carter's Clay. Hants 3M 9
**Carterton**. Oxon 3L 19
Carterway Heads. Nmbd 6D 54
Carthew. Corn 6C 4
Carthorpe. N Yor 7M 47
Cartington. Nmbd 1D 54
Cartland. S Lan 5G 59
Cartmel. Cumb 8B 46
Cartmel Fell. Cumb 7C 46
Cartworth. W Yor 7K 41
Carwath. Cumb 7H 53
Carway. Carm 6L 15
Carwinley. Cumb 4J 53
Cascob. Powy 6M 25
**Cas-gwent**. Mon 4D 18
Cash Feus. Fife 7F 66
Cashlie. Per 3J 65
Cashmoor. Dors 4H 9
Cas-Mael. Pemb 4G 15
**Casnewydd**. Newp 114 (5B 18)
Cassington. Oxon 2B 20
Cassop. Dur 8G 55
Castell. Cnwy 4G 33
Castell. Den 4L 33
Castell Hendre. Pemb 4G 15
**Castell-Nedd**. Neat 5G 17
Castell Newydd Emlyn. Carm 2K 15
Castell-y-bwch. Torf 4A 18
Casterton. Cumb 8E 46
Castle. Som 1D 8
Castle Acre. Norf 8E 38
Castle Ashby. Nptn 6F 28
Castlebay. W Isl 6C 74
Castle Bolton. N Yor 6J 47
Castle Bromwich. W Mid 3K 27
Castle Bytham. Linc 8G 37
Castlebythe. Pemb 4G 15
Castle Caereinion. Powy 2L 25
Castle Camps. Cambs 7C 30
Castle Carrock. Cumb 6K 53
Castle Cary. Som 2E 8
Castlecary. N Lan 2F 58
Castlecaulfield. M Ulst 5E 92
Castle Combe. Wilts 6G 19
Castlecraig. High 7J 79
Castledawson. M Ulst 4F 93
Castlederg. Derr 4C 92
Castle Donington. Leics 7B 36
Castle Douglas. Dum 5B 52
Castle Eaton. Swin 4K 19
Castle Eden. Dur 8H 55
**Castleford**. W Yor 5B 42
Castle Frome. Here 7E 26
Castle Green. Surr 7G 21
Castle Green. Warw 4L 27
Castle Gresley. Derbs 8L 35
Castle Heaton. Nmbd 5G 61
Castle Hedingham. Essx 8D 30
Castle Hill. Kent 1C 12
Castle Hill. Suff 7H 31
Castlehill. Per 4F 66
Castlehill. S Lan 4G 59
Castlehill. W Dun 2B 58
Castle Kennedy. Dum 6G 51
Castle Lachlan. Arg 8E 64
Castlemartin. Pemb 7F 14
Castlemilk. Glas 4E 58
Castlemorris. Pemb 3F 14
Castlemorton. Worc 8F 26
Castle O'er. Dum 2G 53
Castle Park. N Yor 4F 48
Castlerigg. Cumb 3A 46
Castle Rising. Norf 7C 38
Castlerock. Caus 2E 92
Castleroe. Caus 2F 93
Castleside. Dur 7D 54
Castlethorpe. Mil 7E 28
Castleton. Abers 6A 72
Castleton. Arg 1H 57
Castleton. Derbs 1K 35
Castleton. G Man 6G 41
Castleton. Mor 3A 72
Castleton. Newp 5A 18
Castleton. N Yor 5D 48
Castleton. Per 6C 66
Castletown. Cumb 8K 53
Castletown. Dors 8E 8
Castletown. High 5C 86
Castletown. IOM 8B 44
Castletown. Tyne 6G 55
Castlewellan. New M 7H 93
Castley. N Yor 3L 41
Caston. Norf 2F 30
Castor. Pet 2J 29
Caswell. Swan 6E 16
Catacol. N Ayr 5J 57
Catbrook. Mon 3D 18
Catchems End. Worc 4F 26
Catchgate. Dur 6E 54
Catcleugh. Nmbd 1M 53
Catcliffe. S Yor 1B 36
Catcott. Som 2B 8
**Caterham**. Surr 8L 21
Catfield. Norf 7K 39
Catfield Common. Norf 7K 39
Catfirth. Shet 2E 90
**Catford**. G Lon 6L 21
Catforth. Lanc 4C 40
Cathcart. Glas 3D 58
Cathedine. Powy 2L 17
Catherine-de-Barnes. W Mid 3K 27
Catherington. Hants 4D 10
Catherston Leweston. Dors 6B 8
Catherton. Shrp 4E 26
Catisfield. Hants 5C 10
Catlodge. High 6G 71
Catlowdy. Cumb 4J 53
Catmore. W Ber 5B 20
Caton. Devn 8G 7
Caton. Lanc 1D 40
Catrine. E Ayr 7D 58
Cat's Ash. Newp 4B 18
Catsfield. E Sus 4D 12
Catsgore. Som 3D 8
Catshill. Worc 4H 27
Cattal. N Yor 2B 42
Cattawade. Suff 8H 31
Catterall. Lanc 3D 40
Catterick. N Yor 6L 47
Catterick Bridge. N Yor 6L 47
Catterick Garrison. N Yor 6K 47
Catterlen. Cumb 8J 53
Catterline. Abers 8H 73
Catterton. N Yor 3C 42
Catteshall. Surr 1G 11
Catthorpe. Leics 4C 28
Cattistock. Dors 6D 8
Catton. Nmbd 6B 54
Catton. N Yor 8A 48
Catwick. E Yor 3J 43
Catworth. Cambs 4H 29
Caudle Green. Glos 2H 19
Caulcott. Oxon 1C 20
Cauldhame. Stir 8L 65
Cauldmill. Bord 8C 60
Cauldon. Staf 5J 35
Cauldon Lowe. Staf 5J 35
Cauldwells. Abers 8G 81
Caulkerbush. Dum 6D 52
Caulside. Dum 3J 53
Caunsall. Worc 3G 27
Caunton. Notts 3E 36
Causewayend. S Lan 6J 59
Causewayhead. Stir 8B 66
Causey Park. Nmbd 2E 54
Caute. Devn 4D 6
Cautley. Cumb 6E 46
Cavendish. Suff 7E 30
Cavendish Bridge. Leics 7B 36
Cavenham. Suff 4D 30
Caversfield. Oxon 1C 20
Caversham. Read 6E 20
Caversham Heights. Read 6E 20
Caverswall. Staf 5H 35
Cawdor. High 1J 71
Cawkwell. Linc 1K 37
Cawood. N Yor 4C 42
Cawsand. Corn 6G 5
Cawston. Norf 7H 39
Cawston. Warw 4B 28
Cawthorne. N Yor 7E 48
Cawthorne. S Yor 7L 41
Cawthorpe. Linc 7H 37
Cawton. N Yor 8D 48
Caxton. Cambs 6L 29
Caynham. Shrp 4D 26
Caythorpe. Linc 5G 37
Caythorpe. Notts 5D 36
Cayton. N Yor 7H 49
Ceallan. W Isl 8K 75
Ceann a Bhaigh. W Isl
on North Uist 7J 75
on Scalpay 4D 76
on South Harris 4C 76
Ceann a Bhàigh. W Isl 5B 76
Ceannacroc Lodge. High 4C 70
Ceann a Deas Loch Baghasdail. W Isl 4D 74
Ceann an Leothaid. High 7H 69
Ceann a Tuath Loch Baghasdail. W Isl 3D 74
Ceann Loch Ailleart. High 7J 69
Ceann Loch Muideirt. High 8J 69
Ceann-na-Cleithe. W Isl 4C 76
Ceann Shìphoirt. W Isl 2D 76
Ceann Tarabhaigh. W Isl 2D 76
Cearsiadar. W Isl 1E 76
Ceathramh Meadhanach. W Isl 6K 75
Cefn Berain. Cnwy 4J 33
Cefn-brith. Cnwy 5J 33
Cefn-bryn-brain. Carm 3G 17
Cefn Bychan. Cphy 5M 17
Cefn-bychan. Flin 4L 33
Cefncaeau. Carm 7M 15
Cefn Canol. Powy 7M 33
Cefn Coch. Powy 2K 25
Cefn-coch. Powy 8L 33
Cefn-coed-y-cymmer. Mer T 4K 17
Cefn Cribwr. B'end 6H 17
Cefn-ddwysarn. Gwyn 7J 33
Cefn Einion. Shrp 3A 26
Cefneithin. Carm 3E 16
Cefn Glas. B'end 6H 17
Cefngorwydd. Powy 8J 25
Cefn Llwyd. Cdgn 4F 24
Cefn-mawr. Wrex 5A 34
Cefn-y-bedd. Flin 4B 34
Cefn-y-coed. Powy 3L 25
Cefn-y-pant. Carm 4H 15
Cegidfa. Powy 1M 25
Ceinewydd. Cdgn 1K 15
Cellan. Cdgn 8F 24
Cellardyke. Fife 7J 67
Cellarhead. Staf 5H 35
Cemaes. IOA 1C 32
Cemmaes. Powy 2H 25
Cemmaes Road. Powy 2H 25
Cenarth. Cdgn 2J 15
Cenin. Gwyn 6D 32
Ceos. W Isl 1E 76
Ceres. Fife 6H 67
Ceri. Powy 4L 25
Cerist. Powy 4J 25
Cerne Abbas. Dors 5E 8
Cerney Wick. Glos 4J 19
Cerrigceinwen. IOA 3D 32
Cerrigydrudion. Cnwy 6J 33
Cess. Norf 8L 39
Cessford. Bord 7E 60
Ceunant. Gwyn 4E 32
Chaceley. Glos 8G 27
Chacewater. Corn 4L 3
Chackmore. Buck 8D 28
Chacombe. Nptn 7B 28
**Chadderton**. G Man 7H 41
Chaddesden. Derb 6A 36
Chaddesden Common. Derb 6A 36
Chaddesley Corbett. Worc 4G 27
Chaddlehanger. Devn 8D 6
Chaddleworth. W Ber 6B 20
Chadlington. Oxon 1M 19
Chadshunt. Warw 6M 27
Chadstone. Nptn 6F 28
Chad Valley. W Mid 3J 27
Chadwell. Leics 7E 36
Chadwell. Shrp 8F 34
Chadwell Heath. G Lon 5A 22
Chadwell St Mary. Thur 6C 22
Chadwick End. W Mid 4L 27
Chadwick Green. Mers 8D 40
Chaffcombe. Som 4B 8
Chafford Hundred. Thur 6C 22
Chagford. Devn 7G 7
Chailey. E Sus 4L 11
Chain Bridge. Linc 5L 37
Chainbridge. Cambs 1M 29
Chainhurst. Kent 1D 12
Chalbury. Dors 5J 9
Chalbury Common. Dors 5J 9
Chaldon. Surr 8L 21
Chaldon Herring. Dors 7F 8
Chale. IOW 8B 10
Chale Green. IOW 8B 10
Chalfont Common. Buck 4H 21
Chalfont St Giles. Buck 4G 21
**Chalfont St Peter**. Buck 5H 21
Chalford. Glos 3G 19
Chalgrove. Oxon 4D 20
Chalk. Kent 6C 22
Chalk End. Essx 2C 22
Chalk Hill. Glos 1K 19
Challaborough. Devn 7J 5
Challacombe. Devn 1F 6
Challister. Shet 1F 90
Challoch. Dum 5J 51
Challock. Kent 8G 23
Chalton. C Beds
nr. Bedford 6J 29
nr. Luton 1H 21
Chalton. Hants 4E 10
Chalvington. E Sus 5B 12
Champany. Falk 2J 59
Chance Inn. Fife 6G 67
Chancery. Cdgn 5E 24
Chandler's Cross. Herts 4H 21
Chandler's Cross. Worc 8F 26
Chandler's Ford. Hants 3B 10
Chanlockfoot. Dum 1B 52
Channel's End. Bed 6J 29
**Channel Tunnel**. Kent 2H 13
Channerwick. Shet 5E 90
Chantry. Som 1F 8
Chantry. Suff 7H 31
Chapel. Cumb 8G 53
Chapel. Fife 8F 66
Chapel Allerton. Som 8C 18
Chapel Allerton. W Yor 4L 41
Chapel Amble. Corn 4B 4
Chapel Brampton. Nptn 5E 28
Chapelbridge. Cambs 2K 29
Chapel Chorlton. Staf 6G 35
Chapel Cleeve. Som 1K 7
Chapel End. C Beds 7H 29
Chapel-en-le-Frith. Derbs 1J 35
Chapelfield. Abers 1L 67
Chapelgate. Linc 7M 37
Chapel Green. Warw
nr. Coventry 3L 27
nr. Southam 5B 28
Chapel Haddlesey. N Yor 5C 42
Chapelhall. N Lan 3F 58
Chapel Hill. Abers 2K 73
Chapel Hill. Linc 4K 37
Chapel Hill. Mon 3D 18
Chapelhill. Per
nr. Glencarse 5F 66
nr. Harrietfield 4D 66
Chapelknowe. Dum 4H 53
Chapel Lawn. Shrp 4B 26
Chapel le Dale. N Yor 8F 46
Chapel Milton. Derbs 1J 35
Chapel of Garioch. Abers 3G 73
Chapel Row. W Ber 7C 20
Chapels. Cumb 6M 45
Chapel St Leonards. Linc 2B 38
Chapel Stile. Cumb 5B 46
Chapelthorpe. W Yor 6M 41
Chapelton. Ang 3K 67
Chapelton. Devn 3E 6
Chapelton. High
nr. Grantown-on-Spey 4K 71
nr. Inverness 8F 78
Chapelton. S Lan 5E 58
Chapel Town. Corn 6A 4
Chapeltown. Bkbn 6F 40
Chapeltown. Mor 3B 72
Chapeltown. New M 7J 93
**Chapeltown**. S Yor 8A 42
Chapmanslade. Wilts 1G 9
Chapmans Well. Devn 6C 6
Chapmore End. Herts 2L 21
Chappel. Essx 1E 22
**Chard**. Som 5B 8
Chard Junction. Dors 5B 8
Chardstock. Devn 5B 8
Charfield. S Glo 4F 18
Charing. Kent 1F 12
Charing Heath. Kent 1F 12
Charing Hill. Kent 8F 22
Charingworth. Glos 8L 27
Charlbury. Oxon 2A 20
Charlcombe. Bath 7F 18
Charlcutt. Wilts 6H 19
Charlecote. Warw 6L 27
Charlemont. Arm 6F 93
Charles. Devn 2F 6
Charlesfield. Dum 5F 52
Charleshill. Surr 1F 10
Charleston. Ang 3G 67
Charleston. Ren 3C 58
Charlestown. Aber 5J 73
Charlestown. Abers 7K 81
Charlestown. Corn 6C 4
Charlestown. Dors 8E 8
Charlestown. Fife 1J 59
Charlestown. G Man 7G 41
Charlestown. High
nr. Gairloch 6K 77
nr. Inverness 1G 71
Charlestown. W Yor 5H 41
Charlestown of Aberlour. Mor 1B 72
Charles Tye. Suff 6G 31
Charlesworth. Derbs 8J 41
Charlton. G Lon 6M 21
Charlton. Hants 1A 10
Charlton. Herts 1J 21
Charlton. Nptn 8C 28
Charlton. Nmbd 3B 54
Charlton. Oxon 5B 20
Charlton. Som
nr. Radstock 8E 18
nr. Shepton Mallet 1E 8
nr. Taunton 3A 8
Charlton. Telf 8D 34
Charlton. W Sus 4F 10
Charlton. Wilts
nr. Malmesbury 5H 19
nr. Pewsey 8K 19
nr. Shaftesbury 3H 9
Charlton. Worc
nr. Evesham 7J 27
nr. Stourport-on-Severn 4G 27
Charlton Abbots. Glos 1J 19
Charlton Adam. Som 3D 8
Charlton All Saints. Wilts 3K 9
Charlton Down. Dors 6E 8
Charlton Horethorne. Som 3E 8
**Charlton Kings**. Glos 1H 19
Charlton Mackrell. Som 3D 8
Charlton Marshall. Dors 5H 9
Charlton Musgrove. Som 3F 8
Charlton-on-Otmoor. Oxon 2C 20
Charlton on the Hill. Dors 5G 9
Charlwood. Hants 2D 10
Charlwood. Surr 1K 11
Charlynch. Som 2M 7
Charminster. Dors 6E 8
Charmouth. Dors 6B 8
Charndon. Buck 1D 20
Charney Bassett. Oxon 4A 20
Charnock Green. Lanc 6D 40
Charnock Richard. Lanc 6D 40
Charsfield. Suff 6J 31
The Chart. Kent 8A 22
Chart Corner. Kent 8D 22
Charter Alley. Hants 8C 20
Charterhouse. Som 8C 18
Charterville Allotments. Oxon 2M 19
Chartham. Kent 8H 23
Chartham Hatch. Kent 8H 23
Chartridge. Buck 3G 21
Chart Sutton. Kent 8D 22
Charvil. Wok 6E 20
Charwelton. Nptn 6C 28
Chase Terrace. Staf 1J 27
Chasetown. Staf 1J 27
Chastleton. Oxon 1L 19
Chasty. Devn 5C 6
Chatburn. Lanc 3F 40
Chatcull. Staf 6F 34
**Chatham**. Medw
**Medway Towns 111** (7D 22)
Chatham Green. Essx 2D 22
Chathill. Nmbd 7J 61
Chatley. Worc 5G 27
Chattenden. Medw 6D 22
Chatteris. Cambs 3L 29
Chattisham. Suff 7G 31
Chatton. Nmbd 7H 61
Chatwall. Shrp 2D 26
Chaulden. Herts 3H 21
Chaul End. C Beds 1H 21
Chawleigh. Devn 4G 7
Chawley. Oxon 3B 20
Chawston. Bed 6J 29
Chawton. Hants 2E 10
Chaxhill. Glos 2F 18
**Cheadle**. G Man 1G 35
**Cheadle**. Staf 5J 35
Cheadle Hulme. G Man 1G 35
Cheam. G Lon 7K 21
Cheapside. Wind 7G 21
Chearsley. Buck 2E 20
Chebsey. Staf 7G 35
Checkendon. Oxon 5D 20
Checkley. Ches E 5F 34
Checkley. Here 8D 26
Checkley. Staf 6J 35
Chedburgh. Suff 6D 30
Cheddar. Som 8C 18
Cheddington. Buck 2G 21
Cheddleton. Staf 4H 35
Cheddon Fitzpaine. Som 3M 7
Chedglow. Wilts 4H 19
Chedgrave. Norf 2K 31
Chedington. Dors 5C 8
Chediston. Suff 4K 31
Chediston Green. Suff 4K 31
Chedworth. Glos 2J 19
Chedzoy. Som 2B 8
Cheeseman's Green. Kent 2G 13
Cheetham Hill. G Man 7G 41
Cheglinch. Devn 1E 6
Cheldon. Devn 4G 7
Chelford. Ches E 2G 35
Chellaston. Derb 6A 36
Chellington. Bed 6G 29
Chelmarsh. Shrp 3F 26
Chelmick. Shrp 2C 26
Chelmondiston. Suff 8J 31
Chelmorton. Derbs 3K 35
**Chelmsford**. Essx 3D 22
**Chelsea**. G Lon 6K 21
Chelsfield. G Lon 7A 22
Chelsham. Surr 8L 21
Chelston. Som 3L 7
Chelsworth. Suff 7F 30
**Cheltenham**. Glos 107 (1H 19)
Chelveston. Nptn 5G 29
Chelvey. N Som 7C 18
Chelwood. Bath 7E 18
Chelwood Common. E Sus 3M 11
Chelwood Gate. E Sus 3M 11
Chelworth. Wilts 4H 19
Chelworth Lower Green. Wilts 4J 19
Chelworth Upper Green. Wilts 4J 19
Chelynch. Som 1E 8
Cheney Longville. Shrp 3C 26
Chenies. Buck 4H 21
**Chepstow**. Mon 4D 18
Chequerfield. W Yor 5B 42
Chequers Corner. Norf 1A 30
Cherhill. Wilts 6J 19
Cherington. Glos 4H 19
Cherington. Warw 8L 27
Cheriton. Devn 1G 7
Cheriton. Hants 3C 10
Cheriton. Kent 2J 13
Cheriton. Pemb 7F 14
Cheriton. Swan 7L 15
Cheriton Bishop. Devn 6G 7
Cheriton Cross. Devn 6G 7
Cheriton Fitzpaine. Devn 5H 7
Cherrington. Telf 7E 34
Cherrybank. Per 5E 66
Cherry Burton. E Yor 3G 43
Cherry Green. Herts 1L 21
Cherry Hinton. Cambs 6A 30
Cherry Willingham. Linc 2H 37
**Chertsey**. Surr 7H 21
Cheselbourne. Dors 6F 8
**Chesham**. Buck 3G 21
Chesham. G Man 6G 41
Chesham Bois. Buck 4G 21
**Cheshunt**. Herts 3L 21
Cheslyn Hay. Staf 1H 27
Chessetts Wood. Warw 4K 27
Chessington. G Lon 7J 21
**Chester**. Ches W 108 (3C 34)
Chesterblade. Som 1E 8
**Chesterfield**. Derbs 2A 36
Chesterfield. Staf 1K 27
Chesterhope. Nmbd 3B 54
**Chester-le-Street**. Dur 6F 54
Chester Moor. Dur 7F 54
Chesters. Bord 8D 60
Chesterton. Cambs
nr. Cambridge 5A 30
nr. Peterborough 2J 29
Chesterton. Glos 3J 19
Chesterton. Oxon 1C 20
Chesterton. Shrp 2F 26
Chesterton. Staf 5G 35
Chesterton Green. Warw 6M 27
Chesterwood. Nmbd 5B 54
Chestfield. Kent 7H 23
Cheston. Devn 6J 5
Cheswardine. Shrp 6F 34
Cheswell. Telf 8F 34
Cheswick. Nmbd 5H 61
Cheswick Green. W Mid 4K 27
Chetnole. Dors 5E 8
Chettiscombe. Devn 4J 7
Chettisham. Cambs 3B 30
Chettle. Dors 4H 9
Chetton. Shrp 2E 26
Chetwode. Buck 1D 20
Chetwynd Aston. Telf 8F 34
Cheveley. Cambs 5C 30
Chevening. Kent 8A 22
Chevington. Suff 6D 30
Chevithorne. Devn 4J 7
Chew Magna. Bath 7D 18
Chew Moor. G Man 7E 40
Chew Stoke. Bath 7D 18
Chewton Keynsham. Bath 7E 18
Chewton Mendip. Som 8D 18
Chichacott. Devn 6F 6
Chicheley. Mil 7G 29
**Chichester**. W Sus 5F 10
Chickerell. Dors 7E 8
Chickering. Suff 4J 31
Chicklade. Wilts 2H 9
Chicksands. C Beds 8J 29
Chickward. Here 6A 26
Chidden. Hants 4D 10
Chiddingfold. Surr 2G 11
Chiddingly. E Sus 4B 12
Chiddingstone. Kent 1B 12
Chiddingstone Causeway. Kent 1B 12
Chiddingstone Hoath. Kent 1A 12
Chideock. Dors 6C 8
Chidgley. Som 2K 7
Chidham. W Sus 5E 10
Chieveley. W Ber 6B 20
Chignal St James. Essx 3C 22
Chignal Smealy. Essx 2C 22
**Chigwell**. Essx 4M 21
Chigwell Row. Essx 4A 22
Chilbolton. Hants 1A 10
Chilcomb. Hants 3C 10
Chilcombe. Dors 6D 8
Chilcompton. Som 8E 18
Chilcote. Leics 8L 35
Childer Thornton. Ches W 2B 34
Child Okeford. Dors 4G 9
Childrey. Oxon 5A 20
Child's Ercall. Shrp 7E 34
Childswickham. Worc 8J 27
Childwall. Mers 1C 34
Childwick Green. Herts 2J 21
Chilfrome. Dors 6D 8
Chilgrove. W Sus 4F 10
Chilham. Kent 8G 23
Chilhampton. Wilts 2J 9
Chilla. Devn 5D 6
Chilland. Hants 2C 10
Chillaton. Devn 7D 6
Chillenden. Kent 8J 23
Chillerton. IOW 7B 10
Chillesford. Suff 6K 31
Chillingham. Nmbd 7H 61
Chillington. Devn 7K 5
Chillington. Som 4B 8
Chilmark. Wilts 2H 9
Chilmington Green. Kent 1F 12
Chilson. Oxon 2M 19
Chilsworthy. Corn 8D 6
Chilsworthy. Devn 5C 6
Chiltern Green. C Beds 2J 21
Chilthorne Domer. Som 4D 8
Chilton. Buck 2D 20
Chilton. Devn 5H 7
Chilton. Dur 3L 47
Chilton. Oxon 5B 20
Chilton Candover. Hants 1C 10
Chilton Cantelo. Som 3D 8
Chilton Foliat. Wilts 6M 19
Chilton Lane. Dur 8G 55
Chilton Polden. Som 2B 8
Chilton Street. Suff 7D 30
Chilton Trinity. Som 2A 8
Chilwell. Notts 6C 36
Chilworth. Hants 4B 10
Chilworth. Surr 1H 11
Chimney. Oxon 3A 20
Chimney Street. Suff 7D 30
Chineham. Hants 8D 20
**Chingford**. G Lon 4L 21
Chinley. Derbs 1J 35
Chinnor. Oxon 3E 20
Chipley. Som 3L 7
Chipnall. Shrp 6F 34
Chippenham. Cambs 5C 30
**Chippenham**. Wilts 6H 19
Chipperfield. Herts 3H 21
Chipping. Herts 8L 29
Chipping. Lanc 3E 40
Chipping Campden. Glos 8K 27
Chipping Hill. Essx 2E 22
Chipping Norton. Oxon 1M 19
Chipping Ongar. Essx 3B 22
**Chipping Sodbury**. S Glo 5F 18
Chipping Warden. Nptn 7B 28
Chipstable. Som 3K 7
Chipstead. Kent 8B 22
Chipstead. Surr 8K 21
Chirbury. Shrp 2A 26
Chirk. Wrex 6A 34
Chirmorie. S Ayr 4H 51
Chirnside. Bord 4F 60
Chirnsidebridge. Bord 4F 60
Chirton. Wilts 8J 19
Chisbridge Cross. Buck 5F 20
Chisbury. Wilts 7L 19
Chiselborough. Som 4C 8
Chiseldon. Swin 6K 19
Chiselhampton. Oxon 4C 20
Chiserley. W Yor 5J 41
**Chislehurst**. G Lon 6M 21
Chislet. Kent 7J 23
Chiswell. Dors 8E 8
Chiswell Green. Herts 3J 21
**Chiswick**. G Lon 6K 21
Chisworth. Derbs 8H 41
Chitcombe. E Sus 3E 12
Chithurst. W Sus 3F 10
Chittering. Cambs 5A 30
Chitterley. Devn 5J 7
Chitterne. Wilts 1H 9
Chittlehamholt. Devn 3F 6
Chittlehampton. Devn 3F 6
Chittoe. Wilts 7H 19
Chivelstone. Devn 8K 5
Chivenor. Devn 2E 6
Chobham. Surr 7G 21
Cholderton. Wilts 1L 9
Cholesbury. Buck 3G 21
Chollerford. Nmbd 4C 54
Chollerton. Nmbd 4C 54
Cholsey. Oxon 5C 20
Cholstrey. Here 6C 26
Chop Gate. N Yor 6C 48
Choppington. Nmbd 3F 54
Chopwell. Tyne 6E 54
Chorley. Ches E 4D 34
**Chorley**. Lanc 6D 40
Chorley. Shrp 3E 26
Chorley. Staf 8J 35
Chorleywood. Herts 4H 21
Chorlton. Ches E 4F 34
Chorlton-cum-Hardy. G Man 8G 41
Chorlton Lane. Ches W 5C 34
Choulton. Shrp 3B 26
Chrishall. Essx 8M 29
Christchurch. Cambs 2A 30
**Christchurch**. Dors 6K 9
Christchurch. Glos 2D 18
Christian Malford. Wilts 6H 19
Christleton. Ches W 3C 34
Christmas Common. Oxon 4E 20
Christon. N Som 8B 18
Christon Bank. Nmbd 7K 61
Christow. Devn 7H 7
Chryston. N Lan 2E 58
Chuck Hatch. E Sus 2A 12
Chudleigh. Devn 8H 7
Chudleigh Knighton. Devn 8H 7
Chulmleigh. Devn 4F 6
Chunal. Derbs 8J 41
Church. Lanc 5F 40
Churcham. Glos 2F 18
Church Aston. Telf 8F 34
Church Brampton. Nptn 5E 28
Church Brough. Cumb 4F 46
Church Broughton. Derbs 6L 35
Church Corner. Suff 3L 31
Church Crookham. Hants 8F 20
Churchdown. Glos 1G 19
Church Eaton. Staf 8G 35
Church End. Cambs
nr. Cambridge 6A 30
nr. Over 4L 29
nr. Sawtry 3K 29
nr. Wisbech 1L 29
Church End. C Beds
nr. Stotfold 8J 29
nr. Totternhoe 1G 21
Church End. E Yor 2H 43
Church End. Essx
nr. Braintree 1D 22
nr. Great Dunmow 1C 22
nr. Saffron Walden 7B 30
Church End. Glos 3F 18
Church End. Hants 8D 20
Church End. Linc
nr. Donington 6K 37
nr. North Somercotes 8M 43
Church End. Norf 8B 38
Church End. Warw
nr. Coleshill 2L 27
nr. Nuneaton 2L 27
Church End. Wilts 6J 19
Churchend. Essx 4G 23
Church Enstone. Oxon 1A 20
Church Fenton. N Yor 4C 42
Church Green. Devn 6L 7
Church Gresley. Derbs 8L 35
Church Hanborough. Oxon 2B 20
Church Hill. Ches W 3E 34
Church Hill. Worc 5J 27
Church Hougham. Kent 1J 13
Church Houses. N Yor 6D 48
Churchill. Devn
nr. Axminster 5B 8
nr. Barnstaple 1E 6
Churchill. N Som 8C 18
Churchill. Oxon 1L 19
Churchill. Worc
nr. Kidderminster 4G 27
nr. Worcester 6H 27
Churchinford. Som 4M 7
Church Knowle. Dors 7H 9
Church Laneham. Notts 2F 36
Church Langley. Essx 3A 22
Church Langton. Leics 2E 28
Church Lawford. Warw 4B 28
Church Lawton. Ches E 4G 35
Church Leigh. Staf 6J 35
Church Lench. Worc 6J 27
Church Mayfield. Staf 5K 35
Church Minshull. Ches E 3E 34
Church Norton. W Sus 6F 10
Churchover. Warw 3C 28
Church Preen. Shrp 2D 26
Church Pulverbatch. Shrp 1C 26
Churchstanton. Som 4L 7
Church Stoke. Powy 2A 26
Churchstow. Devn 7K 5
Church Stowe. Nptn 6D 28
Church Street. Kent 6D 22
Church Stretton. Shrp 2C 26
Church Town. Leics 8A 36
Church Town. N Lin 7E 42
Churchtown. Cumb 7H 53
Churchtown. Derbs 3L 35
Churchtown. Devn 1F 6
Churchtown. IOM 5D 44
Churchtown. Lanc 3C 40
Churchtown. Mers 6B 40
Churchtown. New M 6J 93
Churchtown. Shrp 3A 26
Church Village. Rhon 6K 17
Church Warsop. Notts 3C 36
Church Westcote. Glos 1L 19
Church Wilne. Derbs 6B 36
Churnsike Lodge. Nmbd 4L 53
Churston Ferrers. Torb 6M 5
Churt. Surr 2F 10
Churton. Ches W 4C 34
Churwell. W Yor 5L 41
Chute Standen. Wilts 8M 19
Chwilog. Gwyn 7D 32
Chwitffordd. Flin 3L 33
Chyandour. Corn 5H 3
Cilan Uchaf. Gwyn 8B 32
Cilcain. Flin 4L 33
Cilcennin. Cdgn 6E 24
Cilfrew. Neat 4G 17
Cilfynydd. Rhon 5K 17
Cilgerran. Pemb 2H 15
Cilgeti. Pemb 6H 15
Cilgwyn. Carm 2G 17
Cilgwyn. Pemb 3G 15
Ciliau Aeron. Cdgn 1L 15
Cill Amhlaidh. W Isl 1D 74
Cill Donnain. W Isl 3D 74
Cille a' Bhacstair. High 7E 76
Cille Bhrighde. W Isl 4D 74
Cille Pheadair. W Isl 4D 74
Cilmaengwyn. Neat 4G 17
Cilmeri. Powy 7K 25
Cilmery. Powy 7K 25
Cilrhedyn. Pemb 3J 15
Cilsan. Carm 2E 16
Ciltalgarth. Gwyn 6H 33
Ciltwrch. Powy 8L 25
Cilybebyll. Neat 4G 17
Cilycwm. Carm 8G 25
Cimla. Neat 5G 17
**Cinderford**. Glos 2E 18
Cinderhill. Derbs 5A 36
Cippenham. Slo 5G 21
Cippyn. Pemb 2H 15
Cirbhig. W Isl 7E 82
Circebost. W Isl 8E 82
**Cirencester**. Glos 3J 19
City. Powy 3M 25
City. V Glam 7J 17
The City. Buck 4E 20
City Airport. G Lon 5M 21
City Centre. Stoke
**Stoke 116** (5G 35)
City Dulas. IOA 2D 32
City of Derry Airport. Derr 2D 92
**City of London**. G Lon
**London 113** (5L 21)
Civiltown. Arm 6G 93
Clabby. Ferm 6D 92
Clabhach. Arg 2G 63
Clachaig. Arg 1L 57
Clachaig. High
nr. Kinlochleven 2F 64
nr. Nethy Bridge 4L 71
Clachamish. High 8E 76
Clachan. Arg
on Kintyre 4G 57
on Lismore 3C 64
Clachan. High
nr. Bettyhill 5K 85
nr. Staffin 7F 76
nr. Uig 6F 76
on Raasay 2G 69
Clachan Farm. Arg 6F 64
Clachan na Luib. W Isl 7K 75
Clachan of Campsie. E Dun 2E 58
Clachan of Glendaruel. Arg 1J 57
Clachan-Seil. Arg 6B 64
Clachan Shannda. W Isl 6K 75
Clachan Strachur. Arg 7E 64
Clachbreck. Arg 2G 57
Clachnaharry. High 1G 71
Clachtoll. High 1M 77
Clackmannan. Clac 8C 66
**Clackmannanshire Bridge**. Clac 1H 59
Clackmarras. Mor 8B 80
**Clacton-on-Sea**. Essx 2H 23
Cladach a Chaolais. W Isl 7J 75
Cladach Chairinis. W Isl 8K 75
Cladach Chirceboist. W Isl 7J 75
Cladach Iolaraigh. W Isl 7J 75
Cladich. Arg 5E 64
Cladswell. Worc 6J 27
Clady. Derr 4C 92
Clady. M Ulst 3F 93
Claggan. High
nr. Fort William 8B 70
nr. Lochaline 2B 64
Claigan. High 8D 76
Clandown. Bath 8E 18
Clanfield. Hants 4D 10
Clanfield. Oxon 3L 19
Clanville. Hants 1M 9
Clanville. Som 2E 8
Claonaig. Arg 4H 57
Clapgate. Dors 5J 9
Clapgate. Herts 1M 21
Clapham. Bed 6H 29
Clapham. Devn 7H 7
**Clapham**. G Lon 6K 21
Clapham. N Yor 1F 40
Clapham. W Sus 5H 11
Clap Hill. Kent 2G 13
Clappers. Bord 4G 61
Clappersgate. Cumb 5B 46
Clapphoull. Shet 5E 90
Clapton. Som
nr. Crewkerne 5C 8
nr. Radstock 8E 18
Clapton in Gordano. N Som 6C 18
Clapton-on-the-Hill. Glos 2K 19
Clapworthy. Devn 3F 6
Clara Vale. Tyne 5E 54
Clarbeston. Pemb 4G 15
Clarbeston Road. Pemb 4G 15
Clarborough. Notts 1E 36
Clare. Arm 6G 93
Clare. Suff 7D 30
Clarebrand. Dum 5B 52
Clarencefield. Dum 5E 52
Clarilaw. Bord 8C 60
Clark's Green. Surr 2J 11
Clark's Hill. Linc 7L 37
**Clarkston**. E Ren 4D 58
Clasheddy. High 5J 85
Clashindarroch. Abers 2D 72
Clashmore. High
nr. Dornoch 5H 79
nr. Stoer 8C 84
Clashnessie. High 8C 84
Clashnoir. Mor 3B 72
Clate. Shet 1F 90
Clathick. Per 5B 66
Clathy. Per 6C 66
Clatt. Abers 3E 72
Clatter. Powy 3J 25
Clatterford. IOW 7B 10
Clatworthy. Som 2K 7
Claudy. Derr 3D 92
Claughton. Lanc
nr. Caton 1D 40
nr. Garstang 3D 40
Claughton. Mers 1A 34
Claverdon. Warw 5K 27
Claverham. N Som 7C 18
Clavering. Essx 8A 30
Claverley. Shrp 2F 26
Claverton. Bath 7F 18
Clawdd-côch. V Glam 7K 17
Clawdd-newydd. Den 5K 33
Clawson Hill. Leics 7E 36
Clawton. Devn 6C 6
Claxby. Linc
nr. Alford 2A 38
nr. Market Rasen 8J 43
Claxton. Norf 1K 31
Claxton. N Yor 1D 42
Claybrooke Magna. Leics 3B 28
Claybrooke Parva. Leics 3B 28
Clay Common. Suff 3L 31
Clay Coton. Nptn 4C 28
**Clay Cross**. Derbs 3A 36
Claydon. Oxon 6B 28
Claydon. Suff 6H 31
Clay End. Herts 1L 21
Claygate. Dum 4H 53
Claygate. Kent 1D 12
Claygate. Surr 7J 21
Claygate Cross. Kent 8C 22
Clayhall. Hants 6D 10
Clayhanger. Devn 3K 7
Clayhanger. W Mid 1J 27
Clayhidon. Devn 4L 7
Clay Hill. Bris 6E 18
Clayhill. E Sus 3E 12
Clayhill. Hants 5M 9
Clayhithe. Cambs 5B 30
Clayholes. Ang 4J 67
Clay Lake. Linc 7K 37
Clayock. High 6C 86
Claypits. Glos 3F 18
Claypole. Linc 5F 36
Claythorpe. Linc 2M 37
Clayton. G Man 8G 41
Clayton. S Yor 7B 42
Clayton. Staf 5G 35
Clayton. W Sus 4L 11
Clayton. W Yor 4K 41
Clayton Green. Lanc 5D 40
Clayton-le-Moors. Lanc 4F 40
Clayton-le-Woods. Lanc 5D 40
Clayton West. W Yor 6L 41
Clayworth. Notts 1E 36
Cleadale. High 7F 68
Cleadon. Tyne 5G 55
Clearbrook. Devn 5H 5
Clearwell. Glos 3D 18
Cleasby. N Yor 4L 47
Cleat. Orkn
nr. Braehead 5D 88
nr. St Margaret's Hope 3F 86
Cleatlam. Dur 4K 47
Cleator. Cumb 3K 45
Cleator Moor. Cumb 3K 45
**Cleckheaton**. W Yor 5K 41
Cleedownton. Shrp 3D 26
Cleehill. Shrp 4D 26
Cleekhimin. N Lan 4F 58
Clee St Margaret. Shrp 3D 26
Cleestanton. Shrp 4D 26
**Cleethorpes**. NE Lin 7L 43
Cleeton St Mary. Shrp 4E 26
Cleeve. N Som 7C 18
Cleeve. Oxon 5D 20
Cleeve Hill. Glos 1H 19
Cleeve Prior. Worc 7J 27
Clehonger. Here 8C 26
Cleigh. Arg 5C 64
Cleish. Per 8D 66
Cleland. N Lan 4G 59
Clench Common. Wilts 7K 19
Clenchwarton. Norf 7B 38
Clennell. Nmbd 1C 54
Clent. Worc 4H 27
Cleobury Mortimer. Shrp 4E 26
Cleobury North. Shrp 3E 26
Clephanton. High 8J 79
Clerkhill. High 5K 85
Clestrain. Orkn 1E 86
Clevancy. Wilts 6J 19
**Clevedon**. N Som 6C 18
Cleveley. Oxon 1A 20
**Cleveleys**. Lanc 3B 40
Clevelode. Worc 7G 27
Cleverton. Wilts 5H 19
Clewer. Som 8C 18
Cley next the Sea. Norf 5G 39
Cliaid. W Isl 5C 74
Cliasmol. W Isl 3B 76
Clibberswick. Shet 2L 91
Cliburn. Cumb 3D 46
Cliddesden. Hants 1D 10
Clieves Hills. Lanc 7B 40
Cliff. Warw 2L 27
Cliffburn. Ang 3K 67
Cliffe. Medw 6D 22
Cliffe. N Yor
nr. Darlington 4L 47
nr. Selby 4D 42
Cliff End. E Sus 4E 12
Cliffe Woods. Medw 6D 22
Clifford. Here 8M 25
Clifford. W Yor 3B 42
Clifford Chambers. Warw 6K 27
Clifford's Mesne. Glos 1F 18
Cliffsend. Kent 7K 23
Clifton. Bris 6D 18
Clifton. C Beds 8J 29
Clifton. Cumb 3D 46
Clifton. Derbs 5K 35
Clifton. Devn 1F 6
Clifton. G Man 7F 40
Clifton. Lanc 4C 40
Clifton. Nmbd 3F 54
Clifton. N Yor 3K 41
Clifton. Nott 6C 36
Clifton. Oxon 8B 28
Clifton. S Yor 8C 42
Clifton. Stir 4H 65
Clifton. W Yor 5K 41
Clifton. Worc 7G 27
Clifton. York 2C 42
Clifton Campville. Staf 8L 35
Clifton Hampden. Oxon 4C 20
Clifton Hill. Worc 5F 26
Clifton Reynes. Mil 6G 29
Clifton upon Dunsmore. Warw 4C 28
Clifton upon Teme. Worc 5F 26
Cliftonville. Kent 6K 23
Cliftonville. Norf 6K 39
Climping. W Sus 5G 11
Climpy. S Lan 4H 59
Clink. Som 1F 8
Clint. N Yor 2L 41
Clint Green. Norf 8G 39
Clintmains. Bord 6D 60
Cliobh. W Isl 8D 82
Clipiau. Gwyn 1H 25
Clippesby. Norf 8L 39
Clippings Green. Norf 8G 39
Clipsham. Rut 8G 37
Clipston. Nptn 3E 28
Clipston. Notts 6D 36
Clipstone. Notts 3C 36
**Clitheroe**. Lanc 3F 40
Cliuthar. W Isl 4C 76
Clive. Shrp 7D 34
Clivocast. Shet 3K 91
Clixby. Linc 7H 43
Clocaenog. Den 5K 33
Clochan. Mor 7D 80
Clochforbie. Abers 8H 81
Clock Face. Mers 8D 40
Cloddiau. Powy 2M 25
Cloddymoss. Mor 7K 79
Clodock. Here 1B 18
Cloford. Som 1F 8
Clogh. ME Ant 3G 93
Clogher. M Ulst 6D 92
Cloghmills. Caus 3G 93
Clola. Abers 1K 73
Clonoe. M Ulst 5F 93
Clonvaraghan. New M 6H 93
Clophill. C Beds 8H 29
Clopton. Nptn 3H 29
Clopton Corner. Suff 6J 31
Clopton Green. Suff 6D 30
Closeburn. Dum 2C 52
Close Clark. IOM 7B 44
Closworth. Som 4D 8
Clothall. Herts 8K 29
Clotton. Ches W 3D 34
Clough. G Man 6H 41
Clough. New M 6J 93
Clough. W Yor 6J 41
Cloughey. Ards 6K 93
Clough Foot. W Yor 5H 41
Cloughton. N Yor 6H 49
Cloughton Newlands. N Yor 6H 49
Clousta. Shet 2D 90
Clouston. Orkn 8B 88
Clova. Abers 3D 72
Clova. Ang 8C 72
Clovelly. Devn 3C 6
Clovenfords. Bord 6B 60
Clovenstone. Abers 4G 73
Clovullin. High 1E 64
Clowne. Derbs 2B 36
Clows Top. Worc 4F 26
Cloy. Wrex 5B 34
Cloyfin. Caus 2F 93
Cluanie Inn. High 4A 70
Cluanie Lodge. High 4A 70
Cluddley. Telf 8E 34
Clun. Shrp 3B 26
Y Clun. Neat 4H 17
Clunas. High 1J 71
Clunbury. Shrp 3B 26
Clunderwen. Pemb 5H 15
Clune. High 3H 71
Clunes. High 7C 70
Clungunford. Shrp 4B 26
Clunie. Per 3E 66
Clunton. Shrp 3B 26
Cluny. Fife 8F 66
Clutton. Bath 8E 18
Clutton. Ches W 4C 34
Clwt-y-bont. Gwyn 4E 32
Clwydfagwyr. Mer T 4K 17
Clydach. Mon 3M 17
**Clydach**. Swan 4F 16
Clydach Vale. Rhon 5J 17
**Clydebank**. W Dun 3D 58
Clydey. Pemb 3J 15
Clyffe Pypard. Wilts 6J 19
Clynder. Arg 1M 57
Clyne. Neat 4H 17
Clynelish. High 3J 79
Clynnog-fawr. Gwyn 6D 32
Clyro. Powy 8M 25
Clyst Honiton. Devn 6J 7
Clyst Hydon. Devn 5K 7
Clyst St George. Devn 7J 7
Clyst St Lawrence. Devn 5K 7
Clyst St Mary. Devn 6J 7
Clyth. High 8D 86
Cnip. W Isl 8D 82
Cnoc Amhlaigh. W Isl 8J 83
Cnwcau. Pemb 2J 15
Cnwch Coch. Cdgn 5F 24
Coad's Green. Corn 8B 6
Coagh. M Ulst 5F 93
Coal Aston. Derbs 2A 36
Coalbrookdale. Telf 1E 26
Coalbrookvale. Blae 4L 17
Coalburn. S Lan 6G 59
Coalburns. Tyne 5E 54
Coalcleugh. Nmbd 7B 54
Coaley. Glos 3F 18
Coalford. Abers 6H 73
Coalhall. E Ayr 8C 58
Coalhill. Essx 4D 22
Coalisland. M Ulst 5F 93
Coalpit Heath. S Glo 5E 18
Coal Pool. W Mid 1J 27
Coalport. Telf 1F 26
Coalsnaughton. Clac 8C 66
Coaltown of Balgonie. Fife 8G 67
Coaltown of Wemyss. Fife 8G 67
**Coalville**. Leics 8B 36
Coalway. Glos 2D 18
Coanwood. Nmbd 6L 53
Coat. Som 3C 8
**Coatbridge**. N Lan 3F 58
Coatdyke. N Lan 3F 58
Coate. Swin 5K 19
Coate. Wilts 7J 19
Coates. Cambs 2L 29
Coates. Glos 3H 19
Coates. Linc 1G 37
Coates. W Sus 4G 11
Coatham. Red C 3C 48
Coatham Mundeville. Darl 3L 47
Cobbaton. Devn 3F 6
Coberley. Glos 2H 19
Cobhall Common. Here 8C 26
Cobham. Kent 7C 22
**Cobham**. Surr 8J 21
Cobnash. Here 5C 26
Coburg. Devn 8H 7
Cockayne. N Yor 6D 48
Cockayne Hatley. C Beds 7K 29
Cock Bank. Wrex 5B 34
Cock Bridge. Abers 5B 72
Cockburnspath. Bord 2E 60
Cock Clarks. Essx 3E 22
Cockenzie and Port Seton. E Lot 2B 60
Cockerham. Lanc 2C 40
Cockermouth. Cumb 8F 52
Cockernhoe. Herts 1J 21
Cockfield. Dur 3K 47
Cockfield. Suff 6F 30
Cockfosters. G Lon 4K 21
Cock Gate. Here 5C 26
Cock Green. Essx 2C 22
Cocking. W Sus 4F 10
Cocking Causeway. W Sus 4F 10
Cockington. Torb 5L 5
Cocklake. Som 1C 8
Cocklaw. Abers 1K 73
Cocklaw. Nmbd 4C 54
Cockley Beck. Cumb 4M 45
Cockley Cley. Norf 1D 30
Cockmuir. Abers 8J 81
Cockpole Green. Wok 5E 20
Cockshutford. Shrp 3D 26
Cockshutt. Shrp 7C 34
Cockthorpe. Norf 5F 38
Cockwood. Devn 7J 7
Cockyard. Derbs 2J 35
Cockyard. Here 8C 26
Codda. Corn 8A 6
Coddenham. Suff 6H 31
Coddenham Green. Suff 6H 31

Coddington. *Ches W* 4C 34
Coddington. *Here* 7F 26
Coddington. *Notts* 4F 36
Codford. *Wilts* 2H 9
Codicote. *Herts* 2K 21
Codmore Hill. *W Sus* 3H 11
Codnor. *Derbs* 5B 36
Codrington. *S Glo* 6F 18
**Codsall**. *Staf* 1G 27
Codsall Wood. *Staf* 1G 27
**Coed Duon**. *Cphy* 5L 17
Coedely. *Rhon* 6K 17
Coedglasson. *Powy* 6K 25
Coedkernew. *Newp* 5A 18
Coed Morgan. *Mon* 2B 18
Coedpoeth. *Wrex* 4A 34
Coedway. *Powy* 8B 34
Coed-y-bryn. *Cdgn* 2K 15
Coed-y-paen. *Mon* 4B 18
Coed Ystumgwern. *Gwyn* 8E 32
Coelbren. *Powy* 3H 17
Coffinswell. *Devn* 5L 5
Cofton Hackett. *Worc* 4J 27
Cogan. *V Glam* 7L 17
Cogenhoe. *Nptn* 5F 28
Cogges. *Oxon* 3A 20
Coggeshall. *Essx* 1E 22
Coggeshall Hamlet. *Essx* 1E 22
Coggins Mill. *E Sus* 3B 12
Coignafearn Lodge. *High* 4G 71
Coig Peighinnean. *W Isl* 5J 83
Coig Peighinnean Bhuirgh. *W Isl* 6H 83
Coilleag. *W Isl* 4D 74
Coillemore. *High* 6G 79
Coillore. *High* 2E 68
Coire an Fhuarain. *W Isl* 8F 82
Coity. *B'end* 6J 17
Cokhay Green. *Derbs* 7L 35
Col. *W Isl* 7H 83
Colaboll. *High* 2F 78
Colan. *Corn* 5A 4
Colaton Raleigh. *Devn* 7K 7
Colbost. *High* 1D 68
Colburn. *N Yor* 6K 47
Colby. *Cumb* 3E 46
Colby. *IOM* 7B 44
Colby. *Norf* 6J 39
**Colchester**. *Essx* 1G 23
Cold Ash. *W Ber* 7C 20
Cold Ashby. *Nptn* 4D 28
Cold Ashton. *S Glo* 6F 18
Cold Aston. *Glos* 2K 19
Coldbackie. *High* 6J 85
Cold Blow. *Pemb* 5H 15
Cold Brayfield. *Mil* 6G 29
Cold Cotes. *N Yor* 8F 46
Coldean. *Brig* 5L 11
Coldeast. *Devn* 8H 7
Colden. *W Yor* 5H 41
Colden Common. *Hants* 3B 10
Coldfair Green. *Suff* 5L 31
Coldham. *Cambs* 1M 29
Coldham. *Staf* 1G 27
Cold Hanworth. *Linc* 1H 37
Cold Harbour. *Dors* 6H 9
Coldharbour. *Corn* 4L 3
Coldharbour. *Glos* 3D 18
Coldharbour. *Kent* 8B 22
Coldharbour. *Surr* 1J 11
Cold Hatton. *Telf* 7E 34
Cold Hatton Heath. *Telf* 7E 34
Cold Hesledon. *Dur* 7H 55
Cold Hiendley. *W Yor* 6A 42
Cold Higham. *Nptn* 6D 28
Coldingham. *Bord* 3G 61
Cold Kirby. *N Yor* 7C 48
Coldmeece. *Staf* 6G 35
Cold Northcott. *Corn* 7B 6
Cold Norton. *Essx* 3E 22
Cold Overton. *Leics* 8F 36
Coldrain. *Per* 7D 66
Coldred. *Kent* 1J 13
Coldridge. *Devn* 5F 6
Cold Row. *Lanc* 3B 40
Coldstream. *Bord* 5F 60
Coldwaltham. *W Sus* 4H 11
Coldwell. *Here* 8C 26
Coldwells. *Abers* 2L 73
Coldwells Croft. *Abers* 3E 72
Cole. *Shet* 1D 90
Cole. *Som* 2E 8
Colebatch. *Shrp* 3B 26
Colebrook. *Devn* 5K 7
Colebrooke. *Devn* 6G 7
Coleburn. *Mor* 8B 80
Coleby. *Linc* 3G 37
Coleby. *N Lin* 6F 42
Cole End. *Warw* 3L 27
Coleford. *Devn* 5G 7
**Coleford**. *Glos* 2D 18
Coleford. *Som* 1E 8
Colegate End. *Norf* 3H 31
Cole Green. *Herts* 2K 21
Cole Henley. *Hants* 8B 20
Colehill. *Dors* 5J 9
Coleman Green. *Herts* 2J 21
Coleman's Hatch. *E Sus* 2A 12
Colemere. *Shrp* 6C 34
Colemore. *Hants* 2E 10
Colemore Green. *Shrp* 2F 26
Coleorton. *Leics* 8B 36
**Coleraine**. *Caus* 2F 93
Colerne. *Wilts* 6G 19
Colesbourne. *Glos* 2J 19
Colesden. *Bed* 6J 29
Coles Green. *Worc* 6F 26
Coleshill. *Buck* 4G 21
Coleshill. *Oxon* 4L 19
Coleshill. *Warw* 3L 27
Colestocks. *Devn* 5K 7
Colethrop. *Glos* 2G 19
Coley. *Bath* 8D 18
Colgate. *W Sus* 2K 11
Colinsburgh. *Fife* 7H 67
Colinton. *Edin* 3L 59
Colintraive. *Arg* 2K 57
Colkirk. *Norf* 7F 38
Collace. *Per* 4F 66
Collam. *W Isl* 4C 76
Collaton. *Devn* 8K 5
Collaton St Mary. *Torb* 5L 5
College of Roseisle. *Mor* 7M 79
Collessie. *Fife* 6F 66
Collier Row. *G Lon* 4A 22
Colliers End. *Herts* 1L 21
Collier Street. *Kent* 1D 12
Colliery Row. *Tyne* 7G 55
Collieston. *Abers* 3K 73
Collin. *Dum* 4E 52
Collingbourne Ducis. *Wilts* 8L 19
Collingbourne Kingston. *Wilts* 8L 19
Collingham. *Notts* 3F 36
Collingham. *W Yor* 3A 42
Collingtree. *Nptn* 6E 28
Collins Green. *Warr* 8D 40
Collins Green. *Worc* 6F 26
Colliston. *Ang* 3K 67
Colliton. *Devn* 5K 7
Collydean. *Fife* 7F 66
Collyweston. *Nptn* 1G 29
Colmonell. *S Ayr* 3G 51
Colmworth. *Bed* 6J 29
Colnbrook. *Slo* 6H 21
Colne. *Cambs* 4L 29
**Colne**. *Lanc* 3G 41
Colne Engaine. *Essx* 8E 30
Colney. *Norf* 1H 31
Colney Heath. *Herts* 3K 21
Colney Street. *Herts* 3J 21
Coln Rogers. *Glos* 3J 19
Coln St Aldwyns. *Glos* 3K 19
Coln St Dennis. *Glos* 2J 19
Colpitts Grange. *Nmbd* 6C 54
Colpy. *Abers* 2F 72
Colscott. *Devn* 4C 6
Colsterdale. *N Yor* 7K 47
Colsterworth. *Linc* 7G 37
Colston Bassett. *Notts* 6E 36
Colstoun House. *E Lot* 2C 60
Coltfield. *Mor* 7M 79
Colthouse. *Cumb* 6B 46
Coltishall. *Norf* 8J 39
Coltness. *N Lan* 4G 59
Colton. *Cumb* 7B 46
Colton. *Norf* 1H 31
Colton. *N Yor* 3C 42
Colton. *Staf* 7J 35
Colton. *W Yor* 4A 42
Colt's Hill. *Kent* 1C 12
Col Uarach. *W Isl* 8H 83
Colvend. *Dum* 6C 52
Colvister. *Shet* 4K 91
Colwall. *Here* 7F 26
Colwall Green. *Here* 7F 26
Colwell. *Nmbd* 4C 54
Colwich. *Staf* 7J 35
Colwick. *Notts* 5D 36
Colwinston. *V Glam* 7J 17
Colworth. *W Sus* 5G 11
**Colwyn Bay**. *Cnwy* 3H 33
Colyford. *Devn* 6A 8
Colyton. *Devn* 6M 7
Combe. *Devn* 5K 5
Combe. *Here* 5B 26
Combe. *Oxon* 2B 20
Combe. *W Ber* 7A 20
Combe Almer. *Dors* 6H 9
Combebow. *Devn* 7D 6
Combe Down. *Bath* 7F 18
Combe Fishacre. *Devn* 5L 5
Combe Florey. *Som* 2L 7
Combe Hay. *Bath* 7F 18
Combeinteignhead. *Devn* 8J 7
Combe Martin. *Devn* 1E 6
Combe Moor. *Here* 5B 26
Comber. *Ards* 5J 93
Combe Raleigh. *Devn* 5L 7
Comberbach. *Ches W* 2E 34
Comberford. *Staf* 1K 27
Comberton. *Cambs* 6L 29
Comberton. *Here* 5C 26
Combe St Nicholas. *Som* 4B 8
Combpyne. *Devn* 6A 8
Combridge. *Staf* 6J 35
Combrook. *Warw* 6M 27
Combs. *Derbs* 2J 35
Combs. *Suff* 6G 31
Combs Ford. *Suff* 6G 31
Combwich. *Som* 1A 8
Comers. *Abers* 5F 72
Comhampton. *Worc* 5G 27
Comins Coch. *Cdgn* 4F 24
Comley. *Shrp* 2C 26
Commercial End. *Cambs* 5B 30
Commins. *Powy* 8L 33
Commins Coch. *Powy* 2H 25
The Common. *Wilts*
nr. Salisbury 2L 9
nr. Swindon 5J 19
Commondale. *N Yor* 4D 48
Common End. *Cumb* 2K 45
Common Hill. *Here* 8D 26
Common Moor. *Corn* 5E 4
Common Side. *Derbs* 2M 35
Commonside. *Ches W* 2D 34
Commonside. *Derbs* 5L 35
Compstall. *G Man* 8H 41
Compton. *Devn* 5L 5
Compton. *Hants* 3B 10
Compton. *Staf* 3G 27
Compton. *Surr* 1G 11
Compton. *W Ber* 6C 20
Compton. *W Sus* 4E 10
Compton. *Wilts* 8K 19
Compton Abbas. *Dors* 4G 9
Compton Abdale. *Glos* 2J 19
Compton Bassett. *Wilts* 6J 19
Compton Beauchamp. *Oxon* 5L 19
Compton Bishop. *Som* 8B 18
Compton Chamberlayne. *Wilts* 3J 9
Compton Dando. *Bath* 7E 18
Compton Dundon. *Som* 2C 8
Compton Greenfield. *S Glo* 5D 18
Compton Martin. *Bath* 8D 18
Compton Pauncefoot. *Som* 3E 8
Compton Valence. *Dors* 6D 8
Comrie. *Fife* 1J 59
Comrie. *Per* 5A 66
Conaglen. *High* 1E 64
Conchra. *Arg* 1K 57
Conchra. *High* 3K 69
Conder Green. *Lanc* 2C 40
Conderton. *Worc* 8H 27
Condicote. *Glos* 1K 19
Condorrat. *N Lan* 2F 58
Condover. *Shrp* 1C 26
Coneyhurst. *W Sus* 3J 11
Coneyisland. *New M* 7J 93
Coneysthorpe. *N Yor* 8E 48
Coneythorpe. *N Yor* 2A 42
Coney Weston. *Suff* 4F 30
Conford. *Hants* 2F 10
Congdon's Shop. *Corn* 8B 6
Congerstone. *Leics* 1A 28
Congham. *Norf* 7D 38
**Congleton**. *Ches E* 3G 35
Congl-y-wal. *Gwyn* 6G 33
Congresbury. *N Som* 7C 18
Congreve. *Staf* 8H 35
Conham. *S Glo* 6E 18
Conicaval. *Mor* 8K 79
Coningsby. *Linc* 4K 37
Conington. *Cambs*
nr. Fenstanton 5L 29
nr. Sawtry 3J 29
**Conisbrough**. *S Yor* 8C 42
Conisby. *Arg* 3B 56
Conisholme. *Linc* 8M 43
Coniston. *Cumb* 6B 46
Coniston. *E Yor* 4J 43
Coniston Cold. *N Yor* 2H 41
Conistone. *N Yor* 1H 41
Conlig. *Ards* 5J 93
**Connah's Quay**. *Flin* 2A 34
Connel. *Arg* 4D 64
Connel Park. *E Ayr* 8E 58
Connista. *High* 6F 76
Connor. *ME Ant* 4G 93
Connor Downs. *Corn* 5J 3
Conock. *Wilts* 8J 19
Conon Bridge. *High* 8F 78
Cononley. *N Yor* 3H 41
Cononsyth. *Ang* 3J 67
Conordan. *High* 2G 69
Consall. *Staf* 5H 35
**Consett**. *Dur* 6E 54
Constable Burton. *N Yor* 6K 47
Constantine. *Corn* 6L 3
Constantine Bay. *Corn* 4A 4
Contin. *High* 8E 78
Contullich. *High* 6G 79
Conwy. *Cnwy* 3G 33
Conyer. *Kent* 7F 22
Conyer's Green. *Suff* 5E 30
Cooden. *E Sus* 5D 12
Cooil. *IOM* 7C 44
Cookbury. *Devn* 5D 6
Cookbury Wick. *Devn* 5C 6
Cookham. *Wind* 5F 20
Cookham Dean. *Wind* 5F 20
Cookham Rise. *Wind* 5F 20
Cookhill. *Worc* 6J 27
Cookley. *Suff* 4K 31
Cookley. *Worc* 3G 27
Cookley Green. *Oxon* 4D 20
Cookney. *Abers* 6H 73
Cooksbridge. *E Sus* 4M 11
Cooksey Green. *Worc* 5H 27
Cookshill. *Staf* 5H 35
Cooksmill Green. *Essx* 3C 22
**Cookstown**. *M Ulst* 5F 93
Coolham. *W Sus* 3J 11
Cooling. *Medw* 6D 22
Cooling Street. *Medw* 6D 22
Coombe. *Corn*
nr. Bude 4B 6
nr. St Austell 6B 4
nr. Truro 4M 3
Coombe. *Devn*
nr. Sidmouth 6L 7
nr. Teignmouth 8J 7
Coombe. *Glos* 4F 18
Coombe. *Hants* 3D 10
Coombe. *Wilts* 8K 19
Coombe Bissett. *Wilts* 3K 9
Coombe Hill. *Glos* 1G 19
Coombe Keynes. *Dors* 7G 9
Coombes. *W Sus* 5J 11
Coopersale. *Essx* 3A 22
Coopersale Street. *Essx* 3A 22
Cooper's Corner. *Kent* 1A 12
Cooper Street. *Kent* 8K 23
Cootham. *W Sus* 4H 11
Copalder Corner. *Cambs* 2L 29
Copdock. *Suff* 7H 31
Copford. *Essx* 1F 22
Copford Green. *Essx* 1F 22
Copgrove. *N Yor* 1M 41
Copister. *Shet* 6J 91
Cople. *Bed* 7J 29
Copley. *Dur* 3J 47
Coplow Dale. *Derbs* 2K 35
Copmanthorpe. *York* 3C 42
Copp. *Lanc* 4C 40
Coppathorne. *Corn* 5B 6
Coppenhall. *Ches E* 4F 34
Coppenhall. *Staf* 8H 35
Coppenhall Moss. *Ches E* 4F 34
Copperhouse. *Corn* 5J 3
Coppicegate. *Shrp* 3F 26
Coppingford. *Cambs* 3J 29
Copplestone. *Devn* 5G 7
Coppull. *Lanc* 6D 40
Coppull Moor. *Lanc* 6D 40
Copsale. *W Sus* 3J 11
Copshaw Holm. *Bord* 3J 53
Copster Green. *Lanc* 4E 40
Copston Magna. *Warw* 3B 28
Copt Green. *Warw* 5K 27
Copthall Green. *Essx* 3M 21
Copt Heath. *W Mid* 4K 27
Copt Hewick. *N Yor* 8M 47
Copthill. *Dur* 7B 54
Copthorne. *W Sus* 2L 11
Coptiviney. *Shrp* 6C 34
Copy's Green. *Norf* 6F 38
Copythorne. *Hants* 4M 9
Corbridge. *Nmbd* 5C 54
**Corby**. *Nptn* 3F 28
Corby Glen. *Linc* 7G 37
Cordon. *N Ayr* 6K 57
Coreley. *Shrp* 4E 26
Corfe. *Som* 4M 7
Corfe Castle. *Dors* 7H 9
Corfe Mullen. *Dors* 6H 9
Corfton. *Shrp* 3C 26
Corgarff. *Abers* 5B 72
Corhampton. *Hants* 3D 10
Corkey. *Caus* 2G 93
Corlae. *Dum* 2A 52
Corlannau. *Neat* 5G 17
Corley. *Warw* 3M 27
Corley Ash. *Warw* 3L 27
Corley Moor. *Warw* 3L 27
Cormiston. *S Lan* 6J 59
Cornaa. *IOM* 6D 44
Cornaigbeg. *Arg* 3E 62
Cornaigmore. *Arg*
on Coll 1H 63
on Tiree 3E 62
Corner Row. *Lanc* 4C 40
Corney. *Cumb* 5L 45
Cornforth. *Dur* 8G 55
Cornhill. *Abers* 8E 80
Cornhill. *High* 4F 78
Cornhill-on-Tweed. *Nmbd* 6F 60
Cornholme. *W Yor* 5H 41
Cornish Hall End. *Essx* 8C 30
Cornquoy. *Orkn* 1G 87
Cornriggs. *Dur* 7B 54
Cornsay. *Dur* 7E 54
Cornsay Colliery. *Dur* 7E 54
Corntown. *High* 8F 78
Corntown. *V Glam* 7J 17
Cornwall Airport Newquay. *Corn* 5A 4
Cornwell. *Oxon* 1L 19
Cornwood. *Devn* 6J 5
Cornworthy. *Devn* 6L 5
Corpach. *High* 8A 70
Corpusty. *Norf* 7H 39
Corra. *Dum* 5C 52
Corran. *High*
nr. Arnisdale 1E 64
nr. Fort William 5K 69
Corrany. *IOM* 6D 44
Corribeg. *High* 8L 69
Corrie. *N Ayr* 5K 57
Corrie Common. *Dum* 3G 53
Corriecravie. *N Ayr* 7J 57
Corriekinloch. *High* 1D 78
Corriemoillie. *High* 7D 78
Corrievarkie Lodge. *Per* 8F 70
Corrievorrie. *High* 3H 71
Corrigall. *Orkn* 8C 88
Corrimony. *High* 2D 70
Corringham. *Linc* 8F 42
**Corringham**. *Thur* 5D 22
Corris. *Gwyn* 2G 25
Corris Uchaf. *Gwyn* 2G 25
Corrour Shooting Lodge. *High* 1J 65
Corry. *High* 3H 69
Corrybrough. *High* 3J 71
Corrygills. *N Ayr* 6K 57
Corry of Ardnagrask. *High* 1F 70
Corsback. *High*
nr. Dunnet 4D 86
nr. Halkirk 6D 86
Corscombe. *Dors* 5D 8
Corse. *Abers* 1F 72
Corse. *Glos* 1F 18
Corsehill. *Abers* 8J 81
Corse Lawn. *Worc* 8G 27
Corse of Kinnoir. *Abers* 1E 72
**Corsham**. *Wilts* 6G 19
Corsley. *Wilts* 1G 9
Corsley Heath. *Wilts* 1G 9
Corsock. *Dum* 4B 52
Corston. *Bath* 7E 18
Corston. *Wilts* 5H 19
Corstorphine. *Edin* 2L 59
Cortachy. *Ang* 2G 67
Corton. *Suff* 2M 31
Corton. *Wilts* 1H 9
Corton Denham. *Som* 3E 8
Corwar House. *S Ayr* 3H 51
Corwen. *Den* 6K 33
Coryates. *Dors* 7E 8
Coryton. *Devn* 7D 6
Coryton. *Thur* 5D 22
Cosby. *Leics* 2C 28
Coscote. *Oxon* 5C 20
Coseley. *W Mid* 2H 27
Cosgrove. *Nptn* 7E 28
Cosham. *Port* 5D 10
Cosheston. *Pemb* 6G 15
Coskills. *N Lin* 6H 43
Cosmeston. *V Glam* 8L 17
Cossall. *Notts* 5B 36
Cossington. *Leics* 8D 36
Cossington. *Som* 1B 8
Costa. *Orkn* 7C 88
Costessey. *Norf* 8H 39
Costock. *Notts* 7C 36
Coston. *Leics* 7F 36
Coston. *Norf* 1G 31
Cote. *Oxon* 3A 20
Cotebrook. *Ches W* 3D 34
Cotehill. *Cumb* 6J 53
Cotes. *Cumb* 7C 46
Cotes. *Leics* 7C 36
Cotes. *Staf* 6G 35
Cotesbach. *Leics* 3C 28
Cotes Heath. *Staf* 6G 35
Cotford St Luke. *Som* 3L 7
Cotgrave. *Notts* 6D 36
Cothal. *Abers* 4H 73
Cotham. *Notts* 5E 36
Cothelstone. *Som* 2L 7
Cotheridge. *Worc* 6F 26
Cotherstone. *Dur* 4J 47
Cothill. *Oxon* 4B 20
Cotland. *Mon* 3D 18
Cotleigh. *Devn* 5M 7
Cotmanhay. *Derbs* 5B 36
Coton. *Cambs* 6M 29
Coton. *Nptn* 4D 28
Coton. *Staf*
nr. Gnosall 7G 35
nr. Stone 6H 35
nr. Tamworth 1K 27
Coton Clanford. *Staf* 7G 35
Coton Hayes. *Staf* 6H 35
Coton Hill. *Shrp* 8C 34
Coton in the Clay. *Staf* 7K 35
Coton in the Elms. *Derbs* 8L 35
Cotonwood. *Shrp* 6D 34
Cotonwood. *Staf* 7G 35
Cott. *Devn* 5K 5
Cott. *Orkn* 7F 88
Cottam. *E Yor* 1G 43
Cottam. *Lanc* 4D 40
Cottam. *Notts* 2F 36
Cottartown. *High* 2L 71
Cottarville. *Nptn* 5E 28
Cottenham. *Cambs* 5A 30
Cotterdale. *N Yor* 6G 47
Cottered. *Herts* 1L 21
Cotterstock. *Nptn* 2H 29
Cottesbrooke. *Nptn* 4E 28
Cottesmore. *Rut* 8G 37
Cotteylands. *Devn* 4J 7
Cottingham. *E Yor* 4H 43
Cottingham. *Nptn* 2F 28
Cottingley. *W Yor* 4K 41
Cottisford. *Oxon* 8C 28
Cotton. *Staf* 5J 35
Cotton. *Suff* 5G 31
Cotton End. *Bed* 7H 29
Cottown. *Abers* 1H 73
Cotts. *Devn* 5G 5
Cotwalton. *Staf* 6H 35
Couch's Mill. *Corn* 6D 4
Coughton. *Here* 1D 18
Coughton. *Warw* 5J 27
Coulags. *High* 1L 69
Coulby Newham. *Midd* 4C 48
Coulderton. *Cumb* 4J 45
Coulin Lodge. *High* 8M 77
Coull. *Abers* 5E 72
Coulport. *Arg* 1M 57
**Coulsdon**. *G Lon* 8K 21
Coulston. *Wilts* 8H 19
Coulter. *S Lan* 6J 59
Coultings. *Som* 1M 7
Coulton. *N Yor* 8D 48
Cound. *Shrp* 1D 26
Coundon. *Dur* 3L 47
Coundon Grange. *Dur* 3L 47
Countersett. *N Yor* 7H 47
Countess. *Wilts* 1K 9
Countess Cross. *Essx* 8E 30
Countesthorpe. *Leics* 2C 28
Countisbury. *Devn* 1G 7
Coupar Angus. *Per* 3F 66
Coupe Green. *Lanc* 5D 40
Coupland. *Cumb* 4F 46
Coupland. *Nmbd* 6G 61
Cour. *Arg* 5H 57
Courance. *Dum* 2E 52
Court-at-Street. *Kent* 2G 13
Courteachan. *High* 6H 69
Courteenhall. *Nptn* 6E 28
Court Henry. *Carm* 2E 16
Courtsend. *Essx* 4G 23
Courtway. *Som* 2M 7
Cousland. *Midl* 3A 60
Cousley Wood. *E Sus* 2C 12
Coustonn. *Arg* 2K 57
Cove. *Arg* 1M 57
Cove. *Devn* 4J 7
Cove. *Hants* 8F 20
Cove. *High* 4K 77
Cove. *Bord* 2E 60
Cove Bay. *Aber* 5J 73
Covehithe. *Suff* 3M 31
Coven. *Staf* 1H 27
Coveney. *Cambs* 3A 30
Covenham St Bartholomew. *Linc* 8L 43
Covenham St Mary. *Linc* 8L 43
Coven Heath. *Staf* 1H 27
**Coventry**. *W Mid* 108 (4M 27)
Coverack. *Corn* 7L 3
Coverham. *N Yor* 7K 47
Covesea. *Mor* 6A 80
Covingham. *Swin* 5K 19
Covington. *Cambs* 4H 29
Covington. *S Lan* 6H 59
Cowan Bridge. *Lanc* 8E 46
Cowan Head. *Cumb* 6C 46
Cowbar. *Red C* 4E 48
Cowbeech. *E Sus* 4C 12
Cowbit. *Linc* 8K 37
Cowbridge. *V Glam* 7J 17
Cowden. *Kent* 1A 12
**Cowdenbeath**. *Fife* 8E 66
Cowdenburn. *Bord* 4L 59
Cowdenend. *Fife* 8E 66
Cowers Lane. *Derbs* 5M 35
**Cowes**. *IOW* 6B 10
Cowesby. *N Yor* 7B 48
Cowfold. *W Sus* 3K 11
Cowfords. *Mor* 7C 80
Cowgill. *Cumb* 7F 46
Cowie. *Abers* 7H 73
Cowie. *Stir* 1G 59
Cowlam. *E Yor* 1G 43
Cowley. *Devn* 6J 7
Cowley. *Glos* 2H 19
Cowley. *G Lon* 5H 21
Cowley. *Oxon* 3C 20
Cowley. *Staf* 8G 35
Cowleymoor. *Devn* 4J 7
Cowling. *Lanc* 6D 40
Cowling. *N Yor*
nr. Bedale 7L 47
nr. Glusburn 3H 41
Cowlinge. *Suff* 6D 30
Cowmes. *W Yor* 6K 41
Cowpe. *Lanc* 5G 41
Cowpen. *Nmbd* 3F 54
Cowpen Bewley. *Stoc T* 3B 48
Cowplain. *Hants* 4D 10
Cowshill. *Dur* 7B 54
Cowslip Green. *N Som* 7C 18
Cowstrandburn. *Fife* 8D 66
Cowthorpe. *N Yor* 2B 42
Coxall. *Here* 4B 26
Coxbank. *Ches E* 5E 34
Coxbench. *Derbs* 5A 36
Cox Common. *Suff* 3L 31
Coxford. *Norf* 7E 38
Cox Green. *Surr* 2H 11
Cox Green. *Tyne* 6G 55
Coxgreen. *Staf* 3G 27
Coxheath. *Kent* 8D 22
Coxhoe. *Dur* 8G 55
Coxley. *Som* 1D 8
Coxwold. *N Yor* 8C 48
Coychurch. *B'end* 6J 17
Coylton. *S Ayr* 8C 58
Coylumbridge. *High* 4K 71
Coynach. *Abers* 5D 72
Coynachie. *Abers* 2D 72
Coytrahen. *B'end* 6H 17
Crabbs Cross. *Worc* 5J 27
Crabgate. *Norf* 7G 39
Crab Orchard. *Dors* 5J 9
Crabtree. *W Sus* 3K 11
Crabtree Green. *Wrex* 5B 34
Crackaig. *High* 2K 79
Crackenthorpe. *Cumb* 3E 46
Crackington Haven. *Corn* 2D 4
Crackley. *Staf* 4G 35
Crackley. *Warw* 4L 27
Crackleybank. *Shrp* 8F 34
Crackpot. *N Yor* 6H 47
Cracoe. *N Yor* 1H 41
Craddock. *Devn* 4K 7
Cradhlastadh. *W Isl* 8D 82
Cradley. *Here* 7F 26
Cradley. *W Mid* 3H 27
Cradoc. *Powy* 1K 17
Crafthole. *Corn* 6F 4
Crafton. *Buck* 2F 20
Cragabus. *Arg* 5C 56
Crag Foot. *Lanc* 8C 46
Craggan. *High* 3L 71
Cragganmore. *Mor* 2A 72
Cragganvallie. *High* 2F 70
Craggie. *High* 2J 79
Craggiemore. *High* 2H 71
Cragg Vale. *W Yor* 5J 41
Craghead. *Dur* 6F 54
Crai. *Powy* 2H 17
Craichie. *Ang* 3J 67
Craig. *Arg* 4E 64
Craig. *Dum* 4A 52
Craig. *High*
nr. Achnashellach 1M 69
nr. Lower Diabaig 7J 77
nr. Stromeferry 2K 69
Craiganour Lodge. *Per* 2L 65
**Craigavon**. *Arm* 6G 93
Craigbrack. *Arg* 8F 64
Craig-Cefn-Parc. *Swan* 4F 16
Craigdallie. *Per* 5F 66
Craigdam. *Abers* 2H 73
Craigdarragh. *Derr* 3D 92
Craigdarroch. *E Ayr* 1M 51
Craigdarroch. *High* 8E 78
Craigdhu. *High* 1E 70
Craigearn. *Abers* 4G 73
Craigellachie. *Mor* 1B 72
Craigend. *Per* 5E 66
Craigendoran. *Arg* 1B 58
Craigends. *Ren* 3C 58
Craigenputtock. *Dum* 3B 52
Craigens. *E Ayr* 8D 58
Craighall. *Edin* 2K 59
Craighead. *Fife* 6K 67
Craighouse. *Arg* 3E 56
Craigie. *Abers* 4J 73
Craigie. *D'dee* 4H 67
Craigie. *Per*
nr. Blairgowrie 3E 66
nr. Perth 5E 66
Craigie. *S Ayr* 6C 58
Craigielaw. *E Lot* 2B 60
Craiglemine. *Dum* 8K 51
Craig-llwyn. *Shrp* 8M 33
Craiglockhart. *Edin* 2L 59
Craig Lodge. *Arg* 2K 57
Craigmalloch. *E Ayr* 2K 51
Craigmaud. *Abers* 8H 81
Craigmill. *Stir* 8B 66
Craigmillar. *Edin* 2L 59
Craigmore. *Arg* 3L 57
Craigmuie. *Dum* 3B 52
Craignair. *Dum* 5C 52
Craignant. *Shrp* 6A 34
Craigneuk. *N Lan*
nr. Airdrie 3F 58
nr. Motherwell 4F 58
Craignure. *Arg* 4B 64
Craigo. *Ang* 1K 67
Craigrory. *High* 1G 71
Craigrothie. *Fife* 6G 67
Craigs. *Dum* 4G 53
The Craigs. *High* 4E 78
Craigshill. *W Lot* 3J 59
Craigton. *Aber* 5H 73
Craigton. *Abers* 5G 73
Craigton. *Ang*
nr. Carnoustie 4J 67
nr. Kirriemuir 2G 67
Craigton. *High* 1G 71
Craigtown. *High* 6L 85
Craig-y-Duke. *Neat* 4G 17
Craig-y-nos. *Powy* 3H 17
Craik. *Bord* 1H 53
Crail. *Fife* 7K 67
Crailing. *Bord* 7D 60
Crailinghall. *Bord* 7D 60
Crakehill. *N Yor* 8B 48
Crakemarsh. *Staf* 6J 35
Crambe. *N Yor* 1E 42
Crambeck. *N Yor* 1E 42
**Cramlington**. *Nmbd* 4F 54
Cramond. *Edin* 2K 59
Cramond Bridge. *Edin* 2K 59
Cranage. *Ches E* 3F 34
Cranagh. *Derr* 4D 92
Cranberry. *Staf* 6G 35
Cranborne. *Dors* 4J 9
Cranbourne. *Brac* 6G 21
Cranbrook. *Devn* 6K 7
Cranbrook. *Kent* 2D 12
Cranbrook Common. *Kent* 2D 12
Crane Moor. *S Yor* 7M 41
Crane's Corner. *Norf* 8F 38
Cranfield. *C Beds* 7G 29
Cranford. *G Lon* 6J 21
Cranford St Andrew. *Nptn* 4G 29
Cranford St John. *Nptn* 4G 29
Cranham. *Glos* 2G 19
Cranham. *G Lon* 5B 22
Crank. *Mers* 8D 40
**Cranleigh**. *Surr* 2H 11
Cranley. *Suff* 4H 31
Cranloch. *Mor* 8B 80
Cranmer Green. *Suff* 4G 31
Cranmore. *IOW* 6B 10
Cranmore. *Linc* 1J 29
Crannich. *Arg* 3L 63
Crannoch. *Mor* 8D 80
Cranoe. *Leics* 2E 28
Cransford. *Suff* 5K 31
Cranshaws. *Bord* 3D 60
Cranstal. *IOM* 4D 44
Crantock. *Corn* 2L 3
Cranwell. *Linc* 5H 37
Cranwich. *Norf* 2D 30
Cranworth. *Norf* 1F 30
Craobh Haven. *Arg* 7B 64
Craobhnaclag. *High* 1E 70
Crapstone. *Devn* 5H 5
Crarae. *Arg* 8D 64
Crask. *High*
nr. Bettyhill 5K 85
nr. Lairg 1F 78
Crask of Aigas. *High* 1E 70
Craster. *Nmbd* 7K 61
Craswall. *Here* 8A 26
Cratfield. *Suff* 4K 31
Crathes. *Abers* 6G 73
Crathie. *Abers* 6B 72
Crathie. *High* 6F 70
Crathorne. *N Yor* 5B 48
Craven Arms. *Shrp* 3C 26
Crawcrook. *Tyne* 5E 54
Crawford. *Lanc* 7C 40
Crawford. *S Lan* 7H 59
Crawforddyke. *S Lan* 4G 59
Crawfordjohn. *S Lan* 7G 59
Crawfordsburn. *Ards* 4J 93
Crawick. *Dum* 8F 58
Crawley. *Devn* 5A 8
Crawley. *Hants* 2B 10
Crawley. *Oxon* 2M 19
**Crawley**. *W Sus* 2K 11
Crawley Down. *W Sus* 2L 11
Crawley End. *Essx* 7M 29
Crawley Side. *Dur* 7C 54
Crawshawbooth. *Lanc* 5G 41
Crawton. *Abers* 7H 73
Cray. *N Yor* 8H 47
Cray. *Per* 1E 66
Crayford. *G Lon* 6B 22
Crayke. *N Yor* 8C 48
Craymere Beck. *Norf* 6G 39
Crays Hill. *Essx* 4D 22
Cray's Pond. *Oxon* 5D 20
Crazies Hill. *Wok* 5E 20
Creacombe. *Devn* 4H 7
Creagan. *Arg* 3D 64
Creag Aoil. *High* 8B 70
Creag Ghoraidh. *W Isl* 1D 74
Creaguaineach Lodge. *High* 1H 65
Creamore Bank. *Shrp* 6D 34
Creaton. *Nptn* 4E 28
Creca. *Dum* 4G 53
Credenhill. *Here* 7C 26
Crediton. *Devn* 5H 7
Creebridge. *Dum* 5K 51
Creech. *Dors* 7H 9
Creech Heathfield. *Som* 3A 8
Creech St Michael. *Som* 3A 8
Creed. *Corn* 7B 4
Creekmoor. *Pool* 6H 9
Creekmouth. *G Lon* 5A 22
Creeting St Mary. *Suff* 6G 31
Creeting St Peter. *Suff* 6G 31
Creeton. *Linc* 7H 37
Creetown. *Dum* 6K 51
Creggan. *Ferm* 5E 92
Creggan. *New M* 7F 93
Creggans. *Arg* 7E 64
Cregneash. *IOM* 8A 44
Cregrina. *Powy* 7L 25
Creich. *Arg* 5J 63
Creich. *Fife* 5G 67
Creighton. *Staf* 6J 35
Creigiau. *Card* 6K 17
Cremyll. *Corn* 6G 5
Crendell. *Dors* 4J 9
Crepkill. *High* 1F 68
Cressage. *Shrp* 1D 26
Cressbrook. *Derbs* 2K 35
Cresselly. *Pemb* 6G 15
Cressing. *Essx* 1D 22
Cresswell. *Nmbd* 2F 54
Cresswell. *Staf* 6H 35
Cresswell Quay. *Pemb* 6G 15
Creswell. *Derbs* 2C 36
Creswell Green. *Staf* 8J 35
Cretingham. *Suff* 5J 31
**Crewe**. *Ches E* 4F 34
Crewe-by-Farndon. *Ches W* 4C 34
Crewgreen. *Powy* 8B 34
Crewkerne. *Som* 5C 8
Crews Hill. *G Lon* 3L 21
Crewton. *Derb* 6A 36
Crianlarich. *Stir* 5H 65
Cribbs Causeway. *S Glo* 5D 18
Cribyn. *Cdgn* 1M 15
Criccieth. *Gwyn* 7D 32
Crich. *Derbs* 4A 36
Crichton. *Midl* 3A 60
Crick. *Mon* 4C 18
Crick. *Nptn* 4C 28
Crickadarn. *Powy* 8K 25
Cricket Hill. *Hants* 7F 20
Cricket Malherbie. *Som* 4B 8
Cricket St Thomas. *Som* 5B 8
Crickham. *Som* 1C 8
Crickheath. *Shrp* 7A 34
Crickhowell. *Powy* 3M 17
Cricklade. *Wilts* 4K 19
Cricklewood. *G Lon* 5K 21
Cridling Stubbs. *N Yor* 5C 42
Crieff. *Per* 5B 66
Criftins. *Shrp* 6B 34
Criggion. *Powy* 8A 34
Crigglestone. *W Yor* 6M 41
Crimchard. *Som* 5B 8
Crimdon Park. *Dur* 8H 55
Crimond. *Abers* 8K 81
Crimonmogate. *Abers* 8K 81
Crimplesham. *Norf* 1C 30
Crimscote. *Warw* 7L 27
Crinan. *Arg* 8B 64
Cringleford. *Norf* 1H 31
Crinow. *Pemb* 5H 15
Cripplesease. *Corn* 5J 3
Cripplestyle. *Dors* 4J 9
Cripp's Corner. *E Sus* 3D 12
Croanford. *Corn* 4C 4
Crockenhill. *Kent* 7B 22
Crocker End. *Oxon* 5E 20
Crockerhill. *Hants* 5C 10
Crockernwell. *Devn* 6G 7
Crocker's Ash. *Here* 2D 18
Crockerton. *Wilts* 1G 9
Crocketford. *Dum* 4C 52
Crockey Hill. *York* 3D 42
Crockham Hill. *Kent* 8M 21
Crockhurst Street. *Kent* 1C 12
Crockleford Heath. *Essx* 1G 23
Croeserw. *Neat* 5H 17
Croes-Goch. *Pemb* 3E 14
Croes Hywel. *Mon* 2B 18
Croes-lan. *Cdgn* 2K 15
Croesor. *Gwyn* 6F 32
**Croesoswallt**. *Shrp* 7A 34
Croesyceiliog. *Carm* 5L 15
Croesyceiliog. *Torf* 4B 18
Croes-y-mwyalch. *Torf* 4B 18
Croesywaun. *Gwyn* 5E 32
Croford. *Som* 3L 7
Croft. *Leics* 2C 28
Croft. *Linc* 3B 38
Croft. *Warr* 8E 40
Croftamie. *Stir* 1C 58
Croftfoot. *Glas* 3D 58
Croftmill. *Per* 4B 66
Crofton. *Cumb* 6H 53
Crofton. *W Yor* 6A 42
Crofton. *Wilts* 7L 19
Croft-on-Tees. *N Yor* 5L 47
Crofts. *Dum* 4B 52
Crofts of Benachielt. *High* 8C 86
Crofts of Dipple. *Mor* 8C 80
Crofty. *Swan* 7M 15
Croggan. *Arg* 5B 64
Croglin. *Cumb* 7K 53
Croich. *High* 4E 78
Croick. *High* 6L 85
Croig. *Arg* 2J 63
Cromarty. *High* 7H 79
Crombie. *Fife* 1J 59
Cromdale. *High* 3L 71
Cromer. *Herts* 1K 21
Cromer. *Norf* 5J 39
Cromford. *Derbs* 4L 35
Cromhall. *S Glo* 4E 18
Cromor. *W Isl* 1F 76
Cromra. *High* 7F 70
Cromwell. *Notts* 3E 36
Cronberry. *E Ayr* 7E 58
Crondall. *Hants* 1E 10
The Cronk. *IOM* 5C 44
Cronk-y-Voddy. *IOM* 6C 44
Cronton. *Mers* 1C 34
Crook. *Cumb* 6C 46
Crook. *Dur* 8E 54
Crookdake. *Cumb* 7F 52
Crooke. *G Man* 7D 40
Crookedholm. *E Ayr* 6C 58
Crooked Soley. *Wilts* 6M 19
Crookes. *S Yor* 1M 35
Crookgate Bank. *Dur* 6E 54
Crookhall. *Dur* 6E 54
Crookham. *Nmbd* 6G 61
Crookham. *W Ber* 7C 20
Crookham Village. *Hants* 8E 20
Crooklands. *Cumb* 7D 46
Crook of Devon. *Per* 7D 66
Crookston. *Glas* 3D 58
Cropredy. *Oxon* 7B 28
Cropston. *Leics* 8C 36
Cropthorne. *Worc* 7H 27
Cropton. *N Yor* 7E 48
Cropwell Bishop. *Notts* 6D 36
Cropwell Butler. *Notts* 6D 36
Cros. *W Isl* 5J 83
Crosbie. *N Ayr* 4M 57
Crosbost. *W Isl* 1E 76
Crosby. *Cumb* 8E 52
Crosby. *IOM* 7C 44
**Crosby**. *Mers* 8B 40
Crosby. *N Lin* 6F 42
Crosby Court. *N Yor* 6A 48
Crosby Garrett. *Cumb* 5F 46
Crosby Ravensworth. *Cumb* 4E 46
Crosby Villa. *Cumb* 8E 52
Croscombe. *Som* 1D 8
Crosland Moor. *W Yor* 6K 41
Cross. *Som* 8C 18
Crossaig. *Arg* 4H 57
Crossapol. *Arg* 3E 62
Cross Ash. *Mon* 2C 18
Cross-at-Hand. *Kent* 1D 12
Crossbush. *W Sus* 5H 11
Crosscanonby. *Cumb* 8E 52
Crossdale Street. *Norf* 6J 39
Cross End. *Essx* 8E 30
Crossens. *Mers* 5B 40
Crossford. *Fife* 1J 59
Crossford. *S Lan* 5G 59
Cross Foxes. *Gwyn* 1G 25
Crossgar. *New M* 6J 93
Crossgate. *Orkn* 8D 88
Crossgate. *Staf* 6H 35
Crossgatehall. *E Lot* 3A 60
Cross Gates. *W Yor* 4A 42
Crossgates. *Fife* 1K 59
Crossgates. *N Yor* 7H 49
Crossgates. *Powy* 6K 25
Crossgill. *Lanc* 1D 40
Cross Green. *Devn* 7C 6
Cross Green. *Staf* 1H 27
Cross Green. *Suff*
nr. Cockfield 6E 30
nr. Hitcham 6F 30
Cross Hands. *Carm* 3E 16
Crosshands. *Carm* 4H 15
Crosshands. *E Ayr* 6C 58
Cross Hill. *Derbs* 5B 36
Cross Hill. *Glos* 4D 18
Crosshill. *E Ayr* 7C 58
Crosshill. *Fife* 8E 66
Crosshill. *S Ayr* 1J 51
Cross Hills. *N Yor* 3J 41
Crosshills. *High* 6G 79
Cross Holme. *N Yor* 6C 48
Crosshouse. *E Ayr* 6B 58
Cross Houses. *Shrp* 1D 26
Crossings. *Cumb* 4K 53
Cross in Hand. *E Sus* 3B 12
Cross Inn. *Cdgn*
nr. Aberaeron 6E 24
nr. New Quay 1K 15
Cross Inn. *Rhon* 6K 17
Crosskeys. *Cphy* 5M 17
Crosskirk. *High* 5B 86
Crosslands. *Cumb* 7B 46
Cross Lane Head. *Shrp* 2F 26
Cross Lanes. *Corn* 6K 3
Cross Lanes. *Dur* 4J 47
Cross Lanes. *N Yor* 1C 42
Cross Lanes. *Wrex* 5B 34
Crosslanes. *Shrp* 8B 34
Crosslee. *Ren* 3C 58
Crossmaglen. *New M* 7F 93
Crossmichael. *Dum* 5B 52
Crossmoor. *Lanc* 4C 40
Crossnacreevy. *Lis* 5H 93
Cross Oak. *Powy* 2L 17
Cross of Jackston. *Abers* 2G 73
Cross o' th' Hands. *Derbs* 5L 35
Crossroads. *Abers*
nr. Aberdeen 5J 73
nr. Banchory 6G 73
Crossroads. *E Ayr* 6C 58
Cross Side. *Devn* 3H 7
Cross Street. *Suff* 4H 31
Crosston. *Ang* 2J 67
Cross Town. *Ches E* 2F 34
Crossway. *Mon* 2C 18
Crossway. *Powy* 7K 25
Crossway Green. *Mon* 4D 18
Crossway Green. *Worc* 5G 27
Crossways. *Dors* 7F 8
Crosswell. *Pemb* 3H 15
Crosswood. *Cdgn* 5F 24
Crosthwaite. *Cumb* 6C 46
Croston. *Lanc* 6C 40
Crostwick. *Norf* 8J 39
Crostwight. *Norf* 7K 39
Crothair. *W Isl* 8E 82
Crouch. *Kent* 8C 22
Croucheston. *Wilts* 3J 9
Crouch Hill. *Dors* 4F 8
Croughton. *Nptn* 8C 28
Crovie. *Abers* 7H 81
Crow. *Hants* 5K 9
Crowan. *Corn* 5K 3
**Crowborough**. *E Sus* 2B 12
Crowcombe. *Som* 2L 7
Crowcroft. *Worc* 6F 26
Crowdecote. *Derbs* 3K 35
Crowden. *Derbs* 8J 41
Crowden. *Devn* 6D 6
Crowdhill. *Hants* 4B 10
Crowdon. *N Yor* 6G 49
Crow Edge. *S Yor* 7K 41
Crow End. *Cambs* 6L 29
Crowfield. *Nptn* 7D 28
Crowfield. *Suff* 6H 31
Crow Green. *Essx* 4B 22
Crow Hill. *Here* 1E 18
Crowhurst. *E Sus* 4D 12
Crowhurst. *Surr* 1L 11
Crowhurst Lane End. *Surr* 1L 11
Crowland. *Linc* 8K 37
Crowland. *Suff* 4G 31
Crowlas. *Corn* 5J 3
Crowle. *N Lin* 6E 42
Crowle. *Worc* 6H 27
Crowle Green. *Worc* 6H 27
Crowmarsh Gifford. *Oxon* 5D 20
Crown Corner. *Suff* 4J 31
Crownthorpe. *Norf* 1G 31
Crowntown. *Corn* 5K 3
Crows-an-wra. *Corn* 6G 3
Crowshill. *Norf* 1F 30
**Crowthorne**. *Brac* 7F 20
Crowton. *Ches W* 2D 34
Croxall. *Staf* 8K 35
Croxby. *Linc* 8J 43
Croxdale. *Dur* 8F 54
Croxden. *Staf* 6J 35
Croxley Green. *Herts* 4H 21
Croxton. *Cambs* 5K 29
Croxton. *Norf*
nr. Fakenham 6F 38
nr. Thetford 3E 30
Croxton. *N Lin* 6H 43
Croxton. *Staf* 6F 34
Croxtonbank. *Staf* 6F 34
Croxton Green. *Ches E* 4D 34
Croxton Kerrial. *Leics* 7F 36
Croy. *High* 1H 71
Croy. *N Lan* 2F 58
Croyde. *Devn* 2D 6
Croydon. *Cambs* 7L 29
**Croydon**. *G Lon* 7L 21
Crubenbeg. *High* 6G 71
Crubenmore Lodge. *High* 6G 71
Cruckmeole. *Shrp* 1C 26
Cruckton. *Shrp* 8C 34
Cruden Bay. *Abers* 2K 73
Crudgington. *Telf* 8E 34
Crudie. *Abers* 8G 81
Crudwell. *Wilts* 4H 19
Cruft. *Devn* 6E 6
Crug. *Powy* 5L 25
Crughywel. *Powy* 3M 17
Crugmeer. *Corn* 4B 4
Crugybar. *Carm* 1F 16
Crug-y-byddar. *Powy* 4L 25
Crulabhig. *W Isl* 8E 82
Crumlin. *Ant* 5G 93
Crumlin. *Cphy* 5M 17
Crumpsall. *G Man* 7G 41
Crumpsbrook. *Shrp* 4E 26
Crundale. *Kent* 1G 13
Crundale. *Pemb* 5F 14
Cruwys Morchard. *Devn* 4H 7
Crux Easton. *Hants* 8B 20
Cruxton. *Dors* 6E 8
Crwbin. *Carm* 5L 15
Cryers Hill. *Buck* 4F 20
Crymych. *Pemb* 3H 15
Crynant. *Neat* 4G 17
Crystal Palace. *G Lon* 6L 21
Cuaich. *High* 7G 71
Cuaig. *High* 8J 77
Cuan. *Arg* 6B 64
Cubbington. *Warw* 5M 27
Cubert. *Corn* 3L 3
Cubley. *S Yor* 7L 41
Cubley Common. *Derbs* 6K 35
Cublington. *Buck* 1F 20
Cublington. *Here* 8B 26
Cuckfield. *W Sus* 3L 11
Cucklington. *Som* 3F 8
Cuckney. *Notts* 2C 36
Cuckron. *Shet* 2E 90
Cuddesdon. *Oxon* 3D 20
Cuddington. *Buck* 2E 20
Cuddington. *Ches W* 2E 34
Cuddington Heath. *Ches W* 5C 34
Cuddy Hill. *Lanc* 4C 40
Cudham. *G Lon* 8M 21
Cudlipptown. *Devn* 8E 6
Cudworth. *Som* 4B 8
**Cudworth**. *S Yor* 7A 42
Cudworth. *Surr* 1K 11
Cuerdley Cross. *Warr* 1D 34
Cuffley. *Herts* 3L 21
Cuidhir. *W Isl* 5C 74
Cuidhsiadar. *W Isl* 6J 83
Cuidhtinis. *W Isl* 5B 76
Culbo. *High* 7G 79
Culbokie. *High* 8G 79
Culburnie. *High* 1E 70
Culcabock. *High* 1G 71
Culcavy. *Lis* 5H 93
Culcharry. *High* 8J 79
Culcheth. *Warr* 8E 40
Culduie. *High* 1J 69
Culeave. *High* 4F 78
Culford. *Suff* 4E 30
Culgaith. *Cumb* 3E 46
Culham. *Oxon* 4C 20
Culkein. *High* 8C 84
Culkein Drumbeg. *High* 8D 84
Culkerton. *Glos* 4H 19
Cullaville. *New M* 7F 93
Cullen. *Mor* 7E 80
Cullercoats. *Tyne* 4G 55
Cullicudden. *High* 7G 79
Cullingworth. *W Yor* 4J 41
Cullipool. *Arg* 6B 64
Cullivoe. *Shet* 3K 91
Culloch. *Per* 6A 66
Culloden. *High* 1H 71
Cullompton. *Devn* 5K 7
Cullybackey. *ME Ant* 3G 93
Cullycapple. *Caus* 2F 93
Cullyhanna. *New M* 7F 93
Culm Davy. *Devn* 4L 7
Culmington. *Shrp* 3C 26
Culmore. *Derr* 2D 92
Culmstock. *Devn* 4L 7
Cul na Caepaich. *High* 7H 69
Culnacnoc. *High* 7G 77
Culnacraig. *High* 3A 78
Culnady. *M Ulst* 3F 93
Culrain. *High* 4F 78
Culross. *Fife* 1H 59
Culroy. *S Ayr* 8B 58
Culswick. *Shet* 3C 90
Cults. *Aber* 5H 73
Cults. *Abers* 2E 72
Cults. *Fife* 7G 67
Cultybraggan Camp. *Per* 5A 66
Culver. *Devn* 6H 7
Culverlane. *Devn* 5K 5
Culverstone Green. *Kent* 7C 22
Culverthorpe. *Linc* 5H 37
Culworth. *Nptn* 7C 28
Culzie Lodge. *High* 6F 78
Cumberlow Green. *Herts* 8L 29
**Cumbernauld**. *N Lan* 2F 58
Cumbernauld Village. *N Lan* 2F 58
Cumberworth. *Linc* 2B 38
Cumdivock. *Cumb* 7H 53
Cuminestown. *Abers* 8H 81
Cumledge Mill. *Bord* 4E 60
Cumlewick. *Shet* 5E 90
Cummersdale. *Cumb* 6H 53
Cummertrees. *Dum* 5F 52
Cummingstown. *Mor* 7M 79
Cumnock. *E Ayr* 7D 58
Cumnor. *Oxon* 3B 20
Cumrew. *Cumb* 6K 53
Cumwhinton. *Cumb* 6J 53
Cumwhitton. *Cumb* 6K 53
Cundall. *N Yor* 8B 48
Cunninghamhead. *N Ayr* 5B 58
Cunning Park. *S Ayr* 8B 58
Cunningsburgh. *Shet* 5E 90
Cunnister. *Shet* 4K 91
Cupar. *Fife* 6G 67
Cupar Muir. *Fife* 6G 67
Cupernham. *Hants* 3A 10
Curbar. *Derbs* 2L 35
Curborough. *Staf* 8K 35
Curbridge. *Hants* 4C 10
Curbridge. *Oxon* 3M 19
Curdridge. *Hants* 4C 10
Curdworth. *Warw* 2K 27
Curland. *Som* 4A 8
Curland Common. *Som* 4A 8
Curran. *M Ulst* 4F 93
Curridge. *W Ber* 6B 20
Currie. *Edin* 3K 59
Curry Mallet. *Som* 3B 8
Curry Rivel. *Som* 3B 8
Curtisden Green. *Kent* 1D 12
Curtisknowle. *Devn* 6K 5
Cury. *Corn* 6K 3
Cusgarne. *Corn* 4L 3
Cushendall. *Caus* 2H 93
Cushendun. *Caus* 2H 93
Cusop. *Here* 8M 25
Cusworth. *S Yor* 7C 42
Cutcombe. *Som* 2J 7
Cuthill. *E Lot* 2A 60
Cutiau. *Gwyn* 1F 24
Cutlers Green. *Essx* 8B 30
Cutmadoc. *Corn* 5C 4
Cutnall Green. *Worc* 5G 27
Cutsdean. *Glos* 8J 27
Cutthorpe. *Derbs* 2M 35
Cuttiford's Door. *Som* 4B 8
Cuttivett. *Corn* 5F 4
Cutts. *Shet* 4D 90
Cuttybridge. *Pemb* 5F 14
Cuttyhill. *Abers* 8K 81
Cuxham. *Oxon* 4D 20
Cuxton. *Medw* 7D 22
Cuxwold. *Linc* 7J 43
Cwm. *Blae* 4L 17
Cwm. *Den* 3K 33
Cwm. *Powy* 2A 26
Cwmafan. *Neat* 5G 17
Cwmaman. *Rhon* 5J 17
Cwmann. *Carm* 8E 24
Cwmbach. *Carm* 4J 15
Cwmbach. *Powy* 1L 17
Cwmbach. *Rhon* 4K 17
Cwmbach Llechrhyd. *Powy* 7K 25
Cwmbelan. *Powy* 4J 25
**Cwmbran**. *Torf* 4A 18
Cwmbrwyno. *Cdgn* 4G 25
Cwm Capel. *Carm* 6L 15
Cwmcarn. *Cphy* 5M 17
Cwmcarvan. *Mon* 3C 18
Cwm-celyn. *Blae* 4M 17
Cwmcerdinen. *Swan* 4F 16
Cwm-Cewydd. *Gwyn* 1H 25
Cwm-cou. *Cdgn* 2J 15
Cwmcych. *Pemb* 3J 15
Cwmdare. *Rhon* 4J 17
Cwmdu. *Carm* 1F 16
Cwmdu. *Powy* 2L 17
Cwmduad. *Carm* 3K 15
Cwm Dulais. *Swan* 4F 16
Cwmerfyn. *Cdgn* 4F 24
Cwmfelin. *B'end* 6H 17
Cwmfelin Boeth. *Carm* 5H 15
Cwmfelinfach. *Cphy* 5L 17
Cwmfelin Mynach. *Carm* 4J 15
Cwmffrwd. *Carm* 5L 15
Cwmgiedd. *Powy* 3G 17
Cwmgors. *Neat* 3G 17
Cwmgwili. *Carm* 3E 16
Cwmgwrach. *Neat* 4H 17
Cwmhiraeth. *Carm* 3K 15
Cwmifor. *Carm* 2F 16
Cwmisfael. *Carm* 5L 15
Cwm-Llinau. *Powy* 2H 25
Cwmllynfell. *Neat* 3G 17
Cwm-mawr. *Carm* 5M 15
Cwm-miles. *Carm* 4H 15
Cwmorgan. *Carm* 3J 15
Cwmparc. *Rhon* 5J 17
Cwm Penmachno. *Cnwy* 6G 33
Cwmpennar. *Rhon* 4K 17
Cwm Plysgog. *Pemb* 2H 15
Cwmrhos. *Powy* 2L 17
Cwmsychpant. *Cdgn* 2L 15
Cwmsyfiog. *Cphy* 4L 17
Cwmsymlog. *Cdgn* 4F 24
Cwmtillery. *Blae* 4M 17

Cwm-twrch Isaf. Powy 4G 17
Cwm-twrch Uchaf. Powy 3G 17
Cwmwysg. Powy 2H 17
Cwm-y-glo. Gwyn 4E 32
Cwmyoy. Mon 1B 18
Cwmystwyth. Cdgn 5G 25
Cwrt. Gwyn 2F 24
Cwrtnewydd. Cdgn 2L 15
Cwrt-y-Cadno. Carm 8F 24
Cydweli. Carm 6L 15
Cyffylliog. Den 5K 33
Cymau. Flin 4A 34
Cymer. Neat 5H 17
Cymmer. Neat 5H 17
Cymmer. Rhon 5K 17
Cyncoed. Card 6L 17
Cynghordy. Carm 1H 17
Cynheidre. Carm 6L 15
Cynonville. Neat 5H 17
Cynwyd. Den 6K 33
Cynwyl Elfed. Carm 4K 15
Cywarch. Gwyn 1H 25

## D

Dacre. Cumb 3C 46
Dacre. N Yor 1K 41
Dacre Banks. N Yor 1K 41
Daddry Shield. Dur 8B 54
Dadford. Buck 8D 28
Dadlington. Leics 2B 28
Dafen. Carm 6M 15
Daffy Green. Norf 1F 30
Dagdale. Staf 6J 35
**Dagenham**. G Lon 5A 22
Daggons. Dors 4K 9
Daglingworth. Glos 3H 19
Dagnall. Buck 2G 21
Dagtail End. Worc 5J 27
Dail. Arg 4E 64
Dail Beag. W Isl 7F 82
Dail bho Dheas. W Isl 5H 83
Dailly. S Ayr 1H 51
Dail Mor. W Isl 7F 82
Dairsie. Fife 6H 67
Daisy Bank. W Mid 2J 27
Daisy Hill. G Man 7E 40
Daisy Hill. W Yor 4K 41
Dalabrog. W Isl 3D 74
Dalavich. Arg 6D 64
Dalbeattie. Dum 5C 52
Dalblair. E Ayr 8E 58
Dalbury. Derbs 6L 35
Dalby. IOM 7B 44
Dalby Wolds. Leics 7D 36
Dalchalm. High 3K 79
Dalcharn. High 6J 85
Dalchork. High 2F 78
Dalchreichart. High 4C 70
Dalchruin. Per 6M 65
Dalcross. High 1H 71
Dalderby. Linc 3K 37
Dale. Cumb 7K 53
Dale. Pemb 6E 14
Dale Abbey. Derbs 6B 36
Dalebank. Derbs 3A 36
Dale Bottom. Cumb 3A 46
Dale Head. Cumb 4C 46
Dalehouse. N Yor 4E 48
Dalelia. High 1B 64
Dale of Walls. Shet 2B 90
Dalgarven. N Ayr 5A 58
**Dalgety Bay**. Fife 1K 59
Dalginross. Per 5A 66
Dalguise. Per 3C 66
Dalhalvaig. High 6L 85
Dalham. Suff 5D 30
Dalintart. Arg 5C 64
**Dalkeith**. Midl 3M 59
Dallas. Mor 8M 79
Dalleagles. E Ayr 8D 58
Dall House. Per 2K 65
Dallinghoo. Suff 6J 31
Dallington. E Sus 4C 12
Dallow. N Yor 8K 47
Dalmally. Arg 5F 64
Dalmarnock. Glas 3E 58
Dalmellington. E Ayr 1K 51
Dalmeny. Edin 2K 59
Dalmigavie. High 4H 71
Dalmilling. S Ayr 7B 58
Dalmore. High
nr. Alness 7G 79
nr. Rogart 3H 79
Dalmuir. W Dun 2C 58
Dalmunach. Mor 1B 72
Dalnabreck. High 1B 64
Dalnacardoch Lodge. Per 8H 71
Dalnamein Lodge. Per 1A 66
Dalnaspidal Lodge. Per 8G 71
Dalnatrat. High 2D 64
Dalnavie. High 6G 79
Dalnawillan Lodge. High 7B 86
Dalness. High 2F 64
Dalnessie. High 2G 79
Dalqueich. Per 7D 66
Dalquhairn. S Ayr 2J 51
Dalreavoch. High 3H 79
Dalreoch. Per 6D 66
Dalry. Edin 2L 59
Dalry. N Ayr 5A 58
Dalrymple. E Ayr 8B 58
Dalscote. Nptn 6D 28
Dalserf. S Lan 4G 59
Dalsmirren. Arg 8F 56
Dalston. Cumb 6H 53
Dalswinton. Dum 3D 52
Dalton. Dum 4F 52
Dalton. Lanc 7C 40
Dalton. Nmbd
nr. Hexham 6C 54
nr. Ponteland 4E 54
Dalton. N Yor
nr. Richmond 5K 47
nr. Thirsk 8B 48
Dalton. S Lan 4E 58
Dalton. S Yor 8B 42
Dalton-in-Furness. Cumb 7M 45
Dalton-le-Dale. Dur 7H 55
Dalton Magna. S Yor 8B 42
Dalton-on-Tees. N Yor 5L 47
Dalton Piercy. Hart 8H 55
Daltot. Arg 1G 57
Dalvey. High 2M 71
Dalwhinnie. High 7G 71
Dalwood. Devn 5A 8
Damerham. Hants 4K 9
Damgate. Norf
nr. Acle 1L 31
nr. Martham 8L 39
Dam Green. Norf 3G 31
Damhead. Mor 8L 79
Danaway. Kent 7E 22
Danbury. Essx 3D 22
Danby. N Yor 5E 48
Danby Botton. N Yor 5D 48
Danby Wiske. N Yor 6M 47
Danderhall. Midl 3M 59
Danebank. Ches E 1H 35
Danebridge. Ches E 3H 35
Dane End. Herts 1L 21
Danehill. E Sus 3M 11
Danesford. Shrp 2F 26
Daneshill. Hants 8D 20
Danesmoor. Derbs 3B 36
Danestone. Aber 4J 73
Dangerous Corner. Lanc 6D 40
Daniel's Water. Kent 1F 12
Dan's Castle. Dur 8E 54
Danzey Green. Warw 5K 27
Dapple Heath. Staf 7J 35
Daren. Powy 3M 17
Darenth. Kent 6B 22
Daresbury. Hal 1D 34
Darfield. S Yor 7B 42
Dargate. Kent 7G 23
Dargill. Per 6B 66
Darite. Corn 5E 4
Darkley. Arm 7F 93
Darlaston. W Mid 2H 27
Darley. N Yor 2L 41
Darley Abbey. Derb 6M 35
Darley Bridge. Derbs 3L 35
Darley Dale. Derbs 3L 35
Darley Head. N Yor 2K 41
Darlingscott. Warw 7L 27
**Darlington**. Darl 4L 47
Darliston. Shrp 6D 34
Darlton. Notts 2E 36
Darmsden. Suff 6G 31
Darnall. S Yor 1A 36
Darnford. Abers 6G 73
Darnford. Staf 1K 27
Darnhall. Ches W 3E 34
Darnick. Bord 6C 60
Darowen. Powy 2H 25
Darra. Abers 1G 73
Darracott. Devn 2D 6
Darragh Cross. New M 6J 93
Darras Hall. Nmbd 4E 54
Darrington. W Yor 5B 42
Darrow Green. Norf 3J 31
Darsham. Suff 5L 31
Dartfield. Abers 8K 81
**Dartford**. Kent 6B 22
**Dartford-Thurrock River Crossing**. Kent 6B 22
Dartington. Devn 5K 5
Dartmeet. Devn 8F 6
Dartmouth. Devn 6L 5
**Darton**. S Yor 6M 41
Darvel. E Ayr 6D 58
**Darwen**. Bkbn 5E 40
Dassels. Herts 1L 21
Datchet. Wind 6G 21
Datchworth. Herts 2K 21
Datchworth Green. Herts 2K 21
Daubhill. G Man 7F 40
Dauntsey. Wilts 5H 19
Dauntsey Green. Wilts 5H 19
Dauntsey Lock. Wilts 5H 19
Dava. Mor 2L 71
Davenham. Ches W 2E 34
**Daventry**. Nptn 5C 28
Davidson's Mains. Edin 2L 59
Davidston. High 7H 79
Davidstow. Corn 7A 6
David's Well. Powy 5K 25
Davington. Dum 1G 53
Daviot. Abers 3G 73
Daviot. High 2H 71
Davyhulme. G Man 8F 40
Daw Cross. N Yor 2L 41
Dawdon. Dur 7H 55
Dawesgreen. Surr 1K 11
Dawley. Telf 1E 26
**Dawlish**. Devn 8J 7
Dawlish Warren. Devn 8J 7
Dawn. Cnwy 3H 33
Daws Heath. Essx 5E 22
Dawshill. Worc 6G 27
Daw's House. Corn 7C 6
Dawsmere. Linc 6M 37
Dayhills. Staf 6H 35
Dayhouse Bank. Worc 4H 27
Daylesford. Glos 1L 19
Daywall. Shrp 6A 34
Ddol. Flin 3L 33
Ddol Cownwy. Powy 1K 25
Deadman's Cross. C Beds 7J 29
Deadwater. Nmbd 2L 53
Deaf Hill. Dur 8G 55
**Deal**. Kent 8K 23
Dean. Cumb 2K 45
Dean. Devn
nr. Combe Martin 1F 6
nr. Lynton 1G 7
Dean. Dors 4H 9
Dean. Hants
nr. Bishop's Waltham 4C 10
nr. Winchester 2B 10
Dean. Oxon 1M 19
Dean. Som 1E 8
Dean Bank. Dur 8F 54
Deanburnhaugh. Bord 8A 60
Dean Cross. Devn 1E 6
Deane. Hants 8C 20
Deanich Lodge. High 5D 78
Deanland. Dors 4H 9
Deanlane End. W Sus 4E 10
Dean Park. Shrp 5E 26
Dean Prior. Devn 5K 5
Dean Row. Ches E 1G 35
Deans. W Lot 3J 59
Deanscales. Cumb 2K 45
Deanshanger. Nptn 7E 28
Deanston. Stir 7M 65
Dearham. Cumb 8E 52
**Dearne Valley**. S Yor 7A 42
Debach. Suff 6J 31
Debden. Essx 8B 30
Debden Green. Essx
nr. Loughton 4M 21
nr. Saffron Walden 8B 30
Debenham. Suff 5H 31
Dechmont. W Lot 2J 59
Deddington. Oxon 8B 28
Dedham. Essx 8G 31
Dedham Heath. Essx 8G 31
Deebank. Abers 6F 72
Deene. Nptn 2G 29
Deenethorpe. Nptn 2G 29
Deepcar. S Yor 8L 41
Deepcut. Surr 8G 21
Deepdale. Cumb 7F 46
Deepdale. N Lin 6H 43
Deepdale. N Yor 8G 47
Deeping Gate. Pet 1J 29
Deeping St James. Linc 8J 37
Deeping St Nicholas. Linc 8K 37
Deerhill. Mor 8D 80
Deerhurst. Glos 1G 19
Deerhurst Walton. Glos 1G 19
Deerness. Orkn 1G 87
Defford. Worc 7H 27
Defynnog. Powy 2J 17
Deganwy. Cnwy 3G 33
Deighton. N Yor 5A 48
Deighton. W Yor 6K 41
Deighton. York 3D 42
Deiniolen. Gwyn 4E 32
Delabole. Corn 3C 4
Delamere. Ches W 3D 34
Delfour. High 5J 71
The Dell. Suff 2L 31
Delliefure. High 2L 71
Delly End. Oxon 2A 20
Delny. High 6H 79
Delph. G Man 7H 41
Delves. Dur 7E 54
The Delves. W Mid 2J 27
Delvin End. Essx 8D 30
Dembleby. Linc 6H 37
Demelza. Corn 5B 4
The Den. N Ayr 4B 58
Denaby Main. S Yor 8B 42
Denbeath. Fife 8G 67
Denbigh. Den 4K 33
Denbury. Devn 5L 5
Denby. Derbs 5A 36
Denby Common. Derbs 5B 36
Denby Dale. W Yor 7L 41
Denchworth. Oxon 4A 20
Dendron. Cumb 7M 45
Deneside. Dur 7H 55
Denford. Nptn 4G 29
Dengie. Essx 3F 22
Denham. Buck 5H 21
Denham. Suff
nr. Bury St Edmunds 5D 30
nr. Eye 4H 31
Denham Green. Buck 5H 21
Denham Street. Suff 4H 31
Denhead. Abers
nr. Ellon 2J 73
nr. Strichen 8J 81
Denhead. Fife 6H 67
Denholm. Bord 8C 60
Denholme. W Yor 4J 41
Denholme Clough. W Yor 4J 41
Denholme Gate. W Yor 4J 41
Denio. Gwyn 7C 32
Denmead. Hants 4D 10
Dennington. Suff 5J 31
**Denny**. Falk 1G 59
Denny End. Cambs 5A 30
Dennyloanhead. Falk 1G 59
Den of Lindores. Fife 6F 66
Denshaw. G Man 6H 41
Denside. Abers 6H 73
Densole. Kent 1J 13
Denston. Suff 6D 30
Denstone. Staf 5K 35
Denstroude. Kent 7H 23
Dent. Cumb 7F 46
Denton. Cambs 3J 29
Denton. Darl 4L 47
Denton. E Sus 5A 12
**Denton**. G Man 8H 41
Denton. Kent 1J 13
Denton. Linc 6F 36
Denton. Norf 3J 31
Denton. Nptn 6F 28
Denton. N Yor 3K 41
Denton. Oxon 3C 20
Denver. Norf 1C 30
Denwick. Nmbd 8K 61
Deopham. Norf 1G 31
Deopham Green. Norf 2G 31
Depden. Suff 6D 30
Depden Green. Suff 6D 30
**Deptford**. G Lon 6L 21
Deptford. Wilts 2J 9
**Derby**. Derb 108 (6A 36)
Derbyhaven. IOM 8B 44
Derculich. Per 2B 66
**Dereham**. Norf 8F 38
Deri. Cphy 4L 17
Derril. Devn 5C 6
Derringstone. Kent 1J 13
Derrington. Shrp 2E 26
Derrington. Staf 7G 35
Derriton. Devn 5C 6
**Derry**. Derr 3D 92
Derryboye. New M 6J 93
Derrycrin. M Ulst 5F 93
Derrygonnelly. Ferm 6B 92
Derryguaig. Arg 4K 63
Derry Hill. Wilts 6H 19
Derrykeighan. Caus 2F 93
Derrylin. Ferm 7C 92
Derrymacash. Arm 6G 93
Derrythorpe. N Lin 7F 42
Derrytrasna. Arm 5F 93
Dersingham. Norf 6C 38
Dervaig. Arg 2K 63
Dervock. Caus 2F 93
Derwen. Den 5K 33
Derwen Gam. Cdgn 1L 15
Derwenlas. Powy 3G 25
Desborough. Nptn 3F 28
Desertmartin. M Ulst 4F 93
Desford. Leics 1B 28
Detchant. Nmbd 6H 61
Dethick. Derbs 4M 35
Detling. Kent 8D 22
Deuchar. Ang 1H 67
Deuddwr. Powy 1M 25
Devauden. Mon 4C 18
Devil's Bridge. Cdgn 5G 25
Devitts Green. Warw 2L 27
**Devizes**. Wilts 7J 19
Devonport. Plym 6G 5
Devonside. Clac 8C 66
Devoran. Corn 5L 3
Dewartown. Midl 3A 60
Dewlish. Dors 6F 8
Dewsall Court. Here 8C 26
**Dewsbury**. W Yor 5L 41
Dexbeer. Devn 5B 6
Dhoon. IOM 6D 44
Dhoor. IOM 5D 44
Dhowin. IOM 4D 44
Dial Green. W Sus 3G 11
Dial Post. W Sus 4J 11
The Diamond. M Ulst 5F 93
Dibberford. Dors 5C 8
Dibden. Hants 5B 10
Dibden Purlieu. Hants 5B 10
Dickleburgh. Norf 3H 31
Didbrook. Glos 8J 27
**Didcot**. Oxon 4C 20
Diddington. Cambs 5J 29
Diddlebury. Shrp 3D 26
Didley. Here 8C 26
Didling. W Sus 4F 10
Didmarton. Glos 5G 19
Didsbury. G Man 8G 41
Didworthy. Devn 5J 5
Digby. Linc 4H 37
Digg. High 7F 76
Diggle. G Man 7J 41
Digmoor. Lanc 7C 40
Digswell. Herts 2K 21
Dihewyd. Cdgn 1L 15
Dilham. Norf 7K 39
Dilhorne. Staf 5H 35
Dillarburn. S Lan 5G 59
Dillington. Cambs 5J 29
Dilston. Nmbd 5C 54
Dilston Marsh. Wilts 1G 9
Dilwyn. Here 6C 26
Dimmer. Som 2E 8
Dimple. G Man 6F 40
Dinas. Carm 3J 15
Dinas. Gwyn
nr. Caernarfon 5D 32
nr. Tudweiliog 7B 32
Dinas Cross. Pemb 3G 15
Dinas Dinlle. Gwyn 5D 32
Dinas Mawddwy. Gwyn 1H 25
Dinas Powys. V Glam 7L 17
Dinbych. Den 4K 33
Dinbych-y-Pysgod. Pemb 6H 15
Dinckley. Lanc 4E 40
Dinder. Som 1D 8
Dinedor. Here 8D 26
Dinedor Cross. Here 8D 26
Dingestow. Mon 2C 18
Dingle. Mers 1B 34
Dingleden. Kent 2E 12
Dingleton. Bord 6C 60
Dingley. Nptn 3E 28
Dingwall. High 8F 78
Dinmael. Cnwy 6K 33
Dinnet. Abers 6D 72
Dinnington. Som 4C 8
Dinnington. S Yor 1C 36
Dinnington. Tyne 4F 54
Dinorwig. Gwyn 4E 32
Dinton. Buck 2E 20
Dinton. Wilts 2J 9
Dinworthy. Devn 4C 6
Dipley. Hants 8E 20
Dippen. Arg 6G 57
Dippenhall. Surr 1F 10
Dippertown. Devn 7D 6
Dippin. N Ayr 7K 57
Dipple. S Ayr 1H 51
Diptford. Devn 6K 5
Dipton. Dur 6E 54
Dirleton. E Lot 1C 60
Dirt Pot. Nmbd 7B 54
Discoed. Powy 5A 26
Diseworth. Leics 7B 36
Dishes. Orkn 7F 88
Dishforth. N Yor 8A 48
Disley. Ches E 1H 35
Diss. Norf 4H 31
Disserth. Powy 7K 25
Distington. Cumb 2K 45
Ditchampton. Wilts 2J 9
Ditcheat. Som 2E 8
Ditchingham. Norf 2K 31
Ditchling. E Sus 4L 11
Ditteridge. Wilts 7G 19
Dittisham. Devn 6L 5
Ditton. Hal 1C 34
Ditton. Kent 8D 22
Ditton Green. Cambs 6C 30
Ditton Priors. Shrp 3E 26
Divach. High 3E 70
Dixonfield. High 5C 86
Dixton. Glos 8H 27
Dixton. Mon 2D 18
Dizzard. Corn 6A 6
Doagh. Ant 4H 93
Dobcross. G Man 7H 41
Dobs Hill. Flin 3B 34
Dobson's Bridge. Shrp 6C 34
Dobwalls. Corn 5E 4
Doccombe. Devn 7G 7
Dochgarroch. High 1G 71
Docking. Norf 6D 38
Docklow. Here 6D 26
Dockray. Cumb 3B 46
Doc Penfro. Pemb 6F 14
Dodbrooke. Devn 7K 5
Doddenham. Worc 6F 26
Doddinghurst. Essx 4B 22
Doddington. Cambs 2L 29
Doddington. Kent 8F 22
Doddington. Linc 2G 37
Doddington. Nmbd 6G 61
Doddington. Shrp 4E 26
Doddiscombsleigh. Devn 7H 7
Doddshill. Norf 6D 38
Dodford. Nptn 5D 28
Dodford. Worc 4H 27
Dodington. Som 1L 7
Dodington. S Glo 5F 18
Dodleston. Ches W 3B 34
Dods Leigh. Staf 6J 35
Dodworth. S Yor 7M 41
Doe Lea. Derbs 3B 36
Dogdyke. Linc 4K 37
Dogmersfield. Hants 8E 20
Dogsthorpe. Pet 1K 29
Dog Village. Devn 6J 7
Dolanog. Powy 1K 25
Dolau. Powy 6L 25
Dolau. Rhon 6K 17
Dolbenmaen. Gwyn 6E 32
Doley. Staf 7F 34
Dol-fâch. Powy 2J 25
Dolfach. Powy 5J 25
Dolfor. Powy 4L 25
Dolgarrog. Cnwy 4G 33
Dolgellau. Gwyn 1G 25
Dolgoch. Gwyn 2F 24
Dol-gran. Carm 3L 15
Dolhelfa. Powy 5J 25
Doll. High 3J 79
Dollar. Clac 8C 66
Dolley Green. Powy 5A 26
Dollingstown. Arm 6G 93
Dollwen. Cdgn 4F 24
Dolphin. Flin 3L 33
Dolphinholme. Lanc 2D 40
Dolphinton. S Lan 5K 59
Dolton. Devn 4E 6
Dolwen. Cnwy 3H 33
Dolwyddelan. Cnwy 5G 33
Dol-y-Bont. Cdgn 4F 24
Dolyhir. Powy 7M 25
Domgay. Powy 8A 34
Donagh. Ferm 7C 92
Donaghadee. Ards 5J 93
Donaghcloney. Arm 6G 93
Donaghmore. M Ulst 5E 92
**Doncaster**. S Yor 7C 42
Doncaster Sheffield Airport. S Yor 8D 42
Donhead St Andrew. Wilts 3H 9
Donhead St Mary. Wilts 3H 9
Doniford. Som 1K 7
Donington. Linc 6K 37
Donington. Shrp 1G 27
Donington Eaudike. Linc 6K 37
Donington le Heath. Leics 8B 36
Donington on Bain. Linc 1K 37
Donington South Ing. Linc 6K 37
Donisthorpe. Leics 8M 35
Donkey Street. Kent 2H 13
Donkey Town. Surr 7G 21
Donna Nook. Linc 8M 43
Donnington. Glos 1K 19
Donnington. Here 8F 26
Donnington. Shrp 1D 26
Donnington. Telf 8F 34
Donnington. W Ber 7B 20
Donnington. W Sus 5F 10
Donyatt. Som 4B 8
Doomsday Green. W Sus 3J 11
Doonfoot. S Ayr 8B 58
Doonholm. S Ayr 8B 58
Dorback Lodge. High 4L 71
**Dorchester**. Dors 6E 8
Dorchester on Thames. Oxon 4C 20
Dordon. Warw 1L 27
Dore. S Yor 1M 35
Dores. High 2F 70
**Dorking**. Surr 1J 11
Dorking Tye. Suff 8F 30
Dormansland. Surr 1M 11
Dormans Park. Surr 1L 11
Dormanstown. Red C 3C 48
Dormington. Here 7D 26
Dormston. Worc 6H 27
Dorn. Glos 8L 27
Dorney. Buck 6G 21
Dornie. High 3K 69
Dornoch. High 5H 79
Dornock. Dum 5G 53
Dorrery. High 6B 86
Dorridge. W Mid 4K 27
Dorrington. Linc 4H 37
Dorrington. Shrp 1C 26
Dorsington. Warw 7K 27
Dorstone. Here 7B 26
Dorton. Buck 2D 20
Dosthill. Staf 1L 27
Dotham. IOA 3C 32
Dottery. Dors 6C 8
Doublebois. Corn 5D 4
Dougarie. N Ayr 6H 57
Doughton. Glos 4G 19
Douglas. IOM 7C 44
Douglas. S Lan 6G 59
Douglas Bridge. Derr 4C 92
Douglastown. Ang 3H 67
Douglas Water. S Lan 6G 59
Doulting. Som 1E 8
Dounby. Orkn 7B 88
Doune. High
nr. Kingussie 4J 71
nr. Lairg 3E 78
Doune. Stir 7M 65
Dounie. High
nr. Bonar Bridge 4F 78
nr. Tain 5G 79
Dounreay, Upper & Lower. High 5A 86
Doura. N Ayr 5B 58
Dousland. Devn 5H 5
Dovaston. Shrp 7B 34
Dove Holes. Derbs 2J 35
Dovenby. Cumb 8E 52
**Dover**. Kent 108 (1K 13)
Dovercourt. Essx 8J 31
Doverdale. Worc 5G 27
Doveridge. Derbs 6K 35
Doversgreen. Surr 1K 11
Dowally. Per 3D 66
Dowbridge. Lanc 4C 40
Dowdeswell. Glos 2J 19
Dowlais. Mer T 4K 17
Dowland. Devn 4E 6
Dowlands. Devn 6A 8
Dowles. Worc 4F 26
Dowlesgreen. Wok 7F 20
Dowlish Wake. Som 4B 8
The Down. Shrp 2E 26
Downall Green. Mers 7D 40
Down Ampney. Glos 4K 19
Downderry. Corn
nr. Looe 6F 4
nr. St Austell 6B 4
Downe. G Lon 7M 21
Downend. IOW 7C 10
Downend. S Glo 6E 18
Downend. W Ber 6B 20
Down Field. Cambs 4C 30
Downfield. D'dee 4G 67
Downgate. Corn
nr. Kelly Bray 8C 6
nr. Upton Cross 8B 6
Downham. Essx 4D 22
Downham. Lanc 3F 40
Downham. Nmbd 6F 60
Downham Market. Norf 1C 30
Down Hatherley. Glos 1G 19
Downhead. Som
nr. Frome 1E 8
nr. Yeovil 3D 8
Downhill. Caus 2E 92
Downholland Cross. Lanc 7B 40
Downholme. N Yor 6K 47
Downies. Abers 6J 73
Downley. Buck 4F 20
**Downpatrick**. New M 6J 93
Down St Mary. Devn 5G 7
Downside. Som
nr. Chilcompton 8E 18
nr. Shepton Mallet 1E 8
Downside. Surr 8J 21
Down Thomas. Devn 6H 5
Downton. Hants 6L 9
Downton. Wilts 3K 9
Downton on the Rock. Here 4C 26
Dowsby. Linc 7J 37
Dowsdale. Linc 8K 37
Dowthwaitehead. Cumb 3B 46
Doxey. Staf 7H 35
Doxford. Nmbd 7J 61
Doynton. S Glo 6F 18
Drabblegate. Norf 7J 39
Draethen. Cphy 6M 17
Draffan. S Lan 5F 58
Dragonby. N Lin 6G 43
Dragon's Green. W Sus 3J 11
Drakelow. Worc 3G 27
Drakemyre. N Ayr 4A 58
Drakes Broughton. Worc 7H 27
Drakes Cross. Worc 4J 27
Drakewalls. Corn 8D 6
Draperstown. M Ulst 4E 92
Draughton. Nptn 4E 28
Draughton. N Yor 2J 41
Drax. N Yor 5D 42
Draycot. Oxon 3D 20
Draycote. Warw 4B 28
Draycot Foliat. Swin 6K 19
Draycott. Derbs 6B 36
Draycott. Glos 8K 27
Draycott. Shrp 2G 27
Draycott. Som
nr. Cheddar 8C 18
nr. Yeovil 3D 8
Draycott. Worc 7G 27
Draycott in the Clay. Staf 7K 35
Draycott in the Moors. Staf 5H 35
Drayford. Devn 4G 7
Drayton. Leics 2F 28
Drayton. Linc 6K 37
Drayton. Norf 8H 39
Drayton. Nptn 5C 28
Drayton. Oxon
nr. Abingdon 4B 20
nr. Banbury 7B 28
Drayton. Port 5D 10
Drayton. Som 3C 8
Drayton. Warw 6K 27
Drayton. Worc 4H 27
Drayton Bassett. Staf 1K 27
Drayton Beauchamp. Buck 2G 21
Drayton Parslow. Buck 1F 20
Drayton St Leonard. Oxon 4C 20
Drebley. N Yor 2J 41
Dreenhill. Pemb 5F 14
Y Dref. Gwyn 7D 32
Drefach. Carm
nr. Meidrim 5M 15
nr. Newcastle Emlyn 3K 15
nr. Tumble 4J 15
Drefach. Cdgn 2L 15
Dreghorn. N Ayr 6B 58
Drellingore. Kent 1J 13
Drem. E Lot 2C 60
**Y Drenewydd**. Powy 3L 25
Dreumasdal. W Isl 2D 74
Drewsteignton. Devn 6G 7
Driby. Linc 2L 37
Driffield. E Yor 2H 43
Driffield. Glos 4J 19
Drift. Corn 6H 3
Drigg. Cumb 5K 45
Drighlington. W Yor 5L 41
Drimnin. High 2L 63
Drimpton. Dors 5C 8
Dringhoe. E Yor 2J 43
Drinisiadar. W Isl 4C 76
Drinkstone. Suff 5F 30
Drinkstone Green. Suff 5F 30
Drointon. Staf 7J 35
**Droitwich Spa**. Worc 5G 27
Droman. High 6D 84
Dromara. Lis 6H 93
Dromore. Arm 6H 93
Dromore. Ferm 5C 92
Dron. Per 6E 66
**Dronfield**. Derbs 2A 36
Dronfield Woodhouse. Derbs 2M 35
Drongan. E Ayr 8C 58
Dronley. Ang 4G 67
Droop. Dors 5F 8
Drope. V Glam 7L 17
Droxford. Hants 4D 10
**Droylsden**. G Man 8G 41
Druggers End. Worc 8F 26
Druid. Den 6K 33
Druid's Heath. W Mid 1J 27
Druidston. Pemb 5E 14
Druim. High 8K 79
Druimarbin. High 8A 70
Druim Fhearna. High 4H 69
Druimindarroch. High 7H 69
Druim Saighdinis. W Isl 7K 75
Drum. Per 7D 66
Drumaness. New M 6H 93
Drumaroad. New M 6H 93
Drumbeg. High 8D 84
Drumblade. Abers 1E 72
Drumbo. Lis 5H 93
Drumbuie. Dum 3L 51
Drumbuie. High 2J 69
Drumburgh. Cumb 6G 53
Drumburn. Dum 5D 52
Drumchapel. Glas 2D 58
Drumchardine. High 1F 70
Drumchork. High 5K 77
Drumclog. S Lan 6E 58
Drumeldrie. Fife 7H 67
Drumelzier. Bord 6K 59
Drumfearn. High 4H 69
Drumgask. High 6G 71
Drumgelloch. N Lan 3F 58
Drumgley. Ang 2H 67
Drumguish. High 6H 71
Drumin. Mor 2A 72
Drumindorsair. High 1E 70
Drumintee. New M 7G 93
Drumlamford House. S Ayr 4H 51
Drumlasie. Abers 5F 72
Drumlemble. Arg 8F 56
Drumlithie. Abers 7G 73
Drummoddie. Dum 7J 51
Drummond. High 7G 79
Drummore. Dum 8G 51
Drummuir. Mor 1C 72
Drumnacanvy. Arm 6G 93
Drumnadrochit. High 2F 70
Drumnagorrach. Mor 8E 80
Drumnakilly. Ferm 5D 92
Drumoak. Abers 6G 73
Drumquin. Ferm 5C 92
Drumraighland. Caus 2E 92
Drumrunie. High 3B 78
Drumry. W Dun 2D 58
Drums. Abers 3J 73
Drumsleet. Dum 4D 52
Drumsmittal. High 1G 71
Drums of Park. Abers 8E 80
Drumsturdy. Ang 4H 67
Drumsurn. Caus 3E 92
Drumtochty Castle. Abers 7F 72
Drumuie. High 1F 68
Drumuillie. High 3K 71
Drumvaich. Stir 7L 65
Drumwhindle. Abers 2J 73
Drunkendub. Ang 3K 67
Drury. Flin 3A 34
Drury Square. Norf 8F 38
Drybeck. Cumb 4E 46
Drybridge. Mor 7D 80
Drybridge. N Ayr 6B 58
Drybrook. Glos 2E 18
Drybrook. Here 2D 18
Dryburgh. Bord 6C 60
Dry Doddington. Linc 5F 36
Dry Drayton. Cambs 5L 29
Drym. Corn 5K 3
Drymen. Stir 1C 58
Drymuir. Abers 1J 73
Drynachan Lodge. High 2J 71
Drynie Park. High 8F 78
Drynoch. High 2F 68
Dry Sandford. Oxon 3B 20
Dryslwyn. Carm 2E 16
Dry Street. Essx 5C 22
Dryton. Shrp 1D 26
Dubford. Abers 7G 81
Dubiton. Abers 8F 80
Dubton. Ang 2J 67
Duchally. High 2D 78
Duck End. Essx 1C 22
Duckington. Ches W 4C 34
Ducklington. Oxon 3A 20
Duckmanton. Derbs 2B 36
Duck Street. Hants 1M 9
Dudbridge. Glos 3G 19
Duddenhoe End. Essx 8A 30
Duddingston. Edin 2L 59
Duddington. Nptn 1G 29
Duddleswell. E Sus 3A 12
Duddo. Nmbd 5G 61
Duddon. Ches W 3D 34
Duddon Bridge. Cumb 6L 45
Dudleston. Shrp 6B 34
Dudleston Heath. Shrp 6B 34
Dudley. Tyne 4F 54
**Dudley**. W Mid 3H 27
Dudston. Shrp 3M 25
Dudwells. Pemb 4F 14
Duffield. Derbs 5M 35
Duffryn. Neat 5H 17
Dufftown. Mor 1C 72
Duffus. Mor 7A 80
Dufton. Cumb 3E 46
Duggleby. N Yor 1F 42
Duirinish. High 2J 69
Duisdalemore. High 4H 69
Duisdeil Mòr. High 4H 69
Duisky. High 8M 69
Dukesfield. Nmbd 6C 54
Dukestown. Blae 4L 17
**Dukinfield**. G Man 8H 41
Dulas. IOA 2D 32
Dulcote. Som 1D 8
Dulford. Devn 5K 7
Dull. Per 3B 66
Dullatur. N Lan 2F 58
Dullingham. Cambs 6C 30
Dullingham Ley. Cambs 6C 30
Dulnain Bridge. High 3K 71
Duloe. Bed 5J 29
Duloe. Corn 6E 4
Dulverton. Som 3J 7
Dulwich. G Lon 6L 21
**Dumbarton**. W Dun 2C 58
Dumbleton. Glos 8J 27
Dumfin. Arg 1B 58
**Dumfries**. Dum 108 (4D 52)
Dumgoyne. Stir 1D 58
Dummer. Hants 1C 10
Dumpford. W Sus 3F 10
Dun. Ang 1K 67
Dunadry. Ant 4G 93
Dunaghy. Caus 2F 93
Dunagoil. Arg 4K 57
Dunalastair. Per 2M 65
Dunan. High 3G 69
Dunball. Som 1B 8
Dunbar. E Lot 2D 60
Dunbeath. High 1A 80
Dunbeg. Arg 4C 64
Dunblane. Stir 7A 66
Dunbog. Fife 6F 66
Dunbridge. Hants 3M 9
Duncanston. Abers 3E 72
Duncanston. High 8F 78
Dun Charlabhaigh. W Isl 7E 82
Dunchideock. Devn 7H 7
Dunchurch. Warw 4B 28
Duncote. Nptn 6D 28
Duncow. Dum 3D 52
Duncrievie. Per 7E 66
Duncton. W Sus 4G 11
**Dundee**. D'dee 108 (4H 67)
Dundee Airport. D'dee 5G 67
Dundon. Som 2C 8
**Dundonald**. Lis 5J 93
Dundonald. S Ayr 6B 58
Dundonnell. High 5A 78
Dundraw. Cumb 7G 53
Dundreggan. High 4D 70
Dundrennan. Dum 7B 52
Dundridge. Hants 4C 10
Dundrod. Lis 5H 93
Dundrum. New M 7J 93
Dundry. N Som 7D 18
Dunecht. Abers 5G 73
**Dunfermline**. Fife 1J 59
Dunford Bridge. S Yor 7K 41
**Dungannon**. M Ulst 5E 92
Dungate. Kent 8F 22
Dunge. Wilts 8G 19
Dungeness. Kent 4G 13
Dungiven. Caus 3E 92
Dungworth. S Yor 1L 35
Dunham-on-the-Hill. Ches W 2C 34
Dunham-on-Trent. Notts 2F 36
Dunhampton. Worc 5G 27
Dunham Town. G Man 1F 34
Dunham Woodhouses. G Man 1F 34
Dunholme. Linc 2H 37
Dunino. Fife 6J 67
Dunipace. Falk 1G 59
Dunira. Per 5M 65
Dunkeld. Per 3D 66
Dunkerton. Bath 8F 18
Dunkeswell. Devn 5L 7
Dunkeswick. N Yor 3M 41
Dunkirk. Kent 8G 23
Dunkirk. S Glo 5F 18
Dunkirk. Staf 4G 35
Dunkirk. Wilts 7H 19
Dunk's Green. Kent 8C 22
Dunlappie. Ang 1J 67
Dunley. Hants 8B 20
Dunley. Worc 5F 26
Dunlichity Lodge. High 2G 71
Dunlop. E Ayr 5C 58
Dunloy. Caus 3G 93
Dunmaglass Lodge. High 3F 70
Dunmore. Arg 3G 57
Dunmore. Falk 1G 59
Dunmore. High 1F 70
Dunmurry. Bel 5H 93
Dunnamanagh. Derr 3D 92
Dunnaval. New M 7H 93
Dunnet. High 4D 86
Dunnichen. Ang 3J 67
Dunning. Per 6D 66
Dunnington. E Yor 2J 43
Dunnington. Warw 6J 27
Dunnington. York 2D 42
Dunningwell. Cumb 6L 45
Dunnockshaw. Lanc 5G 41
**Dunoon**. Arg 2L 57
Dunphail. Mor 1L 71
Dunragit. Dum 6G 51
Dunrostan. Arg 1G 57
Duns. Bord 4E 60
Dunsby. Linc 7J 37
Dunscar. G Man 6F 40
Dunscore. Dum 3C 52
Dunscroft. S Yor 7D 42
Dunsdale. Red C 4D 48
Dunsden Green. Oxon 6E 20
Dunsfold. Surr 2H 11
Dunsford. Devn 7H 7
Dunshalt. Fife 6F 66
Dunshillock. Abers 1J 73
Dunsley. N Yor 4F 48
Dunsley. Staf 3G 27
Dunsmore. Buck 3F 20
Dunsop Bridge. Lanc 2E 40
**Dunstable**. C Beds 1H 21
Dunstal. Staf 7J 35
Dunstall. Staf 7K 35
Dunstall Green. Suff 5D 30
Dunstall Hill. W Mid 1H 27
Dunstan. Nmbd 8K 61
Dunster. Som 1J 7
Duns Tew. Oxon 1B 20
Dunston. Linc 3H 37
Dunston. Norf 1J 31
Dunston. Staf 8H 35
Dunston. Tyne 5F 54
Dunstone. Devn 6H 5
Dunston Heath. Staf 8H 35
Dunsville. S Yor 7D 42
Dunswell. E Yor 4H 43
Dunsyre. S Lan 5J 59
Dunterton. Devn 8C 6
Duntisbourne Abbots. Glos 3H 19
Duntisbourne Leer. Glos 3H 19
Duntisbourne Rouse. Glos 3H 19
Duntish. Dors 5E 8
Duntocher. W Dun 2C 58
Dunton. Buck 1F 20
Dunton. C Beds 7K 29
Dunton. Norf 6E 38
Dunton Bassett. Leics 2C 28
Dunton Green. Kent 8B 22
Dunton Patch. Norf 6E 38
Duntulm. High 6F 76
Dunure. S Ayr 8A 58
Dunvant. Swan 5E 16
Dunvegan. High 1D 68
Dunwich. Suff 4L 31
Dunwood. Staf 4H 35
Durdar. Cumb 6J 53
Durgates. E Sus 2C 12
**Durham**. Dur 108 (7F 54)
Durham Tees Valley Airport. Darl 4A 48
Durisdeer. Dum 1C 52
Durisdeermill. Dum 1C 52
Durkar. W Yor 6M 41
Durleigh. Som 2A 8
Durley. Hants 4C 10
Durley. Wilts 7L 19
Durley Street. Hants 4C 10
Durlow Common. Here 8E 26
Durnamuck. High 4M 77
Durness. High 5G 85
Durno. Abers 3G 73
Durns Town. Hants 6L 9
Duror. High 2D 64
Durran. Arg 7D 64
Durran. High 5C 86
Durrant Green. Kent 2E 12
Durrants. Hants 4E 10
Durrington. W Sus 5J 11
Durrington. Wilts 1K 9
**Dursley**. Glos 4F 18
Dursley Cross. Glos 2E 18
Durston. Som 3A 8
Durweston. Dors 5G 9
Dury. Shet 2E 90
Duston. Nptn 5E 28
Duthil. High 3K 71
Dutlas. Powy 5M 25
Duton Hill. Essx 1C 22
Dutson. Corn 7C 6
Dutton. Ches W 2D 34
Duxford. Cambs 7A 30
Duxford. Oxon 4A 20
Dwygyfylchi. Cnwy 3G 33
Dwyran. IOA 4D 32
Dyce. Aber 4H 73
Dyffryn. B'end 5H 17
Dyffryn. Carm 4K 15
Dyffryn. Pemb 3F 14
Dyffryn. V Glam 7K 17
Dyffryn Ardudwy. Gwyn 8E 32
Dyffryn Castell. Cdgn 4G 25
Dyffryn Ceidrych. Carm 2G 17
Dyffryn Cellwen. Neat 4H 17
Dyke. Linc 7J 37
Dyke. Mor 8K 79
Dykehead. Ang 1G 67
Dykehead. N Lan 3G 59
Dykehead. Stir 8K 65
Dykend. Ang 2F 66
Dykesfield. Cumb 6H 53
Dylife. Powy 3H 25
Dymchurch. Kent 3H 13
Dymock. Glos 8F 26
Dyrham. S Glo 6F 18
Dysart. Fife 8G 67
Dyserth. Den 3K 33

## E

Eachwick. Nmbd 4E 54
Eadar Dha Fhadhail. W Isl 8D 82
Eagland Hill. Lanc 3C 40
Eagle. Linc 3F 36
Eagle Barnsdale. Linc 3F 36
Eagle Moor. Linc 3F 36
**Eaglescliffe**. Stoc T 4B 48
Eaglesfield. Cumb 2K 45
Eaglesfield. Dum 4G 53
Eaglesham. E Ren 4D 58
Eaglethorpe. Nptn 2H 29
Eagley. G Man 6F 40
Eairy. IOM 7B 44
Eakley Lanes. Mil 6F 28
Eakring. Notts 3D 36
Ealand. N Lin 6E 42
**Ealing**. G Lon 5J 21
Eallabus. Arg 3C 56
Eals. Nmbd 6L 53
Eamont Bridge. Cumb 3D 46
Earby. Lanc 3H 41
Earcroft. Bkbn 5E 40
Eardington. Shrp 2F 26
Eardisland. Here 6C 26
Eardisley. Here 7B 26
Eardiston. Shrp 7B 34
Eardiston. Worc 5E 26
Earith. Cambs 4L 29
Earlais. High 7E 76
Earle. Nmbd 7G 61
Earlesfield. Linc 6G 37
Earlestown. Mers 8D 40
Earley. Wok 6E 20
Earlham. Norf 1H 31
Earlish. High 7E 76
Earls Barton. Nptn 5F 28
Earls Colne. Essx 1E 22
Earls Common. Worc 6H 27
Earl's Croome. Worc 7G 27
Earlsdon. W Mid 4M 27
Earlsferry. Fife 7H 67
Earlsford. Abers 2H 73
Earl's Green. Suff 5G 31
Earlsheaton. W Yor 5L 41
**Earl Shilton**. Leics 2B 28
Earl Soham. Suff 5J 31
Earl Sterndale. Derbs 3J 35
Earlston. E Ayr 6C 58
Earlston. Bord 6C 60
Earl Stonham. Suff 6H 31
Earlstoun. Dum 3M 51
Earlswood. Mon 4C 18
Earlswood. Warw 4K 27
Earlyvale. Bord 4L 59
Earnley. W Sus 6F 10
Earsairidh. W Isl 6D 74
Earsdon. Tyne 4G 55
Earsham. Norf 3K 31
Earsham Street. Suff 4J 31
Earswick. York 2D 42
Eartham. W Sus 5G 11
Earthcott Green. S Glo 5E 18
Easby. N Yor
nr. Great Ayton 5C 48
nr. Richmond 5K 47
Easdale. Arg 6B 64
Easebourne. W Sus 3F 10
Easenhall. Warw 4B 28
Eashing. Surr 1G 11
Easington. Buck 2D 20
Easington. Dur 7H 55
Easington. E Yor 6L 43
Easington. Nmbd 6J 61
Easington. Oxon
nr. Banbury 8B 28
nr. Watlington 4D 20
Easington. Red C 4E 48
Easington Colliery. Dur 7H 55
Easington Lane. Tyne 7G 55
Easingwold. N Yor 8C 48
Eassie. Ang 3G 67
Eassie and Nevay. Ang 3G 67
East Aberthaw. V Glam 8K 17
Eastacombe. Devn 3E 6
Eastacott. Devn 3F 6
East Allington. Devn 7K 5
East Anstey. Devn 3H 7
East Anton. Hants 1A 10
East Appleton. N Yor 6L 47
East Ardsley. W Yor 5M 41
East Ashley. Devn 4F 6
East Ashling. W Sus 5F 10
East Aston. Hants 1B 10
East Ayton. N Yor 7G 49
East Barkwith. Linc 1J 37
East Barnby. N Yor 4F 48
East Barnet. G Lon 4K 21
East Barns. E Lot 2E 60
East Barsham. Norf 6F 38
East Beach. W Sus 6F 10
East Beckham. Norf 6H 39
East Bedfont. G Lon 6H 21
East Bennan. N Ayr 7J 57
East Bergholt. Suff 8G 31
East Bierley. W Yor 5L 41
East Bilney. Norf 8F 38
East Blatchington. E Sus 5A 12
East Bloxworth. Dors 6G 9
East Boldre. Hants 5A 10
East Bolton. Nmbd 8J 61
Eastbourne. Darl 4L 47
**Eastbourne**. E Sus 108 (6C 12)
East Brent. Som 8B 18
East Bridge. Suff 5L 31
East Bridgford. Notts 5D 36
East Briscoe. Dur 4H 47
East Buckland. Devn
nr. Barnstaple 2F 6
nr. Thurlestone 7J 5
East Budleigh. Devn 7K 7
Eastburn. W Yor 3J 41
East Burnham. Buck 5G 21
East Burrafirth. Shet 2D 90
East Burton. Dors 7G 9
Eastbury. Herts 4H 21
Eastbury. W Ber 6M 19
East Butsfield. Dur 7E 54
East Butterleigh. Devn 5J 7
East Butterwick. N Lin 7F 42
Eastby. N Yor 2J 41
East Calder. W Lot 3J 59
East Carleton. Norf 1H 31
East Carlton. Nptn 3F 28
East Carlton. W Yor 3L 41
East Chaldon. Dors 7F 8
East Challow. Oxon 5A 20
East Charleton. Devn 7K 5
East Chelborough. Dors 5D 8
East Chiltington. E Sus 4L 11
East Chinnock. Som 4C 8
East Chisenbury. Wilts 8K 19
Eastchurch. Kent 6F 22
East Clandon. Surr 8H 21
East Claydon. Buck 1E 20
East Clevedon. N Som 6C 18
East Clyne. High 3J 79
East Clyth. High 8D 86
East Coker. Som 4D 8
East Combe. Som 2L 7
Eastcombe. Glos 3G 19
East Common. N Yor 4D 42
East Compton. Som 1E 8
East Cornworthy. Devn 6L 5
Eastcote. G Lon 5J 21
Eastcote. Nptn 6D 28
Eastcote. W Mid 4K 27
Eastcott. Corn 4B 6
Eastcott. Wilts 8J 19
East Cottingwith. E Yor 3E 42
Eastcourt. Wilts
nr. Pewsey 7L 19
nr. Tetbury 4H 19
East Cowes. IOW 6C 10
East Cowick. E Yor 5D 42
East Cowton. N Yor 5M 47
East Cramlington. Nmbd 4F 54
East Cranmore. Som 1E 8
East Creech. Dors 7H 9
East Croachy. High 3G 71
East Dean. E Sus 6B 12
East Dean. Glos 1E 18
East Dean. Hants 3L 9
East Dean. W Sus 4G 11
East Down. Devn 1F 6
East Drayton. Notts 2E 36
East Dundry. N Som 7D 18
East Ella. Hull 5H 43
East End. Cambs 4L 29
East End. Dors 6H 9
East End. E Yor
nr. Ulrome 2J 43
nr. Withernsea 5K 43
East End. Hants
nr. Lymington 6A 10
nr. Newbury 7B 20
East End. Herts 1A 22
East End. Kent
nr. Minster 6F 22
nr. Tenterden 2E 12
East End. N Som 6C 18
East End. Oxon 2A 20
East End. Som 8D 18
East End. Suff 8H 31
Easter Ardross. High 6G 79
Easter Balgedie. Per 7E 66
Easter Balmoral. Abers 6B 72
Easter Brae. High 7G 79
Easter Buckieburn. Stir 1F 58
Easter Compton. S Glo 5D 18
Easter Fearn. High 5G 79
Easter Galcantray. High 1J 71
Eastergate. W Sus 5G 11
Easterhouse. Glas 3E 58
Easter Howgate. Midl 3L 59
Easter Kinkell. High 8F 78
Easter Lednathie. Ang 1G 67
Easter Ogil. Ang 1H 67
Easter Ord. Abers 5H 73
Easter Quarff. Shet 4E 90
Easter Rhynd. Per 6E 66
Easter Skeld. Shet 3D 90
Easter Suddie. High 8G 79
Easterton. Wilts 8J 19
Eastertown. Som 8B 18
Easter Tulloch. Abers 8G 73
East Everleigh. Wilts 8L 19
East Farleigh. Kent 8D 22
East Farndon. Nptn 3E 28
East Ferry. Linc 8F 42
Eastfield. N Lan
nr. Caldercruix 3G 59
nr. Harthill 3G 59
**Eastfield**. N Yor 7H 49
Eastfield. S Lan 3E 58
Eastfield Hall. Nmbd 1F 54
East Fortune. E Lot 2C 60
East Garforth. W Yor 4B 42
East Garston. W Ber 6A 20
Eastgate. Dur 8C 54
Eastgate. Norf 7H 39
East Ginge. Oxon 5B 20
East Gores. Essx 1E 22
East Goscote. Leics 8D 36
East Grafton. Wilts 7L 19
East Green. Suff 6C 30
East Grimstead. Wilts 3L 9
**East Grinstead**. W Sus 2L 11
East Guldeford. E Sus 3F 12
East Haddon. Nptn 5D 28
East Hagbourne. Oxon 5C 20

East Halton. N Lin 5J 43
**East Ham**. G Lon 5M 21
Eastham. Mers 1B 34
Eastham. Worc 5E 26
Eastham Ferry. Mers 1B 34
Easthampstead. Brac 7F 20
Easthampton. Here 5C 26
East Hanney. Oxon 4B 20
East Hanningfield. Essx 3D 22
East Hardwick. W Yor 6B 42
East Harling. Norf 3F 30
East Harlsey. N Yor 6B 48
East Harptree. Bath 8D 18
East Hartford. Nmbd 4F 54
East Harting. W Sus 4F 10
East Hatch. Wilts 3H 9
East Hatley. Cambs 6K 29
Easthaugh. Norf 8G 39
East Hauxwell. N Yor 6K 47
East Haven. Ang 4J 67
Eastheath. Wok 7F 20
East Heckington. Linc 5J 37
East Hedleyhope. Dur 7E 54
East Helmsdale. High 2L 79
East Hendred. Oxon 5B 20
East Heslerton. N Yor 8G 49
East Hoathly. E Sus 4B 12
East Holme. Dors 7G 9
Easthope. Shrp 2D 26
Easthorpe. Essx 1F 22
Easthorpe. Leics 6F 36
East Horrington. Som 1D 8
East Horsley. Surr 8H 21
East Horton. Nmbd 6H 61
Easthouses. Midl 3M 59
East Howe. Bour 6J 9
East Huntspill. Som 1B 8
East Hyde. C Beds 2J 21
East Ilsley. W Ber 5B 20
Eastington. Devn 5G 7
Eastington. Glos
nr. Northleach 2K 19
nr. Stonehouse 3F 18
East Keal. Linc 3L 37
East Kennett. Wilts 7K 19
East Keswick. W Yor 3A 42
**East Kilbride**. S Lan 4E 58
East Kirkby. Linc 3L 37
East Knapton. N Yor 8F 48
East Knighton. Dors 7G 9
East Knowstone. Devn 3H 7
East Knoyle. Wilts 2G 9
East Kyloe. Nmbd 6H 61
East Lambrook. Som 4C 8
East Langdon. Kent 1K 13
East Langton. Leics 2E 28
East Langwell. High 3H 79
East Lavant. W Sus 5F 10
East Lavington. W Sus 4G 11
East Layton. N Yor 5K 47
Eastleach Martin. Glos 3L 19
Eastleach Turville. Glos 3K 19
East Leake. Notts 7C 36
East Learmouth. Nmbd 6F 60
East Leigh. Devn
nr. Crediton 5F 6
nr. Modbury 6J 5
Eastleigh. Devn 3D 6
**Eastleigh**. Hants 4B 10
East Lexham. Norf 8E 38
East Lilburn. Nmbd 7H 61
Eastling. Kent 8F 22
East Linton. E Lot 2C 60
East Liss. Hants 3E 10
East Lockinge. Oxon 5B 20
East Looe. Corn 6E 4
East Lound. N Lin 8E 42
East Lulworth. Dors 7G 9
East Lutton. N Yor 1G 43
East Lydford. Som 2D 8
East Lyng. Som 3B 8
East Mains. Abers 6F 72
East Malling. Kent 8D 22
East Marden. W Sus 4F 10
East Markham. Notts 2E 36
East Marton. N Yor 2H 41
East Meon. Hants 3D 10
East Mersea. Essx 2G 23
East Mey. High 4E 86
East Midlands Airport.
Leics 119 (7B 36)
East Molesey. Surr 7J 21
Eastmoor. Norf 1D 30
East Morden. Dors 6H 9
East Morton. W Yor 3K 41
East Ness. N Yor 8D 48
East Newton. E Yor 4K 43
East Newton. N Yor 8D 48
Eastney. Port 6D 10
Eastnor. Here 8F 26
East Norton. Leics 1E 28
East Nynehead. Som 3L 7
East Oakley. Hants 8C 20
Eastoft. N Lin 6F 42
East Ogwell. Devn 8H 7
Easton. Cambs 4J 29
Easton. Cumb
nr. Burgh by Sands 6G 53
nr. Longtown 4J 53
Easton. Devn 7G 7
Easton. Dors 8E 8
Easton. Hants 2C 10
Easton. Linc 7G 37
Easton. Norf 8H 39
Easton. Som 1D 8
Easton. Suff 6J 31
Easton. Wilts 6G 19
Easton Grey. Wilts 5G 19
Easton-in-Gordano. N Som 6D 18
Easton Maudit. Nptn 6F 28
Easton on the Hill. Nptn 1H 29
Easton Royal. Wilts 7L 19
East Orchard. Dors 4G 9
East Ord. Nmbd 4G 61
East Panson. Devn 6C 6
East Peckham. Kent 1C 12
East Pennard. Som 2D 8
East Perry. Cambs 5J 29
East Pitcorthie. Fife 7J 67
East Portlemouth. Devn 8K 5
East Prawle. Devn 8K 5
East Preston. W Sus 5H 11
East Putford. Devn 4C 6
East Quantoxhead. Som 1L 7
East Rainton. Tyne 7G 55
East Ravendale. NE Lin 8K 43
East Raynham. Norf 7E 38
Eastrea. Cambs 2K 29
East Rhidorroch Lodge.
High 4C 78
Eastriggs. Dum 5G 53
East Rigton. W Yor 3A 42
Eastrington. E Yor 5E 42
East Rounton. N Yor 5B 48
East Row. N Yor 4F 48
East Rudham. Norf 7E 38
East Runton. Norf 5H 39
East Ruston. Norf 7K 39
Eastry. Kent 8K 23
East Saltoun. E Lot 3B 60
East Shaws. Dur 4J 47
East Shefford. W Ber 6A 20
Eastshore. Shet 6D 90
East Sleekburn. Nmbd 3F 54
East Somerton. Norf 8L 39
East Stockwith. Linc 8E 42
East Stoke. Dors 7G 9
East Stoke. Notts 5E 36
East Stoke. Som 4C 8
East Stour. Dors 3G 9
East Stourmouth. Kent 7J 23
East Stowford. Devn 3F 6
East Stratton. Hants 1C 10
East Studdal. Kent 1K 13
East Taphouse. Corn 5D 4
East-the-Water. Devn 3D 6
East Thirston. Nmbd 2E 54
East Tilbury. Thur 6C 22
East Tisted. Hants 2E 10
East Torrington. Linc 1J 37
East Tuddenham. Norf 8G 39
East Tytherley. Hants 3L 9
East Tytherton. Wilts 6H 19
East Village. Devn 5H 7
Eastville. Linc 4M 37
East Wall. Shrp 2D 26
East Walton. Norf 8D 38
East Week. Devn 6F 6
Eastwell. Leics 7E 36
East Wellow. Hants 3M 9
East Wemyss. Fife 8G 67
East Whitburn. W Lot 3H 59
Eastwick. Herts 2M 21
Eastwick. Shet 6H 91
East Williamston. Pemb 6G 15
East Winch. Norf 8C 38
East Winterslow. Wilts 2L 9
East Wittering. W Sus 6E 10
East Witton. N Yor 7K 47
**Eastwood**. Notts 5B 36
Eastwood. S'end 5E 22
East Woodburn. Nmbd 3C 54
Eastwood End. Cambs 2M 29
East Woodhay. Hants 7B 20
East Woodlands. Som 1F 8
East Worldham. Hants 2E 10
East Worlington. Devn 4G 7
East Wretham. Norf 2F 30
East Youlstone. Devn 4B 6
Eathorpe. Warw 5A 28
Eaton. Ches E 3G 35
Eaton. Ches W 3D 34
Eaton. Leics 7E 36
Eaton. Norf
nr. Heacham 6C 38
nr. Norwich 1J 31
Eaton. Notts 2E 36
Eaton. Oxon 3B 20
Eaton. Shrp
nr. Bishop's Castle 3B 26
nr. Church Stretton 3D 26
Eaton Bishop. Here 8C 26
Eaton Bray. C Beds 1G 21
Eaton Constantine. Shrp 1D 26
Eaton Hastings. Oxon 4L 19
**Eaton Socon**. Cambs 6J 29
Eaton upon Tern. Shrp 7E 34
Eau Brink. Norf 8B 38
Eaves Green. W Mid 3L 27
Ebberley Hill. Devn 4E 6
Ebberston. N Yor 7F 48
Ebbesbourne Wake. Wilts 3H 9
Ebblake. Dors 5K 9
Ebbsfleet. Kent 6C 22
**Ebbw Vale**. Blae 4L 17
Ebchester. Dur 6E 54
Ebernoe. W Sus 3G 11
Ebford. Devn 7J 7
Ebley. Glos 3G 19
Ebnal. Ches W 5C 34
Ebrington. Glos 7K 27
Ecchinswell. Hants 8C 20
Ecclefechan. Dum 4F 52
**Eccles**. G Man 8F 40
Eccles. Kent 7D 22
Eccles. Bord 5E 60
Ecclesall. S Yor 1M 35
Ecclesfield. S Yor 8A 42
Eccles Green. Here 7B 26
Eccleshall. Staf 7G 35
Eccleshill. W Yor 4K 41
Ecclesmachan. W Lot 2J 59
Eccles on Sea. Norf 7L 39
Eccles Road. Norf 2G 31
Eccleston. Ches W 3C 34
Eccleston. Lanc 6D 40
Eccleston. Mers 8C 40
Eccup. W Yor 3L 41
Echt. Abers 5G 73
Eckford. Bord 7E 60
Eckington. Derbs 2B 36
Eckington. Worc 7H 27
Ecton. Nptn 5F 28
Edale. Derbs 1K 35
Eday Airport. Orkn 6E 88
Edburton. W Sus 4K 11
Edderside. Cumb 7F 52
Edderton. High 5H 79
Eddington. Kent 7H 23
Eddington. W Ber 7M 19
Eddleston. Bord 5L 59
Eddlewood. S Lan 4F 58
Eden. ME Ant 4J 93
Edenbridge. Kent 1M 11
Edendonich. Arg 5F 64
Edenfield. Lanc 6F 40
Edenhall. Cumb 8K 53
Edenham. Linc 7H 37
Edensor. Derbs 2L 35
Edentaggart. Arg 8H 65
Edenthorpe. S Yor 7D 42
Eden Vale. Dur 8H 55
Edern. Gwyn 7B 32
Ederney. Ferm 5C 92
Edgarley. Som 2D 8
Edgbaston. W Mid 3J 27
Edgcott. Buck 1D 20
Edgcott. Som 2H 7
Edge. Glos 3G 19
Edge. Shrp 1B 26
Edgebolton. Shrp 7D 34
Edge End. Glos 2D 18
Edgefield. Norf 6G 39
Edgefield Street. Norf 6G 39
Edge Green. Ches W 4C 34
Edgehead. Midl 3A 60
Edgeley. Shrp 5D 34
Edgeside. Lanc 5G 41
Edgeworth. Glos 3H 19
Edgiock. Worc 5J 27
Edgmond. Telf 8F 34
Edgmond Marsh. Telf 7F 34
Edgton. Shrp 3B 26
**Edgware**. G Lon 4J 21
Edgworth. Bkbn 6F 40
Edinbane. High 8E 76
**Edinburgh**. Edin 109 (2L 59)
Edinburgh Airport. Edin 2K 59
Edingale. Staf 8L 35
Edingley. Notts 4D 36
Edingthorpe. Norf 6K 39
Edington. Som 2B 8
Edington. Wilts 8H 19
Edingworth. Som 8B 18
Edistone. Devn 3B 6
Edithmead. Som 1B 8
Edith Weston. Rut 1G 29
Edlaston. Derbs 5K 35
Edlesborough. Buck 2G 21
Edlingham. Nmbd 1E 54
Edlington. Linc 2K 37
Edmondsham. Dors 4J 9
Edmondsley. Dur 7F 54
Edmondthorpe. Leics 8F 36
Edmonstone. Orkn 7E 88
Edmonton. Corn 4B 4
**Edmonton**. G Lon 4L 21
Edmundbyers. Dur 6D 54
Ednam. Bord 6E 60
Ednaston. Derbs 5L 35
Edney Common. Essx 3C 22
Edrom. Bord 4F 60
Edstaston. Shrp 6D 34
Edstone. Warw 5K 27
Edwalton. Notts 6C 36
Edwardstone. Suff 7F 30
Edwardsville. Mer T 5K 17
Edwinsford. Carm 1F 16
Edwinstowe. Notts 3D 36
Edworth. C Beds 7K 29
Edwyn Ralph. Here 6E 26
Edzell. Ang 1K 67
Efail-fach. Neat 5G 17
Efail Isaf. Rhon 6K 17
Efailnewydd. Gwyn 7C 32
Efail-rhyd. Powy 8L 33
Efailwen. Carm 4H 15
Efenechtyd. Den 5L 33
Effingham. Surr 8J 21
Effingham Common. Surr 8J 21
Effirth. Shet 2D 90
Efflinch. Staf 8K 35
Efford. Devn 5H 7
Efstigarth. Shet 4J 91
Egbury. Hants 8B 20
Egdon. Worc 6H 27
Egerton. G Man 6F 40
Egerton. Kent 1F 12
Egerton Forstal. Kent 1E 12
Eggborough. N Yor 5C 42
Eggbuckland. Plym 6G 5
Eggesford. Devn 4F 6
Eggington. C Beds 1G 21
Egginton. Derbs 7L 35
Egglescliffe. Stoc T 4B 48
Eggleston. Dur 3H 47
**Egham**. Surr 6H 21
Egham Hythe. Surr 6H 21
Egleton. Rut 1F 28
Eglingham. Nmbd 8J 61
Eglinton. Derr 2D 92
Eglish. M Ulst 6E 92
Egloshayle. Corn 4C 4
Egloskerry. Corn 7B 6
Eglwysbach. Cnwy 3H 33
Eglwys-Brewis. V Glam 8K 17
Eglwys Fach. Cdgn 3F 24
Eglwyswrw. Pemb 3H 15
Egmanton. Notts 3E 36
Egmere. Norf 6F 38
Egremont. Cumb 3K 45
Egremont. Mers 8B 40
Egton. N Yor 5F 48
Egton Bridge. N Yor 5F 48
Egypt. Buck 5G 21
Egypt. Hants 1B 10
Eight Ash Green. Essx 1F 22
Eight Mile Burn. Midl 4K 59
Eignaig. High 3B 64
Eilanreach. High 4K 69
Eildon. Bord 6C 60
Eileanach Lodge. High 7F 78
Eilean Fhlodaigh. W Isl 8K 75
Eilean Iarmain. High 4J 69
Einacleit. W Isl 1C 76
Eisgein. W Isl 2E 76
Eisingrug. Gwyn 7F 32
Elan Village. Powy 6J 25
Elberton. S Glo 5E 18
Elbridge. W Sus 5G 11
Elburton. Plym 6H 5
Elcho. Per 5E 66
Elcombe. Swin 5K 19
Elcot. W Ber 7A 20
Eldernell. Cambs 2L 29
Eldersfield. Worc 8G 27
Elderslie. Ren 3C 58
Elder Street. Essx 8B 30
Eldon. Dur 3L 47
Eldroth. N Yor 1F 40
Eldwick. W Yor 3K 41
Elfhowe. Cumb 6C 46
Elford. Nmbd 6J 61
Elford. Staf 8K 35
Elford Closes. Cambs 4A 30
**Elgin**. Mor 7B 80
Elgol. High 4G 69
Elham. Kent 1H 13
Elie. Fife 7H 67
Eling. Hants 4A 10
Eling. W Ber 6C 20
Elishaw. Nmbd 2B 54
Elizafield. Dum 4E 52
Elkesley. Notts 2D 36
Elkington. Nptn 4D 28
Elkins Green. Essx 3C 22
Elkstone. Glos 2H 19
Ellan. High 3J 71
**Elland**. W Yor 5K 41
Ellary. Arg 2G 57
Ellastone. Staf 5K 35
Ellbridge. Corn 5G 5
Ellel. Lanc 2C 40
Ellemford. Bord 3E 60
Ellenabeich. Arg 6B 64
Ellenborough. Cumb 8E 52
Ellenbrook. Herts 3K 21
Ellenhall. Staf 7G 35
Ellen's Green. Surr 2H 11
Ellerbeck. N Yor 6B 48
Ellerburn. N Yor 7F 48
Ellerby. N Yor 4E 48
Ellerdine. Telf 7E 34
Ellerdine Heath. Telf 7E 34
Ellerhayes. Devn 5J 7
Elleric. Arg 3E 64
Ellerker. E Yor 5G 43
Ellerton. E Yor 4E 42
Ellerton. Shrp 7F 34
Ellerton-on-Swale. N Yor 6L 47
Ellesborough. Buck 3F 20
Ellesmere. Shrp 6C 34
**Ellesmere Port**. Ches W 2C 34
Ellingham. Hants 5K 9
Ellingham. Norf 2K 31
Ellingham. Nmbd 7J 61
Ellingstring. N Yor 7K 47
Ellington. Cambs 4J 29
Ellington. Nmbd 2F 54
Ellington Thorpe. Cambs 4J 29
Elliot. Ang 4K 67
Ellisfield. Hants 1D 10
Ellishadder. High 7G 77
Ellistown. Leics 8B 36
Ellon. Abers 2J 73
Ellonby. Cumb 8J 53
Ellough. Suff 3L 31
Elloughton. E Yor 5G 43
Ellwood. Glos 3D 18
Elm. Cambs 1A 30
Elmbridge. Glos 2G 19
Elmbridge. Worc 5H 27
Elmdon. Essx 8A 30
Elmdon. W Mid 3K 27
Elmdon Heath. W Mid 3K 27
Elmesthorpe. Leics 2B 28
Elmfield. IOW 6D 10
Elm Hill. Dors 3G 9
Elmhurst. Staf 8K 35
Elmley Castle. Worc 7H 27
Elmley Lovett. Worc 5G 27
Elmore. Glos 2F 18
Elmore Back. Glos 2F 18
Elm Park. G Lon 5B 22
Elmscott. Devn 3B 6
Elmsett. Suff 7G 31
Elmstead. Essx 1G 23
Elmstead Heath. Essx 1G 23
Elmstead Market. Essx 1G 23
Elmsted. Kent 1H 13
Elmstone. Kent 7J 23
Elmstone Hardwicke. Glos 1H 19
Elmswell. E Yor 2G 43
Elmswell. Suff 5F 30
Elmton. Derbs 2C 36
Elphin. High 2C 78
Elphinstone. E Lot 2A 60
Elrick. Abers 5H 73
Elrick. Mor 3D 72
Elrig. Dum 7J 51
Elsdon. Nmbd 2C 54
Elsecar. S Yor 8A 42
Elsenham. Essx 1B 22
Elsfield. Oxon 2C 20
Elsham. N Lin 6H 43
Elsing. Norf 8G 39
Elslack. N Yor 3H 41
Elsrickle. S Lan 5J 59
Elstead. Surr 1G 11
Elsted. W Sus 4F 10
Elsted Marsh. W Sus 3F 10
Elsthorpe. Linc 7H 37
Elstob. Dur 3M 47
Elston. Devn 5G 7
Elston. Lanc 4E 40
Elston. Notts 5E 36
Elston. Wilts 1J 9
Elstone. Devn 4F 6
Elstow. Bed 7H 29
Elstree. Herts 4J 21
Elstronwick. E Yor 4K 43
Elswick. Lanc 4C 40
Elswick. Tyne 5F 54
Elsworth. Cambs 5L 29
Elterwater. Cumb 5B 46
**Eltham**. G Lon 6M 21
Eltisley. Cambs 6K 29
Elton. Cambs 2H 29
Elton. Ches W 2C 34
Elton. Derbs 3L 35
Elton. Glos 2F 18
Elton. G Man 6F 40
Elton. Here 4C 26
Elton. Notts 6E 36
Elton. Stoc T 4B 48
Elton Green. Ches W 2C 34
Eltringham. Nmbd 5D 54
Elvanfoot. S Lan 8H 59
Elvaston. Derbs 6B 36
Elveden. Suff 4E 30
Elvetham Heath. Hants 8E 20
Elvingston. E Lot 2B 60
Elvington. Kent 8J 23
Elvington. York 3E 42
Elwick. Hart 8H 55
Elwick. Nmbd 6J 61
Elworth. Ches E 3F 34
Elworth. Dors 7D 8
Elworthy. Som 2K 7
**Ely**. Cambs 3B 30
Ely. Card 7L 17
Emberton. Mil 7F 28
Embleton. Cumb 8F 52
Embleton. Hart 3B 48
Embleton. Nmbd 7K 61
Embo. High 4J 79
Emborough. Som 8E 18
Embo Street. High 4J 79
Embsay. N Yor 2J 41
Emery Down. Hants 5L 9
Emley. W Yor 6L 41
Emmbrook. Wok 7E 20
Emmer Green. Read 6E 20
Emmington. Oxon 3E 20
Emneth. Norf 1A 30
Emneth Hungate. Norf 1B 30
Empingham. Rut 1G 29
Empshott. Hants 2E 10
**Emsworth**. Hants 5E 10
Enborne. W Ber 7B 20
Enborne Row. W Ber 7B 20
Enchmarsh. Shrp 2D 26
Enderby. Leics 2C 28
Endmoor. Cumb 7D 46
Endon. Staf 4H 35
Endon Bank. Staf 4H 35
**Enfield**. G Lon 4L 21
Enfield Wash. G Lon 4L 21
Enford. Wilts 8K 19
Engine Common. S Glo 5E 18
Englefield. W Ber 6D 20
Englefield Green. Surr 6G 21
Englesea-brook. Ches E 4F 34
English Bicknor. Glos 2D 18
Englishcombe. Bath 7F 18
English Frankton. Shrp 7C 34
Enham Alamein. Hants 1A 10
Enmore. Som 2M 7
Ennerdale Bridge. Cumb 3K 45
Enniscaven. Corn 6B 4
**Enniskillen**. Ferm 6C 92
Enoch. Dum 1C 52
Enochdhu. Per 1D 66
Ensay. Arg 3J 63
Ensbury. Bour 6J 9
Ensdon. Shrp 8C 34
Ensis. Devn 3E 6
Enson. Staf 7H 35
Enstone. Oxon 1A 20
Enterkinfoot. Dum 1C 52
Enville. Staf 3G 27
Eolaigearraidh. W Isl 5D 74
Eorabus. Arg 5J 63
Eoropaidh. W Isl 5J 83
Epney. Glos 2F 18
Epperstone. Notts 5D 36
**Epping**. Essx 3A 22
Epping Green. Essx 3M 21
Epping Green. Herts 3K 21
Epping Upland. Essx 3M 21
Eppleby. N Yor 4K 47
Eppleworth. E Yor 4H 43
**Epsom**. Surr 7K 21
Epwell. Oxon 7A 28
Epworth. N Lin 7E 42
Epworth Turbary. N Lin 7E 42
Erbistock. Wrex 5B 34
Erbusaig. High 3J 69
Erchless Castle. High 1E 70
Erdington. W Mid 2K 27
Eredine. Arg 7D 64
Erganagh. Derr 4C 92
Eriboll. High 6G 85
Ericstane. Dum 8J 59
Eridge Green. E Sus 2B 12
Erines. Arg 2H 57
Eriswell. Suff 4D 30
**Erith**. G Lon 6B 22
Erlestoke. Wilts 8H 19
Ermine. Linc 2G 37
Ermington. Devn 6J 5
Ernesettle. Plym 6G 5
Erpingham. Norf 6H 39
Erriott Wood. Kent 8F 22
Errogie. High 3F 70
Errol. Per 5F 66
Errol Station. Per 5F 66
**Erskine**. Ren 2C 58
**Erskine Bridge**. Ren 2C 58
Ervie. Dum 5F 50
Erwarton. Suff 8J 31
Erwood. Powy 8K 25
Eryholme. N Yor 5M 47
Eryrys. Den 5M 33
Escalls. Corn 6G 3
Escomb. Dur 8E 54
Escrick. N Yor 3D 42
Esgair. Carm
nr. Carmarthen 4K 15
nr. St Clears 5J 15
Esgairgeiliog. Powy 2G 25
Esh. Dur 7E 54
**Esher**. Surr 7J 21
Esholt. W Yor 3K 41
Eshott. Nmbd 2F 54
Eshton. N Yor 2H 41
Esh Winning. Dur 7E 54
Eskadale. High 2E 70
Eskbank. Midl 3M 59
Eskdale Green. Cumb 4L 45
Eskdalemuir. Dum 2G 53
Eskham. Linc 8L 43
Esknish. Arg 3C 56
Esk Valley. N Yor 5F 48
Eslington Hall. Nmbd 8H 61
Esprick. Lanc 4C 40
Essendine. Rut 8H 37
Essendon. Herts 3K 21
Essich. High 2G 71
Essington. Staf 1H 27
**Eston**. Red C 4C 48
Estover. Plym 6H 5
Eswick. Shet 2E 90
Etal. Nmbd 6G 61
Etchilhampton. Wilts 7J 19
Etchingham. E Sus 3D 12
Etchinghill. Kent 2H 13
Etchinghill. Staf 8J 35
Etherley Dene. Dur 3K 47
Ethie Haven. Ang 3K 67
Etling Green. Norf 8G 39
Etloe. Glos 3E 18
**Eton**. Wind 6G 21
Eton Wick. Wind 6G 21
Etteridge. High 6G 71
Ettersgill. Dur 3G 47
Ettiley Heath. Ches E 3F 34
Ettington. Warw 7L 27
Etton. E Yor 3G 43
Etton. Pet 1J 29
Ettrick. Bord 8L 59
Ettrickbridge. Bord 7A 60
Etwall. Derbs 6L 35
Eudon Burnell. Shrp 3F 26
Eudon George. Shrp 3E 26
Euston. Suff 4E 30
Euxton. Lanc 6D 40
Evanstown. B'end 6J 17
Evanton. High 7G 79
Evedon. Linc 5H 37
Evelix. High 4H 79
Evendine. Here 7F 26
Evenjobb. Powy 5A 26
Evenley. Nptn 8C 28
Evenlode. Glos 1L 19
Even Swindon. Swin 5K 19
Evenwood. Dur 3K 47
Evenwood Gate. Dur 3K 47
Everbay. Orkn 7F 88
Evercreech. Som 2E 8
Everdon. Nptn 6C 28
Everingham. E Yor 3F 42
Everleigh. Wilts 8L 19
Everley. N Yor 7G 49
Eversholt. C Beds 8G 29
Evershot. Dors 5D 8
Eversley. Hants 7E 20
Eversley Centre. Hants 7E 20
Eversley Cross. Hants 7E 20
Everthorpe. E Yor 4G 43
Everton. C Beds 6K 29
Everton. Hants 6L 9
Everton. Mers 8B 40
Everton. Notts 8D 42
Evertown. Dum 4H 53
Evesbatch. Here 7E 26
**Evesham**. Worc 7J 27
Evington. Leic 1D 28
Ewden Village. S Yor 8L 41
Ewdness. Shrp 2F 26
**Ewell**. Surr 7K 21
Ewell Minnis. Kent 1J 13
Ewelme. Oxon 4D 20
Ewen. Glos 4J 19
Ewenny. V Glam 7J 17
Ewerby. Linc 5J 37
Ewes. Dum 2H 53
Ewesley. Nmbd 2D 54
Ewhurst. Surr 1H 11
Ewhurst Green. E Sus 3D 12
Ewhurst Green. Surr 2H 11
Ewlo. Flin 3A 34
Ewloe. Flin 3A 34
Ewood Bridge. Lanc 5F 40
Eworthy. Devn 6D 6
Ewshot. Hants 8F 20
Ewyas Harold. Here 1B 18
Exbourne. Devn 5F 6
Exbury. Hants 5B 10
Exceat. E Sus 6B 12
Exebridge. Som 3J 7
Exelby. N Yor 7L 47
**Exeter**. Devn 109 (6J 7)
Exeter Airport. Devn 6K 7
Exford. Som 2H 7
Exfords Green. Shrp 1C 26
Exhall. Warw 6K 27
Exlade Street. Oxon 5D 20
Exminster. Devn 7J 7
**Exmouth**. Devn 7K 7
Exnaboe. Shet 6D 90
Exning. Suff 5C 30
Exton. Devn 7J 7
Exton. Hants 3D 10
Exton. Rut 8G 37
Exton. Som 2J 7
Exwick. Devn 6J 7
Eyam. Derbs 2L 35
Eydon. Nptn 6C 28
Eye. Here 5C 26
Eye. Pet 1K 29
Eye. Suff 4H 31
Eye Green. Pet 1K 29
Eyemouth. Bord 3G 61
Eyeworth. C Beds 7K 29
Eyhorne Street. Kent 8E 22
Eyke. Suff 6K 31
Eynesbury. Cambs 6J 29
Eynort. High 3E 68
Eynsford. Kent 7B 22
Eynsham. Oxon 3B 20
Eyre. High
on Isle of Skye 8F 76
on Raasay 2G 69
Eythorne. Kent 1J 13
Eyton. Here 5C 26
Eyton. Shrp
nr. Bishop's Castle 3B 26
nr. Shrewsbury 8B 34
Eyton. Wrex 5B 34
Eyton on Severn. Shrp 1D 26
Eyton upon the Weald Moors.
Telf 8E 34

## F

Faccombe. Hants 8A 20
Faceby. N Yor 5B 48
Faddiley. Ches E 4D 34
Fadmoor. N Yor 7D 48
Fagwyr. Swan 4F 16
Faichem. High 5C 70
Faifley. W Dun 2D 58
Fail. S Ayr 7C 58
Failand. N Som 6D 18
Failford. S Ayr 7C 58
**Failsworth**. G Man 7H 41
Fairbourne. Gwyn 1F 24
Fairbourne Heath. Kent 8E 22
Fairburn. N Yor 5B 42
Fairfield. Derbs 2J 35
Fairfield. Kent 3F 12
Fairfield. Worc
nr. Bromsgrove 4H 27
nr. Evesham 7J 27
Fairford. Glos 3K 19
Fair Green. Norf 8C 38
Fair Hill. Cumb 8K 53
Fairhill. S Lan 4F 58
Fair Isle Airport. Shet 2M 89
Fairlands. Surr 8G 21
Fairlie. N Ayr 4M 57
Fairlight. E Sus 4E 12
Fairlight Cove. E Sus 4E 12
Fairmile. Devn 6K 7
Fairmile. Surr 7J 21
Fairmilehead. Edin 3L 59
Fair Oak. Devn 4K 7
Fair Oak. Hants
nr. Eastleigh 4B 10
nr. Kingsclere 7C 20
Fairoak. Staf 6F 34
Fair Oak Green. Hants 7D 20
Fairseat. Kent 7C 22
Fairstead. Essx 2D 22
Fairstead. Norf 8C 38
Fairwarp. E Sus 3A 12
Fairwater. Card 7L 17
Fairy Cross. Devn 3D 6
Fakenham. Norf 6F 38
Fakenham Magna. Suff 4F 30
Fala. Midl 3B 60
Fala Dam. Midl 3B 60
Falcon. Here 8E 26
Faldingworth. Linc 1H 37
Falfield. S Glo 4E 18
Y Fali. IOA 3B 32
Falkenham. Suff 8J 31
**Falkirk**. Falk 1G 59
Falkland. Fife 7F 66
Fallin. Stir 8B 66
Fallowfield. G Man 8G 41
Falmer. E Sus 5L 11
**Falmouth**. Corn 5M 3
Falsgrave. N Yor 7H 49
Falstone. Nmbd 3M 53
Fanagmore. High 7D 84
Fancott. C Beds 1H 21
Fanellan. High 1E 70
Fangdale Beck. N Yor 6C 48
Fangfoss. E Yor 2E 42
Fankerton. Falk 1F 58
Fanmore. Arg 3K 63
Fanner's Green. Essx 2C 22
Fannich Lodge. High 7C 78
Fans. Bord 5D 60
Farcet. Cambs 2K 29
Far Cotton. Nptn 6E 28
**Fareham**. Hants 5C 10
Farewell. Staf 8J 35
Far Forest. Worc 4F 26
Farforth. Linc 2L 37
Far Green. Glos 3F 18
Far Hoarcross. Staf 7K 35
Faringdon. Oxon 4L 19
Farington. Lanc 5D 40
Farlam. Cumb 6K 53
Farleigh. N Som 7C 18
Farleigh. Surr 7L 21
Farleigh Hungerford. Som 8G 19
Farleigh Wallop. Hants 1D 10
Farleigh Wick. Wilts 7G 19
Farlesthorpe. Linc 2A 38
Farleton. Cumb 7D 46
Farleton. Lanc 1D 40
Farley. High 1E 70
Farley. Shrp
nr. Shrewsbury 1B 26
nr. Telford 1E 26
Farley. Staf 5J 35
Farley. Wilts 3L 9
Farley Green. Suff 6D 30
Farley Green. Surr 1H 11
Farley Hill. Wok 7E 20
Farley's End. Glos 2F 18
Farlington. N Yor 1D 42
Farlington. Port 5D 10
Farlow. Shrp 3E 26
Farmborough. Bath 7E 18
Farmcote. Glos 1J 19
Farmcote. Shrp 2F 26
Farmington. Glos 2K 19
Far Moor. G Man 7D 40
Farmoor. Oxon 3B 20
Farmtown. Mor 8E 80
Farnah Green. Derbs 5M 35
Farnborough. G Lon 7M 21
**Farnborough**. Hants 8F 20
Farnborough. Warw 7B 28
Farnborough. W Ber 5B 20
Farncombe. Surr 1G 11
Farndish. Bed 5G 29
Farndon. Ches W 4C 34
Farndon. Notts 4E 36
Farnell. Ang 2K 67
Farnham. Dors 4H 9
Farnham. Essx 1A 22
Farnham. N Yor 1A 42
Farnham. Suff 5K 31
**Farnham**. Surr 1F 10
Farnham Common. Buck 5G 21
Farnham Green. Essx 1A 22
Farnham Royal. Buck 5G 21
Farnhill. N Yor 3J 41
Farningham. Kent 7B 22
Farnley. N Yor 3L 41
Farnley Tyas. W Yor 6K 41
Farnsfield. Notts 4D 36
**Farnworth**. G Man 7F 40
Farnworth. Hal 1D 34
Far Oakridge. Glos 3H 19
Farr. High
nr. Bettyhill 5K 85
nr. Inverness 2G 71
nr. Kingussie 5J 71
Farraline. High 3F 70
Farringdon. Devn 6K 7
Farrington. Dors 4G 9
Farrington Gurney. Bath 8E 18
Far Sawrey. Cumb 6B 46
Farsley. W Yor 4L 41
Farthinghoe. Nptn 8C 28
Farthingstone. Nptn 6D 28
Farthorpe. Linc 2K 37
Fartown. W Yor 6K 41
Farway. Devn 6L 7
Fasag. High 8K 77
Fascadale. High 8G 69
Fasnacloich. Arg 3E 64
Fassfern. High 8M 69
Fatfield. Tyne 6G 55
Faugh. Cumb 6K 53
Fauld. Staf 7K 35
Fauldhouse. W Lot 3H 59
Faulkbourne. Essx 2D 22
Faulkland. Som 8F 18
Fauls. Shrp 6D 34
Faverdale. Darl 4L 47
**Faversham**. Kent 7G 23
Fawdington. N Yor 8B 48
Fawfieldhead. Staf 3J 35
Fawkham Green. Kent 7B 22
Fawler. Oxon 2A 20
Fawley. Buck 5E 20
**Fawley**. Hants 5B 10
Fawley. W Ber 5A 20
Fawley Chapel. Here 1D 18
Fawton. Corn 5D 4
Faxfleet. E Yor 5F 42
Faygate. W Sus 2K 11
Fazakerley. Mers 8B 40
Fazeley. Staf 1K 27
Feagour. High 6F 70
Fearann Dhomhnaill. High 5H 69
Fearby. N Yor 7K 47
Fearn. High 6J 79
Fearnan. Per 3M 65
Fearnbeg. High 8J 77
Fearnhead. Warr 8E 40
Fearnmore. High 7J 77
Featherstone. Staf 1H 27
**Featherstone**. W Yor 5B 42
Featherstone Castle. Nmbd 5L 53
Feckenham. Worc 5J 27
Feeny. Caus 3E 92
Feering. Essx 1E 22
Feetham. N Yor 6H 47
Feizor. N Yor 1F 40
Felbridge. Surr 2L 11
Felbrigg. Norf 6J 39
Felcourt. Surr 1L 11
Felden. Herts 3H 21
Felhampton. Shrp 3C 26
Felindre. Carm
nr. Llandeilo 2E 16
nr. Llandovery 1F 16
nr. Newcastle Emlyn 3K 15
Felindre. Powy 4L 25
Felindre. Swan 4F 16
Felindre Farchog. Pemb 3H 15
Felinfach. Cdgn 1M 15
Felinfach. Powy 1K 17
Felinfoel. Carm 6M 15
Felingwmisaf. Carm 4M 15
Felingwmuchaf. Carm 4M 15
Y Felinheli. Gwyn 4E 32
Felin Newydd. Powy
nr. Newtown 2K 25
nr. Oswestry 8M 33
Felin Wnda. Cdgn 2K 15
Felinwynt. Cdgn 1J 15
Felixkirk. N Yor 7B 48
**Felixstowe**. Suff 8J 31
Felixstowe Ferry. Suff 8K 31
Felkington. Nmbd 5G 61
Fell End. Cumb 6F 46
**Felling**. Tyne 5F 54
Fell Side. Cumb 8H 53
Felmersham. Bed 6G 29
Felmingham. Norf 7J 39
Felpham. W Sus 6G 11
Felsham. Suff 6F 30
Felsted. Essx 1C 22
**Feltham**. G Lon 6J 21
Felthamhill. Surr 6H 21
Felthorpe. Norf 8H 39
Felton. Here 7D 26
Felton. N Som 7D 18
Felton. Nmbd 1E 54
Felton Butler. Shrp 8B 34
Feltwell. Norf 2D 30
Fenay Bridge. W Yor 6K 41
Fence. Lanc 4G 41
Fence Houses. Tyne 6G 55
Fencott. Oxon 2C 20
Fen Ditton. Cambs 5A 30
Fen Drayton. Cambs 5L 29
Fen End. Linc 7K 37
Fen End. W Mid 4L 27
Fenham. Nmbd 5H 61
Fenham. Tyne 5F 54
Fenhouses. Linc 5K 37
Feniscowles. Bkbn 5E 40
Feniton. Devn 6K 7
Fenn Green. Shrp 3F 26
**Y Fenni**. Mon 2B 18
Fenn's Bank. Wrex 6D 34
Fenn Street. Medw 6D 22
Fenny Bentley. Derbs 4K 35
Fenny Bridges. Devn 6L 7
Fenny Compton. Warw 6B 28
Fenny Drayton. Leics 2M 27
Fenny Stratford. Mil 8F 28
Fenrother. Nmbd 2E 54
Fenstanton. Cambs 5L 29
Fen Street. Norf 2G 31
Fenton. Cambs 4L 29
Fenton. Cumb 6K 53
Fenton. Linc
nr. Caythorpe 4F 36
nr. Saxilby 2F 36
Fenton. Nmbd 6G 61
Fenton. Notts 1E 36
Fenton. Stoke 5G 35
Fentonadle. Corn 4C 4
Fenton Barns. E Lot 1C 60
Fenwick. E Ayr 5C 58
Fenwick. Nmbd
nr. Berwick-upon-Tweed
5H 61
nr. Hexham 4D 54
Fenwick. S Yor 6C 42
Feochaig. Arg 8G 57
Feock. Corn 5M 3
Feolin Ferry. Arg 3D 56
Feorlan. Arg 1B 50
Ferindonald. High 5H 69
Feriniquarrie. High 8C 76
Fern. Ang 1H 67
**Ferndale**. Rhon 5J 17
**Ferndown**. Dors 5J 9
Ferness. High 1K 71
Fernham. Oxon 4L 19
Fernhill. W Sus 1L 11
Fernhill Heath. Worc 6G 27
Fernhurst. W Sus 3F 10
Fernieflatt. Abers 8H 73
Ferniegair. S Lan 4F 58
Fernilea. High 2E 68
Fernilee. Derbs 2J 35
Ferrensby. N Yor 1A 42
Ferriby Sluice. N Lin 5G 43
Ferring. W Sus 5H 11
Ferrybridge. W Yor 5B 42
Ferryden. Ang 2L 67
Ferry Hill. Cambs 3L 29
Ferryhill. Aber 5J 73
**Ferryhill**. Dur 8F 54
Ferryhill Station. Dur 8G 55
Ferryside. Carm 5K 15
Ferryton. High 7G 79
Fersfield. Norf 3G 31
Fersit. High 8D 70
Y Ferwig. Cdgn 2H 15
Feshiebridge. High 5J 71
Fetcham. Surr 8J 21
Fetterangus. Abers 8J 81
Fettercairn. Abers 8F 72
Fewcott. Oxon 1C 20
Fewston. N Yor 2K 41
Ffairfach. Carm 2F 16
Ffair Rhos. Cdgn 6G 25
Ffaldybrenin. Carm 8F 24
Ffarmers. Carm 8F 24
Ffawyddog. Powy 3M 17
**Y Fflint**. Flin 3M 33
Ffodun. Powy 2M 25
Ffont-y-gari. V Glam 8K 17
Y Ffor. Gwyn 7C 32
Fforest. Carm 4E 16
Fforest-fach. Swan 5F 16
Fforest Goch. Neat 4G 17
Ffostrasol. Cdgn 2K 15
Ffos-y-ffin. Cdgn 6D 24
Ffrith. Flin 4A 34
Ffwl-y-mwn. V Glam 8K 17
Ffynnon-ddrain. Carm 4L 15
Ffynnongroyw. Flin 2L 33
Ffynnon Gynydd. Powy 8L 25
Ffynnon-oer. Cdgn 1M 15
Fiag Lodge. High 1E 78
Fidden. Arg 5J 63
Fiddington. Glos 8H 27
Fiddington. Som 1M 7
Fiddleford. Dors 4G 9
Fiddlers Hamlet. Essx 3A 22
Field. Staf 6J 35
Field Assarts. Oxon 2M 19
Field Broughton. Cumb 7B 46
Field Dalling. Norf 6G 39
Field Head. Leics 1B 28
Fieldhead. Cumb 8J 53
Fifehead Magdalen. Dors 3F 8
Fifehead Neville. Dors 4F 8
Fifehead St Quintin. Dors 4F 8
Fife Keith. Mor 8D 80
Fifield. Oxon 2L 19
Fifield. Wilts 8K 19
Fifield. Wind 6G 21
Fifield Bavant. Wilts 3J 9
Figheldean. Wilts 1K 9
Filby. Norf 8L 39
Filey. N Yor 7J 49
Filford. Dors 6C 8
Filgrave. Mil 7F 28
Filkins. Oxon 3L 19
Filleigh. Devn
nr. Crediton 4G 7
nr. South Molton 3F 6
Fillingham. Linc 1G 37
Fillongley. Warw 3L 27
Filton. S Glo 6E 18
Fimber. E Yor 1F 42
Finavon. Ang 2H 67
Fincham. Norf 1C 30
Finchampstead. Wok 7E 20
Fincharn. Arg 7D 64
Finchdean. Hants 4E 10
Finchingfield. Essx 8C 30
**Finchley**. G Lon 4K 21
Findern. Derbs 6M 35
Findhorn. Mor 7L 79
Findhorn Bridge. High 3J 71
Findochty. Mor 7D 80
Findo Gask. Per 5D 66
Findon. Abers 6J 73
Findon. W Sus 5J 11
Findon Mains. High 7G 79
Findon Valley. W Sus 5J 11
Finedon. Nptn 4G 29
Fingal Street. Suff 4J 31
Fingest. Buck 4E 20
Finghall. N Yor 7K 47
Fingland. Cumb 6G 53
Fingland. Dum 8F 58
Finglesham. Kent 8K 23
Fingringhoe. Essx 1G 23
Finiskaig. High 6K 69
Finmere. Oxon 8D 28
Finnart. Per 2K 65
Finningham. Suff 5G 31
Finningley. S Yor 8D 42
Finnygaud. Abers 8F 80
**Finsbury**. G Lon 5L 21
Finstall. Worc 5H 27
Finsthwaite. Cumb 7B 46
Finstock. Oxon 2A 20
Finstown. Orkn 8C 88
Fintona. Ferm 5D 92
Fintry. Abers 8G 81
Fintry. D'dee 4H 67
Fintry. Stir 1E 58
Finvoy. Caus 3F 93
Finwood. Warw 5K 27
Finzean. Abers 6F 72
Fionnphort. Arg 5J 63
Fionnsabhagh. W Isl 5B 76
Firbeck. S Yor 1C 36
Firby. N Yor
nr. Bedale 7L 47
nr. Malton 1E 42
Firgrove. G Man 6H 41
Firle. E Sus 5A 12
Firsby. Linc 3A 38
Firsdown. Wilts 2L 9
First Coast. High 4L 77
Firth. Shet 6J 91
Fir Tree. Dur 8E 54
Fishbourne. IOW 6C 10
Fishbourne. W Sus 5F 10
Fishburn. Dur 8G 55
Fishcross. Clac 8B 66
Fisherford. Abers 2F 72
Fisherrow. E Lot 2M 59
Fisher's Pond. Hants 3B 10
Fisher's Row. Lanc 3C 40
Fisherstreet. W Sus 2G 11
Fisherton. High 8H 79
Fisherton. S Ayr 8A 58
Fisherton de la Mere. Wilts 2H 9
Fishguard. Pemb 3F 14
Fishlake. S Yor 6D 42
Fishley. Norf 8L 39
Fishnish. Arg 3A 64
Fishpond Bottom. Dors 6B 8
Fishponds. Bris 6E 18
Fishpool. Glos 1E 18
Fishpool. G Man 6G 41
Fishpools. Powy 6L 25
Fishtoft. Linc 5L 37
Fishtoft Drove. Linc 5L 37
Fishwick. Bord 4G 61
Fiskavaig. High 2E 68
Fiskerton. Linc 2H 37
Fiskerton. Notts 4E 36
Fitch. Shet 3D 90
Fitling. E Yor 4K 43
Fittleton. Wilts 1K 9
Fittleworth. W Sus 4H 11
Fitton End. Cambs 8M 37
Fitz. Shrp 8C 34
Fitzhead. Som 3L 7
Fitzwilliam. W Yor 6B 42
Fiunary. High 3M 63
Five Ash Down. E Sus 3A 12
Five Ashes. E Sus 3B 12
Five Bells. Som 1K 7
Five Bridges. Here 7E 26
Fivehead. Som 3B 8
Fivelanes. Corn 7B 6
Fivemiletown. M Ulst 6D 92
Five Oak Green. Kent 1C 12
Five Oaks. W Sus 3H 11
Five Roads. Carm 6L 15
Five Ways. Warw 4L 27
Flack's Green. Essx 2D 22
Flackwell Heath. Buck 5F 20
Fladbury. Worc 7H 27
Fladda. Shet 5H 91
Fladdabister. Shet 4E 90
Flagg. Derbs 3K 35
Flamborough. E Yor 8K 49
Flamstead. Herts 2H 21
Flansham. W Sus 5G 11
Flasby. N Yor 2H 41
Flash. Staf 3J 35
Flashader. High 8E 76
The Flatt. Cumb 4K 53
Flaunden. Herts 3H 21
Flawborough. Notts 5E 36
Flawith. N Yor 1B 42
Flax Bourton. N Som 7D 18
Flaxby. N Yor 2A 42
Flaxholme. Derbs 5M 35
Flaxley. Glos 2E 18
Flaxley Green. Staf 8J 35
Flaxpool. Som 2L 7
Flaxton. N Yor 1D 42
Fleck. Shet 6D 90
Fleckney. Leics 2D 28
Flecknoe. Warw 5C 28
Fledborough. Notts 2F 36
Fleet. Dors 7E 8
**Fleet**. Hants
nr. Farnborough 8F 20
Fleet. Hants
nr. South Hayling 5E 10
Fleet. Linc 7L 37
Fleet Hargate. Linc 7L 37
Fleetville. Herts 3J 21
**Fleetwood**. Lanc 3B 40
Fleggburgh. Norf 8L 39
Fleisirin. W Isl 8J 83
Flemingston. V Glam 8K 17
Flemington. S Lan
nr. Glasgow 3E 58
nr. Strathaven 5F 58
Flempton. Suff 5E 30
Fleoideabhagh. W Isl 5B 76
Fletcher's Green. Kent 1B 12
Fletchertown. Cumb 7G 53
Fletching. E Sus 3M 11
Fleuchary. High 4H 79
Flexbury. Corn 5B 6
Flexford. Surr 1G 11
Flimby. Cumb 8E 52
Flimwell. E Sus 2D 12
**Flint**. Flin 3M 33
Flintham. Notts 5E 36
Flint Mountain. Flin 3M 33
Flinton. E Yor 4K 43
Flintsham. Here 6B 26
Flishinghurst. Kent 2D 12
Flitcham. Norf 7D 38
Flitton. C Beds 8H 29
**Flitwick**. C Beds 8H 29
Flixborough. N Lin 6F 42
Flixton. G Man 8F 40
Flixton. N Yor 8H 49
Flixton. Suff 3K 31
Flockton. W Yor 6L 41
Flodden. Nmbd 6G 61
Flodigarry. High 6F 76
Flood's Ferry. Cambs 2L 29
Flookburgh. Cumb 8B 46
Flordon. Norf 2H 31
Flore. Nptn 5D 28
Flotterton. Nmbd 1C 54
Flowton. Suff 7G 31
Flushing. Abers 1K 73
Flushing. Corn 5M 3
Fluxton. Devn 6K 7
Flyford Flavell. Worc 6H 27
Fobbing. Thur 5D 22
Fochabers. Mor 8C 80
Fochriw. Cphy 4L 17
Fockerby. N Lin 6F 42
Fodderty. High 8F 78
Foddington. Som 3D 8
Foel. Powy 1J 25
Foffarty. Ang 3H 67
Foggathorpe. E Yor 4E 42
Fogo. Bord 5E 60
Fogorig. Bord 5E 60
Foindle. High 7D 84
Folda. Ang 1E 66
Fole. Staf 6J 35
Foleshill. W Mid 3A 28
Foley Park. Worc 4G 27
Folke. Dors 4E 8
**Folkestone**. Kent 109 (2J 13)
Folkingham. Linc 6H 37
Folkington. E Sus 5B 12
Folksworth. Cambs 3J 29
Folkton. N Yor 8H 49
Folla Rule. Abers 2G 73
Follifoot. N Yor 2M 41
The Folly. Herts 2J 21
Folly Cross. Devn 5D 6
Folly Gate. Devn 6E 6
Fonmon. V Glam 8K 17
Fonthill Bishop. Wilts 2H 9
Fonthill Gifford. Wilts 2H 9
Fontmell Magna. Dors 4G 9
Fontwell. W Sus 5G 11
Font-y-gary. V Glam 8K 17
Foodieash. Fife 6G 67
Foolow. Derbs 2K 35
Footdee. Aber 5J 73
Footherley. Staf 1K 27
Foots Cray. G Lon 6A 22
Forbestown. Abers 4C 72
Force Forge. Cumb 6B 46
Force Mills. Cumb 6B 46
Forcett. N Yor 4K 47
Ford. Arg 7C 64
Ford. Buck 3E 20
Ford. Derbs 1B 36
Ford. Devn
nr. Bideford 3D 6
nr. Holbeton 6J 5
nr. Salcombe 7K 5
Ford. Glos 1J 19

Ford. *Nmbd* 6G **61**
Ford. *Plym* 6G **5**
Ford. *Shrp* 8C **34**
Ford. *Som*
nr. Wells 8D **18**
nr. Wiveliscombe 3K **7**
Ford. *Staf* 4J **35**
Ford. *W Sus* 5H **11**
Ford. *Wilts*
nr. Chippenham 6G **19**
nr. Salisbury 2K **9**
Forda. *Devn* 2D **6**
Ford Barton. *Devn* 4J **7**
Fordcombe. *Kent* 1B **12**
Fordell. *Fife* 1K **59**
Forden. *Powy* 2M **25**
Ford End. *Essx* 2C **22**
Forder Green. *Devn* 5K **5**
Ford Green. *Lanc* 3C **40**
Fordham. *Cambs* 4C **30**
Fordham. *Essx* 1F **22**
Fordham. *Norf* 2C **30**
Fordham Heath. *Essx* 1F **22**
Ford Heath. *Shrp* 8C **34**
Fordhouses. *W Mid* 1H **27**
Fordie. *Per* 5A **66**
Fordingbridge. *Hants* 4K **9**
Fordington. *Linc* 2M **37**
Fordon. *E Yor* 8H **49**
Fordoun. *Abers* 8G **73**
Ford Street. *Essx* 1F **22**
Ford Street. *Som* 4L **7**
Fordton. *Devn* 6H **7**
Fordwells. *Oxon* 2M **19**
Fordwich. *Kent* 8H **23**
Fordyce. *Abers* 7E **80**
Forebridge. *Staf* 7H **35**
Foreglen. *Caus* 3E **92**
Foremark. *Derbs* 7M **35**
Forest. *N Yor* 5L **47**
Forestburn Gate. *Nmbd* 2D **54**
Foresterseat. *Mor* 8A **80**
Forest Green. *Glos* 4G **19**
Forest Green. *Surr* 1J **11**
Forest Hall. *Cumb* 5D **46**
Forest Head. *Cumb* 6K **53**
Forest Hill. *Oxon* 3C **20**
Forest-in-Teesdale. *Dur* 3G **47**
Forest Lodge. *Per* 8K **71**
Forest Mill. *Clac* 8C **66**
Forest Row. *E Sus* 2M **11**
Forestside. *W Sus* 4E **10**
Forest Town. *Notts* 3C **36**
**Forfar**. *Ang* 2H **67**
Forgandenny. *Per* 6D **66**
Forge. *Powy* 3G **25**
The Forge. *Here* 6B **26**
Forge Side. *Torf* 4M **17**
Forgewood. *N Lan* 4F **58**
Forgie. *Mor* 8C **80**
Forgue. *Abers* 1F **72**
Forkill. *New M* 7G **93**
**Formby**. *Mers* 7B **40**
Forncett End. *Norf* 2H **31**
Forncett St Mary. *Norf* 2H **31**
Forncett St Peter. *Norf* 2H **31**
Forneth. *Per* 3D **66**
Fornham All Saints. *Suff* 5E **30**
Fornham St Martin. *Suff* 5E **30**
Forres. *Mor* 8L **79**
Forrestfield. *N Lan* 3G **59**
Forrest Lodge. *Dum* 3L **51**
Forsbrook. *Staf* 5H **35**
Forse. *High* 8D **86**
Forsinard. *High* 7L **85**
Forss. *High* 5B **86**
The Forstal. *Kent* 2G **13**
Forston. *Dors* 6E **8**
Fort Augustus. *High* 5D **70**
Forteviot. *Per* 6D **66**
Fort George. *High* 8H **79**
Forth. *S Lan* 4H **59**
Forthampton. *Glos* 8G **27**
Forthay. *Glos* 4F **18**
Fortingall. *Per* 3M **65**
Fort Matilda. *Inv* 2A **58**
Forton. *Hants* 1B **10**
Forton. *Lanc* 2C **40**
Forton. *Shrp* 8C **34**
Forton. *Som* 5B **8**
Forton. *Staf* 7F **34**
Forton Heath. *Shrp* 8C **34**
Fortrie. *Abers* 1F **72**
Fortrose. *High* 8H **79**
Fortuneswell. *Dors* 8E **8**
**Fort William**. *High* 8B **70**
Forty Green. *Buck* 4G **21**
Forty Hill. *G Lon* 4L **21**
Forward Green. *Suff* 6G **31**
Fosbury. *Wilts* 8M **19**
Foscot. *Oxon* 1L **19**
Fosdyke. *Linc* 6L **37**
Foss. *Per* 2A **66**
Fossebridge. *Glos* 2J **19**
Foster Street. *Essx* 3A **22**
Foston. *Derbs* 6K **35**
Foston. *Leics* 2D **28**
Foston. *Linc* 5F **36**
Foston. *N Yor* 1D **42**
Foston on the Wolds. *E Yor* 2J **43**
Fotherby. *Linc* 8L **43**
Fothergill. *Cumb* 8E **52**
Fotheringhay. *Nptn* 2H **29**
Foubister. *Orkn* 1G **87**
Foula Airport. *Shet* 4B **90**
Foul Anchor. *Cambs* 8A **38**
Foulbridge. *Cumb* 7J **53**
Foulden. *Norf* 2D **30**
Foulden. *Bord* 4G **61**
Foul Mile. *E Sus* 4C **12**
Foulridge. *Lanc* 3G **41**
Foulsham. *Norf* 7G **39**
Fountainhall. *Bord* 5B **60**
The Four Alls. *Shrp* 6E **34**
Four Ashes. *Staf*
nr. Cannock 1H **27**
nr. Kinver 3G **27**
Four Ashes. *Suff* 4G **31**
Four Crosses. *Powy*
nr. Llanerfyl 2K **25**
nr. Llanymynech 8A **34**
Four Crosses. *Staf* 1H **27**
Four Elms. *Kent* 1A **12**
Four Forks. *Som* 2M **7**
Four Gotes. *Cambs* 8A **38**
Four Lane End. *S Yor* 7L **41**
Four Lane Ends. *Lanc* 2D **40**
Four Lanes. *Corn* 5K **3**
Fourlanes End. *Ches E* 4G **35**
Four Marks. *Hants* 2D **10**
Four Mile Bridge. *IOA* 3B **32**
Four Oaks. *E Sus* 3E **12**
Four Oaks. *Glos* 1E **18**
Four Oaks. *W Mid* 3L **27**
Four Roads. *Carm* 6L **15**
Four Roads. *IOM* 8B **44**
Fourstones. *Nmbd* 5B **54**
Four Throws. *Kent* 3D **12**
Fovant. *Wilts* 3J **9**
Foveran. *Abers* 3J **73**
Fowey. *Corn* 6D **4**
Fowlershill. *Aber* 4J **73**
Fowley Common. *Warr* 8E **40**
Fowlis. *Ang* 4G **67**
Fowlis Wester. *Per* 5C **66**
Fowlmere. *Cambs* 7M **29**
Fownhope. *Here* 8D **26**
Fox Corner. *Surr* 8G **21**
Foxcote. *Glos* 2J **19**
Foxcote. *Som* 8F **18**
Foxdale. *IOM* 7B **44**
Foxearth. *Essx* 7E **30**
Foxfield. *Cumb* 6M **45**
Foxham. *Wilts* 6H **19**
Fox Hatch. *Essx* 4B **22**
Foxhole. *Corn* 6B **4**
Foxholes. *N Yor* 8H **49**
Foxhunt Green. *E Sus* 4B **12**
Fox Lane. *Hants* 8F **20**
Foxley. *Norf* 7G **39**
Foxley. *Nptn* 6D **28**
Foxley. *Wilts* 5G **19**
Foxlydiate. *Worc* 5J **27**
Fox Street. *Essx* 1G **23**
Foxt. *Staf* 5J **35**
Foxton. *Cambs* 7M **29**
Foxton. *Dur* 3A **48**
Foxton. *Leics* 3D **28**
Foxton. *N Yor* 6B **48**
Foxup. *N Yor* 8G **47**
Foxwist Green. *Ches W* 3E **34**
Foxwood. *Shrp* 4E **26**
Foy. *Here* 1D **18**
Foyers. *High* 3E **70**
Foynesfield. *High* 8J **79**
Fraddam. *Corn* 5J **3**
Fraddon. *Corn* 6B **4**
Fradley. *Staf* 8K **35**
Fradley South. *Staf* 8K **35**
Fradswell. *Staf* 6H **35**
Fraisthorpe. *E Yor* 1J **43**
Framfield. *E Sus* 3A **12**
Framingham Earl. *Norf* 1J **31**
Framingham Pigot. *Norf* 1J **31**
Framlingham. *Suff* 5J **31**
Frampton. *Dors* 6E **8**
Frampton. *Linc* 6L **37**
Frampton Cotterell. *S Glo* 5E **18**
Frampton Mansell. *Glos* 3H **19**
Frampton on Severn. *Glos* 3F **18**
Frampton West End. *Linc* 5K **37**
Framsden. *Suff* 6H **31**
Framwellgate Moor. *Dur* 7F **54**
Franche. *Worc* 4G **27**
Frandley. *Ches W* 2E **34**
Frankby. *Mers* 2M **33**
Frankfort. *Norf* 7K **39**
Frankley. *Worc* 3H **27**
Frank's Bridge. *Powy* 7L **25**
Frankton. *Warw* 4B **28**
Frankwell. *Shrp* 8C **34**
Frant. *E Sus* 2B **12**
**Fraserburgh**. *Abers* 7J **81**
Frating Green. *Essx* 1G **23**
Fratton. *Port* 5D **10**
Freathy. *Corn* 6G **5**
Freckenham. *Suff* 4C **30**
Freckleton. *Lanc* 5C **40**
Freeby. *Leics* 7F **36**
Freefolk Priors. *Hants* 1B **10**
Freehay. *Staf* 5J **35**
Freeland. *Oxon* 2B **20**
Freester. *Shet* 2E **90**
Freethorpe. *Norf* 1L **31**
Freiston. *Linc* 5L **37**
Freiston Shore. *Linc* 5L **37**
Fremington. *Devn* 2E **6**
Fremington. *N Yor* 6J **47**
Frenchay. *S Glo* 6E **18**
Frenchbeer. *Devn* 7F **6**
Frenich. *Stir* 7J **65**
Frensham. *Surr* 1F **10**
Frenze. *Norf* 3H **31**
Fresgoe. *High* 5A **86**
Freshfield. *Mers* 7A **40**
Freshford. *Bath* 7F **18**
Freshwater. *IOW* 7M **9**
Freshwater Bay. *IOW* 7M **9**
Freshwater East. *Pemb* 7G **15**
Fressingfield. *Suff* 4J **31**
Freston. *Suff* 8H **31**
Freswick. *High* 5E **86**
Fretherne. *Glos* 3F **18**
Frettenham. *Norf* 8J **39**
Freuchie. *Fife* 7F **66**
Freystrop. *Pemb* 5F **14**
Friar's Gate. *E Sus* 2A **12**
Friar Waddon. *Dors* 7E **8**
Friday Bridge. *Cambs* 1A **30**
Friday Street. *E Sus* 5C **12**
Friday Street. *Surr* 1J **11**
Fridaythorpe. *E Yor* 2F **42**
Friden. *Derbs* 3K **35**
Friern Barnet. *G Lon* 4K **21**
Friesthorpe. *Linc* 1H **37**
Frieston. *Linc* 5G **37**
Frieth. *Buck* 4E **20**
Friezeland. *Notts* 4B **36**
Frilford. *Oxon* 4B **20**
Frilsham. *W Ber* 6C **20**
**Frimley**. *Surr* 8F **20**
Frimley Green. *Surr* 8F **20**
Frindsbury. *Medw* 7D **22**
Fring. *Norf* 6D **38**
Fringford. *Oxon* 1D **20**
Frinsted. *Kent* 8E **22**
**Frinton-on-Sea**. *Essx* 2J **23**
Friockheim. *Ang* 3J **67**
Friog. *Gwyn* 1F **24**
Frisby. *Leics* 1E **28**
Frisby on the Wreake.
*Leics* 8D **36**
Friskney. *Linc* 4A **38**
Friskney Eaudyke. *Linc* 4A **38**
Friston. *E Sus* 6B **12**
Friston. *Suff* 5L **31**
Fritchley. *Derbs* 4A **36**
Fritham. *Hants* 4L **9**
Frith Bank. *Linc* 5L **37**
Frith Common. *Worc* 5E **26**
Frithelstock. *Devn* 4D **6**
Frithelstock Stone. *Devn* 4D **6**
Frithsden. *Herts* 3H **21**
Frithville. *Linc* 4L **37**
Frittenden. *Kent* 1E **12**
Frittiscombe. *Devn* 7L **5**
Fritton. *Norf*
nr. Great Yarmouth 1L **31**
nr. Long Stratton 2J **31**
Fritwell. *Oxon* 1C **20**
Frizinghall. *W Yor* 4K **41**
Frizington. *Cumb* 3K **45**
Frobost. *W Isl* 3D **74**
Frocester. *Glos* 3F **18**
Frochas. *Powy* 2L **25**
Frodesley. *Shrp* 1D **26**
Frodingham. *N Lin* 6G **43**
Frodsham. *Ches W* 2D **34**
Froggatt. *Derbs* 2L **35**
Froghall. *Staf* 5J **35**
Frogham. *Hants* 4K **9**
Frogham. *Kent* 8J **23**
Frogmore. *Devn* 7K **5**
**Frogmore**. *Hants* 7F **20**
Frogmore. *Herts* 3J **21**
Frognall. *Linc* 8J **37**
Frogshall. *Norf* 6J **39**
Frogwell. *Corn* 5F **4**
Frolesworth. *Leics* 2C **28**
**Frome**. *Som* 1F **8**
Fromefield. *Som* 1F **8**
Frome St Quintin. *Dors* 5D **8**
Fromes Hill. *Here* 7E **26**
Fron. *Gwyn* 7C **32**
Fron. *Powy*
nr. Llandrindod Wells 6K **25**
nr. Newtown 3L **25**
nr. Welshpool 2M **25**
Y Fron. *Gwyn* 5E **32**
Froncysyllte. *Wrex* 5A **34**
Frongoch. *Gwyn* 7J **33**
Fron Isaf. *Wrex* 5A **34**
Fronoleu. *Gwyn* 7G **33**
Frosterley. *Dur* 8D **54**
Frotoft. *Orkn* 7D **88**
Froxfield. *C Beds* 8G **29**
Froxfield. *Wilts* 7L **19**
Froxfield Green. *Hants* 3E **10**
Fryern Hill. *Hants* 3B **10**
Fryerning. *Essx* 3C **22**
Fryton. *N Yor* 8D **48**
Fugglestone St Peter. *Wilts* 2K **9**
Fulbeck. *Linc* 4G **37**
Fulbourn. *Cambs* 6B **30**
Fulbrook. *Oxon* 2L **19**
Fulflood. *Hants* 2B **10**
Fulford. *Som* 3M **7**
Fulford. *Staf* 6H **35**
Fulford. *York* 3D **42**
**Fulham**. *G Lon* 6K **21**
Fulking. *W Sus* 4K **11**
Fuller's Moor. *Ches W* 4C **34**
Fuller Street. *Essx* 2D **22**
Fullerton. *Hants* 2A **10**
Fulletby. *Linc* 2K **37**
Full Sutton. *E Yor* 2E **42**
Fullwood. *E Ayr* 4C **58**
Fulmer. *Buck* 5G **21**
Fulmodestone. *Norf* 6F **38**
Fulnetby. *Linc* 2H **37**
Fulney. *Linc* 7K **37**
Fulstow. *Linc* 8L **43**
Fulthorpe. *Stoc T* 3B **48**
Fulwell. *Tyne* 6G **55**
Fulwood. *Lanc* 4D **40**
Fulwood. *Notts* 4B **36**
Fulwood. *Som* 4M **7**
Fulwood. *S Yor* 1L **35**
Fundenhall. *Norf* 2H **31**
Funtington. *W Sus* 5F **10**
Funtley. *Hants* 5C **10**
Funzie. *Shet* 4L **91**
Furley. *Devn* 5A **8**
Furnace. *Arg* 7E **64**
Furnace. *Carm* 6M **15**
Furnace. *Cdgn* 3F **24**
Furner's Green. *E Sus* 3M **11**
Furness Vale. *Derbs* 1J **35**
Furneux Pelham. *Herts* 1M **21**
Furzebrook. *Dors* 7H **9**
Furzehill. *Devn* 1G **7**
Furzehill. *Dors* 5J **9**
Furzeley Corner. *Hants* 4D **10**
Furzey Lodge. *Hants* 5A **10**
Furzley. *Hants* 4L **9**
Fyfield. *Essx* 3B **22**
Fyfield. *Glos* 3L **19**
Fyfield. *Hants* 1L **9**
Fyfield. *Oxon* 4B **20**
Fyfield. *Wilts* 7K **19**
**The Fylde**. *Lanc* 4B **40**
Fylingthorpe. *N Yor* 5G **49**
Fyning. *W Sus* 3F **10**
Fyvie. *Abers* 2G **73**

## G

Gabhsann bho Dheas.
*W Isl* 6H **83**
Gabhsann bho Thuath.
*W Isl* 6H **83**
Gabroc Hill. *E Ayr* 4C **58**
Gadbrook. *Surr* 1K **11**
Gaddesby. *Leics* 8D **36**
Gadfa. *IOA* 2D **32**
Gadgirth. *S Ayr* 7C **58**
Gaer. *Powy* 2L **17**
Gaerwen. *IOA* 3D **32**
Gagingwell. *Oxon* 1B **20**
Gaick Lodge. *High* 7H **71**
Gailey. *Staf* 8H **35**
Gainford. *Dur* 4K **47**
**Gainsborough**. *Linc* 8F **42**
Gainsborough. *Suff* 7H **31**
Gainsford End. *Essx* 8D **30**
Gairletter. *Arg* 1L **57**
Gairloch. *Abers* 5G **73**
Gairloch. *High* 6K **77**
Gairlochy. *High* 7B **70**
Gairney Bank. *Per* 8E **66**
Gairnshiel Lodge. *Abers* 5B **72**
Gaisgill. *Cumb* 5E **46**
Gaitsgill. *Cumb* 7H **53**
**Galashiels**. *Bord* 6B **60**
Galgate. *Lanc* 2C **40**
Galgorm. *ME Ant* 3G **93**
Galhampton. *Som* 3E **8**
Gallatown. *Fife* 8F **66**
Galley Common. *Warw* 2M **27**
Galleyend. *Essx* 3D **22**
Galleywood. *Essx* 3D **22**
Gallin. *Per* 3K **65**
Gallowfauld. *Ang* 3H **67**
Gallowhill. *Per* 4E **66**
Gallowhill. *Ren* 3C **58**
Gallowhills. *Abers* 8K **81**
Gallows Green. *Staf* 5J **35**
Gallows Green. *Worc* 5H **27**
Gallowstree Common.
*Oxon* 5D **20**
Galltair. *High* 3K **69**
Gallt Melyd. *Den* 2K **33**
Galmington. *Som* 3M **7**
Galmisdale. *High* 7F **68**
Galmpton. *Devn* 7J **5**
Galmpton. *Torb* 6L **5**
Galmpton Warborough. *Torb* 6L **5**
Galphay. *N Yor* 8L **47**
Galston. *E Ayr* 6C **58**
Galton. *Dors* 7F **8**
Galtrigill. *High* 8C **76**
Gamblesby. *Cumb* 8L **53**
Gamblestown. *Arm* 6G **93**
Gamelsby. *Cumb* 6G **53**
Gamesley. *Derbs* 8J **41**
Gamlingay. *Cambs* 6K **29**
Gamlingay Cinques. *Cambs* 6K **29**
Gamlingay Great Heath.
*Cambs* 6K **29**
Gammaton. *Devn* 3D **6**
Gammersgill. *N Yor* 7J **47**
Gamston. *Notts*
nr. Nottingham 6D **36**
nr. Retford 2E **36**
Ganarew. *Here* 2D **18**
Ganavan. *Arg* 4C **64**
Ganborough. *Glos* 1K **19**
Gang. *Corn* 5F **4**
Ganllwyd. *Gwyn* 8G **33**
Gannochy. *Ang* 8E **72**
Gannochy. *Per* 5E **66**
Gansclet. *High* 7E **86**
Ganstead. *E Yor* 4J **43**
Ganthorpe. *N Yor* 8D **48**
Ganton. *N Yor* 8G **49**
Gants Hill. *G Lon* 5M **21**
Gappah. *Devn* 8H **7**
Garafad. *High* 7F **76**
Garboldisham. *Norf* 3G **31**
Garden City. *Flin* 3B **34**
Gardeners Green. *Wok* 7F **20**
Gardenstown. *Abers* 7H **81**
Garden Village. *S Yor* 8L **41**
Garden Village. *Swan* 5E **16**
Garderhouse. *Shet* 3D **90**
Gardham. *E Yor* 3G **43**
Gardie. *Shet*
on Papa Stour 1B **90**
on Unst 2L **91**
Gardie Ho. *Shet* 3E **90**
Gare Hill. *Wilts* 1F **8**
Garelochhead. *Arg* 8G **65**
Garford. *Oxon* 4B **20**
**Garforth**. *W Yor* 4B **42**
Gargrave. *N Yor* 2H **41**
Gargunnock. *Stir* 8M **65**
Garleffin. *S Ayr* 3F **50**
Garlieston. *Dum* 7K **51**
Garlinge Green. *Kent* 8H **23**
Garlogie. *Abers* 5G **73**
Garmelow. *Staf* 7F **34**
Garmond. *Abers* 8H **81**
Garmondsway. *Dur* 8G **55**
Garmony. *Arg* 3A **64**
Garmouth. *Mor* 7C **80**
Garmston. *Shrp* 1E **26**
Garnant. *Carm* 3F **16**
Garndiffaith. *Torf* 3A **18**
Garndolbenmaen. *Gwyn* 6D **32**
Garnett Bridge. *Cumb* 6D **46**
Garnfadryn. *Gwyn* 7B **32**
Garnkirk. *N Lan* 3E **58**
Garnlydan. *Blae* 3L **17**
Garnsgate. *Linc* 7M **37**
Garnswllt. *Swan* 4F **16**
Garn yr Erw. *Torf* 3M **17**
Garrabost. *W Isl* 8J **83**
Garrallan. *E Ayr* 8D **58**
Garras. *Corn* 6L **3**
Garreg. *Gwyn* 6F **32**
Garrigill. *Cumb* 7M **53**
Garrison. *Ferm* 6A **92**
Garriston. *N Yor* 6K **47**
Garrogie Lodge. *High* 4F **70**
Garros. *High* 7F **76**
Garrow. *Per* 3B **66**
Garsdale. *Cumb* 7F **46**
Garsdale Head. *Cumb* 6F **46**
Garsdon. *Wilts* 5H **19**
Garshall Green. *Staf* 6H **35**
Garsington. *Oxon* 3C **20**
Garstang. *Lanc* 3C **40**
Garston. *Mers* 1C **34**
Garswood. *Mers* 8D **40**
Gartcosh. *N Lan* 3E **58**
Garth. *B'end* 5H **17**
Garth. *Cdgn* 4F **24**
Garth. *Gwyn* 7E **32**
Garth. *IOM* 7C **44**
Garth. *Powy*
nr. Builth Wells 8J **25**
nr. Knighton 4A **26**
Garth. *Shet*
nr. Sandness 2C **90**
nr. Skellister 2E **90**
Garth. *Wrex* 5A **34**
Garthamlock. *Glas* 3E **58**
Garthbrengy. *Powy* 1K **17**
Gartheli. *Cdgn* 7E **24**
Garthmyl. *Powy* 3L **25**
Garthorpe. *Leics* 7F **36**
Garthorpe. *N Lin* 6F **42**
Garth Owen. *Powy* 3L **25**
Garth Place. *Cphy* 6L **17**
Garth Row. *Cumb* 6D **46**
Gartly. *Abers* 2E **72**
Gartmore. *Stir* 8K **65**
Gartness. *N Lan* 3F **58**
Gartness. *Stir* 1D **58**
Gartocharn. *W Dun* 1C **58**
Garton. *E Yor* 4K **43**
Garton-on-the-Wolds.
*E Yor* 2G **43**
Gartsherrie. *N Lan* 3F **58**
Gartymore. *High* 2L **79**
Garvagh. *Caus* 3F **93**
Garvaghy. *Ferm* 5D **92**
Garvald. *E Lot* 2C **60**
Garvamore. *High* 6F **70**
Garvard. *Arg* 8J **63**
Garvault. *High* 8K **85**
Garve. *High* 7D **78**
Garvestone. *Norf* 1G **31**
Garvetagh. *Derr* 4C **92**
Garvie. *Arg* 8E **64**
Garvock. *Abers* 8G **73**
Garvock. *Inv* 2A **58**
Garway. *Here* 1C **18**
Garway Common. *Here* 1C **18**
Garway Hill. *Here* 1C **18**
Garwick. *Linc* 5J **37**
Gaskan. *High* 8K **69**
Gasper. *Wilts* 2F **8**
Gastard. *Wilts* 7G **19**
Gasthorpe. *Norf* 3F **30**
Gatcombe. *IOW* 7B **10**
Gateacre. *Mers* 1C **34**
Gatebeck. *Cumb* 7D **46**
Gate Burton. *Linc* 1F **36**
Gateforth. *N Yor* 5C **42**
Gatehead. *E Ayr* 6B **58**
Gate Helmsley. *N Yor* 2D **42**
Gatehouse. *Nmbd* 3A **54**
Gatehouse of Fleet. *Dum* 6M **51**
Gatelawbridge. *Dum* 2D **52**
Gateley. *Norf* 7F **38**
Gatenby. *N Yor* 7M **47**
Gatesgarth. *Cumb* 3L **45**
**Gateshead**. *Tyne* 5F **54**
Gatesheath. *Ches W* 3C **34**
Gateside. *Ang*
nr. Forfar 3H **67**
nr. Kirriemuir 3G **67**
Gateside. *Fife* 7E **66**
Gateside. *N Ayr* 4B **58**
Gathurst. *G Man* 7D **40**
**Gatley**. *G Man* 1G **35**
Gatton. *Surr* 8K **21**
Gattonside. *Bord* 6C **60**
Gatwick Airport.
*W Sus* **119** (1K **11**)
Gaufron. *Powy* 6J **25**
Gaulby. *Leics* 1D **28**
Gauldry. *Fife* 5G **67**
Gaultree. *Norf* 1A **30**
Gaunt's Common. *Dors* 5J **9**
Gaunt's Earthcott. *S Glo* 5E **18**
Gautby. *Linc* 2J **37**
Gavinton. *Bord* 4E **60**
Gawber. *S Yor* 7M **41**
Gawcott. *Buck* 8D **28**
Gawsworth. *Ches E* 3G **35**
Gawthorpe. *W Yor* 5L **41**
Gawthrop. *Cumb* 7E **46**
Gawthwaite. *Cumb* 7A **46**
Gay Bowers. *Essx* 3D **22**
Gaydon. *Warw* 6A **28**
Gayfield. *Orkn* 4D **88**
Gayhurst. *Mil* 7F **28**
Gayle. *N Yor* 7G **47**
Gayles. *N Yor* 5K **47**
Gay Street. *W Sus* 3H **11**
Gayton. *Mers* 1A **34**
Gayton. *Norf* 8D **38**
Gayton. *Nptn* 6E **28**
Gayton. *Staf* 7H **35**
Gayton le Marsh. *Linc* 1M **37**
Gayton le Wold. *Linc* 1K **37**
Gayton Thorpe. *Norf* 8D **38**
Gaywood. *Norf* 7C **38**
Gazeley. *Suff* 5D **30**
Geanies. *High* 6J **79**
Gearraidh Bhailteas. *W Isl* 3D **74**
Gearraidh Bhaird. *W Isl* 2E **76**
Gearraidh ma Monadh.
*W Isl* 4D **74**
Gearraidh na h-Aibhne.
*W Isl* 8F **82**
Geary. *High* 7D **76**
Geddes. *High* 8J **79**
Gedding. *Suff* 6F **30**
Geddington. *Nptn* 3F **28**
Gedintailor. *High* 2G **69**
Gedling. *Notts* 5D **36**
Gedney. *Linc* 7M **37**
Gedney Broadgate. *Linc* 7M **37**
Gedney Drove End. *Linc* 7A **38**
Gedney Dyke. *Linc* 7M **37**
Gedney Hill. *Linc* 8L **37**
Gee Cross. *G Man* 8H **41**
Geeston. *Rut* 1G **29**
Geilston. *Arg* 2B **58**
Geirinis. *W Isl* 1D **74**
Geise. *High* 5C **86**
Geisiadar. *W Isl* 8E **82**
Gelder Shiel. *Abers* 7B **72**
Geldeston. *Norf* 2K **31**
Gell. *Cnwy* 4H **33**
Gelli. *Pemb* 5G **15**
Gelli. *Rhon* 5J **17**
Gellifor. *Den* 4L **33**
**Gelligaer**. *Cphy* 5L **17**
Y Gelli Gandryll. *Powy* 8M **25**
Gellilydan. *Gwyn* 7F **32**
Gellinudd. *Neat* 4G **17**
Gellyburn. *Per* 4D **66**
Gellywen. *Carm* 4J **15**
Gelston. *Dum* 6B **52**
Gelston. *Linc* 5G **37**
Gembling. *E Yor* 2J **43**
Geneva. *Cdgn* 1L **15**
Gentleshaw. *Staf* 8J **35**
Geocrab. *W Isl* 4C **76**
George Best Belfast City Airport.
*Bel* 5H **93**
George Green. *Buck* 5G **21**
Georgeham. *Devn* 2D **6**
George Nympton. *Devn* 3G **7**
Georgetown. *Blae* 4L **17**
Georgetown. *Ren* 3C **58**
Georth. *Orkn* 7C **88**
Gerlan. *Gwyn* 4F **32**
Germansweek. *Devn* 6D **6**
Germoe. *Corn* 6J **3**
Gerrans. *Corn* 8A **4**
Gerrard's Bromley. *Staf* 6F **34**
**Gerrards Cross**. *Buck* 5G **21**
Gerston. *High* 6C **86**
Gestingthorpe. *Essx* 8E **30**
Gethsemane. *Pemb* 2G **15**
Geuffordd. *Powy* 1M **25**
Gibraltar. *Buck* 2E **20**
Gibraltar. *Linc* 4B **38**
Gibraltar. *Suff* 6H **31**
Gibsmere. *Notts* 5E **36**
Giddeahall. *Wilts* 6G **19**
Gidea Park. *G Lon* 5B **22**
Gidleigh. *Devn* 7F **6**
**Giffnock**. *E Ren* 4D **58**
Gifford. *E Lot* 3C **60**
Giffordtown. *Fife* 6F **66**
Giggetty. *Staf* 2G **27**
Giggleswick. *N Yor* 1G **41**
Gignog. *Pemb* 4E **14**
Gilberdyke. *E Yor* 5F **42**
Gilbert's End. *Worc* 7G **27**
Gilbert's Green. *Warw* 4K **27**
Gilchriston. *E Lot* 3B **60**
Gilcrux. *Cumb* 8F **52**
Gildersome. *W Yor* 5L **41**
Gildingwells. *S Yor* 1C **36**
Gilesgate Moor. *Dur* 7F **54**
Gileston. *V Glam* 8K **17**
Gilfach. *Cphy* 5L **17**
Gilfach Goch. *Rhon* 6J **17**
Gilfachreda. *Cdgn* 1L **15**
Gilford. *Arm* 6G **93**
Gilgarran. *Cumb* 2K **45**
Gillamoor. *N Yor* 6D **48**
Gillan. *Corn* 6L **3**
Gillar's Green. *Mers* 8C **40**
Gillen. *High* 8D **76**
Gilling East. *N Yor* 8D **48**
Gillingham. *Dors* 3G **9**
**Gillingham**. *Medw*
**Medway Towns 111** (7D **22**)
Gillingham. *Norf* 2L **31**
Gilling West. *N Yor* 5K **47**
Gillock. *High* 6D **86**
Gillow Heath. *Staf* 4G **35**
Gills. *High* 4E **86**
Gill's Green. *Kent* 2D **12**
Gilmanscleuch. *Bord* 7M **59**
Gilmerton. *Edin* 3L **59**
Gilmerton. *Per* 5B **66**
Gilmonby. *Dur* 4H **47**
Gilmorton. *Leics* 3C **28**
Gilsland. *Nmbd* 5L **53**
Gilsland Spa. *Cumb* 5L **53**
Gilston. *Bord* 4B **60**
Giltbrook. *Notts* 5B **36**
Gilwern. *Mon* 3M **17**
Gimingham. *Norf* 6J **39**
Giosla. *W Isl* 1C **76**
Gipping. *Suff* 5G **31**
Gipsey Bridge. *Linc* 5K **37**
Gipton. *W Yor* 4M **41**
Girdle Toll. *N Ayr* 5B **58**
Girlsta. *Shet* 2E **90**
Girsby. *N Yor* 5A **48**
Girthon. *Dum* 6M **51**
Girton. *Cambs* 5M **29**
Girton. *Notts* 3F **36**
Girvan. *S Ayr* 2G **51**
Gisburn. *Lanc* 3G **41**
Gisleham. *Suff* 3M **31**
Gislingham. *Suff* 4G **31**
Gissing. *Norf* 3H **31**
Gittisham. *Devn* 6L **7**
Gladestry. *Powy* 7M **25**
Gladsmuir. *E Lot* 2B **60**
Glaichbea. *High* 2F **70**
Glais. *Swan* 4G **17**
Glaisdale. *N Yor* 5E **48**
Glame. *High* 1G **69**
Glamis. *Ang* 3G **67**
Glanaman. *Carm* 3F **16**
Glan-Conwy. *Cnwy* 5H **33**
Glandford. *Norf* 5G **39**
Glan Duar. *Carm* 2M **15**
Glandwr. *Blae* 4M **17**
Glandwr. *Pemb* 4H **15**
Glan-Dwyfach. *Gwyn* 6D **32**
Glandy Cross. *Carm* 4H **15**
Glandyfi. *Cdgn* 3F **24**
Glangrwyney. *Powy* 3M **17**
Glanmule. *Powy* 3L **25**
Glan-rhyd. *Pemb* 3H **15**
Glan-rhyd. *Powy* 4G **17**
Glanrhyd. *Gwyn* 7B **32**
Glanrhyd. *Pemb* 2H **15**
Glanton. *Nmbd* 8H **61**
Glanton Pyke. *Nmbd* 8H **61**
Glanvilles Wootton. *Dors* 5E **8**
Glan-y-don. *Flin* 3L **33**
Glan-y-nant. *Powy* 4J **25**
Glan-yr-afon. *Gwyn* 6K **33**
Glan-yr-afon. *IOA* 2F **32**
Glan-yr-afon. *Powy* 2K **25**
Glan-y-wern. *Gwyn* 7F **32**
Glapthorn. *Nptn* 2H **29**
Glapwell. *Derbs* 3B **36**
Glarryford. *ME Ant* 3G **93**
Glas Aird. *Arg* 8J **63**
Glas-allt Shiel. *Abers* 7B **72**
Glasbury. *Powy* 1L **17**
Glaschoil. *High* 2L **71**
Glascoed. *Den* 3J **33**
Glascoed. *Mon* 3B **18**
Glascote. *Staf* 1L **27**
Glascwm. *Powy* 7L **25**
Glasfryn. *Cnwy*
5J **33** **Glasgow**. *Glas* **109** (3D **58**)
Glasgow Airport. *Ren* **119** (3C **58**)
Glasgow Prestwick Airport.
*S Ayr* 7B **58**
Glashvin. *High* 7F **76**
Glasinfryn. *Gwyn* 4E **32**
Glas na Cardaich. *High* 6H **69**
Glasnacardoch. *High* 6H **69**
Glasnakille. *High* 4G **69**
Glaspwll. *Cdgn* 3G **25**
Glassburn. *High* 2D **70**
Glassenbury. *Kent* 2D **12**
Glasserton. *Dum* 8K **51**
Glassford. *S Lan* 5F **58**
Glassgreen. *Mor* 7B **80**
Glasshouse. *Glos* 1F **18**
Glasshouses. *N Yor* 1K **41**
Glasson. *Cumb* 5G **53**
Glasson. *Lanc* 2C **40**
Glassonby. *Cumb* 8K **53**
Glasswater. *New M* 6J **93**
Glasterlaw. *Ang* 2J **67**
Glaston. *Rut* 1F **28**
Glastonbury. *Som* 2C **8**
Glatton. *Cambs* 3J **29**
Glazebrook. *Warr* 8E **40**
Glazebury. *Warr* 8E **40**
Glazeley. *Shrp* 3F **26**
Gleadless. *S Yor* 1A **36**
Gleadsmoss. *Ches E* 3G **35**
Gleann Dail bho Dheas.
*W Isl* 4D **74**
Gleann Tholastaidh. *W Isl* 7J **83**
Gleann Uige. *High* 8H **69**
Gleaston. *Cumb* 8A **46**
Glebe. *Derr* 4C **92**
Glecknabae. *Arg* 3K **57**
Gledrid. *Shrp* 6A **34**
Gleiniant. *Powy* 3J **25**
Glemsford. *Suff* 7E **30**
Glen. *Dum* 6L **51**
Glenancross. *High* 6H **69**
Glenanne. *Arm* 7F **93**
Glenariff. *Caus* 2H **93**
Glenarm. *ME Ant* 3H **93**
Glen Auldyn. *IOM* 5D **44**
Glenavy. *Lis* 5G **93**
Glenbarr. *Arg* 6F **56**
Glenbeg. *High* 1L **63**
Glen Bernisdale. *High* 1F **68**
Glenbervie. *Abers* 7G **73**
Glenboig. *N Lan* 3F **58**
Glenborrodale. *High* 1M **63**
Glenbranter. *Arg* 8F **64**
Glenbreck. *Bord* 7J **59**
Glenbrein Lodge. *High* 4E **70**
Glenbrittle. *High* 3F **68**
Glenbuchat Lodge. *Abers* 4C **72**
Glenbuck. *E Ayr* 7F **58**
Glenburn. *Ren* 3C **58**
Glencalvie Lodge. *High* 5E **78**
Glencaple. *Dum* 5D **52**
Glencarron Lodge. *High* 8A **78**
Glencarse. *Per* 5E **66**
Glencassley Castle. *High* 3E **78**
Glencat. *Abers* 6E **72**
Glencoe. *High* 2F **64**
Glen Cottage. *High* 7H **69**
Glencraig. *Fife* 8E **66**
Glendale. *High* 1C **68**
Glendevon. *Per* 7C **66**
Glendoebeg. *High* 5E **70**
Glendoick. *Per* 5F **66**
Glendoune. *S Ayr* 2G **51**
Glenduckie. *Fife* 6F **66**
Gleneagles. *Per* 7C **66**
Glenegedale. *Arg* 4C **56**
Glenegedale Lots. *Arg* 4C **56**
Glenelg. *High* 4K **69**
Glenernie. *Mor* 1L **71**
Glenesslin. *Dum* 3C **52**
Glenfarg. *Per* 6E **66**
Glenfarquhar Lodge. *Abers* 7G **73**
Glenferness Mains. *High* 1K **71**
Glenfeshie Lodge. *High* 6J **71**
Glenfiddich Lodge. *Mor* 2C **72**
Glenfield. *Leics* 1C **28**
Glenfinnan. *High* 7L **69**
Glenfintaig Lodge. *High* 7C **70**
Glenfoot. *Per* 6E **66**
Glenfyne Lodge. *Arg* 6G **65**
Glengap. *Dum* 6A **52**
Glengarnock. *N Ayr* 4B **58**
Glengolly. *High* 5C **86**
Glengorm Castle. *Arg* 2K **63**
Glengormley. *Ant* 4H **93**
Glengrasco. *High* 1F **68**
Glenhead Farm. *Ang* 1F **66**
Glenholm. *Bord* 6K **59**
Glen House. *Bord* 6L **59**
Glenhurich. *High* 1C **64**
Glenkerry. *Bord* 8L **59**
Glenkiln. *Dum* 4C **52**
Glenkindie. *Abers* 4D **72**
Glenkinglass Lodge. *Arg* 4F **64**
Glenkirk. *Bord* 7J **59**
Glenlean. *Arg* 1K **57**
Glenlee. *Dum* 3M **51**
Glenleraig. *High* 8D **84**
Glenlichorn. *Per* 6A **66**
Glenlivet. *Mor* 3A **72**
Glenlochar. *Dum* 5B **52**
Glenlochsie Lodge. *Per* 8L **71**
Glenluce. *Dum* 6G **51**
Glenmarksie. *High* 8D **78**
Glenmassan. *Arg* 1L **57**
Glenmavis. *N Lan* 3F **58**
Glen Maye. *IOM* 7B **44**
Glenmazeran Lodge. *High* 3H **71**
Glenmidge. *Dum* 3C **52**
Glen Mona. *IOM* 6D **44**
Glenmore. *High*
nr. Glenborrodale 1L **63**
nr. Kingussie 5K **71**
on Isle of Skye 1F **68**
Glenmoy. *Ang* 1H **67**
Glennoe. *Arg* 4E **64**
Glen of Coachford. *Abers* 1D **72**
Glenogil. *Ang* 1H **67**
Glen Parva. *Leics* 2C **28**
Glenprosen Village. *Ang* 1G **67**
Glenree. *N Ayr* 7J **57**
Glenridding. *Cumb* 4B **46**
Glenrosa. *N Ayr* 6K **57**
**Glenrothes**. *Fife* 7F **66**
Glensanda. *High* 3C **64**
Glensaugh. *Abers* 8F **72**
Glenshero Lodge. *High* 6F **70**
Glensluain. *Arg* 8E **64**
Glenstockadale. *Dum* 5F **50**
Glenstriven. *Arg* 2K **57**
Glen Tanar House. *Abers* 6D **72**
Glentham. *Linc* 8H **43**
Glenton. *Abers* 3F **72**
Glentress. *Bord* 6L **59**
Glentromie Lodge. *High* 6H **71**
Glentrool Lodge. *Dum* 3K **51**
Glentrool Village. *Dum* 4J **51**
Glentruim House. *High* 6G **71**
Glentworth. *Linc* 1G **37**
Glenuig. *High* 8H **69**
Glen View. *New M* 7G **93**
Glen Village. *Falk* 2G **59**
Glen Vine. *IOM* 7C **44**
Glenwhilly. *Dum* 4G **51**
Glenzierfoot. *Dum* 4H **53**
Glespin. *S Lan* 7G **59**
Gletness. *Shet* 2E **90**
Glewstone. *Here* 1D **18**
Glib Cheois. *W Isl* 1E **76**
Glinton. *Pet* 1J **29**
Glooston. *Leics* 2E **28**
**Glossop**. *Derbs* 8J **41**
Gloster Hill. *Nmbd* 1F **54**
**Gloucester**. *Glos* **109** (2G **19**)
Gloucestershire Airport.
*Glos* 1G **19**
Gloup. *Shet* 3K **91**
Glusburn. *N Yor* 3J **41**
Glutt Lodge. *High* 8A **86**
Glutton Bridge. *Derbs* 3J **35**
Gluvian. *Corn* 5B **4**
Glympton. *Oxon* 1B **20**
Glyn. *Cnwy* 3H **33**
Glynarthen. *Cdgn* 2K **15**
Glynbrochan. *Powy* 4J **25**
Glyn Ceiriog. *Wrex* 7M **33**
Glyncoch. *Rhon* 5K **17**
Glyncorrwg. *Neat* 5H **17**
Glynde. *E Sus* 5A **12**
Glyndebourne. *E Sus* 4A **12**
Glyndyfrdwy. *Den* 6L **33**
**Glyn Ebwy**. *Blae* 4L **17**
Glynllan. *B'end* 6J **17**
Glynn. *ME Ant* 4J **93**
Glyn-neath. *Neat* 4H **17**
Glynogwr. *B'end* 6J **17**
Glyntaff. *Rhon* 6K **17**
Glyntawe. *Powy* 3H **17**
Glynteg. *Carm* 3K **15**
Gnosall. *Staf* 7G **35**
Gnosall Heath. *Staf* 7G **35**
Goadby. *Leics* 2E **28**
Goadby Marwood. *Leics* 7E **36**
Goatacre. *Wilts* 6J **19**
Goathill. *Dors* 4E **8**
Goathland. *N Yor* 5F **48**
Goathurst. *Som* 2A **8**
Goathurst Common. *Kent* 8A **22**
Goat Lees. *Kent* 1G **13**
Gobernuisgach Lodge. *High* 7G **85**
Gobernuisgeach. *High* 8A **86**
Gobhaig. *W Isl* 3B **76**
Gobowen. *Shrp* 6B **34**
**Godalming**. *Surr* 1G **11**
Goddard's Corner. *Suff* 5J **31**
Goddard's Green. *Kent*
nr. Benenden 2E **12**
nr. Cranbrook 2D **12**
Goddards' Green. *W Sus* 3K **11**
Godford Cross. *Devn* 5L **7**
Godleybrook. *Staf* 5H **35**
Godmanchester. *Cambs* 4K **29**
Godmanstone. *Dors* 6E **8**
Godmersham. *Kent* 8G **23**
Godolphin Cross. *Corn* 5K **3**
Godre'r-graig. *Neat* 4G **17**
Godshill. *Hants* 4K **9**
Godshill. *IOW* 7C **10**
Godstone. *Staf* 6J **35**
Godstone. *Surr* 8L **21**
Goetre. *Mon* 3B **18**
Goff's Oak. *Herts* 3L **21**
Gogar. *Edin* 2K **59**
Goginan. *Cdgn* 4F **24**
Golan. *Gwyn* 6E **32**
Golant. *Corn* 6D **4**
Golberdon. *Corn* 8C **6**
**Golborne**. *G Man* 8E **40**
Golcar. *W Yor* 6J **41**
Goldcliff. *Newp* 5B **18**
Golden Cross. *E Sus* 4B **12**
Golden Green. *Kent* 1C **12**
Golden Grove. *Carm* 3E **16**
Golden Grove. *N Yor* 5F **48**
Golden Hill. *Pemb* 4F **14**
Goldenhill. *Stoke* 4G **35**
Golden Pot. *Hants* 1E **10**
Golden Valley. *Glos* 1H **19**
Golders Green. *G Lon* 5K **21**
Goldhanger. *Essx* 3F **22**
Gold Hill. *Norf* 2B **30**
Golding. *Shrp* 1D **26**
Goldington. *Bed* 6H **29**
Goldsborough. *N Yor*
nr. Harrogate 2A **42**
nr. Whitby 4F **48**
Goldsithney. *Corn* 5J **3**
Goldstone. *Kent* 7J **23**
Goldstone. *Shrp* 7F **34**
Goldthorpe. *S Yor* 7B **42**
Goldworthy. *Devn* 3C **6**
Golfa. *Powy* 8L **33**
Gollanfield. *High* 8J **79**
Gollinglith Foot. *N Yor* 7K **47**
Golsoncott. *Som* 2K **7**
Golspie. *High* 4J **79**
Gomeldon. *Wilts* 2K **9**
Gomersal. *W Yor* 5L **41**
Gometra House. *Arg* 3J **63**
Gomshall. *Surr* 1H **11**
Gonalston. *Notts* 5D **36**
Gonerby Hill Foot. *Linc* 6G **37**
Gonfirth. *Shet* 1D **90**
Good Easter. *Essx* 2C **22**
Gooderstone. *Norf* 1D **30**
Goodleigh. *Devn* 2F **6**
Goodmanham. *E Yor* 3F **42**
Goodmayes. *G Lon* 5A **22**
Goodnestone. *Kent*
nr. Aylesham 8J **23**
nr. Faversham 7G **23**
Goodrich. *Here* 2D **18**
Goodrington. *Torb* 6L **5**
Goodshaw. *Lanc* 5G **41**
Goodshaw Fold. *Lanc* 5G **41**
Goodstone. *Devn* 8G **7**
Goodwick. *Pemb* 3F **14**
Goodworth Clatford. *Hants* 1A **10**
**Goole**. *E Yor* 5E **42**
Goom's Hill. *Worc* 6J **27**
Goonabarn. *Corn* 6B **4**
Goonbell. *Corn* 4L **3**
Goonhavern. *Corn* 3L **3**
Goonlaze. *Corn* 5L **3**
Goonvrea. *Corn* 4L **3**
Goose Green. *Cumb* 7D **46**
Goose Green. *S Glo* 5F **18**
Gooseham. *Corn* 4B **6**
Goosewell. *Plym* 6H **5**
Goosey. *Oxon* 4A **20**
Goosnargh. *Lanc* 4D **40**
Goostrey. *Ches E* 2F **34**
Gorcott Hill. *Warw* 5J **27**
Gord. *Shet* 5E **90**
Gordon. *Bord* 5D **60**
Gordonbush. *High* 3J **79**
Gordonstown. *Abers*
nr. Cornhill 8E **80**
nr. Fyvie 2G **73**
Gorebridge. *Midl* 3M **59**
Gorefield. *Cambs* 8M **37**
Gores. *Wilts* 8K **19**
Gorgie. *Edin* 2L **59**
Goring. *Oxon* 5D **20**
Goring-by-Sea. *W Sus* 5J **11**
Goring Heath. *Oxon* 6D **20**
Gorleston-on-Sea. *Norf* 1M **31**
Gornalwood. *W Mid* 2H **27**
Gorran Churchtown. *Corn* 7B **4**
Gorran Haven. *Corn* 7C **4**
Gorran High Lanes. *Corn* 7B **4**
Gors. *Cdgn* 5F **24**
Gorsedd. *Flin* 3L **33**
**Gorseinon**. *Swan* 5E **16**
Gorseness. *Orkn* 8D **88**
Gorseybank. *Derbs* 4L **35**
Gorsgoch. *Cdgn* 1L **15**
Gorslas. *Carm* 3E **16**
Gorsley. *Glos* 1E **18**
Gorsley Common. *Here* 1E **18**
Gorstan. *High* 7D **78**
Gorstella. *Ches W* 3B **34**
Gorsty Common. *Here* 8C **26**
Gorsty Hill. *Staf* 7K **35**
Gortantaoid. *Arg* 2C **56**
Gorteneorn. *High* 1M **63**
Gortenfern. *High* 1M **63**
Gortin. *Ferm* 4D **92**
Gortnahey. *Caus* 3E **92**
Gorton. *G Man* 8G **41**
Gosbeck. *Suff* 6H **31**
Gosberton. *Linc* 6K **37**
Gosberton Cheal. *Linc* 7K **37**
Gosberton Clough. *Linc* 7J **37**
Goseley Dale. *Derbs* 7M **35**
Gosfield. *Essx* 1D **22**
Gosford. *Oxon* 2C **20**
Gosforth. *Cumb* 4K **45**
**Gosforth**. *Tyne* 5F **54**
Gosmore. *Herts* 1J **21**
Gospel End. *Staf* 2G **27**
**Gosport**. *Hants* 6D **10**
Gossabrough. *Shet* 5K **91**
Gossington. *Glos* 3F **18**
Gossops Green. *W Sus* 2K **11**
Goswick. *Nmbd* 5H **61**
Gotham. *Notts* 6C **36**
Gotherington. *Glos* 1H **19**
Gott. *Arg* 3F **62**
Gott. *Shet* 3E **90**
Goudhurst. *Kent* 2D **12**
Goulceby. *Linc* 2K **37**
Gourdon. *Abers* 8H **73**
Gourock. *Inv* 2M **57**
Govan. *Glas* 3D **58**
Govanhill. *Glas* 3D **58**
Goverton. *Notts* 5E **36**
Goveton. *Devn* 7K **5**
Govilon. *Mon* 2A **18**
Gowanhill. *Abers* 7K **81**
Gowdall. *E Yor* 5D **42**
Gowdystown. *Arm* 6G **93**
Gowerton. *Swan* 5E **16**
Gowkhall. *Fife* 1J **59**
Gowthorpe. *E Yor* 2E **42**
Goxhill. *E Yor* 3J **43**
Goxhill. *N Lin* 5J **43**
Goxhill Haven. *N Lin* 5J **43**
Goytre. *Neat* 6G **17**
Grabhair. *W Isl* 2E **76**
Graby. *Linc* 7H **37**
Gracehill. *ME Ant* 3G **93**
Graffham. *W Sus* 4G **11**
Grafham. *Cambs* 5J **29**
Grafham. *Surr* 1H **11**
Grafton. *Here* 8C **26**
Grafton. *N Yor* 1B **42**
Grafton. *Oxon* 3L **19**
Grafton. *Shrp* 8C **34**
Grafton. *Worc*
nr. Evesham 8H **27**
nr. Leominster 5D **26**
Grafton Flyford. *Worc* 6H **27**
Grafton Regis. *Nptn* 7E **28**
Grafton Underwood. *Nptn* 3G **29**
Grafty Green. *Kent* 1E **12**
Graianrhyd. *Den* 5M **33**
Graig. *Carm* 6L **15**
Graig. *Cnwy* 3H **33**
Graig. *Den* 3K **33**
Graig-fechan. *Den* 5L **33**
Graig Penllyn. *V Glam* 7J **17**
Grain. *Medw* 6E **22**
Grainsby. *Linc* 8K **43**
Grainthorpe. *Linc* 8L **43**
Grainthorpe Fen. *Linc* 8L **43**
Graiselound. *N Lin* 8E **42**
Gramasdail. *W Isl* 8K **75**
Grampound. *Corn* 7B **4**
Grampound Road. *Corn* 6B **4**
Granborough. *Buck* 1E **20**
Granby. *Notts* 6E **36**
Grandborough. *Warw* 5B **28**
Grandpont. *Oxon* 3C **20**
Grandtully. *Per* 2C **66**
Grange. *Cumb* 4A **46**
Grange. *E Ayr* 6C **58**
Grange. *Here* 4C **26**
Grange. *Mers* 2M **33**
Grange. *Per* 5F **66**
The Grange. *N Yor* 6C **48**
Grange Corner. *ME Ant* 4G **93**
Grange Crossroads. *Mor* 8D **80**
Grange Hill. *Essx* 4M **21**
Grangemill. *Derbs* 4L **35**
Grange Moor. *W Yor* 6L **41**
**Grangemouth**. *Falk* 1H **59**
Grange of Lindores. *Fife* 6F **66**
Grange-over-Sands. *Cumb* 8C **46**
Grangepans. *Falk* 1J **59**
Grange Park. *New M* 6J **93**
Grangetown. *Card* 7L **17**
Grangetown. *Red C* 3C **48**
Grange Villa. *Dur* 6F **54**
Granish. *High* 4J **71**
Gransmoor. *E Yor* 2J **43**
Granston. *Pemb* 3E **14**
Grantchester. *Cambs* 6M **29**
**Grantham**. *Linc* 6G **37**
Grantley. *N Yor* 1L **41**
Grantlodge. *Abers* 4G **73**
Granton. *Edin* 2L **59**
Grantown-on-Spey. *High* 3L **71**
Grantshouse. *Bord* 3F **60**
Grappenhall. *Warr* 1E **34**
Grasby. *Linc* 7H **43**
Grasmere. *Cumb* 5B **46**
Grasscroft. *G Man* 7H **41**
Grassendale. *Mers* 1B **34**
Grassgarth. *Cumb* 7H **53**
Grassholme. *Dur* 3H **47**
Grassington. *N Yor* 1J **41**
Grassmoor. *Derbs* 3B **36**
Grassthorpe. *Notts* 3E **36**
Grateley. *Hants* 1L **9**
Gratton. *Devn* 4C **6**
Gratton. *Staf* 4H **35**
Gratwich. *Staf* 6J **35**
Graveley. *Cambs* 5K **29**
Graveley. *Herts* 1K **21**
Gravelhill. *Shrp* 8C **34**
Gravel Hole. *G Man* 7H **41**
Gravelly Hill. *W Mid* 2K **27**
Graven. *Shet* 6J **91**
Graveney. *Kent* 7G **23**
**Gravesend**. *Kent* 6C **22**
Grayingham. *Linc* 8G **43**
Grayrigg. *Cumb* 6D **46**
**Grays**. *Thur* 6C **22**
Grayshott. *Hants* 2F **10**
Grayson Green. *Cumb* 2J **45**
Grayswood. *Surr* 2G **11**
Graythorp. *Hart* 3C **48**
Grazeley. *Wok* 7D **20**
Grealin. *High* 7G **77**
Greasbrough. *S Yor* 8B **42**
**Greasby**. *Mers* 1A **34**
Great Abington. *Cambs* 7B **30**
Great Addington. *Nptn* 4G **29**
Great Alne. *Warw* 6K **27**
Great Altcar. *Lanc* 7B **40**
Great Amwell. *Herts* 2L **21**
Great Asby. *Cumb* 4E **46**
Great Ashfield. *Suff* 5F **30**
Great Ayton. *N Yor* 4C **48**
Great Baddow. *Essx* 3D **22**
Great Bardfield. *Essx* 8C **30**
Great Barford. *Bed* 6J **29**
Great Barr. *W Mid* 2J **27**
Great Barrington. *Glos* 2L **19**
Great Barrow. *Ches W* 3C **34**
Great Barton. *Suff* 5E **30**
Great Barugh. *N Yor* 8E **48**
Great Bavington. *Nmbd* 3C **54**
Great Bealings. *Suff* 7J **31**
Great Bedwyn. *Wilts* 7L **19**
Great Bentley. *Essx* 1H **23**
Great Billing. *Nptn* 5F **28**
Great Bircham. *Norf* 6D **38**
Great Blakenham. *Suff* 6H **31**
Great Blencow. *Cumb* 8J **53**
Great Bolas. *Telf* 7E **34**
Great Bookham. *Surr* 8J **21**
Great Bosullow. *Corn* 5H **3**
Great Bourton. *Oxon* 7B **28**
Great Bowden. *Leics* 3E **28**
Great Bradley. *Suff* 6C **30**
Great Braxted. *Essx* 2E **22**
Great Bricett. *Suff* 6G **31**
Great Brickhill. *Buck* 8G **29**
Great Bridgeford. *Staf* 7G **35**
Great Brington. *Nptn* 5D **28**
Great Bromley. *Essx* 1G **23**
Great Broughton. *Cumb* 8E **52**
Great Broughton. *N Yor* 5C **48**
Great Budworth. *Ches W* 2E **34**
Great Burdon. *Darl* 4M **47**
Great Burstead. *Essx* 4C **22**
Great Busby. *N Yor* 5C **48**
Great Canfield. *Essx* 2B **22**
Great Carlton. *Linc* 1M **37**
Great Casterton. *Rut* 1G **29**
Great Chalfield. *Wilts* 7G **19**
Great Chart. *Kent* 1F **12**
Great Chatwell. *Staf* 8F **34**
Great Chesterford. *Essx* 7B **30**
Great Cheverell. *Wilts* 8H **19**
Great Chilton. *Dur* 8F **54**
Great Chishill. *Cambs* 8M **29**
Great Clacton. *Essx* 2H **23**
Great Cliff. *W Yor* 6M **41**
Great Clifton. *Cumb* 2K **45**
Great Coates. *NE Lin* 6K **43**
Great Comberton. *Worc* 7H **27**
Great Corby. *Cumb* 6J **53**
Great Cornard. *Suff* 7E **30**
Great Cowden. *E Yor* 3K **43**
Great Coxwell. *Oxon* 4L **19**
Great Crakehall. *N Yor* 6L **47**
Great Cransley. *Nptn* 4F **28**
Great Cressingham. *Norf* 1E **30**
Great Crosby. *Mers* 7B **40**
Great Cubley. *Derbs* 6K **35**
Great Dalby. *Leics* 8E **36**
Great Doddington. *Nptn* 5F **28**
Great Doward. *Here* 2D **18**
Great Dunham. *Norf* 8E **38**
Great Dunmow. *Essx* 1C **22**
Great Durnford. *Wilts* 2K **9**
Great Easton. *Essx* 1C **22**
Great Easton. *Leics* 2F **28**
Great Eccleston. *Lanc* 3C **40**
Great Edstone. *N Yor* 7E **48**
Great Ellingham. *Norf* 2G **31**
Great Elm. *Som* 1F **8**
Great Eppleton. *Tyne* 7G **55**
Great Eversden. *Cambs* 6L **29**
Great Fencote. *N Yor* 6L **47**
Great Finborough. *Suff* 6G **31**
Greatford. *Linc* 8H **37**
Great Fransham. *Norf* 8E **38**
Great Gaddesden. *Herts* 2H **21**
Great Gate. *Staf* 5J **35**
Great Gidding. *Cambs* 3J **29**
Great Givendale. *E Yor* 2F **42**
Great Glemham. *Suff* 5K **31**
Great Glen. *Leics* 2D **28**
Great Gonerby. *Linc* 6F **36**
Great Gransden. *Cambs* 6K **29**
Great Green. *Norf* 3J **31**
Great Green. *Suff*
nr. Lavenham 6F **30**
nr. Palgrave 4H **31**
Great Habton. *N Yor* 8E **48**
Great Hale. *Linc* 5J **37**
Great Hallingbury. *Essx* 2B **22**
Greatham. *Hants* 2E **10**
Greatham. *Hart* 3B **48**
Greatham. *W Sus* 4H **11**
Great Hampden. *Buck* 3F **20**
Great Harrowden. *Nptn* 4F **28**
**Great Harwood**. *Lanc* 4F **40**
Great Haseley. *Oxon* 3D **20**
Great Hatfield. *E Yor* 3J **43**
Great Haywood. *Staf* 7H **35**
Great Heath. *W Mid* 3M **27**
Great Heck. *N Yor* 5C **42**
Great Henny. *Essx* 8E **30**
Great Hinton. *Wilts* 8H **19**
Great Hockham. *Norf* 2F **30**

Great Holland. Essx 2J 23
Great Horkesley. Essx 8F 30
Great Hormead. Herts 8M 29
Great Horton. W Yor 4K 41
Great Horwood. Buck 8E 28
Great Houghton. Nptn 6E 28
Great Houghton. S Yor 7B 42
Great Hucklow. Derbs 2K 35
Great Kelk. E Yor 2J 43
Great Kendale. E Yor 1H 43
Great Kimble. Buck 3F 20
Great Kingshill. Buck 4F 20
Great Langdale. Cumb 5A 46
Great Langton. N Yor 6L 47
Great Leighs. Essx 2D 22
Great Limber. Linc 7J 43
Great Linford. Mil 7F 28
Great Livermere. Suff 4E 30
Great Longstone. Derbs 2L 35
Great Lumley. Dur 7F 54
Great Lyth. Shrp 1C 26
**Great Malvern**. Worc 7F 26
Great Maplestead. Essx 8E 30
Great Marton. Bkpl 4B 40
Great Massingham. Norf 7D 38
Great Melton. Norf 1H 31
Great Milton. Oxon 3D 20
Great Missenden. Buck 3F 20
Great Mitton. Lanc 4F 40
Great Mongeham. Kent 8K 23
Great Moulton. Norf 2H 31
Great Munden. Herts 1L 21
Great Musgrave. Cumb 4F 46
Great Ness. Shrp 8B 34
Great Notley. Essx 1D 22
Great Oak. Mon 3B 18
Great Oakley. Essx 1H 23
Great Oakley. Nptn 3F 28
Great Offley. Herts 1J 21
Great Ormside. Cumb 4F 46
Great Orton. Cumb 6H 53
Great Ouseburn. N Yor 1B 42
Great Oxendon. Nptn 3E 28
Great Oxney Green. Essx 3C 22
Great Parndon. Essx 3M 21
Great Paxton. Cambs 5K 29
Great Plumpton. Lanc 4B 40
Great Plumstead. Norf 8K 39
Great Ponton. Linc 6G 37
Great Potheridge. Devn 4E 6
Great Preston. W Yor 5B 42
Great Raveley. Cambs 3K 29
Great Rissington. Glos 2K 19
Great Rollright. Oxon 8M 27
Great Ryburgh. Norf 7F 38
Great Ryle. Nmbd 8H 61
Great Ryton. Shrp 1C 26
Great Saling. Essx 1D 22
Great Salkeld. Cumb 8K 53
Great Sampford. Essx 8C 30
**Great Sankey**. Warr 1D 34
Great Saredon. Staf 1H 27
Great Saxham. Suff 5D 30
Great Shefford. W Ber 6A 20
Great Shelford. Cambs 6A 30
Great Shoddesden. Hants 1L 9
Great Smeaton. N Yor 5M 47
Great Snoring. Norf 6F 38
Great Somerford. Wilts 5H 19
Great Stainton. Darl 3M 47
Great Stambridge. Essx 4E 22
Great Staughton. Cambs 5J 29
Great Steeping. Linc 3M 37
Great Stonar. Kent 8K 23
Greatstone-on-Sea. Kent 3G 13
Great Strickland. Cumb 3D 46
Great Stukeley. Cambs 4K 29
Great Sturton. Linc 2K 37
Great Sutton. Ches W 2B 34
Great Sutton. Shrp 3D 26
Great Swinburne. Nmbd 4C 54
Great Tew. Oxon 1A 20
Great Tey. Essx 1E 22
Great Thirkleby. N Yor 8B 48
Great Thorness. IOW 6B 10
Great Thurlow. Suff 6C 30
Great Torr. Devn 7J 5
Great Torrington. Devn 4D 6
Great Tosson. Nmbd 1D 54
Great Totham North. Essx 2E 22
Great Totham South. Essx 2E 22
Great Tows. Linc 8K 43
Great Urswick. Cumb 8A 46
Great Wakering. Essx 5F 22
Great Waldingfield. Suff 7F 30
Great Walsingham. Norf 6F 38
Great Waltham. Essx 2C 22
Great Warley. Essx 4B 22
Great Washbourne. Glos 8H 27
Great Wenham. Suff 8G 31
Great Whelnetham. Suff 6E 30
Great Whittington. Nmbd 4D 54
Great Wigborough. Essx 2F 22
Great Wilbraham. Cambs 6B 30
Great Wilne. Derbs 6B 36
Great Wishford. Wilts 2J 9
Great Witchingham. Norf 7H 39
Great Witcombe. Glos 2H 19
Great Witley. Worc 5F 26
Great Wolford. Warw 8L 27
Greatworth. Nptn 7C 28
Great Wratting. Suff 7C 30
Great Wymondley. Herts 1K 21
**Great Wyrley**. Staf 1H 27
Great Wytheford. Shrp 8D 34
**Great Yarmouth**. Norf 1M 31
Great Yeldham. Essx 8D 30
Grebby. Linc 3M 37
Greeba Castle. IOM 6C 44
The Green. Cumb 6L 45
The Green. Wilts 2G 9
Greenbank. Shet 3K 91
Greenbottom. Corn 4L 3
Greenburn. W Lot 3H 59
Greencastle. Ferm 4D 92
Greencroft. Dur 6E 54
Greendown. Som 8D 18
Greendykes. Nmbd 7H 61
Green End. Bed
nr. Bedford 7H 29
nr. Little Staughton 5J 29
Green End. Herts
nr. Buntingford 8L 29
nr. Stevenage 1L 21
Green End. N Yor 5F 48
Green End. Warw 3L 27
Greenfield. Arg 8G 65
Greenfield. C Beds 8H 29
Greenfield. Flin 3L 33
Greenfield. G Man 7H 41
Greenfield. Oxon 4E 20
Greenfoot. N Lan 3F 58
**Greenford**. G Lon 5J 21
Greengairs. N Lan 2F 58
Greengate. Norf 8G 39
Greengill. Cumb 8F 52
Greenhalgh. Lanc 4C 40
Greenham. Dors 5C 8
Greenham. Som 3K 7
Greenham. W Ber 7B 20
Green Hammerton. N Yor 2B 42
Greenhaugh. Nmbd 3A 54
Greenhead. Nmbd 5L 53
Green Heath. Staf 8H 35
Greenhill. Dum 4F 52
Greenhill. Falk 2G 59
Greenhill. Kent 7H 23
Greenhill. S Yor 1M 35
Greenhill. Worc 4G 27
Greenhills. N Ayr 4B 58
Greenhithe. Kent 6B 22
Greenholm. E Ayr 6D 58
Greenhow Hill. N Yor 1K 41
Greenigoe. Orkn 1F 86
Greenisland. ME Ant 4H 93
Greenland. High 5D 86
Greenland Mains. High 5D 86
Greenlands. Worc 5J 27
Green Lane. Shrp 7E 34
Green Lane. Worc 5J 27
Greenlaw. Bord 5E 60
Greenlea. Dum 4E 52
Greenloaning. Per 7B 66
Greenmount. G Man 6F 40
Greenmow. Shet 5E 90
**Greenock**. Inv 2A 58
Greenock Mains. E Ayr 7E 58
Greenodd. Cumb 7B 46
Green Ore. Som 8D 18
Greenrow. Cumb 6F 52
Greens. Abers 1H 73
Greensgate. Norf 8H 39
Greenside. Tyne 5E 54
Greensidehill. Nmbd 8G 61
Greens Norton. Nptn 7D 28
Greenstead Green. Essx 1E 22
Greensted Green. Essx 3B 22
Green Street. Herts 4J 21
Green Street. Suff 4H 31
Green Street Green. G Lon 7A 22
Green Street Green. Kent 6B 22
Greenstreet Green. Suff 7G 31
Green Tye. Herts 2M 21
Greenwall. Orkn 1G 87
Greenway. Pemb 3G 15
Greenway. V Glam 7K 17
Greenwell. Cumb 6K 53
**Greenwich**. G Lon 6L 21
Greet. Glos 8J 27
Greete. Shrp 4D 26
Greetham. Linc 2L 37
Greetham. Rut 8G 37
Greetland. W Yor 5J 41
Gregson Lane. Lanc 5D 40
Grein. W Isl 5C 74
Greinetobht. W Isl 6K 75
Greinton. Som 2C 8
Gremista. Shet 3E 90
Grenaby. IOM 7B 44
Grendon. Nptn 5F 28
Grendon. Warw 2L 27
Grendon Common. Warw 2L 27
Grendon Green. Here 6D 26
Grendon Underwood. Buck 1D 20
Grenofen. Devn 8D 6
Grenoside. S Yor 8M 41
Greosabhagh. W Isl 4C 76
Gresford. Wrex 4B 34
Gresham. Norf 6H 39
Greshornish. High 8E 76
Gressenhall. Norf 8F 38
Gressingham. Lanc 1D 40
Greta Bridge. Dur 4J 47
Gretna. Dum 5H 53
Gretna Green. Dum 5H 53
Gretton. Glos 8J 27
Gretton. Nptn 2G 29
Gretton. Shrp 2D 26
Grewelthorpe. N Yor 8L 47
Greyabbey. Ards 5J 93
Greygarth. N Yor 8K 47
Grey Green. N Lin 7E 42
Greylake. Som 2B 8
Greysouthen. Cumb 2K 45
Greysteel. Caus 2D 92
Greystoke. Cumb 8J 53
Greystoke Gill. Cumb 3C 46
Greystone. Ang 3J 67
Greystones. S Yor 1M 35
Greywell. Hants 8E 20
Griais. W Isl 7H 83
Grianan. W Isl 8H 83
Gribthorpe. E Yor 4E 42
Gribun. Arg 4K 63
Griff. Warw 3A 28
Griffithstown. Torf 4A 18
Griffydam. Leics 8B 36
Griggs Green. Hants 2F 10
Grimbister. Orkn 8C 88
Grimeford Village. Lanc 6E 40
Grimeston. Orkn 8C 88
Grimethorpe. S Yor 7B 42
Griminis. W Isl
on Benbecula 8J 75
on North Uist 6J 75
Grimister. Shet 4J 91
Grimley. Worc 5G 27
Grimness. Orkn 2F 86
Grimoldby. Linc 1L 37
Grimpo. Shrp 7B 34
Grimsargh. Lanc 4D 40
Grimsbury. Oxon 7B 28
**Grimsby**. NE Lin 7K 43
Grimscote. Nptn 6D 28
Grimscott. Corn 5B 6
Grimshaw. Bkbn 5F 40
Grimshaw Green. Lanc 6C 40
Grimsthorpe. Linc 7H 37
Grimston. E Yor 4K 43
Grimston. Leics 7D 36
Grimston. Norf 7D 38
Grimston. York 2D 42
Grimstone. Dors 6E 8
Grimstone End. Suff 5F 30
Grinacombe Moor. Devn 6D 6
Grindale. E Yor 8J 49
Grindhill. Devn 6D 6
Grindiscol. Shet 4E 90
Grindle. Shrp 1F 26
Grindleford. Derbs 2L 35
Grindleton. Lanc 3F 40
Grindley. Staf 7J 35
Grindley Brook. Shrp 5D 34
Grindlow. Derbs 2K 35
Grindon. Nmbd 5G 61
Grindon. Staf 4J 35
Gringley on the Hill. Notts 8E 42
Grinsdale. Cumb 6H 53
Grinshill. Shrp 7D 34
Grinton. N Yor 6J 47
Griomsidar. W Isl 1F 76
Grishipoll. Arg 2G 63
Grisling Common. E Sus 3M 11
Gristhorpe. N Yor 7H 49
Griston. Norf 2F 30
Gritley. Orkn 1G 87
Grittenham. Wilts 5J 19
Grittleton. Wilts 5G 19
Grizebeck. Cumb 6M 45
Grizedale. Cumb 6B 46
Grobister. Orkn 7F 88
Grobsness. Shet 1D 90
Groby. Leics 1C 28
Groes. Cnwy 4K 33
Groes. Neat 6G 17
Groes-faen. Rhon 6K 17
Groesffordd. Gwyn 7B 32
Groesffordd. Powy 2K 17
Groeslon. Gwyn 5D 32
Groes-lwyd. Powy 1M 25
Groes-wen. Cphy 6L 17
Grogport. Arg 5H 57
Groigearraidh. W Isl 1D 74
Gromford. Suff 6K 31
Gronant. Flin 2K 33
Groombridge. E Sus 2B 12
Groomsport. Ards 4J 93
Grosmont. Mon 1C 18
Grosmont. N Yor 5F 48
Groton. Suff 7F 30
Grove. Dors 8E 8
Grove. Kent 7J 23
Grove. Notts 2E 36
Grove. Oxon 4A 20
The Grove. Dum 4D 52
The Grove. Worc 7G 27
Grovehill. E Yor 4H 43
Grove Park. G Lon 6M 21
Grovesend. Swan 4E 16
Grub Street. Staf 7F 34
Grudie. High 7D 78
Gruids. High 3F 78
Gruinard House. High 4L 77
Gruinart. Arg 3B 56
Grulinbeg. Arg 3B 56
Gruline. Arg 3L 63
Grummore. High 8J 85
Grundisburgh. Suff 6J 31
Gruting. Shet 3C 90
Grutness. Shet 7E 90
Gualachulain. High 3F 64
Gualin House. High 6F 84
Guardbridge. Fife 6H 67
Guarlford. Worc 7G 27
Guay. Per 3D 66
Gubblecote. Herts 2G 21
Guestling Green. E Sus 4E 12
Guestling Thorn. E Sus 4E 12
Guestwick. Norf 7G 39
Guestwick Green. Norf 7G 39
Guide. Bkbn 5F 40
Guide Post. Nmbd 3F 54
Guilden Down. Shrp 3B 26
Guilden Morden. Cambs 7K 29
Guilden Sutton. Ches W 3C 34
**Guildford**. Surr 109 (1G 11)
Guildtown. Per 4E 66
Guilsborough. Nptn 4D 28
Guilsfield. Powy 1M 25
Guineaford. Devn 2E 6
**Guisborough**. Red C 4D 48
Guiseley. W Yor 3K 41
Guist. Norf 7F 38
Guiting Power. Glos 1J 19
Gulberwick. Shet 4E 90
Gulladuff. M Ulst 4F 93
Gullane. E Lot 1B 60
Gulling Green. Suff 6E 30
Gulval. Corn 5H 3
Gulworthy. Devn 8D 6
Gumfreston. Pemb 6H 15
Gumley. Leics 2D 28
Gunby. E Yor 4E 42
Gunby. Linc 7G 37
Gundleton. Hants 2D 10
Gun Green. Kent 2D 12
Gun Hill. E Sus 4B 12
Gunn. Devn 2F 6
Gunnerside. N Yor 6H 47
Gunnerton. Nmbd 4C 54
Gunness. N Lin 6F 42
Gunnislake. Corn 8D 6
Gunnista. Shet 3E 90
Gunsgreenhill. Bord 3G 61
Gunstone. Staf 1G 27
Gunthorpe. Norf 6G 39
Gunthorpe. N Lin 8F 42
Gunthorpe. Notts 5D 36
Gunthorpe. Pet 1J 29
Gunville. IOW 7B 10
Gupworthy. Som 2J 7
Gurnard. IOW 6B 10
Gurney Slade. Som 1E 8
Gurnos. Powy 4G 17
Gussage All Saints. Dors 4J 9
Gussage St Andrew. Dors 4H 9
Gussage St Michael. Dors 4H 9
Guston. Kent 1K 13
Gutcher. Shet 4K 91
Guthram Gowt. Linc 7J 37
Guthrie. Ang 2J 67
Guyhirn. Cambs 1M 29
Guyhirn Gull. Cambs 1L 29
Guy's Head. Linc 7A 38
Guy's Marsh. Dors 3G 9
Guyzance. Nmbd 1F 54
Gwaelod-y-garth. Card 6L 17
Gwaenynog Bach. Den 4K 33
Gwaenysgor. Flin 2K 33
Gwalchmai. IOA 3C 32
Gwastad. Pemb 4G 15
Gwaun-Cae-Gurwen. Neat 3G 17
Gwbert. Cdgn 2H 15
Gweek. Corn 6L 3
Gwehelog. Mon 3B 18
Gwenddwr. Powy 8K 25
Gwennap. Corn 4L 3
Gwenter. Corn 7L 3
Gwernaffield. Flin 4M 33
Gwernesney. Mon 3C 18
Gwernogle. Carm 3M 15
Gwern-y-go. Powy 3M 25
Gwernymynydd. Flin 4M 33
Gwersyllt. Wrex 4B 34
Gwespyr. Flin 2L 33
Gwinear. Corn 5J 3
Gwithian. Corn 4J 3
Gwredog. IOA 2D 32
Gwyddelwern. Den 6K 33
Gwyddgrug. Carm 3L 15
Gwynfryn. Wrex 4A 34
Gwystre. Powy 6K 25
Gwytherin. Cnwy 4H 33
Gyfelia. Wrex 5B 34
Gyffin. Cnwy 3G 33


## H


Haa of Houlland. Shet 3K 91
Habberley. Shrp 1C 26
Habblesthorpe. Notts 1E 36
Habergham. Lanc 4G 41
Habin. W Sus 3F 10
Habrough. NE Lin 6J 43
Haceby. Linc 6H 37
Hacheston. Suff 6K 31
Hackenthorpe. S Yor 1B 36
Hackford. Norf 1G 31
Hackforth. N Yor 6L 47
Hackland. Orkn 7C 88
Hackleton. Nptn 6F 28
Hackman's Gate. Worc 4G 27
Hackness. N Yor 6G 49
Hackness. Orkn 2E 86
**Hackney**. G Lon 5L 21
Hackthorn. Linc 1G 37
Hackthorpe. Cumb 3D 46
Haclait. W Isl 1E 74
Haconby. Linc 7J 37
Hadden. Bord 6E 60
Haddenham. Buck 3E 20
Haddenham. Cambs 4A 30
Haddenham End Field.
Cambs 4A 30
Haddington. E Lot 2C 60
Haddington. Linc 3G 37
Haddiscoe. Norf 2L 31
Haddo. Abers 2H 73
Haddon. Cambs 2J 29
Hademore. Staf 1K 27
Hadfield. Derbs 8J 41
Hadham Cross. Herts 2M 21
Hadham Ford. Herts 1M 21
Hadleigh. Essx 5E 22
Hadleigh. Suff 7G 31
Hadleigh Heath. Suff 7F 30
Hadley. Telf 8E 34
Hadley. Worc 5G 27
Hadley End. Staf 7K 35
Hadley Wood. G Lon 4K 21
Hadlow. Kent 1C 12
Hadlow Down. E Sus 3B 12
Hadnall. Shrp 7D 34
Hadstock. Essx 7B 30
Hadston. Nmbd 1F 54
Hady. Derbs 2A 36
Hadzor. Worc 5H 27
Haffenden Quarter. Kent 1E 12
Haggate. Lanc 4G 41
Haggbeck. Cumb 4J 53
Haggersta. Shet 3D 90
Haggerston. Nmbd 5H 61
Haggrister. Shet 6H 91
Hagley. Here 7D 26
Hagley. Worc 3H 27
Hagnaby. Linc 3L 37
Hagworthingham. Linc 3L 37
Haigh. G Man 7E 40
Haigh Moor. W Yor 5L 41
Haighton Green. Lanc 4D 40
Haile. Cumb 4K 45
Hailes. Glos 8J 27
Hailey. Herts 2L 21
Hailey. Oxon 2A 20
**Hailsham**. E Sus 5B 12
Hail Weston. Cambs 5J 29
Hainault. G Lon 4A 22
Hainford. Norf 8J 39
Hainton. Linc 1J 37
Hainworth. W Yor 4J 41
Haisthorpe. E Yor 1J 43
Hakin. Pemb 6E 14
Halam. Notts 4D 36
Halbeath. Fife 1K 59
Halberton. Devn 4K 7
Halcro. High 5D 86
Hale. Cumb 8D 46
**Hale**. G Man 1F 34
Hale. Hal 1C 34
Hale. Hants 4K 9
Hale. Surr 1F 10
Hale Bank. Hal 1C 34
Halebarns. G Man 1F 34
Hales. Norf 2K 31
Hales. Staf 6F 34
Halesgate. Linc 7L 37
Hales Green. Derbs 5K 35
**Halesowen**. W Mid 3H 27
Hale Street. Kent 1C 12
Halesworth. Suff 4K 31
Halewood. Mers 1C 34
Halford. Shrp 3C 26
Halford. Warw 7L 27
Halfpenny. Cumb 7D 46
Halfpenny Furze. Carm 5J 15
Halfpenny Green. Staf 2G 27
Halfway. Carm
nr. Llandeilo 1F 16
nr. Llandovery 1H 17
Halfway. S Yor 1B 36
Halfway. W Ber 7B 20
Halfway House. Shrp 8B 34
Halfway Houses. Kent 6F 22
Halgabron. Corn 3C 4
**Halifax**. W Yor 5J 41
Halistra. High 8D 76
Halket. E Ayr 4C 58
Halkirk. High 6C 86
Halkyn. Flin 3M 33
Hall. E Ren 4C 58
Hallam Fields. Derbs 5B 36
Halland. E Sus 4B 12
The Hallands. N Lin 5H 43
Hallaton. Leics 2E 28
Hallatrow. Bath 8E 18
Hallbank. Cumb 6E 46
Hallbankgate. Cumb 6K 53
Hall Dunnerdale. Cumb 5M 45
Hallen. S Glo 5D 18
Hall End. Bed 7H 29
Hallgarth. Dur 7G 55
Hall Green. Ches E 4G 35
Hall Green. Norf 3H 31
Hall Green. W Mid 3K 27
Hall Green. W Yor 6M 41
Hall Green. Wrex 5C 34
Halliburton. Bord 5D 60
Hallin. High 8D 76
Halling. Medw 7D 22
Hallington. Linc 1L 37
Hallington. Nmbd 4C 54
Halloughton. Notts 4D 36
Hallow. Worc 6G 27
Hallow Heath. Worc 6G 27
Hallowsgate. Ches W 3D 34
Hallsands. Devn 8L 5
Hall's Green. Herts 1K 21
Hallspill. Devn 3D 6
Hallthwaites. Cumb 6L 45
Hall Waberthwaite. Cumb 5L 45
Hallwood Green. Glos 8E 26
Hallworthy. Corn 7A 6
Hallyne. Bord 5K 59
Halmer End. Staf 5G 35
Halmond's Frome. Here 7E 26
Halmore. Glos 3E 18
Halnaker. W Sus 5G 11
Halsall. Lanc 6B 40
Halse. Nptn 7C 28
Halse. Som 3L 7
Halsetown. Corn 5J 3
Halsham. E Yor 5K 43
Halsinger. Devn 2E 6
**Halstead**. Essx 8E 30
Halstead. Kent 7A 22
Halstead. Leics 1E 28
Halstock. Dors 5D 8
Halsway. Som 2L 7
Haltcliff Bridge. Cumb 8H 53
Haltham. Linc 3K 37
Haltoft End. Linc 5L 37
Halton. Buck 3F 20
Halton. Hal 1D 34
Halton. Lanc 1D 40
Halton. Nmbd 5C 54
Halton. W Yor 4A 42
Halton. Wrex 6B 34
Halton East. N Yor 2J 41
Halton Fenside. Linc 3M 37
Halton Gill. N Yor 8G 47
Halton Holegate. Linc 3M 37
Halton Lea Gate. Nmbd 6L 53
Halton Moor. W Yor 4M 41
Halton Shields. Nmbd 5D 54
Halton West. N Yor 2G 41
Haltwhistle. Nmbd 5M 53
Halvergate. Norf 1L 31
Halwell. Devn 6K 5
Halwill. Devn 6D 6
Halwill Junction. Devn 6D 6
Ham. Devn 5M 7
Ham. Glos 4E 18
Ham. G Lon 6J 21
Ham. High 4D 86
Ham. Kent 8K 23
Ham. Plym 6G 5
Ham. Shet 4B 90
Ham. Som
nr. Ilminster 4A 8
nr. Taunton 3A 8
nr. Wellington 3L 7
Ham. Wilts 7M 19
Hambleden. Buck 5E 20
Hambledon. Hants 4D 10
Hambledon. Surr 2G 11
Hamble-le-Rice. Hants 5B 10
Hambleton. Lanc 3B 40
Hambleton. N Yor 4C 42
Hambridge. Som 3B 8
Hambrook. S Glo 6E 18
Hambrook. W Sus 5E 10
Ham Common. Dors 3G 9
Hameringham. Linc 3L 37
Hamerton. Cambs 4J 29
Ham Green. Here 7F 26
Ham Green. Kent 7E 22
Ham Green. N Som 6D 18
Ham Green. Worc 5J 27
Ham Hill. Kent 7C 22
Hamilton. Leic 1D 28
**Hamilton**. S Lan 4F 58
Hamiltonsbawn. Arm 6F 93
Hamister. Shet 1F 90
Hammer. W Sus 2F 10
**Hammersmith**. G Lon 6K 21
Hammerwich. Staf 1J 27
Hammerwood. E Sus 2M 11
Hammill. Kent 8J 23
Hammond Street. Herts 3L 21
Hammoon. Dors 4G 9
Hamnavoe. Shet
nr. Braehoulland 5G 91
nr. Burland 4D 90
nr. Lunna 6J 91
on Yell 5J 91
Hamp. Som 2B 8
Hampden Park. E Sus 5B 12
Hampen. Glos 2J 19
Hamperden End. Essx 8B 30
Hamperley. Shrp 3C 26
Hampnett. Glos 2J 19
Hampole. S Yor 6C 42
Hampreston. Dors 6J 9
**Hampstead**. G Lon 5K 21
Hampstead Norreys. W Ber 6C 20
Hampsthwaite. N Yor 2L 41
Hampton. Devn 6A 8
Hampton. G Lon 6J 21
Hampton. Kent 7H 23
Hampton. Shrp 3F 26
Hampton. Swin 4K 19
Hampton. Worc 7J 27
Hampton Bishop. Here 8D 26
Hampton Fields. Glos 4G 19
Hampton Hargate. Pet 2J 29
Hampton Heath. Ches W 5D 34
Hampton in Arden. W Mid 3L 27
Hampton Loade. Shrp 3F 26
Hampton Lovett. Worc 5G 27
Hampton Lucy. Warw 6L 27
Hampton Magna. Warw 5L 27
Hampton on the Hill. Warw 5L 27
Hampton Poyle. Oxon 2C 20
Hampton Wick. G Lon 7J 21
Hamptworth. Wilts 4L 9
Hamrow. Norf 7F 38
Hamsey. E Sus 4M 11
Hamsey Green. Surr 8L 21
Hamstall Ridware. Staf 8K 35
Hamstead. IOW 6B 10
Hamstead. W Mid 2J 27
Hamstead Marshall. W Ber 7B 20
Hamsterley. Dur
nr. Consett 6E 54
nr. Wolsingham 8E 54
Hamsterley Mill. Dur 6E 54
Ham Street. Som 2D 8
Hamstreet. Kent 2G 13
Hamworthy. Pool 6H 9
Hanbury. Staf 7K 35
Hanbury. Worc 5H 27
Hanbury Woodend. Staf 7K 35
Hanby. Linc 6H 37
Hanchurch. Staf 5G 35
Hand and Pen. Devn 6K 7
Handbridge. Ches W 3C 34
Handcross. W Sus 2K 11
Handforth. Ches E 1G 35
Handley. Ches W 4C 34
Handley. Derbs 3A 36
Handsacre. Staf 8J 35
Handsworth. S Yor 1B 36
Handsworth. W Mid 2J 27
Handy Cross. Buck 4F 20
Hanford. Dors 4G 9
Hanford. Stoke 5G 35
Hangersley. Hants 5K 9
Hanging Houghton. Nptn 4E 28
Hanging Langford. Wilts 2J 9
Hangleton. Brig 5K 11
Hangleton. W Sus 5H 11
Hanham. S Glo 6E 18
Hanham Green. S Glo 6E 18
Hankelow. Ches E 5E 34
Hankerton. Wilts 4H 19
Hankham. E Sus 5C 12
**Hanley**. Stoke **Stoke 116** (5G 35)
Hanley Castle. Worc 7G 27
Hanley Childe. Worc 5E 26
Hanley Swan. Worc 7G 27
Hanley William. Worc 5E 26
Hanlith. N Yor 1H 41
Hanmer. Wrex 6C 34
Hannaborough. Devn 5E 6
Hannaford. Devn 3F 6
Hannah. Linc 2B 38
Hannington. Hants 8C 20
Hannington. Nptn 4F 28
Hannington. Swin 4K 19
Hannington Wick. Swin 4K 19
Hanscombe End. C Beds 8J 29
Hanslope. Mil 7F 28
Hanthorpe. Linc 7H 37
Hanwell. G Lon 5J 21
Hanwell. Oxon 7B 28
Hanwood. Shrp 1C 26
Hanworth. G Lon 6J 21
Hanworth. Norf 6H 39
Happas. Ang 3H 67
Happendon. S Lan 6G 59
Happisburgh. Norf 6K 39
Happisburgh Common.
Norf 7K 39
Hapsford. Ches W 2C 34
Hapton. Lanc 4F 40
Hapton. Norf 2H 31
Harberton. Devn 6K 5
Harbertonford. Devn 6K 5
Harbledown. Kent 8H 23
Harborne. W Mid 3J 27
Harborough Magna. Warw 4B 28
Harbottle. Nmbd 1C 54
Harbourneford. Devn 5K 5
Harbours Hill. Worc 5H 27
Harbridge. Hants 4K 9
Harbury. Warw 5A 28
Harby. Leics 6E 36
Harby. Notts 2F 36
Harcombe. Devn 6L 7
Harcombe Bottom. Devn 6B 8
Harcourt. Corn 5M 3
Harden. W Yor 4J 41
Hardenhuish. Wilts 6H 19
Hardgate. Abers 5G 73
Hardgate. Dum 5C 52
Hardham. W Sus 4H 11
Hardingham. Norf 1G 31
Hardingstone. Nptn 6E 28
Hardings Wood. Staf 4G 35
Hardington. Som 8F 18
Hardington Mandeville. Som 4D 8
Hardington Marsh. Som 5D 8
Hardington Moor. Som 4D 8
Hardley. Hants 5B 10
Hardley Street. Norf 1K 31
Hardmead. Mil 7G 29
Hardraw. N Yor 6G 47
Hardstoft. Derbs 3B 36
Hardway. Hants 5D 10
Hardway. Som 2F 8
Hardwick. Buck 2F 20
Hardwick. Cambs 6L 29
Hardwick. Norf 3J 31
Hardwick. Nptn 5F 28
Hardwick. Oxon
nr. Bicester 1C 20
nr. Witney 3A 20
Hardwick. Shrp 2B 26
Hardwick. S Yor 1B 36
Hardwick. Stoc T 3B 48
Hardwick. W Mid 2J 27
Hardwicke. Glos
nr. Cheltenham 1H 19
nr. Gloucester 2F 18
Hardwicke. Here 7A 26
Hardwick Village. Notts 2D 36
Hardy's Green. Essx 1F 22
Hare. Som 4A 8
Hareby. Linc 3L 37
Hareden. Lanc 2E 40
Harefield. G Lon 4H 21
Hare Green. Essx 1G 23
Hare Hatch. Wok 6F 20
Harehill. Derbs 6K 35
Harehills. W Yor 4M 41
Harehope. Nmbd 7H 61
Harelaw. Dum 4J 53
Harelaw. Dur 6E 54
Hareplain. Kent 2E 12
Haresceugh. Cumb 7L 53
Harescombe. Glos 2G 19
Haresfield. Glos 2G 19
Haresfinch. Mers 8D 40
Hareshaw. N Lan 3G 59
Hare Street. Essx 3M 21
Hare Street. Herts 1L 21
Harewood. W Yor 3M 41
Harewood End. Here 1D 18
Harford. Devn 6J 5
Hargate. Norf 2H 31
Hargatewall. Derbs 2K 35
Hargrave. Ches W 3C 34
Hargrave. Nptn 4H 29
Hargrave. Suff 6D 30
Harker. Cumb 5H 53
Harkland. Shet 5J 91
Harkstead. Suff 8H 31
Harlaston. Staf 8L 35
Harlaxton. Linc 6F 36
Harlech. Gwyn 7E 32
Harlequin. Notts 6D 36
Harlescott. Shrp 8D 34
Harleston. Devn 7K 5
Harleston. Norf 3J 31
Harleston. Suff 5G 31
Harlestone. Nptn 5E 28
Harley. Shrp 1D 26
Harley. S Yor 8A 42
Harling Road. Norf 3F 30
Harlington. C Beds 8H 29
Harlington. G Lon 6H 21
Harlington. S Yor 7B 42
Harlosh. High 1D 68
**Harlow**. Essx 2M 21
Harlow Hill. Nmbd 5D 54
Harlsey Castle. N Yor 6B 48
Harlthorpe. E Yor 4E 42
Harlton. Cambs 6L 29
Harlyn Bay. Corn 4A 4
Harman's Cross. Dors 7H 9
Harmby. N Yor 7K 47
Harmer Green. Herts 2K 21
Harmer Hill. Shrp 7C 34
Harmondsworth. G Lon 6H 21
Harmston. Linc 3G 37
Harnage. Shrp 1D 26
Harnham. Nmbd 3D 54
Harnham. Wilts 3K 9
Harnhill. Glos 3J 19
Harold Hill. G Lon 4B 22
Haroldston West. Pemb 5E 14
Haroldswick. Shet 2L 91
Harold Wood. G Lon 4B 22
Harome. N Yor 7D 48
**Harpenden**. Herts 2J 21
Harpford. Devn 6K 7
Harpham. E Yor 1H 43
Harpley. Norf 7D 38
Harpley. Worc 5E 26
Harpole. Nptn 5D 28
Harpsdale. High 6C 86
Harpsden. Oxon 5E 20
Harpswell. Linc 1G 37
Harpurhey. G Man 7G 41
Harpur Hill. Derbs 2J 35
Harraby. Cumb 6J 53
Harracott. Devn 3E 6
Harrapool. High 3H 69
Harrapul. High 3H 69
Harrietfield. Per 5C 66
Harrietsham. Kent 8E 22
Harrington. Cumb 2J 45
Harrington. Linc 2L 37
Harrington. Nptn 3E 28
Harringworth. Nptn 2G 29
Harriseahead. Staf 4G 35
Harriston. Cumb 7F 52
**Harrogate**. N Yor 110 (2M 41)
Harrold. Bed 6G 29
Harrop Dale. G Man 7J 41
**Harrow**. G Lon 5J 21
Harrowbarrow. Corn 5F 4
Harrowden. Bed 7H 29
Harrowgate Hill. Darl 4L 47
Harrow on the Hill. G Lon 5J 21
Harrow Weald. G Lon 4J 21
Harry Stoke. S Glo 6E 18
Harston. Cambs 6M 29
Harston. Leics 6F 36
Harswell. E Yor 3F 42
Hart. Hart 8H 55
Hartburn. Nmbd 3D 54
Hartburn. Stoc T 4B 48
Hartest. Suff 6E 30
Hartfield. E Sus 2A 12
Hartford. Cambs 4K 29
Hartford. Ches W 2E 34
Hartford. Som 3J 7
Hartford Bridge. Hants 8E 20
Hartford End. Essx 2C 22
Harthill. Ches W 4D 34
Harthill. N Lan 3H 59
Harthill. S Yor 1B 36
Hartington. Derbs 3K 35
Hartland. Devn 3B 6
Hartland Quay. Devn 3B 6
Hartle. Worc 4H 27
Hartlebury. Worc 4G 27
**Hartlepool**. Hart 8J 55
Hartley. Cumb 5F 46
Hartley. Kent
nr. Cranbrook 2D 12
nr. Dartford 7C 22
Hartley. Nmbd 4G 55
Hartley Green. Staf 7H 35
Hartley Mauditt. Hants 2E 10
Hartley Wespall. Hants 8D 20
Hartley Wintney. Hants 8E 20
Hartlip. Kent 7E 22
Hartmount Holdings. High 6H 79
Hartoft End. N Yor 6E 48
Harton. N Yor 1E 42
Harton. Shrp 3C 26
Harton. Tyne 5G 55
Hartpury. Glos 1G 19
Hartshead. W Yor 5K 41
**Hartshill**. Warw 2M 27
Hartshorne. Derbs 7M 35
Hartsop. Cumb 4C 46
Hart Station. Hart 8H 55
Hartswell. Som 3K 7
Hartwell. Nptn 6E 28
Hartwood. Lanc 6D 40
Hartwood. N Lan 4G 59
Harvel. Kent 7C 22
Harvington. Worc
nr. Evesham 7J 27
nr. Kidderminster 4G 27
Harwell. Oxon 5B 20
**Harwich**. Essx 118 (8J 31)
Harwood. Dur 8B 54
Harwood. G Man 6F 40
Harwood Dale. N Yor 6G 49
Harworth. Notts 8D 42
Hascombe. Surr 2G 11
Haselbech. Nptn 4E 28
Haselbury Plucknett. Som 4C 8
Haseley. Warw 5L 27
Hasfield. Glos 1G 19
Hasguard. Pemb 6E 14
Haskayne. Lanc 7B 40
Hasketon. Suff 6J 31
Hasland. Derbs 3A 36
**Haslemere**. Surr 2G 11
**Haslingden**. Lanc 5F 40
Haslingfield. Cambs 6M 29
Haslington. Ches E 4F 34
Hassall. Ches E 4F 34
Hassall Green. Ches E 4F 34
Hassell Street. Kent 1G 13
Hassendean. Bord 7C 60
Hassingham. Norf 1K 31
Hassness. Cumb 3L 45
Hassocks. W Sus 4L 11
Hassop. Derbs 2L 35
Haster. High 6E 86
Hasthorpe. Linc 3A 38
Hastigrow. High 5D 86
Hastingleigh. Kent 1G 13
**Hastings**. E Sus 5E 12
Hastingwood. Essx 3A 22
Hastoe. Herts 3G 21
Haston. Shrp 7D 34
Haswell. Dur 7G 55
Haswell Plough. Dur 7G 55
Hatch. C Beds 7J 29
Hatch Beauchamp. Som 3B 8
Hatch End. G Lon 4J 21
Hatch Green. Som 4B 8
Hatching Green. Herts 2J 21
Hatchmere. Ches W 2D 34
Hatch Warren. Hants 1D 10
Hatcliffe. NE Lin 7K 43
Hatfield. Here 6D 26
**Hatfield**. Herts 3K 21
**Hatfield**. S Yor 7D 42
Hatfield. Worc 6G 27
Hatfield Broad Oak. Essx 2B 22
Hatfield Garden Village.
Herts 3K 21
Hatfield Heath. Essx 2B 22
Hatfield Hyde. Herts 2K 21
Hatfield Peverel. Essx 2D 22
Hatfield Woodhouse. S Yor 7D 42
Hatford. Oxon 4M 19
Hatherden. Hants 8M 19
Hatherleigh. Devn 5E 6
Hathern. Leics 7B 36
Hatherop. Glos 3K 19
Hathersage. Derbs 1L 35
Hathersage Booths. Derbs 1L 35
Hatherton. Ches E 5E 34
Hatherton. Staf 8H 35
Hatley St George. Cambs 6K 29
Hatt. Corn 5F 4
Hattersley. G Man 8H 41
Hattingley. Hants 2D 10
Hatton. Abers 2K 73
Hatton. Derbs 6L 35
Hatton. G Lon 6H 21
Hatton. Linc 2J 37
Hatton. Shrp 2C 26
Hatton. Warr 1E 34
Hatton. Warw 5L 27
Hattoncrook. Abers 3H 73
Hatton Heath. Ches W 3C 34
Hatton of Fintray. Abers 4H 73
Haugh. E Ayr 7C 58
Haugh. Linc 2M 37
Haugham. Linc 1L 37
Haugh Head. Nmbd 7H 61
Haughley. Suff 5G 31
Haughley Green. Suff 5G 31
Haugh of Ballechin. Per 2C 66
Haugh of Glass. Mor 2D 72
Haugh of Urr. Dum 5C 52
Haughton. Ches E 4D 34
Haughton. Notts 2D 36
Haughton. Shrp
nr. Bridgnorth 2E 26
nr. Oswestry 7B 34
nr. Shifnal 1F 26
nr. Shrewsbury 8D 34
Haughton. Staf 7G 35
Haughton Green. G Man 8H 41
Haughton le Skerne. Darl 4M 47
Haultwick. Herts 1L 21
Haunn. Arg 3J 63
Haunn. W Isl 4D 74
Haunton. Staf 8L 35
Hauxton. Cambs 6M 29
Havannah. Ches E 3G 35
**Havant**. Hants 5E 10
Haven. Here 6C 26
The Haven. W Sus 2H 11
Haven Bank. Linc 4K 37
Havenstreet. IOW 6C 10
Havercroft. W Yor 6A 42
**Haverfordwest**. Pemb 5F 14
**Haverhill**. Suff 7C 30
Haverigg. Cumb 7L 45
Havering-Atte-Bower.
G Lon 4B 22
Havering's Grove. Essx 4C 22
Haversham. Mil 7F 28
Haverthwaite. Cumb 7B 46
Haverton Hill. Stoc T 3B 48
Havyatt. Som 2D 8
**Hawarden**. Flin 3B 34
Hawbridge. Worc 7H 27
Hawcoat. Cumb 7M 45
Hawcross. Glos 8F 26
Hawen. Cdgn 2K 15
Hawes. N Yor 7G 47
Hawes Green. Norf 2J 31
**Hawick**. Bord 8C 60
Hawkchurch. Devn 5B 8
Hawkedon. Suff 6D 30
Hawkenbury. Kent 1E 12
Hawkeridge. Wilts 8G 19
Hawkerland. Devn 7K 7
Hawkesbury. S Glo 5F 18
Hawkesbury. Warw 3A 28
Hawkesbury Upton. S Glo 5F 18
Hawkes End. W Mid 3L 27
Hawk Green. G Man 1H 35
Hawkhurst. Kent 2D 12
Hawkhurst Common. E Sus 4B 12
Hawkinge. Kent 1J 13
Hawkley. Hants 3E 10
Hawkridge. Som 2H 7
Hawksdale. Cumb 7H 53
Hawkshaw. G Man 6F 40
Hawkshead. Cumb 6B 46
Hawkshead Hill. Cumb 6B 46
Hawkswick. N Yor 8H 47
Hawksworth. Notts 5E 36
Hawksworth. W Yor 3K 41
Hawkwell. Essx 4E 22
Hawley. Hants 8F 20
Hawley. Kent 6B 22
Hawling. Glos 1J 19
Hawnby. N Yor 7C 48
Haworth. W Yor 4J 41
Hawstead. Suff 6E 30
Hawthorn. Dur 7H 55
Hawthorn Hill. Brac 6F 20
Hawthorn Hill. Linc 4K 37
Hawthorpe. Linc 7H 37
Hawton. Notts 4E 36
**Haxby**. York 2D 42
Haxey. N Lin 8E 42
Haybridge. Shrp 4E 26
Haybridge. Som 1D 8
**Haydock**. Mers 8D 40
Haydon. Bath 8E 18
Haydon. Dors 4E 8
Haydon. Som 3A 8
Haydon Bridge. Nmbd 5B 54
Haydon Wick. Swin 5K 19
Haye. Corn 5F 4
Hayes. G Lon
nr. Bromley 7M 21
**Hayes**. G Lon
nr. Uxbridge 5H 21
Hayfield. Derbs 1J 35
Hay Green. Norf 8B 38
Hayhill. E Ayr 8C 58
Haylands. IOW 6C 10
Hayle. Corn 5J 3
Hayley Green. W Mid 3H 27
**Hayling Island**. Hants 6E 10
Hayne. Devn 5H 7
Haynes. C Beds 7H 29
Haynes West End. C Beds 7H 29
Hay-on-Wye. Powy 8M 25
Hayscastle. Pemb 4E 14
Hayscastle Cross. Pemb 4F 14
Hayshead. Ang 3K 67
Hay Street. Herts 1L 21
Hayton. Aber 5J 73
Hayton. Cumb
nr. Aspatria 7F 52
nr. Brampton 6K 53
Hayton. E Yor 3F 42
Hayton. Notts 1E 36
Hayton's Bent. Shrp 3D 26
Haytor Vale. Devn 8G 7
Haytown. Devn 4C 6
**Haywards Heath**. W Sus 3L 11
Haywood. S Lan 4H 59
Hazelbank. S Lan 5G 59
Hazelbury Bryan. Dors 5F 8
Hazeleigh. Essx 3E 22
Hazeley. Hants 8E 20
**Hazel Grove**. G Man 1H 35
Hazelhead. S Yor 7K 41
Hazelslade. Staf 8J 35
Hazel Street. Kent 2C 12
Hazelton Walls. Fife 5G 67
Hazelwood. Derbs 5M 35
Hazlemere. Buck 4F 20
Hazler. Shrp 2C 26
Hazlerigg. Tyne 4F 54
Hazles. Staf 5J 35
Hazleton. Glos 2J 19
Hazon. Nmbd 1E 54
Heacham. Norf 6C 38
Headbourne Worthy. Hants 2B 10
Headcorn. Kent 1E 12
Headingley. W Yor 4L 41
Headington. Oxon 3C 20
Headlam. Dur 4K 47
Headless Cross. Worc 5J 27
Headley. Hants
nr. Haslemere 2F 10
nr. Kingsclere 7C 20
Headley. Surr 8K 21
Headley Down. Hants 2F 10
Headley Heath. Worc 4J 27
Headley Park. Bris 7D 18
Head of Muir. Falk 1G 59
Headon. Notts 2E 36
Heads Nook. Cumb 6J 53
Heage. Derbs 4A 36
Healaugh. N Yor
nr. Grinton 6J 47
nr. York 3C 42
Heald Green. G Man 1G 35
Heale. Devn 1F 6
Healey. G Man 6G 41
Healey. Nmbd 6D 54
Healey. N Yor 7K 47
Healeyfield. Dur 7D 54
Healing. NE Lin 6K 43
Heamoor. Corn 5H 3
Heanish. Arg 3F 62
**Heanor**. Derbs 5B 36
Heanton Punchardon. Devn 2E 6
Heapham. Linc 1F 36
Heartsease. Powy 6L 25
Heasley Mill. Devn 2G 7
Heaste. High 4H 69
Heath. Derbs 3B 36
The Heath. Norf
nr. Buxton 7J 39
nr. Fakenham 7F 38
nr. Hevingham 7H 39
The Heath. Staf 6J 35
The Heath. Suff 8H 31
Heath and Reach. C Beds 1G 21
Heath Common. W Sus 4J 11
Heathcote. Derbs 3K 35
Heath Cross. Devn 6G 7
Heathencote. Nptn 7E 28
Heath End. Hants 7C 20
Heath End. Leics 7A 36
Heath End. W Mid 1J 27
Heather. Leics 8A 36
Heatherfield. High 1F 68
Heatherton. Derb 6M 35
Heathfield. Cambs 7A 30
Heathfield. Cumb 7F 52
Heathfield. Devn 8H 7
Heathfield. E Sus 3B 12
Heathfield. Ren 3B 58
Heathfield. Som
nr. Lydeard St Lawrence 2L 7
nr. Norton Fitzwarren 3L 7
Heath Green. Worc 4J 27
Heathhall. Dum 4D 52
Heath Hayes. Staf 8J 35
Heath Hill. Shrp 8F 34
Heath House. Som 1C 8
Heathrow Airport. G Lon 119 (6H 21)
Heathstock. Devn 5M 7
Heathton. Shrp 2G 27
Heathtop. Derbs 6L 35
Heath Town. W Mid 2H 27
Heatley. Staf 7J 35
Heatley. Warr 1F 34
Heaton. Lanc 1C 40
Heaton. Staf 3H 35
Heaton. Tyne 5F 54
Heaton. W Yor 4K 41
Heaton Moor. G Man 8G 41
Heaton's Bridge. Lanc 6C 40
Heaverham. Kent 8B 22
Heavitree. Devn 6J 7
**Hebburn**. Tyne 5G 55
Hebden. N Yor 1J 41
Hebden Bridge. W Yor 5H 41
Hebden Green. Ches W 3E 34
Hebing End. Herts 1L 21
Hebron. Carm 4H 15
Hebron. Nmbd 3E 54
Heck. Dum 3E 52
Heckdyke. Notts 8E 42
Heckfield. Hants 7E 20
Heckfield Green. Suff 4H 31
Heckfordbridge. Essx 1F 22
Heckington. Linc 5J 37
**Heckmondwike**. W Yor 5L 41
Heddington. Wilts 7H 19
Heddle. Orkn 8C 88
Heddon. Devn 3F 6
Heddon-on-the-Wall. Nmbd 5E 54
Hedenham. Norf 2K 31
**Hedge End**. Hants 4B 10
Hedgerley. Buck 5G 21
Hedging. Som 3B 8
Hedley on the Hill. Nmbd 6D 54
Hednesford. Staf 8J 35
Hedon. E Yor 5J 43
Hegdon Hill. Here 6D 26
Heglibister. Shet 2D 90
Heighington. Darl 3L 47
Heighington. Linc 3H 37
Heightington. Worc 4F 26
Heights of Brae. High 7F 78
Heights of Fodderty. High 7F 78
Heights of Kinlochewe.
High 7A 78
Heiton. Bord 6E 60
Hele. Devn
nr. Exeter 5J 7
nr. Holsworthy 6C 6
nr. Ilfracombe 1E 6
Hele. Torb 5M 5
Helen's Bay. Ards 4J 93
**Helensburgh**. Arg 1A 58
Helford. Corn 6L 3
Helhoughton. Norf 7E 38
Helions Bumpstead. Essx 7C 30
Helland. Corn 4C 4
Helland. Som 3B 8
Hellandbridge. Corn 4C 4
Hellesdon. Norf 8J 39
Hellesveor. Corn 4J 3
Hellidon. Nptn 6C 28
Hellifield. N Yor 2G 41
Hellingly. E Sus 4B 12
Hellington. Norf 1K 31
Hellister. Shet 3D 90
Helmdon. Nptn 7C 28
Helmingham. Suff 6H 31
Helmington Row. Dur 8E 54
Helmsdale. High 2L 79
Helmshore. Lanc 5F 40
Helmsley. N Yor 7D 48
Helperby. N Yor 1B 42
Helperthorpe. N Yor 8G 49
Helpringham. Linc 5J 37
Helpston. Pet 1J 29
Helsby. Ches W 2C 34
Helsey. Linc 2B 38
Helston. Corn 6K 3
Helstone. Corn 3C 4
Helton. Cumb 3D 46
Helwith. N Yor 5J 47
Helwith Bridge. N Yor 1G 41
Helygain. Flin 3M 33
The Hem. Shrp 1F 26
Hemblington. Norf 8K 39
**Hemel Hempstead**. Herts 3H 21
Hemerdon. Devn 6H 5
Hemingbrough. N Yor 4D 42
Hemingby. Linc 2K 37
Hemingfield. S Yor 7A 42
Hemingford Abbots.
Cambs 4K 29
Hemingford Grey. Cambs 4K 29
Hemingstone. Suff 6H 31
Hemington. Leics 7B 36
Hemington. Nptn 3H 29
Hemington. Som 8F 18
Hemley. Suff 7J 31
Hemlington. Midd 4B 48
Hempholme. E Yor 2H 43
Hempnall. Norf 2J 31
Hempnall Green. Norf 2J 31
Hempriggs. High 7E 86
Hemp's Green. Essx 1F 22
Hempstead. Essx 8C 30
Hempstead. Medw 7D 22
Hempstead. Norf
nr. Holt 6H 39
nr. Stalham 7L 39
Hempsted. Glos 2G 19
Hempton. Norf 7F 38
Hempton. Oxon 8B 28
Hemsby. Norf 8L 39
Hemswell. Linc 8G 43
Hemswell Cliff. Linc 1G 37
Hemsworth. Dors 5H 9
**Hemsworth**. W Yor 6B 42
Hemyock. Devn 4L 7
Henallt. Carm 4L 15
Henbury. Bris 6D 18
Henbury. Ches E 2G 35
Hendomen. Powy 3M 25

**Hendon**. G Lon 5K 21
Hendon. Tyne 6H 55
Hendra. Corn 6B 4
Hendre. B'end 6J 17
Hendreforgan. Rhon 6J 17
Hendy. Carm 4E 16
Heneglwys. IOA 3D 32
Henfeddau Fawr. Pemb 3J 15
Henfield. S Glo 6E 18
Henfield. W Sus 4K 11
Henford. Devn 6C 6
Hengoed. Cphy 5L 17
Hengoed. Shrp 6A 34
Hengrave. Suff 5E 30
Henham. Essx 1B 22
Heniarth. Powy 2L 25
Henlade. Som 3A 8
Henley. Dors 5E 8
Henley. Shrp
nr. Church Stretton 3C 26
nr. Ludlow 4D 26
Henley. Som 2C 8
Henley. Suff 6H 31
Henley. W Sus 3F 10
Henley Down. E Sus 4D 12
Henley-in-Arden. Warw 5K 27
**Henley-on-Thames**. Oxon 5E 20
Henley Street. Kent 7C 22
Henllan. Cdgn 2K 15
Henllan. Den 4K 33
Henllan. Mon 1A 18
Henllan Amgoed. Carm 5H 15
Henllys. Torf 4A 18
Henlow. C Beds 8J 29
Hennock. Devn 7H 7
Henny Street. Essx 8E 30
Henryd. Cnwy 3G 33
Henry's Moat. Pemb 4G 15
Hensall. N Yor 5C 42
Henshaw. Nmbd 5A 54
Hensingham. Cumb 3J 45
Henstead. Suff 3L 31
Hensting. Hants 3B 10
Henstridge. Som 4F 8
Henstridge Ash. Som 3F 8
Henstridge Bowden. Som 3E 8
Henstridge Marsh. Som 3F 8
Henton. Oxon 3E 20
Henton. Som 1C 8
Henwood. Corn 8B 6
Heogan. Shet 3E 90
Heolgerrig. Mer T 4K 17
Heol Senni. Powy 2J 17
Heol-y-Cyw. B'end 6J 17
Hepburn. Nmbd 7H 61
Hepple. Nmbd 1C 54
Hepscott. Nmbd 3F 54
Heptonstall. W Yor 5H 41
Hepworth. Suff 4F 30
Hepworth. W Yor 7K 41
Herbrandston. Pemb 6E 14
**Hereford**. Here 8D 26
Heribusta. High 6F 76
Heriot. Bord 4B 60
Hermiston. Edin 2K 59
Hermitage. Dors 5E 8
Hermitage. Bord 2K 53
Hermitage. W Ber 6C 20
Hermitage. W Sus 5E 10
Hermon. Carm
nr. Llandeilo 2F 16
nr. Newcastle Emlyn 3K 15
Hermon. IOA 4C 32
Hermon. Pemb 3J 15
Herne. Kent 7H 23
**Herne Bay**. Kent 7H 23
Herne Common. Kent 7H 23
Herne Pound. Kent 8C 22
Herner. Devn 3E 6
Hernhill. Kent 7G 23
Herodsfoot. Corn 5E 4
Heronden. Kent 8J 23
Herongate. Essx 4C 22
Heronsford. S Ayr 3G 51
Heronsgate. Herts 4H 21
Heron's Ghyll. E Sus 3A 12
Herra. Shet 4L 91
Herriard. Hants 1D 10
Herringfleet. Suff 2L 31
Herringswell. Suff 5D 30
Herrington. Tyne 6G 55
Hersden. Kent 7J 23
Hersham. Corn 5B 6
Hersham. Surr 7J 21
Herstmonceux. E Sus 4C 12
Herston. Dors 8J 9
Herston. Orkn 2F 86
**Hertford**. Herts 2L 21
Hertford Heath. Herts 2L 21
Hertingfordbury. Herts 2L 21
Hesketh. Lanc 5C 40
Hesketh Bank. Lanc 5C 40
Hesketh Lane. Lanc 3E 40
Hesket Newmarket. Cumb 8H 53
Heskin Green. Lanc 6D 40
Hesleden. Dur 8H 55
Hesleyside. Nmbd 3B 54
Heslington. York 2D 42
Hessay. York 2C 42
Hessenford. Corn 6F 4
Hessett. Suff 5F 30
Hessilhead. N Ayr 4B 58
Hessle. E Yor 5H 43
Hestaford. Shet 2C 90
Hest Bank. Lanc 1C 40
Hester's Way. Glos 1H 19
Hestinsetter. Shet 3C 90
Heston. G Lon 6J 21
Hestwall. Orkn 8B 88
**Heswall**. Mers 1A 34
Hethe. Oxon 1C 20
Hethelpit Cross. Glos 1F 18
Hethersett. Norf 1H 31
Hethersgill. Cumb 5J 53
Hetherside. Cumb 5J 53
Hethpool. Nmbd 7F 60
Hett. Dur 8F 54
Hetton. N Yor 2H 41
**Hetton-le-Hole**. Tyne 7G 55
Hetton Steads. Nmbd 6H 61
Heugh. Nmbd 4D 54
Heugh-head. Abers 4C 72
Heveningham. Suff 4K 31
Hever. Kent 1A 12
Heversham. Cumb 7C 46
Hevingham. Norf 7H 39
Hewas Water. Corn 7B 4
Hewelsfield. Glos 3D 18
Hewish. N Som 7C 18
Hewish. Som 5C 8
Hewood. Dors 5B 8
Heworth. York 2D 42
**Hexham**. Nmbd 5C 54
Hextable. Kent 6B 22
Hexton. Herts 8J 29
Hexworthy. Devn 8F 6
Heybridge. Essx
nr. Brentwood 4C 22
nr. Maldon 3E 22
Heybridge Basin. Essx 3E 22
Heybrook Bay. Devn 7G 5
Heydon. Cambs 7M 29
Heydon. Norf 7H 39
Heydour. Linc 6H 37
Heylipol. Arg 3E 62
Heyop. Powy 5M 25
Heysham. Lanc 1C 40
Heyshott. W Sus 4F 10
Heytesbury. Wilts 1H 9
Heythrop. Oxon 1A 20
**Heywood**. G Man 6G 41
Heywood. Wilts 8G 19
Hibaldstow. N Lin 7G 43
Hickleton. S Yor 7B 42
Hickling. Norf 7L 39
Hickling. Notts 7D 36
Hickling Green. Norf 7L 39
Hickling Heath. Norf 7L 39
Hickstead. W Sus 3K 11
Hidcote Bartrim. Glos 7K 27
Hidcote Boyce. Glos 7K 27
Higford. Shrp 1F 26
High Ackworth. W Yor 6B 42
Higham. Derbs 4A 36
Higham. Kent 6D 22
Higham. Lanc 4G 41
Higham. S Yor 7M 41
Higham. Suff
nr. Ipswich 8G 31
nr. Newmarket 5D 30
Higham Dykes. Nmbd 4E 54
Higham Ferrers. Nptn 5G 29
Higham Gobion. C Beds 8J 29
Higham on the Hill. Leics 2A 28
Highampton. Devn 5D 6
Higham Wood. Kent 1C 12
High Angerton. Nmbd 3D 54
High Auldgirth. Dum 3D 52
High Bankhill. Cumb 7K 53
High Banton. N Lan 1F 58
High Barnet. G Lon 4K 21
High Beech. Essx 4M 21
High Bentham. N Yor 1E 40
High Bickington. Devn 3F 6
High Biggins. Cumb 8D 46
High Birkwith. N Yor 8F 46
High Blantyre. S Lan 4E 58
High Bonnybridge. Falk 2G 59
High Borrans. Cumb 5C 46
High Bradfield. S Yor 8L 41
High Bray. Devn 2F 6
Highbridge. Cumb 7H 53
Highbridge. High 7C 70
Highbridge. Som 1B 8
Highbrook. W Sus 2L 11
High Brooms. Kent 1B 12
High Bullen. Devn 3E 6
Highburton. W Yor 6K 41
Highbury. Som 1E 8
High Buston. Nmbd 1F 54
High Callerton. Nmbd 4E 54
High Carlingill. Cumb 5E 46
High Catton. E Yor 2E 42
High Church. Nmbd 3E 54
Highclere. Hants 7B 20
Highcliffe. Dors 6L 9
High Cogges. Oxon 3A 20
High Common. Norf 1F 30
High Coniscliffe. Darl 4L 47
High Crosby. Cumb 6J 53
High Cross. Hants 3E 10
High Cross. Herts 2L 21
High Easter. Essx 2C 22
High Eggborough. N Yor 5C 42
High Ellington. N Yor 7K 47
Higher Alham. Som 1E 8
Higher Ansty. Dors 5F 8
Higher Ashton. Devn 7H 7
Higher Ballam. Lanc 4B 40
Higher Bartle. Lanc 4D 40
Higher Bockhampton. Dors 6F 8
Higher Bojewyan. Corn 5G 3
High Ercall. Telf 8D 34
Higher Cheriton. Devn 5L 7
Higher Clovelly. Devn 3C 6
Higher Compton. Plym 6G 5
Higher Dean. Devn 5K 5
Higher Dinting. Derbs 8J 41
Higher Dunstone. Devn 8G 7
Higher End. G Man 7D 40
Higherford. Lanc 3G 41
Higher Gabwell. Devn 5M 5
Higher Halstock Leigh. Dors 5D 8
Higher Heysham. Lanc 1C 40
Higher Hurdsfield. Ches E 2H 35
Higher Kingcombe. Dors 6D 8
Higher Kinnerton. Flin 3B 34
Higher Melcombe. Dors 5F 8
Higher Penwortham. Lanc 5D 40
Higher Porthpean. Corn 6C 4
Higher Poynton. Ches E 1H 35
Higher Shotton. Flin 3B 34
Higher Shurlach. Ches W 2E 34
Higher Slade. Devn 1E 6
Higher Tale. Devn 5K 7
Higher Town. IOS 1H 3
Higher Town. Som 1J 7
Highertown. Corn 4M 3
Higher Vexford. Som 2L 7
Higher Walton. Lanc 5D 40
Higher Walton. Warr 1D 34
Higher Whatcombe. Dors 5G 9
Higher Wheelton. Lanc 5E 40
Higher Whiteleigh. Corn 6B 6
Higher Whitley. Ches W 1E 34
Higher Wincham. Ches W 2E 34
Higher Wraxall. Dors 5D 8
Higher Wych. Ches W 5C 34
Higher Yalberton. Torb 6L 5
High Etherley. Dur 3K 47
High Ferry. Linc 5L 37
Highfield. E Yor 4E 42
Highfield. N Ayr 4B 58
Highfield. Tyne 6E 54
Highfields Caldecote.
Cambs 6L 29
High Gallowhill. E Dun 2E 58
High Garrett. Essx 1D 22
Highgate. G Lon 5K 21
Highgate. N Ayr 4B 58
Highgate. Powy 3L 25
High Grange. Dur 8E 54
High Green. Cumb 5C 46
High Green. Norf 1H 31
High Green. Shrp 3F 26
High Green. S Yor 8M 41
High Green. W Yor 6K 41
High Green. Worc 7G 27
Highgreen Manor. Nmbd 2B 54
High Halden. Kent 2E 12
High Halstow. Medw 6D 22
High Ham. Som 2C 8
High Harrington. Cumb 2K 45
High Haswell. Dur 7G 55
High Hatton. Shrp 7E 34
High Hawsker. N Yor 5G 49
High Hesket. Cumb 7J 53
High Hesleden. Dur 8H 55
High Hoyland. S Yor 6L 41
High Hunsley. E Yor 4G 43
High Hurstwood. E Sus 3A 12
High Hutton. N Yor 1E 42
High Ireby. Cumb 8G 53
High Keil. Arg 1B 50
High Kelling. Norf 6H 39
High Kilburn. N Yor 8C 48
High Knipe. Cumb 4D 46
High Lands. Dur 3K 47
The Highlands. Shrp 3E 26
High Lane. G Man 1H 35
High Lane. Worc 5E 26
Highlane. Ches E 3G 35
Highlane. Derbs 1B 36
High Laver. Essx 3B 22
Highlaws. Cumb 7F 52
Highleadon. Glos 1F 18
High Legh. Ches E 1F 34
Highleigh. W Sus 6F 10
High Leven. Stoc T 4B 48
Highley. Shrp 3F 26
High Littleton. Bath 8E 18
High Longthwaite. Cumb 7G 53
High Lorton. Cumb 2L 45
High Marishes. N Yor 8F 48
High Marnham. Notts 2F 36
High Melton. S Yor 7C 42
High Mickley. Nmbd 5D 54
High Moor. Lanc 6D 40
Highmoor. Cumb 7G 53
Highmoor. Oxon 5E 20
Highmoor Cross. Oxon 5E 20
Highmoor Hill. Mon 5C 18
Highnam. Glos 2F 18
High Newport. Tyne 6G 55
High Newton. Cumb 7C 46
High Newton-by-the-Sea.
Nmbd 7K 61
High Nibthwaite. Cumb 7A 46
High Offley. Staf 7F 34
High Ongar. Essx 3B 22
High Onn. Staf 8G 35
High Orchard. Glos 2G 19
High Park. Mers 6B 40
High Roding. Essx 2C 22
High Row. Cumb 8H 53
High Salvington. W Sus 5J 11
High Scales. Cumb 7F 52
High Shaw. N Yor 6G 47
High Shincliffe. Dur 7F 54
High Side. Cumb 8G 53
High Spen. Tyne 5E 54
Highsted. Kent 7F 22
High Stoop. Dur 7E 54
High Street. Corn 6B 4
High Street. Suff
nr. Aldeburgh 6L 31
nr. Bungay 3K 31
nr. Yoxford 4L 31
High Street Green. Suff 6G 31
Highstreet Green. Essx 8D 30
Highstreet Green. Surr 2G 11
Hightae. Dum 4E 52
High Throston. Hart 8H 55
High Town. Staf 8H 35
Hightown. Ches E 3G 35
Hightown. Mers 7A 40
Hightown Green. Suff 6F 30
High Toynton. Linc 3K 37
High Trewhitt. Nmbd 1D 54
High Valleyfield. Fife 1J 59
Highway. Here 7C 26
Highweek. Devn 8H 7
High Westwood. Dur 6E 54
Highwood. Staf 6J 35
Highwood. Worc 5E 26
High Worsall. N Yor 5A 48
Highworth. Swin 4L 19
High Wray. Cumb 6B 46
High Wych. Herts 2A 22
**High Wycombe**. Buck 4F 20
Hilborough. Norf 1E 30
Hilcott. Wilts 8K 19
Hildenborough. Kent 1B 12
Hildersham. Cambs 7B 30
Hilderstone. Staf 6H 35
Hilderthorpe. E Yor 1J 43
Hilfield. Dors 5E 8
Hilgay. Norf 2C 30
Hill. S Glo 4E 18
Hill. Warw 5B 28
Hill. Worc 7H 27
The Hill. Cumb 6L 45
Hillam. N Yor 5C 42
Hillbeck. Cumb 4F 46
Hillberry. IOM 7C 44
Hillborough. Kent 7J 23
Hillbourne. Pool 6J 9
Hillbrae. Abers
nr. Aberchirder 1F 72
nr. Inverurie 3G 73
nr. Methlick 2H 73
Hill Brow. Hants 3E 10
Hillbutts. Dors 5H 9
Hillcliffane. Derbs 5L 35
Hillcommon. Som 3L 7
Hill Deverill. Wilts 1G 9
Hilldyke. Linc 5L 37
Hill End. Dur 8D 54
Hill End. Fife 8D 66
Hill End. N Yor 2J 41
Hillend. Fife 1K 59
Hillend. N Lan 3G 59
Hillend. Shrp 2G 27
Hillend. Swan 7L 15
Hillersland. Glos 2D 18
Hillerton. Devn 6G 7
Hillesden. Buck 1D 20
Hillesley. Glos 5F 18
Hillfarrance. Som 3L 7
Hill Gate. Here 1C 18
Hill Green. Essx 8A 30
Hill Green. W Ber 6B 20
Hillhall. Lis 5H 93
Hill Head. Hants 5C 10
Hillhead. Abers 2E 72
Hillhead. Devn 6M 5
Hillhead. S Ayr 8C 58
Hillhead of Auchentumb.
Abers 8J 81
Hilliard's Cross. Staf 8K 35
Hilliclay. High 5C 86
Hillingdon. G Lon 5H 21
Hillington. Glas 3D 58
Hillington. Norf 7D 38
Hillmorton. Warw 4C 28
Hill of Beath. Fife 8E 66
Hill of Fearn. High 6J 79
Hill of Fiddes. Abers 3J 73
Hill of Keillor. Ang 3F 66
Hill of Overbrae. Abers 7H 81
Hill Ridware. Staf 8J 35
Hillsborough. Lis 6H 93
Hillsborough. S Yor 8M 41
Hill Side. W Yor 6K 41
Hillside. Abers 6J 73
Hillside. Ang 1L 67
Hillside. Devn 5K 5
Hillside. Mers 6B 40
Hillside. Orkn 7C 88
Hillside. Shet 1E 90
Hillside. Shrp 3E 26
Hillside. Worc 5F 26
Hillside of Prieston. Ang 4G 67
Hill Somersal. Derbs 6K 35
Hillstown. Derbs 3B 36
Hillstreet. Hants 4M 9
Hillswick. Shet 6G 91
Hill Top. Dur
nr. Barnard Castle 3H 47
nr. Durham 7F 54
nr. Stanley 6E 54
Hilltown. New M 7H 93
Hill View. Dors 6H 9
Hillwell. Shet 6D 90
Hill Wootton. Warw 5M 27
Hillyland. Per 5D 66
Hilmarton. Wilts 6J 19
Hilperton. Wilts 8G 19
Hilperton Marsh. Wilts 8G 19
Hilsea. Port 5D 10
Hilston. E Yor 4K 43
Hiltingbury. Hants 3B 10
Hilton. Cambs 5K 29
Hilton. Cumb 3F 46
Hilton. Derbs 6L 35
Hilton. Dors 5F 8
Hilton. Dur 3K 47
Hilton. High 5H 79
Hilton. Shrp 2F 26
Hilton. Staf 1J 27
Hilton. Stoc T 4B 48
Hilton of Cadboll. High 6J 79
Himbleton. Worc 6H 27
Himley. Staf 2G 27
Hincaster. Cumb 7D 46
Hinchwick. Glos 1K 19
**Hinckley**. Leics 2B 28
Hinderclay. Suff 4G 31
Hinderwell. N Yor 4E 48
Hindford. Shrp 6B 34
Hindhead. Surr 2F 10
**Hindley**. G Man 7E 40
Hindley. Nmbd 6D 54
Hindley Green. G Man 7E 40
Hindlip. Worc 6G 27
Hindolveston. Norf 7G 39
Hindon. Wilts 2H 9
Hindringham. Norf 6F 38
Hingham. Norf 1G 31
Hinksford. Staf 3G 27
Hinstock. Shrp 7E 34
Hintlesham. Suff 7G 31
Hinton. Hants 6L 9
Hinton. Here 8B 26
Hinton. Nptn 6C 28
Hinton. Shrp 1C 26
Hinton. S Glo 6F 18
Hinton Ampner. Hants 3C 10
Hinton Blewett. Bath 8D 18
Hinton Charterhouse. Bath 8F 18
Hinton-in-the-Hedges. Nptn 8C 28
Hinton Martell. Dors 5J 9
Hinton on the Green. Worc 7J 27
Hinton Parva. Swin 5L 19
Hinton St George. Som 4C 8
Hinton St Mary. Dors 4F 8
Hinton Waldrist. Oxon 4A 20
Hints. Shrp 4E 26
Hints. Staf 1K 27
Hinwick. Bed 5G 29
Hinxhill. Kent 1G 13
Hinxton. Cambs 7A 30
Hinxworth. Herts 7K 29
Hipley. Hants 4D 10
Hipperholme. W Yor 5K 41
Hipsburn. Nmbd 8K 61
Hipswell. N Yor 6K 47
Hiraeth. Carm 4H 15
Hirn. Abers 5G 73
Hirnant. Powy 8K 33
Hirst. N Lan 3G 59
Hirst. Nmbd 3F 54
Hirst Courtney. N Yor 5D 42
Hirwaen. Den 4L 33
Hirwaun. Rhon 4J 17
Hiscott. Devn 3E 6
Histon. Cambs 5M 29
Hitcham. Suff 6F 30
**Hitchin**. Herts 1J 21
Hittisleigh. Devn 6G 7
Hittisleigh Barton. Devn 6G 7
Hive. E Yor 4F 42
Hixon. Staf 7J 35
Hoaden. Kent 8J 23
Hoar Cross. Staf 7K 35
Hoarwithy. Here 1D 18
Hoath. Kent 7J 23
Yr Hôb. Flin 4B 34
Hobarris. Shrp 4B 26
Hobbister. Orkn 1E 86
Hobbles Green. Suff 6D 30
Hobbs Cross. Essx 4A 22
Hobkirk. Bord 8C 60
Hobson. Dur 6E 54
Hoby. Leics 8D 36
Hockering. Norf 8G 39
Hockering Heath. Norf 8G 39
Hockerton. Notts 4E 36
**Hockley**. Essx 4E 22
Hockley. Staf 1L 27
Hockley. W Mid 4L 27
Hockley Heath. W Mid 4K 27
Hockliffe. C Beds 1G 21
Hockwold cum Wilton.
Norf 3D 30
Hockworthy. Devn 4K 7
**Hoddesdon**. Herts 3L 21
Hoddlesden. Bkbn 5F 40
Hoddomcross. Dum 4F 52
Hodgeston. Pemb 7G 15
Hodley. Powy 3L 25
Hodnet. Shrp 7E 34
Hodsoll Street. Kent 7C 22
Hodson. Swin 5K 19
Hodthorpe. Derbs 2C 36
Hoe. Norf 8F 38
The Hoe. Plym 6G 5
Hoe Gate. Hants 4D 10
Hoff. Cumb 4E 46
Hoffleet Stow. Linc 6K 37
Hogaland. Shet 6H 91
Hogben's Hill. Kent 8G 23
Hoggard's Green. Suff 6E 30
Hoggeston. Buck 1F 20
Hoggrill's End. Warw 2L 27
Hogha Gearraidh. W Isl 6J 75
Hoghton. Lanc 5E 40
Hoghton Bottoms. Lanc 5E 40
Hognaston. Derbs 4L 35
Hogsthorpe. Linc 2B 38
Hogstock. Dors 5H 9
Holbeach. Linc 7L 37
Holbeach Bank. Linc 7L 37
Holbeach Clough. Linc 7L 37
Holbeach Drove. Linc 8L 37
Holbeach Hurn. Linc 7L 37
Holbeach St Johns. Linc 8L 37
Holbeach St Marks. Linc 6L 37
Holbeach St Matthew. Linc 6M 37
Holbeck. Notts 2C 36
Holbeck. W Yor 4L 41
Holbeck Woodhouse. Notts 2C 36
Holberrow Green. Worc 6J 27
Holbeton. Devn 6J 5
Holborn. G Lon 5L 21
Holbrook. Derbs 5A 36
Holbrook. S Yor 1B 36
Holbrook. Suff 8H 31
Holburn. Nmbd 6H 61
Holbury. Hants 5B 10
Holcombe. Devn 8J 7
Holcombe. G Man 6F 40
Holcombe. Som 1E 8
Holcombe Brook. G Man 6F 40
Holcombe Rogus. Devn 4K 7
Holcot. Nptn 5E 28
Holden. Lanc 3F 40
Holdenby. Nptn 5D 28
Holder's Green. Essx 1C 22
Holdgate. Shrp 3D 26
Holdingham. Linc 5H 37
Holditch. Dors 5B 8
Holemoor. Devn 5D 6
Hole Street. W Sus 4J 11
Holford. Som 1L 7
Holker. Cumb 8B 46
Holkham. Norf 5E 38
Hollacombe. Devn 5C 6
Holland. Orkn
on Papa Westray 4D 88
on Stronsay 7F 88
Holland Fen. Linc 5K 37
Holland Lees. Lanc 7D 40
Holland-on-Sea. Essx 2J 23
Holland Park. W Mid 1J 27
Hollandstoun. Orkn 4G 89
Hollesley. Suff 7K 31
Hollinfare. Warr 8E 40
Hollingbourne. Kent 8E 22
Hollingbury. Brig 5L 11
Hollingdon. Buck 1F 20
Hollingrove. E Sus 3C 12
Hollington. Derbs 6L 35
Hollington. E Sus 4D 12
Hollington. Staf 6J 35
Hollington Grove. Derbs 6L 35
Hollingwood. Derbs 2B 36
Hollingworth. G Man 8J 41
Hollins. Derbs 2M 35
Hollins. G Man
nr. Bury 7G 41
nr. Middleton 7G 41
Hollinsclough. Staf 3J 35
Hollinswood. Telf 1F 26
Hollinthorpe. W Yor 4A 42
Hollinwood. G Man 7H 41
Hollinwood. Shrp 6D 34
Hollocombe. Devn 4F 6
Holloway. Derbs 4M 35
Hollowell. Nptn 4D 28
Hollow Meadows. S Yor 1L 35
Hollows. Dum 4H 53
Hollybush. Cphy 4L 17
Hollybush. E Ayr 8B 58
Hollybush. Worc 8F 26
Holly End. Norf 1A 30
Holly Hill. N Yor 5K 47
Hollyhurst. Shrp 5D 34
Hollym. E Yor 5L 43
Hollywood. Worc 4J 27
Holmacott. Devn 3E 6
Holmbridge. W Yor 7K 41
Holmbury St Mary. Surr 1J 11
Holmbush. Corn 6C 4
Holmcroft. Staf 7H 35
Holme. Cambs 3J 29
Holme. Cumb 8D 46
Holme. N Lin 7G 43
Holme. N Yor 7A 48
Holme. Notts 4F 36
Holme. W Yor 7K 41
Holmebridge. Dors 7G 9
Holme Chapel. Lanc 5G 41
Holme Hale. Norf 1E 30
Holme Lacy. Here 8D 26
Holme Marsh. Here 6B 26
Holmend. Dum 1E 52
Holme next the Sea. Norf 5D 38
Holme-on-Spalding-Moor.
E Yor 4F 42
Holme on the Wolds. E Yor 3G 43
Holme Pierrepont. Notts 6D 36
Holmer. Here 7D 26
Holmer Green. Buck 4G 21
Holmes. Lanc 6C 40
Holme St Cuthbert. Cumb 7F 52
Holmes Chapel. Ches E 3F 34
Holmesfield. Derbs 2M 35
Holmeswood. Lanc 6C 40
Holmewood. Derbs 3B 36
**Holmfirth**. W Yor 7K 41
Holmhead. E Ayr 7D 58
Holmisdale. High 1C 68
Holm of Drumlanrig. Dum 2C 52
Holmpton. E Yor 5L 43
Holmrook. Cumb 5K 45
Holmsgarth. Shet 3E 90
Holmside. Dur 7F 54
Holmwrangle. Cumb 7K 53
Holne. Devn 5K 5
Holsworthy. Devn 5C 6
Holsworthy Beacon. Devn 5C 6
Holt. Dors 5J 9
Holt. Norf 6G 39
Holt. Wilts 7G 19
Holt. Worc 5G 27
Holt. Wrex 4C 34
Holtby. York 2D 42
Holt End. Hants 2D 10
Holt End. Worc 5J 27
Holt Fleet. Worc 5G 27
Holt Green. Lanc 7B 40
Holt Heath. Dors 5J 9
Holt Heath. Worc 5G 27
Holton. Oxon 3C 20
Holton. Som 3E 8
Holton. Suff 4K 31
Holton cum Beckering. Linc 1J 37
Holton Heath. Dors 6H 9
Holton le Clay. Linc 7K 43
Holton le Moor. Linc 8H 43
Holton St Mary. Suff 8G 31
Holt Pound. Hants 1F 10
Holtsmere End. Herts 2H 21
Holtye. E Sus 2A 12
Holwell. Dors 4F 8
Holwell. Herts 8J 29
Holwell. Leics 7E 36
Holwell. Oxon 3L 19
Holwell. Som 1F 8
Holwick. Dur 3H 47
Holworth. Dors 7F 8
Holybourne. Hants 1E 10
Holy City. Devn 5B 8
Holy Cross. Worc 4H 27
Holyfield. Essx 3L 21
**Holyhead**. IOA 2B 32
Holy Island. Nmbd 5J 61
Holymoorside. Derbs 3M 35
Holyport. Wind 6F 20
Holystone. Nmbd 1C 54
Holytown. N Lan 3F 58
Holywell. Cambs 4L 29
Holywell. Corn 3L 3
Holywell. Dors 5D 8
Holywell. Flin 3L 33
Holywell. Glos 4F 18
Holywell. Nmbd 4G 55
Holywell. Warw 5K 27
Holywell Green. W Yor 6J 41
Holywell Lake. Som 3L 7
Holywell Row. Suff 4D 30
**Holywood**. Ards 5J 93
Holywood. Dum 3D 52
Homer. Shrp 1E 26
Homer Green. Mers 7B 40
Homersfield. Suff 3J 31
Hom Green. Here 1D 18
Homington. Wilts 3K 9
Honeyborough. Pemb 6F 14
Honeybourne. Worc 7K 27
Honeychurch. Devn 5F 6
Honeydon. Bed 6J 29
Honey Hill. Kent 7H 23
Honey Street. Wilts 7K 19
Honey Tye. Suff 8F 30
Honeywick. C Beds 1G 21
Honiley. Warw 4L 27
Honing. Norf 7K 39
Honingham. Norf 8H 39
Honington. Linc 5G 37
Honington. Suff 4F 30
Honington. Warw 7L 27
Honiton. Devn 5L 7
Honley. W Yor 6K 41
Honnington. Telf 8F 34
Hoo. Suff 6J 31
Hoobrook. Worc 4G 27
Hood Green. S Yor 7M 41
Hooe. E Sus 5C 12
Hooe. Plym 6H 5
Hooe Common. E Sus 4C 12
Hoo Green. Ches E 1F 34
Hoohill. Bkpl 4B 40
Hook. Cambs 2M 29
Hook. E Yor 5E 42
Hook. G Lon 7J 21
Hook. Hants
nr. Basingstoke 8E 20
nr. Fareham 5C 10
Hook. Pemb 5F 14
Hook. Wilts 5J 19
Hook-a-Gate. Shrp 1C 26
Hook Bank. Worc 7G 27
Hooke. Dors 5D 8
Hooker Gate. Tyne 6E 54
Hookgate. Staf 6F 34
Hook Green. Kent
nr. Lamberhurst 2C 12
nr. Meopham 7C 22
nr. Southfleet 6C 22
Hook Norton. Oxon 8A 28
Hook's Cross. Herts 1K 21
Hook Street. Glos 4E 18
Hookway. Devn 6H 7
Hookwood. Surr 1K 11
Hoole. Ches W 3C 34
Hooley. Surr 8K 21
Hooley Bridge. G Man 6G 41
Hooley Brow. G Man 6G 41
Hoo St Werburgh. Medw 6D 22
Hooton. Ches W 2B 34
Hooton Levitt. S Yor 8C 42
Hooton Pagnell. S Yor 7B 42
Hooton Roberts. S Yor 8B 42
Hoove. Shet 3D 90
Hope. Derbs 1K 35
Hope. Flin 4B 34
Hope. High 5G 85
Hope. Powy 1A 26
Hope. Shrp 1B 26
Hope. Staf 4K 35
Hope Bagot. Shrp 4D 26
Hope Bowdler. Shrp 2C 26
Hopedale. Staf 4K 35
Hope Green. Ches E 1H 35
Hopeman. Mor 7M 79
Hope Mansell. Here 2E 18
Hopesay. Shrp 3B 26
Hope's Green. Essx 5D 22
Hopetown. W Yor 5A 42
Hope under Dinmore. Here 6D 26
Hopley's Green. Here 6B 26
Hopperton. N Yor 2B 42
Hop Pole. Linc 8J 37
Hopstone. Shrp 2F 26
Hopton. Derbs 4L 35
Hopton. Powy 3M 25
Hopton. Shrp
nr. Oswestry 7B 34
nr. Wem 7D 34
Hopton. Staf 7H 35
Hopton. Suff 4F 30
Hopton Cangeford. Shrp 3D 26
Hopton Castle. Shrp 4B 26
Hopton Heath. Staf 7H 35
Hoptonheath. Shrp 4B 26
Hopton on Sea. Norf 1M 31
Hopton Wafers. Shrp 4E 26
Hopwas. Staf 1K 27
Hopwood. Worc 4J 27
Horam. E Sus 4B 12
Horbling. Linc 6J 37
Horbury. W Yor 6L 41
Horcott. Glos 3K 19
Horden. Dur 7H 55
Horderley. Shrp 3C 26
Hordle. Hants 6L 9
Hordley. Shrp 6B 34
Horeb. Carm
nr. Brechfa 4M 15
nr. Llanelli 6L 15
Horeb. Cdgn 2K 15
Horfield. Bris 6D 18
Horgabost. W Isl 4B 76
Horham. Suff 4J 31
Horkstow. N Lin 6G 43
Horley. Oxon 7B 28
**Horley**. Surr 1K 11
Horn Ash. Dors 5B 8
Hornblotton Green. Som 2D 8
Hornby. Lanc 1D 40
Hornby. N Yor
nr. Appleton Wiske 5A 48
nr. Catterick Garrison 6L 47
Horncastle. Linc 3K 37
**Hornchurch**. G Lon 5B 22
Horncliffe. Nmbd 5G 61
Horndean. Hants 4E 10
Horndean. Bord 5F 60
Horndon. Devn 7E 6
Horndon on the Hill. Thur 5C 22
Horne. Surr 1L 11
Horner. Som 1J 7
Horning. Norf 8K 39
Horninghold. Leics 2F 28
Horninglow. Staf 7L 35
Horningsea. Cambs 5A 30
Horningsham. Wilts 1G 9
Horningtoft. Norf 7F 38
Hornsbury. Som 4B 8
Hornsby. Cumb 6K 53
Hornsbygate. Cumb 6K 53
Horns Corner. Kent 3D 12
Horns Cross. Devn 3C 6
Hornsea. E Yor 3K 43
Hornsea Burton. E Yor 3K 43
**Hornsey**. G Lon 5L 21
Hornton. Oxon 7A 28
Horpit. Swin 5L 19
Horrabridge. Devn 5H 5
Horringer. Suff 5E 30
Horringford. IOW 7C 10
Horrocks Fold. G Man 6F 40
Horrocksford. Lanc 3F 40
Horsbrugh Ford. Bord 6L 59
Horsebridge. Devn 8D 6
Horsebridge. Hants 2M 9
Horsebrook. Staf 8G 35
Horsecastle. N Som 7C 18
Horsehay. Telf 1E 26
Horseheath. Cambs 7C 30
Horsehouse. N Yor 7J 47
Horsell. Surr 8G 21
Horseman's Green. Wrex 5C 34
Horsenden. Buck 3E 20
Horseway. Cambs 3M 29
Horsey. Norf 7L 39
Horsey. Som 2B 8
Horsford. Norf 8H 39
**Horsforth**. W Yor 4L 41
**Horsham**. W Sus 2J 11
Horsham. Worc 6F 26
Horsham St Faith. Norf 8J 39
Horsington. Linc 3J 37
Horsington. Som 3F 8
Horsley. Derbs 5A 36
Horsley. Glos 4G 19
Horsley. Nmbd
nr. Prudhoe 5D 54
nr. Rochester 2B 54
Horsley Cross. Essx 1H 23
Horsleycross Street. Essx 1H 23
Horsleyhill. Bord 8C 60
Horsleyhope. Dur 7D 54
Horsley Woodhouse. Derbs 5A 36
Horsmonden. Kent 1C 12
Horspath. Oxon 3C 20
Horstead. Norf 8J 39
Horsted Keynes. W Sus 3L 11
Horton. Buck 2G 21
Horton. Dors 5J 9
Horton. Lanc 2G 41
Horton. Nptn 6F 28
Horton. Shrp 6C 34
Horton. Som 4B 8
Horton. S Glo 5F 18
Horton. Staf 4H 35
Horton. Swan 8L 15
Horton. Wilts 7J 19
Horton. Wind 6H 21
Horton Cross. Som 4B 8
Horton-cum-Studley. Oxon 2C 20
Horton Grange. Nmbd 4F 54
Horton Green. Ches W 5C 34
Horton Heath. Hants 4B 10
Horton in Ribblesdale.
N Yor 8G 47
Horton Kirby. Kent 7B 22
Hortonwood. Telf 8E 34
**Horwich**. G Man 6E 40
Horwich End. Derbs 1J 35
Horwood. Devn 3E 6
Hoscar. Lanc 6C 40
Hose. Leics 7E 36
Hosh. Per 5B 66
Hosta. W Isl 6J 75
Hoswick. Shet 5E 90
Hotham. E Yor 4F 42
Hothfield. Kent 1F 12
Hoton. Leics 7C 36
Houbie. Shet 4L 91
Hough. Arg 3E 62
Hough. Ches E
nr. Crewe 4F 34
nr. Wilmslow 2G 35
Hougham. Linc 5F 36
Hough Green. Hal 1C 34
Hough-on-the-Hill. Linc 5G 37
Houghton. Cambs 4K 29
Houghton. Cumb 6J 53
Houghton. Hants 2M 9
Houghton. Nmbd 5E 54
Houghton. Pemb 6F 14
Houghton. W Sus 4H 11
Houghton Bank. Darl 3L 47
Houghton Conquest.
C Beds 7H 29
Houghton Green. E Sus 3F 12
Houghton-le-Side. Darl 3L 47
**Houghton-le-Spring**. Tyne 6G 55
Houghton on the Hill. Leics 1D 28
Houghton Regis. C Beds 1H 21
Houghton St Giles. Norf 6F 38
Houlland. Shet
on Mainland 2D 90
on Yell 6K 91
Houlsyke. N Yor 5E 48
Houlton. Warw 4C 28
Hound. Hants 5B 10
Hound Green. Hants 8E 20
Houndslow. Bord 5D 60
Houndsmoor. Som 3L 7
Houndwood. Bord 3F 60
Hounsdown. Hants 4M 9
**Hounslow**. G Lon 6J 21
Housabister. Shet 2E 90
Housay. Shet 6L 91
Househill. High 8J 79
Housetter. Shet 5H 91
Houss. Shet 4D 90
Houston. Ren 3C 58
Housty. High 8C 86
Houton. Orkn 1E 86
**Hove**. Brig 106 (5K 11)
Hoveringham. Notts 5D 36
Hoveton. Norf 8K 39
Hovingham. N Yor 8D 48
How. Cumb 6K 53
How Caple. Here 8E 26
Howden. E Yor 5E 42
Howden-le-Wear. Dur 8E 54
Howe. High 5E 86
Howe. Norf 1J 31
Howe. N Yor 7A 48
The Howe. Cumb 7C 46
The Howe. IOM 8A 44
Howe Green. Essx 3D 22
Howe Green. Warw 3M 27
Howegreen. Essx 3E 22
Howell. Linc 5J 37
How End. C Beds 7H 29
Howe of Teuchar. Abers 1G 73
Howes. Dum 5F 52
Howe Street. Essx
nr. Chelmsford 2C 22
nr. Finchingfield 8C 30
Howey. Powy 7K 25
Howgate. Midl 4L 59
Howgill. Lanc 3G 41
Howgill. N Yor 2J 41
How Green. Kent 1A 12
How Hill. Norf 8K 39
Howick. Nmbd 8K 61
Howle. Telf 7E 34
Howle Hill. Here 1E 18
Howleigh. Som 4M 7
Howlett End. Essx 8B 30
Howley. Som 5A 8
Howley. Warr 1E 34
Hownam. Bord 8E 60
Howsham. N Lin 7H 43
Howsham. N Yor 1E 42
Howtel. Nmbd 6F 60
Howt Green. Kent 7E 22
Howton. Here 1C 18
Howwood. Ren 3B 58
Hoxne. Suff 4H 31
**Hoylake**. Mers 2M 33
**Hoyland**. S Yor 7A 42
Hoylandswaine. S Yor 7L 41
Hoyle. W Sus 4G 11
Hubberholme. N Yor 8H 47
Hubberston. Pemb 6E 14
Hubbert's Bridge. Linc 5K 37
Huby. N Yor
nr. Harrogate 3L 41
nr. York 1C 42
Hucclecote. Glos 2G 19
Hucking. Kent 8E 22
**Hucknall**. Notts 5C 36
**Huddersfield**. W Yor 6K 41
Huddington. Worc 6H 27
Huddlesford. Staf 1K 27
Hudswell. N Yor 5K 47
Huggate. E Yor 2F 42
Hugglescote. Leics 8B 36
Hughenden Valley. Buck 4F 20
Hughley. Shrp 2D 26
Hughton. High 1E 70
Hugh Town. IOS 1H 3
Hugus. Corn 4L 3
Huish. Devn 4E 6
Huish. Wilts 7K 19
Huish Champflower. Som 3K 7
Huish Episcopi. Som 3C 8
Huisinis. W Isl 2A 76
Hulcote. Nptn 7E 28
Hulcott. Buck 2F 20
Hulham. Devn 7K 7
**Hull**. Hull
**Kingston upon Hull 110** (5J 43)
Hulland. Derbs 5L 35
Hulland Moss. Derbs 5L 35
Hulland Ward. Derbs 5L 35
Hullavington. Wilts 5G 19
Hullbridge. Essx 4E 22
Hulme. G Man 8G 41
Hulme. Staf 5H 35
Hulme End. Staf 4K 35
Hulme Walfield. Ches E 3G 35
Hulverstone. IOW 7A 10
Hulver Street. Suff 3L 31
Humber. Devn 8J 7
Humber. Here 6D 26
**Humber Bridge**. N Lin 5H 43
Humberside Airport. N Lin 6H 43
Humberston. NE Lin 7L 43
Humberstone. Leic 1D 28
Humbie. E Lot 3B 60
Humbleton. E Yor 4K 43
Humbleton. Nmbd 7G 61
Humby. Linc 6H 37
Hume. Bord 5E 60
Humshaugh. Nmbd 4C 54
Huna. High 4E 86
Huncoat. Lanc 4F 40
Huncote. Leics 2C 28
Hundall. Derbs 2A 36
Hunderthwaite. Dur 3H 47
Hundleby. Linc 3L 37
Hundle Houses. Linc 4K 37
Hundleton. Pemb 6F 14
Hundon. Suff 7D 30
The Hundred. Here 5D 26
Hundred Acres. Hants 4C 10
Hundred House. Powy 7L 25
Hungarton. Leics 1D 28
Hungerford. Hants 4K 9
Hungerford. Shrp 3D 26
Hungerford. Som 1K 7
Hungerford. W Ber 7M 19
Hungerford Newtown.
W Ber 6A 20
Hunger Hill. G Man 7E 40
Hungerton. Linc 6F 36
Hungladder. High 6E 76
Hungryhatton. Shrp 7E 34
Hunmanby. N Yor 8H 49
Hunmanby Sands. N Yor 8J 49
Hunningham. Warw 5A 28
Hunnington. Worc 3H 27
Hunny Hill. IOW 7B 10
Hunsdon. Herts 2M 21
Hunsdonbury. Herts 2M 21
Hunsingore. N Yor 2B 42
Hunslet. W Yor 4M 41
Hunslet Carr. W Yor 4M 41
Hunsonby. Cumb 8K 53
Hunspow. High 4D 86
Hunstanton. Norf 5C 38
Hunstanworth. Dur 7C 54
Hunston. Suff 5F 30
Hunston. W Sus 5F 10
Hunstrete. Bath 7E 18
Hunt End. Worc 5J 27
Hunterfield. Midl 3M 59
Hunters Forstal. Kent 7H 23
Hunter's Quay. Arg 2L 57
Huntham. Som 3B 8
Hunthill Lodge. Ang 8D 72
**Huntingdon**. Cambs 4K 29
Huntingfield. Suff 4K 31
Huntingford. Wilts 3G 9
Huntington. Ches W 3C 34
Huntington. E Lot 2B 60
Huntington. Here 6A 26
Huntington. Staf 8H 35
Huntington. Telf 1E 26
Huntington. York 2D 42
Huntingtower. Per 5D 66
Huntley. Glos 2F 18
Huntley. Staf 5J 35
Huntly. Abers 2E 72
Huntlywood. Bord 5D 60
Hunton. Hants 2B 10
Hunton. Kent 1D 12
Hunton. N Yor 6K 47
Hunton Bridge. Herts 4H 21
Hunt's Corner. Norf 3G 31
Huntscott. Som 1J 7
Hunt's Cross. Mers 1C 34
Hunts Green. Warw 2K 27
Huntsham. Devn 3K 7
Huntshaw. Devn 3E 6
Huntspill. Som 1B 8
Huntstile. Som 2A 8
Huntworth. Som 2B 8
Hunwick. Dur 8E 54
Hunworth. Norf 6G 39
Hurcott. Som
nr. Ilminster 4B 8
nr. Somerton 3D 8
Hurdcott. Wilts 2K 9
Hurdley. Powy 2A 26
Hurdsfield. Ches E 2H 35
Hurlet. Glas 3D 58
Hurley. Warw 2L 27
Hurley. Wind 5F 20
Hurlford. E Ayr 6C 58
Hurliness. Orkn 3D 86
Hurlston Green. Lanc 6C 40
Hurn. Dors 6K 9
Hursey. Dors 5C 8
Hursley. Hants 3B 10
Hurst. G Man 7H 41
Hurst. N Yor 5J 47
Hurst. Som 4C 8
Hurst. Wok 6E 20
Hurstbourne Priors. Hants 1B 10
Hurstbourne Tarrant. Hants 8A 20
Hurst Green. Ches E 5D 34
Hurst Green. E Sus 3D 12
Hurst Green. Essx 2G 23
Hurst Green. Lanc 4E 40
Hurst Green. Surr 8L 21
Hurstley. Here 7B 26
Hurstpierpoint. W Sus 4K 11
Hurstway Common. Here 7B 26
Hurst Wickham. W Sus 4K 11
Hurstwood. Lanc 4G 41
Hurtmore. Surr 1G 11
Hurworth-on-Tees. Darl 4M 47
Hurworth Place. Darl 5L 47
Hury. Dur 4H 47
Husbands Bosworth. Leics 3D 28
Husborne Crawley. C Beds 8G 29
Husthwaite. N Yor 8C 48
Hutcherleigh. Devn 6K 5
Hut Green. N Yor 5C 42
Huthwaite. Notts 4B 36
Huttoft. Linc 2B 38
Hutton. Cumb 3C 46
Hutton. E Yor 2H 43
Hutton. Essx 4C 22
Hutton. Lanc 5C 40
Hutton. N Som 8B 18
Hutton. Bord 4G 61
Hutton Bonville. N Yor 5M 47
Hutton Buscel. N Yor 7G 49
Hutton Conyers. N Yor 8M 47
Hutton Cranswick. E Yor 2H 43
Hutton End. Cumb 8J 53
Hutton Gate. Red C 4C 48
Hutton Henry. Dur 8H 55
Hutton-le-Hole. N Yor 7E 48
Hutton Magna. Dur 4K 47
Hutton Mulgrave. N Yor 5F 48
Hutton Roof. Cumb
nr. Kirkby Lonsdale 8D 46
nr. Penrith 8H 53
Hutton Rudby. N Yor 5B 48
Huttons Ambo. N Yor 1E 42
Hutton Sessay. N Yor 8B 48
Hutton Village. Red C 4D 48
Hutton Wandesley. N Yor 2C 42
Huxham. Devn 6J 7
Huxham Green. Som 2D 8
Huxley. Ches W 3D 34
Huxter. Shet
on Mainland 2B 90
on Whalsay 1F 90
**Huyton**. Mers 8C 40
**Hwlffordd**. Pemb 5F 14
Hycemoor. Cumb 6K 45
Hyde. Glos
nr. Stroud 3G 19
nr. Winchcombe 1J 19
**Hyde**. G Man 8H 41
Hyde Heath. Buck 3G 21
Hyde Lea. Staf 8H 35
Hyde Park. S Yor 7C 42
Hydestile. Surr 1G 11
Hyndford Bridge. S Lan 5H 59
Hynish. Arg 4E 62
Hyssington. Powy 2B 26
**Hythe**. Hants 5B 10
**Hythe**. Kent 2H 13
Hythe End. Wind 6H 21
Hythie. Abers 8K 81
Hyton. Cumb 6K 45

## I

Ianstown. Mor 7D 80
Iarsiadar. W Isl 8E 82
Ibberton. Dors 5F 8
Ible. Derbs 4L 35
Ibrox. Glas 3D 58
Ibsley. Hants 5K 9
Ibstock. Leics 8B 36
Ibstone. Buck 4E 20
Ibthorpe. Hants 8A 20
Iburndale. N Yor 5F 48
Ibworth. Hants 8C 20
Icelton. N Som 7B 18
Ichrachan. Arg 4E 64
Ickburgh. Norf 2E 30
Ickenham. G Lon 5H 21
Ickenthwaite. Cumb 7B 46
Ickford. Buck 3D 20
Ickham. Kent 8J 23
Ickleford. Herts 8J 29
Icklesham. E Sus 4E 12
Ickleton. Cambs 7A 30
Icklingham. Suff 4D 30
Ickwell. C Beds 7J 29
Icomb. Glos 1L 19
Idbury. Oxon 2L 19
Iddesleigh. Devn 5E 6
Ide. Devn 6H 7
Ideford. Devn 8H 7
Ide Hill. Kent 8A 22
Iden. E Sus 3F 12
Iden Green. Kent
nr. Benenden 2E 12
nr. Goudhurst 2D 12
Idle. W Yor 4K 41
Idless. Corn 4M 3
Idlicote. Warw 7L 27
Idmiston. Wilts 2K 9
Idole. Carm 5L 15
Idridgehay. Derbs 5L 35
Idrigill. High 7E 76
Idstone. Oxon 5L 19
Iffley. Oxon 3C 20
Ifield. W Sus 2K 11
Ifieldwood. W Sus 2K 11
Ifold. W Sus 2H 11
Iford. E Sus 5M 11
Ifton Heath. Shrp 6B 34
Ightfield. Shrp 6D 34
Ightham. Kent 8B 22
Iken. Suff 6L 31
Ilam. Staf 4K 35
Ilchester. Som 3D 8
Ilderton. Nmbd 7H 61
**Ilford**. G Lon 5M 21
Ilford. Som 4B 8
**Ilfracombe**. Devn 1E 6
**Ilkeston**. Derbs 5B 36
Ilketshall St Andrew. Suff 3K 31
Ilketshall St Lawrence. Suff 3K 31
Ilketshall St Margaret. Suff 3K 31
**Ilkley**. W Yor 3K 41
Illand. Corn 8B 6
Illey. W Mid 3H 27
Illidge Green. Ches E 3F 34
Illington. Norf 3F 30
Illingworth. W Yor 5J 41
Illogan. Corn 4K 3
Illogan Highway. Corn 4K 3
Illston on the Hill. Leics 2E 28
Ilmer. Buck 3E 20
Ilmington. Warw 7L 27
Ilminster. Som 4B 8
Ilsington. Devn 8G 7
Ilsington. Dors 6F 8
Ilston. Swan 5E 16
Ilton. N Yor 8K 47
Ilton. Som 4B 8
Imachar. N Ayr 5H 57
Imber. Wilts 1H 9
**Immingham**. NE Lin 6J 43
Immingham Dock. NE Lin 6K 43
Impington. Cambs 5M 29
Ince. Ches W 2C 34
Ince Blundell. Mers 7B 40
**Ince-in-Makerfield**. G Man 7D 40
Inchbae Lodge. High 7E 78
Inchbare. Ang 1K 67
Inchberry. Mor 8C 80
Inchbraoch. Ang 2L 67
Inchbrook. Glos 3G 19

Incheril. High 7M 77
Inchinnan. Ren 3C 58
Inchlaggan. High 5B 70
Inchmichael. Per 5F 66
Inchnadamph. High 1C 78
Inchree. High 1E 64
Inchture. Per 5F 66
Inchyra. Per 5E 66
Indian Queens. Corn 6B 4
Ingatestone. Essx 4C 22
Ingbirchworth. S Yor 7L 41
Ingestre. Staf 7H 35
Ingham. Linc 1G 37
Ingham. Norf 7K 39
Ingham. Suff 4E 30
Ingham Corner. Norf 7K 39
Ingleborough. Norf 8A 38
Ingleby. Derbs 7M 35
Ingleby Arncliffe. N Yor 5B 48
Ingleby Barwick. Stoc T 4B 48
Ingleby Greenhow. N Yor 5C 48
Ingleigh Green. Devn 5F 6
Inglemire. Hull 4H 43
Inglesbatch. Bath 7F 18
Ingleton. Dur 3K 47
Ingleton. N Yor 8E 46
Inglewhite. Lanc 3D 40
Ingoe. Nmbd 4D 54
Ingol. Lanc 4D 40
Ingoldisthorpe. Norf 6C 38
Ingoldmells. Linc 3B 38
Ingoldsby. Linc 6H 37
Ingon. Warw 6L 27
Ingram. Nmbd 8H 61
Ingrave. Essx 4C 22
Ingrow. W Yor 4J 41
Ings. Cumb 6C 46
Ingst. S Glo 5D 18
Ingthorpe. Rut 1G 29
Ingworth. Norf 7H 39
Inishrush. M Ulst 3F 93
Inkberrow. Worc 6J 27
Inkford. Worc 4J 27
Inkpen. W Ber 7A 20
Inkstack. High 4D 86
Innellan. Arg 3L 57
Inner Hope. Devn 8J 5
Innerleith. Fife 6F 66
Innerleithen. Bord 6M 59
Innerleven. Fife 7G 67
Innermessan. Dum 5F 50
Innerwick. E Lot 2E 60
Innerwick. Per 3K 65
Innsworth. Glos 1G 19
Insch. Abers 3F 72
Insh. High 5J 71
Inshegra. High 6E 84
Inshore. High 4F 84
Inskip. Lanc 4C 40
Instow. Devn 2D 6
Intwood. Norf 1H 31
Inver. Abers 6B 72
Inver. High 5J 79
Inver. Per 3D 66
Inverailort. High 7J 69
Inveralligin. High 8K 77
Inverallochy. Abers 7K 81
Inveramsay. Abers 3G 73
Inveran. High 4F 78
Inveraray. Arg 7E 64
Inverarish. High 2G 69
Inverarity. Ang 3H 67
Inverarnan. Stir 6H 65
Inverarnie. High 2G 71
Inverbeg. Arg 8H 65
Inverbervie. Abers 8H 73
Inverboyndie. Abers 7F 80
Invercassley. High 3E 78
Invercharnan. High 3F 64
Inverchoran. High 8C 78
Invercreran. Arg 3E 64
Inverdruie. High 4K 71
Inverebrie. Abers 2J 73
Invereck. Arg 1L 57
Inveresk. E Lot 2M 59
Inveresragan. Arg 4D 64
Inverey. Abers 7L 71
Inverfarigaig. High 3F 70
Invergarry. High 5D 70
Invergeldie. Per 5M 65
Invergordon. High 7H 79
Invergowrie. Per 4G 67
Inverguseran. High 5J 69
Inverharroch. Mor 2C 72
Inverie. High 5J 69
Inverinan. Arg 6D 64
Inverinate. High 3L 69
Inverkeilor. Ang 3K 67
**Inverkeithing**. Fife 1K 59
Inverkeithny. Abers 1F 72
Inverkip. Inv 2M 57
Inverkirkaig. High 2A 78
Inverlael. High 5B 78
Inverliever Lodge. Arg 7C 64
Inverliver. Arg 4E 64
Inverlochlarig. Stir 6J 65
Inverlochy. High 8B 70
Inverlussa. Arg 1F 56
Inver Mallie. High 7B 70
Invermarkie. Abers 2D 72
Invermoriston. High 4E 70
Invernaver. High 5K 85
Inverneil House. Arg 1H 57
**Inverness**. High 110 (1G 71)
Inverness Airport. High 8H 79
Invernettie. Abers 1L 73
Inverpolly Lodge. High 2A 78
Inverquhomery. Abers 1K 73
Inverroy. High 7C 70
Inversanda. High 2D 64
Invershiel. High 4L 69
Invershin. High 4F 78
Invershore. High 8D 86
Inversnaid. Stir 7H 65
Inverugie. Abers 1L 73
Inveruglas. Arg 7H 65
**Inverurie**. Abers 3G 73
Invervar. Per 3L 65
Inverythan. Abers 1G 73
Inwardleigh. Devn 6E 6
Inworth. Essx 2E 22
Iochdar. W Isl 1D 74
Iping. W Sus 3F 10
Ipplepen. Devn 5L 5
Ipsden. Oxon 5D 20
Ipstones. Staf 5J 35
**Ipswich**. Suff 110 (7H 31)
Irby. Mers 1A 34
Irby in the Marsh. Linc 3A 38
Irby upon Humber. NE Lin 7J 43
Irchester. Nptn 5G 29
Ireby. Cumb 8G 53
Ireby. Lanc 8E 46
Ireland. Shet 5D 90
Ireleth. Cumb 7M 45
Ireshopeburn. Dur 8B 54
Ireton Wood. Derbs 5L 35
**Irlam**. G Man 8F 40
Irnham. Linc 7H 37
Iron Acton. S Glo 5E 18
Iron Bridge. Cambs 2A 30
Ironbridge. Telf 1E 26
Iron Cross. Warw 6J 27
Ironville. Derbs 4B 36
Irstead. Norf 7K 39
Irthington. Cumb 5J 53
Irthlingborough. Nptn 4G 29
Irton. N Yor 7H 49
**Irvine**. N Ayr 6B 58
Irvine Mains. N Ayr 6B 58
Irvinestown. Ferm 6C 92
Isabella Pit. Nmbd 3G 55
Isauld. High 5A 86
Isbister. Orkn 8C 88
Isbister. Shet
on Mainland 4H 91
on Whalsay 1F 90
Isfield. E Sus 4A 12
Isham. Nptn 4F 28
Island Carr. N Lin 7G 43
Islay Airport. Arg 4C 56
Isle Abbotts. Som 3B 8
Isle Brewers. Som 3B 8
Isleham. Cambs 4C 30
Isle of Man Airport. IOM 8B 44
**Isle of Thanet**. Kent 7K 23
Isle of Whithorn. Dum 8K 51
**Isle of Wight**. IOW 7B 10
Isleornsay. High 4J 69
Islesburgh. Shet 1D 90
Isles of Scilly Airport. IOS 1H 3
Islesteps. Dum 4D 52
**Isleworth**. G Lon 6J 21
Isley Walton. Leics 7B 36
Islibhig. W Isl 1A 76
**Islington**. G Lon 5L 21
Islington. Telf 7F 34
Islip. Nptn 4G 29
Islip. Oxon 2C 20
Isombridge. Telf 8E 34
Istead Rise. Kent 7C 22
Itchen. Sotn 4B 10
Itchen Abbas. Hants 2C 10
Itchenor. W Sus 5E 10
Itchen Stoke. Hants 2C 10
Itchingfield. W Sus 3J 11
Itchington. S Glo 5E 18
Itlaw. Abers 8F 80
Itteringham. Norf 6H 39
Itteringham Common. Norf 7H 39
Itton. Devn 6F 6
Itton Common. Mon 4C 18
Ivegill. Cumb 7J 53
Ivelet. N Yor 6H 47
Iverchaolain. Arg 2K 57
Iver Heath. Buck 5H 21
Iveston. Dur 6E 54
Ivetsey Bank. Staf 8G 35
Ivinghoe. Buck 2G 21
Ivinghoe Aston. Buck 2G 21
Ivington. Here 6C 26
Ivington Green. Here 6C 26
Ivybridge. Devn 6J 5
Ivychurch. Kent 3G 13
Ivy Hatch. Kent 8B 22
Ivy Todd. Norf 1E 30
Iwade. Kent 7F 22
Iwerne Courtney. Dors 4G 9
Iwerne Minster. Dors 4G 9
Ixworth. Suff 4F 30
Ixworth Thorpe. Suff 4F 30


## J


Jackfield. Shrp 1E 26
Jack Hill. N Yor 2K 41
Jacksdale. Notts 4B 36
Jackton. S Lan 4D 58
Jacobstow. Corn 6A 6
Jacobstowe. Devn 5E 6
Jacobs Well. Surr 8G 21
Jameston. Pemb 7G 15
Jamestown. Dum 2H 53
Jamestown. Fife 1K 59
Jamestown. High 8E 78
Jamestown. W Dun 1B 58
Janetstown. High
nr. Thurso 5B 86
nr. Wick 6E 86
**Jarrow**. Tyne 5G 55
Jarvis Brook. E Sus 3B 12
Jasper's Green. Essx 1D 22
Jaywick. Essx 2H 23
Jedburgh. Bord 7D 60
Jeffreyston. Pemb 6G 15
Jemimaville. High 7H 79
Jenkins Park. High 5D 70
Jersey Marine. Neat 5G 17
Jesmond. Tyne 5F 54
Jevington. E Sus 5B 12
Jingle Street. Mon 2C 18
Jockey End. Herts 2H 21
Jodrell Bank. Ches E 2F 34
Johnby. Cumb 8J 53
John O'Gaunts. W Yor 5M 41
John o' Groats. High 4E 86
John's Cross. E Sus 3D 12
Johnshaven. Abers 1L 67
Johnson Street. Norf 8K 39
Johnston. Pemb 5F 14
**Johnstone**. Ren 3C 58
Johnstonebridge. Dum 2E 52
Johnstown. Carm 5L 15
Johnstown. Wrex 5B 34
Jonesborough. New M 7G 93
Joppa. Edin 2M 59
Joppa. S Ayr 8C 58
Jordan Green. Norf 7G 39
Jordans. Buck 4G 21
Jordanston. Pemb 3F 14
Jump. S Yor 7A 42
Jumpers Common. Dors 6K 9
Juniper. Nmbd 6C 54
Juniper Green. Edin 3K 59
Jurby East. IOM 5C 44
Jurby West. IOM 5C 44
Jury's Gap. E Sus 4F 12


## K


Kaber. Cumb 4F 46
Kaimend. S Lan 5H 59
Kaimes. Edin 3L 59
Kaimrig End. Bord 5J 59
Kames. Arg 2J 57
Kames. E Ayr 7E 58
Katesbridge. Arm 6H 93
Kea. Corn 4M 3
Keadby. N Lin 6F 42
Keady. Arm 7F 93
Keal Cotes. Linc 3L 37
Kearsley. G Man 7F 40
Kearsney. Kent 1J 13
Kearstwick. Cumb 7E 46
Kearton. N Yor 6H 47
Kearvaig. High 4E 84
Keasden. N Yor 1F 40
Keason. Corn 5F 4
Keckwick. Hal 1D 34
Keddington. Linc 1L 37
Keddington Corner. Linc 1L 37
Kedington. Suff 7D 30
Kedleston. Derbs 5M 35
Kedlock Feus. Fife 6G 67
Keekle. Cumb 3K 45
Keelby. Linc 6J 43
Keele. Staf 5G 35
Keeley Green. Bed 7H 29
Keeston. Pemb 5F 14
Keevil. Wilts 8H 19
Kegworth. Leics 7B 36
Kehelland. Corn 4K 3
Keig. Abers 4F 72
**Keighley**. W Yor 3J 41
Keilarsbrae. Clac 8B 66
Keillmore. Arg 1F 56
Keillor. Per 3F 66
Keillour. Per 5C 66
Keills. Arg 3D 56
Keiloch. Abers 6A 72
Keils. Arg 3E 56
Keinton Mandeville. Som 2D 8
Keir Mill. Dum 2C 52
Keirsleywell Row. Nmbd 6A 54
Keisby. Linc 7H 37
Keisley. Cumb 3F 46
Keiss. High 5E 86
Keith. Mor 8D 80
Keith Inch. Abers 1L 73
Kelbrook. Lanc 3H 41
Kelby. Linc 5H 37
Keld. Cumb 4D 46
Keld. N Yor 5G 47
Keldholme. N Yor 7E 48
Kelfield. N Lin 7F 42
Kelfield. N Yor 4C 42
Kelham. Notts 4E 36
Kellacott. Devn 7D 6
Kellan. Arg 3L 63
Kellas. Ang 4H 67
Kellas. Mor 8A 80
Kellaton. Devn 8L 5
Kelleth. Cumb 5E 46
Kelling. Norf 5G 39
Kellingley. N Yor 5C 42
Kellington. N Yor 5C 42
Kelloe. Dur 8G 55
Kelloholm. Dum 8F 58
Kells. Cumb 3J 45
Kells. ME Ant 4G 93
Kelly. Devn 7C 6
Kelly Bray. Corn 8C 6
Kelmarsh. Nptn 4E 28
Kelmscott. Oxon 4L 19
Kelsale. Suff 5K 31
Kelsall. Ches W 3D 34
Kelshall. Herts 8L 29
Kelsick. Cumb 6F 52
Kelso. Bord 6E 60
Kelstedge. Derbs 3M 35
Kelstern. Linc 8K 43
Kelsterton. Flin 2A 34
Kelston. Bath 7F 18
Keltneyburn. Per 3A 66
Kelton. Dum 4D 52
Kelton Hill. Dum 6B 52
Kelty. Fife 8E 66
Kelvedon. Essx 2E 22
Kelvedon Hatch. Essx 4B 22
Kelvinside. Glas 3D 58
Kelynack. Corn 5G 3
Kemback. Fife 6H 67
Kemberton. Shrp 1F 26
Kemble. Glos 4H 19
Kemerton. Worc 8H 27
Kemeys Commander. Mon 3B 18
Kemnay. Abers 4G 73
Kempe's Corner. Kent 1G 13
Kempley. Glos 1E 18
Kempley Green. Glos 1E 18
Kempsey. Worc 7G 27
Kempsford. Glos 4K 19
Kemps Green. Warw 4K 27
Kempshott. Hants 1D 10
**Kempston**. Bed 7H 29
Kempston Hardwick. Bed 7H 29
Kempton. Shrp 3B 26
Kemp Town. Brig 5L 11
Kemsing. Kent 8B 22
Kemsley. Kent 7F 22
Kenardington. Kent 2F 12
Kenchester. Here 7C 26
Kencot. Oxon 3L 19
**Kendal**. Cumb 6D 46
Kendleshire. S Glo 6E 18
Kendray. S Yor 7A 42
Kenfig. B'end 6H 17
Kenfig Hill. B'end 6H 17
Kengharair. Arg 3K 63
**Kenilworth**. Warw 4L 27
Kenknock. Stir 4J 65
Kenley. G Lon 8L 21
Kenley. Shrp 1D 26
Kenmore. High 8J 77
Kenmore. Per 3A 66
Kenn. Devn 7J 7
Kenn. N Som 7C 18
Kennacraig. Arg 3H 57
Kenneggy Downs. Corn 6J 3
Kennerleigh. Devn 5H 7
Kennet. Clac 8C 66
Kennethmont. Abers 3E 72
Kennett. Cambs 5D 30
Kennford. Devn 7J 7
Kenninghall. Norf 3G 31
Kennington. Kent 1G 13
Kennington. Oxon 3C 20
Kennoway. Fife 7G 67
Kennyhill. Suff 4C 30
Kennythorpe. N Yor 1E 42
Kenovay. Arg 3E 62
Kensaleyre. High 8F 76
**Kensington**. G Lon 6K 21
Kenstone. Shrp 7D 34
Kensworth. C Beds 2H 21
Kensworth Common.
C Beds 2H 21
Kentallen. High 2E 64
Kentchurch. Here 1C 18
Kentford. Suff 5D 30
Kentisbeare. Devn 5K 7
Kentisbury. Devn 1F 6
Kentisbury Ford. Devn 1F 6
Kentmere. Cumb 5C 46
Kenton. Devn 7J 7
Kenton. G Lon 5J 21
Kenton. Suff 5H 31
Kenton Bankfoot. Tyne 5F 54
Kentra. High 1M 63
Kentrigg. Cumb 6D 46
Kents Bank. Cumb 8B 46
Kent's Green. Glos 1F 18
Kent's Oak. Hants 3M 9
Kent Street. E Sus 4D 12
Kent Street. Kent 8C 22
Kent Street. W Sus 3K 11
Kenwick. Shrp 6C 34
Kenwyn. Corn 4M 3
Kenyon. Warr 8E 40
Keoldale. High 5F 84
Keppoch. High 3L 69
Kepwick. N Yor 6B 48
Keresley. W Mid 3M 27
Keresley Newland. Warw 3M 27
Keristal. IOM 7C 44
Kerne Bridge. Here 2D 18
Kerridge. Ches E 2H 35
Kerris. Corn 6H 3
Kerrow. High 2D 70
Kerry. Powy 4L 25
Kerrycroy. Arg 3L 57
Kerry's Gate. Here 8B 26
Kersall. Notts 3E 36
Kersbrook. Devn 7K 7
Kerse. Ren 4B 58
Kersey. Suff 7G 31
Kershopefoot. Cumb 3J 53
Kersoe. Worc 7H 27
Kerswell. Devn 5K 7
Kerswell Green. Worc 7G 27
Kesgrave. Suff 7J 31
Kesh. Ferm 5B 92
Kessingland. Suff 3M 31
Kessingland Beach. Suff 3M 31
Kestle. Corn 7B 4
Kestle Mill. Corn 6A 4
Keston. G Lon 7M 21
Keswick. Cumb 3A 46
Keswick. Norf
nr. North Walsham 6K 39
nr. Norwich 1J 31
Ketsby. Linc 2L 37
**Kettering**. Nptn 4F 28
Ketteringham. Norf 1H 31
Kettins. Per 4F 66
Kettlebaston. Suff 6F 30
Kettlebridge. Fife 7G 67
Kettlebrook. Staf 1L 27
Kettleburgh. Suff 5J 31
Kettleholm. Dum 4F 52
Kettleness. N Yor 4F 48
Kettleshulme. Ches E 2H 35
Kettlesing. N Yor 2L 41
Kettlesing Bottom. N Yor 2L 41
Kettlestone. Norf 6F 38
Kettlethorpe. Linc 2F 36
Kettletoft. Orkn 6F 88
Kettlewell. N Yor 8H 47
Ketton. Rut 1G 29
Kew. G Lon 6J 21
Kewaigue. IOM 7C 44
Kewstoke. N Som 7B 18
Kexbrough. S Yor 7L 41
Kexby. Linc 1F 36
Kexby. York 2E 42
Keyford. Som 1F 8
Key Green. Ches E 3G 35
Key Green. N Yor 5F 48
Keyham. Leics 1D 28
Keyhaven. Hants 6M 9
Keyhead. Abers 8K 81
Keyingham. E Yor 5K 43
Keymer. W Sus 4L 11
**Keynsham**. Bath 7E 18
Keysoe. Bed 5H 29
Keysoe Row. Bed 5H 29
Key's Toft. Linc 4A 38
Keyston. Cambs 4H 29
Key Street. Kent 7E 22
Keyworth. Notts 6D 36
Kibblesworth. Tyne 6F 54
Kibworth Beauchamp.
Leics 2D 28
Kibworth Harcourt. Leics 2D 28
Kidbrooke. G Lon 6M 21
Kidburngill. Cumb 2K 45
Kiddemore Green. Staf 1G 27
**Kidderminster**. Worc 4G 27
Kiddington. Oxon 1B 20
Kidd's Moor. Norf 1H 31
**Kidlington**. Oxon 2B 20
Kidmore End. Oxon 6D 20
Kidnal. Ches W 5C 34
**Kidsgrove**. Staf 4G 35
Kidstones. N Yor 7H 47
Kidwelly. Carm 6L 15
Kiel Crofts. Arg 4D 64
Kielder. Nmbd 2L 53
Kilbagie. Fife 8C 66
Kilbarchan. Ren 3C 58
Kilbeg. High 5H 69
Kilberry. Arg 3G 57
Kilbirnie. N Ayr 4B 58
Kilbride. Arg 5C 64
Kilbride. High 3G 69
Kilbucho Place. Bord 6J 59
Kilburn. Derbs 5A 36
Kilburn. G Lon 5K 21
Kilburn. N Yor 8C 48
Kilby. Leics 2D 28
Kilchattan. Arg 8J 63
Kilchattan Bay. Arg 4L 57
Kilchenzie. Arg 7F 56
Kilcheran. Arg 4C 64
Kilchiaran. Arg 3B 56
Kilchoan. High
nr. Inverie 6J 69
nr. Tobermory 1K 63
Kilchoman. Arg 3B 56
Kilchrenan. Arg 5E 64
Kilclief. New M 6J 93
Kilconquhar. Fife 7H 67
Kilcoo. New M 7H 93
Kilcot. Glos 1E 18
Kilcoy. High 8F 78
Kilcreggan. Arg 1M 57
Kildale. N Yor 5D 48
Kildary. High 6H 79
Kildermorie Lodge. High 6F 78
Kildonan. Dum 6F 50
Kildonan. High
nr. Helmsdale 1K 79
on Isle of Skye 8E 76
Kildonan. N Ayr 7K 57
Kildonnan. High 7F 68
Kildrummy. Abers 4D 72
Kildwick. N Yor 3J 41
Kilfillan. Dum 6H 51
Kilfinan. Arg 2J 57
Kilfinnan. High 6C 70
Kilgetty. Pemb 6H 15
Kilgour. Fife 7F 66
Kilgrammie. S Ayr 1H 51
Kilham. E Yor 1H 43
Kilham. Nmbd 6F 60
Kilkeel. New M 7H 93
Kilkenneth. Arg 3E 62
Kilkhampton. Corn 4B 6
Killadeas. Ferm 6C 92
Killamarsh. Derbs 1B 36
Killandrist. Arg 3C 64
Killay. Swan 5F 16
Killean. Arg 5F 56
Killearn. Stir 1D 58
Killeen. M Ulst 5F 93
Killellan. Arg 8F 56
Killen. Derr 4C 92
Killen. High 8G 79
Killerby. Darl 4K 47
Killeter. Derr 4C 92
Killichonan. Per 2K 65
Killiechronan. Arg 3L 63
Killiecrankie. Per 1C 66
Killilan. High 2L 69
Killimster. High 6E 86
Killin. Stir 4K 65
Killinchy. Ards 5J 93
Killinghall. N Yor 2L 41
Killington. Cumb 7E 46
**Killingworth**. Tyne 4F 54
Killin Lodge. High 5F 70
Killinochonoch. Arg 8C 64
Killochyett. Bord 5B 60
Killough. New M 7J 93
Killowen. New M 7G 93
Killundine. High 3L 63
Killylea. Arm 6E 92
Killyleagh. New M 6J 93
Killyrammer. Caus 2F 93
Kilmacolm. Inv 3B 58
Kilmahog. Stir 7L 65
Kilmahumaig. Arg 8B 64
Kilmalieu. High 2C 64
Kilmaluag. High 6F 76
Kilmany. Fife 5G 67
Kilmarie. High 4G 69
**Kilmarnock**. E Ayr 110 (6C 58)
Kilmaron. Fife 6G 67
Kilmartin. Arg 8C 64
Kilmaurs. E Ayr 5C 58
Kilmelford. Arg 6C 64
Kilmeny. Arg 3C 56
Kilmersdon. Som 8E 18
Kilmeston. Hants 3C 10
Kilmichael Glassary. Arg 8C 64
Kilmichael of Inverlussa.
Arg 1G 57
Kilmington. Devn 6A 8
Kilmington. Wilts 2F 8
Kilmoluaig. Arg 3E 62
Kilmorack. High 1E 70
Kilmore. Arg 5C 64
Kilmore. Arm 6F 93
Kilmore. High 5H 69
Kilmore. New M 6J 93
Kilmory. Arg 2G 57
Kilmory. High
nr. Kilchoan 8G 69
on Rùm 5E 68
Kilmory. N Ayr 7J 57
Kilmory Lodge. Arg 7B 64
Kilmote. High 2K 79
Kilmuir. High
nr. Dunvegan 1D 68
nr. Invergordon 6H 79
nr. Inverness 1G 71
nr. Uig 6E 76
Kilmun. Arg 1L 57
Kilnave. Arg 2B 56
Kilncadzow. S Lan 5G 59
Kilndown. Kent 2D 12
Kiln Green. Here 2E 18
Kiln Green. Wok 6F 20
Kilnhill. Cumb 8G 53
Kilnhurst. S Yor 8B 42
Kilninian. Arg 3J 63
Kilninver. Arg 5C 64
Kiln Pit Hill. Nmbd 6D 54
Kilnsea. E Yor 6M 43
Kilnsey. N Yor 1H 41
Kilnwick. E Yor 3G 43
Kiloran. Arg 8J 63
Kilpatrick. N Ayr 7J 57
Kilpeck. Here 8C 26
Kilpin. E Yor 5E 42
Kilpin Pike. E Yor 5E 42
Kilrea. Caus 3F 93
Kilrenny. Fife 7J 67
Kilsby. Nptn 4C 28
Kilspindie. Per 5F 66
**Kilsyth**. N Lan 2F 58
Kiltarlity. High 1F 70
Kilton. Som 1L 7
Kilton Thorpe. Red C 4D 48
Kilvaxter. High 7E 76
Kilve. Som 1L 7
Kilvington. Notts 5F 36
**Kilwinning**. N Ayr 5A 58
Kimberley. Norf 1G 31
**Kimberley**. Notts 5B 36
Kimblesworth. Dur 7F 54
Kimble Wick. Buck 3F 20
Kimbolton. Cambs 5H 29
Kimbolton. Here 5D 26
Kimcote. Leics 3C 28
Kimmeridge. Dors 8H 9
Kimmerston. Nmbd 6G 61
Kimpton. Hants 1L 9
Kimpton. Herts 2J 21
Kinallen. Arm 6H 93
Kinawley. Ferm 7C 92
Kinbeachie. High 7G 79
Kinbrace. High 8L 85
Kinbuck. Stir 7A 66
Kincaple. Fife 6H 67
Kincardine. Fife 1H 59
Kincardine. High 5G 79
**Kincardine Bridge**. Falk 1H 59
Kincardine O'Neil. Abers 6E 72
Kinchrackine. Arg 5F 64
Kincorth. Aber 5J 73
Kincraig. High 5J 71
Kincraigie. Per 3C 66
Kindallachan. Per 2C 66
Kineton. Glos 1J 19
Kineton. Warw 6M 27
Kinfauns. Per 5E 66
Kingairloch. High 2C 64
Kingarth. Arg 4K 57
Kingcoed. Mon 3C 18
King Edward. Abers 8G 81
Kingerby. Linc 8H 43
Kingham. Oxon 1L 19
Kingholm Quay. Dum 4D 52
Kinghorn. Fife 1L 59
Kingie. High 5B 70
Kinglassie. Fife 8F 66
Kingledores. Bord 7K 59
King o' Muirs. Clac 8B 66
Kingoodie. Per 5G 67
King's Acre. Here 7C 26
Kingsand. Corn 6G 5
Kingsash. Buck 3F 20
Kingsbarns. Fife 6J 67
Kingsbridge. Devn 7K 5
Kingsbridge. Som 2J 7
King's Bromley. Staf 8K 35
Kingsburgh. High 8E 76
Kingsbury. G Lon 5J 21
Kingsbury. Warw 2L 27
Kingsbury Episcopi. Som 3C 8
Kings Caple. Here 1D 18
Kingscavil. W Lot 2J 59
Kingsclere. Hants 8C 20
King's Cliffe. Nptn 2H 29
Kings Clipstone. Notts 3D 36
Kingscote. Glos 4G 19
Kingscott. Devn 4E 6
Kings Coughton. Warw 6J 27
Kingscross. N Ayr 7K 57
Kingsdon. Som 3D 8
Kingsdown. Kent 1K 13
Kingsdown. Swin 5K 19
Kingsdown. Wilts 7G 19
Kingseat. Fife 8E 66
Kingsey. Buck 3E 20
Kingsfold. Lanc 5D 40
Kingsfold. W Sus 2J 11
Kingsford. E Ayr 5C 58
Kingsford. Worc 3G 27
Kingsforth. N Lin 6H 43
Kingsgate. Kent 6K 23
King's Green. Glos 8F 26
Kingshall Street. Suff 5F 30
Kingsheanton. Devn 2E 6
King's Heath. W Mid 3J 27
Kings Hill. Kent 8C 22
Kingsholm. Glos 2G 19
Kingshouse. High 2G 65
Kingshouse. Stir 5K 65
Kingshurst. W Mid 3K 27
Kingskerswell. Devn 5L 5
Kingskettle. Fife 7G 67
Kingsland. Here 5C 26
Kingsland. IOA 2B 32
Kings Langley. Herts 3H 21
Kingsley. Ches W 2D 34
Kingsley. Hants 2E 10
Kingsley. Staf 5J 35
Kingsley Green. W Sus 2F 10
Kingsley Holt. Staf 5J 35
**King's Lynn**. Norf 7C 38
King's Meaburn. Cumb 3E 46
Kings Moss. Mers 7D 40
Kings Muir. Bord 6L 59
Kingsmuir. Ang 3H 67
Kingsmuir. Fife 7J 67
King's Newnham. Warw 4B 28
King's Newton. Derbs 7A 36
Kingsnorth. Kent 2G 13
Kingsnorth. Medw 6E 22
King's Norton. Leics 1D 28
Kings Norton. W Mid 4J 27
King's Nympton. Devn 4F 6
King's Pyon. Here 6C 26
Kings Ripton. Cambs 4K 29
King's Somborne. Hants 2A 10
King's Stag. Dors 4F 8
King's Stanley. Glos 3G 19
King's Sutton. Nptn 8B 28
Kingstanding. W Mid 2J 27
Kingsteignton. Devn 8H 7
Kingsteps. High 8K 79
King Sterndale. Derbs 2J 35
King's Thorn. Here 8D 26
Kingsthorpe. Nptn 5E 28
Kingston. Cambs 6L 29
Kingston. Devn 7J 5
Kingston. Dors
nr. Sturminster Newton 5F 8
nr. Swanage 8H 9
Kingston. E Lot 1C 60
Kingston. Hants 5K 9
Kingston. IOW 7B 10
Kingston. Kent 8H 23
Kingston. Mor 7C 80
Kingston. W Sus 5H 11
Kingston Bagpuize. Oxon 4B 20
Kingston Blount. Oxon 4E 20
Kingston by Sea. W Sus 5K 11
Kingston Deverill. Wilts 2G 9
Kingstone. Here 8C 26
Kingstone. Som 4B 8
Kingstone. Staf 7J 35
Kingston Lisle. Oxon 5M 19
Kingston Maurward. Dors 6F 8
Kingston near Lewes.
E Sus 5L 11
Kingston on Soar. Notts 7C 36
Kingston Russell. Dors 6D 8
Kingston St Mary. Som 3M 7
Kingston Seymour. N Som 7C 18
Kingston Stert. Oxon 3E 20
**Kingston upon Hull**.
Hull 110 (5J 43)
**Kingston upon Thames**.
G Lon 7J 21
King's Walden. Herts 1J 21
Kingswear. Devn 6L 5
Kingswells. Aber 5H 73
Kingswinford. W Mid 3G 27
Kingswood. Buck 2D 20
Kingswood. Glos 4F 18
Kingswood. Here 6A 26
Kingswood. Kent 8E 22
Kingswood. Per 4D 66
Kingswood. Powy 2M 25
Kingswood. Som 2L 7
**Kingswood**. S Glo 6E 18
Kingswood. Surr 8K 21
Kingswood. Warw 4K 27
Kingswood Common. Staf 1G 27
Kings Worthy. Hants 2B 10
Kingthorpe. Linc 2J 37
Kington. Here 6A 26
Kington. S Glo 4E 18
Kington. Worc 6H 27
Kington Langley. Wilts 6H 19
Kington Magna. Dors 3F 8
Kington St Michael. Wilts 6H 19
Kingussie. High 5H 71
Kingweston. Som 2D 8
Kinharrachie. Abers 2J 73
Kinhrive. High 6G 79
Kinkell Bridge. Per 6C 66
Kinknockie. Abers 1K 73
Kinkry Hill. Cumb 4K 53
Kinlet. Shrp 3F 26
Kinloch. High
nr. Lochaline 2A 64
nr. Loch More 8F 84
on Rùm 6E 68
Kinloch. Per 3E 66
Kinlochard. Stir 7J 65
Kinlochbervie. High 6E 84
Kinlocheil. High 8L 69
Kinlochewe. High 7M 77
Kinloch Hourn. High 5L 69
Kinloch Laggan. High 7F 70
Kinlochleven. High 1F 64
Kinloch Lodge. High 6H 85
Kinlochmoidart. High 8J 69
Kinlochmore. High 1F 64
Kinloch Rannoch. Per 2L 65
Kinlochspelve. Arg 5A 64
Kinloid. High 7H 69
Kinloss. Mor 7L 79
Kinmel Bay. Cnwy 2J 33
Kinmuck. Abers 4H 73
Kinnadie. Abers 1J 73
Kinnaird. Per 5F 66
Kinneff. Abers 8H 73
Kinnelhead. Dum 1E 52
Kinnell. Ang 2K 67
Kinnerley. Shrp 7B 34
Kinnernie. Abers 5G 73
Kinnersley. Here 7B 26
Kinnersley. Worc 7G 27
Kinnerton. Powy 6M 25
Kinnerton. Shrp 2B 26
Kinnesswood. Per 7E 66
Kinninvie. Dur 3J 47
Kinnordy. Ang 2G 67
Kinoulton. Notts 6D 36
Kinross. Per 7E 66
Kinrossie. Per 4E 66
Kinsbourne Green. Herts 2J 21
Kinsey Heath. Ches E 5E 34
Kinsham. Here 5B 26
Kinsham. Worc 8H 27
Kinsley. W Yor 6B 42
Kinson. Bour 6J 9
Kintbury. W Ber 7A 20
Kintessack. Mor 7L 79
Kintillo. Per 6E 66
Kinton. Here 4C 26
Kinton. Shrp 8B 34
Kintore. Abers 4G 73
Kintour. Arg 4D 56
Kintra. Arg 5J 63
Kintraw. Arg 7C 64
Kinveachy. High 4K 71
Kinver. Staf 3G 27
Kinwarton. Warw 6K 27
Kiplingcotes. E Yor 3G 43
Kippax. W Yor 4B 42
Kippen. Stir 8L 65
Kippford. Dum 6C 52
Kipping's Cross. Kent 1C 12
Kirbister. Orkn
nr. Hobbister 1E 86
nr. Quholm 8B 88
Kirbuster. Orkn 7F 88
Kirby Bedon. Norf 1J 31
Kirby Bellars. Leics 8E 36
Kirby Cane. Norf 2K 31
Kirby Cross. Essx 1J 23
Kirby Fields. Leics 1C 28
Kirby Green. Norf 2K 31
Kirby Grindalythe. N Yor 1G 43
Kirby Hill. N Yor
nr. Richmond 5K 47
nr. Ripon 1A 42
Kirby Knowle. N Yor 7B 48
Kirby-le-Soken. Essx 1J 23
Kirby Misperton. N Yor 8E 48
Kirby Muxloe. Leics 1C 28
Kirby Sigston. N Yor 6B 48
Kirby Underdale. E Yor 2F 42
Kirby Wiske. N Yor 7A 48
Kircubbin. Ards 5K 93
Kirdford. W Sus 3H 11
Kirk. High 6D 86
Kirkabister. Shet
on Bressay 4E 90
on Mainland 2E 90
Kirkandrews. Dum 7M 51
Kirkandrews-on-Eden.
Cumb 6H 53
Kirkapol. Arg 3F 62
Kirkbampton. Cumb 6H 53
Kirkbean. Dum 6D 52
Kirk Bramwith. S Yor 6D 42
Kirkbride. Cumb 6G 53
Kirkbridge. N Yor 6L 47
Kirkbuddo. Ang 3J 67
Kirkburn. E Yor 2G 43
Kirkburton. W Yor 6K 41
Kirkby. Linc 8H 43
**Kirkby**. Mers 8C 40
Kirkby. N Yor 5C 48
Kirkby Fenside. Linc 3L 37
Kirkby Fleetham. N Yor 6L 47
Kirkby Green. Linc 4H 37
**Kirkby-in-Ashfield**. Notts 4C 36
Kirkby-in-Furness. Cumb 6M 45
Kirkby la Thorpe. Linc 5J 37
Kirkby Lonsdale. Cumb 8E 46
Kirkby Malham. N Yor 1G 41
Kirkby Mallory. Leics 1B 28
Kirkby Malzeard. N Yor 8L 47
Kirkby Mills. N Yor 7E 48
Kirkbymoorside. N Yor 7D 48
Kirkby on Bain. Linc 3K 37
Kirkby Overblow. N Yor 3M 41
Kirkby Stephen. Cumb 5F 46
Kirkby Thore. Cumb 3E 46
Kirkby Underwood. Linc 7H 37
Kirkby Wharfe. N Yor 3C 42
**Kirkcaldy**. Fife 8F 66
Kirkcambeck. Cumb 5K 53
Kirkcolm. Dum 5F 50
Kirkconnel. Dum 8F 58
Kirkconnell. Dum 5D 52
Kirkcowan. Dum 5J 51
Kirkcudbright. Dum 6A 52
Kirkdale. Mers 8B 40
Kirk Deighton. N Yor 2A 42
Kirk Ella. E Yor 5H 43
Kirkfieldbank. S Lan 5G 59
Kirkforthar Feus. Fife 7F 66
Kirkgunzeon. Dum 5C 52
Kirk Hallam. Derbs 5B 36
Kirkham. Lanc 4C 40
Kirkham. N Yor 1E 42
Kirkhamgate. W Yor 5L 41
Kirk Hammerton. N Yor 2B 42
Kirkharle. Nmbd 3D 54
Kirkheaton. Nmbd 4D 54
Kirkheaton. W Yor 6K 41
Kirkhill. Ang 1K 67
Kirkhill. High 1F 70
Kirkhope. S Lan 1D 52
Kirkhouse. Bord 6M 59
Kirkibost. High 4G 69
Kirkinch. Ang 3G 67
Kirkinner. Dum 6K 51
**Kirkintilloch**. E Dun 2E 58
Kirk Ireton. Derbs 4L 35
Kirkland. Cumb
nr. Cleator Moor 3K 45
nr. Penrith 8L 53
nr. Wigton 7G 53
Kirkland. Dum
nr. Kirkconnel 8F 58
nr. Moniaive 2C 52
Kirkland Guards. Cumb 7F 52
Kirk Langley. Derbs 6L 35
Kirklauchline. Dum 6F 50
Kirkleatham. Red C 3C 48
Kirklevington. Stoc T 5B 48
Kirkley. Suff 2M 31
Kirklington. N Yor 7M 47
Kirklington. Notts 4D 36
Kirklinton. Cumb 5J 53
Kirkliston. Edin 2K 59
Kirkmabreck. Dum 6K 51
Kirkmaiden. Dum 8G 51
Kirk Merrington. Dur 8F 54
Kirk Michael. IOM 5C 44
Kirkmichael. Per 1D 66
Kirkmichael. S Ayr 1J 51
Kirkmuirhill. S Lan 5F 58
Kirknewton. Nmbd 6G 61
Kirknewton. W Lot 3K 59
Kirkney. Abers 2E 72
Kirk of Shotts. N Lan 3G 59
Kirkoswald. Cumb 7K 53
Kirkoswald. S Ayr 1H 51
Kirkpatrick. Dum 2D 52
Kirkpatrick Durham. Dum 4B 52
Kirkpatrick-Fleming. Dum 4G 53
**Kirk Sandall**. S Yor 7D 42
Kirksanton. Cumb 6L 45
Kirk Smeaton. N Yor 6C 42
Kirkstall. W Yor 4L 41
Kirkstile. Dum 2H 53
Kirkstyle. High 4E 86
Kirkthorpe. W Yor 5A 42
Kirkton. Abers
nr. Alford 4F 72
nr. Insch 3F 72
nr. Turriff 1H 73
Kirkton. Ang
nr. Dundee 4H 67
nr. Forfar 3H 67
nr. Tarfside 7D 72
Kirkton. Dum 3D 52
Kirkton. Fife 5G 67
Kirkton. High
nr. Golspie 4H 79
nr. Kyle of Lochalsh 3K 69
nr. Lochcarron 1L 69
Kirkton. Bord 8C 60
Kirkton. S Lan 7H 59
Kirktonhill. W Dun 2B 58
Kirkton Manor. Bord 6L 59
Kirkton of Airlie. Ang 2G 67
Kirkton of Auchterhouse.
Ang 4G 67
Kirkton of Bourtie. Abers 3H 73
Kirkton of Collace. Per 4E 66
Kirkton of Craig. Ang 2L 67
Kirkton of Culsalmond.
Abers 2F 72
Kirkton of Durris. Abers 6G 73
Kirkton of Glenbuchat.
Abers 4C 72
Kirkton of Glenisla. Ang 1F 66
Kirkton of Kingoldrum. Ang 2G 67
Kirkton of Largo. Fife 7H 67
Kirkton of Lethendy. Per 3E 66
Kirkton of Logie Buchan.
Abers 3J 73
Kirkton of Maryculter.
Abers 6H 73
Kirkton of Menmuir. Ang 1J 67
Kirkton of Monikie. Ang 4J 67
Kirkton of Oyne. Abers 3F 72
Kirkton of Rayne. Abers 2F 72
Kirkton of Skene. Abers 5H 73
Kirktown. Abers
nr. Fraserburgh 7J 81
nr. Peterhead 8K 81
Kirktown of Alvah. Abers 7F 80
Kirktown of Auchterless.
Abers 1G 73
Kirktown of Deskford. Mor 7E 80
Kirktown of Fetteresso.
Abers 7H 73
Kirktown of Mortlach. Mor 2C 72
Kirktown of Slains. Abers 3K 73
Kirkurd. Bord 5K 59
Kirkwall. Orkn 8D 88
Kirkwall Airport. Orkn 1F 86
Kirkwhelpington. Nmbd 3C 54
Kirk Yetholm. Bord 7F 60
Kirmington. N Lin 6J 43
Kirmond le Mire. Linc 8J 43
Kirn. Arg 2L 57
Kirriemuir. Ang 2G 67
Kirstead Green. Norf 2J 31
Kirtlebridge. Dum 4G 53
Kirtleton. Dum 4G 53
Kirtling. Cambs 6C 30
Kirtling Green. Cambs 6C 30
Kirtlington. Oxon 2C 20
Kirtomy. High 5K 85
Kirton. Linc 6L 37
Kirton. Notts 3D 36
Kirton. Suff 8J 31
Kirton End. Linc 5K 37
Kirton Holme. Linc 5K 37
Kirton in Lindsey. N Lin 8G 43
Kishorn. High 1K 69
Kislingbury. Nptn 6D 28
Kites Hardwick. Warw 5B 28
Kittisford. Som 3K 7
Kittle. Swan 6E 16
Kittybrewster. Aber 5J 73
Kitwood. Hants 2D 10
Kivernoll. Here 8C 26
Kiveton Park. S Yor 1B 36
Knaith. Linc 1F 36
Knaith Park. Linc 1F 36
Knaphill. Surr 8G 21
Knapp. Hants 3B 10
Knapp. Per 4F 66
Knapp. Som 3B 8
Knapperfield. High 6D 86
Knapton. Norf 6K 39
Knapton. York 2C 42
Knapton Green. Here 6C 26
Knapwell. Cambs 5L 29
**Knaresborough**. N Yor 2A 42
Knarsdale. Nmbd 6L 53
Knatts Valley. Kent 7B 22
Knaven. Abers 1H 73
Knayton. N Yor 7B 48
Knebworth. Herts 1K 21
Knedlington. E Yor 5E 42
Kneesall. Notts 3E 36
Kneesworth. Cambs 7L 29
Kneeton. Notts 5E 36
Knelston. Swan 8L 15
Knenhall. Staf 6H 35
Knightacott. Devn 2F 6
Knightcote. Warw 6B 28
Knightcott. N Som 8B 18
Knightley. Staf 7G 35
Knightley Dale. Staf 7G 35
Knightlow Hill. Warw 4B 28
Knighton. Devn 7H 5
Knighton. Dors 4E 8
Knighton. Leic 1C 28
Knighton. Powy 4A 26
Knighton. Som 1L 7
Knighton. Staf
nr. Eccleshall 7F 34
nr. Woore 5F 34
Knighton. Wilts 6L 19
Knighton. Worc 6J 27
Knighton Common. Worc 4E 26
Knight's End. Cambs 2M 29
Knightswood. Glas 3D 58
Knightwick. Worc 6F 26
Knill. Here 5A 26
Knipton. Leics 6F 36
Knitsley. Dur 7E 54
Kniveton. Derbs 4L 35
Knock. Arg 4L 63
Knock. Cumb 3E 46
Knock. Mor 8E 80
Knockally. High 1M 79
Knockan. Arg 5K 63
Knockan. High 2C 78
Knockandhu. Mor 3B 72
Knockando. Mor 1A 72
Knockarthur. High 3H 79
Knockbain. High 8G 79
Knockbreck. High 7D 76
Knockcloghrim. M Ulst 4F 93
Knockdee. High 5C 86
Knockdolian. S Ayr 3G 51
Knockdon. S Ayr 8B 58
Knockdown. Glos 5G 19
Knockenbaird. Abers 3F 72
Knockenkelly. N Ayr 7K 57
Knockentiber. E Ayr 6B 58
Knockfarrel. High 8F 78
Knockglass. High 5B 86
Knockholt. Kent 8A 22
Knockholt Pound. Kent 8A 22
Knockie Lodge. High 4E 70
Knockin. Shrp 7B 34
Knockinlaw. E Ayr 6C 58
Knockinnon. High 8C 86
Knocknacarry. Caus 2H 93
Knockrome. Arg 2E 56
Knocksharry. IOM 6B 44
Knockshinnoch. E Ayr 8C 58
Knockvennie. Dum 4B 52
Knockvologan. Arg 6J 63
Knodishall. Suff 5L 31
Knole. Som 3C 8
Knollbury. Mon 5C 18
Knolls Green. Ches E 2G 35
Knolton. Wrex 6B 34
Knook. Wilts 1H 9
Knossington. Leics 1F 28
Knott. High 8E 76
Knott End-on-Sea. Lanc 3B 40
Knotting. Bed 5H 29
Knotting Green. Bed 5H 29
**Knottingley**. W Yor 5B 42
Knotts. Cumb 3C 46
Knotty Ash. Mers 8C 40
Knotty Green. Buck 4G 21
Knowbury. Shrp 4D 26
Knowe. Dum 4J 51
Knowefield. Cumb 6J 53
Knowehead. Dum 2M 51
Knowes. E Lot 2D 60
Knowesgate. Nmbd 3C 54
Knoweside. S Ayr 8A 58
Knowes of Elrick. Abers 8F 80
Knowle. Bris 6E 18
Knowle. Devn
nr. Braunton 2D 6
nr. Budleigh Salterton 7K 7
nr. Crediton 5G 7
Knowle. Shrp 4D 26
**Knowle**. W Mid 4K 27
Knowle Green. Lanc 4E 40
Knowle St Giles. Som 4B 8
Knowlesands. Shrp 2F 26
Knowle Village. Hants 5C 10
Knowl Hill. Wind 6F 20
Knowlton. Kent 8J 23
Knowsley. Mers 8C 40
Knowstone. Devn 3H 7
Knucklas. Powy 4A 26
Knuston. Nptn 5G 29
**Knutsford**. Ches E 2F 34
Knypersley. Staf 4G 35
Krumlin. W Yor 6J 41
Kuggar. Corn 7L 3
Kyleakin. High 3J 69
Kyle of Lochalsh. High 3J 69
Kylerhea. High 3J 69
Kylesku. High 8E 84
Kyles Lodge. W Isl 5A 76
Kylesmorar. High 6K 69
Kylestrome. High 8E 84
Kymin. Mon 2D 18
Kynaston. Here 8E 26
Kynaston. Shrp 7B 34
Kynnersley. Telf 8E 34
Kyre Green. Worc 5E 26
Kyre Park. Worc 5E 26
Kyrewood. Worc 5E 26


## L


Labost. W Isl 7F 82
Lacasaidh. W Isl 1E 76
Lacasdail. W Isl 8H 83
Laceby. NE Lin 7K 43
Lacey Green. Buck 3F 20
Lach Dennis. Ches W 2F 34
Lache. Ches W 3B 34
Lack. Ferm 5C 92
Lackagh. Caus 3E 92
Lackford. Suff 4D 30
Lacock. Wilts 7H 19
Ladbroke. Warw 6B 28
Laddingford. Kent 1C 12
Lade Bank. Linc 4L 37
Ladock. Corn 6A 4
Lady. Orkn 5F 88
Ladybank. Fife 6G 67
Ladycross. Corn 7C 6
Lady Green. Mers 7B 40
Lady Hall. Cumb 6L 45
Ladykirk. Bord 5F 60
Ladysford. Abers 7J 81
Ladywood. W Mid 3J 27
Ladywood. Worc 5G 27
Laga. High 1M 63
Lagavulin. Arg 5D 56
Lagg. Arg 2E 56
Lagg. N Ayr 7J 57
Laggan. Arg 4B 56
Laggan. High
nr. Fort Augustus 6C 70
nr. Newtonmore 6G 71
Laggan. Mor 2C 72
Lagganlia. High 5J 71
Lagganulva. Arg 3K 63
Laghey Corner. M Ulst 5F 93
Laglingarten. Arg 7F 64
Lagness. W Sus 5F 10
Laid. High 6G 85
Laide. High 4K 77
Laigh Fenwick. E Ayr 5C 58
Laindon. Essx 5C 22
Lairg. High 3F 78
Lairg Muir. High 3F 78
Laithes. Cumb 8J 53
Laithkirk. Dur 3H 47
Lake. Devn 2E 6
Lake. IOW 7C 10
Lake. Wilts 2K 9
Lakenham. Norf 1J 31
Lakenheath. Suff 3D 30
Lakesend. Norf 2B 30
Lakeside. Cumb 7B 46
Laleham. Surr 7H 21
Laleston. B'end 6H 17
Lamancha. Bord 4L 59
Lamarsh. Essx 8E 30
Lamas. Norf 7J 39
Lamb Corner. Essx 8G 31
Lambden. Bord 5E 60
Lamberhead Green. G Man 7D 40
Lamberhurst. Kent 2C 12
Lamberhurst Quarter. Kent 2C 12
Lamberton. Bord 4G 61
**Lambeth**. G Lon 6L 21
Lambfell Moar. IOM 6B 44
Lambhill. Glas 3D 58
Lambley. Nmbd 6L 53
Lambley. Notts 5D 36
Lambourn. W Ber 6M 19
Lambourne End. Essx 4A 22
Lambourn Woodlands.
W Ber 6M 19
Lambs Green. Dors 6H 9
Lambs Green. W Sus 2K 11
Lambston. Pemb 5F 14
Lamellion. Corn 5E 4
Lamerton. Devn 8D 6
Lamesley. Tyne 6F 54
Laminess. Orkn 6F 88
Lamington. High 6H 79
Lamington. S Lan 6H 59
Lamlash. N Ayr 6K 57
Lamonby. Cumb 8J 53
Lamorick. Corn 5C 4
Lamorna. Corn 6H 3
Lamorran. Corn 7A 4
Lampeter. Cdgn 8E 24
Lampeter Velfrey. Pemb 5H 15
Lamphey. Pemb 6G 15
Lamplugh. Cumb 2K 45
Lamport. Nptn 4E 28
Lamyatt. Som 2E 8
Lana. Devn
nr. Ashwater 6C 6
nr. Holsworthy 5C 6
Lanark. S Lan 5G 59

Lanarth. Corn 6L 3
Lancaster. Lanc 1C 40
Lanchester. Dur 7E 54
Lancing. W Sus 5J 11
Landbeach. Cambs 5A 30
Landcross. Devn 3D 6
Landerberry. Abers 5G 73
Landford. Wilts 4L 9
Land Gate. G Man 7D 40
Landhallow. High 8C 86
Landimore. Swan 7L 15
Landkey. Devn 2E 6
Landkey Newland. Devn 2E 6
Landore. Swan 5F 16
Landport. Port 5D 10
Landrake. Corn 5F 4
Landscove. Devn 5K 5
Land's End Airport. Corn 6G 3
Landshipping. Pemb 5G 15
Landulph. Corn 5G 5
Landywood. Staf 1H 27
Lane. Corn 2M 3
Laneast. Corn 7B 6
Lane Bottom. Lanc 4G 41
Lane End. Buck 4F 20
Lane End. Hants 3C 10
Lane End. IOW 7D 10
Lane End. Wilts 1G 9
Lane Ends. Derbs 6L 35
Lane Ends. Dur 8E 54
Lane Ends. Lanc 2F 40
Laneham. Notts 2F 36
Lane Head. Dur
nr. Hutton Magna 4K 47
nr. Woodland 3J 47
Lane Head. G Man 8E 40
Lane Head. W Yor 7K 41
Lanehead. Dur 7B 54
Lanehead. Nmbd 3A 54
Lane Heads. Lanc 4C 40
Lanercost. Cumb 5K 53
Laneshaw Bridge. Lanc 3H 41
Laney Green. Staf 1H 27
Langais. W Isl 7K 75
Langal. High 1B 64
Langar. Notts 6E 36
Langbank. Ren 2B 58
Langbar. N Yor 2J 41
Langburnshiels. Bord 1K 53
Langcliffe. N Yor 1G 41
Langdale End. N Yor 6G 49
Langdon. Corn 6B 6
Langdon Beck. Dur 8B 54
Langdon Cross. Corn 7C 6
Langdon Hills. Essx 5C 22
Langdown. Hants 5B 10
Langdyke. Fife 7G 67
Langenhoe. Essx 2G 23
Langford. C Beds 7J 29
Langford. Devn 5K 7
Langford. Essx 3E 22
Langford. Notts 4F 36
Langford. Oxon 3L 19
Langford. Som 3M 7
Langford Budville. Som 3L 7
Langham. Dors 3F 8
Langham. Essx 8G 31
Langham. Norf 5G 39
Langham. Rut 8F 36
Langham. Suff 5F 30
Langho. Lanc 4F 40
Langholm. Dum 3H 53
Langland. Swan 6F 16
Langleeford. Nmbd 7G 61
Langley. Ches E 2H 35
Langley. Derbs 5B 36
Langley. Essx 8M 29
Langley. Glos 1J 19
Langley. Hants 5B 10
Langley. Herts 1K 21
Langley. Kent 8E 22
Langley. Nmbd 5B 54
Langley. Slo 6H 21
Langley. Som 3K 7
Langley. Warw 5K 27
Langley. W Sus 3F 10
Langley Burrell. Wilts 6H 19
Langleybury. Herts 3H 21
Langley Common. Derbs 6L 35
Langley Green. Derbs 6L 35
Langley Green. Norf 1K 31
Langley Green. Warw 5K 27
Langley Green. W Sus 2K 11
Langley Heath. Kent 8E 22
Langley Marsh. Som 3K 7
Langley Moor. Dur 7F 54
Langley Park. Dur 7F 54
Langley Street. Norf 1K 31
Langney. E Sus 5C 12
Langold. Notts 1C 36
Langore. Corn 7B 6
Langport. Som 3C 8
Langrick. Linc 5K 37
Langridge. Bath 7F 18
Langridgeford. Devn 3E 6
Langrigg. Cumb 7F 52
Langrish. Hants 3E 10
Langsett. S Yor 7L 41
Langshaw. Bord 6C 60
Langstone. Hants 5E 10
Langthorne. N Yor 6L 47
Langthorpe. N Yor 1A 42
Langthwaite. N Yor 5J 47
Langtoft. E Yor 1H 43
Langtoft. Linc 8J 37
Langton. Dur 4K 47
Langton. Linc
nr. Horncastle 3K 37
nr. Spilsby 2L 37
Langton. N Yor 1E 42
Langton by Wragby. Linc 2J 37
Langton Green. Kent 2B 12
Langton Herring. Dors 7E 8
Langton Long Blandford.
Dors 5G 9
Langton Matravers. Dors 8H 9
Langtree. Devn 4D 6
Langwathby. Cumb 8K 53
Langwith. Derbs 2C 36
Langworth. Linc 2H 37
Lanivet. Corn 5C 4
Lanjeth. Corn 6B 4
Lank. Corn 4C 4
Lanlivery. Corn 6C 4
Lanner. Corn 5L 3
Lanreath. Corn 6D 4
Lansallos. Corn 6D 4
Lansdown. Bath 7F 18
Lansdown. Glos 1H 19
Lanteglos Highway. Corn 6D 4
Lanton. Nmbd 6G 61
Lanton. Bord 7D 60
Lapford. Devn 5G 7
Lapford Cross. Devn 5G 7
Laphroaig. Arg 5C 56
Lapley. Staf 8G 35
Lapworth. Warw 4K 27
Larachbeg. High 3A 64
Larbert. Falk 1G 59
Larden Green. Ches E 4D 34
Larel. High 6C 86
Largie. Abers 2F 72
Largiemore. Arg 1J 57
Largoward. Fife 7H 67
Largs. N Ayr 4M 57
Largue. Abers 1F 72
Largybeg. N Ayr 7K 57
Largymeanoch. N Ayr 7K 57
Largymore. N Ayr 7K 57
Larkfield. Inv 2M 57
Larkfield. Kent 8D 22
Larkhall. Bath 7F 18
Larkhall. S Lan 4F 58
Larkhill. Wilts 1K 9
Larling. Norf 3F 30
Larne. ME Ant 3J 93
Larport. Here 8D 26
Lartington. Dur 4J 47
Lary. Abers 5C 72
Lasham. Hants 1D 10
Lashenden. Kent 1E 12
Lasswade. Midl 3M 59
Lastingham. N Yor 6E 48
Latchford. Herts 1L 21
Latchford. Oxon 3D 20
Latchingdon. Essx 3E 22
Latchley. Corn 8D 6
Latchmere Green. Hants 8D 20
Lathbury. Mil 7F 28
Latheron. High 8C 86
Latheronwheel. High 8C 86
Lathom. Lanc 7C 40
Lathones. Fife 7H 67
Latimer. Buck 4H 21
Latteridge. S Glo 5E 18
Lattiford. Som 3E 8
Latton. Wilts 4J 19
Laudale House. High 2B 64
Lauder. Bord 5C 60
Laugharne. Carm 5K 15
Laughterton. Linc 2F 36
Laughton. E Sus 4B 12
Laughton. Leics 3D 28
Laughton. Linc
nr. Gainsborough 8F 42
nr. Grantham 6H 37
Laughton Common. S Yor 1C 36
Laughton en le Morthen.
S Yor 1C 36
Launcells. Corn 5B 6
Launceston. Corn 7C 6
Launcherley. Som 1D 8
Launton. Oxon 1D 20
Laurelvale. Arm 6G 93
Laurencekirk. Abers 8G 73
Laurieston. Dum 5A 52
Laurieston. Falk 2H 59
Lavendon. Mil 6G 29
Lavenham. Suff 7F 30
Laverhay. Dum 2F 52
Laversdale. Cumb 5J 53
Laverstock. Wilts 2K 9
Laverstoke. Hants 1B 10
Laverton. Glos 8J 27
Laverton. N Yor 8L 47
Laverton. Som 8F 18
Lavister. Wrex 4B 34
Law. S Lan 4G 59
Lawers. Per 4L 65
Lawford. Essx 8G 31
Lawhitton. Corn 7C 6
Lawkland. N Yor 1F 40
Lawley. Telf 1E 26
Lawnhead. Staf 7G 35
Lawrencetown. Arm 6G 93
Lawrenny. Pemb 6G 15
Lawshall. Suff 6E 30
Lawton. Here 6C 26
Laxey. IOM 6D 44
Laxfield. Suff 4J 31
Laxfirth. Shet 2E 90
Laxo. Shet 1E 90
Laxton. E Yor 5E 42
Laxton. Nptn 2G 29
Laxton. Notts 3E 36
Laycock. W Yor 3J 41
Layer Breton. Essx 2F 22
Layer-de-la-Haye. Essx 1F 22
Layer Marney. Essx 2F 22
Laymore. Dors 5B 8
Laysters Pole. Here 5D 26
Layter's Green. Buck 4G 21
Laytham. E Yor 4E 42
Lazenby. Red C 4C 48
Lazonby. Cumb 8K 53
Lea. Derbs 4M 35
Lea. Here 1E 18
Lea. Linc 1F 36
Lea. Shrp
nr. Bishop's Castle 3B 26
nr. Shrewsbury 1C 26
Lea. Wilts 5H 19
Leabrooks. Derbs 4B 36
Leac a Li. W Isl 4C 76
Leachd. Arg 8E 64
Leachkin. High 1G 71
Leachpool. Pemb 5F 14
Leadburn. Midl 4L 59
Leadenham. Linc 4G 37
Leaden Roding. Essx 2B 22
Leaderfoot. Bord 6C 60
Leadgate. Cumb 7M 53
Leadgate. Dur 6E 54
Leadgate. Nmbd 6E 54
Leadhills. S Lan 8G 59
Leadingcross Green. Kent 8E 22
Lea End. Worc 4J 27
Leafield. Oxon 2M 19
Leagrave. Lutn 1H 21
Lea Hall. W Mid 3K 27
Lea Heath. Staf 7J 35
Leake. N Yor 6B 48
Leake Common Side. Linc 4L 37
Leake Fold Hill. Linc 4M 37
Leake Hurn's End. Linc 5M 37
Lealholm. N Yor 5E 48
Lealt. Arg 8A 64
Lealt. High 7G 77
Leam. Derbs 2L 35
Lea Marston. Warw 2L 27
Leamington Hastings.
Warw 5B 28
Leamington Spa, Royal.
Warw 5M 27
Leamonsley. Staf 1K 27
Leamside. Dur 7G 55
Leargybreck. Arg 2E 56
Lease Rigg. N Yor 5F 48
Leasgill. Cumb 7C 46
Leasingham. Linc 5H 37
Leasingthorne. Dur 8F 54
Leasowe. Mers 8A 40
Leatherhead. Surr 8J 21
Leathley. N Yor 3L 41
Leaths. Dum 5B 52
Leaton. Shrp 8C 34
Leaton. Telf 8E 34
Lea Town. Lanc 4C 40
Leaveland. Kent 8G 23
Leavenheath. Suff 8F 30
Leavening. N Yor 1E 42
Leaves Green. G Lon 7M 21
Lea Yeat. Cumb 7F 46
Leazes. Dur 6E 54
Lebberston. N Yor 7H 49
Lechlade on Thames. Glos 4L 19
Leck. Lanc 8E 46
Leckford. Hants 2A 10
Leckfurin. High 6K 85
Leckgruinart. Arg 3B 56
Leckhampstead. Buck 8E 28
Leckhampstead. W Ber 6B 20
Leckhampton. Glos 2H 19
Leckmelm. High 4B 78
Leckwith. V Glam 7L 17
Leconfield. E Yor 3H 43
Ledaig. Arg 4D 64
Ledburn. Buck 1G 21
Ledbury. Here 8F 26
Ledgemoor. Here 6C 26
Ledgowan. High 8B 78
Ledicot. Here 5C 26
Ledmore. High 2C 78
Lednabirichen. High 4H 79
Lednagullin. High 5L 85
Ledsham. Ches W 2B 34
Ledsham. W Yor 5B 42
Ledston. W Yor 5B 42
Ledstone. Devn 7K 5
Ledwell. Oxon 1B 20
Lee. Devn
nr. Ilfracombe 1D 6
nr. South Molton 3H 7
Lee. G Lon 6L 21
Lee. Hants 4A 10
Lee. Lanc 2D 40
Lee. Shrp 6C 34
The Lee. Buck 3G 21
Leeans. Shet 3D 90
Leebotten. Shet 5E 90
Leebotwood. Shrp 2C 26
Lee Brockhurst. Shrp 7D 34
Leece. Cumb 8M 45
Leechpool. Mon 5D 18
Lee Clump. Buck 3G 21
Leeds. Kent 8E 22
Leeds. W Yor 110 (4L 41)
Leeds Bradford Airport.
W Yor 3L 41
Leedstown. Corn 5K 3
Leegomery. Telf 8E 34
Lee Head. Derbs 8J 41
Leek. Staf 4H 35
Leekbrook. Staf 4H 35
Leek Wootton. Warw 5L 27
Lee Mill. Devn 6H 5
Leeming. N Yor 7L 47
Leeming Bar. N Yor 6L 47
Lee Moor. Devn 5H 5
Lee Moor. W Yor 5M 41
Lee-on-the-Solent. Hants 5C 10
Lees. Derbs 6L 35
Lees. G Man 7H 41
Lees. W Yor 4J 41
The Lees. Kent 8G 23
Leeswood. Flin 3A 34
Leetown. Per 5F 66
Leftwich. Ches W 2E 34
Legbourne. Linc 1L 37
Legburthwaite. Cumb 4B 46
Legerwood. Bord 5C 60
Legsby. Linc 1J 37
Leicester. Leic 110 (1C 28)
Leicester Forest East. Leics 1C 28
Leigh. Dors 5E 8
Leigh. G Man 7E 40
Leigh. Kent 1B 12
Leigh. Shrp 1B 26
Leigh. Surr 1K 11
Leigh. Wilts 4J 19
Leigh. Worc 6F 26
The Leigh. Glos 1G 19
Leigham. Plym 6H 5
Leigh Beck. Essx 5E 22
Leigh Common. Som 3F 8
Leigh Delamere. Wilts 6G 19
Leigh Green. Kent 2F 12
Leighland Chapel. Som 2K 7
Leigh-on-Sea. S'end 5E 22
Leigh Park. Hants 5E 10
Leigh Sinton. Worc 6F 26
Leighterton. Glos 4G 19
Leighton. N Yor 8K 47
Leighton. Powy 2M 25
Leighton. Shrp 1E 26
Leighton. Som 1F 8
Leighton Bromswold.
Cambs 4J 29
Leighton Buzzard. C Beds 1G 21
Leigh-upon-Mendip. Som 1E 8
Leinthall Earls. Here 5C 26
Leinthall Starkes. Here 5C 26
Leintwardine. Here 4C 26
Leire. Leics 2C 28
Leirinmore. High 5G 85
Leishmore. High 1E 70
Leiston. Suff 5L 31
Leitfie. Per 3F 66
Leith. Edin 2L 59
Leitholm. Bord 5E 60
Leitrim. New M 7H 93
Lelant. Corn 5J 3
Lelant Downs. Corn 5J 3
Lelley. E Yor 4K 43
Lem Hill. Shrp 4F 26
Lemington. Tyne 5E 54
Lempitlaw. Bord 6E 60
Lemsford. Herts 2K 21
Lenacre. Cumb 7E 46
Lenchie. Abers 2E 72
Lenchwick. Worc 7J 27
Lendalfoot. S Ayr 3G 51
Lendrick. Stir 7K 65
Lenham. Kent 8E 22
Lenham Heath. Kent 1F 12
Lenimore. N Ayr 5H 57
Lennel. Bord 5F 60
Lennoxtown. E Dun 2E 58
Lenton. Linc 6H 37
Lentran. High 1F 70
Lenwade. Norf 8G 39
Lenzie. E Dun 2E 58
Leochel Cushnie. Abers 4E 72
Leogh. Shet 2M 89
Leominster. Here 6C 26
Leonard Stanley. Glos 3G 19
Lepe. Hants 6B 10
Lephenstrath. Arg 1B 50
Lephin. High 1C 68
Lephinchapel. Arg 8D 64
Lephinmore. Arg 8D 64
Leppington. N Yor 1E 42
Lepton. W Yor 6L 41
Lerryn. Corn 6D 4
Lerwick. Shet 3E 90
Lerwick (Tingwall) Airport.
Shet 3E 90
Lesbury. Nmbd 8K 61
Leslie. Abers 3E 72
Leslie. Fife 7F 66
Lesmahagow. S Lan 6G 59
Lesnewth. Corn 2D 4
Lessingham. Norf 7K 39
Lessonhall. Cumb 6G 53
Leswalt. Dum 5F 50
Letchmore Heath. Herts 4J 21
Letchworth Garden City.
Herts 8K 29
Letcombe Bassett. Oxon 5A 20
Letcombe Regis. Oxon 5A 20
Letham. Ang 3J 67
Letham. Falk 1G 59
Letham. Fife 6G 67
Lethanhill. E Ayr 8C 58
Lethenty. Abers 1H 73
Letheringham. Suff 6J 31
Letheringsett. Norf 6G 39
Lettaford. Devn 7G 7
Lettan. Orkn 5G 89
Letter. Abers 4G 73
Letterewe. High 6L 77
Letterfearn. High 3K 69
Lettermore. Arg 3K 63
Letters. High 5B 78
Lettershendoney. Derr 3D 92
Letterston. Pemb 4F 14
Letton. Here
nr. Kington 7B 26
nr. Leintwardine 4B 26
Letty Green. Herts 2K 21
Letwell. S Yor 1C 36
Leuchars. Fife 5H 67
Leumrabhagh. W Isl 2E 76
Leusdon. Devn 8G 7
Levaneap. Shet 1E 90
Levedale. Staf 8G 35
Leven. E Yor 3J 43
Leven. Fife 7G 67
Levencorroch. N Ayr 7K 57
Levenhall. E Lot 2A 60
Levens. Cumb 7C 46
Levens Green. Herts 1L 21
Levenshulme. G Man 8G 41
Levenwick. Shet 5E 90
Leverburgh. W Isl 5B 76
Leverington. Cambs 8M 37
Leverton. Linc 5L 37
Leverton. W Ber 6M 19
Leverton Lucasgate. Linc 5M 37
Leverton Outgate. Linc 5M 37
Levington. Suff 8J 31
Levisham. N Yor 6F 48
Levishie. High 4E 70
Lew. Oxon 3M 19
Lewaigue. IOM 5D 44
Lewannick. Corn 7B 6
Lewdown. Devn 7D 6
Lewes. E Sus 4M 11
Leweston. Pemb 4F 14
Lewisham. G Lon 6L 21
Lewiston. High 3F 70
Lewistown. B'end 6J 17
Lewknor. Oxon 4E 20
Leworthy. Devn
nr. Barnstaple 2F 6
nr. Holsworthy 5C 6
Lewson Street. Kent 7F 22
Lewthorn Cross. Devn 8G 7
Lewtrenchard. Devn 7D 6
Ley. Corn 5D 4
Leybourne. Kent 8C 22
Leyburn. N Yor 6K 47
Leycett. Staf 5F 34
Leyfields. Staf 1L 27
Ley Green. Herts 1J 21
Ley Hill. Buck 3G 21
Leyland. Lanc 5D 40
Leylodge. Abers 4G 73
Leymoor. W Yor 6K 41
Leys. Per 4F 66
Leysdown-on-Sea. Kent 6G 23
Leysmill. Ang 3K 67
Leyton. G Lon 5L 21
Leytonstone. G Lon 5M 21
Lezant. Corn 8C 6
Leziate. Norf 8C 38
Lhanbryde. Mor 7B 80
The Lhen. IOM 4C 44
Liatrie. High 2C 70
Libanus. Powy 2J 17
Libberton. S Lan 5H 59
Libbery. Worc 6H 27
Liberton. Edin 3L 59
Liceasto. W Isl 4C 76
Lichfield. Staf 1K 27
Lickey. Worc 4H 27
Lickey End. Worc 4H 27
Lickfold. W Sus 3G 11
Liddaton. Devn 7D 6
Liddington. Swin 5L 19
Liddle. Orkn 3F 86
Lidgate. Suff 6D 30
Lidgett. Notts 3D 36
Lidham Hill. E Sus 4E 12
Lidlington. C Beds 8G 29
Lidsey. W Sus 5G 11
Lidstone. Oxon 1A 20
Lienassie. High 3L 69
Liff. Ang 4G 67
Lifford. W Mid 3J 27
Lifton. Devn 7C 6
Liftondown. Devn 7C 6
Lighthorne. Warw 6M 27
Light Oaks. Stoke 4H 35
Lightwater. Surr 7G 21
Lightwood. Staf 5J 35
Lightwood. Stoke 5H 35
Lightwood Green. Ches E 5E 34
Lightwood Green. Wrex 5B 34
Lilbourne. Nptn 4C 28
Lilburn Tower. Nmbd 7H 61
Lillesdon. Som 3B 8
Lilleshall. Telf 8F 34
Lilley. Herts 1J 21
Lilliesleaf. Bord 7C 60
Lillingstone Dayrell. Buck 8E 28
Lillingstone Lovell. Buck 7E 28
Lillington. Dors 4E 8
Lilstock. Som 1L 7
Lilybank. Inv 2B 58
Lilyhurst. Shrp 8F 34
Limavady. Caus 2E 92
Limbrick. Lanc 6E 40
Limbury. Lutn 1H 21
Limekilnburn. S Lan 4F 58
Limekilns. Fife 1J 59
Limerigg. Falk 2G 59
Limestone Brae. Nmbd 7A 54
Lime Street. Worc 8G 27
Limington. Som 3D 8
Limpenhoe. Norf 1K 31
Limpley Stoke. Wilts 7F 18
Limpsfield. Surr 8M 21
Limpsfield Chart. Surr 8M 21
Linburn. W Lot 3K 59
Linby. Notts 4C 36
Linchmere. W Sus 2F 10
Lincluden. Dum 4D 52
Lincoln. Linc 111 (2G 37)
Lincomb. Worc 5G 27
Lindale. Cumb 7C 46
Lindal in Furness. Cumb 8A 46
Lindean. Bord 6B 60
Linden. Glos 2G 19
Lindfield. W Sus 3L 11
Lindford. Hants 2F 10
Lindores. Fife 6F 66
Lindridge. Worc 5E 26
Lindsell. Essx 1C 22
Lindsey. Suff 7F 30
Lindsey Tye. Suff 7F 30
Linford. Hants 5K 9
Linford. Thur 6C 22
Lingague. IOM 7B 44
Lingdale. Red C 4D 48
Lingen. Here 5B 26
Lingfield. Surr 1L 11
Lingreabhagh. W Isl 5B 76
Lingwood. Norf 1K 31
Lingy Close. Cumb 6H 53
Linicro. High 7E 76
Linkend. Worc 8G 27
Linkenholt. Hants 8A 20
Linkinhorne. Corn 8C 6
Linklater. Orkn 3F 86
Linksness. Orkn 8E 88
Linktown. Fife 8F 66
Linkwood. Mor 7B 80
Linley. Shrp
nr. Bishop's Castle 2B 26
nr. Bridgnorth 2E 26
Linley Green. Here 6E 26
Linlithgow. W Lot 2H 59
Linlithgow Bridge. Falk 2H 59
Linneraineach. High 3B 78
Linshiels. Nmbd 1B 54
Linsiadar. W Isl 8F 82
Linsidemore. High 4F 78
Linslade. C Beds 1G 21
Linstead Parva. Suff 4K 31
Linstock. Cumb 6J 53
Linthwaite. W Yor 6K 41
Lintlaw. Bord 4F 60
Lintmill. Mor 7E 80
Linton. Cambs 7B 30
Linton. Derbs 8L 35
Linton. Here 1E 18
Linton. Kent 1D 12
Linton. N Yor 1H 41
Linton. Bord 7E 60
Linton. W Yor 3A 42
Linton Colliery. Nmbd 2F 54
Linton Hill. Here 1E 18
Linton-on-Ouse. N Yor 1B 42
Lintzford. Dur 6E 54
Lintzgarth. Dur 7C 54
Linwood. Hants 5K 9
Linwood. Linc 1J 37
Linwood. Ren 3C 58
Lionacleit. W Isl 1D 74
Lionacro. High 7E 76
Lionacuidhe. W Isl 1D 74
Lional. W Isl 5J 83
Liphook. Hants 2F 10
Lipley. Shrp 6F 34
Lipyeate. Som 8E 18
Liquo. N Lan 4G 59
Lisbane. Ards 5J 93
Lisbellaw. Ferm 6C 92
Lisburn. Lis 5H 93
Liscard. Mers 8B 40
Liscolman. Caus 2F 93
Liscombe. Som 2H 7
Lishahawley. Derr 2D 92
Liskeard. Corn 5E 4
Lislea. New M 7G 93
Lisle Court. Hants 6M 9
Lisnarick. Ferm 6B 92
Lisnaskea. Ferm 7C 92
Liss. Hants 3E 10
Lissett. E Yor 2J 43
Liss Forest. Hants 3E 10
Lissington. Linc 1J 37
Liston. Essx 7E 30
Listooder. New M 6J 93
Lisvane. Card 6L 17
Liswerry. Newp 5B 18
Litcham. Norf 8E 38
Litchard. B'end 6J 17
Litchborough. Nptn 6D 28
Litchfield. Hants 8B 20
Litherland. Mers 8B 40
Litlington. Cambs 7L 29
Litlington. E Sus 5B 12
Littemill. Nmbd 8K 61
Litterty. Abers 8G 81
Little Abington. Cambs 7B 30
Little Addington. Nptn 4G 29
Little Airmyn. N Yor 5E 42
Little Alne. Warw 5K 27
Little Ardo. Abers 2H 73
Little Asby. Cumb 5E 46
Little Aston. Staf 1J 27
Little Atherfield. IOW 7B 10
Little Ayton. N Yor 4C 48
Little Baddow. Essx 3D 22
Little Badminton. S Glo 5G 19
Little Ballinluig. Per 2C 66
Little Bampton. Cumb 6G 53
Little Bardfield. Essx 8C 30
Little Barford. Bed 6J 29
Little Barningham. Norf 6H 39
Little Barrington. Glos 2L 19
Little Barrow. Ches W 3C 34
Little Barugh. N Yor 8E 48
Little Bavington. Nmbd 4C 54
Little Bealings. Suff 7J 31
Littlebeck. Cumb 4E 46
Little Bedwyn. Wilts 7L 19
Little Bentley. Essx 1H 23
Little Berkhamsted. Herts 3K 21
Little Billing. Nptn 5F 28
Little Billington. C Beds 1G 21
Little Birch. Here 8D 26
Little Bispham. Bkpl 3B 40
Little Blakenham. Suff 7H 31
Little Blencow. Cumb 8J 53
Little Bognor. W Sus 3H 11
Little Bolas. Shrp 7E 34
Little Bollington. Ches E 1F 34
Little Bookham. Surr 8J 21
Littleborough. Devn 4H 7
Littleborough. G Man 6H 41
Littleborough. Notts 1F 36
Littlebourne. Kent 8J 23
Little Bourton. Oxon 7B 28
Little Bowden. Leics 3E 28
Little Bradley. Suff 6C 30
Little Brampton. Shrp 3B 26
Little Brechin. Ang 1J 67
Littlebredy. Dors 7D 8
Little Brickhill. Mil 8G 29
Little Bridgeford. Staf 7G 35
Little Brington. Nptn 5D 28
Little Bromley. Essx 1G 23
Little Broughton. Cumb 8E 52
Little Budworth. Ches W 3D 34
Little Burstead. Essx 4C 22
Little Burton. E Yor 3J 43
Littlebury. Essx 8B 30
Littlebury Green. Essx 8A 30
Little Bytham. Linc 8H 37
Little Canfield. Essx 1B 22
Little Canford. Dors 6J 9
Little Carlton. Linc 1L 37
Little Carlton. Notts 4E 36
Little Casterton. Rut 1H 29
Little Catwick. E Yor 3J 43
Little Catworth. Cambs 4J 29
Little Cawthorpe. Linc 1L 37
Little Chalfont. Buck 4G 21
Little Chart. Kent 1F 12
Little Chesterford. Essx 7B 30
Little Cheverell. Wilts 8H 19
Little Chishill. Cambs 8M 29
Little Clacton. Essx 2H 23
Little Clanfield. Oxon 3L 19
Little Clifton. Cumb 2K 45
Little Coates. NE Lin 7K 43
Little Comberton. Worc 7H 27
Little Common. E Sus 5D 12
Little Compton. Warw 8L 27
Little Cornard. Suff 8E 30
Littlecote. Buck 1F 20
Littlecott. Wilts 8K 19
Little Cowarne. Here 6E 26
Little Coxwell. Oxon 4L 19
Little Crakehall. N Yor 6L 47
Little Crawley. Mil 7G 29
Little Creich. High 5G 79
Little Cressingham. Norf 1E 30
Little Crosby. Mers 7B 40
Little Crosthwaite. Cumb 2M 45
Little Cubley. Derbs 6K 35
Little Dalby. Leics 8E 36
Little Dawley. Telf 1E 26
Littledean. Glos 2E 18
Little Dens. Abers 1K 73
Little Dewchurch. Here 8D 26
Little Ditton. Cambs 6C 30
Little Down. Hants 8A 20
Little Downham. Cambs 3B 30
Little Drayton. Shrp 6E 34
Little Driffield. E Yor 2H 43
Little Dunham. Norf 8E 38
Little Dunkeld. Per 3D 66
Little Dunmow. Essx 1C 22
Little Easton. Essx 1C 22
Little Eaton. Derbs 5A 36
Little Eccleston. Lanc 3C 40
Little Ellingham. Norf 2G 31
Little Elm. Som 1F 8
Little End. Essx 3B 22
Little Everdon. Nptn 6C 28
Little Eversden. Cambs 6L 29
Little Faringdon. Oxon 3L 19
Little Fencote. N Yor 6L 47
Little Fenton. N Yor 4C 42
Littleferry. High 4J 79
Little Fransham. Norf 8F 38
Little Gaddesden. Herts 2G 21
Little Garway. Here 1C 18
Little Gidding. Cambs 3J 29
Little Glemham. Suff 6K 31
Little Glenshee. Per 4C 66
Little Gransden. Cambs 6K 29
Little Green. Suff 4G 31
Little Green. Wrex 5C 34
Little Grimsby. Linc 8L 43
Little Habton. N Yor 8E 48
Little Hadham. Herts 1M 21
Little Hale. Linc 5J 37
Little Hallingbury. Essx 2A 22
Littleham. Devn
nr. Bideford 3D 6
nr. Exmouth 7K 7
Little Hampden. Buck 3F 20
Littlehampton. W Sus 5H 11
Little Haresfield. Glos 3G 19
Little Harrowden. Nptn 4F 28
Little Haseley. Oxon 3D 20
Little Hatfield. E Yor 3J 43
Little Hautbois. Norf 7J 39
Little Haven. Pemb 5E 14
Little Hay. Staf 1K 27
Little Hayfield. Derbs 1J 35
Little Haywood. Staf 7J 35
Little Heath. W Mid 3M 27
Little Heck. N Yor 5C 42
Littlehempston. Devn 5L 5
Little Herbert's. Glos 2H 19
Little Hereford. Here 5D 26
Little Horkesley. Essx 8F 30
Little Hormead. Herts 1L 21
Little Horsted. E Sus 4A 12
Little Horton. W Yor 4K 41
Little Horwood. Buck 8E 28
Little Houghton. Nptn 6F 28
Little Houghton. S Yor 7B 42
Littlehoughton. Nmbd 8K 61
Little Hucklow. Derbs 2K 35
Little Hulton. G Man 7F 40
Little Irchester. Nptn 5G 29
Little Kelk. E Yor 1H 43
Little Kimble. Buck 3F 20
Little Kineton. Warw 6M 27
Little Kingshill. Buck 4F 20
Little Langdale. Cumb 5B 46
Little Langford. Wilts 2J 9
Little Laver. Essx 3B 22
Little Lawford. Warw 4B 28
Little Leigh. Ches W 2E 34
Little Leighs. Essx 2D 22
Little Leven. E Yor 3H 43
Little Lever. G Man 7F 40
Little Linford. Mil 7F 28
Little London. Buck 2D 20
Little London. E Sus 4B 12
Little London. Hants
nr. Andover 1A 10
nr. Basingstoke 8D 20
Little London. Linc
nr. Long Sutton 7M 37
nr. Spalding 7K 37
Little London. Norf
nr. North Walsham 6J 39
nr. Northwold 2D 30
nr. Saxthorpe 6H 39
nr. Southery 2C 30
Little London. Powy 4K 25
Little Longstone. Derbs 2K 35
Little Malvern. Worc 7F 26
Little Maplestead. Essx 8E 30
Little Marcle. Here 8E 26
Little Marlow. Buck 5F 20
Little Massingham. Norf 7D 38
Little Melton. Norf 1H 31
Little Mill. Mon 3B 18
Littlemill. Abers 6C 72
Littlemill. E Ayr 8C 58
Littlemill. High 1K 71
Little Milton. Oxon 3D 20
Little Missenden. Buck 4G 21
Littlemoor. Derbs 3A 36
Littlemoor. Dors 7E 8
Littlemore. Oxon 3C 20
Little Mountain. Flin 3A 34
Little Musgrave. Cumb 4F 46
Little Ness. Shrp 8C 34
Little Neston. Ches W 2A 34
Little Newcastle. Pemb 4F 14
Little Newsham. Dur 4K 47
Little Oakley. Essx 1J 23
Little Oakley. Nptn 3F 28
Little Onn. Staf 8G 35
Little Ormside. Cumb 4F 46
Little Orton. Cumb 6H 53
Little Orton. Leics 1M 27
Little Ouse. Cambs 3C 30
Little Ouseburn. N Yor 1B 42
Littleover. Derb 6M 35
Little Packington. Warw 3L 27
Little Paxton. Cambs 5J 29
Little Petherick. Corn 4B 4
Little Plumpton. Lanc 4B 40
Little Plumstead. Norf 8K 39
Little Ponton. Linc 6G 37
Littleport. Cambs 3B 30
Little Posbrook. Hants 5C 10
Little Potheridge. Devn 4E 6
Little Preston. Nptn 6C 28
Little Raveley. Cambs 4K 29
Little Reynoldston. Swan 8L 15
Little Ribston. N Yor 2A 42
Little Rissington. Glos 2K 19
Little Rogart. High 3H 79
Little Rollright. Oxon 8L 27
Little Ryburgh. Norf 7F 38
Little Ryle. Nmbd 8H 61
Little Ryton. Shrp 1C 26
Little Salkeld. Cumb 8K 53
Little Sampford. Essx 8C 30
Little Sandhurst. Brac 7F 20
Little Saredon. Staf 1H 27
Little Saxham. Suff 5D 30
Little Scatwell. High 8D 78
Little Shelford. Cambs 6A 30
Little Shoddesden. Hants 1L 9
Little Singleton. Lanc 4B 40
Little Smeaton. N Yor 6C 42
Little Snoring. Norf 6F 38
Little Sodbury. S Glo 5F 18
Little Somborne. Hants 2A 10
Little Somerford. Wilts 5H 19
Little Soudley. Shrp 7F 34
Little Stainforth. N Yor 1G 41
Little Stainton. Darl 4M 47
Little Stanney. Ches W 2C 34
Little Staughton. Bed 5J 29
Little Steeping. Linc 3M 37
Littlester. Shet 5K 91
Little Stoke. Staf 6H 35
Littlestone-on-Sea. Kent 3G 13
Little Stonham. Suff 5H 31
Little Stretton. Leics 1D 28
Little Stretton. Shrp 2C 26
Little Strickland. Cumb 4D 46
Little Stukeley. Cambs 4K 29
Little Sugnall. Staf 6G 35
Little Sutton. Ches W 2B 34
Little Sutton. Linc 7A 38
Little Swinburne. Nmbd 4C 54
Little Tew. Oxon 1A 20
Little Tey. Essx 1E 22
Little Thetford. Cambs 4B 30
Little Thirkleby. N Yor 8B 48
Little Thornage. Norf 6G 39
Little Thornton. Lanc 3B 40
Little Thorpe. W Yor 5K 41
Littlethorpe. Leics 2C 28
Littlethorpe. N Yor 1M 41
Little Thurlow. Suff 6C 30
Little Thurrock. Thur 6C 22
Littleton. Ches W 3C 34
Littleton. Hants 2B 10
Littleton. Som 2C 8
Littleton. Surr
nr. Guildford 1G 11
nr. Staines 7H 21
Littleton Drew. Wilts 5G 19
Littleton Pannell. Wilts 8J 19
Littleton-upon-Severn.
S Glo 5D 18
Little Torboll. High 4H 79
Little Torrington. Devn 4D 6
Little Totham. Essx 2E 22
Little Town. Cumb 3M 45
Little Town. Lanc 4E 40
Littletown. Dur 7G 55
Littletown. High 5H 79
Little Twycross. Leics 1M 27
Little Urswick. Cumb 8A 46
Little Wakering. Essx 5F 22
Little Walden. Essx 7B 30
Little Waldingfield. Suff 7F 30
Little Walsingham. Norf 6F 38
Little Waltham. Essx 2D 22
Little Warley. Essx 4C 22
Little Weighton. E Yor 4G 43
Little Wenham. Suff 8G 31
Little Wenlock. Telf 1E 26
Little Whelnetham. Suff 5E 30
Little Whittingham Green.
Suff 4J 31
Littlewick Green. Wind 6F 20
Little Wilbraham. Cambs 6B 30
Littlewindsor. Dors 5C 8
Little Wisbeach. Linc 6J 37
Little Witcombe. Glos 2H 19
Little Witley. Worc 5F 26
Little Wittenham. Oxon 4C 20
Little Wolford. Warw 8L 27
Littleworth. Bed 7H 29
Littleworth. Glos 8K 27
Littleworth. Oxon 4M 19
Littleworth. Staf
nr. Cannock 8J 35
nr. Eccleshall 7F 34
nr. Stafford 7H 35
Littleworth. W Sus 3J 11
Littleworth. Worc
nr. Redditch 5H 27
nr. Worcester 6G 27
Little Wratting. Suff 7C 30
Little Wymondley. Herts 1K 21
Little Wyrley. Staf 1J 27
Little Yeldham. Essx 8D 30
Littley Green. Essx 2C 22
Litton. Derbs 2K 35
Litton. N Yor 8H 47
Litton. Som 8D 18
Litton Cheney. Dors 6D 8
Liurbost. W Isl 1E 76
Liverpool. Mers 111 (8B 40)
Liverpool John Lennon Airport.
Mers 1C 34
Liversedge. W Yor 5K 41
Liverton. Devn 8H 7
Liverton. Red C 4E 48
Liverton Mines. Red C 4E 48
Livingston. W Lot 3J 59
Livingston Village. W Lot 3J 59
Lixwm. Flin 3L 33
Lizard. Corn 7L 3
Llaingoch. IOA 2B 32
Llaithddu. Powy 4K 25
Llampha. V Glam 7J 17
Llan. Powy 2H 25
Llanaber. Gwyn 1F 24
Llanaelhaearn. Gwyn 6C 32
Llanaeron. Cdgn 6D 24
Llanafan. Cdgn 5F 24
Llanafan-fawr. Powy 7J 25
Llanafan-fechan. Powy 7J 25
Llanallgo. IOA 2D 32
Llanandras. Powy 5B 26
Llananno. Powy 5K 25
Llanarmon. Gwyn 7D 32
Llanarmon Dyffryn Ceiriog.
Wrex 7L 33
Llanarmon-yn-Ial. Den 5L 33
Llanarth. Cdgn 1L 15
Llanarth. Mon 2B 18
Llanarthne. Carm 4M 15
Llanasa. Flin 2L 33
Llanbabo. IOA 2C 32
Llanbadarn Fawr. Cdgn 4F 24
Llanbadarn Fynydd. Powy 5L 25
Llanbadarn-y-garreg. Powy 8L 25
Llanbadoc. Mon 3B 18
Llanbadrig. IOA 1C 32
Llanbeder. Newp 4B 18
Llanbedr. Gwyn 8E 32
Llanbedr. Powy
nr. Crickhowell 2M 17
nr. Hay-on-Wye 8L 25
Llanbedr-Dyffryn-Clwyd.
Den 5L 33
Llanbedrgoch. IOA 2E 32
Llanbedrog. Gwyn 7C 32
Llanbedr Pont Steffan.
Cdgn 8E 24
Llanbedr-y-cennin. Cnwy 4G 33
Llanberis. Gwyn 4E 32
Llanbethery. V Glam 8K 17
Llanbister. Powy 5L 25
Llanblethian. V Glam 7J 17
Llanboidy. Carm 4J 15
Llanbradach. Cphy 5L 17
Llanbrynmair. Powy 2H 25
Llanbydderi. V Glam 8K 17
Llancadle. V Glam 8K 17
Llancarfan. V Glam 7K 17
Llancatal. V Glam 8K 17
Llancayo. Mon 3B 18
Llancloudy. Here 1C 18
Llancoch. Powy 5M 25
Llancynfelyn. Cdgn 3F 24
Llandaff. Card 7L 17
Llandanwg. Gwyn 8E 32
Llandarcy. Neat 5G 17
Llandawke. Carm 5J 15
Llanddaniel Fab. IOA 3D 32
Llanddarog. Carm 5M 15
Llanddeiniol. Cdgn 5E 24
Llanddeiniolen. Gwyn 4E 32
Llandderfel. Gwyn 7J 33
Llanddeusant. Carm 2G 17
Llanddeusant. IOA 2C 32
Llanddew. Powy 1K 17
Llanddewi. Swan 8L 15
Llanddewi Brefi. Cdgn 7F 24
Llanddewi'r Cwm. Powy 8K 25
Llanddewi Rhydderch. Mon 2B 18
Llanddewi Velfrey. Pemb 5H 15
Llanddewi Ystradenni.
Powy 6L 25
Llanddoged. Cnwy 4H 33
Llanddona. IOA 3E 32
Llanddowror. Carm 5J 15
Llanddulas. Cnwy 3J 33
Llanddwywe. Gwyn 8E 32
Llanddyfnan. IOA 3E 32
Llandecwyn. Gwyn 7F 32
Llandefaelog Fach. Powy 1K 17
Llandefaelog-tre'r-graig.
Powy 1L 17
Llandefalle. Powy 1L 17
Llandegfan. IOA 3E 32
Llandegla. Den 5L 33
Llandegley. Powy 6L 25
Llandegveth. Mon 4B 18
Llandeilo. Carm 2F 16
Llandeilo Graban. Powy 8K 25
Llandeilo'r Fan. Powy 1H 17
Llandeloy. Pemb 4E 14
Llandenny. Mon 3C 18
Llandevaud. Newp 4C 18
Llandevenny. Mon 5C 18
Llandilo. Pemb 4H 15
Llandinabo. Here 1D 18
Llandinam. Powy 4K 25
Llandissilio. Pemb 4H 15
Llandogo. Mon 3D 18
Llandough. V Glam
nr. Cowbridge 7J 17
nr. Penarth 7L 17
Llandovery. Carm 1G 17
Llandow. V Glam 7J 17
Llandre. Cdgn 4F 24
Llandrillo. Den 7K 33
Llandrillo-yn-Rhos. Cnwy 2H 33
Llandrindod. Powy 6K 25
Llandrindod Wells. Powy 6K 25
Llandrinio. Powy 8A 34
Llandudno. Cnwy 2G 33
Llandudno Junction. Cnwy 3G 33
Llandudoch. Pemb 2H 15
Llandw. V Glam 7J 17
Llandwrog. Gwyn 5D 32
Llandybie. Carm 3F 16
Llandyfaelog. Carm 5L 15
Llandyfan. Carm 3F 16
Llandyfriog. Cdgn 2K 15
Llandyfrydog. IOA 2D 32
Llandygai. Gwyn 3F 32
Llandygwydd. Cdgn 2J 15
Llandynan. Den 6L 33
Llandyrnog. Den 4L 33
Llandysilio. Powy 8A 34
Llandyssil. Powy 3L 25
Llandysul. Cdgn 2L 15
Llanedeyrn. Card 6M 17
Llaneglwys. Powy 1K 17
Llanegryn. Gwyn 2F 24
Llanegwad. Carm 4M 15
Llaneilian. IOA 1D 32
Llanelian-yn-Rhos. Cnwy 3H 33
Llanelidan. Den 5L 33
Llanelieu. Powy 1L 17
Llanellen. Mon 2B 18
Llanelli. Carm 7M 15
Llanelltyd. Gwyn 1G 25
Llanelly. Mon 3M 17
Llanelly Hill. Mon 3M 17
Llanelwedd. Powy 7K 25
Llan-Elwy. Den 3K 33
Llanenddwyn. Gwyn 8E 32
Llanengan. Gwyn 8B 32
Llanerch. Powy 2B 26
Llanerchymedd. IOA 2D 32
Llanerfyl. Powy 2K 25
Llaneuddog. IOA 2D 32
Llanfachraeth. IOA 2C 32
Llanfachreth. Gwyn 8G 33
Llanfaelog. IOA 3C 32
Llanfaelrhys. Gwyn 8B 32
Llanfaenor. Mon 2C 18
Llanfaes. IOA 3F 32
Llanfaes. Powy 2K 17
Llanfaethlu. IOA 2C 32
Llanfaglan. Gwyn 4D 32
Llanfair. Gwyn 8E 32
Llanfair. Here 7A 26
Llanfair Caereinion. Powy 2L 25
Llanfair Clydogau. Cdgn 7F 24
Llanfair Dyffryn Clwyd. Den 5L 33
Llanfairfechan. Cnwy 3F 32
Llanfair-Nant-Gwyn. Pemb 3H 15
Llanfair Pwllgwyngyll. IOA 3E 32
Llanfair Talhaiarn. Cnwy 3J 33
Llanfair Waterdine. Shrp 5M 25
Llanfair-ym-Muallt. Powy 7K 25
Llanfairyneubwll. IOA 3C 32
Llanfairynghornwy. IOA 1C 32
Llanfallteg. Carm 5H 15
Llanfallteg West. Carm 5H 15
Llanfaredd. Powy 7K 25
Llanfarian. Cdgn 5E 24
Llanfechain. Powy 8L 33
Llanfechell. IOA 1C 32
Llanfendigaid. Gwyn 2E 24
Llanferres. Den 4L 33
Llan Ffestiniog. Gwyn 6G 33
Llanfflewyn. IOA 2C 32
Llanfihangel-ar-Arth. Carm 3L 15
Llanfihangel Glyn Myfyr.
Cnwy 6J 33
Llanfihangel Nant Bran.
Powy 1J 17
Llanfihangel-Nant-Melan.
Powy 7L 25
Llanfihangel near Rogiet.
Mon 5C 18
Llanfihangel Rhydithon.
Powy 6L 25
Llanfihangel Tal-y-llyn.
Powy 2L 17
Llanfihangel-uwch-Gwili.
Carm 4L 15
Llanfihangel-y-Creuddyn.
Cdgn 5F 24
Llanfihangel-yng-Ngwynfa.
Powy 1K 25
Llanfihangel yn Nhowyn.
IOA 3C 32
Llanfihangel-y-pennant.
Gwyn nr. Golan 6E 32
nr. Tywyn 2F 24
Llanfihangel-y-traethau.
Gwyn 7E 32
Llanfilo. Powy 1L 17
Llanfleiddan. V Glam 7J 17
Llanfoist. Mon 2A 18
Llanfor. Gwyn 7J 33
Llanfrechfa. Torf 4B 18
Llanfrothen. Gwyn 6F 32
Llanfrynach. Powy 2K 17
Llanfwrog. Den 5L 33
Llanfwrog. IOA 2C 32
Llanfyllin. Powy 1L 25
Llanfynydd. Carm 2E 16
Llanfynydd. Flin 4A 34
Llanfyrnach. Pemb 3J 15
Llangadfan. Powy 1K 25
Llangadog. Carm
nr. Llandovery 2G 17
nr. Llanelli 6L 15
Llangadwaladr. IOA 4C 32
Llangadwaladr. Powy 7L 33
Llangaffo. IOA 4D 32
Llangain. Carm 5K 15
Llangammarch Wells. Powy 8J 25
Llangan. V Glam 7J 17
Llangarron. Here 1D 18
Llangasty-Talyllyn. Powy 2L 17
Llangathen. Carm 2E 16
Llangattock. Powy 3M 17
Llangattock Lingoed. Mon 1B 18
Llangattock-Vibon-Avel.
Mon 2C 18
Llangedwyn. Powy 8L 33
Llangefni. IOA 3D 32
Llangeinor. B'end 6J 17
Llangeitho. Cdgn 7F 24
Llangeler. Carm 3K 15
Llangelynin. Gwyn 2E 24
Llangendeirne. Carm 5L 15
Llangennech. Carm 4E 16
Llangennith. Swan 7L 15
Llangenny. Powy 3M 17
Llangernyw. Cnwy 4H 33
Llangian. Gwyn 8B 32
Llangiwg. Neat 4G 17
Llangloffan. Pemb 3F 14
Llanglydwen. Carm 4H 15
Llangoed. IOA 3F 32
Llangoedmor. Cdgn 2H 15
Llangollen. Den 6M 33
Llangolman. Pemb 4H 15
Llangorse. Powy 2L 17
Llangorwen. Cdgn 4F 24
Llangovan. Mon 3C 18
Llangower. Gwyn 7J 33
Llangranog. Cdgn 1K 15
Llangristiolus. IOA 3D 32
Llangrove. Here 2D 18
Llangua. Mon 1B 18
Llangunllo. Powy 5M 25
Llangunnor. Carm 4L 15
Llangurig. Powy 5J 25
Llangwm. Cnwy 6J 33
Llangwm. Mon 3C 18
Llangwm. Pemb 6F 14
Llangwm-isaf. Mon 3C 18
Llangwnnadl. Gwyn 7B 32
Llangwyfan. Den 4L 33
Llangwyfan-isaf. IOA 4C 32
Llangwyllog. IOA 3D 32
Llangwyryfon. Cdgn 5F 24
Llangybi. Cdgn 7F 24
Llangybi. Gwyn 6D 32
Llangybi. Mon 4B 18
Llangyfelach. Swan 5F 16
Llangynhafal. Den 4L 33
Llangynidr. Powy 3L 17
Llangynin. Carm 5J 15
Llangynog. Carm 5K 15
Llangynog. Powy 8K 33
Llangynwyd. B'end 6H 17
Llanhamlach. Powy 2K 17
Llanharan. Rhon 6K 17
Llanharry. Rhon 6K 17
Llanhennock. Mon 4B 18
Llanhilleth. Blae 4M 17
Llanidloes. Powy 4J 25
Llaniestyn. Gwyn 7B 32
Llanigon. Powy 8M 25
Llanilar. Cdgn 5F 24
Llanilid. Rhon 6J 17
Llanilltud Fawr. V Glam 8J 17
Llanishen. Card 6L 17
Llanishen. Mon 3C 18
Llanllawddog. Carm 4L 15
Llanllechid. Gwyn 4F 32
Llanllowell. Mon 4B 18
Llanllugan. Powy 2K 25
Llanllwch. Carm 5K 15
Llanllwchaiarn. Powy 3L 25
Llanllwni. Carm 3L 15
Llanllyfni. Gwyn 5D 32
Llanmadoc. Swan 7L 15
Llanmaes. V Glam 8J 17
Llanmartin. Newp 5B 18
Llanmerwig. Powy 3L 25
Llanmihangel. V Glam 7J 17
Llan-mill. Pemb 5H 15
Llanmiloe. Carm 6J 15
Llanmorlais. Swan 7M 15
Llannefydd. Cnwy 3J 33
Llan-non. Cdgn 6E 24
Llannon. Carm 6M 15
Llannor. Gwyn 7C 32
Llanover. Mon 3B 18
Llanpumsaint. Carm 4L 15
Llanrhaeadr. Den 4K 33
Llanrhaeadr-ym-Mochnant.
Powy 8L 33
Llanrhian. Pemb 3E 14
Llanrhidian. Swan 7L 15
Llanrhos. Cnwy 2G 33
Llanrhyddlad. IOA 2C 32
Llanrhystud. Cdgn 6E 24
Llanrothal. Here 2C 18
Llanrug. Gwyn 4E 32
Llanrumney. Card 6M 17
Llanrwst. Cnwy 4G 33
Llansadurnen. Carm 5J 15
Llansadwrn. Carm 1F 16
Llansadwrn. IOA 3E 32
Llansaint. Carm 6K 15
Llansamlet. Swan 5F 16
Llansanffraid Glan Conwy.
Cnwy 3H 33

Llansannan. Cnwy 4J 33
Llansannor. V Glam 7J 17
Llansantffraed. Cdgn 6E 24
Llansantffraed. Powy 2L 17
Llansantffraed Cwmdeuddwr. Powy 6J 25
Llansantffraed-in-Elwel. Powy 7K 25
Llansantffraid-ym-Mechain. Powy 8M 33
Llansawel. Carm 1F 16
Llansawel. Neat 5G 17
Llansilin. Powy 8M 33
Llansoy. Mon 3C 18
Llanspyddid. Powy 2K 17
Llanstadwell. Pemb 6F 14
Llansteffan. Carm 5K 15
Llanstephan. Powy 8L 25
Llantarnam. Torf 4B 18
Llanteg. Pemb 5H 15
Llanthony. Mon 1A 18
Llantilio Crossenny. Mon 2B 18
Llantilio Pertholey. Mon 2B 18
Llantood. Pemb 2H 15
Llantrisant. Mon 4B 18
Llantrisant. Rhon 6K 17
Llantrithyd. V Glam 7K 17
Llantwit Fardre. Rhon 6K 17
**Llantwit Major**. V Glam 8J 17
Llanuwchllyn. Gwyn 7H 33
Llanvaches. Newp 4C 18
Llanvair Discoed. Mon 4C 18
Llanvapley. Mon 2B 18
Llanvetherine. Mon 2B 18
Llanveynoe. Here 8B 26
Llanvihangel Crucorney. Mon 1B 18
Llanvihangel Gobion. Mon 3B 18
Llanvihangel Ystern-Llewern. Mon 2C 18
Llanwarne. Here 1D 18
Llanwddyn. Powy 1K 25
Llanwenarth. Mon 2A 18
Llanwenog. Cdgn 2L 15
Llanwern. Newp 5B 18
Llanwinio. Carm 4J 15
Llanwnda. Gwyn 5D 32
Llanwnda. Pemb 3F 14
Llanwnnen. Cdgn 2M 15
Llanwnog. Powy 3K 25
Llanwrda. Carm 1G 17
Llanwrin. Powy 2G 25
Llanwrthwl. Powy 6J 25
Llanwrtud. Powy 8H 25
Llanwrtyd. Powy 8H 25
Llanwrtyd Wells. Powy 8H 25
Llanwyddelan. Powy 2K 25
Llanyblodwel. Shrp 8M 33
Llanybri. Carm 5K 15
Llanybydder. Carm 2M 15
Llanycefn. Pemb 4G 15
Llanychaer. Pemb 3F 14
Llanycil. Gwyn 7J 33
Llanymawddwy. Gwyn 1J 25
Llanymddyfri. Carm 1G 17
Llanymynech. Powy 7A 34
Llanynghenedl. IOA 2C 32
Llanynys. Den 4L 33
Llan-y-pwll. Wrex 4B 34
Llanyrafon. Torf 4B 18
Llanyre. Powy 6K 25
Llanystumdwy. Gwyn 7D 32
Llanywern. Powy 2L 17
Llawhaden. Pemb 5G 15
Llawndy. Flin 2L 33
Llawnt. Shrp 6A 34
Llawr Dref. Gwyn 8B 32
Llawryglyn. Powy 3J 25
Llay. Wrex 4B 34
Llechfaen. Powy 2K 17
Llechryd. Cphy 4L 17
Llechryd. Cdgn 2J 15
Llechrydau. Wrex 7M 33
Lledrod. Cdgn 5F 24
Llethrid. Swan 7M 15
Llidiad-Nenog. Carm 3M 15
Llidiardau. Gwyn 7H 33
Llidiart y Parc. Den 6L 33
Llithfaen. Gwyn 6C 32
Lloc. Flin 3L 33
Llong. Flin 3A 34
Llowes. Powy 8L 25
Lloyney. Powy 5M 25
Llundain-fach. Cdgn 7E 24
Llwydcoed. Rhon 4J 17
Llwyncelyn. Cdgn 1L 15
Llwyncelyn. Swan 4F 16
Llwyndafydd. Cdgn 1K 15
Llwynderw. Powy 2M 25
Llwyn-du. Mon 2A 18
Llwyngwril. Gwyn 2E 24
Llwynhendy. Carm 7M 15
Llwynmawr. Wrex 7M 33
Llwyn-on Village. Mer T 3K 17
Llwyn-têg. Carm 4E 16
Llwyn-y-brain. Carm 5H 15
Llwynygog. Powy 3H 25
Llwyn-y-groes. Cdgn 7E 24
Llwynypia. Rhon 5J 17
Llynclys. Shrp 7A 34
Llynfaes. IOA 3D 32
Llysfaen. Cnwy 3H 33
Llyswen. Powy 1L 17
Llysworney. V Glam 7J 17
Llys-y-fran. Pemb 4G 15
Llywel. Powy 1H 17
Llywernog. Cdgn 4G 25
Loan. Falk 2H 59
Loanend. Nmbd 4G 61
Loanhead. Midl 3L 59
Loaningfoot. Dum 6D 52
Loanreoch. High 6G 79
Loans. S Ayr 6B 58
Loansdean. Nmbd 3E 54
Lobb. Devn 2D 6
Lobhillcross. Devn 7D 6
Lochaber. Mor 8L 79
Loch a Charnain. W Isl 1E 74
Loch a Ghainmhich. W Isl 1D 76
Lochailort. High 7J 69
Lochaline. High 3A 64
Lochans. Dum 6F 50
Locharbriggs. Dum 3D 52
Lochardil. High 1G 71
Lochassynt Lodge. High 1B 78
Lochavich. Arg 6D 64
Lochawe. Arg 5F 64
Loch Baghasdail. W Isl 4D 74
Lochboisdale. W Isl 4D 74
Lochbuie. Arg 5M 63
Lochcarron. High 2K 69
Loch Choire Lodge. High 8J 85
Lochdochart House. Stir 5J 65
Lochdon. Arg 4B 64
Lochearnhead. Stir 5K 65
Lochee. D'dee 4G 67
Lochend. High
nr. Inverness 2F 70
nr. Thurso 5D 86
Locherben. Dum 2D 52
Loch Euphort. W Isl 7K 75
Lochfoot. Dum 4C 52
Lochgair. Arg 8D 64
Lochgarthside. High 4F 70
Lochgelly. Fife 8E 66
Lochgilphead. Arg 1H 57
Lochgoilhead. Arg 7F 64
Loch Head. Dum 7J 51
Lochhill. Mor 7B 80
Lochindorb Lodge. High 2K 71
Lochinver. High 1A 78
Lochlane. Per 5B 66
**Loch Lomond**. Arg 7H 65
Loch Loyal Lodge. High 7J 85
Lochluichart. High 7D 78
Lochmaben. Dum 3E 52
Lochmaddy. W Isl 7L 75
Loch nam Madadh. W Isl 7L 75
Lochore. Fife 8E 66
Lochportain. W Isl 6L 75
Lochranza. N Ayr 4J 57
Loch Sgioport. W Isl 2E 74
Lochside. Abers 1L 67
Lochside. High
nr. Achentoul 8L 85
nr. Nairn 8J 79
Lochslin. High 5J 79
Lochstack Lodge. High 7E 84
Lochton. Abers 6G 73
Lochty. Fife 7J 67
Lochuisge. High 2B 64
Lochussie. High 8E 78
Lochwinnoch. Ren 4B 58
Lochyside. High 8B 70
Lockengate. Corn 5C 4
Lockerbie. Dum 3F 52
Lockeridge. Wilts 7K 19
Lockerley. Hants 3L 9
Lockhills. Cumb 7K 53
Locking. N Som 8B 18
Lockington. E Yor 3G 43
Lockington. Leics 7B 36
Lockleywood. Shrp 7E 34
Locksgreen. IOW 6B 10
**Locks Heath**. Hants 5C 10
Lockton. N Yor 6F 48
Loddington. Leics 1E 28
Loddington. Nptn 4F 28
Loddiswell. Devn 7K 5
Loddon. Norf 2K 31
Lode. Cambs 5B 30
Loders. Dors 6C 8
Lodsworth. W Sus 3G 11
Lofthouse. N Yor 8K 47
Lofthouse. W Yor 5M 41
Lofthouse Gate. W Yor 5M 41
Loftus. Red C 4E 48
Logan. E Ayr 7D 58
Loganlea. W Lot 3H 59
Logaston. Here 6B 26
Loggerheads. Den 4L 33
Loggerheads. Staf 6F 34
Loggie. High 4B 78
Logie. Ang 1K 67
Logie. Fife 5H 67
Logie. Mor 8L 79
Logie Coldstone. Abers 5D 72
Logie Pert. Ang 1K 67
Logierait. Per 2C 66
Login. Carm 4H 15
Lolworth. Cambs 5L 29
Lonbain. High 8H 77
Londesborough. E Yor 3F 42
**London**. G Lon 112-113 (5L 21)
London Apprentice. Corn 6C 4
London Ashford Airport. Kent 3G 13
London City Airport. G Lon 5M 21
London Colney. Herts 3J 21
**Londonderry**. Derr 3D 92
Londonderry. N Yor 7M 47
London Gatwick Airport. W Sus 119 (1K 11)
London Heathrow Airport. G Lon 119 (6H 21)
London Luton Airport. Lutn 119 (1J 21)
London Southend Airport. Essx 5E 22
London Stansted Airport. Essx 119 (1B 22)
Londonthorpe. Linc 6G 37
Londubh. High 5K 77
Lone. High 7F 84
Lonemore. High
nr. Dornoch 5H 79
nr. Gairloch 6J 77
Long Ashton. N Som 6D 18
Long Bank. Worc 4F 26
Longbar. N Ayr 4B 58
Long Bennington. Linc 5F 36
**Longbenton**. Tyne 5F 54
Longborough. Glos 1K 19
Long Bredy. Dors 6D 8
Longbridge. Warw 5L 27
Longbridge. W Mid 4J 27
Longbridge Deverill. Wilts 1G 9
Long Buckby. Nptn 5D 28
Long Buckby Wharf. Nptn 5D 28
Longburgh. Cumb 6H 53
Longburton. Dors 4E 8
Long Clawson. Leics 7E 36
Longcliffe. Derbs 4L 35
Long Common. Hants 4C 10
Long Compton. Staf 7G 35
Long Compton. Warw 8L 27
Longcot. Oxon 4L 19
Long Crendon. Buck 3D 20
Long Crichel. Dors 4H 9
Longcroft. Cumb 6G 53
Longcroft. Falk 2F 58
Longcross. Surr 7G 21
Longdale. Cumb 5E 46
Longdales. Cumb 7K 53
Longden. Shrp 1C 26
Longden Common. Shrp 1C 26
Long Ditton. Surr 7J 21
Longdon. Staf 8J 35
Longdon. Worc 8G 27
Longdon Green. Staf 8J 35
Longdon on Tern. Telf 8E 34
Longdown. Devn 6H 7
Longdowns. Corn 5L 3
Long Drax. N Yor 5D 42
Long Duckmanton. Derbs 2B 36
**Long Eaton**. Derbs 6B 36
Longfield. Kent 7C 22
Longfield. Shet 6D 90
Longfield Hill. Kent 7C 22
Longford. Derbs 6L 35
Longford. Glos 1G 19
Longford. G Lon 6H 21
Longford. Shrp 6E 34
Longford. Telf 8F 34
Longford. W Mid 3A 28
Longforgan. Per 4G 67
Longformacus. Bord 4D 60
Longframlington. Nmbd 1E 54
Long Gardens. Essx 8E 30
Long Green. Ches W 2C 34
Long Green. Worc 8G 27
Longham. Dors 6J 9
Longham. Norf 8F 38
Long Hanborough. Oxon 2B 20
Longhedge. Wilts 1G 9
Longhill. Abers 8K 81
Longhirst. Nmbd 3F 54
Longhope. Glos 2E 18
Longhope. Orkn 2E 86
Longhorsley. Nmbd 2E 54
Longhoughton. Nmbd 8K 61
Long Itchington. Warw 5B 28
Longlands. Cumb 8G 53
Long Lane. Telf 8E 34
Longlane. Derbs 6L 35
Longlane. W Ber 6B 20
Long Lawford. Warw 4B 28
Long Lease. N Yor 5G 49
Longley Green. Worc 6F 26
Long Load. Som 3C 8
Longmanhill. Abers 7G 81
Long Marston. Herts 2F 20
Long Marston. N Yor 2C 42
Long Marston. Warw 7K 27
Long Marton. Cumb 3E 46
Long Meadow. Cambs 5B 30
Long Meadowend. Shrp 3C 26
Long Melford. Suff 7E 30
Longmoor Camp. Hants 2E 10
Longmorn. Mor 8B 80
Longmoss. Ches E 2G 35
Long Newnton. Glos 4H 19
Long Newton. Stoc T 4A 48
Longnewton. Bord 7C 60
Longney. Glos 2F 18
Longniddry. E Lot 2B 60
Longnor. Shrp 1C 26
Longnor. Staf
nr. Leek 3J 35
nr. Stafford 8G 35
Longparish. Hants 1B 10
Longpark. Cumb 5J 53
Long Preston. N Yor 2G 41
Longridge. Lanc 4E 40
Longridge. Staf 8H 35
Longridge. W Lot 3H 59
Longriggend. N Lan 2G 59
Long Riston. E Yor 3J 43
Longrock. Corn 5J 3
Longsdon. Staf 4H 35
Longshaw. G Man 7D 40
Longshaw. Staf 5J 35
Longside. Abers 1K 73
Longslow. Shrp 6E 34
Longstanton. Cambs 5L 29
Longstock. Hants 2A 10
Longstowe. Cambs 6L 29
Long Stratton. Norf 2H 31
Long Street. Mil 7E 28
Longstreet. Wilts 8K 19
Long Sutton. Hants 1E 10
Long Sutton. Linc 7M 37
Long Sutton. Som 3C 8
Longthorpe. Pet 2J 29
Long Thurlow. Suff 5G 31
Longthwaite. Cumb 3C 46
**Longton**. Lanc 5C 40
Longton. Stoke 5H 35
Longtown. Cumb 5H 53
Longtown. Here 1B 18
Longville in the Dale. Shrp 2D 26
Long Whatton. Leics 7B 36
Longwick. Buck 3E 20
Long Wittenham. Oxon 4C 20
Longwitton. Nmbd 3D 54
Longworth. Oxon 4A 20
Longyester. E Lot 3C 60
Lonmore. High 1D 68
Looe. Corn 6E 4
Loose. Kent 8D 22
Loosegate. Linc 7L 37
Loosley Row. Buck 3F 20
Lopcombe Corner. Wilts 2L 9
Lopen. Som 4C 8
Loppington. Shrp 7C 34
Lorbottle. Nmbd 1D 54
Lordington. W Sus 5E 10
Loscoe. Derbs 5B 36
Loscombe. Dors 6D 8
Losgaintir. W Isl 4B 76
Lossiemouth. Mor 7B 80
Lossit. Arg 4A 56
Lostock Gralam. Ches W 2E 34
Lostock Green. Ches W 2E 34
Lostock Hall. Lanc 5D 40
Lostock Junction. G Man 7E 40
Lostwithiel. Corn 6D 4
Lothbeg. High 2K 79
Lothersdale. N Yor 3H 41
Lothianbridge. Midl 3M 59
Lothianburn. Midl 3L 59
Lothmore. High 2K 79
Lottisham. Som 2D 8
Loudwater. Buck 4G 21
**Loughborough**. Leics 8C 36
Loughbrickland. Arm 6G 93
Loughgall. Arm 6F 93
Loughguile. Caus 2G 93
Loughinisland. New M 6J 93
Loughmacrory. Ferm 5D 92
Loughor. Swan 5E 16
Loughries. Ards 5J 93
**Loughton**. Essx 4M 21
Loughton. Mil 8F 28
Loughton. Shrp 3E 26
Lound. Linc 8H 37
Lound. Notts 1D 36
Lound. Suff 2M 31
Lount. Leics 8A 36
The Loup. M Ulst 4F 93
**Louth**. Linc 1L 37
Love Clough. Lanc 5G 41
Lovedean. Hants 4D 10
Lover. Wilts 3L 9
Loversall. S Yor 8C 42
Loves Green. Essx 3C 22
Loveston. Pemb 6G 15
Lovington. Som 2D 8
Low Ackworth. W Yor 6B 42
Low Angerton. Nmbd 3D 54
Low Ardwell. Dum 7F 50
Low Ballochdowan. S Ayr 4F 50
Lowbands. Glos 8F 26
Low Barlings. Linc 2H 37
Low Bell End. N Yor 6E 48
Low Bentham. N Yor 1E 40
Low Borrowbridge. Cumb 5E 46
Low Bradfield. S Yor 8L 41
Low Bradley. N Yor 3J 41
Low Braithwaite. Cumb 7J 53
Low Brunton. Nmbd 4C 54
Low Burnham. N Lin 7E 42
Lowca. Cumb 2J 45
Low Catton. E Yor 2E 42
Low Coniscliffe. Darl 4L 47
Low Coylton. S Ayr 8C 58
Low Crosby. Cumb 6J 53
Low Dalby. N Yor 7F 48
Lowdham. Notts 5D 36
Low Dinsdale. Darl 4M 47
Lowe. Shrp 6D 34
Low Ellington. N Yor 7L 47
Lower Amble. Corn 4B 4
Lower Ansty. Dors 5F 8
Lower Arboll. High 5J 79
Lower Arncott. Oxon 2D 20
Lower Ashton. Devn 7H 7
Lower Assendon. Oxon 5E 20
Lower Auchenreath. Mor 7C 80
Lower Badcall. High 7D 84
Lower Ballam. Lanc 4B 40
Lower Ballinderry. Lis 5G 93
Lower Basildon. W Ber 6D 20
Lower Beeding. W Sus 3K 11
Lower Benefield. Nptn 3G 29
Lower Bentley. Worc 5H 27
Lower Beobridge. Shrp 2F 26
Lower Bockhampton. Dors 6F 8
Lower Boddington. Nptn 6B 28
Lower Bordean. Hants 3D 10
Lower Brailes. Warw 8M 27
Lower Breakish. High 3H 69
Lower Broadheath. Worc 6G 27
Lower Brynamman. Neat 3G 17
Lower Bullingham. Here 8D 26
Lower Bullington. Hants 1B 10
Lower Burgate. Hants 4K 9
Lower Cam. Glos 3F 18
Lower Catesby. Nptn 6C 28
Lower Chapel. Powy 1K 17
Lower Cheriton. Devn 5L 7
Lower Chicksgrove. Wilts 2H 9
Lower Chute. Wilts 8M 19
Lower Clopton. Warw 6K 27
Lower Common. Hants 1D 10
Lower Crossings. Derbs 1J 35
Lower Cumberworth. W Yor 7L 41
Lower Darwen. Bkbn 5E 40
Lower Dean. Bed 5H 29
Lower Dean. Devn 5K 5
Lower Diabaig. High 7J 77
Lower Dicker. E Sus 4B 12
Lower Dounreay. High 5A 86
Lower Down. Shrp 3B 26
Lower Dunsforth. N Yor 1B 42
Lower East Carleton. Norf 1H 31
Lower Egleton. Here 7E 26
Lower Ellastone. Staf 5K 35
Lower End. Nptn 5F 28
Lower Everleigh. Wilts 8K 19
Lower Eype. Dors 6C 8
Lower Failand. N Som 6D 18
Lower Faintree. Shrp 3E 26
Lower Farringdon. Hants 2E 10
Lower Foxdale. IOM 7B 44
Lower Frankton. Shrp 6B 34
Lower Froyle. Hants 1E 10
Lower Gabwell. Devn 5M 5
Lower Gledfield. High 4F 78
Lower Godney. Som 1C 8
Lower Gravenhurst. C Beds 8J 29
Lower Green. Essx 8M 29
Lower Green. Norf 6F 38
Lower Green. W Ber 7A 20
Lower Halstow. Kent 7E 22
Lower Hardres. Kent 8H 23
Lower Hardwick. Here 6C 26
Lower Hartshay. Derbs 4A 36
Lower Hawthwaite. Cumb 6M 45
Lower Haysden. Kent 1B 12
Lower Hayton. Shrp 3D 26
Lower Hergest. Here 6A 26
Lower Heyford. Oxon 1B 20
Lower Heysham. Lanc 1C 40
Lower Higham. Kent 6D 22
Lower Holbrook. Suff 8H 31
Lower Holditch. Dors 5B 8
Lower Hordley. Shrp 7B 34
Lower Horncroft. W Sus 4H 11
Lower Horsebridge. E Sus 4B 12
Lower Kilcott. Glos 5F 18
Lower Killeyan. Arg 5B 56
Lower Kingcombe. Dors 6D 8
Lower Kingswood. Surr 8K 21
Lower Kinnerton. Ches W 3B 34
Lower Langford. N Som 7C 18
Lower Largo. Fife 7H 67
Lower Layham. Suff 7G 31
Lower Ledwyche. Shrp 4D 26
Lower Leigh. Staf 6J 35
Lower Lemington. Glos 8L 27
Lower Lenie. High 3F 70
Lower Ley. Glos 2F 18
Lower Llanfadog. Powy 6J 25
Lower Lode. Glos 8G 27
Lower Lovacott. Devn 3E 6
Lower Loxhore. Devn 2F 6
Lower Loxley. Staf 6J 35
Lower Lydbrook. Glos 2D 18
Lower Lye. Here 5C 26
Lower Machen. Newp 6M 17
Lower Maes-coed. Here 8B 26
Lower Meend. Glos 3D 18
Lower Midway. Derbs 7M 35
Lower Milovaig. High 8C 76
Lower Moor. Worc 7H 27
Lower Morton. S Glo 4E 18
Lower Mountain. Flin 4B 34
Lower Nazeing. Essx 3L 21
Lower Netchwood. Shrp 2E 26
Lower Nyland. Dors 3F 8
Lower Oakfield. Fife 8E 66
Lower Oddington. Glos 1L 19
Lower Ollach. High 2G 69
Lower Penarth. V Glam 8L 17
Lower Penn. Staf 2G 27
Lower Pennington. Hants 6M 9
Lower Peover. Ches W 2F 34
Lower Pilsley. Derbs 3B 36
Lower Pitkerrie. High 6J 79
Lower Place. G Man 6H 41
Lower Quinton. Warw 7K 27
Lower Rainham. Medw 7E 22
Lower Raydon. Suff 8G 31
Lower Seagry. Wilts 5H 19
Lower Shelton. C Beds 7G 29
Lower Shiplake. Oxon 6E 20
Lower Shuckburgh. Warw 5B 28
Lower Sketty. Swan 5F 16
Lower Slade. Devn 1E 6
Lower Slaughter. Glos 1K 19
Lower Soudley. Glos 2E 18
Lower Stanton St Quintin. Wilts 5H 19
Lower Stoke. Medw 6E 22
Lower Stondon. C Beds 8J 29
Lower Stonnall. Staf 1J 27
Lower Stow Bedon. Norf 2F 30
Lower Street. Norf 6J 39
Lower Strensham. Worc 7H 27
Lower Sundon. C Beds 1H 21
Lower Swanwick. Hants 5B 10
Lower Swell. Glos 1K 19
Lower Tale. Devn 5K 7
Lower Tean. Staf 6J 35
Lower Thurlton. Norf 2L 31
Lower Thurnham. Lanc 2C 40
Lower Thurvaston. Derbs 6L 35
Lower Town. Here 7E 26
Lower Town. IOS 1H 3
Lower Town. Pemb 3F 14
Lowertown. Corn 6K 3
Lowertown. Orkn 2F 86
Lower Tysoe. Warw 7M 27
Lower Upham. Hants 4C 10
Lower Upnor. Medw 6D 22
Lower Vexford. Som 2L 7
Lower Walton. Warr 1E 34
Lower Wear. Devn 7J 7
Lower Weare. Som 8C 18
Lower Welson. Here 6A 26
Lower Whatcombe. Dors 5G 9
Lower Whitley. Ches W 2E 34
Lower Wield. Hants 1D 10
Lower Withington. Ches E 3G 35
Lower Woodend. Buck 5F 20
Lower Woodford. Wilts 2K 9
Lower Wraxall. Dors 5D 8
Lower Wych. Ches W 5C 34
Lower Wyche. Worc 7F 26
Lowesby. Leics 1E 28
**Lowestoft**. Suff 2M 31
Loweswater. Cumb 2L 45
Low Etherley. Dur 3K 47
Lowfield Heath. W Sus 1K 11
Lowford. Hants 4B 10
Low Fulney. Linc 7K 37
Low Gate. Nmbd 5C 54
Lowgill. Cumb 6E 46
Lowgill. Lanc 1E 40
Low Grantley. N Yor 8L 47
Low Green. N Yor 2L 41
Low Habberley. Worc 4G 27
Low Ham. Som 3C 8
Low Hameringham. Linc 3L 37
Low Hawsker. N Yor 5G 49
Low Hesket. Cumb 7J 53
Low Hesleyhurst. Nmbd 2D 54
Lowick. Cumb 7A 46
Lowick. Nptn 3G 29
Lowick. Nmbd 6H 61
Lowick Bridge. Cumb 7A 46
Lowick Green. Cumb 7A 46
Low Knipe. Cumb 3D 46
Low Leighton. Derbs 1J 35
Low Lorton. Cumb 2L 45
Low Marishes. N Yor 8F 48
Low Marnham. Notts 3F 36
Low Mill. N Yor 6D 48
Low Moor. Lanc 3F 40
Low Moor. W Yor 5K 41
Low Moorsley. Tyne 7G 55
Low Newton-by-the-Sea. Nmbd 7K 61
Lownie Moor. Ang 3H 67
Lowood. Bord 6C 60
Low Row. Cumb
nr. Brampton 5K 53
nr. Wigton 7F 52
Low Row. N Yor 6H 47
Lowsonford. Warw 5K 27
Low Street. Norf 1G 31
Lowther. Cumb 3D 46
Lowthorpe. E Yor 1H 43
Lowton. Devn 5F 6
Lowton. G Man 8E 40
Lowton. Som 4L 7
Lowton Common. G Man 8E 40
Low Torry. Fife 1J 59
Low Toynton. Linc 2K 37
Low Valleyfield. Fife 1H 59
Low Westwood. Dur 6E 54
Low Whinnow. Cumb 6H 53
Low Wood. Cumb 7B 46
Low Worsall. N Yor 5A 48
Low Wray. Cumb 5B 46
Loxbeare. Devn 4J 7
Loxhill. Surr 2H 11
Loxhore. Devn 2F 6
Loxley. S Yor 1M 35
Loxley. Warw 6L 27
Loxley Green. Staf 6J 35
Loxton. N Som 8B 18
Loxwood. W Sus 2H 11
Lubcroy. High 3D 78
Lubenham. Leics 3E 28
Lubinvullin. High 5H 85
Luccombe. Som 1J 7
Luccombe Village. IOW 7C 10
Lucker. Nmbd 6J 61
Luckett. Corn 8C 6
Luckington. Wilts 5G 19
Lucklawhill. Fife 5H 67
Luckwell Bridge. Som 2J 7
Lucton. Here 5C 26
Ludag. W Isl 4D 74
Ludborough. Linc 8K 43
Ludchurch. Pemb 5H 15
Luddenden. W Yor 5J 41
Luddenden Foot. W Yor 5J 41
Luddenham. Kent 7F 22
Ludderburn. Cumb 6C 46
Luddesdown. Kent 7C 22
Luddington. N Lin 6F 42
Luddington. Warw 6K 27
Luddington in the Brook. Nptn 3J 29
Ludford. Linc 1J 37
Ludford. Shrp 4D 26
Ludgershall. Buck 2D 20
Ludgershall. Wilts 8L 19
Ludgvan. Corn 5J 3
Ludham. Norf 8K 39
Ludlow. Shrp 4D 26
Ludstone. Shrp 2G 27
Ludwell. Wilts 3H 9
Ludworth. Dur 7G 55
Luffenhall. Herts 1K 21
Luffincott. Devn 6C 6
Lugar. E Ayr 7D 58
Luggate Burn. E Lot 2D 60
Lugg Green. Here 5C 26
Luggiebank. N Lan 2F 58
Lugton. E Ayr 4C 58
Lugwardine. Here 7D 26
Luib. High 3G 69
Luib. Stir 5J 65
Lulham. Here 7C 26
Lullington. Derbs 8L 35
Lullington. E Sus 5B 12
Lullington. Som 8F 18
Lulsgate Bottom. N Som 7D 18
Lulsley. Worc 6F 26
Lulworth Camp. Dors 7G 9
Lumb. Lanc 5G 41
Lumby. N Yor 4B 42
Lumphanan. Abers 5E 72
Lumphinnans. Fife 8E 66
Lumsdaine. Bord 3F 60
Lumsden. Abers 3D 72
Lunan. Ang 2K 67
Lunanhead. Ang 2H 67
Luncarty. Per 5D 66
Lund. E Yor 3G 43
Lund. N Yor 4D 42
Lundie. Ang 4F 66
Lundin Links. Fife 7H 67
Lundy Green. Norf 2J 31
Lunna. Shet 1E 90
Lunning. Shet 1F 90
Lunnon. Swan 8M 15
Lunsford. Kent 8C 22
Lunsford's Cross. E Sus 4D 12
Lunt. Mers 7B 40
Luppitt. Devn 5L 7
Lupridge. Devn 6K 5
Lupset. W Yor 6M 41
Lupton. Cumb 7D 46
**Lurgan**. Arm 6G 93
Lurganare. New M 7G 93
Lurgashall. W Sus 3G 11
Lurley. Devn 4J 7
Lusby. Linc 3L 37
Luscombe. Devn 6K 5
Luson. Devn 7J 5
Luss. Arg 8H 65
Lussagiven. Arg 1F 56
Lusta. High 8D 76
Lustleigh. Devn 7G 7
Luston. Here 5C 26
Luthermuir. Abers 1K 67
Luthrie. Fife 6G 67
Lutley. Staf 3G 27
Luton. Devn
nr. Honiton 5K 7
nr. Teignmouth 8J 7
**Luton**. Lutn 1H 21
Luton Airport. Lutn 119 (1J 21)
Lutterworth. Leics 3C 28
Lutton. Devn
nr. Ivybridge 6H 5
nr. South Brent 5J 5
Lutton. Linc 7M 37
Lutton. Nptn 3J 29
Lutton Gowts. Linc 7M 37
Lutworthy. Devn 4G 7
Luxborough. Som 2J 7
Luxley. Glos 1E 18
Luxulyan. Corn 6C 4
Lybster. High 8D 86
Lydbury North. Shrp 3B 26
Lydcott. Devn 2F 6
Lydd. Kent 3G 13
Lydd Airport. Kent 3G 13
Lydden. Kent
nr. Dover 1J 13
nr. Margate 7K 23
Lyddington. Rut 2F 28
Lydd-on-Sea. Kent 3G 13
Lydeard St Lawrence. Som 2L 7
Lyde Green. Hants 8E 20
Lydford. Devn 7E 6
Lydford Fair Place. Som 2D 8
Lydgate. G Man 7H 41
Lydgate. W Yor 5H 41
Lydham. Shrp 2B 26
Lydiard Millicent. Wilts 5J 19
Lydiate. Mers 7B 40
Lydiate Ash. Worc 4H 27
Lydlinch. Dors 4F 8
Lydmarsh. Som 5B 8
Lydney. Glos 3E 18
Lydstep. Pemb 7G 15
Lye. W Mid 3H 27
The Lye. Shrp 2E 26
Lye Green. Buck 3G 21
Lye Green. E Sus 2B 12
Lye Head. Worc 4F 26
Lyford. Oxon 4A 20
Lyham. Nmbd 6H 61
Lylestone. N Ayr 5B 58
Lymbridge Green. Kent 1H 13
Lyme Regis. Dors 6B 8
Lyminge. Kent 1H 13
**Lymington**. Hants 6M 9
Lyminster. W Sus 5H 11
**Lymm**. Warr 1E 34
Lymore. Hants 6L 9
Lympne. Kent 2H 13
Lympsham. Som 8B 18
Lympstone. Devn 7J 7
Lynaberack Lodge. High 6H 71
Lynbridge. Devn 1G 7
Lynch. Som 1J 7
Lynchat. High 5H 71
Lynch Green. Norf 1H 31
Lyndhurst. Hants 5M 9
Lyndon. Rut 1G 29
Lyne. Bord 5L 59
Lyne. Surr 7H 21
Lyneal. Shrp 6C 34
Lyne Down. Here 8E 26
Lyneham. Oxon 1L 19
Lyneham. Wilts 6J 19
Lyneholmeford. Cumb 4K 53
Lynemouth. Nmbd 2F 54
Lyne of Gorthleck. High 3F 70
Lyne of Skene. Abers 4G 73
Lynesack. Dur 3J 47
Lyness. Orkn 2E 86
Lyng. Norf 8G 39
Lyngate. Norf
nr. North Walsham 6J 39
nr. Worstead 7K 39
Lynmouth. Devn 1G 7
Lynn. Staf 1J 27
Lynn. Telf 8F 34
Lynsted. Kent 7F 22
Lynstone. Corn 5B 6
Lynton. Devn 1G 7
Lynwilg. High 4J 71
Lyon's Gate. Dors 5E 8
Lyonshall. Here 6B 26
Lytchett Matravers. Dors 6H 9
Lytchett Minster. Dors 6H 9
Lyth. High 5D 86
Lytham. Lanc 5B 40
**Lytham St Anne's**. Lanc 5B 40
Lythe. N Yor 4F 48
Lythes. Orkn 3F 86
Lythmore. High 5B 86


## M


Mabe Burnthouse. Corn 5L 3
Mabie. Dum 4D 52
Mablethorpe. Linc 1B 38
Macbiehill. Bord 4K 59
**Macclesfield**. Ches E 2H 35
Macclesfield Forest. Ches E 2H 35
Macduff. Abers 7G 81
Machan. S Lan 4F 58
Macharioch. Arg 1C 50
Machen. Cphy 6M 17
Machrie. N Ayr 6H 57
Machrihanish. Arg 7F 56
Machroes. Gwyn 8C 32
Machynlleth. Powy 2G 25
Mackerye End. Herts 2J 21
Mackworth. Derb 6M 35
Macmerry. E Lot 2B 60
Macosquin. Caus 2F 93
Madderty. Per 5C 66
Maddington. Wilts 1J 9
Maddiston. Falk 2H 59
Madehurst. W Sus 4G 11
Madeley. Staf 5F 34
Madeley. Telf 1E 26
Madeley Heath. Staf 5F 34
Madeley Heath. Worc 4H 27
Madford. Devn 4L 7
Madingley. Cambs 5L 29
Madley. Here 8C 26
Madresfield. Worc 7G 27
Madron. Corn 5H 3
Maenaddwyn. IOA 2D 32
Maenclochog. Pemb 4G 15
Maendy. V Glam 7K 17
Maenporth. Corn 6L 3
Maentwrog. Gwyn 6F 32
Maen-y-groes. Cdgn 1K 15
Maer. Staf 6F 34
Maerdy. Carm 2F 16
Maerdy. Cnwy 6K 33
Maerdy. Rhon 5J 17
Maesbrook. Shrp 7B 34
Maesbury. Shrp 7B 34
Maesbury Marsh. Shrp 7B 34
Maes-glas. Flin 3L 33
Maesgwyn-Isaf. Powy 1L 25
Maeshafn. Den 4M 33
Maes Llyn. Cdgn 2K 15
Maesmynis. Powy 8K 25
**Maesteg**. B'end 5H 17
Maestir. Cdgn 8E 24
Maesybont. Carm 3E 16
Maesycrugiau. Carm 2L 15
Maesycwmmer. Cphy 5L 17
Maesyrhandir. Powy 3K 25
Magdalen Laver. Essx 3B 22
Maggieknockater. Mor 1C 72
Maghaberry. Lis 5G 93
Magham Down. E Sus 4C 12
Maghera. M Ulst 3F 93
Maghera. New M 7H 93
Magherafelt. M Ulst 4F 93
Magheralin. Arm 6G 93
Magheramason. Derr 3C 92
Magheraveely. Ferm 7D 92
Maghery. Arm 5F 93
**Maghull**. Mers 7B 40
Magna Park. Leics 3C 28
Magor. Mon 5C 18
Magpie Green. Suff 4G 31
Maguiresbridge. Ferm 7C 92
Magwyr. Mon 5C 18
Maidenbower. W Sus 2K 11
Maiden Bradley. Wilts 2G 9
Maidencombe. Torb 5M 5
Maidenhayne. Devn 6A 8
**Maidenhead**. Wind 5F 20
Maiden Law. Dur 7E 54
Maiden Newton. Dors 6D 8
Maidens. S Ayr 1H 51
Maiden's Green. Brac 6F 20
Maidensgrove. Oxon 5E 20
Maidenwell. Corn 4D 4
Maidenwell. Linc 2L 37
Maiden Wells. Pemb 7F 14
Maidford. Nptn 6D 28
Maids Moreton. Buck 8E 28
**Maidstone**. Kent 8D 22
Maidwell. Nptn 4E 28
Mail. Shet 5E 90
Maindee. Newp 5B 18
Mainsforth. Dur 8G 55
Mains of Auchindachy. Mor 1D 72
Mains of Auchnagatt. Abers 1J 73
Mains of Drum. Abers 6H 73
Mains of Edingight. Mor 8E 80
Mainsriddle. Dum 6D 52
Mainstone. Shrp 3A 26
Maisemore. Glos 1G 19
Major's Green. Worc 4K 27
Makeney. Derbs 5A 36
Makerstoun. Bord 6D 60
Malacleit. W Isl 6J 75
Malaig. High 6H 69
Malaig Bheag. High 6H 69
Malborough. Devn 8K 5
Malcoff. Derbs 1J 35
Malcolmburn. Mor 8C 80
Malden Rushett. G Lon 7J 21
**Maldon**. Essx 3E 22
Malham. N Yor 1H 41
Maligar. High 7F 76
Malinslee. Telf 1E 26
Mallaig. High 6H 69
Malleny Mills. Edin 3K 59
Mallows Green. Essx 1A 22
Malltraeth. IOA 4D 32
Mallusk. Ant 4H 93
Mallwyd. Gwyn 1H 25
Malmesbury. Wilts 5H 19
Malmsmead. Devn 1G 7
Malpas. Ches W 5C 34
Malpas. Corn 4M 3
Malpas. Newp 4B 18
Malswick. Glos 1F 18
**Maltby**. S Yor 8C 42
Maltby. Stoc T 4B 48
Maltby le Marsh. Linc 1A 38
Malt Lane. Arg 7E 64
Maltman's Hill. Kent 1F 12
Malton. N Yor 8E 48
Malvern Link. Worc 7F 26
Malvern Wells. Worc 7F 26
Mamble. Worc 4E 26
Mamhilad. Mon 3B 18
Manaccan. Corn 6L 3
Manafon. Powy 2L 25
Manais. W Isl 5C 76
Manaton. Devn 7G 7
Manby. Linc 1L 37
Mancetter. Warw 2M 27
**Manchester**. G Man 111 (8G 41)
Manchester Airport. G Man 119 (1G 35)
Mancot. Flin 3B 34
Manea. Cambs 3A 30
Maney. W Mid 2K 27
Manfield. N Yor 4L 47
**Mangotsfield**. S Glo 6E 18
Mangurstadh. W Isl 8D 82
Mankinholes. W Yor 5H 41
Manley. Ches W 2D 34
Manmoel. Cphy 4L 17
Mannal. Arg 3E 62
Mannerston. Falk 2J 59
Manningford Bohune. Wilts 8K 19
Manningford Bruce. Wilts 8K 19
Manningham. W Yor 4K 41
Mannings Heath. W Sus 3K 11
Mannington. Dors 5J 9
Manningtree. Essx 8H 31
Mannofield. Aber 5J 73
Manorbier. Pemb 7G 15
Manorbier Newton. Pemb 7G 15
Manordeilo. Carm 2F 16
Manorowen. Pemb 3F 14
Manor Park. G Lon 5M 21
Mansell Gamage. Here 7B 26
Mansell Lacy. Here 7C 26
Mansergh. Cumb 7E 46
Mansewood. Glas 3D 58
Mansfield. E Ayr 8E 58
**Mansfield**. Notts 3C 36
**Mansfield Woodhouse**. Notts 3C 36
Mansriggs. Cumb 7A 46
Manston. Dors 4G 9
Manston. Kent 7K 23
Manston. W Yor 4A 42
Manswood. Dors 5H 9
Manthorpe. Linc
nr. Bourne 8H 37
nr. Grantham 6G 37
Manton. N Lin 7G 43
Manton. Notts 2C 36
Manton. Rut 1F 28
Manton. Wilts 7K 19
Manuden. Essx 1A 22
Maperton. Som 3E 8
Maplebeck. Notts 3E 36
Maple Cross. Herts 4H 21
Mapledurham. Oxon 6D 20
Mapledurwell. Hants 8D 20
Maplehurst. W Sus 3J 11
Maplescombe. Kent 7B 22
Mapleton. Derbs 5K 35
Mapperley. Derbs 5B 36
Mapperley. Nott 5C 36
Mapperley Park. Nott 5C 36
Mapperton. Dors
nr. Beaminster 6D 8
nr. Poole 6H 9
Mappleborough Green. Warw 5J 27
Mappleton. E Yor 3K 43
Mapplewell. S Yor 7M 41
Mappowder. Dors 5F 8
Maraig. W Isl 3D 76
Marazion. Corn 5J 3
Marbhig. W Isl 2F 76
Marbury. Ches E 5D 34
**March**. Cambs 2M 29
Marcham. Oxon 4B 20
Marchamley. Shrp 7D 34
Marchington. Staf 6K 35
Marchington Woodlands. Staf 7K 35
Marchwiel. Wrex 5B 34
Marchwood. Hants 4A 10
Marcross. V Glam 8J 17
Marden. Here 7D 26
Marden. Kent 1D 12
Marden. Wilts 8J 19
Marden Beech. Kent 1D 12
Marden Thorn. Kent 1D 12
Mardu. Shrp 3A 26
Mardy. Mon 2B 18
Marefield. Leics 1E 28
Mareham le Fen. Linc 3K 37
Mareham on the Hill. Linc 3K 37
Marehay. Derbs 5B 36
Marehill. W Sus 4H 11
Maresfield. E Sus 3A 12
Marfleet. Hull 5J 43
Marford. Wrex 4B 34
Margam. Neat 6G 17
Margaret Marsh. Dors 4G 9
Margaret Roding. Essx 2B 22
Margaretting. Essx 3C 22
Margaretting Tye. Essx 3C 22
**Margate**. Kent 6K 23
Margery. Surr 8K 21
Margnaheglish. N Ayr 6K 57
Marham. Norf 1D 30
Marhamchurch. Corn 5B 6
Marholm. Pet 1J 29
Marian Cwm. Den 3K 33
Mariandyrys. IOA 2F 32
Marian-glas. IOA 2E 32
Mariansleigh. Devn 3G 7
Marian-y-de. Gwyn 7C 32
Marian-y-mor. Gwyn 7C 32
Marine Town. Kent 6F 22
Marishader. High 7F 76
Marjoriebanks. Dum 3E 52
Mark. Dum 6G 51
Mark. Som 1B 8
Markbeech. Kent 1A 12
Markby. Linc 2A 38
Mark Causeway. Som 1B 8
Mark Cross. E Sus 2B 12
Markeaton. Derb 6M 35
Market Bosworth. Leics 1B 28
**Market Deeping**. Linc 8J 37
Market Drayton. Shrp 6E 34
Market End. Warw 3M 27
**Market Harborough**. Leics 3E 28
Markethill. Arm 7F 93
Markethill. Per 4F 66
Market Lavington. Wilts 8J 19
Market Overton. Rut 8F 36
Market Rasen. Linc 1J 37
Market Stainton. Linc 1K 37
Market Weighton. E Yor 3F 42
Market Weston. Suff 4F 30
Markfield. Leics 8B 36
Markham. Cphy 4L 17
Markinch. Fife 7F 66
Markington. N Yor 1L 41
Marksbury. Bath 7E 18
Mark's Corner. IOW 6B 10
Marks Tey. Essx 1F 22
Markwell. Corn 6F 4
Markyate. Herts 2H 21
Marlborough. Wilts 7K 19
Marlcliff. Warw 6J 27
Marldon. Devn 5L 5
Marle Green. E Sus 4B 12
Marlesford. Suff 6K 31
Marley Green. Ches E 5D 34
Marley Hill. Tyne 6F 54
Marlingford. Norf 1H 31
Mar Lodge. Abers 7L 71
Marloes. Pemb 6D 14
**Marlow**. Buck 5F 20
Marlow. Here 4B 26
Marlow Bottom. Buck 5F 20
Marlow Common. Buck 5F 20
Marlpit Hill. Kent 1M 11
Marlpits. E Sus 3M 11
Marlpool. Derbs 5B 36
Marnhull. Dors 4F 8
Marnoch. Abers 8E 80
Marnock. N Lan 3F 58
**Marple**. G Man 1H 35
Marr. S Yor 7C 42
Marrel. High 2L 79
Marrick. N Yor 6J 47
Marrister. Shet 1F 90
Marros. Carm 6J 15
Marsden. Tyne 5G 55
Marsden. W Yor 6J 41
Marsett. N Yor 7H 47
Marsh. Buck 3F 20
Marsh. Devn 4A 8
The Marsh. Powy 2B 26
The Marsh. Shrp 7E 34
Marshall Meadows. Nmbd 4G 61
Marshalsea. Dors 5B 8
Marshalswick. Herts 3J 21
Marsham. Norf 7H 39
Marshaw. Lanc 2D 40
Marsh Baldon. Oxon 4C 20
Marsh Benham. W Ber 7B 20
Marshborough. Kent 8K 23
Marshbrook. Shrp 3C 26
Marshchapel. Linc 8L 43
Marshfield. Newp 5A 18
Marshfield. S Glo 6F 18
Marshgate. Corn 6A 6
Marsh Gibbon. Buck 1D 20
Marsh Green. Devn 6K 7
Marsh Green. Kent 1M 11
Marsh Green. Staf 4G 35
Marsh Green. Telf 8E 34
Marsh Lane. Derbs 2B 36
Marsh Side. Norf 5D 38
Marshside. Kent 7J 23
Marshside. Mers 6B 40
Marsh Street. Som 1J 7
Marshwood. Dors 6B 8
Marske. N Yor 5K 47
Marske-by-the-Sea. Red C 3D 48
Marston. Ches W 2E 34
Marston. Here 6B 26
Marston. Linc 5F 36
Marston. Oxon 3C 20
Marston. Staf
nr. Stafford 7H 35
nr. Wheaton Aston 8G 35
Marston. Warw 2L 27
Marston. Wilts 8H 19
Marston Doles. Warw 6B 28
Marston Green. W Mid 3K 27
Marston Hill. Glos 4K 19
Marston Jabbett. Warw 3A 28
Marston Magna. Som 3D 8
Marston Meysey. Wilts 4K 19
Marston Montgomery. Derbs 6K 35
Marston Moretaine. C Beds 7G 29
Marston on Dove. Derbs 7L 35
Marston St Lawrence. Nptn 7C 28
Marston Stannett. Here 6D 26
Marston Trussell. Nptn 3D 28
Marstow. Here 2D 18
Marsworth. Buck 2G 21
Marten. Wilts 8L 19
Marthall. Ches E 2G 35
Martham. Norf 8L 39
Marthwaite. Cumb 6E 46
Martin. Hants 4J 9
Martin. Kent 1K 13
Martin. Linc
nr. Horncastle 3K 37
nr. Metheringham 4J 37
Martindale. Cumb 4C 46
Martin Dales. Linc 3J 37
Martin Drove End. Hants 3J 9
Martinhoe. Devn 1F 6
Martinhoe Cross. Devn 1F 6
Martin Hussingtree. Worc 5G 27
Martin Mill. Kent 1K 13
Martinscroft. Warr 1E 34
Martin's Moss. Ches E 3G 35
Martinstown. Dors 7E 8
Martinstown. ME Ant 3G 93
Martlesham. Suff 7J 31
Martlesham Heath. Suff 7J 31
Martletwy. Pemb 5G 15
Martley. Worc 5F 26
Martock. Som 4C 8
Marton. Ches E 3G 35
Marton. Cumb 7M 45
Marton. E Yor
nr. Bridlington 1K 43
nr. Hull 4J 43
Marton. Linc 1F 36
Marton. Midd 4C 48
Marton. N Yor
nr. Boroughbridge 1B 42
nr. Pickering 7E 48
Marton. Shrp
nr. Myddle 7C 34
nr. Worthen 1A 26
Marton. Warw 5B 28
Marton Abbey. N Yor 1C 42
Marton-le-Moor. N Yor 8A 48
Martyr's Green. Surr 8H 21
Martyr Worthy. Hants 2C 10
Marwick. Orkn 7B 88
Marwood. Devn 2E 6
Marybank. High
nr. Dingwall 8E 78
nr. Invergordon 6H 79
Maryburgh. High 8F 78
Maryfield. Corn 6G 5
Maryhill. Glas 3D 58
Marykirk. Abers 1K 67
**Marylebone**. G Lon 5K 21
Marylebone. G Man 7D 40
Marypark. Mor 2A 72
**Maryport**. Cumb 8E 52
Maryport. Dum 8G 51
Marystow. Devn 7D 6
Mary Tavy. Devn 8E 6
Maryton. Ang
nr. Kirriemuir 2G 67
nr. Montrose 2K 67
Marywell. Abers 6E 72
Marywell. Ang 3K 67
Masham. N Yor 7L 47
Mashbury. Essx 2C 22
Masongill. N Yor 8E 46
Masons Lodge. Abers 5H 73
Mastin Moor. Derbs 2B 36
Mastrick. Aber 5J 73
Matching. Essx 2B 22
Matching Green. Essx 2B 22
Matching Tye. Essx 2B 22
Matfen. Nmbd 4D 54
Matfield. Kent 1C 12
Mathern. Mon 4D 18
Mathon. Here 7F 26
Mathry. Pemb 3E 14
Matlaske. Norf 6H 39
**Matlock**. Derbs 4L 35
Matlock Bath. Derbs 4L 35
Matterdale End. Cumb 3B 46
Mattersey. Notts 1D 36
Mattersey Thorpe. Notts 1D 36
Mattingley. Hants 8E 20
Mattishall. Norf 8G 39
Mattishall Burgh. Norf 8G 39
Mauchline. E Ayr 7C 58
Maud. Abers 1J 73
Maudlin. Corn 5C 4
Maugersbury. Glos 1K 19
Maughold. IOM 5D 44
Maulden. C Beds 8H 29
Maulds Meaburn. Cumb 4E 46
Maunby. N Yor 7A 48
Maund Bryan. Here 6D 26
Mautby. Norf 8L 39
Mavesyn Ridware. Staf 8J 35
Mavis Enderby. Linc 3L 37
Mawbray. Cumb 7E 52
Mawdesley. Lanc 6C 40
Mawdlam. B'end 6H 17
Mawgan. Corn 6L 3
Mawgan Porth. Corn 2M 3
Maw Green. Ches E 4F 34
Mawla. Corn 4L 3
Mawnan. Corn 6L 3
Mawnan Smith. Corn 6L 3
Mawsley Village. Nptn 4E 28
Mawthorpe. Linc 2A 38
Maxey. Pet 1J 29
Maxstoke. Warw 3L 27
Maxted Street. Kent 1H 13
Maxton. Kent 1J 13
Maxton. Bord 6D 60
Maxwellheugh. Bord 6E 60
Maxwelltown. Dum 4D 52
Maxworthy. Corn 6B 6
Mayals. Swan 6F 16
Maybole. S Ayr 8B 58
Maybush. Sotn 4A 10
Maydown. Derr 3D 92
Mayes Green. Surr 2J 11
Mayfield. E Sus 3B 12
**Mayfield**. Midl 3A 60
Mayfield. Per 5D 66
Mayfield. Staf 5K 35
Mayford. Surr 8G 21
Mayhill. Swan 5F 16
Mayland. Essx 3F 22
Maylandsea. Essx 3F 22
Maynard's Green. E Sus 4B 12
Mayobridge. New M 7G 93
Maypole. IOS 1H 3
Maypole. Kent 7J 23
Maypole. Mon 2C 18
Maypole Green. Norf 2L 31
Maypole Green. Suff 6F 30
Maywick. Shet 5D 90
Mazetown. Lis 5H 93
Mead. Devn 4B 6
Meadgate. Bath 8E 18

Meadle. *Buck* 3F 20
Meadowbank. *Ches W* 3E 34
Meadowfield. *Dur* 8F 54
Meadow Green. *Here* 6F 26
Meadowmill. *E Lot* 2B 60
Meadows. *Nott* 6C 36
Meadowtown. *Shrp* 1B 26
Meadwell. *Devn* 7D 6
Meaford. *Staf* 6G 35
Mealabost. *W Isl*
nr. Borgh 6H 83
nr. Stornoway 8H 83
Mealasta. *W Isl* 1A 76
Meal Bank. *Cumb* 6D 46
Mealrigg. *Cumb* 7F 52
Mealsgate. *Cumb* 7G 53
Meanwood. *W Yor* 4L 41
Mearbeck. *N Yor* 1G 41
Meare. *Som* 1C 8
Meare Green. *Som*
nr. Curry Mallet 3A 8
nr. Stoke St Gregory 3B 8
Mears Ashby. *Nptn* 5F 28
Measham. *Leics* 8M 35
Meath Green. *Surr* 1K 11
Meathop. *Cumb* 7C 46
Meaux. *E Yor* 4H 43
Meavy. *Devn* 5H 5
Medbourne. *Leics* 2E 28
Medburn. *Nmbd* 4E 54
Meddon. *Devn* 4B 6
Meden Vale. *Notts* 3C 36
Medlam. *Linc* 4L 37
Medlicott. *Shrp* 2C 26
Medmenham. *Buck* 5F 20
Medomsley. *Dur* 6E 54
Medstead. *Hants* 2D 10
**Medway Towns**.
*Medw* 111 (7D 22)
Meerbrook. *Staf* 3H 35
Meer End. *W Mid* 4L 27
Meers Bridge. *Linc* 1A 38
Meesden. *Herts* 8M 29
Meeson. *Telf* 7E 34
Meeth. *Devn* 5E 6
Meeting Green. *Suff* 6D 30
Meeting House Hill. *Norf* 7K 39
Meidrim. *Carm* 4J 15
Meifod. *Powy* 1L 25
Meigh. *New M* 7G 93
Meigle. *Per* 3F 66
Meikle Earnock. *S Lan* 4F 58
Meikle Kilchattan Butts.
*Arg* 4K 57
Meikleour. *Per* 4E 66
Meikle Tarty. *Abers* 3J 73
Meikle Wartle. *Abers* 2G 73
Meinciau. *Carm* 5L 15
Meir. *Stoke* 5H 35
Meir Heath. *Staf* 5H 35
Melbourn. *Cambs* 7L 29
Melbourne. *Derbs* 7A 36
Melbourne. *E Yor* 3E 42
Melbury Abbas. *Dors* 3G 9
Melbury Bubb. *Dors* 5D 8
Melbury Osmond. *Dors* 5D 8
Melbury Sampford. *Dors* 5D 8
Melby. *Shet* 2B 90
Melchbourne. *Bed* 5H 29
Melcombe Bingham. *Dors* 5F 8
Melcombe Regis. *Dors* 7E 8
Meldon. *Devn* 6E 6
Meldon. *Nmbd* 3E 54
Meldreth. *Cambs* 7L 29
Melfort. *Arg* 6C 64
Melgarve. *High* 6E 70
Meliden. *Den* 2K 33
Melinbyrhedyn. *Powy* 3H 25
Melincourt. *Neat* 4H 17
Melin-y-coed. *Cnwy* 4H 33
Melin-y-ddol. *Powy* 2K 25
Melin-y-wig. *Den* 6K 33
Melkington. *Nmbd* 5F 60
Melkinthorpe. *Cumb* 3D 46
Melkridge. *Nmbd* 5M 53
**Melksham**. *Wilts* 7H 19
Mellangaun. *High* 5K 77
Melldalloch. *Arg* 2J 57
Mellguards. *Cumb* 7J 53
Melling. *Lanc* 8D 46
Melling. *Mers* 7B 40
Melling Mount. *Mers* 7C 40
Mellis. *Suff* 4G 31
Mellon Charles. *High* 4K 77
Mellon Udrigle. *High* 4K 77
Mellor. *G Man* 1H 35
Mellor. *Lanc* 4E 40
Mellor Brook. *Lanc* 4E 40
Mells. *Som* 1F 8
Melmerby. *Cumb* 8L 53
Melmerby. *N Yor*
nr. Middleham 7J 47
nr. Ripon 8M 47
Melplash. *Dors* 6C 8
Melrose. *Bord* 6C 60
Melsetter. *Orkn* 3D 86
Melsonby. *N Yor* 5K 47
Meltham. *W Yor* 6K 41
Meltham Mills. *W Yor* 6K 41
Melton. *E Yor* 5G 43
Melton. *Suff* 6J 31
Meltonby. *E Yor* 2E 42
Melton Constable. *Norf* 6G 39
**Melton Mowbray**. *Leics* 8E 36
Melton Ross. *N Lin* 6H 43
Melvaig. *High* 5J 77
Melverley. *Shrp* 8B 34
Melverley Green. *Shrp* 8B 34
Melvich. *High* 5L 85
Membury. *Devn* 5A 8
Memsie. *Abers* 7J 81
Memus. *Ang* 2H 67
Menabilly. *Corn* 6C 4
Menai Bridge. *IOA* 3E 32
Mendham. *Suff* 3J 31
Mendlesham. *Suff* 5H 31
Mendlesham Green. *Suff* 5G 31
Menethorpe. *N Yor* 1E 42
Menheniot. *Corn* 5E 4
Menithwood. *Worc* 5F 26
Menna. *Corn* 6B 4
Mennock. *Dum* 1C 52
Menston. *W Yor* 3K 41
Menstrie. *Clac* 8B 66
Menthorpe. *N Yor* 4E 42
Mentmore. *Buck* 2G 21
Meole Brace. *Shrp* 8C 34
Meols. *Mers* 1M 33
Meon. *Hants* 5C 10
Meonstoke. *Hants* 3D 10
Meopham. *Kent* 7C 22
Meopham Green. *Kent* 7C 22
Meopham Station. *Kent* 7C 22
Mepal. *Cambs* 3M 29
Meppershall. *C Beds* 8J 29
Merbach. *Here* 7B 26
Mercaston. *Derbs* 5L 35
Merchiston. *Edin* 2L 59
Mere. *Ches E* 1F 34
Mere. *Wilts* 2G 9
Mere Brow. *Lanc* 6C 40
Mereclough. *Lanc* 4G 41
Mere Green. *W Mid* 2K 27
Mere Green. *Worc* 5H 27
Mere Heath. *Ches W* 2E 34
Mereside. *Bkpl* 4B 40
Meretown. *Staf* 7F 34
Mereworth. *Kent* 8C 22
Meriden. *W Mid* 3L 27
Merkadale. *High* 2E 68
Merkland. *S Ayr* 2H 51
Merkland Lodge. *High* 1D 78
Merley. *Pool* 6J 9
Merlin's Bridge. *Pemb* 5F 14
Merridge. *Som* 2M 7
Merrington. *Shrp* 7C 34
Merrion. *Pemb* 7F 14
Merriott. *Som* 4C 8
Merrivale. *Devn* 8E 6
Merrow. *Surr* 8H 21
Merrybent. *Darl* 4L 47
Merry Lees. *Leics* 1B 28
Merrymeet. *Corn* 5E 4
Mersham. *Kent* 2G 13
Merstham. *Surr* 8K 21
Merston. *W Sus* 5F 10
Merstone. *IOW* 7C 10
Merther. *Corn* 7A 4
Merthyr. *Carm* 4K 15
Merthyr Cynog. *Powy* 1J 17
Merthyr Dyfan. *V Glam* 7L 17
Merthyr Mawr. *B'end* 7H 17
**Merthyr Tudful**. *Mer T* 4K 17
**Merthyr Tydfil**. *Mer T* 4K 17
Merthyr Vale. *Mer T* 5K 17
Merton. *Devn* 4E 6
**Merton**. *G Lon* 7K 21
Merton. *Norf* 2F 30
Merton. *Oxon* 2C 20
Meshaw. *Devn* 4G 7
Messing. *Essx* 2E 22
Messingham. *N Lin* 7F 42
Metcombe. *Devn* 6K 7
Metfield. *Suff* 3J 31
Metherell. *Corn* 5G 5
Metheringham. *Linc* 3H 37
Methil. *Fife* 8G 67
Methilhill. *Fife* 8G 67
Methley. *W Yor* 5A 42
Methley Junction. *W Yor* 5A 42
Methlick. *Abers* 2H 73
Methven. *Per* 5D 66
Methwold. *Norf* 2D 30
Methwold Hythe. *Norf* 2D 30
Mettingham. *Suff* 3K 31
Metton. *Norf* 6H 39
Mevagissey. *Corn* 7C 4
**Mexborough**. *S Yor* 7B 42
Mey. *High* 4D 86
Meysey Hampton. *Glos* 4K 19
Miabhag. *W Isl* 4C 76
Miabhaig. *W Isl*
nr. Cliasmol 3B 76
nr. Timsgearraidh 8D 82
Mial. *High* 6J 77
Michaelchurch. *Here* 1D 18
Michaelchurch Escley. *Here* 8B 26
Michaelchurch-on-Arrow.
*Powy* 7M 25
Michaelston-le-Pit. *V Glam* 7L 17
Michaelston-y-Fedw. *Newp* 6M 17
Michaelstow. *Corn* 4C 4
Michelcombe. *Devn* 5J 5
Micheldever. *Hants* 2C 10
Micheldever Station. *Hants* 1C 10
Michelmersh. *Hants* 3M 9
Mickfield. *Suff* 5H 31
Micklebring. *S Yor* 8C 42
Mickleby. *N Yor* 4F 48
Micklefield. *W Yor* 4B 42
Micklefield Green. *Herts* 4H 21
Mickleham. *Surr* 8J 21
Mickleover. *Derb* 6M 35
Micklethwaite. *Cumb* 6G 53
Micklethwaite. *W Yor* 3K 41
Mickleton. *Dur* 3H 47
Mickleton. *Glos* 7K 27
Mickletown. *W Yor* 5A 42
Mickle Trafford. *Ches W* 3C 34
Mickley. *N Yor* 8L 47
Mickley Green. *Suff* 6E 30
Mickley Square. *Nmbd* 5D 54
Mid Ardlaw. *Abers* 7J 81
Midbea. *Orkn* 5D 88
Mid Beltie. *Abers* 5F 72
Mid Calder. *W Lot* 3J 59
Mid Clyth. *High* 8D 86
Middle Assendon. *Oxon* 5E 20
Middle Aston. *Oxon* 1B 20
Middle Barton. *Oxon* 1B 20
Middlebie. *Dum* 4G 53
Middle Chinnock. *Som* 4C 8
Middle Claydon. *Buck* 1E 20
Middlecliffe. *S Yor* 7B 42
Middlecott. *Devn* 7G 7
Middle Drums. *Ang* 2J 67
Middle Duntisbourne. *Glos* 3H 19
Middle Essie. *Abers* 8K 81
Middleforth Green. *Lanc* 5D 40
Middleham. *N Yor* 7K 47
Middle Handley. *Derbs* 2B 36
Middle Harling. *Norf* 3F 30
Middlehope. *Shrp* 3C 26
Middle Littleton. *Worc* 7J 27
Middle Maes-coed. *Here* 8B 26
Middlemarsh. *Dors* 5E 8
Middle Marwood. *Devn* 2E 6
Middle Mayfield. *Staf* 5K 35
Middlemoor. *Devn* 8D 6
Middlemuir. *Abers*
nr. New Deer 1H 73
nr. Strichen 8J 81
Middle Rainton. *Tyne* 7G 55
Middle Rasen. *Linc* 1H 37
The Middles. *Dur* 6F 54
**Middlesbrough**.
*Midd* 111 (4B 48)
Middlesceugh. *Cumb* 7H 53
Middleshaw. *Cumb* 7D 46
Middlesmoor. *N Yor* 8J 47
Middlestone. *Dur* 8F 54
Middlestone Moor. *Dur* 8F 54
Middle Stoughton. *Som* 1C 8
Middlestown. *W Yor* 6L 41
Middle Street. *Glos* 3F 18
Middle Taphouse. *Corn* 5D 4
Middleton. *Ang* 3J 67
Middleton. *Arg* 3E 62
Middleton. *Cumb* 7E 46
Middleton. *Derbs*
nr. Bakewell 3K 35
nr. Wirksworth 4L 35
Middleton. *Essx* 8E 30
**Middleton**. *G Man* 7G 41
Middleton. *Hants* 1B 10
Middleton. *Hart* 8J 55
Middleton. *Here* 5D 26
Middleton. *IOW* 7M 9
Middleton. *Lanc* 2C 40
Middleton. *Midl* 4A 60
Middleton. *Norf* 8C 38
Middleton. *Nptn* 3F 28
Middleton. *Nmbd*
nr. Belford 6J 61
nr. Morpeth 3D 54
Middleton. *N Yor*
nr. Ilkley 3K 41
nr. Pickering 7E 48
Middleton. *Per* 7E 66
Middleton. *Shrp*
nr. Ludlow 4D 26
nr. Oswestry 7B 34
Middleton. *Suff* 5L 31
Middleton. *Swan* 8L 15
Middleton. *Warw* 2K 27
Middleton. *W Yor* 5L 41
Middleton Cheney. *Nptn* 7C 28
Middleton Green. *Staf* 6H 35
Middleton-in-Teesdale. *Dur* 3H 47
Middleton One Row. *Darl* 4A 48
Middleton-on-Leven. *N Yor* 5B 48
Middleton-on-Sea. *W Sus* 5G 11
Middleton on the Hill.
*Here* 5D 26
Middleton-on-the-Wolds.
*E Yor* 3G 43
Middleton Priors. *Shrp* 2E 26
Middleton Quernhow.
*N Yor* 8M 47
Middleton St George. *Darl* 4M 47
Middleton Scriven. *Shrp* 3E 26
Middleton Stoney. *Oxon* 1C 20
Middleton Tyas. *N Yor* 5L 47
Middle Town. *IOS* 1H 3
Middletown. *Arm* 7E 92
Middletown. *Cumb* 4J 45
Middletown. *Powy* 8B 34
Middle Tysoe. *Warw* 7M 27
Middle Wallop. *Hants* 2L 9
**Middlewich**. *Ches E* 3F 34
Middle Winterslow. *Wilts* 2L 9
Middlewood. *Corn* 8B 6
Middlewood. *S Yor* 8M 41
Middle Woodford. *Wilts* 2K 9
Middlewood Green. *Suff* 5G 31
Middleyard. *Glos* 3G 19
Middlezoy. *Som* 2B 8
Middridge. *Dur* 3L 47
Midelney. *Som* 3C 8
Midfield. *High* 5H 85
Midford. *Bath* 7F 18
Mid Garrary. *Dum* 4L 51
Midge Hall. *Lanc* 5D 40
Midgeholme. *Cumb* 6L 53
Midgham. *W Ber* 7C 20
Midgley. *W Yor*
nr. Halifax 5J 41
nr. Horbury 6L 41
Mid Ho. *Shet* 4K 91
Midhopestones. *S Yor* 8L 41
Midhurst. *W Sus* 3F 10
Mid Kirkton. *N Ayr* 4L 57
Mid Lambrook. *Som* 4C 8
Midland. *Orkn* 1E 86
Mid Lavant. *W Sus* 5F 10
Midlem. *Bord* 7C 60
Midney. *Som* 3D 8
**Midsomer Norton**. *Bath* 8E 18
Midton. *Inv* 2M 57
Midtown. *High*
nr. Poolewe 5K 77
nr. Tongue 5H 85
Midville. *Linc* 4L 37
Mid Walls. *Shet* 3B 90
Mid Yell. *Shet* 4K 91
Migdale. *High* 4G 79
Migvie. *Abers* 5D 72
Milborne Port. *Som* 4E 8
Milborne St Andrew. *Dors* 6G 9
Milborne Wick. *Som* 3E 8
Milbourne. *Nmbd* 4E 54
Milbourne. *Wilts* 5H 19
Milburn. *Cumb* 3E 46
Milbury Heath. *S Glo* 4E 18
Milby. *N Yor* 1B 42
Milcombe. *Oxon* 8B 28
Milden. *Suff* 7F 30
**Mildenhall**. *Suff* 4D 30
Mildenhall. *Wilts* 7L 19
Milebrook. *Powy* 4B 26
Milebush. *Kent* 1D 12
Mile End. *Cambs* 3C 30
Mile End. *Essx* 1F 22
Mileham. *Norf* 8F 38
Mile Oak. *Brig* 5K 11
Miles Green. *Staf* 4G 35
Miles Hope. *Here* 5D 26
Milesmark. *Fife* 1J 59
Mile Town. *Kent* 6F 22
Milfield. *Nmbd* 6G 61
Milford. *Arm* 6F 93
Milford. *Derbs* 5A 36
Milford. *Devn* 3B 6
Milford. *Powy* 3K 25
Milford. *Staf* 7H 35
Milford. *Surr* 1G 11
**Milford Haven**. *Pemb* 6F 14
Milford on Sea. *Hants* 6L 9
Milkwall. *Glos* 3D 18
Milkwell. *Wilts* 3H 9
Milland. *W Sus* 3F 10
Mill Bank. *W Yor* 5J 41
Millbank. *Ant* 4H 93
Millbank. *High* 5C 86
Millbay. *ME Ant* 4J 93
Millbeck. *Cumb* 3A 46
Millbounds. *Orkn* 6E 88
Millbreck. *Abers* 1K 73
Millbridge. *Surr* 1F 10
Millbrook. *C Beds* 8H 29
Millbrook. *Corn* 6G 5
Millbrook. *G Man* 8H 41
Millbrook. *ME Ant* 3H 93
Millbrook. *Sotn* 4A 10
Mill Common. *Suff* 3L 31
Mill Corner. *E Sus* 3E 12
Milldale. *Staf* 4K 35
Millden Lodge. *Ang* 8E 72
Milldens. *Ang* 2J 67
Millearn. *Per* 6C 66
Mill End. *Buck* 5E 20
Mill End. *Cambs* 6C 30
Mill End. *Glos* 2K 19
Mill End. *Herts* 8L 29
Millend. *Glos* 4F 18
Millerhill. *Midl* 3M 59
Miller's Dale. *Derbs* 2K 35
Millers Green. *Derbs* 4L 35
Millerston. *Glas* 3E 58
Millfield. *Abers* 6D 72
Millfield. *Pet* 1J 29
Millgate. *Lanc* 6G 41
Mill Green. *Essx* 3C 22
Mill Green. *Norf* 3H 31
Mill Green. *Shrp* 7E 34
Mill Green. *Staf* 7J 35
Mill Green. *Suff* 7F 30
Millhalf. *Here* 7A 26
Millhall. *E Ren* 4D 58
Millhayes. *Devn*
nr. Honiton 5M 7
nr. Wellington 4L 7
Millhead. *Lanc* 8C 46
Millheugh. *S Lan* 4F 58
Mill Hill. *Bkbn* 5E 40
Mill Hill. *G Lon* 4K 21
Millholme. *Cumb* 6D 46
Millhouse. *Arg* 2J 57
Millhouse. *Cumb* 8H 53
Millhousebridge. *Dum* 3F 52
Millhouses. *S Yor* 1M 35
Millikenpark. *Ren* 3C 58
Millington. *E Yor* 2F 42
Millington Green. *Derbs* 5L 35
Millisle. *Ards* 5J 93
Mill Knowe. *Arg* 7G 57
Mill Lane. *Hants* 8E 20
Millmeece. *Staf* 6G 35
Mill of Craigievar. *Abers* 4E 72
Mill of Fintray. *Abers* 4H 73
Mill of Haldane. *W Dun* 1C 58
Millom. *Cumb* 6L 45
Millow. *C Beds* 7K 29
Millpool. *Corn* 4D 4
Millport. *N Ayr* 4L 57
Mill Side. *Cumb* 7C 46
Mill Street. *Norf*
nr. Lyng 8G 39
nr. Swanton Morley 8G 39
Millthorpe. *Derbs* 2M 35
Millthorpe. *Linc* 6J 37
Millthrop. *Cumb* 6E 46
Milltimber. *Aber* 5H 73
Mill Town. *Ant* 4G 93
Milltown. *Abers*
nr. Corgarff 5B 72
nr. Lumsden 4D 72
Milltown. *Ant* 4G 93
Milltown. *Arm*
nr. Banbridge 6G 93
nr. Coalisland 5F 93
nr. Richhill 6F 93
Milltown. *Corn* 6D 4
Milltown. *Derbs* 3A 36
Milltown. *Devn* 2E 6
Milltown. *Dum* 4H 53
Milltown of Aberdalgie.
*Per* 5D 66
Milltown of Auchindoun.
*Mor* 1C 72
Milltown of Campfield.
*Abers* 5F 72
Milltown of Edinvillie. *Mor* 1B 72
Milltown of Rothiemay.
*Mor* 1E 72
Milltown of Towie. *Abers* 4D 72
Milnacraig. *Ang* 2F 66
Milnathort. *Per* 7E 66
**Milngavie**. *E Dun* 2D 58
Milnholm. *Stir* 1F 58
**Milnrow**. *G Man* 6H 41
Milnthorpe. *Cumb* 7C 46
Milnthorpe. *W Yor* 6M 41
Milson. *Shrp* 4E 26
Milstead. *Kent* 8F 22
Milston. *Wilts* 1K 9
Milthorpe. *Nptn* 7C 28
Milton. *Ang* 3G 67
Milton. *Cambs* 5A 30
Milton. *Cumb*
nr. Brampton 5K 53
nr. Crooklands 7D 46
Milton. *Derbs* 7M 35
Milton. *Dum*
nr. Crocketford 4C 52
nr. Glenluce 6H 51
Milton. *Glas* 3D 58
Milton. *High*
nr. Achnasheen 8D 78
nr. Applecross 1J 69
nr. Drumnadrochit 2E 70
nr. Invergordon 6H 79
nr. Inverness 1F 70
nr. Wick 6E 86
Milton. *Mor*
nr. Cullen 7E 80
nr. Tomintoul 4A 72
Milton. *N Som* 7B 18
Milton. *Notts* 2E 36
Milton. *Oxon*
nr. Bloxham 8B 28
nr. Didcot 4B 20
Milton. *Pemb* 6G 15
Milton. *Port* 6D 10
Milton. *Som* 3C 8
Milton. *S Ayr* 7C 58
Milton. *Stir*
nr. Aberfoyle 7K 65
nr. Drymen 8J 65
Milton. *Stoke* 4H 35
Milton. *W Dun* 2C 58
Milton Abbas. *Dors* 5G 9
Milton Abbot. *Devn* 8D 6
Milton Auchlossan. *Abers* 5E 72
Milton Bridge. *Midl* 3L 59
Milton Bryan. *C Beds* 8G 29
Milton Clevedon. *Som* 2E 8
Milton Coldwells. *Abers* 2J 73
Milton Combe. *Devn* 5G 5
Milton Common. *Oxon* 3D 20
Milton Damerel. *Devn* 4C 6
Miltonduff. *Mor* 7A 80
Milton End. *Glos* 3K 19
Milton Ernest. *Bed* 6H 29
Milton Green. *Ches W* 4C 34
Milton Hill. *Devn* 8J 7
Milton Hill. *Oxon* 4B 20
**Milton Keynes**. *Mil* 114 (8F 28)
Milton Keynes Village. *Mil* 8F 28
Milton Lilbourne. *Wilts* 7K 19
Milton Malsor. *Nptn* 6E 28
Milton Morenish. *Per* 4L 65
Milton of Auchinhove.
*Abers* 5E 72
Milton of Balgonie. *Fife* 7G 67
Milton of Barras. *Abers* 8H 73
Milton of Campsie. *E Dun* 2E 58
Milton of Cultoquhey. *Per* 5B 66
Milton of Cushnie. *Abers* 4E 72
Milton of Finavon. *Ang* 2H 67
Milton of Gollanfield. *High* 8H 79
Milton of Lesmore. *Abers* 3D 72
Milton of Leys. *High* 1G 71
Milton of Tullich. *Abers* 6C 72
Milton on Stour. *Dors* 3F 8
Milton Regis. *Kent* 7E 22
Milton Street. *E Sus* 5B 12
Milton-under-Wychwood.
*Oxon* 2L 19
Milverton. *Som* 3L 7
Milverton. *Warw* 5M 27
Milwich. *Staf* 6H 35
Mimbridge. *Surr* 7G 21
Minard. *Arg* 8D 64
Minchington. *Dors* 4H 9
Minchinhampton. *Glos* 3G 19
Mindrum. *Nmbd* 6F 60
Minehead. *Som* 1J 7
Minera. *Wrex* 4A 34
Minerstown. *New M* 7J 93
Minety. *Wilts* 4J 19
Minffordd. *Gwyn* 7E 32
Mingarrypark. *High* 1A 64
Mingary. *High* 1L 63
Mingearraidh. *W Isl* 3D 74
Miningsby. *Linc* 3L 37
Minions. *Corn* 8B 6
Minishant. *S Ayr* 8B 58
Minllyn. *Gwyn* 1H 25
Minnigaff. *Dum* 5K 51
Minorca. *IOM* 6D 44
Minskip. *N Yor* 1A 42
Minstead. *Hants* 4L 9
Minsted. *W Sus* 3F 10
Minster. *Kent*
nr. Ramsgate 7K 23
**Minster**. *Kent*
nr. Sheerness 6F 22
Minsteracres. *Nmbd* 6D 54
Minsterley. *Shrp* 1B 26
Minster Lovell. *Oxon* 2M 19
Minsterworth. *Glos* 2F 18
Minterne Magna. *Dors* 5E 8
Minterne Parva. *Dors* 5E 8
Minting. *Linc* 2J 37
Mintlaw. *Abers* 1K 73
Minto. *Bord* 7C 60
Minton. *Shrp* 2C 26
Minwear. *Pemb* 5G 15
Minworth. *W Mid* 2K 27
Miodar. *Arg* 3F 62
Mirbister. *Orkn* 7C 88
Mirehouse. *Cumb* 3J 45
Mireland. *High* 5E 86
**Mirfield**. *W Yor* 6L 41
Miserden. *Glos* 3H 19
Miskin. *Rhon* 6K 17
Misson. *Notts* 8D 42
Misterton. *Leics* 3C 28
Misterton. *Notts* 8E 42
Misterton. *Som* 5C 8
Mistley. *Essx* 8H 31
Mistley Heath. *Essx* 8H 31
**Mitcham**. *G Lon* 7K 21
Mitcheldean. *Glos* 2E 18
Mitchell. *Corn* 6A 4
Mitchel Troy. *Mon* 2C 18
Mitcheltroy Common. *Mon* 3C 18
Mitford. *Nmbd* 3E 54
Mithian. *Corn* 3L 3
Mitton. *Staf* 8G 35
Mixbury. *Oxon* 8D 28
Mixenden. *W Yor* 5J 41
Mixon. *Staf* 4J 35
Moaness. *Orkn* 1D 86
Moarfield. *Shet* 3K 91
Moat. *Cumb* 4J 53
Moats Tye. *Suff* 6G 31
Mobberley. *Ches E* 2F 34
Mobberley. *Staf* 5J 35
Moccas. *Here* 7B 26
Mochdre. *Cnwy* 3H 33
Mochdre. *Powy* 4K 25
Mochrum. *Dum* 7J 51
Mockbeggar. *Hants* 5K 9
Mockerkin. *Cumb* 2K 45
Modbury. *Devn* 6J 5
Moddershall. *Staf* 6H 35
Modsarie. *High* 5J 85
Moelfre. *Cnwy* 3J 33
Moelfre. *IOA* 2E 32
Moelfre. *Powy* 8L 33
Moffat. *Dum* 1E 52
Moggerhanger. *C Beds* 7J 29
Mogworthy. *Devn* 4H 7
Moira. *Leics* 8M 35
Moira. *Lis* 5G 93
Molash. *Kent* 8G 23
Mol-chlach. *High* 4F 68
Mold. *Flin* 4M 33
Molehill Green. *Essx* 1B 22
Molescroft. *E Yor* 3H 43
Molesden. *Nmbd* 3E 54
Molesworth. *Cambs* 4H 29
Moll. *High* 3G 69
Molland. *Devn* 3H 7
Mollington. *Ches W* 2B 34
Mollington. *Oxon* 7B 28
Mollinsburn. *N Lan* 2F 58
Monachty. *Cdgn* 6E 24
Monachyle. *Stir* 6J 65
Monar Lodge. *High* 1C 70
Monaughty. *Powy* 6M 25
Monea. *Ferm* 6B 92
Monewden. *Suff* 6J 31
Moneydie. *Per* 5D 66
Moneyglass. *Ant* 4G 93
Moneymore. *M Ulst* 4F 93
Moneyneany. *M Ulst* 4E 92
Moneyreagh. *Lis* 5J 93
Moneyrow Green. *Wind* 6F 20
Moneyslane. *Arm* 7H 93
Moniaive. *Dum* 2B 52
Monifieth. *Ang* 4J 67
Monikie. *Ang* 4J 67
Monimail. *Fife* 6F 66
Monington. *Pemb* 2H 15
Monk Bretton. *S Yor* 7A 42
Monken Hadley. *G Lon* 4K 21
Monk Fryston. *N Yor* 5C 42
Monk Hesleden. *Dur* 8H 55
Monkhide. *Here* 7E 26
Monkhill. *Cumb* 6H 53
Monkhopton. *Shrp* 2E 26
Monkland. *Here* 6C 26
Monkleigh. *Devn* 3D 6
Monknash. *V Glam* 7J 17
Monkokehampton. *Devn* 5E 6
Monkseaton. *Tyne* 4G 55
Monks Eleigh. *Suff* 7F 30
Monk's Gate. *W Sus* 3K 11
Monk's Heath. *Ches E* 2G 35
Monk Sherborne. *Hants* 8D 20
Monkshill. *Abers* 1G 73
Monksilver. *Som* 2K 7
Monks Kirby. *Warw* 3B 28
Monk Soham. *Suff* 5J 31
Monk Soham Green. *Suff* 5J 31
Monkspath. *W Mid* 4K 27
Monks Risborough. *Buck* 3F 20
Monksthorpe. *Linc* 3M 37
Monkstown. *Ant* 4H 93
Monk Street. *Essx* 1C 22
Monkswood. *Mon* 3B 18
Monkton. *Devn* 5L 7
Monkton. *Kent* 7J 23
Monkton. *Pemb* 6F 14
Monkton. *S Ayr* 7B 58
Monkton Combe. *Bath* 7F 18
Monkton Deverill. *Wilts* 2G 9
Monkton Farleigh. *Wilts* 7G 19
Monkton Heathfield. *Som* 3A 8
Monktonhill. *S Ayr* 7B 58
Monkton Up Wimborne.
*Dors* 4J 9
Monkton Wyld. *Dors* 6B 8
Monkwearmouth. *Tyne* 6G 55
Monkwood. *Dors* 6C 8
Monkwood. *Hants* 2D 10
Monmarsh. *Here* 7D 26
Monmouth. *Mon* 2D 18
Monnington on Wye. *Here* 7B 26
Monreith. *Dum* 7J 51
Montacute. *Som* 4C 8
Monteith. *Arm* 6G 93
Montford. *Arg* 3L 57
Montford. *Shrp* 8C 34
Montford Bridge. *Shrp* 8C 34
Montgarrie. *Abers* 4E 72
Montgarswood. *E Ayr* 7D 58
Montgomery. *Powy* 3M 25
Montgreenan. *N Ayr* 5B 58
Montrave. *Fife* 7G 67
**Montrose**. *Ang* 2L 67
Monxton. *Hants* 1M 9
Monyash. *Derbs* 3K 35
Monymusk. *Abers* 4F 72
Monzie. *Per* 5B 66
Moodiesburn. *N Lan* 2E 58
Moon's Green. *Kent* 3E 12
Moonzie. *Fife* 6G 67
Moor. *Som* 4C 8
The Moor. *Kent* 3D 12
Moor Allerton. *W Yor* 4L 41
Moorbath. *Dors* 6C 8
Moorbrae. *Shet* 5J 91
Moorby. *Linc* 3K 37
Moorcot. *Here* 6B 26
Moor Crichel. *Dors* 5H 9
Moor Cross. *Devn* 6J 5
Moordown. *Bour* 6J 9
Moore. *Hal* 1D 34
Moor End. *E Yor* 4F 42
Moorend. *Dum* 4G 53
Moorend. *Glos*
nr. Dursley 3F 18
nr. Gloucester 2G 19
Moorends. *S Yor* 6D 42
Moorfields. *ME Ant* 4G 93
Moorgate. *S Yor* 8B 42
Moor Green. *Wilts* 7G 19
Moorgreen. *Hants* 4B 10
Moorgreen. *Notts* 5B 36
Moorhaigh. *Notts* 3C 36
Moorhall. *Derbs* 2M 35
Moorhampton. *Here* 7B 26
Moorhouse. *Cumb*
nr. Carlisle 6H 53
nr. Wigton 6G 53
Moorhouse. *Notts* 3E 36
Moorhouse. *Surr* 8M 21
Moorhouses. *Linc* 4K 37
Moorland. *Som* 2B 8
Moorlinch. *Som* 2C 8
Moor Monkton. *N Yor* 2C 42
Moor of Granary. *Mor* 8L 79
Moor Row. *Cumb*
nr. Whitehaven 3K 45
nr. Wigton 7G 53
Moorsholm. *Red C* 4D 48
Moorside. *Dors* 4F 8
Moorside. *G Man* 7H 41
Moortown. *Devn* 6C 6
Moortown. *Hants* 5K 9
Moortown. *IOW* 7B 10
Moortown. *Linc* 8H 43
Moortown. *M Ulst* 5F 93
Moortown. *Telf* 8E 34
Moortown. *W Yor* 4M 41
Morangie. *High* 5H 79
Morar. *High* 6H 69
Morborne. *Cambs* 2J 29
Morchard Bishop. *Devn* 5G 7
Morcombelake. *Dors* 6C 8
Morcott. *Rut* 1G 29
Morda. *Shrp* 7A 34
**Morden**. *G Lon* 7K 21
Mordiford. *Here* 8D 26
Mordon. *Dur* 3M 47
More. *Shrp* 2B 26
Morebath. *Devn* 3J 7
Morebattle. *Bord* 7E 60
**Morecambe**. *Lanc* 1C 40
Morefield. *High* 4B 78
Moreleigh. *Devn* 6K 5
Morenish. *Per* 4K 65
Moresby Parks. *Cumb* 3J 45
Morestead. *Hants* 3C 10
Moreton. *Dors* 7G 9
Moreton. *Essx* 3B 22
Moreton. *Here* 5D 26
**Moreton**. *Mers* 8A 40
Moreton. *Oxon* 3D 20
Moreton. *Staf* 8F 34
Moreton Corbet. *Shrp* 7D 34
Moretonhampstead. *Devn* 7G 7
Moreton-in-Marsh. *Glos* 8L 27
Moreton Jeffries. *Here* 7E 26
Moreton Morrell. *Warw* 6M 27
Moreton on Lugg. *Here* 7D 26
Moreton Pinkney. *Nptn* 7C 28
Moreton Say. *Shrp* 6E 34
Moreton Valence. *Glos* 3F 18
Morfa. *Cdgn* 1K 15
Morfa Bach. *Carm* 5K 15
Morfa Bychan. *Gwyn* 7E 32
Morfa Glas. *Neat* 4H 17
Morfa Nefyn. *Gwyn* 6B 32
Morganstown. *Card* 6L 17
Morgan's Vale. *Wilts* 3K 9
Morham. *E Lot* 2C 60
Moriah. *Cdgn* 5F 24
Morland. *Cumb* 3D 46
Morley. *Ches E* 1G 35
Morley. *Derbs* 5A 36
Morley. *Dur* 3K 47
**Morley**. *W Yor* 5L 41
Morley St Botolph. *Norf* 2G 31
Morningside. *Edin* 2L 59
Morningside. *N Lan* 4G 59
Morningthorpe. *Norf* 2J 31
**Morpeth**. *Nmbd* 3F 54
Morrey. *Staf* 8K 35
Morridge Side. *Staf* 4J 35
Morridge Top. *Staf* 3J 35
Morrington. *Dum* 3C 52
Morris Green. *Essx* 8D 30
Morriston. *Swan* 5F 16
Morston. *Norf* 5G 39
Mortehoe. *Devn* 1D 6
Morthen. *S Yor* 1B 36
Mortimer. *W Ber* 7D 20
Mortimer's Cross. *Here* 5C 26
Mortimer West End. *Hants* 7D 20
Mortomley. *S Yor* 8M 41
Morton. *Cumb*
nr. Calthwaite 8J 53
nr. Carlisle 6H 53
Morton. *Derbs* 3B 36
Morton. *Linc*
nr. Bourne 7H 37
nr. Gainsborough 8F 42
nr. Lincoln 3F 36
Morton. *Norf* 8H 39
Morton. *Notts* 4E 36
Morton. *Shrp* 7A 34
Morton. *S Glo* 4E 18
Morton Bagot. *Warw* 5K 27
Morton Mill. *Shrp* 7D 34
Morton-on-Swale. *N Yor* 6M 47
Morton Tinmouth. *Dur* 3K 47
Morvah. *Corn* 5H 3
Morval. *Corn* 6E 4
Morvich. *High*
nr. Golspie 3H 79
nr. Shiel Bridge 3L 69
Morvil. *Pemb* 3G 15
Morville. *Shrp* 2E 26
Morwenstow. *Corn* 4B 6
Morwick. *Nmbd* 1F 54
**Mosborough**. *S Yor* 1B 36
Moscow. *E Ayr* 5C 58
Mose. *Shrp* 2F 26
Mosedale. *Cumb* 8H 53
Moseley. *W Mid*
nr. Birmingham 3J 27
nr. Wolverhampton 1H 27
Moseley. *Worc* 6G 27
Moss. *Arg* 3E 62
Moss. *High* 1A 64
Moss. *S Yor* 6C 42
Moss. *Wrex* 4B 34
Mossatt. *Abers* 4D 72
Moss Bank. *Mers* 8D 40
Mossbank. *Shet* 6J 91
Mossblown. *S Ayr* 7C 58
Mossbrow. *G Man* 1F 34
Mossburnford. *Bord* 8D 60
Mossdale. *Dum* 4A 52
Mossedge. *Cumb* 5J 53
Mossend. *N Lan* 3F 58
Mossgate. *Staf* 6H 35
Moss Lane. *Ches E* 2H 35
Mossley. *Ant* 4H 93
Mossley. *Ches E* 3G 35
**Mossley**. *G Man* 7H 41
Mossley Hill. *Mers* 1B 34
Moss of Barmuckity. *Mor* 7B 80
Mosspark. *Glas* 3D 58
Mosspaul. *Bord* 2J 53
Moss Side. *Cumb* 6F 52
Moss Side. *G Man* 8G 41
Moss Side. *Lanc*
nr. Blackpool 4B 40
nr. Preston 5D 40
Moss Side. *Mers* 7B 40
Moss-Side. *Caus* 2G 93
Moss-side. *High* 8J 79
Moss-side of Cairness.
*Abers* 7K 81
Mosstodloch. *Mor* 7C 80
Mosswood. *Nmbd* 6D 54
Mossy Lea. *Lanc* 6D 40
Mosterton. *Dors* 5C 8
Moston. *Shrp* 7D 34
Moston Green. *Ches E* 3F 34
Mostyn. *Flin* 2L 33
Mostyn Quay. *Flin* 2L 33
Motcombe. *Dors* 3G 9
Mothecombe. *Devn* 7J 5
Motherby. *Cumb* 3C 46
**Motherwell**. *N Lan* 4F 58
Mottingham. *G Lon* 6M 21
Mottisfont. *Hants* 3M 9
Mottistone. *IOW* 7B 10
**Mottram in Longdendale**.
*G Man* 8H 41
Mottram St Andrew.
*Ches E* 2G 35
Mott's Mill. *E Sus* 2B 12
Mouldsworth. *Ches W* 2D 34
Moulin. *Per* 2C 66
Moulsecoomb. *Brig* 5L 11
Moulsford. *Oxon* 5C 20
Moulsoe. *Mil* 7G 29
Moulton. *Ches W* 3E 34
Moulton. *Linc* 7L 37
Moulton. *Nptn* 5E 28
Moulton. *N Yor* 5L 47
Moulton. *Suff* 5C 30
Moulton. *V Glam* 7K 17
Moulton Chapel. *Linc* 8K 37
Moulton Eaugate. *Linc* 8L 37
Moulton St Mary. *Norf* 1K 31
Moulton Seas End. *Linc* 7L 37
Mount. *Corn*
nr. Bodmin 5D 4
nr. Newquay 3L 3
**Mountain Ash**. *Rhon* 5K 17
Mountain Cross. *Bord* 5K 59
Mountain Street. *Kent* 8G 23
Mountain Water. *Pemb* 4F 14
Mount Ambrose. *Corn* 4L 3
Mountbenger. *Bord* 7M 59
Mountblow. *W Dun* 2C 58
Mount Bures. *Essx* 8F 30
Mountfield. *E Sus* 3D 12
Mountfield. *Ferm* 5D 92
Mountgerald. *High* 7F 78
Mount Hawke. *Corn* 4L 3
Mount High. *High* 7G 79
Mountjoy. *Corn* 5A 4
Mountjoy. *Ferm* 5D 92
Mount Lothian. *Midl* 4L 59
Mountnessing. *Essx* 4C 22
Mountnorris. *Arm* 7F 93
Mounton. *Mon* 4D 18
Mount Pleasant. *Buck* 8D 28
Mount Pleasant. *Ches E* 4G 35
Mount Pleasant. *Derbs*
nr. Derby 5M 35
nr. Swadlincote 8L 35
Mount Pleasant. *E Sus* 4M 11
Mount Pleasant. *Hants* 6L 9
Mount Pleasant. *Norf* 2F 30
Mount Skippett. *Oxon* 2A 20
Mountsorrel. *Leics* 8C 36
Mount Stuart. *Arg* 4L 57
Mousehole. *Corn* 6H 3
Mouswald. *Dum* 4E 52
Mow Cop. *Ches E* 4G 35
Mowden. *Darl* 4L 47
Mowhaugh. *Bord* 7F 60
Mowmacre Hill. *Leic* 1C 28
Mowsley. *Leics* 3D 28
Moy. *High* 2H 71
Moy. *M Ulst* 6F 93
Moygashel. *M Ulst* 5F 93
Moylgrove. *Pemb* 2H 15
Moy Lodge. *High* 7E 70
Muasdale. *Arg* 5F 56
Muchalls. *Abers* 6J 73
Much Birch. *Here* 8D 26
Much Cowarne. *Here* 7E 26
Much Dewchurch. *Here* 8C 26
Muchelney. *Som* 3C 8
Muchelney Ham. *Som* 3C 8
Much Hadham. *Herts* 2M 21
Much Hoole. *Lanc* 5C 40
Muchlarnick. *Corn* 6E 4
Much Marcle. *Here* 8E 26
Muchrachd. *High* 2C 70
Much Wenlock. *Shrp* 1E 26
Mucking. *Thur* 5C 22
Muckle Breck. *Shet* 1F 90
Muckleford. *Dors* 6E 8
Mucklestone. *Staf* 6F 34
Muckleton. *Norf* 6E 38
Muckleton. *Shrp* 7D 34
Muckley. *Shrp* 2E 26
Muckley Corner. *Staf* 1J 27
Muckton. *Linc* 1L 37
Mudale. *High* 8H 85
Muddiford. *Devn* 2E 6
Mudeford. *Dors* 6K 9
Mudford. *Som* 4D 8
Mudgley. *Som* 1C 8
Mugdock. *Stir* 2D 58
Mugeary. *High* 2F 68
Muggington. *Derbs* 5L 35
Muggintonlane End. *Derbs* 5L 35
Muggleswick. *Dur* 6D 54
Mugswell. *Surr* 8K 21
Muie. *High* 3G 79
Muirden. *Abers* 8G 81
Muirdrum. *Ang* 4J 67
Muiredge. *Per* 5F 66
Muirend. *Glas* 3D 58
Muirhead. *Ang* 4G 67
Muirhead. *Fife* 7F 66
Muirhead. *N Lan* 3E 58
Muirhouses. *Falk* 1J 59
Muirkirk. *E Ayr* 7E 58
Muir of Alford. *Abers* 4E 72
Muir of Fairburn. *High* 8E 78
Muir of Fowlis. *Abers* 4E 72
Muir of Miltonduff. *Mor* 8A 80
Muir of Ord. *High* 8F 78
Muir of Tarradale. *High* 8F 78
Muirshearlich. *High* 7B 70
Muirtack. *Abers* 2J 73
Muirton. *High* 7H 79
Muirton. *Per* 5E 66
Muirton of Ardblair. *Per* 3E 66
Muirtown. *Per* 6C 66
Muiryfold. *Abers* 8G 81
Muker. *N Yor* 6H 47
Mulbarton. *Norf* 1H 31
Mulben. *Mor* 8C 80
Mulindry. *Arg* 4C 56
Mulla. *Shet* 1E 90
Mullach Charlabhaigh.
*W Isl* 7F 82
Mullacott. *Devn* 1E 6
Mullaghbane. *New M* 7F 93
Mullaghboy. *ME Ant* 3J 93
Mullaghglass. *New M* 7G 93
Mullion. *Corn* 7K 3
Mullion Cove. *Corn* 7K 3
Mumbles. *Swan* 6F 16
Mumby. *Linc* 2B 38
Munderfield Row. *Here* 6E 26
Munderfield Stocks. *Here* 6E 26
Mundesley. *Norf* 6K 39
Mundford. *Norf* 2E 30
Mundham. *Norf* 2K 31
Mundon. *Essx* 3E 22
Munerigie. *High* 5C 70
Muness. *Shet* 3L 91
Mungasdale. *High* 4L 77
Mungrisdale. *Cumb* 8H 53
Munlochy. *High* 8G 79
Munsley. *Here* 7E 26
Munslow. *Shrp* 3D 26
Murchington. *Devn* 7F 6
Murcot. *Worc* 7J 27
Murcott. *Oxon* 2C 20
Murdishaw. *Hal* 1D 34
Murieston. *W Lot* 3J 59
Murkle. *High* 5C 86
Murlaggan. *High* 6M 69
Murra. *Orkn* 1D 86
The Murray. *S Lan* 4E 58
Murrayfield. *Edin* 2L 59
Murrell Green. *Hants* 8E 20
Murroes. *Ang* 4H 67
Murrow. *Cambs* 1L 29
Mursley. *Buck* 1F 20
Murthly. *Per* 4D 66
Murton. *Cumb* 3F 46
Murton. *Dur* 7G 55
Murton. *Nmbd* 5G 61
Murton. *Swan* 6E 16
Murton. *York* 2D 42
Musbury. *Devn* 6A 8
Muscoates. *N Yor* 7D 48
Muscott. *Nptn* 5D 28
**Musselburgh**. *E Lot* 2M 59
Muston. *Leics* 6F 36
Muston. *N Yor* 8H 49
Mustow Green. *Worc* 4G 27
Muswell Hill. *G Lon* 5K 21
Mutehill. *Dum* 7A 52
Mutford. *Suff* 3L 31
Muthill. *Per* 6B 66
Mutterton. *Devn* 5K 7
Muxton. *Telf* 8F 34
Mwmbwls. *Swan* 6F 16
Mybster. *High* 6C 86
Myddfai. *Carm* 1G 17
Myddle. *Shrp* 7C 34
Mydroilyn. *Cdgn* 1L 15
Myerscough. *Lanc* 4C 40
Mylor Bridge. *Corn* 5M 3
Mylor Churchtown. *Corn* 5M 3
Mynachlog-ddu. *Pemb* 3H 15
Mynydd-bach. *Mon* 4C 18
Mynydd Isa. *Flin* 3A 34
Mynyddislwyn. *Cphy* 5L 17
Mynydd Llandegai. *Gwyn* 4F 32
Mynydd Mechell. *IOA* 1C 32
Mynydd-y-briw. *Powy* 8L 33
Mynyddygarreg. *Carm* 6L 15
Mynytho. *Gwyn* 7C 32
Myrebird. *Abers* 6G 73
Myrelandhorn. *High* 6D 86
Mytchett. *Surr* 8F 20
The Mythe. *Glos* 8G 27
Mytholmroyd. *W Yor* 5J 41
Myton-on-Swale. *N Yor* 1B 42
Mytton. *Shrp* 8C 34

## N

Naast. *High* 5K 77
Na Buirgh. *W Isl* 4B 76
Naburn. *York* 3C 42
Nab Wood. *W Yor* 4K 41
Nackington. *Kent* 8H 23
Nacton. *Suff* 7J 31
Nafferton. *E Yor* 2H 43
Na Gearrannan. *W Isl* 7E 82
Nailbridge. *Glos* 2E 18
Nailsbourne. *Som* 3M 7
**Nailsea**. *N Som* 6C 18
Nailstone. *Leics* 1B 28
Nailsworth. *Glos* 4G 19
Nairn. *High* 8J 79
Nalderswood. *Surr* 1K 11
Nancegollan. *Corn* 5K 3
Nancledra. *Corn* 5H 3
Nangreaves. *G Man* 6G 41
Nanhyfer. *Pemb* 3G 15
Nannerch. *Flin* 4L 33
Nanpantan. *Leics* 8C 36
Nanpean. *Corn* 6B 4
Nansledan M2 3
Nanstallon. *Corn* 5C 4
Nant-ddu. *Powy* 3K 17
Nanternis. *Cdgn* 1K 15
Nantgaredig. *Carm* 4L 15
Nantgarw. *Rhon* 6L 17
Nant Glas. *Powy* 6J 25
Nantglyn. *Den* 4K 33
Nantgwyn. *Powy* 5J 25
Nantlle. *Gwyn* 5E 32
Nantmawr. *Shrp* 7A 34
Nantmel. *Powy* 6K 25
Nantmor. *Gwyn* 6F 32
Nant Peris. *Gwyn* 5F 32
**Nantwich**. *Ches E* 4E 34
Nant-y-bai. *Carm* 8G 25
Nant-y-bwch. *Blae* 3L 17
Nant-y-Derry. *Mon* 3B 18
Nant-y-dugoed. *Powy* 1J 25
Nant-y-felin. *Cnwy* 3F 32
Nantyffyllon. *B'end* 5H 17
Nantyglo. *Blae* 3L 17
Nant-y-meichiaid. *Powy* 1L 25
Nant-y-moel. *B'end* 5J 17
Nant-y-pandy. *Cnwy* 3F 32
Naphill. *Buck* 4F 20
Nappa. *N Yor* 2G 41
Napton on the Hill. *Warw* 5B 28
Narberth. *Pemb* 5H 15
Narberth Bridge. *Pemb* 5H 15
Narborough. *Leics* 2C 28
Narborough. *Norf* 8D 38
Narkurs. *Corn* 6F 4
The Narth. *Mon* 3D 18
Narthwaite. *Cumb* 6F 46
Nasareth. *Gwyn* 5D 32
Naseby. *Nptn* 4D 28
Nash. *Buck* 8E 28
Nash. *Here* 5B 26
Nash. *Kent* 8J 23
Nash. *Newp* 5B 18
Nash. *Shrp* 4E 26
Nash Lee. *Buck* 3F 20
Nassington. *Nptn* 2H 29
Nasty. *Herts* 1L 21
Natcott. *Devn* 3B 6
Nateby. *Cumb* 5F 46
Nateby. *Lanc* 3C 40
Nately Scures. *Hants* 8E 20
Natland. *Cumb* 7D 46
Naughton. *Suff* 7G 31
Naunton. *Glos* 1K 19
Naunton. *Worc* 8G 27
Naunton Beauchamp. *Worc* 6H 27
Navenby. *Linc* 4G 37
Navestock. *Essx* 4B 22
Navestock Side. *Essx* 4B 22
Navidale. *High* 2L 79
Nawton. *N Yor* 7D 48
Nayland. *Suff* 8F 30
Nazeing. *Essx* 3M 21
Neacroft. *Hants* 6K 9
Nealhouse. *Cumb* 6H 53
Neal's Green. *Warw* 3M 27
Near Sawrey. *Cumb* 6B 46
Neasden. *G Lon* 5K 21
Neasham. *Darl* 4M 47
**Neath**. *Neat* 5G 17
Neath Abbey. *Neat* 5G 17
Neatishead. *Norf* 7K 39
Neaton. *Norf* 1F 30
Nebo. *Cdgn* 6E 24
Nebo. *Cnwy* 5H 33
Nebo. *Gwyn* 5D 32
Nebo. *IOA* 1D 32
Necton. *Norf* 1E 30
Nedd. *High* 8D 84
Nedderton. *Nmbd* 3F 54
Nedging. *Suff* 7G 31
Nedging Tye. *Suff* 7G 31
Needham. *Norf* 3J 31
Needham Market. *Suff* 6G 31
Needham Street. *Suff* 5D 30
Needingworth. *Cambs* 4L 29
Needwood. *Staf* 7K 35
Neen Savage. *Shrp* 4E 26
Neen Sollars. *Shrp* 4E 26
Neenton. *Shrp* 3E 26
Nefyn. *Gwyn* 6C 32
Neilston. *E Ren* 4C 58
Neithrop. *Oxon* 7B 28
Nelly Andrews Green.
*Powy* 1A 26
Nelson. *Cphy* 5L 17
**Nelson**. *Lanc* 4G 41
Nelson Village. *Nmbd* 4F 54
Nemphlar. *S Lan* 5G 59
Nempnett Thrubwell. *Bath* 7D 18
Nene Terrace. *Linc* 1K 29
Nenthall. *Cumb* 7A 54
Nenthead. *Cumb* 7A 54
Nenthorn. *Bord* 6D 60
Nercwys. *Flin* 4M 33
Neribus. *Arg* 4B 56
Nerston. *S Lan* 4E 58
Nesbit. *Nmbd* 6G 61
Nesfield. *N Yor* 3J 41
Ness. *Ches W* 2B 34
Nesscliffe. *Shrp* 8B 34
Ness of Tenston. *Orkn* 8B 88
**Neston**. *Ches W* 2A 34
Neston. *Wilts* 7G 19
Nethanfoot. *S Lan* 5G 59
Nether Alderley. *Ches E* 2G 35
Netheravon. *Wilts* 1K 9
Nether Blainslie. *Bord* 5C 60
Netherbrae. *Abers* 8G 81
Netherbrough. *Orkn* 8C 88
Nether Broughton. *Leics* 7D 36
Netherburn. *S Lan* 5G 59
Nether Burrow. *Lanc* 8E 46
Netherbury. *Dors* 6C 8
Netherby. *Cumb* 4H 53
Nether Careston. *Ang* 2J 67
Nether Cerne. *Dors* 6E 8
Nether Compton. *Dors* 4D 8
Nethercote. *Glos* 1K 19
Nethercote. *Warw* 5C 28
Nethercott. *Devn* 2D 6
Nethercott. *Oxon* 1B 20
Nether Dallachy. *Mor* 7C 80
Nether Durdie. *Per* 5F 66
Nether End. *Derbs* 2L 35
Netherend. *Glos* 3D 18
Nether Exe. *Devn* 5J 7
Netherfield. *E Sus* 4D 12
Netherfield. *Notts* 5D 36
Nethergate. *Norf* 7G 39
Netherhampton. *Wilts* 3K 9
Nether Handley. *Derbs* 2B 36
Nether Haugh. *S Yor* 8B 42
Nether Heage. *Derbs* 4A 36
Nether Heyford. *Nptn* 6D 28
Netherhouses. *Cumb* 7A 46
Nether Howcleugh. *S Lan* 8J 59
Nether Kellet. *Lanc* 1D 40
Nether Kinmundy. *Abers* 1K 73
Netherland Green. *Staf* 6K 35
Nether Langwith. *Notts* 2C 36
Netherlaw. *Dum* 7B 52
Netherley. *Abers* 6H 73
Nethermill. *Dum* 3E 52
Nethermills. *Mor* 8E 80
Nether Moor. *Derbs* 3A 36
Nether Padley. *Derbs* 2L 35
Netherplace. *E Ren* 4D 58
Nether Poppleton. *York* 2C 42
Netherseal. *Derbs* 8L 35
Nether Silton. *N Yor* 6B 48
Nether Stowey. *Som* 2L 7
Nether Street. *Essx* 2B 22
Netherstreet. *Wilts* 7H 19
Netherthird. *E Ayr* 8D 58
Netherthong. *W Yor* 7K 41
Netherton. *Ang* 2J 67
Netherton. *Cumb* 8E 52
Netherton. *Devn* 8H 7
Netherton. *Hants* 8A 20
Netherton. *Here* 1D 18
Netherton. *Mers* 8B 40
Netherton. *N Lan* 4F 58
Netherton. *Nmbd* 1C 54
Netherton. *Per* 2E 66
Netherton. *Shrp* 3F 26
Netherton. *Stir* 2D 58
Netherton. *W Mid* 3H 27
Netherton. *W Yor*
nr. Armitage Bridge 6K 41
nr. Horbury 6L 41
Netherton. *Worc* 7H 27
Nethertown. *Cumb* 4J 45
Nethertown. *High* 4E 86
Nethertown. *Staf* 8K 35
Nether Urquhart. *Fife* 7E 66
Nether Wallop. *Hants* 2M 9
Nether Wasdale. *Cumb* 4L 45
Nether Welton. *Cumb* 7H 53

Nether Westcote. Glos 1L 19
Nether Whitacre. Warw 2L 27
Nether Winchendon. Buck 2E 20
Netherwitton. Nmbd 2E 54
Nether Worton. Oxon 8B 28
Nethy Bridge. High 3L 71
Netley. Shrp 1C 26
Netley Abbey. Hants 5B 10
Netley Marsh. Hants 4M 9
Nettlebed. Oxon 5E 20
Nettlebridge. Som 1E 8
Nettlecombe. Dors 6D 8
Nettlecombe. IOW 8C 10
Nettleden. Herts 2H 21
Nettleham. Linc 2H 37
Nettlestead. Kent 8C 22
Nettlestead Green. Kent 8C 22
Nettlestone. IOW 6D 10
Nettlesworth. Dur 7F 54
Nettleton. Linc 7J 43
Nettleton. Wilts 6G 19
Netton. Devn 7H 5
Netton. Wilts 2K 9
Neuadd. Powy 2K 25
The Neuk. Abers 6G 73
Nevendon. Essx 4D 22
Nevern. Pemb 3G 15
New Abbey. Dum 5D 52
New Aberdour. Abers 7H 81
**New Addington**. G Lon 7L 21
Newall. W Yor 3L 41
New Alresford. Hants 2C 10
New Alyth. Per 3F 66
Newark. Orkn 5G 89
Newark. Pet 1K 29
**Newark-on-Trent**. Notts 4E 36
New Arley. Warw 3L 27
Newarthill. N Lan 4F 58
New Ash Green. Kent 7C 22
New Balderton. Notts 4F 36
New Barn. Kent 7C 22
New Barnetby. N Lin 6H 43
Newbattle. Midl 3M 59
New Bewick. Nmbd 7H 61
Newbie. Dum 5F 52
Newbiggin. Cumb
nr. Appleby 3E 46
nr. Barrow-in-Furness 8M 45
nr. Cumrew 7K 53
nr. Penrith 3C 46
nr. Seascale 5K 45
Newbiggin. Dur
nr. Consett 7E 54
nr. Holwick 3H 47
Newbiggin. Nmbd 7C 54
Newbiggin. N Yor
nr. Askrigg 6H 47
nr. Filey 7J 49
nr. Thoralby 7H 47
Newbiggin-by-the-Sea. Nmbd 3G 55
Newbigging. Ang
nr. Monikie 4H 67
nr. Newtyle 3F 66
nr. Tealing 4H 67
Newbigging. Edin 2K 59
Newbigging. S Lan 5J 59
Newbiggin-on-Lune. Cumb 5F 46
Newbold. Derbs 2A 36
Newbold. Leics 8B 36
Newbold on Avon. Warw 4B 28
Newbold on Stour. Warw 7L 27
Newbold Pacey. Warw 6L 27
Newbold Verdon. Leics 1B 28
New Bolingbroke. Linc 4L 37
Newborough. IOA 4D 32
Newborough. Pet 1K 29
Newborough. Staf 7K 35
Newbottle. Nptn 8C 28
Newbottle. Tyne 6G 55
New Boultham. Linc 2G 37
Newbourne. Suff 7J 31
New Brancepeth. Dur 7F 54
New Bridge. Dum 4D 52
Newbridge. Cphy 5M 17
Newbridge. Cdgn 1M 15
Newbridge. Corn 5H 3
Newbridge. Edin 2K 59
Newbridge. Hants 4L 9
Newbridge. IOW 7B 10
Newbridge. N Yor 7F 48
Newbridge. Pemb 3F 14
Newbridge. Wrex 5A 34
Newbridge Green. Worc 8G 27
Newbridge-on-Usk. Mon 4B 18
Newbridge on Wye. Powy 7K 25
New Brighton. Flin 3A 34
New Brighton. Hants 5E 10
New Brighton. Mers 8B 40
New Brinsley. Notts 4B 36
Newbrough. Nmbd 5B 54
New Broughton. Wrex 4B 34
New Buckenham. Norf 2G 31
New Buildings. Derr 3D 92
Newbuildings. Devn 5G 7
Newburgh. Abers 3J 73
Newburgh. Fife 6F 66
Newburgh. Lanc 6C 40
**Newburn**. Tyne 5E 54
**Newbury**. W Ber 7B 20
Newbury. Wilts 1G 9
Newby. Cumb 3D 46
Newby. N Yor
nr. Ingleton 8F 46
nr. Scarborough 7H 49
nr. Stokesley 4C 48
Newby Bridge. Cumb 7B 46
Newby Cote. N Yor 8F 46
Newby East. Cumb 6J 53
Newby Head. Cumb 3D 46
New Byth. Abers 8H 81
Newby West. Cumb 6H 53
Newby Wiske. N Yor 7A 48
Newcastle. Ards 6K 93
Newcastle. B'end 6H 17
Newcastle. Mon 2C 18
Newcastle. New M 7H 93
Newcastle. Shrp 4M 25
Newcastle Emlyn. Carm 2K 15
Newcastle International Airport. Tyne 4E 54
Newcastleton. Bord 3J 53
**Newcastle-under-Lyme**. Staf 5G 35
**Newcastle upon Tyne**. Tyne 111 (5F 54)
Newchapel. Pemb 3J 15
Newchapel. Powy 4J 25
Newchapel. Staf 4G 35
Newchapel. Surr 1L 11
New Cheriton. Hants 3C 10
Newchurch. Carm 4K 15
Newchurch. Here 6B 26
Newchurch. IOW 7C 10
Newchurch. Kent 2G 13
Newchurch. Lanc 5G 41
Newchurch. Mon 4C 18
Newchurch. Powy 7M 25
Newchurch. Staf 7K 35
Newchurch in Pendle. Lanc 4G 41
New Costessey. Norf 8H 39
Newcott. Devn 5M 7
New Cowper. Cumb 7F 52
Newcraighall. Edin 2M 59
New Crofton. W Yor 6A 42
New Cross. Cdgn 5F 24
New Cross. Som 4C 8
New Cumnock. E Ayr 8E 58
New Deer. Abers 1H 73
New Denham. Buck 5H 21
Newdigate. Surr 1J 11
New Duston. Nptn 5E 28
New Earswick. York 2D 42
New Edlington. S Yor 8C 42
New Elgin. Mor 7B 80
New Ellerby. E Yor 4J 43
Newell Green. Brac 6F 20
New Eltham. G Lon 6M 21
New End. Warw 5K 27
New End. Worc 6J 27
Newenden. Kent 3E 12
New England. Essx 7D 30
New England. Pet 1J 29
Newent. Glos 1F 18
New Ferry. Mers 1B 34
Newfield. Dur
nr. Chester-le-Street 6F 54
nr. Willington 8F 54
Newfound. Hants 8C 20
New Fryston. W Yor 5B 42
Newgale. Pemb 4E 14
New Galloway. Dum 4M 51
Newgate. Norf 5G 39
Newgate Street. Herts 3L 21
New Greens. Herts 3J 21
New Grimsby. IOS 1G 3
New Hainford. Norf 8J 39
Newhall. Ches E 5E 34
Newhall. Derbs 7L 35
Newham. Nmbd 7J 61
New Hartley. Nmbd 4G 55
Newhaven. Derbs 3K 35
**Newhaven**. E Sus 118 (5M 11)
Newhaven. Edin 2L 59
New Haw. Surr 7H 21
New Hedges. Pemb 6H 15
New Herrington. Tyne 6G 55
Newhey. G Man 6H 41
New Holkham. Norf 6E 38
New Holland. N Lin 5H 43
Newholm. N Yor 4F 48
New Houghton. Derbs 3C 36
New Houghton. Norf 7D 38
Newhouse. N Lan 3F 58
New Houses. N Yor 8G 47
New Hutton. Cumb 6D 46
New Hythe. Kent 8D 22
Newick. E Sus 3M 11
Newingreen. Kent 2H 13
Newington. Edin 2L 59
Newington. Kent
nr. Folkestone 2H 13
nr. Sittingbourne 7E 22
Newington. Notts 8D 42
Newington. Oxon 4D 20
Newington Bagpath. Glos 4G 19
New Inn. Carm 3L 15
New Inn. Mon 3C 18
New Inn. N Yor 8G 47
New Inn. Torf 4B 18
New Invention. Shrp 4A 26
New Kelso. High 1L 69
New Lanark. S Lan 5G 59
Newland. Glos 3D 18
Newland. Hull 4H 43
Newland. N Yor 5D 42
Newland. Som 2H 7
Newland. Worc 7F 26
Newlandrig. Midl 3A 60
Newlands. Cumb 8H 53
Newlands. High 1H 71
Newlands. Nmbd 6D 54
Newlands. Staf 7J 35
Newlands of Geise. High 5B 86
Newlands of Tynet. Mor 7C 80
Newlands Park. IOA 2B 32
New Lane. Lanc 6C 40
New Lane End. Warr 8E 40
New Langholm. Dum 3H 53
New Leake. Linc 4M 37
New Leeds. Abers 8J 81
New Lenton. Nott 6C 36
New Longton. Lanc 5D 40
Newlot. Orkn 8E 88
New Luce. Dum 5G 51
Newlyn. Corn 6H 3
Newmachar. Abers 4H 73
Newmains. N Lan 4G 59
New Mains of Ury. Abers 7H 73
**New Malden**. G Lon 7K 21
Newman's Green. Suff 7E 30
**Newmarket**. Suff 5C 30
Newmarket. W Isl 8H 83
New Marske. Red C 3D 48
New Marton. Shrp 6B 34
New Micklefield. W Yor 4B 42
New Mill. Abers 1G 73
New Mill. Corn 5H 3
New Mill. Herts 2G 21
New Mill. W Yor 7K 41
New Mill. Wilts 7K 19
Newmill. Ant 4H 93
Newmill. Mor 8D 80
Newmill. Bord 8B 60
Newmillerdam. W Yor 6M 41
New Mills. Corn 6A 4
New Mills. Derbs 1J 35
New Mills. Mon 3D 18
New Mills. Powy 2K 25
Newmills. Arm 6G 93
Newmills. Fife 1J 59
Newmills. High 7G 79
Newmills. M Ulst 5F 93
Newmiln. Per 4E 66
Newmilns. E Ayr 6D 58
**New Milton**. Hants 6L 9
New Mistley. Essx 8H 31
New Moat. Pemb 4G 15
Newmore. High
nr. Dingwall 8F 78
nr. Invergordon 6G 79
Newnham. Cambs 6M 29
Newnham. Glos 2E 18
Newnham. Hants 8E 20
Newnham. Herts 8K 29
Newnham. Kent 8F 22
Newnham. Nptn 6C 28
Newnham. Warw 5K 27
Newnham Bridge. Worc 5E 26
New Ollerton. Notts 3D 36
New Oscott. W Mid 2J 27
New Park. N Yor 2L 41
Newpark. Fife 6H 67
New Pitsligo. Abers 8H 81
New Polzeath. Corn 4B 4
Newport. Corn 7C 6
Newport. Devn 2E 6
Newport. E Yor 4F 42
Newport. Essx 8B 30
Newport. Glos 4E 18
Newport. High 1M 79
**Newport**. IOW 7C 10
**Newport**. Newp 114 (5B 18)
Newport. Norf 8M 39
Newport. Pemb 3G 15
Newport. Som 3B 8
**Newport**. Telf 8F 34
Newport-on-Tay. Fife 5H 67
**Newport Pagnell**. Mil 7F 28
Newpound Common. W Sus 3H 11
New Prestwick. S Ayr 7B 58
New Quay. Cdgn 1K 15
**Newquay**. Corn 2M 3
Newquay Cornwall Airport. Corn 5A 4
New Rackheath. Norf 8J 39
New Radnor. Powy 6M 25
New Rent. Cumb 8J 53
New Ridley. Nmbd 6D 54
New Romney. Kent 3G 13
**New Rossington**. S Yor 8D 42
New Row. Cdgn 5G 25
**Newry**. New M 7G 93
New Sauchie. Clac 8B 66
Newsbank. Ches E 3G 35
Newseat. Abers 2G 73
Newsham. Lanc 4D 40
Newsham. Nmbd 4G 55
Newsham. N Yor
nr. Richmond 4K 47
nr. Thirsk 7A 48
New Sharlston. W Yor 5A 42
Newsholme. E Yor 5E 42
Newsholme. Lanc 2G 41
New Shoreston. Nmbd 6J 61
New Springs. G Man 7D 40
Newstead. Notts 4C 36
Newstead. Bord 6C 60
New Stevenston. N Lan 4F 58
New Street. Here 6B 26
Newstreet Lane. Shrp 6E 34
New Swanage. Dors 7J 9
New Swannington. Leics 8B 36
Newthorpe. N Yor 4B 42
Newthorpe. Notts 5B 36
Newton. Arg 8E 64
Newton. B'end 7H 17
Newton. Cambs
nr. Cambridge 7M 29
nr. Wisbech 8M 37
Newton. Ches W
nr. Chester 3C 34
nr. Tattenhall 4D 34
Newton. Cumb 7M 45
Newton. Derbs 4B 36
Newton. Dors 4F 8
Newton. Dum
nr. Annan 4G 53
nr. Moffat 2F 52
Newton. G Man 8H 41
Newton. Here
nr. Ewyas Harold 8B 26
nr. Leominster 6D 26
Newton. High
nr. Cromarty 7H 79
nr. Inverness 1H 71
nr. Kylestrome 8E 84
nr. Wick 7E 86
Newton. Lanc
nr. Blackpool 4B 40
nr. Carnforth 8D 46
nr. Clitheroe 2E 40
Newton. Linc 6H 37
Newton. Mers 2M 33
Newton. Mor 7A 80
Newton. Norf 8E 38
Newton. Nptn 3F 28
Newton. Nmbd 5D 54
Newton. Notts 5D 36
Newton. Bord 7D 60
Newton. Shet 4D 90
Newton. Shrp
nr. Bridgnorth 2F 26
nr. Wem 6C 34
Newton. Som 2L 7
Newton. S Lan
nr. Glasgow 3E 58
nr. Lanark 6H 59
Newton. Staf 7J 35
Newton. Suff 7F 30
Newton. Swan 6F 16
Newton. Warw 4C 28
Newton. W Lot 2J 59
Newton. Wilts 3L 9
**Newton Abbot**. Devn 8H 7
Newtonairds. Dum 3C 52
Newton Arlosh. Cumb 6G 53
**Newton Aycliffe**. Dur 3L 47
Newton Bewley. Hart 3B 48
Newton Blossomville. Mil 6G 29
Newton Bromswold. Nptn 5G 29
Newton Burgoland. Leics 1A 28
Newton by Toft. Linc 1H 37
Newton Ferrers. Devn 7H 5
Newton Flotman. Norf 2J 31
Newtongrange. Midl 3M 59
Newton Green. Mon 4D 18
Newton Hall. Dur 7F 54
Newton Hall. Nmbd 5D 54
Newton Harcourt. Leics 2D 28
Newton Heath. G Man 7G 41
Newton Hill. W Yor 5M 41
Newtonhill. Abers 6J 73
Newtonhill. High 1F 70
Newton Ketton. Darl 3M 47
Newton Kyme. N Yor 3B 42
**Newton-le-Willows**. Mers 8D 40
Newton-le-Willows. N Yor 7L 47
Newton Longville. Buck 8F 28
**Newton Mearns**. E Ren 4D 58
Newtonmore. High 6H 71
Newton Morrell. N Yor 5L 47
Newton Mulgrave. N Yor 4E 48
Newton of Ardtoe. High 8H 69
Newton of Balcanquhal. Per 6E 66
Newton of Beltrees. Ren 4B 58
Newton of Falkland. Fife 7F 66
Newton of Mountblairy. Abers 8F 80
Newton of Pitcairns. Per 6D 66
Newton-on-Ouse. N Yor 2C 42
Newton-on-Rawcliffe. N Yor 6F 48
Newton on the Hill. Shrp 7C 34
Newton-on-the-Moor. Nmbd 1E 54
Newton on Trent. Linc 2F 36
Newton Poppleford. Devn 7K 7
Newton Purcell. Oxon 8D 28
Newton Regis. Warw 1L 27
Newton Reigny. Cumb 8J 53
Newton Rigg. Cumb 8J 53
Newton St Cyres. Devn 6H 7
Newton St Faith. Norf 8J 39
Newton St Loe. Bath 7F 18
Newton St Petrock. Devn 4D 6
Newton Solney. Derbs 7L 35
Newton Stacey. Hants 1B 10
Newton Stewart. Dum 5K 51
Newton Toney. Wilts 1L 9
Newton Tony. Wilts 1L 9
Newton Tracey. Devn 3E 6
Newton under Roseberry. Red C 4C 48
Newton upon Ayr. S Ayr 7B 58
Newton upon Derwent. E Yor 3E 42
Newton Valence. Hants 2E 10
Newton-with-Scales. Lanc 4C 40
New Town. Dors 4H 9
New Town. E Lot 2B 60
New Town. Lutn 1H 21
New Town. W Yor 5B 42
Newtown. Abers 7G 81
Newtown. Cambs 5H 29
Newtown. Corn 8B 6
Newtown. Cumb
nr. Aspatria 7E 52
nr. Brampton 5K 53
nr. Penrith 3D 46
Newtown. Derbs 1H 35
Newtown. Devn 3G 7
Newtown. Dors 5C 8
Newtown. Falk 1H 59
Newtown. Glos
nr. Lydney 3E 18
nr. Tewkesbury 8H 27
Newtown. Hants
nr. Bishop's Waltham 4C 10
nr. Liphook 2F 10
nr. Lyndhurst 4L 9
nr. Newbury 7B 20
nr. Romsey 3M 9
nr. Warsash 5B 10
nr. Wickham 4D 10
Newtown. Here
nr. Little Dewchurch 8D 26
nr. Stretton Grandison 7E 26
Newtown. High 5D 70
Newtown. IOM 7C 44
Newtown. IOW 6B 10
Newtown. Lanc 6D 40
Newtown. Nmbd
nr. Rothbury 1D 54
nr. Wooler 7H 61
Newtown. Pool 6J 9
**Newtown**. Powy 3L 25
Newtown. Rhon 5K 17
Newtown. Shet 5J 91
Newtown. Shrp 6C 34
Newtown. Som 4A 8
Newtown. Staf
nr. Biddulph 3H 35
nr. Cannock 1H 27
nr. Longnor 3J 35
Newtown. Wilts 3H 9
**Newtownabbey**. Ant 4H 93
**Newtownards**. Ards 5J 93
Newtownbutler. Ferm 7D 92
Newtown-Crommelin. ME Ant 3G 93
Newtownhamilton. New M 7F 93
Newtown-in-St Martin. Corn 6L 3
Newtown Linford. Leics 1C 28
Newtown St Boswells. Bord 6C 60
Newtownstewart. Derr 4D 92
Newtown Unthank. Leics 1B 28
New Tredegar. Cphy 4L 17
Newtyle. Ang 3F 66
New Village. E Yor 4H 43
New Village. S Yor 7C 42
New Walsoken. Cambs 1A 30
New Waltham. NE Lin 7K 43
New Winton. E Lot 2B 60
New World. Cambs 2L 29
New Yatt. Oxon 2A 20
Newyears Green. G Lon 5H 21
New York. Linc 4K 37
New York. Tyne 4G 55
Nextend. Here 6B 26
Neyland. Pemb 6F 14
Nib Heath. Shrp 8C 34
Nicholashayne. Devn 4L 7
Nicholaston. Swan 8M 15
Nidd. N Yor 1M 41
Niddrie. Edin 2M 59
Niddry. W Lot 2J 59
Nigg. Aber 5J 73
Nigg. High 6J 79
Nigg Ferry. High 7H 79
Nightcott. Som 3H 7
Nimmer. Som 4B 8
Nine Ashes. Essx 3B 22
Ninebanks. Nmbd 6A 54
Nine Elms. Swin 5K 19
Ninemile Bar. Dum 4C 52
Nine Mile Burn. Midl 4K 59
Ninfield. E Sus 4D 12
Ningwood. IOW 7B 10
Nisbet. Bord 7D 60
Nisbet Hill. Bord 4E 60
Niton. IOW 8C 10
Nitshill. Glas 3D 58
Niwbwrch. IOA 4D 32
Nixon's Corner. Derr 3D 92
Noak Hill. G Lon 4B 22
Nobold. Shrp 8C 34
Nobottle. Nptn 5D 28
Nocton. Linc 3H 37
Nogdam End. Norf 1K 31
Noke. Oxon 2C 20
Nolton. Pemb 5E 14
Nolton Haven. Pemb 5E 14
No Man's Heath. Ches W 5D 34
No Man's Heath. Warw 1L 27
Nomansland. Devn 4H 7
Nomansland. Wilts 4L 9
Noneley. Shrp 7C 34
Noness. Shet 5E 90
Nonikiln. High 6G 79
Nonington. Kent 8J 23
Nook. Cumb
nr. Longtown 4J 53
nr. Milnthorpe 7D 46
Noranside. Ang 1H 67
Norbreck. Bkpl 3B 40
Norbridge. Here 7F 26
Norbury. Ches E 5D 34
Norbury. Derbs 5K 35
Norbury. Shrp 2B 26
Norbury. Staf 7F 34
Norby. N Yor 7B 48
Norby. Shet 2B 90
Norcross. Lanc 3B 40
Nordelph. Norf 1B 30
Norden. G Man 6G 41
Nordley. Shrp 2E 26
Norham. Nmbd 5G 61
Norland Town. W Yor 5J 41
Norley. Ches W 2D 34
Norleywood. Hants 6A 10
Normanby. N Lin 6F 42
Normanby. N Yor 7E 48
Normanby. Red C 4C 48
Normanby-by-Spital. Linc 1H 37
Normanby le Wold. Linc 8J 43
Norman Cross. Cambs 2J 29
Normandy. Surr 8G 21
Norman's Bay. E Sus 5C 12
Norman's Green. Devn 5K 7
Normanton. Derb 6M 35
Normanton. Leics 5F 36
Normanton. Notts 4E 36
**Normanton**. W Yor 5A 42
Normanton le Heath. Leics 8A 36
Normanton-on-Cliffe. Linc 5G 37
Normanton on Soar. Notts 7C 36
Normanton-on-the-Wolds. Notts 6D 36
Normanton on Trent. Notts 3E 36
Normoss. Lanc 4B 40
Norrington Common. Wilts 7G 19
Norris Green. Mers 8B 40
Norris Hill. Leics 8M 35
Norristhorpe. W Yor 5L 41
Northacre. Norf 2F 30
Northall. Buck 1G 21
**Northallerton**. N Yor 6A 48
Northam. Devn 3D 6
Northam. Sotn 4B 10
**Northampton**. Nptn 114 (5E 28)
North Anston. S Yor 1C 36
North Ascot. Brac 7G 21
North Aston. Oxon 1B 20
Northaw. Herts 3K 21
Northay. Som 4A 8
North Baddesley. Hants 3A 10
North Balfern. Dum 6K 51
North Ballachulish. High 1E 64
North Barrow. Som 3E 8
North Barsham. Norf 6F 38
Northbeck. Linc 5H 37
North Benfleet. Essx 5D 22
North Bersted. W Sus 5G 11
North Berwick. E Lot 1C 60
North Bitchburn. Dur 8E 54
North Blyth. Nmbd 3G 55
North Boarhunt. Hants 4D 10
North Bockhampton. Dors 6K 9
Northborough. Pet 1J 29
Northbourne. Kent 8K 23
Northbourne. Oxon 5C 20
North Bovey. Devn 7G 7
North Bowood. Dors 6C 8
North Bradley. Wilts 8G 19
North Brentor. Devn 7D 6
North Brewham. Som 2F 8
Northbrook. Oxon 1B 20
North Brook End. Cambs 7K 29
North Broomhill. Nmbd 1F 54
North Buckland. Devn 1D 6
North Burlingham. Norf 8K 39
North Cadbury. Som 3E 8
North Carlton. Linc 2G 37
North Cave. E Yor 4F 42
North Cerney. Glos 3J 19
North Chailey. E Sus 3L 11
Northchapel. W Sus 3G 11
North Charford. Hants 4K 9
North Charlton. Nmbd 7J 61
North Cheriton. Som 3E 8
North Chideock. Dors 6C 8
Northchurch. Herts 3G 21
North Cliffe. E Yor 4F 42
North Clifton. Notts 2F 36
North Close. Dur 8F 54
North Cockerington. Linc 8L 43
North Coker. Som 4D 8
North Collafirth. Shet 5H 91
North Common. E Sus 3L 11
North Commonty. Abers 1H 73
North Coombe. Devn 4H 7
North Cornelly. B'end 6H 17
North Cotes. Linc 7L 43
Northcott. Devn
nr. Boyton 6C 6
nr. Culmstock 4K 7
Northcourt. Oxon 4C 20
North Cove. Suff 3L 31
North Cowton. N Yor 5L 47
North Craigo. Ang 1K 67
North Crawley. Mil 7G 29
North Cray. G Lon 6A 22
North Creake. Norf 6E 38
North Curry. Som 3B 8
North Dalton. E Yor 2G 43
North Deighton. N Yor 2A 42
North Dronley. Ang 4G 67
North Duffield. N Yor 4D 42
Northdyke. Orkn 7B 88
Northedge. Derbs 3A 36
North Elkington. Linc 8K 43
North Elmham. Norf 7F 38
North Elmsall. W Yor 6B 42
North End. E Yor 4K 43
North End. Essx
nr. Great Dunmow 2C 22
nr. Great Yeldham 8D 30
North End. Hants 7B 20
North End. Leics 8C 36
North End. Linc 5K 37
North End. Norf 2F 30
North End. N Som 7C 18
North End. Port 5D 10
North End. W Sus 5J 11
North End. Wilts 4J 19
Northend. Buck 4E 20
Northend. Warw 6A 28
North Erradale. High 5J 77
North Evington. Leic 1D 28
North Fambridge. Essx 4E 22
North Fearns. High 2G 69
North Featherstone. W Yor 5B 42
North Feorline. N Ayr 7J 57
North Ferriby. E Yor 5G 43
Northfield. Aber 5H 73
Northfield. E Yor 5H 43
Northfield. Som 2A 8
Northfield. W Mid 4J 27
**Northfleet**. Kent 6C 22
North Frodingham. E Yor 2J 43
Northgate. Linc 7J 37
North Gluss. Shet 6H 91
North Gorley. Hants 4K 9
North Green. Norf 3J 31
North Green. Suff
nr. Framlingham 5K 31
nr. Halesworth 4K 31
nr. Saxmundham 5K 31
North Greetwell. Linc 2H 37
North Grimston. N Yor 1F 42
North Halling. Medw 7D 22
North Hayling. Hants 5E 10
North Hazelrigg. Nmbd 6H 61
North Heasley. Devn 2G 7
North Heath. W Sus 3H 11
North Hill. Corn 8B 6
North Holmwood. Surr 1J 11
North Huish. Devn 6K 5
North Hykeham. Linc 3G 37
Northiam. E Sus 3E 12
Northill. C Beds 7J 29
Northington. Hants 2C 10
North Kelsey. Linc 7H 43
North Kelsey Moor. Linc 7H 43
North Kessock. High 1G 71
North Killingholme. N Lin 6J 43
North Kilvington. N Yor 7B 48
North Kilworth. Leics 3D 28
North Kyme. Linc 4J 37
North Lancing. W Sus 5J 11
Northlands. Linc 4L 37
Northleach. Glos 2K 19
North Lee. Buck 3F 20
North Lees. N Yor 8L 47
North Leigh. Kent 1H 13
North Leigh. Oxon 2A 20
Northleigh. Devn
nr. Barnstaple 2F 6
nr. Honiton 6L 7
North Leverton. Notts 1E 36
Northlew. Devn 6E 6
North Littleton. Worc 7J 27
North Lopham. Norf 3G 31
North Luffenham. Rut 1G 29
North Marden. W Sus 4F 10
North Marston. Buck 1E 20
North Middleton. Midl 4A 60
North Middleton. Nmbd 7H 61
North Molton. Devn 3G 7
North Moor. N Yor 7G 49
Northmoor. Oxon 3B 20
Northmoor Green. Som 2B 8
North Moreton. Oxon 5C 20
Northmuir. Ang 2G 67
North Mundham. W Sus 5F 10
North Murie. Per 5F 66
North Muskham. Notts 4E 36
North Ness. Orkn 2E 86
North Newbald. E Yor 4G 43
North Newington. Oxon 8B 28
North Newnton. Wilts 8K 19
North Newton. Som 2A 8
Northney. Hants 5E 10
North Nibley. Glos 4F 18
North Oakley. Hants 8C 20
North Ockendon. G Lon 5B 22
**Northolt**. G Lon 5J 21
Northop. Flin 4M 33
Northop Hall. Flin 3A 34
North Ormesby. Midd 4C 48
North Ormsby. Linc 8K 43
Northorpe. Linc
nr. Bourne 8H 37
nr. Donington 6K 37
nr. Gainsborough 8F 42
North Otterington. N Yor 7A 48
Northover. Som
nr. Glastonbury 2C 8
nr. Yeovil 3D 8
North Owersby. Linc 8H 43
Northowram. W Yor 5K 41
North Perrott. Som 5C 8
North Petherton. Som 2A 8
North Petherwin. Corn 7B 6
North Pickenham. Norf 1E 30
North Piddle. Worc 6H 27
North Poorton. Dors 6D 8
North Port. Arg 5E 64
Northport. Dors 7H 9
North Queensferry. Fife 1K 59
North Radworthy. Devn 2G 7
North Rauceby. Linc 5H 37
Northrepps. Norf 6J 39
North Rigton. N Yor 3L 41
North Rode. Ches E 3G 35
North Roe. Shet 5H 91
North Ronaldsay Airport. Orkn 4G 89
North Row. Cumb 8G 53
North Runcton. Norf 8C 38
North Sannox. N Ayr 5K 57
North Scale. Cumb 7L 45
North Scarle. Linc 3F 36
North Seaton. Nmbd 3F 54
North Seaton Colliery. Nmbd 3F 54
North Sheen. G Lon 6J 21
North Shian. Arg 3D 64
**North Shields**. Tyne 5G 55
North Shoebury. S'end 5F 22
North Shore. Bkpl 4B 40
North Side. Cumb 2K 45
North Skelton. Red C 4D 48
North Somercotes. Linc 8M 43
North Stainley. N Yor 8L 47
North Stainmore. Cumb 4G 47
North Stifford. Thur 5C 22
North Stoke. Bath 7F 18
North Stoke. Oxon 5D 20
North Stoke. W Sus 4H 11
Northstowe. Cambs 5M 29
North Street. Hants 2D 10
North Street. Kent 8G 23
North Street. Medw 6E 22
North Street. W Ber 6D 20
North Sunderland. Nmbd 6K 61
North Tamerton. Corn 6C 6
North Tawton. Devn 5F 6
North Thoresby. Linc 8K 43
North Tidworth. Wilts 1L 9
North Town. Devn 5E 6
North Town. Shet 6D 90
Northtown. Orkn 2F 86
North Tuddenham. Norf 8G 39
North Walbottle. Tyne 5E 54
Northwall. Orkn 5G 89
North Walney. Cumb 8L 45
**North Walsham**. Norf 6J 39
North Waltham. Hants 1C 10
North Warnborough. Hants 8E 20
North Water Bridge. Ang 1K 67
North Watten. High 6D 86
Northway. Glos 8H 27
Northway. Swan 6E 16
North Weald Bassett. Essx 3B 22
North Weston. N Som 6C 18
North Weston. Oxon 3D 20
North Wheatley. Notts 1E 36
North Whilborough. Devn 5L 5
**Northwich**. Ches W 2E 34
North Wick. Bath 7D 18
Northwick. Som 1B 8
Northwick. S Glo 5D 18
North Widcombe. Bath 8D 18
North Willingham. Linc 1J 37
**North Wingfield**. Derbs 3B 36
North Witham. Linc 7G 37
Northwold. Norf 2D 30
Northwood. Derbs 3L 35
**Northwood**. G Lon 4H 21
Northwood. IOW 6B 10
Northwood. Kent 7K 23
Northwood. Shrp 6C 34
Northwood. Stoke 5G 35
Northwood Green. Glos 2F 18
North Wootton. Dors 4E 8
North Wootton. Norf 7C 38
North Wootton. Som 1D 8
North Wraxall. Wilts 6G 19
North Wroughton. Swin 5K 19
North Yardhope. Nmbd 1C 54
Norton. Devn 6L 5
Norton. Glos 1G 19
Norton. Hal 1D 34
Norton. Herts 8K 29
Norton. IOW 7M 9
Norton. Mon 1C 18
Norton. Nptn 5D 28
Norton. Notts 2C 36
Norton. Powy 5B 26
Norton. Shrp
nr. Ludlow 3C 26
nr. Madeley 1F 26
nr. Shrewsbury 1D 26
Norton. S Yor
nr. Askern 6C 42
nr. Sheffield 1A 36
Norton. Stoc T 3B 48
Norton. Suff 5F 30
Norton. Swan 6F 16
Norton. W Sus
nr. Selsey 6F 10
nr. Westergate 5G 11
Norton. Wilts 5G 19
Norton. Worc
nr. Evesham 7J 27
nr. Worcester 6G 27
Norton Bavant. Wilts 1H 9
Norton Bridge. Staf 6G 35
Norton Canes. Staf 1J 27
Norton Canon. Here 7B 26
Norton Corner. Norf 7G 39
Norton Disney. Linc 4F 36
Norton East. Staf 1J 27
Norton Ferris. Wilts 2F 8
Norton Fitzwarren. Som 3M 7
Norton Green. IOW 7M 9
Norton Green. Stoke 4H 35
Norton Hawkfield. Bath 7D 18
Norton Heath. Essx 3B 22
Norton in Hales. Shrp 6F 34
Norton in the Moors. Stoke 4G 35
Norton-Juxta-Twycross. Leics 1M 27
Norton-le-Clay. N Yor 8B 48
Norton Lindsey. Warw 5L 27
Norton Little Green. Suff 5F 30
Norton Malreward. Bath 7E 18
Norton Mandeville. Essx 3B 22
Norton-on-Derwent. N Yor 8E 48
Norton St Philip. Som 8F 18
Norton Subcourse. Norf 2L 31
Norton sub Hamdon. Som 4C 8
Norton Woodseats. S Yor 1A 36
Norwell. Notts 3E 36
Norwell Woodhouse. Notts 3E 36
**Norwich**. Norf 114 (1J 31)
Norwich Airport. Norf 8J 39
Norwick. Shet 2L 91
Norwood. Derbs 1B 36
Norwood Green. W Yor 5K 41
Norwood Hill. Surr 1K 11
Norwood Park. Som 2D 8
Norwoodside. Cambs 2M 29
Noseley. Leics 2E 28
Noss. Shet 6D 90
Noss Mayo. Devn 7H 5
Nosterfield. N Yor 7L 47
Nostie. High 3K 69
Notgrove. Glos 1K 19
Nottage. B'end 7H 17
**Nottingham**. Nott 114 (5C 36)
Nottington. Dors 7E 8
Notton. Dors 6E 8
Notton. W Yor 6M 41
Notton. Wilts 7H 19
Nounsley. Essx 2D 22
Noutard's Green. Worc 5F 26
Nox. Shrp 8C 34
Noyadd Trefawr. Cdgn 2J 15
Nuffield. Oxon 5D 20
Nunburnholme. E Yor 3F 42
Nuncargate. Notts 4C 36
Nunclose. Cumb 7J 53
**Nuneaton**. Warw 2A 28
Nuneham Courtenay. Oxon 4C 20
Nun Monkton. N Yor 2C 42
Nunnerie. S Lan 8H 59
Nunney. Som 1F 8
Nunnington. N Yor 8D 48
Nunnykirk. Nmbd 2D 54
Nunsthorpe. NE Lin 7K 43
Nunthorpe. Midd 4C 48
Nunthorpe. York 2C 42
Nunton. Wilts 3K 9
Nunwick. Nmbd 4B 54
Nunwick. N Yor 8M 47
Nupend. Glos 3F 18
Nursling. Hants 4A 10
Nursted. Hants 3E 10
Nursteed. Wilts 7J 19
Nurston. V Glam 8K 17
Nutbourne. W Sus
nr. Chichester 5E 10
nr. Pulborough 4H 11
Nutfield. Surr 8L 21
Nuthall. Notts 5C 36
Nuthampstead. Herts 8M 29
Nuthurst. Warw 4K 27
Nuthurst. W Sus 3J 11
Nutley. E Sus 3M 11
Nuttall. G Man 6F 40
Nutwell. S Yor 7D 42
Nybster. High 5E 86
Nyetimber. W Sus 6F 10
Nyewood. W Sus 3F 10
Nymet Rowland. Devn 5G 7
Nymet Tracey. Devn 5G 7
Nympsfield. Glos 3G 19
Nynehead. Som 3L 7
Nyton. W Sus 5G 11


## O


**Oadby**. Leics 1D 28
Oad Street. Kent 7E 22
Oakamoor. Staf 5J 35
Oakbank. Arg 4B 64
Oakbank. W Lot 3J 59
Oakdale. Cphy 5L 17
Oakdale. Pool 6J 9
Oake. Som 3L 7
Oaken. Staf 1G 27
Oakenclough. Lanc 3D 40
Oakengates. Telf 8E 34
Oakenholt. Flin 2A 34
Oakenshaw. Dur 8F 54
Oakenshaw. W Yor 5K 41
Oakerthorpe. Derbs 4A 36
Oakford. Cdgn 1L 15
Oakford. Devn 3J 7
Oakfordbridge. Devn 3J 7
Oakgrove. Ches E 3H 35
Oakham. Rut 1F 28
Oakhanger. Ches E 4F 34
Oakhanger. Hants 2E 10
Oakhill. Som 1E 8
Oakington. Cambs 5M 29
Oaklands. Powy 7K 25
Oakle Street. Glos 2F 18
Oakley. Bed 6H 29
Oakley. Buck 2D 20
Oakley. Fife 1J 59
Oakley. Hants 8C 20
Oakley. Suff 4H 31
Oakley Green. Wind 6G 21
Oakley Park. Powy 4J 25
Oakmere. Ches W 3D 34
Oakridge Lynch. Glos 3H 19
Oaks. Shrp 1C 26
Oaksey. Wilts 4H 19
Oaks Green. Derbs 6K 35
Oakshaw Ford. Cumb 4K 53
Oakshott. Hants 3E 10
Oakthorpe. Leics 8M 35
Oak Tree. Darl 4A 48
Oakwood. Derb 6A 36
Oakwood. W Yor 4M 41
Oakwoodhill. Surr 2J 11
Oakworth. W Yor 4J 41
Oape. High 3E 78
Oare. Kent 7G 23
Oare. Som 1H 7
Oare. W Ber 6C 20
Oare. Wilts 7K 19
Oareford. Som 1H 7
Oasby. Linc 6H 37
Oath. Som 3B 8
Oathlaw. Ang 2H 67
Oatlands. N Yor 2M 41
**Oban**. Arg 115 (5C 64)
Oban. W Isl 3C 76
Oborne. Dors 4E 8
Obsdale. High 7G 79
Obthorpe. Linc 8H 37
Occlestone Green. Ches W 3E 34
Occold. Suff 4H 31
Ochiltree. E Ayr 7D 58
Ochtermuthill. Per 6B 66
Ochtertyre. Per 5B 66
Ockbrook. Derbs 6B 36
Ockeridge. Worc 5F 26
Ockham. Surr 8H 21
Ockle. High 8G 69
Ockley. Surr 1J 11
Ocle Pychard. Here 7D 26
Octofad. Arg 4B 56
Octomore. Arg 4B 56
Octon. E Yor 1H 43
Odcombe. Som 4D 8
Odd Down. Bath 7F 18
Oddingley. Worc 6H 27
Oddington. Oxon 2C 20
Oddsta. Shet 4K 91
Odell. Bed 6G 29
Odie. Orkn 7F 88
Odiham. Hants 8E 20
Odsey. Cambs 8K 29
Odstock. Wilts 3K 9
Odstone. Leics 1A 28
Offchurch. Warw 5A 28
Offenham. Worc 7J 27
Offenham Cross. Worc 7J 27
Offerton. G Man 1H 35
Offerton. Tyne 6G 55
Offham. E Sus 4L 11
Offham. Kent 8C 22
Offham. W Sus 5H 11
Offleyhay. Staf 7G 35
Offley Hoo. Herts 1J 21
Offleymarsh. Staf 7F 34
Offord Cluny. Cambs 5K 29
Offord D'Arcy. Cambs 5K 29
Offton. Suff 7G 31
Offwell. Devn 6L 7
Ogbourne Maizey. Wilts 6K 19
Ogbourne St Andrew. Wilts 6K 19
Ogbourne St George. Wilts 6L 19
Ogden. G Man 6H 41
Ogle. Nmbd 4E 54
Ogmore. V Glam 7H 17
Ogmore-by-Sea. V Glam 7H 17
Ogmore Vale. B'end 5J 17
Okeford Fitzpaine. Dors 4G 9
Okehampton. Devn 6E 6
Okehampton Camp. Devn 6E 6
Okraquoy. Shet 4E 90
Okus. Swin 5K 19
Old. Nptn 4E 28
Old Aberdeen. Aber 5J 73
Old Alresford. Hants 2C 10
Oldany. High 8D 84
Old Arley. Warw 2L 27
Old Basford. Nott 5C 36
Old Basing. Hants 8D 20
Oldberrow. Warw 5K 27
Old Bewick. Nmbd 7H 61
Old Bexley. G Lon 6A 22
Old Blair. Per 1B 66
Old Bolingbroke. Linc 3L 37
Oldborough. Devn 5G 7
Old Brampton. Derbs 2M 35
Old Bridge of Tilt. Per 1B 66
Old Bridge of Urr. Dum 5B 52
Old Brumby. N Lin 7F 42
Old Buckenham. Norf 2G 31
Old Burghclere. Hants 8B 20
Oldbury. Shrp 2F 26
Oldbury. Warw 2M 27
**Oldbury**. W Mid 3H 27
Oldbury-on-Severn. S Glo 4E 18
Oldbury on the Hill. Glos 5G 19
Old Byland. N Yor 7C 48
Old Cassop. Dur 8G 55
Oldcastle. Mon 1B 18
Oldcastle Heath. Ches W 5C 34
Old Catton. Norf 8J 39
Old Clee. NE Lin 7K 43
Old Cleeve. Som 1K 7
Old Colwyn. Cnwy 3H 33
Oldcotes. Notts 1C 36
Old Coulsdon. G Lon 8L 21
Old Dailly. S Ayr 2H 51
Old Dalby. Leics 7D 36
Old Dam. Derbs 2K 35
Old Deer. Abers 1J 73
Old Dilton. Wilts 1G 9
Old Down. S Glo 5E 18
Oldeamere. Cambs 2L 29
Old Edlington. S Yor 8C 42
Old Eldon. Dur 3L 47
Old Ellerby. E Yor 4J 43
Old Fallings. W Mid 1H 27
Oldfallow. Staf 8H 35
Old Felixstowe. Suff 8K 31
Oldfield. Shrp 3E 26
Oldfield. Worc 5G 27
Old Fletton. Pet 2J 29
Oldford. Som 8F 18
Old Forge. Here 2D 18
Old Glossop. Derbs 8J 41
Old Goole. E Yor 5E 42
Old Gore. Here 1E 18
Old Graitney. Dum 5H 53
Old Grimsby. IOS 1G 3
Oldhall. High 6D 86
Old Hall Street. Norf 6K 39
**Oldham**. G Man 7H 41
Oldhamstocks. E Lot 2E 60
Old Heathfield. E Sus 3B 12
Old Hill. W Mid 3H 27
Old Hunstanton. Norf 5C 38
Oldhurst. Cambs 4K 29
Old Hutton. Cumb 7D 46
Old Kea. Corn 4M 3
Old Kilpatrick. W Dun 2C 58
Old Kinnernie. Abers 5G 73
Old Knebworth. Herts 1K 21
Oldland. S Glo 6E 18
Old Laxey. IOM 6D 44
Old Leake. Linc 4M 37
Old Lenton. Nott 6C 36
Old Llanberis. Gwyn 5F 32
Old Malton. N Yor 8E 48
Oldmeldrum. Abers 3H 73
Old Micklefield. W Yor 4B 42
Old Mill. Corn 8C 6
Oldmixon. N Som 8B 18
Old Monkland. N Lan 3F 58
Old Newton. Suff 5G 31
Old Park. Telf 1E 26
Old Pentland. Midl 3L 59
Old Philpstoun. W Lot 2J 59
Old Quarrington. Dur 8G 55
Old Radnor. Powy 6A 26
Old Rayne. Abers 3F 72
Oldridge. Devn 6H 7
Old Romney. Kent 3G 13
Old Scone. Per 5E 66
Oldshore Beg. High 6D 84
Oldshoremore. High 6E 84
Old Snydale. W Yor 5B 42
Old Sodbury. S Glo 5F 18
Old Somerby. Linc 6G 37
Old Spital. Dur 4H 47
Oldstead. N Yor 7C 48
Old Stratford. Nptn 7E 28
Old Swan. Mers 8B 40
Old Swarland. Nmbd 1E 54
Old Tebay. Cumb 5E 46
Old Town. Cumb 7J 53
Old Town. E Sus 6B 12
Old Town. IOS 1H 3
Old Town. Nmbd 2B 54
Oldtown. High 5F 78
Old Trafford. G Man 8G 41
Old Tupton. Derbs 3A 36
Oldwall. Cumb 5J 53
Oldwalls. Swan 7L 15
Old Warden. C Beds 7J 29
Oldways End. Som 3H 7
Old Westhall. Abers 3F 72
Old Weston. Cambs 4H 29
Oldwhat. Abers 8H 81
Old Windsor. Wind 6G 21
Old Wives Lees. Kent 8G 23
Old Woking. Surr 8H 21
Oldwood Common. Worc 5D 26
Old Woodstock. Oxon 2B 20
Olgrinmore. High 6B 86
Oliver's Battery. Hants 3B 10
Ollaberry. Shet 5H 91
Ollerton. Ches E 2F 34
Ollerton. Notts 3D 36
Ollerton. Shrp 7E 34
Olmarch. Cdgn 7F 24
Olmstead Green. Cambs 7C 30
Olney. Mil 6F 28
Olrig. High 5C 86
Olton. W Mid 3K 27
Olveston. S Glo 5E 18
**Omagh**. Ferm 5D 92
Ombersley. Worc 5G 27
Ompton. Notts 3D 36
Omunsgarth. Shet 3D 90
onchan. IOM 7D 44
onecote. Staf 4J 35
onehouse. Suff 6G 31
onen. Mon 2C 18
ongar Hill. Norf 7B 38
ongar Street. Here 5B 26
onibury. Shrp 4C 26
onich. High 1E 64
onllwyn. Neat 3H 17
onneley. Staf 5F 34
onslow Green. Essx 2C 22
onslow Village. Surr 1G 11
onthank. E Ayr 6C 58
Openwoodgate. Derbs 5A 36
Opinan. High
nr. Gairloch 6J 77
nr. Laide 4K 77
Orasaigh. W Isl 2E 76
Orbost. High 1D 68
Orby. Linc 3A 38
Orchard Hill. Devn 3D 6
Orchard Portman. Som 3M 7
Orcheston. Wilts 1J 9
Orcop. Here 1C 18
Orcop Hill. Here 1C 18
Ord. High 4H 69
Ordale. Shet 3L 91
Ordhead. Abers 4F 72
Ordie. Abers 5D 72
Ordiquish. Mor 8C 80
Ordley. Nmbd 6C 54
Ordsall. Notts 2E 36
Ore. E Sus 4E 12
Oreton. Shrp 3E 26
Orford. Suff 7L 31
Orford. Warr 8E 40
Organford. Dors 6H 9
Orgil. Orkn 1D 86
Orgreave. Staf 8K 35
Oridge Street. Glos 1F 18
Orlestone. Kent 2F 12
Orleton. Here 5C 26
Orleton. Worc 5E 26
Orleton Common. Here 5C 26
Orlingbury. Nptn 4F 28
Ormacleit. W Isl 2D 74
Ormathwaite. Cumb 3A 46
Ormesby. Red C 4C 48
Ormesby St Margaret. Norf 8L 39
Ormesby St Michael. Norf 8L 39
Ormiscaig. High 4K 77
Ormiston. E Lot 3B 60
Ormsaigbeg. High 1K 63
Ormsaigmore. High 1K 63
Ormsary. Arg 2G 57
Ormsgill. Cumb 7L 45
**Ormskirk**. Lanc 7C 40
Orphir. Orkn 1E 86
**Orpington**. G Lon 7A 22
**Orrell**. G Man 7D 40
Orrell. Mers 8B 40
Orrisdale. IOM 5C 44
Orsett. Thur 5C 22
Orslow. Staf 8G 35
Orston. Notts 5E 36
Orthwaite. Cumb 8G 53
Orton. Cumb 5E 46
Orton. Mor 8C 80
Orton. Nptn 4F 28
Orton. Staf 2G 27
Orton Longueville. Pet 2J 29
Orton-on-the-Hill. Leics 1M 27
Orton Waterville. Pet 2J 29
Orton Wistow. Pet 2J 29
Orwell. Cambs 6L 29
Osbaldeston. Lanc 4E 40
Osbaldwick. York 2D 42
Osbaston. Leics 1B 28
Osbaston. Shrp 7B 34
Osbournby. Linc 6H 37
Osclay. High 8D 86
Oscroft. Ches W 3D 34
Ose. High 1E 68
Osgathorpe. Leics 8B 36
Osgodby. Linc 8H 43
Osgodby. N Yor
nr. Scarborough 7H 49
nr. Selby 4D 42
Oskaig. High 2G 69
Oskamull. Arg 4K 63
Osleston. Derbs 6L 35
Osmaston. Derb 6A 36
Osmaston. Derbs 5L 35
Osmington. Dors 7F 8
Osmington Mills. Dors 7F 8
Osmondthorpe. W Yor 4M 41
Osmondwall. Orkn 3E 86
Osmotherley. N Yor 6B 48
Osnaburgh. Fife 6H 67
Ospisdale. High 5H 79
Ospringe. Kent 7G 23
**Ossett**. W Yor 5L 41
Ossington. Notts 3E 36
Ostend. Essx 4F 22
Ostend. Norf 6K 39
Osterley. G Lon 6J 21
Oswaldkirk. N Yor 8D 48
**Oswaldtwistle**. Lanc 5F 40
**Oswestry**. Shrp 7A 34
Otby. Linc 8J 43
Otford. Kent 8B 22
Otham. Kent 8D 22
Otherton. Staf 8H 35

Othery. Som 2B 8
Otley. Suff 6J 31
**Otley**. W Yor 3L 41
Otterbourne. Hants 3B 10
Otterburn. Nmbd 2B 54
Otterburn. N Yor 2G 41
Otterburn Camp. Nmbd 2B 54
Otterburn Hall. Nmbd 2B 54
Otter Ferry. Arg 1J 57
Otterford. Som 4M 7
Otterham. Corn 6A 6
Otterhampton. Som 1M 7
Otterham Quay. Medw 7E 22
Ottershaw. Surr 7H 21
Otterspool. Mers 1B 34
Otterswick. Shet 5K 91
Otterton. Devn 7K 7
Otterwood. Hants 5B 10
Ottery St Mary. Devn 6K 7
Ottinge. Kent 1H 13
Ottringham. E Yor 5K 43
Oughterby. Cumb 6G 53
Oughtershaw. N Yor 7G 47
Oughterside. Cumb 7F 52
Oughtibridge. S Yor 8M 41
Oughtrington. Warr 1E 34
Oulston. N Yor 8C 48
Oulton. Cumb 6G 53
Oulton. Norf 7H 39
Oulton. Staf
nr. Gnosall Heath 7F 34
nr. Stone 6H 35
Oulton. Suff 2M 31
Oulton. W Yor 5A 42
Oulton Broad. Suff 2M 31
Oulton Street. Norf 7H 39
Oundle. Nptn 3H 29
Ousby. Cumb 8L 53
Ousdale. High 2L 79
Ousden. Suff 6D 30
Ousefleet. E Yor 5F 42
Ouston. Dur 6F 54
Ouston. Nmbd
nr. Bearsbridge 6A 54
nr. Stamfordham 4D 54
Outer Hope. Devn 7J 5
Outertown. Orkn 8B 88
Outgate. Cumb 6B 46
Outhgill. Cumb 5F 46
Outlands. Staf 6F 34
Outlane. W Yor 6J 41
Out Newton. E Yor 5L 43
Out Rawcliffe. Lanc 3C 40
Outwell. Norf 1B 30
Outwick. Hants 4K 9
Outwood. Surr 1L 11
Outwood. W Yor 5M 41
Outwood. Worc 4H 27
Outwoods. Leics 8B 36
Outwoods. Staf 8F 34
Ouzlewell Green. W Yor 5M 41
Ovenden. W Yor 5J 41
Over. Cambs 4L 29
Over. Ches W 3E 34
Over. Glos 2G 19
Over. S Glo 5D 18
Overbister. Orkn 5F 88
Over Burrows. Derbs 6L 35
Overbury. Worc 8H 27
Overcombe. Dors 7E 8
Over Compton. Dors 4D 8
Over End. Cambs 2H 29
Over Finlarg. Ang 3H 67
Over Green. Warw 2K 27
Overgreen. Derbs 2M 35
Over Haddon. Derbs 3L 35
Over Hulton. G Man 7E 40
Over Kellet. Lanc 8D 46
Over Kiddington. Oxon 1B 20
Overleigh. Som 2C 8
Overley. Staf 8K 35
Over Monnow. Mon 2D 18
Over Norton. Oxon 1M 19
Over Peover. Ches E 2F 34
Overpool. Ches W 2B 34
Overscaig. High 1E 78
Overseal. Derbs 8L 35
Over Silton. N Yor 6B 48
Oversland. Kent 8G 23
Overstone. Nptn 5F 28
Over Stowey. Som 2L 7
Overstrand. Norf 5J 39
Over Stratton. Som 4C 8
Over Street. Wilts 2J 9
Overthorpe. Nptn 7B 28
Overton. Aber 4H 73
Overton. Ches W 2D 34
Overton. Hants 1C 10
Overton. High 8D 86
Overton. Lanc 2C 40
Overton. N Yor 2C 42
Overton. Shrp
nr. Bridgnorth 3E 26
nr. Ludlow 4D 26
Overton. Swan 8L 15
Overton. W Yor 6L 41
Overton. Wrex 5B 34
Overtown. Lanc 8E 46
Overtown. N Lan 4G 59
Overtown. Swin 6K 19
Over Wallop. Hants 2L 9
Over Whitacre. Warw 2L 27
Over Worton. Oxon 1B 20
Oving. Buck 1E 20
Oving. W Sus 5G 11
Ovingdean. Brig 5L 11
Ovingham. Nmbd 5D 54
Ovington. Dur 4K 47
Ovington. Essx 7D 30
Ovington. Hants 2C 10
Ovington. Norf 1F 30
Ovington. Nmbd 5D 54
Owen's Bank. Staf 7L 35
Ower. Hants
nr. Holbury 5B 10
nr. Totton 4M 9
Owermoigne. Dors 7F 8
Owlbury. Shrp 2B 26
Owler Bar. Derbs 2L 35
Owlerton. S Yor 8M 41
Owlsmoor. Brac 7F 20
Owlswick. Buck 3E 20
Owmby. Linc 7H 43
Owmby-by-Spital. Linc 1H 37
Ownham. W Ber 6B 20
Owrytn. Wrex 5B 34
Owslebury. Hants 3C 10
Owston. Leics 1E 28
Owston. S Yor 6C 42
Owston Ferry. N Lin 7F 42
Owstwick. E Yor 4K 43
Owthorne. E Yor 5L 43
Owthorpe. Notts 6D 36
Owton Manor. Hart 3B 48
Oxborough. Norf 1D 30
Oxbridge. Dors 6C 8
Oxcombe. Linc 2L 37
Oxen End. Essx 1C 22
Oxenhall. Glos 1F 18
Oxenholme. Cumb 6D 46
Oxenhope. W Yor 4J 41
Oxen Park. Cumb 7B 46
Oxenpill. Som 1C 8
Oxenton. Glos 8H 27
Oxenwood. Wilts 8M 19
**Oxford**. Oxon 114 (3C 20)
Oxgangs. Edin 3L 59
Oxhey. Herts 4J 21
Oxhill. Warw 7M 27
Oxley. W Mid 1H 27
Oxley Green. Essx 2F 22
Oxley's Green. E Sus 3C 12
Oxlode. Cambs 3A 30
Oxnam. Bord 8E 60
Oxshott. Surr 7J 21
Oxspring. S Yor 7L 41
**Oxted**. Surr 8L 21
Oxton. Mers 1B 34
Oxton. N Yor 3C 42
Oxton. Notts 4D 36
Oxton. Bord 4B 60
Oxwich. Swan 8L 15
Oxwich Green. Swan 8L 15
Oxwick. Norf 7F 38
Oykel Bridge. High 3D 78
Oyne. Abers 3F 72
Oystermouth. Swan 6F 16
Ozleworth. Glos 4F 18

**P**

Pabail Iarach. W Isl 8J 83
Pabail Uarach. W Isl 8J 83
Pachesham Park. Surr 8J 21
Packers Hill. Dors 4F 8
Packington. Leics 8A 36
Packmoor. Stoke 4G 35
Packmores. Warw 5L 27
Packwood. W Mid 4K 27
Packwood Gullet. W Mid 4K 27
Padanaram. Ang 2H 67
Padbury. Buck 8E 28
**Paddington**. G Lon 5K 21
Paddington. Warr 1E 34
Paddlesworth. Kent 2H 13
Paddock. Kent 8F 22
Paddockhole. Dum 3G 53
Paddock Wood. Kent 1C 12
Paddolgreen. Shrp 6D 34
Padeswood. Flin 3A 34
**Padiham**. Lanc 4F 40
Padside. N Yor 2K 41
Padson. Devn 6E 6
Padstow. Corn 4B 4
Padworth. W Ber 7D 20
Page Bank. Dur 8F 54
Pagham. W Sus 6F 10
Paglesham Churchend. Essx 4F 22
Paglesham Eastend. Essx 4F 22
Paibeil. W Isl
on North Uist 7J 75
on Taransay 4B 76
Paiblesgearraidh. W Isl 7J 75
**Paignton**. Torb 5L 5
Pailton. Warw 3B 28
Paine's Corner. E Sus 3C 12
Painleyhill. Staf 6J 35
Painscastle. Powy 8L 25
Painshawfield. Nmbd 5D 54
Painsthorpe. E Yor 2F 42
Painswick. Glos 3G 19
Painter's Forstal. Kent 8F 22
Painthorpe. W Yor 6M 41
Pairc Shiaboist. W Isl 7F 82
**Paisley**. Ren 3C 58
Pakefield. Suff 2M 31
Pakenham. Suff 5F 30
Pale. Gwyn 7J 33
Palehouse Common. E Sus 4A 12
Palestine. Hants 1L 9
Paley Street. Wind 6F 20
Palgowan. Dum 3J 51
Palgrave. Suff 4H 31
Pallington. Dors 6F 8
Palmarsh. Kent 2H 13
Palmer Moor. Derbs 6K 35
Palmers Cross. W Mid 1G 27
Palmerstown. V Glam 8L 17
Palnackie. Dum 6C 52
Palnure. Dum 5K 51
Palterton. Derbs 3B 36
Pamber End. Hants 8D 20
Pamber Green. Hants 8D 20
Pamber Heath. Hants 7D 20
Pamington. Glos 8H 27
Pamphill. Dors 5H 9
Pampisford. Cambs 7A 30
Panborough. Som 1C 8
Panbride. Ang 4J 67
Pancrasweek. Devn 5B 6
Pandy. Gwyn
nr. Bala 7H 33
nr. Tywyn 2F 24
Pandy. Mon 1B 18
Pandy. Powy 2J 25
Pandy. Wrex 7L 33
Pandy Tudur. Cnwy 4H 33
Panfield. Essx 1D 22
Pangbourne. W Ber 6D 20
Pannal. N Yor 2M 41
Pannal Ash. N Yor 2L 41
Pannanich. Abers 6C 72
Pant. Shrp 7A 34
Pant. Wrex 5A 34
Pantasaph. Flin 3L 33
Pant Glas. Gwyn 6D 32
Pant-glas. Shrp 6A 34
Pantgwyn. Carm 2E 16
Pantgwyn. Cdgn 2J 15
Pant-lasau. Swan 4F 16
Panton. Linc 2J 37
Pant-pastynog. Den 4K 33
Pantperthog. Gwyn 2G 25
Pant-teg. Carm 4L 15
Pant-y-Caws. Carm 4H 15
Pant-y-dwr. Powy 5J 25
Pant-y-ffridd. Powy 2L 25
Pantyffynnon. Carm 3F 16
Pantygasseg. Torf 3A 18
Pant-y-llyn. Carm 3F 16
Pant-yr-awel. B'end 6J 17
Pant y Wacco. Flin 3L 33
Panxworth. Norf 8K 39
Papa Stour Airport. Shet 2B 90
Papa Westray Airport. Orkn 4D 88
Papcastle. Cumb 8F 52
Papigoe. High 6E 86
Papil. Shet 4D 90
Papple. E Lot 2C 60
Papplewick. Notts 4C 36
Papworth Everard. Cambs 5K 29
Papworth St Agnes. Cambs 5K 29
Par. Corn 6C 4
Paramour Street. Kent 7J 23
Parbold. Lanc 6C 40
Parbrook. Som 2D 8
Parbrook. W Sus 3H 11
Parc. Gwyn 7H 33
Parcllyn. Cdgn 1J 15
Parc-Seymour. Newp 4C 18
Pardown. Hants 1C 10
Pardshaw. Cumb 2K 45
Parham. Suff 5K 31
Park. Abers 6G 73
Park. Arg 3D 64
Park. Derr 3D 92
Park. Dum 2D 52
Park Bottom. Corn 4K 3
Parkburn. Abers 2G 73
Park Corner. E Sus 2B 12
Park Corner. Oxon 5D 20
Park End. Nmbd 4B 54
Parkend. Glos 3E 18
Parkeston. Essx 8J 31
Parkfield. Corn 5F 4
Park Gate. Hants 5C 10
Park Gate. Worc 4H 27
Parkgate. Ant 4H 93
Parkgate. Ches W 2A 34
Parkgate. Cumb 7G 53
Parkgate. Dum 3E 52
Parkgate. Surr 1K 11
Parkhall. W Dun 2C 58
Parkham. Devn 3C 6
Parkham Ash. Devn 3C 6
Parkhead. Cumb 7H 53
Parkhead. Glas 3E 58
Park Hill. Mers 7C 40
Parkhouse. Mon 3D 18
Parkhurst. IOW 6B 10
Park Lane. G Man 7F 40
Park Lane. Staf 1G 27
Park Mill. W Yor 6L 41
Parkmill. Swan 8M 15
Parkneuk. Abers 8G 73
Parkside. N Lan 4G 59
Parkstone. Pool 6J 9
Park Street. Herts 3J 21
Park Street. W Sus 2J 11
Park Town. Oxon 3C 20
Park Village. Nmbd 5L 53
Parkway. Here 8F 26
Parley Cross. Dors 6J 9
Parmoor. Buck 5E 20
Parr. Mers 8D 40
Parracombe. Devn 1F 6
Parrog. Pemb 3G 15
Parsonage Green. Essx 2D 22
Parsonby. Cumb 8F 52
Parson Cross. S Yor 8M 41
Parson Drove. Cambs 1L 29
Partick. Glas 3D 58
Partington. G Man 8F 40
Partney. Linc 3M 37
Parton. Cumb
nr. Whitehaven 2J 45
nr. Wigton 6G 53
Parton. Dum 4A 52
Partridge Green. W Sus 4J 11
Parwich. Derbs 4K 35
Passenham. Nptn 8E 28
Passfield. Hants 2F 10
Passingford Bridge. Essx 4B 22
Paston. Norf 6K 39
Pasturefields. Staf 7H 35
Patchacott. Devn 6D 6
Patcham. Brig 5L 11
Patchetts Green. Herts 4J 21
Patching. W Sus 5H 11
Patchole. Devn 1F 6
Patchway. S Glo 5E 18
Pateley Bridge. N Yor 1K 41
Pathe. Som 2B 8
Pathfinder Village. Devn 6H 7
Pathhead. Abers 1L 67
Pathhead. E Ayr 8E 58
Pathhead. Fife 8F 66
Pathhead. Midl 3A 60
Pathlow. Warw 6K 27
Path of Condie. Per 6D 66
Pathstruie. Per 6D 66
Patmore Heath. Herts 1M 21
Patna. E Ayr 8C 58
Patney. Wilts 8J 19
Patrick. IOM 6B 44
Patrick Brompton. N Yor 6L 47
Patrington. E Yor 5L 43
Patrington Haven. E Yor 5L 43
Patrixbourne. Kent 8H 23
Patterdale. Cumb 4B 46
Pattiesmuir. Fife 1J 59
Pattingham. Staf 2G 27
Pattishall. Nptn 6D 28
Pattiswick. Essx 1E 22
Patton Bridge. Cumb 6D 46
Paul. Corn 6H 3
Paulerspury. Nptn 7E 28
Paull. E Yor 5J 43
Paulton. Bath 8E 18
Pauperhaugh. Nmbd 2E 54
Pave Lane. Telf 8F 34
Pavenham. Bed 6G 29
Pawlett. Som 1A 8
Pawston. Nmbd 6F 60
Paxford. Glos 8K 27
Paxton. Bord 4G 61
Payhembury. Devn 5K 7
Paythorne. Lanc 2G 41
Payton. Som 3L 7
**Peacehaven**. E Sus 5M 11
Peak Dale. Derbs 2J 35
Peak Forest. Derbs 2K 35
Peak Hill. Linc 8K 37
Peakirk. Pet 1J 29
Pearsie. Ang 2G 67
Peasedown St John. Bath 8F 18
Peaseland Green. Norf 8G 39
Peasemore. W Ber 6B 20
Peasenhall. Suff 5K 31
Pease Pottage. W Sus 2K 11
Peaslake. Surr 1H 11
Peasley Cross. Mers 8D 40
Peasmarsh. E Sus 3E 12
Peasmarsh. Som 4B 8
Peasmarsh. Surr 1G 11
Peaston. E Lot 3B 60
Peastonbank. E Lot 3B 60
Peathill. Abers 7J 81
Peat Inn. Fife 7H 67
Peatling Magna. Leics 2C 28
Peatling Parva. Leics 3C 28
Peaton. Arg 1M 57
Peaton. Shrp 3D 26
Peats Corner. Suff 5H 31
Pebmarsh. Essx 8E 30
Pebworth. Worc 7K 27
Pecket Well. W Yor 5H 41
Peckforton. Ches E 4D 34
Peckham Bush. Kent 8C 22
Peckleton. Leics 1B 28
Pedair-ffordd. Powy 8L 33
Pedham. Norf 8K 39
Pedlinge. Kent 2H 13
Pedmore. W Mid 3H 27
Pedwell. Som 2C 8
Peebles. Bord 5L 59
Peel. IOM 6B 44
Peel. Bord 6B 60
Peel Common. Hants 5C 10
Peening Quarter. Kent 3E 12
Peggs Green. Leics 8B 36
Pegsdon. C Beds 8J 29
Pegswood. Nmbd 3F 54
Peinchorran. High 2G 69
Peinlich. High 8F 76
Pelaw. Tyne 5F 54
Pelcomb Bridge. Pemb 5F 14
Pelcomb Cross. Pemb 5F 14
Peldon. Essx 2F 22
**Pelsall**. W Mid 1J 27
Pelton. Dur 6F 54
Pelutho. Cumb 7F 52
Pelynt. Corn 6E 4
Pemberton. Carm 6M 15
Pembrey. Carm 6L 15
Pembridge. Here 6B 26
Pembroke. Pemb 6F 14
Pembroke Dock. Pemb 118 (6F 14)
Pembroke Ferry. Pemb 6F 14
Pembury. Kent 1C 12
Penallt. Mon 2D 18
Penally. Pemb 7H 15
Penalt. Here 1D 18
Penalum. Pemb 7H 15
Penare. Corn 7B 4
**Penarth**. V Glam 7L 17
Penbeagle. Corn 5J 3
Penberth. Corn 6H 3
Pen-bont Rhydybeddau. Cdgn 4F 24
Penbryn. Cdgn 1J 15
Pencader. Carm 3L 15
Pen-cae. Cdgn 1L 15
Pencaenewydd. Gwyn 6D 32
Pencaerau. Neat 5G 17
Pencaitland. E Lot 3B 60
Pencarnisiog. IOA 3C 32
Pencarreg. Carm 2M 15
Pencarrow. Corn 3D 4
Pencelli. Powy 2K 17
Pen-clawdd. Swan 7M 15
Pencoed. B'end 6J 17
Pencombe. Here 6D 26
Pencraig. Here 1D 18
Pencraig. Powy 8K 33
Pendeen. Corn 5G 3
Pendeford. W Mid 1G 27
Penderyn. Rhon 4J 17
Pendine. Carm 6J 15
**Pendlebury**. G Man 7F 40
Pendleton. G Man 8G 41
Pendleton. Lanc 4F 40
Pendock. Worc 8F 26
Pendoggett. Corn 4C 4
Pendomer. Som 4D 8
Pendoylan. V Glam 7K 17
Pendre. B'end 6J 17
Penegoes. Powy 2G 25
Penelewey. Corn 4M 3
Penffordd. Pemb 4G 15
Penffordd-Lâs. Powy 3H 25
Penfro. Pemb 6F 14
Pengam. Cphy 5L 17
Pengam. Card 7M 17
**Penge**. G Lon 7L 21
Pengelly. Corn 3C 4
Pengenffordd. Powy 1L 17
Pengersick. Corn 6J 3
Pengorffwysfa. IOA 1D 32
Pengover Green. Corn 5E 4
Pengwern. Den 3K 33
Penhale. Corn
nr. Mullion 7K 3
nr. St Austell 6B 4
Penhale Camp. Corn 3L 3
Penhallow. Corn 3L 3
Penhalvean. Corn 5L 3
Penhelig. Gwyn 3F 24
Penhill. Swin 5K 19
Penhow. Newp 4C 18
Penhurst. E Sus 4C 12
Peniarth. Gwyn 2F 24
**Penicuik**. Midl 3L 59
Peniel. Carm 4L 15
Penifiler. High 1F 68
Peninver. Arg 7G 57
Penisa'r Waun. Gwyn 4E 32
Penistone. S Yor 7L 41
Penketh. Warr 1D 34
Penkill. S Ayr 2H 51
Penkridge. Staf 8H 35
Penley. Wrex 6C 34
Penllech. Gwyn 7B 32
Penllergaer. Swan 5F 16
Pen-llyn. IOA 2C 32
Penmachno. Cnwy 5G 33
Penmaen. Swan 8M 15
Penmaenmawr. Cnwy 3G 33
Penmaenpool. Gwyn 1F 24
Penmaen Rhos. Cnwy 3H 33
Pen-marc. V Glam 8K 17
Penmark. V Glam 8K 17
Penmarth. Corn 5L 3
Penmon. IOA 2F 32
Penmorfa. Gwyn 6E 32
Penmynydd. IOA 3E 32
Penn. Buck 4G 21
Penn. Dors 6B 8
Penn. W Mid 2G 27
Pennal. Gwyn 2G 25
Pennan. Abers 7H 81
Pennant. Cdgn 6E 24
Pennant. Den 7K 33
Pennant. Gwyn 8J 33
Pennant. Powy 3H 25
Pennant Melangell. Powy 8K 33
Pennar. Pemb 6F 14
Pennard. Swan 6E 16
Pennerley. Shrp 2B 26
Pennington. Cumb 8A 46
Pennington. G Man 8E 40
Pennington. Hants 6M 9
Pennorth. Powy 2L 17
Penn Street. Buck 4G 21
Pennsylvania. Devn 6J 7
Pennsylvania. S Glo 6F 18
Penny Bridge. Cumb 7B 46
Pennycross. Plym 6G 5
Pennygate. Norf 7K 39
Pennyghael. Arg 5L 63
Penny Hill. Linc 7L 37
Pennylands. Lanc 7C 40
Pennymoor. Devn 4H 7
Pennyvenie. E Ayr 1K 51
Pennywell. Tyne 6G 55
Penparc. Cdgn 2J 15
Penparcau. Cdgn 4E 24
Pen-pedair-heol. Cphy 5L 17
Penperlleni. Mon 3B 18
Penpillick. Corn 6C 4
Penpol. Corn 5M 3
Penpoll. Corn 6D 4
Penponds. Corn 5K 3
Penpont. Corn 4C 4
Penpont. Dum 2C 52
Penpont. Powy 2J 17
Penprysg. B'end 6J 17
Penquit. Devn 6J 5
Penrherber. Carm 3J 15
Penrhiw. Pemb 2J 15
Penrhiwceiber. Rhon 5K 17
Pen-Rhiw-fawr. Neat 3G 17
Penrhiw-llan. Cdgn 2K 15
Penrhiw-pal. Cdgn 2K 15
Penrhos. Gwyn 7C 32
Penrhos. Here 6B 26
Penrhos. IOA 2B 32
Penrhos. Mon 2C 18
Penrhos. Powy 3H 17
Penrhos Garnedd. Gwyn 3E 32
Penrhyn. IOA 1C 32
Penrhyn Bay. Cnwy 2H 33
Penrhyn-coch. Cdgn 4F 24
Penrhyndeudraeth. Gwyn 7F 32
Penrhyn-side. Cnwy 2H 33
Penrice. Swan 8L 15
**Penrith**. Cumb 3D 46
Penrose. Corn 4A 4
Penruddock. Cumb 3C 46
Penryn. Corn 5L 3
Pen-sarn. Carm 5L 15
Pen-sarn. Gwyn 8E 32
Pensax. Worc 5F 26
Pensby. Mers 1A 34
Penselwood. Som 2F 8
Pensford. Bath 7E 18
Pensham. Worc 7H 27
Penshaw. Tyne 6G 55
Penshurst. Kent 1B 12
Pensilva. Corn 5E 4
Pensnett. W Mid 3H 27
Penston. E Lot 2B 60
Penstone. Devn 5G 7
Pentewan. Corn 7C 4
Pentir. Gwyn 4E 32
Pentire. Corn 2L 3
Pentlepoir. Pemb 6H 15
Pentlow. Essx 7E 30
Pentney. Norf 8D 38
Penton Mewsey. Hants 1M 9
Pentraeth. IOA 3E 32
Pentre. Powy
nr. Church Stoke 2A 26
nr. Kerry 4L 25
nr. Mochdre 4K 25
Pentre. Rhon 5J 17
Pentre. Shrp 8B 34
Pentre. Wrex
nr. Chirk 5A 34
nr. Llanarmon Dyffryn Ceiriog 7L 33
Pentre-bach. Cdgn 2M 15
Pentre-bach. Powy 1J 17
Pentrebach. Carm 1H 17
Pentrebach. Mer T 4K 17
Pentrebach. Swan 4F 16
Pentre Berw. IOA 3D 32
Pentre-bont. Cnwy 5G 33
Pentrecagal. Carm 2K 15
Pentre-celyn. Den 5L 33
Pentre-clawdd. Shrp 6A 34
Pentreclwydau. Neat 4H 17
Pentre-cwrt. Carm 3K 15
Pentre Dolau Honddu. Powy 8J 25
Pentre-dwr. Swan 5F 16
Pentrefelin. Carm 2E 16
Pentrefelin. Cdgn 8F 24
Pentrefelin. Cnwy 3H 33
Pentrefelin. Gwyn 7E 32
Pentrefoelas. Cnwy 5H 33
Pentre Galar. Pemb 3H 15
Pentregat. Cdgn 1K 15
Pentre Gwenlais. Carm 3F 16
Pentre Gwynfryn. Gwyn 8E 32
Pentre Halkyn. Flin 3M 33
Pentre Hodre. Shrp 4B 26
Pentre-Llanrhaeadr. Den 4K 33
Pentre Llifior. Powy 3L 25
Pentrellwyn. IOA 2E 32
Pentre-llwyn-llwyd. Powy 7J 25
Pentre-llyn-cymmer. Cnwy 5J 33
Pentre Meyrick. V Glam 7J 17
Pentre-piod. Gwyn 7H 33
Pentre-poeth. Newp 5A 18
Pentre'r beirdd. Powy 1L 25
Pentre'r-felin. Powy 1J 17
Pentre-tafarn-y-fedw. Cnwy 4H 33
Pentre-ty-gwyn. Carm 1H 17
Pentre-uchaf. Gwyn 7C 32
Pentrich. Derbs 4A 36
Pentridge. Dors 4J 9
Pen-twyn. Cphy 4M 17
Pentwyn. Cphy 4L 17
Pentwyn. Card 6M 17
Pentyrch. Card 6L 17
Pentywyn. Carm 6J 15
Penuwch. Cdgn 6E 24
Penwithick. Corn 6C 4
Penwyllt. Powy 3H 17
Pen-y-banc. Carm 2F 16
Penybanc. Carm 3F 16
Pen-y-bont. Carm 4K 15
Pen-y-bont. Powy 8M 33
Penybont. Powy 6L 25
**Pen-y-Bont Ar Ogwr**. B'end 6J 17
Penybontfawr. Powy 8K 33
Pen-y-bryn. Pemb 2H 15
Pen-y-bryn. Wrex 5A 34
Penybryn. Cphy 5L 17
Pen-y-cae. Powy 3H 17
Penycae. Wrex 5A 34
Pen-y-cae mawr. Mon 4C 18
Penycaerau. Gwyn 8A 32
Pen-y-cefn. Flin 3L 33
Pen-y-clawdd. Mon 3C 18
Pen-y-coedcae. Rhon 6K 17
Penycwm. Pemb 4E 14
Pen-y-Darren. Mer T 4K 17
Pen-y-fai. B'end 6H 17
Pen-y-ffordd. Flin 2L 33
Penyffordd. Flin 3B 34
Penyffridd. Gwyn 5E 32
Pen-y-garn. Cdgn 4F 24
Pen-y-garnedd. IOA 3E 32
Penygarnedd. Powy 8L 33
Pen-y-graig. Gwyn 7B 32
Penygraig. Rhon 5J 17
Penygraigwen. IOA 2D 32
Pen-y-groes. Carm 3E 16
Penygroes. Gwyn 5D 32
Penygroes. Pemb 3H 15
Pen-y-Mynydd. Carm 6L 15
Penymynydd. Flin 3B 34
Pen-yr-heol. Mon 2C 18
Penyrheol. Cphy 6L 17
Penyrheol. Swan 5E 16
Penysarn. IOA 1D 32
Pen-y-stryt. Den 5L 33
Penywaun. Rhon 4J 17
**Penzance**. Corn 5H 3
Peopleton. Worc 6H 27
Peover Heath. Ches E 2F 34
Peper Harow. Surr 1G 11
Peplow. Shrp 7E 34
Pepper Arden. N Yor 5L 47
Perceton. N Ayr 5B 58
Percyhorner. Abers 7J 81
Perham Down. Wilts 1L 9
Periton. Som 1J 7
Perkinsville. Dur 6F 54
Perlethorpe. Notts 2D 36
Perranarworthal. Corn 5L 3
Perranporth. Corn 3L 3
Perranuthnoe. Corn 6J 3
Perranwell. Corn 5L 3
Perranzabuloe. Corn 3L 3
Perrott's Brook. Glos 3J 19
Perry. W Mid 2J 27
Perry Barr. W Mid 2J 27
Perry Crofts. Staf 1L 27
Perry Green. Essx 1E 22
Perry Green. Herts 2M 21
Perry Green. Wilts 5H 19
Perry Street. Kent 6C 22
Perry Street. Som 5B 8
Perrywood. Kent 8G 23
Pershall. Staf 7G 35
Pershore. Worc 7H 27
Pertenhall. Bed 5H 29
**Perth**. Per 115 (5E 66)
Perthy. Shrp 6B 34
Perton. Staf 2G 27
Pertwood. Wilts 2G 9
**Peterborough**. Pet 115 (2J 29)
Peterburn. High 5J 77
Peterchurch. Here 8B 26
Peterculter. Aber 5H 73
**Peterhead**. Abers 1L 73
**Peterlee**. Dur 7H 55
**Petersfield**. Hants 3E 10
Petersfinger. Wilts 3K 9
Peters Green. Herts 2J 21
Peters Marland. Devn 4D 6
Peterstone Wentlooge. Newp 5A 18
Peterston-super-Ely. V Glam 7K 17
Peterstow. Here 1D 18
Peters Village. Kent 7D 22
Peter Tavy. Devn 8E 6
Petertown. Orkn 1E 86
Petham. Kent 8H 23
Petherwin Gate. Corn 7B 6
Petrockstowe. Devn 5E 6
Petsoe End. Mil 7F 28
Pett. E Sus 4E 12
Pettaugh. Suff 6H 31
Pett Bottom. Kent 8H 23
Petteridge. Kent 1C 12
Pettinain. S Lan 5H 59
Pettistree. Suff 6J 31
Petton. Devn 3K 7
Petton. Shrp 7C 34
Petts Wood. G Lon 7M 21
Pettycur. Fife 1L 59
Pettywell. Norf 7G 39
Petworth. W Sus 3G 11
Pevensey. E Sus 5C 12
Pevensey Bay. E Sus 5C 12
Pewsey. Wilts 7K 19
Pheasants Hill. Buck 5E 20
Philadelphia. Tyne 6G 55
Philham. Devn 3B 6
Philiphaugh. Bord 7B 60
Phillack. Corn 5J 3
Philleigh. Corn 8A 4
Philpstoun. W Lot 2J 59
Phocle Green. Here 1E 18
Phoenix Green. Hants 8E 20
Pibsbury. Som 3C 8
Pibwrlwyd. Carm 5L 15
Pica. Cumb 2K 45
Piccadilly. Warw 2L 27
Piccadilly Corner. Norf 3J 31
Piccotts End. Herts 3H 21
Pickering. N Yor 7E 48
Picket Piece. Hants 1A 10
Picket Post. Hants 5K 9
Pickford. W Mid 3L 27
Pickhill. N Yor 7M 47
Picklenash. Glos 1F 18
Picklescott. Shrp 2C 26
Pickletillem. Fife 5H 67
Pickmere. Ches E 2E 34
Pickstock. Telf 7F 34
Pickwell. Devn 1D 6
Pickwell. Leics 8E 36
Pickworth. Linc 6H 37
Pickworth. Rut 8G 37
Picton. Ches W 2C 34
Picton. Flin 2L 33
Picton. N Yor 5B 48
Pict's Hill. Som 3C 8
Piddinghoe. E Sus 5M 11
Piddington. Buck 4F 20
Piddington. Nptn 6F 28
Piddington. Oxon 2D 20
Piddlehinton. Dors 6F 8
Piddletrenthide. Dors 5F 8
Pidley. Cambs 4L 29
Pidney. Dors 5F 8
Pie Corner. Here 5E 26
Piercebridge. Darl 4L 47
Pierowall. Orkn 5D 88
Pigdon. Nmbd 3E 54
Pightley. Som 2M 7
Pikehall. Derbs 4K 35
Pikeshill. Hants 5L 9
Pilford. Dors 5J 9
Pilgrims Hatch. Essx 4B 22
Pilham. Linc 8F 42
Pill. N Som 6D 18
The Pill. Mon 5C 18
Pillaton. Corn 5F 4
Pillaton. Staf 8H 35
Pillerton Hersey. Warw 7M 27
Pillerton Priors. Warw 7L 27
Pilleth. Powy 5A 26
Pilley. Hants 6M 9
Pilley. S Yor 7M 41
Pillgwenlly. Newp 5B 18
Pilling. Lanc 3C 40
Pilling Lane. Lanc 3B 40
Pillowell. Glos 3E 18
Pillwell. Dors 4F 8
Pilning. S Glo 5D 18
Pilsbury. Derbs 3K 35
Pilsdon. Dors 6C 8
Pilsgate. Pet 1H 29
Pilsley. Derbs
nr. Bakewell 2L 35
nr. Clay Cross 3B 36
Pilson Green. Norf 8K 39
Piltdown. E Sus 3M 11
Pilton. Edin 2L 59
Pilton. Nptn 3H 29
Pilton. Rut 1G 29
Pilton. Som 1D 8
Pilton Green. Swan 8L 15
Pimperne. Dors 5H 9
Pinchbeck. Linc 7K 37
Pinchbeck Bars. Linc 7J 37
Pinchbeck West. Linc 7K 37
Pinfold. Lanc 6B 40
Pinford End. Suff 6E 30
Pinged. Carm 6L 15
Pinhoe. Devn 6J 7
Pinkerton. E Lot 2E 60
Pinkneys Green. Wind 5F 20
Pinley. W Mid 4A 28
Pinley Green. Warw 5L 27
Pinmill. Suff 8J 31
Pinmore. S Ayr 2H 51
**Pinner**. G Lon 5J 21
Pins Green. Worc 7F 26
Pinsley Green. Ches E 5D 34
Pinvin. Worc 7H 27
Pinwherry. S Ayr 3G 51
Pinxton. Derbs 4B 36
Pipe and Lyde. Here 7D 26
Pipe Aston. Here 4C 26
Pipe Gate. Shrp 5F 34
Pipehill. Staf 1J 27
Piperhill. High 8J 79
Pipe Ridware. Staf 8J 35
Pipers Pool. Corn 7B 6
Pipewell. Nptn 3F 28
Pippacott. Devn 2E 6
Pipton. Powy 1L 17
Pirbright. Surr 8G 21
Pirnmill. N Ayr 5H 57
Pirton. Herts 8J 29
Pirton. Worc 7G 27
Pisgah. Stir 7A 66
Pishill. Oxon 5E 20
Pistyll. Gwyn 6C 32
Pitagowan. Per 1B 66
Pitcairn. Per 2B 66
Pitcairngreen. Per 5D 66
Pitcalnie. High 6J 79
Pitcaple. Abers 3G 73
Pitchcombe. Glos 3G 19
Pitchcott. Buck 1E 20
Pitchford. Shrp 1D 26
Pitch Green. Buck 3E 20
Pitch Place. Surr 8G 21
Pitcombe. Som 2E 8
Pitcox. E Lot 2D 60
Pitcur. Per 4F 66
Pitfichie. Abers 4F 72
Pitgrudy. High 4H 79
Pitkennedy. Ang 2J 67
Pitlessie. Fife 7G 67
Pitlochry. Per 2C 66
Pitmachie. Abers 3F 72
Pitmaduthy. High 6H 79
Pitmedden. Abers 3H 73
Pitminster. Som 4M 7
Pitnacree. Per 2C 66
Pitney. Som 3C 8
Pitroddie. Per 5F 66
Pitscottie. Fife 6H 67
Pitsea. Essx 5D 22
Pitsford. Nptn 5E 28
Pitsford Hill. Som 2L 7
Pitsmoor. S Yor 1A 36
Pitstone. Buck 2G 21
Pitt. Hants 3B 10
Pitt Court. Glos 4F 18
Pittentrail. High 3H 79
Pittenweem. Fife 7J 67
Pittington. Dur 7G 55
Pitton. Swan 8L 15
Pitton. Wilts 2L 9
Pittswood. Kent 1C 12
Pittulie. Abers 7J 81
Pittville. Glos 1H 19
Pitversie. Per 6E 66
Pity Me. Dur 7F 54
Pityme. Corn 4B 4
Pixey Green. Suff 4J 31
Pixley. Here 8E 26
Place Newton. N Yor 8F 48
Plaidy. Abers 8G 81
Plaidy. Corn 6E 4
Plain Dealings. Pemb 5G 15
Plains. N Lan 3F 58
Plainsfield. Som 2L 7
Plaish. Shrp 2D 26
Plaistow. Here 8E 26
Plaistow. W Sus 2H 11
Plaitford. Wilts 4L 9
Plastow Green. Hants 7C 20
Plas yn Cefn. Den 3K 33
The Platt. E Sus 2B 12
Platt Bridge. G Man 7E 40
Platt Lane. Shrp 6D 34
Platts Common. S Yor 7A 42
Platt's Heath. Kent 8E 22
Plawsworth. Dur 7F 54
Plaxtol. Kent 8C 22
Playden. E Sus 3F 12
Playford. Suff 7J 31
Play Hatch. Oxon 6E 20
Playing Place. Corn 4M 3
Playley Green. Glos 8F 26
Plealey. Shrp 1C 26
Plean. Stir 1G 59
Pleasington. Bkbn 5E 40
Pleasley. Derbs 3C 36
Pledgdon Green. Essx 1B 22
Plenmeller. Nmbd 5M 53
Pleshey. Essx 2C 22
Plockton. High 2K 69
Plocrapol. W Isl 4C 76
Ploughfield. Here 7B 26
Plowden. Shrp 3B 26
Ploxgreen. Shrp 1B 26
Pluckley. Kent 1F 12
Plucks Gutter. Kent 7J 23
Plumbland. Cumb 8F 52
Plumbridge. Derr 4D 92
Plumgarths. Cumb 6C 46
Plumley. Ches E 2F 34
Plummers Plain. W Sus 3K 11
Plumpton. Cumb 8J 53
Plumpton. E Sus 4L 11
Plumpton. Nptn 7C 28
Plumpton Foot. Cumb 8J 53
Plumpton Green. E Sus 4L 11
Plumpton Head. Cumb 8K 53
Plumstead. G Lon 6M 21
Plumstead. Norf 6H 39
Plumtree. Notts 6D 36
Plumtree Park. Notts 6D 36
Plungar. Leics 6E 36
Plush. Dors 5F 8
Plushabridge. Corn 8C 6
Plwmp. Cdgn 1K 15
**Plymouth**. Plym 115 (6G 5)
Plympton. Plym 6H 5
Plymstock. Plym 6H 5
Plymtree. Devn 5K 7
Pockley. N Yor 7D 48
Pocklington. E Yor 3F 42
Pode Hole. Linc 7K 37
Podimore. Som 3D 8
Podington. Bed 5G 29
Podmore. Staf 6F 34
Poffley End. Oxon 2A 20
Point Clear. Essx 2G 23
Pointon. Linc 6J 37
Pokesdown. Bour 6K 9
Polbae. Dum 4H 51
Polbain. High 3M 77
Polbathic. Corn 6F 4
Polbeth. W Lot 3J 59
Polbrock. Corn 5C 4
Polchar. High 5J 71
Polebrook. Nptn 3H 29
Pole Elm. Worc 7G 27
Polegate. E Sus 5B 12
Pole Moor. W Yor 6J 41
Poles. High 4H 79
Polesworth. Warw 1L 27
Polglass. High 3M 77
Polgooth. Corn 6B 4
Poling. W Sus 5H 11
Poling Corner. W Sus 5H 11
Polio. High 6H 79
Polkerris. Corn 6C 4
Polla. High 6F 84
Pollard Street. Norf 6K 39
Pollicott. Buck 2E 20
Pollington. E Yor 6D 42
Polloch. High 1B 64
Pollok. Glas 3D 58
Pollokshaws. Glas 3D 58
Pollokshields. Glas 3D 58
Polmaily. High 2E 70
Polmassick. Corn 7B 4
**Polmont**. Falk 2H 59
Polnessan. E Ayr 8C 58
Polnish. High 7J 69
Polperro. Corn 6E 4
Polruan. Corn 6D 4
Polscoe. Corn 5D 4
Polsham. Som 1D 8
Polskeoch. Dum 1A 52
Polstead. Suff 8F 30
Polstead Heath. Suff 7F 30
Poltesco. Corn 7L 3
Poltimore. Devn 6J 7
Polton. Midl 3L 59
Polwarth. Bord 4E 60
Polyphant. Corn 7B 6
Polzeath. Corn 4B 4
Pomeroy. M Ulst 5E 92
Ponde. Powy 1L 17
Pondersbridge. Cambs 2K 29
Ponders End. G Lon 4L 21
Pond Street. Essx 8A 30
Pondtail. Hants 8F 20
Ponsanooth. Corn 5L 3
Ponsongath. Corn 7L 3
Ponsworthy. Devn 8G 7
Pontamman. Carm 3F 16
Pontantwn. Carm 5L 15
**Pontardawe**. Neat 4G 17
Pontarddulais. Swan 4E 16
Pontarfynach. Cdgn 5G 25
Pont-ar-gothi. Carm 4M 15
Pont ar Hydfer. Powy 2H 17
Pontarllechau. Carm 2G 17
Pontarsais. Carm 4L 15
Pontblyddyn. Flin 3A 34
Pontbren Llwyd. Rhon 4J 17
Pont-Cyfyng. Cnwy 5G 33
Pontdolgoch. Powy 3K 25
**Pontefract**. W Yor 5B 42
**Ponteland**. Nmbd 4E 54
Ponterwyd. Cdgn 4G 25
Pontesbury. Shrp 1C 26
Pontesford. Shrp 1C 26
Pontfadog. Wrex 7M 33
Pont-Faen. Shrp 6A 34
Pont-faen. Powy 1J 17
Pontfaen. Pemb 3G 15
Pontgarreg. Cdgn 1K 15
Pont-Henri. Carm 6L 15
Ponthir. Torf 4B 18
Ponthirwaun. Cdgn 2J 15
Pont-iets. Carm 6L 15
Pontllanfraith. Cphy 5L 17
Pontlliw. Swan 4F 16
Pont Llogel. Powy 1K 25
Pontllyfni. Gwyn 5D 32
Pontlottyn. Cphy 4L 17
Pontneddfechan. Powy 4J 17
Pont-newydd. Carm 6L 15
Pont-newydd. Flin 4L 33
Pontnewydd. Torf 4A 18
Ponton. Shet 2D 90
Pont Pen-y-benglog. Gwyn 4F 32
Pontrhydfendigaid. Cdgn 6G 25
Pont Rhyd-y-cyff. B'end 6H 17
Pontrhydyfen. Neat 5G 17
Pont-rhyd-y-groes. Cdgn 5G 25
Pontrhydyrun. Torf 4A 18
Pont-Rhythallt. Gwyn 4E 32
Pontrilas. Here 1B 18
Pontrilas Road. Here 1B 18
Pontrobert. Powy 1L 25
Pont-rug. Gwyn 4E 32
Ponts Green. E Sus 4C 12
Pontshill. Here 1E 18
Pont-Sian. Cdgn 2L 15
Pontsticill. Mer T 3K 17
Pont-Walby. Neat 4H 17
Pontwelly. Carm 3L 15
Pontwgan. Cnwy 3G 33
Pontyates. Carm 6L 15
Pontyberem. Carm 5M 15
Pontybodkin. Flin 4A 34
Pontyclun. Rhon 6K 17
Pontycymer. B'end 5J 17
Pontyglazier. Pemb 3H 15
Pontygwaith. Rhon 5K 17
Pont-y-pant. Cnwy 5G 33
**Pontypool**. Torf 4A 18
**Pontypridd**. Rhon 6K 17
**Pontypwl**. Torf 4A 18
Pontywaun. Cphy 5M 17
Pooksgreen. Hants 4A 10
Pool. Corn 4K 3
Pool. W Yor 3L 41
Poole. N Yor 5B 42
**Poole**. Pool 118 (6J 9)
Poole. Som 3L 7
Poole Keynes. Glos 4H 19
Poolend. Staf 4H 35
Poolewe. High 5K 77
Pooley Bridge. Cumb 3C 46
Poolfold. Staf 4G 35
Pool Head. Here 6D 26
Pool Hey. Lanc 6B 40
Poolhill. Glos 1F 18
Poolmill. Here 1D 18
Pool o' Muckhart. Clac 7D 66
Pool Quay. Powy 8A 34
Poolsbrook. Derbs 2B 36
Pool Street. Essx 8D 30
Pootings. Kent 1A 12
Pope Hill. Pemb 5F 14
Pope's Hill. Glos 2E 18
Popeswood. Brac 7F 20
Popham. Hants 1C 10
**Poplar**. G Lon 5L 21
Popley. Hants 8D 20
Porchfield. IOW 6B 10
Porin. High 8D 78
Poringland. Norf 1J 31
Porkellis. Corn 5K 3
Porlock. Som 1H 7
Porlock Weir. Som 1H 7
Portachoillan. Arg 4G 57
Port Adhair Bheinn na Faoghla. W Isl 8J 75
Port Adhair Thirlodh. Arg 3F 62
**Portadown**. Arm 6G 93
Portaferry. Ards 6J 93
Port Ann. Arg 1J 57
Port Appin. Arg 3D 64
Port Asgaig. Arg 3D 56
Port Askaig. Arg 3D 56
Portavadie. Arg 3J 57
Portavogie. Ards 5K 93
Portballintrae. Caus 1F 93
Port Bannatyne. Arg 3K 57
Portbury. N Som 6D 18
Port Carlisle. Cumb 5G 53
Port Charlotte. Arg 4B 56
Portchester. Hants 5D 10
Port Clarence. Stoc T 3B 48
Port Driseach. Arg 2J 57
Port Dundas. Glas 3D 58
Port Ellen. Arg 5C 56
Port Elphinstone. Abers 3G 73
Portencalzie. Dum 4F 50
Portencross. N Ayr 5L 57
Port Erin. IOM 8A 44
Port Erroll. Abers 2K 73
Porter's Fen Corner. Norf 1B 30
Portesham. Dors 7E 8
Portessie. Mor 7D 80
Port e Vullen. IOM 5D 44
Port-Eynon. Swan 8L 15
Portfield. Som 3C 8
Portfield Gate. Pemb 5F 14
Portgate. Devn 7D 6
Port Gaverne. Corn 3C 4
**Port Glasgow**. Inv 2B 58
Portglenone. ME Ant 3F 93
Portgordon. Mor 7C 80
Portgower. High 2L 79
Porth. Corn 2M 3
Porth. Rhon 5K 17
Porthaethwy. IOA 3E 32
Porthallow. Corn
nr. Looe 6E 4
nr. St Keverne 6L 3
**Porthcawl**. B'end 7H 17
Porthceri. V Glam 8K 17
Porthcothan. Corn 4A 4
Porthcurno. Corn 6G 3
Port Henderson. High 6J 77
Porthgain. Pemb 3E 14
Porthgwarra. Corn 6G 3
Porthill. Shrp 8C 34
Porthkerry. V Glam 8K 17
Porthleven. Corn 6K 3
Porthllechog. IOA 1D 32
Porthmadog. Gwyn 7E 32
Porthmeor. Corn 5H 3
Porth Navas. Corn 6L 3
Portholland. Corn 7B 4
Porthoustock. Corn 6M 3
Porthtowan. Corn 4K 3
Porth Tywyn. Carm 6L 15
Porth-y-felin. IOA 2B 32
Porthyrhyd. Carm
nr. Carmarthen 5M 15
nr. Llandovery 1G 17
Porth-y-waen. Shrp 7A 34
Portincaple. Arg 8G 65
Portington. E Yor 4E 42
Portinnisherrich. Arg 6D 64
Portinscale. Cumb 3A 46
Port Isaac. Corn 3B 4
**Portishead**. N Som 6C 18
Portknockie. Mor 7D 80
Port Lamont. Arg 2K 57
Portlethen. Abers 6J 73
Portlethen Village. Abers 6J 73
Portling. Dum 6C 52
Port Lion. Pemb 6F 14
Portloe. Corn 8B 4
Port Logan. Dum 7F 50
Portmahomack. High 5K 79
Portmead. Swan 5F 16
Portmeirion. Gwyn 7E 32
Portmellon. Corn 7C 4
Port Mholair. W Isl 8J 83
Port Mor. High 8F 68
Portmore. Hants 6M 9
Port Mulgrave. N Yor 4E 48
Portnacroish. Arg 3D 64
Portnahaven. Arg 4A 56
Portnalong. High 2E 68
Portnaluchaig. High 7H 69
Portnancon. High 5G 85
Port Nan Giuran. W Isl 8J 83
Port nan Long. W Isl 6K 75
Port Nis. W Isl 5J 83
Portobello. Edin 2M 59
Portobello. W Yor 6M 41
Port of Menteith. Stir 7K 65
Porton. Wilts 2K 9
Portormin. High 1A 80
Portpatrick. Dum 6F 50
Port Quin. Corn 3B 4
Port Ramsay. Arg 3C 64
Portreath. Corn 4K 3
Portree. High 1F 68
Port Righ. High 1F 68
Portrush. Caus 2F 93
Port St Mary. IOM 8B 44
Portscatho. Corn 8A 4
Portsea. Port 5D 10
Port Seton. E Lot 2B 60
Portskerra. High 5L 85
Portskewett. Mon 5D 18
**Portslade-by-Sea**. Brig 5K 11
**Portsmouth**. Port 115 (5D 10)
Portsmouth. W Yor 5H 41
Port Soderick. IOM 7C 44
Port Solent. Port 5D 10
Portsonachan. Arg 5E 64
Portsoy. Abers 7E 80
Portstewart. Caus 2F 93
Port Sunlight. Mers 1B 34
Portswood. Sotn 4B 10
**Port Talbot**. Neat 6G 17
Porttannachy. Mor 7C 80
Port Tennant. Swan 5F 16
Portuairk. High 1K 63
Portway. Here 7C 26
Portway. Worc 4J 27
Port Wemyss. Arg 4A 56
Port William. Dum 7J 51
Portwrinkle. Corn 6F 4
Poslingford. Suff 7D 30
Postbridge. Devn 8F 6
Postcombe. Oxon 4E 20
Post Green. Dors 6H 9
Postling. Kent 2H 13
Postlip. Glos 1J 19
Post-Mawr. Cdgn 1L 15
Postwick. Norf 1J 31
Potarch. Abers 6F 72
Potsgrove. C Beds 1G 21
Potten End. Herts 3H 21
Potter Brompton. N Yor 8G 49
Pottergate Street. Norf 2H 31
Potterhanworth. Linc 3H 37
Potterhanworth Booths. Linc 3H 37
Potter Heigham. Norf 8L 39
Potter Hill. Leics 7E 36
**The Potteries**. Stoke 5G 35
Potterne. Wilts 8H 19
Potterne Wick. Wilts 8J 19
Potternewton. W Yor 4M 41
**Potters Bar**. Herts 3K 21
Potters Brook. Lanc 2C 40
Potter's Cross. Staf 3G 27
Potters Crouch. Herts 3J 21
Potter Somersal. Derbs 6K 35
Potterspury. Nptn 7E 28
Potter Street. Essx 3A 22
Potterton. Abers 4J 73
Potthorpe. Norf 7F 38
Pottle Street. Wilts 1G 9
Potto. N Yor 5B 48
Potton. C Beds 7K 29
Pott Row. Norf 7D 38
Pott Shrigley. Ches E 2H 35
Poughill. Corn 5B 6
Poughill. Devn 5H 7
Poulner. Hants 5K 9
Poulshot. Wilts 8H 19
Poulton. Glos 3K 19
**Poulton-le-Fylde**. Lanc 4B 40
Pound Bank. Worc 4F 26
Poundbury. Dors 6E 8
Poundfield. E Sus 2B 12
Poundgate. E Sus 3A 12
Pound Green. E Sus 3B 12
Pound Green. Suff 6D 30
Pound Hill. W Sus 2K 11

Poundland. S Ayr 3G 51
Poundon. Buck 1D 20
Poundsgate. Devn 8G 7
Poundstock. Corn 6B 6
Pound Street. Hants 7B 20
Pounsley. E Sus 3B 12
Powburn. Nmbd 8H 61
Powderham. Devn 7J 7
Powerstock. Dors 6D 8
Powfoot. Dum 5F 52
Powick. Worc 6G 27
Powmill. Per 8D 66
Poxwell. Dors 7F 8
Poyle. Slo 6H 21
Poynings. W Sus 4K 11
Poyntington. Dors 3E 8
**Poynton**. Ches E 1H 35
Poynton. Telf 8D 34
Poynton Green. Telf 8D 34
Poyntz Pass. Arm 7G 93
Poystreet Green. Suff 6F 30
Praa Sands. Corn 6J 3
Pratt's Bottom. G Lon 7A 22
Praze-an-Beeble. Corn 5K 3
Prees. Shrp 6D 34
Preesall. Lanc 3B 40
Preesall Park. Lanc 3B 40
Prees Green. Shrp 6D 34
Prees Higher Heath. Shrp 6D 34
Prendergast. Pemb 5F 14
Prendwick. Nmbd 8H 61
Pren-gwyn. Cdgn 2L 15
Prenteg. Gwyn 6E 32
Prenton. Mers 1B 34
**Prescot**. Mers 8C 40
Prescott. Devn 4K 7
Prescott. Shrp 7C 34
Preshute. Wilts 7K 19
Pressen. Nmbd 6F 60
**Prestatyn**. Den 2K 33
Prestbury. Ches E 2H 35
Prestbury. Glos 1H 19
Presteigne. Powy 5B 26
Presthope. Shrp 2D 26
Prestleigh. Som 1E 8
Preston. Brig 5L 11
Preston. Devn 8H 7
Preston. Dors 7F 8
Preston. E Lot
 nr. East Linton 2C 60
 nr. Prestonpans 2A 60
Preston. E Yor 4J 43
Preston. Glos 3J 19
Preston. Herts 1J 21
Preston. Kent
 nr. Canterbury 7J 23
 nr. Faversham 7G 23
**Preston**. Lanc 115 (5D 40)
Preston. Nmbd 7J 61
Preston. Rut 1F 28
Preston. Bord 4E 60
Preston. Shrp 8D 34
Preston. Suff 6F 30
Preston. Wilts
 nr. Aldbourne 6L 19
 nr. Lyneham 6J 19
Preston Bagot. Warw 5K 27
Preston Bissett. Buck 1D 20
Preston Bowyer. Som 3L 7
Preston Brockhurst. Shrp 7D 34
Preston Brook. Hal 1D 34
Preston Candover. Hants 1D 10
Preston Capes. Nptn 6C 28
Preston Cross. Glos 8E 26
Preston Gubbals. Shrp 8C 34
Preston-le-Skerne. Dur 3M 47
Preston Marsh. Here 7D 26
Prestonmill. Dum 6D 52
Preston on Stour. Warw 7L 27
Preston on the Hill. Hal 1D 34
Preston on Wye. Here 7B 26
Prestonpans. E Lot 2A 60
Preston Plucknett. Som 4D 8
Preston-under-Scar. N Yor 6J 47
Preston upon the Weald Moors.
 Telf 8E 34
Preston Wynne. Here 7D 26
**Prestwich**. G Man 7G 41
Prestwick. Nmbd 4E 54
**Prestwick**. S Ayr 7B 58
Prestwold. Leics 7C 36
Prestwood. Buck 3F 20
Prestwood. Staf 5K 35
Price Town. B'end 5J 17
Prickwillow. Cambs 3B 30
Priddy. Som 8D 18
Priestcliffe. Derbs 2K 35
Priesthill. Glas 3D 58
Priest Hutton. Lanc 8D 46
Priestland. E Ayr 6D 58
Priest Weston. Shrp 2A 26
Priestwood. Brac 6F 20
Priestwood. Kent 7C 22
Primethorpe. Leics 2C 28
Primrose Green. Norf 8G 39
Primrose Hill. Glos 3E 18
Primrose Hill. Lanc 7B 40
Primrose Valley. N Yor 8J 49
Primsidemill. Bord 7F 60
Princes Gate. Pemb 5H 15
Princes Risborough. Buck 3F 20
Princethorpe. Warw 4B 28
Princetown. Devn 8E 6
Prinsted. W Sus 5E 10
Prion. Den 4K 33
Prior Muir. Fife 6J 67
Prior's Frome. Here 8D 26
Priors Halton. Shrp 4C 26
Priors Hardwick. Warw 6B 28
Priorslee. Telf 8F 34
Priors Marston. Warw 6B 28
Prior's Norton. Glos 1G 19
The Priory. W Ber 7M 19
Priory Wood. Here 7A 26
Priston. Bath 7E 18
Pristow Green. Norf 3H 31
Prittlewell. S'end 5E 22
Privett. Hants 3D 10
Prixford. Devn 2E 6
Probus. Corn 7A 4
Prospect. Cumb 7F 52
Prospect Village. Staf 8J 35
Provanmill. Glas 3E 58
**Prudhoe**. Nmbd 5D 54
Publow. Bath 7E 18
Puckeridge. Herts 1L 21
Puckington. Som 4B 8
Pucklechurch. S Glo 6E 18
Puckrup. Glos 8G 27
Puddinglake. Ches W 3F 34
Puddington. Ches W 2B 34
Puddington. Devn 4H 7
Puddlebrook. Glos 2E 18
Puddledock. Norf 2G 31
Puddletown. Dors 6F 8
Pudleston. Here 6D 26
**Pudsey**. W Yor 4L 41
Pulborough. W Sus 4H 11
Puleston. Telf 7F 34
Pulford. Ches W 4B 34
Pulham. Dors 5F 8
Pulham Market. Norf 3H 31
Pulham St Mary. Norf 3J 31
Pulley. Shrp 1C 26
Pulloxhill. C Beds 8H 29
Pulpit Hill. Arg 5C 64
Pulverbatch. Shrp 1C 26
Pumpherston. W Lot 3J 59
Pumsaint. Carm 8F 24
Puncheston. Pemb 4G 15
Puncknowle. Dors 7D 8
Punnett's Town. E Sus 3C 12
Purbrook. Hants 5D 10
Purfleet-on-Thames. Thur 6B 22
Puriton. Som 1B 8
Purleigh. Essx 3E 22
**Purley**. G Lon 7L 21
Purley on Thames. W Ber 6D 20
Purlogue. Shrp 4A 26
Purl's Bridge. Cambs 3A 30
Purse Caundle. Dors 4E 8
Purslow. Shrp 3B 26
Purston Jaglin. W Yor 6B 42
Purtington. Som 5B 8
Purton. Glos
 nr. Lydney 3E 18
 nr. Sharpness 3E 18
Purton. Wilts 5J 19
Purton Stoke. Wilts 4J 19
Pury End. Nptn 7E 28
Pusey. Oxon 4A 20
Putley. Here 8E 26
**Putney**. G Lon 6K 21
Putsborough. Devn 1D 6
Puttenham. Herts 2F 20
Puttenham. Surr 1G 11
Puttock End. Essx 7E 30
Puttock's End. Essx 2B 22
Puxey. Dors 4F 8
Puxton. N Som 7C 18
Pwll. Carm 6L 15
Pwll. Powy 2L 25
Pwllcrochan. Pemb 6F 14
Pwll-glas. Den 5L 33
Pwllgloyw. Powy 1K 17
Pwllheli. Gwyn 7C 32
Pwllmeyric. Mon 4D 18
Pwlltrap. Carm 5J 15
Pwll-y-glaw. Neat 5G 17
Pyecombe. W Sus 4K 11
Pye Corner. Herts 2M 21
Pye Corner. Newp 5B 18
Pye Green. Staf 8H 35
Pyewipe. NE Lin 6K 43
**Pyle**. B'end 6H 17
Pyle. IOW 8B 10
Pyle Hill. Surr 8G 21
Pylle. Som 2E 8
Pymoor. Cambs 3A 30
Pymore. Dors 6C 8
Pyrford. Surr 8H 21
Pyrford Village. Surr 8H 21
Pyrton. Oxon 4D 20
Pytchley. Nptn 4F 28
Pyworthy. Devn 5C 6

## Q

Quabbs. Shrp 4M 25
Quadring. Linc 6K 37
Quadring Eaudike. Linc 6K 37
Quainton. Buck 1E 20
Quaking Houses. Dur 6E 54
Quarley. Hants 1L 9
Quarndon. Derbs 5M 35
Quarrendon. Buck 2F 20
Quarrier's Village. Inv 3B 58
Quarrington. Linc 5H 37
Quarrington Hill. Dur 8G 55
The Quarry. Glos 4F 18
Quarry Bank. W Mid 3H 27
Quarrywood. Mor 7A 80
Quartalehouse. Abers 1J 73
Quarter. N Ayr 3L 57
Quarter. S Lan 4F 58
Quatford. Shrp 2F 26
Quatt. Shrp 3F 26
Quebec. Dur 7E 54
Quedgeley. Glos 2G 19
Queen Adelaide. Cambs 3B 30
Queenborough. Kent 6F 22
Queen Camel. Som 3D 8
Queen Charlton. Bath 7E 18
Queen Dart. Devn 4H 7
Queenhill. Worc 8G 27
Queen Oak. Dors 2F 8
Queensbury. W Yor 4K 41
Queensferry. Flin 3B 34
**Queensferry Crossing**. Edin 2K 59
Queenstown. Bkpl 4B 40
Queen Street. Kent 1C 12
Queenzieburn. N Lan 2E 58
Quemerford. Wilts 7J 19
Quendale. Shet 6D 90
Quendon. Essx 8B 30
Queniborough. Leics 8D 36
Quenington. Glos 3K 19
Quernmore. Lanc 1D 40
Quethiock. Corn 5F 4
Quholm. Orkn 8B 88
Quick's Green. W Ber 6C 20
Quidenham. Norf 3G 31
Quidhampton. Hants 8C 20
Quidhampton. Wilts 2K 9
Quilquox. Abers 2J 73
Quina Brook. Shrp 6D 34
Quindry. Orkn 2F 86
Quine's Hill. IOM 7C 44
Quinton. Nptn 6E 28
Quinton. W Mid 3H 27
Quintrell Downs. Corn 2M 3
Quixhill. Staf 5K 35
Quoditch. Devn 6D 6
Quorn. Leics 8C 36
Quorndon. Leics 8C 36
Quothquan. S Lan 6H 59
Quoyloo. Orkn 7B 88
Quoyness. Orkn 1D 86
Quoys. Shet
 on Mainland 1E 90
 on Unst 2L 91

## R

Rableyheath. Herts 2K 21
Raby. Cumb 6F 52
Raby. Mers 2B 34
Rachan Mill. Bord 6K 59
Rachub. Gwyn 4F 32
Rack End. Oxon 3B 20
Rackenford. Devn 4H 7
Rackham. W Sus 4H 11
Rackheath. Norf 8J 39
Racks. Dum 4E 52
Rackwick. Orkn
 on Hoy 2D 86
 on Westray 5D 88
Radbourne. Derbs 6L 35
**Radcliffe**. G Man 7F 40
Radcliffe. Nmbd 1F 54
Radcliffe on Trent. Notts 6D 36
Radclive. Buck 8D 28
Radernie. Fife 7H 67
Radfall. Kent 7H 23
Radford. Bath 8E 18
Radford. Nott 5C 36
Radford. Oxon 1B 20
Radford. W Mid 3M 27
Radford. Worc 6J 27
Radford Semele. Warw 5M 27
Radipole. Dors 7E 8
Radlett. Herts 4J 21
Radley. Oxon 4C 20
Radnage. Buck 4E 20
**Radstock**. Bath 8E 18
Radstone. Nptn 7C 28
Radway. Warw 7A 28
Radway Green. Ches E 4F 34
Radwell. Bed 6H 29
Radwell. Herts 8K 29
Radwinter. Essx 8C 30
Radyr. Card 6L 17
RAF Coltishall. Norf 7J 39
Rafford. Mor 8L 79
Raffrey. New M 6J 93
Ragdale. Leics 8D 36
Ragdon. Shrp 2C 26
Ragged Appleshaw. Hants 1M 9
Raggra. High 7E 86
Raglan. Mon 3C 18
Ragnall. Notts 2F 36
Raholp. New M 6J 93
Raigbeg. High 3J 71
Rainford. Mers 7C 40
Rainford Junction. Mers 7C 40
**Rainham**. G Lon 5B 22
Rainham. Medw 7E 22
Rainhill. Mers 8C 40
Rainow. Ches E 2H 35
Rainton. N Yor 8A 48
Rainworth. Notts 4C 36
Raisbeck. Cumb 5E 46
Raise. Cumb 7M 53
Rait. Per 5F 66
Raithby. Linc 1L 37
Raithby by Spilsby. Linc 3L 37
Raithwaite. N Yor 4F 48
Rake. W Sus 3F 10
Rake End. Staf 8J 35
Rakeway. Staf 5J 35
Rakewood. G Man 6H 41
Ralia. High 6H 71
Ram Alley. Wilts 7L 19
Ramasaig. High 1C 68
Rame. Corn
 nr. Millbrook 7G 5
 nr. Penryn 5L 3
Ram Lane. Kent 1F 12
Ramnageo. Shet 3L 91
Rampisham. Dors 5D 8
Rampside. Cumb 8M 45
Rampton. Cambs 5M 29
Rampton. Notts 2E 36
**Ramsbottom**. G Man 6F 40
Ramsburn. Mor 8E 80
Ramsbury. Wilts 6L 19
Ramscraigs. High 1M 79
Ramsdean. Hants 3E 10
Ramsdell. Hants 8C 20
Ramsden. Oxon 2A 20
Ramsden. Worc 7H 27
Ramsden Bellhouse. Essx 4D 22
Ramsden Heath. Essx 4D 22
Ramsey. Cambs 3K 29
Ramsey. Essx 8J 31
Ramsey. IOM 5D 44
Ramsey Forty Foot. Cambs 3L 29
Ramsey Heights. Cambs 3K 29
Ramsey Island. Essx 3F 22
Ramsey Mereside. Cambs 3K 29
Ramsey St Mary's. Cambs 3K 29
**Ramsgate**. Kent 7K 23
Ramsgill. N Yor 8K 47
Ramshaw. Dur 7C 54
Ramshorn. Staf 5J 35
Ramsley. Devn 6F 6
Ramsnest Common. Surr 2G 11
Ramstone. Abers 4F 72
Ranais. W Isl 1F 76
Ranby. Linc 2K 37
Ranby. Notts 1D 36
Rand. Linc 2J 37
Randalstown. Ant 4G 93
Randwick. Glos 3G 19
Ranfurly. Ren 3B 58
Rangag. High 7C 86
Rangemore. Staf 7K 35
Rangeworthy. S Glo 5E 18
Rankinston. E Ayr 8C 58
Rank's Green. Essx 2D 22
Ranmore Common. Surr 8J 21
Rannoch Station. Per 2J 65
Ranochan. High 7K 69
Ranskill. Notts 1D 36
Ranton. Staf 7G 35
Ranton Green. Staf 7G 35
Ranworth. Norf 8K 39
Raploch. Stir 8A 66
Rapness. Orkn 5E 88
Rapps. Som 4B 8
Rascal Moor. E Yor 4F 42
Rascarrel. Dum 7B 52
Rasharkin. Caus 3F 93
Rashfield. Arg 1L 57
Rashwood. Worc 5H 27
Raskelf. N Yor 8B 48
Rassau. Blae 3L 17
Rastrick. W Yor 5K 41
Ratagan. High 4L 69
Ratby. Leics 1C 28
Ratcliffe Culey. Leics 2M 27
Ratcliffe on Soar. Notts 7B 36
Ratcliffe on the Wreake.
 Leics 8D 36
Rathen. Abers 7K 81
Rathfriland. Arm 7G 93
Rathillet. Fife 5G 67
Rathmell. N Yor 1G 41
Ratho. Edin 2K 59
Ratho Station. Edin 2K 59
Rathven. Mor 7D 80
Ratley. Hants 3M 9
Ratley. Warw 7A 28
Ratlinghope. Shrp 2C 26
Rattar. High 4D 86
Ratten Row. Cumb 7H 53
Ratten Row. Lanc 3C 40
Rattery. Devn 5K 5
Rattlesden. Suff 6F 30
Ratton Village. E Sus 5B 12
Rattray. Abers 8K 81
Rattray. Per 3E 66
Raughton. Cumb 7H 53
Raughton Head. Cumb 7H 53
Raunds. Nptn 4G 29
Ravenfield. S Yor 8B 42
Ravenfield Common. S Yor 8B 42
Ravenglass. Cumb 5K 45
Ravenhills Green. Worc 6F 26
Raveningham. Norf 2K 31
Ravenscar. N Yor 5G 49
Ravensdale. IOM 5C 44
Ravensden. Bed 6H 29
Ravenseat. N Yor 5G 47
Ravenshead. Notts 4C 36
Ravensmoor. Ches E 4E 34
Ravensthorpe. Nptn 4D 28
Ravensthorpe. W Yor 5L 41
Ravenstone. Leics 8B 36
Ravenstone. Mil 6F 28
Ravenstonedale. Cumb 5F 46
Ravenstown. Cumb 8B 46
Ravenstruther. S Lan 5H 59
Ravensworth. N Yor 5K 47
Ravernet. Lis 5H 93
Raw. N Yor 5G 49
Rawcliffe. E Yor 5D 42
Rawcliffe. York 2C 42
Rawcliffe Bridge. E Yor 5D 42
Rawdon. W Yor 4L 41
Rawgreen. Nmbd 6C 54
**Rawmarsh**. S Yor 8B 42
Rawnsley. Staf 8J 35
Rawreth. Essx 4D 22
Rawridge. Devn 5M 7
Rawson Green. Derbs 5A 36
**Rawtenstall**. Lanc 5G 41
Raydon. Suff 8G 31
Raylees. Nmbd 2C 54
**Rayleigh**. Essx 4E 22
Raymond's Hill. Devn 6B 8
Rayne. Essx 1D 22
Rayners Lane. G Lon 5J 21
Reach. Cambs 5B 30
Read. Lanc 4F 40
**Reading**. Read 115 (6E 20)
Reading Green. Suff 4H 31
Reading Street. Kent 2F 12
Readymoney. Corn 6D 4
Reagill. Cumb 4E 46
Rearquhar. High 4H 79
Rearsby. Leics 8D 36
Reasby. Linc 2H 37
Reaseheath. Ches E 4E 34
Reaster. High 5D 86
Reawick. Shet 3D 90
Reay. High 5A 86
Rechullin. High 8K 77
Reculver. Kent 7J 23
Redberth. Pemb 6G 15
Redbourn. Herts 2J 21
Redbourne. N Lin 7G 43
Redbrook. Glos 3D 18
Redbrook. Wrex 5D 34
Redburn. High 1K 71
Redburn. Nmbd 5A 54
**Redcar**. Red C 3D 48
Redcastle. High 1F 70
Redcliffe Bay. N Som 6C 18
Red Dial. Cumb 7G 53
Redding. Falk 2H 59
Reddingmuirhead. Falk 2H 59
The Reddings. Glos 1H 19
Reddish. G Man 8G 41
**Redditch**. Worc 5J 27
Rede. Suff 6E 30
Redenhall. Norf 3J 31
Redesdale Camp. Nmbd 2B 54
Redesmouth. Nmbd 3B 54
Redford. Ang 3J 67
Redford. Dur 8D 54
Redford. W Sus 3F 10
Redfordgreen. Bord 8A 60
Redgate. Corn 5E 4
Redgrave. Suff 4G 31
Red Hill. Warw 6K 27
Red Hill. W Yor 5B 42
Redhill. Abers 5G 73
Redhill. Herts 8K 29
Redhill. N Som 7D 18
Redhill. Shrp 8F 34
**Redhill**. Surr 8K 21
Redhouses. Arg 3C 56
Redisham. Suff 3L 31
Redland. Bris 6D 18
Redland. Orkn 7C 88
Redlingfield. Suff 4H 31
Red Lodge. Suff 4C 30
Redlynch. Som 2F 8
Redlynch. Wilts 3L 9
Redmain. Cumb 8F 52
Redmarley. Worc 5F 26
Redmarley D'Abitot. Glos 8F 26
Redmarshall. Stoc T 3A 48
Redmile. Leics 6E 36
Redmire. N Yor 6J 47
Rednal. Shrp 7B 34
Redpath. Bord 6C 60
Redpoint. High 7J 77
Red Post. Corn 5B 6
Red Rock. G Man 7D 40
Red Roses. Carm 5J 15
Red Row. Nmbd 2F 54
**Redruth**. Corn 4L 3
Red Street. Staf 4G 35
Redvales. G Man 7G 41
Red Wharf Bay. IOA 2E 32
Redwick. Newp 5C 18
Redwick. S Glo 5D 18
Redworth. Darl 3L 47
Reed. Herts 8L 29
Reed End. Herts 8L 29
Reedham. Linc 4K 37
Reedham. Norf 1L 31
Reedness. E Yor 5F 42
Reeds Beck. Linc 3K 37
Reemshill. Abers 1G 73
Reepham. Linc 2H 37
Reepham. Norf 7G 39
Reeth. N Yor 6J 47
Regaby. IOM 5D 44
Regil. N Som 7D 18
Regoul. High 8J 79
Reiff. High 2L 77
**Reigate**. Surr 8K 21
Reighton. N Yor 8J 49
Reilth. Shrp 3A 26
Reinigeadal. W Isl 3D 76
Reisque. Abers 4H 73
Reiss. High 6E 86
Rejerrah. Corn 3L 3
Releath. Corn 5K 3
Relubbus. Corn 5J 3
Relugas. Mor 1K 71
Remenham. Wok 5E 20
Remenham Hill. Wok 5E 20
Rempstone. Notts 7C 36
Rendcomb. Glos 3J 19
Rendham. Suff 5K 31
Rendlesham. Suff 6K 31
**Renfrew**. Ren 3D 58
Renhold. Bed 6H 29
Renishaw. Derbs 2B 36
Rennington. Nmbd 8K 61
Renton. W Dun 2B 58
Renwick. Cumb 7K 53
Repps. Norf 8L 39
Repton. Derbs 7M 35
Rescassa. Corn 7B 4
Rescobie. Ang 2J 67
Rescorla. Corn
 nr. Penwithick 6C 4
 nr. Sticker 7B 4
Resipole. High 1B 64
Resolfen. Neat 4H 17
Resolis. High 7G 79
Resolven. Neat 4H 17
Rest and be thankful. Arg 7G 65
Reston. Bord 3F 60
Restrop. Wilts 5J 19
**Retford**. Notts 1E 36
Retire. Corn 5C 4
Rettendon. Essx 4D 22
Revesby. Linc 3K 37
Rew. Devn 8K 5
Rewe. Devn 6J 7
Rew Street. IOW 6B 10
Rexon. Devn 7D 6
Reybridge. Wilts 7H 19
Reydon. Suff 4M 31
Reymerston. Norf 1G 31
Reynalton. Pemb 6G 15
Reynoldston. Swan 8L 15
Rezare. Corn 8C 6
Rhadyr. Mon 3B 18
Rhaeadr Gwy. Powy 6J 25
Rhandirmwyn. Carm 8G 25
Rhayader. Powy 6J 25
Rheindown. High 1F 70
Rhemore. High 2L 63
Rhenetra. High 8F 76
Rhewl. Den
 nr. Llangollen 6L 33
 nr. Ruthin 4L 33
Rhewl. Shrp 6B 34
Rhewl-Mostyn. Flin 2L 33
Rhian. High 2F 78
Rhian Breck. High 3F 78
Rhicarn. High 1A 78
Rhiconich. High 6E 84
Rhicullen. High 6G 79
Rhidorroch. High 4B 78
Rhifail. High 7K 85
Rhigos. Rhon 4J 17
Rhilochan. High 3H 79
Rhiroy. High 5B 78
Rhitongue. High 6J 85
Rhiw. Gwyn 8B 32
Rhiwabon. Wrex 5B 34
Rhiwbina. Card 6L 17
Rhiwbryfdir. Gwyn 6F 32
Rhiwderin. Newp 5A 18
Rhiwlas. Gwyn
 nr. Bala 7J 33
 nr. Bangor 4E 32
Rhiwlas. Powy 7L 33
Rhodes. G Man 7G 41
Rhodesia. Notts 1C 36
Rhodes Minnis. Kent 1H 13
Rhodiad-y-Brenin. Pemb 4D 14
**Rhondda**. Rhon 5J 17
Rhonehouse. Dum 6B 52
Rhoose. V Glam 8K 17
Rhos. Carm 3K 15
Rhos. Neat 4G 17
The Rhos. Pemb 5G 15
Rhosaman. Carm 3G 17
Rhoscefnhir. IOA 3E 32
Rhoscolyn. IOA 3B 32
Rhos Common. Powy 8A 34
Rhoscrowther. Pemb 6F 14
Rhos-ddu. Gwyn 7B 32
Rhosdylluan. Gwyn 8H 33
Rhosesmor. Flin 4M 33
Rhos-fawr. Gwyn 7C 32
Rhosgadfan. Gwyn 5E 32
Rhosgoch. IOA 2D 32
Rhosgoch. Powy 8L 25
Rhos Haminiog. Cdgn 6E 24
Rhos-hill. Pemb 2H 15
Rhoshirwaun. Gwyn 8A 32
Rhoslan. Gwyn 6D 32
Rhoslefain. Gwyn 2E 24
**Rhosllanerchrugog**. Wrex 5A 34
Rhôs Lligwy. IOA 2D 32
Rhosmaen. Carm 2F 16
Rhosmeirch. IOA 3D 32
Rhosneigr. IOA 3C 32
Rhôs-on-Sea. Cnwy 2H 33
Rhossili. Swan 8L 15
Rhosson. Pemb 4D 14
Rhostrenwfa. IOA 3D 32
Rhostryfan. Gwyn 5D 32
Rhostyllen. Wrex 5B 34
Rhoswiel. Shrp 6A 34
Rhosybol. IOA 2D 32
Rhos-y-brithdir. Powy 8L 33
Rhos-y-garth. Cdgn 5F 24
Rhos-y-gwaliau. Gwyn 7J 33
Rhos-y-llan. Gwyn 7B 32
Rhos-y-meirch. Powy 5A 26
Rhu. Arg 1A 58
Rhuallt. Den 3K 33
Rhubha Stoer. High 8C 84
Rhubodach. Arg 2K 57
Rhuddall Heath. Ches W 3D 34
Rhuddlan. Cdgn 2L 15
Rhuddlan. Den 3K 33
Rhue. High 4A 78
Rhulen. Powy 8L 25
Rhunahaorine. Arg 5G 57
Rhuthun. Den 5L 33
Rhuvoult. High 6E 84
Y Rhws. V Glam 8K 17
Rhyd. Gwyn 6F 32
**Rhydaman**. Carm 3F 16
Rhydargaeau. Carm 4L 15
Rhydcymerau. Carm 1E 16
Rhydd. Worc 7G 27
Rhyd-Ddu. Gwyn 5E 32
Rhydding. Neat 5G 17
Rhydfudr. Cdgn 6E 24
Rhydlanfair. Cnwy 5H 33
Rhydlewis. Cdgn 2K 15
Rhydlios. Gwyn 7A 32
Rhydlydan. Cnwy 5H 33
Rhyd-meirionydd. Cdgn 4F 24
Rhydowen. Cdgn 2L 15
Rhyd-Rosser. Cdgn 6E 24
Rhydspence. Here 8M 25
Rhydtalog. Flin 5M 33
Rhyd-uchaf. Gwyn 7J 33
Rhydwyn. IOA 2C 32
Rhyd-y-clafdy. Gwyn 7C 32
Rhydycroesau. Powy 7M 33
Rhydyfelin. Cdgn 5E 24
Rhydyfelin. Rhon 6K 17
Rhyd-y-foel. Cnwy 3J 33
Rhyd-y-fro. Neat 4G 17
Rhydymain. Gwyn 8H 33
Rhyd-y-meudwy. Den 5L 33
Rhydymwyn. Flin 4M 33
Rhyd-yr-onen. Gwyn 2F 24
Rhyd-y-sarn. Gwyn 6F 32
**Rhyl**. Den 2K 33
Rhymney. Cphy 4L 17
Rhymni. Cphy 4L 17
Rhynd. Per 5E 66
Rhynie. Abers 3D 72
Ribbesford. Worc 4F 26
Ribbleton. Lanc 4D 40
Ribby. Lanc 4C 40
Ribchester. Lanc 4E 40
Riber. Derbs 4M 35
Ribigill. High 6H 85
Riby. Linc 7J 43
Riccall. N Yor 4D 42
Riccarton. E Ayr 6C 58
Richards Castle. Here 5C 26
Richborough Port. Kent 7K 23
Richhill. Arm 6F 93
Richings Park. Buck 6H 21
**Richmond**. G Lon 6J 21
Richmond. N Yor 5K 47
Rickarton. Abers 7H 73
Rickerby. Cumb 6J 53
Rickerscote. Staf 7H 35
Rickford. N Som 8C 18
Rickham. Devn 8K 5
Rickinghall. Suff 4G 31
Rickleton. Tyne 6F 54
Rickling. Essx 8A 30
Rickling Green. Essx 1B 22
**Rickmansworth**. Herts 4H 21
Riddings. Derbs 4B 36
Riddlecombe. Devn 4F 6
Riddlesden. W Yor 3J 41
Ridge. Dors 7H 9
Ridge. Herts 3K 21
Ridge. Wilts 2H 9
Ridgebourne. Powy 6K 25
Ridge Lane. Warw 2L 27
Ridgeway. Derbs
 nr. Alfreton 4A 36
 nr. Sheffield 1B 36
Ridgeway. Staf 4G 35
Ridgeway Cross. Here 7F 26
Ridgeway Moor. Derbs 1B 36
Ridgewell. Essx 7D 30
Ridgewood. E Sus 3A 12
Ridgmont. C Beds 8G 29
Ridgwardine. Shrp 6E 34
Riding Mill. Nmbd 5D 54
Ridley. Kent 7C 22
Ridley. Nmbd 5A 54
Ridlington. Norf 6K 39
Ridlington. Rut 1F 28
Ridsdale. Nmbd 3C 54
Riemore Lodge. Per 3D 66
Rievaulx. N Yor 7C 48
Rift House. Hart 8H 55
Rigg. Dum 5G 53
Riggend. N Lan 2F 58
Rigsby. Linc 2M 37
Rigside. S Lan 6G 59
Riley Green. Lanc 5E 40
Rileyhill. Staf 8K 35
Rilla Mill. Corn 8B 6
Rillington. N Yor 8F 48
Rimington. Lanc 3G 41
Rimpton. Som 3E 8
Rimsdale. High 7K 85
Rimswell. E Yor 5L 43
Ringasta. Shet 6D 90
Ringford. Dum 6A 52
Ringing Hill. Leics 8B 36
Ringinglow. S Yor 1L 35
Ringland. Norf 8H 39
Ringlestone. Kent 8E 22
Ringmer. E Sus 4M 11
Ringmore. Devn
 nr. Kingsbridge 7J 5
 nr. Teignmouth 8J 7
Ring o' Bells. Lanc 6C 40
Ring's End. Cambs 1L 29
Ringsfield. Suff 3L 31
Ringsfield Corner. Suff 3L 31
Ringshall. Buck 2G 21
Ringshall. Suff 6G 31
Ringshall Stocks. Suff 6G 31
Ringstead. Norf 5D 38
Ringstead. Nptn 4G 29
**Ringwood**. Hants 5K 9
Ringwould. Kent 1K 13
Rinmore. Abers 4D 72
Rinnigill. Orkn 2E 86
Rinsey. Corn 6J 3
Riof. W Isl 8E 82
Ripe. E Sus 4B 12
**Ripley**. Derbs 4B 36
Ripley. Hants 6K 9
Ripley. N Yor 1L 41
Ripley. Surr 8H 21
Riplingham. E Yor 4G 43
**Ripon**. N Yor 8M 47
Rippingale. Linc 7H 37
Ripple. Kent 1K 13
Ripple. Worc 8G 27
Ripponden. W Yor 6J 41
Rireavach. High 4M 77
Risabus. Arg 5C 56
Risbury. Here 6D 26
Risby. E Yor 4H 43
Risby. N Lin 6G 43
Risby. Suff 5D 30
**Risca**. Cphy 5M 17
Rise. E Yor 3J 43
Riseden. E Sus 2C 12
Riseden. Kent 2D 12
Rise End. Derbs 4L 35
Risegate. Linc 7K 37
Riseholme. Linc 2G 37
Riseley. Bed 5H 29
Riseley. Wok 7E 20
Rishangles. Suff 5H 31
Rishton. Lanc 4F 40
Rishworth. W Yor 6J 41
Risley. Derbs 6B 36
Risley. Warr 8E 40
Risplith. N Yor 1L 41
Rispond. High 5G 85
Rivar. Wilts 7M 19
Rivenhall. Essx 2E 22
Rivenhall End. Essx 2E 22
River. Kent 1J 13
River. W Sus 3G 11
River Bank. Cambs 5B 30
Riverhead. Kent 8B 22
Rivington. Lanc 6E 40
Roach Bridge. Lanc 5D 40
Roachill. Devn 3H 7
Roade. Nptn 6E 28
Road Green. Norf 2J 31
Roadhead. Cumb 4K 53
Roadmeetings. S Lan 5G 59
Roadside. High 5C 86
Roadside of Catterline.
 Abers 8H 73
Roadside of Kinneff. Abers 8H 73
Roadwater. Som 2K 7
Road Weedon. Nptn 6D 28
Roag. High 1D 68
Roa Island. Cumb 8M 45
Roath. Card 7L 17
Roberton. Bord 8B 60
Roberton. S Lan 7H 59
Robertsbridge. E Sus 3D 12
Robertstown. Mor 1B 72
Robertstown. Rhon 4J 17
Roberttown. W Yor 5K 41
Robeston Back. Pemb 5G 15
Robeston Wathen. Pemb 5G 15
Robeston West. Pemb 6E 14
Robin Hood. Lanc 6D 40
Robin Hood. W Yor 5M 41
Robinhood End. Essx 8D 30
Robin Hood's Bay. N Yor 5G 49
Roborough. Devn
 nr. Great Torrington 4E 6
 nr. Plymouth 5H 5
Rob Roy's House. Arg 6F 64
Roby Mill. Lanc 7D 40
Rocester. Staf 6K 35
Roch. Pemb 4E 14
**Rochdale**. G Man 6G 41
Roche. Corn 5B 4
**Rochester**. Medw
 Medway Towns 111 (7D 22)
Rochester. Nmbd 2B 54
**Rochford**. Essx 4E 22
Rock. Corn 4B 4
Rock. Nmbd 7K 61
Rock. W Sus 4J 11
Rock. Worc 4F 26
The Rock. M Ulst 5E 92
Rockbeare. Devn 6K 7
Rockbourne. Hants 4K 9
Rockcliffe. Cumb 5H 53
Rockcliffe. Dum 6C 52
Rockcliffe Cross. Cumb 5H 53
Rock Ferry. Mers 1B 34
Rockfield. High 5K 79
Rockfield. Mon 2C 18
Rockford. Hants 5K 9
Rockgreen. Shrp 4D 26
Rockhampton. S Glo 4E 18
Rockhead. Corn 3C 4
Rockingham. Nptn 2F 28
Rockland All Saints. Norf 2F 30
Rockland St Mary. Norf 1K 31
Rockland St Peter. Norf 2F 30
Rockley. Wilts 6K 19
Rockwell End. Buck 5E 20
Rockwell Green. Som 4L 7
Rodborough. Glos 3G 19
Rodbourne. Wilts 5H 19
Rodd. Here 5B 26
Roddam. Nmbd 7H 61
Rodden. Dors 7E 8
Roddenloft. E Ayr 7C 58
Roddymoor. Dur 8E 54
Rode. Som 8G 19
Rode Heath. Ches E 4G 35
Rodeheath. Ches E 3G 35
Rodel. W Isl 5B 76
Roden. Telf 8D 34
Rodhuish. Som 2K 7
Rodington. Telf 8D 34
Rodington Heath. Telf 8D 34
Rodley. Glos 2F 18
Rodmarton. Glos 4H 19
Rodmell. E Sus 5M 11
Rodmersham. Kent 7F 22
Rodmersham Green. Kent 7F 22
Rodney Stoke. Som 1C 8
Rodsley. Derbs 5L 35
Rodway. Som 2A 8
Rodway. Telf 8E 34
Rodwell. Dors 8E 8
Roecliffe. N Yor 1A 42
Roe Green. Herts 8L 29
Roehampton. G Lon 6K 21
Roesound. Shet 1D 90
Roffey. W Sus 2J 11
Rogart. High 3H 79
Rogate. W Sus 3F 10
Roger Ground. Cumb 6B 46
Rogerstone. Newp 5A 18
Rogiet. Mon 5C 18
Rogue's Alley. Cambs 1L 29
Roke. Oxon 4D 20
Rokemarsh. Oxon 4D 20
Roker. Tyne 6H 55
Rollesby. Norf 8L 39
Rolleston. Leics 1E 28
Rolleston. Notts 4E 36
Rolleston on Dove. Staf 7L 35
Rolston. E Yor 3K 43
Rolvenden. Kent 2E 12
Rolvenden Layne. Kent 2E 12
Romaldkirk. Dur 3H 47
Roman Bank. Shrp 2D 26
Romanby. N Yor 6A 48
Romannobridge. Bord 5K 59
Romansleigh. Devn 3G 7
Romers Common. Worc 5D 26
Romesdal. High 8F 76
Romford. Dors 5J 9
**Romford**. G Lon 5B 22
**Romiley**. G Man 8H 41
**Romsey**. Hants 3A 10
Romsley. Shrp 3F 26
Romsley. Worc 4H 27
Ronague. IOM 7B 44
Ronaldsvoe. Orkn 2F 86
Rookby. Cumb 4G 47
Rookhope. Dur 7C 54
Rooking. Cumb 4C 46
Rookley. IOW 7C 10
Rooks Bridge. Som 8B 18
Rooksey Green. Suff 6F 30
Rook's Nest. Som 2K 7
Rookwood. W Sus 6E 10
Roos. E Yor 4K 43
Roosebeck. Cumb 8M 45
Roosecote. Cumb 8M 45
Rootfield. High 8F 78
Rootham's Green. Bed 6J 29
Rootpark. S Lan 4H 59
Ropley. Hants 2D 10
Ropley Dean. Hants 2D 10
Ropsley. Linc 6G 37
Rora. Abers 8K 81
Rorandle. Abers 4F 72
Rorrington. Shrp 1B 26
Rose. Corn 3L 3
Roseacre. Lanc 4C 40
Rose Ash. Devn 3G 7
Rosebank. S Lan 5G 59
Rosebush. Pemb 4G 15
Rosedale Abbey. N Yor 6E 48
Roseden. Nmbd 7H 61
Rose Green. Essx 1E 22
Rose Green. Suff 7F 30
Rosehall. High 3E 78
Rosehearty. Abers 7J 81
Rose Hill. E Sus 4A 12
Rose Hill. Lanc 4G 41
Rosehill. Shrp
 nr. Market Drayton 6E 34
 nr. Shrewsbury 8C 34
Roseisle. Mor 7M 79
Rosemarket. Pemb 6F 14
Rosemarkie. High 8H 79
Rosemary Lane. Devn 4L 7
Rosemount. Per 3E 66
Rosenannon. Corn 5B 4
Roser's Cross. E Sus 3B 12
Rosevean. Corn 6C 4
Rosewell. Midl 3L 59
Roseworth. Stoc T 3B 48
Roseworthy. Corn 5K 3
Rosgill. Cumb 4D 46
Roshven. High 8J 69
Roskhill. High 1D 68
Roskorwell. Corn 6L 3
Rosley. Cumb 7H 53
Roslin. Midl 3L 59
Rosliston. Derbs 8L 35
Rosneath. Arg 1A 58
Ross. Dum 7M 51
Ross. Nmbd 6J 61
Ross. Per 5A 66
Ross. Bord 3G 61
**Rossendale**. Lanc 5F 40
Rossett. Wrex 4B 34
Rossington. S Yor 8D 42
Rosskeen. High 7G 79
Rossland. Ren 2C 58
Rosslea. Ferm 7D 92
**Ross-on-Wye**. Here 1E 18
Roster. High 8D 86
Rostherne. Ches E 1F 34
Rostholme. S Yor 7C 42
Rosthwaite. Cumb 4A 46
Roston. Derbs 5K 35
Rostrevor. New M 7G 93
Rosudgeon. Corn 6J 3
Rosyth. Fife 1K 59
Rothbury. Nmbd 1D 54
Rotherby. Leics 8D 36
Rotherfield. E Sus 3B 12
Rotherfield Greys. Oxon 5E 20
Rotherfield Peppard. Oxon 5E 20
**Rotherham**. S Yor 8B 42
Rothersthorpe. Nptn 6E 28
Rotherwick. Hants 8E 20
Rothes. Mor 1B 72
Rothesay. Arg 3K 57
Rothienorman. Abers 2G 73
Rothiesholm. Orkn 7F 88
Rothley. Leics 8C 36
Rothley. Nmbd 3D 54
Rothwell. Linc 8J 43
Rothwell. Nptn 3F 28
**Rothwell**. W Yor 5M 41
Rotsea. E Yor 2H 43
Rottal. Ang 1G 67
Rotten End. Suff 5K 31
Rotten Row. Norf 8G 39
Rotten Row. W Ber 6C 20
Rotten Row. W Mid 4K 27
**Rottingdean**. Brig 5L 11
Rottington. Cumb 3J 45
Roud. IOW 7C 10
Rougham. Norf 7E 38
Rougham. Suff 5F 30
Rough Close. Staf 6H 35
Rough Common. Kent 8H 23
Roughcote. Staf 5H 35
Roughfort. Ant 4H 93
Rough Haugh. High 7K 85
Rough Hay. Staf 7L 35
Roughlee. Lanc 3G 41
Roughley. W Mid 2K 27
Roughsike. Cumb 4K 53
Roughton. Linc 3K 37
Roughton. Norf 6J 39
Roughton. Shrp 2F 26
Roundbush Green. Essx 2B 22
Roundham. Som 5C 8
Roundhay. W Yor 4M 41
Round Hill. Torb 5L 5
Roundhurst. W Sus 2G 11
Round Maple. Suff 7F 30
Round Oak. Shrp 3B 26
Roundstreet Common.
 W Sus 3H 11
Roundthwaite. Cumb 5E 46
Roundway. Wilts 7J 19
Roundyhill. Ang 2G 67
Rousdon. Devn 6A 8
Rousham. Oxon 1B 20
Rousky. Ferm 4D 92
Rous Lench. Worc 6J 27
Routh. E Yor 3H 43
Rout's Green. Buck 4E 20
Row. Corn 4C 4
Row. Cumb
 nr. Kendal 7C 46
 nr. Penrith 8L 53
The Row. Lanc 8C 46
Rowanburn. Dum 4J 53
Rowanhill. Abers 8K 81
Rowardennan. Stir 8H 65
Rowarth. Derbs 1J 35
Row Ash. Hants 4C 10
Rowberrow. Som 8C 18
Rowde. Wilts 7H 19
Rowden. Devn 6F 6
Rowen. Cnwy 3G 33
Rowfoot. Nmbd 5L 53
Row Green. Essx 1D 22
Row Heath. Essx 2H 23
Rowhedge. Essx 1G 23
Rowhook. W Sus 2J 11
Rowington. Warw 5L 27
Rowland. Derbs 2L 35
Rowlands Castle. Hants 4E 10
Rowlands Gill. Tyne 6E 54
Rowledge. Hants 1F 10
Rowley. Dur 7D 54
Rowley. E Yor 4G 43
Rowley. Shrp 1B 26
Rowley Hill. W Yor 6K 41
Rowley Regis. W Mid 3H 27
Rowlstone. Here 1B 18
Rowly. Surr 1H 11
Rowner. Hants 5C 10
Rowney Green. Worc 4J 27
Rownhams. Hants 4A 10
Rowrah. Cumb 3K 45
Rowsham. Buck 2F 20
Rowsley. Derbs 3L 35
Rowstock. Oxon 5B 20
Rowston. Linc 4H 37
Rowthorne. Derbs 3B 36
Rowton. Ches W 3C 34
Rowton. Shrp
 nr. Ludlow 3C 26
 nr. Shrewsbury 8B 34
Rowton. Telf 8E 34
Row Town. Surr 7H 21
Roxburgh. Bord 6E 60
Roxby. N Lin 6G 43
Roxby. N Yor 4E 48
Roxhill. Ant 4G 93
Roxton. Bed 6J 29
Roxwell. Essx 3C 22
**Royal Leamington Spa**.
 Warw 5M 27
Royal Oak. Darl 3L 47
Royal Oak. Lanc 7C 40
Royal Oak. N Yor 8J 49
Royal's Green. Ches E 5E 34
**Royal Sutton Coldfield**.
 W Mid 2K 27
**Royal Tunbridge Wells**.
 Kent 2B 12
**Royal Wootton Bassett**.
 Wilts 5J 19
Roybridge. High 7C 70
Roydon. Essx 2M 21
Roydon. Norf
 nr. Diss 3G 31
 nr. King's Lynn 7D 38
Roydon Hamlet. Essx 3M 21
**Royston**. Herts 7L 29
**Royston**. S Yor 6A 42
Royston Water. Som 4M 7
**Royton**. G Man 7H 41
Ruabon. Wrex 5B 34
Ruaig. Arg 3F 62
Ruan High Lanes. Corn 8B 4
Ruan Lanihorne. Corn 7A 4
Ruan Major. Corn 7L 3
Ruan Minor. Corn 7L 3
Ruarach. High 3L 69
Ruardean. Glos 2E 18
Ruardean Hill. Glos 2E 18
Ruardean Woodside. Glos 2E 18
Rubane. Ards 5K 93
Rubery. Worc 4H 27
Ruchazie. Glas 3E 58
Ruckcroft. Cumb 7K 53
Ruckinge. Kent 2G 13
Ruckland. Linc 2L 37
Rucklers Lane. Herts 3H 21
Ruckley. Shrp 1D 26
Rudbaxton. Pemb 4F 14
Rudby. N Yor 5B 48
Ruddington. Notts 6C 36
Rudford. Glos 1F 18
Rudge. Shrp 2G 27
Rudge. Wilts 8G 19
Rudge Heath. Shrp 2F 26
Rudgeway. S Glo 5E 18
Rudgwick. W Sus 2H 11
Rudhall. Here 1E 18
Rudheath. Ches W 2E 34
Rudley Green. Essx 3E 22
Rudloe. Wilts 6G 19
Rudry. Cphy 6M 17
Rudston. E Yor 1H 43
Rudyard. Staf 4H 35
Rufford. Lanc 6C 40
Rufforth. York 2C 42
**Rugby**. Warw 4C 28
**Rugeley**. Staf 8J 35
Ruglen. S Ayr 1H 51
Ruilick. High 1F 70
Ruisaurie. High 1E 70
Ruishton. Som 3A 8
Ruisigearraidh. W Isl 5L 75
**Ruislip**. G Lon 5H 21
Ruislip Common. G Lon 5H 21
Rumbling Bridge. Per 8D 66
Rumburgh. Suff 3K 31
Rumford. Corn 4A 4
Rumford. Falk 2H 59
Rumney. Card 7M 17
Rumwell. Som 3L 7
**Runcorn**. Hal 1D 34
Runcton. W Sus 5F 10
Runcton Holme. Norf 1C 30
Rundlestone. Devn 8E 6
Runfold. Surr 1F 10
Runhall. Norf 1G 31
Runham. Norf 8L 39
Runnington. Som 3L 7
Runshaw Moor. Lanc 6D 40
Runswick. N Yor 4F 48
Runtaleave. Ang 1F 66
Runwell. Essx 4D 22
Ruscombe. Wok 6E 20
Rushall. Here 8E 26
Rushall. Norf 3H 31
Rushall. W Mid 1J 27
Rushall. Wilts 8K 19
Rushbrooke. Suff 5E 30
Rushbury. Shrp 2D 26
Rushden. Herts 8L 29
**Rushden**. Nptn 5G 29
Rushenden. Kent 6F 22
Rushford. Devn 8D 6
Rushford. Suff 3F 30
Rush Green. Herts 1K 21
Rushlake Green. E Sus 4C 12
Rushmere. Suff 3L 31
Rushmere St Andrew. Suff 7J 31
Rushmoor. Surr 1F 10
Rushock. Worc 4G 27
Rusholme. G Man 8G 41
Rushton. Ches W 3D 34
Rushton. Nptn 3F 28
Rushton. Shrp 1E 26
Rushton Spencer. Staf 3H 35
Rushwick. Worc 6G 27
Rushyford. Dur 3L 47
Ruskie. Stir 7L 65
Ruskington. Linc 4H 37
Rusland. Cumb 7B 46
Rusper. W Sus 2K 11
Ruspidge. Glos 2E 18
Russell's Water. Oxon 5E 20
Russel's Green. Suff 4J 31
Russ Hill. Surr 1K 11
Russland. Orkn 8C 88
Rusthall. Kent 2B 12
Rustington. W Sus 5H 11
Ruston. N Yor 7G 49
Ruston Parva. E Yor 1H 43
Ruswarp. N Yor 5F 48
**Rutherglen**. S Lan 3E 58
Ruthernbridge. Corn 5C 4
Ruthin. Den 5L 33
Ruthin. V Glam 7J 17
Ruthrieston. Aber 5J 73
Ruthven. Abers 1E 72
Ruthven. Ang 3F 66
Ruthven. High
 nr. Inverness 2J 71
 nr. Kingussie 6H 71
Ruthvoes. Corn 5B 4
Ruthwaite. Cumb 8G 53
Ruthwell. Dum 5F 52
Ruxton Green. Here 2D 18
Ruyton-XI-Towns. Shrp 7B 34
Ryal. Nmbd 4D 54
Ryall. Dors 6C 8
Ryall. Worc 7G 27
Ryarsh. Kent 8C 22
Rychraggan. High 2E 70
Rydal. Cumb 5B 46
**Ryde**. IOW 6C 10
Rye. E Sus 3F 12
Ryecroft Gate. Staf 3H 35
Ryeford. Here 1E 18
Rye Foreign. E Sus 3F 12
Rye Harbour. E Sus 4F 12
Ryehill. E Yor 5K 43
Rye Street. Worc 8F 26
Ryhall. Rut 8H 37
Ryhill. W Yor 6A 42
Ryhope. Tyne 6H 55
Ryhope Colliery. Tyne 6H 55
Rylands. Notts 6C 36
Rylstone. N Yor 2H 41
Ryme Intrinseca. Dors 4D 8
Ryther. N Yor 4C 42
Ryton. Glos 8F 26
Ryton. N Yor 8E 48
Ryton. Shrp 1F 26
**Ryton**. Tyne 5E 54
Ryton. Warw 3B 28
Ryton-on-Dunsmore. Warw 4A 28
Ryton Woodside. Tyne 5E 54

## S

Saasaig. High 5H 69
Sabden. Lanc 4F 40
Sacombe. Herts 2L 21
Sacriston. Dur 7F 54
Sadberge. Darl 4M 47
Saddell. Arg 6G 57
Saddington. Leics 2D 28
Saddle Bow. Norf 8C 38
Saddlescombe. W Sus 4K 11
**Saddleworth**. G Man 7H 41
Sadgill. Cumb 5C 46
**Saffron Walden**. Essx 8B 30
Sageston. Pemb 6G 15
Saham Hills. Norf 1F 30
Saham Toney. Norf 1E 30
Saighdinis. W Isl 7K 75
Saighton. Ches W 3C 34
Sain Dunwyd. V Glam 8J 17
Sain Hilari. V Glam 7K 17
St Abbs. Bord 3G 61
St Agnes. Corn 3L 3

**St Albans.** Herts 3J 21
St Allen. Corn 3M 3
**St Andrews.** Fife 6J 67
St Andrews Major. V Glam 7L 17
St Anne's. Lanc 5B 40
St Ann's. Dum 2E 52
St Ann's Chapel. Corn 8D 6
St Ann's Chapel. Devn 7J 5
St Anthony. Corn 8A 4
St Anthony-in-Meneage. Corn 6L 3
St Arvans. Mon 4D 18
**St Asaph.** Den 3K 33
Sain Tathan. V Glam 8K 17
St Athan. V Glam 8K 17
**St Austell.** Corn 6C 4
St Bartholomew's Hill. Wilts 3H 9
St Bees. Cumb 3J 45
St Blazey. Corn 6C 4
St Blazey Gate. Corn 6C 4
St Boswells. Bord 6C 60
St Breock. Corn 4B 4
St Breward. Corn 4C 4
St Briavels. Glos 3D 18
St Brides. Pemb 5D 14
St Brides Major. V Glam 7H 17
St Bride's Netherwent. Mon 5C 18
St Bride's-super-Ely. V Glam 7K 17
St Brides Wentlooge. Newp 5A 18
St Budeaux. Plym 6G 5
Saintbury. Glos 8K 27
St Buryan. Corn 6H 3
St Catherine. Bath 6F 18
St Catherines. Arg 7F 64
St Clears. Carm 5J 15
St Cleer. Corn 5E 4
St Clement. Corn 7A 4
St Clether. Corn 7B 6
St Colmac. Arg 3K 57
St Columb Major. Corn 5B 4
St Columb Minor. Corn 2M 3
St Columb Road. Corn 6B 4
St Combs. Abers 7K 81
St Cross. Hants 3B 10
St Cross South Elmham. Suff 3J 31
St Cyrus. Abers 1L 67
St David's. Per 5C 66
**St Davids.** Pemb 4D 14
St Day. Corn 4L 3
St Dennis. Corn 6B 4
St Dogmaels. Pemb 2H 15
St Dominick. Corn 5F 4
St Donat's. V Glam 8J 17
St Edith's Marsh. Wilts 7H 19
St Endellion. Corn 4B 4
St Enoder. Corn 6A 4
St Erme. Corn 4M 3
St Erney. Corn 6F 4
St Erth. Corn 5J 3
St Erth Praze. Corn 5J 3
St Ervan. Corn 4A 4
St Eval. Corn 5A 4
St Ewe. Corn 7B 4
St Fagans. Card 7L 17
St Fergus. Abers 8K 81
Saintfield. New M 6J 93
St Fillans. Per 5L 65
St Florence. Pemb 6G 15
St Gennys. Corn 6A 6
St George. Cnwy 3J 33
St George's. N Som 7B 18
St Georges. V Glam 7K 17
St George's Hill. Surr 7H 21
St Germans. Corn 6F 4
St Giles in the Wood. Devn 4E 6
St Giles on the Heath. Devn 6C 6
St Giles's Hill. Hants 3B 10
St Gluvias. Corn 5L 3
St Harmon. Powy 5J 25
St Helena. Warw 1L 27
St Helen Auckland. Dur 3K 47
St Helen's. E Sus 4E 12
St Helens. Cumb 8E 52
St Helens. IOW 7D 10
**St Helens.** Mers 8D 40
St Hilary. Corn 5J 3
St Hilary. V Glam 7K 17
Saint Hill. Devn 5K 7
Saint Hill. W Sus 2L 11
St Illtyd. Blae 4M 17
St Ippolyts. Herts 1J 21
St Ishmael. Carm 6K 15
St Ishmael's. Pemb 6E 14
St Issey. Corn 4B 4
St Ive. Corn 5F 4
**St Ives.** Cambs 4L 29
**St Ives.** Corn 4J 3
St Ives. Dors 5K 9
St James' End. Nptn 5E 28
St James South Elmham. Suff 3K 31
St Jidgey. Corn 5B 4
St John. Corn 6G 5
St John's. IOM 6B 44
St John's. Worc 6G 27
St John's Chapel. Devn 3E 6
St John's Chapel. Dur 8B 54
St John's Fen End. Norf 8B 38
St John's Town of Dalry. Dum 3M 51
St Judes. IOM 5C 44
St Just. Corn 5G 3
St Just in Roseland. Corn 8A 4
St Katherines. Abers 2G 73
St Keverne. Corn 6L 3
St Kew. Corn 4C 4
St Kew Highway. Corn 4C 4
St Keyne. Corn 5E 4
St Lawrence. Corn 5C 4
St Lawrence. Essx 3F 22
St Lawrence. IOW 8C 10
St Leonards. Buck 3G 21
St Leonards. Dors 5K 9
St Leonards. E Sus 5D 12
St Levan. Corn 6G 3
St Lythans. V Glam 7L 17
St Mabyn. Corn 4C 4
St Madoes. Per 5E 66
St Margaret's. Herts 2H 21
St Margaret's. Wilts 7L 19
St Margarets. Here 8B 26
St Margarets. Herts 2L 21
St Margaret's at Cliffe. Kent 1K 13
St Margaret's Hope. Orkn 2F 86
St Margaret South Elmham. Suff 3K 31
St Mark's. IOM 7B 44
St Martin. Corn
nr. Helston 6L 3
nr. Looe 6E 4
St Martin's. Shrp 6B 34
St Martins. Per 4E 66
St Mary Bourne. Hants 8B 20
St Mary Church. V Glam 7K 17
St Marychurch. Torb 5M 5
St Mary Cray. G Lon 7A 22
St Mary Hill. V Glam 7J 17
St Mary Hoo. Medw 6E 22
St Mary in the Marsh. Kent 3G 13
St Mary's. Orkn 1F 86
St Mary's Airport. IOS 1H 3
St Mary's Bay. Kent 3G 13
St Marys Platt. Kent 8C 22
St Maughan's Green. Mon 2C 18
St Mawes. Corn 5M 3
St Mawgan. Corn 5A 4
St Mellion. Corn 5F 4
St Mellons. Card 6M 17
St Merryn. Corn 4A 4
St Mewan. Corn 6B 4
St Michael Caerhays. Corn 7B 4
St Michael Penkevil. Corn 7A 4
St Michaels. Kent 2E 12
St Michaels. Torb 6L 5
St Michaels. Worc 5D 26
St Michael's on Wyre. Lanc 3C 40
St Michael South Elmham. Suff 3K 31
St Minver. Corn 4B 4
St Monans. Fife 7J 67
St Neot. Corn 5D 4
**St Neots.** Cambs 5J 29
St Newlyn East. Corn 3M 3
St Nicholas. Pemb 3E 14
St Nicholas. V Glam 7K 17
St Nicholas at Wade. Kent 7J 23
St Nicholas South Elmham. Suff 3K 31
St Ninians. Stir 8A 66
St Olaves. Norf 2L 31
St Osyth. Essx 2H 23
St Osyth Heath. Essx 2H 23
St Owen's Cross. Here 1D 18
St Paul's Cray. G Lon 7A 22
St Paul's Walden. Herts 1J 21
St Peter's. Kent 7K 23
St Peter The Great. Worc 6G 27
St Petrox. Pemb 7F 14
St Pinnock. Corn 5E 4
St Quivox. S Ayr 7B 58
St Ruan. Corn 7L 3
St Stephen. Corn 6B 4
St Stephens. Corn
nr. Launceston 7C 6
nr. Saltash 6G 5
St Teath. Corn 3C 4
St Thomas. Devn 6J 7
St Thomas. Swan 5F 16
St Tudy. Corn 4C 4
St Twynnells. Pemb 7F 14
St Veep. Corn 6D 4
St Vigeans. Ang 3K 67
St Wenn. Corn 5B 4
St Weonards. Here 1C 18
St Winnolls. Corn 6F 4
St Winnow. Corn 6D 4
Salcombe. Devn 8K 5
Salcombe Regis. Devn 7L 7
Salcott. Essx 2F 22
**Sale.** G Man 8F 40
Saleby. Linc 2A 38
Sale Green. Worc 6H 27
Salehurst. E Sus 3D 12
Salem. Carm 2F 16
Salem. Cdgn 4F 24
Salen. Arg 3L 63
Salen. High 1A 64
Salesbury. Lanc 4E 40
Saleway. Worc 6H 27
Salford. C Beds 8G 29
**Salford.** G Man **Manchester 111 (8G 41)**
Salford. Oxon 1L 19
Salford Priors. Warw 6J 27
Salfords. Surr 1K 11
Salhouse. Norf 8K 39
Saligo. Arg 3B 56
Saline. Fife 8D 66
**Salisbury.** Wilts 115 (2K 9)
Salkeld Dykes. Cumb 8K 53
Sallachan. High 1D 64
Sallachy. High
nr. Lairg 3F 78
nr. Stromeferry 2L 69
Salle. Norf 7H 39
Salmonby. Linc 2L 37
Salmond's Muir. Ang 4J 67
Salperton. Glos 1J 19
Salph End. Bed 6H 29
Salsburgh. N Lan 3G 59
Salt. Staf 7H 35
Salta. Cumb 7E 52
Saltaire. W Yor 4K 41
**Saltash.** Corn 6G 5
Saltburn. High 7H 79
Saltburn-by-the-Sea. Red C 3D 48
Saltby. Leics 7F 36
Saltcoats. Cumb 5K 45
**Saltcoats.** N Ayr 5M 57
**Saltdean.** Brig 5L 11
Salt End. E Yor 5J 43
Salter. Lanc 1E 40
Salterforth. Lanc 3G 41
Salters Lode. Norf 1B 30
Salterswall. Ches W 3E 34
Salterton. Wilts 2K 9
Saltfleet. Linc 8M 43
Saltfleetby All Saints. Linc 1A 38
Saltfleetby St Clements. Linc 1A 38
Saltfleetby St Peter. Linc 1M 37
Saltford. Bath 7E 18
Salthouse. Norf 5G 39
Saltmarshe. E Yor 5E 42
Saltness. Orkn 3D 86
Saltness. Shet 3C 90
Saltney. Flin 3B 34
Salton. N Yor 8E 48
Saltrens. Devn 3D 6
Saltwick. Nmbd 4E 54
Saltwood. Kent 2H 13
Salum. Arg 3F 62
Salwarpe. Worc 5G 27
Salwayash. Dors 6C 8
Samalaman. High 8H 69
Sambourne. Warw 5J 27
Sambourne. Wilts 1G 9
Sambrook. Telf 7F 34
Samhla. W Isl 7J 75
Samlesbury. Lanc 4D 40
Samlesbury Bottoms. Lanc 5E 40
Sampford Arundel. Som 4L 7
Sampford Brett. Som 1K 7
Sampford Courtenay. Devn 5F 6
Sampford Peverell. Devn 4K 7
Sampford Spiney. Devn 8E 6
Samsonslane. Orkn 7F 88
Samuelston. E Lot 2B 60
Sanaigmore. Arg 2B 56
Sancreed. Corn 6H 3
Sancton. E Yor 4G 43
Sand. High 4L 77
Sand. Shet 3D 90
Sand. Som 1C 8
Sandaig. Arg 3E 62
Sandaig. High 5J 69
Sandale. Cumb 7G 53
Sandal Magna. W Yor 6M 41
Sandavore. High 7F 68
Sanday Airport. Orkn 5F 88
**Sandbach.** Ches E 3F 34
Sandbank. Arg 1L 57
Sandbanks. Pool 7J 9
Sandend. Abers 7E 80
Sanderstead. G Lon 7L 21
Sandfields. Neat 5G 17
Sandford. Cumb 4F 46
Sandford. Devn 5H 7
Sandford. Dors 7H 9
Sandford. Hants 5K 9
Sandford. IOW 7C 10
Sandford. N Som 8C 18
Sandford. Shrp
nr. Oswestry 7B 34
nr. Whitchurch 6D 34
Sandford. S Lan 5F 58
Sandfordhill. Abers 1M 73
Sandford-on-Thames. Oxon 3C 20
Sandford Orcas. Dors 3E 8
Sandford St Martin. Oxon 1B 20
Sandgate. Kent 2H 13
Sandgreen. Dum 7L 51
Sandhaven. Abers 7J 81
Sandhead. Dum 6F 50
Sandhill. Cambs 3B 30
Sandhills. Dors 4E 8
Sandhills. Oxon 3C 20
Sandhills. Surr 2G 11
Sandhoe. Nmbd 5C 54
Sand Hole. E Yor 4F 42
Sandholes. M Ulst 5E 92
Sandholme. E Yor 4F 42
Sandholme. Linc 6L 37
**Sandhurst.** Brac 7F 20
Sandhurst. Glos 1G 19
Sandhurst. Kent 3D 12
Sandhurst Cross. Kent 3D 12
Sand Hutton. N Yor 2D 42
Sandhutton. N Yor 7A 48
Sandiacre. Derbs 6B 36
Sandilands. Linc 1B 38
Sandiway. Ches W 2E 34
Sandleheath. Hants 4K 9
Sandling. Kent 8D 22
Sandlow Green. Ches E 3F 34
Sandness. Shet 2B 90
Sandon. Essx 3D 22
Sandon. Herts 8L 29
Sandon. Staf 7H 35
Sandonbank. Staf 7H 35
**Sandown.** IOW 7C 10
Sandplace. Corn 6E 4
Sandridge. Herts 2J 21
Sandringham. Norf 7C 38
The Sands. Surr 1F 10
Sandsend. N Yor 4F 48
Sandside. Cumb 8B 46
Sandsound. Shet 3D 90
Sandtoft. N Lin 7E 42
Sandvoe. Shet 4H 91
Sandway. Kent 8E 22
Sandwich. Kent 8K 23
Sandwick. Cumb 4C 46
Sandwick. Orkn
on Mainland 8B 88
on South Ronaldsay 3F 86
Sandwick. Shet
on Mainland 5E 90
on Whalsay 1F 90
Sandwith. Cumb 3J 45
Sandy. Carm 6L 15
Sandy. C Beds 7J 29
Sandy Bank. Linc 4K 37
Sandycroft. Flin 3B 34
Sandy Cross. Here 6E 26
Sandygate. Devn 8H 7
Sandygate. IOM 5C 44
Sandy Haven. Pemb 6E 14
Sandyhills. Dum 6C 52
Sandylands. Lanc 1C 40
Sandy Lane. Wilts 7H 19
Sandylane. Swan 6E 16
Sandystones. Bord 7C 60
Sandyway. Here 1C 18
Sangobeg. High 5G 85
Sangomore. High 5G 85
Sankyn's Green. Worc 5F 26
Sanna. High 1K 63
Sanndabhaig. W Isl
on Isle of Lewis 8H 83
on South Uist 1E 74
Sannox. N Ayr 5K 57
Sanquhar. Dum 8F 58
Santon. Cumb 4K 45
Santon Bridge. Cumb 4L 45
Santon Downham. Suff 3E 30
Sapcote. Leics 2B 28
Sapey Common. Here 5F 26
Sapiston. Suff 4F 30
Sapley. Cambs 4K 29
Sapperton. Derbs 6K 35
Sapperton. Glos 3H 19
Sapperton. Linc 6H 37
Saracen's Head. Linc 7L 37
Sarclet. High 7E 86
Sardis. Carm 4E 16
Sardis. Pemb
nr. Milford Haven 6F 14
nr. Tenby 6H 15
Sarisbury Green. Hants 5C 10
Sarn. B'end 6J 17
Sarn. Powy 3M 25
Sarnau. Carm 5K 15
Sarnau. Cdgn 1K 15
Sarnau. Gwyn 7J 33
Sarnau. Powy
nr. Brecon 1K 17
nr. Welshpool 1M 25
Sarn Bach. Gwyn 8C 32
Sarnesfield. Here 6B 26
Sarn Meyllteyrn. Gwyn 7B 32
Saron. Carm
nr. Ammanford 3F 16
nr. Newcastle Emlyn 3K 15
Saron. Gwyn
nr. Bethel 4E 32
nr. Bontnewydd 5D 32
Sarratt. Herts 4H 21
Sarre. Kent 7J 23
Sarsden. Oxon 1L 19
Satley. Dur 7E 54
Satron. N Yor 6H 47
Satterleigh. Devn 3F 6
Satterthwaite. Cumb 6B 46
Satwell. Oxon 5E 20
Sauchen. Abers 4F 72
Saucher. Per 4E 66
Saughall. Ches W 2B 34
Saughtree. Bord 2K 53
Saul. Glos 3F 18
Saul. New M 6J 93
Saundby. Notts 1E 36
Saundersfoot. Pemb 6H 15
Saunderton. Buck 3E 20
Saunderton Lee. Buck 4F 20
Saunton. Devn 2D 6
Sausthorpe. Linc 3L 37
Saval. High 3F 78
Saverley Green. Staf 6H 35
Sawbridge. Warw 5C 28
**Sawbridgeworth.** Herts 2A 22
Sawdon. N Yor 7G 49
Sawley. Derbs 6B 36
Sawley. Lanc 3F 40
Sawley. N Yor 1L 41
Sawston. Cambs 7A 30
Sawtry. Cambs 3J 29
Saxby. Leics 8F 36
Saxby. Linc 1H 37
Saxby All Saints. N Lin 6G 43
Saxelbye. Leics 7E 36
Saxham Street. Suff 5G 31
Saxilby. Linc 2F 36
Saxlingham. Norf 6G 39
Saxlingham Green. Norf 2J 31
Saxlingham Nethergate. Norf 2J 31
Saxlingham Thorpe. Norf 2J 31
Saxmundham. Suff 5K 31
Saxondale. Notts 5D 36
Saxon Street. Cambs 6C 30
Saxtead. Suff 5J 31
Saxtead Green. Suff 5J 31
Saxthorpe. Norf 6H 39
Saxton. N Yor 4B 42
Sayers Common. W Sus 4K 11
Scackleton. N Yor 8D 48
Scadabhagh. W Isl 4C 76
Scaddy. New M 6J 93
Scaftworth. Notts 8D 42
Scagglethorpe. N Yor 8F 48
Scaitcliffe. Lanc 5F 40
Scaladal. W Isl 2C 76
Scalasaig. Arg 8J 63
Scalby. E Yor 5F 42
Scalby. N Yor 6H 49
Scalby Mills. N Yor 6H 49
Scaldwell. Nptn 4E 28
Scaleby. Cumb 5J 53
Scaleby Hill. Cumb 5J 53
Scale Houses. Cumb 7K 53
Scales. Cumb
nr. Barrow-in-Furness 8A 46
nr. Keswick 3B 46
Scalford. Leics 7E 36
Scaling. N Yor 4E 48
Scaling Dam. Red C 4E 48
Scalloway. Shet 4E 90
Scalpaigh. W Isl 4D 76
Scalpay House. High 3H 69
Scamblesby. Linc 2K 37
Scamodale. High 8K 69
Scampston. N Yor 8F 48
Scampton. Linc 2G 37
Scaniport. High 2G 71
Scapa. Orkn 1F 86
Scapegoat Hill. W Yor 6J 41
Scar. Orkn 5F 88
Scarasta. W Isl 4B 76
**Scarborough.** N Yor 7H 49
Scarcliffe. Derbs 3B 36
Scarcroft. W Yor 3A 42
Scarfskerry. High 4D 86
Scargill. Dur 4J 47
Scarinish. Arg 3F 62
Scarisbrick. Lanc 6B 40
Scarning. Norf 8F 38
Scarrington. Notts 5E 36
Scarth Hill. Lanc 7C 40
Scartho. NE Lin 7K 43
Scarva. Arm 6G 93
Scarvister. Shet 3D 90
Scatness. Shet 7D 90
Scatwell. High 8D 78
Scaur. Dum 6C 52
Scawby. N Lin 7G 43
Scawby Brook. N Lin 7G 43
Scawsby. S Yor 7C 42
Scawton. N Yor 7C 48
Scaynes Hill. W Sus 3L 11
Scethrog. Powy 2L 17
Scholar Green. Ches E 4G 35
Scholes. G Man 7D 40
Scholes. W Yor
nr. Bradford 5K 41
nr. Holmfirth 7K 41
nr. Leeds 4A 42
Scholey Hill. W Yor 5A 42
School Aycliffe. Darl 3L 47
School Green. Ches W 3E 34
School Green. Essx 8D 30
Scissett. W Yor 6L 41
Scleddau. Pemb 3F 14
Scofton. Notts 1D 36
Scole. Norf 4H 31
Scollogstown. New M 7J 93
Scolpaig. W Isl 6J 75
Scolton. Pemb 4F 14
Scone. Per 5E 66
Scoonie. Fife 7G 67
Scoraig. High 4M 77
Scorborough. E Yor 3H 43
Scorrier. Corn 4L 3
Scorriton. Devn 5K 5
Scorton. Lanc 3D 40
Scorton. N Yor 5L 47
Sco Ruston. Norf 7J 39
Scotbheinn. W Isl 8K 75
Scotby. Cumb 6J 53
**Scotch Corner.** N Yor 5K 47
Scotch Street. Arm 6F 93
Scot Hay. Staf 5F 34
Scothern. Linc 2H 37
Scotland End. Oxon 8A 28
Scotlandwell. Per 7E 66
Scot Lane End. G Man 7E 40
Scotsburn. High 6H 79
Scotsburn. Mor 7B 80
Scotsdike. Cumb 4H 53
Scot's Gap. Nmbd 3D 54
Scotstoun. Glas 3D 58
Scotstown. High 1C 64
Scotswood. Tyne 5F 54
Scottas. High 5J 69
Scotter. Linc 7F 42
Scotterthorpe. Linc 7F 42
Scottlethorpe. Linc 7H 37
Scotton. Linc 8F 42
Scotton. N Yor
nr. Catterick Garrison 6K 47
nr. Harrogate 2M 41
Scottow. Norf 7J 39
Scoulton. Norf 1F 30
Scounslow Green. Staf 7J 35
Scourie. High 7D 84
Scourie More. High 7D 84
Scousburgh. Shet 6D 90
Scout Green. Cumb 5D 46
Scouthead. G Man 7H 41
Scrabster. High 4B 86
Scrafield. Linc 3L 37
Scrainwood. Nmbd 1C 54
Scrane End. Linc 5L 37
Scraptoft. Leics 1D 28
Scratby. Norf 8M 39
Scrayingham. N Yor 1E 42
Scredington. Linc 5H 37
Scremby. Linc 3M 37
Scremerston. Nmbd 5H 61
Screveton. Notts 5E 36
Scrivelsby. Linc 3K 37
Scriven. N Yor 2A 42
Scronkey. Lanc 3C 40
Scrooby. Notts 8D 42
Scropton. Derbs 6K 35
Scrub Hill. Linc 4K 37
Scruton. N Yor 6L 47
Scuggate. Cumb 4J 53
Sculamus. High 3H 69
Sculcoates. Hull 4H 43
Sculthorpe. Norf 6F 38
**Scunthorpe.** N Lin 6F 42
Scurlage. Swan 8L 15
Sea. Som 4B 8
Seaborough. Dors 5C 8
Seabridge. Staf 5G 35
Seabrook. Kent 2H 13
Seaburn. Tyne 5H 55
Seacombe. Mers 8B 40
Seacroft. Linc 3B 38
Seacroft. W Yor 4M 41
Seadyke. Linc 6L 37
Seafield. High 5K 79
Seafield. Midl 3L 59
Seafield. S Ayr 7B 58
Seafield. W Lot 3J 59
**Seaford.** E Sus 6A 12
Seaforde. New M 6J 93
Seaforth. Mers 8B 40
Seagrave. Leics 8D 36
**Seaham.** Dur 7H 55
Seahouses. Nmbd 6K 61
Seal. Kent 8B 22
Sealand. Flin 3B 34
Seale. Surr 1F 10
Seamer. N Yor
nr. Scarborough 7H 49
nr. Stokesley 4B 48
Seamill. N Ayr 5M 57
Sea Mills. Bris 6D 18
Sea Palling. Norf 7L 39
Searby. Linc 7H 43
Seasalter. Kent 7G 23
Seascale. Cumb 4K 45
Seaside. Per 5F 66
Seater. High 5E 86
Seathorne. Linc 3B 38
Seathwaite. Cumb
nr. Buttermere 3M 45
nr. Ulpha 5M 45
Seatle. Cumb 7B 46
Seatoller. Cumb 3M 45
Seaton. Corn 6F 4
Seaton. Cumb 8E 52
Seaton. Devn 6M 7
Seaton. Dur 7G 55
Seaton. E Yor 3J 43
Seaton. Nmbd 4G 55
Seaton. Rut 2G 29
Seaton Burn. Tyne 4F 54
Seaton Carew. Hart 3C 48
Seaton Delaval. Nmbd 4G 55
Seaton Junction. Devn 6A 8
Seaton Ross. E Yor 3E 42
Seaton Sluice. Nmbd 4G 55
Seatown. Abers 7E 80
Seatown. Dors 6C 8
Seatown. Mor
nr. Cullen 7E 80
nr. Lossiemouth 6B 80
Seave Green. N Yor 5D 48
Seaview. IOW 6D 10
Seaville. Cumb 6F 52
Seavington St Mary. Som 4C 8
Seavington St Michael. Som 4C 8
Seawick. Essx 2H 23
Sebastopol. Torf 4A 18
Sebergham. Cumb 7H 53
Seckington. Warw 1L 27
Second Coast. High 4L 77
Sedbergh. Cumb 6E 46
Sedbury. Glos 4D 18
Sedbusk. N Yor 6G 47
Sedgeberrow. Worc 8J 27
Sedgebrook. Linc 6F 36
Sedgefield. Dur 3A 48
Sedgeford. Norf 6D 38
Sedgehill. Wilts 3G 9
Sedgley. W Mid 2H 27
Sedgwick. Cumb 7D 46
Sedlescombe. E Sus 4D 12
Seend. Wilts 7H 19
Seend Cleeve. Wilts 7H 19
Seer Green. Buck 4G 21
Seething. Norf 2K 31
Sefster. Shet 2D 90
Sefton. Mers 7B 40
Sefton Park. Mers 1B 34
Segensworth. Hants 5C 10
Seggat. Abers 1G 73
Seghill. Nmbd 4F 54
Seifton. Shrp 3C 26
Seighford. Staf 7G 35
Seilebost. W Isl 4B 76
Seisdon. Staf 2G 27
Seisiadar. W Isl 8J 83
Selattyn. Shrp 6A 34
Selborne. Hants 2E 10
**Selby.** N Yor 4D 42
Selham. W Sus 3G 11
Selkirk. Bord 7B 60
Sellack. Here 1D 18
Sellafirth. Shet 4K 91
Sellick's Green. Som 4M 7
Sellindge. Kent 2H 13
Selling. Kent 8G 23
Sells Green. Wilts 7H 19
Selly Oak. W Mid 3J 27
Selmeston. E Sus 5B 12
Selsdon. G Lon 7L 21
Selsey. W Sus 6F 10
Selsfield Common. W Sus 2L 11
Selside. Cumb 6D 46
Selside. N Yor 8F 46
Selsley. Glos 3G 19
Selsted. Kent 1J 13
Selston. Notts 4B 36
Selworthy. Som 1J 7
Semblister. Shet 2D 90
Semer. Suff 7G 31
Semington. Wilts 7G 19
Semley. Wilts 3G 9
Sempringham. Linc 6J 37
Send. Surr 8H 21
Send Marsh. Surr 8H 21
Senghenydd. Cphy 5L 17
Sennen. Corn 6G 3
Sennen Cove. Corn 6G 3
Sennybridge. Powy 2J 17
Serlby. Notts 1D 36
Sessay. N Yor 8B 48
Setchey. Norf 8C 38
Setley. Hants 5M 9
Setter. Shet 5J 91
Settiscarth. Orkn 8C 88
Settle. N Yor 1G 41
Settrington. N Yor 8F 48
Seven Ash. Som 2L 7
Sevenhampton. Glos 1J 19
Sevenhampton. Swin 4L 19
**Sevenoaks.** Kent 8B 22
Sevenoaks Weald. Kent 8B 22
Seven Sisters. Neat 4H 17
Seven Springs. Glos 2H 19
Severn Beach. S Glo 5D 18
Severn Stoke. Worc 7G 27
Sevington. Kent 1G 13
Sewards End. Essx 8B 30
Sewardstone. Essx 4L 21
Sewell. C Beds 1G 21
Sewerby. E Yor 1K 43
Seworgan. Corn 5L 3
Sewstern. Leics 7F 36
Sgallairidh. W Isl 6C 74
Sgarasta Mhor. W Isl 4B 76
Sgiogarstaigh. W Isl 5J 83
Sgreadan. Arg 8J 63
Shabbington. Buck 3D 20
Shackerley. Shrp 1G 27
Shackerstone. Leics 1A 28
Shackleford. Surr 1G 11
Shadforth. Dur 7G 55
Shadingfield. Suff 3L 31
Shadoxhurst. Kent 2F 12
Shadsworth. Bkbn 5F 40
Shadwell. Norf 3F 30
Shadwell. W Yor 4M 41
Shaftesbury. Dors 3G 9
Shafton. S Yor 6A 42
Shafton Two Gates. S Yor 6A 42
Shaggs. Dors 7G 9
Shakesfield. Glos 8E 26
Shalbourne. Wilts 7M 19
Shalcombe. IOW 7A 10
Shalden. Hants 1D 10
Shaldon. Devn 8J 7
Shalfleet. IOW 7B 10
Shalford. Essx 1D 22
Shalford. Surr 1H 11
Shalford Green. Essx 1D 22
Shallowford. Devn 1G 7
Shallowford. Staf 7G 35
Shalmsford Street. Kent 8G 23
Shalstone. Buck 8D 28
Shamley Green. Surr 1H 11
Shandon. Arg 1A 58
Shandwick. High 6J 79
Shangton. Leics 2E 28
Shankhouse. Nmbd 4F 54
**Shanklin.** IOW 7C 10
Shannochie. N Ayr 7J 57
Shap. Cumb 4D 46
Shapwick. Dors 5H 9
Shapwick. Som 2C 8
Shardlow. Derbs 6B 36
Shareshill. Staf 1H 27
Sharlston. W Yor 6A 42
Sharlston Common. W Yor 6A 42
Sharnal Street. Medw 6D 22
Sharnbrook. Bed 6G 29
Sharneyford. Lanc 5G 41
Sharnford. Leics 2B 28
Sharnhill Green. Dors 5F 8
Sharoe Green. Lanc 4D 40
Sharow. N Yor 8M 47
Sharpenhoe. C Beds 8H 29
Sharperton. Nmbd 1C 54
Sharpness. Glos 3E 18
Sharp Street. Norf 7K 39
Sharpthorne. W Sus 2L 11
Sharrington. Norf 6G 39
Shatterford. Worc 3F 26
Shatton. Derbs 1K 35
Shaugh Prior. Devn 5H 5
Shavington. Ches E 4F 34
**Shaw.** G Man 7H 41
Shaw. W Ber 7B 20
Shaw. Wilts 7G 19
Shawbirch. Telf 8E 34
Shawbury. Shrp 7D 34
Shawell. Leics 3C 28
Shawford. Hants 3B 10
Shawforth. Lanc 5G 41
Shaw Green. Lanc 6D 40
Shawhead. Dum 4C 52
Shaw Mills. N Yor 1L 41
Shawwood. E Ayr 7D 58
Shearington. Dum 5E 52
Shearsby. Leics 2D 28
Shearston. Som 2A 8
Shebbear. Devn 5D 6
Shebdon. Staf 7F 34
Shebster. High 5B 86
Sheddocksley. Aber 5H 73
Shedfield. Hants 4C 10
Shedog. N Ayr 6J 57
Sheen. Staf 3K 35
Sheepbridge. Derbs 2A 36
Sheep Hill. Dur 6E 54
Sheepscar. W Yor 4M 41
Sheepscombe. Glos 2G 19
Sheepstor. Devn 5H 5
Sheepwash. Devn 5D 6
Sheepwash. Nmbd 3F 54
Sheepway. N Som 6C 18
Sheepy Magna. Leics 1M 27
Sheepy Parva. Leics 1M 27
Sheering. Essx 2B 22
**Sheerness.** Kent 6F 22
Sheerwater. Surr 7H 21
Sheet. Hants 3E 10
**Sheffield.** S Yor 116 (1A 36)
Sheffield Bottom. W Ber 7D 20
Sheffield Green. E Sus 3M 11
Shefford. C Beds 8J 29
Shefford Woodlands. W Ber 6A 20
Sheigra. High 5D 84
Sheinton. Shrp 1E 26
Shelderton. Shrp 4C 26
Sheldon. Derbs 3K 35
Sheldon. Devn 5L 7
Sheldon. W Mid 3K 27
Sheldwich. Kent 8G 23
Sheldwich Lees. Kent 8G 23
Shelf. W Yor 5K 41
Shelfanger. Norf 3H 31
Shelfield. Warw 5K 27
Shelfield. W Mid 1J 27
Shelford. Notts 5D 36
Shelford. Warw 3B 28
Shell. Worc 6H 27
Shelley. Suff 8G 31
Shelley. W Yor 6L 41
Shell Green. Hal 1D 34
Shellingford. Oxon 4M 19
Shellow Bowells. Essx 3C 22
Shelsley Beauchamp. Worc 5F 26
Shelsley Walsh. Worc 5F 26
Shelthorpe. Leics 8C 36
Shelton. Bed 5H 29
Shelton. Norf 2J 31
Shelton. Notts 5E 36
Shelton. Shrp 8C 34
Shelton Green. Norf 2J 31
Shelton Lock. Derb 6A 36
Shelve. Shrp 2B 26
Shelwick. Here 7D 26
Shelwick Green. Here 7D 26
Shenfield. Essx 4C 22
Shenington. Oxon 7A 28
Shenley. Herts 3J 21
Shenley Brook End. Mil 8F 28
Shenleybury. Herts 3J 21
Shenley Church End. Mil 8F 28
Shenmore. Here 8B 26
Shennanton. Dum 5J 51
Shenstone. Staf 1K 27
Shenstone. Worc 4G 27
Shenstone Woodend. Staf 1K 27
Shenton. Leics 1A 28
Shenval. Mor 3B 72
Shepeau Stow. Linc 8L 37
Shephall. Herts 1K 21
Shepherd's Bush. G Lon 5K 21
Shepherd's Gate. Norf 8B 38
Shepherd's Green. Oxon 5E 20
Shepherd's Port. Norf 6C 38
Shepherdswell. Kent 1J 13
Shepley. W Yor 7K 41
Sheppardstown. High 7C 86
Shepperdine. S Glo 4E 18
Shepperton. Surr 7H 21
Shepreth. Cambs 7L 29
**Shepshed.** Leics 8B 36
Shepton Beauchamp. Som 4C 8
Shepton Mallet. Som 1E 8
Shepton Montague. Som 2E 8
Shepway. Kent 8D 22
Sheraton. Dur 8H 55
Sherborne. Dors 4E 8
Sherborne. Glos 2K 19
Sherborne. Som 8D 18
Sherborne Causeway. Dors 3G 9
Sherborne St John. Hants 8D 20
Sherbourne. Warw 5L 27
Sherburn. Dur 7G 55
Sherburn. N Yor 8G 49
Sherburn Hill. Dur 7G 55
Sherburn in Elmet. N Yor 4B 42
Shere. Surr 1H 11
Shereford. Norf 7E 38
Sherfield English. Hants 3L 9
Sherfield on Loddon. Hants 8D 20
Sherford. Devn 7K 5
Sherford. Dors 6H 9
Sheriffhales. Shrp 8F 34
Sheriff Hutton. N Yor 1D 42
Sheriffston. Mor 7B 80
Sheringham. Norf 5H 39
Sherington. Mil 7F 28
Shermanbury. W Sus 4K 11
Shernal Green. Worc 5H 27
Shernborne. Norf 6D 38
Sherrington. Wilts 2H 9
Sherston. Wilts 5G 19
Sherwood. Nott 5C 36
Sherwood Green. Devn 3E 6
Shettleston. Glas 3E 58
Shevington. G Man 7D 40
Shevington Moor. G Man 6D 40
Shevington Vale. G Man 7D 40
Sheviock. Corn 6F 4
Shide. IOW 7B 10
Shiel Bridge. High 4L 69
Shieldaig. High
nr. Charlestown 6K 77
nr. Torridon 8K 77
Shieldhill. Dum 3E 52
Shieldhill. Falk 2G 59
Shieldhill. S Lan 5J 59
Shieldmuir. N Lan 4F 58
Shielfoot. High 8H 69
Shielhill. Abers 8K 81
Shielhill. Ang 2H 67
Shifnal. Shrp 1F 26
Shilbottle. Nmbd 1E 54
**Shildon.** Dur 3L 47
Shillford. E Ren 4C 58
Shillingford. Devn 3J 7
Shillingford. Oxon 4C 20
Shillingford St George. Devn 7J 7
Shillingstone. Dors 4G 9
Shillington. C Beds 8J 29
Shillmoor. Nmbd 1B 54
Shilton. Oxon 3L 19
Shilton. Warw 3B 28
Shilvinghampton. Dors 7E 8
Shilvington. Nmbd 3E 54
Shimpling. Norf 3H 31
Shimpling. Suff 6E 30
Shimpling Street. Suff 6E 30
Shincliffe. Dur 7F 54
Shiney Row. Tyne 6G 55
Shinfield. Wok 7E 20
Shingay. Cambs 7L 29
Shingham. Norf 1D 30
Shingle Street. Suff 7K 31
Shinner's Bridge. Devn 5K 5
Shinness. High 2F 78
Shipbourne. Kent 8B 22
Shipdham. Norf 1F 30
Shipham. Som 8C 18
Shiphay. Torb 5L 5
Shiplake. Oxon 6E 20
Shipley. Derbs 5B 36
Shipley. Nmbd 8J 61
Shipley. Shrp 2G 27
Shipley. W Sus 3J 11
**Shipley.** W Yor 4K 41
Shipley Bridge. Surr 1L 11
Shipmeadow. Suff 3K 31
Shippon. Oxon 4B 20
Shipston-on-Stour. Warw 7L 27
Shipton. Buck 1E 20
Shipton. Glos 2J 19
Shipton. N Yor 2C 42
Shipton. Shrp 2D 26
Shipton Bellinger. Hants 1L 9
Shipton Gorge. Dors 6C 8
Shipton Green. W Sus 6F 10
Shipton Moyne. Glos 5G 19
Shipton-on-Cherwell. Oxon 2B 20
Shiptonthorpe. E Yor 3F 42
Shipton-under-Wychwood. Oxon 2L 19
Shirburn. Oxon 4D 20
Shirdley Hill. Lanc 6B 40
Shire. Cumb 8L 53
**Shirebrook.** Derbs 3C 36
Shiregreen. S Yor 8A 42
Shirehampton. Bris 6D 18
Shiremoor. Tyne 4G 55
Shirenewton. Mon 4C 18
Shireoaks. Notts 1C 36
Shires Mill. Fife 1J 59
Shirkoak. Kent 2F 12
Shirland. Derbs 4A 36
Shirley. Derbs 5L 35
Shirley. Sotn 4B 10
Shirley. W Mid 4K 27
Shirleywich. Staf 7H 35
Shirl Heath. Here 6C 26
Shirrell Heath. Hants 4C 10
Shirwell. Devn 2E 6
Shiskine. N Ayr 7J 57
Shobdon. Here 5B 26
Shobnall. Staf 7L 35
Shobrooke. Devn 5H 7
Shoby. Leics 7D 36
Shocklach. Ches W 5C 34
Shoeburyness. S'end 5F 22
Sholden. Kent 8K 23
Sholing. Sotn 4B 10
Sholver. G Man 7H 41
Shoot Hill. Shrp 8C 34
Shop. Corn
nr. Bude 4B 6
nr. Padstow 4A 4
Shop. Devn 4C 6
Shopford. Cumb 4K 53
**Shoreditch.** G Lon 5L 21
Shoreditch. Som 3M 7
Shoregill. Cumb 5F 46
Shoreham. Kent 7B 22
**Shoreham-by-Sea.** W Sus 5K 11
Shoresdean. Nmbd 5G 61
Shoreswood. Nmbd 5G 61
Shorncote. Glos 4J 19
Shorne. Kent 6C 22
Shorne Ridgeway. Kent 6C 22
Shortacombe. Devn 7E 6
Shortbridge. E Sus 3A 12
Shortgate. E Sus 4A 12
Short Green. Norf 3G 31
Shorthampton. Oxon 1M 19
Short Heath. Derbs 8M 35
Short Heath. W Mid
nr. Erdington 2J 27
nr. Wednesfield 1H 27
Shortlanesend. Corn 4M 3
Shorton. Torb 5L 5
Shortstown. Bed 7H 29
Shortwood. S Glo 6E 18
Shorwell. IOW 7B 10
Shoscombe. Bath 8F 18
Shotesham. Norf 2J 31
Shotgate. Essx 4D 22
Shotley. Suff 8J 31
Shotley Bridge. Dur 6D 54
Shotleyfield. Nmbd 6D 54
Shotley Gate. Suff 8J 31
Shottenden. Kent 8G 23
Shottermill. Surr 2F 10
Shottery. Warw 6K 27
Shotteswell. Warw 7B 28
Shottisham. Suff 7K 31
Shottle. Derbs 5M 35
Shotton. Dur
nr. Peterlee 8H 55
nr. Sedgefield 3A 48
**Shotton.** Flin 3B 34
Shotton. Nmbd
nr. Morpeth 4F 54
nr. Town Yetholm 6F 60
Shotton Colliery. Dur 7G 55
Shotts. N Lan 3G 59
Shotwick. Ches W 2B 34
Shouldham. Norf 1C 30
Shouldham Thorpe. Norf 1C 30
Shoulton. Worc 6G 27
Shrawardine. Shrp 8C 34
Shrawley. Worc 5G 27
Shreding Green. Buck 5H 21
Shrewley. Warw 5L 27
**Shrewsbury.** Shrp 116 (8C 34)
Shrewton. Wilts 1J 9
Shrigley. New M 6J 93
Shripney. W Sus 5G 11
Shrivenham. Oxon 5L 19
Shropham. Norf 2F 30
Shroton. Dors 4G 9
Shrub End. Essx 1F 22
Shucknall. Here 7D 26
Shudy Camps. Cambs 7C 30
Shulishadermor. High 1F 68
Shulista. High 6F 76
Shurdington. Glos 2H 19
Shurlock Row. Wind 6F 20
Shurrery. High 6B 86
Shurton. Som 1M 7
Shustoke. Warw 2L 27
Shute. Devn
nr. Axminster 6A 8
nr. Crediton 5H 7
Shutford. Oxon 7A 28
Shut Heath. Staf 7G 35
Shuthonger. Glos 8G 27
Shutlanehead. Staf 5G 35
Shutlanger. Nptn 6E 28
Shutt Green. Staf 1G 27
Shuttington. Warw 1L 27
Shuttlewood. Derbs 2B 36
Shuttleworth. G Man 6G 41
Siabost. W Isl 7F 82
Siabost bho Dheas. W Isl 7F 82
Siabost bho Thuath. W Isl 7F 82
Siadar. W Isl 6G 83
Siadar Iarach. W Isl 6G 83
Siadar Uarach. W Isl 6G 83
Sibbaldbie. Dum 3F 52
Sibbertoft. Nptn 3D 28
Sibdon Carwood. Shrp 3C 26
Sibertswold. Kent 1J 13
Sibford Ferris. Oxon 8A 28
Sibford Gower. Oxon 8A 28
Sible Hedingham. Essx 8D 30
Sibsey. Linc 4L 37
Sibsey Fen Side. Linc 4L 37
Sibson. Cambs 2H 29
Sibson. Leics 1A 28
Sibster. High 6E 86
Sibthorpe. Notts 5E 36
Sicklesmere. Suff 5E 30
Sicklinghall. N Yor 3A 42
Sid. Devn 7L 7
Sidbury. Devn 6L 7
Sidbury. Shrp 3E 26
Sidcot. N Som 8C 18
**Sidcup.** G Lon 6A 22
Siddick. Cumb 8E 52
Siddington. Ches E 2G 35
Siddington. Glos 4J 19
Side of the Moor. G Man 6F 40
Sidestrand. Norf 6J 39
Sidford. Devn 6L 7
Sidlesham. W Sus 6F 10
Sidley. E Sus 5D 12
Sidlow. Surr 1K 11
**Sidmouth.** Devn 7L 7
Sigford. Devn 8G 7
Sigglesthorne. E Yor 3J 43
Sighthill. Edin 2K 59
Sigingstone. V Glam 7J 17
Signet. Oxon 2L 19
Silchester. Hants 7D 20
Sildinis. W Isl 2D 76
Sileby. Leics 8D 36
Silecroft. Cumb 6L 45
Silfield. Norf 2H 31
Silian. Cdgn 7E 24
Silkstone. S Yor 7L 41
Silkstone Common. S Yor 7L 41
Silksworth. Tyne 6G 55
Silk Willoughby. Linc 5H 37
Silloth. Cumb 6F 52
Sills. Nmbd 1B 54
Sillyearn. Mor 8E 80
Silpho. N Yor 6G 49
Silsden. W Yor 3J 41
Silsoe. C Beds 8H 29
Silverbank. Abers 6G 73
Silverbridge. New M 7F 93
Silverburn. Midl 3L 59
Silverdale. Lanc 8C 46
Silverdale. Staf 5G 35
Silverdale Green. Lanc 8C 46
Silver End. Essx 2E 22
Silver End. W Mid 3H 27
Silvergate. Norf 7H 39
Silver Green. Norf 2J 31
Silverhillocks. Abers 7G 81
Silverley's Green. Suff 4J 31
Silverstone. Nptn 7D 28
Silverton. Devn 5J 7
Silverton. W Dun 2C 58
Silvington. Shrp 4E 26
Simm's Cross. Hal 1D 34
Simm's Lane End. Mers 7D 40
Simonburn. Nmbd 4B 54
Simonsbath. Som 2G 7
Simonstone. Lanc 4F 40
Simprim. Bord 5F 60
Simpson. Pemb 5E 14
Simpson Cross. Pemb 5E 14
Sinclairston. E Ayr 8C 58
Sinclairtown. Fife 8G 67
Sinderby. N Yor 7M 47
Sinderhope. Nmbd 6B 54
Sindlesham. Wok 7E 20
Sinfin. Derb 6M 35
Singleborough. Buck 8E 28
Singleton. Kent 1F 12
Singleton. Lanc 4B 40
Singleton. W Sus 4F 10
Singlewell. Kent 6C 22
Sinkhurst Green. Kent 1E 12
Sinnahard. Abers 4D 72
Sinnington. N Yor 7E 48
Sinton Green. Worc 5G 27
Sion Mills. Derr 4C 92
Sipson. G Lon 6H 21
Sirhowy. Blae 3L 17
Sisland. Norf 2K 31
Sissinghurst. Kent 2D 12
Siston. S Glo 6E 18
Sithney. Corn 6K 3
**Sittingbourne.** Kent 7F 22
Six Ashes. Staf 3F 26
Six Bells. Blae 4M 17
Six Hills. Leics 7D 36
Sixhills. Linc 1J 37
Six Mile Bottom. Cambs 6B 30
Sixmilecross. Ferm 5D 92
Sixpenny Handley. Dors 4H 9
Sizewell. Suff 5L 31
Skail. High 7K 85
Skaill. Orkn 8B 88
Skaills. Orkn 1G 87
Skares. E Ayr 8D 58
Skateraw. E Lot 2E 60
Skaw. Shet 1F 90
Skeabost. High 1F 68
Skeabrae. Orkn 7B 88
Skeeby. N Yor 5K 47
Skeffington. Leics 1E 28
Skeffling. E Yor 6L 43
Skegby. Notts
nr. Mansfield 3B 36
nr. Tuxford 2E 36
**Skegness.** Linc 3C 38
Skelberry. Shet
nr. Boddam 6D 90
nr. Housetter 5H 91
Skelbo. High 4H 79
Skelbo Street. High 4H 79
Skelbrooke. S Yor 6C 42
Skeldyke. Linc 6L 37
Skelfhill. Bord 1J 53
Skellingthorpe. Linc 2G 37
Skellister. Shet 2E 90
Skellorn Green. Ches E 1H 35
Skellow. S Yor 6C 42
Skelmanthorpe. W Yor 6L 41
**Skelmersdale.** Lanc 7C 40
Skelmorlie. N Ayr 3L 57
Skelpick. High 6K 85
Skelton. Cumb 8J 53
Skelton. E Yor 5E 42
Skelton. N Yor
nr. Richmond 5J 47
nr. Ripon 1A 42
Skelton. Red C 4D 48
Skelton. York 2C 42
Skelton Green. Red C 4D 48
Skelwick. Orkn 5D 88
Skelwith Bridge. Cumb 5B 46
Skendleby. Linc 3M 37
Skendleby Psalter. Linc 2M 37
Skenfrith. Mon 1C 18
Skerne. E Yor 2H 43
Skeroblingarry. Arg 7G 57
Skerray. High 5J 85
Skerricha. High 6E 84
Skerries Airport. Shet 6L 91
Skerton. Lanc 1C 40
Sketchley. Leics 2B 28
Sketty. Swan 5F 16
Skewen. Neat 5G 17
Skewsby. N Yor 8D 48
Skeyton. Norf 7J 39
Skeyton Corner. Norf 7J 39
Skiall. High 5B 86
Skidbrooke. Linc 8M 43
Skidbrooke North End. Linc 8M 43
Skidby. E Yor 4H 43
Skilgate. Som 3J 7
Skillington. Linc 7F 36
Skinburness. Cumb 6F 52
Skinflats. Falk 1H 59
Skinidin. High 1D 68
Skinnet. High 5H 85
Skinningrove. Red C 4E 48
Skipness. Arg 4H 57
Skippool. Lanc 3B 40
Skiprigg. Cumb 7H 53
Skipsea. E Yor 2J 43
Skipsea Brough. E Yor 2J 43
**Skipton.** N Yor 2H 41
Skipton-on-Swale. N Yor 8A 48
Skipwith. N Yor 4D 42
Skirbeck. Linc 5L 37
Skirbeck Quarter. Linc 5L 37
Skirlaugh. E Yor 4J 43
Skirling. Bord 6J 59
Skirmett. Buck 4E 20
Skirpenbeck. E Yor 2E 42
Skirwith. Cumb 8L 53
Skirwith. N Yor 8F 46
Skirza. High 5E 86
Skitby. Cumb 5J 53
Skitham. Lanc 3C 40
Skittle Green. Buck 3E 20
Skroo. Shet 2M 89
Skulamus. High 3H 69
Skullomie. High 5J 85
Skyborry Green. Shrp 4A 26
Skye Green. Essx 1E 22
Skye of Curr. High 3K 71
Slack. W Yor 5H 41
The Slack. Dur 3K 47
Slackhall. Derbs 1J 35
Slack Head. Cumb 8C 46
Slackhead. Mor 7D 80
Slackholme End. Linc 2B 38
Slacks of Cairnbanno. Abers 1H 73
Slad. Glos 3G 19
Slade. Swan 8L 15
The Slade. W Ber 7C 20
Slade End. Oxon 4C 20
Slade Field. Cambs 3L 29
Slade Green. G Lon 6B 22
Slade Heath. Staf 1H 27
Slade Hooton. S Yor 1C 36
Sladesbridge. Corn 4C 4
Slaggyford. Nmbd 6L 53
Slaidburn. Lanc 2F 40
Slaid Hill. W Yor 3M 41

Slaithwaite. W Yor 6J 41
Slaley. Derbs 4L 35
Slaley. Nmbd 6C 54
Slamannan. Falk 2G 59
Slapton. Buck 1G 21
Slapton. Devn 7L 5
Slapton. Nptn 7D 28
Slattocks. G Man 7G 41
Slaugham. W Sus 3K 11
Slaughterbridge. Corn 3D 4
Slaughterford. Wilts 6G 19
Slawston. Leics 2E 28
Sleaford. Hants 2F 10
**Sleaford**. Linc 5H 37
Sleagill. Cumb 4D 46
Sleap. Shrp 7C 34
Sledmere. E Yor 1G 43
Sleightholme. Dur 4H 47
Sleights. N Yor 5F 48
Slepe. Dors 6H 9
Slickly. High 5D 86
Sliddery. N Ayr 7J 57
Sligachan. High 3F 68
Slimbridge. Glos 3F 18
Slindon. Staf 6G 35
Slindon. W Sus 5G 11
Slinfold. W Sus 2J 11
Slingsby. N Yor 8D 48
Slip End. C Beds 2H 21
Slipton. Nptn 4G 29
Slitting Mill. Staf 8J 35
Slochd. High 3J 71
Slockavullin. Arg 8C 64
Sloley. Norf 7J 39
Sloncombe. Devn 7G 7
Sloothby. Linc 2A 38
**Slough**. Slo 6G 21
Slough Green. Som 3A 8
Slough Green. W Sus 3K 11
Sluggan. High 3J 71
Slyne. Lanc 1C 40
Smailholm. Bord 6D 60
Smallbridge. G Man 6H 41
Smallbrook. Devn 6H 7
Smallburgh. Norf 7K 39
Smallburn. E Ayr 7E 58
Smalldale. Derbs 2J 35
Small Dole. W Sus 4K 11
Smalley. Derbs 5B 36
Smallfield. Surr 1L 11
Small Heath. W Mid 3J 27
Smallholm. Dum 4F 52
Small Hythe. Kent 2E 12
Smallrice. Staf 6H 35
Smallridge. Devn 5B 8
Smallwood Hey. Lanc 3B 40
Smallworth. Norf 3G 31
Smannell. Hants 1A 10
Smardale. Cumb 5F 46
Smarden. Kent 1E 12
Smarden Bell. Kent 1E 12
Smart's Hill. Kent 1B 12
Smeatharpe. Devn 4M 7
Smeeth. Kent 2G 13
The Smeeth. Norf 8B 38
Smeeton Westerby. Leics 2D 28
Smeircleit. W Isl 4D 74
Smerral. High 8C 86
Smestow. Staf 2G 27
**Smethwick**. W Mid 3J 27
Smirisary. High 8H 69
Smisby. Derbs 8M 35
Smitham Hill. Bath 8D 18
Smith End Green. Worc 6F 26
Smithfield. Cumb 5J 53
Smith Green. Lanc 2C 40
The Smithies. Shrp 2E 26
Smithincott. Devn 4K 7
Smith's Green. Essx 1B 22
Smithstown. High 6J 77
Smithton. High 1H 71
Smithwood Green. Suff 6F 30
Smithy Bridge. G Man 6H 41
Smithy Green. Ches E 2F 34
Smithy Lane Ends. Lanc 6C 40
Smockington. Leics 3B 28
Smoogro. Orkn 1E 86
Smythe's Green. Essx 2F 22
Snaigow House. Per 3D 66
Snailbeach. Shrp 1B 26
Snailwell. Cambs 5C 30
Snainton. N Yor 7G 49
Snaith. E Yor 5D 42
Snape. N Yor 7L 47
Snape. Suff 6K 31
Snape Green. Lanc 6B 40
Snapper. Devn 2E 6
Snarestone. Leics 1M 27
Snarford. Linc 1H 37
Snargate. Kent 3F 12
Snave. Kent 3G 13
Sneachill. Worc 6H 27
Snead. Powy 2B 26
Snead Common. Worc 5F 26
Sneaton. N Yor 5F 48
Sneatonthorpe. N Yor 5G 49
Snelland. Linc 1H 37
Snelston. Derbs 5K 35
Snetterton. Norf 2F 30
Snettisham. Norf 6C 38
Snibston. Leics 8B 36
Sniseabhal. W Isl 2D 74
Snitter. Nmbd 1D 54
Snitterby. Linc 8G 43
Snitterfield. Warw 6L 27
Snitton. Shrp 4D 26
Snodhill. Here 7B 26
Snodland. Kent 7D 22
Snods Edge. Nmbd 6D 54
Snowshill. Glos 8J 27
Snow Street. Norf 3G 31
Snydale. W Yor 5B 42
Soake. Hants 4D 10
Soar. Carm 2F 16
Soar. Gwyn 7F 32
Soar. IOA 3C 32
Soar. Powy 1J 17
Soberton. Hants 4D 10
Soberton Heath. Hants 4D 10
Sockbridge. Cumb 3D 46
Sockburn. Darl 5M 47
Sodom. Den 3K 33
Sodom. Shet 1F 90
Soham. Cambs 4B 30
Soham Cotes. Cambs 4B 30
Solas. W Isl 6K 75
Soldon Cross. Devn 4C 6
Soldridge. Hants 2D 10
Solent Breezes. Hants 5C 10
Sole Street. Kent
nr. Meopham 7C 22
nr. Waltham 1G 13
**Solihull**. W Mid 3K 27
Sollers Dilwyn. Here 6C 26
Sollers Hope. Here 8E 26
Sollom. Lanc 6C 40
Solva. Pemb 4D 14
Somerby. Leics 8E 36
Somerby. Linc 7H 43
Somercotes. Derbs 4B 36
Somerford. Dors 6K 9
Somerford. Staf 1G 27
Somerford Keynes. Glos 4J 19
Somerley. W Sus 6F 10
Somerleyton. Suff 2L 31
Somersal Herbert. Derbs 6K 35
Somersby. Linc 2L 37
Somersham. Cambs 4L 29
Somersham. Suff 7G 31
Somerton. Oxon 1B 20
Somerton. Som 3C 8
Somerton. Suff 6E 30
**Sompting**. W Sus 5J 11
Sonning. Wok 6E 20
Sonning Common. Oxon 5E 20
Sonning Eye. Oxon 6E 20
Sookholme. Notts 3C 36
Sopley. Hants 6K 9
Sopworth. Wilts 5G 19
Sorbie. Dum 7K 51
Sordale. High 5C 86
Sorisdale. Arg 1H 63
Sorn. E Ayr 7D 58
Sornhill. E Ayr 6D 58
Sortat. High 5D 86
Sotby. Linc 2K 37
Sots Hole. Linc 3J 37
Sotterley. Suff 3L 31
Soudley. Shrp
nr. Church Stretton 2C 26
nr. Market Drayton 7F 34
Soughton. Flin 4M 33
Soulbury. Buck 1F 20
Soulby. Cumb
nr. Appleby 4F 46
nr. Penrith 3C 46
Souldern. Oxon 8C 28
Souldrop. Bed 5G 29
Sound. Ches E 5E 34
Sound. Shet
nr. Lerwick 3E 90
nr. Tresta 2D 90
Soundwell. S Glo 6E 18
Sourhope. Bord 7F 60
Sourin. Orkn 6D 88
Sour Nook. Cumb 7H 53
Sourton. Devn 6E 6
Soutergate. Cumb 6M 45
South Acre. Norf 8E 38
**Southall**. G Lon 6J 21
South Allington. Devn 8K 5
South Alloa. Falk 8B 66
Southam. Glos 1H 19
Southam. Warw 5B 28
South Ambersham. W Sus 3G 11
**Southampton**. Sotn 116 (4B 10)
Southampton Airport.
Hants 4B 10
Southannan. N Ayr 4M 57
South Anston. S Yor 1C 36
South Ascot. Wind 7G 21
South Baddesley. Hants 6A 10
South Balfern. Dum 6K 51
South Ballachulish. High 2E 64
**South Bank**. Red C 3C 48
South Barrow. Som 3E 8
**South Benfleet**. Essx 5D 22
South Bents. Tyne 5H 55
South Bersted. W Sus 5G 11
Southborough. Kent 1B 12
Southbourne. Bour 6K 9
Southbourne. W Sus 5E 10
South Bowood. Dors 6C 8
South Brent. Devn 6J 5
South Brewham. Som 2F 8
South Broomage. Falk 1G 59
South Broomhill. Nmbd 2F 54
Southburgh. Norf 1F 30
South Burlingham. Norf 1K 31
Southburn. E Yor 2G 43
South Cadbury. Som 3E 8
South Carlton. Linc 2G 37
South Cave. E Yor 4G 43
South Cerney. Glos 4J 19
South Chailey. E Sus 4L 11
South Chard. Som 5B 8
South Charlton. Nmbd 7J 61
South Cheriton. Som 3E 8
South Church. Dur 3L 47
Southchurch. S'end 5F 22
South Cleatlam. Dur 4K 47
South Cliffe. E Yor 4F 42
South Clifton. Notts 2F 36
South Clunes. High 1F 70
South Cockerington. Linc 1L 37
South Common. Devn 5B 8
South Cornelly. B'end 6H 17
Southcott. Devn
nr. Great Torrington 4D 6
nr. Okehampton 6E 6
Southcott. Wilts 8K 19
Southcourt. Buck 2F 20
South Cove. Suff 3L 31
South Creagan. Arg 3D 64
South Creake. Norf 6E 38
South Crosland. W Yor 6K 41
South Croxton. Leics 8D 36
South Dalton. E Yor 3G 43
South Darenth. Kent 7B 22
Southdean. Bord 1L 53
Southdown. Bath 7F 18
South Duffield. N Yor 4D 42
Southease. E Sus 5M 11
South Elkington. Linc 1K 37
South Elmsall. W Yor 6B 42
South End. Cumb 8M 45
South End. N Lin 5J 43
Southend. Arg 1B 50
Southend. Glos 4F 18
Southend. W Ber 6C 20
Southend Airport. Essx 5E 22
**Southend-on-Sea**. S'end 5E 22
Southerfield. Cumb 7F 52
Southerhouse. Shet 4D 90
Southerly. Devn 7E 6
Southernden. Kent 1E 12
Southerndown. V Glam 7H 17
Southerness. Dum 6D 52
South Erradale. High 6J 77
Southerton. Devn 6K 7
Southery. Norf 2C 30
Southey Green. Essx 8D 30
South Fambridge. Essx 4E 22
South Fawley. W Ber 5A 20
South Feorline. N Ayr 7J 57
South Ferriby. N Lin 5G 43
South Field. E Yor 5H 43
Southfleet. Kent 6C 22
South Garvan. High 8L 69
Southgate. Cdgn 4E 24
**Southgate**. G Lon 4L 21
Southgate. Norf
nr. Aylsham 7H 39
nr. Fakenham 6E 38
Southgate. Swan 6E 16
South Gluss. Shet 6H 91
South Godstone. Surr 1L 11
South Gorley. Hants 4K 9
South Green. Essx
nr. Billericay 4C 22
nr. Colchester 2G 23
South Green. Kent 7E 22
South Hanningfield. Essx 4D 22
South Harting. W Sus 4E 10
South Hayling. Hants 6E 10
South Hazelrigg. Nmbd 6H 61
South Heath. Buck 3G 21
South Heath. Essx 2H 23
South Heighton. E Sus 5M 11
South Hetton. Dur 7G 55
South Hiendley. W Yor 6A 42
South Hill. Corn 8C 6
South Hill. Som 3C 8
South Hinksey. Oxon 3C 20
South Hole. Devn 3B 6
South Holme. N Yor 8E 48
South Holmwood. Surr 1J 11
South Hornchurch. G Lon 5B 22
South Huish. Devn 7J 5
South Hykeham. Linc 3G 37
South Hylton. Tyne 6G 55
Southill. C Beds 7J 29
Southington. Hants 1C 10
South Kelsey. Linc 8H 43
South Kessock. High 1G 71
South Killingholme. N Lin 6J 43
South Kilvington. N Yor 7B 48
South Kilworth. Leics 3D 28
South Kirkby. W Yor 6B 42
South Kirkton. Abers 5G 73
South Knighton. Devn 8H 7
South Kyme. Linc 5J 37
South Lancing. W Sus 5J 11
South Ledaig. Arg 4D 64
South Leigh. Oxon 3A 20
Southleigh. Devn 6M 7
South Leverton. Notts 1E 36
South Littleton. Worc 7J 27
South Lopham. Norf 3G 31
South Luffenham. Rut 1G 29
South Malling. E Sus 4M 11
South Marston. Swin 5K 19
South Middleton. Nmbd 7G 61
South Milford. N Yor 4B 42
South Milton. Devn 7K 5
South Mimms. Herts 3K 21
Southminster. Essx 4F 22
South Molton. Devn 3G 7
South Moor. Dur 6E 54
Southmoor. Oxon 4A 20
South Moreton. Oxon 5C 20
South Mundham. W Sus 5F 10
South Muskham. Notts 4E 36
South Newbald. E Yor 4G 43
South Newington. Oxon 8B 28
South Newsham. Nmbd 4G 55
South Newton. N Ayr 4J 57
South Newton. Wilts 2J 9
South Normanton. Derbs 4B 36
South Norwood. G Lon 7L 21
South Nutfield. Surr 1L 11
**South Ockendon**. Thur 5B 22
Southoe. Cambs 5J 29
Southolt. Suff 5H 31
South Ormsby. Linc 2L 37
Southorpe. Pet 1H 29
South Otterington. N Yor 7A 48
South Owersby. Linc 8H 43
Southowram. W Yor 5K 41
**South Oxhey**. Herts 4J 21
South Perrott. Dors 5C 8
South Petherton. Som 4C 8
South Petherwin. Corn 7C 6
South Pickenham. Norf 1E 30
South Pool. Devn 7K 5
South Poorton. Dors 6D 8
South Port. Arg 5E 64
**Southport**. Mers 6B 40
Southpunds. Shet 6E 90
South Queensferry. Edin 2K 59
South Radworthy. Devn 2G 7
South Rauceby. Linc 5H 37
South Raynham. Norf 7E 38
Southrepps. Norf 6J 39
South Reston. Linc 1M 37
Southrey. Linc 3J 37
Southrop. Glos 3K 19
Southrope. Hants 1D 10
South Runcton. Norf 1C 30
South Scarle. Notts 3F 36
Southsea. Port 6D 10
**South Shields**. Tyne 5G 55
South Shore. Bkpl 4B 40
Southside. Orkn 7E 88
South Somercotes. Linc 8M 43
South Stainley. N Yor 1M 41
South Stainmore. Cumb 4G 47
South Stifford. Thur 6B 22
South Stoke. Bath 7F 18
South Stoke. Oxon 5C 20
South Stoke. W Sus 5H 11
South Street. E Sus 4L 11
South Street. Kent
nr. Faversham 8G 23
nr. Whitstable 7H 23
South Tawton. Devn 6F 6
South Thoresby. Linc 2M 37
South Tidworth. Wilts 1L 9
South Town. Devn 7J 7
South Town. Hants 2D 10
Southtown. Norf 1M 31
Southtown. Orkn 2F 86
South View. Shet 3D 90
Southwaite. Cumb 7J 53
South Walsham. Norf 8K 39
South Warnborough. Hants 1E 10
Southwater. W Sus 3J 11
Southwater Street. W Sus 3J 11
Southway. Som 1D 8
South Weald. Essx 4B 22
South Weirs. Hants 5L 9
Southwell. Dors 8E 8
Southwell. Notts 4E 36
South Weston. Oxon 4E 20
South Wheatley. Corn 6B 6
South Wheatley. Notts 1E 36
Southwick. Hants 5D 10
Southwick. Nptn 2H 29
Southwick. Tyne 6G 55
**Southwick**. W Sus 5K 11
Southwick. Wilts 8G 19
South Widcombe. Bath 8D 18
South Wigston. Leics 2C 28
South Willingham. Linc 1J 37
South Wingfield. Derbs 4A 36
South Witham. Linc 8G 37
Southwold. Suff 4M 31
South Wonston. Hants 2B 10
Southwood. Norf 1K 31
Southwood. Som 2D 8
**South Woodham Ferrers**.
Essx 4E 22
South Wootton. Norf 7C 38
South Wraxall. Wilts 7G 19
South Zeal. Devn 6F 6
Soval Lodge. W Isl 1E 76
Sowerby. N Yor 7B 48
Sowerby. W Yor 5J 41
Sowerby Bridge. W Yor 5J 41
Sowerby Row. Cumb 7H 53
Sower Carr. Lanc 3B 40
Sowley Green. Suff 6D 30
Sowood. W Yor 6J 41
Sowton. Devn 6J 7
Soyal. High 4F 78
Soyland Town. W Yor 5J 41
The Spa. New M 6H 93
Spacey Houses. N Yor 2M 41
Spa Common. Norf 6J 39
**Spalding**. Linc 7K 37
Spaldington. E Yor 4E 42
Spaldwick. Cambs 4J 29
Spalford. Notts 3F 36
Spamount. Derr 4C 92
Spanby. Linc 6H 37
Sparham. Norf 8G 39
Sparhamhill. Norf 8G 39
Spark Bridge. Cumb 7B 46
Sparket. Cumb 3C 46
Sparkford. Som 3E 8
Sparkwell. Devn 6H 5
Sparrow Green. Norf 8F 38
Sparrowpit. Derbs 1J 35
Sparrow's Green. E Sus 2C 12
Sparsholt. Hants 2B 10
Sparsholt. Oxon 5M 19
Spartylea. Nmbd 7B 54
Spath. Staf 6J 35
Spaunton. N Yor 7E 48
Spaxton. Som 2M 7
Spean Bridge. High 7C 70
Spear Hill. W Sus 4J 11
Speen. Buck 4F 20
Speen. W Ber 7B 20
Speeton. N Yor 8J 49
Speke. Mers 1C 34
Speldhurst. Kent 1B 12
Spellbrook. Herts 2A 22
Spelsbury. Oxon 1A 20
Spencers Wood. Wok 7E 20
Spennithorne. N Yor 7K 47
**Spennymoor**. Dur 8F 54
Spernall. Warw 5J 27
Sperrin. Derr 4E 92
Spetchley. Worc 6G 27
Spetisbury. Dors 5H 9
Spexhall. Suff 3K 31
Speybank. High 5J 71
Spey Bay. Mor 7C 80
Speybridge. High 3L 71
Speyview. Mor 1B 72
Spilsby. Linc 3M 37
Spindlestone. Nmbd 6J 61
Spinkhill. Derbs 2B 36
Spinney Hills. Leic 1D 28
Spinningdale. High 5G 79
Spital. Mers 1B 34
Spitalhill. Derbs 5K 35
Spital in the Street. Linc 8G 43
Spithurst. E Sus 4M 11
Spittal. Dum 6J 51
Spittal. E Lot 2B 60
Spittal. High 6C 86
Spittal. Nmbd 4H 61
Spittal. Pemb 4F 14
Spittalfield. Per 3E 66
Spittal of Glenmuick. Abers 7C 72
Spittal of Glenshee. Per 8M 71
Spittal-on-Rule. Bord 7C 60
Spixworth. Norf 8J 39
Splatt. Corn 7B 6
Spofforth. N Yor 2A 42
Spondon. Derb 6B 36
Spon End. W Mid 4M 27
Spooner Row. Norf 2G 31
Sporle. Norf 8E 38
Spott. E Lot 2D 60
Spratton. Nptn 4E 28
Spreakley. Surr 1F 10
Spreyton. Devn 6G 7
Spridlington. Linc 1H 37
Springburn. Glas 3E 58
Springfield. Dum 5H 53
Springfield. Ferm 6B 92
Springfield. Fife 6G 67
Springfield. High 7G 79
Springfield. W Mid 3J 27
Spring Hill. W Mid 2G 27
Springhill. Staf 1H 27
Springholm. Dum 5C 52
Springside. N Ayr 6B 58
Springthorpe. Linc 1F 36
Spring Vale. IOW 6D 10
Spring Valley. IOM 7C 44
Springwell. Tyne 6F 54
Sproatley. E Yor 4J 43
Sproston Green. Ches W 3F 34
Sprotbrough. S Yor 7C 42
Sproughton. Suff 7H 31
Sprouston. Bord 6E 60
Sprowston. Norf 8J 39
Sproxton. Leics 7F 36
Sproxton. N Yor 7D 48
Sprunston. Cumb 7J 53
Spurstow. Ches E 4D 34
Squires Gate. Bkpl 4B 40
Sraid Ruadh. Arg 3E 62
Srannda. W Isl 5B 76
Sron an t-Sithein. High 1C 64
Sronphadruig Lodge. Per 8H 71
Sruth Mor. W Isl 7L 75
Stableford. Shrp 2F 26
Stackhouse. N Yor 1G 41
Stackpole. Pemb 7F 14
Stackpole Elidor. Pemb 7F 14
Stacksford. Norf 2G 31
Stacksteads. Lanc 5G 41
Staddiscombe. Plym 6H 5
Staddlethorpe. E Yor 5F 42
Staddon. Devn 5C 6
Stadhampton. Oxon 4D 20
Stadhlaigearraidh. W Isl 2D 74
Stafainn. High 7F 76
Staffield. Cumb 7K 53
Staffin. High 7F 76
**Stafford**. Staf 7H 35
Stafford Park. Telf 1F 26
Stagden Cross. Essx 2C 22
Stagsden. Bed 7G 29
Stag's Head. Devn 3F 6
Stainburn. Cumb 2K 45
Stainburn. N Yor 3L 41
Stainby. Linc 7G 37
Staincliffe. W Yor 5L 41
Staincross. S Yor 6M 41
Staindrop. Dur 3K 47
**Staines-upon-Thames**.
Surr 6H 21
Stainfield. Linc
nr. Bourne 7H 37
nr. Lincoln 2J 37
Stainforth. N Yor 1G 41
Stainforth. S Yor 6D 42
Staining. Lanc 4B 40
Stainland. W Yor 6J 41
Stainsacre. N Yor 5G 49
Stainton. Cumb
nr. Carlisle 6H 53
nr. Kendal 7D 46
nr. Penrith 3C 46
Stainton. Dur 4J 47
Stainton. Midd 4B 48
Stainton. N Yor 6K 47
Stainton. S Yor 8C 42
Stainton by Langworth.
Linc 2H 37
Staintondale. N Yor 6G 49
Stainton le Vale. Linc 8J 43
Stainton with Adgarley.
Cumb 8A 46
Stair. Cumb 2M 45
Stair. E Ayr 7C 58
Stairhaven. Dum 6H 51
Staithes. N Yor 4E 48
Stakeford. Nmbd 3F 54
Stake Pool. Lanc 3C 40
Stakes. Hants 5D 10
Stalbridge. Dors 4F 8
Stalbridge Weston. Dors 4F 8
Stalham. Norf 7K 39
Stalham Green. Norf 7K 39
Stalisfield Green. Kent 8F 22
Stallen. Dors 4E 8
Stallingborough. NE Lin 6K 43
Stalling Busk. N Yor 7H 47
Stallington. Staf 6H 35
Stalmine. Lanc 3B 40
**Stalybridge**. G Man 8H 41
Stambourne. Essx 8D 30
**Stamford**. Linc 1H 29
Stamford. Nmbd 8K 61
Stamford Bridge. Ches W 3C 34
Stamford Bridge. E Yor 2E 42
Stamfordham. Nmbd 4D 54
Stamperland. E Ren 4D 58
Stanah. Lanc 3B 40
Stanborough. Herts 2K 21
Stanbridge. C Beds 1G 21
Stanbridge. Dors 5J 9
Stanbury. W Yor 4J 41
Stand. N Lan 3F 58
Standburn. Falk 2H 59
Standeford. Staf 1H 27
Standen. Kent 1E 12
Standen Street. Kent 2E 12
Standerwick. Som 8G 19
Standford. Hants 2F 10
Standford Bridge. Telf 7F 34
Standingstone. Cumb 7G 53
Standish. Glos 3G 19
**Standish**. G Man 6D 40
Standish Lower Ground.
G Man 7D 40
Standlake. Oxon 3A 20
Standon. Hants 3B 10
Standon. Herts 1L 21
Standon. Staf 6G 35
Standon Green End. Herts 2L 21
Stane. N Lan 4G 59
Stanecastle. N Ayr 6B 58
Stanfield. Norf 7F 38
Stanfield. Suff 6D 30
Stanford. C Beds 7J 29
Stanford. Kent 2H 13
Stanford Bishop. Here 6E 26
Stanford Bridge. Worc 5F 26
Stanford Dingley. W Ber 6C 20
Stanford in the Vale. Oxon 4M 19
**Stanford-le-Hope**. Thur 5C 22
Stanford on Avon. Nptn 4C 28
Stanford on Soar. Notts 7C 36
Stanford on Teme. Worc 5F 26
Stanford Rivers. Essx 3B 22
Stanfree. Derbs 2B 36
Stanghow. Red C 4D 48
Stanground. Pet 2K 29
Stanhoe. Norf 6E 38
Stanhope. Dur 8C 54
Stanhope. Bord 7K 59
Stanion. Nptn 3G 29
Stanley. Derbs 5B 36
**Stanley**. Dur 6E 54
Stanley. Per 4E 66
Stanley. Shrp 3F 26
Stanley. Staf 4H 35
**Stanley**. W Yor 5M 41
Stanley Common. Derbs 5B 36
Stanley Crook. Dur 8E 54
Stanley Hill. Here 7E 26
Stanlow. Ches W 2C 34
Stanmer. Brig 5L 11
**Stanmore**. G Lon 4J 21
Stanmore. Hants 3B 10
Stanmore. W Ber 6B 20
Stannersburn. Nmbd 3M 53
Stanningfield. Suff 6E 30
Stannington. Nmbd 4F 54
Stannington. S Yor 1M 35
Stansbatch. Here 5B 26
Stanshope. Staf 4K 35
Stanstead. Suff 7E 30
Stanstead Abbotts. Herts 2L 21
Stansted. Kent 7C 22
Stansted Airport. Essx 119 (1B 22)
Stansted Mountfitchet.
Essx 1B 22
Stanthorne. Ches W 3E 34
Stanton. Derbs 8L 35
Stanton. Glos 8J 27
Stanton. Nmbd 2E 54
Stanton. Staf 5K 35
Stanton. Suff 4F 30
Stanton by Bridge. Derbs 7A 36
Stanton-by-Dale. Derbs 6B 36
Stanton Chare. Suff 4F 30
Stanton Drew. Bath 7D 18
Stanton Fitzwarren. Swin 4K 19
Stanton Harcourt. Oxon 3B 20
Stanton Hill. Notts 3B 36
Stanton in Peak. Derbs 3L 35
Stanton Lacy. Shrp 4C 26
Stanton Long. Shrp 2D 26
Stanton-on-the-Wolds.
Notts 6D 36
Stanton Prior. Bath 7E 18
Stanton St Bernard. Wilts 7J 19
Stanton St John. Oxon 3C 20
Stanton St Quintin. Wilts 6H 19
Stanton Street. Suff 5F 30
Stanton under Bardon.
Leics 8B 36
Stanton upon Hine Heath.
Shrp 7D 34
Stanton Wick. Bath 7E 18
Stanwardine in the Fields.
Shrp 7C 34
Stanwardine in the Wood.
Shrp 7C 34
Stanway. Essx 1F 22
Stanway. Glos 8J 27
Stanwell. Surr 6H 21
Stanwell Green. Suff 4H 31
Stanwell Moor. Surr 6H 21
Stanwick. Nptn 4G 29
Stanydale. Shet 2C 90
Staoinebrig. W Isl 2D 74
Stape. N Yor 6E 48
Stapehill. Dors 5J 9
Stapeley. Ches E 5E 34
Stapenhill. Staf 7L 35
Staple. Kent 8J 23
Staple Cross. Devn 3K 7
Staplecross. E Sus 3D 12
Staplefield. W Sus 3K 11
Staple Fitzpaine. Som 4A 8
Stapleford. Cambs 6A 30
Stapleford. Herts 2L 21
Stapleford. Leics 8F 36
Stapleford. Linc 4F 36
**Stapleford**. Notts 6B 36
Stapleford. Wilts 2J 9
Stapleford Abbotts. Essx 4B 22
Stapleford Tawney. Essx 4B 22
Staplegrove. Som 3M 7
Staplehay. Som 3M 7
Staple Hill. S Glo 6E 18
Staplehurst. Kent 1D 12
Staplers. IOW 7C 10
Stapleton. Bris 6E 18
Stapleton. Cumb 4K 53
Stapleton. Here 5B 26
Stapleton. Leics 2B 28
Stapleton. N Yor 4L 47
Stapleton. Shrp 1C 26
Stapleton. Som 3C 8
Stapley. Som 4L 7
Staploe. Bed 5J 29
Staplow. Here 7E 26
Star. Fife 7G 67
Star. Pemb 3J 15
Starbeck. N Yor 2M 41
Starbotton. N Yor 8H 47
Starcross. Devn 7J 7
Stareton. Warw 4M 27
Starkholmes. Derbs 4M 35
Starling. G Man 6F 40
Starling's Green. Essx 8A 30
Starston. Norf 3J 31
Start. Devn 7L 5
Startforth. Dur 4J 47
Start Hill. Essx 1B 22
Startley. Wilts 5H 19
Stathe. Som 3B 8
Stathern. Leics 6E 36
Station Town. Dur 8H 55
Staughton Green. Cambs 5J 29
Staughton Highway.
Cambs 5J 29
Staunton. Glos
nr. Cheltenham 1F 18
nr. Monmouth 2D 18
Staunton in the Vale.
Notts 5F 36
Staunton on Arrow. Here 5B 26
Staunton on Wye. Here 7B 26
Staveley. Cumb 6C 46
**Staveley**. Derbs 2B 36
Staveley. N Yor 1A 42
Staveley-in-Cartmel. Cumb 7B 46
Staverton. Devn 5K 5
Staverton. Glos 1G 19
Staverton. Nptn 5C 28
Staverton. Wilts 7G 19
Stawell. Som 2B 8
Stawley. Som 3K 7
Staxigoe. High 6E 86
Staxton. N Yor 8H 49
Staylittle. Powy 3H 25
Staynall. Lanc 3B 40
Staythorpe. Notts 4E 36
Stean. N Yor 8J 47
Stearsby. N Yor 8D 48
Steart. Som 1A 8
Stebbing. Essx 1C 22
Stebbing Green. Essx 1C 22
Stedham. W Sus 3F 10
Steel. Nmbd 6C 54
Steel Cross. E Sus 2B 12
Steelend. Fife 8D 66
Steele Road. Bord 2K 53
Steel Heath. Shrp 6D 34
Steen's Bridge. Here 6D 26
Steep. Hants 3E 10
Steep Lane. W Yor 5J 41
Steeple. Dors 7H 9
Steeple. Essx 3F 22
Steeple Ashton. Wilts 8H 19
Steeple Aston. Oxon 1B 20
Steeple Barton. Oxon 1B 20
Steeple Bumpstead. Essx 7C 30
Steeple Claydon. Buck 1D 20
Steeple Gidding. Cambs 3J 29
Steeple Langford. Wilts 2J 9
Steeple Morden. Cambs 7K 29
Steeton. W Yor 3J 41
Stein. High 8D 76
Steinmanhill. Abers 1G 73
Stelling Minnis. Kent 1H 13
Stembridge. Som 3C 8
Stemster. High
nr. Halkirk 5C 86
nr. Westfield 5B 86
Stenalees. Corn 6C 4
Stenhill. Devn 4K 7
Stenhouse. Edin 2L 59
**Stenhousemuir**. Falk 1G 59
Stenigot. Linc 1K 37
Stenscholl. High 7F 76
Stenso. Orkn 7C 88
Stenson. Derbs 7M 35
Stenson Fields. Derbs 6M 35
Stenton. E Lot 2D 60
Stenwith. Linc 6F 36
Steòrnabhagh. W Isl 8H 83
Stepaside. Pemb 6H 15
Stepford. Dum 3C 52
**Stepney**. G Lon 5L 21
Steppingley. C Beds 8H 29
Stepps. N Lan 3E 58
Sterndale Moor. Derbs 3K 35
Sternfield. Suff 5K 31
Stert. Wilts 8J 19
Stetchworth. Cambs 6C 30
**Stevenage**. Herts 1K 21
**Stevenston**. N Ayr 5A 58
Stevenstone. Devn 4E 6
Steventon. Hants 1C 10
Steventon. Oxon 4B 20
Steventon End. Essx 7B 30
Stevington. Bed 6G 29
Stewartby. Bed 7H 29
Stewarton. Arg 8F 56
Stewarton. E Ayr 5C 58
Stewartstown. M Ulst 5F 93
Stewkley. Buck 1F 20
Stewkley Dean. Buck 1F 20
Stewley. Som 4B 8
Stewton. Linc 1L 37
Steyning. W Sus 4J 11
Steynton. Pemb 6F 14
Stibb. Corn 4B 6
Stibbard. Norf 7F 38
Stibb Cross. Devn 4D 6
Stibb Green. Wilts 7L 19
Stibbington. Cambs 2H 29
Stichill. Bord 6E 60
Sticker. Corn 6B 4
Stickford. Linc 3L 37
Sticklepath. Devn 6F 6
Sticklinch. Som 2D 8
Stickling Green. Essx 8A 30
Stickney. Linc 4L 37
Stiffkey. Norf 5F 38
Stifford's Bridge. Here 7F 26
Stileway. Som 1C 8
Stillingfleet. N Yor 3C 42
Stillington. N Yor 1C 42
Stillington. Stoc T 3A 48
Stilton. Cambs 3J 29
Stinchcombe. Glos 4F 18
Stinsford. Dors 6F 8
Stiperstones. Shrp 1B 26
Stirchley. Telf 1F 26
Stirchley. W Mid 3J 27
Stirling. Abers 1L 73
**Stirling**. Stir 116 (8A 66)
Stirton. N Yor 2H 41
Stisted. Essx 1D 22
Stitchcombe. Wilts 7L 19
Stithians. Corn 5L 3
Stittenham. High 6G 79
Stivichall. W Mid 4M 27
Stixwould. Linc 3J 37
Stoak. Ches W 2C 34
Stobo. Bord 6K 59
Stobo Castle. Bord 6K 59
Stoborough. Dors 7H 9
Stoborough Green. Dors 7H 9
Stobs Castle. Bord 1K 53
Stobswood. Nmbd 2F 54
Stock. Essx 4C 22
Stockbridge. Hants 2A 10
Stockbridge. W Yor 3J 41
Stockbury. Kent 7E 22
Stockcross. W Ber 7B 20
Stockdalewath. Cumb 7H 53
Stocker's Head. Kent 8F 22
Stockerston. Leics 2F 28
Stock Green. Worc 6H 27
Stocking. Here 8E 26
Stockingford. Warw 2M 27
Stocking Green. Essx 8B 30
Stocking Pelham. Herts 1A 22
Stockland. Devn 5M 7
Stockland Bristol. Som 1M 7
Stockleigh English. Devn 5H 7
Stockleigh Pomeroy. Devn 5H 7
Stockley. Wilts 7J 19
Stocklinch. Som 4B 8
**Stockport**. G Man 1G 35
The Stocks. Kent 3F 12
**Stocksbridge**. S Yor 8L 41
Stocksfield. Nmbd 5D 54
Stockstreet. Essx 1E 22
Stockton. Here 5D 26
Stockton. Norf 2K 31
Stockton. Shrp
nr. Bridgnorth 2F 26
nr. Chirbury 1A 26
Stockton. Telf 8F 34
Stockton. Warw 5B 28
Stockton. Wilts 2H 9
Stockton Brook. Staf 4H 35
Stockton Cross. Here 5D 26
Stockton Heath. Warr 1E 34
**Stockton-on-Tees**. Stoc T 4B 48
Stockton on Teme. Worc 5F 26
Stockton-on-the-Forest.
York 2D 42
Stockwell Heath. Staf 7J 35
Stock Wood. Worc 6J 27
Stockwood. Bris 7E 18
Stodmarsh. Kent 7J 23
Stody. Norf 6G 39
Stoer. High 1M 77
Stoford. Som 4D 8
Stoford. Wilts 2J 9
Stogumber. Som 2K 7
Stogursey. Som 1M 7
Stoke. Devn 3B 6
Stoke. Hants
nr. Andover 8B 20
nr. South Hayling 5E 10
Stoke. Medw 6E 22
Stoke. W Mid 4A 28
Stoke Abbott. Dors 5C 8
Stoke Albany. Nptn 3F 28
Stoke Ash. Suff 4H 31
Stoke Bardolph. Notts 5D 36
Stoke Bliss. Worc 5E 26
Stoke Bruerne. Nptn 7E 28
Stoke by Clare. Suff 7D 30
Stoke-by-Nayland. Suff 8F 30
Stoke Canon. Devn 6J 7
Stoke Charity. Hants 2B 10
Stoke Climsland. Corn 8C 6
Stoke Cross. Here 6E 26
Stoke D'Abernon. Surr 8J 21
Stoke Doyle. Nptn 3H 29
Stoke Dry. Rut 2F 28
Stoke Edith. Here 7E 26
Stoke Farthing. Wilts 3J 9
Stoke Ferry. Norf 1D 30
Stoke Fleming. Devn 7L 5
Stokeford. Dors 7G 9
Stoke Gabriel. Devn 6L 5
Stoke Gifford. S Glo 6E 18
Stoke Golding. Leics 2A 28
Stoke Goldington. Mil 7F 28
Stokeham. Notts 2E 36
Stoke Hammond. Buck 1F 20
Stoke Heath. Shrp 7E 34
Stoke Holy Cross. Norf 1J 31
Stokeinteignhead. Devn 8J 7
Stoke Lacy. Here 7E 26
Stoke Lyne. Oxon 1C 20
Stoke Mandeville. Buck 2F 20
Stokenchurch. Buck 4E 20
**Stoke Newington**. G Lon 5L 21
Stokenham. Devn 7L 5
Stoke on Tern. Shrp 7E 34
**Stoke-on-Trent**.
Stoke 116 (5G 35)
Stoke Orchard. Glos 1H 19
Stoke Pero. Som 1H 7
Stoke Poges. Buck 5G 21
Stoke Prior. Here 6D 26
Stoke Prior. Worc 5H 27
Stoke Rivers. Devn 2F 6
Stoke Rochford. Linc 7G 37
Stoke Row. Oxon 5D 20
Stoke St Gregory. Som 3B 8
Stoke St Mary. Som 3A 8
Stoke St Michael. Som 1E 8
Stoke St Milborough. Shrp 3D 26
Stokesay. Shrp 3C 26
Stokesby. Norf 8L 39
Stokesley. N Yor 5C 48
Stoke sub Hamdon. Som 4C 8
Stoke Talmage. Oxon 4D 20
Stoke Town. Stoke 116 (5G 35)
Stoke Trister. Som 3F 8
Stoke Wake. Dors 5F 8
Stolford. Som 1M 7
Stondon Massey. Essx 3B 22
Stone. Buck 2E 20
Stone. Glos 4E 18
Stone. Kent 6B 22
Stone. Som 2D 8
**Stone**. Staf 6H 35
Stone. Worc 4G 27
Stonea. Cambs 2A 30
Stoneacton. Shrp 2D 26
Stone Allerton. Som 8C 18
Ston Easton. Som 8E 18
Stonebridge. N Som 8B 18
Stonebridge. Surr 1J 11
Stone Bridge Corner. Pet 1K 29
Stonebroom. Derbs 4B 36
Stonebyres Holdings.
S Lan 5G 59
Stone Chair. W Yor 5K 41
Stone Cross. E Sus 5C 12
Stone Cross. Kent 2B 12
Stone-edge Batch. N Som 6C 18
Stoneferry. Hull 4H 43
Stonefield. Arg 4D 64
Stonefield. S Lan 4E 58
Stonegate. E Sus 3C 12
Stonegate. N Yor 5E 48
Stonegrave. N Yor 8D 48
Stonehall. Worc 7G 27
Stonehaugh. Nmbd 4A 54
**Stonehaven**. Abers 7H 73
Stone Heath. Staf 6H 35
Stone Hill. Kent 2G 13
Stone House. Cumb 7F 46
Stonehouse. Glos 3G 19
Stonehouse. Nmbd 6L 53
Stonehouse. S Lan 5F 58
Stone in Oxney. Kent 3F 12
Stoneleigh. Warw 4M 27
Stoneley Green. Ches E 4E 34
Stonely. Cambs 5J 29
Stonepits. Worc 6J 27
Stoner Hill. Hants 3E 10
Stonesby. Leics 7F 36
Stonesfield. Oxon 2A 20
Stones Green. Essx 1H 23
Stone Street. Kent 8B 22
Stone Street. Suff
nr. Boxford 8F 30
nr. Halesworth 3K 31
Stonethwaite. Cumb 4A 46
Stoneyburn. W Lot 3H 59
Stoney Cross. Hants 4L 9
Stoneyford. Devn 5K 7
Stoneygate. Leic 1D 28
Stoneyhills. Essx 4F 22
Stoneykirk. Dum 6F 50
Stoney Middleton. Derbs 2L 35
Stoney Stanton. Leics 2B 28
Stoney Stoke. Som 2F 8
Stoney Stratton. Som 2E 8
Stoney Stretton. Shrp 1B 26
Stoneywood. Aber 4H 73
Stonham Aspal. Suff 6H 31
Stonnall. Staf 1J 27
Stonor. Oxon 5E 20
Stonton Wyville. Leics 2E 28
Stonybreck. Shet 2M 89
Stony Cross. Devn 3E 6
Stony Cross. Here
nr. Great Malvern 7F 26
nr. Leominster 5D 26
Stonyford. Lis 5H 93
Stony Houghton. Derbs 3B 36
Stony Stratford. Mil 7E 28
Stoodleigh. Devn
nr. Barnstaple 2F 6
nr. Tiverton 4J 7
Stopham. W Sus 4H 11
Stopsley. Lutn 1J 21
Stoptide. Corn 4B 4
Storeton. Mers 1B 34
Stormontfield. Per 5E 66
Stornoway. W Isl 8H 83
Stornoway Airport. W Isl 8H 83
Storridge. Here 7F 26
Storrington. W Sus 4H 11
Storrs. Cumb 6B 46
Storth. Cumb 7C 46
Storwood. E Yor 3E 42
Stotfield. Mor 6B 80
Stotfold. C Beds 8K 29
Stottesdon. Shrp 3E 26
Stoughton. Leics 1D 28
Stoughton. Surr 8G 21
Stoughton. W Sus 4F 10
Stoul. High 6J 69
Stoulton. Worc 7H 27
**Stourbridge**. W Mid 3G 27
Stourpaine. Dors 5G 9
**Stourport-on-Severn**.
Worc 4G 27
Stour Provost. Dors 3F 8
Stour Row. Dors 3G 9
Stourton. Staf 3G 27
Stourton. Warw 8L 27
Stourton. W Yor 4M 41
Stourton. Wilts 2F 8
Stourton Caundle. Dors 4F 8
Stove. Orkn 6F 88
Stove. Shet 5E 90
Stoven. Suff 3L 31
Stow. Linc
nr. Billingborough 6H 37
nr. Gainsborough 1F 36
Stow. Bord 5B 60
Stow Bardolph. Norf 1C 30
Stow Bedon. Norf 2F 30
Stowbridge. Norf 1C 30
Stow cum Quy. Cambs 5B 30
Stowe. Glos 3D 18
Stowe. Shrp 4B 26
Stowe. Staf 8K 35
Stowe-by-Chartley. Staf 7J 35
Stowell. Som 3E 8
Stowey. Bath 8D 18
Stowford. Devn
nr. Colaton Raleigh 7K 7
nr. Combe Martin 1F 6
nr. Tavistock 7D 6
Stowlangtoft. Suff 5F 30
Stow Longa. Cambs 4J 29
Stow Maries. Essx 4E 22
**Stowmarket**. Suff 6G 31
Stow-on-the-Wold. Glos 1K 19
Stowting. Kent 1H 13
Stowupland. Suff 6G 31
Straad. Arg 3K 57
**Strabane**. Derr 4C 92
Strachan. Abers 6F 72
Stradbroke. Suff 4J 31
Stradishall. Suff 6D 30
Stradsett. Norf 1C 30
Stragglethorpe. Linc 4G 37
Stragglethorpe. Notts 6D 36
Straid. Ant 4H 93
Straid. ME Ant 4G 93
Straid. S Ayr 2G 51
Straight Soley. Wilts 6M 19
Straiton. Midl 3L 59
Straiton. S Ayr 1J 51
Straloch. Per 1D 66
Stramshall. Staf 6J 35
Strang. IOM 7C 44
Strangford. Here 1D 18
Strangford. New M 6J 93
Stranocum. Caus 2G 93
**Stranraer**. Dum 5F 50
Strata Florida. Cdgn 6G 25
Stratfield Mortimer. W Ber 7D 20
Stratfield Saye. Hants 7D 20
Stratfield Turgis. Hants 8D 20
**Stratford**. G Lon 5L 21
Stratford. Worc 8G 27
Stratford St Andrew. Suff 5K 31
Stratford St Mary. Suff 8G 31
Stratford sub Castle. Wilts 2K 9
Stratford Tony. Wilts 3J 9
**Stratford-upon-Avon**.
Warw 116 (6L 27)
Strath. High
nr. Gairloch 6J 77
nr. Wick 6D 86
Strathan. High
nr. Fort William 6L 69
nr. Lochinver 1A 78
nr. Tongue 5H 85
Strathan Skerray. High 5J 85
Strathaven. S Lan 5F 58
Strathblane. Stir 2D 58
Strathcanaird. High 3B 78
Strathcarron. High 1L 69
Strathcoil. Arg 4A 64
Strathdon. Abers 4C 72
Strathkinness. Fife 6H 67
Strathmashie House. High 6F 70
Strathmiglo. Fife 6F 66
Strathmore Lodge. High 7C 86
Strathpeffer. High 8E 78
Strathrannoch. High 6D 78
Strathtay. Per 2C 66
Strathvaich Lodge. High 6D 78
Strathwhillan. N Ayr 6K 57
Strathy. High
nr. Invergordon 6G 79
nr. Melvich 5L 85
Strathyre. Stir 6K 65
Stratton. Corn 5B 6
Stratton. Dors 6E 8
Stratton. Glos 3J 19
Stratton Audley. Oxon 1D 20
Stratton-on-the-Fosse.
Som 8E 18
Stratton St Margaret. Swin 5K 19
Stratton St Michael. Norf 2J 31
Stratton Strawless. Norf 7J 39
Stravithie. Fife 6J 67
Straw. M Ulst 4E 92
Stream. Som 2K 7
Streat. E Sus 4L 11
**Streatham**. G Lon 6L 21
Streatley. C Beds 1H 21
Streatley. W Ber 5C 20
Street. Corn 6B 6
Street. Lanc 2D 40
Street. N Yor 5E 48
Street. Som
nr. Chard 5B 8
**Street**. Som
nr. Glastonbury 2C 8
Street Ash. Som 4A 8
Street Dinas. Shrp 6B 34
Street End. Kent 8H 23
Street End. W Sus 6F 10
Streetgate. Tyne 6F 54
Streethay. Staf 8K 35
Streethouse. W Yor 5A 42
Streetlam. N Yor 6M 47
Street Lane. Derbs 5A 36
Streetly. W Mid 2J 27
Streetly End. Cambs 7C 30
Street on the Fosse. Som 2E 8
Strefford. Shrp 3C 26
Strelley. Notts 5C 36
Strensall. York 1D 42
Strensall Camp. York 2D 42
Stretcholt. Som 1A 8
Strete. Devn 7L 5
**Stretford**. G Man 8G 41
Stretford. Here 6D 26
Strethall. Essx 8A 30
Stretham. Cambs 4B 30
Stretton. Ches W 4C 34
Stretton. Derbs 3A 36
Stretton. Rut 8G 37
Stretton. Staf
nr. Brewood 8G 35
nr. Burton upon Trent 7L 35
Stretton. Warr 1E 34
Stretton en le Field. Leics 8M 35
Stretton Grandison. Here 7E 26
Stretton Heath. Shrp 8B 34
Stretton-on-Dunsmore.
Warw 4B 28
Stretton-on-Fosse. Warw 8L 27
Stretton Sugwas. Here 7C 26
Stretton under Fosse.
Warw 3B 28
Stretton Westwood. Shrp 2D 26
Strichen. Abers 8J 81
Strines. G Man 1H 35
Stringston. Som 1L 7
Strixton. Nptn 5G 29
Stroanfreggan. Dum 2M 51
Stroat. Glos 4D 18
Stromeferry. High 2K 69
Stromemore. High 2K 69
Stromness. Orkn 1D 86
Stronachie. Per 7D 66
Stronachlachar. Stir 6J 65
Stronchreggan. High 8A 70
Strone. Arg 1L 57
Strone. High
nr. Drumnadrochit 3F 70
nr. Kingussie 5H 71
Stronenaba. High 7C 70
Stronganess. Shet 3K 91
Stronmilchan. Arg 5F 64
Stronsay Airport. Orkn 7F 88
Strontian. High 1C 64
Strood. Kent 2E 12
**Strood**. Medw 7D 22
Strood Green. Surr 1K 11
Strood Green. W Sus
nr. Billingshurst 3H 11
nr. Horsham 2J 11
Strothers Dale. Nmbd 6C 54
**Stroud**. Glos 3G 19
Stroud. Hants 3E 10
Stroud Green. Essx 4E 22
Stroxton. Linc 6G 37
Struan. High 2E 68
Struan. Per 1B 66
Struanmore. High 2E 68
Strubby. Linc 1A 38
Strugg's Hill. Linc 6K 37
Strumpshaw. Norf 1K 31
Strutherhill. S Lan 4F 58
Struy. High 2E 70
Stryd. IOA 2B 32
Stryt-issa. Wrex 5A 34
Stuartfield. Abers 1J 73
**Stubbington**. Hants 5C 10
Stubbins. Lanc 6F 40
Stubble Green. Cumb 5K 45
Stubb's Cross. Kent 2F 12
Stubbs Green. Norf 2K 31
Stubhampton. Dors 4H 9
Stubton. Linc 5F 36
Stubwood. Staf 6J 35
Stuckton. Hants 4K 9
Studham. C Beds 2H 21
Studland. Dors 7J 9
Studley. Warw 5J 27
Studley. Wilts 6H 19
Studley Roger. N Yor 8L 47
Stuntney. Cambs 4B 30
Stunts Green. E Sus 4C 12
Sturbridge. Staf 6G 35
Sturgate. Linc 1F 36
Sturmer. Essx 7C 30
Sturminster Marshall. Dors 5H 9
Sturminster Newton. Dors 4F 8
Sturry. Kent 7H 23
Sturton. N Lin 7G 43
Sturton by Stow. Linc 1F 36
Sturton le Steeple. Notts 1E 36
Stuston. Suff 4H 31
Stutton. N Yor 3B 42
Stutton. Suff 8H 31
Styal. Ches E 1G 35
Stydd. Lanc 4E 40
Styrrup. Notts 8D 42
Suainebost. W Isl 5J 83
Suardail. W Isl 8H 83
Succoth. Abers 2D 72
Succoth. Arg 7G 65
Suckley. Worc 6F 26
Suckley Knowl. Worc 6F 26
Sudborough. Nptn 3G 29
Sudbourne. Suff 6L 31

Sudbrook. Linc 5G 37
Sudbrook. Mon 5D 18
Sudbrooke. Linc 2H 37
Sudbury. Derbs 6K 35
**Sudbury**. Suff 7E 30
Sudgrove. Glos 3H 19
Suffield. Norf 6J 39
Suffield. N Yor 6G 49
Sugnall. Staf 6F 34
Sugwas Pool. Here 7C 26
Suisnish. High 2G 69
Sulaisiadar. W Isl 8J 83
Sùlaisiadar Mòr. High 1F 68
Sulby. IOM 5C 44
Sulgrave. Nptn 7C 28
Sulham. W Ber 6D 20
Sulhamstead. W Ber 7D 20
Sullington. W Sus 4H 11
Sullom. Shet 6H 91
Sully. V Glam 8L 17
Sumburgh. Shet 7E 90
Sumburgh Airport. Shet 6D 90
Summer Bridge. N Yor 1L 41
Summercourt. Corn 6A 4
Summergangs. Hull 4J 43
Summer Hill. W Mid 2H 27
Summerhill. Aber 5J 73
Summerhill. Pemb 6H 15
Summerhouse. Darl 4L 47
Summersdale. W Sus 5F 10
Summerseat. G Man 6F 40
Summit. G Man 6H 41
**Sunbury**. Surr 7J 21
Sunderland. Cumb 8F 52
Sunderland. Lanc 2C 40
**Sunderland**. Tyne 116 (6G 55)
Sunderland Bridge. Dur 8F 54
Sundon Park. Lutn 1H 21
Sundridge. Kent 8A 22
Sunk Island. E Yor 6K 43
Sunningdale. Wind 7G 21
Sunninghill. Wind 7G 21
Sunningwell. Oxon 3B 20
Sunniside. Dur 8E 54
Sunniside. Tyne 6F 54
Sunny Bank. Cumb 6A 46
Sunny Hill. Derb 6M 35
Sunnyhurst. Bkbn 5E 40
Sunnylaw. Stir 8A 66
Sunnymead. Oxon 3C 20
Sunnyside. S Yor 8B 42
Sunnyside. W Sus 2L 11
Sunton. Wilts 8L 19
**Surbiton**. G Lon 7J 21
Surby. IOM 7B 44
Surfleet. Linc 7K 37
Surfleet Seas End. Linc 7K 37
Surlingham. Norf 1K 31
Surrex. Essx 1E 22
Sustead. Norf 6H 39
Susworth. Linc 7F 42
Sutcombe. Devn 4C 6
Suton. Norf 2G 31
Sutors of Cromarty. High 7J 79
Sutterby. Linc 2L 37
Sutterton. Linc 6K 37
Sutterton Dowdyke. Linc 6K 37
Sutton. Buck 6H 21
Sutton. Cambs 4M 29
Sutton. C Beds 7K 29
Sutton. E Sus 6A 12
**Sutton**. G Lon 7K 21
Sutton. Kent 1K 13
Sutton. Norf 7K 39
Sutton. Notts 6E 36
Sutton. Oxon 3B 20
Sutton. Pemb 5F 14
Sutton. Pet 2H 29
Sutton. Shrp
  nr. Bridgnorth 3F 26
  nr. Market Drayton 6E 34
  nr. Oswestry 7B 34
  nr. Shrewsbury 8D 34
Sutton. Som 2E 8
Sutton. S Yor 6C 42
Sutton. Staf 7F 34
Sutton. Suff 7K 31
Sutton. W Sus 4G 11
Sutton. Worc 5E 26
Sutton Abinger. Surr 1J 11
Sutton at Hone. Kent 6B 22
Sutton Bassett. Nptn 2E 28
Sutton Benger. Wilts 6H 19
Sutton Bingham. Som 4D 8
Sutton Bonington. Notts 7C 36
Sutton Bridge. Linc 7A 38
Sutton Cheney. Leics 1B 28
**Sutton Coldfield, Royal**.
  W Mid 2K 27
Sutton Corner. Linc 7M 37
Sutton Courtenay. Oxon 4C 20
Sutton Crosses. Linc 7M 37
Sutton cum Lound. Notts 1D 36
Sutton Gault. Cambs 4M 29
Sutton Grange. N Yor 8L 47
Sutton Green. Surr 8H 21
Sutton Howgrave. N Yor 8M 47
**Sutton in Ashfield**. Notts 4B 36
Sutton-in-Craven. N Yor 3J 41
Sutton Ings. Hull 4J 43
Sutton in the Elms. Leics 2C 28
Sutton Lane Ends. Ches E 2H 35
Sutton Leach. Mers 8D 40
Sutton Maddock. Shrp 1F 26
Sutton Mallet. Som 2B 8
Sutton Mandeville. Wilts 3H 9
Sutton Montis. Som 3E 8
Sutton on Hull. Hull 4J 43
Sutton on Sea. Linc 1B 38
Sutton-on-the-Forest.
  N Yor 1C 42
Sutton on the Hill. Derbs 6L 35
Sutton on Trent. Notts 3E 36
Sutton Poyntz. Dors 7F 8
Sutton St Edmund. Linc 8L 37
Sutton St Edmund's Common.
  Linc 1L 29
Sutton St James. Linc 8L 37
Sutton St Michael. Here 7D 26
Sutton St Nicholas. Here 7D 26
Sutton Scarsdale. Derbs 3B 36
Sutton Scotney. Hants 2B 10
Sutton-under-Brailes.
  Warw 8M 27
Sutton-under-Whitestonecliffe.
  N Yor 7B 48
Sutton upon Derwent.
  E Yor 3E 42
Sutton Valence. Kent 1E 12
Sutton Veny. Wilts 1H 9
Sutton Waldron. Dors 4G 9
Sutton Weaver. Ches W 2D 34
Swaby. Linc 2L 37
**Swadlincote**. Derbs 8L 35
Swaffham. Norf 1E 30
Swaffham Bulbeck. Cambs 5B 30
Swaffham Prior. Cambs 5B 30
Swafield. Norf 6J 39
Swainby. N Yor 5B 48
Swainshill. Here 7C 26
Swainsthorpe. Norf 1J 31
Swainswick. Bath 7F 18
Swalcliffe. Oxon 8A 28
Swalecliffe. Kent 7H 23
Swallow. Linc 7J 43
Swallow Beck. Linc 3G 37
Swallowcliffe. Wilts 3H 9
Swallowfield. Wok 7E 20
Swallownest. S Yor 1B 36
Swampton. Hants 8B 20
**Swanage**. Dors 8J 9
Swanbister. Orkn 1E 86
Swanbourne. Buck 1F 20
Swanbridge. V Glam 8L 17
Swan Green. Ches W 2F 34
Swanland. E Yor 5G 43
**Swanley**. Kent 7B 22
Swanmore. Hants 4C 10
Swannington. Leics 8B 36
Swannington. Norf 8H 39
Swanpool. Linc 3G 37
Swanscombe. Kent 6C 22
**Swansea**. Swan 117 (5F 16)
Swan Street. Essx 1E 22
Swanton Abbott. Norf 7J 39
Swanton Morley. Norf 8G 39
Swanton Novers. Norf 6G 39
Swanton Street. Kent 8E 22
Swanwick. Derbs 4B 36
Swanwick. Hants 5C 10
Swanwick Green. Ches E 5D 34
Swarby. Linc 5H 37
Swardeston. Norf 1J 31
Swarister. Shet 5K 91
Swarkestone. Derbs 7A 36
Swarland. Nmbd 1E 54
Swarraton. Hants 2C 10
Swartha. W Yor 3J 41
Swarthmoor. Cumb 8A 46
Swaton. Linc 6J 37
Swatragh. M Ulst 3F 93
Swavesey. Cambs 5L 29
Sway. Hants 6L 9
Swayfield. Linc 7G 37
Swaythling. Sotn 4B 10
Sweet Green. Worc 5E 26
Sweetham. Devn 6H 7
Sweetholme. Cumb 4D 46
Sweets. Corn 6A 6
Sweetshouse. Corn 5C 4
Swefling. Suff 5K 31
Swell. Som 3B 8
Swepstone. Leics 8A 36
Swerford. Oxon 8A 28
Swettenham. Ches E 3G 35
Swetton. N Yor 8K 47
Swffryd. Blae 5M 17
Swiftsden. E Sus 3D 12
Swilland. Suff 6H 31
Swillington. W Yor 4A 42
Swimbridge. Devn 3F 6
Swimbridge Newland. Devn 2F 6
Swinbrook. Oxon 2L 19
Swincliffe. N Yor 2L 41
Swincliffe. W Yor 5L 41
Swinderby. Linc 3F 36
Swindon. Glos 1H 19
Swindon. Nmbd 2C 54
Swindon. Staf 2G 27
**Swindon**. Swin 117 (5K 19)
Swine. E Yor 4J 43
Swinefleet. E Yor 5E 42
Swineford. S Glo 7E 18
Swineshead. Bed 5H 29
Swineshead. Linc 5K 37
Swineshead Bridge. Linc 5K 37
Swiney. High 8D 86
Swinford. Leics 4C 28
Swinford. Oxon 3B 20
Swingate. Notts 5C 36
Swingbrow. Cambs 3L 29
Swingfield Minnis. Kent 1J 13
Swingfield Street. Kent 1J 13
Swingleton Green. Suff 7F 30
Swinhill. S Lan 5F 58
Swinhoe. Nmbd 7K 61
Swinhope. Linc 8K 43
Swinister. Shet 5H 91
Swinithwaite. N Yor 7J 47
Swinmore Common. Here 7E 26
Swinscoe. Staf 5K 35
Swinside Hall. Bord 8E 60
Swinstead. Linc 7H 37
**Swinton**. G Man 7F 40
Swinton. N Yor
  nr. Malton 8E 48
  nr. Masham 8L 47
Swinton. Bord 5F 60
**Swinton**. S Yor 8B 42
Swithland. Leics 8C 36
Swordale. High 7F 78
Swordly. High 5K 85
Sworton Heath. Ches E 1E 34
Swyddffynnon. Cdgn 6F 24
Swynnerton. Staf 6G 35
Swyre. Dors 7D 8
Sycharth. Powy 8M 33
Sychdyn. Flin 4M 33
Sychnant. Powy 5J 25
Sychtyn. Powy 2J 25
Syde. Glos 2H 19
Sydenham. G Lon 6L 21
Sydenham. Oxon 3E 20
Sydenham. Som 2B 8
Sydenham Damerel. Devn 8D 6
Syderstone. Norf 6E 38
Sydling St Nicholas. Dors 6E 8
Sydmonton. Hants 8B 20
Sydney. Ches E 4F 34
Syerston. Notts 5E 36
Syke. G Man 6G 41
Sykehouse. S Yor 6D 42
Sykes. Lanc 2E 40
Syleham. Suff 4J 31
Sylen. Carm 6M 15
Sylfaen. Powy 2L 25
Symbister. Shet 1F 90
Symington. S Ayr 6B 58
Symington. S Lan 6H 59
Symondsbury. Dors 6C 8
Symonds Yat. Here 2D 18
Synod Inn. Cdgn 1L 15
Syre. High 7J 85
Syreford. Glos 1J 19
Syresham. Nptn 7D 28
Syston. Leics 8D 36
Syston. Linc 5G 37
Sytchampton. Worc 5G 27
Sywell. Nptn 5F 28


## T


Tabost. W Isl
  nr. Cearsiadar 2E 76
  nr. Suainebost 5J 83
Tachbrook Mallory. Warw 5M 27
Tackley. Oxon 1B 20
Tacleit. W Isl 8E 82
Tacolneston. Norf 2H 31
Tadcaster. N Yor 3B 42
Taddington. Derbs 2K 35
Taddington. Glos 8J 27
Taddiport. Devn 4D 6
**Tadley**. Hants 7D 20
Tadlow. Cambs 7K 29
Tadmarton. Oxon 8A 28
Tadwick. Bath 6F 18
**Tadworth**. Surr 8K 21
Tafarnaubach. Blae 3L 17
Tafarn-y-bwlch. Pemb 3G 15
Tafarn-y-Gelyn. Den 4L 33
Taff's Well. Rhon 6L 17
Tafolwern. Powy 2H 25
Tai-bach. Powy 8L 33
Taibach. Neat 6G 17
Taigh a Ghearraidh. W Isl 6J 75
Taigh Bhuirgh. W Isl 4B 76
Tain. High
  nr. Invergordon 5H 79
  nr. Thurso 5D 86
Tai-Nant. Wrex 5A 34
Tai'n Lon. Gwyn 5D 32
Tairbeart. W Isl 4C 76
Tairgwaith. Neat 3G 17
Takeley. Essx 1B 22
Takeley Street. Essx 1B 22
Talachddu. Powy 1K 17
Talacre. Flin 2L 33
Talardd. Gwyn 8H 33
Talaton. Devn 6K 7
Talbenny. Pemb 5E 14
Talbot Green. Rhon 6K 17
Taleford. Devn 6K 7
Talerddig. Powy 2J 25
Talgarreg. Cdgn 1L 15
Talgarth. Powy 1L 17
Talisker. High 2E 68
Talke. Staf 4G 35
Talkin. Cumb 6K 53
Talladale. High 6L 77
Talla Linnfoots. Bord 7K 59
Tallaminnock. S Ayr 2J 51
Tallarn Green. Wrex 5C 34
Tallentire. Cumb 8F 52
Talley. Carm 1F 16
Tallington. Linc 1H 29
Talmine. High 5H 85
Talog. Carm 4K 15
Talsarn. Carm 2G 17
Talsarn. Cdgn 1M 15
Talsarnau. Gwyn 7F 32
Talskiddy. Corn 5B 4
Talwrn. IOA 3D 32
Talwrn. Wrex 5A 34
Tal-y-Bont. Cnwy 4G 33
Tal-y-bont. Cdgn 4F 24
Tal-y-bont. Gwyn
  nr. Bangor 3F 32
  nr. Barmouth 8E 32
Talybont-on-Usk. Powy 2L 17
Tal-y-cafn. Cnwy 3G 33
Tal-y-coed. Mon 2C 18
Tal-y-llyn. Gwyn 2G 25
Talyllyn. Powy 2L 17
Talysarn. Gwyn 5D 32
Tal-y-waenydd. Gwyn 6F 32
Talywain. Torf 3A 18
Tal-y-Wern. Powy 2H 25
Tamerton Foliot. Plym 5G 5
Tamlaght. Ferm 6C 92
Tamlaght O'Crilly. M Ulst 3F 93
Tamnamore. M Ulst 5F 93
**Tamworth**. Staf 1L 27
Tamworth Green. Linc 5L 37
Tandlehill. Ren 3C 58
Tandragee. Arm 6G 93
Tandridge. Surr 8L 21
Tanerdy. Carm 4L 15
Tanfield. Dur 6E 54
Tanfield Lea. Dur 6E 54
Tangasdal. W Isl 5C 74
Tang Hall. York 2D 42
Tangiers. Pemb 5F 14
Tangley. Hants 8M 19
Tangmere. W Sus 5G 11
Tangwick. Shet 6G 91
Tankerness. Orkn 1G 87
Tankersley. S Yor 8M 41
Tankerton. Kent 7H 23
Tan-lan. Cnwy 4G 33
Tan-lan. Gwyn 6F 32
Tannach. High 7E 86
Tannadice. Ang 2H 67
Tanner's Green. Worc 4J 27
Tannington. Suff 5J 31
Tannochside. N Lan 3F 58
Tan Office Green. Suff 6D 30
Tansley. Derbs 4M 35
Tansley Knoll. Derbs 3M 35
Tansor. Nptn 2H 29
Tantobie. Dur 6E 54
Tanton. N Yor 4C 48
Tanvats. Linc 3J 37
Tanworth-in-Arden. Warw 4K 27
Tan-y-bwlch. Gwyn 6F 32
Tan-y-fron. Cnwy 4J 33
Tanyfron. Wrex 4A 34
Tanygrisiau. Gwyn 6F 32
Tan-y-groes. Cdgn 2J 15
Tan-y-pistyll. Powy 8K 33
Tan-yr-allt. Den 2K 33
Taobh a Chaolais. W Isl 4D 74
Taobh a Deas Loch Aineort.
  W Isl 3D 74
Taobh a Ghlinne. W Isl 2E 76
Taobh a Tuath Loch Aineort.
  W Isl 3D 74
Taplow. Buck 5G 21
Tapton. Derbs 2A 36
Tarbert. Arg
  on Jura 1F 56
  on Kintyre 3H 57
Tarbert. W Isl 4C 76
Tarbet. Arg 7H 65
Tarbet. High
  nr. Mallaig 6J 69
  nr. Scourie 7D 84
Tarbock Green. Mers 1C 34
Tarbolton. S Ayr 7C 58
Tarbrax. S Lan 4J 59
Tardebigge. Worc 5H 27
Tarfside. Ang 8D 72
Tarland. Abers 5D 72
Tarleton. Lanc 5C 40
Tarlogie. High 5H 79
Tarlscough. Lanc 6C 40
Tarlton. Glos 4H 19
Tarnbrook. Lanc 2D 40
Tarnock. Som 8B 18
Tarns. Cumb 7F 52
Tarporley. Ches W 3D 34
Tarpots. Essx 5D 22
Tarr. Som 2L 7
Tarrant Crawford. Dors 5H 9
Tarrant Gunville. Dors 4H 9
Tarrant Hinton. Dors 4H 9
Tarrant Keyneston. Dors 5H 9
Tarrant Launceston. Dors 5H 9
Tarrant Monkton. Dors 5H 9
Tarrant Rawston. Dors 5H 9
Tarrant Rushton. Dors 5H 9
Tarrel. High 5J 79
Tarring Neville. E Sus 5M 11
Tarrington. Here 7E 26
Tarsappie. Per 5E 66
Tarscabhaig. High 5G 69
Tarskavaig. High 5G 69
Tarves. Abers 2H 73
Tarvie. High 8E 78
Tarvin. Ches W 3C 34
Tasburgh. Norf 2J 31
Tasley. Shrp 2E 26
Tassagh. Arm 7F 93
Taston. Oxon 1A 20
Tatenhill. Staf 7L 35
Tathall End. Mil 7F 28
Tatham. Lanc 1E 40
Tathwell. Linc 1L 37
Tatling End. Buck 5H 21
Tatsfield. Surr 8M 21
Tattenhall. Ches W 4C 34
Tatterford. Norf 7E 38
Tattersett. Norf 6E 38
Tattershall. Linc 4K 37
Tattershall Bridge. Linc 4J 37
Tattershall Thorpe. Linc 4K 37
Tattingstone. Suff 8H 31
Tattingstone White Horse.
  Suff 8H 31
Tattle Bank. Warw 5K 27
Tatworth. Som 5B 8
**Taunton**. Som 117 (3M 7)
**Taverham**. Norf 8H 39
Taverners Green. Essx 2B 22
Tavernspite. Pemb 5H 15
**Tavistock**. Devn 8D 6
Tavool House. Arg 5K 63
Taw Green. Devn 6F 6
Tawstock. Devn 3E 6
Taxal. Derbs 1J 35
Tayinloan. Arg 5F 56
Taynish. Arg 1G 57
Taynton. Glos 1F 18
Taynton. Oxon 2L 19
Taynuilt. Arg 4E 64
Tayport. Fife 5H 67
**Tay Road Bridge**. D'dee 5H 67
Tayvallich. Arg 1G 57
Tealby. Linc 8J 43
Tealing. Ang 4H 67
Teams. Tyne 5F 54
Teangue. High 5H 69
Teanna Mhachair. W Isl 7J 75
Tebay. Cumb 5E 46
Tebworth. C Beds 1G 21
Tedburn St Mary. Devn 6H 7
Teddington. Glos 8H 27
**Teddington**. G Lon 6J 21
Tedsmore. Shrp 7B 34
Tedstone Delamere. Here 6E 26
Tedstone Wafer. Here 6E 26
Teemore. Ferm 7C 92
Teesport. Red C 3C 48
**Teesside**. Stoc T 3C 48
Teeton. Nptn 4D 28
Teffont Evias. Wilts 2H 9
Teffont Magna. Wilts 2H 9
Tegryn. Pemb 3J 15
Teigh. Rut 8F 36
Teigncombe. Devn 7F 6
Teigngrace. Devn 8H 7
Teignmouth. Devn 8J 7
**Telford**. Telf 8E 34
Telham. E Sus 4D 12
Tellisford. Som 8G 19
Telscombe. E Sus 5M 11
Telscombe Cliffs. E Sus 5L 11
Tempar. Per 2L 65
Templand. Dum 3E 52
Temple. Corn 4D 4
Temple. Glas 3D 58
Temple. Midl 4M 59
Temple Balsall. W Mid 4L 27
Temple Bar. Carm 3E 16
Temple Bar. Cdgn 1M 15
Temple Cloud. Bath 8E 18
Templecombe. Som 3F 8
Temple Ewell. Kent 1J 13
Temple Grafton. Warw 6K 27
Temple Guiting. Glos 1J 19
Templehall. Fife 8F 66
Temple Hirst. N Yor 5D 42
Temple Normanton. Derbs 3B 36
Templepatrick. Ant 4H 93
Temple Sowerby. Cumb 3E 46
Templeton. Devn 4H 7
Templeton. Pemb 5H 15
Templeton. W Ber 7A 20
Templetown. Dur 7E 54
Tempo. Ferm 6C 92
Tempsford. C Beds 6J 29
Tenandry. Per 1C 66
Tenbury Wells. Worc 5D 26
Tenby. Pemb 6H 15
Tendring. Essx 1H 23
Tendring Green. Essx 1H 23
Tenga. Arg 3L 63
Ten Mile Bank. Norf 2C 30
Tenterden. Kent 2E 12
Terfyn. Cnwy 3J 33
Terhill. Som 2L 7
Terling. Essx 2D 22
Termon Rock. Ferm 5E 92
Ternhill. Shrp 6E 34
Terregles. Dum 4D 52
Terrick. Buck 3F 20
Terrington. N Yor 8D 48
Terrington St Clement. Norf 7B 38
Terrington St John. Norf 8B 38
Terry's Green. Warw 4K 27
Teston. Kent 8D 22
Testwood. Hants 4M 9
Tetbury. Glos 4G 19
Tetbury Upton. Glos 4G 19
Tetchill. Shrp 6B 34
Tetcott. Devn 6C 6
Tetford. Linc 2L 37
Tetney. Linc 7L 43
Tetney Lock. Linc 7L 43
Tetsworth. Oxon 3D 20
Tettenhall. W Mid 1G 27
Teversal. Notts 3B 36
Teversham. Cambs 6A 30
Teviothead. Bord 1J 53
Tewel. Abers 7H 73
Tewin. Herts 2K 21
**Tewkesbury**. Glos 8G 27
Teynham. Kent 7F 22
Teynham Street. Kent 7F 22
Thackthwaite. Cumb 3C 46
Thakeham. W Sus 4J 11
**Thame**. Oxon 3E 20
Thames Ditton. Surr 7J 21
Thames Haven. Thur 5D 22
Thamesmead. G Lon 5A 22
**Thamesport**. Medw 6E 22
Thanington Without. Kent 8H 23
Thankerton. S Lan 6H 59
Tharston. Norf 2H 31
**Thatcham**. W Ber 7C 20
Thatto Heath. Mers 8D 40
Thaxted. Essx 8C 30
Theakston. N Yor 7M 47
Thealby. N Lin 6F 42
Theale. Som 1C 8
Theale. W Ber 6D 20
Thearne. E Yor 4H 43
Theberton. Suff 5L 31
Theddingworth. Leics 3D 28
Theddlethorpe All Saints.
  Linc 1A 38
Theddlethorpe St Helen.
  Linc 1A 38
Thelbridge Barton. Devn 4G 7
Thelnetham. Suff 4G 31
Thelveton. Norf 3H 31
Thelwall. Warr 1E 34
Themelthorpe. Norf 7G 39
Thenford. Nptn 7C 28
Therfield. Herts 8L 29
Thetford. Linc 8J 37
**Thetford**. Norf 3E 30
Thethwaite. Cumb 7H 53
Theydon Bois. Essx 4M 21
Thick Hollins. W Yor 6K 41
Thickwood. Wilts 6G 19
Thimbleby. Linc 3K 37
Thimbleby. N Yor 6B 48
Thingwall. Mers 1A 34
Thirlby. N Yor 7B 48
Thirlestane. Bord 5C 60
Thirn. N Yor 7L 47
Thirsk. N Yor 7B 48
Thirtleby. E Yor 4J 43
Thistleton. Lanc 4C 40
Thistleton. Rut 8G 37
Thistley Green. Suff 4C 30
Thixendale. N Yor 1F 42
Thockrington. Nmbd 4C 54
Tholomas Drove. Cambs 1M 29
Tholthorpe. N Yor 1B 42
Thomas Chapel. Pemb 6H 15
Thomas Close. Cumb 7J 53
Thomastown. Abers 1G 73
Thomastown. Rhon 6K 17
Thompson. Norf 2F 30
Thomshill. Mor 8B 80
Thong. Kent 6C 22
Thongsbridge. W Yor 7K 41
Thoralby. N Yor 7J 47
Thoresby. Notts 2D 36
Thoresway. Linc 8J 43
Thorganby. Linc 8K 43
Thorganby. N Yor 3D 42
Thorgill. N Yor 6E 48
Thorington. Suff 4L 31
Thorington Street. Suff 8G 31
Thorlby. N Yor 2H 41
Thorley. Herts 2A 22
Thorley Street. Herts 2A 22
Thorley Street. IOW 7A 10
Thormanby. N Yor 8B 48
Thorn. Powy 5A 26
**Thornaby-on-Tees**. Stoc T 4B 48
Thornage. Norf 6G 39
Thornborough. Buck 8E 28
Thornborough. N Yor 8L 47
Thornbury. Devn 5D 6
Thornbury. Here 6E 26
**Thornbury**. S Glo 4E 18
Thornby. Cumb 6G 53
Thornby. Nptn 4D 28
Thorncliffe. Staf 4J 35
Thorncombe. Dors 5B 8
Thorncombe Street. Surr 1G 11
Thorncote Green. C Beds 7J 29
Thorndon. Suff 5H 31
Thorndon Cross. Devn 6E 6
**Thorne**. S Yor 6D 42
Thornehillhead. Devn 4D 6
Thorner. W Yor 3A 42
Thorne St Margaret. Som 3K 7
Thorney. Notts 2F 36
Thorney. Pet 1K 29
Thorney. Som 3C 8
Thorney Hill. Hants 6K 9
Thorney Toll. Cambs 1L 29
Thornfalcon. Som 3A 8
Thornford. Dors 4E 8
Thorngrafton. Nmbd 5A 54
Thorngrove. Som 2B 8
Thorngumbald. E Yor 5K 43
Thornham. Norf 5D 38
Thornham Magna. Suff 4H 31
Thornham Parva. Suff 4H 31
Thornhaugh. Pet 1H 29
Thornhill. Cphy 6L 17
Thornhill. Cumb 4K 45
Thornhill. Derbs 1K 35
Thornhill. Dum 2C 52
Thornhill. Sotn 4B 10
Thornhill. Stir 8L 65
Thornhill. W Yor 6L 41
Thornhill Lees. W Yor 6L 41
Thornhills. W Yor 5K 41
Thornholme. E Yor 1J 43
Thornicombe. Dors 5G 9
Thornington. Nmbd 6F 60
Thornley. Dur
  nr. Durham 8G 55
  nr. Tow Law 8E 54
Thornley Gate. Nmbd 6B 54
Thornliebank. E Ren 3D 58
Thornroan. Abers 2H 73
Thorns. Suff 6D 30
Thornsett. Derbs 1J 35
Thornthwaite. Cumb 2M 45
Thornthwaite. N Yor 2K 41
Thornton. Ang 3G 67
Thornton. Buck 8E 28
Thornton. E Yor 3E 42
Thornton. Fife 8F 66
**Thornton**. Lanc 3B 40
Thornton. Leics 1B 28
Thornton. Linc 3K 37
Thornton. Mers 7B 40
Thornton. Midd 4B 48
Thornton. Nmbd 5G 61
Thornton. Pemb 6F 14
Thornton. W Yor 4J 41
Thornton Curtis. N Lin 6H 43
Thorntonhall. S Lan 4D 58
Thornton Heath. G Lon 7L 21
Thornton Hough. Mers 1B 34
Thornton-in-Craven. N Yor 3H 41
Thornton in Lonsdale.
  N Yor 8E 46
Thornton-le-Beans. N Yor 6A 48
Thornton-le-Clay. N Yor 1D 42
Thornton-le-Dale. N Yor 7F 48
Thornton le Moor. Linc 8H 43
Thornton-le-Moor. N Yor 7A 48
Thornton-le-Moors.
  Ches W 2C 34
Thornton-le-Street. N Yor 7B 48
Thorntonloch. E Lot 2E 60
Thornton Rust. N Yor 7H 47
Thornton Steward. N Yor 7K 47
Thornton Watlass. N Yor 7L 47
Thornwood Common. Essx 3A 22
Thornythwaite. Cumb 3B 46
Thoroton. Notts 5E 36
Thorp Arch. W Yor 3B 42
Thorpe. Derbs 4K 35
Thorpe. E Yor 3G 43
Thorpe. Linc 1A 38
Thorpe. Norf 2L 31
Thorpe. N Yor 1J 41
Thorpe. Notts 5E 36
Thorpe. Surr 7H 21
Thorpe Abbotts. Norf 4H 31
Thorpe Acre. Leics 7C 36
Thorpe Arnold. Leics 7E 36
Thorpe Audlin. W Yor 6B 42
Thorpe Bassett. N Yor 8F 48
Thorpe Bay. S'end 5F 22
Thorpe by Water. Rut 2F 28
Thorpe Common. S Yor 8A 42
Thorpe Common. Suff 8J 31
Thorpe Constantine. Staf 1L 27
Thorpe End. Norf 8J 39
Thorpe Fendike. Linc 3A 38
Thorpe Green. Essx 1H 23
Thorpe Green. Suff 6F 30
Thorpe Hall. N Yor 8C 48
Thorpe Hamlet. Norf 1J 31
Thorpe Hesley. S Yor 8A 42
Thorpe in Balne. S Yor 6C 42
Thorpe in the Fallows. Linc 1G 37
Thorpe Langton. Leics 2E 28
Thorpe Larches. Dur 3A 48
Thorpe Latimer. Linc 5J 37
Thorpe-le-Soken. Essx 1H 23
Thorpe le Street. E Yor 3F 42
Thorpe Malsor. Nptn 4F 28
Thorpe Mandeville. Nptn 7C 28
Thorpe Market. Norf 6J 39
Thorpe Marriott. Norf 8H 39
Thorpe Morieux. Suff 6F 30
Thorpeness. Suff 6L 31
Thorpe on the Hill. Linc 3G 37
Thorpe on the Hill. W Yor 5M 41
Thorpe St Andrew. Norf 1J 31
Thorpe St Peter. Linc 3A 38
Thorpe Salvin. S Yor 1C 36
Thorpe Satchville. Leics 8E 36
Thorpe Thewles. Stoc T 3A 48
Thorpe Tilney. Linc 4J 37
Thorpe Underwood. N Yor 2B 42
Thorpe Waterville. Nptn 3H 29
Thorpe Willoughby. N Yor 4C 42
Thorpland. Norf 1C 30
Thorrington. Essx 1G 23
Thorverton. Devn 5J 7
Thrandeston. Suff 4H 31
Thrapston. Nptn 4G 29
Thrashbush. N Lan 3F 58
Threapland. Cumb 8F 52
Threapland. N Yor 1H 41
Threapwood. Ches W 5C 34
Threapwood. Staf 5J 35
Three Ashes. Here 1D 18
Three Bridges. Linc 1M 37
Three Bridges. W Sus 2K 11
Three Burrows. Corn 4L 3
Three Chimneys. Kent 2E 12
Three Cocks. Powy 1L 17
Three Crosses. Swan 5E 16
Three Cups Corner. E Sus 3C 12
Threehammer Common.
  Norf 7K 39
Three Holes. Norf 1B 30
Threekingham. Linc 6H 37
Three Leg Cross. E Sus 2C 12
Three Legged Cross. Dors 5J 9
Three Mile Cross. Wok 7E 20
Threemilestone. Corn 4L 3
Three Oaks. E Sus 4E 12
Threlkeld. Cumb 3B 46
Threshfield. N Yor 1H 41
Thrigby. Norf 8L 39
Thringarth. Dur 3H 47
Thringstone. Leics 8B 36
Thrintoft. N Yor 6M 47
Thriplow. Cambs 7M 29
Throckenholt. Linc 1L 29
Throcking. Herts 8L 29
Throckley. Tyne 5E 54
Throckmorton. Worc 7H 27
Throop. Bour 6K 9
Throphill. Nmbd 3E 54
Thropton. Nmbd 1D 54
Throsk. Stir 8B 66
Througham. Glos 3H 19
Throughgate. Dum 3C 52
Throwleigh. Devn 6F 6
Throwley. Kent 8F 22
Throwley Forstal. Kent 8F 22
Throxenby. N Yor 7H 49
Thrumpton. Notts 6C 36
Thrumster. High 7E 86
Thrunton. Nmbd 8H 61
Thrupp. Glos 3G 19
Thrupp. Oxon 2B 20
Thrushelton. Devn 7D 6
Thrushgill. Lanc 1E 40
Thrussington. Leics 8D 36
Thruxton. Hants 1L 9
Thruxton. Here 8C 26
Thrybergh. S Yor 8B 42
Thulston. Derbs 6B 36
Thundergay. N Ayr 5H 57
Thundersley. Essx 5D 22
Thundridge. Herts 2L 21
Thurcaston. Leics 8C 36
Thurcroft. S Yor 1B 36
Thurdon. Corn 4B 6
Thurgarton. Norf 6H 39
Thurgarton. Notts 5D 36
Thurgoland. S Yor 7L 41
Thurlaston. Leics 2C 28
Thurlaston. Warw 4B 28
Thurlbear. Som 3A 8
Thurlby. Linc
  nr. Alford 2A 38
  nr. Baston 8J 37
  nr. Lincoln 3G 37
Thurleigh. Bed 6H 29
Thurlestone. Devn 7J 5
Thurloxton. Som 2A 8
Thurlstone. S Yor 7L 41
Thurlton. Norf 2L 31
Thurmaston. Leics 1D 28
Thurnby. Leics 1D 28
Thurne. Norf 8L 39
Thurnham. Kent 8E 22
Thurning. Norf 7G 39
Thurning. Nptn 3H 29
Thurnscoe. S Yor 7B 42
Thursby. Cumb 6H 53
Thursford. Norf 6F 38
Thursford Green. Norf 6F 38
Thursley. Surr 2G 11
Thurso. High 5C 86
Thurso East. High 5C 86
Thurstaston. Mers 2M 33
Thurston. Suff 5F 30
Thurston End. Suff 6D 30
Thurstonfield. Cumb 6H 53
Thurstonland. W Yor 6K 41
Thurton. Norf 1K 31
Thurvaston. Derbs
  nr. Ashbourne 6K 35
  nr. Derby 6L 35
Thuxton. Norf 1G 31
Thwaite. Dur 4J 47
Thwaite. N Yor 6G 47
Thwaite. Suff 5H 31
Thwaite Head. Cumb 6B 46
Thwaites. W Yor 3J 41
Thwaite St Mary. Norf 2K 31
Thwing. E Yor 8H 49
Tibbermore. Per 5D 66
Tibberton. Glos 1F 18
Tibberton. Telf 7E 34
Tibberton. Worc 6H 27
Tibenham. Norf 3H 31
Tibshelf. Derbs 3B 36
Tibthorpe. E Yor 2G 43
Ticehurst. E Sus 2C 12
Tichborne. Hants 2C 10
Tickencote. Rut 1G 29
Tickenham. N Som 6C 18
Tickhill. S Yor 8C 42
Ticklerton. Shrp 2C 26
Ticknall. Derbs 7A 36
Tickton. E Yor 3H 43
Tidbury Green. W Mid 4K 27
Tidcombe. Wilts 8L 19
Tiddington. Oxon 3D 20
Tiddington. Warw 6L 27
Tiddleywink. Wilts 6G 19
Tidebrook. E Sus 3C 12
Tideford. Corn 6F 4
Tideford Cross. Corn 5F 4
Tidenham. Glos 4D 18
Tideswell. Derbs 2K 35
Tidmarsh. W Ber 6D 20
Tidmington. Warw 8L 27
Tidpit. Hants 4J 9
Tidworth. Wilts 1L 9
Tidworth Camp. Wilts 1L 9
Tiers Cross. Pemb 5F 14
Tiffield. Nptn 6D 28
Tifty. Abers 1G 73
Tigerton. Ang 1J 67
Tighnabruaich. Arg 2J 57
Tigley. Devn 5K 5
Tilbrook. Cambs 5H 29
**Tilbury**. Thur 6C 22
Tilbury Green. Essx 7D 30
Tilbury Juxta Clare. Essx 7D 30
Tile Hill. W Mid 4L 27
Tilehurst. Read 6D 20
Tilford. Surr 1F 10
Tilgate Forest Row. W Sus 2K 11
Tillathrowie. Abers 2D 72
Tillers Green. Glos 8E 26
Tillery. Abers 3J 73
Tilley. Shrp 7D 34
Tillicoultry. Clac 8C 66
Tillingham. Essx 3F 22
Tillington. Here 7C 26
Tillington. W Sus 3G 11
Tillington Common. Here 7C 26
Tillybirloch. Abers 5F 72
Tillyfourie. Abers 4F 72
Tilmanstone. Kent 8K 23
Tilney All Saints. Norf 8B 38
Tilney Fen End. Norf 8B 38
Tilney High End. Norf 8B 38
Tilney St Lawrence. Norf 8B 38
Tilshead. Wilts 1J 9
Tilstock. Shrp 6D 34
Tilston. Ches W 4C 34
Tilstone Fearnall. Ches W 3D 34
Tilsworth. C Beds 1G 21
Tilton on the Hill. Leics 1E 28
Tiltups End. Glos 4G 19
Timberland. Linc 4J 37
Timbersbrook. Ches E 3G 35
Timberscombe. Som 1J 7
Timble. N Yor 2K 41
Timperley. G Man 1F 34
Timsbury. Bath 8E 18
Timsbury. Hants 3M 9
Timsgearraidh. W Isl 8D 82
Timworth Green. Suff 5E 30
Tincleton. Dors 6F 8
Tindale. Cumb 6L 53
Tindale Crescent. Dur 3L 47
Tingewick. Buck 8D 28
Tingrith. C Beds 8H 29
Tingwall. Orkn 7D 88
Tinhay. Devn 7C 6
Tinshill. W Yor 4L 41
Tinsley. S Yor 8B 42
Tinsley Green. W Sus 2K 11
Tintagel. Corn 3C 4
Tintern. Mon 3D 18
Tintinhull. Som 4C 8
Tintwistle. Derbs 8J 41
Tinwald. Dum 3E 52
Tinwell. Rut 1H 29
Tippacott. Devn 1G 7
Tipperty. Abers 3J 73
Tipps End. Cambs 2B 30
Tiptoe. Hants 6L 9
Tipton. W Mid 2H 27
Tipton St John. Devn 6K 7
Tiptree. Essx 2E 22
Tiptree Heath. Essx 2E 22
Tirabad. Powy 8H 25
Tircoed Forest Village.
  Swan 4F 16
Tiree Airport. Arg 3F 62
Tirinie. Per 1B 66
Tirley. Glos 1G 19
Tiroran. Arg 5K 63
Tir-Phil. Cphy 4L 17
Tirril. Cumb 3D 46
Tirryside. High 2F 78
Tir-y-dail. Carm 3F 16
Tisbury. Wilts 3H 9
Tisman's Common. W Sus 2H 11
Tissington. Derbs 4K 35
Titchberry. Devn 3B 6
Titchfield. Hants 5C 10
Titchmarsh. Nptn 4H 29
Titchwell. Norf 5D 38
Tithby. Notts 6D 36
Titley. Here 6B 26
Titlington. Nmbd 8H 61
Titsey. Surr 8M 21
Titson. Corn 5B 6
Tittensor. Staf 6G 35
Tittleshall. Norf 7E 38
Titton. Worc 5G 27
Tiverton. Ches W 3D 34
**Tiverton**. Devn 4J 7
Tivetshall St Margaret.
  Norf 3H 31
Tivetshall St Mary. Norf 3H 31
Tivington. Som 1J 7
Tixall. Staf 7H 35
Tixover. Rut 1G 29
Toab. Orkn 1G 87
Toab. Shet 6D 90
Toadmoor. Derbs 4A 36
Tobermore. M Ulst 4F 93
Tobermory. Arg 2L 63
Toberonochy. Arg 7B 64
Tobha Beag. W Isl 2D 74
Tobha-Beag. W Isl 6A 76
Tobha Mor. W Isl 2D 74
Tobhtarol. W Isl 8E 82
Tobson. W Isl 8E 82
Tocabhaig. High 4H 69
Tocher. Abers 2F 72
Tockenham. Wilts 6J 19
Tockenham Wick. Wilts 5J 19
Tockholes. Bkbn 5E 40
Tockington. S Glo 5E 18
Tockwith. N Yor 2B 42
Todber. Dors 3G 9
Todding. Here 4C 26
Toddington. C Beds 1H 21
Toddington. Glos 8J 27
Todenham. Glos 8L 27
Todhills. Cumb 5H 53
**Todmorden**. W Yor 5H 41
Todwick. S Yor 1B 36
Toft. Cambs 6L 29
Toft. Linc 8H 37
Toft Hill. Dur 3K 47
Toft Monks. Norf 2L 31
Toft next Newton. Linc 1H 37
Toftrees. Norf 7E 38
Tofts. High 5E 86
Toftwood. Norf 8F 38
Togston. Nmbd 1F 54
Tokavaig. High 4H 69
Tokers Green. Oxon 6E 20
Tolastadh a Chaolais. W Isl 8E 82
Tolladine. Worc 6G 27
Tolland. Som 2L 7
Tollard Farnham. Dors 4H 9
Tollard Royal. Wilts 4H 9
Toll Bar. S Yor 7C 42
Toller Fratrum. Dors 6D 8
Toller Porcorum. Dors 6D 8
Tollerton. N Yor 1C 42
Tollerton. Notts 6D 36
Toller Whelme. Dors 5D 8
Tollesbury. Essx 2F 22
Tolleshunt D'Arcy. Essx 2F 22
Tolleshunt Knights. Essx 2F 22
Tolleshunt Major. Essx 2F 22
Tollie. High 8F 78
Tollie Farm. High 6K 77
Tolm. W Isl 8H 83
Tolpuddle. Dors 6F 8
Tolstadh bho Thuath. W Isl 7J 83
Tolworth. G Lon 7J 21
Tomachlaggan. Mor 3A 72
Tomaknock. Per 5B 66
Tomatin. High 3J 71
Tombuidhe. Arg 7E 64
Tomdoun. High 5B 70
Tomich. High
  nr. Cannich 3D 70
  nr. Invergordon 6H 79
  nr. Lairg 3G 79
Tomintoul. Mor 4A 72
Tomnavoulin. Mor 3B 72
Tomsléibhe. Arg 4M 63
Ton. Mon 4B 18
**Tonbridge**. Kent 1B 12
Tondu. B'end 6H 17
Tonedale. Som 3L 7
Tonfanau. Gwyn 2E 24
Tong. Shrp 1F 26
Tonge. Leics 7B 36
Tong Forge. Shrp 1F 26
Tongham. Surr 1F 10
Tongland. Dum 6A 52
Tong Norton. Shrp 1F 26
Tongue. High 6H 85
Tongue End. Linc 8J 37
Tongwynlais. Card 6L 17
Tonmawr. Neat 5H 17
Tonna. Neat 5G 17
Tonnau. Neat 5G 17
Ton Pentre. Rhon 5J 17
Ton-Teg. Rhon 6K 17
Tonwell. Herts 2L 21
Tonypandy. Rhon 5J 17
Tonyrefail. Rhon 6K 17
Toome. Ant 4F 93
Toot Baldon. Oxon 3C 20
Toot Hill. Essx 3B 22
Toothill. Hants 4A 10
Topcliffe. N Yor 8B 48
Topcliffe. W Yor 5L 41
Topcroft. Norf 2J 31
Topcroft Street. Norf 2J 31
Toppesfield. Essx 8D 30
Toppings. G Man 6F 40
Toprow. Norf 2H 31
Topsham. Devn 7J 7
**Torbay**. Torb 5M 5
Torbeg. N Ayr 7H 57
Torbothie. N Lan 4G 59
Torbryan. Devn 5L 5
Torcross. Devn 7L 5
Tore. High 8G 79
Torgyle. High 4D 70
Torinturk. Arg 3H 57
Torksey. Linc 2F 36
Torlum. W Isl 8J 75
Torlundy. High 8B 70
Tormarton. S Glo 6F 18
Tormitchell. S Ayr 2H 51
Tormore. High 5H 69
Tormore. N Ayr 6H 57
Tornagrain. High 1H 71
Tornaveen. Abers 5F 72
Torness. High 3F 70
Toronto. Dur 8E 54
Torpenhow. Cumb 8G 53
Torphichen. W Lot 2H 59
Torphins. Abers 5F 72
Torpoint. Corn 6G 5
**Torquay**. Torb 5M 5
Torr. Devn 6H 5
Torra. Arg 4C 56
Torran. High 1G 69
Torrance. E Dun 2E 58
Torrans. Arg 5K 63
Torranyard. N Ayr 5B 58
Torre. Som 2K 7
Torre. Torb 5M 5
Torridon. High 8L 77
Torrin. High 3G 69
Torrisdale. Arg 6G 57
Torrisdale. High 5J 85
Torrish. High 2K 79
Torrisholme. Lanc 1C 40
Torroble. High 3F 78
Torroy. High 4F 78
Torry. Aber 5J 73
Torryburn. Fife 1J 59
Torthorwald. Dum 4E 52
Tortington. W Sus 5H 11
Tortworth. S Glo 4F 18
Torvaig. High 1F 68
Torver. Cumb 6A 46
Torwood. Falk 1G 59
Torworth. Notts 1D 36
Toscaig. High 2J 69
Toseland. Cambs 5K 29
Tosside. N Yor 2F 40
Tostock. Suff 5F 30
Totaig. High 8C 76
Totardor. High 2E 68
Tote. High 1F 68
Totegan. High 5L 85
Tothill. Linc 1M 37
Totland. IOW 7M 9
Totley. S Yor 2M 35
Totnell. Dors 5E 8
Totnes. Devn 5L 5
Toton. Notts 6B 36
Totronald. Arg 2G 63
Totscore. High 7E 76
**Tottenham**. G Lon 4L 21
Tottenhill. Norf 8C 38
Tottenhill Row. Norf 8C 38
Totteridge. G Lon 4K 21
Totternhoe. C Beds 1G 21
Tottington. G Man 6F 40
**Totton**. Hants 4A 10
Touchen-end. Wind 6F 20
Toulvaddie. High 5J 79
The Towans. Corn 5J 3
Toward. Arg 3L 57
Towcester. Nptn 7D 28
Towednack. Corn 5H 3
Tower End. Norf 8C 38
Tower Hill. Mers 7C 40
Tower Hill. W Sus 3J 11
Towersey. Oxon 3E 20
Towie. Abers 4D 72
Towiemore. Mor 1C 72
Tow Law. Dur 8E 54
The Town. IOS 1G 3
Town End. Cambs 2M 29
Town End. Cumb
  nr. Ambleside 5C 46
  nr. Kirkby Thore 3E 46
  nr. Lindale 7C 46
  nr. Newby Bridge 7B 46
Town End. Mers 1C 34
Townend. W Dun 2C 58
Townfield. Dur 7C 54
Towngate. Cumb 7K 53
Towngate. Linc 8J 37
Town Green. Lanc 7C 40
Town Head. Cumb
  nr. Grasmere 5B 46
  nr. Great Asby 4E 46
Townhead. Cumb
  nr. Lazonby 8K 53
  nr. Maryport 8E 52
  nr. Ousby 8L 53
Townhead. Dum 7A 52
Townhead of Greenlaw.
  Dum 5B 52
Townhill. Fife 1K 59
Townhill. Swan 5F 16
Townjoy. M Ulst 5F 93
Town Kelloe. Dur 8G 55
Town Littleworth. E Sus 4M 11
Town Row. E Sus 2B 12
Towns End. Hants 8C 20
Townsend. Herts 3J 21
Townshend. Corn 5J 3
Town Street. Suff 3D 30
Town Yetholm. Bord 7F 60
Towthorpe. E Yor 1G 43
Towthorpe. York 2D 42
Towton. N Yor 4B 42
Towyn. Cnwy 3J 33
Toxteth. Mers 1B 34
Toynton All Saints. Linc 3L 37
Toynton Fen Side. Linc 3L 37
Toynton St Peter. Linc 3M 37
Toy's Hill. Kent 8A 22
Trabboch. E Ayr 7C 58
Traboe. Corn 6L 3
Tradespark. High 8J 79
Tradespark. Orkn 1F 86
Trafford Park. G Man 8F 40
Trallong. Powy 2J 17
Y Trallwng. Powy 2M 25
Tranent. E Lot 2B 60
Tranmere. Mers 1B 34
Trantlebeg. High 6L 85
Trantlemore. High 6L 85
Tranwell. Nmbd 3E 54
Trapp. Carm 3F 16
Traquair. Bord 6M 59
Trash Green. W Ber 7D 20
Trawden. Lanc 4H 41
Trawscoed. Powy 1K 17
Trawsfynydd. Gwyn 7G 33
Trawsgoed. Cdgn 5F 24
Treaddow. Here 1D 18
Trealaw. Rhon 5K 17
Treales. Lanc 4C 40
Trearddur. IOA 3B 32
Treaslane. High 8E 76
Treator. Corn 4B 4
Trebanog. Rhon 5K 17
Trebanos. Neat 4G 17
Trebarber. Corn 5A 4
Trebartha. Corn 8B 6
Trebarwith. Corn 3C 4
Trebetherick. Corn 4B 4
Treborough. Som 2K 7
Trebudannon. Corn 5A 4
Trebullett. Corn 8C 6
Treburley. Corn 8C 6
Treburrick. Corn 4A 4
Trebyan. Corn 5C 4
Trecastle. Powy 2H 17
Trecenydd. Cphy 6L 17
Trecott. Devn 5F 6
Trecwn. Pemb 3F 14
Trecynon. Rhon 4J 17
Tredaule. Corn 7B 6
Tredavoe. Corn 6H 3
**Tredegar**. Blae 4L 17
Trederwen. Powy 8A 34
Tredington. Glos 1H 19
Tredington. Warw 7L 27
Tredinnick. Corn
  nr. Bodmin 5D 4
  nr. Looe 6E 4
  nr. Padstow 4B 4
Tredogan. V Glam 8K 17
Tredomen. Powy 1L 17
Tredunnock. Mon 4B 18
Tredustan. Powy 1L 17
Treen. Corn
  nr. Land's End 6G 3
  nr. St Ives 5H 3
Treeton. S Yor 1B 36
Trefaldwyn. Powy 3M 25
Trefasser. Pemb 3E 14
Trefdraeth. IOA 3D 32
Trefdraeth. Pemb 3G 15
Trefecca. Powy 1L 17
Trefechan. Mer T 4K 17
Trefeglwys. Powy 3J 25
Trefenter. Cdgn 6F 24
Treffgarne. Pemb 4F 14
Treffynnon. Flin 3L 33
Treffynnon. Pemb 4E 14
Trefil. Blae 3L 17
Trefilan. Cdgn 1M 15
Trefin. Pemb 3E 14
Treflach. Shrp 7A 34
Trefnant. Den 3K 33
Trefonen. Shrp 7A 34
Trefor. Gwyn 6C 32
Trefor. IOA 2C 32
Treforest. Rhon 6K 17
Trefrew. Corn 3D 4
Trefriw. Cnwy 4G 33
Tref-y-Clawdd. Powy 4A 26
Trefynwy. Mon 2D 18
Tregada. Corn 7C 6
Tregadillett. Corn 7B 6
Tregare. Mon 2C 18
Tregarne. Corn 6L 3
Tregaron. Cdgn 7F 24
Tregarth. Gwyn 4F 32
Tregear. Corn 6A 4
Tregeare. Corn 7B 6
Tregeiriog. Wrex 7L 33
Tregele. IOA 1C 32
Tregeseal. Corn 5G 3
Tregiskey. Corn 7C 4
Tregole. Corn 6A 6
Tregolwyn. V Glam 7J 17
Tregonetha. Corn 5B 4
Tregonhawke. Corn 6G 5
Tregony. Corn 7B 4
Tregoodwell. Corn 3D 4
Tregorrick. Corn 6C 4
Tregoss. Corn 5B 4
Tregowris. Corn 6L 3

Tregoyd. Powy 1L 17
Tregrehan Mills. Corn 6C 4
Tre-groes. Cdgn 2L 15
Treguilon. Corn 5C 4
Tregurrian. Corn 5A 4
Tregynon. Powy 3K 25
Trehafod. Rhon 5K 17
Trehan. Corn 6G 5
**Treharris**. Mer T 5K 17
Treherbert. Rhon 5J 17
Trehunist. Corn 5F 4
Trekenner. Corn 8C 6
Trekenning. Corn 5B 4
Treknow. Corn 3C 4
Trelales. B'end 6H 17
Trelan. Corn 7L 3
Trelash. Corn 6A 6
Trelassick. Corn 6A 4
Trelawnyd. Flin 3K 33
Trelech. Carm 3J 15
Treleddyd-fawr. Pemb 4D 14
Trelewis. Mer T 5L 17
Treligga. Corn 3C 4
Trelights. Corn 4B 4
Trelill. Corn 4C 4
Trelissick. Corn 5M 3
Trellech. Mon 3D 18
Trelleck Grange. Mon 3C 18
Trelogan. Flin 2L 33
Trelystan. Powy 1A 26
Tremadog. Gwyn 6E 32
Tremail. Corn 7A 6
Tremain. Cdgn 2J 15
Tremaine. Corn 7B 6
Tremar. Corn 5E 4
Trematon. Corn 6F 4
Tremeirchion. Den 3K 33
Tremore. Corn 5C 4
Tremorfa. Card 7M 17
Trenance. Corn
nr. Newquay 5A 4
nr. Padstow 4B 4
Trenarren. Corn 7C 4
Trench. Telf 8E 34
Trencreek. Corn 2M 3
Trendeal. Corn 6A 4
Trenear. Corn 5K 3
Treneglos. Corn 7B 6
Trenewan. Corn 6D 4
Trengune. Corn 6A 6
Trent. Dors 4D 8
Trentham. Stoke 5G 35
Trentishoe. Devn 1F 6
Trentlock. Derbs 6B 36
Treoes. V Glam 7J 17
Treorchy. Rhon 5J 17
Treorci. Rhon 5J 17
Tre'r-ddol. Cdgn 3F 24
Tre'r llai. Powy 2M 25
Trerulefoot. Corn 6F 4
Tresaith. Cdgn 1J 15
Trescott. Staf 2G 27
Trescowe. Corn 5J 3
Tresham. Glos 4F 18
Tresigin. V Glam 7J 17
Tresillian. Corn 7A 4
Tresimwn. V Glam 7K 17
Tresinney. Corn 3D 4
Treskillard. Corn 5K 3
Treskinnick Cross. Corn 6B 6
Tresmeer. Corn 7B 6
Tresparrett. Corn 2D 4
Tresparrett Posts. Corn 6A 6
Tressady. High 3G 79
Tressait. Per 1B 66
Tresta. Shet
on Fetlar 4L 91
on Mainland 2D 90
Treswell. Notts 2E 36
Treswithian. Corn 5K 3
Tre Taliesin. Cdgn 3F 24
Trethomas. Cphy 6L 17
Trethosa. Corn 6B 4
Trethurgy. Corn 6C 4
Tretio. Pemb 4D 14
Tretire. Here 1D 18
Tretower. Powy 2L 17
Treuddyn. Flin 4A 34
Trevadlock. Corn 8B 6
Trevalga. Corn 3C 4
Trevalyn. Wrex 4B 34
Trevance. Corn 4B 4
Trevanger. Corn 4B 4
Trevanson. Corn 4B 4
Trevarrack. Corn 5H 3
Trevarren. Corn 5B 4
Trevarrian. Corn 5A 4
Trevarrick. Corn 7B 4
Trevaughan. Carm
nr. Carmarthen 4L 15
nr. Whitland 5H 15
Treveighan. Corn 4C 4
Trevellas. Corn 3L 3
Trevelmond. Corn 5E 4
Treverva. Corn 5M 3
Trevescan. Corn 6G 3
Trevethin. Torf 3A 18
Trevia. Corn 3C 4
Trevigro. Corn 5F 4
Trevilley. Corn 6G 3
Treviscoe. Corn 6B 4
Trevivian. Corn 7A 6
Trevone. Corn 4A 4
Trevor. Wrex 5A 34
Trevor Uchaf. Den 6M 33
Trew. Corn 6K 3
Trewalder. Corn 3C 4
Trewarlett. Corn 7C 6
Trewarmett. Corn 3C 4
Trewassa. Corn 3D 4
Treween. Corn 7B 6
Trewellard. Corn 5G 3
Trewen. Corn 7B 6
Trewennack. Corn 6K 3
Trewern. Powy 8A 34
Trewetha. Corn 4C 4
Trewidland. Corn 6E 4
Trewint. Corn 6A 6
Trewithian. Corn 8A 4
Trewoofe. Corn 6H 3
Trewoon. Corn 6B 4
Treworthal. Corn 8A 4
Trewyddel. Pemb 2H 15
Treyarnon. Corn 4A 4
Treyford. W Sus 4F 10
Triangle. Staf 1J 27
Triangle. W Yor 5J 41
Trickett's Cross. Dors 5J 9
Trillick. Ferm 6C 92
Trimdon. Dur 8G 55
Trimdon Colliery. Dur 8G 55
Trimdon Grange. Dur 8G 55
Trimingham. Norf 6J 39
Trimley Lower Street.
Suff 8J 31
Trimley St Martin. Suff 8J 31
Trimley St Mary. Suff 8J 31
Trimpley. Worc 4F 26
Trimsaran. Carm 6L 15
Trimstone. Devn 1E 6
Trinafour. Per 1M 65
Trinant. Cphy 5M 17
**Tring**. Herts 2G 21
Trinity. Ang 1K 67
Trinity. Edin 2L 59
Triscombe. Som 2L 7
Trislaig. High 8A 70
Trispen. Corn 3M 3
Tritlington. Nmbd 2F 54
Trochry. Per 3C 66
Troedrhiwdalar. Powy 7J 25
Troedrhiwfuwch. Cphy 4L 17
Troedrhiw-gwair. Blae 4L 17
Troedyraur. Cdgn 2K 15
Troedyrhiw. Mer T 4K 17
Trondavoe. Shet 6H 91
Troon. Corn 5K 3
**Troon**. S Ayr 6B 58
Troqueer. Dum 4D 52
Troston. Suff 4E 30
Trottiscliffe. Kent 7C 22
Trotton. W Sus 3F 10
Troutbeck. Cumb
nr. Ambleside 5C 46
nr. Penrith 3B 46
Troutbeck Bridge. Cumb 5C 46
Troway. Derbs 2A 36
**Trowbridge**. Wilts 8G 19
Trowell. Notts 6B 36
Trowle Common. Wilts 8G 19
Trowley Bottom. Herts 2H 21
Trowse Newton. Norf 1J 31
Trudoxhill. Som 1F 8
Trull. Som 3M 7
Trumaisgearraidh. W Isl 6K 75
Trumpan. High 7D 76
Trumpet. Here 8E 26
Trumpington. Cambs 6M 29
Trumps Green. Surr 7G 21
Trunch. Norf 6J 39
Trunnah. Lanc 3B 40
**Truro**. Corn 4M 3
Trusham. Devn 7H 7
Trusley. Derbs 6L 35
Trusthorpe. Linc 1B 38
Tryfil. IOA 2D 32
Trysull. Staf 2G 27
Tubney. Oxon 4B 20
Tuckenhay. Devn 6L 5
Tuckhill. Shrp 3F 26
Tuckingmill. Corn 4K 3
Tuckton. Bour 6K 9
Tuddenham. Suff 4D 30
Tuddenham St Martin.
Suff 7H 31
Tudeley. Kent 1C 12
Tudhoe. Dur 8F 54
Tudhoe Grange. Dur 8F 54
Tudorville. Here 1D 18
Tudweiliog. Gwyn 7B 32
Tuesley. Surr 1G 11
Tufton. Hants 1B 10
Tufton. Pemb 4G 15
Tugby. Leics 1E 28
Tugford. Shrp 3D 26
Tughall. Nmbd 7K 61
Tulchan. Per 5C 66
Tullibardine. Per 6C 66
Tullibody. Clac 8B 66
Tullich. Arg 6E 64
Tullich. High
nr. Lochcarron 1L 69
nr. Tain 6J 79
Tullich. Mor 1C 72
Tullich Muir. High 6H 79
Tulliemet. Per 2C 66
Tulloch. Abers 2H 73
Tulloch. High
nr. Bonar Bridge 4G 79
nr. Fort William 7D 70
nr. Grantown-on-Spey 4K 71
Tulloch. Per 5D 66
Tullochgorm. Arg 8D 64
Tullybeagles Lodge. Per 4D 66
Tullyhogue. M Ulst 5F 93
Tullymurdoch. Per 2F 66
Tullynessle. Abers 4E 72
Tumble. Carm 5M 15
Tumbler's Green. Essx 1E 22
Tumby. Linc 3K 37
Tumby Woodside. Linc 4K 37
Tummel Bridge. Per 2A 66
**Tunbridge Wells, Royal**.
Kent 2B 12
Tunga. W Isl 8H 83
Tungate. Norf 7J 39
Tunley. Bath 8E 18
Tunstall. E Yor 4L 43
Tunstall. Kent 7E 22
Tunstall. Lanc 8E 46
Tunstall. Norf 1L 31
Tunstall. N Yor 6L 47
Tunstall. Staf 7F 34
Tunstall. Stoke 4G 35
Tunstall. Suff 6K 31
Tunstall. Tyne 6G 55
Tunstead. Derbs 2K 35
Tunstead. Norf 7J 39
Tunstead Milton. Derbs 1J 35
Tunworth. Hants 1D 10
Tupsley. Here 7D 26
Tupton. Derbs 3A 36
Turfholm. S Lan 6G 59
Turfmoor. Devn 5A 8
Turgis Green. Hants 8D 20
Turkdean. Glos 2K 19
Turkey Island. Hants 4C 10
Tur Langton. Leics 2E 28
Turleigh. Wilts 7G 19
Turlin Moor. Pool 6H 9
Turnastone. Here 8B 26
Turnberry. S Ayr 1H 51
Turnchapel. Plym 6G 5
Turnditch. Derbs 5L 35
Turners Hill. W Sus 2L 11
Turners Puddle. Dors 6G 9
Turnford. Herts 3L 21
Turnhouse. Edin 2K 59
Turnworth. Dors 5G 9
Turriff. Abers 1G 73
Tursdale. Dur 8G 55
Turton Bottoms. Bkbn 6F 40
Turtory. Mor 1E 72
Turves Green. W Mid 4J 27
Turvey. Bed 6G 29
Turville. Buck 4E 20
Turville Heath. Buck 4E 20
Turweston. Buck 8D 28
Tushielaw. Bord 8M 59
Tutbury. Staf 7L 35
Tutnall. Worc 4H 27
Tutshill. Glos 4D 18
Tuttington. Norf 7J 39
Tutts Clump. W Ber 6C 20
Tutwell. Corn 8C 6
Tuxford. Notts 2E 36
Twatt. Orkn 7B 88
Twatt. Shet 2D 90
Twechar. E Dun 2E 58
Tweedale. Telf 1F 26
Tweedbank. Bord 6C 60
Tweedmouth. Nmbd 4G 61
Tweedsmuir. Bord 7J 59
Twelveheads. Corn 4L 3
Twemlow Green. Ches E 3F 34
Twenty. Linc 7J 37
Twerton. Bath 7F 18
**Twickenham**. G Lon 6J 21
Twigworth. Glos 1G 19
Twineham. W Sus 4K 11
Twinhoe. Bath 8F 18
Twinstead. Essx 8E 30
Twinstead Green. Essx 8E 30
Twiss Green. Warr 8E 40
Twiston. Lanc 3G 41
Twitchen. Devn 2G 7
Twitchen. Shrp 4B 26
Two Bridges. Devn 8F 6
Two Bridges. Glos 3E 18
Two Dales. Derbs 3L 35
Two Gates. Staf 1L 27
Two Mile Oak. Devn 5L 5
Twycross. Leics 1M 27
Twyford. Buck 1D 20
Twyford. Derbs 7M 35
Twyford. Dors 4G 9
Twyford. Hants 3B 10
Twyford. Leics 8E 36
Twyford. Norf 7G 39
Twyford. Wok 6E 20
Twyford Common. Here 8D 26
Twynholm. Dum 6A 52
Twyning. Glos 8G 27
Twyning Green. Glos 8H 27
Twynllanan. Carm 2G 17
Twyn-y-Sheriff. Mon 3C 18
Twywell. Nptn 4G 29
Tyberton. Here 8B 26
Tyburn. W Mid 2K 27
Tyby. Norf 7G 39
Tycroes. Carm 3F 16
Tycrwyn. Powy 1L 25
**Tyddewi**. Pemb 4D 14
Tydd Gote. Linc 8A 38
Tydd St Giles. Cambs 8M 37
Tydd St Mary. Linc 8M 37
Tye. Hants 5E 10
Tye Green. Essx
nr. Bishop's Stortford 1B 22
nr. Braintree 1D 22
nr. Saffron Walden 8B 30
Tyersal. W Yor 4K 41
Ty Issa. Powy 7L 33
**Tyldesley**. G Man 7E 40
Tyler Hill. Kent 7H 23
Tyler's Green. Essx 3B 22
Tylers Green. Buck 4F 20
Tylorstown. Rhon 5K 17
Tylwch. Powy 4J 25
Y Tymbl. Carm 5M 15
Tynan. Arm 6E 92
Ty-nant. Cnwy 6J 33
Tyndrum. Stir 4H 65
Tyneham. Dors 7G 9
Tynehead. Midl 4A 60
**Tynemouth**. Tyne 5G 55
**Tyneside**. Tyne 5F 54
**Tyne Tunnel**. Tyne 5G 55
Tynewydd. Rhon 5J 17
Tyninghame. E Lot 2D 60
Tynron. Dum 2C 52
Ty'n-y-bryn. Rhon 6K 17
Tyn-y-celyn. Wrex 7L 33
Tyn-y-cwm. Swan 4F 16
Tyn-y-ffridd. Powy 7L 33
Tynygongl. IOA 2E 32
Tynygraig. Cdgn 6F 24
Ty'n-y-groes. Cnwy 3G 33
Ty'n-yr-eithin. Cdgn 6F 24
Tyn-y-rhyd. Powy 1K 25
Tyn-y-wern. Powy 8K 33
Tyrie. Abers 7J 81
Tyringham. Mil 7F 28
Tythecott. Devn 4D 6
Tythegston. B'end 7H 17
Tytherington. Ches E 2H 35
Tytherington. Som 1F 8
Tytherington. S Glo 5E 18
Tytherington. Wilts 1H 9
Tytherleigh. Devn 5B 8
Tywardreath. Corn 6C 4
Tywardreath Highway. Corn 6C 4
Tywyn. Cnwy 3G 33
Tywyn. Gwyn 2E 24


## U


Uachdar. W Isl 8K 75
Uags. High 2J 69
Ubbeston Green. Suff 4K 31
Ubley. Bath 8D 18
Uckerby. N Yor 5L 47
**Uckfield**. E Sus 3A 12
Uckinghall. Worc 8G 27
Uckington. Glos 1H 19
Uckington. Shrp 1D 26
Uddingston. S Lan 3E 58
Uddington. S Lan 6G 59
Udimore. E Sus 4E 12
Udny Green. Abers 3H 73
Udny Station. Abers 3J 73
Udston. S Lan 4E 58
Udstonhead. S Lan 5F 58
Uffcott. Wilts 6K 19
Uffculme. Devn 4K 7
Uffington. Linc 1H 29
Uffington. Oxon 5M 19
Uffington. Shrp 8D 34
Ufford. Pet 1H 29
Ufford. Suff 6J 31
Ufton. Warw 5A 28
Ufton Nervet. W Ber 7D 20
Ugadale. Arg 7G 57
Ugborough. Devn 6J 5
Ugford. Wilts 2J 9
Uggeshall. Suff 3L 31
Ugglebarnby. N Yor 5F 48
Ugley. Essx 1B 22
Ugley Green. Essx 1B 22
Ugthorpe. N Yor 4E 48
Uidh. W Isl 6C 74
Uig. Arg 2J 63
Uig. High
nr. Balgown 7E 76
nr. Dunvegan 8C 76
Uigshader. High 1F 68
Uisken. Arg 6J 63
Ulbster. High 7E 86
Ulcat Row. Cumb 3C 46
Ulceby. Linc 2M 37
Ulceby. N Lin 6J 43
Ulceby Skitter. N Lin 6J 43
Ulcombe. Kent 1E 12
Uldale. Cumb 8G 53
Uley. Glos 4F 18
Ulgham. Nmbd 2F 54
Ullapool. High 4B 78
Ullenhall. Warw 5K 27
Ulleskelf. N Yor 4C 42
Ullesthorpe. Leics 3C 28
Ulley. S Yor 1B 36
Ullingswick. Here 8D 26
Ullinish. High 2E 68
Ullock. Cumb 2K 45
Ulpha. Cumb 5L 45
Ulrome. E Yor 2J 43
Ulsta. Shet 5J 91
Ulting. Essx 3E 22
Ulva House. Arg 4K 63
**Ulverston**. Cumb 8A 46
Ulwell. Dors 7J 9
Umberleigh. Devn 3F 6
Unapool. High 8E 84
Underbarrow. Cumb 6C 46
Undercliffe. W Yor 4K 41
Underdale. Shrp 8D 34
Underhoull. Shet 3K 91
Underriver. Kent 8B 22
Under Tofts. S Yor 1M 35
Underton. Shrp 2E 26
Underwood. Newp 5B 18
Underwood. Notts 4B 36
Underwood. Plym 6H 5
Undley. Suff 3C 30
Undy. Mon 5C 18
Union Mills. IOM 7C 44
Union Street. E Sus 2D 12
Unstone. Derbs 2A 36
Unstone Green. Derbs 2A 36
Unthank. Cumb
nr. Carlisle 7H 53
nr. Gamblesby 7L 53
nr. Penrith 8J 53
Unthank End. Cumb 8J 53
Upavon. Wilts 8K 19
Up Cerne. Dors 5E 8
Upchurch. Kent 7E 22
Upcott. Devn 5E 6
Upcott. Here 6B 26
Upend. Cambs 6C 30
Up Exe. Devn 5J 7
Upgate. Norf 8H 39
Upgate Street. Norf 2G 31
Uphall. Dors 5D 8
Uphall. W Lot 2J 59
Uphall Station. W Lot 2J 59
Upham. Devn 5H 7
Upham. Hants 3C 10
Uphampton. Here 5B 26
Uphampton. Worc 5G 27
Up Hatherley. Glos 1H 19
Uphill. N Som 8B 18
Up Holland. Lanc 7D 40
Uplawmoor. E Ren 4C 58
Upleadon. Glos 1F 18
Upleatham. Red C 4D 48
Uplees. Kent 7G 23
Uploders. Dors 6D 8
Uplowman. Devn 4K 7
Uplyme. Devn 6B 8
Up Marden. W Sus 4E 10
**Upminster**. G Lon 5B 22
Up Nately. Hants 8D 20
Upottery. Devn 5M 7
Uppat. High 3J 79
Upper Affcot. Shrp 3C 26
Upper Arley. Worc 3F 26
Upper Armley. W Yor 4L 41
Upper Arncott. Oxon 2D 20
Upper Astrop. Nptn 8C 28
Upper Badcall. High 7D 84
Upper Ballinderry. Lis 5G 93
Upper Bangor. Gwyn 3E 32
Upper Basildon. W Ber 6C 20
Upper Batley. W Yor 5L 41
Upper Beeding. W Sus 4J 11
Upper Benefield. Nptn 3G 29
Upper Bentley. Worc 5H 27
Upper Bighouse. High 6L 85
Upper Boddam. Abers 2F 72
Upper Boddington. Nptn 6B 28
Upper Bogside. Mor 8B 80
Upper Booth. Derbs 1K 35
Upper Borth. Cdgn 4F 24
Upper Boyndlie. Abers 7J 81
Upper Brailes. Warw 7M 27
Upper Breinton. Here 7C 26
Upper Broughton. Notts 7D 36
Upper Brynamman. Carm 3G 17
Upper Bucklebury. W Ber 7C 20
Upper Bullington. Hants 1B 10
Upper Burgate. Hants 4K 9
Upper Caldecote. C Beds 7J 29
Upper Canterton. Hants 4L 9
Upper Catesby. Nptn 6C 28
Upper Chapel. Powy 8K 25
Upper Cheddon. Som 3M 7
Upper Chicksgrove. Wilts 3H 9
Upper Church Village.
Rhon 6K 17
Upper Chute. Wilts 8L 19
Upper Clatford. Hants 1A 10
Upper Coberley. Glos 2H 19
Upper Coedcae. Torf 3A 18
Upper Cound. Shrp 1D 26
Upper Cudworth. S Yor 7A 42
Upper Cumberworth.
W Yor 7L 41
Upper Cuttlehill. Abers 1D 72
Upper Cwmbran. Torf 4A 18
Upper Dallachy. Mor 7C 80
Upper Dean. Bed 5H 29
Upper Denby. W Yor 7L 41
Upper Derraid. High 2L 71
Upper Diabaig. High 7K 77
Upper Dicker. E Sus 5B 12
Upper Dinchope. Shrp 3C 26
Upper Dochcarty. High 7F 78
Upper Dounreay. High 5A 86
Upper Dovercourt. Essx 8J 31
Upper Dunsforth. N Yor 1B 42
Upper Dunsley. Herts 2G 21
Upper Eastern Green.
W Mid 3L 27
Upper Elkstone. Staf 4J 35
Upper Ellastone. Staf 5K 35
Upper End. Derbs 2J 35
Upper Enham. Hants 1A 10
Upper Farmcote. Shrp 2F 26
Upper Farringdon. Hants 2E 10
Upper Framilode. Glos 2F 18
Upper Froyle. Hants 1E 10
Upper Gills. High 4E 86
Upper Glenfintaig. High 7C 70
Upper Godney. Som 1C 8
Upper Gravenhurst. C Beds 8J 29
Upper Green. Essx 8M 29
Upper Green. W Ber 7A 20
Upper Green. W Yor 5L 41
Upper Grove Common.
Here 1D 18
Upper Hackney. Derbs 3L 35
Upper Hale. Surr 1F 10
Upper Halliford. Surr 7H 21
Upper Halling. Medw 7C 22
Upper Hambleton. Rut 1G 29
Upper Hardres Court.
Kent 8H 23
Upper Hardwick. Here 6C 26
Upper Hartfield. E Sus 2A 12
Upper Haugh. S Yor 8B 42
Upper Hayton. Shrp 3D 26
Upper Heath. Shrp 3D 26
Upper Hellesdon. Norf 8J 39
Upper Helmsley. N Yor 2D 42
Upper Hengoed. Shrp 7A 34
Upper Hergest. Here 6A 26
Upper Heyford. Nptn 6D 28
Upper Heyford. Oxon 1B 20
Upper Hill. Here 6C 26
Upper Hindhope. Bord 1A 54
Upper Hopton. W Yor 6K 41
Upper Howsell. Worc 7F 26
Upper Hulme. Staf 3J 35
Upper Inglesham. Swin 4L 19
Upper Kilcott. S Glo 5F 18
Upper Killay. Swan 5L 15
Upper Kirkton. Abers 2G 73
Upper Kirkton. N Ayr 4L 57
Upper Knockando. Mor 1A 72
Upper Knockchoilum.
High 4E 70
Upper Lambourn. W Ber 5M 19
Upperlands. M Ulst 3F 93
Upper Langford. N Som 8C 18
Upper Langwith. Derbs 3C 36
Upper Largo. Fife 7H 67
Upper Latheron. High 8C 86
Upper Layham. Suff 7G 31
Upper Leigh. Staf 6J 35
Upper Lenie. High 3F 70
Upper Lochton. Abers 6F 72
Upper Longdon. Staf 8J 35
Upper Longwood. Shrp 1E 26
Upper Lybster. High 8D 86
Upper Lydbrook. Glos 2E 18
Upper Lye. Here 5B 26
Upper Maes-coed. Here 8B 26
Upper Midway. Derbs 7L 35
Uppermill. G Man 7H 41
Upper Millichope. Shrp 3D 26
Upper Milovaig. High 1C 68
Upper Minety. Wilts 4J 19
Upper Mitton. Worc 4G 27
Upper Nash. Pemb 6G 15
Upper Neepaback. Shet 5K 91
Upper Netchwood. Shrp 2E 26
Upper Nobut. Staf 6J 35
Upper North Dean. Buck 4F 20
Upper Norwood. W Sus 4G 11
Upper Nyland. Dors 3F 8
Upper Oddington. Glos 1L 19
Upper Ollach. High 2G 69
Upper Outwoods. Staf 7L 35
Upper Padley. Derbs 2L 35
Upper Pennington. Hants 6M 9
Upper Poppleton. York 2C 42
Upper Quinton. Warw 7K 27
Upper Rissington. Glos 2L 19
Upper Rochford. Worc 5E 26
Upper Rusko. Dum 5L 51
Upper Sandaig. High 4J 69
Upper Sanday. Orkn 1G 87
Upper Sapey. Here 5E 26
Upper Seagry. Wilts 5H 19
Upper Shelton. C Beds 7G 29
Upper Sheringham. Norf 5H 39
Upper Skelmorlie. N Ayr 3L 57
Upper Slaughter. Glos 1K 19
Upper Sonachan. Arg 5E 64
Upper Soudley. Glos 2E 18
Upper Staploe. Bed 6J 29
Upper Stoke. Norf 1J 31
Upper Stondon. C Beds 8J 29
Upper Stowe. Nptn 6D 28
Upper Street. Hants 4K 9
Upper Street. Norf
nr. Horning 8K 39
nr. Hoveton 8K 39
Upper Street. Suff 8H 31
Upper Strensham. Worc 8H 27
Upper Studley. Wilts 8G 19
Upper Sundon. C Beds 1H 21
Upper Swell. Glos 1K 19
Upper Tankersley. S Yor 8M 41
Upper Tean. Staf 6J 35
Upperthong. W Yor 7K 41
Upperthorpe. N Lin 7E 42
Upper Thurnham. Lanc 2C 40
Upper Tillyrie. Per 7E 66
Upperton. W Sus 3G 11
Upper Tooting. G Lon 6K 21
Upper Town. Derbs
nr. Bonsall 4L 35
nr. Hognaston 4L 35
Upper Town. Here 7D 26
Upper Town. N Som 7D 18
Uppertown. Derbs 3M 35
Uppertown. High 4E 86
Uppertown. Nmbd 4B 54
Uppertown. Orkn 2F 86
Upper Tysoe. Warw 7M 27
Upper Upham. Wilts 6L 19
Upper Upnor. Medw 6D 22
Upper Urquhart. Fife 7E 66
Upper Wardington. Oxon 7B 28
Upper Weald. Mil 8E 28
Upper Weedon. Nptn 6D 28
Upper Wellingham. E Sus 4M 11
Upper Whiston. S Yor 1B 36
Upper Wield. Hants 2D 10
Upper Winchendon.
Buck 2E 20
Upperwood. Derbs 4L 35
Upper Woodford. Wilts 2K 9
Upper Wootton. Hants 8C 20
Upper Wraxall. Wilts 6G 19
Upper Wyche. Worc 7F 26
Uppincott. Devn 5H 7
Uppingham. Rut 2F 28
Uppington. Shrp 1E 26
Upsall. N Yor 7B 48
Upsettlington. Bord 5F 60
Upshire. Essx 3M 21
Up Somborne. Hants 2A 10
Upstreet. Kent 7J 23
Up Sydling. Dors 5E 8
Upthorpe. Suff 4F 30
Upton. Buck 2E 20
Upton. Cambs 4J 29
Upton. Ches W 3C 34
Upton. Corn
nr. Bude 5B 6
nr. Liskeard 8B 6
Upton. Cumb 8H 53
Upton. Devn
nr. Honiton 5K 7
nr. Kingsbridge 7K 5
Upton. Dors
nr. Poole 6H 9
nr. Weymouth 7F 8
Upton. E Yor 2J 43
Upton. Hants
nr. Andover 8A 20
nr. Southampton 4A 10
Upton. IOW 6C 10
Upton. Leics 2A 28
Upton. Linc 1F 36
Upton. Mers 1A 34
Upton. Norf 8K 39
Upton. Nptn 5E 28
Upton. Notts
nr. Retford 2E 36
nr. Southwell 4E 36
Upton. Oxon 5C 20
Upton. Pemb 6G 15
Upton. Pet 1J 29
Upton. Slo 6G 21
Upton. Som
nr. Somerton 3C 8
nr. Wiveliscombe 3J 7
Upton. Warw 6K 27
Upton. W Yor 6B 42
Upton. Wilts 2G 9
Upton Bishop. Here 1E 18
Upton Cheyney. S Glo 7E 18
Upton Cressett. Shrp 2E 26
Upton Crews. Here 1E 18
Upton Cross. Corn 8B 6
Upton End. C Beds 8J 29
Upton Grey. Hants 1D 10
Upton Heath. Ches W 3C 34
Upton Hellions. Devn 5H 7
Upton Lovell. Wilts 1H 9
Upton Magna. Shrp 8D 34
Upton Noble. Som 2F 8
Upton Pyne. Devn 6J 7
Upton St Leonards. Glos 2G 19
Upton Scudamore. Wilts 1G 9
Upton Snodsbury. Worc 6H 27
Upton upon Severn. Worc 7G 27
Upton Warren. Worc 5H 27
Upwaltham. W Sus 4G 11
Upware. Cambs 4B 30
Upwell. Norf 1B 30
Upwey. Dors 7E 8
Upwick Green. Herts 1A 22
Upwood. Cambs 3K 29
Urafirth. Shet 6H 91
Uragaig. Arg 8J 63
Urchany. High 1J 71
Urchfont. Wilts 8J 19
Urdimarsh. Here 7D 26
Ure. Shet 6G 91
Ure Bank. N Yor 8M 47
Urgha. W Isl 4C 76
Urlay Nook. Stoc T 4B 48
**Urmston**. G Man 8F 40
Urquhart. Mor 7B 80
Urra. N Yor 5C 48
Urray. High 8F 78
Usan. Ang 2L 67
Ushaw Moor. Dur 7F 54
Usk. Mon 3B 18
Usselby. Linc 8H 43
Usworth. Tyne 6G 55
Utkinton. Ches W 3D 34
Uton. Devn 6H 7
Utterby. Linc 8L 43
**Uttoxeter**. Staf 6J 35
Uwchmynydd. Gwyn 8A 32
**Uxbridge**. G Lon 5H 21
Uyeasound. Shet 3K 91
Uzmaston. Pemb 5F 14


## V


Valley. IOA 3B 32
Valley End. Surr 7G 21
Valley Truckle. Corn 3D 4
Valsgarth. Shet 2L 91
Valtos. High 7G 77
Van. Powy 4J 25
Vange. Essx 5D 22
Varteg. Torf 3A 18
Vatsetter. Shet 5K 91
Vatten. High 1D 68
Vaul. Arg 3F 62
The Vauld. Here 7D 26
Vaynor. Mer T 3K 17
Veensgarth. Shet 3E 90
Velindre. Powy 1L 17
Vellow. Som 2K 7
Velly. Devn 3B 6
Veness. Orkn 7E 88
Venhay. Devn 4G 7
Venn. Devn 7K 5
Venngreen. Devn 4C 6
Vennington. Shrp 1B 26
Venn Ottery. Devn 6K 7
Venn's Green. Here 7D 26
Venny Tedburn. Devn 6H 7
Venterdon. Corn 8C 6
Ventnor. IOW 8C 10
Vernham Dean. Hants 8M 19
Vernham Street. Hants 8M 19
Vernolds Common. Shrp 3C 26
Verwood. Dors 5J 9
Veryan. Corn 8B 4
Veryan Green. Corn 8B 4
Vicarage. Devn 7M 7
Vickerstown. Cumb 8L 45
Victoria. Corn 5B 4
Victoria Bridge. Derr 4C 92
Vidlin. Shet 1E 90
**Viewpark**. N Lan 3F 58
Vigo. W Mid 1J 27
Vigo Village. Kent 7C 22
Vinehall Street. E Sus 3D 12
Vine's Cross. E Sus 4B 12
Viney Hill. Glos 3E 18
Virginia Water. Surr 7G 21
Virginstow. Devn 6C 6
Vobster. Som 1F 8
Voe. Shet
nr. Hillside 1E 90
nr. Swinister 5H 91
Vole. Som 1B 8
Vowchurch. Here 8B 26
Voxter. Shet 6H 91
Voy. Orkn 8B 88
Vulcan Village. Mers 8D 40


## W


Waberthwaite. Cumb 5L 45
Wackerfield. Dur 3K 47
Wacton. Norf 2H 31
Wadbister. Shet 3E 90
Wadborough. Worc 7H 27
Wadbrook. Devn 5B 8
Waddesdon. Buck 2E 20
Waddeton. Devn 6L 5
Waddicar. Mers 8B 40
Waddingham. Linc 8G 43
Waddington. Lanc 3F 40
Waddington. Linc 3G 37
Waddon. Devn 8H 7
Wadebridge. Corn 4B 4
Wadeford. Som 4B 8
Wadenhoe. Nptn 3H 29
Wadesmill. Herts 2L 21
Wadhurst. E Sus 2C 12
Wadshelf. Derbs 2M 35
Wadsley. S Yor 8M 41
Wadsley Bridge. S Yor 8M 41
Wadswick. Wilts 7G 19
Wadwick. Hants 8B 20
Wadworth. S Yor 8C 42
Waen. Den
nr. Llandymog 4L 33
nr. Nantglyn 4J 33
Waen. Powy 3J 25
Waen Fach. Powy 1M 25
Waen Goleugoed. Den 3K 33
Wag. High 1L 79
Wainfleet All Saints. Linc 4A 38
Wainfleet Bank. Linc 4A 38
Wainfleet St Mary. Linc 4A 38
Wainhouse Corner. Corn 6A 6
Wainscott. Medw 6D 22
Wainstalls. W Yor 5J 41
Waitby. Cumb 5F 46
Waithe. Linc 7K 43
**Wakefield**. W Yor 5M 41
Wakerley. Nptn 2G 29
Wakes Colne. Essx 1E 22
Walberswick. Suff 4L 31
Walberton. W Sus 5G 11
Walbottle. Tyne 5E 54
Walby. Cumb 5J 53
Walcombe. Som 1D 8
Walcot. Linc 6H 37
Walcot. N Lin 5F 42
Walcot. Swin 5K 19
Walcot. Telf 8D 34
Walcot. Warw 6K 27
Walcote. Leics 3C 28
Walcot Green. Norf 3H 31
Walcott. Linc 4J 37
Walcott. Norf 6K 39
Walden. N Yor 7J 47
Walden Head. N Yor 7H 47
Walden Stubbs. N Yor 6C 42
Walderslade. Medw 7D 22
Walderton. W Sus 4E 10
Walditch. Dors 6C 8
Waldley. Derbs 6K 35
Waldridge. Dur 6F 54
Waldringfield. Suff 7J 31
Waldron. E Sus 4B 12
Wales. S Yor 1B 36
Walesby. Linc 8J 43
Walesby. Notts 2D 36
Walford. Here
nr. Leintwardine 4B 26
nr. Ross-on-Wye 1D 18
Walford. Shrp 7C 34
Walford. Staf 6G 35
Walford Heath. Shrp 8C 34
Walgherton. Ches E 5E 34
Walgrave. Nptn 4F 28
Walhampton. Hants 6M 9
**Walkden**. G Man 7F 40
Walker. Tyne 5F 54
Walkerburn. Bord 6A 60
Walker Fold. Lanc 3E 40
Walkeringham. Notts 8E 42
Walkerith. Linc 8E 42
Walkern. Herts 1K 21
Walker's Green. Here 7D 26
Walkerton. Fife 7F 66
Walkerville. N Yor 6L 47
Walkford. Dors 6L 9
Walkhampton. Devn 5H 5
Walkington. E Yor 4G 43
Walkley. S Yor 1M 35
Walk Mill. Lanc 4G 41
Wall. Corn 5K 3
Wall. Nmbd 5C 54
Wall. Staf 1K 27
Wallaceton. Dum 3C 52
Wallacetown. Shet 2D 90
Wallacetown. S Ayr
nr. Ayr 7B 58
nr. Dailly 1H 51
Wallands Park. E Sus 4M 11
**Wallasey**. Mers 8A 40
Wallaston Green. Pemb 6F 14
Wallbrook. W Mid 2H 27
Wallcrouch. E Sus 2C 12
Wall End. Cumb 6M 45
Wallend. Medw 6E 22
Wall Heath. W Mid 3G 27
Wallingford. Oxon 5D 20
**Wallington**. G Lon 7K 21
Wallington. Hants 5C 10
Wallington. Herts 8K 29
Wallis. Pemb 4G 15
Wallisdown. Bour 6J 9
Walliswood. Surr 2J 11
Wall Nook. Dur 7F 54
Walls. Shet 3C 90
**Wallsend**. Tyne 5G 55
Wallsworth. Glos 1G 19
Wall under Heywood. Shrp 2D 26
Wallyford. E Lot 2A 60
Walmer. Kent 8K 23
Walmer Bridge. Lanc 5C 40
Walmersley. G Man 6G 41
Walmley. W Mid 2K 27
Walnut Grove. Per 5E 66
Walpole. Suff 4K 31
Walpole Cross Keys. Norf 8B 38
Walpole Gate. Norf 8B 38
Walpole Highway. Norf 8B 38
Walpole Marsh. Norf 8A 38
Walpole St Andrew. Norf 8B 38
Walpole St Peter. Norf 8B 38
**Walsall**. W Mid 2J 27
Walsall Wood. W Mid 1J 27
Walsden. W Yor 5H 41
Walsgrave on Sowe.
W Mid 3A 28
Walsham le Willows. Suff 4G 31
Walshaw. G Man 6F 40
Walshford. N Yor 2B 42
Walsoken. Norf 8A 38
Walston. S Lan 5J 59
Walsworth. Herts 8J 29
Walter's Ash. Buck 4F 20
Walterston. V Glam 7K 17
Walterstone. Here 1B 18
Waltham. Kent 1H 13
Waltham. NE Lin 7K 43
**Waltham Abbey**. Essx 3L 21
Waltham Chase. Hants 4C 10
Waltham Cross. Herts 3L 21
Waltham on the Wolds.
Leics 7F 36
Waltham St Lawrence.
Wind 6F 20
Waltham's Cross. Essx 8C 30
**Walthamstow**. G Lon 5L 21
Walton. Cumb 5K 53
Walton. Derbs 3A 36
Walton. Leics 3C 28
Walton. Mers 8B 40
Walton. Mil 8F 28
Walton. Pet 1J 29
Walton. Powy 6A 26
Walton. Som 2C 8
Walton. Staf
nr. Eccleshall 7G 35
nr. Stone 6G 35
Walton. Suff 8J 31
Walton. Telf 8D 34
Walton. Warw 6L 27
Walton. W Yor
nr. Wakefield 6A 42
nr. Wetherby 3B 42
Walton Cardiff. Glos 8H 27
Walton East. Pemb 4G 15
Walton Elm. Dors 4F 8
Walton Highway. Norf 8A 38
Walton in Gordano. N Som 6C 18
Walton-le-Dale. Lanc 5D 40
**Walton-on-Thames**. Surr 7J 21
Walton on the Hill. Surr 8K 21
Walton-on-the-Hill. Staf 7H 35
**Walton-on-the-Naze**. Essx 1J 23
Walton on the Wolds. Leics 8C 36
Walton-on-Trent. Derbs 8L 35
Walton West. Pemb 5E 14
Walwick. Nmbd 4C 54
Walworth. Darl 4L 47
Walworth Gate. Darl 3L 47
Walwyn's Castle. Pemb 5E 14
Wambrook. Som 5A 8
Wampool. Cumb 6G 53
Wanborough. Surr 1G 11
Wanborough. Swin 5L 19
Wandel. S Lan 7H 59
**Wandsworth**. G Lon 6K 21
Wangford. Suff
nr. Lakenheath 3D 30
nr. Southwold 4L 31
Wanlip. Leics 8C 36
Wanlockhead. Dum 8G 59
Wannock. E Sus 5B 12
Wansford. E Yor 2H 43
Wansford. Pet 2H 29
Wanshurst Green. Kent 1D 12
**Wanstead**. G Lon 5M 21
Wanstrow. Som 1F 8
Wanswell. Glos 3E 18
Wantage. Oxon 5B 20
Wapley. S Glo 6F 18
Wappenbury. Warw 5A 28
Wappenham. Nptn 7D 28
Warbleton. E Sus 4C 12
Warblington. Hants 5E 10
Warborough. Oxon 4C 20
Warboys. Cambs 3L 29
Warbreck. Bkpl 4B 40
Warbstow. Corn 6B 6
Warburton. G Man 1F 34
Warcop. Cumb 4F 46
Warden. Kent 6G 23
Warden. Nmbd 5C 54
Ward End. W Mid 3K 27
Ward Green. Suff 5G 31
Ward Green Cross. Lanc 4E 40
Wardhedges. C Beds 8H 29
Wardhouse. Abers 2E 72
Wardington. Oxon 7B 28
Wardle. Ches E 4E 34
Wardle. G Man 6H 41
Wardley. Rut 1F 28
Wardley. W Sus 3F 10
Wardlow. Derbs 2K 35
Wardsend. Ches E 1H 35
Wardy Hill. Cambs 3A 30
**Ware**. Herts 2L 21
Ware. Kent 7J 23
Wareham. Dors 7H 9
Warehorne. Kent 2F 12
Warenford. Nmbd 7J 61
Waren Mill. Nmbd 6J 61
Warenton. Nmbd 6J 61
Wareside. Herts 2L 21
Waresley. Cambs 6K 29
Waresley. Worc 5G 27
Warfield. Brac 6F 20
Warfleet. Devn 6L 5
Wargate. Linc 6K 37
Wargrave. Wok 6E 20
Warham. Norf 5F 38
Waringsford. Arm 6H 93
Waringstown. Arm 6G 93
Wark. Nmbd
nr. Coldstream 6F 60
nr. Hexham 4B 54
Warkleigh. Devn 3F 6
Warkton. Nptn 4F 28
Warkworth. Nptn 7B 28
Warkworth. Nmbd 1F 54
Warlaby. N Yor 6M 47
Warland. W Yor 5H 41
Warleggan. Corn 5D 4
**Warlingham**. Surr 8L 21
Warmanbie. Dum 5F 52
Warmfield. W Yor 5A 42
Warmingham. Ches E 3F 34
Warminghurst. W Sus 4J 11
Warmington. Nptn 2H 29
Warmington. Warw 7B 28
**Warminster**. Wilts 1G 9
Warmley. S Glo 6E 18
Warmsworth. S Yor 7C 42
Warmwell. Dors 7F 8
Warndon. Worc 6G 27
Warners End. Herts 3H 21
Warnford. Hants 3D 10
Warnham. W Sus 2J 11
Warningcamp. W Sus 5H 11
Warninglid. W Sus 3K 11
Warren. Ches E 2G 35
Warren. Pemb 7F 14
Warrenby. Red C 3C 48
Warren Corner. Hants
nr. Aldershot 1F 10
nr. Petersfield 3E 10
Warrenpoint. New M 7G 93
Warren Row. Wind 5F 20
Warren Street. Kent 8F 22
Warrington. Mil 6F 28
**Warrington**. Warr 1E 34
Warsash. Hants 5B 10
Warse. High 4E 86
Warslow. Staf 4J 35
**Warsop**. Notts 3C 36
Warsop Vale. Notts 3C 36
Warter. E Yor 2F 42
Warthermarske. N Yor 8L 47
Warthill. N Yor 2D 42
Wartling. E Sus 5C 12
Wartnaby. Leics 7E 36
Warton. Lanc
nr. Carnforth 8C 46
nr. Freckleton 5C 40
Warton. Nmbd 1D 54
Warton. Warw 1L 27
**Warwick**. Warw 5L 27
Warwick Bridge. Cumb 6J 53
Warwick-on-Eden. Cumb 6J 53
Warwick Wold. Surr 8L 21
Wasbister. Orkn 6C 88
Wasdale Head. Cumb 4L 45
Wash. Derbs 1J 35
Washaway. Corn 5C 4
Washbourne. Devn 6K 5
Washbrook. Suff 7H 31
Wash Common. W Ber 7B 20
Washerwall. Staf 5H 35
Washfield. Devn 4J 7
Washfold. N Yor 5J 47
Washford. Som 1K 7
Washford Pyne. Devn 4H 7
Washingborough. Linc 2H 37
**Washington**. Tyne 6G 55
Washington. W Sus 4J 11
Washington Village. Tyne 6G 55
Waskerley. Dur 7D 54
Wasperton. Warw 6L 27
Wasp Green. Surr 1L 11
Wasps Nest. Linc 3H 37
Wass. N Yor 8C 48
Watchet. Som 1K 7
Watchfield. Oxon 4L 19
Watchgate. Cumb 6D 46
Watchhill. Cumb 7F 52
Watcombe. Torb 5M 5
Watendlath. Cumb 4A 46
Water. Devn 7G 7
Water. Lanc 5G 41
Waterbeach. Cambs 5A 30
Waterbeach. W Sus 5F 10
Waterbeck. Dum 4G 53
Waterditch. Hants 6K 9
Water End. C Beds 8H 29
Water End. E Yor 4E 42
Water End. Essx 7B 30
Water End. Herts
nr. Hatfield 3K 21
nr. Hemel Hempstead 2H 21
Waterfall. Staf 4J 35
Waterfoot. Caus 2H 93
Waterfoot. E Ren 4D 58
Waterfoot. Lanc 5G 41
Waterford. Herts 2L 21
Water Fryston. W Yor 5B 42
Waterhead. Cumb 5B 46
Waterhead. E Ayr 8D 58
Waterhead. S Ayr 2J 51
Waterheads. Bord 4L 59
Waterhouses. Dur 7E 54
Waterhouses. Staf 4J 35
Wateringbury. Kent 8C 22
Waterlane. Glos 3H 19
Waterlip. Som 1E 8
Waterloo. Cphy 6L 17
Waterloo. Corn 4D 4
Waterloo. Here 7B 26
Waterloo. High 3H 69
Waterloo. Mers 8B 40
Waterloo. Norf 8J 39
Waterloo. N Lan 4G 59
Waterloo. Pemb 6F 14
Waterloo. Per 4D 66
Waterloo. Pool 6J 9
Waterloo. Shrp 6C 34
**Waterlooville**. Hants 5D 10
Watermead. Buck 2F 20
Watermillock. Cumb 3C 46
Water Newton. Cambs 2J 29
Water Orton. Warw 2K 27
Waterperry. Oxon 3D 20
Waterrow. Som 3K 7
Watersfield. W Sus 4H 11
Waterside. Buck 3G 21
Waterside. Cambs 4C 30
Waterside. Cumb 7G 53
Waterside. E Ayr
nr. Ayr 1K 51
nr. Kilmarnock 5C 58
Waterside. E Dun 2E 58
Waterstein. High 1C 68
Waterstock. Oxon 3D 20
Waterston. Pemb 6F 14
Water Stratford. Buck 8D 28
Waters Upton. Telf 8E 34
Water Yeat. Cumb 7A 46
**Watford**. Herts 4J 21
Watford. Nptn 5D 28
Wath. Cumb 5E 46
Wath. N Yor
nr. Pateley Bridge 1K 41
nr. Ripon 8M 47
Wath Brow. Cumb 3K 45
**Wath upon Dearne**. S Yor 7B 42
Watlington. Norf 8C 38
Watlington. Oxon 4D 20
Watten. High 6D 86
Wattisfield. Suff 4G 31
Wattisham. Suff 6G 31
Wattlesborough Heath.
Shrp 8B 34
Watton. Dors 6C 8
Watton. E Yor 2H 43
Watton. Norf 1F 30
Watton at Stone. Herts 2K 21
Wattston. N Lan 2F 58
Wattstown. Rhon 5K 17
Wattsville. Cphy 5M 17
Wauldby. E Yor 5G 43
Waulkmill. Abers 6F 72
Waun. Powy 1M 25
Y Waun. Wrex 6A 34
Waunarlwydd. Swan 5F 16
Waun Fawr. Cdgn 4F 24
Waunfawr. Gwyn 5E 32
Waungilwen. Carm 3K 15
Waun-Lwyd. Blae 4L 17
Waun y Clyn. Carm 6L 15
Wavendon. Mil 8G 29
Waverbridge. Cumb 7G 53
Waverley. Surr 1F 10
Waverton. Ches W 3C 34
Waverton. Cumb 7G 53
Wavertree. Mers 1B 34
Wawne. E Yor 4H 43
Waxham. Norf 7L 39
Waxholme. E Yor 5L 43
Wayford. Som 5C 8
Way Head. Cambs 3A 30
Waytown. Dors 6C 8
Way Village. Devn 4H 7
Wdig. Pemb 3F 14
Wealdstone. G Lon 5J 21
Weardley. W Yor 3L 41
Weare. Som 8C 18
Weare Giffard. Devn 3D 6
Wearhead. Dur 8B 54
Wearne. Som 3C 8
Weasdale. Cumb 5E 46
Weasenham All Saints.
Norf 7E 38
Weasenham St Peter. Norf 7E 38
Weaverham. Ches W 2E 34
Weaverthorpe. N Yor 8G 49
Webheath. Worc 5J 27
Webton. Here 8C 26
Wedderlairs. Abers 2H 73
Weddington. Warw 2A 28
Wedhampton. Wilts 8J 19
Wedmore. Som 1C 8
Wednesbury. W Mid 2H 27
Wednesfield. W Mid 1H 27
Weecar. Notts 3F 36
Weedon. Buck 2F 20
Weedon Bec. Nptn 6D 28
Weedon Lois. Nptn 7D 28
Weeford. Staf 1K 27
Week. Devn
nr. Barnstaple 3E 6
nr. Okehampton 5F 6
nr. South Molton 4G 7
nr. Totnes 5K 5
Week. Som 2J 7
Weeke. Devn 5G 7
Weeke. Hants 2B 10
Week Green. Corn 6B 6
Weekley. Nptn 3F 28
Week St Mary. Corn 6B 6
Weel. E Yor 4H 43
Weeley. Essx 1H 23
Weeley Heath. Essx 1H 23
Weem. Per 3B 66
Weeping Cross. Staf 7H 35
Weethly. Warw 6J 27
Weeting. Norf 3D 30
Weeton. E Yor 5L 43
Weeton. Lanc 4B 40
Weeton. N Yor 3L 41
Weetwood Hall. Nmbd 7H 61
Weir. Lanc 5G 41
Welborne. Norf 8G 39
Welbourn. Linc 4G 37
Welburn. N Yor
nr. Kirkbymoorside 7D 48
nr. Malton 1E 42
Welbury. N Yor 5A 48
Welby. Linc 6G 37
Welches Dam. Cambs 3A 30
Welcombe. Devn 4B 6
Weld Bank. Lanc 6D 40
Weldon. Nptn 3G 29
Weldon. Nmbd 2E 54

Welford. Nptn 3D 28
Welford. W Ber 6B 20
Welford-on-Avon. Warw 6K 27
Welham. Leics 2E 28
Welham. Notts 1E 36
Welham Green. Herts 3K 21
Well. Hants 1E 10
Well. Linc 2M 37
Well. N Yor 7L 47
Welland. Worc 7F 26
Wellbank. Ang 4H 67
Well Bottom. Dors 4H 9
Welldale. Dum 5F 52
Wellesbourne. Warw 6L 27
Well Hill. Kent 7A 22
Wellhouse. W Ber 6C 20
Welling. G Lon 6A 22
**Wellingborough**. Nptn 5F 28
Wellingham. Norf 7E 38
Wellingore. Linc 4G 37
Wellington. Cumb 4K 45
Wellington. Here 7C 26
**Wellington**. Som 3L 7
Wellington. Telf 8E 34
Wellington Heath. Here 7F 26
Wellow. Bath 8F 18
Wellow. IOW 7A 10
Wellow. Notts 3D 36
Wellpond Green. Herts 1M 21
**Wells**. Som 1D 8
Wellsborough. Leics 1A 28
Wells Green. Ches E 4E 34
Wells-next-the-Sea. Norf 5F 38
Wellswood. Torb 5M 5
Wellwood. Fife 1J 59
Welney. Norf 2B 30
Welsford. Devn 3B 6
Welshampton. Shrp 6C 34
Welsh End. Shrp 6D 34
Welsh Frankton. Shrp 6B 34
Welsh Hook. Pemb 4F 14
Welsh Newton. Here 2C 18
Welsh Newton Common.
Here 2D 18
Welshpool. Powy 2M 25
Welsh St Donats. V Glam 7K 17
Welton. Bath 8E 18
Welton. Cumb 7H 53
Welton. E Yor 5G 43
Welton. Linc 1H 37
Welton. Nptn 5C 28
Welton Hill. Linc 1H 37
Welton le Marsh. Linc 3A 38
Welton le Wold. Linc 1K 37
Welwick. E Yor 5L 43
Welwyn. Herts 2K 21
**Welwyn Garden City**.
Herts 2K 21
Wem. Shrp 7D 34
Wembdon. Som 2A 8
**Wembley**. G Lon 5J 21
Wembury. Devn 7H 5
Wembworthy. Devn 5F 6
Wemyss Bay. Inv 2L 57
Wenallt. Cdgn 5F 24
Wenallt. Gwyn 6J 33
Wendens Ambo. Essx 8B 30
Wendlebury. Oxon 2C 20
Wendling. Norf 8F 38
Wendover. Buck 3F 20
Wendron. Corn 5K 3
Wendy. Cambs 7L 29
Wenfordbridge. Corn 4C 4
Wenhaston. Suff 4L 31
Wennington. Cambs 4K 29
Wennington. G Lon 5B 22
Wennington. Lanc 8E 46
Wensley. Derbs 3L 35
Wensley. N Yor 7J 47
Wentbridge. W Yor 6B 42
Wentnor. Shrp 2B 26
Wentworth. Cambs 4A 30
Wentworth. S Yor 8A 42
Wenvoe. V Glam 7L 17
Weobley. Here 6C 26
Weobley Marsh. Here 6C 26
Wepham. W Sus 5H 11
Wereham. Norf 1C 30
Wergs. W Mid 1G 27
Wern. Gwyn 6E 32
Wern. Powy
nr. Brecon 3L 17
nr. Guilsfield 8A 34
nr. Llangadfan 1J 25
nr. Llanymynech 7A 34
Wernffrwd. Swan 7M 15
Wernyrheolydd. Mon 2B 18
Werrington. Corn 7C 6
Werrington. Pet 1J 29
Werrington. Staf 5H 35
Wervin. Ches W 2C 34
Wesham. Lanc 4C 40
Wessington. Derbs 4A 36
West Aberthaw. V Glam 8K 17
West Acre. Norf 8D 38
West Allerdean. Nmbd 5G 61
West Alvington. Devn 7K 5
West Amesbury. Wilts 1K 9
West Anstey. Devn 3H 7
West Appleton. N Yor 6L 47
West Ardsley. W Yor 5L 41
West Arthurlie. E Ren 4C 58
West Ashby. Linc 2K 37
West Ashling. W Sus 5F 10
West Ashton. Wilts 8G 19
West Auckland. Dur 3K 47
West Ayton. N Yor 7H 49
West Bagborough. Som 2L 7
West Bank. Hal 1D 34
West Barkwith. Linc 1J 37
West Barnby. N Yor 4F 48
West Barns. E Lot 2D 60
West Barsham. Norf 6F 38
West Bay. Dors 6C 8
West Beckham. Norf 6H 39
West Bennan. N Ayr 7J 57
Westbere. Kent 7H 23
West Bergholt. Essx 1F 22
West Bexington. Dors 7D 8
West Bilney. Norf 8D 38
West Blackdene. Dur 8B 54
West Blatchington. Brig 5K 11
Westborough. Linc 5F 36
Westbourne. Bour 6J 9
Westbourne. W Sus 5E 10
West Bowling. W Yor 4K 41
West Brabourne. Kent 1G 13
West Bradford. Lanc 3F 40
West Bradley. Som 2D 8
West Bretton. W Yor 6L 41
**West Bridgford**. Notts 6C 36
West Briggs. Norf 8C 38
**West Bromwich**. W Mid 2J 27
Westbrook. Here 7A 26
Westbrook. Kent 6K 23
Westbrook. Wilts 7H 19
West Buckland. Devn
nr. Barnstaple 2F 6
nr. Thurlestone 7J 5
West Buckland. Som 3L 7
West Burnside. Abers 8G 73
West Burrafirth. Shet 2C 90
West Burton. N Yor 7J 47
West Burton. W Sus 4H 11
Westbury. Buck 8D 28
Westbury. Shrp 1B 26
**Westbury**. Wilts 8G 19
Westbury Leigh. Wilts 8G 19
Westbury-on-Severn. Glos 2F 18
Westbury on Trym. Bris 6D 18
Westbury-sub-Mendip.
Som 1D 8
West Butsfield. Dur 7E 54
West Butterwick. N Lin 7F 42
Westby. Linc 7G 37
West Byfleet. Surr 7H 21
West Caister. Norf 8M 39
West Calder. W Lot 3J 59
West Camel. Som 3D 8
West Carr. N Lin 7E 42
West Chaldon. Dors 7F 8
West Challow. Oxon 5A 20
West Charleton. Devn 7K 5
West Chelborough. Dors 5D 8
West Chevington. Nmbd 2F 54
West Chiltington. W Sus 4H 11
West Chiltington Common.
W Sus 4H 11
West Chinnock. Som 4C 8
West Chisenbury. Wilts 8K 19
West Clandon. Surr 8H 21
West Cliffe. Kent 1K 13
Westcliff-on-Sea. S'end 5E 22
West Clyne. High 3J 79
West Coker. Som 4D 8
Westcombe. Som
nr. Evercreech 2E 8
nr. Somerton 3C 8
West Compton. Dors 6D 8
West Compton. Som 1D 8
West Cornforth. Dur 8G 55
Westcot. Oxon 5M 19
Westcott. Buck 2E 20
Westcott. Devn 5K 7
Westcott. Surr 1J 11
Westcott Barton. Oxon 1B 20
West Cowick. E Yor 5D 42
West Cranmore. Som 1E 8
West Croftmore. High 4K 71
West Cross. Swan 6F 16
West Cullerlie. Abers 5G 73
West Culvennan. Dum 5H 51
West Curry. Corn 6B 6
West Curthwaite. Cumb 7H 53
West Dean. W Sus 4F 10
West Dean. Wilts 3L 9
Westdean. E Sus 6B 12
West Deeping. Linc 1J 29
West Derby. Mers 8B 40
West Dereham. Norf 1C 30
West Down. Devn 1E 6
Westdowns. Corn 3C 4
**West Drayton**. G Lon 6H 21
West Drayton. Notts 2E 36
West Dunnet. High 4D 86
West Ella. E Yor 5H 43
West End. Bed 6G 29
West End. Cambs 2M 29
West End. Dors 5H 9
West End. E Yor
nr. Kilham 1H 43
nr. Preston 4J 43
nr. South Cove 4G 43
nr. Ulrome 2J 43
**West End**. G Lon 5K 21
West End. Hants 4B 10
West End. Herts 3K 21
West End. Kent 7H 23
West End. Lanc 1C 40
West End. Linc 5L 37
West End. Norf 8M 39
West End. N Som 7C 18
West End. N Yor 2K 41
West End. S Glo 5F 18
West End. S Lan 5H 59
West End. Surr 7G 21
West End. Wilts 3H 9
West End. Wind 6F 20
West End Green. Hants 7D 20
Westenhanger. Kent 2H 13
Wester Aberchalder. High 4F 70
Wester Balgedie. Per 7E 66
Wester Brae. High 7G 79
Wester Culbeuchly. Abers 7F 80
Westerdale. High 6C 86
Westerdale. N Yor 5D 48
Wester Dechmont. W Lot 2J 59
Wester Fearn. High 5G 79
Westerfield. Suff 7H 31
Wester Galcantray. High 1J 71
Westergate. W Sus 5G 11
Wester Gruinards. High 4F 78
Westerham. Kent 8M 21
Westerleigh. S Glo 6F 18
Westerloch. High 6E 86
Wester Mandally. High 5E 70
Wester Quarff. Shet 4E 90
Wester Rarichie. High 6J 79
Wester Shian. Per 4B 66
Wester Skeld. Shet 3C 90
Westerton. Ang 2K 67
Westerton. Dur 8F 54
Westerton. W Sus 5F 10
Westerwick. Shet 3C 90
West Farleigh. Kent 8D 22
West Farndon. Nptn 6C 28
West Felton. Shrp 7B 34
Westfield. Cumb 2J 45
Westfield. E Sus 4E 12
Westfield. High 5B 86
Westfield. Norf 1F 30
Westfield. N Lan 2F 58
Westfield. W Lot 2H 59
Westfields. Dors 5F 8
Westfields of Rattray.
Per 3E 66
West Fleetham. Nmbd 7J 61
Westford. Som 3L 7
West Garforth. W Yor 4A 42
Westgate. Dur 8C 54
Westgate. Norf 5F 38
Westgate. N Lin 7E 42
Westgate on Sea. Kent 6K 23
West Ginge. Oxon 5B 20
West Grafton. Wilts 7L 19
West Green. Hants 8E 20
West Grimstead. Wilts 3L 9
West Grinstead. W Sus 3J 11
West Haddlesey. N Yor 5C 42
West Haddon. Nptn 4D 28
West Hagbourne. Oxon 5C 20
West Hagley. Worc 3H 27
West Hall. Cumb 5K 53
Westhall. Suff 3L 31
West Hallam. Derbs 5B 36
Westhall Terrace. Ang 4H 67
West Halton. N Lin 5G 43
**West Ham**. G Lon 5L 21
Westham. Dors 8E 8
Westham. E Sus 5C 12
Westham. Som 1C 8
Westhampnett. W Sus 5F 10
West Handley. Derbs 2A 36
West Hanney. Oxon 4B 20
West Hanningfield. Essx 4D 22
West Hardwick. W Yor 6B 42
West Harptree. Bath 8D 18
West Harting. W Sus 3E 10
West Harton. Tyne 5G 55
West Hatch. Som 3A 8
Westhay. Som 1C 8
West Head. Norf 1B 30
Westhead. Lanc 7C 40
West Heath. Hants
nr. Basingstoke 8C 20
nr. Farnborough 8F 20
West Helmsdale. High 2L 79
West Hendred. Oxon 5B 20
West Heogaland. Shet 6G 91
West Heslerton. N Yor 8G 49
West Hewish. N Som 7B 18
Westhide. Here 7D 26
West Hill. Devn 6K 7
West Hill. E Yor 1J 43
West Hill. N Som 6C 18
West Hill. W Sus 2L 11
Westhill. Abers 5H 73
Westhill. High 1H 71
West Hoathly. W Sus 2L 11
West Holme. Dors 7G 9
Westhope. Here 6C 26
Westhope. Shrp 3C 26
West Horndon. Essx 5C 22
Westhorp. Nptn 6C 28
Westhorpe. Linc 6K 37
Westhorpe. Suff 5G 31
West Horrington. Som 1D 8
West Horsley. Surr 8H 21
West Horton. Nmbd 6H 61
West Hougham. Kent 1J 13
**Westhoughton**. G Man 7E 40
West Houlland. Shet 2C 90
Westhouse. N Yor 8E 46
Westhouses. Derbs 4B 36
West Howe. Bour 6J 9
Westhumble. Surr 8J 21
West Huntspill. Som 1B 8
West Hyde. Herts 4H 21
West Hynish. Arg 4E 62
West Hythe. Kent 2H 13
West Ilsley. W Ber 5B 20
Westing. Shet 3K 91
West Keal. Linc 3L 37
West Kennett. Wilts 7K 19
West Kilbride. N Ayr 5M 57
West Kingsdown. Kent 7B 22
West Kington. Wilts 6G 19
**West Kirby**. Mers 2M 33
West Knapton. N Yor 8F 48
West Knighton. Dors 7F 8
West Knoyle. Wilts 2G 9
West Kyloe. Nmbd 5H 61
Westlake. Devn 6J 5
West Lambrook. Som 4C 8
West Langdon. Kent 1K 13
West Langwell. High 3G 79
West Lavington. W Sus 3F 10
West Lavington. Wilts 8J 19
West Layton. N Yor 5K 47
West Leake. Notts 7C 36
West Learmouth. Nmbd 6F 60
West Leigh. Devn 5F 6
Westleigh. Devn
nr. Bideford 3D 6
nr. Tiverton 4K 7
Westleigh. G Man 7E 40
West Leith. Herts 2G 21
Westleton. Suff 5L 31
West Lexham. Norf 8E 38
Westley. Shrp 1B 26
Westley. Suff 5E 30
Westley Waterless.
Cambs 6C 30
West Lilling. N Yor 1D 42
West Lingo. Fife 7H 67
Westlington. Buck 2E 20
West Linton. Bord 4K 59
Westlinton. Cumb 5H 53
West Littleton. S Glo 6F 18
West Looe. Corn 6E 4
West Lulworth. Dors 7G 9
West Lutton. N Yor 1G 43
West Lydford. Som 2D 8
West Lyng. Som 3B 8
West Lynn. Norf 8C 38
West Mains. Per 6C 66
West Malling. Kent 8C 22
West Malvern. Worc 7F 26
Westmancote. Worc 8H 27
West Marden. W Sus 4E 10
West Markham. Notts 2E 36
West Marsh. NE Lin 7K 43
Westmarsh. Kent 7J 23
West Marton. N Yor 2G 41
West Meon. Hants 3D 10
West Mersea. Essx 2G 23
Westmeston. E Sus 4L 11
Westmill. Herts
nr. Buntingford 1L 21
nr. Hitchin 8J 29
West Milton. Dors 6D 8
**Westminster**. G Lon 6K 21
West Molesey. Surr 7J 21
West Monkton. Som 3A 8
Westmoor End. Cumb 8E 52
West Moors. Dors 5J 9
West Morden. Dors 6H 9
West Muir. Ang 1J 67
Westmuir. Ang 2G 67
West Murkle. High 5C 86
West Ness. N Yor 8D 48
Westness. Orkn 7C 88
West Newton. E Yor 4J 43
West Newton. Norf 7C 38
West Newton. Som 3A 8
Westnewton. Cumb 7F 52
Westnewton. Nmbd 6G 61
West Norwood. G Lon 6L 21
Westoe. Tyne 5G 55
West Ogwell. Devn 5L 5
Weston. Bath 7F 18
Weston. Ches E
nr. Crewe 4F 34
nr. Macclesfield 2G 35
Weston. Devn
nr. Honiton 5L 7
nr. Sidmouth 7L 7
Weston. Dors
nr. Weymouth 8E 8
nr. Yeovil 5D 8
Weston. Hal 1D 34
Weston. Hants 3E 10
Weston. Here 6B 26
Weston. Herts 8K 29
Weston. Linc 7K 37
Weston. Nptn 7C 28
Weston. Notts 3E 36
Weston. Shrp
nr. Bridgnorth 2D 26
nr. Knighton 4B 26
nr. Wem 7D 34
Weston. S Lan 5J 59
Weston. Staf 7H 35
Weston. Suff 3L 31
Weston. W Ber 6A 20
Weston Bampfylde. Som 3E 8
Weston Beggard. Here 7D 26
Westonbirt. Glos 5G 19
Weston by Welland. Nptn 2E 28
Weston Colville. Cambs 6C 30
Westoncommon. Shrp 7C 34
Weston Coyney. Stoke 5H 35
Weston Ditch. Suff 4C 30
Weston Favell. Nptn 5E 28
Weston Green. Cambs 6C 30
Weston Green. Norf 8H 39
Weston Heath. Shrp 8F 34
Weston Hills. Linc 8K 37
Weston in Arden. Warw 3A 28
Westoning. C Beds 8H 29
Weston in Gordano. N Som 6C 18
Weston Jones. Staf 7F 34
Weston Longville. Norf 8H 39
Weston Lullingfields. Shrp 7C 34
Weston-on-Avon. Warw 6K 27
Weston-on-the-Green.
Oxon 2C 20
Weston-on-Trent. Derbs 7B 36
Weston Patrick. Hants 1D 10
Weston Rhyn. Shrp 6A 34
Weston-sub-Edge. Glos 7K 27
**Weston-super-Mare**.
N Som 7B 18
Weston Town. Som 1F 8
Weston Turville. Buck 2F 20
Weston under Lizard. Staf 8G 35
Weston under Penyard.
Here 1E 18
Weston under Wetherley.
Warw 5A 28
Weston Underwood. Derbs 5L 35
Weston Underwood. Mil 6F 28
Westonzoyland. Som 2B 8
West Orchard. Dors 4G 9
West Overton. Wilts 7K 19
Westow. N Yor 1E 42
Westown. Per 5F 66
West Panson. Devn 6C 6
West Park. Hart 8H 55
West Parley. Dors 6J 9
West Peckham. Kent 8C 22
West Pelton. Dur 6F 54
West Pennard. Som 2D 8
West Pentire. Corn 2L 3
West Perry. Cambs 5J 29
West Pitcorthie. Fife 7J 67
West Plean. Stir 1G 59
West Poringland. Norf 1J 31
West Porlock. Som 1H 7
Westport. Som 4B 8
West Putford. Devn 4C 6
West Quantoxhead. Som 1L 7
Westra. V Glam 7L 17
West Rainton. Dur 7G 55
West Rasen. Linc 1H 37
West Ravendale. NE Lin 8K 43
Westray Airport. Orkn 4D 88
West Raynham. Norf 7E 38
Westrigg. W Lot 3H 59
West Rounton. N Yor 5B 48
West Row. Suff 4C 30
West Rudham. Norf 7E 38
West Runton. Norf 5H 39
Westruther. Bord 4D 60
Westry. Cambs 2L 29
West Saltoun. E Lot 3B 60
West Sandford. Devn 5H 7
West Sandwick. Shet 5J 91
West Scrafton. N Yor 7J 47
Westside. Orkn 7C 88
West Sleekburn. Nmbd 3F 54
West Somerton. Norf 8L 39
West Stafford. Dors 7F 8
West Stockwith. Notts 8E 42
West Stoke. W Sus 5F 10
West Stonesdale. N Yor 5G 47
West Stoughton. Som 1C 8
West Stour. Dors 3F 8
West Stourmouth. Kent 7J 23
West Stow. Suff 4E 30
West Stowell. Wilts 7K 19
West Strathan. High 5H 85
West Stratton. Hants 1C 10
West Street. Kent 8F 22
West Tanfield. N Yor 8L 47
West Taphouse. Corn 5D 4
West Tarbert. Arg 3H 57
West Thirston. Nmbd 1E 54
West Thorney. W Sus 5E 10
West Thurrock. Thur 6B 22
West Tilbury. Thur 6C 22
West Tisted. Hants 3D 10
West Tofts. Norf 2E 30
West Torrington. Linc 1J 37
West Town. Bath 7D 18
West Town. Hants 6E 10
West Town. N Som 7C 18
West Tytherley. Hants 3L 9
West Tytherton. Wilts 6H 19
West View. Hart 8H 55
Westville. Notts 5C 36
West Walton. Norf 8A 38
Westward. Cumb 7G 53
Westward Ho!. Devn 3D 6
Westwell. Kent 1F 12
Westwell. Oxon 3L 19
Westwell Leacon. Kent 1F 12
West Wellow. Hants 4L 9
West Wemyss. Fife 8G 67
West Wick. N Som 7B 18
Westwick. Cambs 5M 29
Westwick. Dur 4J 47
Westwick. Norf 7J 39
West Wickham. Cambs 7C 30
West Wickham. G Lon 7L 21
West Williamston. Pemb 6G 15
West Willoughby. Linc 5G 37
West Winch. Norf 8C 38
West Winterslow. Wilts 2L 9
West Wittering. W Sus 6E 10
West Witton. N Yor 7J 47
Westwood. Devn 6K 7
Westwood. Kent 7K 23
Westwood. Pet 1J 29
Westwood. S Lan 4E 58
Westwood. Wilts 8G 19
West Woodburn. Nmbd 3B 54
West Woodhay. W Ber 7A 20
West Woodlands. Som 1F 8
West Woodside. Cumb 7H 53
Westwoodside. N Lin 8E 42
West Worldham. Hants 2E 10
West Worlington. Devn 4G 7
West Worthing. W Sus 5J 11
West Wratting. Cambs 6C 30
West Wycombe. Buck 4F 20
West Wylam. Nmbd 5E 54
West Yatton. Wilts 6G 19
West Yell. Shet 5J 91
West Youlstone. Corn 4B 6
Wetheral. Cumb 6J 53
Wetherby. W Yor 3B 42
Wetherden. Suff 5G 31
Wetheringsett. Suff 5H 31
Wethersfield. Essx 8D 30
Wethersta. Shet 1D 90
Wetherup Street. Suff 5H 31
Wetley Rocks. Staf 5H 35
Wettenhall. Ches E 3E 34
Wetton. Staf 4K 35
Wetwang. E Yor 2G 43
Wetwood. Staf 6F 34
Wexcombe. Wilts 8L 19
Wexham Street. Buck 5G 21
Weybourne. Norf 5H 39
Weybourne. Surr 1F 10
Weybread. Suff 3J 31
**Weybridge**. Surr 7H 21
Weycroft. Devn 6B 8
Weydale. High 5C 86
Weyhill. Hants 1M 9
**Weymouth**. Dors 118 (8E 8)
Weythel. Powy 7M 25
Whaddon. Buck 8F 28
Whaddon. Cambs 7L 29
Whaddon. Glos 2G 19
Whaddon. Wilts 3K 9
Whale. Cumb 3D 46
Whaley. Derbs 2C 36
Whaley Bridge. Derbs 1J 35
Whaley Thorns. Derbs 2C 36
Whalley. Lanc 4F 40
Whalton. Nmbd 3E 54
Whaplode. Linc 7L 37
Whaplode Drove. Linc 8L 37
Whaplode St Catherine.
Linc 7L 37
Wharfe. N Yor 1F 40
Wharles. Lanc 4C 40
Wharley End. C Beds 7G 29
Wharncliffe Side. S Yor 8L 41
Wharram-le-Street. N Yor 1F 42
Wharton. Ches W 3E 34
Wharton. Here 6D 26
Whashton. N Yor 5K 47
Whasset. Cumb 7D 46
Whatcote. Warw 7M 27
Whateley. Warw 2L 27
Whatfield. Suff 7G 31
Whatley. Som
nr. Chard 5B 8
nr. Frome 1F 8
Whatlington. E Sus 4E 12
Whatmore. Shrp 4E 26
Whatstandwell. Derbs 4M 35
Whatton. Notts 6E 36
Whauphill. Dum 7K 51
Whaw. N Yor 5H 47
Wheatacre. Norf 2L 31
Wheatcroft. Derbs 4A 36
Wheathampstead. Herts 2J 21
Wheathill. Shrp 3E 26
Wheatley. Devn 6H 7
Wheatley. Hants 1E 10
Wheatley. Oxon 3D 20
Wheatley. S Yor 7C 42
Wheatley. W Yor 5J 41
Wheatley Hill. Dur 8G 55
Wheatley Lane. Lanc 4G 41
Wheatley Park. S Yor 7C 42
Wheaton Aston. Staf 8G 35
Wheatstone Park. Staf 1G 27
Wheddon Cross. Som 2J 7
Wheelerstreet. Surr 1G 11
Wheelock. Ches E 4F 34
Wheelock Heath. Ches E 4F 34
Wheelton. Lanc 5E 40
Wheldrake. York 3D 42
Whelford. Glos 4K 19
Whelpley Hill. Buck 3G 21
Whelpo. Cumb 8H 53
Whelston. Flin 3M 33
Whenby. N Yor 1D 42
Whepstead. Suff 6E 30
Wherstead. Suff 7H 31
Wherwell. Hants 1A 10
Wheston. Derbs 2K 35
Whetsted. Kent 1C 12
Whetstone. G Lon 4K 21
Whetstone. Leics 2C 28
Whicham. Cumb 7L 45
Whichford. Warw 8M 27
**Whickham**. Tyne 5F 54
Whiddon. Devn 5D 6
Whiddon Down. Devn 6F 6
Whigstreet. Ang 3H 67
Whilton. Nptn 5D 28
Whimble. Devn 5C 6
Whimple. Devn 6K 7
Whimpwell Green. Norf 7K 39
Whinburgh. Norf 1G 31
Whin Lane End. Lanc 3B 40
Whinney Hill. Stoc T 4A 48
Whinnyfold. Abers 2K 73
Whippingham. IOW 6C 10
Whipsnade. C Beds 2H 21
Whipton. Devn 6J 7
Whirlow. S Yor 1M 35
Whisby. Linc 3G 37
Whissendine. Rut 8F 36
Whissonsett. Norf 7F 38
Whisterfield. Ches E 2G 35
Whistley Green. Wok 6E 20
Whiston. Mers 8C 40
Whiston. Nptn 5F 28
Whiston. S Yor 8B 42
Whiston. Staf
nr. Cheadle 5J 35
nr. Penkridge 8G 35
Whiston Cross. Shrp 1F 26
Whiston Eaves. Staf 5J 35
Whitacre Heath. Warw 2L 27
Whitbeck. Cumb 6L 45
Whitbourne. Here 6F 26
Whitburn. Tyne 5H 55
**Whitburn**. W Lot 3H 59
Whitburn Colliery. Tyne 5H 55
Whitby. Ches W 2B 34
**Whitby**. N Yor 4F 48
Whitbyheath. Ches W 2B 34
Whitchester. Bord 4E 60
Whitchurch. Bath 7E 18
Whitchurch. Buck 1E 20
Whitchurch. Card 7L 17
Whitchurch. Devn 8D 6
Whitchurch. Hants 1B 10
Whitchurch. Here 2D 18
Whitchurch. Pemb 4D 14
Whitchurch. Shrp 5D 34
Whitchurch Canonicorum.
Dors 6B 8
Whitchurch Hill. Oxon 6D 20
Whitchurch-on-Thames.
Oxon 6D 20
Whitcombe. Dors 7F 8
Whitcot. Shrp 2B 26
Whitcott Keysett. Shrp 3A 26
Whiteabbey. Ant 4H 93
Whiteash Green. Essx 8D 30
Whitebog. High 7H 79
Whitebridge. High 4E 70
Whitebrook. Mon 3D 18
Whitecairns. Abers 4J 73
Whitechapel. Lanc 3D 40
Whitechurch. Pemb 3H 15
White Colne. Essx 1E 22
White Coppice. Lanc 6E 40
White Corries. High 2G 65
Whitecraig. E Lot 2A 60
Whitecroft. Glos 3E 18
White Cross. Corn 6K 3
Whitecross. Corn 4B 4
Whitecross. Falk 2H 59
Whitecross. New M 7F 93
White End. Worc 8G 27
Whiteface. High 5H 79
Whitefarland. N Ayr 5H 57
Whitefaulds. S Ayr 1H 51
Whitefield. Dors 6H 9
**Whitefield**. G Man 7G 41
Whitefield. Som 3K 7
Whiteford. Abers 3G 73
Whitegate. Ches W 3E 34
Whitehall. Devn 4L 7
Whitehall. Hants 8E 20
Whitehall. Orkn 7F 88
Whitehall. W Sus 3J 11
**Whitehaven**. Cumb 3J 45
Whitehead. ME Ant 4J 93
Whitehill. Hants 2E 10
Whitehill. N Ayr 4A 58
Whitehills. Abers 7F 80
Whitehills. Ang 2H 67
White Horse Common.
Norf 7K 39
Whitehough. Derbs 1J 35
Whitehouse. Abers 4F 72
Whitehouse. Arg 3H 57
Whiteinch. Glas 3D 58
Whitekirk. E Lot 1C 60
White Kirkley. Dur 8D 54
White Lackington. Dors 6F 8
Whitelackington. Som 4B 8
White Ladies Aston. Worc 6H 27
White Lee. W Yor 5L 41
Whiteley. Hants 5C 10
Whiteley Bank. IOW 7C 10
Whiteley Village. Surr 7H 21
Whitemans Green. W Sus 3L 11
White Mill. Carm 4L 15
Whitemire. Mor 8K 79
Whitemoor. Corn 6B 4
Whitenap. Hants 3A 10
Whiteness. Shet 3E 90
White Notley. Essx 2D 22
Whiteoak Green. Oxon 2M 19
Whiteparish. Wilts 3L 9
White Pit. Linc 2L 37
Whiterashes. Abers 4J 73
Whiterock. Ards 5J 93
White Rocks. Here 1C 18
White Roding. Essx 2B 22
Whiterow. High 7E 86
Whiterow. Mor 8L 79
Whiteshill. Glos 3G 19
Whiteside. Nmbd 5M 53
Whiteside. W Lot 3H 59
Whitesmith. E Sus 4B 12
Whitestaunton. Som 4A 8
White Stone. Here 7D 26
Whitestone. Abers 6F 72
Whitestone. Devn 6H 7
Whitestones. Abers 8H 81
Whitestreet Green. Suff 8F 30
Whitewall Corner. N Yor 8E 48
White Waltham. Wind 6F 20
Whiteway. Glos 2H 19
Whitewell. Lanc 3E 40
Whitewell Bottom. Lanc 5G 41
Whiteworks. Devn 8F 6
Whitewreath. Mor 8B 80
Whitfield. D'dee 4H 67
Whitfield. Kent 1K 13
Whitfield. Nptn 8D 28
Whitfield. Nmbd 6A 54
Whitfield. S Glo 4E 18
Whitford. Devn 6A 8
Whitford. Flin 3L 33
Whitgift. E Yor 5F 42
Whitgreave. Staf 7G 35
Whithorn. Dum 7K 51
Whiting Bay. N Ayr 7K 57
Whitington. Norf 2D 30
Whitkirk. W Yor 4A 42
Whitland. Carm 5J 15
Whitleigh. Plym 6G 5
Whitletts. S Ayr 7B 58
Whitley. N Yor 5C 42
Whitley. Wilts 7G 19
**Whitley Bay**. Tyne 4G 55
Whitley Chapel. Nmbd 6C 54
Whitley Heath. Staf 7G 35
Whitley Lower. W Yor 6L 41
Whitley Thorpe. N Yor 5C 42
Whitlock's End. W Mid 4K 27
Whitminster. Glos 3F 18
Whitmore. Dors 5J 9
Whitmore. Staf 5G 35
Whitnage. Devn 4K 7
Whitnash. Warw 5M 27
Whitney. Here 8A 26
Whitrigg. Cumb
nr. Kirkbride 6G 53
nr. Torpenhow 8G 53
Whitsbury. Hants 4K 9
Whitsome. Bord 4F 60
Whitson. Newp 5B 18
**Whitstable**. Kent 7H 23
Whitstone. Corn 6B 6
Whittingham. Nmbd 8H 61
Whittingslow. Shrp 3C 26
Whittington. Derbs 2B 36
Whittington. Glos 1J 19
Whittington. Lanc 8E 46
Whittington. Norf 2D 30
Whittington. Shrp 6B 34
Whittington. Staf
nr. Kinver 3G 27
nr. Lichfield 1K 27
Whittington. Warw 2L 27
Whittington. Worc 6G 27
Whittington Barracks. Staf 1K 27
Whittlebury. Nptn 7D 28
Whittleford. Warw 2M 27
Whittle-le-Woods. Lanc 5D 40
**Whittlesey**. Cambs 2K 29
Whittlesford. Cambs 7A 30
Whittlestone Head. Bkbn 6F 40
Whitton. N Lin 5G 43
Whitton. Nmbd 1D 54
Whitton. Powy 5A 26
Whitton. Bord 7E 60
Whitton. Shrp 4D 26
Whitton. Stoc T 3A 48
Whittonditch. Wilts 6L 19
Whittonstall. Nmbd 6D 54
Whitway. Hants 8B 20
Whitwell. Derbs 2C 36
Whitwell. Herts 1J 21
Whitwell. IOW 8C 10
Whitwell. N Yor 6L 47
Whitwell. Rut 1G 29
Whitwell-on-the-Hill. N Yor 1E 42
Whitwick. Leics 8B 36
Whitwood. W Yor 5B 42
Whitworth. Lanc 6G 41
Whixall. Shrp 6D 34
Whixley. N Yor 2B 42
Whoberley. W Mid 4M 27
Whorlton. Dur 4K 47
Whorlton. N Yor 5B 48
Whygate. Nmbd 4M 53
Whyle. Here 5D 26
Whyteleafe. Surr 8L 21
Wibdon. Glos 4D 18
Wibtoft. Warw 3B 28
Wichenford. Worc 5F 26
Wichling. Kent 8F 22
Wick. Bour 6K 9
Wick. Devn 5L 7
**Wick**. High 6E 86
Wick. Shet
on Mainland 4E 90
on Unst 3K 91
Wick. Som
nr. Bridgwater 1M 7
nr. Burnham-on-Sea 8B 18
nr. Somerton 3C 8
Wick. S Glo 6F 18
Wick. V Glam 7J 17
Wick. W Sus 5H 11
Wick. Wilts 3K 9
Wick. Worc 7H 27
Wick Airport. High 6E 86
Wicken. Cambs 4B 30
Wicken. Nptn 8E 28
Wicken Bonhunt. Essx 8A 30
Wickenby. Linc 1H 37
Wicken Green Village. Norf 6E 38
Wickersley. S Yor 8B 42
Wicker Street Green. Suff 7F 30
**Wickford**. Essx 4D 22
Wickham. Hants 4C 10
Wickham. W Ber 6A 20
Wickham Bishops. Essx 2E 22
Wickhambreaux. Kent 8J 23
Wickhambrook. Suff 6D 30
Wickhamford. Worc 7J 27
Wickham Green. Suff 5G 31
Wickham Heath. W Ber 7B 20
Wickham Market. Suff 6K 31
Wickhampton. Norf 1L 31
Wickham St Paul. Essx 8E 30
Wickham Skeith. Suff 5G 31
Wickham Street. Suff 5G 31
Wick Hill. Wok 7E 20
Wicklewood. Norf 1G 31
Wickmere. Norf 6H 39
Wick St Lawrence. N Som 7B 18
Wickwar. S Glo 5F 18
Widdington. Essx 8B 30
Widdrington. Nmbd 2F 54
Widdrington Station. Nmbd 2F 54
Widecombe in the Moor.
Devn 8G 7
Widegates. Corn 6E 4
Widemouth Bay. Corn 5B 6
Wide Open. Tyne 4F 54
Widewall. Orkn 2F 86
Widford. Essx 3C 22
Widford. Herts 2M 21
Widham. Wilts 5J 19
Widmer End. Buck 4F 20
Widmerpool. Notts 7D 36
**Widnes**. Hal 1D 34
Widworthy. Devn 6M 7
**Wigan**. G Man 7D 40
Wigbeth. Dors 5J 9
Wigborough. Som 4C 8
Wiggaton. Devn 6L 7
Wiggenhall St Germans.
Norf 8B 38
Wiggenhall St Mary Magdalen.
Norf 8B 38
Wiggenhall St Mary the Virgin.
Norf 8B 38
Wiggenhall St Peter. Norf 8C 38
Wiggens Green. Essx 7C 30
Wigginton. Herts 2G 21
Wigginton. Oxon 8A 28
Wigginton. Staf 1L 27
Wigginton. York 2C 42
Wigglesworth. N Yor 2G 41
Wiggonby. Cumb 6G 53
Wiggonholt. W Sus 4H 11
Wighill. N Yor 3B 42
Wighton. Norf 6F 38
Wightwick. W Mid 2G 27
Wigley. Hants 4M 9
Wigmore. Here 5C 26
Wigmore. Medw 7D 22
Wigsley. Notts 2F 36
Wigsthorpe. Nptn 3H 29
**Wigston**. Leics 2D 28
Wigtoft. Linc 6K 37
Wigton. Cumb 7G 53
Wigtown. Dum 6K 51
Wike. W Yor 3M 41
Wilbarston. Nptn 3F 28
Wilberfoss. E Yor 2E 42
Wilburton. Cambs 4A 30
Wilby. Norf 3G 31
Wilby. Nptn 5F 28
Wilby. Suff 4J 31
Wilcot. Wilts 7K 19
Wilcott. Shrp 8B 34
Wilcove. Corn 6G 5
Wildboarclough. Ches E 3H 35
Wilden. Bed 6H 29
Wilden. Worc 4G 27
Wildern. Hants 4B 10
Wilderspool. Warr 1E 34
Wilde Street. Suff 4D 30
Wildhern. Hants 8A 20
Wildmanbridge. S Lan 4G 59
Wildmoor. Worc 4H 27
Wildsworth. Linc 8F 42
Wildwood. Staf 7H 35
Wilford. Nott 6C 36
Wilkesley. Ches E 5E 34
Wilkhaven. High 5K 79
Wilkieston. W Lot 3K 59
Wilksby. Linc 3K 37
Willand. Devn 4K 7
Willaston. Ches E 4E 34
Willaston. Ches W 2B 34
Willaston. IOM 7C 44
Willen. Mil 7F 28
Willenhall. W Mid
nr. Coventry 4A 28
nr. Wolverhampton 2H 27
Willerby. E Yor 4H 43
Willerby. N Yor 8H 49
Willersey. Glos 8K 27
Willersley. Here 7B 26
Willesborough. Kent 1G 13
Willesborough Lees. Kent 1G 13
**Willesden**. G Lon 5K 21
Willesley. Wilts 5G 19
Willett. Som 2L 7
Willey. Shrp 2E 26
Willey. Warw 3B 28
Willey Green. Surr 8G 21
Williamscot. Oxon 7B 28
Williamsetter. Shet 5D 90
Willian. Herts 8K 29
Willingale. Essx 3B 22
Willingdon. E Sus 5B 12
Willingham. Cambs 4M 29
Willingham by Stow. Linc 1F 36
Willingham Green. Cambs 6C 30
Willington. Bed 7J 29
Willington. Derbs 7L 35
Willington. Dur 8E 54
Willington. Tyne 5G 55
Willington. Warw 8L 27
Willington Corner. Ches W 3D 34
Willisham Tye. Suff 6G 31
Willitoft. E Yor 4E 42
Williton. Som 1K 7
Willoughbridge. Staf 5F 34
Willoughby. Linc 2A 38
Willoughby. Warw 5C 28
Willoughby-on-the-Wolds.
Notts 7D 36
Willoughby Waterleys.
Leics 2C 28
Willoughton. Linc 8G 43
Willow Green. Worc 6F 26
Willows Green. Essx 2D 22
Willsbridge. S Glo 6E 18
Willslock. Staf 6J 35
Wilmcote. Warw 6K 27
Wilmington. Bath 7E 18
Wilmington. Devn 6M 7
Wilmington. E Sus 5B 12
Wilmington. Kent 6B 22
**Wilmslow**. Ches E 1G 35
Wilnecote. Staf 1L 27
Wilney Green. Norf 3G 31
Wilpshire. Lanc 4E 40
Wilsden. W Yor 4J 41
Wilsford. Linc 5H 37
Wilsford. Wilts
nr. Amesbury 2K 9
nr. Devizes 8J 19
Wilsill. N Yor 1K 41
Wilsley Green. Kent 2D 12
Wilson. Here 1D 18
Wilson. Leics 7B 36
Wilsontown. S Lan 4H 59
Wilstead. Bed 7H 29
Wilsthorpe. E Yor 1J 43
Wilsthorpe. Linc 8H 37
Wilstone. Herts 2G 21
Wilton. Cumb 3K 45
Wilton. N Yor 7F 48
Wilton. Red C 4C 48
Wilton. Bord 8C 60
Wilton. Wilts
nr. Marlborough 7L 19
nr. Salisbury 2J 9
Wimbish. Essx 8B 30
Wimbish Green. Essx 8C 30
Wimblebury. Staf 8J 35
**Wimbledon**. G Lon 6K 21
Wimblington. Cambs 2M 29
Wimboldsley. Ches W 3E 34
**Wimborne Minster**. Dors 6J 9
Wimborne St Giles. Dors 4J 9
Wimbotsham. Norf 1C 30
Wimpole. Cambs 6L 29
Wimpstone. Warw 7L 27
Wincanton. Som 3F 8
Winceby. Linc 3L 37
Wincham. Ches W 2E 34
Winchburgh. W Lot 2J 59
Winchcombe. Glos 1J 19
Winchelsea. E Sus 4F 12
Winchelsea Beach. E Sus 4F 12
**Winchester**. Hants 117 (3B 10)
Winchet Hill. Kent 1D 12
Winchfield. Hants 8E 20
Winchmore Hill. Buck 4G 21
Winchmore Hill. G Lon 4L 21
Wincle. Ches E 3H 35
Windermere. Cumb 6C 46
Winderton. Warw 7M 27
Windhill. High 1F 70
Windle Hill. Ches W 2B 34
Windlesham. Surr 7G 21
Windley. Derbs 5M 35
Windmill. Derbs 2K 35
Windmill Hill. E Sus 4C 12
Windmill Hill. Som 4B 8
Windrush. Glos 2K 19
**Windsor**. Wind 117 (6G 21)
Windsor Green. Suff 6E 30
Windyedge. Abers 6H 73
Windygates. Fife 7G 67
Windyharbour. Ches E 2G 35
Windyknowe. W Lot 3H 59
Wineham. W Sus 3K 11
Winestead. E Yor 5L 43
Winfarthing. Norf 3H 31
Winford. IOW 7C 10
Winford. N Som 7D 18
Winforton. Here 7A 26
Winfrith Newburgh. Dors 7G 9
Wing. Buck 1F 20
Wing. Rut 1F 28
Wingate. Dur 8H 55
Wingates. G Man 7E 40
Wingates. Nmbd 2E 54
Wingerworth. Derbs 3A 36
Wingfield. C Beds 1H 21
Wingfield. Suff 4J 31
Wingfield. Wilts 8G 19
Wingfield Park. Derbs 4A 36
Wingham. Kent 8J 23
Wingmore. Kent 1H 13
Wingrave. Buck 2F 20
Winkburn. Notts 4E 36
Winkfield. Brac 6G 21
Winkfield Row. Brac 6F 20
Winkhill. Staf 4J 35
Winklebury. Hants 8D 20
Winkleigh. Devn 5F 6
Winksley. N Yor 8L 47
Winkton. Dors 6K 9
Winlaton. Tyne 5E 54
Winlaton Mill. Tyne 5E 54
Winless. High 6E 86
Winmarleigh. Lanc 3C 40
Winnal Common. Here 8C 26
Winnard's Perch. Corn 5B 4
Winnersh. Wok 6E 20
Winnington. Ches W 2E 34
Winnington. Staf 6F 34
Winnothdale. Staf 5J 35
Winscales. Cumb 2K 45
Winscombe. N Som 8C 18
**Winsford**. Ches W 3E 34
Winsford. Som 2J 7
Winsham. Devn 2D 6
Winsham. Som 5B 8
Winshill. Staf 7L 35
Winsh-wen. Swan 5G 17
Winskill. Cumb 8K 53
Winslade. Hants 1D 10
Winsley. Wilts 7G 19
Winslow. Buck 1E 20
Winson. Glos 3J 19
Winson Green. W Mid 3J 27
Winsor. Hants 4M 9
Winster. Cumb 6C 46
Winster. Derbs 3L 35
Winston. Dur 4K 47
Winston. Suff 5H 31
Winstone. Glos 3H 19
Winswell. Devn 4D 6
Winterborne Clenston. Dors 5G 9
Winterborne Herringston.
Dors 7E 8
Winterborne Houghton.
Dors 5G 9
Winterborne Kingston. Dors 6G 9
Winterborne Monkton. Dors 7E 8
Winterborne St Martin. Dors 7E 8
Winterborne Stickland. Dors 5G 9
Winterborne Whitechurch.
Dors 5G 9
Winterborne Zelston. Dors 6G 9
Winterbourne. S Glo 5E 18
Winterbourne. W Ber 6B 20
Winterbourne Abbas. Dors 6E 8
Winterbourne Bassett.
Wilts 6K 19
Winterbourne Dauntsey.
Wilts 2K 9
Winterbourne Earls. Wilts 2K 9
Winterbourne Gunner. Wilts 2K 9
Winterbourne Monkton.
Wilts 6K 19
Winterbourne Steepleton.
Dors 7E 8
Winterbourne Stoke.
Wilts 1J 9
Winterbrook. Oxon 5D 20
Winterburn. N Yor 2H 41
Winter Gardens. Essx 5D 22
Winterhay Green. Som 4B 8
Winteringham. N Lin 5G 43
Winterley. Ches E 4F 34
Wintersett. W Yor 6A 42
Winterton. N Lin 6G 43
Winterton-on-Sea. Norf 8L 39
Winthorpe. Linc 3B 38
Winthorpe. Notts 4F 36
Winton. Bour 6J 9
Winton. Cumb 4F 46
Winton. E Sus 5B 12
Wintringham. N Yor 8F 48
Winwick. Cambs 3J 29
Winwick. Nptn 4D 28
Winwick. Warr 8E 40
Wirksworth. Derbs 4L 35
Wirswall. Ches E 5D 34
**Wisbech**. Cambs 8A 38
Wisbech St Mary. Cambs 1M 29
Wisborough Green. W Sus 3H 11
Wiseton. Notts 1E 36
**Wishaw**. N Lan 4F 58
Wishaw. Warw 2K 27
Wisley. Surr 8H 21
Wispington. Linc 2K 37
Wissenden. Kent 1F 12
Wissett. Suff 4K 31
Wistanstow. Shrp 3C 26
Wistanswick. Shrp 7E 34
Wistaston. Ches E 4E 34
Wiston. Pemb 5G 15
Wiston. S Lan 6H 59
Wiston. W Sus 4J 11
Wistow. Cambs 3K 29
Wistow. N Yor 4C 42
Wiswell. Lanc 4F 40
Witcham. Cambs 3A 30
Witchampton. Dors 5H 9
Witchford. Cambs 4B 30
**Witham**. Essx 2E 22
Witham Friary. Som 1F 8
Witham on the Hill. Linc 8H 37
Witham St Hughs. Linc 3F 36
Withcall. Linc 1K 37
Witherenden Hill. E Sus 3C 12
Withergate. Norf 7J 39
Witheridge. Devn 4H 7
Witheridge Hill. Oxon 5D 20
Witherley. Leics 2M 27
Withermarsh Green. Suff 8G 31
Withern. Linc 1M 37
Withernsea. E Yor 5L 43
Withernwick. E Yor 3J 43
Withersdale Street. Suff 3J 31
Withersfield. Suff 7C 30
Witherslack. Cumb 7C 46
Withiel. Corn 5B 4
Withiel Florey. Som 2J 7
Withington. Glos 2J 19
Withington. G Man 8G 41
Withington. Here 7D 26
Withington. Shrp 8D 34
Withington. Staf 6J 35
Withington Green. Ches E 2G 35
Withington Marsh. Here 7D 26
Withleigh. Devn 4J 7
Withnell. Lanc 5E 40
Withnell Fold. Lanc 5E 40
Withybrook. Warw 3B 28
Withycombe. Som 1K 7
Withycombe Raleigh. Devn 7K 7
Withyham. E Sus 2A 12
Withypool. Som 2H 7
Witley. Surr 1G 11
Witnesham. Suff 6H 31
**Witney**. Oxon 2A 20
Wittering. Pet 1H 29
Wittersham. Kent 3F 12
Witton. Norf 1K 31
Witton. Worc 5G 27
Witton Bridge. Norf 6K 39
Witton Gilbert. Dur 7F 54
Witton-le-Wear. Dur 8E 54
Witton Park. Dur 8E 54
Wiveliscombe. Som 3K 7
Wivelrod. Hants 2D 10
Wivelsfield. E Sus 3L 11
Wivelsfield Green. E Sus 4L 11
Wivenhoe. Essx 1G 23
Wiveton. Norf 5G 39
Wix. Essx 1H 23
Wixford. Warw 6J 27
Wixhill. Shrp 7D 34
Wixoe. Suff 7D 30
Woburn. C Beds 8G 29
Woburn Sands. Mil 8G 29
**Woking**. Surr 8H 21
**Wokingham**. Wok 7F 20
Wolborough. Devn 8H 7
Woldingham. Surr 8L 21
Wold Newton. E Yor 8H 49
Wold Newton. NE Lin 8K 43
Wolferlow. Here 5E 26
Wolferton. Norf 7C 38
Wolfhill. Per 4E 66
Wolf's Castle. Pemb 4F 14
Wolfsdale. Pemb 4F 14
Wolgarston. Staf 8H 35
Wollaston. Nptn 5G 29
Wollaston. Shrp 8B 34
Wollaston. W Mid 3G 27
Wollaton. Nott 5C 36
Wollerton. Shrp 7E 34
Wollescote. W Mid 3H 27
Wolseley Bridge. Staf 7J 35
Wolsingham. Dur 8D 54
Wolstanton. Staf 5G 35
Wolston. Warw 4B 28
Wolsty. Cumb 6F 52
Wolterton. Norf 6H 39
Wolvercote. Oxon 3C 20
**Wolverhampton**.
W Mid 117 (2H 27)
Wolverley. Shrp 6C 34
Wolverley. Worc 4G 27
Wolverton. Hants 8C 20
Wolverton. Mil 7F 28
Wolverton. Warw 5L 27
Wolverton. Wilts 2F 8
Wolverton Common. Hants 8C 20
Wolvesnewton. Mon 4C 18
Wolvey. Warw 3B 28
Wolvey Heath. Warw 3B 28
Wolviston. Stoc T 3B 48
Womaston. Powy 5A 26
Wombleton. N Yor 7D 48
Wombourne. Staf 2G 27
**Wombwell**. S Yor 7A 42
Womenswold. Kent 8J 23
Womersley. N Yor 6C 42
Wonersh. Surr 1H 11
Wonston. Dors 5F 8

Wonston. *Hants* 2B **10**
Wooburn. *Buck* 5G **21**
Wooburn Green. *Buck* 5G **21**
Wood. *Pemb* 4E **14**
Woodacott. *Devn* 5C **6**
Woodale. *N Yor* 8J **47**
Woodall. *S Yor* 1B **36**
Woodbank. *Ches W* 2B **34**
Woodbastwick. *Norf* 8K **39**
Woodbeck. *Notts* 2E **36**
Woodborough. *Notts* 5D **36**
Woodborough. *Wilts* 8K **19**
Woodbridge. *Devn* 6L **7**
Woodbridge. *Dors* 4F **8**
**Woodbridge**. *Suff* 7J **31**
Wood Burcote. *Nptn* 7D **28**
Woodbury. *Devn* 7K **7**
Woodbury Salterton. *Devn* 7K **7**
Woodchester. *Glos* 3G **19**
Woodchurch. *Kent* 2F **12**
Woodchurch. *Mers* 1A **34**
Woodcock Heath. *Staf* 7J **35**
Woodcombe. *Som* 1J **7**
Woodcote. *Oxon* 5D **20**
Woodcote Green. *Worc* 4H **27**
Woodcott. *Hants* 8B **20**
Woodcroft. *Glos* 4D **18**
Woodcutts. *Dors* 4H **9**
Wood Dalling. *Norf* 7G **39**
Woodditton. *Cambs* 6C **30**
Wood Eaton. *Staf* 8G **35**
Woodeaton. *Oxon* 2C **20**
Wood End. *Bed* 5H **29**
Wood End. *Herts* 1L **21**
Wood End. *Warw*
nr. Bedworth 3L **27**
nr. Dordon 2L **27**
nr. Tanworth-in-Arden 4K **27**
Woodend. *Cumb* 5L **45**
Woodend. *Nptn* 7D **28**
Woodend. *Staf* 7K **35**
Woodend. *W Sus* 5F **10**
Wood Enderby. *Linc* 3K **37**
Woodend Green. *Essx* 1B **22**
Woodfalls. *Wilts* 3K **9**
Woodfield. *Oxon* 1C **20**
Woodfields. *Lanc* 4E **40**
Woodford. *Corn* 4B **6**
Woodford. *Devn* 6K **5**
Woodford. *Glos* 4E **18**
**Woodford**. *G Lon* 4L **21**
Woodford. *G Man* 1G **35**
Woodford. *Nptn* 4G **29**
Woodford. *Plym* 6H **5**
Woodford Green. *G Lon* 4M **21**
Woodford Halse. *Nptn* 6C **28**
Woodgate. *Norf* 8G **39**
Woodgate. *W Mid* 3H **27**
Woodgate. *W Sus* 5G **11**
Woodgate. *Worc* 5H **27**
**Wood Green**. *G Lon* 4K **21**
Woodgreen. *Hants* 4K **9**
Woodgreen. *Oxon* 2A **20**
Woodhall. *Inv* 2B **58**
Woodhall. *Linc* 3K **37**
Woodhall. *N Yor* 6H **47**
Woodhall Spa. *Linc* 3J **37**
Woodham. *Surr* 7H **21**
Woodham Ferrers. *Essx* 4D **22**
Woodham Mortimer. *Essx* 3E **22**
Woodham Walter. *Essx* 3E **22**
Woodhaven. *Fife* 5H **67**
Wood Hayes. *W Mid* 1H **27**
Woodhead. *Abers*
nr. Fraserburgh 7J **81**
nr. Fyvie 2G **73**
Woodhill. *N Som* 6C **18**
Woodhill. *Shrp* 3F **26**
Woodhill. *Som* 3B **8**
Woodhorn. *Nmbd* 3F **54**
Woodhouse. *Leics* 8C **36**
Woodhouse. *S Yor* 1B **36**
Woodhouse. *W Yor*
nr. Leeds 4L **41**
nr. Normanton 5A **42**
Woodhouse Eaves. *Leics* 8C **36**
Woodhouses. *Ches W* 2D **34**
Woodhouses. *G Man*
nr. Failsworth 7H **41**
nr. Sale 8F **40**
Woodhouses. *Staf* 8K **35**
Woodhuish. *Devn* 6M **5**
Woodhurst. *Cambs* 4L **29**
Woodingdean. *Brig* 5L **11**
Woodland. *Devn* 5K **5**
Woodland. *Dur* 3J **47**
Woodland Head. *Devn* 6G **7**
Woodlands. *Abers* 6G **73**
Woodlands. *Dors* 5J **9**
Woodlands. *Hants* 4M **9**
Woodlands. *Kent* 7B **22**
Woodlands. *N Yor* 2M **41**
Woodlands. *S Yor* 7C **42**
Woodlands Park. *Wind* 6F **20**
Woodlands St Mary. *W Ber* 6M **19**
Woodlane. *Shrp* 7E **34**
Woodlane. *Staf* 7K **35**
Woodleigh. *Devn* 7K **5**
Woodlesford. *W Yor* 5A **42**
Woodley. *G Man* 8H **41**
Woodley. *Wok* 6E **20**
Woodmancote. *Glos*
nr. Cheltenham 1H **19**
nr. Cirencester 3J **19**
Woodmancote. *W Sus*
nr. Chichester 5E **10**
nr. Henfield 4K **11**
Woodmancote. *Worc* 7H **27**
Woodmancott. *Hants* 1C **10**
Woodmansey. *E Yor* 4H **43**
Woodmansgreen. *W Sus* 3F **10**
Woodmansterne. *Surr* 8K **21**
Woodmanton. *Devn* 7K **7**
Woodmill. *Staf* 7K **35**
Woodminton. *Wilts* 3J **9**
Woodnesborough. *Kent* 8K **23**
Woodnewton. *Nptn* 2H **29**
Woodnook. *Linc* 6G **37**
Wood Norton. *Norf* 7G **39**
Woodplumpton. *Lanc* 4D **40**
Woodrising. *Norf* 1F **30**
Wood Row. *W Yor* 5A **42**
Woodrow. *Cumb* 7G **53**
Woodrow. *Dors*
nr. Fifehead Neville 4F **8**
nr. Hazelbury Bryan 5F **8**
Woods Eaves. *Here* 7A **26**
Woodseaves. *Shrp* 6E **34**
Woodseaves. *Staf* 7G **35**
Woodsend. *Wilts* 6L **19**
Woodsetts. *S Yor* 1C **36**
Woodsford. *Dors* 6F **8**
Wood's Green. *E Sus* 2C **12**
Woodshaw. *Wilts* 5J **19**
Woodside. *Aber* 5J **73**
Woodside. *Brac* 6G **21**
Woodside. *Derbs* 5A **36**
Woodside. *Dum* 4E **52**
Woodside. *Dur* 3K **47**
Woodside. *Fife* 7H **67**
Woodside. *Herts* 3K **21**
Woodside. *Per* 4F **66**
Wood Stanway. *Glos* 8J **27**
Woodstock. *Oxon* 2B **20**
Woodstock Slop. *Pemb* 4G **15**
Woodston. *Pet* 2J **29**
Wood Street. *Norf* 7K **39**
Wood Street Village. *Surr* 8G **21**
Woodthorpe. *Derbs* 2B **36**
Woodthorpe. *Leics* 8C **36**
Woodthorpe. *Linc* 1M **37**
Woodthorpe. *Notts* 5C **36**
Woodthorpe. *York* 3C **42**
Woodton. *Norf* 2J **31**
Woodtown. *Devn*
nr. Bideford 3D **6**
nr. Littleham 3D **6**
Woodvale. *Mers* 6B **40**
Woodville. *Derbs* 8M **35**
Woodwalton. *Cambs* 3K **29**
Woodwick. *Orkn* 7C **88**
Woodyates. *Dors* 4J **9**
Woody Bay. *Devn* 1F **6**
Woofferton. *Shrp* 5D **26**
Wookey. *Som* 1D **8**
Wookey Hole. *Som* 1D **8**
Wool. *Dors* 7G **9**
Woolacombe. *Devn* 1D **6**
Woolage Green. *Kent* 1J **13**
Woolage Village. *Kent* 8J **23**
Woolaston. *Glos* 4D **18**
Woolavington. *Som* 1B **8**
Woolbeding. *W Sus* 3F **10**
Woolcotts. *Som* 2J **7**
Wooldale. *W Yor* 7K **41**
Wooler. *Nmbd* 7G **61**
Woolfardisworthy. *Devn*
nr. Bideford 3C **6**
nr. Crediton 5H **7**
Woolfords. *S Lan* 4J **59**
Woolgarston. *Dors* 7H **9**
Woolhampton. *W Ber* 7C **20**
Woolhope. *Here* 8E **26**
Woolland. *Dors* 5F **8**
Woollard. *Bath* 7E **18**
Woolley. *Bath* 7F **18**
Woolley. *Cambs* 4J **29**
Woolley. *Corn* 4B **6**
Woolley. *Derbs* 3A **36**
Woolley. *W Yor* 6M **41**
Woolley Green. *Wilts* 7G **19**
Woolmere Green. *Worc* 5H **27**
Woolmer Green. *Herts* 2K **21**
Woolminstone. *Som* 5C **8**
Woolpit. *Suff* 5F **30**
Woolridge. *Glos* 1G **19**
Woolscott. *Warw* 5B **28**
Woolsery. *Devn* 3C **6**
Woolsington. *Tyne* 5E **54**
Woolstaston. *Shrp* 2C **26**
Woolsthorpe By Belvoir. *Linc* 6F **36**
Woolsthorpe-by-Colsterworth. *Linc* 7G **37**
Woolston. *Devn* 7K **5**
Woolston. *Shrp*
nr. Church Stretton 3C **26**
nr. Oswestry 7B **34**
Woolston. *Som* 3E **8**
Woolston. *Sotn* 4B **10**
Woolston. *Warr* 1E **34**
Woolstone. *Glos* 8H **27**
Woolstone. *Oxon* 5L **19**
Woolston Green. *Devn* 5K **5**
Woolton. *Mers* 1C **34**
Woolton Hill. *Hants* 7B **20**
Woolverstone. *Suff* 8H **31**
Woolverton. *Som* 8F **18**
Woolwell. *Devn* 5H **5**
**Woolwich**. *G Lon* 6M **21**
Woonton. *Here*
nr. Kington 6B **26**
nr. Leominster 5D **26**
Wooperton. *Nmbd* 7H **61**
Woore. *Shrp* 5F **34**
Wooth. *Dors* 6C **8**
Wooton. *Shrp* 3F **26**
Wootton. *Bed* 7H **29**
Wootton. *Hants* 6L **9**
Wootton. *IOW* 6C **10**
Wootton. *Kent* 1J **13**
Wootton. *Nptn* 6E **28**
Wootton. *N Lin* 6H **43**
Wootton. *Oxon*
nr. Abingdon 3B **20**
nr. Woodstock 2B **20**
Wootton. *Shrp*
nr. Ludlow 4C **26**
nr. Oswestry 7B **34**
Wootton. *Staf*
nr. Eccleshall 7G **35**
nr. Ellastone 5K **35**
**Wootton Bassett, Royal**. *Wilts* 5J **19**
Wootton Bridge. *IOW* 6C **10**
Wootton Common. *IOW* 6C **10**
Wootton Courtenay. *Som* 1J **7**
Wootton Fitzpaine. *Dors* 6B **8**
Wootton Rivers. *Wilts* 7K **19**
Wootton St Lawrence. *Hants* 8C **20**
Wootton Wawen. *Warw* 5K **27**
**Worcester**. *Worc* **117** (6G **27**)
Worcester Park. *G Lon* 7K **21**
Wordsley. *W Mid* 3G **27**
Worfield. *Shrp* 2F **26**
Work. *Orkn* 8D **88**
Workhouse Green. *Suff* 8F **30**
**Workington**. *Cumb* 2J **45**
**Worksop**. *Notts* 2C **36**
Worlaby. *N Lin* 6H **43**
World's End. *W Ber* 6B **20**
World's End. *W Sus* 4L **11**
Worlds End. *Hants* 4D **10**
Worlds End. *W Mid* 3K **27**
Worldsend. *Shrp* 2C **26**
Worle. *N Som* 7B **18**
Worleston. *Ches E* 4E **34**
Worlingham. *Suff* 3L **31**
Worlington. *Suff* 4C **30**
Worlingworth. *Suff* 5J **31**
Wormbridge. *Here* 8C **26**
Wormegay. *Norf* 8C **38**
Wormelow Tump. *Here* 8C **26**
Wormhill. *Derbs* 2K **35**
Wormingford. *Essx* 8F **30**
Worminghall. *Buck* 3D **20**
Wormington. *Glos* 8J **27**
Worminster. *Som* 1D **8**
Wormit. *Fife* 5G **67**
Wormleighton. *Warw* 6B **28**
Wormley. *Herts* 3L **21**
Wormley. *Surr* 2G **11**
Wormshill. *Kent* 8E **22**
Wormsley. *Here* 7C **26**
Worplesdon. *Surr* 8G **21**
Worrall. *S Yor* 8M **41**
**Worsbrough**. *S Yor* 7A **42**
Worsley. *G Man* 7F **40**
Worstead. *Norf* 7K **39**
Worsthorne. *Lanc* 4G **41**
Worston. *Lanc* 3F **40**
Worth. *Kent* 8K **23**
Worth. *W Sus* 2K **11**
Wortham. *Suff* 4G **31**
Worthen. *Shrp* 1B **26**
Worthenbury. *Wrex* 5C **34**
Worthing. *Norf* 8F **38**
**Worthing**. *W Sus* 5J **11**
Worthington. *Leics* 7B **36**
Worth Matravers. *Dors* 8H **9**
Worting. *Hants* 8D **20**
Wortley. *Glos* 4F **18**
Wortley. *S Yor* 8M **41**
Wortley. *W Yor* 4L **41**
Worton. *N Yor* 7H **47**
Worton. *Wilts* 8H **19**
Wortwell. *Norf* 3J **31**
Wotherton. *Shrp* 1A **26**
Wothorpe. *Pet* 1H **29**
Wotter. *Devn* 5H **5**
Wotton. *Glos* 2G **19**
Wotton. *Surr* 1J **11**
Wotton-under-Edge. *Glos* 4F **18**
Wotton Underwood. *Buck* 2D **20**
Wouldham. *Kent* 7D **22**
Wrabness. *Essx* 8H **31**
Wrafton. *Devn* 2D **6**
Wragby. *Linc* 2J **37**
Wragby. *W Yor* 6B **42**
Wramplingham. *Norf* 1H **31**
Wrangbrook. *W Yor* 6B **42**
Wrangle. *Linc* 4M **37**
Wrangle Lowgate. *Linc* 4M **37**
Wrangway. *Som* 4L **7**
Wrantage. *Som* 3B **8**
Wrawby. *N Lin* 7H **43**
Wraxall. *N Som* 6C **18**
Wraxall. *Som* 2E **8**
Wray. *Lanc* 1E **40**
Wraysbury. *Wind* 6H **21**
Wrayton. *Lanc* 8E **46**
Wrea Green. *Lanc* 4B **40**
Wreay. *Cumb*
nr. Carlisle 7J **53**
nr. Penrith 3C **46**
Wrecclesham. *Surr* 1F **10**
**Wrecsam**. *Wrex* 4B **34**
Wrekenton. *Tyne* 6F **54**
Wrelton. *N Yor* 7E **48**
Wrenbury. *Ches E* 5D **34**
Wreningham. *Norf* 2H **31**
Wrentham. *Suff* 3L **31**
Wrenthorpe. *W Yor* 5M **41**
Wrentnall. *Shrp* 1C **26**
Wressle. *E Yor* 4E **42**
Wressle. *N Lin* 7G **43**
Wrestlingworth. *C Beds* 7K **29**
Wretton. *Norf* 2C **30**
**Wrexham**. *Wrex* 4B **34**
Wreyland. *Devn* 7G **7**
Wrickton. *Shrp* 3E **26**
Wrightington Bar. *Lanc* 6D **40**
Wright's Green. *Essx* 2B **22**
Wrinehill. *Staf* 5F **34**
Wrington. *N Som* 7C **18**
Writtle. *Essx* 3C **22**
Wrockwardine. *Telf* 8E **34**
Wroot. *N Lin* 7E **42**
Wrotham. *Kent* 8C **22**
Wrotham Heath. *Kent* 8C **22**
Wroughton. *Swin* 5K **19**
Wroxall. *IOW* 7C **10**
Wroxall. *Warw* 4L **27**
Wroxeter. *Shrp* 1D **26**
Wroxham. *Norf* 8K **39**
Wroxton. *Oxon* 7B **28**
Wyaston. *Derbs* 5K **35**
Wyatt's Green. *Essx* 4B **22**
Wybers Wood. *NE Lin* 7K **43**
Wyberton. *Linc* 5L **37**
Wyboston. *Bed* 6J **29**
Wybunbury. *Ches E* 5E **34**
Wychbold. *Worc* 5H **27**
Wych Cross. *E Sus* 2M **11**
Wychnor. *Staf* 8K **35**
Wychnor Bridges. *Staf* 8K **35**
Wyck. *Hants* 2E **10**
Wyck Hill. *Glos* 1K **19**
Wyck Rissington. *Glos* 1K **19**
Wycliffe. *Dur* 4K **47**
Wycombe Marsh. *Buck* 4F **20**
Yr Wyddgrug. *Flin* 4M **33**
Wyddial. *Herts* 8L **29**
Wye. *Kent* 1G **13**
Wyesham. *Mon* 2D **18**
Wyfold. *Oxon* 5D **20**
Wyfordby. *Leics* 8E **36**
The Wyke. *Shrp* 1F **26**
Wyke. *Devn* 6H **7**
Wyke. *Dors* 3F **8**
Wyke. *Shrp* 1E **26**
Wyke. *Surr* 8G **21**
Wyke. *W Yor* 5K **41**
Wyke Champflower. *Som* 2E **8**
Wykeham. *Linc* 7K **37**
Wykeham. *N Yor*
nr. Malton 8F **48**
nr. Scarborough 7G **49**
Wyken. *Shrp* 2F **26**
Wyken. *W Mid* 3A **28**
Wyke Regis. *Dors* 8E **8**
Wykey. *Shrp* 7B **34**
Wykin. *Leics* 2B **28**
Wylam. *Nmbd* 5E **54**
Wylde Green. *W Mid* 2K **27**
Wylye. *Wilts* 2J **9**
Wymering. *Port* 5D **10**
Wymeswold. *Leics* 7D **36**
Wymington. *Bed* 5G **29**
Wymondham. *Leics* 8F **36**
**Wymondham**. *Norf* 1H **31**
Wyndham. *B'end* 5J **17**
Wynford Eagle. *Dors* 6D **8**
Wyng. *Orkn* 2E **86**
Wynyard Village. *Stoc T* 3B **48**
Wyre Piddle. *Worc* 7H **27**
Wysall. *Notts* 7D **36**
Wyson. *Here* 5D **26**
Wythall. *Worc* 4J **27**
Wytham. *Oxon* 3B **20**
Wythenshawe. *G Man* 1G **35**
Wythop Mill. *Cumb* 2L **45**
Wyton. *Cambs* 4K **29**
Wyton. *E Yor* 4J **43**
Wyverstone. *Suff* 5G **31**
Wyverstone Street. *Suff* 5G **31**
Wyville. *Linc* 7F **36**
Wyvis Lodge. *High* 6E **78**


## Y


Yaddlethorpe. *N Lin* 7F **42**
Yafford. *IOW* 7B **10**
Yafforth. *N Yor* 6M **47**
Yalding. *Kent* 8C **22**
Yanley. *N Som* 7D **18**
Yanwath. *Cumb* 3D **46**
Yanworth. *Glos* 2J **19**
Yapham. *E Yor* 2E **42**
Yapton. *W Sus* 5G **11**
Yarburgh. *Linc* 8L **43**
Yarcombe. *Devn* 5M **7**
Yarde. *Som* 2K **7**
Yardley. *W Mid* 3K **27**
Yardley Gobion. *Nptn* 7E **28**
Yardley Hastings. *Nptn* 6F **28**
Yardley Wood. *W Mid* 3K **27**
Yardro. *Powy* 7M **25**
Yarhampton. *Worc* 5F **26**
Yarkhill. *Here* 7E **26**
Yarlet. *Staf* 7H **35**
Yarley. *Som* 1D **8**
Yarlington. *Som* 3E **8**
Yarm. *Stoc T* 4B **48**
Yarmouth. *IOW* 7A **10**
Yarnbrook. *Wilts* 8G **19**
Yarnfield. *Staf* 6G **35**
Yarnscombe. *Devn* 3E **6**
Yarnton. *Oxon* 2B **20**
Yarpole. *Here* 5C **26**
Yarrow. *Nmbd* 3M **53**
Yarrow. *Bord* 7A **60**
Yarrow. *Som* 1B **8**
Yarrow Feus. *Bord* 7M **59**
Yarrow Ford. *Bord* 6B **60**
Yarsop. *Here* 7C **26**
Yarwell. *Nptn* 2H **29**
Yate. *S Glo* 5F **18**
**Yateley**. *Hants* 7F **20**
Yatesbury. *Wilts* 6J **19**
Yattendon. *W Ber* 6C **20**
Yatton. *Here*
nr. Leominster 5C **26**
nr. Ross-on-Wye 8E **26**
Yatton. *N Som* 7C **18**
Yatton Keynell. *Wilts* 6G **19**
Yaverland. *IOW* 7D **10**
Yawl. *Devn* 6B **8**
Yaxham. *Norf* 8G **39**
Yaxley. *Cambs* 2J **29**
Yaxley. *Suff* 4H **31**
Yazor. *Here* 7C **26**
Yeading. *G Lon* 5J **21**
Yeadon. *W Yor* 3L **41**
Yealand Conyers. *Lanc* 8D **46**
Yealand Redmayne. *Lanc* 8D **46**
Yealand Storrs. *Lanc* 8C **46**
Yealmpton. *Devn* 6H **5**
Yearby. *Red C* 3D **48**
Yearngill. *Cumb* 7F **52**
Yearsett. *Here* 6F **26**
Yearsley. *N Yor* 8C **48**
Yeaton. *Shrp* 8C **34**
Yeaveley. *Derbs* 5K **35**
Yeavering. *Nmbd* 6G **61**
Yedingham. *N Yor* 8F **48**
Yeldersley Hollies. *Derbs* 5L **35**
Yelford. *Oxon* 3A **20**
Yelland. *Devn* 2D **6**
Yelling. *Cambs* 5K **29**
Yelsted. *Kent* 7E **22**
Yelvertoft. *Nptn* 4C **28**
Yelverton. *Devn* 5H **5**
Yelverton. *Norf* 1J **31**
Yenston. *Som* 3F **8**
Yeoford. *Devn* 6G **7**
Yeolmbridge. *Corn* 7C **6**
Yeo Mill. *Devn* 3H **7**
**Yeovil**. *Som* 4D **8**
Yeovil Marsh. *Som* 4D **8**
Yeovilton. *Som* 3D **8**
Yerbeston. *Pemb* 6G **15**
Yesnaby. *Orkn* 8B **88**
Yetlington. *Nmbd* 1D **54**
Yetminster. *Dors* 4D **8**
Yett. *N Lan* 4F **58**
Yett. *S Ayr* 7C **58**
Yettington. *Devn* 7K **7**
Yetts o' Muckhart. *Clac* 7D **66**
Yielden. *Bed* 5H **29**
Yieldshields. *S Lan* 4G **59**
Yiewsley. *G Lon* 5H **21**
Yinstay. *Orkn* 8E **88**
Ynysboeth. *Rhon* 5K **17**
Ynysddu. *Cphy* 5L **17**
Ynysforgan. *Swan* 5F **16**
Ynyshir. *Rhon* 5K **17**
Ynyslas. *Cdgn* 3F **24**
Ynysmaerdy. *Rhon* 6K **17**
Ynysmeudwy. *Neat* 4G **17**
Ynystawe. *Swan* 4F **16**
Ynys-wen. *Rhon* 5J **17**
Ynyswen. *Powy* 3H **17**
Ynys y Barri. *V Glam* 8L **17**
Ynysybwl. *Rhon* 5K **17**
Ynysymaerdy. *Neat* 5G **17**
Yockenthwaite. *N Yor* 8H **47**
Yockleton. *Shrp* 8C **34**
Yokefleet. *E Yor* 5F **42**
Yoker. *Glas* 3D **58**
Yonder Bognie. *Abers* 1E **72**
Yonderton. *Abers* 2J **73**
**York**. *York* **117** (2D **42**)
Yorkletts. *Kent* 7G **23**
Yorkley. *Glos* 3E **18**
Yorton. *Shrp* 7D **34**
Yorton Heath. *Shrp* 7D **34**
Youlgreave. *Derbs* 3L **35**
Youlthorpe. *E Yor* 2E **42**
Youlton. *N Yor* 1B **42**
Young's End. *Essx* 2D **22**
Young Wood. *Linc* 2J **37**
Yoxall. *Staf* 8K **35**
Yoxford. *Suff* 5K **31**
Ysbyty Cynfyn. *Cdgn* 5G **25**
Ysbyty Ifan. *Cnwy* 6H **33**
Ysbyty Ystwyth. *Cdgn* 5G **25**
Ysceifiog. *Flin* 3L **33**
Yspitty. *Carm* 5E **16**
Ystalyfera. *Neat* 4G **17**
Ystrad. *Rhon* 5J **17**
Ystrad Aeron. *Cdgn* 1M **15**
Ystradfellte. *Powy* 3J **17**
Ystradffin. *Carm* 8G **25**
Ystradgynlais. *Powy* 3G **17**
Ystradmeurig. *Cdgn* 6G **25**
Ystrad Mynach. *Cphy* 5L **17**
Ystradowen. *Carm* 3G **17**
Ystradowen. *V Glam* 7K **17**
Ystumtuen. *Cdgn* 5G **25**
Ythanbank. *Abers* 2J **73**
Ythanwells. *Abers* 2F **72**


## Z


Zeal Monachorum. *Devn* 5G **7**
Zeals. *Wilts* 2F **8**
Zelah. *Corn* 3M **3**
Zennor. *Corn* 5H **3**
Zouch. *Notts* 7C **36**



Published by Geographers' A-Z Map Company Limited
An imprint of HarperCollins Publishers
Westerhill Road
Bishopbriggs
Glasgow
G64 2QT

www.az.co.uk
a-z.maps@harpercollins.co.uk

HarperCollinsPublishers
1st Floor, Watermarque Building, Ringsend Road, Dublin 4, Ireland

37th edition 2022





Base relief by Geo-Innovations, © www.geoinnovations.co.uk





A catalogue record for this book is available from the British Library.

ISBN 978-0-00-852870-6

10 9 8 7 6 5 4 3 2 1

Printed in Italy

# INDEX TO SELECTED PLACES OF INTEREST

(1) A strict alphabetical order is used e.g. Benmore Botanic Gdn. follows Ben Macdui but precedes Ben Nevis.

(2) Places of Interest which fall on City and Town Centre maps are referenced first to the detailed map page, followed by the main map page if appropriate. The name of the map is included if it is not clear from the index entry.
e.g. Ashmolean Mus. of Art & Archaeology (OX1 2PH)....Oxford 114 (3C 20)

(3) Entries in italics are not named on the map but are shown with a symbol only.
e.g. *Aberdour Castle (KY3 0XA)*....1K 59

**SAT NAV POSTCODES**

Postcodes are shown to assist Sat Nav users and are included on this basis.
It should be noted that postcodes have been selected by their proximity to the Place of Interest and that they may not form part of the actual postal address. Drivers should follow the Tourist Brown Signs when available.

**ABBREVIATIONS USED IN THIS INDEX**

Centre : Cen. Garden : Gdn. Gardens : Gdns. Museum : Mus. National : Nat. Park : Pk.

## A


Abbeydale Industrial Hamlet (S7 2QW)....1M 35
Abbey House Mus. (LS5 3EH)....4L 41
*Abbot Hall Art Gallery. (LA9 5AL)*....6D 46
Abbotsbury Subtropical Gdns. (DT3 4LA)....7D 8
Abbotsbury Swannery (DT3 4JG)....7D 8
Abbotsford (TD6 9BQ)....6C 60
Aberdeen Maritime Mus. (AB11 5BY)....106 (5J 73)
*Aberdour Castle. (KY3 0XA)*....1K 59
Aberdulais Falls (SA10 8EU)....4G 17
Aberglasney Gdns. (SA32 8QH)....2E 16
Abernethy Round Tower (PH2 9RT)....6E 66
*Aberystwyth Castle. (SY23 1DZ)*....4E 24
Acorn Bank Gdn. & Watermill (CA10 1SP)....3E 46
*Acton Burnell Castle. (SY5 7PF)*....1D 26
Acton Scott Historic Working Farm (SY6 6QN)....3C 26
Adlington Hall (SK10 4LF)....1H 35
Africa Alive! (NR33 7TF)....3M 31
Aintree Racecourse (L9 5AS)....8B 40
Aira Force (CA11 0JX)....3C 46
A la Ronde (EX8 5BD)....7K 7
Alby Gdns. (NR11 7QE)....6J 39
Aldeburgh Mus. (IP15 5DS)....6L 31
Alfred Corry Mus. (IP18 6NB)....4M 31
Alfriston Clergy House (BN26 5TL)....5B 12
Alloa Tower (FK10 1PP)....8B 66
*Alnwick Castle. (NE66 1NQ)*....8J 61
*Alnwick Gdn. (NE66 1YU)*....8J 61
Althorp (NN7 4HQ)....5D 28
Alton Towers (ST10 4DB)....5J 35
Amberley Mus. & Heritage Cen. (BN18 9LT)....4H 11
The American Mus. in Britain (BA2 7BD)....7F 18
Angel of the North (NE9 6PG)....6F 54
Anglesey Abbey & Lode Mill (CB25 9EJ)....5B 30
Anne Hathaway's Cottage (CV37 9HH)....6K 27
Antonine Wall, Rough Castle (FK4 2AA)....2G 59
Antony (PL11 2QA)....6G 5
Appuldurcombe House (PO38 3EW)....7C 10
Arbeia Roman Fort & Mus. (NE33 2BB)....5G 55
*Arbroath Abbey. (DD11 1JQ)*....3K 67
Arbury Hall (CV10 7PT)....3M 27
Arbuthnott House Gdn. (AB30 1PA)....8G 73
Ardkinglas Woodland Gdns. (PA26 8BG)....6F 64
Ardnamurchan Point (PH36 4LN)....1J 63
Ardress House (BT62 1SQ)....6F 93
Arduaine Gdn. (PA34 4XQ)....6B 64
Ardwell Gdns. (DG9 9LY)....7G 51
The Argory (BT71 6NA)....6F 93
Argyll's Lodging (FK8 1EG)....Stirling 116 (8A 66)
Arley Hall & Gdns. (CW9 6NA)....1E 34
Arlington Court (EX31 4LP)....2F 6
Arlington Row (GL7 5NJ)....3K 19
Armadale Castle Gdns. (IV45 8RS)....5H 69
*Armagh County Mus. (BT61 9BE)*....6F 93
Armagh Planetarium (BT61 9DB)....6F 93
Arniston House (EH23 4RY)....4M 59
*Arundel Castle. (BN18 9AB)*....5H 11
Arundel Wetland Cen. (BN18 9PB)....5H 11
Ascot Racecourse (SL5 7JX)....7G 21
Ascott (LU7 0PT)....1F 20
*Ashby-de-la-Zouch Castle. (LE65 1BR)*....8A 36
Ashdown Forest (TN7 4EU)....2A 12
Ashdown House (RG17 8RE)....5L 19
Ashmolean Mus. of Art & Archaeology (OX1 2PH)....Oxford 114 (3C 20)
*Astley Hall Mus. & Art Gallery. (PR7 1NP)*....6D 40
Athelhampton House & Gdns. (DT2 7LG)....6F 8
Attingham Pk. (SY4 4TP)....1D 26
Auchingarrich Wildlife Cen. (PH6 2JE)....6A 66
*Auckland Castle. (DL14 7NP)*....8F 54
Audley End House & Gdns. (CB11 4JF)....8B 30
Avebury (SN8 1RE)....6K 19
Avoncroft Mus. of Historic Buildings (B60 4JR)....5H 27
Avon Valley Adventure & Wildlife Pk. (BS31 1TP)....7E 18
Avon Valley Railway (BS30 6HD)....6E 18
Aydon Castle (NE45 5PJ)....5C 54
Ayr Racecourse (KA8 0JE)....7B 58
Ayscoughfee Hall Mus. & Gdns. (PE11 2RA)....7K 37
Aysgarth Falls (DL8 3SR)....7J 47
*Ayton Castle (Eyemouth). (TD14 5RD)*....3G 61


## B


Bachelors' Club (KA5 5RB)....7C 58
*Baconsthorpe Castle. (NR25 6PS)*....6H 39
Baddesley Clinton (B93 0DQ)....4K 27
Bala Lake Railway (LL23 7DD)....7H 33
Ballindalloch Castle (AB37 9AX)....2A 72
Balmoral Castle (AB35 5TB)....6B 72
Balvaird Castle (PH2 9PY)....6E 66
Balvenie Castle (AB55 4DH)....1C 72
*Bamburgh Castle. (NE69 7DF)*....6J 61
*Bangor Cathedral. (LL57 1DN)*....3E 32
Banham Zoo (NR16 2HE)....3G 31
Bannockburn Battle Site (FK7 0PL)....8A 66
Barbara Hepworth Mus. & Sculpture Gdn. (TR26 1AD)....4J 3
*Barnard Castle. (DL12 8PR)*....4J 47
Barnsdale Gdns. (LE15 8AH)....8G 37
Barrington Court (TA19 0NQ)....4B 8
Basildon Pk. (RG8 9NR)....6D 20
Basing House (RG24 8AE)....8D 20
Basingwerk Abbey (CH8 7GH)....3L 33
Bateman's (TN19 7DS)....3C 12
Bath Abbey (BA1 1LT)....106 (7F 18)
Bath Assembly Rooms (BA1 2QH)....106
Battle Abbey (TN33 0AD)....4D 12
The Battlefield Line Railway (CV13 0BS)....1A 28
The Battle of Britain Memorial (CT18 7JJ)....2J 13
Battle of Britain Memorial Flight Visitors Cen. (LN4 4SY)....4K 37
Battle of Hastings Site (TN33 0AD)....4D 12
Bayham Abbey (TN3 8BG)....2C 12
Beachy Head (BN20 7YA)....6B 12
Beamish (DH9 0RG)....6F 54
The Beatles Story (L3 4AD)....Liverpool 111
Beaulieu Abbey (SO42 7ZN)....5A 10
Beauly Priory (IV4 7BL)....1F 70
*Beaumaris Castle. (LL58 8AP)*....3F 32
Beck Isle Mus. (YO18 8DU)....7E 48
Bedgebury National Pinetum (TN17 2SL)....2D 12
Bedruthan Steps (PL27 7UW)....5A 4
*Beeston Castle & Woodland Pk. (CW6 9TX)*....4D 34
Bekonscot Model Village & Railway (HP9 2PL)....4G 21
Belfast Castle (BT15 5GR)....5H 93
Belfast Zoological Gdns. (BT36 7PN)....4H 93
Belgrave Hall Mus. & Gdns. (LE4 5PE)....1C 28
Belleek Pottery (BT93 3FY)....6A 92
Belmont House & Gdns. (ME13 0HH)....8F 22
Belsay Hall, Castle & Gdns. (NE20 0DX)....4D 54
Belton House (NG32 2LS)....6G 37
Belvoir Castle (NG32 1PD)....6F 36
Beningbrough Hall & Gdns. (YO30 1DD)....2C 42
Benington Lordship Gdns. (SG2 7BS)....1K 21
Ben Lawers (PH15 2PA)....3L 65
Ben Lomond (FK8 3TR)....7H 65
Ben Macdui (PH22 1RB)....6K 71
Benmore Botanic Gdn. (PA23 8QU)....1L 57
Ben Nevis (PH33 6SY)....8B 70
Benthall Hall (TF12 5RX)....1E 26
Berkeley Castle (GL13 9BQ)....4E 18
Berkhamsted Castle (HP4 1LJ)....3G 21
Berney Arms Windmill (NR31 9HU)....1L 31
Berrington Hall (HR6 0DW)....5D 26
Berry Pomeroy Castle (TQ9 6LJ)....5L 5
Bessie Surtees House (NE1 3JF)....Newcastle upon Tyne 111
Beverley Minster (HU17 0DP)....4H 43
Bicton Gdns. (EX9 7BJ)....7K 7
Biddulph Grange Gdn. (ST8 7SD)....4G 35
Big Ben (SW1A 2PW)....London 113
Bignor Roman Villa (RH20 1PH)....4G 11
Big Pit National Coal Mus. (NP4 9XP)....4M 17
Binham Priory (NR21 0DJ)....5F 38
Birmingham Mus. & Art Gallery (B3 3DH)....106
Bishop's Waltham Palace (SO32 1DP)....4C 10
*Black Country Living Mus. (DY1 4SQ)*....2H 27
Blackgang Chine (PO38 2HN)....8B 10
Blackhouse (HS2 9DB)....7G 83
Blackness Castle (EH49 7NH)....1J 59
Blackpool Pleasure Beach (FY4 1EZ)....4B 40
Blackpool Zoo (FY3 8PP)....4B 40
The Blackwell Arts & Crafts House (LA23 3JR)....6C 46
Blaenavon Ironworks (NP4 9RJ)....4M 17
*Blaenavon World Heritage Cen. (NP4 9AS)*....4M 17
Blair Castle (PH18 5TL)....1B 66
Blair Drummond Safari & Adventure Pk. (FK9 4UR)....8M 65
Blakeney Point (NR25 7SA)....5G 39
Blakesley Hall (B25 8RN)....3K 27
Blenheim Palace (OX20 1PX)....2B 20
Bletchley Pk. (MK3 6EB)....8F 28
Blickling Estate (NR11 6NF)....7H 39
Blists Hill Victorian Town (TF7 5DS)....1E 26
Bluebell Railway (TN22 3QL)....3L 11
Blue John Cavern (S33 8WP)....1K 35
Blue Reef Aquarium
Newquay (TR7 1DU)....2M 3
Hastings (TN34 3DW)....5E 12
Portsmouth (PO5 3PB)....115 (6D 10)
Tynemouth (NE30 4JF)....4G 55
Boath Doocot (IV12 5TD)....8K 79
Bodelwyddan Castle (LL18 5YA)....3J 33
*Bodiam Castle. (TN32 5UA)*....3D 12
Bodleian Library (OX1 3BG)....Oxford 114
Bodmin & Wenford Railway (PL31 1AQ)....5C 4
Bodmin Moor (PL15 7TN)....8A 6
Bodnant Gdn. (LL28 5RE)....3H 33
Bodrhyddan Hall (LL18 5SB)....3K 33
Bolingbroke Castle (PE23 4HH)....3L 37
*Bolsover Castle. (S44 6PR)*....2B 36
Bolton Castle (DL8 4ET)....6J 47
Bolton Priory (BD23 6AL)....2J 41
Bonawe Historic Iron Furnace (PA35 1JQ)....4E 64
Bo'ness & Kinneil Railway (EH51 9AQ)....1H 59
Booth Mus. of Natural History (BN1 5AA)....Brighton & Hove 106 (5K 11)
Borde Hill Gdn. (RH16 1XP)....3L 11
Borth Wild Animal Kingdom (SY24 5NA)....4F 24
Boscobel House (ST19 9AR)....1G 27
*Boston Stump. (PE21 6NQ)*....5L 37
Bosworth Field Battle Site (CV13 0AB)....1A 28
Bothwell Castle (G71 8BL)....4E 58
Boughton House (NN14 1BJ)....3G 29
*Bowes Castle. (DL12 9LE)*....4H 47
Bowes Mus. (DL12 8NP)....4J 47
Bowhill House & Country Estate (TD7 5ET)....7B 60
Bowood House & Gdns. (SN11 0LZ)....7H 19
Box Hill (KT20 7LF)....8J 21
Braemar Castle (AB35 5XR)....6A 72
Bramall Hall (SK7 3NX)....1G 35
*Bramber Castle. (BN44 3FJ)*....4J 11
Bramham Pk. (LS23 6ND)....3B 42
Brands Hatch (DA3 8NG)....7B 22
Brantwood (LA21 8AD)....6B 46
Breamore House (SP6 2DF)....4K 9
Brean Down (TA8 2RS)....8A 18
Brecon Beacons Nat. Pk. (CF44 9JG)....2J 17
Brecon Mountain Railway (CF48 2UP)....3K 17
Bressingham Steam & Gdns. (IP22 2AB)....3G 31
Brimham Rocks (HG3 4DW)....1L 41
Brindley Mill & The James Brindley Mus. (ST13 8FA)....4H 35
Brinkburn Priory (NE65 8AR)....2E 54
Bristol Aquarium (BS1 5TT)....107
Bristol Cathedral (BS1 5TJ)....107 (6D 18)
Bristol Zoo Gdns. (BS8 3HA)....107 (6D 18)
Britannia Bridge (LL61 5YH)....3E 32
British Airways i360 (BN1 2LN)....Brighton & Hove 106 (5L 11)
British Golf Mus. (KY16 9AB)....6J 67
British in India Mus. (BB9 8AD)....4G 41
British Library (NW1 2DB)....London 113
British Motor Mus. (CV35 0BJ)....6M 27
British Mus. (WC1B 3DG)....London 113
Broadlands (SO51 9ZD)....3A 10
Broads Nat. Pk. (NR3 1BJ)....1L 31
Broadway Tower (WR12 7LB)....8K 27
Brobury House Gdns. (HR3 6BS)....7B 26
Brockhampton Estate (WR6 5TB)....6E 26
Brockhole, Lake District Visitor Cen. (LA23 1LJ)....5B 46
Brodick Castle & Gdn. (KA27 8HY)....6K 57
Brodie Castle (IV36 2TE)....8L 79
Brodsworth Hall & Gdns. (DN5 7XJ)....7C 42
Brogdale (ME13 8XU)....8G 23
Bronllys Castle (LD3 0HL)....1L 17
Brontë Parsonage Mus. (BD22 8DR)....4J 41
*Broseley Pipeworks. (TF12 5LX)*....1E 26
*Brougham Castle. (CA10 2AA)*....3D 46
*Brough Castle. (CA17 4EJ)*....4F 46
Broughton Castle (OX15 5EB)....8B 28
Broughton House & Gdn. (DG6 4JX)....6A 52
Brownsea Island (BH13 7EE)....7J 9
Bruce's Stone (DG7 3SQ)....4L 51
Brunel's SS Great Britain (BS1 6TY)....Bristol 107
Bubblecar Mus. (PE22 7AW)....5K 37
Buckfast Abbey (TQ11 0EE)....5K 5
Buckingham Palace (SW1A 1AA)....London 113
Buckland Abbey (PL20 6EY)....5G 5
Buckler's Hard Maritime Mus. (SO42 7XB)....6B 10
Buildwas Abbey (TF8 7BW)....1E 26
*Bungay Castle. (NR35 1DD)*....3K 31
Bure Valley Railway (NR11 6BW)....7J 39
Burford House Gdns. (WR15 8HQ)....5D 26
Burghley (PE9 3JY)....1H 29
Burleigh Castle (KY13 9TD)....7E 66
Burnby Hall Gdns. & Mus. (YO42 2QF)....3F 42
Burns House Mus. (KA5 5BZ)....7C 58
Burton Agnes Hall (YO25 4ND)....1J 43
Burton Constable Hall (HU11 4LN)....4J 43
Buscot Pk. (SN7 8BU)....4L 19
Butser Ancient Farm (PO8 0QF)....4E 10
The Buttertubs (DL11 6DR)....6G 47
Buxton Pavilion Gdns. (SK17 6XN)....2J 35
Byland Abbey (YO61 4BD)....8C 48


## C


Cadair Idris (LL40 1TN)....1F 24
Cadbury World (B30 1JR)....3J 27
Caerlaverock Castle (DG1 4RU)....5E 52
Caerleon Roman Fortress (NP18 1AY)....4B 18
*Caernarfon Castle. (LL55 2AY)*....4D 32
*Caerphilly Castle. (CF83 1JD)*....6L 17
Cairngorms Nat. Pk. (PH26 3HG)....5K 71
Cairnpapple Hill (EH48 4NW)....2H 59
Caister Castle (NR30 5SN)....8M 39
Calanais Standing Stones (HS2 9DY)....8F 82
Caldey Island (SA70 7UH)....7H 15
*Caldicot Castle. (NP26 5JB)*....5C 18
Caledonian Railway (DD9 7AF)....2K 67
Calke Abbey (DE73 7LE)....7A 36
*Calshot Castle. (SO45 1BR)*....5B 10
Camber Castle (TN31 7TB)....4F 12
Cambo Gdns. (KY16 8QD)....6K 67
Cambridge University Botanic Gdn. (CB2 1JE)....107 (6A 30)
Camperdown Wildlife Cen. (DD2 4TF)....4G 67
Canal Mus. (NN12 7SE)....6E 28
Cannock Chase (WS12 4PW)....8H 35
Cannon Hall Mus. (S75 4AT)....7L 41
Canons Ashby House (NN11 3SD)....6C 28
Canterbury Cathedral (CT1 2EH)....107 (8H 23)
Capesthorne Hall (SK11 9JY)....2G 35
Cape Wrath (IV27 4QQ)....4E 84
Captain Cook Schoolroom Mus. (TS9 6NB)....4C 48
Cardiff Castle (CF10 3RB)....107 (7L 17)
Cardoness Castle (DG7 2EH)....6L 51
*Carew Castle. (SA70 8SL)*....6G 15
Carisbrooke Castle & Mus. (PO30 1XY)....7B 10
Carlisle Castle (CA3 8UR)....107 (6H 53)
Carlisle Cathedral (CA3 8TZ)....107 (6H 53)
Carlyle's Birthplace (DG11 3DG)....4F 52
Carnasserie Castle (PA31 8RQ)....7C 64
Carn Euny Ancient Village (TR20 8RB)....6H 3
Carnfunnock Country Pk. (BT40 2QG)....3H 93
Carreg Cennen Castle & Farm (SA19 6UA)....3F 16
Carrick-a-Rede Rope Bridge (BT54 6LS)....1G 93
Carrickfergus Castle (BT38 7BG)....4J 93
Carsluith Castle (DG8 7DY)....6K 51
Cartmel Priory (LA11 6QQ)....8B 46
*Castell Coch. (CF15 7JQ)*....6L 17
Castell Dinas Bran (LL20 8DY)....6M 33
Castell y Bere (LL36 9TP)....2F 24
*Castle Acre Castle. (PE32 2XB)*....8E 38
Castle Acre Priory (PE32 2AA)....8E 38
Castle & Gdns. of Mey (KW14 8XH)....4D 86
Castle Campbell & Gdn. (FK14 7PP)....8C 66
Castle Coole (BT74 6JY)....6C 92
Castle Drogo (EX6 6PB)....6G 7
Castle Fraser (AB51 7LD)....4G 73
Castle Howard (YO60 7DA)....8E 48
Castle Kennedy Gdns. (DG9 8SJ)....5G 51
Castle Leod (IV14 9AA)....8E 78
Castle Menzies (PH15 2JD)....3B 66
Castlerigg Stone Circle (CA12 4RN)....3A 46
*Castle Rising Castle. (PE31 6AH)*....7C 38
Castle Ward (BT30 7LS)....6J 93
*Catalyst Science Discovery Cen. (WA8 0DF)*....1D 34
*Cawdor Castle. (IV12 5RD)*....1J 71
Cerne Giant (DT2 7TS)....5E 8
Chanonry Point (IV10 8SD)....8H 79
Charlecote Pk. (CV35 9ER)....6L 27
Charleston (BN8 6LL)....5A 12
Chartwell (TN16 1PS)....8A 22
Chastleton House (GL56 0SU)....1L 19
Chatsworth House (DE45 1PP)....2L 35
Chavenage House (GL8 8XP)....4G 19
Cheddar Gorge (BS40 7XT)....8C 18
Chedworth Roman Villa (GL54 3LJ)....2J 19
Cheltenham Racecourse (GL50 4SH)....1H 19
Chenies Manor House & Gdns. (WD3 6ER)....4H 21
Chepstow Castle (NP16 5EZ)....4D 18
Chepstow Racecourse (NP16 6EG)....4D 18
Chesil Beach (DT3 4ED)....7E 8
Chessington World of Adventures (KT9 2NE)....7J 21
Chester Cathedral (CH1 2HU)....108 (3C 34)
Chester Roman Amphitheatre (CH1 1RF)....108
Chesters Roman Fort & Mus. (NE46 4EU)....4C 54
Chester Zoo (CH2 1LH)....2C 34
*Chichester Cathedral. (PO19 1PX)*....5F 10
Chiddingstone Castle (TN8 7AD)....1A 12
*Chillingham Castle. (NE66 5NJ)*....7H 61
Chillingham Wild Cattle (NE66 5NJ)....7H 61
Chillington Hall (WV8 1RE)....1G 27
Chiltern Hills (RG9 6DR)....5D 20
Chiltern Open Air Mus. (HP8 4AB)....4H 21
Chirk Castle (LL14 5AF)....6A 34
Cholmondeley Castle Gdns. (SY14 8AH)....4D 34
*Christchurch Castle & Norman House (BH23 1BW)*....6K 9
Churnet Valley Railway (ST13 7EE)....4H 35
Chysauster Ancient Village (TR20 8XA)....5H 3
*Cilgerran Castle. (SA43 2SF)*....2H 15
Cissbury Ring (BN14 0SQ)....5J 11
Clandon Pk. (GU4 7RQ)....8H 21
Claremont Landscape Gdn. (KT10 9JG)....7J 21
Claydon (MK18 2EY)....1E 20
Clearwell Caves (GL16 8JR)....3D 18
Cleeve Abbey (TA23 0PS)....1K 7
Clevedon Court (BS21 6QU)....6C 18
Clifford's Tower (YO1 9SA)....York 117 (2D 42)
Clifton Suspension Bridge (BS8 3PA)....Bristol 107
Cliveden (SL6 0JA)....5G 21
Clouds Hill (BH20 7NQ)....6G 9
Clumber Pk. (S80 3BX)....2D 36
*Clun Castle. (SY7 8JR)*....3A 26
Clyde Muirshiel Regional Pk. (PA10 2PZ)....3A 58
Coalbrookdale Mus. of Iron (TF8 7DQ)....1E 26
Coalport China Mus. (TF8 7HT)....1E 26
Coed y Brenin Visitor Cen. (LL40 2HZ)....8G 33
Coggeshall Grange Barn (CO6 1RE)....1E 22
*Coity Castle. (CF35 6AU)*....6J 17
Colby Woodland Gdn. (SA67 8PP)....6H 15
*Colchester Castle Mus. (CO1 1TJ)*....1G 23
Colchester Zoo (CO3 0SL)....1F 22
Coleridge Cottage (TA5 1NQ)....2L 7
Coleton Fishacre (TQ6 0EQ)....6M 5
Colour Experience (BD1 2PW)....Bradford 106
Colzium Walled Gdn. (G65 0PY)....2F 58
Combe Martin Wildlife & Dinosaur Pk. (EX34 0NG)....1E 6
Compton Acres (BH13 7ES)....7J 9
*Compton Castle. (TQ3 1TA)*....5L 5
Compton Verney (CV35 9HZ)....6M 27
*Conisbrough Castle. (DN12 3BU)*....8C 42
Conishead Priory (LA12 9QQ)....8B 46
Conkers (DE12 6GA)....8M 35
Constable Burton Hall Gdns. (DL8 5LJ)....6K 47
*Conwy Castle. (LL32 8LD)*....3G 33
*Coombes & Churnet Nature Reserve. (ST13 7NN)*....4J 35
Corbridge Roman Town (NE45 5NT)....5C 54
Corfe Castle (BH20 5EZ)....7H 9
Corgarff Castle (AB36 8YP)....5B 72
Corinium Mus. (GL7 2BX)....3J 19
Cornish Seal Sanctuary (TR12 6UG)....6L 3
Corrieshalloch Gorge (IV23 2PJ)....6C 78
Corsham Court (SN13 0BZ)....6G 19
Cotehele (PL12 6TA)....5G 5
Coton Manor Gdn. (NN6 8RQ)....4D 28
Cotswold Farm Pk. (GL54 5UG)....1K 19
Cotswold Hills (GL8 8NU)....4H 19
Cotswold Water Pk. (GL7 5TL)....4J 19
Cottesbrooke Hall & Gdns. (NN6 8PF)....4E 28
Cotton Mechanical Music Mus. (IP14 4QN)....5G 31
Coughton Court (B49 5JA)....5J 27
The Courts Gdn. (BA14 6RR)....7G 19
Coventry Cathedral (CV1 5AB)....108 (4M 27)
Coventry Transport Mus. (CV1 1JD)....108 (4M 27)
Cowdray House (GU29 9AL)....3F 10
Cragside (NE65 7PX)....1D 54
Craigievar Castle (AB33 8JF)....5E 72
*Craigmillar Castle. (EH16 4SY)*....2L 59
Craignethan Castle (ML11 9PL)....5G 59
Craigston Castle (AB53 5PX)....8G 81
Cranborne Manor Gdns. (BH21 5PS)....4J 9
Cranwell Aviation Heritage Cen. (NG34 8QR)....5H 37
Crarae Gdn. (PA32 8YA)....8D 64
Crathes Castle, Gdn. & Estate (AB31 5QJ)....6G 73
Creswell Crags (S80 3LH)....2C 36
Crewe Heritage Cen. (CW1 2DD)....4F 34
*Criccieth Castle. (LL52 0DP)*....7D 32
Crichton Castle (EH37 5XA)....3A 60
Crich Tramway Village (DE4 5DP)....4M 35
Croft Castle (HR6 9PW)....5C 26
Croft Circuit (DL2 2PL)....5L 47
Crom (BT92 8AP)....7C 92
Cromford Mill (DE4 3RQ)....4L 35
Cromwell Mus. (PE29 3LF)....4K 29
Crookston Castle (G53 5RR)....3D 58
Croome (WR8 9JS)....7G 27
Crossraguel Abbey (KA19 8HQ)....1H 51
Croxden Abbey (ST14 5JG)....6J 35
Croxteth Hall (L12 0HB)....8C 40
Cruachan Power Station (PA33 1AN)....5E 64
Culloden Battlefield Visitor Cen. (IV2 5EU)....1H 71
Culloden Battle Site (IV2 5EU)....1H 71
Culross Palace (KY12 8JH)....1H 59
Culzean Castle (KA19 8LE)....8M 57
Curraghs Wildlife Pk. (IM7 5EA)....5C 44
*Cusworth Hall. (DN5 7TU)*....7C 42
Cymer Abbey (LL40 2HE)....1G 25


## D


Dales Countryside Mus. (DL8 3NT)....6G 47
Dallas Dhu Historic Distillery (IV36 2RR)....8L 79
Dalmeny House (EH30 9TQ)....2K 59
Darby Houses (TF8 7DQ)....1E 26
Dartington Crystal (EX38 7AN)....4D 6
Dartington Hall Gdns. (TQ9 6EL)....5L 5
Dartmoor Nat. Pk. (TQ13 9JQ)....7E 6
Dartmoor Zoo (PL7 5DG)....6H 5
Dartmouth Castle (TQ6 0JN)....6L 5
Dartmouth Steam Railway (TQ4 6AF)....6L 5
Dawyck Botanic Gdn. (EH45 9JU)....6K 59
*Deal Castle. (CT14 7BA)*....8K 23
Dean Castle (KA3 1XB)....6C 58
Dean Forest Railway (GL15 4ET)....3E 18
Deene Pk. (NN17 3EW)....2G 29
The Deep (HU1 4DP)....Kingston upon Hull 110 (5J 43)
Deep Sea World (KY11 1JR)....1K 59
Delamere Forest Pk. (CW8 2JD)....2D 34
Delgatie Castle (AB53 5TD)....8G 81
The Den & The Glen (AB12 5FT)....6H 73
*Denbigh Castle. (LL16 3NB)*....4K 33
*Derrymore House. (BT35 7EF)*....7G 93
Devil's Dyke (BN45 7DE)....4K 11
Devil's Punch Bowl (GU26 6AB)....2F 10
Dewa Roman Experience (CH1 1NL)....Chester 108
DH Lawrence Birthplace Mus. (NG16 3AW)....5B 36
Dickens House Mus. (CT10 1QS)....7K 23
Didcot Railway Cen. (OX11 7NJ)....4C 20
Dinefwr Castle (SA19 6PF)....2F 16
Dinefwr Pk. (SA19 6RT)....2F 16
Dinorwig Power Station (LL55 4UR)....5E 32
Dinosaur Adventure (NR9 5JW)....8H 39
The Dinosaur Mus. (DT1 1EW)....6E 8
*Dirleton Castle & Gdn. (EH39 5ER)*....1C 60
Discovery Mus. (NE1 4JA)....Newcastle upon Tyne 111 (5F 54)
Discovery Point, Dundee (DD1 4XA)....108
Dock Mus. (LA14 2PW)....8L 45
Doddington Hall & Gdns. (LN6 4RU)....2F 36
Doddington Place Gdns. (ME9 0BB)....8F 22
Dolaucothi Gold Mines (SA19 8RR)....1F 16
Dolbadarn Castle (LL55 4SU)....5E 32
Dolforwyn Castle (SY15 6JH)....3L 25
*Dolwyddelan Castle. (LL25 0JD)*....5G 33
Doncaster Racecourse (DN2 6BB)....7D 42
Donington Pk. (DE74 2RP)....7B 36
*Donnington Castle. (RG14 2LE)*....7B 20
Dorfold Hall (CW5 8LD)....4E 34
Dorothy Clive Gdn. (TF9 4EU)....6F 34
*Doune Castle. (FK16 6EA)*....7M 65
Dove Cottage (LA22 9SH)....5B 46
Dovedale (DE6 1NL)....4K 35
Dover Castle (CT16 1HU)....108 (1K 13)
Downhill Demesne (BT51 4RP)....2E 92
Down House (BR6 7JT)....7M 21
Dozmary Pool (PL15 7TP)....8A 6
Drayton Manor Theme Pk. (B78 3TW)....1K 27
Drum Castle & Gdn. (AB31 5EY)....5G 73
Drumlanrig Castle (DG3 4AQ)....2C 52
Drummond Gdns. (PH5 2AA)....6B 66
Drusillas (BN26 5QS)....5B 12
Dryburgh Abbey (TD6 0RQ)....6C 60
*Dryslwyn Castle. (SA32 8JQ)*....2E 16
Duart Castle (PA64 6AP)....4B 64
Dudmaston Estate (WV15 6QN)....3F 26
Duff House Country Gallery (AB45 3SX)....7F 80
Duffus Castle (IV30 5RH)....7A 80
The Dukeries (S80 3BT)....2D 36
Dumbarton Castle (G82 1JJ)....2C 58
*Dunblane Cathedral. (FK15 0AQ)*....7A 66
Dun Carloway (HS2 9AZ)....7E 82
Duncombe Pk. (YO62 5EB)....7D 48
*Dundonald Castle. (KA2 9HD)*....6B 58
Dundrennan Abbey (DG6 4QH)....7B 52
*Dunfermline Abbey. (KY12 7PE)*....1J 59
Dungeon Ghyll Force (LA22 9JY)....5A 46
Dunge Valley Rhododendron Gdns. (SK23 7RF)....2H 35
Dunham Massey (WA14 4SJ)....1F 34
*Dunkeld Cathedral. (PH8 0AW)*....3D 66
Dunkery Beacon (TA24 7AT)....1H 7
Dunnet Head (KW14 8XS)....4D 86
Dunninald (DD10 9TD)....2L 67
Dunnottar Castle (AB39 2TL)....7H 73
Dunrobin Castle (KW10 6SF)....3J 79
Dunstaffnage Castle (PA37 1PZ)....4C 64
Dunstanburgh Castle (NE66 3TG)....7K 61
*Dunster Castle. (TA24 6SL)*....1J 7
Dunvegan Castle (IV55 8WF)....1D 68
Durdle Door (BH20 5PU)....7G 9
Durham Cathedral (DH1 3EH)....108 (7F 54)
Dyffryn Gdns. (CF5 6SU)....7K 17
Dylan Thomas Boathouse (SA33 4SD)....5K 15
Dynamic Earth (EH8 8AS)....Edinburgh 109
Dyrham Pk., Gloucestershire (SN14 8ER)....6F 18


## E


Eagle Heights Wildlife Pk. (DA4 0JB)....7B 22
Easby Abbey (DL10 7JU)....5K 47
East Anglian Railway Mus. (CO6 2DS)....1E 22
East Bergholt Place Gdn. (CO7 6UP)....8G 31
East Kent Railway (CT15 7PD)....1J 13
East Lambrook Manor Gdns. (TA13 5HH)....4C 8
East Lancashire Railway (BB4 6AG)....5G 41
Eastnor Castle (HR8 1RD)....8F 26
East Pool Mine (TR15 3NP)....4K 3
East Riddlesden Hall (BD20 5EL)....3J 41
East Somerset Railway (BA4 4QP)....1E 8
Eden Project (PL24 2SG)....6C 4
Edinburgh Castle (EH1 2NG)....109 (2L 59)
Edinburgh St Giles' Cathedral (EH1 1RE)....109 (2L 59)
*Edinburgh Zoo. (EH12 6TS)*....2L 59
Edzell Castle & Gdn. (DD9 7UE)....1J 67
Egglestone Abbey (DL12 9TN)....4J 47
Eilean Donan Castle (IV40 8DX)....3K 69
*Elcho Castle. (PH2 8QQ)*....5E 66
Electric Mountain (LL55 4UR)....4E 32
Elgar's Birthplace (WR2 6RH)....6G 27
*Elgin Cathedral. (IV30 1EL)*....7B 80
Eltham Palace & Gdns. (SE9 5QE)....6M 21
Elton Hall House & Gdns. (PE8 6SH)....2H 29
*Ely Cathedral. (CB7 4DL)*....3B 30
Embsay & Bolton Abbey Steam Railway (BD23 6AF)....2J 41
Emmetts Gdn. (TN14 6BA)....8A 22
Enginuity (TF8 7DQ)....1E 26
Epping Ongar Railway (CM5 9BN)....3B 22
Epsom Downs Racecourse (KT18 5LQ)....8K 21
Erddig (LL13 0YT)....5B 34
*Etal Castle. (TD12 4TN)*....6G 61
*Eureka! The National Children's Mus. (HX1 2NE)*....5J 41
Euston Hall (IP24 2QW)....4E 30
*Ewloe Castle. (CH5 3BZ)*....3A 34
Exbury Gdns. (SO45 1AZ)....5B 10
Exeter Cathedral (EX1 1HS)....109 (6J 7)
Exmoor Nat. Pk. (TA22 9HL)....2H 7
Exploris Aquarium (BT22 1NZ)....6J 93
Eyam Hall (S32 5QW)....2L 35
*Eye Castle. (IP23 7AP)*....4H 31
*Eynsford Castle. (DA4 0AA)*....7B 22


## F


Fairbourne Steam Railway (LL38 2PZ)....1F 24
Fairhaven Woodland & Water Gdn. (NR13 6DZ)....8K 39
Falkirk Wheel (FK1 4RS)....1G 59
Falkland Palace (KY15 7BU)....7F 66
Falls of Glomach (IV40 8DS)....3M 69
*Farleigh Hungerford Castle. (BA2 7RS)*....8F 18
Farmland Mus. & Denny Abbey (CB25 9PQ)....5A 30
Farnborough Hall (OX17 1DU)....7B 28
Farne Islands (NE68 7SY)....6K 61
*Farnham Castle Keep. (GU9 0AE)*....1F 10
Felbrigg Hall (NR11 8PR)....6H 39
Fell Foot Pk. (LA12 8NN)....7B 46
Ferniehirst Castle (TD8 6NX)....8D 60
Ffestiniog Railway (LL49 9NF)....6F 32
Fiddleford Manor (DT10 2BU)....4G 9
Finchale Priory (DH1 5SH)....7F 54
Finch Foundry (EX20 2NW)....6F 6
Fingal's Cave (PA73 6NA)....4J 63
Finlaystone Country Estate (PA14 6TJ)....2B 58
Firle Place (BN8 6LP)....5A 12
The Firs (WR2 6RH)....6G 27
Fishbourne Roman Palace & Gdns. (PO19 3QR)....5F 10
Fitzwilliam Mus. (CB2 1RB)....Cambridge 107 (6M 29)
Five Sisters of Kintail (IV40 8HQ)....4L 69
Flambards (TR13 0QA)....6K 3
Flamingo Land (YO17 6UX)....8E 48
Fleet Air Arm Mus. (BA22 8HT)....3D 8
*Flint Castle. (CH6 5PE)*....3M 33
Floors Castle & Gdns. (TD5 7SF)....6E 60
Florence Court (BT92 1DB)....7B 92
*Fonmon Castle. (CF62 3ZN)*....8K 17
Forde Abbey & Gdns. (TA20 4LU)....5B 8
*Ford Green Hall. (ST6 1NG)*....4G 35
Forest of Dean (GL15 4SL)....3E 18
Fort George (IV2 7TD)....8H 79
Forth Bridge (EH30 9TB)....1K 59
Fort Nelson (Royal Armouries) (PO17 6AN)....5D 10
Fountains Abbey & Studley Royal Water Gdn. (HG4 3DY)....1L 41
Foxfield Steam Railway (ST11 9BG)....5H 35
Foxton Locks (LE16 7RA)....3E 28
*Framlingham Castle. (IP13 9BP)*....5J 31
Froghall Wharf (ST10 2HH)....5J 35
Furness Abbey (LA13 0PG)....7M 45
Furzey Gdns. (SO43 7GL)....4L 9
Fyne Court (TA5 2EQ)....2M 7
*Fyvie Castle. (AB53 8JS)*....2G 73


## G


Gainsborough Old Hall (DN21 2NB)....8F 42
Gainsborough's House (CO10 2EU)....7E 30
Gallery of Modern Art, Glasgow (G1 3AH)....109
Galloway Forest Pk. (DG8 6TA)....3K 51

Galloway House Gdns. (DG8 8HF) 7K 51
The Gdn. House (PL20 7LQ) 5G 5
Gawsworth Hall (SK11 9RN) 3G 35
Gawthorpe Hall (BB12 8UA) 4G 41
Geevor Tin Mine Mus. (TR19 7EW) 5G 3
George Stephenson's Birthplace
(NE41 8BP) 5E 54
The Georgian House (EH2 4DR) **Edinburgh 109**
Giant's Causeway (BT57 8SU) 1F 93
Gibside (NE16 6BG) 6E 54
Gilbert White's House (GU34 3JH) 2E 10
Gisborough Priory (TS14 6BU) 4D 48
*Gladstone Pottery Mus. (ST3 1PQ) 5H 35*
Gladstone's Land (EH1 2NT) **Edinburgh 109**
Glamis Castle (DD8 1QJ) 3G 67
*Glasgow St Mary's Episcopal Cathedral.*
*(G4 9JB) 3D 58*
Glastonbury Abbey (BA6 9EL) 2D 8
Glastonbury Tor (BA6 8BG) 2D 8
Glenarn (G84 8LL) 1A 58
Glenbuchat Castle (AB36 8TN) 4C 72
Glencoe Gorge (PH50 4SG) 2F 64
Glendurgan Gdn. (TR11 5JZ) 6L 3
Glenfinnan Monument (PH37 4LT) 7L 69
Glenluce Abbey (DG8 0LW) 6G 51
Glenmore Forest Pk. (PH22 1QT) 4K 71
Glenwhan Gdns. (DG9 8PH) 6G 51
Gloucester Cathedral (GL1 2LR) 109 (2G 19)
Gloucestershire Warwickshire Steam Railway
(GL54 5DT) 8J 27
Gloucester Waterways Mus.
(GL1 2EH) 109 (2G 19)
Glynde Place (BN8 6SX) 5A 12
Godinton House & Gdns. (TN23 3BP) 1F 12
Godolphin (TR13 9RE) 5K 3
Goodnestone Pk. Gdns. (CT3 1PL) 8J 23
*Goodrich Castle. (HR9 6HY) 1D 18*
Goodwood House (PO18 0PX) 5F 10
Goodwood Racecourse (PO18 0PS) 4F 10
Gordale Scar (BD23 4DL) 1H 41
Grampian Transport Mus. (AB33 8AE) 4E 72
The Grange at Northington (SO24 9TG) 2C 10
Graves Gallery
(S1 1XZ) **Sheffield 116** (1A 36)
Gray's Printing Press (BT82 8AU) 4C 92
Graythwaite Hall Gdns. (LA12 8BA) 6B 46
Great Central Railway (LE11 1RW) 8C 36
Great Central Railway (Nottingham)
(NG11 6NX) 6C 36
Great Chalfield Manor & Gdn.
(SN12 8NH) 7G 19
Great Comp Gdn. (TN15 8QS) 8C 22
Great Dixter (TN31 6PH) 3E 12
Great North Mus.: Hancock
(NE2 4PT) **Newcastle upon Tyne 111**
Greenbank House & Gdn. (G76 8RB) 4D 58
Greenknowe Tower (TD3 6JL) 5D 60
Greenway (TQ5 0ES) 6L 5
Gretna Green Famous Blacksmith's Shop
(DG16 5EA) 5H 53
Grey Mare's Tail Waterfall, Moffat
(DG10 9LH) 8K 59
Greys Court (RG9 4PG) 5E 20
Grimes Graves (IP26 5DE) 2E 30
*Grimsby Fishing Heritage Cen. (DN31 1UZ) 7K 43*
Grimspound (PL20 6TB) 7G 7
Grimsthorpe Castle (PE10 0LZ) 7H 37
Grizedale Forest (LA22 0QJ) 6B 46
Groombridge Place Gdns. (TN3 9QG) 2B 12
Grove Mus. (IM8 3UA) 5D 44
Guildhall, Lavenham (CO10 9QZ) 7F 30
*Gulliver's Kingdom, Matlock Bath.*
*(DE4 3PG) 4L 35*
Gulliver's Land, Milton Keynes
(MK15 0DT) 114 (8F 28)
Gulliver's World, Warrington (WA5 9YZ) 8D 40
Gunby Hall (PE23 5SS) 3A 38
Gwydir Castle (LL26 0PN) 4H 33

## H

Haddo House (AB41 7EQ) 2H 73
Haddon Hall (DE45 1LA) 3L 35
Hadleigh Castle (SS7 2AR) 5E 22
Hadrian's Wall, Winshields (NE47 7AW) 5M 53
Hailes Abbey (GL54 5PB) 1J 19
Hailes Castle (EH41 3SB) 2C 60
*Hall i' th' Wood Mus. (BL1 8UA) 6F 40*
Hall Place & Gdns. (DA5 1PQ) 6B 22
*Hamerton Zoo Pk. (PE28 5RE) 3J 29*
Ham House & Gdn. (TW10 7RS) 6J 21
Hammerwood Pk. (RH19 3QE) 2M 11
Hampden Pk. (G42 9AY) 3D 58
Hampton Court Castle & Gdns.
(HR6 0PN) 6D 26
Hampton Court Palace (KT8 9AU) 7J 21
Hanbury Hall (WR9 7EA) 5H 27
Hardknott Roman Fort (LA20 6EQ) 4M 45
Hardwick Hall (S44 5QJ) 3B 36
Hardy Monument (DT2 9HY) 7E 8
Hardy's Cottage (DT2 8QJ) 6F 8
Hare Hill (SK10 4QA) 2G 35
Harewood House (LS17 9LG) 3M 41
*Harlech Castle. (LL46 2YH) 7E 32*
The Harley Gallery (S80 3LW) 2C 36
Hartland Abbey & Gdns. (EX39 6DT) 3B 6
Harvington Hall (DY10 4LR) 4G 27
Harwich Redoubt (CO12 3NL) 8J 31
Hatchlands Pk. (GU4 7RT) 8H 21
Hatfield House (AL9 5NQ) 3K 21
Haughmond Abbey (SY4 4RW) 8D 34
*Haverfordwest Castle. (SA61 2BW) 5F 14*
*Haverfordwest Priory. (SA61 1RN) 5F 14*
Hawk Conservancy Trust (SP11 8DY) 1M 9
Haydock Pk. Racecourse (WA12 0HQ) 8D 40
Head of Steam – Darlington Railway Mus.
(DL3 6ST) 4L 47
Heale Gdns. (SP4 6NT) 2K 9
Heaton Hall (M25 2SW) 7G 41
Hedingham Castle (CO9 3DJ) 8D 30
Heights of Abraham (DE4 3PB) 4L 35
Hellens (HR8 2LY) 8E 26
Helmingham Hall Gdns. (IP14 6EF) 6H 31
Helmshore Mills Textile Mus. (BB4 4NP) 5F 40
*Helmsley Castle. (YO62 5AB) 7D 48*
Helvellyn (CA12 4TP) 4B 46
*Heptonstall Mus. (HX7 7PL) 5H 41*
*Hereford Cathedral. (HR1 2NG) 8D 26*
Hereford Cider Mus. (HR4 0LW) 8D 26
Hergest Croft Gdns. (HR5 3EG) 6A 26
Hermitage Castle (TD9 0LU) 2K 53
Herstmonceux Castle & Gdns.
(BN27 1RN) 4C 12
Hestercombe (TA2 8LG) 3M 7
Hever Castle & Gdns. (TN8 7NG) 1A 12
Hexham Abbey (NE46 3NB) 5C 54
Hidcote (GL55 6LR) 7K 27
High Beeches Gdns. (RH17 6HQ) 2K 11
Highclere Castle (RG20 9RN) 8B 20
Highland Folk Mus. (PH20 1AY) 6H 71
Highland Wildlife Pk. (PH21 1NL) 5J 71
The Hill House (G84 9AJ) 1A 58
Hill of Tarvit Mansionhouse & Gdns.
(KY15 5PB) 6G 67
Hill Top (LA22 0LF) 6B 46
*Hinton Ampner. (SO24 0LA) 3C 10*
Hirsel (TD12 4LP) 5F 60
The Historic Dockyard Chatham
(ME4 4TZ) **Medway Towns 111** (7D 22)
HMS Victory (PO1 3LJ) **Portsmouth 115**
HMS Warrior 1860 (PO1 3QX) **Portsmouth 115**
Hodnet Hall Gdns. (TF9 3NN) 7E 34
Hoghton Tower (PR5 0SH) 5E 40
Hog's Back (GU3 1AQ) 1G 11
(BA2 4DB) **Bath 106** (7F 18)
Holdenby House Gdns. & Falconry Cen.
(NN6 8DJ) 5D 28
Holehird Gdns. (LA23 1NP) 5C 46
Holker Hall & Gdns. (LA11 7PL) 8B 46
Holkham Hall (NR23 1AB) 5E 38
Hollycombe Steam in the Country
(GU30 7LP) 3F 10
Holst Birthplace Mus.
(GL52 2AY) **Cheltenham 107** (1H 19)
Holy Jesus Hospital
(NE1 2AS) **Newcastle upon Tyne 111**
Holyrood Abbey (EH8 8DX) **Edinburgh 109** (2L 59)
Hopetoun (EH30 9SL) 2J 59
Hop Farm Family Pk. (TN12 6PY) 1C 12
Houghton Hall (PE31 6TZ) 7D 38
Houghton House (MK45 2EZ) 8H 29
Houghton Lodge Gdns. (SO20 6LQ) 2M 9
House of Dun (DD10 9LQ) 2K 67
House of Manannan Mus. (IM5 1TA) 6B 44
House of the Binns (EH49 7NA) 1J 59
Houses of Parliament (SW1A 0RS) **London 113**
Housesteads Roman Fort & Mus.
(NE47 6NN) 5A 54
Hoveton Hall Gdns. (NR12 8RJ) 7K 39
Hovingham Hall (YO62 4LU) 8D 48
Howick Hall Gdns. (NE66 3LB) 8K 61
Howletts Wild Animal Pk. (CT4 5EL) 8H 23
Hughenden Manor (HP14 4LA) 4F 20
Hugh Miller Mus. & Birthplace Cottage
(IV11 8XA) 7H 79
Hunstanton Sea Life Sanctuary (PE36 5BH) 5C 38
*Hunterian Mus. & Art Gallery. (G12 8QQ) 3D 58*
Huntingtower Castle (PH1 3JL) 5D 66
*Huntly Castle. (AB54 4SH) 1E 72*
Hurst Castle (SO41 0TP) 7M 9
Hutton-in-the-Forest (CA11 9TH) 8J 53
Hylands House & Gdns. (CM2 8WQ) 3C 22

## I

Ickworth (IP29 5QE) 5E 30
Iford Manor (Peto Gdn.) (BA15 2BA) 8G 19
Ightham Mote (TN15 0NT) 8B 22
Ilam Pk. (DE6 2AZ) 4K 35
Ilfracombe Aquarium (EX34 9EQ) 1E 6
Imperial War Mus. Duxford (CB22 4QR) 7A 30
Imperial War Mus. London, Main Mus.
(SE1 6HZ) 113
*Imperial War Mus. North. (M17 1TZ) 8G 41*
Inchcolm Abbey (KY3 0XR) 1K 59
Inchmahome Priory (FK8 3RD) 7K 65
Ingatestone Hall (CM4 9NS) 4C 22
International Bomber Command Cen.
(LN4 2HQ) 3G 37
International Cen. for Birds of Prey
(GL18 1JJ) 1F 18
*Inveraray Castle. (PA32 8XE) 7E 64*
Inveresk Lodge Gdn. (EH21 7TE) 2M 59
Inverewe Gdn. (IV22 2LG) 5K 77
Inverlochy Castle (PH33 6TQ) 8B 70
Inverness Mus. & Art Gallery
(IV2 3EB) 110 (1G 71)
Iona (PA76 6SP) 5H 63
*Iron Bridge. (TF8 7JP) 1E 26*
Isel Hall (CA13 0QG) 8F 52
Isle of Man Steam Railway (IM1 4LL) 7C 44
Isle of Wight Steam Railway (PO33 4DS) 7C 10
Ivinghoe Beacon (LU6 2EG) 2G 21
Izaak Walton's Cottage (ST15 0PA) 7G 35

## J

Jackfield Tile Mus. (TF8 7ND) 1E 26
Jane Austen's House Mus. (GU34 1SD) 2E 10
Jarlshof Prehistoric & Norse Settlement
(ZE3 9JN) 7D 90
Jedburgh Abbey (TD8 6JQ) 8D 60
Jervaulx Abbey (HG4 4PH) 7K 47
JM Barrie's Birthplace (DD8 4BX) 2G 67
Jodrell Bank Discovery Cen. (SK11 9DL) 2F 34
Jorvik Viking Cen. (YO1 9WT) **York 117** (2D 42)

## K

Kedleston Hall (DE22 5JH) 5M 35
Keighley & Worth Valley Railway
(BD22 8NJ) 4J 41
Kelburn Castle & Country Cen.
(KA29 0BE) 4M 57
Keld Chapel (CA10 3QF) 4D 46
Kelham Island Mus. (S3 8RY) **Sheffield 116**
Kellie Castle & Gdn. (KY10 2RF) 7J 67
Kelmarsh Hall & Gdns. (NN6 9LY) 4E 28
Kelmscott Manor (GL7 3HJ) 4L 19
Kelso Abbey (TD5 7BB) 6E 60
*Kelvingrove Art Gallery & Mus. (G3 8AG) 3D 58*
Kempton Pk. Racecourse (TW16 5AE) 6J 21
*Kenilworth Castle. (CV8 1NE) 4L 27*
Kent & East Sussex Railway (TN30 6HE) 3E 12
Kentwell (CO10 9BA) 7E 30
Kenwood House (NW3 7JR) 5K 21
*Keswick Mus. & Gallery. (CA12 4NF) 3A 46*
*Kidwelly Castle. (SA17 5BQ) 6L 15*
Kielder Water & Forest Pk. (NE48 1QZ) 3L 53
Kiftsgate Court Gdns. (GL55 6LN) 7K 27
Kilchurn Castle (PA33 1AF) 5F 64
Kildrummy Castle (AB33 8RA) 4D 72
Killerton (EX5 3LE) 5J 7
Kilmartin Glen Prehistoric Sites
(PA31 8RQ) 8C 64
Kilmartin House Mus. (PA31 8RQ) 8C 64
Kinder Scout (S33 7ZJ) 1J 35
King's College Chapel
(CB2 1TN) **Cambridge 107** (6A 30)
Kingston Bagpuize House (OX13 5AX) 4B 20
Kingston Lacy (BH21 4EA) 5H 9
*Kingston Maurward Gdns. & Animal Pk.*
*(DT2 8PY) 6F 8*
Kinnersley Castle (HR3 6QF) 8B 26
Kiplin Hall (DL10 6AT) 6L 47
Kirby Hall (NN17 3EN) 2G 29
*Kirby Muxloe Castle. (LE9 2DH) 1C 28*
Kirkham Priory (YO60 7JS) 1E 42
Kirklees Light Railway (HD8 9XJ) 6L 41
Kirkstall Abbey (LS5 3EH) 4L 41
*Kirkwall Cathedral. (KW15 1JF) 8D 88*
*Knaresborough Castle. (HG5 8BB) 2M 41*
Knebworth House (SG3 6PY) 1K 21
Knightshayes (EX16 7RQ) 4J 7
Knockhill Motor Circuit (KY12 9TF) 8D 66
Knole (TN15 0RP) 8B 22
Knoll Gdns. (BH21 7ND) 5J 9
Knowsley Safari Pk. (L34 4AN) 8C 40

## L

Lacock Abbey (SN15 2LG) 7H 19
*Lady Lever Art Gallery. (CH62 5EQ) 1B 34*
The Lady of the North (NE23 8AU) 4F 54
Laing Art Gallery
(NE1 8AG) **Newcastle upon Tyne 111**
Lake District Nat. Pk. (LA9 7RL) 4B 46
Lakeside & Haverthwaite Railway
(LA12 8AL) 7B 46
Lamb House (TN31 7ES) 3F 12
Lamphey Bishop's Palace (SA71 5NT) 6G 15
Lamport Hall & Gdns. (NN6 9HD) 4E 28
Landmark Forest Adventure Pk.
(PH23 3AJ) 3K 71
Land's End (TR19 7AA) 6G 3
Lanercost Priory (CA8 2HQ) 5K 53
Langdale Pikes (LA22 9JY) 5A 46
Langley Chapel (SY5 7HU) 2D 26
Lanhydrock (PL30 5AD) 5C 4
Lappa Valley Steam Railway (TR8 5LX) 3M 3
Larmer Tree Gdns. (SP5 5PZ) 4H 9
*Laugharne Castle. (SA33 4SA) 5K 15*
*Launceston Castle. (PL15 7DR) 7C 6*
Launceston Steam Railway (PL15 8DA) 7C 6
Lauriston Castle (EH4 5QD) 2L 59
Laxey Wheel (IM4 7NL) 6D 44
Layer Marney Tower (CO5 9US) 2F 22
Leeds Castle (ME17 1PL) 8E 22
Leeds City Mus. (LS1 3AA) 110
Legoland (SL4 4AY) 6G 21
Leighton Buzzard Railway (LU7 4TN) 1G 21
Leighton Hall (LA5 9ST) 8D 46
Leiston Abbey (IP16 4TD) 5L 31
Leith Hall (AB54 4NQ) 3E 72
Leith Hill (RH5 6LX) 1J 11
Lennoxlove House (EH41 4NZ) 2C 60
Leonardslee Gdns. (RH13 6PP) 3K 11
Levant Mine & Beam Engine (TR19 7SX) 5G 3
Levens Hall (LA8 0PD) 7C 46
*Lewes Castle. (BN7 1YE) 4M 11*
*Lichfield Cathedral. (WS13 7LD) 8K 35*
Life (NE1 4EP) **Newcastle upon Tyne 111**
Lightwater Valley (HG4 3HT) 8L 47
Lilleshall Abbey (TF10 9HW) 8F 34
Lincoln Castle (LN1 3AA) 111 (2G 37)
Lincoln Cathedral (LN2 1PZ) 111 (2G 37)
Lincolnshire Road Transport Mus.
(LN6 3QT) 3G 37
Lindisfarne (TD15 2SF) 5J 61
Lindisfarne Castle (TD15 2SH) 5J 61
Lindisfarne Priory (TD15 2RX) 5J 61
Linlithgow Palace (EH49 7AL) 2J 59
Linton Zoo (CB21 4XN) 7B 30
Little Clarendon (SP3 5DZ) 2J 9
Little Malvern Court (WR14 4JN) 7F 26
Little Moreton Hall (CW12 4SD) 4G 35
*Liverpool Cathedral Church of Christ.*
*(L1 7AZ) 1B 34*
Liverpool Metropolitan RC Cathedral of Christ the
King (L3 5TQ) 111 (8B 40)
Lizard Point (TR12 7NU) 7L 3
Llanberis Lake Railway (LL55 3HB) 4E 32
Llanerchaeron (SA48 8DG) 6D 24
Llangollen Railway (LL20 7AJ) 6L 33
*Llansteffan Castle. (SA33 5JX) 5K 15*
*Llawhaden Castle. (SA67 8HL) 5G 15*
Llechwedd Slate Caverns (LL41 3NB) 6G 33
Llywernog Silver-Lead Mine (SY23 3AB) 4G 25
Lochalsh Woodland Gdn. (IV40 8DN) 3J 69
Loch Doon Castle (KA6 7QE) 2K 51
Lochleven Castle (KY13 8ET) 7E 66
Loch Lomond (G83 8PA) 8H 65
Loch Lomond & The Trossachs Nat. Pk.
(FK8 3UA) 6J 65
*Lochmaben Castle. (DG11 1JE) 3E 52*
Loch Ness Cen. & Exhibition (IV63 6TU) 2F 70
Locomotion (DL4 1PQ) 3L 47
The Lodge Nature Reserve (SG19 2DL) 7J 29
Lodge Pk. (GL54 3PP) 2K 19
Logan Botanic Gdn. (DG9 9ND) 7F 50
Logan Fish Pond & Marine Life Cen.
(DG9 9NF) 7F 50
London Dungeon (SE1 2SZ) 113
London Eye (SE1 7PB) 113
London Film Mus. (WC2E 7BN) 113
London Zoo (NW1 4RY) 112 (5K 21)
Long Cross Victorian Gdns. (PL29 3TF) 4B 4
Longleat Safari & Adventure Pk.
(BA12 7NW) 1G 9
Long Mynd (SY7 8BH) 2C 26
Longthorpe Tower (PE3 6SU) 2J 29
*Longtown Castle. (HR2 0LE) 1B 18*
*Lord Leycester Hospital & The Master's Gdn.*
*(CV34 4BH) 5L 27*
Loseley Pk. (GU3 1HS) 1G 11
The Lost Gdns. of Heligan (PL26 6EN) 7B 4
Lotherton Hall (LS25 3EB) 4B 42
Lough Neagh Discovery Cen. (BT66 6NJ) 5G 93
Loughwood Meeting House (EX13 7DU) 6A 8
*Ludgershall Castle. (SP11 9QS) 8L 19*
*Ludlow Castle. (SY8 1AY) 4D 26*
Lullingstone Castle & World Gdn.
(DA4 0JA) 7B 22
Lullingstone Roman Villa (DA4 0JA) 7B 22
Lulworth Castle & Pk. (BH20 5QS) 7G 9
Lundy Island (EX39 2LY) 1A 6
Lyddington Bede House (LE15 9LZ) 2F 28
*Lydford Castle & Saxon Town. (EX20 4BH) 7E 6*
Lydford Gorge (EX20 4BH) 7E 6
Lydiard House & Pk. (SN5 3PA) 5K 19
Lydney Pk. Gdns. (GL15 6BU) 3E 18
Lyme Pk. (SK12 2NX) 1H 35
Lytes Cary Manor (TA11 7HU) 3D 8
Lyveden New Bield (PE8 5AT) 3G 29

## M

Macclesfield Silk Mus. (SK11 6PD) 2H 35
Macduff Marine Aquarium (AB44 1SL) 7G 81
MacLellan's Castle (DG6 4JD) 6A 52
Madame Tussaud's (NW1 5LR) **London 112**
Maeshowe Chambered Cairn (KW16 3HQ) 8C 88
Magna Science Adventure Cen.
(S60 1DX) 8B 42
Maiden Castle (DT2 9PP) 7E 8
The Major Oak, Sherwood Forest Country Pk.
(NG21 9HN) 3D 36
Malham Cove (BD23 4DJ) 1G 41
Malham Tarn (BD24 9PU) 1G 41
Malleny Gdn. (EH14 7AF) 3K 59
*Malton Mus. (YO17 7LP) 8E 48*
Malvern Hills (HR8 1EN) 8F 26
Manchester Art Gallery (M2 3JL) 111
Manderston (TD11 3PP) 4F 60
Mannington Gdns. (NR11 7BB) 6H 39
*Manorbier Castle. (SA70 7SY) 7G 15*
Manx Electric Railway (IM2 4NR) 5D 44
Manx Mus. (IM1 3LY) 7C 44
Mapledurham House (RG4 7TR) 6D 20
Marble Arch Caves Global Geopark
(BT92 1EW) 7B 92
Marble Hill House (TW1 2NL) 6J 21
Markenfield Hall (HG4 3AD) 1L 41
*Mar Lodge Estate. (AB35 5YJ) 7L 71*
Martin Mere Wetland Cen. (L40 0TA) 6C 40
Marwell Wildlife (SO21 1JH) 3C 10
Marwood Hill Gdns. (EX31 4EB) 2E 6
Mary Arden's Farm (CV37 9UN) 6K 27
Mary, Queen of Scots' Visitor Cen.
(TD8 6EN) 7D 60
Mary Rose Mus. (PO1 3LJ) **Portsmouth 115**
Max Gate (DT1 2AB) 6F 8
M&D's Scotland Theme Pk. (ML1 3RT) 4F 58
The Medieval Bishop's Palace
(LN2 1PU) **Lincoln 111**
Megginch Castle Gdns. (PH2 7SW) 5F 66
Melbourne Hall & Gdns. (DE73 8EN) 7A 36
Melford Hall (CO10 9AA) 7E 30
Mellerstain House (TD3 6LG) 6D 60
*Melrose Abbey. (TD6 9LG) 6C 60*
Menai Suspension Bridge (LL59 5HH) 3E 32
Mendip Hills (BS40 7XS) 8C 18
Merriments Gdns. (TN19 7RA) 3D 12
(L3 4AQ) **Liverpool 111** (1B 34)
Mertoun Gdns. (TD6 0EA) 6D 60
Michelham Priory (BN27 3QS) 5B 12
*Middleham Castle, Middleham. (DL8 4QR) 7K 47*
Midland Railway Cen. (DE5 3QZ) 4B 36
Mid-Norfolk Railway (NR19 1DF) 1G 31
Millennium Coastal Pk. (SA15 2LG) 7L 15
Milton Manor House (OX14 4EN) 4B 20
Milton's Cottage (HP8 4JH) 4G 21
Minack Theatre (TR19 6JU) 6G 3
Minsmere (IP17 3BY) 5L 31
Minterne House & Gdns. (DT2 7AU) 5E 8
Mirehouse (CA12 4QE) 2M 45
Misarden Pk. Gdns. (GL6 7JA) 3H 19
Mr Straw's House (S81 0JG) 1C 36
Mistley Towers (CO11 1ET) 8H 31
Mompesson House
(SP1 2EL) **Salisbury 115** (3K 9)
Monk Bretton Priory (S71 5QE) 7A 42
Monkey Forest at Trentham (ST4 8AY) 6G 35
Monkey Sanctuary (PL13 1NZ) 6E 4
Monkey World (BH20 6HH) 7G 9
Monk's House (BN7 3HF) 5M 11
Montacute House (TA15 6XP) 4C 8
Monteviot House (TD8 6UH) 7D 60
*Montgomery Castle. (SY15 6HN) 3M 25*
*Moreton Corbet Castle. (SY4 4DW) 7D 34*
Morwellham Quay (PL19 8JL) 5G 5
*Moseley Old Hall. (WV10 7HY) 1H 27*
Mother Shipton's Cave (HG5 8DD) 2M 41
Mottisfont (SO51 0LP) 3M 9
Mount Edgcumbe House (PL10 1HZ) 6G 5
Mount Ephraim Gdns. (ME13 9TX) 7G 23
Mountfitchet Castle (CM24 8SP) 1B 22
Mount Grace Priory (DL6 3JG) 6B 48
Mount Stewart House & Gdns. (BT22 2AD) 5J 93
*Mount Stuart. (PA20 9LR) 4L 57*
Muchelney Abbey (TA10 0DQ) 3C 8
Muchelney Priest's House (TA10 0DQ) 3C 8
Mull of Kintyre (PA28 6RU) 1A 50
Muncaster Castle (CA18 1RQ) 5L 45
Murlough Nat. Nature Reserve (BT33 0NQ) 7J 93
Mus. of Army Flying (SO20 8DY) 2M 9
Mus. of East Anglian Life (IP14 1DL) 6G 31
*Mus. of Lakeland Life & Industry. (LA9 5AL) 6D 46*
Mus. of Lincolnshire Life
(LN1 3LY) **Lincoln 111** (2G 37)
Mus. of London (EC2Y 5HN) 113
Mus. of Royal Worcester
(WR1 2ND) 117 (6G 27)
Mus. of Scottish Lighthouses
(AB43 9DU) 7J 81
Mus. of The Gorge (TF8 7NH) 1E 26
Mus. of the Isles (IV45 8RS) 5H 69
Mus. of the Jewellery Quarter
(B18 6HA) **Birmingham 106**

## N

National Botanic Gdn. of Wales
(SA32 8HG) 5M 15
National Coal Mining Mus. for England
(WF4 4RH) 6L 41
National Coracle Cen. (SA38 9JL) 2J 15
National Exhibition Cen. (NEC) (B40 1NT) 3K 27
National Football Mus.
(M4 3BG) **Manchester 111**
The National Forest (DE12 6HZ) 8M 35
National Gallery (WC2N 5DN) **London 113**
National Glass Cen. (SR6 0GL) 6H 55
National Heritage Cen. for Horseracing & Sporting
Art (CB8 8JL) 5C 30
National Marine Aquarium
(PL4 0LF) **Plymouth 115**
*National Maritime Mus. (SE10 9NF) 6L 21*
*National Maritime Mus. Cornwall.*
*(TR11 3QY) 5M 3*
National Memorial Arboretum (DE13 7AR) 8K 35
National Mining Mus. Scotland
(EH22 4QN) 3M 59
National Motorcycle Mus. (B92 0EJ) 3L 27
The National Motor Mus. (SO42 7ZN) 5A 10
National Mus. Cardiff
(CF10 3NP) 107 (7L 17)
National Mus. of Flight (EH39 5LF) 2C 60
National Mus. of Rural Life Scotland
(G76 9HR) 4E 58
National Mus. of Scotland
(EH1 1JF) **Edinburgh 109** (2L 59)
National Mus. of the Royal Navy
(PO1 3NH) **Portsmouth 115**
National Portrait Gallery
(WC2H 0HE) **London 113**
National Railway Mus., York
(YO26 4XJ) 117 (2C 42)
*National Roman Legion Mus. (NP18 1AE) 4B 18*
National Science & Media Mus.
(BD1 1NQ) **Bradford 106** (4K 41)
National Sea Life Cen.
(B1 2HL) **Birmingham 106**
National Showcaves Cen. for Wales
(SA9 1GJ) 3H 17
National Slate Mus. (LL55 4TY) 4E 32
National Space Cen. (LE4 5NS) 1C 28
National Waterfront Mus.
(SA1 3RD) **Swansea 117** (5F 16)
National Waterways Mus. (CH65 4FW) 2C 34
National Wool Mus. (SA44 5UP) 3K 15
Natural History Mus., London (SW7 5BD) 112
Natural History Mus. at Tring
(HP23 6AP) 2G 21
Neath Abbey (SA10 7DW) 5G 17
The Needles (PO39 0JH) 7L 9
Nene Valley Railway (PE8 6LR) 2J 29
Ness Botanic Gdns. (CH64 4AY) 2B 34
Nessieland (IV63 6TU) 2F 70
Nether Winchendon House (HP18 0DY) 2E 20
Netley Abbey (SO31 5HB) 5B 10
New Abbey Corn Mill (DG2 8DX) 5D 52
Newark Air Mus. (NG24 2NY) 4F 36
Newark Castle, Port Glasgow (PA14 5NG) 2B 58
*Newark Castle, Newark-on-Trent.*
*(NG24 1BN) 4E 36*
Newark Pk. (GL12 7PZ) 4F 18
*The New Art Gallery Walsall. (WS2 8LG) 2J 27*
Newburgh Priory (YO61 4AS) 8C 48
Newbury Racecourse (RG14 7NZ) 7B 20
Newby Hall & Gdns. (HG4 5AE) 1A 42
*Newcastle Castle, Bridgend. (CF31 4JW) 6H 17*
Newcastle Upon Tyne Castle Keep (NE1 1RQ) 111
New Forest Nat. Pk. (SO43 7BD) 4L 9
New Lanark World Heritage Site
(ML11 9DB) 5G 59
*Newmarket Racecourse. (CB8 0TG) 5C 30*
*Newquay Zoo. (TR7 2LZ) 2M 3*
Newstead Abbey (NG15 8NA) 4C 36
Nine Ladies Stone Circle (DE4 2LF) 3L 35
Norfolk Broads Nat. Pk. (NR3 1BJ) 1L 31
Norfolk Lavender (PE31 7JE) 6C 38
*Norham Castle. (TD15 2LL) 5G 61*
Normanby Hall Mus. (DN15 9HU) 6F 42
North Downs (GU10 5QE) 8J 21
North Norfolk Railway (NR26 8RA) 5H 39
Northumberlandia, the Lady of the North
(NE23 8AU) 4F 54
Northumberland Nat. Pk. (NE46 1BS) 2B 54
North York Moors Nat. Pk. (YO18 8RN) 6D 48
North Yorkshire Moors Railway (YO18 7AJ) 7F 48
Norton Conyers (HG4 5EQ) 8M 47
Norton Priory Mus. & Gdns.
(WA7 1SX) 1D 34
(NR1 3JU) 114 (1J 31)
Norwich Cathedral (NR1 4DH) 114 (1J 31)
Nostell Priory (WF4 1QE) 6B 42
Nuffield Place (RG9 5RX) 5D 20
*Nunney Castle. (BA11 4LN) 1F 9*
Nunnington Hall (YO62 5UY) 8D 48
Nymans (RH17 6EB) 3K 11

## O

Oakham Castle (LE15 6DR) 1F 28
*Oakwell Hall. (WF17 9LG) 5L 41*
Oakwood Theme Pk. (SA67 8DE) 5G 15
The Observatory Science Cen. (BN27 1RN) 4C 12
Oceanarium (BH2 5AA) **Bournemouth 106**
Offa's Dyke, Brockweir (NP16 7NQ) 3D 18
*Okehampton Castle. (EX20 1JA) 6E 6*
Old Beaupre Castle (CF71 7LT) 7K 17
Old Gorhambury House (AL3 6AH) 3J 21
Old Oswestry Hill Fort (SY10 7AA) 6A 34
Old Sarum (SP1 3SD) 2K 9
Old Wardour Castle (SP3 6RR) 3H 9
Old Winchester Hill Hill Fort (GU32 1HN) 3D 10
*Orford Castle & Mus. (IP12 2NF) 7L 31*
Orford Ness (IP12 2NU) 7L 31
Ormesby Hall (TS7 9AS) 4C 48
Osborne House (PO32 6JX) 6C 10
*Osterley Pk. & House. (TW7 4RB) 6J 21*
Oulton Pk. Circuit (CW6 9BW) 3D 34
Overbeck's (TQ8 8LW) 8K 5
Owletts (DA12 3AP) 7C 22
Oxburgh Hall (PE33 9PS) 1D 30
Oxford Christ Church Cathedral
(OX1 4JF) 114 (3C 20)
Oxford Island Nat. Nature Reserve
(BT66 6NJ) 5G 93
*Oxwich Castle. (SA3 1LU) 8L 15*
Oystermouth Castle (SA3 5TA) 6F 16

## P

Packwood House (B94 6AT) 4K 27
Paignton Zoo (TQ4 7EU) 6L 5
Painshill Pk. (KT11 1JE) 8H 21
Painswick Rococo Gdn. (GL6 6TH) 2G 19
Palace of Holyroodhouse
(EH8 8DX) **Edinburgh 109** (2L 59)
Papplewick Pumping Station (NG15 9AJ) 4C 36
Paradise Pk. Wildlife Sanctuary (TR27 4HB) 5J 3
Paradise Wildlife Pk. (EN10 7QZ) 3L 21
Parcevall Hall Gdns. (BD23 6DE) 1J 41
Parham (RH20 4HS) 4H 11
Pashley Manor Gdns. (TN5 7HE) 3D 12
Patterson's Spade Mill (BT39 0AP) 4H 93
Paultons Pk. (SO51 6AL) 4M 9
*Paxton House. (TD15 1SZ) 4G 61*
Paycocke's House & Gdn. (CO6 1NS) 1E 22
Peak Cavern (S33 8WS) 1K 35
Peak District Nat. Pk. (DE45 1AE) 1K 35
Peak Rail (DE4 3NA) 3L 35
Peckover House & Gdn. (PE13 1JR) 1A 30
*Peel Castle. (IM5 1AB) 6B 44*
*Pembroke Castle. (SA71 4LA) 6F 14*
Pembrokeshire Coast Nat. Pk. (SA41 3XD) 6E 14
Pencarrow (PL30 3AG) 4C 4
Pendennis Castle (TR11 4LP) 5M 3
Penrhyn Castle (LL57 4HN) 3F 32
*Penrith Castle. (CA11 7JB) 3D 46*
Penshurst Place & Gdns. (TN11 8DG) 1B 12
Peover Hall (WA16 9HW) 2F 34
Perth Mus. & Art Gallery (PH1 5LB) 115
Peterborough St Peter's Cathedral
(PE1 1XZ) 115 (2J 29)
Petworth House & Pk. (GU28 0AE) 3G 11
*Pevensey Castle. (BN24 5LE) 5C 12*
Peveril Castle (S33 8WQ) 1K 35
Pickering Castle (YO18 7AX) 7F 48
Picton Castle (SA62 4AS) 5G 15
Piel Castle (LA13 0QN) 8M 45
Pistyll Rhaeadr (SY10 0BZ) 8K 33
Pitmedden Gdn. (AB41 7PD) 3H 73
Pitt Rivers Mus. (OX1 3PP) **Oxford 114** (3C 20)
Plantasia, Swansea (SA1 2AL) 117
Plas Brondanw Gdns. (LL48 6SW) 6F 32
Plas Newydd, Llangollen (LL20 8AW) 6M 33
Plas Newydd, Llanfair Pwllgwyngyll
(LL61 6DQ) 4E 32
Plas yn Rhiw (LL53 8AB) 8B 32
Pleasurewood Hills (NR32 5DZ) 2M 31
Poldark Mine (TR13 0ES) 5K 3
Polesden Lacey (RH5 6BD) 8J 21
Pollok House (G43 1AT) 3D 58
Pontcysyllte Aqueduct (LL20 7YS) 5A 34
*Portchester Castle. (PO16 9QW) 5D 10*
Portland Castle (DT5 1AZ) 8E 8
Port Lympne Reserve (CT21 4PD) 2H 13
Portsmouth Historic Dockyard
(PO1 3LJ) 115 (5D 10)
The Potteries Mus. & Art Gallery (ST1 3DW) 116
*Powderham Castle. (EX6 8JQ) 7J 7*
Powis Castle & Gdn. (SY21 8RF) 2M 25
The Prebendal Manor House (PE8 6QG) 2H 29
Prestongrange Mus. (EH32 9RX) 2A 60
*Preston Manor. (BN1 6SD) 5L 11*
Preston Mill & Phantassie Doocot
(EH40 3DS) 2C 60
Preston Tower, Prestonpans (EH32 9NN) 2A 60
Preston Tower, Chathill (NE67 5DH) 7J 61
Prideaux Place (PL28 8RP) 4B 4
Principality Stadium (CF10 1NS) **Cardiff 107**
Prior Pk. Landscape Gdn. (BA2 5AH) 7F 18
Provan Hall (G34 9NJ) 3E 58
Prudhoe Castle (NE42 6NA) 5D 54

## Q

Quantock Hills (TA4 4AP) 2L 7
Quarry Bank Mill (SK9 4LA) 1G 35
Quebec House (TN16 1TD) 8M 21
Queen Elizabeth Country Pk. (PO8 0QE) 4E 10
Queen Elizabeth Forest Pk. (FK8 3UZ) 8J 65
Queen Elizabeth Olympic Pk. (E20 2ST) 5L 21
Quex House & Gdns. (CT7 0BH) 7K 23

## R

Raby Castle (DL2 3AH) 3K 47
RAF Holmpton (HU19 2RG) 5L 43
RAF Mus. Cosford (TF11 8UP) 1F 26
RAF Mus. London (NW9 5LL) 4K 21
Raglan Castle (NP15 2BT) 3C 18
Ragley (B49 5NJ) 6J 27
Ramsey Island (SA62 6SA) 4C 14
Ravenglass & Eskdale Railway
(CA18 1SW) 5L 45
Raveningham Gdns. (NR14 6NS) 2K 31
Ravenscraig Castle (KY1 2AZ) 8F 66
Reculver Towers (CT6 6SX) 7J 23
Red House (DA6 8JF) 6A 22

Renishaw Hall & Gdns. (S21 3WB) ... 2B **36**
Restoration House, Rochester (ME1 1RF) ... **Medway Towns 111**
Restormel Castle (PL22 0HN) ... 5D **4**
Revolution House (S41 9LA) ... 2A **36**
Rheged Cen. (CA11 0DQ) ... 3C **46**
Rheidol Power Station (SY23 3NF) ... 5G **25**
Rhossili Bay (SA3 1PR) ... 8L **15**
RHS Gdn. Harlow Carr (HG3 1QB) ... 2L **41**
RHS Gdn. Hyde Hall (CM3 8ET) ... 4D **22**
RHS Gdn. Rosemoor (EX38 8PH) ... 4E **6**
RHS Gdn. Wisley (GU23 6QB) ... 8H **21**
*Rhuddlan Castle. (LL18 5AD)* ... 3K ***33***
Ribchester Roman Mus. (PR3 3XS) ... 4E **40**
*Richmond Castle. (DL10 4QW)* ... 5K ***47***
Rievaulx Abbey (YO62 5LB) ... 7C **48**
Rievaulx Terrace (YO62 5LJ) ... 7C **48**
Ripley Castle (HG3 3AY) ... 1L **41**
*Ripon Cathedral. (HG4 1QT)* ... 8M ***47***
River & Rowing Mus. (RG9 1BF) ... 5E **20**
*Riverside Mus., Mus. of Transport & Travel. (G3 8RS)* ... 3D ***58***
Robert Burns Birthplace Mus. (KA7 4PY) ... 8B **58**
Robert Burns House (DG1 2PS) ... **Dumfries 108** (4D **52**)
Roche Abbey (S66 8NW) ... 1C **36**
Rochester Castle (ME1 1SW) ... **Medway Towns 111** (7D **22**)
Rochester Cathedral (ME1 1SX) ... **Medway Towns 111** (7D **22**)
Rockbourne Roman Villa (SP6 3PG) ... 4K **9**
Rockingham Castle (LE16 8TH) ... 2F **28**
Rockingham Motor Speedway (NN17 5AF) ... 2G **29**
Rocks by Rail (LE15 7BX) ... 8F **36**
Rode Hall & Gdns. (ST7 3QP) ... 4G **35**
Rodmarton Manor (GL7 6PF) ... 4H **19**
Rokeby Pk. (DL12 9RZ) ... 4J **47**
Rollright Stones (OX7 5QB) ... 8L **27**
Roman Army Mus. (CA8 7JB) ... 5L **53**
Roman Baths (BA1 1LZ) ... **Bath 106** (7F **18**)
The Roman Painted House (CT17 9AJ) ... **Dover 108**
Roman Vindolanda (NE47 7JN) ... 5A **54**
Romney, Hythe & Dymchurch Railway (TN28 8PL) ... 3G **13**
Roseberry Topping (TS9 6QX) ... 4C **48**
*Rothesay Castle. (PA20 0DA)* ... 3K ***57***
Rothiemurchus Cen. (PH22 1QH) ... 4K **71**
Rousham House & Gdns. (OX25 4QX) ... 1B **20**
Rowallane Gdn. (BT24 7JA) ... 6J **93**
Royal Academy of Arts (Burlington House) (W1J 0BD) ... **London 113**
*Royal Albert Bridge. (PL12 4GT)* ... 6G ***5***
The Royal Armouries Mus. (LS10 1LT) ... **Leeds 110**
Royal Botanic Gdn. (EH3 5LR) ... 2L **59**
Royal Botanic Gdns., Kew (TW9 3AB) ... 6J **21**
Royal Cornwall Mus. (TR1 2SJ) ... 4M **3**
Royal Crown Derby Mus. (DE23 8JZ) ... **108** (6A **36**)
Royal Mint Mus. (CF72 8YT) ... 6K **17**
Royal Navy Submarine Mus. (PO12 2AS) ... 6D **10**
Royal Pavilion (BN1 1EE) ... **Brighton & Hove 106** (5L **11**)
Royal Pump Room Mus. (HG1 2RY) ... **Harrogate 110** (2L **41**)
Royal Yacht Britannia (EH6 6JJ) ... 2L **59**
Ruddington Framework Knitters Mus. (NG11 6HE) ... 6C **36**
Rufford Abbey (NG22 9DF) ... 3D **36**
Rufford Old Hall (L40 1SG) ... 6C **40**
Rufus Stone (SO43 7HN) ... 4L **9**
Rushton Triangular Lodge (NN14 1RP) ... 3F **28**
Russell-Cotes Art Gallery & Mus. (BH1 3AA) ... **Bournemouth 106** (6J **9**)
Rutland County Mus. (LE15 6HW) ... 1F **28**
Rydal Mount & Gdns. (LA22 9LU) ... 5B **46**
Ryedale Folk Mus. (YO62 6UA) ... 6E **48**
Ryton Gdns. (CV8 3LG) ... 4B **28**


## S


Saatchi Gallery (SW3 4RY) ... **London 112**
Sainsbury Cen. for Visual Arts (NR4 7TJ) ... 1H **31**
St Abb's Head (TD14 5QF) ... 3G **61**
*St Albans Cathedral. (AL1 1BY)* ... 3J ***21***
St Andrews Aquarium (KY16 9AS) ... 6J **67**
*St Andrews Cathedral. (KY16 9QL)* ... 6J ***67***
St Augustine's Abbey, Canterbury (CT1 1PF) ... **107** (8H **23**)
*St Columbs Cathedral, Londonderry. (BT48 6RQ)* ... 3D ***92***
*St David's Cathedral. (SA62 6RD)* ... 4D ***14***
St Dogmaels Abbey (SA43 3JH) ... 2H **15**
St Edmunds Abbey, Bury St Edmunds (IP33 1RS) ... 5E **30**
St Fagans National Mus. of History (CF5 6XB) ... 7L **17**
St John's Jerusalem (DA4 9HQ) ... 6B **22**
St Mary's House & Gdns. (BN44 3WE) ... 4J **11**
St Mawes Castle (TR2 5DE) ... 5M **3**
St Michael's Mount (TR17 0HS) ... 6J **3**
The St Patrick Cen. (BT30 6LZ) ... 6J **93**
*St Patrick's Cathedral, Armagh. (BT61 7QX)* ... 6F ***93***
St Paul's Cathedral (EC4M 8AE) ... **London 113**
Salford Mus. & Art Gallery (M5 4WU) ... **Manchester 111** (8G **41**)
Salisbury Cathedral (SP1 2EG) ... **115** (3K **9**)
*Saltaire World Heritage Village. (BD18 4PL)* ... 4K ***41***
Saltram (PL7 1UH) ... 6H **5**
Samlesbury Hall (PR5 0UP) ... 4E **40**
Sandford Orcas Manor House (DT9 4SB) ... 3E **8**
Sandham Memorial Chapel (RG20 9JT) ... 7B **20**
Sandown Pk. Racecourse (KT10 9AJ) ... 7J **21**
Sandringham (PE35 6EP) ... 7C **38**
Sandwich Wildlife Pk. (CT13 0DD) ... 8K **23**
Sarehole Mill (B13 0BD) ... 3J **27**
The Savill Gdn. (SL4 2HT) ... 6G **21**
Sawley Abbey (BB7 4LE) ... 3F **40**
Saxtead Green Post Mill (IP13 9QQ) ... 5J **31**
Scafell Pike (CA20 1EX) ... 4M **45**
Scampston Hall (YO17 8NG) ... 8F **48**
*Scarborough Castle. (YO11 1HY)* ... 7H ***49***
Science & Industry Mus. (M3 4FP) ... **Manchester 111**
Science Mus. (SW7 2DD) ... **London 112**
Scone Palace (PH2 6BD) ... 5E **66**
Scotch Whisky Experience (EH1 2NE) ... **Edinburgh 109**
Scotney Castle (TN3 8JN) ... 2C **12**
Scotstarvit Tower (KY15 5PA) ... 6G **67**
Scottish Deer Cen. (KY15 4NQ) ... 6G **67**
Scottish Exhibition & Conference Cen. (G3 8YW) ... **Glasgow 109**
Scottish Fisheries Mus. (KY10 3AB) ... 7J **67**
Scottish Industrial Railway Cen. (KA6 7JF) ... 1K **51**
Scottish Maritime Mus. (KA12 8QE) ... 6B **58**
Scottish National Gallery (EH2 2EL) ... **Edinburgh 109**
*Scottish National Gallery of Modern Art. (EH4 3DR)* ... 2L ***59***
Scottish National Portrait Gallery (EH2 1JD) ... **Edinburgh 109**
Scottish Parliament (EH99 1SP) ... **Edinburgh 109**
Scottish Sea Life Sanctuary (PA37 1SE) ... 3D **64**
Sea Life, Blackpool (FY1 5AA) ... **106**
Sea Life, Brighton (BN2 1TB) ... **Brighton & Hove 106** (5L **11**)
Sea Life, Great Yarmouth (NR30 3AH) ... 1M **31**
Sea Life, Loch Lomond (Glasgow) (G83 8QL) ... 1B **58**
Sea Life, London (SE1 7PB) ... **113**
Sea Life, Scarborough (YO12 6RP) ... 6H **49**
Sea Life, Southend-on-Sea (SS1 2ER) ... 5E **22**
Sea Life, Weymouth (DT4 7SX) ... 7E **8**
SeaQuarium, Rhyl (LL18 3AF) ... 2K **33**
SeaQuarium, Weston (BS23 1BE) ... 7B **18**
Seaton Delaval Hall (NE26 4QR) ... 4G **55**
Seaton Tramway (EX12 2NQ) ... 6A **8**
Selby Abbey (YO8 4PF) ... 4D **42**
Selly Manor (B30 2AD) ... 3J **27**
Severn Bridge (BS35 4BL) ... 4D **18**
Severn Valley Railway (DY12 1BE) ... 3F **26**
Sewerby Hall & Gdns. (YO15 1EA) ... 1K **43**
Sezincote (GL56 9AW) ... 8K **27**
Shaftesbury Abbey Mus. & Gdns. (SP7 8JR) ... 3G **9**
Shakespeare's Birthplace (CV37 6QW) ... **Stratford 116**
Shandy Hall (YO61 4AD) ... 8C **48**
Shap Abbey (CA10 3NB) ... 4D **46**
Shaw's Corner (AL6 9BX) ... 2J **21**
Sheffield Pk. & Gdn. (TN22 3QX) ... 3M **11**
Shepreth Wildlife Pk. (SG8 6PZ) ... 7L **29**
Sherborne Castle (DT9 5NR) ... 4E **8**
Sherborne Old Castle (DT9 3SA) ... 4E **8**
Sherwood Forest (NG21 9HN) ... 4C **36**
*Shibden Hall. (HX3 6XG)* ... 5K ***41***
Shipton Hall (TF13 6JZ) ... 2D **26**
Shoe Mus. (BA16 0EQ) ... 2C **8**
Shrewsbury Castle (SY1 2AT) ... **116** (8C **34**)
Shugborough (ST17 0XB) ... 7H **35**
Shute Barton (EX13 7PT) ... 6A **8**
The Shuttleworth Collection (SG18 9EP) ... 7J **29**
Silbury Hill (SN8 1QH) ... 7K **19**
Silverstone Circuit (NN12 8TN) ... 7D **28**
Sir Harold Hillier Gdns. (SO51 0QA) ... 3A **10**
Sir Walter Scott's Courtroom (TD7 4BT) ... 7B **60**
Sissinghurst Castle Gdn. (TN17 2AB) ... 2E **12**
Sizergh Castle & Gdn. (LA8 8AE) ... 7C **46**
Skara Brae Prehistoric Village (KW16 3LR) ... 8B **88**
*Skenfrith Castle. (NP7 8UH)* ... 1C ***18***
Skiddaw (CA12 4QE) ... 3A **46**
Skipness Castle (PA29 6XU) ... 4J **57**
*Skipton Castle. (BD23 1AW)* ... 2H ***41***
Skokholm Island (SA62 3BL) ... 6D **14**
Skomer Island (SA62 3BL) ... 6D **14**
Sledmere House (YO25 3XG) ... 1G **43**
*Slimbridge Wetland Cen. (GL2 7BT)* ... 3F ***18***
Smailholm Tower (TD5 7PG) ... 6D **60**
Smallhythe Place (TN30 7NG) ... 3F **12**
Snaefell Mountain Railway (IM4 7NL) ... 6D **44**
Snowdonia Nat. Pk. (LL48 6LF) ... 7G **33**
Snowdon Mountain Railway (LL55 4TY) ... 5F **32**
Snowdon Summit (LL55 4UL) ... 5F **32**
Snowshill Manor & Gdn. (WR12 7JU) ... 8J **27**
Somerleyton Hall (NR32 5QQ) ... 2L **31**
Somerset Heritage Cen. (TA2 6SF) ... 3M **7**
Souter Lighthouse (SR6 7NH) ... 5H **55**
South Devon Railway (TQ11 0DZ) ... 5K **5**
South Downs Nat. Pk. (GU29 9SB) ... 5K **11**
South Tynedale Railway (CA9 3JB) ... 7M **53**
Southwell Minster (NG25 0HD) ... 4E **36**
Spa Valley Railway (TN2 5QY) ... 2B **12**
Speedwell Cavern (S33 8WA) ... 1K **35**
Speke Hall Gdn. & Estate (L24 1XD) ... 1C **34**
Spetchley Pk. Gdns. (WR5 1RR) ... 6G **27**
Spinnaker Tower (PO1 3TN) ... **Portsmouth 115** (6D **10**)
Spinners Gdn. (SO41 5QE) ... 6M **9**
Spofforth Castle (HG3 1DA) ... 2A **42**
Springhill (BT45 7NQ) ... 4F **93**
Sprivers Gdn. (TN12 8DR) ... 1C **12**
Spurn Head (HU12 0UG) ... 6M **43**
Spynie Palace (IV30 5QG) ... 7B **80**
Squerryes (TN16 1SJ) ... 8M **21**
*Stafford Castle. (ST16 1DJ)* ... 7H ***35***
Stagshaw Gdns. (LA22 0HE) ... 5B **46**
Stanage Edge (S33 0AD) ... 1L **35**
Standen (RH19 4NE) ... 2L **11**
Stanford Hall (LE17 6DH) ... 4C **28**
Stansted Pk. (PO9 6DX) ... 5E **10**
Stanway House & Fountain (GL54 5PQ) ... 8J **27**
Staunton Harold Church (LE65 1RT) ... 7A **36**
STEAM Mus. of the Great Western Railway (SN2 2EY) ... 5K **19**
Stirling Castle (FK8 1EJ) ... **116** (8A **66**)
Stoke Pk. Pavilions (NN12 7RZ) ... 7E **28**
*Stokesay Castle. (SY7 9AH)* ... 3C ***26***
Stoke-sub-Hamdon Priory (TA14 6QP) ... 4C **8**
Stoneacre (ME15 8RS) ... 8E **22**
Stonehenge (SP4 7DE) ... 1K **9**
Stoneleigh Abbey (CV8 2LF) ... 4M **27**
Stonor (RG9 6HF) ... 5E **20**
Stott Pk. Bobbin Mill (LA12 8AX) ... 7B **46**
Stourhead (BA12 6QD) ... 2F **8**
Stowe House (MK18 5EH) ... 8D **28**
Stowe Landscape Gdns. (MK18 5EH) ... 8D **28**
Strata Florida Abbey (SY25 6BJ) ... 6G **25**
Stratfield Saye House (RG7 2BZ) ... 7D **20**
*Strathaven Castle. (ML10 6QS)* ... 5F ***58***
Strathspey Railway (PH22 1PY) ... 4K **71**
Strawberry Hill (TW1 4ST) ... 6J **21**
Strome Castle (IV54 8YJ) ... 2K **69**
Sudbury Hall (DE6 5HT) ... 6K **35**
Sudeley Castle (GL54 5JD) ... 1J **19**
Sufton Court (HR1 4LU) ... 8D **26**
Sulgrave Manor (OX17 2SD) ... 7C **28**
Summerlee Mus. of Scottish Industrial Life (ML5 1QD) ... 3F **58**
Sundown Adventureland (DN22 0HX) ... 2E **36**
Sutton Hoo (IP12 3DJ) ... 7J **31**
Sutton Pk. (YO61 1DP) ... 1C **42**
Sutton Scarsdale Hall (S44 5UT) ... 3B **36**
*Sutton Valence Castle. (ME17 3DA)* ... 1E ***12***
Swaledale Mus. (DL11 6QT) ... 6J **47**
Swallow Falls (LL24 0DH) ... 5G **33**
Swansea RC Cathedral (SA1 2BX) ... **117** (5F **16**)
Sweetheart Abbey (DG2 8BU) ... 5D **52**
Swindon & Cricklade Railway (SN25 2DA) ... 4K **19**


## T


The Swiss Gdn. (SG18 9ER) ... 7J **29**
Syon Pk. (TW8 8JF) ... 6J **21**
Tabley House (WA16 0HB) ... 2F **34**
Talley Abbey (SA19 7AX) ... 1F **16**
Talyllyn Railway (LL36 9EY) ... 2F **24**
*Tamworth Castle. (B79 7NA)* ... 1L ***27***
Tank Mus. (BH20 6JG) ... 7G **9**
Tantallon Castle (EH39 5PN) ... 1C **60**
Tarn Hows (LA22 0PR) ... 6B **46**
Tar Tunnel (TF8 7HS) ... 1E **26**
Tate Britain (SW1P 4RG) ... **London 113**
Tate Liverpool (L3 4BB) ... **111** (1B **34**)
Tate Modern (SE1 9TG) ... **London 113**
Tate St Ives (TR26 1TG) ... 4J **3**
Tattershall Castle (LN4 4NR) ... 4K **37**
Tatton Pk. (WA16 6QN) ... 1F **34**
Tay Forest Pk. (PH17 2QG) ... 2K **65**
Teifi Valley Railway (SA44 5TD) ... 2K **15**
Temple Newsam House (LS15 0AE) ... 4A **42**
*Tenby Castle. (SA70 7BP)* ... 6H ***15***
Thames Barrier (SE18 5NJ) ... 6M **21**
Thetford Forest Pk. (IP26 5DB) ... 2E **30**
Thetford Priory (IP24 1AZ) ... 3E **30**
Thirlestane Castle (TD2 6RU) ... 5C **60**
Thoresby Gallery (NG22 9EP) ... 2D **36**
Thornham Walled Gdn. (IP23 8HH) ... 4H **31**
Thornton Abbey & Gatehouse (DN39 6TU) ... 6J **43**
Thorpe Pk. (KT16 8PN) ... 7H **21**
Thorp Perrow Arboretum (DL8 2PR) ... 7L **47**
Threave Castle (DG7 2AB) ... 5B **52**
Threave Gdn. (DG7 1RX) ... 5B **52**
Thrigby Hall Wildlife Gdns. (NR29 3DR) ... 8L **39**
Thruxton Circuit (SP11 8PW) ... 1L **9**
Thursford Collection (NR21 0AS) ... 6F **38**
Tilbury Fort (RM18 7NR) ... 6C **22**
Tintagel Castle (PL34 0HE) ... 3C **4**
*Tintagel Visitor Cen. (PL34 0AJ)* ... 3C ***4***
Tintern Abbey (NP16 6SH) ... 3D **18**
Tintinhull Gdn. (BA22 8QL) ... 3D **8**
Titanic Belfast (BT3 9EP) ... 5H **93**
Titchfield Abbey (PO15 5RA) ... 5C **10**
*Tiverton Castle. (EX16 6RP)* ... 4J ***7***
Tolpuddle Martyrs Mus. (DT2 7EH) ... 6F **8**
Tolquhon Castle (AB41 7LP) ... 3H **73**
Torridon Countryside Cen. (IV22 2EW) ... 8L **77**
*Totnes Castle. (TQ9 5NU)* ... 5L ***5***
Tower Bridge (SE1 2UP) ... **London 113**
The Tower of London (EC3N 4AB) ... **113**
Towneley Hall (Art Gallery & Mus.) (BB11 3RQ) ... 4G **41**
Townend (LA23 1LB) ... 5C **46**
Traquair House (EH44 6PW) ... 6M **59**
Treasurer's House, Martock (TA12 6JL) ... 4C **8**
Treasurer's House, York (YO1 7JL) ... **117**
Trebah Gdn. (TR11 5JZ) ... 6L **3**
Tredegar House (NP10 8YW) ... 5A **18**
Tregrehan Gdn. (PL24 2SJ) ... 6C **4**
Trelissick Gdn. (TR3 6QL) ... 5M **3**
Trengwainton Gdn. (TR20 8RZ) ... 5H **3**
Trentham Gdns. (ST4 8NF) ... 5G **35**
Trerice (TR8 4PG) ... 3M **3**
Tresco Abbey Gdns. (TR24 0QQ) ... 1G **3**
*Tretower Castle. (NP8 1RF)* ... 2L ***17***
Trewithen (TR2 4DD) ... 7B **4**
Tropical Birdland (LE9 9GN) ... 1B **28**
The Trossachs (FK17 8HZ) ... 7K **65**
Tudor Merchant's House (SA70 7BX) ... 6H **15**
Tudor World (CV37 6EE) ... **Stratford 116**
Turner Contemporary (CT9 1HG) ... 6K **23**
Turton Tower (BL7 0HG) ... 6F **40**
*Tutbury Castle. (DE13 9JF)* ... 7L ***35***
Twycross Zoo (CV9 3PX) ... 1M **27**
Ty Mawr Wybrnant (LL25 0HJ) ... 5G **33**
*Tynemouth Castle. (NE30 4BZ)* ... 5G ***55***
Tyntesfield (BS48 1NT) ... 6D **18**


## U


Uffington White Horse (SN7 7QJ) ... 5M **19**
Ugbrooke (TQ13 0AD) ... 8H **7**
Ulster American Folk Pk. (BT78 5QU) ... 5D **92**
Ulster Folk & Transport Mus. (BT18 0EU) ... 4J **93**
Ulster Mus. (BT9 5AB) ... 5H **93**
Upnor Castle (ME2 4XG) ... 6D **22**
Uppark (GU31 5QR) ... 4E **10**
Upton Castle Gdns. (SA72 4SE) ... 6G **15**
Upton House & Gdns. (OX15 6HT) ... 7A **28**
Urquhart Castle (IV63 6XJ) ... 3F **70**
Usher Gallery (LN2 1NN) ... **Lincoln 111**
*Usk Castle. (NP15 1SD)* ... 3B ***18***
Vale of Rheidol Railway (SY23 1PG) ... 5F **24**


## V


Valle Crucis Abbey (LL20 8DT) ... 6M **33**
The Valley Gdns. (SL4 2HT) ... 7G **21**
V&A Mus. of Design, Dundee (DD1 4QB) ... **108** (5H **67**)
Veddw House Gdn. (NP16 6PH) ... 4C **18**
*Verulamium Mus. (AL3 4SW)* ... 3J ***21***
Victoria & Albert Mus. (SW7 2RL) ... **London 112**
The Vyne (RG24 9HL) ... 8D **20**


## W


W5 Discovery Cen. (BT3 9QQ) ... 5H **93**
Waddesdon Manor (HP18 0JH) ... 2E **20**
Wakehurst Place (RH17 6TN) ... 2L **11**
Walker Art Gallery (L3 8EL) ... **Liverpool 111** (8B **40**)
Wallington (NE61 4AR) ... 3D **54**
Walmer Castle & Gdns. (CT14 7LJ) ... 1K **13**
Walsingham Abbey (NR22 6BL) ... 6F **38**
*Warkworth Castle. (NE65 0UJ)* ... 1F ***54***
*Warwick Castle. (CV34 4QX)* ... 5L ***27***
*Washington Old Hall. (NE38 7LE)* ... 6G ***55***
Watercress Line (SO24 9JG) ... 2D **10**
Watermouth Castle (EX34 9SL) ... 1E **6**
Waterperry Gdns. (OX33 1JZ) ... 3D **20**
Watersmeet (EX35 6NT) ... 1G **7**
Weald & Downland Living Mus. (PO18 0EU) ... 4F **10**
Weaver Hall Mus. & Workhouse (CW9 8AB) ... 2E **34**
Weaver's Cottage (PA10 2JG) ... 3B **58**
Wedgwood Visitor Cen. (ST12 9ER) ... 6G **35**
The Weir (HR4 7QF) ... 7C **26**
Wellbrook Beetling Mill (BT80 9RY) ... 5E **92**
Wells & Walsingham Light Railway (NR23 1QB) ... 5F **38**
*Wells Cathedral. (BA5 2UE)* ... 1D ***8***
Welney Wetland Cen. (PE14 9TN) ... 2B **30**
Welsh Highland Heritage Railway (LL49 9DY) ... 7E **32**
Welsh Highland Railway (LL54 5UP) ... 5E **32**
Welsh Mountain Zoo (LL28 5UY) ... 3H **33**
Welshpool & Llanfair Light Railway (SY21 0SF) ... 2L **25**
Wembley Stadium (HA9 0WS) ... 5J **21**
Wenlock Edge (SY7 9JH) ... 3C **26**
Wenlock Priory (TF13 6HS) ... 1E **26**
Wentworth Castle Gdns. (S75 3ET) ... 7M **41**
Weobley Castle (SA3 1HB) ... 7L **15**
Weoley Castle (B29 5RX) ... 3J **27**
Wesley Cottage (PL15 7TG) ... 7B **6**
Westbury Court Gdn. (GL14 1PD) ... 2F **18**
West Green House Gdns. (RG27 8JB) ... 8E **20**
West Highland Mus. (PH33 6AJ) ... 8B **70**
West Midland Safari & Leisure Pk. (DY12 1LF) ... 4G **27**
Westminster Abbey (SW1P 3PA) ... **London 113**
Westminster RC Cathedral (SW1P 1QH) ... **London 113**
Westonbirt National Arboretum (GL8 8QS) ... 5G **19**
Weston Pk. (TF11 8LE) ... 8G **35**
West Somerset Railway (TA24 5BG) ... 3L **7**
Westwood Manor (BA15 2AF) ... 8G **19**
West Wycombe Pk. (HP14 3AJ) ... 4F **20**
Wetlands Animal Pk. (DN22 8SB) ... 1D **36**
Whalley Abbey (BB7 9TN) ... 4F **40**
Wheal Martyn (PL26 8XG) ... 6C **4**
Whipsnade Tree Cathedral (LU6 2LL) ... 2H **21**
Whipsnade Zoo (LU6 2LF) ... 2H **21**
Whitby Abbey (YO22 4JT) ... 4G **49**
White Castle (NP7 8UD) ... 2B **18**
White Horse Hill (SN7 7QJ) ... 5M **19**
White Scar Cave (LA6 3AW) ... 8F **46**
Whithorn Priory & Mus. (DG8 8PY) ... 7K **51**
Whitmore Hall (ST5 5HW) ... 5G **35**
*Whitworth Art Gallery. (M15 6ER)* ... 8G ***41***
Wicken Fen National Nature Reserve (CB7 5YG) ... 4B **30**
Wicksteed Pk. (NN15 6NJ) ... 4F **28**
Wightwick Manor & Gdns. (WV6 8EE) ... 2G **27**
*Wigmore Castle. (HR6 9UJ)* ... 5C ***26***
Wilberforce House Mus. (HU1 1NE) ... **Kingston upon Hull 110** (5J **43**)
Wilderhope Manor (TF13 6EG) ... 2D **26**
Wildwood Escot (EX11 1LU) ... 6K **7**
Wilton House (SP2 0BJ) ... 2J **9**
Wimbledon Lawn Tennis Mus. (SW19 5HP) ... 6K **21**
Wimpole Hall & Gdns. (SG8 0BW) ... 6L **29**
Winchester Cathedral (SO23 9LS) ... **117** (3B **10**)
Windmill Hill Neolithic Camp (SN4 9NW) ... 6J **19**
Windsor Castle (SL4 1NJ) ... **117** (6G **21**)
Wingfield Manor (DE55 7NH) ... 4A **36**
Winkworth Arboretum (GU8 4AD) ... 1G **11**
Winter Gdn. (S1 2PP) ... **Sheffield 116**
Witley Court & Gdns. (WR6 6JT) ... 5F **26**
Woburn Abbey (MK17 9WA) ... 8G **29**
Woburn Safari Pk. (MK17 9QN) ... 8G **29**
The Wolds, Yorkshire (YO25 9EN) ... 2G **43**
The Wolds, Lincolnshire (LN8 6BL) ... 8K **43**
Wolfeton House (DT2 9QN) ... 6E **8**
Wollaton Hall (NG8 2AE) ... 6C **36**
The Wolseley Cen. (ST17 0WT) ... 7J **35**
Wolvesey Castle (SO23 9NB) ... **Winchester 117**
Woodchester Mansion (GL10 3TS) ... 3G **19**
Woodhenge (SP4 7AR) ... 1K **9**
Wookey Hole (BA5 1BB) ... 1D **8**
Woolsthorpe Manor (NG33 5PD) ... 7G **37**
Worcester Cathedral (WR1 2LH) ... **117** (6G **27**)
Worcestershire County Mus. (DY11 7XZ) ... 4G **27**
Wordsworth House (CA13 9RX) ... 8F **52**
The Wordsworth Mus. & Art Gallery (LA22 9SH) ... 5B **46**
Wotton House Landscape Gdns. (HP18 0SB) ... 2D **20**
Wrest Pk. (MK45 4HR) ... 8H **29**
*Wrexham RC Cathedral. (LL11 1RB)* ... 4B ***34***
Wroxeter Roman City (SY5 6PH) ... 1D **26**
Wroxton Abbey Gdns. (OX15 6PX) ... 7B **28**
Wylfa Visitor Cen. (LL67 0DH) ... 1C **32**
Wyre Forest (DY14 9UH) ... 4F **26**
*Wythenshawe Hall. (M23 0AB)* ... 1G ***35***


## Y


Yarmouth Castle (PO41 0PB) ... 7A **10**
York Art Gallery (YO1 7EW) ... **117**
York Castle Mus. (YO1 9RY) ... **117** (2D **42**)
York Minster (YO1 7JN) ... **117** (2D **42**)
York Racecourse (YO23 1EX) ... 3C **42**
Yorkshire Dales Nat. Pk. (BD23 5LB) ... 8G **47**
Yorkshire Mus. (YO30 7DR) ... **117**
Yorkshire Sculpture Pk. (WF4 4LG) ... 6L **41**